Berlin Transit

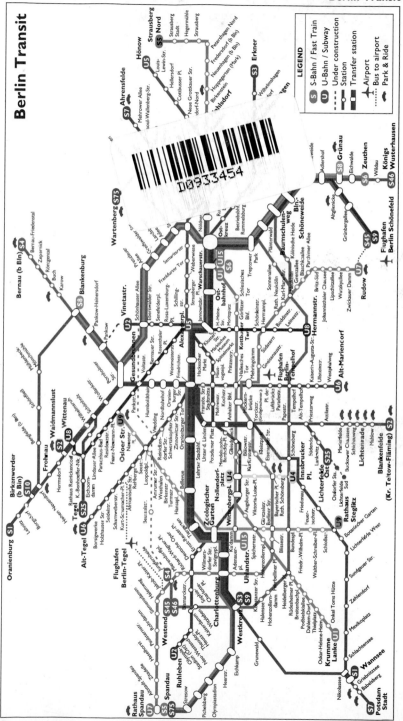

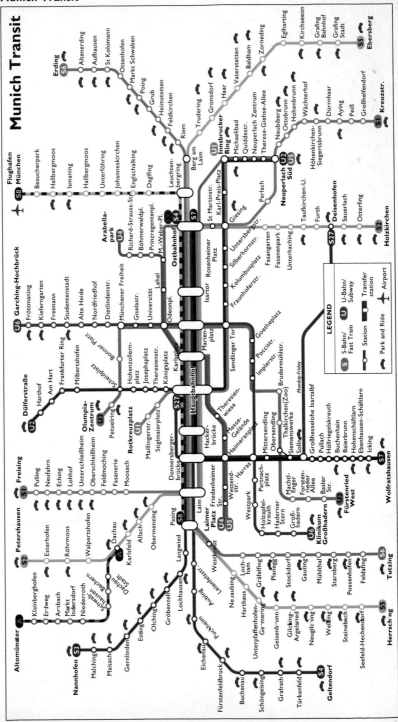

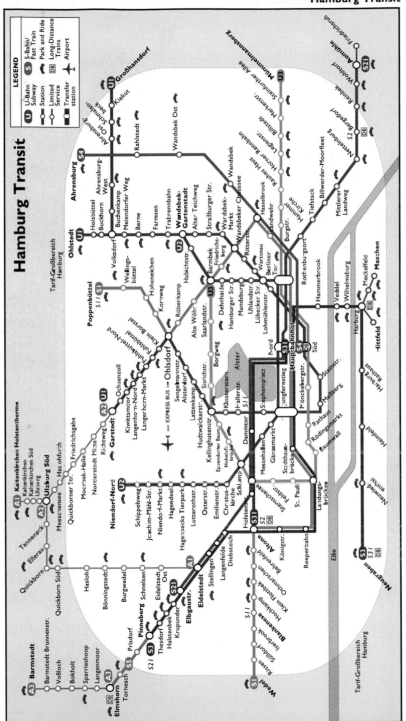

Hamburg Transit

Frankfurt Transit

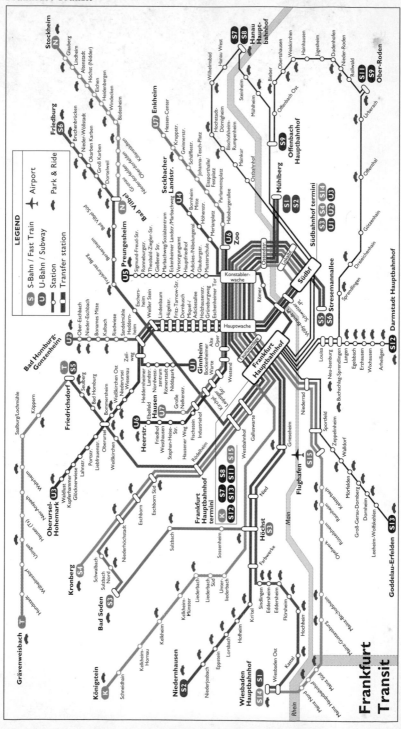

LET'S GO
Germany

■ Let's Go writers travel on your budget.

"Guides that penetrate the veneer of the holiday brochures and mine the grit of real life."
　　　　　　　　　　　　　　　　　　　　　　　　　　—The Economist

"The writers seem to have experienced every rooster-packed bus and lunar-surfaced mattress about which they write."
　　　　　　　　　　　　　　　　　　　　　　　　　　—The New York Times

"All the dirt, dirt cheap."
　　　　　　　　　　　　　　　　　　　　　　　　　　—People

■ Great for independent travelers.

"The guides are aimed not only at young budget travelers but at the independent traveler, a sort of streetwise cookbook for traveling alone."
　　　　　　　　　　　　　　　　　　　　　　　　　　—The New York Times

"Flush with candor and irreverence, chock full of budget travel advice."
　　　　　　　　　　　　　　　　　　　　　　　　　　—The Des Moines Register

"An indispensable resource. *Let's Go*'s practical information can be used by every traveler."
　　　　　　　　　　　　　　　　　　　　　　　　　　—The Chattanooga Free Press

■ Let's Go is completely revised each year.

"Only *Let's Go* has the zeal to annually update every title on its list."
　　　　　　　　　　　　　　　　　　　　　　　　　　—The Boston Globe

"Unbeatable: good sight-seeing advice; up-to-date info on restaurants, hotels, and inns; a commitment to money-saving travel; and a wry style that brightens nearly every page."
　　　　　　　　　　　　　　　　　　　　　　　　　　—The Washington Post

■ All the important information you need.

"*Let's Go* authors provide a comedic element while still providing concise information and thorough coverage of the country. Anything you need to know about budget traveling is detailed in this book."
　　　　　　　　　　　　　　　　　　　　　　　　　　—The Chicago Sun-Times

"Value-packed, unbeatable, accurate, and comprehensive."
　　　　　　　　　　　　　　　　　　　　　　　　　　—Los Angeles Times

Let's Go Publications

Let's Go: Alaska & the Pacific Northwest 1999
Let's Go: Australia 1999
Let's Go: Austria & Switzerland 1999
Let's Go: Britain & Ireland 1999
Let's Go: California 1999
Let's Go: Central America 1999
Let's Go: Eastern Europe 1999
Let's Go: Ecuador & the Galápagos Islands 1999
Let's Go: Europe 1999
Let's Go: France 1999
Let's Go: Germany 1999
Let's Go: Greece 1999 **New title!**
Let's Go: India & Nepal 1999
Let's Go: Ireland 1999
Let's Go: Israel & Egypt 1999
Let's Go: Italy 1999
Let's Go: London 1999
Let's Go: Mexico 1999
Let's Go: New York City 1999
Let's Go: New Zealand 1999
Let's Go: Paris 1999
Let's Go: Rome 1999
Let's Go: South Africa 1999 **New title!**
Let's Go: Southeast Asia 1999
Let's Go: Spain & Portugal 1999
Let's Go: Turkey 1999 **New title!**
Let's Go: USA 1999
Let's Go: Washington, D.C. 1999

Let's Go Map Guides

Amsterdam	Madrid
Berlin	New Orleans
Boston	New York City
Chicago	Paris
Florence	Rome
London	San Francisco
Los Angeles	Washington, D.C.

Coming Soon: Prague, Seattle

Let's Go Publications

Let's Go Germany 1999

Douglas Muller
Editor

Erica A. Silverstein
Anna M. Schneider-Mayerson
Associate Editors

Researcher-Writers:
Kata Gellen
Max Hirsh
Jamie L. Jones
Winnie Li
Dáša Pejchar
Mike Weller

St. Martin's Press ※ New York

HELPING LET'S GO

If you want to share your discoveries, suggestions, or corrections, please drop us a line. We read every piece of correspondence, whether a postcard, a 10-page email, or a coconut. Please note that mail received after May 1999 may be too late for the 2000 book, but will be kept for future editions. **Address mail to:**

Let's Go: Germany
67 Mount Auburn Street
Cambridge, MA 02138
USA

Visit Let's Go at **http://www.letsgo.com**, or send email to:

feedback@letsgo.com
Subject: "Let's Go: Germany"

In addition to the invaluable travel advice our readers share with us, many are kind enough to offer their services as researchers or editors. Unfortunately, our charter enables us to employ only currently enrolled Harvard-Radcliffe students.

Maps by David Lindroth copyright © 1999, 1998, 1997, 1996, 1995, 1994, 1993, 1992, 1991, 1990, 1989, 1988 by St. Martin's Press, Inc.

Distributed outside the USA and Canada by Macmillan.

ISBN: 0-312-19483-8

First edition
10 9 8 7 6 5 4 3 2 1

Let's Go: Germany is written by Let's Go Publications, 67 Mount Auburn Street, Cambridge, MA 02138, USA.

Let's Go® and the thumb logo are trademarks of Let's Go, Inc. Printed in the USA on recycled paper with biodegradable soy ink.

Contents

How to Use This Book

Welcome to **Budget Travel 1999: Let's Go Germany.** All you travel freshmen may fancy yourself ready for big-league backpacking, European rail-riding, and all sorts of other fancy-schmancy activities, but you've got one thing comin': namely this book, a crash course on the finer points of budget travel in Germany. If you stay awake through the whole class, you will find yourself transformed into one savvy traveler in the land of Teuton. Whether bustin' a move in the clubs of Berlin or bustin' your boots on the slopes of the Alps, **Let's Go Germany** promises to guide you through this beautiful, compelling, and very often bizarre land.

Open your text immediately to the **Essentials** section, which has been painstakingly researched to- prepare you for departure and orient you upon arrival. Read up on passport and visa information, how to snag the best deals in budget airfare, and how to handle everyday life as a visitor to Germany. Our trained experts have done their homework, infiltrating the very fabric of German society to discover the skinny on concerns of women, gays and lesbians, and others with specific interests (including vegetarians!). Indeed, we cover all of the hard facts—health, safety, money matters, transportation, and camping and the outdoors, among others.

We've also got a section specially designed for you humanities majors: **History and Culture.** Here, we trace German history from the age of the Neanderthals to the Berlin Wall and its fall. **This Year in Germany** lets you skip your news-reading by giving you the plot summary of the past year's events. Bach, Hegel, and Goethe live on in the sections on **Music, Philosophy,** and **Literature.** We'll break for lunch with **Food and Drink,** then get it on German-style according to the guidelines in **Social Life.**

Break's over—back to class. We will now address the subject at hand: the actual descriptions of the cities, towns, and regions you will encounter on your journey. The country is divided into chapters based on *Land,* with Berlin at the beginning, followed by the eastern *Länder,* moving counter-clockwise to end up in Bavaria. Each city is divided into easily understood sections. **Orientation and Practical Information** tells you where to go for resources and how to get there. **Food and Accommodations** fills your tummy and puts you to bed; these sections are ranked, starting with the teacher's pet establishments. **Sights** leads you from Romanesque cathedrals to bizarre postmodern sculptures, helping you work your way through Germany's rich historical and cultural offerings. **Nightlife and Entertainment** first gets you cultured, with listings of drama, film, and musical offerings, and then lets you go wild, teaching you to party like it's 1999.

The **Let's Go Picks** comprise Germany's touristic honor roll; give them your attention, as they truly shine. The **Appendix** teaches you a little *Deutsch* and gives you useful weather, distance, and communications information. Lastly, a note on **how not to use this book.** Although we provide tons of necessary information, you should put the guide aside from time to time and simply explore on your own. Doing this will guarantee you an A+ adventure.

A NOTE TO OUR READERS

Maps

Color Maps

Germany: Chapters

DENMARK

Baltic Sea

North Sea

Schleswig-Holstein and Hamburg
pp. 246-272

Hamburg

Mecklenburg-Vorpommern
pp. 229-245

NETHER-LANDS

Bremen

POLAND

Niedersachsen (Lower Saxony)
pp. 273-317

Hannover

Brandenburg
pp. 132-142

Berlin
pp. 85-131

Nordrhein-Westfalen (North Rhine-Westphalia)
pp. 318-359

Düsseldorf

Köln (Cologne)

Bonn

BEL.

Sachsen-Anhalt (Saxony-Anhalt)
pp. 207-228

Hessen (Hesse)
pp. 360-387

Thüringen (Thuringia)
pp. 178-206

Sachsen (Saxony)
pp. 143-177

Dresden

Frankfurt-am-Main

CZECH REPUBLIC

Rheinland-Pfalz (Rhineland-Palatinate)
pp. 388-411

LUX.

Heidelberg

Nürnberg (Nuremberg)

Baden-Württemberg
pp. 412-470

Stuttgart

Bayern (Bavaria)
pp. 471-570

FRANCE

Freiburg

München (Munich)

AUSTRIA

SWITZERLAND

IX

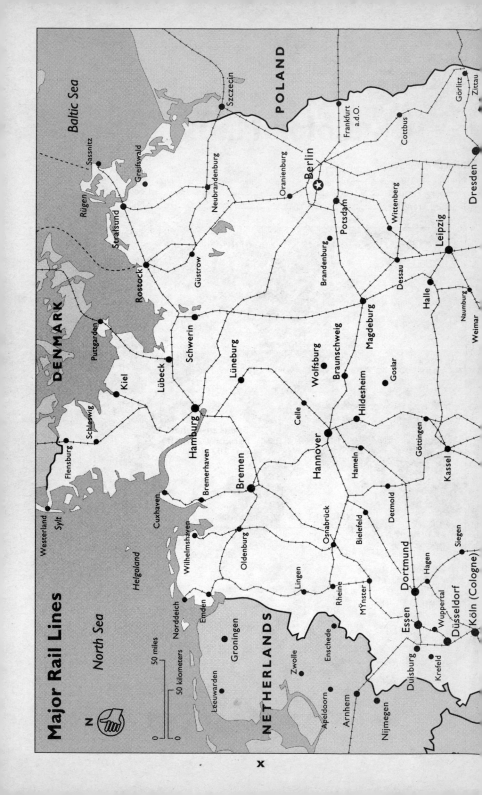

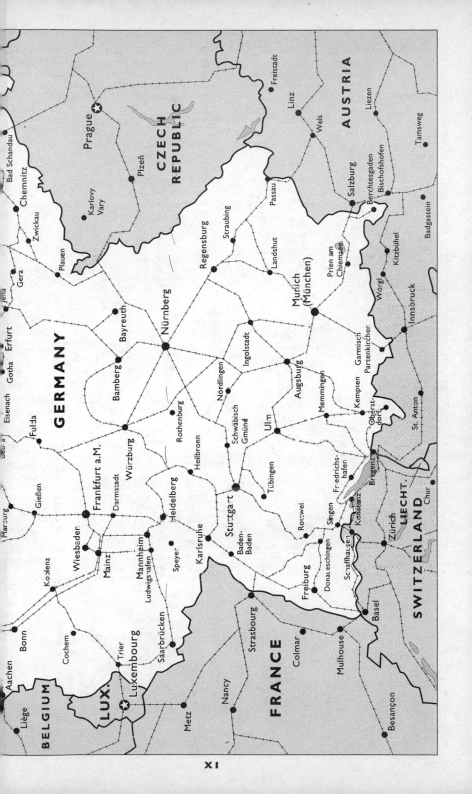

Germany

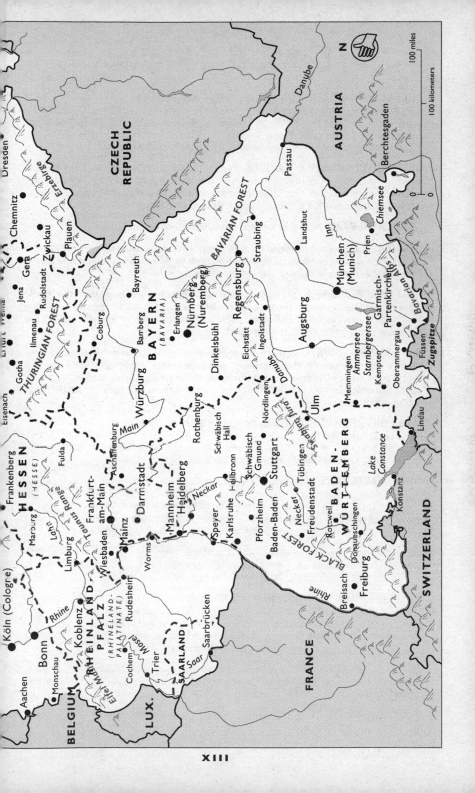

Let's Go Picks

BEST ACCOMMODATIONS: **Jugendherberge Burg Stahleck** in Bacharach, which occupies a gorgeously restored castle perched high above the Rhine, continues its reign as the primo DJH hostel in the nation (p. 394). In Berlin, check out **The Backpacker** hostel (p. 98) or the **Hotel Transit** (p. 101); in Munich, rest your weary feet at "**The Tent**" (Jugendlager Kapuzinerhölzl) or **4 you München** (p. 482).

BEST BOOTY-SHAKIN' LOCATIONS: Berlin, *Berlin*, and **Berlin**. **The Love Parade** gets the whole city busy during the second weekend in July, but Berlin's year-round offerings are just as fab. Our favorites are **Insel der Jugend** (p. 127) and **SO36** (p. 125). In Munich, work it at the mammoth **Kunstpark Ost** (p. 496).

BEST CATHEDRAL: Now and forever, the **Kölner Dom** is king (p. 324).

BEST CASTLE: **Neuschwanstein** (p. 508), Disney World's model for Cinderella's castle, is dreamy, while the crumbling **Burg Rheinfels** (p. 394) offers a unique chance for solo castle exploration through subterranean passages.

BEST BEACHES: **Sylt** (p. 271) is Germany's ritzy beach resort *par excellence*, while some of the lesser-visited of the **East Frisian islands** (p. 313) are serene and desolately beautiful. Watch out for "**FKK**" **signs;** these indicate beaches where you can get the *complete* tan. You know what we mean.

BEST ALPINE TOWN: **Garmisch-Partenkirchen** (p. 500), in the shadow of Germany's tallest mountain, the Zugspitze, welcomes visitors with all the fixings of a world-class winter-Olympics city without all those pesky Olympians—they left in 1936. Garmisch-Partenkirchen features two great hostels and tons of climbing and skiing opportunities.

MOST UNIQUE MUSEUM: Hands down, the **ZAM** (Zentrum für Außergewöhnliche Museen; Center for Unusual Museums) in Munich wins this title (p. 492). The museum houses a variety of truly bizarre collections, from the Sisi Museum to the questionably tasteful, and therefore mad fun, Chamberpot Museum.

BEST TRAVEL SERVICES: Alan Wissenberg's **EurAide** office in the Munich *Hauptbahnhof* is a godsend (p. 478). Wissenberg, an American emigré, knows anything and everything about travel in Germany. The folks at **DERTravel Services** (p. 39) can get you equipped to ride the rails of Deutsche Bahn. The **German National Tourist Office** (p. 1) will shower you with infinite amounts of helpful information.

BEST HIKING TRAIL: The **Pforzheim-Basel Westweg** cuts a gorgeous 280km path through the mountains and valleys of the Schwarzwald (p. 470), while the **Rennsteig** winds through the Thüringer Wald for 168km (p. 197).

BEST UNIQUELY GERMAN PHENOMENON: Every sin is satisfied at the everything-but-the-kitchen-sink nightlife complexes that sprout up in almost every large German city. These always include bars, clubs, cafes, and restaurants, sometimes even cinemas (see **Cine Citta,** in Nürnberg, p. 558) and, on one very rare occasion, an indoor climbing wall (see **Gerber III,** in Weimar, p. 184).

BEST CELEBRATION: Weimar's year-long **birthday party for Goethe** and its much-touted title as "**Europe's Cultural Capital**" will keep the city full of art, culture, and rowdy partying 'til the end of the century (p. 178).

BEST BATHROOM: The black lighting in the john at the **Quasimodo** club in Berlin (p. 124) makes peeing an adventure—turn to the Nightlife section to see why!

Essentials

PLANNING YOUR TRIP

A fun and inexpensive trip to Germany requires preparation. For better or for worse, there is a sprawling industry designed to help you and other travelers. The many organizations listed below, especially national tourist offices, will send you daunting mounds of literature. Dive in and plan a trip tailored to your specific interests. You can design a historical, hiking, even a beer tour of Germany. The possibilities are endless. Resist the urge to see everything, as a madcap schedule will detract from your enjoyment. If you try to see Berlin, Munich, and Köln in a week, you'll come away with only vague memories of train stations and youth hostels. Similarly, choose your traveling companions carefully—traveling with a group of friends may effectively insulate you from genuine intimacy with local culture. On the other hand, they will share food and lodging costs, provide extra safety in numbers, and often serve as invaluable sources of energy and comfort. Along your journey, you are certain to meet many fascinating people; a lone traveler is never truly alone. Make sure to use the information provided by *Let's Go* and other sources to assemble your "support system," both in terms of what you bring and the arrangements you make. It's been said that all you really need are time and money, but on a budget voyage you don't want to waste either due to lack of planning.

■ When to Go

In July and August, temperatures, airfares, and tempers rise right along with the number of tourists. In winter months, some hostels hibernate and museum hours may be abbreviated. The cloudy, temperate months of May, June, and September are perhaps your best bet. But bear in mind that many school field trips to historic sites take place in June, and that youth hostels may be inundated with schoolchildren. Winter sports gear up in November and continue through April; high season for skiing hits in mid-December to mid-January and February to March. Germans head to vacation spots *en masse* with the onset of school vacations; airports and train stations are jammed and the traffic on the *Autobahn* can be measured in meters per hour. The staggering of vacation periods among the federal states has alleviated the crunch a tad, but you should still avoid trekking across Germany the day after school lets out, or risk being buried by throngs. See the **Appendix,** p. 571, for further holiday and weather information.

■ Useful Information

GOVERNMENT INFORMATION OFFICES

These official German outposts in your native country can be a great help in planning your trip; have them send you information and brochures before you leave. The **German National Tourist Offices** distribute useful publications such as *Travel Tips, Camping in Germany,* and *Youth Hostels.*

Australia: German-Australian Chamber of Industry and Commerce, P.O. Box A 980, Sydney South, NSW 1235 (tel. (02) 9267 8148; fax 9267 9035).

Canada: 175 Bloor St. East, North Tower, Suite 604, Toronto, Ont. M4W 3R8 (tel. (416) 968-1570; fax 968-1986; email germanto@idirect.com).

South Africa: 22 Girton Road, Parktown, P.O. Box 10883, Johannesburg 2000 (tel. (011) 643 16 15; fax 484 27 50).

U.K.: 34 Belgrave Square, London SW1X 8QB (tel. (0171) 493 0080; fax 824 1566; email@infoctr; http://www.german-embassy.org.uk).
U.S.: New York, 122 East 42nd St., 52nd Fl., 10168-0072 (tel. (212) 661-7200; fax 661-7174; email gntony@aol.com; http://www.germany-tourism.de); **Los Angeles,** 11766 Wilshire Blvd., Ste. 750, 90025 (tel. (310) 575-9799; fax 575-1565; email gntolax@aol.com). The **German Information Center,** 950 Third Ave., New York, NY 10022 (tel. (212) 888-9840; fax 752-6691; email gic1@ix.netcom.com). Publishes *This Week in Germany,* a free newspaper for Americans available both via standard mail and email.

TRAVEL ORGANIZATIONS

Council on International Educational Exchange (CIEE), 205 East 42nd St., New York, NY 10017-5706 (tel. (888)-COUNCIL (268-6245); fax (212) 822-2699; http://www.ciee.org). A private, not-for-profit organization, Council administers work, volunteer, academic, internship, and professional programs around the world. They also offer identity cards (including the ISIC and the GO25) and a range of publications, among them the useful magazine *Student Travels* (free).
Federation of International Youth Travel Organizations (FIYTO), Bredgade 25H, DK-1260 Copenhagen K, Denmark (tel. (45) 33 33 96 00; fax 33 93 96 76; email mailbox@fiyto.org; http://www.fiyto.org), is an international organization promoting educational, cultural, and social travel for young people. Member organizations include language schools, educational travel companies, national tourist boards, accommodation centers, and other suppliers of travel services to youth and students. FIYTO sponsors the GO25 Card (http://www.go25.org).
International Student Travel Confederation, Herengracht 479, 1017 BS Amsterdam, The Netherlands (tel. (31) 20 421 2800; fax 20 421 2810; email istcinfo@istc.org; http://www.istc.org) The ISTC is a nonprofit confederation of student travel organizations whose focus is to develop, promote, and facilitate travel among young people and students. Member organizations include International Student Surface Travel Association (ISSTA), Student Air Travel Association (SATA), IASIS Travel Insurance, the International Association for Educational and Work Exchange Programs (IAEWEP), and the International Student Identity Card Association (ISIC).

USEFUL PUBLICATIONS

The publications we list here should be useful in preparation for your trip. If you're interested in books on culture or history, see **Further Reading,** p. 70.

Atlantik-Brücke, Adenauerallee 131, 53113 Bonn (tel. (0228) 21 41 60; fax 21 46 59). Devoted to promoting mutual understanding (hence "Atlantic Bridge"), it publishes *These Strange German Ways*—a must for any American planning on living in Germany—as well as *Meet United Germany, German Holidays and Folk Customs,* and *Speaking Out: Jewish Voices from United Germany.* Order the books from the Hamburg office (tel. (040) 600 7022).
Bon Voyage!, 2069 W. Bullard Ave., Fresno, CA 93711-1200 (tel. (800) 995-9716, from abroad (209) 447-8441; fax 266-6460; email 70754.3511@compuserve.com). Annual mail-order catalogue offers a range of products. Books, travel accessories, luggage, electrical converters, maps, and videos. All merchandise may be returned for exchange or refund within 30 days of purchase, and prices are guaranteed (lower advertised prices will be matched and merchandise shipped free).
The College Connection, Inc., 1295 Prospect St. Suite B, La Jolla, CA 92037 (tel. (619) 551-9770; fax 551-9987; email eurailnow@aol.com). Publishes *The Passport,* a booklet listing hints about every aspect of traveling and studying abroad. This booklet is free to *Let's Go* readers; send your request by email or fax only. The College Rail Connection, a division of the College Connection, sells railpasses with student discounts.
Culture Shock! Germany, published by Graphic Arts Publishing Company, P.O. Box 10306, Portland, OR 97296-0306 (tel. (503) 226-2402). Part of the *Culture*

That "ß" Thing,
Plus a Few Necessary German Words

In your travels, it is useful to pick up a number of words for common tourist attractions and services, even if you speak no German. *Let's Go Germany: 1999* uses a fair number of German words in the text without translation. To read some of them, and many of the titles and phrases in the book, you need to be let in on the mysterious secret of the "ß," a special consonant which Germans call an "ess-tset." **It is pronounced exactly like a double "S"** in English; hence, *Straße*, the German word for street, is pronounced "SHTRAH-ssuh." Meißen, a small town in Sachsen, is pronounced "MIGH-ssen." For details on the future of the "ess-tset," see **The Woeful Decline of the ß,** p. 535. With that aside, here is a list of the most essential German tourist terms that you will see used (all over the place) in this text:

die Altstadt (AHLT-shtaht) = **old city,** the historic section of town
der Dom (DOME) = **cathedral**
der Hauptbahnhof (HAUWPT-bahn-hohf) = a town or city's **main train station**
die Jugendherberge (YOO-gent-hair-BARE-guh) = **youth hostel**
die Kirche (KEER-hkuh) = **church**
die Kneipe (k'NIGH-puh) = a **bar** for students or young people
die Mensa (MAIN-zah) = **cafeteria** (often at a university)
das Münster (MYOON-stuh) = **cathedral**
die Pension (PAHN-tzee-OHN) = small, cheap, often family-run **hotel**
das Privatzimmer (pree-VAHT-tsim-mer) = a **private room,** in a home
das Rathaus (RAHT-house) = **town hall,** often located in the *Altstadt*
das Schloß (SHLOSS) = **castle**
das Imperium schlägt zurück = **The Empire Strikes Back**

Shock! series. A readable low-down on living in *Deutschland* that isn't afraid to hold your hand.

Forsyth Travel Library, Inc., 1750 East 131st Street, P.O. Box 480800, Kansas City, MO 64148 (tel. (800) 367-7984; fax (816) 942-6969; email forsyth@avi.net; http://www.forsyth.com). A mail-order service that stocks a wide range of maps and guides for rail and ferry travel in Europe; also sells rail tickets and passes, and offers reservation services. Sells the *Thomas Cook European Timetable* for trains, a complete guide to European train departures and arrivals (US$28, or US$39 with full map of European train routes; postage US$4.50 for Priority shipping). Call or write for a free catalogue, or visit their web site.

Hunter Publishing, P.O. Box 7816, Edison, NJ 08818 (tel. (908) 225-1900; fax 417-0482; email hunterpub@emi.net; http://www.hunterpublishing.com). Has an extensive catalogue of travel guides, language learning tapes, and quality maps, among them *Charming Small Hotel Guides* to Germany and other countries (each US$15).

Transitions Abroad, P.O. Box 1300, 18 Hulst Rd., Amherst, MA 01004-1300 (tel. (800) 293-0373; fax. 256-0373; email trabroad@aol.com; http://transabroad.com). Invaluable magazine lists publications and resources for overseas study, work, and volunteering (US$25 for 6 issues, single copy US$6.25). Also publishes *The Alternative Travel Directory,* a comprehensive guide to living, learning, and working overseas (US$20; postage $4).

INTERNET RESOURCES

Today, people can make their own airline, hotel, hostel, or car rental reservations on the Internet and communicate with others abroad. **NetTravel: How Travelers Use the Internet,** by Michael Shapiro, is a thorough and informative guide to all aspects of travel planning through the Internet (US$25). **Search engines** (services that search for web pages under specific subjects) can significantly aid the search process. **Lycos** (http://a2z.lycos.com), **Alta Vista** (http://www.altavista.digi-

tal.com), and **Excite** (http://www.excite.com) are among the most popular. **Yahoo!** is a slightly more organized search engine; check out its travel links at http://www.yahoo.com/Recreation/Travel. Another good way to explore is to find a good site and go from there, through links from one web page to another. A search tool for Germany is http://www.yahoo.de. Check out the **Let's Go web site** (http://www.letsgo.com) to find our newsletter, information about our books, and an always-current list of links. *Let's Go* lists web sites specific to certain aspects of travel throughout the Essentials chapter. Or, you can try some of our favorites sites directly:

The CIA World Factbook (http://www.odci.gov/cia/publications/factbook/index.html) has tons of vital statistics on Germany. Check it out for an overview of Germany's economy, or an explanation of its system of government.

City.Net (http://city.net/countries/germany) links into tourist information servers in numerous cities. Information on sights, entertainment, and accommodations.

Cybercafé Guide (http://www.cyberiacafe.net/cyberia/guide/ccafe.htm) can help you find cybercafes worldwide.

Foreign Language for Travelers (http://www.travlang.com) can help you brush up on your German.

German Information Center (http://germany-info.org/index.htm) in New York provides a wealth of information about Germany and German culture, plus great links to other sites pertaining to specific issues such as travel planning.

German Tourist Board (http://www.germany-tourism.de) delivers the lowdown on city information, major festivals and cultural events, and tourist tips.

Internet Resources for Germany (http://www.goethe.de/uk/saf/eninet.htm), produced by the Goethe-Institut, explores every nook and cranny of the *Infoautobahn* in Germany, including newspapers, fellowships and academic pursuits, cultural information, and insights into travel and accommodations.

Microsoft Expedia (http://expedia.msn.com) has everything you'd ever need to make travel plans on the web—compare flight fares, look at maps, make reservations. FareTracker, a free service within Expedia, sends you monthly emails about the cheapest fares to any destination.

Shoestring Travel (http://www.stratpub.com) is a budget travel e-zine featuring listings of home exchanges, links, and accommodations information.

Lowestfare.com (http://www.lowestfare.com) provides a search engine that locates the lowest priced ticket on a regularly scheduled flight.

TravelHUB (http://www.travelhub.com) is a great site for cheap travel deals.

▓ Documents and Formalities

All applications should be filed several weeks or months in advance of your planned departure date. Remember that you are relying on government agencies to complete these transactions. Try to apply as early as possible; Demand for passports is highest between January and August

When you travel, always carry on your person two or more forms of identification, including at least one photo ID. A passport combined with a driver's license or birth certificate usually serves as adequate proof of your identity and citizenship. Many establishments, especially banks, require several IDs before cashing traveler's checks. Never carry all your forms of ID together, however—you risk being left entirely without ID or funds in case of theft or loss. Also carry several extra passport-size photos that you can attach to IDs or railpasses you will eventually acquire. If you are planning an extended stay, register your passport with the nearest embassy or consulate.

GERMAN EMBASSIES AND CONSULATES

The German embassy or consulate in your home country can supply you with legal information concerning your trip, arrange for visas, and direct you to a wealth of other information about tourism, education, and employment in Germany.

Australia, in **Canberra** at 119 Empire Circuit, Yarralumla, ACT 2600 (tel. (02) 6270 1911; fax 6270 1951); **Consulates: Melbourne,** South Yarra, Vic., 480 Punt Rd., 3141 (tel. (03) 9828 6888; fax 9820 2414); **Sydney,** 13 Trelawney St., Woollahra, N.S.W. 2025 (tel. (02) 9328 7733; fax 9327 9649).

Canada, 1 Waverly St., Ottawa, Ont. K2P OT8 (tel. (613) 232-1101; fax 594-9330; email 100566.2620@compuserve.com). **Consulates: Montréal,** 1250 René-Lévesque Ouest, Suite 4315, H3B 4X1 (tel. (514) 931-2277; fax 931-7239); other consulates in Toronto and Vancouver.

Ireland, 31 Trimleston Ave., Booterstown, Blackrock, Co. Dublin (tel. (01) 269 30 11 or 269 31 23; fax 269 39 46).

New Zealand, 90-92 Hobson St., Thorndon, Wellington (tel. (04) 473 6063; fax 473 6069).

South Africa, 180 Blackwood St., Arcadia, Pretoria 0083 (tel. (012) 427 8900; fax 343 9401). **Consulate: Cape Town,** 825 St. Martini Gardens, Queen Victoria St., 8001 (tel. (021) 24 24 10; fax 24 94 03).

U.K., 23 Belgrave Sq., London SW1X 8PZ (tel. (0171) 824 1300; fax 824 1435; email mail@german-embassy.org.uk). **Consulates: Manchester,** Westminster House, 11 Portlant St., M60 1HY (tel. (0161) 237 5255; fax 237 5244); **Edinburgh,** 16 Eglinton Crescent, EH12 5DG, Scotland (tel. (0131) 337 2323; fax 346 1578).

U.S., 4645 Reservoir Rd. NW, Washington, D.C. 20007-1998 (tel. (202) 298-4000; fax 298-4249; http://www.germany-info.org). **Consulates: New York,** 871 U.N. Plaza, 10017 (tel. (212) 610-9700; fax 610-9702); **Los Angeles,** 6222 Wilshire Blvd., Ste. 500, 90048 (tel. (213) 930-2703; fax 930-2805); other consulates in Atlanta, Boston, Chicago, Detroit, Houston, Miami, San Francisco, and Seattle.

PASSPORTS

Carry a photocopy of your passport separate from your actual passport, and leave another copy at home. This will help prove your citizenship and facilitate the issuing of a new passport if you lose the original document. Consulates also recommend that you carry an expired passport or an official copy of your birth certificate in a part of your baggage separate from other documents.

If you do lose your passport, immediately notify the local police and the nearest embassy or consulate of your home government. To expedite its replacement, you will need to know all information previously recorded and show identification and proof of citizenship. A replacement may take weeks to process, and it may be valid only for a limited time. Any visas stamped in your old passport will be irretrievably lost. In an emergency, ask for immediate temporary traveling papers that will permit you to re-enter your home country.

Your passport is a public document belonging to your nation's government. You may have to surrender it to a foreign government official, but if you don't get it back in a reasonable amount of time, inform the nearest mission of your home country.

Australia Citizens must apply for a passport in person at a post office, a passport office, or an Australian diplomatic mission overseas. An appointment may be necessary. Adult passports cost AUS$120 (for a 32 page passport) or AUS$180 (64 page), and a child's is AUS$60 (32 page) or AUS$90 (64 page). For more info, call toll-free (in Australia) 13 12 32, or visit http://www.austemb.org.

Canada Application forms are available at all passport offices, Canadian missions, many travel agencies, and Northern Stores in northern communities. Citizens may apply in person at any of 28 regional Passport Offices across Canada. Passports cost CDN$60, plus a CDN$25 consular fee, are valid for 5 years, and are not renewable. Processing takes approximately 5 business days for applications in-person; allow three weeks for mail delivery. For additional info, contact the **Canadian Passport Office,** Department of Foreign Affairs and International Trade, Ottawa, ON, K1A 0G3 (tel. (613) 994-3500; http://www.dfait-maeci.gc.ca/passport). Travelers may also call (800) 567-6868 (24hr.).

Ireland Citizens can apply for a passport by mail to either the **Department of Foreign Affairs,** Passport Office, Setanta Centre, Molesworth St., Dublin 2 (tel. (01)

671 1633; fax 671 1092), or the Passport Office, **Irish Life Building,** 1A South Mall, Cork (tel. (021) 272 525; fax 275 7770). Obtain an application at a local Garda station or request one from a passport office. The new Passport Express Service, available through post offices, allows citizens to get a passport in 2 weeks for an extra IR£3. Passports cost IR£45 and are valid for 5 years. Citizens under 18 or over 65 can request a 3-year passport, which costs IR£10.

New Zealand Application forms for passports are available from travel agents and Department of Internal Affairs Link Centres. Applications may also be forwarded to the Passport Office, P.O. Box 10526, Wellington, New Zealand. Standard processing time in New Zealand is 10 working days. The fees are adult NZ$80, and children under 16 NZ$40. An **urgent passport service** is also available for an extra NZ$80. Children's passports are valid for up to 5 years. An adult's passport is valid for up to 10 years. More information is available on the internet at http://www.govt.nz/agency_info/forms.shtml.

South Africa Citizens can apply for a passport at any **Home Affairs Office** or **South African Mission.** Tourist passports, valid for 10 years, cost SAR80. Children under 16 must be issued their own passports, valid for 5 years, which cost SAR60. If a passport is needed in a hurry, an **emergency passport** may be issued for SAR50. An application for a permanent passport must accompany the emergency passport application. Time for the completion of an application is normally 3 months or more from the time of submission. Citizens are urged to renew their passports soon to avoid the expected glut of applications as 2000 approaches. For further information, contact the nearest Department of Home Affairs Office.

United Kingdom British citizens, British Dependent Territories citizens, British Nationals (overseas), British subjects, and British Overseas citizens may apply for a **full passport,** valid for 10 years (5 years if under 16). Application forms are available at passport offices, main post offices, many travel agents, and branches of Lloyds Bank and Artac World Choice. Apply by mail or in person (for an additional UK£10) to one of the passport offices, located in London, Liverpool, Newport, Peterborough, Glasgow, or Belfast. The fee is UK£31, UK£11 for children under 16. The London office offers same-day, walk-in rush service; arrive early. The U.K. Passport Agency can be reached by phone at (0990) 21 04 10.

United States Citizens may apply for a passport at any federal or state **courthouse** or **post office** authorized to accept passport applications, or at a **U.S. Passport Agency.** You must apply in person if this is your first passport, if you're under age 18, or if your current passport is more than 12 years old or was issued before your 18th birthday. Passports are valid for 10 years (5 years if under 18) and cost US$65 (under 18 US$40). Passports may be **renewed** by mail or in person for US$55. Processing takes 3-4 weeks. **Rush service** is available for a surcharge of US$30 with proof of departure within 10 working days (e.g., an airplane ticket or itinerary), or for travelers leaving in 2-3 weeks who require visas. For more info, contact the U.S. Passport Information's **24-hour recorded message** (tel. (202) 647-0518). Additional information is available through the Bureau of Consular Affairs at http://travel.state.gov, or through the State Department at http://www.state.gov.

ENTRANCE REQUIREMENTS AND VISAS

Citizens of **Australia, Canada, Ireland, New Zealand, the U.K., and the U.S.** do not need to obtain a visa ahead of time to enter Germany, unless they wish to work there. These citizens need to carry only a valid passport in order to remain for up to three months. **Citizens of the EU** don't need visas. **South African citizens** require a visa. Contact the nearest German Consulate General for more information. If your travels extend beyond Germany, remember that some other countries in Europe require a visa. Carry proof of your **financial independence**, such as a visa to the next country on your itinerary, a return air ticket, enough money to cover the cost of your living expenses, etc.

If you wish to stay longer than three months, apply for a visa at the German embassy or consulate in your home country well before your departure. You may also apply for an extended-stay visa at a local aliens' authority after entry. You must obtain a work permit before seeking temporary employment in Germany, presuming you have already obtained a residence permit from a local immigration office (see **Work and Volunteer,** p. 21). You should apply for these permits at least eight weeks in advance.

CUSTOMS: ENTERING GERMANY

> *Don't mention the war!*
>
> —Basil Fawlty (John Cleese)

Unless you plan to import a BMW or a barnyard beast, you will probably pass right through the customs barrier with minimal ado. Germany prohibits or restricts the importation of firearms, explosives, ammunition, fireworks, controlled substances, many plants and animals, lottery tickets, and obscene literature or films. To prevent problems with transporting **prescription drugs,** ensure that the bottles are clearly marked, and carry a copy of your prescription to show customs officials. When dealing with customs officers, do your utmost to be polite and look responsible.

Gifts and commodities for personal use are allowed into Germany with the following regulations: Citizens of the European Union (EU) countries can bring up to 300 **cigarettes** into Germany; travelers from outside the EU can bring 200. Germany allows 1.5 liters of **alcoholic beverages** above 22 proof for EU members, 1 liter for travelers from outside the EU. No one under age 17 is entitled to these allowances. Coffee can be imported up to 1000g by EU members and up to 500g by travelers from outside the EU. There are no regulations on the import or export of currency. The total value of goods imported from the EU cannot exceed DM1235, while goods from outside the EU cannot exceed DM115. You can obtain more details from the German Consulate General in your own country.

CUSTOMS: GOING HOME

Upon returning home, you must declare all articles you acquired abroad and pay a **duty** on the value of those articles that exceed the allowance established by your country's customs service. Goods and gifts purchased at **duty-free** shops abroad are not exempt from duty or sales tax at your point of return; you must declare these items as well. "Duty-free" merely means that you need not pay a tax in the country of purchase.

Australia Citizens may import AUS$400 (under 18 AUS$200) of goods duty-free, in addition to 1.125L alcohol and 250 cigarettes or 250g tobacco. You must be over 18 to import alcohol or tobacco. There is no limit to the amount of Australian and/ or foreign cash that may be brought into or taken out of the country, but amounts of AUS$10,000 or more, or the equivalent in foreign currency, must be reported. All foodstuffs and animal products must be declared on arrival. For info, contact the Regional Director, Australian Customs Service, GPO Box 8, Sydney NSW 2001 (tel. (02) 9213 2000; fax 9213 4000), or visit http://www.customs.gov.au.

Canada Citizens who remain abroad for at least 1 week may bring back up to CDN$500 worth of goods duty-free any time. Citizens or residents who travel for a period between 48 hours and 6 days can bring back up to CDN$200. Both of these exemptions may include tobacco and alcohol. You are permitted to ship goods except tobacco and alcohol home under the CDN$500 exemption as long as you declare them when you arrive. Goods under the CDN$200 exemption, as well as all alcohol and tobacco, must be in your hand or checked luggage. Citizens of legal age (which varies by province) may import in-person up to 200 cigarettes, 50 cigars or cigarillos, 200g loose tobacco, 1.14L wine or alcohol, and 24 355mL cans/ bottles of beer; the value of these products is included in the CDN$200 or CDN$500. For more information, write Canadian Customs, 2265 St. Laurent Blvd., Ottawa, Ontario K1G 4K3 (tel. (613) 993-0534), phone the 24-hr. Automated Customs Information Service at (800) 461-9999, or visit Revenue Canada at http://www.revcan.ca.

Ireland Citizens must declare everything in excess of IR£142 (IR£73 per traveler under 15 years of age) obtained outside the EU or duty- and tax-free in the EU above the following allowances: 200 cigarettes, 100 cigarillos, 50 cigars, or 250g tobacco; 1L liquor or 2L wine; 2L still wine; 50mL perfume; and 250mL toilet water. Goods obtained duty- and tax-paid in another EU country up to a value of IR£460 (IR£115 per traveler under 15) will not be subject to additional customs duties. Travelers under 17 may not import tobacco or alcohol. For more information, contact The Revenue Commissioners, Dublin Castle (tel. (01) 679 27 77; fax 671 20 21; email taxes@iol.ie; http://www.revenue.ie) or The Collector of Customs and Excise, The Custom House, Dublin 1.

New Zealand Citizens may import up to NZ$700 worth of goods duty-free if they are intended for personal use or are unsolicited gifts. The concession is 200 cigarettes (1 carton) or 250g tobacco or 50 cigars or a combination of all 3 not to exceed 250g. You may also bring in 4.5L of beer or wine and 1.125L of liquor. Only travelers over 17 may import tobacco or alcohol. For more information, contact New Zealand Customs, 50 Anzac Ave., Box 29, Auckland (tel. (09) 377 35 20; fax 309 29 78).

South Africa Citizens may import duty-free: 400 cigarettes, 50 cigars, 250g tobacco, 2L wine, 1L of spirits, 250mL toilet water, and 50mL perfume, and other consumable items up to a value of SAR500. Goods up to a value of SAR10,000 over and above this duty-free allowance are dutiable at 20%; such goods are also exempted from payment of VAT. Items acquired abroad and sent to the Republic as unaccompanied baggage do not qualify for any allowances. You may not export or import South African bank notes in excess of SAR25000. Free pamphlet *South African Customs Information,* available in airports or from the Commissioner for Customs and Excise, Private Bag X47, Pretoria 0001 (tel. (12) 314 99 11; fax 328 64 78) is helpful.

United Kingdom Citizens or visitors arriving in the U.K. from outside the EU must declare goods in excess of the following allowances: 200 cigarettes or 100 cigarillos or 50 cigars or 250g tobacco; still table wine (2L); strong liqueurs over 22% volume (1L), or fortified or sparkling wine, other liqueurs (2L); perfume (60 cc/mL); toilet water (250 cc/mL); and UK£145 worth of all other goods including gifts and souvenirs. You must be over 17 to import liquor or tobacco. These allowances also apply to duty-free purchases within the EU, except for the last category, other goods, which then has an allowance of UK£75. Goods obtained duty and tax paid for personal use (regulated according to set guide levels) within the EU do not require any further customs duty. More information is available from Her Majesty's Customs and Excise, Custom House, Nettleton Rd., Heathrow Airport, Hounslow, Middlesex TW6 2LA (tel. (0181) 910 3602/3566; fax 910 3765) and on the Web at http://www.open.gov.uk.

United States Citizens may import US$400 worth of accompanying goods duty-free and must pay a 10% tax on the next US$1000. You must declare all purchases, so have sales slips ready. The US$400 personal exemption covers goods purchased for personal or household use (this includes gifts) and cannot include more than 100 cigars, 200 cigarettes (1 carton), and 1L of wine or liquor. You must be over 21 to bring liquor into the U.S. If you mail home personal goods of U.S. origin, you can avoid duty charges by marking the package "American goods returned." For more information, consult the brochure *Know Before You Go,* available from the U.S. Customs Service, Box 7407, Washington, D.C. 20044 (tel. (202) 927-6724), or visit the Web (http://www.customs.ustreas.gov).

YOUTH, STUDENT, AND TEACHER I.D.

The **International Student Identity Card (ISIC)** is the most widely accepted form of student identification. Used properly, this card can procure you discounts for sights, theaters, museums, accommodations, meals, train, ferry, bus, and airplane transportation, and other services. Present the card wherever you go, and ask about discounts even when none are advertised. It also provides insurance benefits, including US$100 per day of in-hospital sickness for a maximum of 60 days, and US$3000 accident-related medical reimbursement for each accident (see **Insurance,** p. 19). In addition, cardholders have access to a toll-free 24-hour ISIC helpline whose multilingual staff can provide assistance in medical, legal, and financial emergencies overseas (tel. (800) 626-2427 in the U.S. and Canada; elsewhere call collect (44) 181 666 9025 or (0181) 666 9025 from the U.K.).

Many student travel agencies around the world issue ISICs, including STA Travel in Australia and New Zealand; Travel CUTS and via the web (http://www.isic-canada.org) in Canada; USIT in Ireland and Northern Ireland; SASTS in South Africa; Campus Travel and STA Travel in the U.K.; Council Travel, Let's Go Travel, STA Travel, and via the web (http://www.ciee.org/idcards/index.htm) in the U.S.; and any of the other organizations under the auspices of the International Student Travel Confederation (ISTC). When you apply for the card, request a copy of the *International Student Identity Card Handbook,* which lists by country some of the available discounts. You can also write to Council for a copy. The card is valid up to 15 months, from the most recent September to December of the following year, and costs US$20, CDN$15 or AUS$15. Applicants must be at least 12 years old and degree-seeking students of a secondary or post-secondary school. Because of the proliferation of phony ISICs, many services require other proof of student identity, such as a signed letter from the registrar attesting to your student status and stamped with the school seal or your actual school ID. The **International Teacher Identity Card (ITIC)** offers the same insurance coverage, and similar but limited discounts. The fee is US$20, UK£5, or AUS$13. For more information on these cards, email the organization or consult their web site (email isicinfo@istc.org; http://www.istc.org).

Federation of International Youth Travel Organizations (FIYTO) issues a discount card to travelers who are under 26 but not students. Known as the **GO25 Card,** this one-year card offers many of the same benefits as the ISIC, and most organizations that sell the ISIC also sell the GO25 Card. A brochure that lists discounts is free when you purchase the card. To apply, you will need a passport, valid driver's license, or copy of a birth certificate; and a passport-sized photo with your name printed on the back. The fee is US$20. Information is available on the web at http://www.ciee.org, or by contacting Travel CUTS in Canada, STA Travel in the U.K., Council Travel in the U.S., or FIYTO headquarters in Denmark (see **Travel Agencies,** p. 29).

DRIVING PERMITS AND CAR INSURANCE

If you plan to drive a car while abroad, you should have an **International Driving Permit (IDP),** though Germany allows travelers with a valid American or Canadian license to drive for one year, with certain stipulations (see **By Car,** p. 42). Most car rental agencies don't require the permit. It may be a good idea to get one anyway, in case you're in a situation (an accident or stranded in a smaller town) where the police do not know English.

Your IDP, valid for one year, must be issued in your own country before you depart. You must be 18 years old and include one or two photos, a current local license, an additional form of identification, and a fee with the application. Once on the road, a valid driver's license from your home country must always accompany the IDP. Australians can obtain an IDP by contacting their local **Royal Automobile Club (RAC),** the **National Royal Motorist Association (NRMA)** if in NSW or the ACT, where a permit can be obtained for AUS$15. An application can be obtained at http://www.rac.com.au, by calling (08) 9421-4271, or faxing 9221-1887. Canadian license holders can obtain an IDP (CDN$10) through any **Canadian Automobile Association (CAA)** branch office in Canada, by writing to CAA, 1145 Hunt Club Rd., Suite 200, K1V 0Y3 Canada. (tel. (613) 247-0117, ext. 2025, fax 247-0118), or on the web at http://www.caa.ca. Irish citizens should drop into their nearest **Automobile Association (AA)** office where an IDP can be picked up for IR£4, or phone (1) 283-3555 (fax 283-3660) for a postal application form. In New Zealand, contact your local **Automobile Association (AA),** or their main office at P.O. Box 5, Auckland (tel. (9) 377-4660; fax 302-2037); procedural information is also available at http://www.nzaa.co.nz. IDPs cost NZ$8, plus NZ$2 for return postage if mailed from abroad. In South Africa visit your local **Automobile Association of South Africa** office, where IDPs can be picked up for SAR28.50, or for more information phone (11) 799 1000, fax 799 1010, or write to P.O. Box 596, 2000 Johannesburg. In the U.K. IDPs are UK£4 and you can either visit your local **AA Shop;** call (01256) 49 39 32 (if abroad, fax (44) (1256) 460 750), or write to AA 5 Star Post Link, Freepost, Copenhagen Court, 8 New St., Basingstroke RG21 7BA, and order a postal application form (allow 2-3 weeks). For further information, call (44) (0990) 44 88 66, or visit http://www.theaa.co.uk/travel. U.S. license holders can obtain an IDP (US$10) at any **American Automobile Association (AAA)** office or by writing to AAA Florida, Travel Agency Services Department, 1000 AAA Dr. (mail stop 28), Heathrow, FL 32746 (tel. (407) 444-4245; fax 444-4247). You do not have to be a member of AAA to receive an IDP.

Most credit cards cover standard **insurance.** If you rent, lease, or borrow a car, you will need a **green card,** or **International Insurance Certificate,** to prove that you have liability insurance. Obtain it through the car rental agency; most include coverage in their prices. If you lease a car, you can obtain a green card from the dealer. Some travel agents offer the card; it may also be available at border crossings. Verify whether your auto insurance applies abroad; even if it does, you will still need a green card to certify this to foreign officials. If you have a collision abroad, the accident will show up on your domestic records if you report it to your insurance company.

■ Money Matters

US$1 = 1.80 Deutschmark (DM)	**1DM= US$0.56**
CDN$1 = 1.16DM	**1DM = CDN$0.86**
AUS$1 = 1.05DM	**1DM = AUS$0.96**
IR£ = 2.51DM	**1DM = IR£0.40**
NZ$1 = 0.89DM	**1DM = NZ$1.13**
SAR1 = 0.28DM	**1DM = SAR3.54**
UK£1 = 2.94DM	**1DM = UK£0.34**

The above exchange rates are from late August 1998. The *Deutsche Mark* or *Deutschmark* (abbreviated DM, occasionally M) is the unit of currency in Germany. It is one of the most stable and respected currencies in the world; indeed, in most markets in Eastern Europe, "hard currency" means U.S. dollars and DM exclusively. One DM equals 100 *Pfennig* (Pf). Coins come in 1, 2, 5, 10, and 50Pf, and DM1, 2, and 5 amounts. Bills come in DM5, 10, 20, 50, 100, 200, 500, and 1000 denominations. Although some (especially Americans) may think of minted metal disks as inconsequential pieces of aluminum, remember that a DM5 coin can easily buy you a meal. To make sure you're not getting duped, accept only those bills that contain embedded silver strips. Old East German currency lost all but sentimental value in July 1990.

CURRENCY AND EXCHANGE

If you stay in hostels and prepare your own food, expect to spend anywhere from US$20-30 per person daily in Germany. Transportation will increase these figures. Don't sacrifice your health or safety for a cheaper tab. If you plan to travel for more than a couple of days, you will need to keep handy a larger amount of cash than usual. Carrying money around with you, even in a money belt, is risky but necessary. Personal checks from home will probably not be acceptable no matter how many forms of identification you have, and even traveler's checks may not be acceptable in some locations. Members can cash personal checks at AmEx offices worldwide.

It is cheaper to buy domestic currency than to buy foreign, so as a rule you should convert money after arriving in Germany. However, converting some money before you go will allow you to zip through the airport while others languish in exchange lines. It's a good idea to carry enough *Deutschmarks* to last for the first 24 to 72 hours of a trip to avoid getting stuck with no money after banking hours or on a holiday. Travelers living in the U.S. can get foreign currency from the comfort of home; contact **Capital Foreign Exchange** on the East Coast (toll-free (888) 842-0880; fax (202) 842-8008), or on the West Coast, **International Currency Express** (toll-free (888) 278-6628; fax (310) 278-6410). They will deliver foreign currency (for over 120 countries) or traveler's checks (see **Traveler's Checks,** below) overnight (US$15) or second-day (US$12) at competitive exchange rates.

Watch out for commission rates and check newspapers to get the standard rate of exchange. Banks generally have the best rates, although sometimes tourist offices or exchange kiosks are decent. Stick to banks or bureaux de change that have only a 5% margin between their buy and sell prices. Be sure that both prices are listed. Since you lose money with every transaction, convert in large sums, but don't convert more than you need since it also costs money to change it back to your home currency, or to a new one.

If you are using traveler's checks or bills, be sure to carry some in small denominations (US$50 or less), especially for times when you are forced to exchange money at disadvantageous rates. However, it is a good idea to carry a range of denominations since charges may be levied per check cashed, depending on location.

TRAVELER'S CHECKS

Traveler's checks are one of the safest and least troublesome means of carrying funds, as they can be refunded if stolen. Several agencies and many banks sell them, usually for face value plus a small percentage commission. (Members of the American Automobile Association, and some banks and credit unions, can get American Express checks commission-free; see **Driving Permits and Car Insurance,** p. 10). **American Express** and **Visa** are the most widely recognized, though other major checks are sold, exchanged, cashed, and refunded almost as easily. In small towns, traveler's checks are less readily accepted than in cities with large tourist industries. Still, there will probably be at least one place in every town where you can exchange them for local currency. Try to order early, especially for large requests.

Each agency provides refunds **if your checks are lost or stolen,** and many provide additional services. (You may need a police report verifying the loss or theft.) Ask about toll-free refund hotlines (in the countries you're visiting), emergency message services, and stolen credit card assistance when you buy your checks.

Expect some red tape and delay if traveler's checks are lost or stolen. For a speedy refund, keep your check receipts separate from your checks and store them in a safe place or with a traveling companion, record check numbers when you cash them and leave a list of check numbers with someone at home, also ask for a list of refund centers when you buy your checks (American Express and Bank of America have over 40,000 centers worldwide). Keep a separate supply of cash or traveler's checks for emergencies. Never countersign your checks until you are ready to cash them, and always bring your passport with you when you plan to use the checks.

Buying traveler's checks in the currency of the country you're visiting can be either wise or futile. In some countries (the U.S., for example) checks are accepted as readily as cash; in others, Germany included, they are only beginning to gain acceptance. Depending on fluctuations in currency, you may gain or lose money by converting your currency beforehand.

American Express: Call (800) 25 19 02 in Australia; in New Zealand (0800) 44 10 68; in the U.K. (0800) 52 13 13; in the U.S. and Canada (800) 221-7282). Elsewhere, call U.S. collect (801) 964-6665. American Express traveler's checks are now available in 10 currencies, including Deutschmarks. They are the most widely recognized worldwide and the easiest to replace if lost or stolen. Checks can be purchased for a small fee (1-4%) at American Express Travel Service Offices, banks, and American Automobile Association offices (AAA members can buy the checks commission-free). Cardmembers can also buy checks at American Express Dispensers at Travel Service Offices at airports, or order them by phone (tel. (800) ORDER-TC (673-3782)). American Express offices cash their checks commission-free, although they often offer slightly worse rates than banks. You can also buy *Cheques for Two* which can be signed by either of two people travelling together. Request the American Express booklet "Traveler's Companion," which lists travel office addresses and stolen check hotlines for Europe. Visit their online travel office (http://www.aexp.com).

Citicorp: Call (800) 645-6556 in the U.S. and Canada; in Europe, the Middle East, or Africa (44) 171 508 7007; from elsewhere call U.S. collect (813) 623-1709. Sells both Citicorp and Citicorp Visa traveler's checks in U.S., Australian, and Canadian, British, German, Spanish, and Japanese currencies. Commission is 1-2% on check purchases. Citicorp's World Courier Service guarantees hand-delivery of traveler's checks when a refund location is not convenient. Call 24hr. a day, 7 days a week.

Thomas Cook MasterCard: For 24-hr. cashing or refund assistance: from the U.S., Canada or Caribbean call (800) 223-7373; from the U.K. call (0800) 622 101 toll-free or (01733) 318 950 collect; from anywhere else call (44) 1733 318 950 collect. Offers checks in German marks and ECUs. Commission 2% for purchases. Thomas Cook offices will cash checks commission-free; banks will make a commission charge. Thomas Cook MasterCard Traveler's Checks are also available from **Capital Foreign Exchange** (see **Currency and Exchange,** p. 11) in German marks.

Visa: Call (800) 227-6811 in the U.S.; in the U.K. (0800) 895 078; from anywhere else in the world call (44) (1733) 318 949 and reverse the charges. Any of the above numbers can tell you the location of their nearest office. Any type of Visa traveler's checks can be reported lost at the Visa number.

CREDIT CARDS

Credit cards are not always useful to the budget traveler in Germany, as many establishments will not accept them, although pricey establishments accept them all too willingly. Still, major credit cards—**MasterCard** and **Visa** are the most welcomed— can be used to extract *Deutschmarks* from associated banks and teller machines throughout Germany. Credit card companies get the wholesale exchange rate, which is generally 5% better than the retail rate used by banks and even better than that used by other currency exchange establishments. You will be charged ruinous interest rates if you don't pay off the bill quickly, so be careful when using this service. **American Express** cards also work in some ATMs, as well as at AmEx offices and major airports. All such machines require a **Personal Identification Number (PIN),** which credit cards in the United States do not usually carry. Ask your credit card company for a PIN before you leave; without it, you will be unable to withdraw cash with your credit card outside the U.S. MasterCard and Visa have different names elsewhere ("EuroCard" or "Access" for MasterCard, "Carte Bleue" or "Barclaycard" for Visa).

Credit cards are also invaluable in an emergency—an unexpected hospital bill or ticket home or the loss of traveler's checks—that may leave you temporarily without other resources. Furthermore, credit cards offer an array of other services, from insurance to emergency assistance, that depend completely on the issuer.

American Express (tel. (800) 843-2273) has a US$55 annual fee but offers a number of helpful services. AmEx cardholders can cash personal checks at AmEx offices outside the U.S., and Global Assist, a 24-hr. hotline with medical and legal assistance in emergencies, is also available (tel. (800) 554-2639 in U.S. and Canada; from abroad call U.S. collect (202) 554-2639). Cardholders can use the American Express Travel Service; benefits include assistance in changing airline, hotel, and car rental reservations, baggage loss and flight insurance, sending mailgrams and international cables, and holding your mail at one of the more than 1700 American Express offices around the world.

CASH CARDS

Cash cards—popularly called **ATM** (Automated Teller Machine) cards—are widespread in Germany (including Eastern Germany). Depending on the system that your bank at home uses, you can probably access your own personal bank account whenever you need money. Look at the back of your ATM card for symbols of compatible networks. Happily, ATMs get the same wholesale exchange rate as credit cards. Despite these perks, do some research before relying too heavily on automation. There is often a limit on the amount of money you can withdraw per day (usually about US$500, depending on the type of card and account), and computer networks sometimes fail. Memorize your PIN code in numeric form since machines outside the U.S. and Canada often don't have letters on their keys. Also, if your PIN is longer than four digits, ask your bank whether the first four digits will work, or whether you need a new number.

The two major international money networks are **Cirrus** (U.S. tel. (800) 4-CIRRUS (424-7787)) and **PLUS** (U.S. tel. (800) 843-7587 for the "Voice Response Unit Locator"). Cirrus has cash machines in 80 countries and territories. It charges US$3-5 to withdraw non-domestically depending on your bank. PLUS covers 115 countries. Carrying one card for each network will provide maximum coverage. To find locations of ATMs around the world, go to http://www.mastercard.com/atm.

GETTING MONEY FROM HOME

One way to get money from home is to bring an **American Express** card. AmEx allows its cardholders to draw cash from their checking accounts at any of its major offices and many of its representatives' offices, up to US$1000 every 21 days (no service charge, no interest). Avoid cashing checks in foreign currencies; they usually take weeks and a US$30 fee to clear. Money can also be wired abroad through international money transfer services operated by **Western Union** (tel. (800) 325-6000). The rates for sending cash are generally US$10-11 cheaper than with a credit card, and the money is usually available in the country you're sending it to within an hour, although this may vary.

Some people choose to send money abroad in cash via **Federal Express** to avoid transmission fees and taxes. FedEx is reasonably reliable; however, this method may be illegal, involves an element of risk, and requires that you remain at a legitimate address for a day or two to wait for the money's arrival. In general, it may be safer to swallow the cost of wire transmission and preserve your peace of mind.

In emergencies, U.S. citizens can have money sent via the State Department's **Overseas Citizens Service, American Citizens Services,** Consular Affairs, Room 4811, U.S. Department of State, Washington, D.C. 20520 (tel. (202) 647-5225; nights, Sundays, and holidays 647-4000; fax (on demand only) 647-3000; http://travel.state.gov on the web; email ca@his.com). For a fee of US$15, the State Department will forward money within hours to the nearest consular office, which will disburse it according to instructions. The office serves only Americans in the direst of straits abroad; non-American travelers should contact their embassies for information on wiring cash.

TAXES

For large purchases, you may be eligible for a refund of **VAT** (Germany's 15% Value-Added Tax). Acquire a Tax Free Shopping Check at the time of purchase and consult German customs when leaving the country (and before checking the goods). You may also obtain a stamp on your VAT refund form at a German embassy or consulate in your home country, but only if there is no possibility for doing so when leaving Germany—you must present the items, sales slips, and your passport. Upon returning home, you must declare all articles you acquired abroad and pay a duty on the value of those articles that exceed the allowance established by your country's customs service.

TIPPING AND BARGAINING

Germans generally round up to the nearest *Mark* when tipping. However, tipping is not practiced as liberally as it is elsewhere—most Germans only tip in restaurants and beer halls, or when they are the beneficiary of a service, such as a taxi ride. It is common to tip as much as 5-10% in fancier restaurants, especially if the service is exceptional. Note that tips in Germany are not left lying on the table, but handed directly to the server. If you don't want any change, say *"Das stimmt so."* As a rule, Germans never bargain, and posted prices are not negotiable.

■ Safety and Security

PERSONAL SAFETY

Tourists are particularly vulnerable to crime for two reasons: they often carry large amounts of cash and they are not as street savvy as locals. To prevent easy theft, don't keep all of your valuables (money, important documents) in one place. Respecting local customs (in many cases, dressing more conservatively) may placate would-be hecklers. Familiarize yourself with your surroundings before setting out; if you must check a map on the streets, duck into a cafe or shop.

When exploring a new city, extra vigilance is wise but there is no need for panic. Find out about unsafe areas from tourist information, from the manager of your hotel or hostel, or from a local whom you trust. You may want to carry a **whistle** to scare off attackers or attract attention. Especially if you are traveling alone, be sure that someone at home knows your itinerary and **never admit that you're traveling alone**. When walking at night, stick to busy, well-lit streets and avoid dark alleyways. Do not attempt to cross through parks, parking lots, or other large, deserted areas. A blissfully isolated beach can become a treacherous nightmare as night falls. Memorize the emergency number of the city or area—the number to contact the **police** in Germany is generally **110**.

> **Safety Warning!** Violent crime is less common in Germany than in most countries, but it exists, especially in big cities like Frankfurt and Berlin, as well as economically depressed regions of the east. Most of Germany's neo-Nazis and skinheads subscribe to the traditional skinhead uniform of flight jackets worn over white shortsleeve shirts and tight jeans rolled up high to reveal high-cut combat boots. Skinheads also tend to follow a **shoelace code**, with white supremacists and neo-Nazis wearing white laces while anti-gay skinheads wear pink laces. Left-wing, anti-Nazi "S.H.A.R.P.s" (Skinheads Against Racial Prejudice) also exist; they favor red laces.

Whenever possible, *Let's Go* warns of unsafe neighborhoods and areas, but you should exercise your own judgment and intuition about the safety of your environs. Buildings in disrepair, vacant lots, and unpopulated areas are all bad signs. The distribution of people can reveal a great deal about the relative safety of the area; look for children playing, women walking in the open, and other signs of an active community. Keep in mind that a district can change character drastically between blocks. If you feel uncomfortable, leave as quickly and directly as you can, but don't allow fear of the unknown to turn you into a hermit.

If you are using a **car**, learn local driving signals. Motor vehicle crashes are a leading cause of travel deaths in many parts of the world. Wearing a seatbelt is law in Germany. Children under 40 lbs. (18kg) should ride only in a specially-designed carseat, available for a small fee from most car rental agencies. Study route maps before you hit the road; some roads have poor (or nonexistent) shoulders, few gas stations, and roaming animals. If you plan on spending a lot of time on the road, you may want to bring spare parts. Be sure to park your vehicle in a garage or well-traveled area.

Sleeping in your car is one of the most dangerous (and often illegal) ways to get your rest. If your car breaks down, wait for the police to assist you. If you must sleep in your car, do so as close to a police station or a 24-hour service station as possible. Sleeping out in the open can be even more dangerous—camping is recommended only in official, supervised campsites or in wilderness backcountry.

Let's Go does not recommend hitchhiking under any circumstances, especially for women—see **Getting There,** p. 45 for more information.

There is no sure-fire set of precautions that will protect you from all of the situations you might encounter when you travel. A good self-defense course will give you more concrete ways to react to different types of aggression. **Impact, Prepare,** and **Model Mugging** can refer you to local self-defense courses in the United States (tel. (800) 345-5425), Vancouver, Canada (tel. (604) 878-3838), and Zurich, Switzerland (tel. (41) (1) 261 2423). Workshop and course prices range from US$50-500. Women's and men's courses are offered.

FINANCIAL SECURITY

Among the more colorful aspects of large cities are **con artists.** Con artists and hustlers often work in groups, and children are among the most effective. They possess an innumerable range of ruses. Be aware of certain classics: sob stories that require money, rolls of bills "found" on the street, mustard spilled (or saliva spit) onto your shoulder distracting you for enough time to snatch your bag. Be especially suspicious in unexpected situations. Do not respond or make eye contact, walk quickly away, and keep a solid grip on your belongings. Contact the police if a hustler is particularly insistent or aggressive.

Don't put a wallet with money in your back pocket. Never count your money in public and carry as little as possible. If you carry a purse, buy a sturdy one with a secure clasp, and carry it crosswise on the side, away from the street with the clasp against you. Secure packs with small combination padlocks which slip through the two zippers. (Even these precautions do not always suffice: moped riders who snatch purses and backpacks sometimes tote knives to cut the straps). A **money belt** is the best way to carry cash; you can buy one at most camping supply stores or through the Forsyth Travel Library (see **Useful Publications,** p. 3). A nylon, zippered pouch with belt that sits inside the waist of your pants or skirt combines convenience and security. A **neck pouch** is equally safe, although far less accessible. Refrain from pulling out your neck pouch in public; if you must, be very discreet. Avoid keeping anything precious in a large waist-pack (even if it's worn on your stomach): your valuables will be highly visible and easy to steal.

In city crowds and especially on public transportation, pick-pockets are amazingly deft. If someone stands uncomfortably close to you on the U-Bahn, move to another car and hold your bags tightly. Also, be alert in public telephone booths. If you must say your calling card number, do so very quietly; if you punch it in, make sure no one can look over your shoulder. **Photocopies** of important documents allow you to recover them in case they are lost or filched. Carry one copy separate from the documents and leave another copy at home. Keep some money separate from the rest to use in an emergency. Label every piece of luggage both inside and out.

Be particularly careful on **buses** and **trains.** Carry your backpack in front of you where you can see it, don't check baggage on trains, and don't trust anyone to "watch your bag for a second." Thieves thrive on trains; professionals wait for tourists to fall asleep and then carry off everything they can. When traveling in pairs, sleep in alternating shifts; when alone, use good judgment in selecting a train compartment: never stay in an empty one, and use a lock to secure your pack to the luggage rack. Keep important documents and other valuables on your person and try to sleep on top bunks with your luggage stored above you (if not in bed with you).

Never leave your belongings unattended; crime occurs in even the most demure-looking hostel or hotel. If you feel unsafe, look for places with either a curfew or a night attendant. *Let's Go* lists locker availability in hostels and train stations, but you'll need your own padlock. Lockers are useful if you plan on sleeping outdoors or don't want to lug everything with you, but don't store valuables in them. When possible, keep anything you couldn't bear to lose at home.

If you travel by **car,** try not to leave valuable possessions—such as radios or luggage—in it while you are away. If your tape deck or radio is removable, hide it in the trunk or take it with you. If it isn't, at least conceal it under something else. Similarly, hide baggage in the trunk.

Travel Assistance International by Worldwide Assistance Services, Inc. offers year-long frequent traveler packages (see **Insurance,** p. 19). The **American Society of Travel Agents** provides extensive informational resources, both at their web site (http://www.astanet.com) and in their free brochure, *Travel Safety.* You can obtain a copy by sending a request and self-addressed, stamped envelope to them at 1101 King St., Suite 200, Alexandria, VA 22314.

DRUGS AND ALCOHOL

Avoid **public drunkenness;** it can jeopardize your safety and earn the disdain of locals. The drinking age in Germany is 16 for beer and wine and 18 for spirits, although it is skimpily enforced. The maximum permissible blood alcohol level while driving in Germany is less than 0.08%.

Needless to say, **illegal drugs** are best avoided altogether; the average sentence for possession outside the U.S. is about seven years. Buying or selling narcotics may lead to a prison sentence. Familiarize yourself with Germany's laws as you are subject to these laws and not to those of your home country. In 1994, the German High Court ruled that while possession of marijuana or hashish was still illegal, possession of "small quantities for personal consumption" was not prosecutable. Each *Land* has interpreted the quantities involved in "personal consumption" differently, with possession of 3 to 30 grams *de facto* decriminalized at the time at which this book was written. The more liberal states, notably Berlin and Hamburg, tend toward the higher end of this spectrum, while the more conservative states of Bayern and the former East afford less leniency. Those interested should find out what the latest law is, including what quantities of possession are acceptable in the various *Länder,* before filling a backpack with hash bricks.

The worst thing you can possibly do is carry drugs across an international border; not only could you end up in prison, you could be blessed with a "Drug Trafficker" stamp on your passport for the rest of your life. If arrested, call your country's consulate. Embassies may not be willing to help those arrested on drug charges. Make sure you get a statement and prescription from your doctor if you'll be carrying insulin, syringes, or any other **prescription drugs.** Refuse to carry even an apparent nun's excess luggage onto a plane; you're more likely to wind up in jail for possession of drugs than in heaven.

▦ Health

Common sense is the simplest prescription for good health while you travel: Mother *Let's Go* says to eat well and drink and sleep enough. Drinking lots of fluids can often prevent dehydration and constipation, and wearing sturdy shoes and clean socks, as well as using talcum powder, can help keep your feet dry and comfortable. To minimize the effects of jet lag, "reset" your body's clock by adopting the time of your destination while still on the plane. Time zone adjustment is usually two to three days.

BEFORE YOU GO

Although no amount of planning can guarantee an accident-free trip, preparation can help minimize the likelihood of contracting a disease and maximize the chances of receiving effective health-care in the event of an emergency.

For minor health problems, bring a compact first-aid kit, including bandages, aspirin or other pain killer, antibiotic cream, a thermometer, a Swiss Army knife with tweezers, moleskin, a decongestant for colds, motion sickness remedy, medicine for diarrhea or stomach problems, sunscreen, insect repellent, and burn ointment.

In your passport, write the names of any people you wish to be contacted in case of a medical emergency, and also list any allergies or medical conditions you would want doctors to be aware of. If you wear glasses or contact lenses, carry an extra prescription and pair of glasses or arrange to have your doctor or a family member send a replacement pair in an emergency. Allergy sufferers should find out if their conditions are likely to be aggravated in the regions they plan to visit, and obtain a full supply of any necessary medication before the trip, since matching a prescription to a foreign equivalent is not always easy, safe, or possible. To get a prescription filled in Germany you must go to an *Apotheke;* a *Drogerie* sells only toilet articles. Most German cities have a rotating all-night pharmacy schedule to ensure that services are available 24 hours a day. Check the **Practical Information** section for each particular city for the location of the major pharmacy. In dire straits, check the front door of the *Apotheke* nearest a city's train station for a schedule of rotating all-night pharmacies. Carry up-to-date, legible prescriptions or a statement from your doctor, especially if you use insulin, a syringe, or a narcotic. While traveling, be sure to keep all medication with you in your carry-on luggage.

Currently, Germany has no vaccination requirements for foreigners entering the country. The following organizations will provide information on more general health concerns: The **United States Centers for Disease Control and Prevention,** an excellent source of information for travelers around the world, maintains an international fax information service for travelers. Call 1 (888) 232-3299 and select an international travel directory; the requested information will be faxed to you. Similar information is available from the CDC website at http://www.cdc.gov. The **United States State Department** compiles Consular Information Sheets on health, entry requirements, and other issues for all countries of the world. Particularly helpful is the website at http://travel.state.gov. For quick information on travel warnings, call the **Overseas Citizens' Services** (tel. (202) 647-5225).

Diabetics can contact the **American Diabetes Association,** 1660 Duke St., Alexandria, VA 22314 (tel. (800) 232-3472) to receive copies of the article "Travel and Diabetes" and a diabetic ID card, which carries messages in 18 languages explaining the carrier's diabetic status. For more general health information, contact the **American Red Cross.** The ARC publishes a First-Aid and Safety Handbook (US$5) available for purchase by calling or writing to the American Red Cross, 285 Columbus Ave., Boston, MA 02116-5114 (tel. (800) 564-1234; M-F 8:30am-4:30pm).

Medical care is readily available in Germany, but if you are concerned about being able to access medical support or English-speaking doctors while traveling, consider **Global Emergency Medical Services (GEMS).** GEMS has a product called *MedPass,* which provides 24-hour international medical assistance and support coordinated through registered nurses who have online access to your medical information, your primary physician, and a worldwide network of screened, credentialed English-speaking doctors and hospitals. Subscribers also receive a personal medical record that contains vital information in case of emergencies. For more information call (800) 860-1111 (8:30am-5:30pm); fax (770) 475-0058; or write: 2001 Westside Dr., #120, Alpharetta, GA 30201.

HOT AND COLD

To prevent **heat exhaustion,** drink lots of non-alcoholic fluids and lie down indoors if you feel awful. Continuous heat stress can eventually lead to **heatstroke,** characterized by rising body temperature, a severe headache, and cessation of sweating. Wear a hat, sunglasses, and a lightweight longsleeved shirt to avoid heatstroke. Sufferers should be cooled off with wet towels and taken to a doctor as soon as possible.

Always drink enough liquids to keep your urine clear. Alcoholic beverages are dehydrating, as are coffee, strong tea, and caffeinated sodas. If you'll be sweating a lot, be sure to eat enough salty food to prevent electrolyte depletion, which causes severe headaches. Less debilitating, but still dangerous, is **sunburn**. If you're prone to sunburn, bring sunscreen with you and apply it liberally and often to avoid burns and risk of skin cancer. If you get sunburned, drink more fluids than usual.

Travelers to **high altitudes** must allow their bodies a couple of days to adjust to lower oxygen levels in the air before exerting themselves. Also be careful about alcohol, especially if you're used to U.S. standards for beer—German brews and liquors tend to pack more punch than a smooth, cold Colt 45, and at high altitudes where the air has less oxygen, any alcohol will do you in quickly.

SEXUAL CONCERNS

Women on the pill should bring enough medicine to allow for possible loss or extended stays. Bring a prescription, since forms of the pill vary a good deal. The sponge is probably too bulky to be worthwhile on the road. Women who use a diaphragm should have enough contraceptive jelly on hand. Condoms *(Kondom)* are widely available in Germany; however, you might want to bring a supply of your favorite national brand. Health professionals recommend the use of latex condoms to prevent HIV transmission. If you are HIV-positive, call (202) 647-1488 for country-specific entry requirements or write to the Bureau of Consular Affairs, #6831, Department of State, Washington, D.C. 20520. **Bayern** requires foreigners seeking a residency permit for more than six months to be HIV-negative, and they do not accept the results of tests taken abroad. For more information on AIDS, call the **U.S. Centers for Disease Control and Prevention's** 24-hour hotline at (800) 342-2437. In Europe, write to the **World Health Organization**, attn: Global Program on AIDS, Avenue Appia 20, 1211 Geneva 27, Switzerland (tel. (41) (22) 791 21 11, fax 79 10 74 60) for statistical material on AIDS internationally. Or write to the **Bureau of Consular Affairs**, #6831, Department of State, Washington, D.C. 20520. Council's brochure, *Travel Safe: AIDS and International Travel,* is available at all Council Travel offices.

Women overseas who want an **abortion** should contact the **National Abortion Federation Hotline** (tel. (800) 772-9100; M-F 9·30am-12:30pm and 1:30-5:30pm), 1775 Massachusetts Ave. NW, Washington, D.C. 20036. **Abortion** is a complicated legal issue in Germany. It is only available within the first trimester, and not on demand; a woman must indicate a reason, and only certain reasons are accepted. In practice, the restrictions simply necessitate a search for a willing doctor. In 1995, new legislation considerably eased legal barriers to abortion in most of the country. Still, if you find yourself with an unwanted pregnancy in Germany and choose to seek an abortion, be aware of the bureaucracy involved, which is stricter in certain states (notably Bayern) than in others (the northwestern *Länder*). You must consult an officially authorized office (*Schwangerschaftsberatungsstelle*) at least three days before an abortion, as proof of this consultation is essential for the abortion. The German word for abortion is *Abtreibung;* the word for abortion rights is *Abtreibungsrecht.* The "morning after" pill *(das Pille für den Morgen danach)* is available in Germany, but the *Abtreibungspille* (RU486; the French "abortion pill") is not.

■ Insurance

Travel insurance generally covers four basic areas: medical/health problems, property loss, trip cancellation/interruption, and emergency evacuation. Beware of unnecessary travel coverage—your regular insurance policies may well extend to travel-related medical problems and property loss. Additional property coverage may be unnecessary unless you are traveling with items of great value. However, you may consider purchasing travel insurance, especially if the cost of potential trip cancellation/interruption or emergency medical evacuation is greater than you can absorb.

Medical insurance (especially university policies) often covers costs incurred abroad, check with your provider. **Medicare's** very limited "foreign travel" coverage for Americans is valid only in Canada and Mexico. Canadians should check with the provincial Ministry of Health or Health Plan Headquarters for details about extent of coverage. Australia has Reciprocal Health Care Agreements (RHCAs) with several countries; Germany is not one of them. The Commonwealth Department of Health and Family Services can provide more information. Your **homeowners' insurance** (or your family's coverage) often covers theft during travel. Homeowners are generally covered against loss of travel documents (passport, plane ticket, railpass, etc.) up to US$500.

ISIC and **ITIC** provide basic insurance benefits, including US$100 per day of in-hospital sickness for a maximum of 60 days, and US$3000 of accident-related medical reimbursement (see **Youth, Student, and Teacher Identification,** p. 9). Cardholders have access to a toll-free 24-hour helpline whose multilingual staff can provide assistance in medical, legal, and financial emergencies overseas (tel. (800) 626-2427 in the U.S. and Canada; elsewhere call the U.S. collect (713) 267-2525). Most **American Express** cardholders receive automatic car rental (collision and theft, but not liability) insurance.

Insurance companies usually require a copy of the police report for thefts, or evidence of having paid medical expenses (doctor's statements, receipts) before they will honor a claim, and may have time limits on filing for reimbursement. Always carry policy numbers and proof of insurance. Check with each insurance carrier for specific restrictions and policies. Most of the carriers listed below have 24-hour hotlines.

Access America, 6600 West Broad St., P.O. Box 11188, Richmond, VA 23230 (tel. (800) 284-8300; fax (804) 673-1491). Covers trip cancellation/interruption, on-the-spot hospital admittance costs, emergency medical evacuation, sickness, and baggage loss. 24hr. hotline (if abroad, call the hotline collect at (804) 673-1159 or (800) 654-1908).

Avi International, 30 Rue de Mogador, 75009 Paris, France (tel. 33 (0) 1 44 63 51 86; fax 33 (0) 1 40 82 90 35). Caters primarily to the international youth traveler, covering emergency travel expenses, medical/accident, dental, liability, and baggage loss. 24-hr. hotline.

Globalcare Travel Insurance, 220 Broadway, Lynnfield, MA 01940 (tel. (800) 821-2488; fax (617) 592-7720); email global@nebc.mv.com; http://nebc.mv.com/glo balcare. Complete medical, legal, emergency, and travel-related services. On-the-spot payments and special student programs, including benefits for trip cancellation and interruption. GTI waives pre-existing medical conditions, and provides coverage for the bankruptcy or default of cruise lines, airlines, or tour operators. Also included at no extra charge is a Worldwide Collision Damage Provision.

■ Alternatives to Tourism

STUDY

Foreign study programs vary tremendously in expense, academic quality, living conditions, degree of contact with local students, and exposure to culture and language. There is a plethora of exchange programs for high school students. Most American undergraduates enroll in programs sponsored by U.S. universities, and many colleges staff offices that give advice and information on study abroad. Ask for the names of recent participants in the programs, and get in touch with them. Even basic language skills might be sufficient to allow direct enrollment in German universities, which are far cheaper than those in North America (and vastly less expensive than a study abroad program).

Council sponsors over 40 study abroad programs throughout the world. Contact them for more information (see **Travel Organizations,** p. 2).

Deutscher Akademischer Austauschdienst (DAAD), 950 3rd Ave., 19th Fl., New York NY 10022 (tel. (212) 758-3223; email daadny@daad.org; http://www.daad.org); in Germany, Kennedyallee 50, 53175 Bonn. Information on language instruction, exchanges, and the wealth of scholarships for study in Germany. The place to contact if you want to enroll in a German university; distributes applications and the valuable *Academic Study in the Federal Republic of Germany.*

Experiment in International Living, Summer Programs, Kipling Rd., P.O. Box 676, Brattleboro, VT 05302 (tel. (800) 345-2929; fax (802) 258-3428; email eil@worldlearning.org; http://www.worldlearning.org). Founded in 1932, it offers cross-cultural, educational homestays, community service, ecological adventure, and language training in Europe. Programs are 3-5 weeks long.

Goethe-Institut, Helene-Weber-Allee 1, 80637 München (tel. (089) 15 92 10; fax 15 92 14 50; mailing address Postfach 190419, 80604 München; email zv@goethe.de; http://www.goethe.de), runs numerous language programs in Germany and abroad; it also orchestrates high school exchange programs in Germany. For information on these programs and on their many cultural offerings, contact your local branch (**Australia,** Canberra City, Melbourne, Sydney; **Canada,** Montreal, Toronto, Vancouver; **Ireland,** Dublin; **New Zealand,** Wellington; **U.K.,** Glasgow, London, Manchester, York; **U.S.,** New York, Washington, D.C., Boston, Atlanta, San Francisco, Los Angeles, Seattle) or write to the main office.

Peterson's, P.O. Box 2123, Princeton, NJ 08543-2123 (tel. (800) 338-3282; fax (609) 243-9150; http://www.petersons.com). Their comprehensive *Study Abroad* annual guide lists programs in countries worldwide and provides essential information on the study abroad experience in general. Purchase a copy at your local bookstore (US$27) or call their toll-free number in the U.S. 20% off the list price when you order through their online bookstore, http://bookstore.petersons.com.

WORK AND VOLUNTEER

There's no better way to submerge yourself in a foreign culture than to become part of its economy. It's easy to find a **temporary job,** but it will rarely be glamorous and may not even pay for your plane fare. Officially, you can hold a job in Germany only with a **work permit.** Your employer must obtain this document, usually by demonstrating that you have skills that locals lack—not the easiest of tasks. There are, however, ways to make it easier. Be an au pair; advertise to teach English. Many permitless agricultural workers reportedly go untroubled by local authorities. European Union citizens can work in any EU country, and if your parents were born in an EU country, you may be able to claim dual citizenship or at least the right to a work permit. (Beware of Germany's obligatory military or public service duty.) Students should check with their university's foreign language departments, which may have connections to job openings abroad.

If you are a full-time student at a U.S. university, the simplest way to get a job abroad is through work permit programs run by **Council on International Educational Exchange (Council)** and its member organizations. For a US$225 application fee, Council can procure three- to six-month work permits (and a handbook to help you find work and housing) for Germany. Positions require evidence of language skill. Contact Council for more information (see **Study,** p. 21). Vacation Work Publications publishes *Work Your Way Around the World* (UK£11, UK£2.50 postage, UK£1.50 within U.K) to help you (see below).

With unemployment rising, Germany's days as a mecca for unskilled foreign workers are over. The German government maintains a series of federally run employment offices, the **Bundesanstalt für Arbeit,** throughout the country. Foreign applications are directed to the central office at Feuerbachstr. 42-6, 60325 Frankfurt am Main. The office tends to treat EU citizens with specific skills more favorably than those from other countries. The youth division is a bit more welcoming for foreign students ages 18-30 seeking summer employment; jobs frequently involve manual labor.

The best tips on jobs for foreigners often come from other travelers, so be alert and inquisitive. Some follow the grape harvest in the fall—mostly in France, but also in Germany's Mosel Valley. Menial jobs can be found anywhere in Europe; ski resorts leave much of the gruntwork to foreigners. Ask at pubs, cafes, restaurants, and hotels. Be sure to be aware of your rights as an employee; should a crafty national try to refuse payment at the end of the season, it'll help if you have a written confirmation of your agreement. Youth hostels often provide room and board to travelers willing to stay a while and help run the place. Consider a job **teaching English.** Post a sign in markets or learning centers stating that you are a native speaker, and scan the classifieds of local newspapers. It may be your only option in eastern Germany. Organizations in the U.S. will place you in a (low-paying) teaching job; professional positions are harder to get. Most European schools require at least a bachelor's degree and training in teaching English as a foreign language. In addition to those resources listed below, **Transitions Abroad** (see p. 3) is a fantastic publisher of books and magazines, offering information on all aspects of studying, working, and living abroad.

Surrey Books, 230 E. Ohio St., Chicago, IL 60611 (tel. (800) 326-4430; fax (312) 751-7330; email SurreyBk@aol.com, http://www.surreybooks.com) publishes *How to Get a Job in Europe: The Insider's Guide* (1995 edition US$18).

Vacation Work Publications, 9 Park End St., Oxford OX1 1HJ, UK (tel. (01865) 24 19 78; fax 79 08 85; http://www.vacationwork.co.uk). Publishes a wide variety of guides and directories with job listings and info for the working traveler. Write for a catalogue of their publications.

The following **au pair** agencies can help you find work in Germany.

Childcare International, Ltd., Trafalgar House, Grenville Place, London NW7 3SA, U.K. (tel. (0181) 906 31 16; fax 906 34 61; email office@childint.demon.co.uk; http://www.childint.demon.co.uk). Offers au pair positions in Germany and elsewhere. Placements are 6-12 months with some available summer positions. Member of the International Au Pair Association.

InterExchange, 161 Sixth Ave., New York, NY 10013 (tel. (212) 924-0446; fax 924-0575; email interex@earthlink.net) provides information on international work, au pair programs, and au pair positions in Germany and Europe.

Volunteer jobs are readily available almost everywhere. You may receive room and board in exchange for your labor; the work can be fascinating (or tedious). You can sometimes avoid the high application fees charged by the organizations that arrange placement by contacting the individual workcamps directly; check with the organizations. Listings in Vacation Work Publications's *International Directory of Voluntary Work* (UK£9; postage UK£2.50) can be helpful (see below).

Council offers **International Volunteer Projects,** 205 E. 42nd St., New York, NY 10017 (tel. (888) COUNCIL (268-6245); fax (212) 822-2699; email info@ciee.org; http://www.ciee.org). These are 2-4 week environmental or community service summer projects in over 30 countries, including Germany. Participants must be at least 18 years old. Minimum US$275 placement fee; additional fees may apply.

Service Civil International Voluntary Service (SCI-VS), 5474 Walnut Level Rd., Crozet, VA 22932 (tel. (804) 823-1826; fax 823-5027; email sciivsusa@igc.apc.org). Arranges placement in work programs in Germany (ages 18 and over). Local organizations sponsor groups for physical or social work. Registration fees US$50-250.

Volunteers for Peace, 43 Tiffany Rd., Belmont, VT 05730 (tel. (802) 259-2759; fax 259-2922; email vfp@vfp.org; http://www.vfp.org). A nonprofit, U.N.-sanctioned organization that arranges speedy placement in more than 1000 2-3 week workcamps comprising 10-15 people. US$195 per workcamp, including meals and accommodations, but not transportation. Up-to-date listings in the annual International Workcamp Directory (US$15). Free newsletter.

Willing Workers on Organic Farms (WWOOF) operates in most west European countries, including Germany, and Australia, New Zealand, and Ghana. Membership in WWOOF allows you to receive room and board at an organic farm in exchange for labor. Those interested in WWOOF-ing in Germany can join WWOOF International (US$10; apply to Dept.: Members Beau Champ, 24610 Montpeyroux, France) or become a member of WWOOF in Germany by writing Miriam Wittmann, Postfach 210259, 01263 Dresden, Germany. Membership costs DM30.

▓ Specific Concerns

WOMEN TRAVELERS

Women exploring on their own inevitably face additional safety concerns, but these warnings and suggestions should not discourage women from traveling alone. Trust your instincts: if you'd feel better somewhere else, move on. Always carry extra money for a phone call, bus, or taxi. You might consider staying in hostels that offer single rooms that lock from the inside or in religious organizations that offer rooms for women only. Communal showers in some hostels are safer than others. Stick to centrally located accommodations and avoid solitary late-night excursions. **Hitchhiking** is never safe for lone women, or even for two women traveling together. It's a good idea to choose train compartments occupied by other women or couples.

When in a foreign country, the less you look like a tourist, the better off you'll be. Look as if you know where you're going (even when you don't) and consider approaching women or couples for directions if you're lost or feel uncomfortable. In general, dress conservatively, especially in rural areas. You must be over 18 to purchase and use various pocket-sized containers of mace (DM12-18), available in many knife and scissors stores. Yes, knife and scissors stores.

Memorize the emergency numbers in Germany—police: **110** and ambulance: **112**. If you spend time in cities, you may be harassed no matter how you're dressed. Your best answer to verbal harassment is no answer at all (a reaction is what the harasser wants). Wearing a conspicuous **wedding band** may help prevent such incidents. If need be, turn to an older woman for help in an uncomfortable situation. Unlike in some parts of southern Europe, catcalls and whistling are not acceptable behavior in Germany—you can feel comfortable rebuking your harasser. Loudly saying *"Laß mich in Ruhe!"* ("Leave me alone!"; LAHSS MEEKH EEN ROOH-eh) should suffice. German standards of public behavior are fairly reserved, and you can often rebuff a harasser by calling the attention of passersby to his behavior. A **Model Mugging** course will not only prepare you for a potential mugging, but will also raise your level of awareness of your surroundings as well as your confidence (see **Safety and Security,** p. 15). The following books provide advice for female travelers:

Women Travel: Adventures, Advice & Experience by Miranda Davies and Natania Jansz (Penguin, US$16.95). Essays by women travelers in several foreign countries plus a decent bibliography and resource index. The sequel, *More Women Travel,* costs US$15. Both from Rough Guides, 375 Hudson St., 3rd Fl., New York, NY 10014 (tel. (212) 366-2348; fax 414-3395; email rough@panix.com; http://www.roughguides.com/women).

Women's Travel in Your Pocket, Ferrari Guides, P.O. Box 37887, Phoenix, AZ 85069 (tel. (602) 863-2408; email ferrari@q-net.com; http://www.q-net.com), an annual guide for women (especially lesbians) traveling worldwide. Hotels, night life, dining, shopping, organizations, group tours, cruises, outdoor adventure and lesbian events (US$14, plus shipping).

A Foxy Old Woman's Guide to Traveling Alone, by Jay Ben-Lesser (Crossing Press, US $10.95). Info, informal advice, and a resource list on solo travel on a low-to-medium budget.

OLDER TRAVELERS

Senior citizens are eligible for a wide range of discounts on transportation, museums, movies, theaters, concerts, restaurants, and accommodations. If you don't see a senior citizen price listed, ask, and you may be delightfully surprised. Agencies for senior group travel are growing in enrollment and popularity. Try **ElderTreks** (597 Markham St., Toronto, Ontario, M6G 2L7, tel. (800) 741-7956 or (416) 588-5000; fax 588-9839; email passages@inforamp.net; http://www.eldertreks.com) or **Walking the World** (P.O. Box 1186, Fort Collins, CO 80522; tel. (970) 498-0500; fax 498-9100; email walktworld@aol.com), which sends trips to North America, Europe, New Zealand, Asia, Central America, and the Galapagos.

The Globe Pequot Press, P.O. Box 833, Old Saybrook, CT 06475-0833 (tel. (800) 243-0495; fax (860) 820-2329; email info@globe-piquot.com). Publishes *Europe the European Way: A Traveler's Guide to Living Affordably in the World's Great Cities* (US $14), which offers general hints for the budget-conscious senior considering a long stay or retiring abroad.

Pilot Books, 127 Sterling Ave., P.O. Box 2102, Greenport, NY 11944 (tel. (516) 477-1094 or (800) 79-PILOT (797-4568); fax (516) 477-0978; email feedback@pilotbooks.com; http://www.pilotbooks.com). Publishes a large number of helpful guides including *Doctor's Guide to Protecting Your Health Before, During, and After International Travel* (US$10, postage US$2) and *Have Grandchildren, Will Travel* (US $10, postage US$2). Call or write for a complete list of titles.

No Problem! Worldwise Tips for Mature Adventurers, by Janice Kenyon. Advice and info on insurance, finances, security, health, and packing. Useful appendices. US$16 from Orca Book Publishers, P.O. Box 468, Custer, WA 98240-0468.

BISEXUAL, GAY, AND LESBIAN TRAVELERS

Germany is quite tolerant of homosexuality, though not quite as accepting as the Netherlands. The German word for gay is *Schwul,* for lesbian *Lesben.* Let's Go provides information on local bisexual, gay, and lesbian culture in **Practical Information** listings and **Entertainment** sections of city descriptions. In general, the larger the city and the farther north you travel, the more tolerant the attitudes toward bisexual, gay, and lesbian travelers. Berlin is the major center of gay life in Germany, followed by

Hamburg, Frankfurt, Köln, and Munich. Women should look for *Frauencafes* and *Frauenkneipen*. It should be stressed that while such cafes are for women only, they are *not* for lesbians only. The local *Frauenbuchladen* (women's bookstores) are good resources. Local **AIDS-Hilfe** are not just AIDS helplines; in fact, AIDS-Hilfe offices tend to find bisexual, gay, and lesbian resources and nightlife.

Gay Europe. A gay guide providing a quick look at gay life in countries throughout Europe, including restaurants, clubs, and beaches. Introductions to each country cover laws and gay-friendliness. Available in bookstores. Perigee Books, US$14.

Spartacus International Gay Guide (US$32.95), published by Bruno Gmünder Verlag GmbH, Leuschnerdamm 31, 10999 Berlin (tel. (030) 615 0030; fax 615 9007; email bgvtravel@aol.com). Lists bars, restaurants, hotels, and bookstores around the world catering to gays; the Germany section is particularly comprehensive. Available in bookstores and in the U.S. by mail from Lambda Rising, 1625 Connecticut Ave. NW, Washington, D.C., 20009-1013 (tel. (202) 462-6969). Bruno Gmünder also publishes travel guides for gay men to Berlin, Stuttgart, Hamburg, Munich, Köln, Düsseldorf, and Frankfurt.

Giovanni's Room, 345 S. 12th St., Philadelphia, PA 19107 (tel. (215) 923-2960; fax 923-0813; email giophilp@netaxs.com). An international feminist, lesbian, and gay bookstore with mail-order service that carries the publications listed here; they accept email orders as well.

International Gay and Lesbian Travel Association, 4331 N. Federal Hwy., Suite 304, Fort Lauderdale, FL 33308 (tel. (954) 776-2626 or (800) 448-8550; fax (954) 776-3303; email IGLTA@aol.com; http://www.iglta.org). An organization of over 1350 companies serving gay and lesbian travelers worldwide. Call for lists of travel agents, accommodations, and events.

MINORITY TRAVELERS

Germany has a significant minority population composed mainly of ethnic Turks. In addition, there are refugees from Eastern and Southern Europe and, facing increasing hostility, a number of Romany-Sinti people (also known as Gypsies). Eastern Germany also has a number of Vietnamese residents. All the same, conspicuously non-German foreigners may stand out in less-traveled parts of both the East and West.

In certain regions, tourists of color or members of certain religious groups may feel threatened by local residents. Neo-Nazi skinheads in the large cities of former East Germany, as well as in Western Germany, have been known to attack foreigners, especially non-whites. In these areas, common sense will serve you best. Either historical or newly developed discrimination against established minority residents may surface against travelers who are members of these minority groups. Keeping abreast of news of any such attack and then keeping away from the area in which it happened is perhaps the best (and only) real strategy for avoiding trouble.

DISABLED TRAVELERS

By and large, Germany is one of the more accessible countries for travelers with disabilities (*Behinderte* or *Schwerbehinderte*). Germany's excellent public transportation systems make most places easily accessible for both older travelers and for travelers with disabilities; many public transport systems are wheelchair-accessible. The international **wheelchair** icon or a large letter "B" indicates access. Intersections in major cities have audible crossing signals for the blind. Trains have a few seats or an integrated compartment reserved for passengers with disabilities. Almost all EuroCity (EC) trains in and out of Germany have wheelchair facilities. Many platforms can be hard to reach; alternative ones sometimes exist. For more info, contact **Deutsche Bahn** (see **Getting Around: By Train,** p. 37). Those traveling with guide dogs should be aware that Germany requires evidence of rabies vaccination from a licensed veterinarian at least 30 days but not more than 12 months before entering the country. A notarized German translation of this certificate is required.

ESSENTIALS

Information for Disabled Travelers

Facts on File, 11 Penn Plaza, 15th Fl., New York, NY 10001 (tel. (212) 967-8800). Publishers of *Resource Directory for the Disabled,* a reference guide for travelers with disabilities (US$45 plus shipping). Available at bookstores or by mail-order.

Graphic Language Press, P.O. Box 270, Cardiff by the Sea, CA 92007 (tel. (760) 944-9594; email niteowl@cts.com; contact person A. Mackin). Publishes *Wheelchair Through Europe,* a guide covering accessible hotels, transportation, sightseeing and resources for disabled travelers in many European cities. Available for US$12.95 (includes S&H), check payable to Graphic Language Press.

Mobility International USA (MIUSA), P.O. Box 10767, Eugene, OR 97440 (tel. (541) 343-1284 voice and TDD; fax 343-6812; email info@miusa.org; http://www.miusa.org). Sells the 3rd edition of *A World of Options: A Guide to International Educational Exchange, Community Service, and Travel for Persons with Disabilities* (individuals US$35; organizations US$45).

Moss Rehab Hospital Travel Information Service (tel. (215) 456-9600, TDD 456-9602). A telephone information resource center on international travel accessibility and other travel-related concerns for those with disabilities.

Tours or Trips for Disabled Travelers

Directions Unlimited, 720 N. Bedford Rd., Bedford Hills, NY 10507 (tel. (800) 533-5343; in NY (914) 241-1700; fax 241-0243). Specializes in arranging individual and group vacations, tours, and cruises for the physically disabled. Group tours for blind travelers.

Flying Wheels Travel Service, 143 W. Bridge St., Owatonne, MN 55060 (tel. (800) 535-6790; fax 451-1685). Arranges trips in the U.S. and abroad for groups and individuals in wheelchairs or with other sorts of limited mobility.

DIETARY CONCERNS

Although Germany is unapologetically carnivorous, **vegetarianism** has become increasingly popular in the last ten years (see **Food and Drink,** p. 80). Mad cow disease, growing health consciousness, and a blooming alternative scene have all contributed to a decline in meat consumption. Vegetarian restaurants have proliferated in larger cities, while health food shops, such as the well-known **Reformhaus,** provide a large selection of vegetarian and vegan products. *Let's Go* makes an effort to identify restaurants that offer vegetarian choices. Many of these establishments are ethnic restaurants; traditional German restaurants often offer no genuinely vegetarian dishes. Tourist offices often publish lists of vegetarian restaurants. Checking websites before you arrive in Germany will provide you with a wealth of helpful tips.

The International Vegetarian Travel Guide (UK£2) was last published in 1991. Order back copies from the Vegetarian Society of the U.K. (VSUK), Parkdale, Dunham Rd., Altringham, Cheshire WA14 4QG (tel. (0161) 928 0793, fax 926 9182; email: veg@minxnet.co.uk; http://www.vegsoc.org). VSUK also publishes other titles, including *The European Vegetarian Guide to Hotels and Restaurants.* Call or send a self-addressed, stamped envelope for a listing.

The Vegetarian Traveler, P.O. Box 410305, Cambridge, MA 02141, sells a packet of 16 cards in 16 languages including German to be presented in restaurants, explaining your diet restrictions. Specify Vegan (no meat, dairy, or eggs), Lacto (no meat or eggs), or Ovo-Lacto (no meat; eggs or dairy allowed). US$9.95 plus $1 shipping.

The Vegan in Germany Homepage (http://ourworld.compuserve.com/homepages /Felix_touchandgo/homepage.htm) provides an overview of veganism in Germany, shopping advice, and addresses of useful organizations.

European Vegetarian Union, Bluetschwitzerweg 5, CH 9443 Widnau, Switzerland (tel. (41) 71 7226445; email evu@ivu.org; http://www.ivu.org/evu), is an umbrella organization for vegetarian groups throughout Europe. Its website has connections to German resources.

For historic and political reasons, few Jews live in Germany, and the **kosher** offerings are correspondingly small. Your own synagogue or college Hillel should have access to lists of Jewish institutions across the nation. If you are strict in your observance, consider preparing your own food on the road.

The Jewish Travel Guide lists synagogues, kosher restaurants, and Jewish institutions in over 80 countries. Available from Vallentine Mitchell Publishers, Newbury House 890-900, Eastern Ave., Newbury Park, Ilford, Essex, U.K. IG2 7HH (tel. (0181) 599 88 66; fax 599 09 84). It is available in the U.S. (US$15 plus US$3 shipping) from Sepher-Hermon Press, 1265 46th St., Brooklyn, NY 11219 (tel./fax (718) 972-9010; contact person Samuel Gross).

RELIGIOUS TRAVELERS

It is impossible to discuss religion in contemporary Germany without hearing the many voices of past and present: the voices of Holocaust survivors, the voices of neo-Nazis, the voices of the courageous East German pastors who led the peaceful resistance against the communists, and the voice of the modern Basic Law which states that "freedom of faith and conscience as well as freedom of religious or other belief shall be inviolable. The undisturbed practice of religion shall be guaranteed" (paragraph 4). The total Jewish population in Germany today is approximately 40-50,000. The largest Jewish congregations are in Berlin and Frankfurt am Main, which together are home to over 10,000 Jews. An influx of foreign workers has brought along with it a strong Islamic population; today, almost two million Muslims, mostly from Turkey, live in Germany. For information, contact the following organizations.

Protestant: Kirchenamt der Evangelischen Kirche in Deutschland, Herrenhäuserstr. 12, 30419 Hannover (tel. (0511) 279 60; fax 279 67 07; email ekd@ckd.dc).
Catholic: Katholisches Auslandssekretariat der Deutschen Bischofskonferenz Tourismus und Urlauberselsorge, Kaiser-Friedrich-Str. 9 53113 Bonn (tel. (0228) 91 14 30; fax 911 43 33).
Muslim: Islamische Gemeinschaft. **Berlin,** Gesslerstr. 11, 10829 Berlin (tel./fax (030) 788 48 83; email igdmb@aol.com).
Jewish: There are Jewish community centers in each of the following cities: **Berlin,** Fasanenstr. 79-80 (tel. (030) 884 20 30); **Bonn,** Kaiser-Friedrich-Str. 9 (tel. (0228) 21 35 60); **Frankfurt,** Westendstr. 43, 60325 (tel. (069) 740 72 15; **Munich,** Reichenbachstr. 27, 80469 (tel. (089) 202 40 00).

TRAVELERS WITH CHILDREN

Family vacations are recipes for disaster—unless you slow your pace and plan ahead. When deciding where to stay, remember the special needs of young children. If you rent a car, make sure the rental company provides a car seat for younger children. Consider using a papoose-style device to carry your baby on walking trips. Be sure that your child carries some sort of ID in case of an emergency or he or she gets lost, and arrange a reunion spot in case of separation when sight-seeing.

Restaurants often have children's menus and discounts. Virtually all museums and tourist attractions also have a children's rate. Children under two generally fly for 10% of the adult airfare on international flights (this does not necessarily include a seat). International fares are usually discounted 25% for children from two to 11.

The following publications offer tips for adults traveling with children or distractions for the kids themselves.
Backpacking with Babies and Small Children (US$9.95). Published by Wilderness Press, 2440 Bancroft Way, Berkeley, CA 94704 (tel. (800) 443-7227 or (510) 843-8080; fax 548-1355; email wpress@ix.netcom.com; http://wildernesspress.com). The third edition was scheduled for release in August 1998.
Take Your Kids to Europe, by Cynthia W. Harriman (US$16.95, shipping US$3.95). A budget travel guide geared toward families. Published by Globe-Pequot Press, 6 Business Park Rd., Old Saybrook, CT 06475 (tel. (800) 285-4078; fax (860) 395-1418).

How to Take Great Trips with Your Kids, by Sanford and Jane Portnoy (US $9.95, shipping and handling US$3). Advice on how to plan trips geared toward the age of your children, packing, and finding child-friendly accomodations. The Harvard Common Press, 535 Albany St., Boston, MA. 02118 (tel. (888) 657-3755; fax 695-9794).

■ Packing

Plan your packing according to the type of travel you'll be doing (multi-city backpacking tour, week-long stay in one place, etc.) and the area's high and low temperatures. The larger your pack, the more cumbersome it is to carry and to store safely. Before you leave, pack your bag, strap it on, and imagine yourself walking uphill on hot asphalt for the next three hours. A good rule is to **lay out only what you absolutely need, then take half the clothes and twice the money.**

LUGGAGE

If you plan to cover most of your itinerary by foot, or anticipate frequent moves between and around cities, a sturdy **backpack** is unbeatable. Get a pack with a strong, padded hip belt to transfer weight from your shoulders to your hips. Be wary of excessively low-end prices, and don't sacrifice quality. **Internal-frame packs** mold better to your back, maintain a lower center of gravity, and can flex adequately in cases of tricky maneuvering; they're almost always preferable to external-frame packs. Good packs cost anywhere from US$150 to US$420. A **suitcase** or **trunk** is fine if you plan to live in one or two cities and explore from there, but a bad idea if you're going to be moving around a lot. Make sure it has wheels and consider how much it weighs even when empty. Hard-sided luggage is more durable and doesn't wrinkle your clothes, but is also heavier. Soft-sided luggage should have a PVC frame, a strong lining to resist bad weather and rough handling, and triple-stitched seams for durability. Bringing a smaller bag, such as a **backpack** or **rucksack,** lets you leave your big bag behind while sight-seeing.

A **moneybelt** or **neck pouch,** available at any good camping store, guards your money, passport, railpass, and other important articles but can sometimes be uncomfortable and protrusive. The moneybelt should tuck inside the waist of your pants or skirt; you want to hide your valuables, not announce them with a colorful waist-pack. (For more information see **Safety and Security,** p. 15.)

CLOTHING AND FOOTWEAR

When choosing your travel wardrobe, aim for versatility and comfort, and avoid fabrics that wrinkle easily (to test a fabric, hold it tightly in your fist for 20 seconds). In certain clubs, stricter dress codes demand some hipper duds; bring along at least one chic outfit if you plan on living the high life. Always bring a jacket or wool sweater. Well-cushioned **sneakers** are good for walking, though you may want to consider a good waterproofed pair of **hiking boots.** A double pair of socks—light silk or polypropylene inside and thick wool outside—will cushion feet, keep them dry, and help prevent blisters. Bring a pair of flip-flops for protection in the shower. **Rain gear** is a must in Germany. A waterproof jacket and a backpack cover will take care of you and your stuff at a moment's notice. Gore-Tex® is a miracle fabric that's both waterproof and breathable; it's all but mandatory if you plan on hiking. Avoid cotton as outerwear, especially if you will be outdoors a lot.

MISCELLANEOUS

If you plan to stay in **youth hostels,** don't pay the linen charge; make the requisite **sleepsack** yourself. Fold a full size sheet in half the long way, then sew it closed along the open long side and one of the short sides. Sleepsacks can also be bought at any HI outlet store. *Let's Go* attempts to provide information on **laundromats** in the **Practical Information** listings for each city, but sometimes it may be easiest to use a sink to get rid of your stink. Bring a small bar or tube of detergent soap, a rubber squash ball to stop up the sink, and a travel clothes line.

Machines that heat-disinfect **contact lenses** will require a small converter (about US$20) if you are visiting an area with a different current. Consider switching temporarily to a chemical disinfection system, but check with your lens dispenser to see if it's safe to switch. Your preferred brand of contact lens supplies may be rare or expensive. Bring enough saline and cleaner for your entire vacation, or wear glasses; better yet, bring your prescription and buy a pair of German glasses, which, on the whole are perhaps the most stylish in the world. In Germany, **electricity** is 220V AC, enough to fry any 110V North American appliance. 220V electrical appliances don't like 110V current, either. Visit a hardware store for an **adapter** (which changes the shape of the plug) and a **converter** (which changes the voltage). Don't make the mistake of using only an adapter (unless appliance instructions explicitly state otherwise), or you'll melt your radio.

Film is expensive just about everywhere. Bring film from home and, if you will be seriously upset if the pictures are ruined, develop it at home. If you're not a serious photographer, you might want to consider bringing a **disposable camera** or two rather than an expensive permanent one. Despite disclaimers, airport security X-rays *can* fog film, so either buy a lead-lined pouch, sold at camera stores, or ask the security to hand-inspect it. Always pack it in your carry-on luggage.

Other useful items: first aid kit; umbrella; sealable plastic bags; alarm clock; moleskin (for blisters); needle and thread; safety pins; sunglasses; a personal stereo (Walkman) with headphones; pocketknife; plastic water bottle; string (makeshift clothesline and lashing material); towel; padlock; whistle; rubber bands; flashlight; earplugs; insect repellent; electrical tape (for patching tears); clothespins; maps and phrasebooks; tweezers; sunscreen; vitamins.

DRESS FOR SUCCESS

If you will encounter situations that require more than the jeans and T-shirt uniform, remember that elegance is understated. Black is ideal because it is always in fashion and you can't tell if it's been worn five times. If you have the inclination and the room, you might decide to bring an extra pair of shoes so you don't ruin that snazzy outfit, although some say that hiking boots go with everything. Please, *please* don't wear your shiny new German-made leather sandals.

GETTING THERE

■ Budget Travel Agencies

Students and people under 26 ("youth") with proper ID qualify for enticing reduced airfares. These are rarely available from airlines or travel agents, but instead from student travel agencies which negotiate special reduced-rate bulk purchase with the airlines, then resell them to the youth market. Return-date change fees also tend to be low (around US$35 per segment through Council or Let's Go Travel). Most flights are on major airlines, though in peak season some agencies may sell seats on chartered aircraft. Student travel agencies can also help non-students and people over 26, but probably won't be able to get the same low fares.

TRAVEL AGENCIES

Campus Travel, 52 Grosvenor Gardens, London SW1W 0AG (http://www.campus travel.co.uk). 46 branches in the U.K. Student and youth fares on plane, train, boat, and bus travel. Skytrekker, flexible airline tickets. Discount and ID cards for students and youths, travel insurance for students and those under 35, and maps and guides. Telephone booking service: in Europe call (0171) 730 34 02; in North America call (0171) 730 21 01; worldwide call (0171) 730 81 11.

Council Travel (http://www..counciltravel.com), the travel division of Council, is a full-service travel agency specializing in youth and budget travel. They offer discount airfares on scheduled airlines, railpasses, hosteling cards, low-cost accommodations, guidebooks, budget tours, travel gear, and international student (ISIC), youth (GO25), and teacher (ITIC) identity cards. U.S. offices include: Emory Village, 1561 N. Decatur Rd., **Atlanta**, GA 30307 (tel. (404) 377-9997); 2000 Guadalupe, **Austin**, TX 78705 (tel. (512) 472-4931); 273 Newbury St., **Boston**, MA 02116 (tel. (617) 266-1926); 1138 13th St., **Boulder**, CO 80302 (tel. (303) 447-8101); 1153 N. Dearborn, **Chicago**, IL 60610 (tel. (312) 951-0585); 10904 Lindbrook Dr., **Los Angeles**, CA 90024 (tel. (310) 208-3551); 1501 University Ave. SE #300, **Minneapolis**, MN 55414 (tel. (612) 379-2323); 205 E. 42nd St., **New York**, NY 10017 (tel. (212) 822-2700); 953 Garnet Ave., **San Diego**, CA 92109 (tel. (619) 270-6401); 530 Bush St., **San Francisco**, CA 94108 (tel. (415) 421-3473); 1314 NE 43rd St. #210, **Seattle**, WA 98105 (tel. (206) 632-2448); 3300 M St. NW, **Washington, D.C.** 20007 (tel. (202) 337-6464). **For U.S. cities not listed**, call 800-2-COUNCIL (226-8624). Also **London** (tel. (0171) 287 3337), **Paris** (tel. (01) 46 55 55 65), and **Munich** (tel. (089) 39 50 22).

Council Charter, 205 E. 42nd St., New York, NY 10017 (tel. (212) 661-0311; fax 972-0194). Offers a combination of inexpensive charter and scheduled airfares from a variety of U.S. gateways to most major European destinations. One-way fares and open jaws (fly into one city and out of another) are available.

CTS Travel, 220 Kensington High St., W8 (tel. (0171) 937 33 66 for travel in Europe, 937 33 88 for travel world-wide; fax 937 90 27). Tube: High St. Kensington. Also at 44 Goodge St., W1. Tube: Goodge St. Specializes in student/youth travel and discount flights.

Let's Go Travel, Harvard Student Agencies, 17 Holyoke St., Cambridge, MA 02138 (tel. (617) 495-9649; fax 495-7956; email travel@hsa.net; http://hsa.net/travel). Railpasses, HI-AYH memberships, ISICs, ITICs, FIYTO cards, guidebooks (including every *Let's Go* at a substantial discount), maps, bargain flights, and a complete line of budget travel gear. All items available by mail; call or write for a catalogue (or see the catalogue in center of this publication).

Rail Europe Inc., 226 Westchester Ave., White Plains, NY 10604 (tel. (800) 438-7245; fax 432-1329; http://www.raileurope.com). Sells all Eurail products and passes, national railpasses including Brit Rail and German Rail passes, and point-to-point tickets. Up-to-date information on all rail travel in Europe, including Eurostar, the English Channel train.

STA Travel, 6560 Scottsdale Rd. #F100, Scottsdale, AZ 85253 (tel. (800) 777-0112 nationwide; fax (602) 922-0793; http://sta-travel.com). A student and youth travel organization with over 150 offices worldwide offering discount airfares for young travelers, railpasses, accommodations, tours, insurance, and ISICs. Sixteen offices in the U.S. including: 297 Newbury Street, **Boston**, MA 02115 (tel. (617) 266-6014); 429 S. Dearborn St., **Chicago**, IL 60605 (tel. (312) 786-9050; 7202 Melrose Ave.), **Los Angeles**, CA 90046 (tel. (213) 934-8722); 10 Downing St., Ste. G, **New York**, NY 10003 (tel. (212) 627-3111); 4341 University Way NE, **Seattle**, WA 98105 (tel. (206) 633-5000); 2401 Pennsylvania Ave., **Washington, D.C.** 20037 (tel. (202) 887-0912); 51 Grant Ave., **San Francisco**, CA 94108 (tel. (415) 391-8407); 100 Whitten University Center, 1306 Stanford Dr., **Coral Gables**, FL 33146 (tel. (305) 284-1044). In the U.K., 6 Wrights Ln., **London** W8 6TA (tel. (0171) 361 61 61 for European travel). In New Zealand, 10 High St., **Auckland** (tel. (09) 309 97 23). In Australia, 222 Faraday St., **Melbourne** VIC 3050 (tel. (03) 349 69 11).

Travel CUTS (Canadian Universities Travel Services Limited), 187 College St., Toronto, Ont. M5T 1P7 (tel. (416) 979-2406; fax 979-8167; email mail@travelcuts). Canada's national student travel bureau and equivalent of Council, with 40 offices across Canada. Also in the U.K., 295-A Regent St., **London** W1R 7YA (tel. (0171) 637 31 61). Discounted domestic and international airfares open to all; special student fares to all destinations with valid ISIC. Issues ISIC, FIYTO GO25, and HI hostel cards, as well as railpasses. Offers free *Student Traveller* magazine, as well as information on the Student Work Abroad Program (SWAP).

Usit Youth and Student Travel, 19-21 Aston Quay, O'Connell Bridge, Dublin 2 (tel. (01) 677-8117; fax 679-8833). In the U.S.: New York Student Center, 895 Amsterdam Ave., New York, NY, 10025 (tel. (212) 663-5435; email usitny@aol.com). Additional offices in Cork, Galway, Limerick, Waterford, Maynooth, Coleraine, Derry, Athlone, Jordanstown, Belfast, and Greece. Specializes in youth and student travel. Offers low-cost tickets and flexible travel arrangements all over the world. Supplies ISIC and FIYTO GO25 cards in Ireland only.

■ By Plane

The **airline industry** attempts to squeeze every dollar from customers; finding a cheap airfare will be easier if you understand the airlines' systems. The national airline of Germany—**Deutsche Lufthansa** (tel. (800) 645-3880 in the U.S.; (800) 563-5954 in Canada)—serves the most cities, but fares tend to be high. Beside Lufthansa, almost every major American airline offers direct serivce from the east coast to Germany. From Australia and New Zealand, planes take off for Germany via either Asia, Russia, or the United States; the flights via Asia are usually cheaper. Call every toll-free number and don't be afraid to ask about discounts; if you don't ask, it's unlikely they'll be volunteered. Have knowledgeable **travel agents** guide you; better yet, use an agent who specializes in the region you will be traveling.. An agent whose clients fly mostly to Miami will not be the best person to hunt down a bargain flight to Berlin.

Students and others under 26 should never need to pay full price for a ticket. Seniors can also get great deals; many airlines offer senior traveler clubs or airline passes with few restrictions and discounts for their companions as well. Sunday newspapers often have travel sections that list bargain fares from the local airport. Outsmart airline reps with the phone-book-sized *Official Airline Guide* (check your local library; at US$359 per year, the tome costs as much as some flights), a monthly guide listing nearly every scheduled flight in the world (with fares, US$479) and toll-free phone numbers for all the airlines that allow you to call in reservations directly. More accessible is Michael McColl's *The Worldwide Guide to Cheap Airfare* (US$15), a useful guide for finding cheap airfare.

There is also a wealth of travel information to be found on the Internet. The **Air Traveler's Handbook** (http://www.cs.cmu.edu/afs/cs.cmu.edu/user/mkant/Pub lic/Travel/airfare.html) is an excellent source of general information on air travel. **TravelHUB** (http://www.travelhub.com) provides a directory of travel agents that includes a searchable database of fares from over 500 consolidators (see **Ticket Consolidators,** below). Edward Hasbrouck maintains a **Consolidators FAQ** (http://www.travel-library.com/air-travel/consolidators.html) that provides great background on finding cheap international flights. Groups such as the **Air Courier Association** (http://www.aircourier.org) offer information about traveling as a courier and provide up-to-date listings of last-minute opportunities. **Travelocity** (http://www.travelocity.com) operates a searchable online database of published airfares, which you can reserve online.

Most airfares peak between mid-June and early September. Midweek (Monday-Thursday morning) round-trip flights run about US$40-50 cheaper than on weekends; weekend flights, however, are generally less crowded. Traveling from hub to hub (for example, New York, Boston, or London to Berlin) will win a more competitive fare than from smaller cities. Return-date flexibility is usually not an option for the budget traveler; traveling with an "open return" ticket can be pricier than fixing a return date and paying to change it. Whenever flying internationally, pick up your ticket well in advance of the departure date, have the flight confirmed within 72 hours of departure, and arrive at the airport at least three hours before your flight.

COMMERCIAL AIRLINES

The airlines' published airfares should be just the beginning of your search. Even if you pay an airline's lowest published fare, you may waste hundreds of dollars. For the adventurous or the bargain-hungry, there are other, perhaps more inconvenient or time-consuming options. But before shopping around it is a good idea to find out the average commercial price in order to measure just how great a "bargain" you are being offered.

The commercial airlines' lowest regular offer is the **Advance Purchase Excursion Fare (APEX);** specials advertised in newspapers may be cheaper, but have more restrictions and fewer available seats. APEX fares provide you with confirmed reservations and allow "open-jaw" tickets (landing in and returning from different cities). Generally, reservations must be made seven to 21 days in advance, with seven- to 14-day minimum and up to 90-day maximum stay limits, and hefty cancellation and change penalties (fees rise in summer). Book APEX fares early during peak season; by May you will have a hard time getting the departure date you want.

Destinations in Germany, especially Frankfurt, are some of the cheapest and most frequently serviced European cities to reach from North America. Round-trip tickets for flights leaving from New York, Boston, or Washington. D.C. were available for as low as US$300 in 1998. Although such tickets are usually not so cheap, a restricted round-trip APEX ticket from a northeast hub (usually with a one-month maximum stay) costs anywhere from US$400 to US$700. **Icelandair** (tel. (800) 223-5500) tends to offer the cheapest APEX tickets of any transatlantic carrier.

TICKET CONSOLIDATORS

Most airlines in the world are heavily regulated, which means that their published fares may be significantly more expensive than the market price available from a **ticket consolidator.** Ticket consolidators resell unsold tickets on commercial and charter airlines at unpublished fares; a 30-40% price reduction is not uncommon. Consolidator tickets provide the greatest discounts over published fares when you are traveling: on short notice (you bypass advance purchase requirements, since you aren't tangled in airline bureaucracy); on a high-priced trip; to an offbeat destination; or in the peak season, when published fares are jacked way up. There are rarely age constraints or stay limitations, but unlike tickets bought through an airline, you won't be able to use your tickets on another flight if you miss yours, and you will have to go back to the consolidator rather than the airline to get a refund. Keep in mind that these tickets are often for coach seats on connecting (not direct) flights on foreign airlines, and that frequent-flyer miles may not be credited.

Not all consolidators deal with the general public; many only sell tickets through travel agents. **Bucket shops** are retail agencies that specialize in getting cheap tickets. Although ticket prices are marked up slightly, bucket shops generally have access to a larger market than would be available to the public and can also get tickets from wholesale consolidators. Generally, a dealer **specializing** in travel to the country of your destination will provide more options and cheaper tickets. The **Association of Special Fares Agents (ASFA)** maintains a database of specialized dealers for particular regions (http://www.ntsltd.com/asfa). Look for bucket shops' tiny ads in the travel section of weekend papers; in the U.S., the *Sunday New York Times* is a good source; in Australia, use the *Sydney Times.* Kelly Monaghan's *Consolidators: Air Travel's Bargain Basement* is an invaluable source for more information and lists of consolidators (US$8 plus US$3.50 shipping) from the Intrepid Traveler, P.O. Box 438, New York, NY 10034 (email info@intrepidtraveler.com).

Be a smart shopper; check out the competition. Among the many reputable and trustworthy companies are, unfortunately, some shady wheeler-dealers. Contact the local Better Business Bureau to find out how long the company has been in business and its track record. Although not necessary, it is preferable to deal with consolidators close to home so you can visit in person, if necessary. Ask to receive your tickets as quickly as possible so you have time to fix any problems. Get the company's policy in writing: insist on a **receipt** that gives full details about the tickets, refunds, and restrictions, and record who you talked to and when. It may be worth paying with a credit card (despite the 2-5% fee) so you can stop payment if you never receive your tickets. Also, some consolidators give discounts on accommodations and car rental.

Always try to contact specialists in your region, but consider the following agents for general services. For destinations **worldwide,** try **Airfare Busters** (offices in Washington, D.C. (tel. (202) 776-0478), Boca Raton, FL (tel. (561) 994-9590), and Houston, TX (tel. (800) 232-8783); **Pennsylvania Travel,** Paoli, PA (tel. (800) 331-0947); **Cheap Tickets,** offices in Los Angeles, CA, San Francisco, CA, Honolulu, HI, Seattle, WA, and New York, NY, (tel. (800) 377-1000); **Interworld** (tel. (305) 443-4929; fax 443-0351); **Travac** (tel. (800) 872-8800; fax (212) 714-9063; email mail@travac.com; http://www.travac.com). **NOW Voyager,** 74 Varick St. #307, New York, NY 10013 (tel. (212) 431-1616; fax 334-5243; email info@nowvoyagertravel.com; http://www.nowvoyagertravel.com) acts as a consolidator and books discounted international flights, mostly from New York, as well as courier flights (see **Courier Companies and Freighters** below), for an annual fee of US$50. For a processing fee, depending on the number of travelers and the itinerary, **Travel Avenue,** Chicago, IL (tel. (800) 333-3335; fax (312) 876-1254; http://www.travelavenue.com) will search for the lowest international airfare available, including consolidated prices, and will even give you a 5% rebate on fares over US$350. To **Europe,** try **Rebel,** Valencia, CA (tel. (800) 227-3235; fax (805) 294-0981; email travel@rebeltours.com; http://www.rebeltours.com) or Orlando, FL (tel. (800) 732-3588).

STAND-BY FLIGHTS

Airhitch, 2641 Broadway, 3rd Fl., New York, NY 10025 (tel. (800) 326-2009 or (212) 864-2000, fax (212) 864-5489) and Los Angeles, CA (tel. (310) 726-5000), will add a certain thrill to the prospects of when you will leave and where exactly you will end up. Complete flexibility in the dates and cities of arrival and departure is necessary. Flights to Europe cost US$159 each way when departing from the Northeast, US$239 from the West Coast or Northwest, US$209 from the Midwest, and US$189 from the Southeast. Travel within Europe is also possible, with rates ranging from US$79-$139. The snag is that you buy not a ticket, but the promise that you will get to a destination near where you're intending to go within a window of time (usually 5 days) from a location in a region you've specified. You call in before your date range to hear all of your flight options for the next seven days and your probability of boarding. You then decide which flights you want to try to make and present a voucher at the airport which grants you the right to board a flight on a space-available basis. This procedure must be followed again for the return trip. Be aware that you may only receive a monetary refund if all available flights which departed within your date-range from the specified region are full, but future travel credit is always available. There are several offices in Europe, so you can wait to register for your return; the main one is in Paris (tel. (1) 47 00 16 30).

AirTech.Com, 588 Broadway #204, New York, NY 10012 (tel. (212) 219-7000, fax 219-0066; email fly@airtech.com; http://www.airtech.com) offers a very similar service. Their travel window is one to four days. Rates to and from Europe (continually updated; call and verify) are: Northeast US$169; West Coast US$229; Midwest/Southeast US$199. Upon registration and payment, AirTech.Com sends you a FlightPass with a contact date falling soon before your travel window, when you are to call them for flight instructions. Note that the service is one-way—you must go through the same procedure to return—and that no refunds are granted unless the company fails to get you a seat before your travel window expires. AirTech.Com also arranges courier flights and regular confirmed-reserved flights at discount rates.

Be sure to read all the fine print in your agreements with either company—a call to The **Better Business Bureau of New York City** (tel. (900) CALL-BBB; http://bbb.org/newyork/reports) may be worthwhile. Be warned that it is difficult to receive

ESSENTIALS

refunds, and that clients' vouchers will not be honored when an airline fails to receive payment in time.

CHARTER FLIGHTS

Charters are flights a tour operator contracts with an airline (usually one specializing in charters) to fly extra loads of passengers to peak-season destinations. Charters are often cheaper than flights on scheduled airlines, especially during peak seasons, although fare wars, consolidator tickets, and small airlines can often beat charter prices. Some charters operate nonstop, and restrictions on minimum advance-purchase and minimum stay are more lenient. However, charter flights fly less frequently than major airlines, make refunds particularly difficult, and are almost always fully booked. Schedules and itineraries may also change or be cancelled at the last moment (as late as 48 hours before the trip, and without a full refund), and check-in, boarding, and baggage claim are often much slower. As always, pay with a credit card if you can; consider it traveler's insurance against trip interruption.

Many consolidators such as **Interworld, Rebel, Travac,** and **Travel Avenue** (see **Ticket Consolidators** above), also offer charter options. Don't be afraid to call every number and hunt for the best deal. Eleventh-hour **discount clubs** and **fare brokers** offer members savings on travel, including charter flights and tour packages. Research your options carefully. **Last Minute Travel Service,** 100 Sylvan Rd., Woburn, MA 01801 (tel. (800) 527-8646 or (617) 267-9800), specializes in domestic and Carribean packages as well as cruises. It is one of the few travel clubs that doesn't charge a membership fee. **Travelers Advantage,** Stamford, CT (tel. (800) 548-1116; http://www.travelersadvantage.com; US$49 annual fee) specializes in European travel and tour packages. Study these organizations' contracts closely; you don't want to end up with an unwanted overnight layover.

COURIER COMPANIES AND FREIGHTERS

Those who travel light should consider flying internationally as a **courier,** where ridiculously low fares often come at the price of heavy restrictions. The company hiring you will use your checked luggage space for freight; you're usually only allowed to bring carry-ons, though some firms allow you to check luggage, depending on your trip. You are responsible for the safe delivery of the baggage claim slips (given to you by a courier company representative) to the representative waiting for you when you arrive—don't screw up or you will be blacklisted as a courier. You will probably never see the cargo you are transporting—the company handles it all—and airport officials know that couriers are not responsible for the baggage checked for them. Restrictions to watch for: you must be over 21 (18 in some cases), have a valid passport, and procure your own visa (if necessary); most flights are round-trip only with short fixed-length stays (usually one week); only single tickets are issued (but a companion may be able to get a next-day flight); and most flights out of the U.S. are from New York. Round-trip fares to Western Europe from the U.S. range from US$100-400 (during the off-season) to US$200-550 (during the summer); flights to Frankfurt range from US$150-300. Keep in mind that last-minute deals for all courier flights can get you significantly cheaper or even free flights. Becoming a member of the **Air Courier Association** (tel. (800) 282-1202; http://www.aircourier.org) is a good way to start; they give you a listing of all reputable courier brokers and the flights they are offering, along with a hefty courier manual and a bimonthly newsletter of updated opportunities (US$30 one-time fee plus US$28 annual dues). For an annual fee of US$45, the **International Association of Air Travel Couriers,** 8 South J St., P.O. Box 1349, Lake Worth, Florida 33460 (tel. (561) 582-8320; email iaatc@courier.org; http://www.courier.org) informs travelers (via email, fax, and mailings) of courier opportunities worldwide. **NOW Voyager,** 74 Varick St. #307, New York, NY 10013 (tel. (212) 431-1616; fax 334-5243; email info@nowvoyagertravel.com; http://www.now-voyagertravel.com), acts as an agent for many courier flights worldwide primarily from New York and offers special last-minute deals to such cities as London, Paris, Rome, and Frankfurt for as little as US$200 round-trip plus a US$50 registration fee.

(They also act as a consolidator; see **Ticket Consolidators,** p. 32.) Another agent to try is **Halbart Express,** 147-05 176th St., Jamaica, NY 11434 (tel. (718) 656-5000; fax 917-0708; offices in Chicago, Los Angeles, and London).

You can also go directly through courier companies in New York, or check your bookstore, library, or online at http://www.amazon.com for handbooks such as *Air Courier Bargains* (US$15 plus US$3.50 shipping from the Intrepid Traveler, tel. (212) 569-1081; email info@intrepidtraveler.com; http://intrepidtraveler.com). *The Courier Air Travel Handbook* (US$10 plus US$3.50 shipping) explains how to travel as an air courier and contains names, phone numbers, and contact points of courier companies. It can be ordered directly from Bookmasters, Inc., P.O. Box 2039, Mansfield, OH 44905 (tel. (800) 507-2665).

■ By Train

European trains retain the charm and romance their North American counterparts lost long ago, but charm and romance don't satisfy those earthly needs. Bring food and a water bottle; the on-board cafe can be priccy, and train water undrinkable. Lock your compartment door and keep your valuables on your person.

Many train stations have different counters for domestic and international tickets, seat reservations, and info—check before lining up. Even with a railpass, reservations are often required on major lines, and are advisable during the busier holiday seasons; make them at least a few hours in advance at the train station (US$3-10). Use of many of Europe's high speed or quality trains (such as EuroCity and InterCity) requires a supplementary expenditure for those traveling with German rail passes.

For overnight travel, a tight, open bunk called a **couchette** is an affordable luxury (about US$20; reserve at the station several days in advance). Germany offers both youth ticket discounts and youth rail passes. (See **Getting Around,** p. 36.)

■ By Ferry

Travel by boat is a bewitching alternative favored by Europeans but often overlooked by foreigners. Most European ferries are comfortable and well-equipped. You should check in at least two hours early for a prime spot and allow plenty of time for late trains and getting to the port. Fares jump sharply in July and August. Ask for discounts; ISIC holders can often get student fares, and Eurail passholders get many reductions and free trips (check the brochure that comes with your railpass). You'll occasionally have to pay a small port tax (under US$10).

Ferries in the **North** and **Baltic Seas** are reliable and go everywhere. Ferries run from Rostock, Kiel, Lübeck, Hamburg, and Rügen Island to Scandinavia, Russia, and England. Those content with deck passage rarely need to book ahead. If you really have travel time to spare, **Ford's Travel Guides,** 19448 Londelius St., Northridge, CA 91324 (tel. (818) 701-7414; fax 701-7415) lists **freighter companies** that will take passengers worldwide. Ask for their *Freighter Travel Guide and Waterways of the World* (US$16, plus US$2.50 postage if mailed outside the U.S.).

ONCE THERE

■ Tourist Offices

Every German town of any touristic importance is served by a local tourist office. These go by a bewildering variety of names—*Verkehrsamt, Fremdenverkehrsbüro, Verkehrsverein, Fremdenverkehrsverein, Tourist-Information, Gemeindeamt,* and (in spa towns) *Kurverwaltung* or *Kurverein.* To simplify things, most are marked by a standard thick lowercase "**i**" sign. Tourist offices are usually located in the town square or by the main train station—sometimes both. Exploit these offices for city maps (often free), cycling routes and rental options, information on sights and museums, and accommodations lists. Many offices will track down a vacant room for you and make a reservation, sometimes for free, otherwise for DM2-5. While Western German tourist personnel can be relied upon to speak fluent English, their comrades in Eastern Germany often possess nothing more than a rudimentary knowledge of English. *Let's Go* lists tourist offices in the **Practical Information** sections.

■ Embassies and Consulates

If you're seriously ill or in trouble, your embassy can provide a list of doctors or pertinent legal advice, and can also contact your relatives. In *extreme* cases, they can offer emergency financial assistance. Embassies are located in Bonn; consulates can be found in other major cities. For the addresses of consulates not listed here, check the **Practical Information** sections of individual cities.

Australia: Embassy, Bonn, Godesberger Allee 105-107, 53175 (tel. (0228) 810 30; fax 810 31 30). **Consulates, Berlin,** c/o Kempinski Plaza, Uhlandstr. 181-183 (tel. (030) 880 08 80; fax 88 00 88 99). **Frankfurt am Main,** Gutleutstr. 85, 60329 (tel. (069) 273 90 90; fax 23 26 31).

Canada: Embassy, Bonn, Friedrich-Wilhelm-Str. 18, 53113 (tel. (0228) 96 80; fax 968 39 03). **Consulates, Berlin,** Friedrichstr. 95, 10117 (tel. (030) 261 11 61; fax 262 92 06). **Düsseldorf,** Prinz-Georg-Str. 126, 40479 (tel. (0211) 172170). **Hamburg,** ABC-Str. 45, 20354 (tel. (040) 35 55 62 95; fax 35 55 62 94). **Munich,** Tal 29, 80331 (tel. (089) 219 95 70).

Ireland: Embassy, Bonn, Godesberger Allee 119, 53175 (tel. (0228) 81 00 06; fax 37 57 39). **Consulates, Berlin,** Ernst-Reuter-Platz 10, 10587 (tel. (030) 34 80 08 22; fax 34 80 08 63). **Hamburg,** Feldbrunnerstr. 43 (tel. (040) 44 18 62 13). **Munich,** Mauerkircherstr. 1a, 81679 (tel. (089) 98 57 23).

New Zealand: Embassy, Bonn, Bundeskanzlerpl. 2-10, 53113 (tel. (0228) 22 80 70; fax 22 16 87). **Consulate, Hamburg,** Heimhuder Str. 56, 20148 (tel. (040) 442 55 50).

South Africa: Embassy, Bonn, Auf der Hostert 3 (tel. (0228) 820 10; fax 820 11 48). **Consulates, Berlin,** Douglasstr. 9, 14171 (tel. (030) 82 50 11; fax 826 65 43). **Frankfurt,** Ulmenstr. 37 (tel. 719 11 30). **Munich,** Sendlinger-Tor-Platz 5, 80366 (tel. (089) 231 16 30).

U.K.: Embassy, Berlin, Unter Den Linden 32-34, 10117 (tel. (030) 20 18 40; fax: 20 18 41 58). **Consulates, Düsseldorf,** Yorckstr. 19, 40476 (tel. (0211) 944 80). **Frankfurt Am Main,** Bockenheimer Landstr. 42, 60323 (tel. (069) 170 00 20; fax 72 95 53). **Hamburg,** Harvestehuderweg 8a, 20148 (tel./fax (040) 448 03 20). **Munich,** Bürkleinstr. 10, 80538 (tel. (089) 21 10 90). **Stuttgart,** Breitestr. 2, 70173 (tel. (0711) 16 26 90). The **Bonn** embassy has no consular services.

United States: Embassies, Bonn, Deichmanns Aue 29, 53170 (tel. (0228) 33 91; fax 339 20 53). **Berlin,** Clayallee 170, 14195n (tel. (030) 832 92 33). **Düsseldorf,** Kennedydamm 15-17, 40476 (tel. (0211) 47 06 10). **Frankfurt Am Main,** Siesmayerstr. 21, 60323 (tel. (069) 753 50; fax 74 89 38). **Hamburg,** Alsterufer 27, 20354 (tel. (040) 41 17 10; fax 41 76 65). **Leipzig,** Wilhelm-Seyfferth-Str. 4, 04107 (tel. (0341) 21 38 40). **Munich,** Königinstr. 5, 80539 (tel. (089) 288 80).

■ Getting Around

BY PLANE

More than 100 international airlines serve Germany, but flying across the country is generally expensive and unnecessary. Nearly all airlines cater to business travelers and set prices accordingly. The headquarters for **Lufthansa German Airlines,** the national carrier (tel. (0221) 82 60), is at Deutsche Lufthansa AG, Von-Gablenz-Str. 2-6, 50679 Köln. Its air hub is located in Frankfurt am Main; from there, all its destinations can be reached in an average of 50 minutes. Within Germany, the toll-free reservations number is 0180 380 3803. To U.S. residents, Lufthansa (tel. (800) 645-

3880) offers "Discover Europe," a package of three flight coupons that cost US$125-200 each, depending on season and destination; up to six additional tickets cost US$105-175 each. *Let's Go* lists airports and flight information telephone numbers in the **Practical Information** sections of major cities. Usually, S-Bahns or buses run between the airport and the nearest city's main train station.

BY TRAIN

"The trains run on time." It's a cliché, almost a joke, and not infallibly true. At the same time, it brings up an important truth about getting around in Germany—if the trains aren't perfect, they do go almost everywhere a traveler would want to go, with the exception of some very rural areas. In fact, the train system's obligation to run lines to inaccessible areas, even at a loss, is written into Germany's Basic Law. The **Deutsche Bahn** sprung from the integration of the western **Deutsche Bundesbahn (DB)** and old eastern **Deutsche Reichsbahn (DR)**. Integration is still taking place; many connections are as yet incomplete. Moving from west to east, there are significant differences in quality and service. One problem in eastern Germany is connections; on an indirect route, allow about twice as much time as you would in the western parts. Averaging over 120kph, including stops, and connecting some 7000 locations, the DB network is probably Europe's best, and also one of its most expensive, although many discount opportunities exist (see below).

"S-Bahn" trains are commuter rail lines that run from a city's center out to its suburbs; they are frequently integrated with the local subway or streetcar system. "RE" or "RB" trains include a number of rail networks between neighboring cities. "InterRegio" (IR) trains, covering larger networks between cities, are speedy and comfortable. "D" trains are foreign trains that serve international routes. "IC" (InterCity) trains zoom along between major cities every hour. You must purchase a supplementary "IC Zuschlag" to ride an "IC" or "EC" train (DM6 when bought in the station, DM8 on the train). Even the IC yields to the futuristic-looking InterCity Express (ICE) trains, which approach the luxury and speed of an airplane: they run at speeds up to 280kph. For these, railpass users usually do not pay a *Zuschlag,* unless the train requires a mandatory seat reservation fee. Ticketed customers do get hit with a fee.

Most German cities have a **main train station;** in German, **der Hauptbahnhof.** (This is the point referred to when *Let's Go* gives directions "from the station.") In train stations, yellow signs indicate departures *(Abfahrt),* and white signs indicate arrivals *(Ankunft).* The number under *"Gleis"* is the track number.

Second-class travel is pleasant, and compartments are excellent places to meet friendly folks of all ages and nationalities. Larger train stations have different counters for domestic tickets, international tickets, seat reservations, and information; check before lining up. On major lines, reservations are always advisable even if you have a railpass; make them at least a few hours in advance at the train station.

European Railpasses

Buying a railpass is both a popular and sensible option under many circumstances. Ideally conceived, a railpass allows you to jump on any train in Europe, go wherever you want whenever you want, and change your plans at will. With your railpass you will receive a timetable for major routes and a map with details on possible ferry, steamer, bus, car rental, hotel, and **Eurostar** (the high speed train linking London and Paris or Brussels) discounts. In practice, it's not so simple. You still must stand in line to pay for supplements, seat reservations, and couchette reservations, as well as to have your pass validated when you first use it. More importantly, railpasses don't always pay off. For ballpark estimates, consult Rick Steves' *Europe Through the Back Door* newsletter or the **DERTravel** or **RailEurope** railpass brochure for prices of point-to-point tickets. Add them up and compare with railpass prices. If you're under age 26, youth fare tickets are probably a viable option.

Eurailpass remains perhaps the best option for non-EU travelers. Eurailpasses are valid in most of Western Europe except for Britain. Eurailpasses and Europasses are designed by the EU itself, and can be purchased only by non-Europeans almost

exclusively from non-European distributors. These passes must be sold at uniform prices determined by the EU, so no one travel agent is better than another as far as the pass itself is concerned. However, some agents tack on a US$10 handling fee. Also, agents often offer different perks with purchase of a railpass, so shop around to see what you can get.

The first-class **Eurailpass** rarely pays off; it is offered for 15 days (US$538), 21 days (US$698), one month (US$864), two months (US$1224), or three months (US$1512). Those traveling in a group of two to five people might prefer the **Eurail Saverpass,** which allows unlimited first-class travel for 15 days (US$458 per person), 21 days (US$594), one month (US$734), two months (US$1040), or three months (US$1286). Travelers ages 12-25 can buy a **Eurail Youthpass,** good for 15 days (US$376), 21 days (US $489), one month (US$605), two months (US$857), or three months (US $1059) of second-class travel. The two-month pass is most economical. **Eurail Flexipasses** allow limited first-class travel within a two-month period: 10 days (US$634), 15 days (US$836). These prices drop to US$540 and US$710, respectively, when traveling in a group of two to five people. **Youth Flexipasses,** for those under 26 who wish to travel second-class, are available for US$444 or US$585, respectively. Children 4-11 pay half-price, and children under 4 travel free.

The **Europass** combines France, Germany, Italy, Spain, and Switzerland into one plan. With a Europass you can travel in any of these five countries for five to fifteen days within a window of two months. First-class adult prices begin at US$326 and increase incrementally by US$42 for each extra day of travel. With purchase of a first-class ticket you can buy an identical ticket for your traveling partner for 40% off. Second-class youth tickets begin at US$216 and increase incrementally by US$29 for each extra day of travel. Children between the ages of 4-11 travel for half the price of a first-class ticket. You can add associate countries (Austria/Hungary, Belgium/ Luxembourg/Netherlands, Greece Plus (Greece and ADN/HML ferry between Italy and Greece) for a fee: US$60 for 1 associated country; US$90 for 2; US$110 for 3, and US$120 for all 4. The Europass introduces planning complications; you must plan your routes so that they only make use of countries you've "purchased." They're serious about this: if you cut through a country you haven't purchased you will be fined.

You should plan your itinerary before buying a Europass. It will save you money if your travels are confined to between three and five adjacent Western European countries, or if you know that you want to go only to large cities. Europasses are not appropriate if you like to take lots of side trips—you'll waste rail days. If you're tempted to add lots of rail days and associate countries, consider the Eurailpass.

You'll find it easiest to buy a Eurailpass before you arrive in Europe; contact Council Travel, Travel CUTS, STA Travel, Let's Go Travel (see **Budget Travel Agencies,** p. 29), or any of many other travel agents. Only a few places in major European cities sell these passes (at a marked-up price). If you're stuck in Europe and unable to find someone to sell you a Eurailpass, call an American railpass agent, who should send a pass by express mail. Eurailpasses are not refundable once validated; you can get a replacement for a lost pass only if you have purchased insurance on it under the Pass Protection Plan (US$10). All Eurailpasses can be purchased from a travel agent, or from **Rail Europe, Inc.,** 226-230 Westchester Ave., White Plains, NY 10604 (tel. (800) 438-7245; fax (800) 432-1329 in the U.S.; and tel. (800) 361-7245; fax (905) 602-4198 in Canada; http://www.raileurope.com), which also sells point-to-point tickets. They offer special rates for groups of six or more traveling together. **DER-Travel Services,** 9501 W. Devon Ave. #400, Rosemont IL 60018 (tel. (800) 421-2929, fax (800) 282-7474; http://www.dertravel.com) also deals in railpasses and point-to- point tickets.

For EU citizens, there are **InterRail Passes,** for which six months' residence in Europe makes you eligible. There are 8 InterRail zones: A (Rep. of Ireland, Great Britain Passenger Railway, N. Ireland), B (Noreway, Sweden, and Finland), C (Germany, Austria, Denmark, and Switzerland), D (Croatia, Czech Rep., Hungary, Poland, and Slovakia), E (France, Belgium, Netherlands, and Luxembourg), F (Spain, Portugal, and Morocco), G (Italy, Greece, Slovenia, Turkey, and the ADN/HML ferries between Italy and Greece), and H (Bulgaria, Romania, Yugoslavia, and Macedonia). You can buy a pass good for 22 days in one zone (under 26 UK£159, over 26 UK£229), or one month in two zones (UK£209, UK£279), three zones (UK£229, UK£309), or all 8 zones (UK£259, UK£349). For information and ticket sales in Europe contact **Student Travel Center,** 1st Fl. 24 Rupert St., London, W1V7FN (tel. (0171) 437 01 21, 437 63 70, or 434 13 06; fax 734 38 36). Tickets are also available from travel agents or main train stations throughout Europe.

If your travels will be limited to one country, consider a national railpass or regional passes (see **German Railpasses** below). In addition to simple railpasses, many countries (and Europass and Eurail) offer rail-and-drive passes, which combine car rental with rail travel—a good option for travelers who wish both to visit cities accessible by rail and make side trips into the surrounding areas. Several national and regional passes offer companion fares, allowing two adults traveling together 50% off the price of one pass. Some of these passes can be bought only in Europe, some only outside of Europe, and for some it doesn't matter; check with a railpass agent or with national tourist offices.

German Railpasses

Non-Europeans can purchase the tourist-oriented **German Railpass** in their home countries. The pass allows five, 10, or 15 days of rail travel within a four-week period on all DB trains (for info on types of trains, see p. 37). The first-class version costs US$276 for five days, US$434 for 10 days, and US$562 for 15 days in a month. The second-class version costs US$188 for five days, US$304 for 10 days, and US$410 for 15 days. There is also a **German Rail Youth Pass** version, available to non-Europeans age 12-25, which comes only in a second-class version. It costs US$146 for five days, US$200 for 10 days, and US$252 for 15. Travelers ages 4-11 can purchase the railpasses for half the adult prices, while those under four travel free.

There are also several "internal" national railpasses, which can *only* be purchased once you've arrived. For anyone under age 27, a decent deal is the **Tramper-Ticket,** which allows you to pick 10 days of unlimited second-class rail travel in a month on all DB trains (including the ICE), the railroad-run buses *(Bahnbusse),* and the local S-Bahns in cities, all for DM369. The pass is only available between June 15 and October 31.

The **BahnCard** is a great option for those making frequent and extensive use of German trains. It is valid for one year, and gets you a 50% discount on all rail tickets, including the ICE. A second-class BahnCard is a great deal for young travelers: students 26 and under and anyone ages 18 to 22 can get one for DM120; first-class cards are DM240. Seniors over 60 can get BahnCards at the same discounts. Those between ages four and 17 can purchase a second-class BahnCard for DM60, first-class DM120. Normal rates are DM240 second-class; DM480 first-class. Crazier still: since 1995, BahnCards have been used as Visa **credit cards** for some purchases in Germany. (See a DB brochure for details.) Passes are only available at major train stations throughout Germany, and all require a small photo. You may contact **Deutsche Bahn** by making a local call from any city (tel. 194 19; http://www.bahn.de). In the U.S., contact **DER Travel Services** at 9501 W. Devon Ave., Rosemont, IL 60018-4832 (tel. (800) 782-2424; fax (800) 282-7474). The DER branch in Canada is located at 904 The East Mall Etobicoke, Ont. M9B 6K2 (tel. (800) 463-8767; fax (416) 695-1453). Deutsche Bahn's fantastic **website** details the great deals that they concoct, as well as information on connections between cities.

Youth, Student, and Discount Fares

Travelers under 26 can purchase **TwenTickets,** which knock 25% off fares over DM10; be sure to let your ticket agent know your age. A **Schönes Wochenende** ticket offers a fantastic deal for weekend trips. For a single price of DM35, up to five people receive unlimited travel on any of the slower trains (**not** ICE, IC, EC, D, or IR) from 12:01am Saturday until 2am on Monday. Single travelers often find larger groups who are amenable to sharing their ticket, either free or for a fraction of the purchase cost. The **Guten-Abend-Ticket** provides an excellent deal for long-distance night travel. It entitles its holders to travel anywhere (**not** on InterCity Night or CityNight Lines) in Germany between 7pm and 2am. Second-class tickets are DM59, with ICE surcharge DM69; first-class DM99, with ICE surcharge DM109; Friday and Sunday DM15 extra.

Useful Resources

The ultimate reference for planning rail trips is the **Thomas Cook European Timetable** (US$28; US$39 including a map of Europe with all train and ferry routes; postage US$4.50). This timetable, updated regularly, covers all major and most minor train routes in Europe. In the U.S. and Canada, order it from **Forsyth Travel Library** (see **Useful Publications,** p. 2). In Europe find it at any **Thomas Cook Money Exchange Center.** Also from Forsyth is **Traveling Europe's Trains** (US$15) by Jay Burnoose, which includes maps and sightseeing suggestions. The annual **Eurail Guide to Train Travel in the New Europe** (US$15) gives timetables, instructions, and prices for international train trips, daytrips, and excursions in Europe. It is available in most bookstores or from **Houghton Mifflin Co.,** 222 Berkeley St., Boston, MA 02116 (tel. (800) 225-3362; fax (800) 634-7568). The annual railpass special edition of the free Rick Steves's **Europe Through the Back Door** travel newsletter and catalogue, 120 Fourth Ave. N., P.O. Box 2009, Edmonds, WA 98020 (tel. (425) 771-8303; fax 771-0833; email rucksteves@aol.com; http://www.ricksteves.com), provides comparative analyses of European railpasses with national or regional passes and point-to-point tickets. **Hunter Publishing,** P.O. Box 7816, Edison, NJ 08818 (tel. (908) 225-1900; fax 417-0482; email hunterpub@emi.net; http://www.hunterpublishing.com), offers a catalogue of rail atlases and travel guides. The vast online bookstore at **http://www.amazon.com** also sells and ships most of the above titles.

BY BUS

Germany does have a few regions that are inaccessible by train, and some bus lines fill the gaps. Bus services between cities and to small, outlying towns usually run from the *Zentral Omnibus Bahnhof (ZOB),* which is usually close to the main train station. Buses are often slightly more expensive than the train for comparable distances. Check the bulletin boards in university buildings or the classified pages of local magazines for occasional deals. Railpasses are not valid on any buses other than those (relatively few) run by Deutsche Bahn.

Eurolines, 4 Cardiff Rd., Luton LU1 1PP (tel. (01582) 40 45 11; fax (01582) 40 06 94; in London, 52 Grosvenor Gardens, Victoria (tel. (0171) 730 82 35; email welcome@eurolines.uk.com; http://www.eurolines.co.uk), is Europe's largest operator of Europe-wide coach services, including Eastern Europe and Russia. A Eurolines Pass offers unlimited 30-day (UK £199, under 26 and over 60 UK£159) or 60-day (UK£249, under 26 and over 60 UK£199) travel between 30 major tourist destinations. Eurolines also offers **Euro Explorers,** seven complete travel loops throughout Europe with set fares and itineraries. **Eurobus UK Ltd.,** Coldborough House, Market Street, Bracknell, Berkshire RG121JA (tel.(01344) 300 301; fax (01344) 860 780; email info@eurobus.uk.com; http://www.eurobus.uk.com), offers cheap bus trips to 25 major cities in 10 major European countries, including for those between ages 18 and 38. The buses, with English-speaking guides and drivers, stop door-to-door at one hostel or budget hotel per city, and let you hop on and off. Tickets are sold by zone (for any 1 zone US$195, for any two zones US$299, for all three zones US$319). Travelers under 26 are eligible for discounts on all tickets. For purchase in the United States contact Commonwealth Express (tel. (800) EUROBUS (387-6287)); in Canada contact Travel CUTS (see **Budget Travel Agencies,** p. 39).

BY CAR

Cars offer freedom, access to the countryside, and an escape from the town-to-town mentality of trains. Unfortunately, they also insulate you from the *esprit de corps* of rail traveling. Although a single traveler won't save by renting a car, four usually will. If you can't decide between train and car travel, you may benefit from a combination of the two; Rail Europe and other railpass vendors offer rail-and-drive packages for both individual countries and all of Europe. Travel agents may offer other options. Fly-and-drive packages are often available from travel agents or airline/rental agency partnerships and the Deutsche Bahn has a **Rail 'n' Drive Pass.**

Australian, European and U.S.-based **car rental** firms (Alamo, Avis, Budget, Europcar, or Hertz) all have offices in Germany. Tour operators (Auto Europe, Europe By Car, Kemwel Holiday Autos, and Rob Liddiard Travel), can also arrange a rental for you from a European company at its own rates. Multinationals offer greater flexibility, but tour operators often strike better deals. Rentals vary by company, season, and pick-up point; picking up your car in Belgium, Germany or Holland is usually cheaper than renting from Paris. Expect to pay US$80-400 per week, plus tax (5-25%), for a teensy car. Reserve well before leaving for Germany and pay in advance if at all possible. It is almost always significantly less expensive to reserve a car from overseas. Always check if prices quoted include tax and collision insurance; some credit card companies will cover this automatically. Ask about discounts and check the terms of insurance, particularly the size of the deductible. Rates are generally lowest in Belgium, Germany, Holland, and the U.K., and highest in Scandinavia and Eastern Europe. Ask your airline about special fly-and-drive packages; you may get up to a week of free or discounted rental. Minimum age varies, but is usually 21-25. At most agencies, all that's needed to rent a car is a license valid in your country and proof that you've had it for a year.

Try **Alamo** (tel. (800) 522-9696; http://www.goalamo.com); **Auto Europe** (U.S. tel. (800) 223-5555; fax (800) 235-6321; email webmaster@autoeurope.com; http://www.autoeurope.com); **Avis Rent a Car** (U.S. tel. (800) 331-1084; http://www.avis.com); **Budget Rent a Car** (U.S. tel. (800) 472-3325; http://www.budget-rentacar.com); **Europe by Car** (tel. (800) 223-1516 or (212) 581-304; fax (212) 246-1458; in California, (800) 252-9401; http://www.europebycar.com); **Hertz Rent a Car** (tel. (800) 654-3001; http://www.hertz.com); **Kemwel Holiday Autos** (tel. (800) 678-0678; email kha@kemwel.com; http://www.kemwel.com); **Rob Liddiard Travel** (tel. (800) 272-3299 or (818) 980-9133; email liddiard@jps.net).

For longer than 17 days, **leasing** can be cheaper than renting; it is often the only option for those ages 18 to 21. The cheapest leases are agreements to buy the car and then sell it back to the manufacturer at a prearranged price. As far as you're concerned, though, it's like a lease and doesn't entail enormous financial transactions. Leases generally include insurance coverage and are not taxed, though they may include a VAT. The most affordable ones usually originate in Belgium, France, or Germany. Expect to pay at least US$1200 for 60 days. Contact **Auto Europe, Europe by Car, Kemwel Holiday Autos,** or **Rob Liddiard Travel.**

If you're brave and know what you're doing, **buying** a used car or van in Europe and selling it just before you leave can provide the cheapest wheels for longer trips. Check with consulates for import-export laws concerning used vehicles, registration, and safety and emission standards. Camper-vans and motor homes give the advantages of a car without the hassle and expense of finding lodgings. Most of these vehicles are diesel-powered and deliver roughly 24 to 30 mi. per gallon (8.5 to

11km per liter) of diesel fuel, which is cheaper than gas. David Shore and Patty Campbell's **Europe by Van and Motorhome** (US$14; postage US$3, overseas US$6) guides you through the entire process of renting, leasing, buying, and selling vehicles in Britain and on the Continent, including buy-back options, registration, insurance, and dealer listings. To order, contact Shore/Campbell Publications, 1842 Santa Margarita Dr., Fallbrook, CA 92028 (tel./fax (800) 659-5222 or (760) 723-6184; email shorecam@aol.com; http://members.aol.com/europevan).

Eric Bredesen's **Moto-Europa** (US$16; shipping US$5), available from Seren Publishing, 2935 Saint Anne Dr., Dubuque, IA 52001 (tel. (800) 387-6728; fax (319) 583-7853), is a thorough guide to all of these options and includes itinerary suggestions, a motorists' phrasebook, and chapters on leasing and buying vehicles. More general info is available from the **American Automobile Association (AAA)**, Travel Agency Services Dept., 1000 AAA Dr., Heathrow, FL 32746 (tel. (800) 222-4357, (407) 444-4300, or (407) 894-3333; http://www.aaa.com). For regional numbers of the **Canadian Automobile Association (CAA)**, call (800) 222-4357 or go to their website (http://www.caa.ca). Also try the **Automobile Association** of the United Kingdom (tel. (01206) 255678; fax 255916; http://www.theaa.co.uk). The **Australian Automobile Association (AAA)** number in New South Wales is 13 21 32.

Americans and Canadians may drive for one year in Germany with a valid national or international license (see **Driving Permits and Car Insurance**, p. 11). The national license must be officially translated by a German diplomatic office, an international motor vehicle office in the country where the license was issued, or a German automobile club like ADAC. If you are planning to stay in Germany for more than one year, you must obtain a German driver's license, available upon presentation of your national license. Vehicle liability insurance is required by law in Germany. Foreign motorists must present the green international insurance card or purchase temporary insurance at the point of entry.

Yes, Virginia, there really is no speed limit on the **Autobahn**. Germans drive *fast*; before venturing on the road, be *very* familiar with traffic rules and especially signs and symbols. Germans drive on the right side of the road. It is **illegal to pass on the right**, *even on superhighways*. On secondary roads, traffic moves at 80-100kph (62 mph) for passenger cars, and in cities and towns speeds hover around 30-60kph (31 mph). The recommended speed on the *Autobahn* is 130kph (81 mph), but if you drive that slowly in the left lane, cars will loom in your rear-view mirror with lights flashing.

German law requires that both front and back seat passengers wear **seat belts;** motorcycle drivers and riders must wear **helmets** if traveling over 24kph. Children under 12 may not sit in the front seat unless special seats have been installed. Studded snow tires are also *verboten*. The maximum permissible **blood alcohol** content is less than 0.08%, lower than the limit in the U.S. and Australia, and even lower amounts are illegal if you're involved in a violation—basically, if you even *think* of alcohol, you're probably over the limit. Other rules and regulations apply; for more information, contact **Allgemeiner Deutscher Automobil Club e.v. (ADAC)** by mail at: Redaktion ADAC Motorwelt, 81373 München, or visit the office once in Germany at Am Westpark 8, Munich-Sendling (tel. (089) 767 60, emergency tel. 22 22 22; fax 76 76 25 00). Or contact **Automobil Club von Deutschland (AvD)**, Lyoner-Str. 16, 60528 Frankfurt (tel. (069) 660 60, emergency (030) 99 09). ADAC maintains **Straßenwachthilfe** units that patrol the roads and assist disabled vehicles. ADAC will provide **road assistance** free of charge if the damage can be repaired within half an hour; if not, you'll pay repair and towing fees. Orange emergency telephones indicated by blue *Notruf* (emergency call) signs summon the free service. A critically important word is **Stau,** meaning "traffic jam"—Germany has plenty. Local radio stations provide traffic reports.

BY BOAT

River boat and motor boat services abound on many inland waters in Germany. In addition to connecting towns within Germany, many passenger and car ferries make connections to offshore islands (the Frisian Islands, for example) in the North and Baltic Seas. On the Danube, Elbe, Main, Mosel, Neckar, Rhine, Oder, Saale, and Weser rivers you can hop a ferry and enjoy seeing Germany from a new perspective. The Mosel, Rhine, and Danube steamers have been overrun by tourists; less commercial-looking lines can be more alluring. *Let's Go* details schedules in many towns. Be sure to ask about discounts if you're holding any kind of railpass or ISIC. The German Rail Youth Pass qualifies you for this special bonus: free travel on the KD River Day Steamer on the Rhine, Main, and Mosel between selected major cities.

BY BIKE

Today, biking is one of the key elements of the classic budget Eurovoyage. With the proliferation of mountain bikes, you can do some serious natural sight-seeing. Remember that touring involves pedaling both yourself and whatever you store in the panniers (bags which strap to your bike); you should take some reasonably challenging rides at home to prepare yourself before you leave, and have your bike tuned up by a reputable shop. Wear visible clothing, drink plenty of water (even if you're not thirsty), and ride on the same side as the traffic. Learn the international signals for turns and use them. It's good to know how to fix a modern derailleur-equipped mount and change a tire, and practice on your own bike. A few simple tools and a good bike manual will be invaluable. For info about touring routes, consult national tourist offices or any of the numerous books available. **The Mountaineers Books,** 1001 S.W. Klickitat Way #201, Seattle, WA 98134 (tel. (800) 553-4453 or (206) 223-6303; fax 223-6306; mbooks@mountaineers.org) offers Germany-specific tour books.

If you are nervous about striking out on your own, **Blue Marble Travel** (in U.S. tel. (800) 258-8689 or (973) 326-9533; fax 326-8939, in Paris (01) 42 36 02 34; fax 42 21 14 77; http://www.bluemarble.org) offers bike tours designed for folks ages 20-50. **CBT Bicycle Tours** offers one- to seven-week tours, priced around US$95 per day, including all lodging and breakfasts, one-third to one-half of all dinners, complete van support, airport transfers, three staff, and extensive route notes and maps each day. Tours run May through October, with departures every seven to 10 days. In 1999, CBT will visit Germany and other European countries. Contact CBT Bicycle Tours, 415 W. Fullerton, #1003, Chicago, IL 60614 (tel. (800) 736-BIKE (2453) or (773) 404-1710; fax 404-1833; email adventure@cbttours.com; http://www.cbttours.com).

Many airlines will count your bike as your second free piece of luggage; a few charge. The additional or automatic fee runs upward of DM100 each way. Bikes must be packed in a cardboard box with the pedals and front wheel detached; some airlines provide or sell bike boxes at the airport, while others expect you to bring your own. Be aware that bikes can be damaged during transport or that airlines may slap on fees as you attempt to get home. Most ferries let you take your bike for free or a nominal fee. You can always ship your bike on trains, though the cost varies widely.

Riding a bike with a frame pack strapped on it or your back is about as safe as pedaling blindfolded over a sheet of ice; panniers are essential. The first thing to buy, however, is a suitable **bike helmet.** At about US$25-50, they're a better buy than injury or death. U-shaped **Citadel** or **Kryptonite locks** are expensive (from US$8-37), but the companies insure their locks against theft of your bike for one to two years. **Bike Nashbar,** 4111 Simon Rd., Youngstown, OH 44512 (tel. (800) 627-4227 or (330) 788-8832; fax (800) 456-1223; http://www.bikenashbar.com), has excellent prices and cheerfully beats advertised competitors' offers by US$.05. They ship anywhere in the U.S. or Canada.

Renting a bike beats bringing your own if your touring will be confined to one or two regions. *Let's Go* lists bike rental shops for most larger cities and towns. A sturdy if unexciting one-speed model will cost DM12-30 per day; be prepared to lay down a sizable deposit. Some youth hostels rent bicycles for low prices. Bike rentals are also available at approximately 180 train stations throughout the country where German Rail's **Fahrrad am Bahnhof** ("Bikes at the Station") program rents for DM6-10 per day. Usually bikes can be rented from one station and returned at another with a deposit of some kind; ask for details at the station.

Germany makes biking easy with its wealth of trails and bike tours, including some organized through hostels and through the rail system. In urban areas, a bicycle can be one of the most efficient ways to get around. German cities and towns usually have designated bike lanes, sometimes in the street, and sometimes laid out on the sidewalk itself. Pedestrians should look out for tell-tale bike icons or changes in pavement color; it may look like those bikers are on the sidewalk, but they move fast, have right-of-way, and with all the conviction of self-righteous biking zeal, expect you to be the one to get out of the way—quickly.

For information about bike routes, regulations, and maps, contact **Allgemeiner Deutscher Fahrrad-Club**, Postfach 10 77 47, 28077 Bremen (tel. (0421) 34 62 90; fax 346 29 50; email kontakt@adfc.de; http://www.adfc.de). The ADFC is the biggest bicycle club for commuters and touring cyclists and an invaluable source of information and support. A bike tour guidebook, including extensive maps, is available from Deutsches Jugendherbergswerk (DJH); see its address under **Accommodations: Hostels,** p. 49.

BY THUMB

Let's Go strongly urges you to consider seriously the risks before you choose to hitch. We do not recommend hitching as a safe means of transportation, and none of the information presented here is intended to do so.

No one should hitch without careful consideration of the risks involved. Favorable hitching experiences allow you to meet local people, but hitching means entrusting your life to a random person who happens to stop beside you on the road and risking theft, assault, sexual harassment, and unsafe driving. If you're a woman traveling alone, don't hitch. It's just too dangerous. A man and a woman are a safer combination, two men will have a harder time, and three will go nowhere. The choice remains yours.

If you do decide to hitch, where you stand is vital. In the **Practical Information** section of many cities, we list the tram or bus lines that take travelers to strategic points for hitching out. It is illegal to hitch on the *Autobahnen* (expressways). Hitchers must stand in front of the *"Autobahn"* signs at on-ramps, or at **Raststätten** (rest stops) and **Tankstellen** (gas stations). *Autobahn* hitchers will need a good map to navigate the tangled interchanges in the Rhine-Ruhr area, and should pay attention to license plates: B=Berlin, M=Munich, F=Frankfurt, HH=Hamburg. There's also plentiful hitching on the heavily traveled *Bundesstraßen*, scenic secondary roads marked by signs with yellow diamonds.

Finally, success will depend on what one looks like. Successful hitchers travel light and stack their belongings in a compact but visible cluster. Most Europeans signal with an open hand, rather than a thumb; many write their destination on a sign in large, bold letters and draw a smiley-face under it. Drivers prefer hitchers who are neat and wholesome.

Safety issues are always imperative, even for those who are not hitching alone. Safety-minded hitchers avoid getting in the back of a two-door car, and never let go of their backpacks. They will not get into a car that they can't get out of again in a hurry. If they ever feel threatened, they insist on being let off, regardless of where they are. Acting as if they are going to open the car door or vomit on the upholstery will usually get a driver to stop. Hitchhiking at night can be particularly dangerous; experienced hitchers stand in well-lit places, and expect drivers to be leery of nocturnal thumbers (or open-handers).

Many German cities offer a ride service, a cross between hitchhiking and the ride boards common at many universities, which pairs drivers with riders; the fee varies according to destination. **Mitfahrzentralen** (ride-share centers) pair drivers with riders, with a fee to agency (about US$20) and driver (per km). Some belong to nation-wide chains (**CityNetz Mitfahrzentrale** have computerized listings); others are local store-front operations. *Let's Go* lists *Mitfahrzentralen* under the **Practical Information** sections in each city; check the white and yellow pages under *"Mitfahrzentrale."*

BY PUBLIC TRANSPORTATION

Urban public transit is excellent in the west and fairly good in the east. You'll see four types in German cities: **Straßenbahn** (streetcars), **S-Bahn** (commuter rails), **U-Bahn** (subways), and regular **buses**. Eurailpass holders get free passage *only* on the S-Bahn, which, in large cities, doesn't usually go everywhere one needs to go. Berlin, Bonn, Düsseldorf, Frankfurt, Hamburg, Hanover, Köln, München, and Stuttgart have U-Bahn systems. Consider purchasing a day card *(Tageskarte, Tagesnetzkarte)* or multiple-ride ticket *(Mehrfahrkarte or Sammelkarte)*, which usually pay for themselves by the third ride. German subways and commuter rails (and many streetcar and bus systems) operate on an honor system. The usual procedure is to buy your ticket from a kiosk or automat and then **validate** it by inserting the indicated edge into a little upright box marked with an **"E"** *(Entwerten)*. The ticket is then "clicked" and marked with the time at which you validated it. On subways, you must do this *before* getting in the car or, if the box is inside the car, *as soon as you*

ESSENTIALS

enter and before the subway starts moving. Once the doors close and the train gets underway, plainclothed inspectors may appear and thrust an orange badge in your face that says *"Kontrolle."* (The adjectival description of this experience is "being controlled.") If you cannot produce a valid ticket that has been properly cancelled, you will be subject to large fines (DM60 is typical) and immense humiliation. The inspectors don't take excuses; if you can't pay up on the spot, a police officer will meet you at the next stop to take you to jail. English-speaking backpackers have a very bad reputation for *Schwarzfahren* ("black riding," or riding without a ticket), so don't expect any sympathy. If you try the "I didn't understand, I don't speak German" excuse, the inspector will brusquely point out the explanatory signs in English. "I thought my Eurailpass was valid," never works, either. Don't assume that folks ride illegally because you don't see them canceling tickets; when the inspector appears, you'll discover that they're all carrying monthly passes

■ Accommodations

Most local tourist offices distribute extensive listings free of charge and will also reserve a room for a small fee. German National Tourist Offices supply more complete lists of campsites and hotels (see **Government Information Offices, p.** 1).

HOSTELS

> HI-affiliated hostels in **Bayern** generally do not admit guests over age 26, although families with young children are usually allowed even if parents are over 26.

In 1908, a German named Richard Schirmann, believing that life in industrial cities was harmful to the physical and moral development of youth, built the world's first **youth hostel** in Altena—a budget dormitory that would bring travel within the means of poor youth. Germany has been a leader in hosteling ever since, and Schirmann is something of a mythical figure. Fees range from DM15 to DM30 per night and hostels affiliated with one of the associations often have lower rates for members. Some hostels are set in strikingly beautiful castles, others in run-down barracks far from the town center. Hostels are generally dorm-style accommodations, often in single-sex large rooms with bunk beds, although some hostels do offer private rooms for families and couples. They sometimes have kitchens and utensils for your use, bike or moped rentals, storage areas, and laundry facilities. There can be drawbacks: some hostels close during certain daytime "lockout" hours, have a curfew, don't accept reservations, impose a maximum stay, or, less frequently, require that you do chores. There's often little privacy and you may run into more screaming pre-teen groups than you care to remember. Many hostels require sheet sleeping sacks (see **Packing**, p. 28). Sleeping bags are usually prohibited (for sanitary reasons), but almost all hostels provide free blankets.

The **DJH webpage** (http://www.djh.de), has pictures, prices, addresses, and phone numbers for almost every hostel in Germany. **Eurotrip** (http://www.eurotrip.com/accommodation/accommodation.html) has information and reviews on budget hostels and several international hostel associations. The **Internet Guide to Hostelling** (http://www.hostels.com), which provides a directory of hostels from around the world in addition to oodles of information about hostelling and backpacking worldwide.

A **one-year Hostelling International (HI) membership** permits you to stay at youth hostels all over Germany at unbeatable prices. Despite the name, you need not be a youth. Most guests are ages 14 to 26, but hostels are rapidly becoming a resource for all ages (except in Bayern); travelers over 26 pay only a bit more. Many German hostels are open to families. It's best to procure a membership card before you leave home; some hostels do not sell them on the spot. Membership cards are available from some travel agencies and from Hostelling International affiliates.

HI hostels, over 4500 of them, are scattered worldwide and many accept reservations via the International Booking Network (IBN) for a nominal fee. Reservations can be made from any other IBN hostel or via phone. From within the U.S. call (tel. (202) 783-6161); outside call your respective national hostelling organization or check http://www.hiayh.org/ushostel/reserva/ibn3.htm for international IBN booking numbers. HI's umbrella organization's web page (http://www.iyhf.org) lists the web adresses and phone numbers of all national associations and can be a great place to begin researching hostelling in a specific region. Although you can join HI on the road, it is much easier to do so at home. Here are some of the national associations:

Australian Youth Hostels Association (AYHA), Level 3, 10 Mallett St., Camperdown NSW 2050 (tel. (02) 9565 1699; fax 9565 1325; email YHA@yha.org.au; http://www.yha.org.au). Membership AUS$44, renewal AUS$27; under 18 AUS$13.

Hostelling International-Canada (HI-C), 400-205 Catherine St., Ottawa, Ontario K2P 1C3 (tel. (613) 237-7884; fax 237-7868; email info@hostellingintl.ca; http://www.hostellingintl.ca). Maintains 73 hostels throughout Canada. IBN booking centers in Edmonton, Montreal, Ottawa, and Vancouver. Membership packages: 1 year, under 18 CDN$12; 1 year, over 18 CDN$25; 2 years, over 18 CDN$35; lifetime CDN$175.

An Óige (Irish Youth Hostel Association), 61 Mountjoy St., Dublin 7 (tel. (353) 1 830-4555; fax 1 830-5808; email anoige@iol.ie; http://www.irelandyha.org). One-year membership is IR£7.50, under 18 IR£4, family IR£7.50 for each adult with children under 16 free.

Youth Hostels Association of New Zealand (YHANZ), P.O. Box 436, 173 Cashel St., Christchurch 1 (tel. (3) 379 9970; fax 365 4476; email info@yha.org.nz; http:/ /www.yha.org.nz). Annual membership fee NZ$24.

Hostelling International Northern Ireland (HINI), 22-32 Donegall Rd., Belfast BT12 5JN, Northern Ireland (tel. (01232) 32 47 33 or 31 54 35; fax 43 96 99; email info@hini.org.uk; http://www.hini.org.uk). Prices range from UK£8-12. Membership packages: 1 year, UK£7, under 18 UK£3, family UK£14 for up to 6 children; lifetime UK£50.

Scottish Youth Hostels Association (SYHA), 7 Glebe Crescent, Stirling FK8 2JA (tel. (01786) 89 14 00; fax 89 13 33; email syha@syha.org.uk; http://www.syha.org.uk). Membership UK£6, under 18 UK£2.50.

Hostelling International South Africa, P.O. Box 4402, Cape Town 8000 (tel. (021) 24 2511; fax 24 4119; email info@hisa.org.za; http://www.hisa.org.za). Membership SAR50, group SAR120, family SAR100, lifetime SAR250.

Youth Hostels Association of England and Wales (YHA), Trevelyan House, 8 St. Stephen's Hill, St. Albans, Hertfordshire AL1 2DY, England (tel. (01727) 85 52 15; fax 84 41 26; email yhacustomerservices@compuserve.com; http://www.yha.org.uk). Enrollment fees: adults UK£10, under 18 UK£5,UK£10 for one parent with children under 18 enrolled free; UK£140 for lifetime membership.

Hostelling International-American Youth Hostels (HI-AYH), 733 15th St. NW, Suite 840, Washington, D.C. 20005 (tel. (202) 783-6161, ext. 136; fax 783-6171; email hiayhserv@hiayh.org; http://www.hiayh.org). Maintains 35 offices and over 150 hostels in the U.S. Memberships can be purchased at many travel agencies or at the national office in Washington, D.C. One-year membership US$25, under 18 US$10, over 54 US$15, family cards US$35; includes *Hostelling North America: The Official Guide to Hostels in Canada and the United States.*

Hostelling in Germany is overseen by **Deutsches Jugendherbergswerk (DJH)** Postfach 1462, 32704 Detmold, Germany (tel. (05231) 740 10; fax 74 01 84; http://www.djh.de). The DJH has, in recent years, initiated a growing number of *Jugendgästehäuser*, youth guest-houses that are generally more expensive, have more facilities, and attract slightly older guests. The DJH has absorbed hundreds of hostels in Eastern Germany with remarkable efficiency, though some still lack the truly sparkling faciilities of their western counterparts. Still, Germany currently has about **600 hostels**—more than any other nation on Earth.

DJH publishes *Jugendherbergen in Deutschland* (DM14.80), a guide to all federated German hostels, available at German bookstores and major train station newsstands, or by writing to DJH.

HOTELS AND PRIVATE ROOMS

The cheapest hotel-style accommodations are places with *Gasthof, Gästehaus,* or *Hotel-Garni* in the name. Breakfast *(Frühstück)* is almost always included. Rooms in private homes *(Privatzimmer)* or guest houses are widely available and less expensive than hotels or *Pensionen,* though most either require a minimum stay of two or more nights or charge you a fee for staying only one night. Local tourist offices usually handle bookings, either for free or for a DM2-5 fee; in less urban areas, look for signs saying *Zimmer frei* (room available) and just knock. Finding affordable hotel rooms in the New Federal States of the east is generally a challenge. Still, eastern Germany is increasingly developing its own tourist industry, and the prices of its *Pensionen* and hotels are often cheaper than in the west.

Hotels are quite expensive in Germany: rock-bottom for singles is DM30, for doubles DM40-45, and the price is almost never subject to haggling. Budget European hotels might come as a rude shock to pampered North American travelers. A bathroom of your own is a rarity and costs extra when provided. Hot showers may also cost extra.

The best bet for a cheap bed is often a **private room** *(Privatzimmer)* in a home. Costs generally run DM20-40 per person, and usually include warm and personal service. This option works best if you have a rudimentary knowledge of German, since room owners prefer to lay down a few household rules before handing over the keys for the night. Simply apprise the local tourist office of your language abilities (if any) when you ask for a room reference. Travelers over 26 who would otherwise pay senior prices at youth hostels will find these rooms well within budget range.

ALTERNATIVE ACCOMMODATIONS

Mitwohnzentralen in most German cities match people who want to lease apartments from a few days to a couple of months. A number of host networks will help you find accommodations with families throughout Europe. See **Work and Volunteer,** p. 21.

■ Longer Stays

Those planning to remain in Germany for an extended period of time should contact the local **Mitwohnzentrale,** an accommodation-finding office, in the city where they plan to stay. Throughout Germany, *Mitwohnzentralen* match apartments with apartment seekers. The stay can last anywhere from a few days to eternity, depending on the availablity of apartments and the price you are willing to pay. Look under the **Practical Information** listings for each individual city to find the address and phone number of individual *Mitwohnzentralen.* Also check postings in universities, where student housing can offer lodging and utilities for DM200-300 per month. Those seeking employment will need a work permit (see **Alternatives to Tourism,** p. 21).

Those looking to **furnish** an abode would do well to capitalize on the German **Sperrmull** phenomenon. Cities around Germany have appointed days on which residents dispose of their larger garbage in a designated *Platz,* thus producing a gold-mine of free couches, tables, TVs, and more. The local *Stadthaus* has a schedule of these days. Bring a shopping cart to lug the juicier booty, and show up early (6pm the day **before** the official event generally yields successful plundering), as rabid German *Schulkinder* tend to loot the goods on the actual *Sperrmull* day.

Those who wish to open a **bank account** should be careful in selecting a bank; the speed with which German banks provide their customers with **ATM cards** varies widely, as do charges for ATM withdrawals. **Dresdner Bank** and **Deutsche**

Bank tend to provide their customers with the best ATM deals; both are national banks, meaning that account holders can withdraw money without any charge throughout Germany. These banks are also networked for withdrawals in most European countries. Sparkasse has been known to take longer in providing clients with ATM cards.

■ Camping, Hiking, and the Outdoors

Germans love the outdoors, and their enthusiasm is evident in the bounty of campsites that dot the outskirts of even the most major of cities, in the armies of decked-out old folks that hit the trails every Sunday, and in the eagerness with which many younger Germans travel around the world in search of wilderness adventures. Though the offerings in Germany are generally rather tame in comparison to those in Switzerland, Austria, or other more mountainous areas, the facilities for outdoor activities in Germany are among the most well-maintained in the world.

CAMPING

There are about 2600 campsites in Germany, most of which are accessible by public transportation and about 400 of which are open in the winter. If you're prepared to go rustic, camping is the best option. Often, however, campgrounds resemble battlegrounds, with weary travelers and screaming children vying for tiny grassy plots. The money and time expended in getting to the site may eat away at your budget and patience, especially in urban areas. Showers, bathrooms, and a restaurant or store are common. Camping costs DM3-10 per person with an additional charge for tents and vehicles.

Blue signs with a black tent on a white background indicate official sites. **Deutscher Camping-Club e.v. (DCC)**, Mandlstr. 28, 80802 München (tel. (089) 380 14 20), and **Allgemeiner Deutscher Automobil-Club (ADAC)** (see **Getting Around: By Car**, p. 42) have specific info on campgrounds, and the National Tourist Office distributes a free map, *Camping in Germany*, with a full list of campgrounds.

These camping guidebooks should meet the needs of the novice or expert:

Automobile Association, AA Publishing. Orders and enquiries to TBS Frating Distribution Centre, Colchester, Essex, CO7 7DW, U.K. (tel. (01206) 25 56 78; fax 25 59 16; http://www.theaa.co.uk). Publishes a wide range of maps, atlases, and travel guides, including *Camping and Caravanning: Europe* (UK£8). New titles include *Big Road Atlas Europe*. They also offer a *Big Road Atlas* for Germany.

The Caravan Club, East Grinstead House, East Grinstead, West Sussex, RH19 1UA, U.K. (tel. (01342) 32 69 44; fax 41 02 58; http://www.caravanclub.co.uk), produces one of the most detailed English-language guides to campsites in Europe.

Stanfords Ltd., 12-14 Long Acre, London, WC2E 9LP, U.K. (tel (0171) 836 2260; fax 379 4776) supplies maps of just about anywhere, including Germany.

At the core of your necessary equipment is the **sleeping bag,** rated according to the lowest outdoor temperature at which it will still keep you warm. If you're using a sleeping bag for serious camping, you should also have either a foam **pad** or an air mattress; another good alternative is the **Therm-A-Rest,** which is part foam and part air-mattress and inflates to full padding when you unroll it. When selecting a tent, pay close attention to weight, storage size, and floor area. Low-profile dome tents are the best all-around. Good two-person tents start at about US$150, and four-person tents at US$400. A **frame backpack** can double as a bona fide heavy-duty trekking pack (see **Luggage,** p. 28). Other necessities include: **battery-operated lantern, plastic groundcloth** for the floor of your tent, **nylon tarp** for general purposes, a **"stuff sack"** to keep your sleeping bag dry; rain gear; synthetic tops, socks, and underwear; a canteen or water bottle; a camp stove; waterproof matches; Swiss Army knife; and insect repellent. The following outfits can provide you with advice and a wide selection of **camping paraphernalia:**

Campmor, P.O. Box 700, Saddle River, NJ 07458-0700 (tel. (888) CAMPMOR (226-7667), outside the U.S. call (201) 825-8300; email customer-service@camp mor.com; http://www.campmor.com), has a wide selection of name-brand equipment at low prices. One-year guarantee for unused or defective merchandise.

Eastern Mountain Sports (EMS), One Vose Farm Rd., Peterborough, NH 03458 (tel. (603) 924-7231); http://www.emsonline.com; email emsmail@emsonline.com), has stores throughout the U.S. Though slightly higher-priced, they provide excellent service and guaranteed customer satisfaction on most items sold. They don't have a catalogue, and they generally don't take mail or phone orders; call the above number for the branch nearest you.

Recreational Equipment, Inc. (REI) (tel. (800) 426-4840); http://www.rei.com) stocks a comprehensive selection of REI brand and other leading brand equipment, clothing, and footwear for the outdoors. REI has 49 retail stores in the U.S.

Discount Camping, 880 Main North Rd., Pooraka, South Australia 5095, Australia (tel. (08) 8262 3399; fax 8260 6240; http://www.austdiscount.com.au/camping), specializes in tents, but carries other equipment and spare parts.

HIKING

Next to *Fußball,* hiking *(wandern)* is the most popular sport in Germany. Trails wind through the outskirts of every German city, and a national network of long-distance trails links the whole country together. The *Schwarzwald* and the Bavarian Alps are especially well-traversed, as are the Harz Mountains and *die Sächsische Schweiz.* Alpine clubs in Germany provide inexpensive, simple accommodations in splendid settings. The **German Alpine Association,** Von-Kahr-Str. 2-4, 80997 München (tel. (089) 14 00 30; fax 140 03 11), maintains over 9000mi. of trails in the Alps and 252 huts open to all mountaineers. They also offer courses and guided expeditions. **Walking Europe from Top to Bottom** by S. Margolis and G. Harmon details one of Europe's most popular trails (US$11); check your local bookstore for others.

■ Sports

Germany enjoys a long tradition of sports and outdoor recreation and outstanding facilities to boot. The *Vereine* (club) culture, encompassing most sports as well as hiking and crafts, produces almost religious fervor and devotion in many of its members. Nearly every city and town in Germany—especially resort towns—has a swimming pool and a spa. The North and Baltic Sea coasts, as well as the Frisian Islands and Rügen, offer attractive beaches in the warm months. In winter, the German Alps, Harz Mountains, Schwarzwald, and Bayerischer Wald are host to all sorts of snow sports, including skiing, ski-jumping, tobogganing, skating, hockey, and bobsledding. Garmisch-Partenkirchen, in the Bayerische Alpen, sports high-caliber winter Olympics facilities. For more information, contact **German Sports Association,** Haus des Sportes, Otto-Fleck Schneise 12, 60528 Frankfurt am Main (tel. (069) 670 00; fax 67 49 06).

■ Keeping in Touch

MAIL

Germany's postal code system is based on geographic zones, with most cities divided into many postal code zones. Large companies and industries even have their own postal codes. The codes are all five digits long and should precede the German name of the town; when sent from outside of Germany, they should include the prefix "D-" before the code.

Sending Mail to Germany

Mail can be sent to Germany through **Poste Restante** (the international phrase for General Delivery; *Postlagernde Briefe* in German) to any city or town; it's well worth using, generally without any surcharges, and much more reliable than you might think. Mark the envelope "BITTE HALTEN" (hold) and address it, for example: Postlagernde Briefe, für Schtanki-Arsch HO, Hauptpostamt, D-50668 Köln, Germany. The last name should be capitalized and underlined. The mail will go to a special desk in the central post office, unless you specify a post office by street address or postal code. As a rule, it is best to use the largest post office in the area; sometimes, mail will be sent there regardless of what you write on the envelope. When possible, it is usually safer and quicker to send mail express or registered.

When picking up your mail, bring a form of photo ID, preferably a passport. If the clerks insist that there is nothing for you, have them check under your first name as well. *Let's Go* lists post offices and codes in the **Practical Information** section.

American Express travel offices throughout the world will act as a mail service for cardholders if you contact them in advance. Under their free **"Client Letter Service,"** they will hold mail for no more than 30 days, forward upon request, and accept telegrams. Just like *Poste Restante*, the last name of the person to whom the mail is addressed should be capitalized and underlined. Some offices will offer these services to non-cardholders (especially those who have purchased AmEx traveler's checks), but you must call ahead to make sure. Check the **Practical Information** section of the countries you plan to visit; *Let's Go* lists AmEx office locations for most large cities. A complete list is available free from AmEx (tel. (800) 528-4800) in the booklet *Traveler's Companion* or online at http://www.americanexpress.com.

Sending Mail to Germany

Airmail between North America and Germany takes 7 to 10 days. Allow at least two weeks for Australia and New Zealand. Postcards and letters from the U.S. and Canada cost 50¢ and 60¢ respectively. It is *vital* to distinguish your airmail from surface mail by labeling it "airmail." **Global Priority Mail,** a service offered by the U.S. Postal Service, gets your mail there more quickly, and its flat-rate envelope charge makes it cheaper than regular airmail sometimes. To send a letter-sized envelope costs US$3.50, while a larger envelope costs US$6.95. **Federal Express** (U.S. tel. for international operator (800) 247-4747) can get a letter from New York to Berlin in two days for a whopping US$25.50.

Surface mail is by far the cheapest and slowest way to send mail. It takes one to three months to cross the Atlantic—appropriate for sending large quantities of items you won't need to see for a while. When ordering books and materials from abroad, always include one or two International Reply Coupons (IRCs)—a way of providing the postage to cover delivery. IRCs should be available from your local post office as well as abroad (US$1.05).

Sending Mail from Germany

Aerogrammes, printed sheets that fold into envelopes and travel via airmail, are available at post offices. It helps to mark *"Mit Luftpost,"* though *Par Avion* is universally understood. Most post offices will charge exorbitant fees or simply refuse to send Aerogrammes with enclosures. Airmail between Germany and the U.S. averages 7 to 10 days. Allow *at least* two weeks for Australia, New Zealand, and most of Africa. To send a **postcard** to an international destination within Europe costs DM1, and to any other international destination via airmail costs DM2. Domestically within Germany, postcards require DM1. To send a **letter** (up to 20g) to another European country costs DM1.10, to anywhere else in the world via airmail costs DM3, and domestically within Germany DM1.10.

Mail moves significantly faster within western Germany than within the East, and crossovers are slower than either. Still, you can generally get a piece of regular mail from one city in Germany to another overnight. Despite postal unity, it's still slower to mail letters from Eastern Germany. **Mailboxes** are bright yellow.

TELEPHONES

To **call Germany,** first dial the international access code of the country you are in (0011 from Australia, 00 from New Zealand, 09 from South Africa, 00 from the U.K. and Ireland, and 011 from the U.S. and Canada), followed by Germany's country code (49), the city code without the first zero, and then, finally, the local number. For a list of city codes see the **appendix** (p. 573) and the inside back cover.

Within Germany, you can always be sure of finding a **public phone** in a post office. Additionally, phones can be found in the *Hauptbahnhof* in just about every German city. Collect calls are not possible from public phones.

EMERGENCY

Police: tel. 110. **Fire:** tel. 112. **Ambulance:** tel. 112.

Local Calls

If you spend a week or more in Germany, invest in a **Telefonkarte** (telephone card), the most sensible way to make calls from public phones. The cards come in DM12, DM24, and DM50 denominations. Cards are sold in all post offices and at many Deutsche Bahn counters. At some phones, you can also pay by **credit card.**

Inter-City Calls

Inter-city calls entail dialing the city telephone code (including the first zero that appears in the code; see or the inside back cover) and the number. There is no standard length for telephone numbers. The smaller the city, the more digits in the city code *(Vorwahl),* while the telephone number *(Rufnummer)* varies in length. In **Eastern Germany,** the phone system is fluctuating during its integration into the West's. Listings operators dispense information about any German city. The **national information number** is 11 833. For information within the EU, call 00 11 88.

International Calls

You can place **international calls** from most telephones in Germany. To call direct, dial the international access code (00) followed by the country code (1 for the United States or Canada, 61 for Australia, 64 for New Zealand, 44 for the U.K., 353 for Ireland, 27 for South Africa; for other codes, see **International Calling Codes,** p. 572). Next, dial the city or area code and the local number. Country and city codes may sometimes be listed with a zero in front (e.g. 033), but after dialing the international access code, drop successive zeros (with the German access code of 00, e.g., 00 33).

English-speaking operators are available for both local and international assistance. Operators can be reached by dialing the access code specific to Germany. These operators will place **collect calls** for you as well as placing calls with your local **calling card.** To reach AT&T in Germany, dial (0130) 0010; for MCI, dial (0130) 0012; for Sprint, dial (0130) 0013. For more information, call **AT&T** about its **USA-Direct** and **World Connect** services (tel. (888) 288-4685; from abroad call (810) 262-6644 collect), **Sprint** (tel. (800) 877-4646; from abroad, call (913) 624-5335 collect), or **MCI WorldPhone** and **World Reach** (tel. (800) 444-4141). In Canada, contact Bell Canada **Canada Direct** (tel. (800) 565 4708); in the U.K., British Telecom **BT Direct** (tel. (800) 34 51 44); in Ireland, Telecom Éireann **Ireland Direct** (tel.

(800) 250 250); in Australia, Telstra **Australia Direct** (tel. 13 22 00); in New Zealand, **Telecom New Zealand** (tel. 123); and in South Africa, **Telkom South Africa** (tel. 09 03). A **calling card** is probably your best and cheapest bet; the calls (plus a small surcharge) are billed either collect or to the calling card. MCI's WorldPhone also provides access to MCI's **Traveler's Assist,** which gives legal and medical advice, exchange rate information, and translation services. Many other long distance carriers and phone companies provide such travel infromation; contact your phone service provider.

Depending on the service you have previously set up, it may be cheaper to find a pay phone and deposit just enough money to be able to say "Call me" and give your number. In Germany, pay phones marked with a bell allow you to receive calls—the phone number should be printed on the phone. Some companies, seizing upon this "call-me-back" concept, have created callback phone services. Under these plans, you call a specified number, ring once, and hang up. The company's computer calls back and gives you a U.S. dial tone. You can then make as many calls as you want, at rates about 20-60% lower than you'd pay using credit cards or pay phones. This option is most economical for loquacious travelers, as services may include a US$10-25 minimum billing per month. For information and immediate hook-up (with a credit card), call **America Tele-Fone** (tel. (800) 321-5817) or **Telegroup** (tel. (800) 338-0225). (Many of these services are available in some countries; call the toll-free numbers for more information.)

Remember **time differences** when calling. Germany is on Western European Time (*MEZ* in German), one hour ahead of Greenwich Mean Time.

OTHER SERVICES

You can pay to send and receive **faxes** in post offices in Germany. Between May 2 and Oktoberfest, **EurAide**, P.O. Box 2375, Naperville, IL 60567 (U.S. tel. (630) 420-2343; fax 420-2369; http://www.cube.net/kmu/euraide.html), offers **Overseas Access,** a service useful to travelers without a set itinerary. The cost is US$15 per week or US$40 per month plus a US$15 registration fee. To reach you, people call, fax, or use the Internet to leave a message; you receive it by calling Munich whenever you wish, which is cheaper than calling overseas. You may also leave messages for callers to pick up by phone.

Electronic mail (email) is one of the best options, and it is increasingly easy to access world-wide, especially in Germany. Every major city and a surprisingly large number of small towns offer cybercafes or other venues that offer pay-per-use Internet connections; *Let's Go* tries to locate many such establishments. **Traveltales.com** (http://traveltales.com) provides free, web-based email for travelers and maintains a list of over 500 cybercafes throughout the world, travel links, and a travelers' chat room. Other free, web-based email providers include **Hotmail** (http://www.hotmail.com) and **USANET** (http://www.usa.net). Accessing telnet abroad can be difficult, but the web is always easy to find.

History and Culture

Ten years after the fall of the Berlin Wall, the story of Germany still stands as a parable for the story of life in the modern era. Germany's experience encapsulates all of the promises and betrayals of life in the 20th century and exposes the fracture line of Western civilization. It has proven a volatile political arena in the recent past, passing through six political systems in 80 years. Events in Germany facilitated the end of the "long 19th century" in 1914 and the end of the "short 20th century" in 1989, when the fall of the Berlin Wall prompted a quick thawing of the cold war. All the while, the "German Question" has been formulated and re-formulated: is there a distinct "German character" that has informed such a peculiar historical path? There are, to be sure, certain German traits—industriousness, efficiency, and a mystifying refusal to cross the street against the light—but the generations of Germans who have come of age after the war defy the negative stereotype of the humorless, heel-clicking German authoritarian. With no direct link to the gruesome past of their parents and grandparents, many younger Germans have abandoned most things "German" and eagerly embraced the global culture of techno-fueled nightlife, international cuisines, and fast-paced business culture. With America as its strongest influence, Germany has developed into a more multi-faceted, modern society. Of course, problems persist even now, 10 years after reunification, and neo-Nazi sentiment remains visible, especially in the economically depressed areas of the East.

But despite its long history of reactionary politics, Germany has been a perennial wellspring of revolutionaries and innovators—for better and for worse. One of the first heroes of German history, **Charlemagne** (Karl der Große) unified post-Roman Europe under enlightened rule. **Martin Luther** went from small-town German monk to one of the most influential figures in Western history when he authored his *95 Theses*, spawning the Protestant Reformation. Socialist pioneers **Karl Marx** and **Friedrich Engels** equipped the revolutionary groundswell of 19th-century Europe with an ideology and a project whose power has been re-channeled but never defused. And one of the most loathsome figures in history, **Adolf Hitler,** performed deeds—the seizure of power, the conquest of Europe, the **Holocaust**—that defy explanation. This last image, of course, indelibly colors all subsequent German history. Germans must grapple with the wrenching fact that the cradle of **Johann Wolfgang von Goethe** and **Immanuel Kant** also nurtured **Auschwitz** and **Dachau.**

These days Germans are busy trying to come to terms with this schizophrenic history and identity. The Wall had barely come down when West Berlin dilettantes started cracking jokes about putting it back up. The "Wall in the Mind" *(die Mauer im Kopf)* may continue to separate Germans for at least a generation. However, this self-examination is beginning to transform into a more international perspective, as the role of Germany in the global market continues to grow. In the wake of Europe's most recent revolutions, a newly reunited Germany's pivotal position between East and West is even more important than it was during the Cold War, and Germany's own experience with reunification informs today's piecing together of the European Union.

The "Wall in the Mind" (die Mauer im Kopf) may continue to separate Germans for at least a generation

The historical and cultural legacies that Germany has offered posterity over centuries of war and division represent a healthy chunk of Western civilization's collective past. There are always bursts of change which seem to have no precedent. But there are also moments when one seems to be hearing the same story again, to hear the same turns of phrase deployed in different settings, the same insistence and the same denial. It is easy to be caught and lost in what Bertolt Brecht called "this Babylonian confusion of words," the narrative of Germany.

■ History

The amount of conflict and debate involved in the telling of German history is matched by few other national histories. Even the starting point of German history is debatable, as it wasn't until 1871 that Germany became its own nation. Relatives of *Homo sapiens* lived in Germany 50,000 years ago; the first remains identified as **Neanderthal Man** were dug up near Düsseldorf in 1856. However, nominally speaking, "German" history didn't begin until 90BC, when the Roman author Posidonius first applied the word to the peoples that migrated from Southern Scandinavia to central Europe around 1000BC. That's where we pick up the story.

TIMELINE

800	Charlemagne crowned as emperor of the Holy Roman Empire.	1914-18	World War I, concluding with the Treaty of Versailles
1356	Golden Bull splits authority between archbishops and electors in choosing Emperor	1918	Socialist revolution in Berlin; Weimar Republic founded
1358	Hanseatic League founded	1922-23	Hyperinflation; Hitler's Beer Hall *Putsch*
1517	Luther posts 95 Theses, inaugurating the Protestant Reformation	1933	Hitler appointed Chancellor, declares himself *Führer* of 3rd Reich
1618-48	Thirty Years War between Protestants and Catholics, concluding with the Peace of Westphalia	1935	Racial Purity Laws, depriving Jews of German citizenship and prohibiting intercourse between "Aryan" and Jew.
1709	Friedrich the Great establishes Berlin as Prussian capital	1938	Kristallnacht, during which most Jewish property in Germany was destroyed
1774	Goethe's *Sorrows of a Young Werther* ushers in *Sturm-und-Drang*	1939-45	World War II, ending with the Allies' defeat of Germany
1806	Napoleonic Wars begin—decline and fall of the Holy Roman Empire	1942-45	"Final Solution," the attempted extermination of European Jews
1815	Congress of Vienna concludes Napoleonic Wars	1949	Division of Germany into FRG and GDR
1824	Beethoven composes his Ninth Symphony	1953	Rebellion in Berlin crushed by Soviets
1848	Abortive socialist revolution; Marx publishes the *Communist Manifesto*	1961	Berlin Wall constructed
1864-71	Bismarck's wars of unification	1989	Fall of the Berlin Wall
1871	Wilhelm I crowned *Kaiser* of new, unified Germany—2nd Reich	1990	Germany reunifies

EARLY GERMAN HISTORY: 58BC-1517

Early German history is more rightly called early European history, as the concept of a nation of Germany didn't emerge until the 19th century. However, the clans of peoples in the region now known as Germany became a real political entity much earlier, when they were forced to define themselves vis-a-vis the powerful **Roman Republic.** After many years of war with the "barbaric" Germans, the Empire had, by 58BC, expanded its borders to the Rhine River. Five centuries of often antagonistic relations between the tribes and the Empire preceded a series of successive pillages of Rome by Germanic tribes. This resulted in the seizure of the city by the Ostrogoths, and the end of the Roman Empire in 476.

While the southern German tribes were busy wreaking savage mayhem among the well-heeled Romans, **the Franks** began to expand their power into the Rhine Valley. This power reached its zenith three centuries later under the rule of **Charlemagne,** whom Germans know as Karl der Große. On Christmas Day in the year 800, Pope Leo III crowned Chuck **Holy Roman Emperor.** Charlemagne's leadership was far more enlightened than that of other leaders at the time; under his rule, monasteries became centers of learning and knowledge preservation, and commerce within Europe and with the Arab and Byzantine worlds was revived. This Dark Age "renaissance" soon came to an end, however, as invasions from outsiders, insufficient infrastructure, and disputes over power inheritance after Charlemagne's death brought on the Treaty of Verdun in 843, which split the empire into three kingdoms, which became further dismantled through later inter-kingdom feuding. A leader of the Frankish kingdom, **Otto I** pushed the Franks' borders east to the Oder River, earning him the title of Holy Roman Emperor in 962.

Despite the continued existence of the Holy Roman Empire, the relationship between the church and the political leadership deteriorated throughout the next several centuries. Quarrels arose repeatedly until the signing of the **Golden Bull of 1356,** which declared that seven electors—three archbishops and four secular leaders—would approve the selection of each emperor. Large-scale bribing of these electors naturally ensued, clearing the way for the ascent of the **House of Habsburg,** which occupied the throne for the next five centuries with the support of their Austrian domains. Under their leadership, the German nation began to define itself a little more clearly; the **Hanseatic League** banded several German merchant towns together in 1358, and outlying areas of the still-alive Holy Roman Empire, including Italy, slipped out of the Habsburgs' control entirely.

THE REFORMATION AND THE THIRTY YEARS WAR: 1517- 1700

On Halloween Day 1517, **Martin Luther,** a monk and professor of Biblical studies at Wittenberg University in Sachsen, posted his **Ninety-Five Theses** on the door of the city's castle church. The reverberations created by the unleashing of the **Protestant Reformation** persist today. Luther attacked the Roman Catholic Church for the extravagance of the papal court in Rome and its practice of selling **indulgences**—gift certificates for the soul that promised to shorten the owner's stay in purgatory. Luther insisted that salvation came only through God's grace, not through paying fees to lazy Catholic clergy. The stern, indefatigable Luther revolutionized everything he touched; one of the greatest salvos of his war against Catholicism was a **new translation of the Bible,** a document whose publication single-handedly crystallized the patchwork of German dialects into a standard, literary High German language.

The German princes soon adopted Lutheranism, captivated by hopes of stemming the flow of money to Rome without going to Hell for it. Armed conflicts soon erupted. The disturbances quickly became more than just religious conflicts; the serfs rebelled during the **Peasants' Wars** in 1524-1526. The chaos was too much for Luther, who called upon the princes to crush the bands of peasants. But Lutheranism continued to spread throughout Europe. The Habsburg Emperor **Karl V**—the most powerful leader since Charlemagne—declared his intention to uproot the subversive doctrine and destroy those who professed it. However, in the 1555 **Peace of Augsburg,** Karl suspended the **Counter-Reformation** and conceded individual princes the right to choose the religion practiced in his territory, a system that led to a number of absurd overnight conversions and further divided and paralyzed the empire.

Karl's successors did not keep the bargain. When Ferdinand of Styria tried to impose Catholicism on Bohemia, Protestants rebelled, leading to the "smashing" **Defenestration of Prague,** in which the unsuspecting papal legate who was hurled out of a window had his fall broken by a pile of steamy horse dung. The **Thirty Years War** (1618-48) that ensued was a catastrophe for Germany. At least one-third of the Holy Roman Empire population was wiped out, towns were laid to waste,

At least one-third of the population was wiped out in the longest and bloodiest conflict ever to embroil Europe

and famine gripped the population in the longest and bloodiest conflict ever to embroil Europe. The **Peace of Westphalia,** which ended the war, granted 300 princes the right to elect the emperor. The Habsburgs' imperial administration was effectively dismantled. The Holy Roman Empire never had a unified and loyal population; although it lingered for another 150 years, it was a dead institution, and its demise left Germany greatly divided.

THE RISE OF BRANDENBURG-PRUSSIA: 1700-1862

The war indirectly benefited the leaders of **Brandenburg-Prussia.** Friedrich II—known as **Friedrich the Great**—led the consolidation of the heartland of the rising Prussian state. Friedrich is revered in German history as an enlightened ruler, notable for administrative and military skill as well as support of the arts. When Maria Theresa became empress of the Habsburg domains in 1740, Friedrich seized the opportunity to snatch the prosperous province of **Silesia.** By the end of the Seven Years War in 1763, Prussia was viewed as one of Europe's great powers. Friedrich II and his nephew joined forces with Russia and Austria to **divide Poland** in 1772 and link Brandenburg to Prussia physically for the first time.

These skirmishes paled in comparison to the havoc wreaked by France in the wake of the French Revolution. **Napoleon** conquered and disbanded the Holy Roman Empire, fusing hundreds of territories into the **Confederation of the Rhine** in 1806. Despite incorporating hundreds of thousands of German soldiers, Napoleon's armies got bogged down in Russia, and a general rebellion known as the **Wars of Liberation** ejected Napoleon from German territory, culminating in the 1813 Battle of Leipzig. The 1815 **Congress of Vienna** partially restored the pre-war German state system by creating the Austrian-led **German Confederation,** although the princelings didn't return. In 1834, Prussia sponsored the **Zollverein,** a customs union that linked most German territories—except Austria—in a free trade zone.

In 1848, revolution broke out again in France, and the discontent spread rapidly to other parts of Europe. The German Confederation agreed to let an elected assembly decide the future of the confederation. The Frankfurt **National Assembly** drafted a liberal constitution, and invited **Friedrich Wilhelm IV** of Prussia to serve as emperor. In a victory of absolutism over democracy, he spurned the offer, saying that he would not accept a cardboard Bürger King crown created by rabble. The assembly disbanded, and the ensuing revolt in Frankfurt was crushed by the Prussian army.

BISMARCK AND THE SECOND REICH: 1862-1914

In 1862, Prussian King Wilhelm I appointed a worldly aristocrat named **Otto von Bismarck** as Chancellor. History's most successful practitioner of *Realpolitik,* Bismarck exploited a remarkably complex series of alliances and compromises that were more than once dissolved in favor of more violent tactics—"Blut und Eisen" (Blood and Iron), Bismarck liked to point out, were all that mattered in the long run. Bismarck believed strongly in the cause of German unity, and used war to achieve it. This he did often and well. In 1864, he fought Denmark and seized control of Schleswig and Holstein. The fallout from this dispute led to conflict with Austria, which Prussia quashed in 1866 at **Sadowa** (Königgrätz). Viewing Austria as a future ally, Bismarck did not impose a humiliating peace. Instead, he made it clear that Prussia would now dominate German affairs and that Austria should mind its own damn business in the East. In 1867, he disbanded the German Confederation and replaced it with the Prus-

"Blut und Eisen" (Blood and Iron), Bismarck liked to point out, were all that mattered in the long run

sian-dominated **North German Confederation.** Bismarck realized that France would never willingly acquiesce to a fully united Germany under Prussian domination. Through a series of trivial diplomatic slights he suckered France into a misguided declaration of war in 1870; the technologically superior Prussian army and its allies swept through France and trounced the French army at **Sedan,** capturing Emperor Napoleon III. Parisians declared a republic and vowed to carry on the fight. Bismarck gleefully besieged Paris and had Wilhelm crowned **Kaiser of the German Reich** in the Hall of Mirrors at the Palace of Versailles.

With France thus disposed of, Bismarck was free to **unify Germany** on his own terms in 1871. He presented German liberals with an offer they couldn't refuse: unification in exchange for an authoritarian monarchy. The so-called **conservative empire** garnered popular support by promoting an aggressive nationalism and colonialist sentiment. **Naval leagues** formed to agitate for a German navy that could compete with Britain in the race for overseas colonies. Naval construction, however, represented only a tiny fraction of the breakneck **industrialization** that Germany underwent in the last decades of the 19th century. In the space of fewer than 40 years, one of the most backward nations in Europe developed the most advanced industrial base on the continent, but retained a medieval political system unable to handle the new liberal ideals. Many historians have attributed many of the nation's problems in the early 20th century to this belated industrialization.

By the 1870s, reformist sentiment had gained ground in Germany. Led by a burgeoning trade union movement and the newly founded **Social Democratic Party** (*Sozialdemokratische Partei Deutschlands*—SPD), working-class radicalism began to pose a serious threat to the reactionary order. In one of the world's great instances of political Machiavellianism, Bismarck engaged in a long series of initiatives that alternatively revolved around reforms and repression (known as the **Kulturkampf**). Bismarck pioneered **social welfare programs** for the working class such as unemployment insurance, but harshly repressed trade unions and the Social Democrats with the **Anti-Socialist Laws** of 1878. His 1879 **Alliance of Iron and Rye** brought together the two leading conservative forces in society—the industrialists and the agrarian aristocrats. By appeasing potential radical factions with these welfare-like programs and alliances, Bismarck quelled revolt. Facing mounting problems with his own constitution and disputes with the new Chancellor Wilhelm II, Bismarck resigned in 1890.

Such rapid transitions produced tremendous social friction. The numbers of the proletariat exploded, but protectionist tariffs kept food absurdly expensive. Germany accelerated its pattern of foreign adventurism in part to quell unrest at home—a policy derisively known as **"Flucht nach vorn"** (flight to the front). Disputes over colonial issues left Germany diplomatically isolated in Europe, and tension between Germany and its neighbors rose. Meanwhile, democratic opposition began to pose a challenge to the regime. For the *Kaisor* and the elites who supported him, it became clear that dramatic and militaristic action might be required for self-preservation.

WORLD WAR I: 1914-1918

On the eve of WWI, Europe was caught in a complex web of alliances in which a minor dispute could easily escalate into a full-blown continental war. The German General Staff designed the **Schlieffen Plan** to win a war on two fronts: a lightning thrust through Belgium would deliver a knock-out blow to France, whereupon Germany could turn to the east and defeat the Russian Czar before he could mobilize his backward army. As Russia's rail network modernized, German generals saw their window of opportunity closing; they were strongly inclined to mobilize at the first sign of a crisis. That crisis broke out in 1914, when a Serbian nationalist assassinated the Habsburg heir to the Austrian throne, **Archduke Franz-Ferdinand**, in Sarajevo.

Austria marched on Serbia. Russia, playing the champion of its brother Slavs, mobilized. Almost the entire *Reichstag*, including the Social Democratic delegates (who despised the Russian Czar), voted to prepare for war to defend the Austrian allies. The decision received popular support from the young generation of German men who were eager to prove themselves on the battlefield. After Russia ignored an ultimatum to rescind the mobilization, Germany entered the war on the side of Austria, prompting France to mobilize. Germany then declared war on France and demanded that Belgium allow its army to cross its frontier. Belgium refused. Britain, which was treaty-bound to defend Belgian neutrality, declared war on Germany. Germany quickly advanced through Belgium and northern France, and suddenly virtually all of Europe was at war.

The slaughter was magnified by new weapons such as machine-guns, planes, and poison gas

After advancing within 50km of Paris, the German offensive stalled at the **Battle of the Marne.** Four years of agonizing **trench warfare** ensued. The slaughter was staggering, magnified by new weapons such as machine-guns, tanks, planes, flame-throwers, and poison gas. Germany's policy of **unrestricted submarine warfare** on all ships entering European waters provoked the

United States into entering on the side of France and Britain. After England checked the imperial navy in the **Battle of Jutland,** a naval blockade rapidly choked Germany. Coupled with the industrial capacity and fresh armies of the U.S., the blockade allowed the Entente to emerge victorious.

THE WEIMAR REPUBLIC: 1918-1933

In late 1918, with the German army on the brink of collapse, riots and mutinies broke out on the home front. On November 9, 1918, Social Democratic leader **Philipp Scheidemann** declared a republic in Berlin, with **Friedrich Ebert** as its first president. France insisted on a harsh peace in the **Treaty of Versailles** (signed at the spot of Wilhelm's coronation—the Hall of Mirrors at the Palace of Versailles), which imposed staggering reparations payments and a clause ascribing the blame for the war to Germany. The new republican government had little choice but to accept the treaty, as the continuing Allied blockade was starving the country. Even before a constitution was drawn up, the republic was stuck with the stigma of the humiliating treaty; because the *Kaiser* had promised a smashing victory right up to the end, Germans were psychologically unprepared for defeat.

Building on this unsettled sentiment, the newly formed **Communist Party** (*Kommunistische Partei Deutschlands*—KPD) led a revolt in Berlin that found some support. The Republic crushed the revolution by appealing to bands of right-wing army veterans called **Freikorps.** In a fit of reactionary fervor, the Freikorps, led by **Wolfgang Kapp,** turned against the government. Workers demonstrated support for the new republic through a general strike, and a force of 50,000-80,000 organized against the coup in the Ruhr industrial area. The republic emerged bruised but intact. Its leaders drew up a constitution in **Weimar;** chosen for its legacy as the birthplace of the German Enlightenment, it now gave its name to a period of intense cultural activity between the world wars.

Outstanding war debts and the burden of reparations produced the staggering **hyperinflation** of 1922-23, during which time the *Reichsmark* sunk from four to 4.2 trillion to the U.S. dollar. Eventually, the Republic achieved a degree of stability with help from the American **Dawes Plan,** and an age of

War debts and the burden of reparations produced the staggering hyperinflation of 1922-23, during which time the Reichsmark sunk from four to 4.2 trillion to the U.S. dollar

relative calm and remarkable artistic production ensued. The old, reactionary order still clung to power in many segments of society: army, police, big business, civil service, and judiciary. When an Austrian corporal named **Adolf Hitler** was arrested for treason after his abortive 1923 **Beer Hall Putsch** uprising in Europe, he was not deported (on the grounds that he "believed he was German") and received the minimum sentence of five years, of which he served only 10 months. During his time in jail, Hitler wrote a book—*Mein Kampf*—and decided that his party, the National Socialist German Workers Party (*Nationalsozialistische Deutsche Arbeiterspartei*—NSDAP), also known as the **Nazis,** would have to seize power by constitutional means. Two aspects of the Weimar constitution, intended to establish a perfectly representative and functional democracy, in fact expedited this process. **Pure proportional representation** encouraged a spectrum of political parties and discouraged stable governments. The infamous **Article 48** (drafted by sociologist Max Weber) gave the Chancellor the power to rule by decree during crises.

The Nazi party expanded its efficient, blindly obedient bureaucracy and nearly quadrupled its membership to 108,000 by 1929. Even so, it was still a fringe party in 1928, receiving only 2.5% of the vote. But when the Great Depression struck in 1929, 25% of the population was unemployed within months. Membership in the NSDAP exploded to more than a million by 1930—the **SA** *(Sturmabteilung),* its paramilitary arm, grew as large as the German army. The Nazis campaigned on an anti-Semitic, xenophobic platform; Hitler failed in a presidential bid against the nearly senile war-hero Hindenburg in 1932, but parliamentary elections made the Nazis the largest party (winning 37% of the seats) in the *Reichstag*. After various political maneuvers,

President Hindenburg reluctantly appointed Hitler Chancellor of a coalition government on January 30, 1933. Completely legally, Hitler had taken over Germany.

THE THIRD REICH: 1933-45

While Hitler now held the most powerful government post, his Nazi party, the largest single party in the coalition government, had difficulty obtaining a majority in the *Reichstag.* But within the first two months of taking control, Hitler convinced the ailing and aging Hindenburg to dissolve the *Reichstag* and call new elections, allowing Hitler to invoke Article 48 and to **rule by decree** for seven weeks. During this reign of terror, he curtailed freedom of the press, authorized his special security arms (the Special State Police, known as the **Gestapo,** the **SA** Storm Troopers, and the **SS** Security Police) as auxiliary police, and brutalized opponents. Politically astute, he seized the opportunity of the mysterious **Reichstag fire** one week prior to the elections, declaring a state of emergency in order to round up opponents, many of whom were relocated to newly built **concentration camps.** In the ensuing election on March 5, 1933, with 44% of the votes, the Nazis once again fell short of a majority. Nonetheless, they arrested and browbeat enough opposing legislators to pass an **Enabling Act** making Hitler **legal dictator** of Germany, authorized to ban all opposition and rule by decree indefinitely. Characteristic humility led Hitler to place himself as a successor to the two previous *Reichs:* the Holy Roman Empire (800-1806) and the German Empire (1871-1918). Nazi party control extended to the smallest details of everyday German life—not just the government, but universities, professional associations, and even chess clubs.

Vilifying the Weimar government as soft and ineffectual, Hitler's platform played on a variety of German anxieties that had accumulated since 1918; these ideas drew strength from notions of anti-Semitism and German racial superiority. Wounded pride over First World War losses and the flailing economy ensured a receptive public. Aided by **Joseph Goebbels,** his propaganda chief, Hitler exploited self-promotion to an insuperable degree; Nazi rallies were masterpieces of political demagoguery and portraits of Hitler and the Nazi emblem, the **swastika,** embellished everything from match covers to fingernails of loyal teeny boppers. "Heil Hitler" and the right arm salute became the legally obligatory greeting.

One of the government's first acts was to institute a **boycott of Jewish businesses** and to expel Jews from professions and the civil service. In 1934, after Hindenburg's death, Hitler appropriated the presidential powers for himself. The following year, the first of the anti Semitic **Racial Purity Laws** deprived Jews of German citizenship. After a respite during the 1936 Berlin Olympics, the program resumed in earnest on November 9, 1938, with **Kristallnacht** (Night of Broken Glass). In that evening alone, Nazis destroyed thousands of Jewish businesses, burned synagogues, killed nearly 100 Jews, and sent at least 20,000 to concentration camps.

> *The Nazis arrested and browbeat enough opposing legislators to pass an Enabling Act making Hitler legal dictator of Germany, authorized to ban all opposition and rule by decree indefinitely*

Hitler directed his wrath at Jews, gypsies, communists, Social Democrats, artists, free-thinkers, gays, and the disabled, as well as anyone who demonstrated any sympathy toward these groups. In some respects, however, the early years of the Third Reich were an improvement over the Weimar era. A massive program of industrialization restored full employment. Hitler abrogated the Versailles Treaty, thus freeing Germany from reparations payments and allowing it to re-arm. Although the *Autobahn* highway project was planned during the republic—as were other improvements for which the Nazis claimed credit—Hitler pushed it in earnest, recognizing its military implications, and then boldly **re-militarized the Rhineland.** Next, Hitler stared down Mussolini and the West to annex Austria—the infamous **Anschluß.** Then he demanded territorial concessions from Czechoslovakia, on the grounds that it served as a home to thousands of ethnic Germans. British Prime Minister Neville Chamberlain assured Hitler in the notorious 1938 **Munich Agreement** that Britain would not interfere with this. Hitler's foreign policy was dominated by one of the fundamental tenets of Nazi ideology: the necessity of acquiring **Lebensraum** (living space) from the "sub-human" Slavs in the East.

WORLD WAR II: 1939-1945

On September 1, 1939, German tanks rolled into eastern neighbor Poland. Britain and France, bound by treaty to defend Poland, immediately declared war on Germany but did not attack. Germany's new tactic of mechanized **Blitzkrieg** (literally, lightning war) quickly crushed Poland. In a month, Poland was vanquished, and Hitler and Stalin divided it under the terms of a secret agreement. On April 9, 1940, Hitler overran Denmark and Norway. A month later, the *Blitzkrieg* roared through the Ardennes Forest of Luxembourg and quickly overwhelmed Belgium, the Netherlands, and France, but the Nazis failed to bomb London into submission in the aerial struggle of the **Battle of Britain.** Preparations for a cross-channel invasion were shelved as Hitler turned his attentions to his most despised enemy, Russia. The German **invasion of the USSR** in June 1941 ended the Hitler-Stalin pact. Despite the Red Army's overwhelming manpower, the invasion came close to success due to the pathetic state of the Soviet officer corps. At the peak of his conquests in late 1941, Hitler held an empire stretching from the Arctic Circle to the Sahara Desert, from the Pyrenees to the Urals. By 1944, his circle of opponents, the Allies, included France, Great Britain, the United States, the USSR, and China.

The Soviets suffered extremely high casualties, but the *Blitzkrieg* faltered in the Russian winter and Hitler sacrificed thousands of German soldiers in his adamant refusal to retreat. The bloody battle of **Stalingrad** was the critical turning point in the East. Hitler committed a second fatal error when he declared war on the United States after ally Japan bombed Pearl Harbor. His attempt to save Mussolini in North Africa led to the Nazi's first battlefield defeats, and soon Germany was retreating on all fronts. The Allied landings in Normandy on **D-Day** (June 6, 1944) preceded an arduous, bloody advance across Western Europe. The Third Reich's final offensive, the **Battle of the Bulge,** failed in December 1944. In March 1945, the Allies crossed the Rhine. The Red Army overcame bitter resistance to take Berlin in April 1945. With Red Army troops overhead, Hitler married Eva Braun just prior to killing himself in his bunker. The Third Reich, which Hitler had boasted would endure for 1000 years, had lasted only 12.

The Third Reich, which Hitler had boasted would endure for 1000 years, had lasted only 12

THE HOLOCAUST

Hitler's twisted ideology regarded history as a series of catastrophic confrontations between racial groups. The German *Volk*, he believed, had to triumph or perish forever. He made no secret of his desire to exterminate all Jews, who, associated with internationalism, communism, pacifism, and democracy, represented the very antithesis of Hitler's fanatic nationalism, militarism, and belief in the myth of the *"Führer."* The Nazis' **"Final Solution to the Jewish problem"** became an appalling exaggeration of the persecution, deprivation, and deportation to which Jews had been subjected since the first days of the *Reich*. Another precedent was the gassing of the handicapped in the 30s. Nevertheless, the mass gassing of Jews in specially constructed **extermination camps** began only in 1942, although **SS** troops who followed the campaign through Russia had earlier staged mass executions. Seven full-fledged extermination camps, **Auschwitz, Buchenwald, Chelmno, Treblinka, Majdanek, Sobibor,** and **Belzec,** plus dozens of nominal "labor" camps such as **Bergen-Belsen, Dachau,** and **Sachsenhausen** were operating before war's end. Some six million Jews, two-thirds of Europe's Jewish population, mostly from Poland and the Soviet Union, were gassed, shot, starved, worked to death, or killed by exposure. Five million other victims— Soviet prisoners of war, Slavs, Gypsies, homosexuals, the mentally retarded, and political opponents—also died in Nazi camps. The atrocities of the Nazi years reach beyond the scope of tragedy and into the realm of inconceivable horror.

How much did the average German know about the Holocaust? No one can say for sure, but it is certain that the vicious persecution and small-scale murder of Jews in pre-war Germany and the "resettlement" of Jews in the east were clear for all to see. However, the Nazis were careful to keep the grisly details of gas chambers and crematoria out of reach, even among the top party leadership. Many Germans who now express horror at the genocide tolerated—or even approved of—the Nazis' earlier expressions of anti-Semitism. Very few were as daring as industrialist Oskar Schindler or the Scholl siblings, who led the "White Rose" student resistance movement.

As the living memory of the Holocaust slowly fades, the aging remains of concentration camps become the most crucial, tangible testimony available to any audience willing to see and listen. Just as a monument can lose its power to shock by becoming too familiar to passersby, so can the very existence of "museums" and guided tours seem to trivialize what occurred at the camps. The very fact that concentration camps are noted as points of interest in many travel guides (including this one) must be recognized as somewhat troubling. If you choose to visit one, keep in mind that while some treat these grounds as "just another stop" on a list of things to see, coming in ignorance and leaving unaffected, many visitors come with a knowledge of the camp's past or perhaps a personal memory of a loved one who perished there.

OCCUPATION AND DIVISION: 1945-1949

Germans call their defeat in the Second World War *Null Stunde*—"Zero Hour"—the moment at which everything began again. Unlike in WWI, Germany's battlefield defeat was total and indisputable. The Allies occupied and partitioned the country: the east under the Soviets, the west under the British and Americans, and Berlin under joint control. The economy was in shambles. Most cities had been bombed into ruin. More than five million German soldiers and civilians died in the war, and millions remained in POW camps. All German territory east of the Oder and Neisse rivers—a quarter of the nation's land—was confiscated and placed under Soviet and Polish administration, while the coal-rich Saarland was put under French control. Ten to twelve million ethnic Germans were expelled from Poland and Sudeten Czechoslovakia; more than two million perished during the exodus. As the details of the Nazi genocidal project became public, "German" became synonymous with "barbaric."

The Allied program for the **Occupation**—demilitarization, democratization, and de-Nazification—proceeded apace, but growing animosity between the Soviets and the Western allies made joint control of Germany increasingly difficult. De-Nazification proceeded in quite disparate ways in East and West, paving the way for total division in 1949. Blaming the structures of bourgeois capitalism for the Nazi nightmare,

> *Germans call their defeat in the Second World War "Nulle Stunde" — "Zero Hour" — the moment at which everything began again*

the Soviets purged only former elites, leaving the common people exempt from most responsibility. The Allies, however, prosecuted Nazis individually, yet often so inadequately that many retained their posts. In 1947, the Western Allies merged their occupation zones into a single economic unit known as **Bizonia** (later Trizonia, after a French occupation zone was carved out of the British and American zones). The Western Allies began rebuilding their zone along the lines of a market economy with the aid of huge cash infusions from the **Marshall Plan.** The Soviets, who suffered immeasurably more in the war than the U.S. or Britain, had neither the desire nor the spare cash to help the East rebuild—they plundered it instead, as allowed by the Potsdam agreement. The Soviet Union carted away everything that wasn't fixed in concrete and a lot of things (such as factories and railroads) that were. The Western Allies ceased their contribution to the Eastern "giant sucking sound" in 1948 and then effectively severed the East's economy from the West's by introducing a new currency to Bizonia, the **Deutschmark.** Although the imposition of the new Mark seemed draconian at the time, most historians agree that it was the single greatest cause of the eventual stabilization of West Germany. The currency reform dispute was the proximate cause of the **Berlin Blockade** and the ultimate **division of Germany** in 1949.

THE FEDERAL REPUBLIC OF GERMANY (FRG)

The Federal Republic of Germany (*Bundesrepublik Deutschland*—FRG) was established as a provisional government of Western Germany on May 24, 1949. The new government set up camp in the sleepy university town of **Bonn**. A **Basic Law,** drawn up under the direction of the Western Allies, safeguarded individual rights and established a system of Federal States. Although similar in many ways to the Weimar Constitution, the Basic Law had significant departures: it made the Chancellor responsible to Parliament, banned anti-democratic parties, renounced militarism, emasculated the presidency, and established a more stable parliamentary system. One of the most visionary paragraphs of the Basic Law was the one that established a Right of Asylum, guaranteeing refuge to any person fleeing persecution. Ratification of the Basic Law, however, did not restore German sovereignty; the Allies retained supreme power over the country.

As the only party untainted by the Third Reich, the **Social Democratic Party** (*Sozialdemokratische Partei Deutschlands*—SPD) seemed poised to dominate post-war German politics. Another new party, the **Free Democratic Party** (*Freidemokratische Partei*—FDP), assembled bourgeois liberals and professionals with several former Nazis. Although the FDP remained small, it acquired power as a coalition partner. A third party, the **Christian Democratic Union** (*Christliche Demokratische Union*—CDU), managed to unite Germany's historically fragmented conservatives and centrists. With former Köln Mayor **Konrad Adenauer** at the helm, the CDU won a small plurality of *Bundestag* seats.

Adenauer, 73 years old when he assumed office, was perhaps the Federal Republic's greatest Chancellor. He unflaggingly pursued the integration of Germany into a unified Europe and, at the same time, the return of German national self-determination. He achieved both of these aims, first in 1951 with West Germany's entrance into the European Coal and Steel Community—the precursor of the modern European Union (EU)—and then in 1955 when the Western Allies recognized West German sovereignty. The idealistic Adenauer also helped to restore the self-esteem and purpose of his defeated people without rekindling nationalism. The speedy recovery of the economy, the **Economic Miracle** (*Wirtschaftswunder*) of the mid-1950s secured the future dominance of the German economy and of the CDU party. Rebuilding progressed rapidly; Germany achieved full employment by the late 1950s and soon began recruiting thousands of foreign **Gastarbeiter** (guest workers). Despite SPD opposition, Adenauer aligned Germany with NATO (North Atlantic Treaty Organization) in a common defense bloc.

The idealistic Adenauer also helped to restore the self-esteem and purpose of his defeated people without rekindling nationalism

The SPD, whose fortunes seemed so promising in 1945, wandered in the electoral wilderness without any bread crumbs for over 20 years. The party's Marxist rhetoric prevented it from expanding beyond a working-class base. In 1961, the SPD jettisoned Marx and found a dynamic young leader in **Willy Brandt,** the charismatic former Berlin mayor who had worked in the anti-Nazi resistance. Germany's first postwar recession in 1967 badly hurt the CDU and the 1969 *Bundestag* elections launched the SPD into power. With Brandt as Chancellor, the **Social-Liberal Coalition** of the SDP and FDP enacted a number of overdue reforms in education, governmental administration, social security, and industrial relations. Its most dramatic policy innovation, however, was in **foreign relations.** Under the old **Hallstein Doctrine,** the Federal Republic refused to recognize the German Democratic Republic, to the point of severing relations with any country that did recognize it. This effectively meant that West Germany was entirely cut off from the entire Eastern Bloc. Under Brandt's **Ostpolitik** (Eastern Policy), the Federal Republic actively sought improved relations with East Germany, the Soviet Union, and other Eastern Bloc nations—a policy symbolized by the famous image of a tearful Brandt dropping to his knees in front of a Polish war memorial. Brandt and his foreign minister concluded several important treaties, including an agreement **normalizing relations** with the GDR. For this, Brandt received the Nobel Peace Prize in 1971.

After Brandt resigned in the wake of a 1974 spy scandal, **Helmut Schmidt** assumed the Chancellorship. West Germany under Schmidt racked up an economic record that was the envy of the industrialized world. Nevertheless, persistent structural problems in heavy industry contributed to **mounting unemployment** and dissatisfaction with the SPD in the late 1970s. In 1982, new partners FDP and CDU formed a government under **Helmut Kohl** after FDP leader **Hans-Dietrich Genscher** abruptly abandoned the Social-Liberal coalition.

Kohl's government pursued a policy of welfare state cutbacks, tight monetary policy, and military cooperation with the U.S. Around the same time, a new political force emerged in Germany: the **Green Party** *(die Grünen)*. By fighting for disarmament and environmentalism and rejecting traditional coalition politics of the Left, the Greens won a surprisingly large following. In 1984, Richard von Weizsäcker of the CDU was elected to the largely symbolic post of Federal President, from which he urged Germans to shoulder fully their moral responsibility for the Third Reich—an implicit rebuke of politicians like Kohl who spoke of "the grace of late birth."

THE GERMAN DEMOCRATIC REPUBLIC (GDR)

When Soviet troops occupied Eastern Germany, a cadre of German Communists who had spent the war in exile came close on their heels. Even before the surrender was signed, these party functionaries began setting up an apparatus to run the Soviet occupation zone. The first party licensed to operate in the Soviet Sector was the **German Communist Party** *(Kommunistische Partei Deutschlands)* under Wilhelm Pieck and Walter Ulbricht, but versions of the Western parties were established shortly afterwards. At first, the German Communists pledged to establish a parliamentary democracy and a distinctively "German path to socialism." However, their dependence on Moscow became apparent. The Social Democrats were forced to join them in a common working-class anti-fascist front, the **Socialist Unity Party** *(Sozialistische Einheitspartei Deutschlands—SED)*.

In Berlin, the Social Democratic Party was permitted to operate freely, and the SED was soundly defeated at the ballot box. The Soviets responded by not holding any more freely contested elections, and future elections required voters to approve or reject a "unity list" of candidates that ensured SED dominance. On October 7, 1949, a People's Congress selected by such methods declared the establishment of the **German Democratic Republic** *(Deutsche Demokratische Republik*—GDR), with the national capital in Berlin. Although the first constitution of the GDR guaranteed civil liberties and paid lip service to parliamentary democracy, these were empty promises. Real power lay in the hands of the SED's *Politbüro* and the party's secretary. Although the SPD was nominally an equal partner in the SED, some 200,000 SPD members were purged.

The German Communists pledged to establish a parliamentary democracy and a distinctively "German path to socialism"

After Stalin's death, political conditions relaxed a bit in the GDR, though the nationalization of industry proceeded without hesitation. Impossibly high work goals, sharpened by the drainage of workers to the West, led to a **workers' revolt** across the GDR on June 17, 1953, which was ruthlessly crushed with the aid of Soviet tanks. In response to the FRG's normalization with the West, the GDR was recognized by the USSR in 1954 and became a member of the **Warsaw Pact** in 1955.

In 1961, the GDR decided to remedy the exodus of skilled young workers to the Federal Republic; although borders to the West had been sealed off, escape through Berlin remained a possibility. On the night of August 12-13, the first, rudimentary barriers of the **Berlin Wall** were laid. The regime called it an "anti-fascist protective wall," but Berliners knew which way the guns were pointed. The time was right for Ulbricht to launch his hard-line **New Economic System** and to establish the GDR's **second constitution** in 1968. This document jettisoned most constitutional rights, already ignored in practice, and abandoned all pretense of parliamentary democracy.

Ulbricht's iron grip on power was broken in 1971 when he ran afoul of his Soviet patrons. His replacement, **Erich Honecker,** was a party functionary even more doctrinaire and colorless than his predecessor. He returned East Germany to unquestioning subservience to the Soviet Union and eliminated all reformist experiments. Relations with the West improved remarkably during the era of Willy Brandt's **Ostpolitik,** and many Westerners were permitted to visit relatives in the GDR for the first time. Despite the scars of the war and the shortcomings of central planning, East Germans were enjoying the highest standard of living in the Eastern Bloc by the late 70s. Nevertheless, the hated secret police, the **Stasi,** maintained a network of hundreds of thousands of agents and paid informants that strove to monitor every citizen.

With the ascension of the *glasnost*-minded **Mikhail Gorbachev** to the leadership of the USSR in 1985, reform began to spread throughout the Eastern Bloc—except in the GDR, which ignored the liberalizing reforms. The foundation for *die Wende* (the turning or the change), as the sudden toppling of the GDR is referred to in Germany, began in May 1989 when Hungary dismantled the barbed-wire border with Austria, giving some 55,000 East Germans a route to the West. By October, Czechoslovakia tolerated a flood of GDR citizens into the West German embassy; thousands emigrated. On October 6, while on a state visit to celebrate the GDR's 40th birthday, Gorbachev publicly reprimanded Honecker and announced that the USSR would not interfere in the GDR's domestic affairs. Dissident groups (supported and protected by the church) such as **New Forum** began to operate more freely, organizing massive **anti-government** demonstrations *(Demos),* which started in Leipzig (see **Leipzig,** p. 169), and spread to Dresden, Berlin, and other cities. The East Germans demanded free elections, freedom of press, and freedom of travel.

Dissident groups began to operate more freely, organizing massive anti-government demonstrations

Faced with rising pressure, Honecker resigned. His successor, **Egon Krenz,** promised reforms. Meanwhile, tens of thousands of GDR citizens—largely young professionals—continued to flee via Czechoslovakia, which completely opened its border with West Germany. The entire GDR Politbüro resigned on November 8, and a day later, a Central Committee spokesperson announced the **opening of all borders to the West,** including the Berlin Wall.

REUNIFICATION AND ITS AFTERMATH: 1989-THE PRESENT

The opening of the Wall did not immediately herald the demise of the GDR or the Communist regime. Elected four days after the opening of the wall, Prime Minister **Hans Modrow** pledged to hold free elections. The constitution was re-written to remove references to the SED's leading role, but the party remained in power and the *Stasi* continued to operate despite pressure. Throughout December, *Demos* continued unabated. Honecker was whisked away to the USSR and the SED renamed itself the **Party of Democratic Socialism (SPD).** The year 1990 began with another ecstatic celebration on top of the Berlin Wall, but the apparent community belied a furious political struggle going on in both Germanies. In the East, opposition parties took shape and assumed positions in the existing government, while the West's political parties scrambled to assert their influence; eventually, all of them linked up with like-minded parties in the GDR in preparation for March **elections.** The SPD was crippled by its expressed reluctance about the prospect of reunification, which inhibited it from making allies in the East. Buoyed by Kohl's success at getting Moscow to assent to unification, the CDU-backed **Alliance for Germany** emerged the winner. In the East, a broad coalition government of non-Communist parties authorized **economic and social union** with the Federal Republic. On **D-Mark Day** (as July 2 was known in the English press), GDR citizens exchanged their worthless Ostmarks for mighty D-Marks. The signing of the **Four-Plus-Two Treaty** by the two Germanies and the four occupying powers on September 12, 1990, signaled the **end of a divided Germany.**

Despite catch-phrases such as *Wiedervereinigung* (reunification), East and West Germany did not unify on an equal basis to create a new nation-state. Rather, East

Germany was absorbed into the institutions and structures of the Federal Republic, leading some to call the union *der Anschluß* (annexation). Under the Basic Law's paragraph 23, any territory had the power to accede, or simply declare themselves ready to be consumed by, the FRG. This was a faster route to unity, and after a great deal of debate, it was the one Germany took. On **October 3, 1990,** the Allies forfeited their occupation rights, the GDR ceased to exist, and Germany became one united, sovereign nation for the first time in 45 years. Germans now distinguish between East and West with the labels **"new federal states"** and **"old federal states."**

Immediately following the quick pace of events in 1989-90, nationalistic euphoria blurred the true state of matters for Germans on both sides of the wall. The inefficient industries and institutions in the East led to massive unemployment and the Federal Republic's worst-ever recession. Many Westerners have resented the inflation and taxes brought on by the cost of rebuilding the new federal states, while Easterners have had to give up the generous social benefits communism afforded them. A rightward-moving political climate in the west pulled the east with it, restricting social programs not only in welfare but also in areas such as abortion.

In the years following, the anger spread to an intense distrust of **foreigners,** especially immigrants from Eastern Europe and the *Gastarbeiter,* some of whom had been living in Germany for decades. German law does not automatically grant citizenship to children born in Germany; parentage is considered the paramount factor. This has become more and more of a troubling point as the children of immigrants grow up in Germany, speak only German, know no other home, but are defined as aliens. The violent attacks on foreigners reached horrible proportions in 1992, when wide-scale assaults were launched against immigrants in Mölln and Rostock, resulting in numerous deaths. In June 1993, an arson attack on the home of a Turkish family in the town of Solingen claimed several lives, including those of young children. Soon after Solingen, the liberal Asylum Law was repealed. Fortunately, the violence has decreased significantly in the past few years.

Nationalistic euphoria blurred the true state of matters for Germans on both sides of the wall

After the dramatic fall of the Berlin Wall in 1989, Kohl and his CDU seemed insurmountable. Carrying their momentum into the first all-German elections, the CDU scored a stunning victory. After that, however, Kohl's popularity plummeted to the point where on one occasion eastern voters pelted him with rotten fruit during a visit, and his party failed to carry his own state in *Land* elections. But the CDU bounced back, and in 1994 it accomplished a hat trick of victories in the elections for President, the European Parliament, and the German Parliament. Kohl's majority is, however, narrow, and dependent on the increasingly marginalized liberal FDP.

Europe, or more specifically the new Germany's place in it, is currently the big political question. The burden of the past makes everyone, including Germans themselves, nervous about German intervention in European foreign policy. The most recent initiative, an attempt to bring about the diplomatic recognition of the splinter states of the former Yugoslavia, ended in disaster; Germany has been content to stick to the sidelines since. The dominant feeling now, promulgated by Kohl's CDU coalition, is that Germany should stay out of foreign policy, acting instead as a large, benign economic machine at the heart of the European Union. But Germany is not Switzerland; such a neutral stance may not always be possible for the most populous and economically powerful nation in Europe. There are thinkers on the political Left, with some support in the Greens and the SPD, who would like to see the unified Germany take on the mission of embodying a "third way," a corrective to the excesses of both Eastern socialism and Western capitalism.

THIS YEAR IN GERMANY

The cute and cartoony, huggable and bubbly **1998 Volkswagen Beetle** stands as a symbol for this year in Germany: it's similar to its past incarnations but is slightly— and oh-so-importantly—different. German nonsmokers continue to get the shaft, as Parliament (not the brand name) rejected a bill that would have granted some relief to non-toking Teutons in a land addicted to nicotine. The measure would have required both smoking and non-smoking areas to be provided in public buildings and workplaces. Although the bill was defeated, it was by a narrower margin than in past efforts: 336-256.

The presence of **neo-Nazis** continued to be a problem, though of a markedly different sort than that which plagued the nation in the years immediately following reunification, when violent attacks on foreigners were severe and fairly pervasive. Today, the movement is attracting a younger set of Germans who take up the neo-Nazi cause to rebel against their parents and against the work-through-the-past mantra that has become aligned, in their minds, with authority. A video of German soldiers making anti-Jewish comments and singing along to right-wing rock songs was discovered by a German cable channel, showing further the extent to which Nazism continues to rear its ugly head. The **German soccer team** continued its historically established path in 1998, as well, losing to World Cup newbies Croatia in a disappointing upset that sparked violence among German hooligans.

Despite this continuity, however, there were a number of noteworthy singular occurrences, among them most prominently the **ICE disaster.** Bound from Munich to Hamburg, ICE train 884 derailed and collapsed into itself, killing almost 100 passengers and injuring 60 more, making it one of the worst high-speed rail disasters ever. A much happier event of note was **the 50th birthday of the Deutschmark.** Established by the occupying allies in the summer of 1948, the Mark most assuredly won't make it another 50 years, as the Euro will usher in a new economic age in 2002. Also celebrating its 50th was the **Berlin Airlift,** still looking good after all these years. A more sobering fifty year mark was reached this year, when the German government finally agreed to pay Eastern European Holocaust survivors $110 million in compensation, a gesture that had been made to Western survivors on a much grander scale ($60 billion) many years earlier. 1998 was also an **election year** in Germany, and though voting will occur too late for us to report the results, the battle looks to be waged mainly between a CDU-CSU coalition platform and the age-old SPD, who are allied this year with **Die Grünen** (the Greens). And don't worry about not hearing the results in a timely fashion: a .125mm thick **fiber-optic cable** stretching from the island of Sylt to New York City will allow 600,000 Germans and Americans to chat it up across the big blue pond simultaneously. *Hallo, Volkswagen! Bitte schicken Sie mir einen roten Beetle!*

FURTHER READING

A great overview for those seeking a broad education in German history from its beginnings to the present is Mary Fulbrook's *Concise History of Germany*. Gordon Craig's *Germany 1866-1945* provides a definitive history of those years. A more general picture of the modern German character can be found in Craig's excellent *The Germans,* an accessible but never simplistic book. Primo Levi's *Survival in Auschwitz* provides a gripping and poignant account of a Holocaust survivor. For an in-depth look at postwar German history, pick up Henry Ashby Turner's *The Two Germanies Since 1945,* or Peter J. Katzenstein's *Policy and Politics in Western Germany*. Ralf Dahrendorf's *Society and Democracy in Germany* is a great treatment of "the German Question." Also, read anything that novelists Günter Grass or Christa Wolf have written on reunification. They criticize the rapidity of the process and the forgetting and abandonment of the historic lessons Germany might have learned in the years since the war. Both are powerful moral voices in contemporary Germany. Their novels are also excellent (see **Literature,** p. 73).

■ Culture

Germany, the Germans like to say, is the land of *"Dichter und Denker"*—the poet and the philosopher. Playwright Bertolt Brecht, with inspired cynicism, claimed that a truer epithet was land of the *"Richter und Henker"*—the judge and the hangman.

While such a scathing inversion may seem a bit too harsh, it reveals the flawed romantic premises upon which the original phrase rests. Far from a lofty pursuit of beauty, German *Kultur* has always echoed with immediate political connotations; the word became charged with nationalism during the Third Reich, when it was used to refer to a celebrated myth of a shared German character. Despite such tendencies, the humanities in Germany have had enormous influence on the development of artistic, literary, and musical trends in all of Europe and the world.

VISUAL ART

The first paintings appeared in Germany in the 8th century, when Irish monks brought the art of illuminating manuscripts to Charlemagne's palace in Aachen. However, it was not until the Renaissance that a distinctively German style of painting came into its own. Although German painting during the late Gothic period was fairly successful, it consisted mainly of religious icons painted on wall panels—a form taken directly from Byzantium. Smitten with Enlightenment thinking, the Renaissance painters of the late 15th and early 16th centuries abandoned purely religious themes in favor of natural scenes and portraiture. **Matthias Grünewald, Hans Holbein the Younger,** and **Lucas Cranach** all helped to sustain this flourishing creative culture; Cranach's bounty of work is scattered throughout towns in east-central Germany. The most renowned of the Renaissance painters in Germany was **Albrecht Dürer,** who worked in painting, drafting, and woodcuts; his work in all three is psychologically dark and masterfully crafted. In the fateful year 1500, on a featureless black background, Dürer painted one of the era's great images—Europe's first self-portrait, in which Dürer portrayed himself as a Christ-like figure.

Although the effects of the Renaissance on the painting of northern Europe were substantial, they were short-lived; from the mid-16th until the mid-18th centuries disunity and conflict brought on by the Reformation led to a 200-year period of relative inactivity in the canvas arts. The **Baroque** and **Rococo** schools of design, imported from France and Italy, were well-received and much-implemented in the construction of churches and palaces, but they prompted little innovation in German painting. It wasn't until the 19th-century movements of **Neoclassicism** and **Romanticism** that work of consequence was again produced. Neoclassicist works consisted mainly of mimicking Roman and Greek sculpture technique and painting posed, poised portraiture with clear lines and Rococo-like backgrounds. This garnered little enthusiasm from German painters, who by and large aligned themselves with the Romantic movement. The Romantics glorified nature and sought unity of man and God, culture and nature, and all such great divides in a style of painting whose blurred lines, softened edges, and infusion of mysticism would inspire spiritual reactions in the viewer. **Caspar David Friedrich,** whose landscapes obsessed over man's solitude amid nature's grandeur, was one of the finest of the Romantic painters. Many of his works capture dramatic, uninhabitable landscapes such as wind-blown cemeteries and the North Sea. The less-bleak **Max Liebermann** began as a master Impressionist and went on to lead the Berlin faction of the **Secession movement** in the 1890s; in two words, decadence and eroticism. This trend became **Jugendstil** (literally, "youth-style"), which rose to popularity in central European cities in the early 20th century.

The early years of the 20th century saw an extraordinary proliferation of artistic genius. The Symbolist tendencies of *Jugendstil* intensified into the larger movement of **German Expressionism,** with a deliberately anti-realist aesthetic that distorted objects and colors to project deeply personal experiences. **Die Brücke** (The Bridge) was the earliest Expressionist consortium, founded in Dresden in 1905 with the aim of making paintings and sculptures that were loud, aggressive, and explicitly "expressive." A 1911 exhibition in Munich entitled **Der Blaue Reiter** (the Blue Rider), led by Russian emigré **Wassily Kandinsky** and named after one of his paintings, was the culmination of creative efforts of a flourishing Munich-based avant-garde. Kandinsky's epoch-making contribution was a series called *Improvisations* painted in 1910-11, considered the first totally **non-representational paintings** in Western civilization. *Der Blaue Reiter* also included **Franz Marc** and **Paul Klee. Max Beckmann** left a large body of Expressionist works (although he shunned the label) focused on the anxieties of a dehumanized culture. The satirical works of **Otto Dix** navigated a tight-rope between Expressionism and Dadaism before embracing the **Neue Sachlichkeit** (New Objectivity) movement and its emphasis on the spectator's (and artist's) role as social critic. The smaller German **Realist** movement devoted itself to bleak, critical works such as **Käthe Kollwitz's** posters for social reform. **Ernst Barlach** infused realism with religious themes, inflaming Nazi censors.

The rise of Nazism drove most Weimar artists and their works into exile. They were either the "wrong" race or religion, or their works were branded "decadent and subversive" and banished from view after the Nazis displayed them in an exhibition to showcase their *Entartete* (degenerate) nature. In contrast to the complex and eclectic banned works, wartime art was strictly and oppressively unified by Nazi ideology. Themes of **Blut und Boden** (Blood and Soil) dominated Nazi visual arts, depicting the mythical union of *völkisch* blood and German soil through idealized images of workers, farmers, and soldiers. A reject from the Vienna School of Art, Hitler favored sterile, bombastic idealism that often made reference to classical and Nordic mythology; especially popular were nude images of the "master race."

Although **Postwar** artistic effort spawned no unified movement *per se*, it was and continues to be one of the defining forces in shaping the world of modern art. Clearly, though, the division between East and West had a substantial impact on the cultural production of the two nations. The art scene in the GDR had a more nuanced history than the Western stereotype of a socialist cultural desert would imply, though it did suffer under government-dictated regulations. After an initial flirtation with liberal tolerance, the ruling SED "Stalinized" the arts. The regime-sponsored orthodox style was known as **Socialist Realism,** exemplified by paintings such as **Lea Grundig's** *Coal and Steel for Peace* and **Otto Nagel's** *Jungpioniere.* The painters **Hans Grundig, Rudolf Bergander,** and **Eva Schulze-Knabe** and the sculptor **Fritz Cremer** (who designed the Buchenwald Memorial) were also leading figures in the movement. Ambiguity had no place in Socialist Realism: the GDR and the SED were glorified, and "bourgeois influence" was repressed.

Postwar art from West Germany incorporated intense performative strategies meant to challenge the relation between art and politics

Postwar art from West Germany incorporated intense performative strategies meant to challenge the relation between art and politics. Much such art has pioneered the destruction of inter-genre boundaries; painting becomes sculpture, architecture becomes performance, everything becomes an "installation." The painters of the **Junge Wilde** (Young Savages), a neo-Expressionist group, surfaced in Berlin in the late 70s, using vivid colors and strong movement. **Josef Beuys** was a charismatic, controversial figure who created deliberately low-brow juxtapositions, such as felt and lard. Today, the best place to view the latest creations of contemporary German artists is at the **documenta,** a much-celebrated summer-long exhibition of contemporary art from around the world that takes place every five years; the next event, documenta 11, will draw hordes to Kassel from June 8th to September 15th, 2002.

ARCHITECTURE AND DESIGN

In the medieval period, violent, highly stylized images and masterworks of carving and glasswork ornamented the quiet, somber lines of the cathedrals. The **Romanesque** period followed, spanning the years 1000 to 1300, with a style of architecture that emerged in direct imitation of antique ruins. Outstanding Romanesque cathedrals can be found at Speyer, Trier, and Mainz. The **Gothic** style gradually replaced the Romanesque from 1300 to 1500. Stained glass filled the windows of Gothic cathedrals with ever more elaborate patterns of divine light in otherwise dark and creepy spaces filled with ornate, vertically oriented decoration. The 14th century was a transitional period that spawned the **Köln Cathedral.**

The Lutheran reforms of the 1550s put a damper on the unrestrained extravagance of cathedrals. Although the **Renaissance** saw fits of church-building, efforts were mostly channelled into secular buildings such as the **Augsburg Rathaus** (town hall) and **Heidelberg Schloß.** Early Baroque shows itself in the **Rathäuser** of Leipzig and Bremen, as well as the **Würzburg Residenz.** Baroque developed quickly into the extravagant ornamentation of **Rococo; **Munich's **Amalienburg Palace** and **Residenztheater** are typical of the hyper-ornate flamboyance of that movement. The French Revolution snuffed out the courtliness that fueled Baroque and Rococo, replacing them with ideals of "noble simplicity" (Einfachheit). These ideals spawned a revival of classical forms, visible in the Prussian buildings along **Unter Den Linden** in Berlin.

Wertheim's Department Store in Berlin and the **Maltidenhöhe** buildings at Darmstadt are two architectural manifestations of **Jugendstil,** the early 20th-century movement of decorative, stylized design (see **Visual Art,** above). **Erich Mendelsohn** later brought the Expressionist aesthetic to architecture, creating curvaceous structures like the **Einstein Tower** in Potsdam, a structure Einstein himself approved with a single word: "Organic." The ideas behind **Neue Sachlichkeit** revolutionized design. **Peter Behrens** pioneered these ideas, designing objects to suit the efficient new materials of industry through unornamented geometric harmonies. **Walter Gropius** designed several sensational buildings with clean forms, flat roofs, and broad windows, all made possible by new concrete-and-steel construction techniques. In 1919 Gropius founded the **Bauhaus,** a ground-breaking school of design that combined theoretical training in the new principles of efficiency with exposure to the realities of mass production. "Form follows function" was its oft-quoted principle. The school moved to **Dessau** in 1925, where Gropius designed the school's new facility, which became the symbol of the modern style. While Bauhaus's sleek, austere lines informed some of the most brilliant designs of the century, the school must also bear some responsibility for the later abuse of its principles: the soulless, box-like skyscrapers and uniform rows of residences that invaded suburbia became the unintended offspring.

While Bauhaus informed some of the most brilliant designs of the century, the school must also bear some responsibility for the later abuse of its principles

Hitler disapproved of the new buildings; he named a design school reject, **Albert Speer,** as his minister of architecture, and commissioned ponderous, Neoclassical buildings intended to last the "Thousand-Year Reich." Many were intended for public rallies, such as the **Congress Hall** and **Stadium** at Nürnberg. The architecture in the GDR created a bizarro *Bauhaus* landscape in sterile, Stalinist style. The overblown buildings lining the then-**Karl-Marx-Allee** in Eastern Berlin represent the apogee of **Socialist Realist** architecture. The East's most noted architect, **Hermann Henselmann,** was a former *Bauhaus* member. As Chief of Architecture in Berlin from 1953 to 1959, he designed several of the sterile edifices on **Alexanderplatz** in Berlin and conceived the plan for the TV tower. The "Sharp Tooth" building at the heart of the former **Karl Marx Universität** in Leipzig bears his bite mark as well.

LITERATURE

From Kafka to Hoffmann, from the *Goethezeit* to contemporary times, German literature has always been motivated by a deep-seated desire to explore the magical and the irrational. Appropriately enough, the very beginnings of German language poetry, which are traceable to sometime before the ninth century, were **magical incantations.** Soon, with the arrival of widespread Christianity, these poems were altered to give them religious themes of piety. In the 10th and 11th centuries, villagers flocked to hear **Spielmänner,** itinerant poet-entertainers, recite tall tales of the exotic or marvelous. At court, nobles amused themselves with chivalric romances. The Anne Rice of the 12th century, **Hartmann von Aue,** wrote the endearing *Der arme Heinrich,* which described a nobleman's leprosy affliction and the fair virgin who (almost— phew!) sacrifices herself to cure his disease. **Wolfram von Eschenbach's** *Parzival* is the seminal story of a noble boy who loses his birthright and then regains it before searching for the Holy Grail.

By the 13th century, popular heroic lyrics developed into full-fledged **epics.** The most famous and popular of these is the **Nibelungenlied,** the story of Prince Siegfried, his wooing of the valkyrie Brunhilde, his murder, and the subsequent downfall of the Burgundians. Shorter lyric forms gave rise to the wandering **Minnesänger,** the greatest of whom was **Walther von der Vogelweide.** Lyrics of this era became an art instead of a means of record-keeping or magic induction, with topics ranging from humorous legend to courtly subjects with an emphasis on originality and form. Although the literature of the following **Reformation** consisted primarily of propagandist prose tracts, Martin Luther's landmark High German **translation of the Bible** brought *Hochdeutsch* to great heights of expression and cemented literary German.

A self-consciously German canon emerged in the 18th century. The dramatist **Gotthold Ephraim Lessing** produced plays that diverged sharply from contemporary French-influenced drama. Lessing broke the ground for the overtly critical and emotional works to come in the series of sub-movements around the turn of the 19th century. The writers of the **Sturm und Drang** (Storm and Stress) movement reacted to the rise of rationalism with a turn to profound and often violent emotion. **Johann Wolfgang von Goethe** was the first major success of this movement, and he remains *the* monumental figure in German literature as a whole; he is often called "the German Shakespeare," though considering Goethe's forays into other interests such as biology and music, "the German Blake" would be more appropriate. His poem "Prometheus," which emphasized the ability of the human being to turn away from God to create his or her own destiny, is a defining work of *Sturm und Drang.* His hugely popular *Die Leiden des jungen Werthers* (The Sorrows of Young Werther) spawned a wave of sentimental *Weltschmerz* (world-weariness). This and other early works virtually ignored the principle of dramatic simplicity, instead opting for psychological works with complicated characters and an unrestrained natural form that had been fostered by **Johann Gottfried Herder.** Herder's insistence on originality of image and on a distinctly national style characterized his literary criticism. **Friedrich Schiller,** Goethe's friend and sometimes literary adversary, also catapulted to continental fame. By the 1790s the *Sturm und Drang* began to metamorphose into a more refined movement balancing feeling and reason, a tendency that gave the period its **Classical** label. Schiller and Goethe composed masterworks in this mature, innovative period just before the full flowering of **Romanticism.** At Weimar, Goethe completed *Faust* and *Wilhelm Meister,* which became a favorite of later Romantics. At the turn of the 19th century, a difficult young poet named **Friedrich Hölderlin** composed sonorous, strangely modern hymns about the disappearance of the Greek gods and the spiritual textures of Germany's hills and rivers. Hölderlin was the college roommate of philosophers Hegel and Schelling; tragedy loomed over his life due to his contemporaries' failure to understand his work and of his gradual descent into madness after 1800. At the same time, the **Brothers Grimm** assembled their famous collection of fairy tales, providing a foundation for German philology. **Heinrich Wilhelm von Kleist** wove pessimistic tales before killing himself; the best known are *Die Marquise von O.* and *Das Erdbeben in Chile.*

Many writers, even during the height of Romanticism, were members of the politicized, anti-mystical **Junges Deutschland** (Young Germany) school banned as subversive by the *Bundesrat* in 1835. **Heinrich Heine** allied with this movement. His *Deutschland: ein Wintermärchen* considers the stultifying climate engendered by political repression. **Georg Büchner** was Heine's counterpart in drama; his *Woyzeck* introduced the first lower-class tragic hero in German literature. Finally, toward the end of the century, the volatile philosopher **Friedrich Nietzsche** took his place among the greatest German writers. In his poetic, apocalyptic discourse *Also Sprach Zarathustra* (Thus Spoke Zarathustra), Nietzsche declared that "God is dead." (For more on Nietzsche, see **Philosophy,** p. 76.)

> **Goethe is often called "the German Shakespeare," though considering Goethe's forays into other interests such as biology and music, "the German Blake" would be more appropriate**

Günter Grass: Literary Superstar

Considered Germany's most celebrated contemporary writer, Günter Grass was born in Danzig in 1927. In the immediate postwar period, he quickly came to prominence in the lively and critical literary Gruppe 47. His brilliant works, *Cat and Mouse, Dog Years,* and *The Tin Drum,* were each uncompromising attempts to come to terms with the horrors of the Nazi experience. With dwarves, toads, and flounders serving as his central characters and an incredible eye for detail, Grass's eccentric and humorous literary style launched his career and catapulted him to fame. Grass has never flinched from his opinion that the writer as intellectual must be actively engaged with the political landscape and democratic process. Grass has applied his versatile, often satirically perverse talents to poetry, essays, plays, and drawings. Since 1989, he has consistently professed a strong, and increasingly isolated, criticism of German unification. With Auschwitz, Grass argues, Germany lost for all time the right to reunify. This radical view is contained in his recent *Two States—One Nation?*

The turn of the century saw a progression into the **Naturalistic** mode, inspired by the work of the French author Emile Zola. In Germany, the movement was based on finding beauty and value in the objects and patterns of everyday life. **Gerhart Hauptmann** and **Theodor Fontane** were the foremost authors of Naturalism. Conversely, the **Symbolist** movement of the early 20th century rejected Naturalism in favor of fleeting, sonorous image-poems; the **George Kreis** (George circle), centered around leading symbolist Stefan George, was a cadre of passionate, like-minded, well-dressed artists. The truly brilliant works of these years were written by Rilke, Hesse, and Mann. **Rainer Maria Rilke** composed supple rhymes and haunting images that captured fragments of experience. His uncanny poems, such as the splendid "Der Panther," expressed the difficulty of finding spirituality in the modern era. **Hermann Hesse** had a similar interest; his *Steppenwolf* considers the plight of modernity and the breakdown of bourgeois identity, while *Siddhartha* describes the enlightenment of the Buddha in an unadorned prose style. **Thomas Mann** carried Symbolism to its purest form with *Der Zauberberg* (The Magic Mountain) and *Doktor Faustus,* two allegorical recountings of Germany's fateful history.

The **Weimar era** marked an intense and magnificent outpouring of artistic expression, producing more masterpieces in less time than any other period in German history. Germany's version of the Parisian "Lost Generation" articulated its disillusionment in the **Neue Sachlichkeit** movement. Its most famous novel was **Erich Maria Remarque's** *Im Westen nichts Neues* (All Quiet on the Western Front), a blunt, uncompromising account of war's horrors which became embroiled in the political turmoil of the era. **Bertolt Brecht's** dramas and poems present humankind in all its grotesque absurdity, and sought to awaken the consciousness of his audience. His *Dreigroschenoper* (Three-Penny Opera) was set to music by Kurt Weill. Inspired by the ferment of Viennese Art Nouveau and nonrepresentational art, **Expressionism** picked up the torch of Symbolism after WWI. The years of the Third Reich yielded little of artistic note; the official attitude toward literature was summed up by Nazi propaganda minister Goebbels, who once sneered, "Whenever I hear the word 'culture,' I reach for my gun." Some 2500 authors went into exile, and others underwent "internal emigration" and ceased to write. The literature that did emerge consisted mainly of anti-Semitic tracts and nationalistic *Heimat* literature.

Nazi propaganda minister Goebbels once sneered, "Whenever I hear the world 'culture,' I reach for my gun"

The experience of war, defeat, and genocide inspired greater social conscience in many Germans. Many authors of the **Social Realist** movement convened formally in 1947 to reform German writing. The resulting coalition, known as **Gruppe 47,** heavily influenced German literature well into the 70s. A major issue for these postwar German authors was how to reclaim their language after its corruption under fascist rule. Gruppe 47's ranks include most of the largest names in contemporary German literature. **Heinrich Böll,** one of the founding members, won the Nobel Prize for Literature in 1972. **Günter Grass** wrote a stunning series of novels relating to recent German history, including *Der Blechtrommel* (The Tin Drum). **Peter Handke** is an on-the-road modern writer; his *Der kurze Brief zum langen Abschied* (The Short Letter at the Long Departure) is set entirely in America. A new school of drama developed through playwrights like **Rolf Hochhuth** *(Die Soldaten)* and **Peter Weiss** *(Marat/Sade).*

The state of letters in the **GDR** was largely determined by the waxing and waning of government control. Many expatriate writers, particularly those with Marxist leanings from before the war (such as Brecht), returned to the East with great hopes. But the communist leadership was not interested in eliciting free artistic expression. The combination of personal danger, the burden of censorship, and simple disillusionment led many immensely talented writers to emigrate, including **Ernst Bloch, Uwe Johnson, Sarah Kirsch,** and **Heiner Kipphardt.** In the 70s and 80s, some East German writers were able to publish in the West, though not at home, and took that option as a middle ground. **Christa Wolf,** one of the most prominent German women writers, voluntarily remained in the GDR. Radical-left GDR playwright **Heiner Müller** shocked audiences throughout the 70s with the disgusted protagonists and stripped-down scenarios of Beckett-esque plays such as *Hamletmachine.* Since reunification, there has been a period of artistic anxiety and occasional malaise; in the former East, many authors are caught up in controversies over complicity with the *Stasi.* The new world of Europe-wide capitalism has filled the shelves of German bookstores with translations of American best-sellers, pushing works by German authors to the wayside.

PHILOSOPHY

Germany's philosophical tradition—one of the most respected in the world—has been characterized by revolutionaries. **Martin Luther** defied the whole Christian establishment, the pompous Pope included, and spawned the Protestant Revolution. **Gottfried Wilhelm Leibniz** gave the world differential and integral calculus, making high school a nuisance. **Immanuel Kant,** the foremost thinker of the Enlightenment, enshrined rational man at the center of his morality. He argued that the commands of morality must be categorical imperatives: they must apply to all rational beings, regardless of their wants and feelings. **Karl Marx** set himself against his contemporary capitalist bourgeois society, by showing that it is based on brutal exploitation of the masses, and conceived of dialectical materialism. He argued that the natural conclusion of history would be a communist society. **Friedrich Nietzsche,** influenced by pessimist *par excellence* **Arthur Schopenhauer,** scorned the mediocrity of the masses, who were ensnared in the hypocritical creeds of Christianity, and made this exaltation the proper task of the "higher man," who exists beyond good and evil:

> *Max Weber, the father of sociology, frightened the world by announcing that we are trapped in a bureaucratic iron cage*

"Not mankind, but superman is the goal." Nietzsche's *Übermensch* has been used and abused repeatedly by evil deed-doers such as Stalin and Hitler. Nietzsche's intensity of thought consumed him prematurely, and he lapsed into *Über*-insanity before kicking the *Über*-bucket in 1900. **Max Weber,** the father of sociology, frightened the world by announcing that we are trapped in a bureaucratic iron-cage—"please, wait in room 101, fill in the pink and blue forms, and stand next to Mr. DeNiro and his friends from *Brazil...*" **Martin Heidegger,** in his mammoth *Being and Time,* articulated a detailed investigation of the relationship between language and metaphysics. Unfortunately, he also aligned himself with the Nazis.

German heroes can be found among the German Idealists, a movement spearheaded by **Johann Gottlieb Fichte** that challenged Kant. While Kant believed that it was impossible to find the truth, Fichte saw human self-consciousness as the primary metaphysical fact through which the philosopher finds his way to the cosmic totality that is "the Absolute" (Swedish vodka?). **Georg Wilhelm Friedrich Hegel** was inspired by Fichte, adding a dialectical twist to the latter's ideas, but, admittedly, he had serious writing difficulties—when asked to encapsulate his philosophical theories in a sentence, he responded with 10 poorly-written volumes of writing. Only our contemporary **Jürgen Habermas**—succeeding **Theodor Adorno, Max Horkheimer, and Walter Benjamin** of the Frankfurt School—lives up to Hegel's muddled style with a true German spirit. Habermas took 3000 pages to say that it is important to talk if there is to be any progress (duh!).

Although philosophy at times seems to diverge from anything logical, Germany has given birth to one of the world's foremost logicians, **Gottlob Frege,** the father of modern mathematical logic. The man behind the man behind phenomenology is **Edmund Husserl,** who strove to make philosophy into a strict science. One of Germany's bad-ass scientists, **Werner Heisenberg,** helped to established quantum mechanics. His grand uncertainty principle tells us that we can't know if a cat in a box is dead or alive…what?! Exasperated, *Let's Go: Germany* seeks solace in…

…FILM

The newborn medium of film exploded onto the German art scene in the **Weimar era** thanks to several brilliant directors. These early German films persist as central elements of all film study. *Das Kabinett des Dr. Caligari* (The Cabinet of Dr. Caligari), an early horror film directed by **Robert Wiene,** plays out a melodrama of autonomy and control against brilliantly expressive sets of painted shadows and tilted walls. **Fritz Lang** produced a remarkable succession of Expressionist films, including *M., Dr. Mabuse der Spieler,* and *Metropolis,* a dark and brutal vision of the techno-fascist city of the future. **Ernst Lubitsch** also produced silent classics, while **F.W. Murnau's** *Nosferatu* crystallized German pathologies of "the other" in his portrayal of the Dracula legend. Meanwhile, **Josef von Sternberg** extended the tradition into sound with his satiric and pathetic *Der blaue Engel* (The Blue Angel), based on Heinrich Mann's novel *Professor Unrath*—it starred the immortal Marlene Dietrich.

Heeding Hitler's prediction that "without motor-cars, sound films, and wireless, (there can be) no victory for National Socialism," propaganda minister **Joseph Goebbels** became a masterful manipulator. Most **Nazi films** fell into two categories: political propaganda and escapism. *Der ewige Jude* (The Eternal Jew) and *Jud Süss* glorified anti-Semitism. The uncanny, masterful propaganda films of **Leni Riefenstahl,** including *Triumph des Willens* (Triumph of the Will), which depicted a Nürnberg Party Rally, and *Olympia,* took the art of the documentary to new heights.

Film has been perhaps the most vigorous artistic medium in postwar Germany. The late 60s and the 70s saw the greatest flood of cinematic excellence. The renaissance began in 1962 with the **Oberhausen Manifesto,** a declaration by independent filmmakers demanding artistic freedom and the right to create the new German feature film; within a few years, the government was granting subsidies to a constellation of young talents. **Rainer Werner Fassbinder** made fatalistic films about individuals corrupted or defeated by society, including a mammoth production of Alfred Döblin's mammoth novel *Berlin Alexanderplatz.* Fassbinder's film *Die Ehe der Maria Braun* (The Marriage of Maria Braun) and **Volker Schlöndorff's** *Der Blechtrommel* (The Tin Drum, based on Grass's novel) were the films that brought the new German wave to a wider, international audience. **Margarethe von Trotta** focused mainly on

> **Film has been perhaps the most vigorous artistic medium in postwar Germany**

women and politics, notably in her film *Die bleierne Zeit* (The Leaden Time). **Wolfgang Petersen** directed *Das Boot* (The Boat), one of the greatest war films ever made. **Werner Herzog's** works, including *Nosferatu,* drew inspiration from the silent films of the 20s in an attempt to revitalize the Expressionism emphasis on oblique cinematic images and very ugly vampires. **Wim Wenders's** "road films," such as *Alice in den Städten* (Alice in the Cities) and the award-winning *Paris, Texas,* examine unconventional relationships and the freedom of life on the road. In 1983, **Edgar Reitz,** a director of the 60s generation, created the 15-hour epic *Heimat* (Home). The film caused a stir in Germany over its questioning of national and regional identities.

East German film was subject to more constraints than other artistic media, owing to the difficulty of producing films without the large-scale financial backing that only the state could provide. Just after the war, directors in the Soviet Zone produced several internationally acclaimed films, among them **Wolfgang Staudte's** *Die Mörder sind unter uns* (The Murderers are Among Us), about a Nazi war criminal who evades detection and goes on to lead the good life, **Kurt Maetzig's** *Ehe im Schatten* (Marriage in the Shadows), and **Erich Engel's** *Affaire Blum* (The Blum Affair). The GDR's ministry of culture operated its own studios, the German Film Corporation (DEFA). **Slatan Dudow** produced the first of DEFA's films, *Unser tägliches Brot* (Our Daily Bread), a paean to the nationalization of industry, and went on to make one of the best East German films, *Stärker als die Nacht* (Stronger than the Night), which tells the story of a communist couple persecuted by the Nazis. After a brief post-Stalinist thaw, few East German films departed from the standard format of socialist heroism or love stories. **Egon Günther's** *Lots Weib* (Lot's Wife), an explicitly feminist exploration of marital breakdown and divorce, was one notable exception. The next year, 1966, saw three major films, Maetzig's *Das Kaninchen bin ich* (The Rabbit is Me), **Frank Vogel's** *Denk bloß nicht, ich heule* (Just Don't Think I'm Crying), and **Frank Beyer's** *Spur der Steine* (Track of Stones). Beyer later made the critically acclaimed *Jakob der Lügner* (Jacob the Liar), which was nominated for an Oscar. Another promising director stifled by the GDR, **Konrad Wolf,** produced such films as *Ich war neunzehn* (I was Nineteen), *Goya,* and *Sonnensucher* (Sun Seekers), the last of which was not permitted to be released until 14 years after its completion. The GDR also devoted a healthy portion of its filmmaking resources to the **documentary** genre. A handful managed to critique the prevailing political situation, although the majority of directors concocted unremarkable films glorifying the Soviet Union and the SED and denouncing the Federal Republic and the United States.

MUSIC

The earliest forms of German music were religious, and written for the Church, but there is also a long-standing tradition of secular music, which hearkens back to the medieval songs of the **Minnesänger,** the German troubadours, whose techniques of singing poetry passed gradually to the **Meistersänger,** commoners who had passed through five ranks from apprentice to *Meister* (Master). Singers remained in local guilds; their instrumental counterparts were the **town-pipers,** whose guilds were the forerunners of modern orchestras. Lutheran hymns applied new polyphonic techniques to folk song forms. The 16th century saw the birth of both the *cantata* and the passion, a work thematizing a saint's transcendence. **Michael Praetorius** and **Johann Pachelbel** (best known for his *Canon in D*) worked in these modes. **Georg Friedrich Händel's** oratorio *Messiah* is now familiar Christmas music throughout the Western world.

Johann Sebastian Bach was the stand-out in a long line of musically successful Bachs. Bach's organ works construct worlds whose meticulous symmetries and regularities reflect a careful spiritual order. In mid-career he produced more secular works; the *Brandenburg Concerti* are famous for their imaginative exploration of the contrast between solo instruments and the chamber orchestra in the Baroque concerto. In 1723, Bach's appointment as cantor of Leipzig's largest church caused him to return to Lutheran religious music; his *St. Matthew Passion* consists of arias and choruses based on Biblical texts. In the latter half of the 18th century, Austrians Franz Josef Haydn, Wolfgang Amadeus Mozart, and their contemporaries rose to the forefront of musical exploration, touting Classical ideals of simplicity and naturalism.

The 19th century was an era of German musical hegemony. **Ludwig van Beethoven's** symphonies and piano sonatas bridged Classicism and Romanticism. He pushed Classical forms to their limits as he focused on rhythmic drives, extremes of musical elements, and intense emotional expressionism. His monumental *Ninth Symphony* and late string quartets were written in the 1820s after he was completely deaf. Beethoven had enormous influence on the Romantic composers who followed him. Inspired by Romantic literature, including lyric poetry and songs, Austrians **Rob-**

ert **Schumann** and **Franz Schubert** composed settings for the poetry of Goethe, Byron, Scott, and Heine. The ethereal work of **Felix Mendelssohn-Bartholdy** is well-represented by his overture to *A Midsummer Night's Dream.* Immigrant **Franz Liszt** pushed piano music and the symphonic form into still further reaches of unorthodox harmony and arrangement. The second generation of Romantic composers included **Johannes Brahms,** who imbued Classical forms with rich Romantic emotion.

Richard Wagner was perhaps the most influential German composer after Beethoven. He composed many of the world's best-known operas—*Tannhäuser, Die Meistersinger, Der Ring des Nibelungen*—in an attempt to revolutionize the form of opera; his vision of *Gesamtkunstwerk* (total work of art) equalized music and text, poetry and philosophy. He envisioned a stream of "endless melody" distinguishing itself through changes in mood or key, or through the reappearance of a *Leitmotiv.* Wagner's plots are highly nationalistic in their celebration of Germanic legend and were easily exploited by German-Aryan supremacists. The center of musical genius shifted to Vienna in the late 19th and early 20th centuries as Romanticism over-ripened into decadence.

The unstable economy of the Weimar Republic and the anti-Romantic backlash encouraged smaller, cheaper musical forms such as jazz. A new movement of *Gebrauchsmusik* (utilitarian music) engendered music for amateur players and film scores. Austrian **Arnold Schönberg** and his disciples **Anton Webern** and **Alban Berg** mastered the possibilities of 12-tone composition and explored the emancipation of dissonance. **Paul Hindemith** headed a group of Neoclassicists influenced by the *Neue Sachlichkeit* and the emphasis on craftsmanship introduced by the *Werkbund* and *Bauhaus.* They embraced the older, variational forms (such as the sonata) most suited to the abstract aesthetic of the time. **Carl Orff,** Hitler's favorite composer, is most noted for his eclectic *Carmina Burana,* a resurrection of bawdy 13th-century lyrics with a bombastic score. Music-hall works prior to WWII bred satiric operettas with songs of the political avant-garde. **Kurt Weill's** partnership with Bertolt Brecht produced such masterpieces of the genre as *Die Dreigroßchenoper* (Three-Penny Opera), whose hit song "Mack the Knife" has been re-recorded by various artists over time, including Louis Armstrong and Ella Fitzgerald.

"Germany is not supposed to be rock 'n' roll country," Rudolf Schenker once remarked about his country's modern music, a pop legacy almost as disgraceful as that of France. Sadly, real rock 'n' roll only makes up a small, albeit benign, tumor on the corpus of German music, a body ill with *Schlager.* One exception is the new hit group Die Ärtzte (The Doctors) whose parody rock style has been taking over German radio. Yet dismissing Germany's pop history as one big pile of putrifax would be ignoring its indispensable contribution—techno. The music blasting from black VWs in German cities, and the music popularized in the U.S. by the Chemical Brothers and Prodigy, derives from the Ur-techno of **Krautrock,** a quintessentially German genre. Krautrock emerged in the 60s with groups like **Neu!** and **Can,** who used primitive keyboards and simple tape loops to create music sounding like stoned people going berserk on dialing pads. **Kraftwerk,** a group of Düsseldorf engineering students designing their own equipment, popularized techno-pop, combining hypnotically catchy melodies with previously unheard of electronic sounds. While they scored an international hit in 1975 with "Autobahn," their huge influence and importance rest on their earlier albums, such as the seminal *The Man Machine.* Krautrock imploded in the late 1970s with the art noise of **Einstürzende Neubauten.** After a decade of musical stagnation in Germany, when glam-rock bands churned out stillborn hits akin to **Scorpions'** attempt at political commentary, "The Winds of Change," **techno** exploded onto the scene in the late 1980s, and it still resounds all over the country.

Dismissing Germany's pop history as one big pile of putrifax would be ignoring its indispensable contribution — techno

In terms of popularity with German *Jugend,* the indelicately named black music comes in second after techno. This mixture of ska, R&B, rap, and soul is all the rage in Germany as youngsters ache more and more to be as American as possible. Next on the German audio-diet is **hardcore.** While American hardcore peaked in the mid-1980s and then fizzled out for a lack of things to be pissed off about, the bleakness of many of the Eastern German cities and the unpopular neo-Nazi renaissance provide German bands with enough holler fodder to support one of the most effervescent hardcore scenes on the planet. The most raging German hardcore bands are **E.G.A.L.** and **Entrails Massacre.**

■ Food and Drink

German cuisine gets bad press. Although it is neither as sophisticated as French cooking nor as sultry as Italian or Hungarian food, *Deutsche Küche* has a robust charm. Meat-and-potatoes lovers especially will find the food in Germany hearty and satisfying. And if the local food is not to your taste, Germany's larger cities offer a wide variety of good ethnic restaurants. Be careful when ordering from a German menu if you don't speak the language; ingredients such as *Aal* (eel), *Blutwurst* (blood sausage), and *Gehirn* (brains) are not uncommon, and may represent an acquired taste. Don't let this deter you from taking risks—brains are probably a lot tastier than you think.

Vegetarians should not fear to enter this land of carnivores. Since the 1980s, vegetarianism has steadily gained popularity in Germany, with a recent rise due to the fear of mad cow disease. Approximately one-fifth of Germany's population now eats little or no meat. While vegetarians may have a rough time in smaller, more rural towns, vegetarian restaurants and dishes abound in the major cities. Be prepared to eat a lot of cheese; vegans will have a more difficult time finding non-dairy options. For more information, see **Dietary Concerns** (p. 26).

The typical German **Frühstück** (breakfast, literally "early piece") is coffee or tea with *Brötchen* (rolls), butter, marmalade, slices of bread, *Wurst* (cold sausage), *Eier* (eggs), and *Käse* (cheese). **Mittagsessen** (lunch) is usually the main meal of the day, consisting of soup, broiled sausage or roasted meat, potatoes or dumplings, and a salad or vegetables. **Abendessen** or **Abendbrot** (supper) is a re-enactment of breakfast, only beer replaces coffee and the selection of meat and cheese is wider. **Dessert** after meals is uncommon, but many Germans indulge in a daily ritual of **Kaffee und Kuchen** (coffee and cakes), a snack analogous to English "tea-time," at 3 or 4pm.

Brains are probably a lot tastier than you think

Brot (bread) is the staff of life in Germany; the country's bakeries produce loaves of astonishing quality and variety. *Vollkornbrot* is whole-wheat (which has a completely different meaning in Germany) and *Roggenbrot* is rye bread. *Schwarzbrot* (black bread) is a dense, dark loaf that's slightly acidic. Go to a *Bäckerei* (bakery) and point to whatever looks good. Generally they sell you the whole loaf; for half, ask for *ein Halbes.* German bread does not contain preservatives and will go stale soon after its purchase. Those traveling on the cheap can ward off hunger for a few dozen *Pfennigs* by entering a bakery and requesting *zwei Brötchen,* a pair of fresh, warm rolls to take out.

Beer and wine (see below) are the meal-time **beverages.** *Saft* (fruit juice), plain or mixed with sparkling water, is an alternative. Germans do not guzzle glasses of water by the dozen as Americans do, although they think it trendy to sip a glass of carbonated mineral water. If you ask for *Wasser* in a restaurant, you get mineral water (which ain't free). For tap water, ask for *Leitungswasser* and expect funny looks.

With very few exceptions **restaurants** expect you to seat yourself. If there are no tables free, ask someone for permission to take a free seat (ask *"Darf ich Platz nehmen?",* pronounced "DAHRF eekh PLAHTS nay-men"). In traditional restaurants, address waiters "Herr Ober," and waitresses (but no one else) as "Fräulein." In a hip *Kneipe* (bar), just say *hallo.* At the table, Germans eat with the fork in the left hand and the knife in the right. While eating, it is polite to keep the tines of your fork pointing down at all times. When you're finished, pay at the table. Ask the server *Zahlen, bitte* ("TSAH-len, BIT-tuh": "check, please"). Taxes *(Mehrwertsteuer)* and service are almost always included in the price, but it is customary to leave a little something extra, usually by rounding up the bill by a Mark.

Eating in restaurants at every meal will quickly drain your budget. One strategy is to stick to the daily *prix-fixe* option, called the *Tagesmenü*. A cheaper option is to buy food in **grocery stores,** which *Let's Go* lists in most cities. German university students eat at cafeterias called **Mensen.** Most *Mensen* (singular *Mensa*) require an ISIC (or charge higher prices for non-students), and some are open only to local students, though travelers often evade this requirement by strolling in as if they belonged. In smaller towns, the best budget option is to stop by a *Bäckerei* (bakery) for bread and garnish it with sausage purchased from a butcher *(Fleischerei* or *Metzgerei).*

Besides bread, the staples of the German diet are *Wurst* (sausage, in myriad varieties), *Schweinefleisch* (pork), *Rindfleisch* (beef), *Kalbsfleisch* (veal), *Huhn* (chicken), *Kartoffeln* (potatoes), and *Eier* (eggs). Dairy products, including *Käse* (cheese) and *Butter*—but especially *Schlagsahne* (whipped cream)—are favorites. Sampling the various **local specialties** around Germany gives a taste of the diverse culinary tradition. Everyone knows *Wiener Schnitzel* (a breaded veal or pork cutlet) and *Sauerkraut* (pickled cabbage), but there's much more to German cuisine. In **Bayern,** *Knödel* (potato and flour dumplings, sometimes filled with meat) are ubiquitous. *Leberknödel* are filled with liver. *Weißwurst* is also a Bavarian specialty; it is a sausage made with milk. It spoils so quickly that it has to be eaten the day it's made. Thüringen and northern Bayern are famed for their succulent grilled *Bratwurst,* the classic, garlicky, roasted sausage eaten with potatoes or bought from a street vendor clasped in a roll. The preferred vehicle for starch in southern Germany is *Spätzle* (noodles), though *Maultaschen* (pasta pockets) are also popular in **Swabia.** German *Pfannkuchen* (pancakes) are much heavier and bigger than the flapjacks back home and come with toppings. *Kaiserschmarren* is a chopped-up pancake with powdered sugar. **Hessians** do amazing things with potatoes, like smothering them in delectable *grüne Soße* (green sauce).

BEER

> Where does the German begin? Where does it end? May a German smoke? The majority says no ... But a German may drink beer, indeed as a true son of Germania's he should drink beer.
>
> —Heinrich Heine

Germans have brewed frothy malt beverages since the 8th century BC, and they've been consuming and exporting them in prodigious quantities ever since. The province of Bayern alone contains about one-fifth of all the breweries in the world. The Germans drink more than 150 liters of beer per person every year, more than any other country. According to legend, the German king Gambrinus invented the modern beer recipe when he threw some hops into fermenting malt. Brewers still honor him. During the Middle Ages, monastic orders refined the art of brewing, imbibing to stave off starvation during long fasts. It wasn't long before the monks' lucrative trade caught the eye of secular lords, who established the first *Hofbraüereien* (court breweries). The variety of beers in Germany boggles the mind. Most beer is **Vollbier,** containing about 4% alcohol. **Export** (5%) is also popular, and stout, tasty **Bockbier** (6.25%) is brewed in the spring. **Doppelbock** is an eye-popping concoction understandably reserved for special occasions. Ordering *"ein Helles"* will get you a light-colored beer, while *"Dunkles"* can look like anything from Coca-Cola to molasses.

Although generalizations are difficult, the average German beer is maltier and more "bread-like" than Czech, Dutch, or American beers. (An affectionate German slang term for beer is *flüßiges Brot,* "liquid bread.")

The province of Bayern alone contains about one-fifth of all the breweries in the world. The Germans drink more that 150 liters of beer per person every year, more than any other country

Among the exceptions is *Pils,* or Pilsner, which is most popular in the north. Its characteristic clarity and bitter taste come from the addition of extra hops. From the south, especially Bayern, comes *Weißbier,* a smooth, refreshing brew. Despite the name, *Weißbier* is not white, but a rich brown. (The name is a corruption of *Weizen-*

Das Reinheitsgebot: Germany's Beer Purity Law

One of the most despised characters in medieval Germany was the shoddy brewer who tried to cut costs by substituting lesser grains for the noble cereal at the heart of beer—barley. In 1516, Duke Wilhelm IV of Bayern decreed that beer could contain only pure water, barley, and hops. Wilhelm's Purity Law *(Reinheitsgebot)* has endured to this day, with minor alterations to permit the cultivation of Bayern's trademark wheat-based beers. The law even applies to imports—none of the filler-laden products of the major American breweries (Samuel Adams is an exception) can be imported into Germany. But with the arrival of the European Union, the law was challenged by other European countries, who saw it as an unfair trade barrier. Now the "impure" foreign beers are being admitted to the market, but to the joy of drinkers worldwide, the German breweries have all reaffirmed their full commitment to the *Reinheitsgebot.*

bier, meaning wheat beer.) The term *Weizenbier* now generally refers to a lighter wheat beer, while *Hefe-Weizen* is wheat beer with a layer of yeast in the bottom. *Faßbier* simply means beer from a barrel. Sampling local brews numbers among the finest of Germany's pleasures. In Köln, one drinks smooth *Kölsch*, an extraordinarily refined, light-colored beer; a Düsseldorf specialty is *Altbier,* a darker top-fermented beer. Berliners are partial to *Berliner Weiße,* a mixture of beer and lime-flavored syrup (or *Berliner Rote* with raspberry syrup). On hot summer days, lightweight drinkers prefer *Radler,* a Bavarian mix containing half beer and half lemon-lime soda. *Diesel* is a mixture of *Bier* and cola that will get your engine started.

The variety of places to drink beer is almost as staggering as the variety of brews. The traditional *Biergarten* consists of outdoor tables under chestnut trees. The broad leaves of the trees originally kept beer barrels cool in the days before refrigeration, until one enterprising brewer figured out that they could do the same thing for beer drinkers. The *Bierkeller* is an indoor version of the *Biergarten,* where local breweries dispense their product. To order "*Ein Bier,*" hold up your thumb, not your index finger. Raise your glass to a *"Prost,"* and drink (for more on Beer Halls in Munich, see **Beer, Beer, and more Beer,** p. 487). Another option for beer drinking is the *Gaststätte,* a simple, local restaurant. It's considered bad form to order only drinks at a *Gaststätte* during mealtimes, but at any other time, friends linger for hours over beers. Many *Gaststätten* have a *Stammtisch* (regulars' table), marked by a flag, where interlopers should not sit. The same group of friends may meet at the *Stammtisch* every week for decades to drink, play cards, and shoot the breeze; keep in mind that your visa has an expiration date. *Kneipen* are bars where young folks hang out.

> *The variety of places to drink beer is almost as staggering as the variety of brews*

WINE AND SPIRITS

Although overshadowed by Germany's more famous export beverage, German wines win over connoisseurs and casual drinkers alike. Virtually all German wines are white, though they vary widely in character. Generally, German wines are sweeter and taste fresher than French, Mediterranean, or Californian wines. Because Germany is the northernmost of the wine-producing countries, the quality of a vineyard's produce can vary considerably with the climate.

The cheapest wines are classified as *Tafelwein* (table wine), while the good stuff (which is still pretty affordable) is *Qualitätswein* (quality wine). The label *Qualitätswein bestimmter Anbaugebiete,* or *Q. b. A.,* designates quality wine from a specific cultivation region. *Qualitätswein mit Prädikat* (quality wine with distinction) denotes an even purer wine derived from a particular varietal grape. The *Prädikat* wines are further subdivided according to the ripeness of the grapes when harvested; from driest to sweetest, they are *Kabinett, Spätlese, Auslese, Beerenauslese, Eiswein,* and *Trockenbeerenauslese.* The grapes that produce the *Trockenbeerenauslese* are left on the vine until they have shriveled into raisins and begun to rot—no kidding.

The major concentrations of viniculture lie along the Rhine and Mosel valleys, along the Main River in Franconia, and in Baden. Rhine wines are bottled in brown glass, all others in green. Of the dozens of varieties, the most famous are *Riesling, Müller-Thurgau,* and *Traminer* (source of *Gewürztraminer*). In wine-producing towns, thirsty travelers can stop by a *Weinstube* to sample the local produce. In Hessen, the beverage of choice is *Äppelwoi* or *Äpfelwein* (apple wine), a hard cider similar in potency to beer. After a meal, many Germans aid their digestion by throwing back a shot of *Schnapps,* distilled from fruits. *Kirschwasser,* a cherry liqueur from the Schwarzwald, is the best known and probably the easiest to stomach, but adventurous sorts can experiment with the sublimely tasty *Black Haus,* a delectable, 100 proof, blackberry *Schnapps* also from the Schwarzwald, which will get you *Haus*ed in a most delightful fashion. Each year, unsuspecting tourists are seduced into buying little green bottles of *Jägermeister,* an herb liqueur slightly more palatable than raw eggs flavored with soap.

■ Media

British dailies, such as the *Times* and *Guardian,* are widely available at newsstands in major cities. The *International Herald Tribune* and the European edition of the *Wall Street Journal* are the most common U.S. papers, though the international edition of *USA Today* has become easier to find in recent years. American and British armed forces maintain English-language radio stations. German-speakers can keep track of things with German language papers both in print and on the web. Stay in touch with world events with the informative, Hamburg-based weekly *Der Spiegel* (http://www.spiegel.de), one of the world's leading news magazines. *Die Zeit* is a witty, left-leaning weekly journal of opinion. The *Frankfurter Allgemeine* is a stodgy newspaper comparable to the *New York Times.* Munich's *Süddeutsche Zeitung* (http://www.sueddeutsche.de) is Germany's best daily paper, though the racy, trashy, semi-rag *Bild Zeitung* (http://www.bild.de) is far more popular. For perspective on *Bild,* read Heinrich Böll's *Lost Honor of Katerina Blum,* an open attack on the tabloid and its distinctive style. Coming at you from Berlin are the liberal *Berliner Tagesspiegel* (http://www.tagesspiegel-berlin.de) and the left-leaning *Tageszeitung* (TAZ).

German television has expanded in the last 10 years. Couch potatoes can now receive more than 25 channels with cable. The government funded stations, ARD and ZDF, are the biggest news stations, followed by state-specific channels. English speakers can indulge in English language channels such as CNN, British NBC, and BBC World. The most popular German channels are RTL+ and SAT1; for laughter-inducing entertainment, watch American TV shows dubbed in German or join the rest of the nation in drooling over Germany's number one prime time soap, *Gute Zeiten, Schlechte Zeiten* (Good Times, Bad Times).

■ Social Life

An afternoon of relaxation at a park in Berlin or a cafe in any college town will teach you more about Germany than one spent in a museum. Many Germans know Americans and Britons only through contact with NATO soldiers, who haven't always made the best impression. Anti-Americanism is sometimes a powerful sentiment among young Germans concerned about what they perceive as the American government's failure to exercise moral leadership in the world. If you are sensitive to this concern, you will find

An afternoon of relaxation at a park in Berlin or a cafe in any college town will teach you more about Germany than one spent in a museum

that most Germans have a passionate interest in the U.S. It is actually rather ironic that despite anti-American sentiment, Germans are obsessed with Americana, and English words and American popular culture are omnipresent in Germany.

HISTORY & CULTURE

Take the time to actually meet people. Although Germans may seem aloof at first, they are not as stand-offish as they first appear. A photo of Walter and Gisela Schmidt who put you up for the night in Laßunsgehendorf will contain more memories than a postcard of the Brandenburg Gate. Europeans in general are sincerely interested in other lands and cultures, but have a very strong sense of their own cultural history; if you insult or belittle it, you'll only seem ignorant (and rude). Above all, don't automatically equate the American, Canadian, British, Australian, etc. way with "better."

The Byzantine rules surrounding German etiquette make Ann Landers look like a gas station attendant. In general, the Germans are much more formal than Americans and Australians, and incredibly big on punctuality (especially to meals). An invitation to a German home is a major courtesy; you should bring something for the hostess. Among the older generations, be careful not to use the informal *"du"* (you) or a first name without being invited to do so. *"Du"* is appropriate when addressing fellow students and friends at a youth hostel, or when addressing children. In all other circumstances, use the formal *"Sie"* for "you," as in the question *"Sprechen Sie Englisch?"* Only waitresses in traditional restaurants are addressed as *"Fräulein"*; address all other women as *Frau* (followed by a name). To find out if someone speaks English (many Germans, particularly in the Western *Länder,* do), humbly ask, *"Sprechen Sie Englisch?"* (SPREH-shen zee AYN-glish?) before launching into a question. Better yet, try to learn a little German and don't be afraid to test your talents. The language is related to English, and you can learn the pronunciation system and some useful phrases in about 15 minutes (see **Appendix: Language,** p. 573). In any case, learn at least two phrases: **please** (*bitte*; BIT-tuh) and **thank you** (*danke;* DAHNK-uh).

Everything you've heard about the Germans' compulsive abidance of law is true. The first time you see a German standing at an intersection in the pouring rain, with no cars in sight, waiting for the "Walk" signal, you'll know what we mean. Jaywalking is only one of the petty offenses that will

The Byzantine rules surrounding German etiquette make Ann Landers look like a gas station attendant

mark you as a foreigner (and subject you to fines); littering is another. Many tourists also do not realize that the bike lanes marked in red between the sidewalk and the road are not for pedestrian use. The younger generation takes matters a bit less seriously. Although **police** are polite and businesslike, they aren't to be messed with. If you fail to treat officers with proper respect (for instance, addressing them with the familiar *"du"* rather than the formal *"Sie"*), they can slap you with on-the-spot fines (see **Insults for Sale,** p. 258). Few officers speak more than a bit of English. The **drinking age** is 16 for beer and 18 for spirits, although both are skimpily enforced; driving under the influence, however, is a severe offense.

Berlin

It has been said that Berliners have experienced more history than any other people in Europe. For 40 years, the divided city personified the undeclared Cold War. Raised in the shadow of global conflict, Berliners responded with a glorious storm of cultural activity and the sort of free-for-all nightlife you might expect from a population that has its back against the wall. With the collapse of the Berlin Wall in 1989, the city suddenly gained the opportunity to reinvent itself. Communist governments fell across Eastern Europe, and Berlin found itself it in a unique position, straddling the border of two distinct but no longer separate worlds. Almost overnight, it became a gateway—*the* gateway—between East and West. Yet at the same time, its two halves were forced to fuse, forming a complex, decentralized metropolis.

Unsurprisingly, the task of reuniting the twin cities is proving to be a difficult one. Plagued by a divisive West-versus-East mentality intensified by the rapidity of reunion, Berliners from both sides of the former divide are palpably less enthusiastic about sharing 'their' city a decade after the myopically euphoric reunification. High unemployment rates, skyrocketing rents, and Berlin's infamous reputation as an *ewige Baustelle*—perpetual construction site—have conspired against the Berliners' initial thrill of reestablishing their city as one of the continent's most prominent cultural and political centers.

Now, as East and West Germany attempt to stitch themselves together, the result will be a new city for a new millennium, redefining Berlin as Germany's cultural center—or so the tourist brochures say. Yet at the heart of the city's current problems is an inability to draw upon a legacy with which to create an innovative, yet historically endowed, national capital. For many people who lived through the horrors of the Second World War, massive construction plans to turn Berlin into a center of intercontinental import are still overwhelmingly redolent of the fascist era; after all, the last man to attempt to exalt the city's virtues was Albert Speer, Hitler's chief architect. Nearly as worrisome is the tendency to attempt to replicate other cities in order to achieve parallel fame. A few years ago, the influential newsmagazine *Der Spiegel* derided this peculiarly German propensity, warning that "Berlin should stop trying to imitate other metropolises such as London and Paris," for "the thirst for glory of a city is even more dangerous than the thirst for glory of an individual."

While Berlin no longer possesses the apocalyptic intensity thrust upon it by the immediate danger of the Cold War, it nonetheless continues to thrive off its omnipresent and chaotic ambivalence toward the future. The threat of nuclear holocaust taught Berliners to live like there was no tomorrow, and this penchant for shortsighted excess continues to manifest itself in all aspects of the city's existence, from its ridiculously grandiose building endeavors to the party-til-dawn atmosphere that reigns in its smoky nightclubs.

Berlin is not pretty; it has neither the architectural glory of Paris nor the densely packed towers of New York. But, to use a phrase once applied to the Rolling Stones, "it's so ugly, it's beautiful." For now, Berlin is a mish-mash of GDR apartment blocks and designer boutiques, decaying pre-war buildings pockmarked with bullet holes and gleaming (yet empty) office complexes. The occasional melancholy of the city's tumultuous past is counteracted by the exhilaration of being on the cutting edge. As Weimar decadent Karl Zuckmayer wrote, "Berlin tasted of the future, and for that one happily accepted the dirt and the coldness as part of the bargain."

🗨 HIGHLIGHTS OF BERLIN

- To see the churned-up center of the **world's largest construction site,** head to **Potsdamer Platz** (see p. 107), where major capitalist corporations are busily reworking the former center of East German communism.
- Stroll the **Straße des 17 Juni** and **Unter den Linden** to enjoy the green serenity of the massive **Tiergarten** and view the **Siegessäule** (see p. 108) and **Brandenburg Gate** (see p. 106).
- Though little of the **Berlin Wall** remains, you can visit **Checkpoint Charlie** (see p. 107) to refresh your memory of the days of divided Berlin and see a preserved 1.3km stretch of the wall at the **East Side Gallery** (see p. 106).
- Vast holdings of art and artifacts are on display at the **Dahlem** museum complex, the **Museuminsel,** and **Schloß Charlottenburg** (see p. 116).
- Berlin's notorious **nightlife** is quite dispersed, but centers on the districts of Kreuzberg, Prenzlauer Berg, and Mitte (see p. 123), with the beginnings of a scene sprouting up in more distant reaches of the former East.

■ History

PRUSSIAN KINGDOM TO WORLD WAR I

Berlin took its time to attain international importance. Populated since the Stone Age, the first mention of a town called "Berlin" appeared in 1237; despite political and economic links, it was not until 1709 that the five towns by the river Spree united into the city of Berlin, capital of the Prussian kingdom. In the 18th century, Berlin flourished under the progressive rule of Friedrich II (the Great), and intellectuals such as Gotthold Ephraim Lessing and Moses Mendelssohn made the growing city a center of the Enlightenment. Nonetheless, Berlin was little more than an ornate garrison town, as Friedrich's penchant for military pomp and circumstance (as well as young officers) turned the city into a series of grandiose parade grounds devoid of civilians. Berlin suffered a decline in the 19th century, as it was conquered by Napoleon and later beset by revolution in 1848. However, it soon became a hotbed of political and economic discontent. In 1871, Berlin became the capital of the German Empire established after Bismarck's wars, but the absence of centralized rule in Germany before that left its mark on the country. Imperial Berlin never became the center of the new nation in the same way that Paris was for France or London for Britain. Munich and Frankfurt remained cultural and commercial rivals, and many Germans felt little affection for the Prussian capital. It was not until the end of WWI and the establishment of the first German Republic that Berlin became the undisputed center of national life.

REVOLUTION AND WEIMAR CULTURE

World War I and the Allied blockade brought about near-starvation conditions in Berlin. A popular uprising led to the *Kaiser's* abdication and Karl Liebknecht's declaration of a socialist republic, with Berlin as capital. Locally, the revolt—led by Liebknecht and Rosa Luxemburg—turned into a full-fledged workers' revolution that wrestled control of the city for several days. The Social Democratic government enlisted the aid of radical right-wing mercenaries, the *Freikorps,* who brutally suppressed the rebellion and murdered Liebknecht and Luxemburg. Political and economic instability continued until 1923, when Chancellor Gustav Stresemann's economic plan and generous loans from the United States improved the situation. Meanwhile, Berlin had become one of the major cultural centers of Europe. Expressionist painting flourished, Bertolt Brecht developed revolutionary new theater techniques, and artists and writers from all over the world flocked to the city. The city's "Golden Twenties," however, ended abruptly with the 1929 economic collapse. Mass unemployment preceded bloody riots, radicalization, political chaos, and the ascent of the Nazis in this period of uncertainty.

CAPITAL OF THE THIRD REICH

When Hitler took power on January 30, 1933, traditionally left-wing "Red Berlin" was not one of his strongholds. He consolidated his control over the city through economic improvements and totalitarian measures, and found plenty of supporters for the savage anti-Semitic pogrom of November 9, 1938, known as *Kristallnacht* (Night of Shattered Glass). Berlin was hit extremely hard during WWII; Allied bombing and the Battle of Berlin leveled one-fifth of the city. With almost all of the healthy men dead or gone, it was Berlin's women, known as the *Trümmerfrauen* (rubble women), who picked up the broken pieces of the city, creating numerous artificial hills out of the tons of rubble strewn across the defeated capital. The pre-war population of 4.3 million sank to 2.8 million. Only 7000 members of Berlin's once-thriving Jewish community of 160,000 survived the Nazi genocide.

After the war, the Allies took control of the city, dividing it into French, British, American, and Soviet sectors under a joint Allied Command. On June 16, 1948, the Soviets withdrew from the joint Command and demanded full control of Berlin. On June 26, they began an 11-month blockade of most land and water routes into the western sectors. The population would have starved were it not for a massive Allied airlift of supplies known as the *Luftbrücke* (air bridge). On May 12, 1949, the Soviets ceded control of the western half of Berlin to the Western Allies.

A DIVIDED CITY

On October 5, 1949, the Soviet-controlled German Democratic Republic *(Deutsche Demokratische Republik)* was formally established, with East Berlin as its capital. The city was thus officially divided. Dissatisfaction was great in East Berlin, and it manifested itself in the workers' uprising of June 17, 1953, when widespread popular demonstrations were crushed under Soviet tanks. One result of the repression was an increase in the number of *Republiksflüchtige* ("Republic-deserters") who emigrated to West Berlin—200,000 in 1960 alone. On the morning of August 13, 1961, the government of the East responded to this exodus of many of its most talented citizens with the almost instantaneous construction of the Berlin Wall, which stopped virtually all interaction between the two halves of the city. The commercial center around Kurfürstendamm was created and nurtured to become *das Schaufenster des Westens* (the store window of the West).

West Berlin remained under joint French, British, and American control. Although there was an elected mayor, final say rested with the Allied commander-in-chief. The city was not officially a part of the Federal Republic of Germany, but had "special status." Although Berlin adopted the resolutions of the Federal Parliament, the municipal Senate still had to approve them, and the Allies retained ultimate authority over the city right up until German reunification in 1990. One perk of this special status was the exemption of West Berliners from military conscription. Thousands of German artists, punks, homosexuals, and left-wing activists moved to Berlin to escape the draft and formed an alternative scene without parallel anywhere in the world. The West German government, determined to make a Cold War showcase of the city, subsidized its economic and cultural life, further enhancing its vitality.

THE WALL OPENS

On November 9, 1989—the 71st anniversary of the proclamation of the Weimar Republic, the 66th anniversary of Hitler's Beer Hall *Putsch,* and the 51st anniversary of *Kristallnacht*—a series of popular demonstrations throughout East Germany, riding on a decade of discontent and a year of rapid change in Eastern Europe, culminated in the opening of the Berlin Wall. The image of jubilant Berliners embracing atop the Brandenburg Gate that night provided one of the most memorable images of the century. Berlin was officially reunited (and Allied authority ended) along with the rest of Germany on October 3, 1990, to widespread celebration. Since then, the euphoria has evaporated. Eastern and Western Berliners have discovered that they don't really like each other as much as they once imagined. Resignation to reconstruction has taken the place of the biting criticism and tasteless jokes that were standard in the early 90s. Eastern Berlin remains politically volatile and economically disadvantaged, and Western Berliners have responded with their own form of xenophobia; in 1995, voters in the western Wedding district voted a handful of far-right nationalists onto the town council. The city is slowly knitting itself back together, but it will be years before residents on both sides of the divide consider themselves citizens of the same city.

Although the first united, freely elected *Bundestag* symbolically convened in Berlin in December of 1990, the June 1991 vote to move the parliament back here did not bode immediate action, with Bonn remaining the seat of the government until September 1999, when the parliament will finally convene in Berlin. When this happens, perhaps the "post-war" era in Berlin will have a definitive endpoint, more than 50 years after World War II, and on the doorstep of the 21st century.

■ Orientation

Berlin surveys the Prussian plains from the northeastern corner of a reunited Germany and is slowly becoming the hub of the national rail network. About four hours southeast of Hamburg by train and eight hours north of Munich (though ICE trains cut down on travel time), Berlin has a web of rail and air connections to other European capitals. The city is well-connected to Eastern European countries—Prague is five hours by rail, Warsaw six hours. Almost all European airlines, Western or Eastern, have frequent service to one of Berlin's three airports.

Berlin is an *immense* conglomeration of what were once two separate and unique cities: the former East, which contains the lion's share of Berlin's landmarks and historic sites, as well as an unfortunate number of pre-fab concrete socialist architectural monsters, and the former West, which functioned for decades as a small, isolated,

Allied-occupied state and is still the commercial heart of united Berlin. As businesses and embassies are starting to move their headquarters to Potsdamer Platz and Mitte, this situation is rapidly changing.

The commercial district of Western Berlin lies at one end of the huge **Tiergarten** park, and is focused around **Bahnhof Zoo** and **Kurfürstendamm** (Ku'damm for short). It is marked by the bombed-out **Kaiser-Wilhelm-Gedächtniskirche**, adjacent to the boxy tower of the **Europa Center**, one of the few "skyscrapers" in Western Berlin. A star of streets radiates from Breitscheidplatz; toward the west run **Hardenbergstraße, Kantstraße,** and the great commercial boulevard of modern Berlin, the renowned and reviled Kurfürstendamm. Down Kantstr. 800m is **Savignyplatz,** home to cafes, restaurants, and *Pensionen*.

The grand, tree-lined **Straße des 17. Juni** runs west-east through the Tiergarten to end at the triumphant **Brandenburg Gate,** which opens out onto **Pariser Platz,** a site of landmark public addresses. Heading south from the Brandenburg Gate and the nearby **Reichstag,** Ebertstraße runs haphazardly through the construction sites to **Potsdamer Platz.** Toward the east, the gate opens onto **Unter den Linden,** Berlin's most famous boulevard and the site of many historic buildings. The *Linden's* broad tree-lined throughway empties into socialist-realist **Alexanderplatz,** the center of the East's growing commercial district and the home of Berlin's most visible landmark, the **Fernsehturm.** Southeast of Mitte lies **Kreuzberg,** a district home to an incongruous mix of radical leftists, Turks, punks, and homosexuals. Once confined to West Berlin's outer limits, Kreuzberg today finds itself bordering reunited Berlin's city center, a fact that is slowly pushing rents up and alternative types out as civil servants from Bonn descend on the area in a wave of gentrification.

The **Spree River** snakes its way from west to east through the center of Berlin; it forms the northern border of the Tiergarten and splits just east of Unter den Linden to close off the **Museumsinsel** (Museum Island), East Berlin's cultural epicenter. The windswept waters of the Wannsee, Tegeler See, and Heiligensee lap against the city's west side, and are connected by narrow canals.

If you're planning to stay more than a few days in Berlin, the blue-and-yellow **Falk Plan** (available at most kiosks and bookstores) is an indispensable and convenient city map that includes a street index and folds open like a book (DM11). Dozens of streets and subway stations in Eastern Berlin were named after Communist heroes and heroines. Many, but not all, have been renamed in a process only recently completed; be sure that your map is up-to-date. In newly united Berlin, many **municipal services** are gradually being joined and coordinated. When services are duplicated in both parts of the city, *Let's Go* lists those in Western Berlin first, then their Eastern counterparts.

> **Safety Warning!** Although Berlin is by far the most tolerant city in Germany in every respect, the economic chaos caused by reunification has, unfortunately, unleashed a new wave of right-wing extremism, particularly in the outer boroughs of Eastern Berlin. While it is unlikely that you will come into contact with neo-Nazi skinheads, it is important for people of color as well as gays and lesbians to take precautions when traveling in the eastern suburbs or on the S-Bahn late at night. Also be aware that all skinheads are not alike: if you run into gangs of shaved-head, leather-toting types in Schöneberg or Kreuzberg, they're more likely to be radical leftists or homosexuals.

■ Practical Information

LONG DISTANCE TRANSPORTATION

Flights: Flughafen Tegel (tel. 41 01 23 06) is Western Berlin's main airport. Take express bus X9 (from Bahnhof Zoo), bus #109 from U-Bahn #7 to "Jakob-Kaiser-Platz," or bus #128 from U-Bahn #6 to "Kurt-Schumacher-Platz." **Flughafen Tempelhof** (tel. 69 51 22 88), the smallest of Berlin's airports, is mostly used for intra-Germany travel and flights within Europe. U-Bahn #6 to "Platz der Luftbrücke."

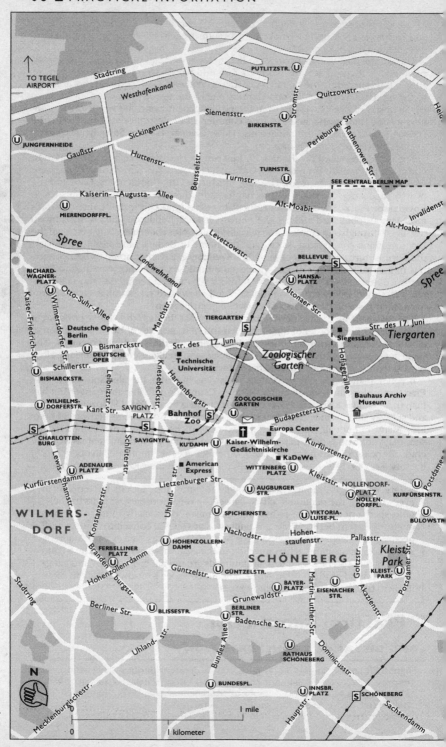

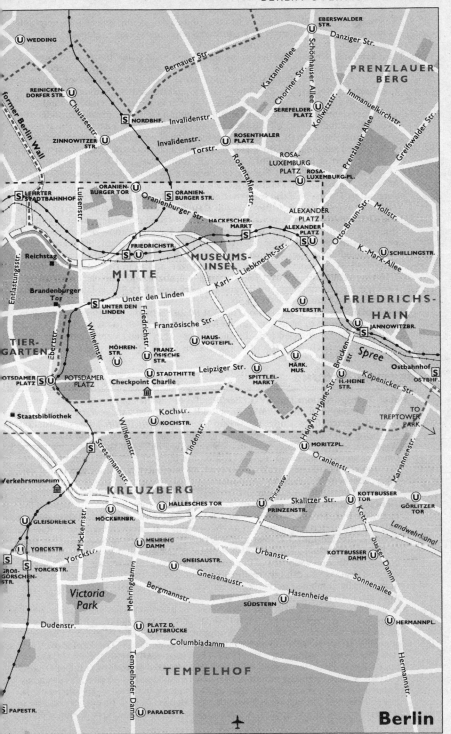

Berlin

Flughafen Schönefeld (tel. 60 91 51 66), southeast of Berlin, is used for interconti-nental flights as well as travel to the former Soviet Union and developing countries. S-Bahn #9 or 45, or bus #171 from U-Bahn #7 to "Rudow."

Train Stations: While construction continues on the *Megabahnhof* of the future at Lehrter Stadtbahnhof, trains to and from Berlin are serviced by **Zoologischer Gar-ten** (almost always called **Bahnhof Zoo**) in the West and **Ostbahnhof** (formerly the *Hauptbahnhof*) in the East. Most trains go to both stations, although some con-nections to cities in the former GDR only stop at Ostbahnhof. Quite a number of trains also connect to **Schönefeld** airport. If coming in late at night it is preferable to arrive at Bahnhof Zoo, as the area around Ostbahnhof can be a little unsavory.

Connections: Hamburg (ICE, 2½hr.); Munich (ICE, 8hr.); Köln (ICE, 5hr.); Frankfurt (ICE, 5hr.); Dresden (ICE, 2hr.); Leipzig (IC, 2hr.); Rostock (IR, 2¾hr.); Amsterdam (ICE, 7hr.); Brussels (ICE, 7½hr.); Paris (ICE, 10hr.); Zurich (ICE, 9hr.); Prague (EC, 5hr.); Kraków (IC, 8½hr.); Warsaw (EC, 6½hr.); Vienna (10hr.); Budapest (13hr.); Moscow (36hr.); and St. Petersburg (36hr.).

Information: Deutsche Bahn Information (tel. 194 19). Be prepared for a long wait. Also long lines at the *Reisezentrum* in **Bahnhof Zoo** (open daily 4:45am-11pm) and **Ostbahnhof.** Both stations have recently installed computers to help you fig-ure out your own itinerary, but there are lines for these, too—*arrive early.* For **recorded information** about departures and arrivals (in German) there are several lines depending on your destination: Hamburg, Rostock, Stralsund and Scandinavia (tel. 01 15 31); Magdeburg, Frankfurt, Hannover, and Köln (tel. 01 15 32); Halle, Erfurt, and Frankfurt (tel. 01 15 33); Leipzig, Nürnberg, and Munich (tel. 01 15 34); Dresden, Czech Republic, Austria, and Hungary (tel. 01 15 35); Poland, Russia, Bal-tic States, and Ukraine (tel. 01 15 36).

Buses: ZOB, the central bus station (tel. 301 80 28), is by the *Funkturm* near Kaiser-damm. U-Bahn #2 to "Kaiserdamm" or S-Bahn #4, 45, or 46 to "Witzleben." Check *Zitty* and *Tip* for deals on long-distance buses—they aren't comfortable but they are often much cheaper than the train. Paris (10hr., DM109 one-way); Vienna (10½hr., DM85 one-way).

GETTING AROUND

Public Transportation: The **BVG** *(Berliner Verkehrsbetriebe)* is arguably the most efficient transportation system in the world, even amidst a massive overhaul of its rail and streetcar lines. Under the slogan *"Freie Bahn für Berlin,"* the construction will bring service in Eastern Berlin up to snuff, reopen closed S-Bahn lines in the West, and improve connections between the two halves of the city as well as to outlying areas in Brandenburg. To cushion the blow, the BVG has put up posters everywhere introducing Berliners to **Max,** an inimitably affable bespectacled car-toon mole who appears on announcements of disruptions to service. In most cases, the worst inconvenience is that you'll wait an extra 30 minutes.

Orientation and Basic Fares: It is impossible to tour Berlin on foot—fortunately, the extensive **bus, Straßenbahn** (streetcar), **U-Bahn** (subway), and **S-Bahn** (surface rail) systems of Berlin will get you to your destination safely and relatively quickly. Berlin is divided into 3 transit zones. Zone A encompasses downtown Berlin, including Tempelhof airport. Almost everything else falls into Zone B, with Zone C containing the outer suburbs of Potsdam, Oranienburg, and Bernau. An AB ticket is the best deal, as you can buy regional Bahn tickets for the outlying areas. A single ticket for the combined network (*Langstrecke* AB or BC, DM3.90, or *Ganzstrecke* ABC, DM4.20) is good for 2hr. after validation.

Special Passes: With the high cost of single tickets, it almost always makes sense to buy a transit pass. A **Tageskarte** (AB DM7.80, ABC DM8.50) is valid from the time of can-cellation until 3am the next day. A **Gruppentageskarte** (AB DM20, ABC DM22.50) allows up to 5 people to travel together on the same ticket. The **WelcomeCard** (DM29) is valid on all lines for 72hr. The **7-Tage-Karte** (AB DM40, ABC DM48) is good for 7 days of travel. For longer stays, an **Umweltkarte Standard** (AB DM99, ABC DM120) is valid during the month of purchase (not necessarily 30 days). You can buy tickets from machines, bus drivers, or ticket windows in the U- and S-Bahn stations. Inspections have increased severely in the past two years, and the cost of cheating is steep (DM60). Children under 6 accompanied by an adult travel free; children under

Central Berlin

BERLIN

MITTE

TIERGARTEN

Tiergarten

former Berlin Wall

Unter den Linden

River Spree

River Spree

N

1/2 mile
1/2 kilometer

Key labels:

ROSA-LUXEMBURG-PLATZ · ROSA-LUXEMBURG-PL. · Karl-Liebknecht-Str. · ALEXANDER-PLATZ · ALEXANDER-PL. · Fernsehturm · MARK. MUS. · Dircksenstr. · Littenstr. · KLOSTERSTR. · Stralauerstr. · Heinrich-Heine-Str. · Inselstr. · Neue Jacobstr. · Annenstr. · Sebastienstr. · Alte Jacobstr. · Stallschreiberstr. · Oranienstr. · Lindenstr. · Ritterstr.

Marienkirche · Rathausstr. · Spandauer Str. · Poststr. · Fischer-Insel · Gertraudenstr. · Breite Str. · SPITTEL-MARKT · SPITTEL-MKT. · Seydelstr. · Kommandantenstr.

HACKESCHER MARKT · Bodemuseum · Pergamon Museum · Alte Nationalgalerie · Berliner Dom · MARX-ENGELS-PLATZ · Werderstr. · Niederwall · Oberwallstr. · HAUS-VOGTEI-PLATZ · Kochstr. · KOCHSTR.

Alte Synagogue · Gr.-Hamburger-Str. · Krausnickstr. · ORANIEN-BURGER STR. · Oranienburger str. · Monbijou-str. · Am Kupfergraben · Humboldt Universität · Staatsoper · BEBEL-PLATZ · Markgrafenstr. · GENDARMEN-MARKT · FRANZÖSISCHE-STR. · Taubenstr. · Mohrenstr. · Krausenstr. · Leipziger Str. · Mauerstr. · Schützenstr. · Checkpoint Charlie · Zimmerstr. · Wilhelmstr.

Rosenthalerstr. · Mulackstr. · Steinstr. · WEINMEISTER STR. · Gipsstr. · Augustr. · Linienstr. · Tucholskystr. · Johannisstr. · Ziegel str. · Bahnhof Friedrichstr. · FRIEDRICHSTR. · Charlotten- str. · Georgenstr. · Am Weidendamm · Mittelstr. · Behrenstr. · STADT-MITTE · MOHREN-STR. · Glinkastr. · Mauerstr. · Martin-Gropius-Bau · Stresemann-str. · Anhalterstr.

Harnoverische Str. · ORANIENBURGER TOR · Friedrichstr. · Reinhardt str. · Schumannstr. · Clara-Zetkin-Str. · Brandenburger Tor · PARISER PLATZ · Potsdamer Str. · POTSDAMER PLATZ · Ebertstr. · Voßstr. · Niederkirchstr.

Philippstr. · Luisenstr. · Schiffbauer · Reichstagufer · Reichstag · Scheidemannstr. · Dorotheenstr. · Str. des 17 Juni

LEHRTER STADTBAHNHOF · Friedrich-List-Ufer · Uter · Lehrter str. · Moltkestr. · Kongresshalle · Soviet Army Memorial · Entlastungsstr. · KEMPERPL. · Bellevue-str. · Margareten str. · Neue Nationalgalerie · Sigismundstr.

BELLEVUE · Invalidenstr. · Alt-Moabit · John-Foster-Dulles-Allee · Str. des 17 Juni · Philharmonie · Kunstgewerbemuseum · Tiergarten str. · Stauffenbergstr. · Hildebrandstr. · Hiroshimastr. · Schöneberger Uter

Werftstr. · Spenerstr. · Paulstr. · Spree weg · GROSSER STERN · Siegessäule · Altonaer Str. · Hofjäger-Allee · Schloß Bellevue · Klingelhöferstr.

Calvinstr. · Melanchtonstr. · Kirchstr. · River Spree · Lützowufer · Köbisstr. · Schniezer-Rauch- str. · Cornelliusstr. · Lützowufer · Wichmannstr. · Klingelhöferstr.

TO ZOOOLOGISCHER GARTEN, KU'DAMM

14 pay a reduced fare. *All tickets must be cancelled in the red or yellow validation box marked "hier entwerten" before boarding to be valid.*

Maps and Information: The **Liniennetz** map can be picked up for free at any tourist office or subway station. The BVG also issues an excellent **Atlas** of the entire city (DM9). For more information, visit the **BVG Pavillon** outside Bahnhof Zoo (tel. 25 62 25 62; open daily 6:30am-10pm) or the **BVG Kundenbüro** at "Turmstr." station on U-Bahn #9 (open M-F 6:30am-8:30pm, Sa 9am-3:30pm).

Night Transport: U- and S-Bahn lines generally do not run from 1-4am, although most S-Bahn lines run once an hour during weekend nights, and the **U9** and **U12** run all night Friday and Saturday. (The U12 line, which only runs Friday and Saturday night, combines the Ruhleben-Gleisdreieck leg of U2 with the Gleisdreieck-Warschauer Str. leg of the U1.) Most regular lines start their final runs by 12:15am. There is an extensive system of **night buses** centered on Bahnhof Zoo that run about every 20-30min.; you can pick up the free *Nachtliniennetz* map at the BVG pavilion. All night bus numbers are preceded by the letter **N.**

Ferries: Stern und Kreis Schiffahrt, Puschkinallee 16-17 (tel. 536 36 00; fax 53 63 60 99), operates ferry services along the Spree Apr.-Oct. Ferries leave from locations throughout the city, including Friedrichstr., Museum Island, the *Dom,* and the Nikolaiviertel. Fares depend on distance traveled (DM3.50-22). Pleasure cruises also available. *Berlin Kombi-Tageskarte* is valid on all regularly scheduled services. For further information, contact tourist office or BVG Pavilion.

Taxis: tel. 21 02 02, 26 10 26, or 690 22. Call at least 15min. in advance. Women may request a female driver.

Car Rental: The **Mietwagenservice,** counter 21 in Bahnhof Zoo's *Reisezentrum* (see above), represents Avis, Hertz, Europacar and Sixt. Most companies also have offices at Tegel airport.

Auto Clubs: ADAC (tel. 018 02 22 22 22). 24hr. breakdown service for members.

Bike Rental: Bahnhof Zoo, next to the lost and found. DM13-23 per day. DM60 for 3 days. DM120 per week. Open daily 6am-11pm. **Herr Beck,** at Goethestr. 7 (tel. 312 19 25), near Ernst-Reuter-Platz. DM12 per day. Mountain bikes DM20 per day. Call for selection and deposit information. Bring passport. No English spoken.

Mitfahrzentrale: City Netz, Joachimstalerstr. 17 (tel. 194 44; fax 882 44 20) has a computerized **ride-share** database. U-Bahn #2 or 9 to "Kurfürstendamm." To Vienna DM79, Paris and Budapest DM109. Open M-F 9am-8pm, Sa-Su 9am-7pm. **Branch offices:** Südstern 2 (tel. 693 60 95), in Kreuzberg. U-Bahn #7 to "Südstern," and Bahnhof Zoo, on the U2 platform (tel. 31 03 31). Both open M-Sa 9am-8pm. **Mitzfahrzentrale Alex,** in the Alexanderplatz U-Bahn station (tel. 241 58 20 or 241 58 21), specializes in Eastern Europe. Open M, W and F 10am-6pm, Th 10am-8pm, Sa-Su 11am-4pm. The **Mitfahrtelephon für Schwule and Lesben,** Yorckstr. 52 (tel. 194 20 or 216 60 21), matches gay and lesbian drivers and passengers. U-Bahn #7 to "Yorckstr." Open M-F 9am-8pm, Sa-Su 10am-4pm. Berlin has many small *Mitzfahrzentralen;* check *Zitty, Tip,* or *030* magazines for addresses and phone numbers.

Hitchhiking: *Let's Go* does not recommend hitchhiking as a safe mode of transportation. Those who hitch west and south (Hannover, Munich, Weimar, Leipzig) take S-Bahn #1 or 7 to "Wannsee," then bus #211 to the *Autobahn* entrance ramp. Those headed north (Hamburg, Rostock) ride U-Bahn #6 to "Alt-Tegel" or S-Bahn #25 to "Tegel," then bus #224; ask the driver to be let out at the "Trampenplatz." Both have crowds, but someone gets picked up every few minutes.

TOURIST OFFICES AND CITY TOURS

Tourist Offices: The headquarters of **Berlin Tourismus** (tel. 25 00 25; fax 25 00 24 24) isn't the office you want to visit once you arrive, but it is nonetheless a useful resource. They will send you information and book rooms. Write to *Berlin Tourismus Marketing GmbH,* Am Karlsbad 11, 10785 Berlin. The other tourist offices do not give out phone numbers, so all inquiries should be directed to the above office. The offices listed below are conveniently located, provide tons of maps and info, and book rooms on the spot. **Europa Center office,** entrance on Budapester Str. From Bahnhof Zoo, walk along Budapester Str. past the Kaiser-Wilhelm-Gedächtniskirche; the office is on the right (5min.). Helpful staff speaks fluent English. Open

M-Sa 8am-10pm, Su 9am-9pm. **Brandenburger Tor office,** S-Bahn #1 or 2 to "Unter den Linden." Open daily 9:30am-6pm. **A.S. Airport-Service,** Flughafen Tegel, Ausgang Haupthalle opposite Gate O. Open daily 5am-10:30pm. **Infopoint Dresdner Bank,** Unter den Linden 17. Open M, W, and F 8:30am-2pm, Tu and Th 8:30am-2pm and 3:30-6pm.

Services: Thanks to recent privatization, the tourist offices no longer provide the plethora of free services and information they used to. However, they all sell a useful city map (DM1) on which sights and transit stations are more clearly marked than on the *Falk Plan.* They book same-day hotel rooms for a DM5 fee—though room prices start at DM50 and rise to stratospheric heights. A free list of hotels and *Pensionen* is available, but most of the rooms listed are not the most economical choices. They also have free copies of the city magazines *030* and (for gays and lesbians) *Siegessäule* and *Sergej,* which have reasonably good entertainment listings. The monthly magazine *Berlin Programm* (DM2.80) lists museums, sights, some restaurants and hotels, and opera, theatre, and classical music schedules. The city's main English language magazine, *Berlin* (DM3.50), has good listings for classical music and opera but little else. Dig *Deutsch?* You're better off buying *Tip* or *Zitty,* which have the most comprehensive listings if you're into film, theater, concerts, clubs, and discos (DM4 each).

Tours: The Walk is one of the best walking tours of Berlin out there. The tour guides are knowledgeable, and you'll appreciate their genuine passion for the city. Tours leave from the taxi stand at *Bahnhof Zoo,* May 25-Oct. 10 daily at 9:45am and 2pm (DM10). **Berlin Walks** (tel. 301 91 94; email berlin_walks@compuserve.com) offers a range of English-language walking tours, including their thorough Discover Berlin tour, and tours of Infamous Third Reich Sites, Jewish Life in Berlin, and Prenzlauer Berg. Tours last about 2½hr. and meet at 9:15, 10am, and 2:30pm in front of the Zoo station (DM15, under 26 DM10). The **Insider Tour** of Berlin hits all of the major sights and enjoys a very good reputation. Tours last 3hr. and leave from the McDonald's by the Zoo station late Mar. to Nov. daily at 10am and 2:30pm (DM15, students DM10). **Rad Zeit,** a monthly pamphlet (available in bike shops and in some cafes), lists bike tours (in German only) of Berlin and the surrounding countryside—a great way to meet people. There is also an **Insider Bike Tour.** It leaves from the same spot as the walking tour (4hr.; DM29, students DM25; May-Sept. daily at 10am and 3pm). **Bus tours** are offered by various companies in English and German, leaving roughly hourly from the Ku'damm near Europa Center and the *Gedächtniskirche.*

BUDGET TRAVEL

STA, Goethestr. 73 (tel. 311 09 50), does the budget travel agency thing. U-Bahn #2 to "Ernst-Reuter-Platz." Open M-W and F 10am-8pm, Th 10am-6pm.

Kilroy Travels, Hardenbergstr. 9 (tel. 313 04 66; fax 312 69 75), across from the Technical University. The friendly staff will cheerfully help you navigate through the intricacies of European planes, trains, and buses. **Branch offices** at: Takustr. 47 (tel. 831 50; fax 832 53 76; U-Bahn #1 to "Dahlem-Dorf"), Nollendorfpl. 7 (tel. 216 30 91; fax 215 92 21; U-Bahn #1, 2, or 4 to "Nollendorfplatz"), Mariannenstr. 7 (tel. 614 68 22; fax 614 99 83; in Kreuzberg; U-Bahn #1 or 8 to "Kotbusser Tor"), Georgenstr., Stadtbahnbogen 184, (in Mitte; S-Bahn or U-Bahn #6 to "Freidrichstr."). All open M-F 10am-6pm, Sa 11am-1pm.

EMBASSIES AND CONSULATES

Berlin's construction plans include a new complex of buildings to house all the foreign embassies. This means that over the next five years, the locations of the embassies and consulates will be in constant flux. For the most updated info, you should contact the Auswärtiges Amt Dienststelle Berlin, 10992, Postfach 610187, or visit them at Wedersches Markt (tel. 20 18 60; fax 20 18 62 52). This is a general office for foreign service.

Australian Consulate: c/o Kempinski Plaza, Uhlandstr. 181-183 (tel. 880 08 80; fax 88 00 88 99). U-Bahn #15 to "Uhlandstr." Open M-F 9am-noon.

Canadian Embassy: Friedrichstr. 95 (tel. 261 11 61; fax 262 92 06). S-Bahn or U-Bahn #6 to "Friedrichstr." Open M-F 8:30am-12:30pm and 1:30-5pm.

Irish Consulate: Ernst-Reuter-Platz 10 (tel. 34 80 08 22; fax 34 80 08 63). U-Bahn #2 to "Ernst-Reuter-Platz" Open M-F 10am-1pm.

New Zealand: citizens should contact their embassy in Bonn.

South African Consulate: Douglasstr. 9 (tel. 82 50 11; fax 826 65 43). Open M-F 9am-noon.

U.K. Embassy: Unter den Linden 32-34 (tel. 20 18 40; fax: 20 18 41 58). S-Bahn #1 or 2 to "Unter den Linden." Open M-F 9am-noon and 2-4pm.

U.S. Citizens Service: Clayallee 170 (tel. 832 92 33; fax 831 49 26). U-Bahn #1 to "Oskar-Helene-Heim." Open M-F 8:30am-noon. Telephone advice available M-F 9am-5pm; after hours, a machine will give you emergency instructions.

U.S. Consulate: Neustädtische Kirchstr. 4-5 (tel. 238 51 74; fax 238 62 90).

GENERAL SERVICES

Currency Exchange: The best rates are usually to be found at the offices that exclusively exchange currency and traveler's checks. The **Wechselstuben** on Breitscheidplatz near the Gedächtniskirche and in the Alexanderplatz train station have good rates and no commission. Open M-F 9am-6pm, Sa 9am-4pm. **Geldwechsel,** Joachimtal Str. 7-9 (tel. 882 63 71) has decent rates and no commission. **Reise-Bank,** at Bahnhof Zoo (tel. 881 71 17; open daily 7:30am-10pm) and Ostbahnhof (tel. 296 43 93; open M-F 7am-10pm, Sa 7am-6pm, Su 8am-4pm). **Berliner Bank,** in Tegel Airport. Open daily 8am-10pm. You can also change money at most **post offices,** which cash traveler's checks for DM6 per check. **Sparkasse** and **Deutsche Bank** have branches everywhere; their ATMs usually accep. Visa and MC (as long as you know your PIN), though only a few still take EuroCard. Sparkasse changes cash free, but charges 1% commission on traveler's checks (with a DM7.50 minimum). **Citibank** has branches with 24hr. ATMs at Kurfürstendamm 72, Wittenbergpl. 1, Wilmersdorfer Str. 133, and Karl-Marx-Allee 153. There's also a Citibank ATM at Tegel Airport.

American Express: Main Office, Uhlandstr. 173 (tel. 88 45 88 21). U-Bahn #15 to "Uhlandstr." Mail held, banking services rendered. No commission for cashing AmEx traveler's checks. On Fridays and Saturdays, expect out-the-door lines of travelers carrying *Let's Go.* Open M-F 9am-5:30pm, Sa 9am-noon. **Branch offices,** Bayreuthstr. 23 (tel. 21 49 83 63). U-Bahn #1 or 2 to "Wittenbergplatz" Traveler's checks cashed and sold, but no mail held. Open M-F 9am-6pm, Sa 10am-1pm. Also at Friedrichstr. 172 (tel. 20 17 40 12). U-Bahn #6 to "Französische Str." Full services. Open M-F 9am-5:30pm, Sa 10am-1pm.

Luggage Storage: In the **Bahnhof Zoo** train station (lockers DM2 per day, larger lockers DM4, 72hr. max.). If all the lockers at Bahnhof Zoo are full, you can check your luggage at the center near the post office for DM4 per piece per day. Open daily 6am-11pm. At the **Hauptbahnhof** (lockers DM2 per day, larger DM4, 72hr. max.). At Bahnhof **Lichtenberg** and S-Bahnhof **Alexanderplatz** (lockers DM2 per day, 24hr. max.).

Lost Property: Zentrales Fundbüro, Platz der Luftbrücke 8 (tel. 69 95). **BVG Fundbüro,** Lorenzweg 5 (tel. 256 230 40). U-Bahn #6 to "Ullsteinstr." For items lost on the bus or U-Bahn. Many, many umbrellas. Open M-Tu and Th 9am-3pm, W 9am-6pm, F 9am-2pm. **Fundbüro Berlin,** Mittelstr. 20 (tel. 29 72 96 12), at the Schönefeld airport train station.

Bookstores: Marga Schoeler Bücherstube, Knesebeckstr. 33 (tel. 881 11 12), at Mommsenstr., betweeen Savignyplatz and the Ku'damm. Large selection of books in English includes politics, history, poetry, lit crit, and fiction. Open M-W 9:30am-7pm, Th-F 9:30am-8pm, Sa 9:30am-4pm. The **British Bookshop,** Mauerstr. 83-84 (tel. 238 46 80), by Checkpoint Charlie. An artfully stocked addition to Berlin's English book club, with well-chosen literature and history sections and English-language newspapers and mags. Open M-F 10am-6pm, Sa 10am-4pm. **Literaturhaus Berlin,** Fasanenstr. 23 (tel. 882 65 52), is in a wonderful old mansion complete with garden and readings of German and international literature. Their resident bookstore, **Kohlhaas & Co.** (tel. 882 50 44), has lots of German paperbacks, and excellent Judaica and Nazi history sections. Open M-F 10am-8pm, Sa 10am-4pm.

Libraries: Staatsbibliothek Preußischer Kulturbesitz, Potsdamer Str. 33 (tel. 26 61), and Unter den Linden 8 (tel. 210 50). 3.5 million books—one for every Berliner—but not all are stored on site. Some can take 2 days to retrieve. Lots of English-language newspapers. The Potsdamer Str. library was built for West Berlin in the 1960s, after the Iron Curtain went down on the original **"Staabi"** on Unter den Linden, next to the Humboldt University. Now Berliners can choose between them—and so can you. Both open M-F 9am-9pm, Sa 9am-5pm.

Cultural Centers: Amerika Haus, Hardenbergstr. 22-24 (tel. 31 00 73 or 31 50 55 70). Library includes English-language books and day-old editions of *The New York Times,* and presents readings by visiting American authors. Offices open M-F 8:30am-5:30pm. Library open Tu and Th 2-8pm, W and F 2-5:30pm. **British Council,** Hardenbergstr. 22 (tel. 31 10 99-0), is next door. Enter through the *Informationszentrum* Berlin, 2nd floor. Office open M-F 9am-12:30pm and 2-5pm. Library open M, W, and F 2-6pm; Tu and Th 2-7pm.

Language Instruction: Goethe Institut, Friedrichstr. 209, 10969 (tel. 25 90 63; fax 25 90 64 00), is the best known and the most expensive. U-Bahn #6 to "Kochstr." All levels of German available. Office open M and Th 9am-2pm and 3-6pm, Tu 9am-2pm and 3-5pm, W and F 9am-2pm. DM1650 for 4 weeks, DM3090 for 8 weeks, 25hr. of instruction per week. **Fokus** *(Forum für Kultur und Sprachen),* Haubachstr. 23, 10585 (tel. 341 47 37), also has a good reputation. U-Bahn #7 to "Richard-Wagner-Platz." DM360 for 4 weeks, 15hr. per week. *Tip* and *Zitty* are filled with ads for other schools and private tutors—check the classifieds under "Unterricht" and shop around.

Laundromat: Wasch Centers at various locations: **Leibnizstr. 72,** in Charlottenburg; U-Bahn #7 to "Wilmersdorfer Str." **Wexstr. 34,** in Schöneberg; U-Bahn #9 to "Bundesplatz" **Bergmannstr. 109,** in Kreuzberg; U-Bahn #7 to "Gniesenaustr." **Behmstr. 12,** in Mitte; S-Bahn #1 or 2, or U-Bahn #8 to "Gesundbrunnen." **Jablonskistr. 21,** in Prenzlauer Berg; U-Bahn #2 to "Eberswalderstr." Wash DM6 per 6kg, soap included. Dry DM2 for 30min. All open daily 6am-11pm. **Waschcenter Schnell und Sauber, Uhlandstr. 61;** U-Bahn #15 to "Uhlandstr." **Torstr. 15,** in Mitte; U-Bahn #8 to "Rosenthaler Platz." **Oderberger Str. 1,** in Prenzlauer Berg; U-Bahn #2 to "Eberswalder Str." **Mehringdamm 32,** in Kreuzberg; U-Bahn #6 to "Mehringdamm." Wash DM6 per 6kg. Open daily 6am-11pm.

Emergency: Police, Platz der Luftbrücke 6 (tel.110 or 69 90). **Ambulance** and **Fire,** tel. 112.

Crisis Lines: Sexual Assault Hotline, tel. 251 28 28. Open Tu and Th 6-9pm, Su noon-2pm. **Schwules Überfall** (gay bashing) hotline and legal help, tel. 216 33 36. Open daily 6-9pm. **Schwulenberatung** (gay men's counseling), tel. 194 46. **Lesbenberatung** (lesbian counseling), tel. 215 20 00. **Drug Crisis,** tel. 192 37. Open M-F 8:30am-10pm, Sa-Su 2-9:30pm. **Frauenkrisentelefon** (women's crisis line), tel. 615 42 43. Open M and Th 10am-noon, Tu-W and F 7-9pm, Sa-Su 5-7pm. **Deutsche AIDS-Hilfe,** Dieffenbachstr. 33 (tel. 690 08 70). English spoken at most crisis lines.

Pharmacies: Europa-Apotheke, Tauentzienstr. 9-12 (tel. 261 41 42), by Europa Center (close to Bahnhof Zoo). Open M-F 9am-8pm, Sa 9am-4pm. **Münz-Apotheke,** Münzstr. 5 (tel. 241 10 83), just off Alexanderplatz. Open M-F 8am-6:30pm, Sa 9am-1pm. Closed *Apotheken* post signs directing you to the nearest open one. For information about late-night pharmacies call 011 41.

Medical Assistance: The American and British embassies have a list of English-speaking doctors and dentists. **Emergency Doctor** (tel. 31 00 31). **Emergency Dentist** (tel. 89 00 43 33).

Internet Access: see **Website,** p. 103.

Post Offices: In the **Bahnhof Zoo** (tel. 311 00 20). Interminable lines, but the best hours. Open M-F 6am-midnight, Sa-Su 8am-midnight. **Poste Restante** (held at window 7) should be addressed: Hauptpostlagernd, Postamt Bahnhof Zoo, 10612 Berlin. Branch office at **Tegel Airport** (tel. 417 84 90). Open M-F 7am-9pm, Sa-Su 8am-8pm. In Eastern Berlin, around the corner from the **Hauptbahnhof,** Postamt Berlin 17, Str. der Pariser Kommune 8-10, 10243 Berlin. Open M-F 7am-9pm, Sa 8am-8pm. Neighborhood branches are everywhere (usually open 9am-6pm, Sa 9am-noon); look for the little yellow "POST" signs.

Telephone Code: 030.

BERLIN

■ Accommodations

Even though tourists mob Berlin during the summer, thanks to the ever-growing hosteling and hotel industry, same-day accommodations aren't impossible to find; but as always, it's best to call ahead. If you plan on visiting during the **Love Parade**, however, you'd better book ahead or plan on dancing all night (see p. 124).

For a DM5 fee, **tourist offices** will find you a room in a hostel, *Pension*, or hotel. Be prepared to pay at least DM70 for a single and DM100 for a double. There are also over 4000 private rooms *(Privatzimmer)* available in the city; the overwhelming majority are controlled by the tourist offices. Expect to pay DM80 for singles, DM100 for doubles, plus a single-night surcharge of DM5. For that price, there's a wide spectrum of locations, comfort levels, and amenities. Press for details, and be sure that they know your language abilities (if any). They often prefer to fill up the *Pensionen* first, so you may have to ask for private rooms.

Although most accommodations are in Western Berlin, the office does have some listings for private rooms in the eastern part of the city. The tourist offices have the pamphlet "Accommodations, Youth Hostels, and Camping Places in Berlin," which lists hostels and inexpensive guest houses and hotels in English and German (DM2). There is also a free list of hotels and pensions, but most places listed are expensive, and the list is very selective.

For longer visits (over 4 days) the various **Mitwohnzentralen** can arrange for you to housesit or sublet someone's apartment. Prices start at DM40 per night, plus a percentage fee, and go down the longer you stay. The **Home Company Mitwohnzentrale,** Joachimstalerstr. 17 (tel. 194 45; U-Bahn #9 or 15 to "Kurfürstendamm") is the biggest (open M-F 9am-6pm, Sa 11am-2pm; AmEx, MC, Visa). **Erste,** Sybelstr. 53 (tel. 324 30 31; fax 324 99 77), tends to be less chaotic (open M-F 9am-8pm, Sa 10am-6pm). U-Bahn #7 to "Adenauerplatz" Usually the **Mitwohnzentralen** require you to pay up front unless you have, or can find a friend who has, a German bank account. Keep fees in mind—for short stays (less than a month) the standard commission is 20% of the final sum while for longer stays the rate is usually 25%, although the monthly prices are lower. Leases in Berlin start at any time—you don't need to wait for a new calendar month.

HOSTELS AND DORMITORY ACCOMMODATIONS

Hostels fill quickly with German school groups (especially in summer and on weekends)—always call ahead. All HI-affiliated hostels are for members only. They tend to attract school groups, and are liable to be overbooked. For an extra DM6, some hostels will give nonmembers a stamp and let you spend the night. To buy an **HI card,** head to Tempelhofer Ufer 32, 10963 Berlin (tel. 264 95 20; fax 262 04 37; open M, W, and F 10am-4pm, Tu and Th 1-6pm). You can call, write, or fax this office to make reservations at any of Berlin's HI hostels. For non-Germans, membership cards cost DM30. You can also purchase the card at any of the HI hostels. HI hostels also have curfews that hinder night-ragers and tend to regulate more strictly. Many hostels accept written or faxed reservations.

Mitte/Friedrichstr.

🐌**The Backpacker,** Chausseestr. 102 (tel. 262 51 40 or 28 39 09 65; fax 28 39 09 35). U-Bahn #6 to "Zinnowitzer Str." Don't be discouraged by the somewhat worn exterior: this hostel has a kitchen, Internet access, bike rentals, 60 beds, and unquantifiable amounts of *style*. The supremely hip staff updates you on nightlife, and is eager to help you with your travel and sight-seeing plans. 5-to-7-bed room DM25, 4-bed room DM28, 3-bed room DM30, 2-bed room DM38 (all prices per person). Sheets DM5. Laundry DM5 per load. Bikes DM10-12 per day. Reduced public transportation day ticket DM5. A superb walking tour in English leaves the hostel daily at 9am and 2pm (4hr., DM10). No curfew. Reception 7am-noon and 1:30-11pm.

Circus, Am Zirkus 2-3 (tel. 28 39 14 33; fax 28 39 14 84; email circus@mind.de). U-Bahn #6 or S-Bahn #1, 2, 3, 5, 7, 9, or 75 to "Friedrichstr." Brand new and close to

Unter den Linden and Oranienburger Str., Circus makes a heroic effort at hostel hipness, offering Internet access, laundry machines, and a disco ball in the lobby. 4-to-5-bed room DM25, 3-bed room DM28. Doubles DM30, singles DM38 (all prices per person). One-time required fee for sheets DM3. Email access is very cheap and bikes are DM12 per day. 24hr. reception. No curfew. The same walking tour that leaves the Backpacker at 9am and 2pm departs from Circus 30min. later.

Kreuzberg

⊛**Die Fabrik,** Schlesische Str. 18 (tel. 611 71 16; fax 617 51 04; email info@diefab rik.com). U-Bahn #1 or 15 to "Schlesisches Tor" or night bus #N65 to "Taborstr." *Pension qua* hostel in a beautifully converted factory with lush green interior within walking distance of Kreuzberg's mad nightlife. The hotel rents **bikes** for DM16 per day. Surprisingly comfortable Mehrbettzimmer sleep-in deal puts you up in a 16-bed room for DM30. Singles DM66; doubles DM94 (honeymoon suite DM110); triples DM120; quads 144. Breakfast in the cafe downstairs DM10. 24hr. reception. Reserve or call ahead. Curfew? Rage all night, little pumpkin.

Hotel Transit, see p. 101.

Schöneberg—Tiergarten

Jugendgästehaus (HI), Kluckstr. 3 (tel. 261 10 97 or 261 10 98; fax 265 03 83). From Kurfürstendamm, bus #129 (direction: "Hermannplatz") to "Gedenkstätte," or U-Bahn #1 to "Kurfürstenstr.," then walk up Potsdamer Str., go left on Pohlstr., and right on Kluckstr. An abstract 8m conceptual "DJH" archway stands in front. While the "art" out front recalls the dark ages of 60s modernism, the 4- and 5-bed rooms are clean and contemporary. DM32, over 26 DM41. Sheets and breakfast included. Key deposit DM10. Lockers and laundry facilities. Reception 1-1:45pm, 2:35-9:45pm, and 10:15pm-midnight. Curfew midnight; stragglers admitted at 12:30 and 1am. Lockout 9am-1pm; ring the bell later. Reservations strongly recommended.

Studentenhotel Berlin, Meiningerstr. 10, 10823 Berlin (tel. 784 67 20; fax 788 15 23). U-Bahn #4: "Rathaus Schöneberg" or U-Bahn #7 to "Eisenacher Str.," or by bus #146 (from Zoo) to "Rathaus Schöneberg," walk right on Freiherr von Stein, then cross Martin-Luther-Str. to Meiningerstr. Barren interior feels like a sanitarium, but same day rooms often available if you call from the station. 4-bed dorms DM37. Singles DM59; doubles DM86. Breakfast included. 24hr. reception. English spoken.

CVJM-Haus, Einemstr. 10 (tel. 264 91 00; fax 261 43 08). U-Bahn #1, 2, or 4 to "Nollendorfplatz" Young men: it's fun to stay at the German YMCA, despite the institutional exterior. Palpably wholesome interior, all in tranquil blue. Conveniently located one block from Nollendorfplatz's gay nightlife. DM40 per person for singles, doubles and dormitory rooms. Quiet time 10pm-7am and 1-3pm. Breakfast included. Reception 8-11am and 4-9pm. You can get a key for curfew-free revelry. Book ahead.

Jugendgästehaus Feurigstraße, Feurigstr. 63 (tel. 781 52 11; fax 788 30 51). U-Bahn #7 to "Kleistpark," or bus #146 or 148. An unadorned brown stucco building in a busy district. 4- and 6-bed rooms that won't cramp your style. 200 beds. Good location for the bars and clubs of Schöneberg. Dorms DM38 (DM27 after August). Singles DM55; doubles with shower DM90. Breakfast included. Sheets DM5 if staying fewer than 3 nights, otherwise free. 24hr. reception. Call from the station.

Bahnhof Zoo

Jugendgästehaus am Zoo, Hardenbergstr. 9a (tel. 312 94 10; fax 401 52 83), opposite the Technical University *Mensa.* Bus #145 to "Steinplatz," or take the short walk from the back exit of Bahnhof Zoo straight down Hardenbergstr. Advantage: it's within spitting distance of the Bahnhof Zoo. Disadvantage: the rooms are spartan and poorly lit. It's on the 5th floor; ride up in the elevator. Small dorms (4-8 beds) DM35. Singles DM47; doubles DM85. Over 26 add DM5 to all prices. 24hr. reception. Check-in 10am. Check-out 9am. No curfew. No reservations, but tends to have room if you call in the morning. Grab a bite to eat at the adjacent Café Hardenberg (see p. 103).

Prenzlauer Berg

Lette'm Sleep Hostel, Lettestr. 7 (tel. 44 73 36 23, fax 44 73 36 25). U-Bahn #2 to "Eberswalder Str." or S-Bahn #4, 8, or 10 to "Prenzlauer Allee." A newcomer to the Berlin backpacking scene, the cleverly named Lette'm Sleep is the first such establishment to open up in Prenzlauer Berg, a few blocks from the Kollwitzplatz cafe scene. Dorm beds DM25-45.

Tegel

Jugendherberge Ernst Reuter (HI), Hermsdorfer Damm 48-50 (tel. 404 16 10; fax 404 59 72). U-Bahn #6 to "Alt-Tegel," then bus #125 or night bus #N25 (direction: "Frohnau/Invalidensiedlung") to "Jugendherberge." Distant from the center in a placid suburb, on the edge of the forest. Lots of school groups necessitate reservations. 6-bed rooms DM26, over 26 DM33. Breakfast and sheets included. DM8 for laundry facilities. Curfew 1am. English spoken. Key deposit DM10. Closed Dec. 3-28.

Jugendgästehaus Tegel, Ziekowstr. 161 (tel. 433 30 46; fax 434 50 63). U-Bahn #6 to "Tegel," then bus #222 or night bus #N22 to "Titusweg." On the north end of town by the Tegel parks. Old brick outside, new and bright inside with linoleum halls. DM37.50. Breakfast and sheets included. Laundry DM5. Reception 7:30am-11pm. No curfew. Same-day rooms sometimes available.

Internationales Jugendcamp Fließtal, Ziekowstr. 161 (tel. 433 86 40). U-Bahn #6 to "Tegel," then bus #222 or night bus #N22 to "Titusweg." Next to and under the same management as Jugendgästehaus Tegel. It's the next best thing to rolling a groovy doobie in your VW van, man. DM10 will get you a blanket and thermal pad under a tent; add DM3 for a summer camp-like cot. Campfire every night. Officially under 27 only, but rules are made for conformists, and they aren't into that sort of thing here. Cheap breakfast buffet DM2-4. Washing machines DM5; no dryers. Reception 5-10pm, but if you come earlier they're happy to lock up your stuff for you. No reservations needed. Open late June to Aug.

Elsewhere in Berlin

Jugendgästehaus Nordufer, Nordufer 28 (tel. 45 19 91 12; fax 452 41 00). U-Bahn #9 to "Westhafen," left over the bridge and left onto Nordufer for about 15min. Away from the center, but on the pretty, blue, swimmable Plötzensee Lake. Some singles, but mostly 4-bed rooms. DM37.50. Breakfast buffet and sheets included. Reception 7am-midnight. No curfew. Swim in the adjacent *Freibad* (swimming pool) for DM5, students DM3.

Jugendgästehaus am Wannsee (HI), Badeweg 1 (tel. 803 20 35; fax 803 59 08). S-Bahn #1 or 3 to "Nikolassee." From the main exit, cross the bridge and head left on Kronprinzessinweg; Badeweg will be on your right after 5min. Far from the center, but Wannsee has its own charm. The tan tile floors, open spaces, white plaster walls, and bright red trim are reminiscent of a municipal swimming pool. 62 4-bed rooms. Toilets shared between 2 rooms, showers between 6. Large groups of jolly kids make it impossible to get a room without booking 2 weeks in advance. DM32, over 26 DM41. Breakfast and sheets included. Key deposit DM20.

HOTELS AND PENSIONEN

Many small *Pensionen* and hotels are within the means of budget travelers, particularly since most establishments listed in *Let's Go* are amenable to *Mehrbettzimmer,* where extra beds are moved into a large double or triple. However, these benefits are really only for groups of three or more; hotels will not usually allow random individuals to crash together (lest an orgy spontaneously erupt). Most affordable hotels are in Western Berlin; the hotels in Mitte are ridiculously expensive, and other areas in the East still lack the facilities to support many visitors. The best places to find cheap rooms are around Savignyplatz and down along Wilmersdorfer Str. and its sidestreets.

Savignyplatz-Charlottenburg

Hotel-Pension Cortina, Kantstr. 140 (tel. 313 90 59; fax 31 73 96). S-Bahn #3, 5, 7, 75, or 9 or bus #149 or X34 to "Savignyplatz." High-ceilinged, bright, convenient, and hospitable. Small singles DM70; doubles DM120, with shower DM130. Extra beds in rooms upon agreement. Breakfast included. 24hr. reception.

Pension Knesebeck, Knesebeckstr. 86 (tel. 312 72 55; fax 313 34 86). S-Bahn #3, 5, 7, or 9 to "Savignyplatz." Just north of the park. Friendly, large *Alt-Berliner* rooms, with faux Baroque stylings come with offerings like couches and sinks. Singles with showers DM80; doubles DM120, with showers DM140; big *Mehrbettzimmer* DM50-60 per person. Hearty buffet-style breakfast included. Laundry machines DM2.50. 24hr. reception. Phone reservations must be confirmed by fax or letter.

Charlottenburger Hof, Stuttgarter Pl. 14 (tel. 32 90 70; fax 323 37 23). S-Bahn #3, 5, 7, or 9 to "Charlottenburg" (across the street) or U-Bahn #7 to "Wilmersdorfer Str." Slick but expensive *Pension* with wall-art: Miró, Klee, and Dalí in the rooms. Spotless modern rooms with phones and TVs, plus a peaceful guest lounge with funky black chairs. Singles DM80-120; doubles DM110-160; quads DM160-220. Shower, bathroom, and TV in all rooms. Nov.-Dec. 20-30% winter discounts. Breakfast in the adjoining **Café Voltaire** (see **Food,** p. 104) DM6. Laundry DM5. Sometimes has same-day space.

Wilmersdorf-Schöneberg

Hotel-Pension München, Güntzelstr. 62 (tel. 857 91 20; fax 85 79 12 22). U-Bahn #9 to "Güntzelstr." *Pension cum* gallery saturated with art by contemporary Berlin artists and sculptures by the owner. Super-clean, white-walled rooms with TVs and phones. Singles DM70, with shower DM110; doubles DM90, with bath DM125. Breakfast DM9. Written reservations are best, but try calling before 2pm.

Hotel Sachsenhof, Motzstr. 7 (tel. 216 20 74; fax 215 82 20). U-Bahn #1, 15, 2, or 4 to "Nollendorfplatz" Small and plainly decorated rooms that are clean and well-furnished in the middle of Nollendorfplatz's gay nightlife scene. Singles DM57, with shower DM65; doubles DM99, with shower DM116, with bath (including an adorable bathtub with feet) DM126-156; DM30 per extra bed. Breakfast DM10. 24hr. reception.

Frauenhotel Artemesia, Brandenburgische Str. 18 (tel. 873 89 05; fax 861 86 53). U-Bahn #7 to "Konstanzer Str." Pricey, but a rare bird—an immaculate, elegant hotel for women only. Rooms celebrate famous women in Berlin's history, while an outdoor terrace provides a damn fine view of contemporary Berlin. The **Artemesia Café** serves breakfast (M-F 7:30-10:30am, Sa-Su 8-11:30am) and evening drinks (5-10pm) to an all-female (straight and lesbian) crowd that really digs Tracy Chapman. Singles DM99, with shower DM149; doubles DM169, with bath DM200; extra beds DM45 per person. Breakfast included. Alternatively, try to get the "last-minute, same-day" specials, with singles from DM79 and doubles from DM129 (without breakfast). Reception 7am-10pm.

Kreuzberg

Pension Kreuzberg, Grossbeerenstr. 64 (tel. 251 13 62; fax 251 06 38). U-Bahn #6 or 7 to "Mehringdamm" or bus #119. Decently priced rooms, small but well-decorated with things abstract in an old but grand building close to the Kreuzberg scene. Watch your head in the doorway to the bathroom. Singles DM65; doubles DM85; *Mehrbettzimmer* DM37 per person. Breakfast DM5. Reception 8am-10pm.

Hotel Transit, Hagelberger Str. 53-54 (tel. 785 50 51; fax 785 96 19). U-Bahn #6 or 7 to "Mehringdamm," or bus #119 or night bus N19 (every 10-15min.). Party hard and crash gently in this stylin' *Pension.* Reception area jams to techno. Big-screen MTV lounge with bar open 24hr. Rooms adorned with sleek, fake *Bauhaus* furnishings and showers. If you anticipate a hangover, you can request breakfast at noon or later. Singles DM90; doubles DM105; triples DM140; quads DM180. Their "Sleep-In" deal allows you to share a *Mehrbettzimmer* with any other traveler for DM33. Breakfast included. 24hr. reception. Curfew? Lockout? Pshaw.

Elsewhere in Berlin

Hotel-Pension Hansablick, Flotowstr. 6 (tel. 390 48 00; fax 392 69 37). S-Bahn #3, 5, 7, 9, or 75 to "Tiergarten." Somewhat pricey, but it's an absolute *Jugendstil* pearl, from the decorative ceilings to the marble entrance and lamps gracing the cobblestone streets in front. Breakfast room like a salon. All rooms have bath, hair dryer, phone, and cable TV. Some have patios from which you can watch ferries on the Spree. Few places like this survived WWII bombing, so call, write, or fax ahead for reservations. Singles DM150; doubles DM175-215. In the low season (July-Aug. and mid.-Nov. to Feb.) singles DM125; doubles DM150-170. Extra bed in the big doubles DM55. 5% discount if you mention *Let's Go.* July-Aug. same-day specials are available but without the *Let's Go* discount. 24hr. reception.

Hamburger Hof, Kinkelstr. 6 (tel. 333 46 02), in the old quarter of Spandau. U-Bahn #7 to "Altstadt Spandau" (second-to-last stop). Easily accessible. A tiny, comfortable hotel with only 18 beds, but so far from the action that they usually have room. Small-town charm, but no English spoken. Diminutive singles DM55; more spacious doubles DM100. Breakfast included.

CAMPING

Deutscher Camping-Club runs the following two major campgrounds in Berlin; both are adjacent to the imaginary line tracing the site of the Berlin Wall. Written reservations can be made by writing the Deutscher Camping-Club Berlin, Geisbergstr. 11, 10777 Berlin. Otherwise, call in advance. Both sites charge DM9.50 per person, DM3.50 per child, and DM7 per tent.

Dreilinden (tel. 805 12 01). S-Bahn #7 to "Griebnitzsee," then walk back between the station and lake. A city campsite, surrounded on 3 sides by the vestiges of the Berlin Wall. The remains of a stretch of the *Autobahn* which fell into disuse after 1949 can be seen through the trees. The site's bar is an old border checkpoint. Open Mar.-Oct.

Kladow, Krampnitzer Weg 111-117 (tel. 365 27 97). U-Bahn #7 to "Rathaus Spandau," then bus #135 to "Alt-Kladow" (the last stop). Switch to bus #234 to "Krampnitzer Weg/Selbitzerstr.," then follow Krampnitzer Weg 200m. A store and restaurant complement the relaxed atmosphere by a swimmable lake. Open year-round.

■ Food

Berlin's cuisine has joined the melting pot, with many delectable international culinary options saving you from the ubiquitous *Würste* and *Schnitzels* of other German cities. While many offerings from the German cuisine are palatable, Berlin's most notable home-grown option is the tasty, sweet **Berliner Weiße mit Schuß,** a concoction of local wheat beer with a shot of syrup. *Rot* (red) is the most popular variety, made with fruity *Himbeer* (raspberry) syrup; *grün* (green) is a bit less palatable to the uninitiated, consisting of a lemony syrup with a piney aftertaste called *Waldmeister.*

Much typical Berlin food is Turkish: almost every street has its own Turkish **Imbiß** or restaurant. The *Imbiß* stands are a lifeline for the late-night partier; most are open ridiculously late, some 24 hours. The *Döner Kebab,* a sandwich of lamb and salad, has cornered the fast-food market, with *Falafel* running a close second. For DM3-5, either makes a small meal. The second wave of immigration has brought quality Indian and Italian restaurants to Berlin.

There is no clear distinction between *Kneipen,* cafes, and restaurants; indeed, cafes often have better food and a livelier atmosphere than restaurants for much more reasonable prices. A gloriously civilized tradition in Berlin cafes is **Frühstück,** breakfast served well into the afternoon, sometimes 24 hours. Leisurely natives read the paper and linger over their fruity, fatty breakfasts; join them and relax with *Milchkaffee.*

Aldi, Plus, Edeka, and **Penny Markt** are the cheapest supermarket chains, followed by the pricier **Bolle, Kaiser's,** and **Reichelt.** Supermarkets are usually open Monday to Friday 9am-6pm, Saturday 9am-2pm, though some chains like Kaiser's are open until as late as 8pm on weekdays and 4pm on Saturday. The best **open-air market** fires up Saturday mornings on Winterfeldtplatz, though almost every neighborhood has one; there's a kaleidoscopic **Turkish market** in Kreuzberg, along Maybachufer on the Landwehrkanal, every Friday. Take U-Bahn #8 to "Schönleinstr."

WESTERN BERLIN

Mensen (University Cafeterias)

Cafeteria Charlottenstraße, Charlottenstr. 55 (tel. 203 09 23 40). U-Bahn #2 to "Sophie-Charlotte-Platz." Conveniently located near Schloß Charlottenburg and its adjacent modern art museums. Meals DM2.55 for students, DM4.50 for others. Salads and grill items also available. Open M-F 9am-2:45pm.

Mensa TU, Hardenbergstr. 34 (tel. 311 22 53). Bus #145 to "Steinplatz," or walk 10min. from Bahnhof Zoo. The mightiest of Berlin's *Mensas*, serving decent food, as well as rather good vegetarian *(Bio Essen)* dishes. Meals DM4-5 for students, others DM6-7. Cafeteria downstairs has longer hours and slightly higher prices. *Mensa* open M-F 11:15am-2:30pm. Cafeteria open M-F 8am-7:45pm.

Bahnhof Zoo-Ku'damm Area

Café Hardenberg, Hardenbergstr. 10 (tel. 312 33 30). Big *belle époque* spot, opposite the TU *Mensa*, but with a lot more atmosphere. Funky music, artsy interior, and lots of students. Breakfast served 9am-5pm (DM4-8). Most entrees well under DM13. Good for a few drinks (grog DM4). Open Su-Th 9am-1am, F-Sa 9am-2am.

Website, Joachimstaler Str. 41 (tel. 88 67 96 30; http://www.vrcafe.de). U-Bahn #9 or 15 to "Kurfürstendamm." Berlin's trendiest cybercafe offers two levels of smoky, black-lit Internet access and virtual reality stations to a mix of cyber-hip Germans and homesick Americans (DM7 per 30min.). Open daily 10am-2am. Across the street at Joachimstaler Str. 5, the **Cyberb@r** in the Karstadt Sport department store has fewer terminals and a less intimate ambience (DM5 per 30min., open M-F 10am-8pm, Sa 9am-4pm).

Restaurant Marché, Kurfürstendamm 14-15 (tel. 882 75 78), just a couple of blocks down from Bahnhof Zoo and the *Gedächtniskirche*. Run by the ubiquitous Mövenpick restaurant company, this place themes itself around a French marketplace (i.e., serve-yourself cafeteria-style dining). The colorful, very *Euro* cafeteria area is full of fresh produce, salads, grilled meats, pour-it-yourself wines, and hot pastries (DM12-25). Free ice water! Open daily 8am-midnight. AmEx, Visa.

KaDeWe, Tauentzienstr. 21-24 (tel. 212 10). U-Bahn #1, 2, or 15 to "Wittenbergplatz." Satiate every desire in the 6th-floor food emporium of this tremendous department store. Bright, beautiful stands happily heaped with cabbage and caviar. An entire wing devoted just to tinned fish. The prices? Ah, but such a joy! Open M-F 9:30am-8pm, Sa 9am-4pm.

Savignyplatz

Schwarzes Café, Kantstr. 148 (tel. 313 80 38; fax 215 29 54), near Savignyplatz. Knotty interior full of trendy young folks. Dark walls, big-band music, and dapper waiters. It's not so cool to pay DM4.20 for 0.2L of apple juice—but hey, they have breakfast at all hours (DM7-15). Open daily 11am-3am.

Mexico Lindo, Kantstr. 134 (tel. 312 82 18), on the corner of Wielandstr. S-Bahn #3, 5, or 7 to "Savignyplatz." Stick with the lunch specials (DM10-13) or pick up some *quesadillas* from the *Imbiß* stand (DM4) and picnic in the park next door; the dinner menu is scrumptious but expensive (DM17.50-30). *Imbiß* open M-F noon-7pm; restaurant opens at 5pm.

Filmbühne am Steinplatz, Hardenbergstr. 12 (tel. 312 65 89). This cafe at one of Berlin's independent cinemas has an eclectic and extensive but generally inexpensive menu. The "Harry & Sally Breakfast" (DM28.50) serves two...or three or four. Vegetarian entrees (DM13). Films daily (DM11, Mondays DM8.50)—they're often subtitled rather than dubbed. Call 312 90 12 for film info. Restaurant open M-Sa 9am-3am, Su 9am-2am.

Schöneberg-Nollendorfplatz

Baharat Falafel, Winterfeldtstr. 37. U-Bahn #1,2, or 4 to "Nollendorfplatz." Perhaps the best falafel in Berlin. Five plump chick-pea balls in a fluffy pita, covered with veggies and heavenly sesame, mango, or chili sauce, for DM5-7. Bright shop with Arab pop and watercolors depicting selfless falafel balls leaping into waiting pita. Open M-Sa 10am-2am, Su 11am-2am. Closed last week in July.

What's a Döner?

When this question was posed to Germany's *Döner* dealers, their response was utter bafflement. After all, everyone knows what a *Döner Kebab* is—chunks of lamb stuffed in a Turkish *Fladenbrot* topped with vegetables and a cucumber-based sauce. Yet where does the name come from? Vendors in northern Germany unanimously insisted that it comes from Berlin and told us not to get any ideas about this being authentic Turkish food. But we learned that the German "Dön" comes from the Turkish word meaning "to turn," and that the meat is thus named a *Döner* because it revolves as it cooks. A *Döner* by any other name simply would not be the same.

Sushi am Winterfeldtplatz, Goltzstr. 24 (tel. 215 49 30). U-Bahn #1, 2, or 4 to "Nollendorfplatz." Standing-room only Japanese cuisine in the heart of Schöneberg. Try the fresh sushi a la carte (DM3-5) or filling lunch platters (including miso soup) for DM15. Open M-Sa noon-1am, Su 3pm-midnight. Delivery available until 1hr. before closing.

Bua Luang, Vorbergstr. 10a (tel. 781 83 81). U-Bahn #7 to "Kleistpark." Mild to spicy Thai food in a quiet residential section of Schöneberg. Feast on the hefty noodle dishes (DM10) or on the delectably spicy Masaman curried tofu (DM8). Open M and W-Su 11am-10pm.

Kurdistan, Uhlandstr. 161 (tel. 883 96 92). U-Bahn #15 to "Uhlandstr." One of Berlin's most exotic and appetizing offerings. Fabulously spiced *Yekawe* (meat with rice, raisins, and cinnamon) DM15. Most entrees DM15-20. Brush up on your Kurdish with one of the grammar books lying around, or challenge the owner to a game of backgammon. Open M-Sa after 5pm.

Café Belmundo, Winterfeldtstr. 36 (tel. 215 20 70), on a street loaded with bohemians. U-Bahn #1 or 2 to "Nollendorfplatz." Young crowd, with outdoor tables and breakfast until 3pm. Sunday breakfast buffet (DM14) until 3pm. Salads DM4.50-10. Open M-Sa 9am-1am, Su 10am-whenever.

Charlottenburg-Tiergarten

⊛Café Voltaire, on Stuttgarter Platz (tel. 324 50 28). S-Bahn #3, 5, 7, or 9 to "Charlottenburg," or U-Bahn #7 to "Wilmersdorfer Str." Cafe-bistro-gallery with a talkative crowd. Close to a whole array of cafes and the *Kino Klick,* at Winterscheidtstr. An extensive menu with great breakfasts (DM6-8; served 5am-3pm). Open daily 24hr.

Ashoka, Alt-Moabit 49 (tel. 393 08 95). U-Bahn #9 to "Turmstr." A friendly, entirely vegetarian, neighborhood Indian place. Huge portions DM6-10, including the exotic and delicious banana curry. Open daily noon-midnight.

Kreuzberg

Amrit, Oranienstr. 202-203 (tel. 612 55 50). U-Bahn #1 or 15 to "Görlitzer Bahnhof." Possibly Berlin's best Indian restaurant, near Kreuzberg's bar and club scene. Fabulous vegetarian dishes like Palak Paneer (DM14) as well as delectably spicy meat entrees. Try the Chicken Saag (DM16). English menu available. Open Su-Th noon-1am, F-Sa noon-2am.

Tibet-Haus, Zossener Str. 19 (tel. 694 89 48). U-Bahn #7 to "Gneisenaustr." This smallish restaurant grooves to the beat of sitar music and Eastern spices. Himalayan delights such as mountain mushrooms roasted in paprika sauce (DM11.50) pique the diner's culinary interest. Tasty chicken with spiced spinach (DM9.50). Open daily noon-midnight. No toilets. Take-out available.

Melek Pastanesi, Oranienstr. 28. U-Bahn #1, 15, or 8 to "Kottbusser Tor." Delicious Turkish pastries sold (almost) around the clock. No specific opening hours, but the bakery is usually open until at least 2am and often later, as it caters to the post-clubbing sugar urge. Baklava DM0.80.

Afroasia, Gneisenaustr. 16 (tel. 693 24 35). U-Bahn #7 to "Gneisenaustr." Brightly lit basement-level hole-in-the-wall serves an eclectic combination of African and Asian specialties prepared individually by the good-humored chef. Among the many delicacies are chicken with peanut sauce (DM8.50) and spicy vegetarian rice and bean plates (DM8). Open M-F noon-10pm, Sa-Su 4-10pm.

Die Rote Harfe, Oranienstr. 13 (tel. 618 44 46), on Heinrichplatz. U-Bahn #1 or 15 to "Görlitzer Bahnhof." Leftists and grizzled types eating solid German food. The *Schweizer Schnitzel* (DM15.90) and the *Algäuer Käsespätzle* (DM9.90) are bound to spark radicalism, even in stodgy old you. 3-course lunch (DM15). Open Su-Th 10am-2am, F-Sa 10am-3am.

Café Abendmahl, Muskauerstr. 9 (tel. 612 51 70). U-Bahn #1 to "Görlitzer Bahnhof." While some of the *Ecce Homo* decorative motifs are a touch overbearing, the restaurant is a favorite for gay and lesbian (and enlightened hetero) Berliners with delicious vegetarian and fish dishes. Substantial salads and artichoke dishes run DM9.50-15.50. Open daily after 6pm.

Café V, Lausitzerpl. 12 (tel. 612 45 05). U-Bahn #1 to "Görlitzer Bahnhof." Berlin's oldest vegetarian restaurant. Try the *Tofu-Würstchen* with scrambled eggs and tomato sauce (DM10.50). Open daily 10am-2am.

EASTERN BERLIN

University Mensa

Humboldt University Mensa, Unter den Linden 6, in the back of the University's main building. The cheapest *Mensa* in Berlin, and conveniently located for sightseeing in Eastern Berlin. Full meals from DM1.50. Student ID required. Open M-F 11:30am-2:30pm.

Oranienburger Straße-Mitte

Trattoria Ossena, Oranienburger Str. 65 (tel. 283 53 48). Surrounded on all sides by Oranienburger Straße's myriad cafes, Ossena serves more substantial fare than the rest in the form of delicious Italian pastas and enormous pizzas. Try the *Pizza Treccose* (artichokes, ham, and mushrooms, DM14) or the *Lasagne con verdura* (vegetarian lasagna; DM14). Open daily from 5pm.

Mendelssohn, Oranienburger Str. 39 (tel 281 78 59). S-Bahn #1, 2, or 25 to "Oranienburger Str." This swank locale serves Macedonian fare in a candlelit setting. Try the *Musaka* (DM12.50), a creamy layered dish of meat and potatoes, or the *Kifli* (DM5.50), a doughy pastry stuffed with goat cheese. Open M-F after 11am, Sa-Su after 9am. Kitchen opens at noon.

Beth Café, Tucholskystr. 40 (tel. 281 31 35), just off Auguststr. S-Bahn #1, 2, or 25 to "Oranienburger Str." A genuine kosher restaurant in the heart of the Scheunenviertel. Serves inexpensive Israeli specialties and a generous selection of kosher wines. Try the falafel (DM4.70) or a bagel with lox and cream cheese (DM4). Other dishes DM5-15. Open Su-Th 11am-10pm, F 9am until 2hr. before shabbat, closed Sat.

Taba, Chausseestr. 106 (tel. 282 67 95). U-Bahn #6 to "Zinnowitzer Str." Big portions of delicious, spicy Mexican and Brazilian food are spiced up further by live salsa music Wednesday. While most of the entrees are DM15-20, you can indulge in great *quesadillas* for DM13.50 or *empanadas* for DM11.50. On W, all entrees are DM10. Open Su-Th from 4pm, Tu-Sa from 6pm.

Käse-König, under the *Fernsehturm* near the Alexanderplatz S-Bahn station. *Incredibly* cheap German food served in a GDR-esque canteen to a mix of students and *Bauarbeiter* (construction workers). Gobble up a *Bockwurst* (DM1) or the daily *Eintopf* (stew, DM3), and wash it down with the generically labelled "Bohemian beer" (DM1.50). Open M-F 9am-6:30pm, Sa 9am-2pm.

Prenzlauer Berg

Die Krähe, Kollwitzstr. 84 (tel. 442 82 91), off Kollwitzplatz. U-Bahn #2 to "Senefelderplatz." Check out the psychedelic "crow" tapestry. Bright crowd orders from changing weekly menu; mighty satisfyin' breakfasts under DM10, whopping salads DM12. The popular Sunday buffet lets you load up until you burst for DM13.50. Open M-Th 5:30pm-2am, F-Sa 5:30pm-3am, Su 10:30am-2am.

Ostwind, Husemannstr. 13 (tel. 441 59 51). U-Bahn #2 to "Senefelderplatz." Chinese food that seeks to bridge the cultural divide between East and West. Prenzlauer hipsters indulge in the dim sum or *Shao-Lin Min* (noodles with tofu, lotus, broccoli, and carrots) for DM12.90. Open M-Th 6pm-1am, F-Sa 10am-1am.

Café-Restaurant Miro, Raumerstr. 29 (tel. 44 73 30 13). U-Bahn #2 to "Eberswalder Str." Generous portions of attractive and delectable Mediterranean cuisine. Soups DM5, large appetizers DM7-9, vegetarian specials DM15-20. Open 10am-whenever.

Village Voice, Ackerstr. 1a (tel. 282 45 50). U-Bahn #8 to "Rosenthaler Platz." Cafe and bar *cum* bookstore trying hard for NYC hipness. Multilingual literature and inexpensive fare; the nachos and tacos beat the campy books. Cafe open M-F 11am-2am, Sa-Su noon-2am; bookstore open M-F 11am-8pm, Sa noon-4pm.

Café Restauration 1900, Husemannstr. 1 (tel. 442 24 94), at Kollwitzplatz. U-Bahn #2 to "Eberswalder Str." Alternative interior on a street decorated in Potemkin-village-esque 19th-century style. Decent food at decent prices. German, French, and Italian wines. Open M-Sa 11am-2am, Su 10am-2am. Kitchen open until midnight.

■ Sights

Berlin can be just as disconcerting in its complexity as it is stunning. For a guide to the city's major neighborhoods, see **Orientation,** p. 88. Below, the sights are organized into five major sections: **Between Eastern and Western** Berlin, **Western** Berlin, **Eastern** Berlin, **Museums,** and the **Outer Boroughs.** Many of central Berlin's major sights lie along the route of **bus #100,** which travels from Bahnhof Zoo to Prenzlauer Berg, passing the Siegessäule, Brandenburg Gate, Unter den Linden, the Berliner Dom, and Alexanderplatz along the way. To add an element of thrill to your sight-seeing expedition, climb up to the second floor of this double-decker bus, and sit in the very first row: the view is unbeatable, and you'll feel like you're on an amusement park ride. Buying individual tickets every time you re-board the bus can get pricey, so you might consider a day pass (DM13) or a 7-day pass (DM40), especially if you'll be using the U- and S-Bahn (see **Getting Around,** p. 92).

■ Between Eastern and Western Berlin

For decades a barricaded gateway to nowhere, today the **Brandenburg Gate** is perhaps the one structure that most symbolizes reunited Berlin. Standing directly in the center of the city, it opens east onto Unter den Linden and west onto the Tiergarten park and Straße des 17. Juni. Built during the reign of Friedrich Wilhelm II as an image of peace, the gate was a symbol of the Cold War east-west division. This locked door embedded in the Berlin Wall did not actually open until December 22, 1989, more than a month after the Wall fell. The images broadcast around the world of East and West Berliners dancing together atop the Wall were all filmed at the Brandenburg Gate, since this section of the wall was the only part with a flat top—everywhere else, the top is curved, preventing would-be escapers from getting a good grip.

The **Berlin Wall** itself is a dinosaur, with only fossil remains still visible. Erected overnight on August 13, 1961 (initially as a fence), the 140km wall separated families and friends, sometimes even running through people's homes. In the early 1970s, a second wall was erected parallel to the first; the space in between them (about the width of a street) became known as the **"death strip."** The 1989 wave of liberalization in other Communist countries and mass demonstrations of East Germans demanding the right to travel freely finally drove the government to open its borders and dismantle the Wall (and itself). Portions of the reinforced concrete structure of the Wall are preserved near the *Ostbahnhof* and by Potsdamer Platz. The longest remaining bit is the brightly painted **East Side Gallery,** a 1.3km stretch of cement slabs that also passes as one of the world's largest open-air art galleries. To get there take S-Bahn #3, 7, or 9 to "Ostbahnhof." The murals are not the remnants of Cold War graffiti, but rather the efforts of an international group of artists who gathered here in 1989 to celebrate the city's openness. The scrawlings of later tourists have been added to their work. Occasionally, late-coming *Mauerspecher* (wall-peckers) nibble at the edges of the Gallery, trying to knock off a chunk for posterity, but most of the pieces you'll see for sale at the tourist stands are fake.

The demolished wall has left an incompletely healed scar across the city center. From the western side, newly planted trees extend the Tiergarten park a few more meters. But the numerous cranes jutting up into the sky on the eastern side have become as much a symbol of Berlin as the TV tower on Alexanderplatz. **Potsdamer Platz**, cut off by the wall, was once a major Berlin transportation hub designed under Friedrich Wilhelm I to approximate Parisian boulevards, with the primary purpose of moving troops quickly. The land surrounding the *Platz* is now a chaotic mess of construction machinery and half-dug foundations. The shiny **InfoBox**, a temporary, bright-red structure near the Potsdamer Platz U- and S-Bahn stations, contains an exhibit describing in exhaustive and enthusiastic detail the future Daimler-Benz-sponsored offices on the site, as well as various railway improvements that will ostensibly make Berlin the transport hub of Europe. The construction was supposed to conclude by 2000, but the date has been pushed back to 2004. You can climb up to the **Dachterrasse** (panoramic platform) for a workout and a spectacular view of the messy construction site, all for only DM2. What a deal. *(Infobox open F-W 9am-7pm, Th 9am-9pm, free; Dachterrasse open daily 9am-10:45pm.)* Near Potsdamer Platz, unmarked and inconspicuous, lies the site of the **Führerbunker,** where Hitler married Eva Braun and then ended his life (or so the government would like to believe). In macabre irony, the actual bunker site is now a playground (behind the record store at Wilhelmstr. 92); tourists looking for it often mistakenly head for the visible bunker at the southern edge of Potsdamer Platz. Plans to restore the bunker were shelved amid fears that the site would become a shrine for the radical right.

Just south of Potsdamer Platz, between the center of Schöneberg and the former no-man's-land surrounding the wall, stands the **Martin-Gropius-Bau**, at Stresemanstr. 110. The decorous edifice was designed by Martin Gropius, a pupil of Schinkel and uncle of *Bauhausmeister* Walter Gropius. There's nothing *Bauhaus*-like about the red-and-white Neoclassical building, though it's more graceful than most Prussian turn-of-the-century fare. Today the building holds a museum of applied and fine arts as well as a dynamic **Jewish Museum** (see **Museums,** p. 118). Across the street from the Martin-Gropius-Bau is the elegant **Abgeordnetenhaus,** Berlin's parliamentary building. The Prussian *Landtag* (state assembly) met in the building from 1899 until 1934, at which point Hitler dissolved the democratic body—in fact, it was in this building that the *Landtag* passed the infamous "Enabling Act," which allowed Hitler to act as dictator. The building has been completely rebuilt, and once again houses the state parliament. You can go in and see one of their sessions, or just check out the exhibit on the history of German democracy (call 23 25 10 61 or 23 25 10 62 for information). Nearby, at Potsdamer Str. 33, across the street from the *Kulturforum* museum complex, funkadelic Modernism rules the exterior of the huge **Staatsbibliothek Preußischer Kulturbesitz** (tel. 26 61), the library that starred in Wim Wenders's *Wings of Desire*—the angels found its main reading room a perfect spot to observe humanity. Good thing they didn't come at exam time, or even they would have had trouble finding a table. *(Open M-F 9am-9pm, Sa 9am-5pm.)*

The door of the **Haus am Checkpoint Charlie,** Friedrichstr. 44 (tel. 251 10 31), is draped with a blood-red Soviet flag. *(Museum open daily 9am-10pm. DM8, students DM5. Films M-F at 5:30 and 7:30pm, Sa-Su at 4:30, 6, and 7pm.)* Take U-Bahn #6 to "Kochstr." or bus #129. A strange, fascinating museum on the site of the famous border crossing point, with an uneasy mixture of blatant Western tourist kitsch and didactic Eastern earnestness, it is still one of Berlin's most popular tourist attractions. On the ground floor, flashiness is the order of the day; an expensive snack bar is crammed against a ticket desk covered with postcards, mugs, posters, books, and "Communist" baubles. Right by the door stands the car in which Johannes Ehret smuggled his girlfriend across the border in 1988. Upstairs you can find out everything you've ever wanted to know about the Wall or various ways of escaping over it, while studying the history of human rights struggles throughout the world. The exhibits are in German, English, French, and Russian. Documentaries and fact-based dramas about the Wall are screened daily in the *Kino* upstairs.

■ Western Berlin

THE REICHSTAG

Just to the north of the Brandenburg Gate sits the imposing, stone-gray **Reichstag** building (tel. 22 73 21 31), former seat of the parliaments of the German Empire and the Weimar Republic, and future home of Germany's governing body, the *Bundestag*. In 1918 Philipp Scheidemann proclaimed a German republic from one of its balconies with the words *"es lebe die deutsche Republik"* ("long live the German Republic"). His move turned out to be wise, since two hours later Karl Liebknecht, in the Imperial Palace a few kilometers away on Unter den Linden, announced a German Socialist Republic, ironically on the site that later supported the parliament of the GDR. (For more on the Imperial Palace, see **Eastern Berlin,** p. 111.) Civil war followed in Berlin and much of the rest of Germany. The government fled to Weimar to draw up a new constitution, but over the course of the next decade the *Reichstag* became the fractured center of the economically troubled Republic. As the Republic declined, Nazi members showed up to sessions in uniform, and on February 28, 1933, a month after Hitler became Chancellor, fire mysteriously broke out in the building. The fire provided a pretext for Hitler to declare a state of emergency, giving the Nazis broad powers to arrest and intimidate opponents before the upcoming elections. The infamous end result was the Enabling Act, which established Hitler as legal dictator and abolished democracy. A conceptual monument outside recalls the 96 members of the Reichstag executed by the Nazis.

In the summer of 1995, the Reichstag metamorphosed into an artsy parcel, when husband-and-wife team **Christo** and **Jeanne-Claude** wrapped the dignified building in 120,000 yards of shimmery metallic fabric. Tourists and residents alike marvelled at the effect, but after three weeks, the cloth came down and less picturesque scaffolding went up as the effort to restore the building for the government's return (set for Sept. 1999) commenced in earnest. The government held a massive design competition for the building's new dome (the original was destroyed in World War II), and decided upon a huge glass dome surrounding a large mirror.

TIERGARTEN AND KURFÜRSTENDAMM

The lush **Tiergarten** in the center of old Berlin is a relief from the neon lights of the Ku'damm to the west and the din and dust of construction work to the east. Spreading over the northeast corner of Western Berlin, the vast landscaped park was formerly used by Prussian monarchs as a hunting ground. As you walk along its canals, notice the old streetlamps; each Prussian city sent one to the capital. In the heart of the Tiergarten, the slender 70m **Siegessäule** (victory column), Straße des 17. Juni, am Großen Stern (tel. 391 29 61), topped by a gilded statue of winged victory, commemorates Prussia's humiliating defeat of France in 1870. *(Open Apr.-Nov. M 1-6pm, Tu-Su 9am-6pm. DM2, students DM1.)* Take bus #100, 187, or 341 to "Großer Stern." In 1938, the Nazis moved the monument from its former spot in front of the *Reichstag* to increase its height and make it more impressive. Climb the monument's 285 steps to the top for a panorama of the city. Radiating out from the column, the **Straße des 17. Juni** bisects the park from west to east. At the eastern end stands the **Soviet Army Memorial** (yes, you're still in Western Berlin) flanked by a pair of giant toy tanks. South of the memorial, Entlastungstr. leads to the highly modern, bright yellow buildings of the **Tiergarten complex,** which includes the Philharmonic, the *"Staabi"* library (see **General Services,** p. 97), and a host of museums (see **Museums,** p. 116).

During the city's division, West Berlin centered around **Bahnhof Zoo,** the only train station in the world to inspire a rock album stadium tour (the U2 subway line runs through the station). At nearby Breitscheidplatz, couched between Budapester Str. and Kurfürstendamm, the shattered **Kaiser-Wilhelm-Gedächtniskirche** (tel. 218 50 23), nicknamed "the rotten tooth" by Berliners, stands as a sobering reminder of the destruction caused during WWII. *(Exhibit open M-Sa 10am-4pm. Church open daily 9am-7pm.)* The shattered tower, its jagged edges silhouetted against the sky, serves as one of Berlin's most striking sights. The church, built in 1852 in a Romanesque/Byzantine style, has an equally striking interior, with colorful mosaics covering the ceiling, floors, and walls. The ruins house an exhibit showing what the church used to look like, as well as shocking photos of the entire city in ruins just after the war. Don't let the cold gray exterior of the adjacent modern church deter you—take a step inside. The enormous octagon-shaped building, erected in the late 1950s, is coated on all eight sides with deep blue stained-glass windows, and the effect is spectacular. In the summer, Berlin's many leftists, foreigners, and young people often gather in front of the church to speak out, sell watches, play bagpipes and sitars (not at the same time), and perform crude imitations of Chancellor Kohl. Stretching several kilometers to the west from Breitscheidplatz, the **Kurfürstendamm** (so damm coo' it's called **Ku'damm**) is Berlin's biggest and fanciest shopping strip, lined with designer boutiques and pricey hotels. The renowned **Zoo** (not the station, but the menagerie) is one of the best in the world, with many animals displayed in open-air habitats instead of cages (main entrance directly across from the train station). *(Open May-Sept. daily 9am-6:30pm; Oct.-Feb. 9am-5pm; Mar.-Apr. 9am-5:30pm. DM12, students DM10.)* The second entrance across from Europa Center is the famous **Elephant Gate,** Budapester Str. 34, a delightfully decorated pagoda of pachyderms. Next door is the excellent **Aquarium,** Budapesterstr. 32, which houses broad collections of insects and reptiles as well as endless tanks of wide-eyed, rainbow-colored fish. *(Open daily 9am-6pm. Aquarium DM12, students DM10. Combination ticket to the zoo and aquarium DM19, students DM16.)* Its pride and joy is its 1000 lb. **Komodo dragon,** the world's largest reptile, a gift to Germany from Indonesia. Check out the psychedelic jellyfish tanks, filled with many translucent sea nettles.

SCHÖNEBERG

Farther south, in the district of Schöneberg, stands the **Rathaus Schöneberg,** where West Berlin's city government convened until the Wall fell. Take U-Bahn #4 to "Rathaus Schöneberg." On June 26, 1963, 1.5 million Berliners swarmed the streets beneath the sleek tower to hear John F. Kennedy reassure them of the Allies' commitment to the city. Kennedy's speech ended with the now-famous words, "All free men, wherever they may live, are citizens of Berlin. And therefore, as a free man, I take pride in the words: *Ich bin ein Berliner.*" Of course, every German understood what Kennedy meant, but for the grammar buffs out there, the prez *did* say he's a jelly doughnut. In 1993, a conceptual art exhibit was set up on the streets near the *Rathaus.* If you look closely, you'll notice some of the street signs have black-and-white placards above them—they state some of the Nazi edicts against Berlin's Jews. A number of these signs can be seen on Grunewaldstr. Not too far away is **Fehrbelliner Platz** (U-Bahn #2 or 7 to "Fehrbelliner Platz"), a standard example of Nazi architecture. These gruesomely regular prison-like blocks were meant to be model apartment houses; try to imagine a city full of them (or just hop on a train to Leipzig).

CHARLOTTENBURG

The borough of Charlottenburg, one of the wealthiest areas in Berlin, includes the area between the Ku'damm and the Spree river; like many of Berlin's neighborhoods, it was once a separate town. **Schloß Charlottenburg,** the vast, bright Baroque palace built by Friedrich I for his second wife, Sophie-Charlotte, presides over a carefully landscaped park on the western edge of the region. *(Open Tu-F 9am-5pm, Sa-Su 10am-5pm. Entire palace complex Tageskarte DM15, students DM10, under 14 free.)* Take U-Bahn #2 to "Sophie-Charlotte-Platz" or bus #145 from the Bahnhof Zoo. The *Schloß*'s many buildings include **Neringbau,** the palace proper, which contains many rooms filled with historical furnishings; the **Schinkel-Pavillion,** a museum dedicated to the Prussian architect; **Belvedere,** a small building housing the royal family's porcelain collection; and the **Mausoleum,** the final resting spot for most of the family. *(Mausoleum open Apr.-Oct. Tu-Su 10am-noon and 1-5pm.)* The **Galerie der Romantik,** a state museum housing Berlin's first-rate collection of German Romantic paintings, is located in a side wing (see **Museums,** p. 116). Seek out the **Palace Gardens** behind the main buildings, with their small lakes, footbridges, fountains, and carefully planted rows of trees. (*Open Tu-Su 6am-9pm. Free.*)

At the western edge of Charlottenburg is the **Olympia Stadion,** one of the more restrained architectural remnants of the Nazi Party. It was erected for the 1936 Olympic Games, in which Jesse Owens, an African-American, triumphed over the Nazis' racial theories by winning four gold medals. Hitler refused to congratulate Owens because of his skin color, but there's now a Jesse-Owens-Allee to the south of the stadium. Film buffs will recognize the complex from Leni Riefenstahl's infamous propaganda film *Olympia.* Take U-Bahn #2 to "Olympia-Stadion (Ost)" or S-Bahn #5 or 75 to "Olympiastadion."

KREUZBERG

Indispensable for a sense of Berlin's famous *alternative Szene,* or counter-culture, is a visit to **Kreuzberg,** an area loaded with cafes and bars. Kreuzberg has long been proud of its diverse population and liberal leanings: this is the place to see anti-Nazi graffiti and left-wing revolutionary slogans (in English, Turkish, Russian, Spanish, and German). During President Reagan's 1985 visit to Berlin, authorities so feared protests from this quarter that they cordoned the whole Kreuzberg district off without warning—an utterly unconstitutional measure. Much of the area was occupied by *Hausbesetzer* (squatters) during the 60s and 70s. A conservative city government decided to forcibly evict the illegal residents in the early 80s, provoking riots and throwing the city into total consternation.

For a look at the district's new, somewhat gentrified face, take U-Bahn #6 or 7 to "Mehringdamm" and wander. Particularly interesting is the area around **Chamissoplatz,** bordered by Bergmannstr. and Fidicinstr. Bergmannstr. features an especially large number of old buildings and second-hand shops as well as excellent used music shops. At night, many bohemian cafes and punk clubs spill onto **Gneisenaustraße,** which heads west from the intersection with Mehringdamm. The cafes and bars on Oranienstr. boast a more radical element; the May Day parades always start on Oranienplatz. Take U-Bahn #1, 15, or 8 to "Kottbusser Tor."

The **Landwehrkanal,** a channel bisecting Kreuzberg, is where Rosa Luxemburg's body was thrown after her murder in 1919. The tree-dotted strip of the canal near Hallesches Tor, **Paul-Linke Ufer,** may be the most beautiful street in Berlin, with its shady terraces and old facades. The east end of Kreuzberg near the old Wall is home to Turkish and Balkan neighborhoods, with a corresponding wealth of ethnic restaurants popular with radicals, students, and shabby genteel gourmets. From the Schlesisches Tor U-Bahn stop, a three-minute walk takes you across the **Oberbaumbrücke,** through a fragment of the wall and into the Friedrichshain district of the former East.

SPANDAU

Spandau is one of the oldest parts of Berlin, reached by taking U-Bahn #7 to "Altstadt Spandau." Many of the old buildings have been restored, including the massive 16th-century **Zitadelle** (citadel), Am Juliusturm (tel. 339 12 12). Take U-Bahn #7 to "Zitadelle," or bus #133. Surrounded on all sides by water so as to be nearly impregnable, the star-shaped enclosure was the anchor of the medieval town. During the war, the Nazis used the fort as a chemical weapons lab, and in 1945 the Allies employed the *Zitadelle* as a prison to hold war criminals before the Nürnberg trials. Despite its grim name and past, the citadel is now a wistful place filled with old field-cannons, statues, and a **medieval history museum.** (*Open Tu-F 9am-5pm, Sa-Su 10am-5pm. DM4, students DM2.*) The thickly fortified *Juliusturm* tower, dating to circa 1200, is Spandau's unofficial symbol. You can catch a boat from near the fort, or take bus #145 to "Johannesstift" (the last stop) into the **Spandau Forest.** Also notable is the exceptionally fine **Rathaus,** which Spandauers defiantly constructed from 1911 to 1913 (at a cost of 3.5 million Marks) in a futile effort to stave off absorption into Berlin. Take U-Bahn #7 to "Rathaus Spandau." **Spandau Prison** was demolished after its last inmate, Hitler's deputy Rudolf Hess, committed suicide in 1987 at age 93. Hess, a devoted party member from the beginning (he participated in the Beer Hall Putsch and took dictation for Hitler's *Mein Kampf*) was an unrepentant Nazi until his death. Lately this unsavory character has made a controversial comeback as a latter-day idol for neo-fascist groups; to Berlin's credit, the local anti-Hess response has been even stronger.

DAHLEM, ZEHLENDORF, AND THE GRÜNEWALD

In the southern suburb of **Dahlem,** Berlin's **Botanischer Garten,** on König-Luise-Platz (tel. 83 00 61 27), is a delight, especially the tropical greenhouses. *(Open daily 9am-9pm. DM6, students DM3.)* Take S-Bahn #1 to "Botanischer Garten." Nearby, a sprawling cultural complex holds several important museums (see **Museums,** p. 116). The even more sprawling *Freie Universität* complex is next door, near the Dahlem-Dorf stop on U-Bahn #1. Dahlem was the center of the former American sector, home to many American military personnel. Although the Allied forces have almost entirely pulled out of Berlin, a strong American presence persists in this area.

West of Dahlem lies **Zehlendorf,** Berlin's ritziest residential district. At the southwestern corner of the district, the **Glienecker Bridge** crosses the Havel into Potsdam and what was once the GDR. Closed to traffic in Cold War days, it is famed as the spot where East and West once exchanged captured spies. The most famous such incident traded American U-2 pilot Gary Powers for Soviet spy Ivanovich Abel. Take bus #116 from the Wannsee bus station to the end of the line.

In summer, clear your head in the nearby **Grünewald,** a 745-acre birch forest. While there, visit the **Jagdschloß,** a restored royal hunting lodge housing a worthwhile collection of European paintings, including works by Rubens, van Dyck, and Cranach. Call the tourist information office for further info.

■ Eastern Berlin

UNTER DEN LINDEN

The Brandenburg Gate opens eastward onto **Unter den Linden,** once one of Europe's best-known boulevards and the spine of old Berlin. All but a few of the venerable buildings near the gate have been destroyed, although a massive reconstruction effort centered around the gate has already revived such pre-war staples as the **Hotel Adlon,** once the premier address for all visiting dignitaries and celebrities. Rebuilding the edifices of the rich and famous wasn't a huge priority in the workers' state; one exception, however, is the imposing **Palais Unter den Linden 7.** The seat of the Russian embassy since 1831, the building was rebuilt to house Soviet comrades after the war, evidenced by the magnificent hammer-and-sickle engravings upstairs. With the end of the Cold War, the *palais* has reverted to being just another embassy, and the huge bust of Lenin that once graced its red star-shaped topiary was quietly removed in 1994. Somewhat ironically, the area is now destined to become the locus of German political power, as the **Bundestag** will soon be housed across the street. Beyond Friedrichstr., many neighboring 18th-century structures have been restored to their original splendor, though the excesses of the GDR days continue to mar the landscape. As the principal thoroughfares of downtown East Berlin, the intersection of Friedrichstr. and Unter den Linden became a proletarian showcase of glitzy hotels and restaurants named after other Communist capitals. From the architectural terror rises the stately **Deutsche Staatsbibliothek** (library), whose shady, ivy-covered courtyard houses a pleasant cafe. *(Open M-F 9am-6pm, Sa 10am-4pm.)* Across the street on the corner of Charlottenstr., the **Deutsche Guggenheim Berlin,** scheduled to open in late 1998, will feature an imposing collection of artworks ranging from Dürer to Picasso. Beyond the library is the H-shaped main building of the **Humboldt Universität,** whose hallowed halls have been filled by the likes of Hegel, Einstein, the Brothers Grimm and Karl Marx. In the wake of the post-1989 internal ideological *Blitzkrieg,* in which "tainted" departments were radically revamped or simply shut down, international scholars have descended upon the university to take part in its dynamic renewal. Nevertheless, or perhaps consequently, Marx and Lenin's greatest hits are available for cheap from the book vendors outside.

In the middle of the boulevard stands the statue of Friedrich the Great atop his horse. The designer despised Fred; rumor has it that he placed the emperor's visage on the horse's behind. Ah, sweet myth. Next door, the **Neue Wache** (new guard house) was designed by Prussian architect Friedrich Schinkel in unrepentant Neoclassical style. Under reconstruction in 1998, it is scheduled to reopen in 1999. During the GDR era, it was known as the **"Monument to the Victims of Fascism and Militarism,"** and, ironically, was guarded by goose-stepping East German soldiers. After reunification, the building closed briefly but was reopened in 1993 as a war memorial. Buried inside are urns filled with earth from the Nazi concentration camps of Buchenwald and Mauthausen as well as from the battlefields of Stalingrad, El Alamein, and Normandy.

Across the way is **Bebelplatz,** where, on May 10, 1933, Nazi students burned nearly 20,000 books by "subversive" authors such as Heinrich Heine and Sigmund Freud—both Jews. A plaque in the center of the square is engraved with Heine's eerily prescient 1820 quote: *"Nur dort wo man Bücher verbrennt, verbrennt man am Ende auch Menschen"* ("Wherever books are burned, ultimately people are also burned").

The building with the curved facade is the **Alte Bibliothek.** Once the royal library, it is now home to the Humboldt's law faculty. On the other side of the square is the handsome **Deutsche Staatsoper,** fully rebuilt after the war from original sketches by Knobelsdorff, the same architect who designed Schloß Sanssouci in Potsdam. The distinctive blue dome at the end of the square belongs to the **St.-Hedwigs-Kathedrale.** Built in 1773 as the first Catholic church erected in Berlin after the Reformation, it was burnt to a crisp by American bombers in 1943. Designed after the Roman Pantheon, the church was rebuilt in the 1950s in high atheist style, such that the interior resembles a socialist nightclub more than a house of worship. On Wednesdays at 3pm, its massive organ erupts with rather frightening tunes.

Back on Unter den Linden, the heavily ornamented **Zeughaus** was once the Prussian Army Hall of Fame and military museum; it has calmed down a bit to become the **Museum of German History** (see **Museums,** p. 119). From the museum you can enter the enclosed courtyard and see the tormented faces of Andreas Schlüter's "Dying Warriors."

GENDARMENMARKT

Berlin's most impressive ensemble of 19th-century buildings is a few blocks south of Unter den Linden at **Gendarmenmarkt,** also known as the French Quarter after it became the main settlement for Protestant Huguenots in the 18th century. During the last week of June and the first week of July, the square transforms into an outdoor stage for open-air classical concerts; call 53 43 53 43 for details. The twin cathedrals **Deutscher Dom** and **Französischer Dom** grace opposite ends of the square. The former houses a *Bundestag*-sponsored exhibition, which traces German political history from despotism to fascism to democracy. *(Open Tu-Su 10am-6pm. Free.)* The latter is home to a small museum chronicling the Huguenot diaspora. *(Open Tu-Sa noon-5pm, Su 11am-5pm. DM3, students DM2.)* In the middle of the square, the Neoclassical **Schauspielhaus,** designed by Schinkel, is Berlin's most elegant concert space, hosting international orchestras and classical performers. Destroyed by an air attack in 1945, it was diligently reconstructed and reopened in 1984.

LUSTGARTEN AND THE MUSEUMINSEL

Unter den Linden, after crossing the Schloßbrücke over the Spree, passes by the **Museuminsel** (Museum Island), the home of four major museums and the **Berliner Dom.** Immediately to the left stands the pillared **Altes Museum,** created by Schinkel, who envisioned Berlin as the "Athens on the Spree." The tubby granite bowl in front was supposed to adorn the main hall, but it didn't fit through the door. The **Lustgarten** in front of the museum is normally a pleasant collection of trees and benches, but for the next few years it will be completely torn up and redesigned to look as it did in the 19th century. Next door, the beautifully bulky, multiple-domed **Berliner Dom** proves that Protestants can go overboard just like Catholics. *(Open daily 9am-7:30pm. Admission to Dom DM5, students DM3. Comprehensive admission to the Dom, tower, and galleries DM8, students DM5. Free organ recitals M, Th, and F at 3pm. Frequent concerts in summer; buy tickets in the church or call 20 45 11 00 for more information.)* Severely damaged by an air raid in 1944, the cathedral, built during the reign of Kaiser Wilhelm II, recently emerged from 20 years of restoration. The ornate gold and jewel encrusted interior, with its distinctively Protestant idols (Calvin, Zwingli, and Luther), is stunning, if tacky to non-believers. There's also the **Kaiserliches Treppenhaus** upstairs, with exhibits of period art and imperial stuff. *(Open M-Sa 9am-8pm, Su noon-8pm. Free.)*

Behind the Altes Museum lie the complex's three other enormous museums: the **Pergamon,** the **Bodemuseum,** and the **Alte Nationalgalerie** (see **Museums,** p. 116). The current **Altes Museum** was once the **Neues Museum,** but when the Altes Museum was bombed, the Neues Museum became the Altes Museum by default. Now the old museum is being restored and is known as the Alte Nationalgalerie, since the Neue Nationalgalerie is in the Tiergarten complex. Across the street, the Lustgarten turns into Marx-Engels-Platz under the glaring, amber-colored **Palast der Republik,** where the GDR parliament met. In 1990, city authorities discovered that the building was full of asbestos and shut it down, and it remains closed as Berliners argue about whether to demolish it. The problems associated with the building itself are further complicated by the fact that the entire square used to be the site of the **Berliner Schloß,** the Hohenzollern family palace. Remarkably, the palace survived the war, although East German authorities demolished it in the 1950s in censure of its royal excess. The **Staatsrat** (Council of the State) currently resides on the site—look for the modern building with a slice of the palace facade embedded in the middle. This section was preserved because Karl Liebknecht proclaimed a German socialist republic from the balcony. The newest plans for the site aim to demolish the *Palast der Republik* and rebuild the facade of the palace with a modern entertainment center behind it, but whether this plan will materialize is anybody's guess. In the mean time, the square is home to a motley crew of *Imbiße* as well as the occasional *Beach-Volleyball* tournament.

Crossing the Liebknecht-Brücke leads you to a small park on the right-hand side of the street; in the middle of the park stands a memorial consisting of steel tablets dedicated to the world-wide workers' struggle against fascism and imperialism. The exhibit is dwarfed by a huge statue of a seated Santa Claus-like Marx and a standing Engels that has become a popular jungle gym for visiting tourist children. The park and the street behind it used to be collectively known as the Marx-Engels Forum; the park has not been renamed, while the street is now called Rathausstr.

ALEXANDERPLATZ AND NIKOLAIVIERTEL

On the other side of the Museumsinsel, Unter den Linden becomes Karl-Liebknecht-Str., and leads into the monolithic **Alexanderplatz.** Formerly the frantic heart of Weimar Berlin, the plaza was transformed in GDR times into an urban wasteland of fountains and pre-fab office buildings, with such socialist monuments as the **Weltzeituhr,** the international clock (so jet-set socialists could check the time in Hanoi and Vladivostok). The undisputed landmark of the district is the **Fernsehturm.** *(Open Mar.-Oct. daily 9am-1am; Nov.-Feb. 10am-midnight. DM8, under 17 DM4.)* The tower, the tallest structure in Berlin, is a truly awkward piece of design intended to show off the new heights achieved through five-year plans. However, the project proved to be somewhat of a flop when it was discovered that the sun's reflection on the tower's amber-tinted windows creates a shadow that looks very much like a crucifix (known as the *Papsts Rache*—the Pope's revenge). The view from the top (the spherical node 203m up the spike) is magnificent. An elevator whisks tourists up and away.

The buildings surrounding the square include some GDR concrete-block classics, including the **Hotel Forum.** In the 1970s, the East German government made a concession to the people's implacable craving for bright lights by erecting some enormous neon signs, thus giving the area around Alexanderplatz the superficial trappings of a Western metropolis: "Chemical Products from Bitterfeld!" and "Medical Instruments of the GDR—Distributed in All the World!" Now nearly all of the buildings have been thoroughly sanitized, but their dreary demeanor remains. In the first post-Communist months, Alexanderplatz was a rough place, the natural meeting ground for antagonistic gangs. But the pedestrians, working Berliners, and tourists. prevailed, though the square is still a poor cousin to West Berlin's Ku'damm. During the day, the square hums with con artists and vendors selling everything from Turkish *Fladenbrot* to black-market cigarettes smuggled from Russia. Around the U- and S-Bahn stations, the picture becomes seedier. Crowds congregate after dusk; watch your pockets.

The **Marienkirche,** a graceful 15th-century church that miraculously withstood Allied bombing, stands on the wide-open plaza in front of the *Fernsehturm.* *(Open M-Th 10am-4pm, Sa-Su noon-4pm, closed F.)* Nearby is the ornately gabled **Rotes Rathaus,** Berlin's famous red-brick town hall. Between 1949 and *die Wende,* it was home to East Berlin's city government; since 1990, the *Oberbürgermeister* and senate of the unified city have had their seats here. Have your own Poseidon adventure in the aquamarine **Neptunbrunnen** in front of the *Rathaus.* A few blocks down Spandauer Str. is the **Nikolaikirche,** whose twin spires mark Berlin's oldest building. *(Open Tu-Su 10am-6pm. DM3, students DM1.)* Inside the 13th-century structure, a small museum documents the early history of the city. The church gives the surrounding **Nikolaiviertel,** a carefully reconstructed *Altstadt,* its name. The Nikolaiviertel's narrow winding streets are popular and crowded; among the two dozen historic buildings is the **Knoblauchhaus,** at Poststr. 23, which houses a small museum documenting the life and times of architect Eduard Knoblauch. *(Open Tu-Su 10am-6pm. DM2, students DM1.)* Nearby is the **Ephraim-Palais,** at the corner of Poststr. and Muhlendamm. *(Open Tu-Su 10am-6pm. DM3, students DM1.)* The Nazis used this Rococo building as a sports museum; now it houses a collection of contemporary art from Berlin artists.

THE SCHEUNENVIERTEL AND ORANIENBURGER STRAßE

Northwest of Alexanderplatz lies the **Scheunenviertel,** once the center of Berlin's Orthodox Jewish community. To get here, take S-Bahn #1,2, or 25 to "Oranienburger Str." or U-Bahn #6 to "Oranienburger Tor." Prior to WWII, Berlin never had any ghettos. Jews lived throughout the city, though during the war they were deported to ghettos in Poland. Wealthier and more assimilated Jews tended to live in Western Berlin while more Orthodox Jews from Eastern Europe settled in the Scheunenviertel. Although evidence of Jewish life in Berlin dates back to the 13th century, the community was expelled in 1573 and not invited back for 100 years. Berlin's first synagogue opened in 1714 near the corner of Rochstr. and Rosenstr. Remarkably, this synagogue was not destroyed during the *Kristallnacht* because of the presence of a post office that had been renting space in the building—however, it was later bombed during the war, never to be reconstructed. The spot is marked by a huge construction site. The former **Jewish welfare office** was located at Rosenstr. 2-4. In the adjacent park, a terracotta memorial was put up in October 1995—on the 54th anniversary of the first deportation of the Berlin Jews. Today the Scheunenviertel is better known for its outdoor cafes and punk clubs than for its historical significance as Berlin's Jewish center, although the past few years have seen the opening of several Judaica-oriented bookstores and kosher restaurants in the area.

The shell of the **Neues Synagoge** stands at Oranienburger Str. 30. This huge, "oriental-style" building was designed by the famous Berlin architect Knoblauch. The synagogue, which seated 3200, was used for worship until 1940, when the Nazis occupied it and used it for storage. This synagogue, amazingly, also survived *Kristallnacht*—the SS torched it, but a local police chief, realizing that the building was a historical monument, ordered the Nazis to extinguish the fire. The synagogue was destroyed by bombing, but its restoration, largely financed by international Jewish organizations, began in 1988. The temple's beautiful gold-laced domes have been reconstructed, and were opened to the public on May 7, 1995—the 50th anniversary of Germany's surrender. Two first-class **exhibits** (tel. 28 40 13 16) are housed here. *(Open Su-Th 10am-6pm, F 10am-2pm. DM5, students DM3.)* **The New Synagogue 1866-1995** display chronicles the synagogue's history; the **Jewish History in Berlin** exhibit documents the history of Jews in Berlin since the 1660s. To enter, you must pass through a metal detector.

At the end of Große Hamburger Str. near the intersection with Monbijoustr. are the remains of the **Alter Jüdischer Friedhof** (Old Jewish Cemetery). Destroyed by the Nazis, the site now contains only the restored gravestone of the Enlightenment philosopher and scholar Moses Mendelssohn; the rest is a quiet park. In front, a plaque marks the site of the **Jüdisches Altersheim,** the Jewish old-age home which after 1942 served as a holding place for Jews before their deportation to concentration camps. Next door, yet another plaque marks the location of Berlin's oldest **Jewish school,** where Moses Mendelssohn taught. Mendelssohn, who was known as "the German Socrates," translated the Hebrew Bible into German, and supported interaction between Berlin's Jewish and non-Jewish communities. Corresponding with his humanist outlook, the school's pupils were half-gentile, half Jewish. The building was reopened as a school in 1992; its student body is still half-and-half.

NORTH MITTE

If any single man personifies the maelstrom of political and aesthetic contradictions that is Berlin, it is **Bertolt Brecht,** who called the city home. "There is a reason to prefer Berlin to other cities," the playwright once declared, "because it is constantly changing. What is bad today can be improved tomorrow." The **Brecht-Haus Berlin,** Chausseestr. 125 (tel. 282 99 16), near the intersection with Schlegelstr., is where Brecht lived and worked from 1953 to 1956. *(Open Tu-Th 9am-noon and 1-4pm, F 9am-noon and 1-3pm. DM4, students DM2. Tours every 30min.)* Take U-Bahn #6 to "Zinnowitzerstr." If you understand German, you should take the guided tour, given in flamboyant Brechtian style. The **Brechtforum** on the second floor sponsors exhibits and lectures on artistic and metropolitan subjects; pick up a schedule. Directly adjacent to Brecht's house, the **Dorotheenstädtischer Friedhof** (cemetery) contains the graves of a host of German luminaries, including Brecht and his wife Helene Wegel. Fichte and Hegel are buried side by side a few yards away; both graves are often festooned with flowers by admirers (or pillaged by frustrated students). At the end of the entrance path, next to the chapel on the right, is a map of grave locations. *(Open May-Aug. daily 8am-8pm; Feb.-Apr. and Sept.-Nov. 8am-6pm; Dec.-Jan. 8am-4pm.)*

PRENZLAUER BERG

Northeast of Oranienburger Str. and Alexanderplatz lies **Prenzlauer Berg,** a former working-class district largely neglected by Eastern Germany's reconstruction efforts. Many of its old buildings are falling apart; others still have shell holes and embedded bullets from World War II. The result is the charm of age and graceful decay, slightly less charming for local residents with bad plumbing and no phones. Don't be surprised, however, at the mind-blowing rate of gentrification underway here; Prenzlauer Berg is one of the most sought-out locales for ex-Kreuzbergers fleeing rent increases. Fancy shops and restaurants are popping up left and right, disturbing this neighborhood's reputation as a mellow, low-key retreat for artists and students. Unlike the loud, raucous scene in Kreuzberg and Mitte, Prenzlauer Berg is still more sedate and cerebral—which is not to say that it isn't lively. The streets here are studded with hip but casual cafes and bars, frequented by an ever-burgeoning crowd.

BERLIN

Especially worthy of a stroll is the restored **Husemannstraße**, home to the **Museum Berliner Arbeiterleben um 1900**, Husemannstr. 12, with a meticulously accurate reproduction of a Berlin working-class family apartment at the turn of the century. *(Open Tu-Th and Sa 10am-6pm, F 10am-3pm. DM2, students DM1.)* Meanwhile, the scene around **Kollwitzplatz** is especially vibrant—a number of cafes have popped up within the past year (see **Food**, p. 105). The statue of artist Käthe Kollwitz has been painted a number of times in the past few years, in acts of affectionate rather than angry vandalism, most notably with big pink polka-dots.

Berlin's Jews found the slightly remote Prenzlauer Berg ideal, slowly gravitating there during the 19th and early 20th centuries. The **Jewish cemetery** on Schönhauser Allee contains the graves of composer Giacomo Meyerbeer and painter Max Liebermann. *(Open M-Th 8am-4pm, F 8am-1pm.)* Take U-Bahn #2 to "Senefelderplatz." Just off Kollwitzplatz stands one of Berlin's loveliest **synagogues**, Rykestr. 53, unharmed during *Kristallnacht* due to its inconspicuous location in a courtyard.

■ Museums

Berlin is one of the world's great museum cities, with collections of art and artifacts encompassing all subjects and eras. The **National Prussian Cultural Foundation** (*Staatliche Museen Preußischer Kulturbesitz* or **SMPK**) runs the four major complexes—Charlottenburg, Dahlem, Museumsinsel, and Tiergarten—that form the hub of the city's museum culture. Since these museums are government-run, their **prices are standardized;** a single admission costs DM4, students DM2. The first Sunday of every month offers free admission. A *Tageskarte* (DM8, students DM4) is valid for all SMPK museums on the day of purchase; the *Wochenkarte* (DM25, students DM12.50) is valid for the whole week. Smaller museums deal with every subject imaginable, from sugar to tarts. **Artery Berlin** is a comprehensive art guide, including museum exhibitions and galleries, as well as a map, available at many museums for DM3.50. **Berlin Programm** also lists museums and some galleries (DM2.80).

MUSEUMINSEL (MUSEUM ISLAND)

The island holds the astoundingly broad treasure hoard of the former GDR in four separate museums. In addition, many exhibits from museums in western Berlin have relocated here recently. Take S-Bahn #3, 5, 7, or 9 to "Hackescher Markt." Unless noted, all Museuminsel museums are open Tuesday through Sunday 9am to 5pm.

Pergamonmuseum, Kupfergraben (tel. 20 35 55 04 or 203 55 00). One of the world's great ancient history museums from the grand old days when archaeology was king and Heinrich Schliemann traversed the world, uncovering the debris of ancient civilizations. The scale of its exhibits is mind-boggling: huge rooms can barely contain the entire Babylonian Ishtar Gate (575 BC), the Roman Market Gate of Miletus, and the majestic Pergamon Altar of Zeus (180 BC). The altar's great frieze (125m long and 2.5m high) depicting the victory of the gods over the giants symbolizes the triumphs of Attalus I. The museum also houses extensive collections of Greek, Assyrian, Islamic, and Far Eastern art. Tours of Pergamon Altar at 11am and 3pm. *Tageskarte* required for entry. Last entry 30min. before closing.

Alte Nationalgalerie, Bodestr. 1-3 (tel. 20 35 52 57). 19th-century art in a beautiful historic building. The collection is mostly German but also includes a sizable number of works by French Impressionist painters. SMPK prices.

Bodemuseum, Monbijoubrücke (tel. 20 35 55 03; fax 200 46 31). A world-class exhibit of Egyptian art, as well as late-Gothic wood sculptures, early Christian art, Byzantine masterpieces, 15th- to 18th-century paintings, and an exhibit on ancient history. The *Kindergalerie* holds interactive exhibits designed for kids, but fun for all. SMPK prices.

Altes Museum, Lustgarten. Converted into a special-exhibit museum, it has recently showcased powerhouse exhibitions of 20th-century avant-garde and political art. Regrettably, a *Tageskarte* for the other museums is not valid here. Exhibits run up to DM10, students DM5. Open Tu-Su 10am-5pm.

TIERGARTEN

Tiergarten-Kulturforum, on Matthäikirchplatz (tel. 20 90 55 55 for all museums), is a complex of museums at the eastern end of the Tiergarten park, near the *Staatsbibliothek* (see **Sights,** p. 111) and Potsdamer Platz. Right now the location is less than ideal; Potsdamer Platz is Europe's biggest construction site, and finding your way around it is quite a task. Bus #129 from the Ku'damm will bring you right to the museum complex; or take U-Bahn #2 or S-Bahn #1, 2, or 25 to "Potsdamer Platz," and walk up Potsdamer Str.; the museums will be on your right, the library on your left.

⊛**Gemäldegalerie** (Painting Gallery) is one of Germany's most famous museums, and rightly so. It houses a stunning and enormous collection by Italian, German, Dutch, and Flemish masters. The world-class collection includes 26 Rembrandts, Bruegel, Vermeer, Raphael, Titian, Botticelli, and Dürer. Open Tu-W and F 10am-6pm, Th 10am-8pm, Sa-Su 11am-6pm. SMPK prices.

Neue Nationalgalerie, Potsdamer Str. 50. This sleek building, designed by Mies van der Rohe, now gives quantity its own quality in a collection devoted to large art displays. Billboard-sized paintings and sculptures heavy enough to make Atlas cry fill the first two floors. The permanent collection includes works by Kokoschka, Barlach, Kirchner, and Beckmann, but these are often put away to make room for special exhibits that wouldn't fit through the door in any other museum. An SMPK *Tageskarte* will get you into the permanent exhibit, but two-thirds of the museum is occupied by special exhibitions (DM12, students DM6). Open Tu-W and F 10am-6pm, Th 10am-8pm, Sa-Su 11am-6pm.

Kunstbibliothek/Kupferstichkabinett, in the same enormous building as the *Gemäldegalerie.* A stellar collection of lithographs and drawings by Renaissance masters, including many Dürers and Botticelli's fantastic illustrations for the *Divine Comedy.* Open Tu-W and F 10am-6pm, Th 10am-8pm, Sa-Su 11am-6pm. SMPK prices.

Kunstgewerbemuseum (Museum of Applied Arts), also in the *Kulturforum* building. A plethora of plates, jugs, and china more or less trace a millennium's advances in dining technology. Hey, if you put it behind glass and shine spotlights on it, it's art. Open Tu-W and F 10am-6pm, Th 10am-8pm, Sa-Su 11am-6pm. SMPK prices.

Musikinstrumenten-Museum (Museum of Musical Instruments), Tiergartenstr. 1 (tel. 25 48 10) Fittingly next door to the Philharmonic, this museum is a must for anyone even remotely interested in classical music. Musical instruments from every period, from 16th-century virginals to Pianolas. You can hear recordings of the period instruments being played. Open Tu-F 9am-5pm, Sa-Su 10am-5pm. DM4, students DM2. Tours Saturday at 11am (DM3).

Raab Galerie, Potsdamer Str. 58 (tel. 261 92 17). A well-kept gallery with thoughtful exhibitions of famous and not-so-famous 20th-century artists Open M-F 10am-7pm, Sa 10am-4pm.

CHARLOTTENBURG

The wide-flung wings of **Schloß Charlottenburg,** Spandauer Damm (tel. 32 09 11), hold several museums set against the romantic *Schloßgarten.* Take U-Bahn #2 to "Sophie-Charlotte-Platz" or take bus #145. The **Kleiner Orangerie** sports special exhibitions. Admission to the historic rooms of the *Schloß* costs DM8 (students DM4), while a *Tageskarte* for the gardens and non-SMPK parts of the *Schloß* costs DM15 (students DM10). For more on the *Schloß* and its grounds, see **Sights** (p. 109).

Ägyptisches Museum (Egyptian Museum), Schloßstr. 70 (tel. 20 90 55 55), across Spandauer Damm from the castle. This stern Neoclassical building houses a fascinating collection of ancient Egyptian art, dramatically lit for the full Indiana Jones effect. The most popular item on display is the stunning 3300-year-old bust of **Queen Nefertiti** (1350 BC), thought to be the most beautiful representation of a woman in the world. Open Tu-F 10am-6pm, Sa-Su 11am-6pm. SMPK prices.

Sammlung Berggruen, Schloßstr. 1 (tel. 20 90 55 55), in an identical building across the street from the Egyptian museum. An incredible collection of Picasso and other modernists with equally impressive special exhibits. Open Tu-F 10am-6pm, Sa-Su 11am-6pm. SMPK ticket valid for permanent and special exhibitions.

⊕**Bröhan Museum,** Schloßstr. 1a (tel. 321 40 29), next door to the Berggruen, features two floors of *Jugendstil* and Art Deco furniture, housewares, and paintings in the sleekest of surroundings. Pieces date from 1889 to 1939. Open Tu-Su 10am-6pm. DM8, students DM4.

Galerie der Romantik (tel. 20 90 55 55) in the palace's *Neuer Flügel* (new wing). It holds the Prussian crown's dynamic collection of 19th-century art. The unquestioned show-stealers are works by early 19th-century Prussian artist Caspar David Friedrich, whose specialty was hypnotically beautiful, bleak landscapes with infinite, looming skies and seas with tiny human figures precariously placed in their midst. Open Tu-F 10am-6pm, Sa-Su 11am-8pm. SMPK prices.

DAHLEM

The **Staatliche Museen Preußischer Kulturbesitz Dahlem** (tel. 20 90 55 55 for all museums) looms near the *Freie Universität*. Take U-Bahn #2 to "Dahlem-Dorf," and follow the signs that say "Museen." Several globe-spanning museums cram into one enormous building, plus another across the street. Pick up a map at the entrance; the museums are laid out very strangely. *All have SMPK prices.*

Museum für Völkerkunde (Ethnography), Lansstr. 8 (tel. 20 90 55 55). Fascinating collections of tools, artifacts, musical instruments, weapons, and clothing from Africa, Polynesia, Central and South America, and Southeast Asia. The Polynesian exhibit climaxes with a giant display of ornately decorated boats, many of which you can climb into. In the African section, you can play the *baláfon* (xylophone). Open Tu-F 10am-6pm, Sa-Su 11am-6pm.

Museum für Volkskunde (Folklore), Im Winkel 6-8 (tel. 20 90 55 55). A hop away from the main Dahlem complex, this museum is dedicated to artifacts of lower- and middle-class life from all over the world over the past 400 years. The exhibit on 50s-80s pop culture is charming—never thought you'd see "Garbage Pail Kids" in a museum, did you? Veronica Vomit lives. Some sections are closed due to renovations. Open Tu-F 10am-6pm, Sa-Su 11am-6pm.

ELSEWHERE IN WESTERN BERLIN

Brücke Museum, Bussardsteig 9 (tel. 831 20 29). From Bahnhof Zoo, bus #249 to "Güntzelstr.," then bus #115 to "Clayallee/Pücklerstr." (30min.; 13 stops). Along with the *Neue Nationalgalerie,* this is *the* Expressionist museum in Berlin, with wildly colorful works by the Expressionist *Brücke* school. Open M and W-Su 11am-5pm. DM7, students DM3.

Martin-Gropius Bau, Stresemannstr. 110 (tel. 25 48 60). S-Bahn #1, 2, or 25 to "Anhalter Bahnhof." Walter Gropius' uncle Martin designed this neo-Renaissance wedding cake as a museum for and tribute to the industrial arts. The building alone is worth the price of admission (DM12, students DM6), but your ticket also entitles you to visit the two museums housed within its ornate walls. The **Berlinische Galerie,** on the second floor, is devoted to rotating exhibits of contemporary German art, much of it very famous, much of it very Picasso. The **Jüdisches Museum,** on the third floor, hosts extremely varied exhibits of painting, sculpture, and design; the only common thread is that the art has something to do with Jews in Germany. Museums open Tu-Su 10am-6pm.

Topographie des Terrors, in back of the Martin-Gropius-Bau, is built on top of the ruins of a Gestapo kitchen; the area used to be the site of the notorious Gestapo headquarters at Prinz-Albrecht-Str. (now Niederkirchnerstr.). Very comprehensive exhibit (in German) details the Nazi party's rise to power and the atrocities that occurred during the war. English guides are available (DM2), but you don't need to understand the captions to be moved by the photographs. Open Tu-Su 10am-6pm. Free. The adjacent **Prinz-Albrecht-Gelände,** a deserted wasteland near the site of the Wall, contains the ruins of Gestapo buildings. Open during daylight hours.

Bauhaus Archiv-Museum für Gestaltung, Klingenhöferstr. 13-14 (tel. 254 00 20). U-Bahn #1, 15, 2, or 4 to "Nollendorfplatz." A building designed by *Bauhaus* founder Walter Gropius that houses a permanent exhibit devoted to the school's development. The temporary exhibits are based around questions of art theory. Open M and W-Su 10am-5pm. DM5, students DM2. Free on Monday.

Museum für Verkehr und Technik (Transportation and Technology Museum), Trebbiner Str. 9 (tel. 25 48 40). U-Bahn #1, 15, or 2 to "Gleisdreieck" or U-Bahn #1, 15, or 7 to "Möckernbrücke." Souvenirs from *Autobahn* speed-devils, medieval printing presses, WWI fighting planes, and an historic brewery filled with historic empties. Combined admission with a yard of antique locomotives down the street. Open Tu-F 9am-6pm, Sa-Su 10am-6pm. DM5, students DM2.

Käthe-Kollwitz-Museum, Fasanenstr. 24 (tel. 882 52 10). U-Bahn #15 to "Uhlandstr." A marvelous collection of works by one of Germany's most prominent modern artists, much of it focusing on the themes of war and poverty. DM6, students DM3. Open M and W-Su 11am-6pm.

Postmuseum Berlin, An der Urania 15 (tel. 21 71 17 17). U-Bahn #1, 15, or 2 to "Wittenbergplatz." Exposes the Post's growth with lots of historic video and techno-fun—play with the toy mail train, light up an historic mail-route map. Open Tu-Su 9am-5pm. Free.

Zucker-Museum, Amrumer Str. 32 (tel. 31 42 75 74), U-Bahn #9 to "Amrumer Str." A cultural history of sugar explores its uses, such as sculpture, records, and alcohol. Yum. Open M-W 11am-5pm, Su 11am-6pm. DM4.50, students DM2 (or a solemn oath never to buy into the myth of cavities).

ELSEWHERE IN EASTERN BERLIN

Märkisches Museum, Am Köllnischen Park 5, at the corner of Märkisches Ufer (tel. 30 86 60). U-Bahn #2 to "Märkisches Museum." A beautiful building on the banks of the Spree River housing a collection of primeval and early Berlin history and lots of applied art. Some exhibitions are closed while the museum gets rebuilt. Open Tu-Su 10am-6pm. DM2, students DM1.

Deutsches Historisches Museum (Museum of German History), Unter den Linden 2, in the former arsenal (tel. 20 30 40). S-Bahn #3, 5, 7, or 9 to "Hackescher Markt." Across from the Museuminsel. Permanent exhibits trace German history from the Neanderthal period to the Nazis, while rotating exhibitions examine the last 50 years. Large quantities of GDR art in the "painting-of-a-happy-faced-worker" vein. Tours (in German) 4-5 times per day. The Zeughaus-Kino on the side shows documentaries and films Tu-Th at 6:15pm and 8:30pm. Open Th-Tu 10am-6pm. Free.

Schinkelmuseum, in the *Friedrichswerdersche Kirche* on Werderstr. (tel. 20 90 55 55), south of Unter den Linden. U-Bahn #2 to "Hausvogteiplatz." 19th-century French and German sculpture in a unique church built by Schinkel. Open Tu-Su 10am-6pm. SMPK ticket.

■ Entertainment

Berlin has one of the most vibrant cultural scenes in the world. Exhibitions, concerts, plays, and dance performances abound, although recent cutbacks in government subsidies have resulted in slightly fewer offerings and higher prices. Nonetheless, Germany still has a generously subsidized art scene, and tickets are usually reasonable, especially with student discounts. Varied festivals celebrating everything from Chinese film to West African music spice up the regular offerings.

You can reserve tickets by calling the box office directly. Always ask about student discounts; most theaters and concert halls offer up to 50% off, but only if you buy at the *Abendkasse* (night box office), which generally opens one hour before a performance begins. Numerous other ticket outlets charge commissions and do not offer student discounts. There are also ticket counters in all **Karstadt** department stores (general tel. 80 60 29 29; fax 80 60 29 22), and in the **KaDeWe** department store, Tauentzienstr. 21 (tel. 217 77 54). All offices charge a 15-18% commission. Remember that while most theaters do accept credit cards, most other ticket outlets don't. Unfortunately, major theaters and operas close from mid-July to late August.

BERLIN

Hekticket, on Hardenbergstr. next to the gigantic Zoo-Palast cineplex (tel. 230 99 30; fax 23 09 82 30), sells last-minute tickets for half-price. Tickets only available for shows posted in the window. Open M-F 9am-8pm, Sa 10am-8pm, Su 4-8pm.

Berliner Festspiele, Budapester Str. 50 (tel. 25 48 92 50; http://www.berliner festspiele.de). Tickets for a variety of shows, concerts, and events. Open M-F 10am-6pm, Su 10am-2pm.

Berlin Ticket, Potsdamer Str. 96 (tel. 23 08 82 30; fax 23 08 82 99).

Theater & Konzertkasse City Center, Kurfürstendamm 16, at the corner of Joachimstaler Str. (tel. 882 65 63; fax 882 65 67).

Theaterkasse Centrum, Meineckestr. 25 (tel. 882 76 11; fax 881 33 32). Open M-F 10am-6:30pm, Sa 10am-2pm.

CONCERTS, OPERA, AND DANCE

Berlin reaches its musical zenith during the fabulous **Berliner Festwochen,** lasting almost the entire month of September and drawing the world's best orchestras and soloists. The **Berliner Jazztage** in November also brings in the crowds. For more information on these events (and tickets, which sell out months in advance), call or write to *Berliner Festspiele* (see above). In mid-July, **Bachtage** (Bach Days) offer an intense week of classical music; every Saturday night in August, **Sommer Festspiele** turns the Ku'damm into a multi-faceted concert hall with punk, steel-drum, and folk groups competing for attention.

In the monthly pamphlets *Konzerte und Theater in Berlin und Brandenburg* (free) and *Berlin Programm* (DM2.80), as well as in the biweekly *Zitty* and *Tip,* you'll find notices of concerts in the courtyard of the old Arsenal on the **Schloßinsel Köpenick** (castle island) or in the parks. The programs for many theaters and opera houses are additionally listed on huge posters in U-Bahn stations. Tickets for the *Philharmonie* and the *Oper* are often impossible to acquire through conventional channels unless you write months in advance. Try standing out in front before performances with a small sign saying *"Suche Karte"* (I seek a ticket)—invariably a few people will try to unload tickets at the last moment. Remember that concert halls and operas close for a few weeks during the summer months.

Berliner Philharmonisches Orchester, Matthäikirchstr. 1 (tel. 25 48 81 32; fax 25 48 81 35). Bus #129 from Ku'damm to "Potsdamer Str." and walk 3 blocks north, or U-Bahn #2 or S-Bahn #1, 2 or 25 to "Potsdamer Platz" and walk up Potsdamer Str. The big yellow asymmetrical building, designed by Scharoun in 1963, is as acoustically perfect within as it is unconventional without. The *Berliner Philharmoniker,* led for decades by the late Herbert von Karajan and currently under the baton of Claudio Abbado, is one of the world's finest orchestras. It is well-nigh impossible to get a seat; check an hour before concert time or write at least 8 weeks in advance. The *Philharmonie* is closed from the end of June until the start of September. Tickets start at DM14 for standing room, DM26 for seats. Ticket office open M-F 3:30-6pm, Sa-Su 11am-2pm. Order tickets by phone, fax, mail, or email (karten buero@philharmonic.sireco.de).

Konzerthaus (Schauspielhaus Gendarmenmarkt), Gendarmenmarkt 2 (tel. 203 09 21 01). U-Bahn #2 or 6 to "Stadtmitte." The opulent home of the Berlin Symphony Orchestra. Call for performance info. Last-minute tickets are somewhat easier to come by. Box office open M-Sa noon-6pm, Su noon-4pm. The orchestra goes on vacation from mid-July to mid-Aug., but the *Deutsches Kammerorchester* continues to perform chamber music in the *Kleiner Saal* of the *Konzerthaus* complex. Order tickets by writing to Deutsches Kammerorchester, Suarezstr. 15, 14057 Berlin; or call 325 42 29; or fax 32 60 86 10.

Deutsche Oper Berlin, Bismarckstr. 35 (tel. 341 02 49 for info, 343 84 01 for tickets). U-Bahn #2 to "Deutsche Oper." Berlin's best opera, featuring newly commissioned works as well as all the German and Italian classics. Student discounts of up to 50% (depending on the price of the ticket) 1 week or less before performance. Tickets DM15-140. Main box office open M-Sa 11am until 1hr. before performance, Su 10am-2pm. Evening tickets available starting 1hr. before performance. For tickets, write to Deutsche Oper Berlin, Richard-Wagner-Str. 10, 10585 Berlin or fax 343

84 55. For program info, write to Deutsche Oper Berlin, Bismarckstr. 35, 10627 Berlin. Closed July-Aug.

Deutsche Staatsoper, Unter den Linden 7 (tel. 20 35 45 55; fax 20 35 44 83). U-Bahn #6 to "Französische Str.," S-Bahn #1, 2, or 25 to "Unter den Linden," or bus #100 or 157. Eastern Berlin's leading opera company, led by Daniel Barenboim (also the conductor of the Chicago Symphony Orchestra). Ballet and classical music, too, although the orchestra fluctuates between good and mediocre. Backstage tours available daily at 11am. Tickets DM18-35, 50% student discount. Box office open M-F 10am-6pm, Sa-Su 2pm-6pm. *Abendkasse* open 1hr. before showtime. Closed mid-July to early Sept.

Komische Oper, Behrenstr. 55-57 (tel. 20 26 03 60; fax 20 26 02 60; http://www.komischeoper.line.de). U-Bahn #6 to "Französische Str," or S-Bahn #1, 2, 25 to "Unter den Linden," or bus #100, 147, 257, or 348. Its reputation was built by famous post-war director Felsenstein, but in recent years zany artistic director Harry Kupfer has revitalized the opera with clever stagings of the classics. Program ranges from Mozart to Gilbert and Sullivan. Tickets DM15-94. 50% student discounts almost always available 2hr. before the show. Box office open M-Sa 11am-7pm, Su 1pm until 1hr. before the performance.

Tanzfabrik, Möckernstr. 68 (tel. 786 58 61). U-Bahn #7 to "Yorckstr." Turn left on Yorckstr., then right onto Möckernstr. Modern dance performances and a center for dance workshops. Box office open M-Th 10am-noon and 5-8pm, F 10am-noon. Tickets DM15. Occasional weekend performances start at 8 or 8:30pm. Often when the main theaters close down for the summer, dance companies take up residence. Check posters at the *Komische Oper* and the *Staatsoper.*

THEATER

Theater listings are available in the monthly pamphlets *Kultur!news* and *Berlin Programm,* as well as in *Zitty* and *Tip.* They are also posted in most U-Bahn stations; look for the yellow posters. In addition to the best German-language theater in the country, Berlin also has a lively English-language theater scene. Look for listings in *Zitty* or *Tip* that say *in englischer Sprache* (in English) next to them. There are a number of privately run companies called "off-theaters" that feature occasional English-language plays. As with concert halls, look out for summer closings (*Theaterferien* or *Sommerpause*); see the introduction to **Entertainment,** p. 119, for box office information. There is an international **Theater Festival** in May.

Deutsches Theater, Schumannstr. 13a (tel. 28 44 12 25). U-Bahn #6 or S-Bahn #1, 2, 25, 3, 5, 7, 75, or 9 to "Friedrichstr." or bus #147 to "Albrechtplatz." The word has spread to Western Berlin: this is the best theater in the country. Max Reinhardt made it great 100 years ago, and it now has innovative productions of the classics and newer works. The repertory runs from Büchner to Mamet to Ibsen. The **Kammerspiel des Deutschen Theaters** (tel. 28 44 12 26) has smaller, controversial productions. Tickets DM15-40, but 50% student discounts often available. Box office open M-Sa noon-6pm, Su 3-6pm.

Hebbel Theater, Stresemannstr. 29 (tel. 25 90 04 27). U-Bahn #1, 15, or 6 to "Hallesches Tor." The most avant of the avant-garde theaters in Berlin, drawing cutting-edge talent from all over the world. Box office open M-Su 4-7pm.

Vaganten Bühne, Kantstr. 12a (tel. 312 45 29). U-Bahn #2 or 9 or S-Bahn #3, 5, 7, 75, or 9 to "Zoologischer Garten." This off-beat hole-in-the-wall near the Ku'damm—the oldest private theater in Berlin—presents a healthy balance of contemporary German plays as well as such existentialist favorites as Sartre's *No Exit,* often in the original language. Tickets DM16-32, students (with ID) DM12. Box office open M 10am-4pm, Tu-F 10am-8pm, Sa 2-8pm.

Friends of Italian Opera, Fidicinstr. 40 (tel. 691 12 11). U-Bahn #6 to "Platz der Luftbrücke." The name is a joking reference to *Some Like It Hot,* and belies its role as Berlin's leading English-language theater, home to the renowned Berliner Grundtheater company as well as a grab-bag of English-language performances with a penchant for the grotesque, ranging from Tennessee Williams to Katherine Anne Porter. Tickets DM15-20. Most shows at 8pm.

BERLIN

Berliner Ensemble, Bertolt-Brecht-Pl. 1 (tel. 28 40 81 55). U-Bahn #6 or S-Bahn #1, 2, 25, 3, 5, 7, 75, or 9 to "Friedrichstr." The famous theater established by Brecht is undergoing a renaissance. Hip repertoire, including Heiner Müller and some young American playwrights, as well as Brecht's own plays. Also some premieres. Tickets DM12-40, 50% student discount available. 1hr. before the show in the *Abendkasse*. Box office open M-Sa 11am-6pm, Su 3-6pm.

Maxim Gorki Theater, Am Festungsgraben 2 (tel. 20 22 11 15). U-Bahn #6 or S-Bahn #1, 2, 25, 3, 5, 7, 75, or 9 to "Friedrichstr.", or bus #100, 157 or 348 to "Deutsche Staatsoper." Excellent contemporary theater with wonderfully varied repertoire—everything from Schiller to Albee. Tickets DM5-25. Box office open M-Sa 1-6:30pm, Su 3-6:30pm.

Die Distel ("The Thistle"), Friedrichstr. 101 (tel. 204 47 04). U-Bahn #6 or S-Bahn #1, 2, 25, 3, 5, 7, 75, or 9 to "Friedrichstr." During GDR days, this was a renowned cabaret for political satire—but reunification has taken the bite out of some of the jokes. Box office open M-F 10am-2pm and 3-6pm, Sa-Su after 4pm.

FILM

Berlin is a movie-lovin' town; it hosts the international **Berlinale** film festival (Feb. 10-21 in 1999), and on any night in Berlin you can choose from 100 different films, many in the original languages. (*"O.F."* next to a movie listing means original version. *"O.m.U."* means original version with German subtitles. Everything else is dubbed.) Check *Tip, Zitty,* or the ubiquitous *Kinoprogramm* posters plastered throughout the city. Numerous cineplexes offer the chance to see dubbed Hollywood blockbusters. **Zoo-Palast,** at Hardenbergstr. 29a (tel. 25 41 47 89), near Bahnhof Zoo, is one of the biggest and most popular, with more than a dozen screens. Mondays, Tuesdays, or Wednesdays are *Kinotage* at most movie theaters, with prices reduced a few Marks. Bring a student ID for discounts.

Freiluftkino. The summer brings a host of outdoor film screenings to Berlin. Two venues show films in English: **Freiluftkino Hasenheide,** at the Sputnik in Hasenheide park, screens anything from silent films to last year's blockbusters. U-Bahn #7 or 8 to "Hermannplatz." **Freiluftkino Kreuzberg,** Mariannenpl. 2 (tel. 238 64 88), screens avant-garde contemporary films. U-Bahn #1, 15, or 8 to "Kottbusser Tor." DM10 for either theater.

Arsenal, Welserstr. 25 (tel. 451 33 56). U-Bahn #1, 15, or 2 to "Wittenbergplatz." Run by the *Freunde der deutschen Kinemathek,* the founders of the *Berlinale,* Arsenal showcases independent films as well as the occasional classic. Frequent appearances by guest directors; a popular meeting place for Berlin's filmmakers.

Odeon, Hauptstr. 116 (tel. 781 26 82). U-Bahn #4 to "Rathaus Schöneberg." Odeon's venue is a mixture of mainstream American and British films with a pseudo-leftist slant. All films shown in English.

Filmtheater Babylon-Mitte, Rosa-Luxemburg-Str. 30 (tel. 242 50 76). U-Bahn #2 to "Rosa-Luxemburg-Platz." Shows classics and art films, often in their original languages. DM8, students DM7. The Kreuzberg **Babylon,** Dresdener Str. 126 (tel. 614 63 16; U-Bahn #1 or 8 to "Kottbuser Tor"), plays offbeat comedies in English with German subtitles.

Blow Up, Immanuelkirchstr. 14 (tel. 442 86 62). S-Bahn #4, 8, or 10 to "Greifswalder Str." Explosive and entertaining—see *Unzipped* followed by a fashion show or catch them when they're showing the eternally cool Bogey flicks. They always screen something in English. DM9, Tu-W DM7.

SHOPPING

When Berlin was a lonely outpost in the Eastern Bloc consumer wilderness, Berliners had no choice but to buy native. Thanks to the captive market, the city accrued a mind-boggling array of things for sale: if a price tag can be put on it, you can buy it in Berlin. The high temple of the consumerist religion is the seven-story **KaDeWe department store** on Wittenbergplatz at Tauentzienstr. 21-24 (tel. 212 10), the largest department store in Europe. (Open M-F 9:30am-8pm, Sa 9am-4pm.) The name is a

German abbreviation of "Department Store of the West" *(Kaufhaus des Westens);* for the tens of thousands of product-starved Easterners who flooded Berlin in the days following the Wall-opening, KaDeWe *was* the West—prompting warnings such as, "OK now, we're going in. Just act normal," as intrepid children stood on the threshold of consumerism. Even Westerners would do well to follow the advice, with the saccharine and pervasive materialism on display alternatively proving awe-inspiring and sickening. (No photography allowed!) The store's food department, sixth floor, has to be seen to be believed (see **Food,** p. 102).

The entire **Kurfürstendamm** is one big shopping district, but the **Ku'damm Eck,** (the corner of Joachimstalerstr.) and **Ku'damm Block** (around Uhlandstr.) are the most notable areas. Bleibtreustr. has stores closer to the budget traveler's reach, while the hagglers around **Brandenburger Tor** will sell you cheap GDR memorabilia—don't accept their stated prices, and don't fool yourself into thinking the relics are authentic; there just aren't *that* many "real" pieces of the Berlin Wall. The intersection of Unter den Linden and Friedrichstr., right down the street from the Brandenburg Gate, was once an important commercial district before the war. Neglected for 50 years by the GDR government, the area lost much of its glory. Nonetheless, the last five years have seen a flourishing of fancy shops and big malls, and many more will pop up over the next two years.

Theodore Sturgeon astutely observed that "90% of everything is crap," and the **flea markets** that regularly fertilize Berlin are no exception. Nevertheless, you can occasionally find the fantastic bargain that makes all the sorting and sifting worthwhile. The market on **Straße des 17. Juni** probably has the best selection of stuff, but the prices are higher than those at a lot of other markets (open Sa-Su 8am-3pm). **Winterfeldmarkt,** by Nollendorfplatz, overflows with food, flowers, and people crooning Dylan tunes over their acoustic guitars (open W and Sa mornings). The market on **Oranienburger Straße** by Tacheles offers works by starving artists and a variety of other nonsensical Dada delights (open Sa-Su 8am-3pm). There is a typical German *Fußgängerzone* (pedestrian zone) on Wilmersdorfer Str. (U-Bahn #7 to "Wilmersdorfer Str." or S-Bahn #3, 5, 7, 75, or 9 to "Charlottenburg"); bakeries, *Döner* joints, trendy clothing shops, and department stores abound.

Zweite Hand (second-hand; DM3.80), an aptly named newspaper appearing at newsstands on Tuesdays, Thursdays, and Saturdays, consists of ads for anything anyone wants to resell, from apartment shares and plane tickets to silk dresses and cats; it also has good deals on **bikes. Bergmannstraße,** in Kreuzberg, is a used clothes and cheap antique shop strip. **Made in Berlin,** Potsdamer Str. 106, generally has funky second-hand stuff, all quite cheap. Get your leather jacket here. Ride U-Bahn #1 to "Kurfürstenstr." Other locations have more used clothing: **Bergmannstr. 102,** and **Ahornstr. 2** (U-Bahn #1, 15, 2, or 4 to "Nollendorfplatz"). A larger selection of used clothes, albeit with less consistent quality, awaits at **Checkpoint,** Mehringdamm 59. Jump on U-Bahn #6 or 7 to "Mehringdamm."

Berlin's largest music store is the enormous **Saturn,** Alexanderpl. 8, located right outside the train station (U-Bahn #2, 5, or 8 or S-Bahn #3, 5, 7, 75, or 9). Most CDs are DM25-30. (Open M-F 9am-8pm, Sa 9am-4pm.) If you're looking for used CDs or LPs, snoop around the streets near the "Schlesisches Tor" U-Bahn stop (lines #1 or 15). A variety of used CDs and records are bought and sold at **Cover,** Turmstr. 52 (tel. 395 87 62), but they're particularly into pop and top-40s music. Take U-Bahn #9 to "Turmstr." (Open M-F 10am-8pm, Sa 10am-4pm.) To complete (or start) your trance, techno, house, and acid collection, head on over to **Flashpoint,** Bornholmer Str. 88 (tel. 44 65 09 59), and Klosterstr. 11. (Open M-W and F noon-7pm, Th noon-8pm, Sa 11am-2pm.)

▓ Nightlife

Berlin's nightlife is absolute madness, a teeming cauldron of debauchery that runs around the clock and threatens to inflict coronaries upon the faint of heart. Bars, clubs, and cafes typically jam until at least 3am and often stay open until daylight; during the weekends, you can literally dance non-stop from Friday night until Monday morning. Take advantage of the night buses from the U-Bahn stations and **U-Bahn #9 and 12,** which run all night on Fridays and Saturdays. The best sources of information about bands and dance venues are the bi-weekly magazines *Tip* (DM4) and the superior *Zitty* (DM4), available at all kiosks and newsagents, and the free *030* that's distributed in all cafes and bars.

In Western Berlin, the best places to look are **Savignyplatz, Nollendorfplatz,** and particularly **Kreuzberg.** The Ku'damm is best avoided at night, unless you enjoy fraternizing with drunken businessmen, middle-aged, unenlightened tourists, and dirty old men who drool at the sight of strip shows. The area west of Zoo, especially Savignyplatz, is rife with cafes and bars as well as a few venues for live music. The main focus of Schöneberg nightlife is around **Nollendorfplatz,** encompassing cafe-*Kneipen* on Winterfeldtplatz, Akazienstr., and Goltzstr., and more bars on Kleiststr. Pushing up against the remains of the Wall is the center of the **Kreuzberg** *Szene*. The scene in East Kreuzberg is wild; in the midst of the heavily Turkish neighborhoods along Oranienstr. between U-Bahn #1 stops "Kottbusser Tor" and "Görlitzer Bahnhof," you'll find a menagerie of radically alternative clubs that range from laid-back to breathtakingly salacious. Farther east lies Schlesisches Tor, home to a more punkish heap of bars, as well as the floating—nay, rocking—club and cafe aboard the **MS Sanssouci.** On the opposite bank of the Spree in Friedrichshain, several clubs have jumped off the capitalist bandwagon and headed East; check out the venues along Mühlenstr. (U-Bahn #1, 12, or 15 to "Warschauer Str.")

As funky as Kreuzberg is, its alterna-charm has become a tad passé as clubs flee to the east and north. While Mercedes-Benz and Sony build their new European headquarters at Potsdamer Platz, speculators have been dumping capital into the surrounding areas, bringing a wave of massive rent increases that have forced nearby clubs to pick up and head deeper into Mitte and Prenzlauer Berg. Rent problems in the west, coupled with a fascinating new "alternative" population, make the East hot. On the other hand, most of the West's clubs are dinosaurs (for example, Metropol and Big Eden), relics of an era when disco was considered a viable weapon against godless communism. Indeed, a military milieu still permeates many Western clubs, which attract divisions of uniformly dressed high school kids to dance on spotless, spit-and-polish shiny dance floors. Some of the more interesting bars abound in the **Scheunenviertel,** especially along **Oranienburger Str.** (not to be confused with Kreuzberg's Oranienstr.) near the synagogue. The **Prenzlauer Berg** area boasts some fun, interesting places along Schönhauser Allee, Kastanienallee, and Kollwitzplatz. Streetlights are sparse on many of the residential streets of the east, making a midnight club crawl a little creepy. Although Eastern Berlin is still safer than most American cities, it's wise to avoid empty alleys and parks and to travel in groups.

If at all possible, try to hit (or, if you're prone to bouts of claustrophobia, avoid) Berlin during the **Love Parade,** usually held in the second weekend of July (see **The Love Parade,** p. 126), when all of Berlin just says "yes" to everything. In that vein, it's also worth mentioning that Berlin has **de-criminalized marijuana possession** of up to eight grams. Smoking in public, however, has not been officially accepted, though it's becoming more common in some clubs. *Let's Go* does not recommend puffing clouds of hash smoke into the face of police officers.

BARS AND CLUBS

This is the section of *Let's Go: Germany* where we dance.

Savigny- and Steinplatz Area

Quasimodo, Kantstr. 12a (tel. 312 80 86; http://www.quasimodo.de). S-Bahn #3, 5, 7, or 9 to "Savignyplatz." This unassuming basement pub with attached *Biergarten* is one of Berlin's most crucial jazz venues, drawing in big names and lively crowds. It's totally dead until 10pm when the shows begin. (An extraordinary fact: the men's bathroom here is lit by fluorescent "black light" bulbs. Why is this extraordinary? Because human urine glows under fluorescent light—make sure you don't dribble!) Cover depends on performance, ranging from free to DM30. Concert tickets available from 5pm or at Kant Kasse ticket service (tel. 313 45 54; fax 312 64 40). Open daily from 8pm.

Big Eden, Kurfürstendamm 202 (tel. 882 61 20). U-Bahn #15 to "Uhlandstr." or U-Bahn #7 to "Adenauerplatz." No paradise: 9 planes of disco inferno. Funked out post-Saturday Night Fever crowd shakes to disco, house, and techno. Cover M-F DM5, Sa-Su DM10. Open daily from 8pm.

Schöneberg

Metropol, Nollendorfpl. 5 (tel. 217 36 80). U-Bahn #1, 15, 2, or 4 to "Nollendorf-platz," or night buses #N5, N19, N26, N48, N52, or N75. 650,000 watts of light! 35,800 watts of sound! Berlin's largest disco sports a hypermodern sushi bar-like motif amid ancient Egyptian pillars. Get down with funk, house, and soul Friday and Saturday nights from 9pm. Cover DM20. Sometimes big-time concerts take place between dances. Concert ticket prices vary; call 215 54 63 for info and prices. Open M-F 11am-3pm and 3:30-6pm.

🄜**Café Bilderbuch,** Akazienstr. 28 (tel. 78 70 60 57). U-Bahn #7 to "Eisenacher Str." This sophisticated jazzy cafe teleports its clientele into a world of flappers and speakeasies. Chill on the plush sofas while sipping a fruity *Berlin Weiße mit Schuß* (DM4.50) or tango the night away at one of the cafe's biweekly *Tanztees*. The tasty brunch baskets, served around the clock, culminate in the sumptuous Sunday buffet (DM15). Open M-Sa 9am-2am, Su 10am-2am.

Kreuzberg

SO 36, Oranienstr. 190 (tel. 61 40 13 06; http://www.SO36.de). U-Bahn #1, 12, or 15 to "Görlitzer Bahnhof" or night bus #N29 to "Heinrichplatz" or N8 to "Adalbertstr." Berlin's only *truly* open club, with a mixed clientele of hip heteros, gays, and lesbians grooving to a mish-mash of wild genres: Mondays are "electric ballroom," a trance party featuring Berlin's up-and-coming DJs and TV screens filled with anime; Thursdays mean a combination of punk, ska, and hip-hop, while weekends run the gamut from techno to live concerts. For other nights see **Gay and Lesbian Berlin,** below. Open after 11pm.

KitKat Club, Glogauerstr. 2 (tel. 611 38 33). U-Bahn #1, 12, or 15 to "Görlitzer Bahnhof" or night bus #N29. Lascivious? The word loses its meaning here. Erotic? This implies innuendo, a quality which has no place on this dance floor. Sex. SEXSEX-SEX. People with varying degrees of clothing, some copulating, some just digging the cool trance music in the jaw-dropping fluorescent interior, leave their inhibitions outside. Cover DM10-20. Open W-Su at 11pm. The Sunday after-hours party (8am-7pm) is popular, free, and more fully clothed. On Thursdays, the club cross-dresses as the **Fuck-Naked Sex Party** for some serious homoerotics (men only!). Not for the faint of heart.

Yaam, Cuvrystr. 50-51 (tel. 617 59 59). U-Bahn #1, 12, or 15 to "Schlesisches Tor" or night bus #N29 or N65. Hip-hop, reggae, and Caribbean beats fill the club's smoky interior. Open F-Su 10pm-late. Cover DM5.

Ex, Mehringhof, Gneisenaustr. 2a (tel. 693 58 00). U-Bahn #6 or 7 to "Mehringdamm" or night bus #N4, N19, or N76. A bar, performance space, and club run by a leftist collective in a steel and concrete courtyard. The commies also cook up an Indian storm bound to cause an intestinal revolution. Curry comrades, attack! Open daily 9pm-late.

Junction Bar, Gneisenaustr. 18 (tel. 694 66 02). U-Bahn #7 to "Gneisenaustr." or night bus #N4 or N19 to "Zossener Str." Live jazz and blues accompany American-style breakfast served until 2:30am. Showtimes at 7:30, 8:30, and 9:30pm, and DJ parties after 1am. Open Su-Th 6pm-3am, F-Sa 5pm-5am.

Sage Club, Brückenstr. 1. U-Bahn #8 to "Heinrich-Heine-Str." or night bus #N8. The latest entry in Berlin's fast-paced dance club arena, Sage Club has dealt a one-two

---

The Love Parade

Every year during the second weekend in July, the Love Parade brings Berlin to its knees—its trains run late, its streets fill with litter, and its otherwise patriotic populace scrambles to the countryside in the wake of a wave of West German teenagers dying their hair, dropping ecstasy, and getting down *en masse*. What started in 1988 as a DJ's birthday party, with only 150 people, has mutated into an annual techno Woodstock, the world's only million-man rave, and a massive corporate event. A huge "parade" takes place on Saturday afternoon, involving a snail-paced procession of tractor-trailers loaded with blasting speakers and topped by gyrating bodies that slowly works it from Ernst-Reuter-Platz to the Brandenburg Gate. The city-wide party turns the Straße des 17 Juni into a riotous dance floor, and the Tiergarten into a garden of original—and sometimes quite creative—sin. To celebrate the licentious atmosphere, the BVG offers a "No-Limit-Ticket," useful for getting around from venue to venue during the weekend's 54 hours of nonstop partying (DM10, condom included). Unless you have a fetish for tall people's hairy and sweaty armpits, the best way to see and enjoy the parade is to be up high (literally, of course)—the porta-potties are supreme watch towers. Club prices skyrocket for the event as the best DJs from Europe are imported for a frantic weekend of beat-thumping madness. It's an experience that you'll never forget, unless you consume something that leaves you in a hazy cloud of oblivion. Keep an ear out for updates on the 1999 event; although past Love Parades have been held in the Tiergarten, the authorities might move it after environmentalists raised concerns about the 750,000 liters of urine which the park must absorb every year. Regardless of the locale, the techno world trembles in eager anticipation of next year's incarnation.

---

punch to its Kreuzberg competitors in cornering the techno and house market. Cover DM10-25. Get into the groove, boy, Th-Su from 11pm.

Oranienburger Straße-Mitte

Tresor/Globus, Leipziger Str. 126a (tel. 229 06 11 or 612 33 64). U-Bahn #2 or S-Bahn #1, 2, or 25 to "Potsdamer Platz" or night bus #N5, N29 or N52. One of the most rocking techno venues in Berlin, packed from wall to wall with enthusiastic ravers. Its 2 dance floors, both sporting rapidly blinking lights and floor-shaking bass, are enough to bring out the epileptic in all of us. **Globus** chills with house, while **Tresor** rocks to techno beats. Cover DM5 on Wednesday, DM10 on Friday, DM15-20 on Saturday. Open W and F-Sa 11pm-6am.

E-Werk, Wilhelmstr. 43 (tel. 617 93 70). U-Bahn #2, S-Bahn #1, 2, or 25, or night bus #N52 to "Potsdamer Platz." After several years' respite from the *Szene*, the world's most famous techno club was scheduled to reopen in late 1998. Whether the club's multi-leveled dance floors will once again be jam-packed on Friday and Saturday nights (to the tune of DM15-20 cover) remains to be seen; call for up-to-date information.

Tacheles, Oranienburger Str. 53-56 (tel. 282 61 85). U-Bahn #6 to "Oranienburger Tor" or S-Bahn #1, 2, or 25 to "Oranienburger Str." or night bus #N6 or N84. A playground for artists, punks, and curious tourists staying in the nearby hostels. Housed in a bombed-out department store and the adjacent courtyard, Tacheles plays host to several art galleries, bars, and vicious raves. The owners have staved off ambitious plans to convert the area into office buildings, but eviction is an omnipresent possibility. Open M-Su 24hr.

Hackesche Höfe, Rosenthaler Str. 40-41. S-Bahn #3, 5, 7, 75, or 9 to "Hackescher Markt." One of the few truly successful attempts to revitalize northern Mitte, the Hackesche Höfe is a series of interconnected courtyards containing restaurants, cafes, clubs, galleries, shops, apartments, and a movie theater. The lively sound of *klezmer* bands vie with street performers for the attention of passersby, while the low-key **Oxymoron** club (tel. 28 39 18 85) serves as a venue for daily jazz concerts (open M and W-Sa after 11pm, Tu after 8:30pm, Su after 10pm).

Café Silberstein, Oranienburger Str. 27 (tel. 281 28 01). S-Bahn #1, 2, or 25 to "Oranienburger Str." Post-everything art decor offers sushi, ambient music, and a hipper than hip clientele. Erica approves. Open M-F after 4pm, Sa after noon.

Prenzlauer Berg

Kulturbrauerei, Knaackstr. 97 (tel. 441 92 69 or 441 92 70). U-Bahn #2 to "Eberswalder Str." Enormous party space located in a former East German brewery. Seven dance spaces, as well as an outdoor stage and cafe, host a variety of concerts and parties throughout the year. Because the venues include everything from hardcore *Ostrock* and disco to techno and reggae, it's best to call ahead. Cover DM3-5, more for special events. Open Th-Su and Tu after 10pm.

Subground, in the **Pfefferberg** club, Schönhauser Allee 176 (tel. 44 38 31 16). U-Bahn #2 to "Senefelderplatz" or night bus #N58. As the name suggests, this club is at ground level. Less mobbed than E-Werk and Tresor, with DJs spinning a varied mix of drum 'n' bass, jungle, and dub, as well as healthy quantities of techno and British house. Cover DM10. Open Th-Sa after 11pm.

Café SowohlAlsAuch, Kollwitzstr. 88 (tel. 442 93 11). U-Bahn #2 to "Senefelderplatz." A comfy coffee bar that serves harder drinks too. Open daily 9am-2am.

Knaack-Klub, Greifswalder Str. 224 (tel. 442 70 60). S-Bahn #4, 8, or 10 to "Greifswalder Str.," then tram #2, 3, or 4. In a perpetual state of musical identity crisis, this club spins hiphop, disco, and 80s music. Mondays are karaoke nights. Cover varies: M free; W DM5; F-Sa DM5 before 10pm, DM10 after 10pm. Open M, F, and Sa from 9pm, W from 11pm.

Elsewhere in Eastern Berlin

⊛**Insel der Jugend,** Alt Treptow 6 (tel. 53 60 80 20). S-Bahn #4, 6, 8, 9, or 10 to "Treptower Park," then bus #166, 167, or 265 or night bus #N65 to "Alt-Treptow." Located in the Spree river, *Insel der Jugend* (island of youth) is not just for kids. Three fiercely decorated floors of dancing have the feel of a fishbowl with fluorescent silver foil and netting all over the place. Very cool. Top 2 floors spin reggae, hip-hop, ska, and house (sometimes all at once), while the frantic techno scene in the basement claims the casualties of the upper floors. An outdoor patio overlooking the trees and river serves as a peaceful venue for smokers. Cover Th-Sa DM5-15. Open W after 7pm, Th after 9pm, F-Sa after 10 pm.

■ Gay and Lesbian Berlin

Berlin is arguably the most open city on the continent. During the Cold War, thousands of homosexuals flocked to Berlin to take part in its left-wing activist scene as well as to avoid West Germany's *Wehrpflicht* (mandatory military service). Even before the war, Berlin was known as a gay metropolis, particularly in the tumultuous 1920s. Traditionally, the social nexus of gay and lesbian life has centered around the **Nollendorfplatz,** the so-called "Pink Village." Christopher Isherwood lived at Nollendorfstr. 17 while writing his collection of stories *Goodbye to Berlin,* later adapted as the musical *Cabaret.* The city's reputation for tolerance was marred by the Nazi persecutions of the 1930s and 40s, when thousands of gay and lesbian Berliners were deported to concentration camps. A marble pink triangle plaque outside the Nollendorfplatz U-Bahn station honors their memory. With the fall of the Wall, Berlin's *Szene* was once again revitalized by the emergence of East Berlin's previously heavily oppressed homosexual community, and many of the new clubs that have opened up in the past few years are situated in the eastern half of the city.

The boisterous history of homosexuality comes out at the **Schwules Museum,** Mehringdamm 61 (tel. 693 11 72; open W-Su 2-6pm; DM7, students DM4). **Spinnboden-Lesbenarchiv,** Anklamerstr. 38 (tel. 448 58 48), tends toward culturally hip lesbian offerings, with exhibits, films, and all kinds of information about current lesbian life (open W and F 2-7pm). Take U-Bahn #8 to "Bernauer Str." **Lesbenberatung,** Kulmerstr. 20a (tel. 215 20 00), offers a library, movie viewings, and counseling on lesbian issues (open Tu and Th 4-7pm, F 2-5pm). Take U-Bahn #7 to "Kleistpark." The gay info center **Mann-o-Meter,** Motzstr. 5 (tel 216 80 08), off Nollendorfplatz, gives out information on nightlife, political activism, and gay or gay-friendly living arrangements. They also offer informal monthly nightly tours for those new to the Berlin scene on the third Friday of every month at 9pm. (Open M-F 5-10pm, Sa-Su 4-10pm.) For up-to-date events listings, pick up a copy of the amazingly comprehensive *Siegessäule* (free), named after one of Berlin's most prominent monuments. Less in-depth but also useful is *Sergej*, a free publication for men. The **Prinz Eisenherz bookstore**, Bleibtreustr. 52 (tel. 313 99 36), has lots of information and books, many in English (open M-W and F 10am-6:30pm, Th 10am-8pm, Sa 10am-4pm). The travel guide *Berlin von Hinten* (Berlin from Behind) costs DM19.80, but details gay life in Berlin extensively in English and German. **Lilith Frauenbuchladen,** Knesebeckstr. 86 (tel. 312 31 02), is a women's bookstore with a focus on lesbian issues (open M-F 10am-6:30pm, Sa 10am-4pm). **Marga Schoeller Bücherstube,** Knesebeckstr. 33 (tel. 881 11 22), offers women's issues books in English. *Blattgold* (DM5 from women's bookstores and some natural food stores) has information and listings for women on a monthly basis. Many of the *Frauencafés* listed are not exclusively lesbian, but do offer an all-woman setting. The second half of June is the high point of the annual queer calendar of events, culminating in the ecstatic, champagne-soaked floats of the **Christopher Street Day (CSD)** parade, a six-hour long street party drawing more than 200,000 people (June 26, 1999). The weekend before CSD sees a smaller but no less jubilant **Lesbisch-schwules Stadtfest** (street fair) at Nollendorfplatz.

Bierhimmel, Oranienstr. 183. U-Bahn #1, 8, or 15 to "Kottbusser Tor." Very popular hangout for Berlin's gays and lesbians. As the name suggests, heavenly beer is in abundance. Open 6pm-late.

Flammende Herzen, Oranienstr. 170 (tel. 615 71 02). U-Bahn #1, 8, or 15 to "Kottbusser Tor." Pleasant cafe frequented by Kreuzberg's gay and lesbian community. People-watch outside or chill in the flaming orange interior. Drinks DM4-8; order at the bar. Open daily from 11am.

Anderes Ufer, Hauptstr. 157 (tel. 784 15 78). U-Bahn #7 to "Kleistpark." A quieter, more relaxed *Kneipe* away from the club scene. Occasional exhibits by local artists adorn the brightly painted interior. Open daily 11am-2am.

SO36, while usually a mixed club (see p. 125), sponsors 4 predominantly queer events. The largest is **Hungrige Herzen** (Wednesdays after 10pm), a jam-packed gay and (somewhat) lesbian trance and drum 'n bass party. Delightful drag queens make the rounds with super-soakers to cool off the flaming crowd. **Café Fatal** (Sundays), has a more relaxed atmosphere, with ballroom dancing from 5pm followed by the obligatory *Schlagerkarusell* at 10pm. The third Friday in every month heralds the coming of **Jane Bond,** a wild party for lesbians and drags (10pm-late), while the second Saturday in the month brings **Gayhane,** a self-described "HomOrientaldancefloor" for a mixed crowd of Turks and Germans.

Die Busche, Mühlenstr. 12. U-Bahn #1, 12, or 15 or S-Bahn #3, 5, 6, 7, 75, or 9 to "Warschauer Str." East Berlin's largest queer disco serves up an incongruous rotation of techno, top 40, and, yes, *Schlager.* Cover DM8-10. Open W and F-Su from 9:30pm. The party gets going around midnight. It *really* gets going around 3am.

Connection, Fuggerstr. 33 (tel. 218 14 32). U-Bahn #1 or 2 to "Wittenbergplatz." Sketchy, sketchy, sketchy. The name says it all. Find your soul mate (well, one-night stand) in the above-ground disco, then head downstairs into the dimly lit labyrinthine **Connection Garage.** You get the picture. Cover DM12 including first drink. Open F-Sa from 11pm.

Café Anal, Muskauer Str. 15 (tel. 618 70 64). U-Bahn #1 to "Görlitzer Bahnhof." Spirited alternative gay and lesbian bar in east Kreuzberg. The decor hovers between Salvador Dalí and Pee-Wee's Playhouse: shiny gold ceiling, stuffed-pumpkin light fixtures, plump multi-colored cushions in corner nooks, seashell-shaped canopy. Monday women only. Open summer daily from 6pm; winter from 8pm.

SchwuZ, Mehringdamm 61 (tel. 694 10 77). U-Bahn #6 or 7 to "Mehringdamm." Cafe *cum* club in southern Kreuzberg with a mostly male clientele. The relaxed *Kneipe* facade belies the intense dance floor scene inside. Ballroom and tango Thursday from 8pm; house, techno, and top 40 Friday-Saturday from 11pm. Cover DM5-10.

MS TitaniCa, on the MS Sanssouci boat off Göbenufer in the Spree River (tel. 611 12 55). U-Bahn #1 or 15 to "Schlesisches Tor." MS Sanssouci's gently swaying cafe transforms once a month into one of Berlin's most swinging lesbian parties (first Friday of the month from 8:30pm). **Schocko-Café,** Mariannenstr. 6 (tel. 615 15 61). U-Bahn #1 or 8 to "Kottbusser Tor." Lesbian central; a cafe with a cultural center upstairs, billiards, and dancing every second Saturday of the month (10pm). Open Su-Th 5pm-1am year-round, plus F-Sa from noon in the summer.

■ The Outer Boroughs

The suburbs of Berlin lie within the *Berliner Außenring,* a massive roundabout of highways and train lines which circles the greater metropolitan area. The towns and city districts listed below are generally accessible by public transportation, and make good afternoon or daytrips. Some of them do lie in the C zone of the BVG transportation system, which means that if you've purchased an AB ticket, you'll have to buy an *Ergänzungsfahrschein* (extension ticket; DM2.50). For excursions to Potsdam, the Spreewald, and Brandenburg, see **Brandenburg** (p. 135).

■ Wannsee

Most Berliners think of the town of Wannsee, on the lake of the same name, as the beach. Wannsee has long stretches of sand along Havelufer Promenade. To reach the lake, take the triangle bus from S-Bahn #1 or 7 to "Wannsee" or "Nikolassee" to "Strandbad Wannsee" (for the beach) or the end of Nikolskoer Weg (for the boats).

Unfortunately, the reputation of the charming village of Wannsee is indelibly tarnished by the memory of the notorious **Wannsee Conference** of January 20, 1942. Leading officials of the SS completed the details for the implementation of the "Final Solution" in the **Wannsee Villa,** Am Großen Wannsee 56, formerly a Gestapo Intelligence Center. In January 1992, the 50th anniversary of the Nazi death-pact, the villa reopened as the **Haus der Wannsee-Konferenz** (tel. 805 00 10), Zehlendorf, an excellent museum with permanent Holocaust exhibits and a documentary film series, as well as a look at the strange history of the villa itself. The villa is discomfitingly lovely, and its grounds offer a dazzling view of the Wannsee. (Open M-F 10am-6pm. Free. Tours and info in English.) Take bus #114 from the S-Bahn station to "Haus der Wannsee-Konferenz." Along the shores of the **Kleiner Wannsee,** the brilliant young author **Heinrich von Kleist** and a terminally ill companion committed suicide in 1811. Kleist's works gained acclaim only after his death.

From Wannsee, ferries also run to the **Pfaueninsel** (Peacock Island; DM10.50), where Friedrich the Great's successor Friedrich Wilhelm II built a *trompe l'oeil* "ruined" castle as a private pleasure house in which he and his mistress could play alone. A flock of the island's namesake fowl roams about the gardens surrounding the castle. From Wannsee, ferries also sail to Tegel, Charlottenburg's Schloßbrücke, Spandau, Potsdam, Werder, and Kladow. Contact **Stern und Kreisschiffahrt** (tel. 536 36 00) or visit them at the Wannsee waterfront near the S-Bahn station.

■ Tegel and Plötzensee

The forest and lake in Tegel are among the most serene in Berlin. You can swim, water-ski, or go boating on the lake (head down Alt Tegelstr.). The forest has been left mostly untouched, with *Wanderwege* (walking paths) to deserted parts of the woods. Take U-Bahn #6 to "Alt-Tegel" or S-Bahn #25 to "Tegel." From the U-Bahn, walk up Karolinenstr. or take buses #133 or 222 two stops to get into the heart of the forest.

An understated yet haunting monument to the victims of Nazism, the **Gedenkstätte Plötzensee** (Plötzensee Memorial; tel. 344 32 26), housed in the former execution chambers of the Third Reich, exhibits documents recording death sentences of "enemies of the people," including the officers who attempted to assassinate Hitler in

1944. (Open Mar.-Sept. daily 8:30am-6pm; Feb. and Oct. 8:30am-5:30pm; Nov. and Jan. 8:30am-4:30pm; Dec. 8:30am-4pm. Free.) More than 2500 people were murdered within these walls. Still visible are the hooks from which victims were hanged. The stone urn in front of the memorial contains soil from Nazi concentration camps. English literature is available at the office. Ride U-Bahn #9 to "Turmstr.," then bus #123 (direction: "Saatwinkler Damm") to "Gedenkstätte Plötzensee."

■ Treptow

The powerful **Sowjetisches Ehrenmal** (Soviet War Memorial) is a mammoth promenade built with marble taken from Hitler's Chancellery. Take S-Bahn #4, 6, 8, 9, or 10 to "Treptower Park." The Soviets dedicated the site in 1948, honoring the millions of Red Army soldiers who fell in what Russians today know as the "Great Patriotic War." Massive granite slabs along the walk are festooned with quotations from Stalin, leading up to colossal bronze figures in the Socialist Realist style, symbolically crushing Nazism underfoot. It's quite moving, despite the pomp. Buried beneath the trees surrounding the monument are the bodies of 5000 unknown Soviet soldiers who were killed during the Battle of Berlin in 1945. The memorial sits in the middle of **Treptower Park,** a spacious forest ideal for morbid picnics. Also in the park is the **Figurentheater,** Puschkinallee 15a, full of figures with wooden expressions on their faces who perform *Märchen* (fairy tales). The neighborhood adjoining the park is known for its pleasant waterside cafes.

■ Lichtenberg

In the suburb of Lichtenberg on Normannenstr. stands perhaps the most hated and feared building of the GDR regime—the headquarters of the East German secret police, the **Staatsicherheit** or **Stasi.** On January 15, 1990, a crowd of 100,000 Berliners stormed and vandalized the building to protest the continued existence of the police state. The building once contained six million individual dossiers on citizens of the GDR, a country of only 16 million people. Since a 1991 law returned the records to their subjects, the "Horror-Files" have rocked Germany, exposing informants—and wrecking careers, marriages, and friendships—at all levels of the political and cultural world. The exhibit displays the offices of Erich Mielke (the loathed Minister for State Security from 1957-1989), surveillance equipment employed by the *Stasi,* and loads of *Stasi* kitsch (including innumerable Lenin busts). The **Forschungs- und Gedenkstätte Normannenstraße,** Ruschestr. 103, Haus 1 (tel. 553 68 54), is the former *Stasi* building and the present day museum, memorial, and research center. (Open Tu-F 11am-6pm, Sa-Su 2-6pm. DM5, students DM3.) Take U-Bahn #5 to "Magdalenenstr." From the station's Ruschestr. exit, walk up Ruschestr., then take a right on Normannenstr.; it's Haus #1 in the complex of office buildings. The museum contains fascinating artifacts, but the history and anecdotes are only written in German. Lichtenberg suffers from severe unemployment and has become a somewhat **dangerous** haven for squatters. When visiting the memorial, be cautious among the remaining emblems of GDR misery. This warning goes for all of the eastern outer boroughs, where right-wing and other disaffected youths sometimes roam.

■ Near Berlin: Oranienburg and Sachsenhausen

The small town of Oranienburg, just north of Berlin, was home to **KZ Sachsenhausen,** a Nazi concentration camp in which more than 100,000 Jews, communists, intellectuals, gypsies, and homosexuals were killed between 1936 and 1945. The **Gedenkstätte Sachsenhausen,** Str. der Nationen 22, 16515 Oranienburg (tel. 80 37 15), was opened by the GDR in 1961. (Open Apr.-Sept. Tu-Su 8:30am-6pm; Oct.-Mar. Tu-Su 8:30am-4:30pm. Free.) Parts of the camp have been preserved in their original forms, including the cell block where particularly "dangerous" prisoners were kept in solitary confinement and tortured daily, and a pathology department where Nazis performed medical experiments on inmates both dead and alive. Only the foundations of Station Z (where prisoners were methodically exterminated) remain, but the windswept grounds convey the horrors that were committed here. A GDR slant is still apparent; the main museum building features Socialist Realist stained-glass windows memorializing "German Anti-Fascist Martyrs." The museums themselves, however, have been totally overhauled recently. The main one hosts special shows of Holocaust-related art, as well as a fascinating permanent textual exhibit (in English and German) on the history of anti-Semitic practices throughout the world. To get to Sachsenhausen, take S-Bahn #1 (direction: "Oranienburg") to the end (40min.). Follow the signs from the station (20min.). The **telephone code** is 03301.

Brandenburg

Surrounding Berlin on all sides, the *Land* of Brandenburg is overshadowed by the sprawling metropolis within it. It was from Brandenburg's forests that the infamous Hohenzollern family emerged to become the wealthy and powerful rulers of Prussia; the stunning palaces in Potsdam stand as reminders of that moment in Brandenburg's past. It is not solely the fancy castles and legacy of riches that attract folks to Brandenburg, but also the pastoral lakes, forests, and canals (yes—canals!) that surround them. The entire region is an easy commute from Berlin, allowing it to provide a soul-saving break from the overloaded circuits of the non-stop metropolis.

🖐 HIGHLIGHTS OF BRANDENBURG

- **Potsdam,** with **Schloß Sanssouci** as its crowning glory, stands as a royally beautiful contrast to the grit of nearby Berlin (see p. 132).
- The winding **canals** of the swampy **Spreewald** make for a sort of rural Venice, with locals using the slow-moving rivers as veritable streets. **Lübbenau** is an excellent base for exploring the woods and waterways (see p. 140).

■ Potsdam

Visitors disappointed by Berlin's distinctly unroyal demeanor can get their fix by taking the S-Bahn to nearby Potsdam, the glittering city of Friedrich II (the Great). While his dad, Friedrich Wilhelm I (a.k.a. "the Soldier King"), wanted to turn Potsdam into a huge garrison, the more eccentric Friedrich II beautified the city. Although most of downtown Potsdam was destroyed in a 20-minute air raid in April 1945, the castle-studded **Sanssouci Park** still stands as a monument to Fred II's (sometimes dubious) aesthetic taste. Potsdam was Germany's "Little Hollywood" from 1921 until WWII, as the suburb of Babelsberg became one of the capitals of the film industry. As the site of the 1945 conference during which the Allies divied up D-land, Potsdam's name became synonymous with Germany's defeat. After serving for 45 years as the home of Communist Party fat cats, the 1000-year-old city finally recovered a sense of dignity in 1991 when Brandenburgers restored its status as the *Land's* capital.

ORIENTATION AND PRACTICAL INFORMATION S-Bahn #7 runs from Berlin to Potsdam-Stadt (30min. from Bahnhof Zoo), which lies in zone C of the Berlin transit system. A BC day ticket is DM7.80; a single ticket in zone C is DM2.80. Potsdam is connected by **rail** to most of Brandenburg. **Bike rental** is available at **City Rad** (tel. 61 90 52), 100m from the Potsdam-Stadt station (May-Sept. M-F 9am-7pm, Sa-Su 9am-8pm; DM20 for 24hr., DM35 for 48hr.). The **tourist office,** Friedrich-Ebert-Str. 5 (tel. 27 55 80; fax 275 58 99), is between the streetcar stops "Alter Markt" and "Platz der Einheit"—all streetcars from the Potsdam-Stadt bus and train station go to one of the two stops. To get to the tourist office, go across the *Lange Brücke* (bridge) and make a right onto Friedrich-Ebert-Str. The office provides a usable city map (Potsdam is also on the more expensive Berlin "Extra" *Falk Plan*) and info on private accommodations, which they'll book for DM5. (Rooms DM20-40 per person. Private bungalows DM35-50 per person. For accommodations info, call 275 58 16. Open Apr.-Oct. M-F 9am-8pm, Sa 9am-6pm, Su 9am-4pm; Nov.-Mar. M-F 10am-6pm, Sa-Su 10am-2pm.) The staff sells public transportation tickets as well. The tourist office has a **branch office** at Brandenburger Str. 18 (tel. 275 58 88; fax 275 58 89), which focuses on ticket sales for concerts, festivals, plays, and other events in Potsdam and Berlin (open M-F 10am-7pm, Sa 10am-2pm).

The tourist office offers three-hour **bus tours** from the **Filmmuseum,** at Schloßstr. 1. (Tours leave Tu-Su at 11am; available in English; DM39 with admission to Sanssouci castle, DM25 without, students DM30.) **City Rad** (see above) offers three- to four-hour **bike tours** every Saturday (11:30am). Tours (DM15, not including bike rental)

Brandenburg and Berlin

can be conducted in English if you ask. The **post office,** 14476 Potsdam, is at Platz der Einheit (open M-F 9am-6pm, Sa 9am-noon). The **telephone code** is 0331.

ACCOMMODATIONS, CAMPING, AND FOOD Potsdam has no hostel— the closest is in Wannsee (see **Berlin,** p. 129), 10 minutes away by S-Bahn. Hotels are scarce, but the tourist office finds private rooms. It also offers a list of campgrounds in the Potsdam area. **Campingplatz Sanssouci/Galsberg,** An der Pirschheide 41 (tel. 556 80), is located on scenic Templiner lake. Take regional train #94 or 95 to "Bahnhof Pirschheide," and head down the lakeside road. (DM9.50 per person, DM3.90 per child; DM2.50-9.90 per tent. Bungalows available for DM45-70. Bike rentals and washing machines also available. Open Apr.-Oct.)

Bright, renovated Brandenburger Str., the local pedestrian zone, encompasses most of the city's restaurants, fast-food stands, and grocery shops—including a bakery that is open on Sunday. The cafes near Brandenburg Gate are lovely but pricey. Similarly, the **Holländisches Viertel** (see **Sights,** below) is lined with chic little cafes, where you can have a civilized afternoon glass of wine or coffee. Less civilized but cheaper is **Pizza Jungle,** Friedrich-Ebert-Str. 22 (tel. 270 12 87), around the corner from Mittelstr., which serves sandwiches for DM4.50, pizzas from DM5, and pasta from DM4. The merchants at the **flea market,** on Bassinplatz, include a number of farmers with fresh produce and fake Levi's (open M-F 9am-6pm). The **Wochenmarkt** takes place in the front yard of the Schloß Charlottenhof (M, W, and F 9am-6pm).

SIGHTS AND ENTERTAINMENT Friedrich the Great's bizarre and authoritarian personality is on display in every manicured square meter of the 600-acre **Sanssouci**

Park. Countless fountains and nude statues line the intersecting footpaths that convey tourists among the park's Baroque castles and exotic pavilions. The largest of the four royal castles, the 200-room **Neues Palais** (tel. 969 42 55), was built by Friedrich to demonstrate Prussia's power and, incidentally, to house his guests. *(Open Apr.-Oct. Su-Th 9am-5pm; Nov.-Mar. Su-Th 9am-4pm. DM6, students DM4, DM2 additional for a tour. A day ticket for DM20, students DM15, will get you into all the castles in Potsdam.)* Inside is the 19th-century **Grottensaal**, a reception room whose ribbed walls glitter with seashells, and the **Schloßtheater** (tel. 29 30 38), which has occasional summer performances of plays, ballets, and concerts. In a macabre reunification gesture, Fred's remains, spirited away in 1945 to a Hohenzollern estate near Tübingen to save them from the Red Army, were brought back to the grounds of Schloß Sanssouci in 1991.

At the other end of the park's long, long **Hauptallee** (central path) stands the main attraction, the Versailles-esque **Schloß Sanssouci** (tel. 969 41 90; streetcar #96 or 98), atop an incredible landscaped hill stair-stepped with garden terraces. *(Open Apr.-Oct. daily 9am-5pm; Feb.-Mar. 9am-4pm; Nov.-Jan. 9am-3pm. DM10, students DM5, or free with a day ticket.)* The orange-tinted palace is small and airy, but richly decorated with figures of Bacchus and other Greek gods; Fred used to go here to escape his wife and drown his sorrows (*sans souci* is French for "without cares"). Unfortunately, visits are not always carefree; reunification has made this truly beautiful sight accessible, and thousands of Western tourists and Hohenzollern groupies (also known as "Ho-hos") are making up for lost time. Tours of the castle in German (strictly limited to 40 people) leave every 20 minutes, but the final tour (5pm) usually sells out by 2pm during the high season. Come early. If you want an English-language tour, go on the one led by the tourist office, but note that it includes only the main *Schloß* (although you're free to wander around afterwards). Inside, the style is cloudlike French Rococo (Fred was an unrepentant Francophile until his dying day)—all pinks and greens with startlingly gaudy gold trim. A high point is the steamy, tropical **Voltairezimmer,** decorated with colorful, carved reliefs of parrots and tropical fruit. Voltaire never stayed at the palace, though; the room was only built in his honor. The library reveals another of Fred's eccentricities: whenever he wanted to read a book, he had five copies printed, one for each of his palaces—in French, of course. By the way, the **"ruins"** the castle overlooks are fake: Fred liked the look of ancient ruins, so he had these built in the style of what's left of the Roman Forum.

Next door is the **Bildergalerie** (tel. 969 41 81), whose brilliant collection of Caravaggio, van Dyck, and Rubens recently opened after extensive restoration with gorgeous results. *(Open mid-May to mid-Oct. Tu-Su 10am-noon and 12:30-5pm; closed 4th Wednesday of each month. DM4, students DM2, or free with a day ticket.)* On the other side of the Schloß Sanssouci are the **Neue Kammern** (royal guest chambers), which also served as a recital hall for the dilettante king. *(Open mid-May to mid-Oct. Sa-Th 10am-noon and 12:30-5pm; Apr. to mid-May and mid-Oct. to early-Nov. Sa-Su only 10am-5pm. DM5 with a tour, DM4 without, students DM2, or free with a day ticket.)* The former ball and festival rooms are lavishly decorated; check out the Hohenzollern porcelain collection in a huge gold-trimmed closet room. Romantic **Schloß Charlottenhof,** whose park surroundings were a Christmas gift from Friedrich Wilhelm III to Friedrich Wilhelm IV, melts into landscaped gardens and grape arbors at the south of the park. Nearby lie the **Römische Bäder** (Roman baths). Overlooking the park from the north, the pseudo-Italian **Orangerie-Schloß** is famous for its 67 dubious Raphael imitations— they replace originals swiped by Napoleon. *(Open mid-May to mid-Oct. 10am-12:30pm and 1-5pm. Closed 4th Thursday of every month. DM6, students DM3, or free with a day ticket.)* The most "exotic" of the park's pavilions is the gold-plated **Chinesisches Teehaus,** complete with a rooftop Buddha toting a parasol. *(DM2, or free with a day ticket.)*

Back in town, the **Brandenburger Tor,** a smaller, vanilla cousin of Berlin's, sits amid traffic flowing through Luisenplatz. From here, Brandenburger Str. leads down to the 19th-century **Kirche St. Peter und Paul,** Bassinpl. (tel. 280 49 42), Potsdam's only Catholic church (tram #92 or 95). One block before the church, Friedrich-Ebert-Str. heads left to the **Holländisches Viertel** (Dutch quarter) and its streets lined with red-brick Dutch-style houses. Now the most sought-after real estate in the city, Mittelstraße offers many quiet cafes. Toward the waterfront on Friedrich-Ebert-Str., the impressive dome of the **Nikolaikirche,** Am Alten Markt (tel. 270 86 02), rises above its neighbors. *(Open M 2-5pm, Tu-Sa 10am-5pm, Su 11:30am-5pm. Vesper music Su at 5pm.)* On closer inspection, the dome and the granite cube it sits on don't seem to match. The interior was renovated a la GDR with glass and sound-tiles that somehow lessen the aesthetic impact. Down Friedrich-Ebert-Str. toward the bridge, the **Filmmuseum,** Breite Str./Schloßstr. (tel. 27 18 10), housed in an old Orangerie (which also served as Freddie's stables), documents Babelsberg's glory days as a film mecca with artifacts like Marlene Dietrich's costumes and a silent film archive. *(Open Tu-Su 10am-6pm. DM4, students DM2. Movies M-F from 2pm, Sa-Su from 3pm. DM7, students DM5.)*

Potsdam's second park, the **Neuer Garten,** nuzzling the Heiligersee, contains several royal residences. The most worthwhile is **Schloß Cecilienhof** (tel. 969 42 44), built in the image of an English country manor. *(Open Tu-Su 9am-noon and 12:30-5pm. DM8 with a tour, DM6 without, students DM4.)* Exhibits document the **Potsdam Treaty,** signed at the palace in 1945. Visitors can see the tacky rooms in which the Allied delegates stayed. Ride Bus #694 to "Cecilienhof," or streetcar #96 to "Platz der Einheit," then streetcar #95 to "Alleestr."

In the beginning of the 19th century, General Yorck brought 500 Russian soldiers to Prussia, and Friedrich Wilhelm III, a great fan of Russian culture, discovered that many of them had singing talent. Unfortunately, by the 1820s, only 12 of the original group were left—the rest died of homesickness. To make up for the depressing atmosphere, Fred III built each soldier an ornate wooden house. The nearby onion-domed **Kapelle Alexander Newski,** designed by Schinkel, was also intended as compensation. To the northeast, the crumbling villas of the Berliner Vorstadt were luxury homes for politicos during the heyday of the GDR. Berliner Str. leads through here to the **Glienicker Brücke** (a.k.a. "The James Bond Bridge"), which used to be swallowed up by the "no man's land" between the GDR and West Berlin. Until 1989, it was used for the exchange of spies. Take streetcar #93-95 to "Burgstr."

Back in the Golden Age of European cinema, the **UFA Fabrik** in nearby Babelsberg was *the* German studio, giving Marlene Dietrich, Hans Alberg, and Leni Riefenstahl their first big breaks; in addition, Fritz Lang made *Metropolis* there. Tragically, apart from the films, few memorials of this era remain. The Disneylandish **Filmstadt Babelsberg,** August-Bebel-Str. 26-52 (tel. 721 27 50), built on the UFA lot, makes a feeble attempt to commemorate the greats of early German cinema, dishing out family fun of the worst sort in the form of video arcades and gift shops. *(Open Apr.-Nov. daily 10am-6pm. DM25, students DM18.)* Hop on S-Bahn #3 or 7 to "Babelsberg," then take bus #690 or 692 to "Ahornstr."

▨ Brandenburg

One-thousand-year-old Brandenburg has long been a reluctant wielder of power; even when it was capital of the province to which it lends its name, it allowed Berlin civic freedom. When Albrecht the Bear ("Grrr...") built the town's cathedral in 1165, the surrounding city became the region's political epicenter. The city's industry took off during the 19th century, when the Brennabor bicycle factory and the Lehmann toy factory first began churning out their wares. Today, Potsdam has officially usurped Brandenburg's political limelight, leaving the town to fade gently into obscurity. Reconstruction of the decaying buildings is proceeding slowly, and the winding cobblestone streets are wistfully quiet.

Brandenburg is surrounded by lush greenery and water. The river Havel, dotted with rowboats, flows gently by the **Dom St. Peter und Paul,** Burghof 11 (tel. 20 03 25), begun in Romanesque style in 1165, completed in Gothic style, and currently being refashioned in late-20th-century-construction-site style, with red bricks swaddled in blue plastic, and hairy construction workers temporarily replacing the removed gargoyles. Before this major overhaul, architect Friedrich Schinkel couldn't resist adding a few touches: the "Schinkel-Rosette" and the window over the entrance. The cathedral's many wings fold off from the center into darkness, ending in little rooms like the 1235 **Bunte Kapelle** (the name means "colorful chapel"). The **Dommuseum** inside displays an array of relics and local-history treasures (open Tu-Sa 10am–4pm, Su noon–4pm; DM3, students DM2). To get to the *Dom* from Neustädter Markt, walk down Neustädtische Fischerstr. for 10min., or take bus A or B to "Domlinden." Back on Neustädter Markt, the **St. Katharinenkirche**, built at the end of the 14th century, is a beautiful example of *Backstein* (glazed brick) Gothic. The carved altar dates back to 1474 (open daily 9:30am–5pm). Both churches offer cultural events: St. Katharinen schedules organ concerts (July and August, Mondays at 7:30pm), and the *Dom* hosts theater in the *Petrikloster* during the summer months. For 500 years, a 6m statue of the legendary hero Roland has stood in front of the **Rathaus**—the GDR-era was just a ripple in time to this medieval symbol of free commerce. Several remaining towers from the 12th-century city walls add historic flavor to the *Altstadt* and the streets around **Neustädter Markt**. Incidentally, *Neustadt* (new town) is a relative term—it was founded in 1196.

Two routes run to Brandenburg from Berlin: you can either hop on trains heading toward Magdeburg and Hannover, or take S-Bahn #3 or 7 to "Potsdam-Stadt," then change to the RB #33 (40min.; DM14 round-trip). The **tourist office**, Hauptstr. 51 (tel. 194 33; fax 22 37 43), is just off Neustädter Markt. To get there from the train station, walk along Große Gartenstr., follow it until it turns into Steinstr., and head left on Hauptstr. Or take streetcar #1, 2, or 9 from the station to "Neustädter Markt." The immensely helpful staff will answer questions and book rooms free of charge. Private rooms run DM30 for singles, DM40 for doubles. The office also supplies cultural and historical information and distributes free maps and brochures in English. (Open M-W and F 9am-7pm, Th 9am-8:30pm, Sa 10am-2pm.) The **telephone code** is 03381.

The **Jugendherberge "Walter Husemann" (HI)**, Hevellerstr. 7 (tel./fax 52 10 40), sits on a tiny island right across from the *Dom's* Domlinden entrance. Bus B also stops near here—get off at "Domlinden," and keep walking for a few blocks. The rustic lakeside locale and old volleyball nets in back transcend backwaterhood; this is charm, *Ossie* style. When the hostel is booked, they've been known to provide overflow housing in tents outside for DM12 per night. (DM18, over 26 DM22. Members only. Breakfast included. Reception 7-9am and 5-7pm. Curfew 10pm, but you can get a key. No English spoken.) **Campingplatz Malge** (tel. 66 31 34) is in the middle of the woods, but only 20 minutes away from the city center. Take Bus B from Neustädter Markt; ask the driver to let you off at the campground. You can rent boats to fish in the nearby lake. (DM6.50 per person. DM6-10 per tent. 2-person bungalows DM30. Showers included. Fishing permits from campground reception or tourist office. Reception 9am-8pm. Open Apr.-Oct.) Inexpensive **restaurants** line the pedestrian area of Hauptstr., which also features a **Spar supermarket**, Hauptstr. 39 (open M-F 8am-6pm, Sa 7-11am), and an open-air **farmers' market** (open daily 8am-6pm) behind the St. Katharinen Church. Delicious, starchy meals await at the appetizingly named **Kartoffel Käfer** (potato beetle), Steinstr. 56 (tel. 22 41 18). It's a short walk from Neustädter Markt, or take bus #9 to "Steinstr./Kino." Substantial meals cost about DM8; *very* substantial meals run DM10-18.

■ Frankfurt an der Oder

When writer **Heinrich von Kleist** was born here in 1777, Frankfurt an der Oder was a sleepy locale—even Kleist couldn't wait to skip town for the greater excitement of Dresden, Paris, and, ultimately, Berlin. Established in 1226 by merchants who found the location on the Oder ideal for trade with Poland and Northern Germany, Frankfurt remained a trading post until the **Universität Viadrina** was established in 1506. The university moved to Wroclaw (Breslau), Poland in 1811, allowing Frankfurt to become a garrison town in the 19th century; consequently, the city was flattened in WWII. After the big sleep of the Communist era, the feeling here is not as much of a town *re*-building as of one building for the first time. In 1991, the Viadrina University returned, quickly coming to represent the youthful energy now surrounding "Frankfurt/O." As Poland becomes an increasingly important trading partner for Germany and the West, Frankfurt an der Oder promises to be a vibrant city in years to come.

ORIENTATION AND PRACTICAL INFORMATION Frankfurt an der Oder is less than an hour from Berlin by frequent **trains.** The city has an extensive and newly revamped public transportation system, but tickets (DM2.20) are only for sale at the SVF houses on the corner of Heilbronner Str. and Karl-Marx-Str., and in front of the *Bahnhof.* The **tourist office,** on the main drag at Karl-Marx-Str. 8a (tel. 32 52 16; fax 225 65), provides maps and information about sights within Frankfurt and the surrounding countryside. From the station, head down the curving Bahnhofstr. and go right at the next major intersection onto Heilbronner Str. A block later, turn left on Karl-Marx-Str. and the office is on the right (15min.). The staff finds private rooms (from DM30 with breakfast) for a fee of DM5 per person and gives out free lists of *Pensionen* and *Privatzimmer.* (Open M-F 10am-noon and 12:30-6pm, Sa 10am-12:30pm; June-Sept. also open on Su 10am-noon.) **Tours** leave from the *Rathaus* on Saturday at 11am (DM5). There is a 24-hour **ATM** in the train station. The main **post office,** 15230 Frankfurt an der Oder, is in a beautiful red brick building on the far right side of Heilbronner Str., at the intersection of Lindenstr. and Logenstr. (open M-F 8am-6pm, Sa 8am-noon). The **telephone code** is 0335.

ACCOMMODATIONS Budget accommodations in Frankfurt an der Oder are sparse and in a state of flux. A *Privatzimmer,* booked through the tourist office, is probably the best option (DM25-45). Otherwise, **Gästehaus Kliestow,** Lebuser Str. 5 (tel. 622 81), provides sufficient and reasonably priced accommodations. Take bus #938 (every 20min.) from the train station to "Kliestow-Mitte," and then continue along in the direction of the bus for five minutes. (Singles DM38, with shower DM55; doubles DM76, with shower DM90. Call ahead.) The **Freizeit- und Campingpark Helenesee** (tel. 55 66 60; fax 556 66 77) provides accommodations and entertainment. Enjoy beaches, boats, and lakeside hiking trails. (Entry for the day DM3, kids and students DM2. Camping DM6 per person, DM4 per student or child; DM6-9 per tent; DM3 per car. Bungalows for four people DM65-75, depending on location and time of year.)

FOOD Aside from the many outdoor food markets and stands, the **Studentenpassage** in the Schmalzgasse, one block down from the tourist office on Karl-Marx-Str., serves good, cheap meals for under DM6 (open M-F 8am-6:30pm, Sa 8am-1pm). Try **Pizzeria Roma,** Lindenstr. 4 (tel. 32 52 59), for Italian fare (DM6-14) in an outdoor sculpture garden (open M-F 9am-11pm, Sa 5-11pm). Afterwards stroll in the cool galleries of the **Haus der Künste,** a Neoclassical building erected in 1787. The **Brunnencafé,** at the corner of Heilbronner Str. and Karl-Marx-Str., serves tasty breakfasts until late in the day (DM5-9.50), and impressive ice cream concoctions (DM8-9). Pack for a picnic on the Oder at **Rewe** supermarket (tel. 404 21), at Johann-Eichorn-Str. and Spartakusring (open M-F 8am-6:30pm, Sa 8am-1pm). Take streetcar #1, 5, 6, or 7 to "Johann-Eichorn-Str." Way cooler, and somewhat cheaper is to cross the bridge from Rosa-Luxemburg-Str. and do lunch in Slubice, Poland (passport required). Given that Slubice's economy seems to be based solely on the sale of **cheap cigarettes** (under DM2 per pack), selling food is a low priority, but there are a few cafes on Robotniczejstr. Most restaurants and stores accept both *Marks* and *Zloty,* but for better prices, convert Marks into Zloty at the exchange stands *(kontor)* on the Polish side.

Eine Straße mit Pommes, bitte!

If ever proof was needed that capitalism has taken over the new *Bundesländer,* the formerly sleepy little town of Blumberg, in Brandenburg, provides it. In an attempt to balance its budget, Blumberg cast its civic pride aside and decided to sell its street names to companies. One of the first takers was none other than the indomitable McDonald's, and other companies are due to follow. It has not been reported whether the renowned burger joint has put in a bid for the large arch in the center of Berlin—Branden*burger* Tor—but in Freiburg (see p. 448), a set of golden arches already graces an old city gate.

BRANDENBURG

SIGHTS Most historical sights in Frankfurt an der Oder are conveniently located within a few blocks of the main Marktplatz. From Karl-Marx-Str. one can easily see the beautiful but scarred **Marienkirche.** Built from 1253 to 1524, the *Marienkirche* was an enormous and spectacular Gothic cathedral that suffered serious damage in WWII. Unfortunately, the deteriorated cathedral is now closed indefinitely while undergoing renovations. If you *really* want to go in, the tourist office can make arrangements.

Brilliant author **Heinrich von Kleist** is the town's claim to fame. After participating in campaigns against the French from 1793 to 1795, he quit the army in 1799, citing the inequality of conditions between officers and enlisted men. Rejecting his noble birthright, he lived as a pauper, writing plays and short stories (the most famous are his novellas *Michael Kohlhaas* and *Die Marquise von O*). Kleist wrote famously complex prose describing bourgeois society with irony and sympathy. Although his works did not find an audience during his lifetime—his scathing eye may have been too much for contemporaries to take—they are now considered classics of German literature. Penniless and dissatisfied, Kleist and a terminally ill friend committed suicide on the shore of the Kleiner Wannsee in Berlin in 1811.

Kleist's birthplace was destroyed during WWII—all that remains is a plaque on an ugly GDR-era apartment block on Große Oderstr., opposite the *Marienkirche.* The **Kleistmuseum,** on Faberstr. 7 (tel. 53 11 55), at the end of Bischofstr., is housed in a small blue building whose three floors feature facts and documents about the Kleist family as well as manuscripts, but very little about Kleist himself. *(Open Tu and Th-Su 10am-5pm, W 10am-8pm. DM4, students DM3. Audio tours in English DM2.)* It's understandable that the museum should be so spare in personal information—when Kleist died, his only possession was a backpack which was sold to pay his debts.

The 13th-century **Rathaus** is a splendid and well-restored brick building with white icing. It houses the permanent exhibition of the **Museum Junge Kunst,** Marktpl. 1, a collection of temporary paintings and sculpture with a focus on modern East German art. *(Open Tu-Su 11am-5pm. DM3, students DM2.)* The **temporary exhibitions** are housed in a gallery at Heilbronner Str. 19. *(Same hours. DM2, students DM1.)*

SPREEWALD (SPREE FOREST)

The Spree River splits apart about 100km southeast of Berlin and branches out over the countryside in an intricate maze of streams, canals, meadows, lakes, and primeval forests stretching over 1000 square kilometers. This is the home of the legendary **Irrlichter,** a sort of German leprechaun who lights the waterways for travelers who lose their way and leads those who refuse to pay to their deaths. Smart travelers now outwit the Irrlichter by warding him off with bright yellow travel guides.

Folklore, tradition, and wildlife have survived here with remarkable harmony in tiny villages and towns first settled in the Middle Ages. Hire a barge, rent a paddle boat, or take to the trails by foot or bicycle to see why locals insist that the Spreewald—not Amsterdam, Stockholm, or St. Petersburg—is the true "Venice of the North." Although the Spreewald lacks the urbanity of its Italian cousin, its canals are in just as constant use: farmers row to their fields and noisy children paddle home from school. The fields and forests teem with owls, kingfishers, otters, and foxes, animals known to most Europeans only through textbooks or television documentaries. In a country infamous for pollution and development, the Spreewald is idyllic.

The region was hit hard by history; the Prussian kings cut down the trees to make furniture, and GDR-era industrial pollution wrought havoc here. However, reunification has brought the mixed blessing of greater environmental protection and hordes of forest-trampling tourists. The Spreewald is now recognized as a *Biosphärreservat* (a biosphere nature reserve) by the U.N. Some sections of the forest are closed to the public; other sections are closed during mating and breeding seasons, but not tourist season. **Guided tours** are offered by reservation, camping spots abound, bicycles can be rented everywhere, and excellent hiking trails and footpaths weave their way through the peaceful forest. Each local tourist office has information on these leisure activities. They won't let you forget, however, that the forest is protected by the government; tourists are urged to be environmentally responsible.

Lübben and Lübbenau, two tiny towns that open up into the labyrinths of canals that snake through the forest, are the most popular tourist destinations and lie within daytrip range of Berlin. Cottbus, close to the Polish border, a bit farther east, offers genuine Sorb culture. The Sorbs, Germany's native Slavic minority, originally settled the Spreewald region (see The Absorbing Sorbs, p. 159), though their presence is not so visible today. If your German is shaky, the Berlin-based Spreewaldbüro, Zwinglistr. 5a (tel. (030) 392 30 22), is your best source of regional information. They speak English and will reserve private rooms. (Open M-F 9am-6pm.) Advance reservations are recommended during the summer. Take U-Bahn #9 to "Turmstr."

■ Lübben

A good base for Spreewald excursions, Lübben is about an hour southeast of Berlin by train or by the Berlin-Cottbus *Autobahn*. The harbor is watched over by the ancient Schloßturm (castle tower), built in the 15th century by the Brandenburg Prince Friedrich II as an imposing defense against invaders. Even WWII, which destroyed 80% of the Altstadt, could not topple the tower.

The *Altstadt's* architectural pride is the newly restored Paul Gerhardt Kirche, named for the most famous German hymn writer since Martin Luther. (Open May-Aug. W 10am-noon and 3-5pm.) Gerhardt is buried inside. The entrance to Lübben's lush green park, Der Hain, is at the end of Breite Str. Near Lübben stands Straupitz, an otherwise forgotten village where Neoclassical architect Karl Friedrich Schinkel erected a strikingly unusual church. Straupitz is accessible by barge or bus.

The Fährmannsverein Lübben/Spreewald, Ernst-von-Houwald-Damm 16 (tel. 71 22), offers boat trips exploring different regions of the Spreewald (open daily 9am-4pm; 1½-8hr., DM4-5 per hr.). Trips depart from the Strandcafé Lübben after 9am; the boats leave when full. Make a left out of the tourist office, and it will be on your left. The Fährmannsverein "Flottes Rudel," Eisenbahnstr. 3 (tel. 82 69), offers boat and barge trips with picnics, starting daily at 9am. Alternatively, rent a boat at Bootsverleih Gebauer (tel. 71 94) on Lindenstr. From the tourist office, go straight and turn right just before you reach the bridge. (Boat rentals from DM7 per hr. per person. Everyone must know how to swim. Lifejackets provided for kids. ID required. Open daily Apr.-Sept. 9am-7pm; Oct.-Mar. 10am-7pm.)

Bike rental is available at the station for DM10 per day (open daily 7am-9pm) or at the Spreewaldinformation office (DM1.50 per hr., DM10 per day, ID deposit required). For a taxi, call 37 16. The office of Spreewaldinformation, Ernst-von-Houwald-Damm 14 (tel. 30 90; fax 25 43) spreads Spreewald love. From the train station, head right on Bahnhofstr., then make a left on Luckauer Str., cross the two bridges, and you'll be on Ernst-von-Houwald Damm. The office is on your right, next door to the castle tower. The staff finds rooms for a DM5 fee. The office charges DM2.50 for a good map, but it's worth avoiding a mapless meander through town. During winter months and after hours, the office posts a list of private rooms just outside the entrance. (Office open M-F 10am-6pm, Sa 10am-4pm, Su 10am-1pm.) The post office waits at Poststr. 4, 15907 Lübben. The telephone code is 03546.

The Jugendherberge Lübben (HI), Zum Wendenfürsten 8 (tel./fax 30 46), is located in the middle of a wheat field on the outskirts of town. Although in the middle of nowhere, the hostel itself is a dream, with cozy 10-bed rooms, nightly entertainment in the form of watching cows stumble into electric fences, and a hip regular crowd of sharply dressed *Schulmädchen*. To get there, turn right off Bahnhofstr. until the end of Luckauer Str., then veer right and take a left onto Eisenbahnstr., cross Pushkinstr., and follow Dorfstr. (DM20, over 26 DM25. Sheets DM6. Reception 9am-7pm. No curfew—not that it really matters.) It takes a good 30 minutes to reach Spreewald-Camping Lübben (tel. 70 53; fax 18 18 15). From the station, turn right on Bahnhofstr., left on Luckauer Str., right on Burgtehnstr., and continue along the footpath to the campground. (DM6 per person; DM5-8 per tent. 4-person cabins

DM30. Reception 7am-10pm. Open mid-Mar. to Oct.) While you're in Lübben, sample the Spreewald's particular pickled delicacies, famous throughout Germany. The **Gurken Paule,** Ernst-von-Houwald-Damm-Str. (tel. 89 81), is an outdoor stand offering the freshest of the Spreewald's unique *Gurken* (cucumber) assortment (*Salzdillgurken*—salty, *Senfgurken*—mustard, *Gewürzgurken*—spicy). Pay around DM0.30 per pickle, or DM5 for a jar. (Open daily 9am-6pm.)

■ Lübbenau

Tiny Lübbenau is the most famous and perhaps the most idyllic of the Spreewald towns. For many tourists (and there are tons), the village serves as a springboard for trips into the **Oberspreewald.** Winding streets of the town center open directly onto the wooded paths and villages of the upper forest. The landscape here is much denser than that above Lübben, and it is intricately interwoven with canals.

PRACTICAL INFORMATION Lübbenau lies 13km past Lübben on the Berlin-Cottbus line. For a **taxi,** call 31 43. **Kowalski,** Poststr. 6 (tel. 28 35), near the station, rents **bikes** (DM10 per day; open M-Sa 9am-6pm). You can rent your own **paddle boat** at **Manfred Franke,** Dammstr. 72 (tel. 27 22; DM3-6 per hr.). To get there from the station, turn right down Bahnhofstr. and left at the next intersection (open Apr.-Oct. daily 8am-7pm). The **tourist office,** Ehm-Welk-Str. 15 (tel. 36 68; fax 467 70), left of the church, provides maps, gives info on bike trails, and finds rooms (DM25-45; open M-F 9am-4pm). In an **emergency,** call 81 91 or 22 22. The **telephone code** is 03542.

ACCOMMODATIONS AND FOOD Even though the closest hostel is in Lübben (10min. by train), finding a room isn't a problem in friendly Lübbenau. Check for *Zimmer frei* signs or knock on the door of **Zimmervermietung-Haus Jerkel,** Max-Plessner-Str. 22 (tel. 436 96), just 10 minutes from the station. Take Poststr. straight, then right on Max-Plessner-Str. The Jerkels offer 14 comfortable beds in their white stone house. They often have same-day rooms, but call ahead. (Doubles DM62, with full bath DM72. Breakfast included.) There are two camping options: directly on the road to Lehde, **Campingplatz "Am Schloßpark"** (tel./fax 35 33) offers 300 plots for tents (DM5-8 per night) with cooking and shower installations on site (DM1-3) and a store with soap, soup, pickles, and other necessities. (DM7 per adult, DM3.50 per child. Bungalows DM55 for up to 4 people, DM14 for trailer spots. Bike rentals DM10 per day, boat rentals DM25 per day. Reception 7am-10pm. Open May-Oct. and sporadically in winter—call ahead.)

For cheap food and pickles, beets, and beans by the barrel, check out the snack bars and stands along the harbor. Toward the campgrounds, the **Café-Garten,** on the Lehde stream (tel. 36 22), is a self-service outdoor cafe with potato salad (DM2.50) or pike filet (DM9.80; open daily 9am-10pm). In town, **Spreewald Idyll,** Spreestr. 13 (tel. 22 51), serves Spreewald specialties (DM7.90-22.80) and salads (DM4-10).

SIGHTS The *Altstadt* is a 10-minute trot from the station. Go straight on Poststr. until you come to the marketplace dominated by the Baroque **Church of St. Nikolai.** *(Open M-F 2-4pm.)* The carved stone pillar in front served as an 18th-century crossroads post marking the distance in *Stunden,* an antique measurement equalling one hour's walk (circa 4.5km). The requisite **Schloß** is now a handsome (but terrifically expensive) hotel and restaurant. The lush castle grounds *(Schloßbezirk)* are open to the public and shelter the **Spreewaldmuseum Lübbenau,** which offers a fascinating overview of Spreewald development and its unique customs. *(Open Apr. to mid-Sept. Tu-Su 10am-6pm; mid.-Sept. to Oct. 10am-5pm. DM3, students DM2.)*

There are two main departure points for **gondola tours** of the forest: the **Großer Hafen** (big harbor) and the **Kleiner Hafen** (little harbor). Follow the signs either from the town center or from the train station. The Großer Hafen offers a larger variety of tours, including two- and three-hour trips to Lehde (DM8.50-10, children half-price). Longer trips (4-8hr.) cost around DM5 per hour; for the same price, you can design your own tour. The boats take on customers starting at 9 or 10am and depart when full, continuing throughout the day (2-7hr.; DM8-14; no English tours, but hilarious if you speak German and can decipher the dialect). From the Kleiner Hafen, at the end of Spreewaldstr., tours leave daily from 9am on and last 1½ to 10 hours. Also at the Kleiner Hafen, a beautiful leafy path begins just over the wooden bridge. **Genossenschaft der Kahnfährleute,** Dammstr. (tel. 22 25), is the biggest boat tour company. *(Open Apr.-Oct. daily 9am-6pm.)* Round-trips to Lehde last three hours and cost DM9 (children DM4.50). A nine-hour tour of the forest costs DM17 (children DM7).

■ Lehde

It's only a hop and a paddle from Lübbenau to **Lehde,** a UNESCO-protected landmark and the most romantic village of the Spreewald, accessible only by foot, bike, or boat. You can drive to the Lehde outskirts, but cars (except those owned by residents) are banned in the village. By foot, it's a 15-minute trek; follow the signs from the Großerhafen. If you're partial to water, take a boat from the harbor. Most farmers here still depend on the canals for access to the world. Check out the **Freilandmuseum Lehde,** where things remain as they were when entire Spreewalder families slept in the same room and newlyweds spent their honeymoons heaving in the hay (open Apr.-Oct. daily 10am-6pm. DM6, students and seniors DM4).

Because Lehde is extremely protective of its landmark status, few guest beds are offered, but a few *Pensionen* cower on the outskirts. Don't expect to stay in Lehde overnight, but if you really want to, talk to the Lübbenau tourist office. Just before you reach the bridge to the museum, you'll see **Zum Fröhlichen Hecht,** Dorfstr. 1 (tel. 27 82), a large cafe, restaurant, and *Biergarten.* Sit upstairs on the wooden benches for a view of the languidly passing boats. Try *Kartoffeln mit Quark* (potatoes with sour curd cheese) in a special Spreewald sauce (DM7) or pickles with a side order of *Schmalz* (lard; DM3), another Spreewald "specialty." Say a prayer for your heart, and dig in. (Open daily 10am-5pm.) The **telephone code** is 03542.

■ Cottbus (Chosebuz)

The second-largest city in Brandenburg, Cottbus dwells in **Niederlausitz** (Lower Lusatia) on the southernmost edge of the Spreewald. Cottbus lacks the small town charm of its neighboring Spreewald villages, but it also falls short (way short) of being a metropolis. The result is a mediocre city with lots of malls and sports bars. However, one interesting feature is that Cottbus's substantial Sorb population is more visible than in other Sorb locales. All street signs are printed in both Sorbian and German, several local Sorbian newspapers and radio stations flourish, and the study of Sorbian is growing popular in local schools.

ORIENTATION AND PRACTICAL INFORMATION Direct trains to Berlin (2hr.) and bus lines to nearby hamlets make Cottbus the nexus for Spreewald tours. The bus station is a 15-minute walk from the train station. Make a left out of the train station, head up the stairs, and make a right onto Bahnhofstr., and then a left onto Marienstr. Or take streetcar #1 from the train station to "Marienstr." (two stops, DM1.30); the bus station is on the right. The **tourist office,** Karl-Marx-Str. 68 (tel. 242 54; fax 79 19 31), like many things in the town, is situated in a mall. They'll find rooms for a DM5 fee, or they'll give you a free list of them. To get there, make a left out of the train station, head up the stairs and turn left over the bridge; follow Bahnhofstr. until it becomes Karl-Marx-Str. at the intersection of Berliner Str. (Open May-Sept. M-F 9am-6pm, Sa-Su 9am-1pm; Oct.-Apr. M-F 9am-6pm, Sa-Su 9:30am-12:30pm.) **Schenker,** Friedrich-Ebert Str. 15 (tel. 330 95), rents **bikes** from DM5 (open M-F 9am-6pm, Sa 9am-noon). The **telephone code** is 0355.

ACCOMMODATIONS Cottbus's youth hostel is conveniently located near the Klosterkirche. From the "Stadthalle" tram stop, head up Berliner Str. toward the *Altstadt,* take a left on Wendestr., and go around the church. **Jugendherberge am Klosterplatz,** Klosterpl. 3 (tel. 225 58; fax 237 98), has clean and modern three- to 10-

BRANDENBURG

bed rooms. (DM20, over 26 DM25. Non-members DM26.50. Breakfast included. Reception M-F 8am-1pm and 7-9pm.) The **Pension** next door, at Klosterpl. 2-3 (tel. 225 58; fax 237 98), is in a historic building embedded in the town wall. (Singles DM50-90; doubles DM85, with shower DM85-130. Breakfast included.)

FOOD The **Wendesches Café,** August-Bebel-Str. 82 (tel. 253 27) serves Sorbian specialties (open M-F 1:30-midnight, Sa-Su 2:30pm-midnight). Romantic atmosphere and a beer await at **Café Altmarkt,** Altmarkt 10 (tel. 310 36; cafe open daily 9am-1am). On the other side of town, **Café Baum,** Marienstr. 6 (tel. 311 20), to the right of the bus station, serves all four food groups: coffee, wine, beer, and ice cream (open M-F, Su 9am-midnight, Sa noon-2pm).

SIGHTS AND ENTERTAINMENT Cottbus, like most East German cities, was severely scarred by WWII. But GDR tract housing has not penetrated the *Altstadt,* which is liberally sprinkled with historic buildings. Heading down Berliner Str., the church on the left is the **Klosterkirche** (tel. 248 25), also known as *Wendische Kirche* (*"Wendisch"* is German for Sorbian). *(Open W and F 10:30am-4:30pm, Sa 10:30am-3:30pm.)* Built in 1300 by Franciscan monks, it is the oldest church in Cottbus. The **Altmarkt** lies a bit farther down Berliner Str. The **Niederlausitzer Apotheke,** Berliner Str. 21 (tel. 239 97), first started dealing drugs in 1573. *(Store open Tu-F 10am-5pm. Obligatory tours Tu-F 11am and 2pm, Sa-Su 2 and 3pm or by appointment. DM4, students DM2.)* The shop still sells herbal teas and other potions, but the back offers a museum with a poison chamber. At the eastern end of the Altmarkt, Sandower Str. leads to the **Oberkirche St. Nikolai,** the largest church in the Niederlausitz and home to frequent concerts by regional orchestras. *(Open M-Sa 10am-5pm, Su 1-5pm. Tickets DM12, students DM6.)* Sorbian culture buffs can head to the **Wendisches Museum** (Sorbian museum), Mühlenstr. 12 (tel. 79 49 30), down Spremburger Str., which houses Sorbian folk art and costumes, including the distinctive headdress. *(Open Tu-F 8:30am-5pm, Sa-Su 2-6pm. DM2, students DM1.)* For more on the Sorbs, see **The Absorbing Sorbs,** p. 159.

Farther down Spremburger Str. lies the strangely named petite **Schloßkirche.** The Huguenots who rebuilt it had no delusions of grandeur. At the end of the street, the *Altstadt* transmogrifies into the *Neustadt.* The 1908 cherub-sprinkled **Staatstheater Cottbus,** Karl-Liebknecht-Str. 23 (tel. 782 41 40), is Europe's only extant example of late-*Jugendstil* architecture. The program includes works by Verdi, Goethe, and Brecht; call 237 61 for tickets. *(Ticket office open Tu-F 10am-6pm, Sa 10am-noon.)* While the inner city is somewhat congested, Cottbus is surrounded by a beautiful landscape. The riverside panorama leads to **Schloß Branitz** (tel. 75 15 21), a Baroque castle built in 1772 by Prince Hermann von Pückler-Muskau, a globetrotter with a love of larger-than-life architecture. *(Open Apr.-Oct. daily 10am-noon and 12:30-6pm; Nov.-Mar. Tu-Su 10am-noon and 12:30-5pm.)* From the *Altstadt,* follow Spremburger Str. to Str.-der-Jugend, bear left at Bautzener Str., turn left at Stadtring, and right at Gustav-Hermann-Str., which leads you to the park. **Branitzer Park,** which surrounds the castle, is peppered with oddities. The landscape in the western park includes several pyramids which will forever bear witness to Pückler-Muskau's Egyptophilia. One appears to float in the center of the lake.

BRANDENBURG

Sachsen (Saxony)

Sachsen is known to foreigners primarily for Leipzig and Dresden, the most fabled cities of Eastern Germany after Berlin, but the entire region provides a fascinating historical stratification that reveals a great deal about life in the former East. The castles around Dresden attest to the bombastic history of Sachsen's prince-electors, while the socialist monuments of Chemnitz and the formless architecture of other major cities depict the colorless world of the GDR. On the eastern edge of Sachsen, Sächsische Schweiz and the Zittauer Gebirge provide a respite from the aesthetic violence done by East Germany's city planners with hiking trails that march through a land of escapism to the borders of the Czech Republic and Poland.

🐝 HIGHLIGHTS OF SACHSEN

- Sometimes called the Florence on the Elbe, **Dresden** is a bumpin' metropolis with strokes of beautiful architecture, a superb nightlife, and a hygiene museum—yes, a **hygiene museum** (see p. 144).
- **Leipzig** fostered East Germany's biggest demonstrations in 1989. Today it harbors an edgy *Uni*-culture scene and one of Europe's grandest old train stations (see p. 169).
- Climbing, hiking, and skiing abound in the several **mountainous regions** of Sachsen: the **Sächsische Schweiz** (see p. 155), the **Erzgebirge** (see p. 165), and the **Vogtland** near Plauen (see p. 167).

Sachsen (Saxony)

SACHSEN

143

■ Dresden

Dresden pulses with a historical intensity that is both vicious and sublime. The city was the cultural capital of pre-war Germany, overseeing many key movements in European history, from the meetings of Goethe, Schiller, and Beethoven in Gottfried Körner's estate to the modern impulses of the 1920s, reflected in the architecture of the Hygiene Museum. Sadly, no matter where you go, you will not be able to forget the Allied bombings of February 1945, which claimed over 50,000 lives and destroyed 75% of the *Altstadt*. Warming up to the efforts of reunification, Dresden today entrances visitors with spectacular ruins amidst an array of world-class museums and partially reconstructed palaces and churches. Reconstruction is scheduled for completion by 2006, the city's 800-year anniversary. However, the expectant energy driving present-day Dresden is not built solely on nostalgic appeals to the past; revitalization and reinvention go hand in hand. The throbbing city emits unprecedented vitality and *Geist* (spirit).

ORIENTATION

The capital of the *Bundesland* of Sachsen, Dresden stands on the Elbe River 80km northwest of the Czech border and 180km south of Berlin. This city of 500,000 people is a major transportation hub between eastern and western Europe.

Dresden is bisected by the Elbe. The *Altstadt* lies on the same side as the *Hauptbahnhof;* the *Neustadt*, to the north, escaped most of the bombing, paradoxically making it one of the oldest parts of the city. South of the *Altstadt* are the contrasting suburbs of Plauen and Strehlen. Many of Dresden's main tourist attractions are centered between the Altmarkt and the Elbe. From there it's a five-minute scenic stroll to the banks of the *Neustadt*. Five immense bridges (Marienbrücke, Augustbrücke, Carolabrücke, Albertbrücke, and the "Blue Wonder" Loschwitzbrücke) connect the city halves. Watch for pickpockets along Pragerstr. and in department stores.

PRACTICAL INFORMATION

Transportation

Flights: Dresden's airport (tel. 88 10) is about 15km from town. The **Airport City Liners** bus (one-way DM8) leaves both stations for the airport every hr.; call 251 82 43 for schedules and information.

Trains: From the **Dresden Hauptbahnhof** (for info, call 194 19 or use the computerized schedule center in the main hall). Travelers shoot off to Leipzig (1½hr., 37 per day), Berlin (2hr., 20 per day), Prague (2½hr., 7 per day), Frankfurt am Main (6hr., 15 per day), Munich (8hr., 18 per day), Warsaw (8-10hr., 5 per day), Budapest (11hr., 2 per day), and Paris (12-15hr., 15 per day). Another station, **Bahnhof Dresden Neustadt,** sits on the other bank of the Elbe and bears a striking resemblance to its mate; trains leave from here for Gorlitz and other eastern cities.

Ferries: The **Sächsische Dampfschiffahrt** (tel. 86 60 90) grooves with a restaurant, band, and dancing. Ships to Pillnitz (2hr., every 2hr. 11am-5pm, DM15), Meißen (2hr., DM7.50), and the Sächsische Schweiz (day pass DM27, under 14 DM16).

Public Transportation: Dresden is sprawling—even if you'll only spend a few days, familiarize yourself with the major bus and streetcar lines. **Punch your ticket as you board.** 4 or fewer stops DM1.30; 1hr. DM2.50; 24hr. pass DM8; weekly pass DM24, students DM15. Tickets and maps are available from friendly *Fahrkarten* dispensers at major stops and from the **Verkehrs-Info** stands outside the *Hauptbahnhof,* Postplatz, Albertplatz, or Pirnaischerplatz. Open M-F 7am-7pm, Sa-Su 8am-4pm. Most major lines run every hr. after midnight. Dresden's **S-Bahn** network reaches from Meißen (DM7.40) to Schöna by the Czech border. Buy tickets from automats in the *Hauptbahnhof* and validate them in the red contraptions; insert the ticket and press *hard*. Harder.

Taxis: tel. 459 81 12.

NEUSTADT

Dr.-Kurt-Fischer-Allee

ALAUNPLATZ

Bischofsweg

ALEXANDER-
PUSCHKIN-
PLATZ

Leipziger Str.

Hansastr.

Grossenhainerstr.

Königsbrückerstr.

Alaunstr.

Rothenburger Str.

Görlitzer Str.

Radebergerstr.

Bautzner Str.

Bahnhof
Neustadt

D
E

Antonstr.

Theresienstr.

Hainstr.

ALBERT
PLATZ

Glacistr.

Bautzner Str.

Hoyersw.str.

Marienbrücke

PALAIS-
PLATZ

Friedrichstr.

Haupstr.

Albertstr.

KÖBIS-
PLATZ

THOMAS-
MÜNTZER-
PLATZ

Ostra-Ufer

Maxstr.

Antonstr.

Goldener
Reiter

Große Meisner Str.

Wigardstr.

Elbe

Käthe-Kollwitz-Ufer

Gruner str.

Ostrallee

Terrassenufer

Augustus
Brücke

Carolabrücke

Albertbrücke

BÖNISCH-
PLATZ

Schweriner
Str.

Semper-
Oper

Hofkirche

Zwinger

AUGUSTUS
PLATZ

Brülsche
Terrasse

Frauenkirche

Terrassenufer

Ziegelstr.

Güntzstr.

GÜNTZ-
PLATZ

Palace of Saxony's
Electors and Kings

Albertinum
Museum

RATHENAU-
PLATZ

Pillnitzer Str.

Marschnerstr.

POST-
PLATZ

Wilsdruffer Str.

Landhaus

PIRNAISCHER
PLATZ

Grunaer Str.

Canalettostr.

TO A

Kreuzkirche

Rathaus

St. Petersburger Str.

F

ALTSTADT

STRAßBURGER
PLATZ

Stübel Allee

STEVN-
PLATZ

Budapester Str.

Reitbahn Str.

Prager Str.

Deutsches
Hygiene-
Museum

LINGER-
PLATZ

Bürger-wiese Parkstr.

Gellert-Lenns-Str.

VOLKSPARK

Ammonstr.

C

WIENER
PLATZ

Zoologischer
Garten

Palais

Hauptbahnhof

Wiener Str.

R.-STRAUSS-
PLATZ

Hauptmannstr.

Wiener Str.

Fritz Löfflerstr.

Uhlandstr.

Strehlenerstr.

N

B

JURI-
GAGARIN-
PLATZ

SPORT-
PLATZ

Reichenbachstr.

STREHLENER
PLATZ

Teplitzerstr.

Münchner Str.

NÜRNBERGER
PLATZ

Zellescher Weg

0   ½ mile

0   ½ kilometer

SACHSEN

Dresden
ACCOMMODATIONS
D City Herberge
F Die Boote
B Herberge Rudi Arnt
C Ibis
A Jugendgästehaus
   Dresden
E Mondpalast

Car Rental: Sixt-Budget, in the Hilton by the Frauenkirche (tel. 864 29 72; fax 495 40 74). Open M-F 7am-8pm, Sa 8am-noon. **Europacar,** in the *Hauptbahnhof* near the Pragerstr. exit. Open M-F 7am-9pm, Sa 8am-7pm, Su 9-11am.

Bike Rental: (tel. 461 32 85) in the *Hauptbahnhof* near the luggage storage. DM10 per day. Open M-F 6am-10pm, Sa 6am-9pm.

Mitfahrzentrale: Antonstr. 41 (tel. 194 40), 400m from *Bahnhof-Neustadt*. DM0.10 per km plus finder's fee. Berlin DM21. Frankfurt am Main DM45. Munich DM43.50. Call 1-2 days in advance. Rides to the old *Bundesländer* are easiest to get. Open M-F 9am-7pm, Sa 9am-1pm, Su 11am-4pm.

Hitchhiking: *Let's Go* does not recommend hitchhiking as a safe mode of transportation. Hitchers stand in front of the *"Autobahn"* signs at on-ramps; otherwise they are heavily fined or smacked by oncoming traffic. To Berlin: streetcar #3 or 6 to "Liststr.," then bus #81 to "Olter." To Prague, Eisenach, or Frankfurt am Main: bus #72 or 76 to their last stops ("Lockwitz" or "Luga," respectively).

Tourist and Financial Services

Tourist Office: Dresden Information, Pragerstr. (tel. 49 19 21 16; http://www.dresden-online.de). Two new tourist offices are slated to open in 1999. The first, on Pragerstr., just across from the *Hauptbahnhof*, will find **private rooms** (DM30-50) or hotel rooms for a DM5 fee, sell theater tickets, and offer guided **tours.** Their free maps cover the sights in a panoply of languages. Open M-F 9am-8pm, Sa 9am-4pm, Su 10am-2pm. Also opening will be an office in the *Schinkelwache*, a small building just in front of the Semper-Oper, in the middle of Dresden's historical center. The **Dresden Card,** available at the tourist office or at DVB public transportation system offices, provides 48hr. of free rides on buses and trains and entry into many major museums (DM26).

Currency Exchange: ReiseBank, in the main hall of the train station. Open M-F 7:30am-7:30pm, Sa 8am-noon and 12:30-4pm, Su 9am-1pm. DM3 charge for cash currency exchange; DM7.50 for traveler's checks. Other banks on Prager Str. After hours, the self-service exchange machine in the *Hauptbahnhof* will do, but the rates are poor.

American Express: Hoyerzwalderstr. 20 (tel. 80 70 30), in front of the Frauenkirche in a booth a bit larger than a shoe box. Money sent, mail held, and other standard AmEx offerings. Open M-F 7:30am-6pm.

Local Services

Luggage Storage and Lockers: At both train stations. Lockers DM2-4. 24hr. storage DM4 per piece. Open M-F 6am-10pm, Sa 6am-9pm.

Bookstore: **Das Internationale Buch,** Kreuzstr. 4 (tel. 495 41 90), directly behind the Kreuzkirche. English books on the 2nd floor. Open M-F 9am-7pm, Sa 9am-2pm.

Library: Haupt- und Musikbibliothek, Freibergerstr. 35 (tel. 864 82 33), in the World Trade Center. A sparkling new library with tons of info, maps, and books about Dresden and Sachsen, plus a cool cafe. Open M-F 10am-7pm, Sa 10am-2pm.

Women's Center: Frauenzentrum "sowieso," Dornblüthstr. 18 (tel. 33 77 09), focuses on women's issues, with a phone line (tel. 281 77 88) for confidential crisis counseling. Office open M 10am-noon, Tu 10am-6pm, F 9am-noon. Women's (straight and lesbian) bar night **"Klara Fall"** Th-F 7pm-midnight.

Gay and Lesbian Organizations: Gerede-Dresdner Lesben, Schwule und alle Anderen, Wienerstr. 41 (tel. 464 02 20), in Haus der Jugend, near the station. Open M and Th 10am-noon, Tu 10am-2pm.

Laundromat: Groove Station, Katharinenstr. 11-13. A laundromat and much, much more. Wash your clothes (DM5-6 per load) while shopping for leather, tattoos, piercings, drinks, or *"Erektionsbekleidung"* (condoms). Open Su-F 11am-2am, Sa 10am-late. Also at **Jugendherberge Rudi Arndt,** in the cellar. DM3-4 per load.

Emergency and Communications

Emergency: Police, tel. 110. **Ambulance and Fire,** tel. 112.

Pharmacy: Throughout the *Alt-* and *Neustadt*. Signs posted indicating open ones.

Post Office: The **Hauptpostamt,** Königbrückerstr. 21/29, 01099 Dresden (tel. 444 10), is in Dresden-Neustadt. Open M-F 8am-6pm, Sa 8am-noon. **Postamt 72,** Pragerstr., 01069 Dresden (tel. 495 41 65), is near the tourist office.

Internet Access: ComPet, Obergraben 7 (tel. 801 18 74), right off the *Neustadt's* Hauptstr. The cafe hosts House and other electronica DJs. 30min. connection DM7. Open daily 11am-midnight.

Telephone Code: 0351.

ACCOMMODATIONS AND CAMPING

If there's one thing that attests to Dresden's status as a city on the rise, it's the state of accommodations. New hotels and hostels are constantly being planned, built, and opened, but come the weekend, it's hard to get a spot in anything with a good location. Planned to open in October 1999 is a 110-bed ship located at Leipziger Str. 57, a 10-minute walk from the *Bahnhof* in Neustadt. For info, inquire at Rudi-Arnt. In regular hotels, though, the situation is just the opposite. The excess of available rooms means that you can often find same-day deals at some of the hotels on Prager Str. For those traveling in small groups, there is a small *Pension* above **Raskolnikow** (see **Food**) that rents rooms at a reasonable rate (triple DM75). The rooms are brand-new, and the owners are flexible about arrangements. The tourist offices can also facilitate stays in private rooms (see p. 146).

Jugendgästehaus Dresden (HI), Maternistr. 22 (tel. 49 26 20; fax 492 62 99), formerly the Hotel-Kongress-Business-Center, is now an authentic glimpse into pre-fab hotel living. Go out the Pragerstr. exit of the *Hauptbahnhof* and turn left, following the streetcar tracks along Annonstr. to Freibergerstr. Turn right and take another quick right onto Maternistr. Everything is as sleek as a GDR bureaucrat's dream. Over 400 beds. Singles, family rooms, and apartment-style rooms available. DM33, over 26 DM38; non-members pay DM5 extra. Breakfast and sheets included. Reception 4-10pm. No curfew.

⊛**Mondpalast Backpacker,** Katharinenstr. 11-13 (tel./fax 804 60 61), a 5min. walk from *Bahnhof-Neustadt,* above Groove Station and DownTown (see p. 151) A hostel created by backpackers for backpackers, located in the heart of the *Neustadt* scene but soundproofed for sweet dreams. The artfully decorated theme rooms, the huge kitchen, the absence of a curfew, and the brand-newness of the whole shebang make it a backpacker's paradise. 4- and 6-bed dorms DM29. Doubles DM70. Sheets included. Bike rentals DM10 per day. 24hr. reception.

Hostel Die Boote, Louisenstr. 20 (tel. 801 33 61; fax 801 33 62). Named after the caves in which Saxon hikers have taken rest for hundreds of years, Die Boote has facilities that are even more sleep-friendly. A renovated apartment building set back in a small courtyard, this new hostel offers 54 beds in immaculate rooms in the middle of the *Neustadt.* Bike rental available. DM27. Breakfast DM8. One-time fee of DM5 for sheets. 24hr. reception. Call ahead.

Jugendherberge Dresden Rudi Arndt (HI), Hübnerstr. 11 (tel. 471 06 67; fax 472 89 59). Streetcar #5 (direction: "Südvorstadt") or 3 (direction: "Plauen") to "Nürnberger Platz." Continue down Nürnbergerstr., turn right onto Hübnerstr.; the hostel is at the first corner on right. Or, from the *Hauptbahnhof,* walk down Fritz-Löffler-Str., bear right onto Münchener Str., turn right onto Nürnberger Str. Walk 1 block, turn left onto Hübnerstr. Central, comfortable, and pacific with a laid-back staff. Crowded 3- to 5-bed rooms don't detract from the convenience. Call, fax, or mail reservations for stays between Mar. and Sept. DM24, over 26 DM29. HI members only. Check-in 3pm-1am. Curfew 1am. One-time linen fee DM5.

City-Herberge, Lignerallee 3 (tel. 485 99 00; fax 485 99 01). From the *Hauptbahnhof,* walk up St. Petersburger Str., crossing over and using the right sidewalk. Turn right at Lignerallee. Central location with access to most major streetcar and bus lines. Practically a hotel, the rooms are crisp and well-appointed, though you have to share bathrooms. The grandiose breakfast buffet makes waking up a treat. Singles DM60; doubles DM80. Breakfast included.

Ibis Hotel, Prager Str. (tel. 48 56 66 61). Three huge hotel skyscrapers on Prager Str., just across the street from the *Hauptbahnhof,* offer summer same-day specials that are a good bargain for people traveling in pairs. Suites for 2 (DM99) come with TV, phone, and shower or bath, but no breakfast. All major credit cards.

Camping: Campingplatz Altfranken, Altfranken (tel. 410 24 00). Only 7km outside of Dresden and 1km from the nearest bus stop. Streetcar #7 to "Julius-Valdrecht," then bus #70 to the end. DM10 per tent. 24hr. reception.

FOOD

Unfortunately, the surge in Dresden tourism has yielded an increase in food prices, particularly in the *Altstadt.* The cheapest eats are at supermarkets or *Imbiß* stands along Pragerstr. The Altmarkt features good Italian and Turkish restaurants. The *Neustadt* area, between Albertplatz and Alunplatz, spawns a new bar every few weeks and clearly rules the roost of quirky ethnic and student-friendly restaurants. The monthly *Spot,* available at the tourist office, details culinary options.

Raskolnikow, Böhmischestr. 34 (tel. 804 57 06). A Dostoevskian haunt in a ramshackle pre-war brownstone. Hidden beneath a sign for *Galerie Erhard.* Russian and Afghan fare (DM8-15)—from goat cheese (DM6) to flaming kippers (DM11.50) to *Srasi* (filled pockets of mashed potatoes, DM12.50). Open daily 10am-2am.

Nordsee, Hauptstr. 14. Just over the bridge from the bustle of the *Theaterplatz,* this chain cooks up every variety of seafood. Cheaper than anything on the other side of the river (meals DM8-14). Open M-F 9am-7pm, Sa 11am-4pm, Su 8am-3pm.

Tio Pepe, Louisenstr. 28 (tel. 803 29 16). If bland German food has gotten you down, savor Tio Pepe's authentic Spanish food, no seasoning omitted. Lather your bread with roasted garlic. Dinners DM15-25. Paella starts at DM15, DM10 for each additional portion. Open daily 11am-2am.

Café Aha, Kreuzstr. 7, across the street from the Kreuzkirche. Yes, some Germans do care about pigs. The upbeat atmosphere celebrates things indigenous and detests things meaty. Try the Quinoa-tofu salad or the Hazelnut soup (DM5.80). Open daily 10am-midnight.

SIGHTS

From the banks of the Elbe, the **Electors of Sachsen** once ruled nearly the whole of central Europe. The extravagant collection of Emperor August the Strong and the magnificent palace he built to house it, the **Zwinger,** once rivaled the Louvre (see **Museums,** p. 149). Today, hordes of tourists flock to view its array of decadent Baroque ornaments. The statues that line the museum grounds are still charred, although workers are busily sandblasting everything back to aesthetic perfection. The northern wing of the palace, a later addition, was designed by Gottfried Semper, revolutionary activist and master architect. Semper's famed Opera House, the **Semper-Oper,** reverberates with the same robust style as the palace wing. *(DM8, students DM5. Believe us, it's worth it.)* Its painstaking restoration, with original techniques affordable only during the GDR-era, has made it one of Dresden's major attractions. The interior is open for tours almost daily. Check the main entrance for tour times (usually mid-day) or call 491 14 96. Many guided **city tours** take off from Theaterplatz for better rates than those offered by the tourist office.

Across from the Zwinger lies the nearly restored **Dresdner Schloß,** the Residential Palace of Sachsen's old time Electors and Emperors. *(Open Tu-Su 10am-6pm. DM5, students and seniors DM3.)* Once the proud home of August the Strong, its restoration has proceeded piecemeal since it was firebombed along with the rest of the *Altstadt* on February 13, 1945. It features a display on the Renaissance and Baroque eras of the palace and the history of its reconstruction. Across the street, the Kempinski Hotel once served as the **Taschenbergpalais,** the home of August the Strong's mistresses. After poor Countess Cosel was banished to Stolpen (see p. 155) it became a residence for princes. A private walkway once connected the *Schloß* to the **Katholische Hofkirche** (Catholic Royal chapel). *(Open M-Th 9am-5pm, F 1-5pm, Sa 10:30am-4pm, Su noon-4pm.)* Adorning the **Fürstenzug** (Procession of Electors), the alley leading to the cathedral entrance is a 105m mosaic in Meißner porcelain tiles tracing Sachsen history since the Middle Ages. If you've been mistaking Friedrich the Earnest for Friedrich the Pugnacious, you may want to stop in here for a quick history lesson. From the Catholic Cathedral, the 16th-century **Brühlische Terrasse** offers a prime photo opportunity of the Elbe. Within its casements, Johann Friedrich Böttger was imprisoned by August the Strong until he finally solved the secret recipe for porcelain (interestingly, Böttger had originally promised he could produce gold). Turn right at the end of the terrace to reach the **Albertinum,** another of Dresden's fabulous museum complexes (see **Museums,** p. 149) that now hosts a courtyard collection of Greek and Roman sculptures. From the Albertinum, a walk to the Neumarkt leads to the ruined shell of the **Frauenkirche,** once a splendid Protestant church, and Dresden's most famous silhouette before construction began to revive the city after the war. The first Protestant celebration of communion in Dresden took place at the **Protestant Kreuzkirche** on the Altmarkt. *(Church open summer M-Tu and Th-F 10am-5:30pm, W and Sa 10am-4:30pm, Su noon-4:30pm; winter M-F 10am-4:30pm, Sa 10am-3:30pm, Su noon-4:30pm. Su services at 9:30am. Free. Tower closes 30min. before the church. DM2, kids DM1.)* Now the fourth church to be erected on the site, its interior is still rough plaster as a reminder of the war's devastation. Some tourists are fortunate enough to catch a performance by the world-famous **Kreuzchor,** a boys choir with a tradition dating back to the 13th century. Climb to the top for a bird's-eye view of the colossal jigsaw puzzle of downtown Dresden.

The main promenade of the **Neustadt,** once *Straße der Befreiung* (Street of Liberation), has been renamed **Hauptstraße** (Main Street) in a surge of nomenclatural genius. The cobblestone pedestrian avenue stretches from the magnificent **Augustus Brücke** over the Elbe past the **Goldener Reiter,** a gold-plated vision of Friedrich August II (a.k.a. August the Strong). The nickname was reputedly an homage to his remarkable (some might say unseemly) virility—legend has it that he fathered over 300 kids, although the official tally sits at 15. At the other end of Hauptstr., **Albertplatz** (formerly Platz der Einheit) is surrounded by handsome 19th-century mansions, and marks the center of the *Neustadt* bar and restaurant scene toward the north and west. Also see the **Dreikönigskirche** (Church of the Three Kings), one of the oldest original structures in the city, farther down Hauptstr. (open daily 10am-6pm).

In the direction of Blasewitz, Loschwitz, and Striesen, you'll find the old haunts of the German romantics. All that remains now of Gottfried Körner's estate is the **Schillerhäuschen,** Schillerstr. 19 (tel. 49 86 60), where Beethoven first heard Schiller's "Ode an die Freude" poem that comprises the finale of his 9th symphony. *(Open May-Sept. Sa-Su 10am-5pm or by appointment. DM1, students and seniors DM0.50.)* This cottage, which now possesses a small collection of Schiller memorabilia, is where Schiller worked. For a taste of Dresden's pre-war atmosphere, venture just a bit farther out to **Blasewitz** and **Loschwitz,** connected by the **Blaues Wunder,** a 19th-century suspension bridge, it is visually resplendent—also the only bridge not destroyed by the SS when the Soviets invaded the city. **Körnerplatz,** on the Loschwitz side, remains one of Dresden's prettiest squares, with its artist-colony ambience still partially intact.

In a particularly dismal section of town, the **Schlachthofringe** (Slaughterhouse Circle) is an original 1910 housing complex. In World War II, the buildings were commandeered as a camp for prisoners of war. Novelist Kurt Vonnegut was imprisoned here during the bombing of Dresden, inspiring his masterpiece *Slaughterhouse Five.* Take streetcar #9 (direction: "Friedrichstadt") to the last stop and walk up (don't do this at night). On the way, you'll pass one of Dresden's architectural oddities, the former **Zigarretenfabrik** (cigarette factory). Keep an eye out for its brown, stained glass dome. Built in 1907, it was modeled on a tobacco factory in Turkey, and now occasionally houses discos.

MUSEUMS

As reconstruction of the Zwinger and the Dresdner **Schloß** nears its end, Dresden's museum exhibits are gradually moving back to their pre-war homes. If you're going to visit the Albertinum, the *Alte Meister* collections, or the Zwinger, a worthwhile

SACHSEN

investment may be the *Tageskarte* (DM12, students and seniors DM7). It covers one-day admission to the Albertinum museums, the *Schloß*, most of the Zwinger and a melange of other sights. Purchase it at any of the major museums.

Zwinger

Gemäldegalerie Alte Meister, Zwinger Palace, Semper Wing (tel. 491 46 19). From the front portal, walk through the main courtyard to the building across the way; the museum is on the left. A world-class collection of paintings from 1500 to 1800. Cranach the Elder's luminous "Adam" and "Eve" paintings, and Rubens's erotically charged "Leda and the Swan" are only a few of the masterpieces. The Canaletto collections commemorate magnificent 18th-century Dresden The 3rd floor displays the pomposity of the august Augusts. Open Tu-Su 10am-6pm. DM7, students and seniors DM4. Free tours Su 4pm.

Rüstkammer (tel. 491 46 19). Across from the *Alte Meister* in the Semper Wing. An exhibit of the royal court's toys, including the knightly apparel that Sachsen electors donned for jousting tournaments. Most of the intricately decorated weapons would have been far too pretty to take into battle. What appears to be a collection of midget armor is, in fact, that of the Wettin (Windsor) family's toddlers. DM3, students and seniors DM2, covered by admission to Gemäldegalerie Alte Meister.

Porzellansammlung (tel. 491 46 19). Entry across from the *Residenzschloß.* The "show-and-tell" centerpiece of Dresden, it traces Sachsen's porcelain industry through outlandishly delicate knick-knacks. Makes you feel like a bull in a china shop. DM3, students and seniors DM2. Open Su-W and F-Sa 10am-6pm.

Mathematisch-Physikalischer Salon (tel. 495 13 64). In the corner of the Zwinger courtyard closest to Postplatz. Europe's oldest "science museum" boasts a collection of historical scientific instruments (globes, clocks, atlases, etc.). Not included in the *Tageskarte.* Open Su-W and F-Sa 9:30am-5pm. DM3, students DM1.50.

Albertinum

Gemäldegalerie der Neuen Meister (tel. 491 46 19). Out with the *alt,* in with the *neu!* A solid ensemble of German and French Impressionists, including many Renoirs and Gauguins, leads into a collection of Expressionists and *"Neue Sachlichkeit"* Modernist works that is hard to match. Otto Dix's renowned "War" triptych steals the show. Open Su-W and F-Sa 10am-6pm. DM7, students and seniors D4.

Grünes Gewölbe, on the second floor of the *Albertinum.* Provides a dazzling collection of the completely gratuitous refinements possessed by the House of Sachsen. A carved cherry pit with 185 tiny heads might be the most decadent miniature you'll ever see. Open Su-W and F-Sa 10am-6pm.

Elsewhere in Dresden

Verkehrsmuseum (Transport Museum), Augustusstr. 1 (tel. 864 40), rolls through the history of German transport, from carriages to bullet trains and BMWs. Open Tu-Su 10am-5pm; last entry at 4:30pm. DM4, students and seniors DM2.

Museum zur Dresdner Frühromantik (Museum of the Early Romantic Period), Hauptstr. 13 (tel. 804 47 60). A small museum with a very thorough *Frühromantik* exhibit. All you ever wanted to know about Weber, Kleist, Friedrich, Wagner, and the Schumanns. Open W-Su 10am-6pm. Last entry 5:30pm. DM3, students DM1.50.

Stadtmuseum, Wilsdrufferstr. 2 (tel. 49 86 60), in the 18th-century Neoclassical **Landhaus,** provides an exhaustive history of Dresden from the 12th century to 1989. The 2nd floor poignantly documents the 1945 fire-bombing, as well as a history of the tumult in 1989, when Dresden's train station served as the primary means of escape into Prague. Upon the closure of the German-Czech border on Oct. 3, violence erupted, and organized resistance quickly sprang up in Dresden, as evidenced by the numerous marching posters from *Montagdemos* on display in the museum. Open Sa-Th 10am-6pm; May-Sept. W to 8pm. DM4, students DM2.

Deutsches Hygienemuseum, Lingnerpl. 1 (tel. 484 60). This ill-named museum long celebrated the health and cleanliness of GDR Germans. Now that the party's over, it exhibits models of our guts. Open Tu and Th-F 9am-5pm, W 9am-8:30pm, Sa-Su 10am-5pm. DM5, students and seniors DM3.

Richard-Wagner-Museum, Richard-Wagner-Str. 6, Gaupa (tel. (03501) 54 82 89). Houses an array of colorful displays on the bombastic and brilliant composer's time in Dresden (1842-49). Frequent concerts. Open Tu-Su 9am-noon and 1-4pm. DM3.

ENTERTAINMENT AND NIGHTLIFE

Dresden's sprawling nightlife provides ample entertainment. Much of the hustle and bustle takes place around Albertplatz in the *Neustadt,* with the big-time bar scene on Alaunstr. This lively area where cool kids of every flavor come to shop during the day and partake in the *Szene* at night, comprises almost a full kilometer, roughly bounded by Königsbrückestr., Bischofsweg, Kamenzerstr., and Albertplatz. At last count over 50 bars were packed into this area. *Kneipen Surfer* provides a list and description of every one. Peruse the back of *SAX* (DM2.50 at the tourist office, or just ask to see one at any bar) to see what concerts and dances are coming up. For centuries, Dresden has been a focal point of theater, opera, and music. The superb **Semper-Oper** has premiered many of Strauss and Wagner's greatest, but tickets are hard to come by. From mid-July to September, many theaters close and students head for the hills, consequently diminishing the offerings. To help fill the gap, the **Filmnächte am Elbufer** (Film Nights on the Elbe) festival in July and August lets you gaze upon an enormous movie screen in the *Neustadt,* with the illuminated *Altstadt* in the background (most shows start at 9:30 or 10pm and cost DM10). A cabaret festival takes place in the first week of October.

Concerts, Opera, and Dance

Sächsische Staatsoper-Semper Oper, Theaterpl. 2 (tel. 491 17 16). See opera's finest in the most majestic of environs. The box office unloads tickets for DM5-10 1hr. before performances, but you have to get lucky; otherwise, call ahead or go to the tourist office for tickets from DM10-85. 50% student and senior discounts. Box office at Schinkelwache, by the opera, open M-W and F 10am-noon and 1-5pm, Th 10am-noon and 1-6pm, Sa 10am-1pm, and 1hr. before performance.

Kulturpalast, Am Altmarkt (tel. 486 60). Home to the **Dresdner Philharmonie** (tel. 486 63 06) as well as other small music groups and dance ensembles. Box office at Schloßstr. 2. Main entrance open M-F 9am-6pm, Sa 10am-2pm.

Staats Operette, Pirnaer Landstr. 131 (tel. 207 99 29). Musical theater from Lerner and Loewe to Sondheim. DM10-34, Tu and Th discount. Ticket office open M 11am-4pm, Tu-F 11am-7pm, Sa 4-7pm, Su 1hr. before shows.

Theater and Cabaret

projekttheater dresden, Louisenstr. 47 (tel. 804 30 41). Experimental theater with an international twist in the heart of the *Neustadt.* So cool they don't use capital letters. Tickets DM20, students DM15. Box office opens at 8pm, shows at 9pm.

Der Herkuleskeule, Sternpl. 1 (tel. 492 55 55). Cabaret with an angry political outlook revels in blasting U.S. culture. Tickets Su-Th DM15-25, F-Sa DM20-30, M-Th student discounts. Box office open M-F 1:30-6pm and 1hr. before performance.

Schauspielhaus, Postpl. (tel. 491 35 67; box office tel. 491 35 55), produces classics from Kleist to Shakespeare. Tickets DM25-40. Box office open M-F 10am-6;30pm, Sa 10am-2pm, and 1hr. before the show.

Schloßtheater, slated to open Jan. 1999. This small ensemble will perform classical works in the Dresdner *Schloß.* Tickets will be available through the Schauspielhaus.

Theater Junge Generation, Meißner Landstr. 4 (tel. 421 45 67). Shakespeare, opera, fairy tales, and more. Tickets DM10-14, 15-50% student discount. Tickets available M-Sa 10am-noon, extra hours W 2-6pm, F 2-7:30pm, or 1hr. before show.

Puppentheater der Stadt Dresden, Leipziger Str. 220 (tel. 84 06 40; fax 840 64 44). Children's performances during the day for young and older folk. DM6, children DM4, family ticket (up to five people) DM18. Occasional evening performance geared more toward adults DM12, students DM10. Box office open 30min. before shows on weekdays, 45min. before shows on weekends.

SACHSEN

Bars and Clubs

AZ Conni, Rudolf-Leonhard-Str. 39 (tel. 804 58 58). Keeping it real in the great tradition of "former" clubs, this one occupies an old Kindergarten, but that doesn't stop the action from getting pretty naughty. The first floor is a nook-filled bar, and the second is a bumpin' dance floor. Tu and Th are dance nights, and weekends frequently bring in concerts. Open daily 9pm until late.

DownTown and Groove Station, Katharinenstr. 11-13 (tel. 801 18 59). *The* place to shake your booty and indulge in Dresden's neon techno scene. One of the few night venues capable of convincing skeptics that some Germans *can* dance. Very popular straight, gay, and lesbian scene. In the upstairs Groove Station (see **Laundromat,** p. 146), patrons numb themselves with drink and get tattooed and/or pierced. DownTown open Th-M 9pm-5am with dancin' on all these days except Sunday; Th-Sa house music, cover DM5-7, Sunday Funk, Monday gay and lesbian.

Scheune, Alaunstr. 36-40 (tel. 802 66 19). The granddaddy of the *Neustadt* bar scene (Dresden's *Kulturzentrum*), in a former youth center. A Pee Wee's Playhouse complete with beer garden that serves decently priced Indian food (DM10-15) cooked by the German Shiva Team. Open Tu-F 7pm-2am, Sa 10am-2pm and 7pm-2am, Su 10am-2pm. The culturally eclectic dance floor invites you to disco to West African roots and Baltic and Yiddish piano songs. Club opens at 8pm.

Studentenklub Bärenzwinger, Brühlischer Garten 1 (tel. 495 51 53), not far from the Albertinum. Head toward the Carolabrücke, but make a sharp left down a little hill just before reaching the streetcar stop. Students congregate in this bizarre tunnel under the Brühlische Terrasse to nurse cheap drinks and partake in the disco action. Some hard core interspersed with canonical American "alternative" racket. Over 18 only. Bring student ID for discounts. Tu, F, Sa are usually dance. Open Tu-Th and Su 8pm-1am, F-Sa 9pm-3am for live shows and dancing. Cover DM8-12.

Straße E, in a partly abandoned industrial complex where all the streets simply have letter names. **Straße E** itself hosts concerts and dance parties, while next door **Bunker** caters to the more morbid, vampire-types. Definitely check in *SAX* before making the trip out Straßenbahn 7 or 8 to "Industriegelände," because the scene really depends on what is being played.

Die Tonne, Am Brauhaus 3 (tel. 802 60 17), boasts an offering of "cool drinks and hot jazz" for slightly more refined (read: twenty-something) entertainment. Performances most nights at 9pm. Cover DM8-20. Free on Monday. Friday is salsa night. Open daily 5pm-1am.

■ Near Dresden: Meißen

Just 30km from Dresden, Meißen sits on the banks of the Elbe as yet another testament to the frivolity of August the Strong. In 1710, the Sachsen emperor developed a severe case of *Porzellankrankheit* (the porcelain "bug"—an affliction that continues to manifest itself in tourists today) and turned the city's defunct *Schloß* into a porcelain-manufacturing base. Those visitors who would otherwise feel little affinity for the craft indulge in a couple of glasses of Meißen's fine wines and soon find themselves toasting the beauty of "white gold" (china, not cocaine). Meißen has a distinct aesthetic advantage over its comrade Dresden; its medieval nooks and crannies were barely scathed by World War II bombs. Meißen is an easy daytrip from Dresden by S-Bahn (45min., one-way DM7.70) or scenic cruise (round-trip from Dresden DM25).

Wander the narrow, romantic alleyways of the *Altstadt* and climb up to the **Albrechtsburg** (tel. 47 07 10), a castle and cathedral overlooking the city. (Open Mar.-Oct. daily 10am-6pm; Nov.-Feb. 10am-5pm; last entry 30min. before closing. DM6, students DM3.) From the Meißen *Bahnhof,* walk straight onto Bahnhofstr. and follow the banks of the Elbe to the Elbbrücke (Elbe bridge). Cross the bridge and continue straight to the Markt and turn right onto Burgstr.; at the end of Burgstr., on Schloßstr., you'll find the stairs that lead to the right up to Albrechtsburg. The castle foundations were first built in 929 to protect the area's Sorb population (see p. 159). The interior was lavishly redecorated in the 15th century, and once again when porcelain profits started pouring in. The fantastically decorated rooms also house an extensive medieval sculpture collection. Next door dwells the **Meißener Dom,** an early Gothic cathedral which ensures that its visitors get their money's worth with four priceless 13th-century **statues** by the Naumburg Master, a triptych by Cranach the Elder, and the beautiful metal grave coverings of the Wettins. (Open Apr.-Oct. daily 9am-6pm; Nov.-Mar. 10am-4pm. Last entry 30min. before closing. DM3.50, students DM2.50. Organ concerts May-Oct. daily noon; DM3, students DM2.)

Meißen's porcelain factory was once more tightly guarded than KGB headquarters for fear that competitors would discover its secret techniques. Porcelain was first discovered here in 1708, and today anyone can tour the **Staatliche Porzellan Manufaktur** at Talstr. 9 (tel 46 82 07). The **Schauhalle** serves as a museum where you can peruse finished products (DM9, students DM7), but the real fun lies in the high-tech tour of the *Schauwerkstatt* (show factory), which shows folks working on different steps of the porcelain-manufacturing process. (English tapes available. Open daily 9am-noon and 1-4:45pm. DM7, students DM5. Open daily 9am-noon and 12:30pm-4:30pm.) Meißen's Gothic **Rathaus** stands alongside the **Frauenkirche,** whose porcelain bells chatter every 15 minutes over the main market square (Frauenkirche open May-Oct. daily 10am-noon and 1-4pm).

A puffed, almost hollow pastry, the *Meißener Fummel* owes its origin to August the Strong. One of his couriers was a spirited sort whose penchant for Meißen wine became known to the king. To keep tabs on his bacchanalian behavior, August ordered the Meißen bakers' guild to create an extremely fragile biscuit. The courier was to carry the *Fummel* with him undamaged when delivering messages. Many *Altstadt* bakeries vend this puffery. For less fluff, try **Zum Kellermeister,** Neugasse 10 (tel. 45 40 88). Most *Schnitzels* run DM5-10 (open M-F 11am-9pm). The farmer's **market** is on the main market (open Tu-F 8am-5pm). In the last weekend of September, Meißen frolics in merriment during its annual **wine festival.**

The **tourist office,** Markt 3 (tel. 45 44 70), is across the *Markt* from the church. Pick up maps or find a room in a private home (DM25-55) for a DM4 fee (open Apr.-Oct. M-F 10am-6pm, Sa-Su 10am-3pm; Nov.-Mar. M-F 9am-5pm). Meißen's **Jugendherberge,** Wilsdrufferstr. 28 (tel. 45 30 65), is a crap shoot—its 45 beds are often booked. Should they have space, they'll put you up in a crowded five-bed room. From the station, cross the Elbe footbridge and take Obergasse to the end where it meets Plosenweg. Turn left and continue uphill until you see the small Edeka Markt; the hostel is across the street. An infrequent bus (line C/C) runs from the train station up the steep hill ("Dr.-Donner-Str."). (DM18. Breakfast included. Sheets DM5. Reception M-F 7am-noon and 4-8pm, Sa-Su 4-8pm.) The **postal code** is 01662. The **telephone code** is 03521.

■ Near Dresden: Moritzburg

Never one to be bashful about leaving his mark on the Sachsen landscape, August the Strong tore down a little palace in 1723 and replaced it with **Schloß Moritzburg** (tel. 87 30; fax 873 11), his titanic hunting lodge of ribaldry. (Open May-Oct. daily 10am-5:30pm; Mar. and Nov. Tu-Su 10am-4:30pm; Apr. Tu-Su 10am-5:30pm; Dec. Tu-Su 10am-3pm. DM7, students and seniors DM4.) The immense *Schloß* lounges arrogantly at the end of Schloßallee on an island in an artificial lake. Inside, lavish rooms and leering deer skulls commemorate the courtly hunting penchant, while the ornately embossed and painted leather wallpaper sets the standard for masculine, animal-killing prowess. A must-see is a portrait of one of Moritzburg's most "beautiful" oxen ever. To get to the *Schloß* from the *Schmalspurbahn* train station, join the pilgrimage out to the left then turn right onto Schloßallee. Near the *Schloß*, the smaller **Fasanenschlößchen** was built by the great-grandson of August the Strong, Friedrich August III. Outside, sculptures of moose in tremendous pain remind you that this, too, is a hunting lodge. Unfortunately, the Fasanenschlößchen is closed indefinitely for repairs; ask the tourist office for more information. From Schloß Moritzburg, follow Meißner Str. to the right until Große Fasanenstr.; the Fasanenschlößchen appears on the left. Farther down Große Fasanenstr., the curious structure peeking out of the forest is the **Leuchtturm** (lighthouse), which once served as a backdrop to the mock sea battles of the decadent princes. Moritzburg is also surrounded by extensive parks in addition to a huge gaming reserve and the **Sächsisches Langestüt** ("Sachsen Stud-Farm"), where animals procreate almost as frequently as did August the Strong—that's over 300 children (see p. 149).

Moritzburg also has a rich art tradition as the place where die Brücke artists resided between 1909 and 1911. It continued to serve as a summer residence for many artists who came back to frolic in the waters. One of Germany's most-celebrated 20th-century artists, **Käthe Kollwitz,** resided in the region for a time. After Kollwitz's home in Berlin was bombed near the end of World War II, Prince Ernst Heinrich von Sachsen offered her a place of retreat here. Though Kollwitz passed away in 1945, only one year after her arrival, her house now holds the **Käthe Kollwitz Gedenkstätte,** Meißner Str. 7. The museum showcases her powerful sculptures, woodcuts, and drawings, starkly and beautifully depicting the cruelty of war and poverty. Pictures and excerpts from her letters and diaries help fill in the gaps about the remarkable woman. (Open Apr.-Oct. Tu-F 11am-5pm, Sa-Su 10am-5pm; Nov.-Mar. Tu-F noon-4pm, Sa-Su 11am-4pm. DM3.50, students DM2.)

The fastest way to Moritzburg from Dresden is by **bus.** Take bus #326 (direction: "Radeburg") from *Bahnhof-Neustadt* to "Mortizburg, Schloß." The return trip runs from "Maritzburg, Markt" on Marktstr. parallel to the Schloßallee. The most scenic route (but also the slowest, bumpiest, and noisiest) is the 110-year old *Schmalspurbahn* (narrow-gauge railway) which leaves from Radebeul-Ost, accessible by the S-Bahn to Meißen (30min., 4 stops; S-Bahn and train DM7.40 each way, students DM5). Moritzburg's **tourist office,** Schloßallee 3b (tel. 854 10; fax 854 20), provides information on guided **tours** of the *Schloßpark,* concerts in the *Schloß,* and horse-and-carriage rentals, and books rooms (DM30-40 per person) for a DM2 fee. (Open May-Oct. M-F 10am-5pm, Sa-Su noon-4pm; Nov.-Apr. M-F 10am-5pm.) Eating in Moritzburg cries out for one thing: picnic. The classical gardens behind the castle provide the perfect backdrop, and they never close. If you forget your basket, there's **Zum Dreispitz,** Schloßallee 5 (tel. 822 00), which offers *Sächsische* meat and mushroom dishes (maybe poached from the stud farm) for DM10-20 (open daily 11am-midnight). The **telephone code** is 035207.

■ Pillnitz

August the Strong must have led a happy life. Among his many castles (almost as numerous as his mistresses), the magnificent gardens of **Schloß Pillnitz** produce a singularly fantastic effect. The strongman inherited the nearly 300-year-old castle in 1694 and generously passed it on to Countess Cosel a few years later—who says diamonds are a girl's best friend? The Countess lived there from 1713 to 1715 until August decided to imprison her in the more poorly furnished Burg Stolpen (see below) and began the extensive remodeling that gave the complex its characteristic look. The turrets of the **Bergpalais** and **Wasserpalais** (modeled on Chinese architectural forms) swim in an amazing setting, surrounded on one side by the Elbe, and on the other by gardens in English, Chinese, and just plain decadent styles. The residences now house Dresden's **Kunstgewerbmuseum** (arts and crafts museum), some modern art displays, and lots of porcelain amidst the sumptuously sensual and suggestively salacious summer-like colors of the courtly rooms. Outside, brilliantly colored flowers heighten the mystical effect of the architecture. Concerts also take place in the garden during the summer; call for info. (Museum open May-Oct. 9:30am-5:30pm. *Bergpalais* and *Kunstgewerbmuseum* closed Mondays, *Wasserpalais* closed Tuesdays. DM3, students and seniors DM2. Grounds open 5am-sunset year round.) To reach Pillnitz from Dresden, take *Straßenbahn* #14 from Pirnaischerplatz (direction: "Kleinzschachwitz") to the last stop (30min.). Get off the *Straßenbahn* and walk toward the banks of the Elbe, where you'll see a ferry shuttling passengers every 15 minutes (DM1.30, children DM1; surcharge DM1 for bicycles, DM5.50 for cars). Bus #85 also runs from Schillerplatz. Alternatively, the **Weiße Flotte** fleet can get you there by boat. Head straight through the main garden to the "Alte Wache" **tourist office** for maps of the surrounding gardens, info, and tours (open daily 10am-6pm).

■ Stolpen

The Sachsen Emperor August the Strong entertained an extensive array of mistresses, but the most well known was the Countess Cosel. As a result of a lovers' quarrel about the king's new mistress and his anti-Protestant stance, she was imprisoned without official sentence in the old castle of Stolpen from 1716 to 1765. Her 49 years of confinement were perhaps made bearable, however, by the spectacular views of Bohemia and Sächsische Schweiz from every window of her lonesome lookout. The 13th-century **Burg Stolpen,** Schloßstr. 10 (tel. 23 40), can be reached from *Neustadt's* Albertplatz by bus #261 (direction: "Sebnitz") to "Stolpen-Ärztehaus" (50min., DM5.40). To find the entrance to the castle, simply start walking uphill, and follow the signs. The heavy stone fortifications and utter lack of adornment seem wholly unrelated to other decadent structures in Sachsen. The first of four courtyards houses a **torture chamber** that should delight any S&M reveler with its maces and handcuffs. If that excites you, go deep into the castle's first tower and find the chamber in which condemned prisoners were left to die. Ah, the romance of European castles. The next two courtyards contain the courtroom, the old castle cannons, the castle tower (which can be climbed), and the castle **chapel and tomb** where Countess Cosel is buried. The **castle well** in the fourth courtyard is the deepest basalt well in the world; it took the castle miners 22 years to find water. (Open daily Apr.-Oct. 9am-5pm; Nov.-Mar. 10am-4pm, weather permitting. Last entrance 30min. before closing. DM6, students and seniors DM4.)

The Stolpen **Tourist Information Center,** Schloßstr. 14a (tel./fax 273 13), offers maps and a list of accommodations (private rooms DM25-35; open Apr.-Sept. daily 9am-5pm; Oct.-Mar. 10am-4pm). **Gar Küche,** on Dresdenerstr., right between the *Markt* and the Nieder Tor, is Stolpen's oldest *Gaststätte,* founded in 1659. They serve *Schnitzel* with veggies and potatoes for DM9. (Open M-Th 10am-2pm and 3:30-10pm, F 10am-2pm and 3-11pm, Sa 11am-11pm, Su 11am-9pm.) Load up on delicious fruity goodness at the **Gemüse am Tor** grocery store next door (open M-F 8:30am-6pm, Sa 8-10am). Stolpen's **postal code** is 01833. The **telephone code** is 035973.

SÄCHSISCHE SCHWEIZ (SAXON SWITZERLAND)

One of Eastern Germany's most beloved holiday destinations, Sächsische Schweiz has become Germany's hottest national park since reunification. The region is "Swiss" because of the stunning landscape—sandstone cliffs emerge from dense vegetation, while sumptuous summits and excellent hiking beckon adventurous tourists. The national park is divided into two regions, the *voderer Teil* and the *hintere Teil;* both are easily accessible from the south with Dresden's S-Bahn #1, which runs along the Elbe River. The **Wanderwege** coil up the hills, into the heart of the park, connecting all towns in the area in a spidery web. The area's vibrant, dense greenery and lovely landscapes make this uniquely beautiful yet inexpensive region a must-see for those convinced that Eastern Germany comes only in shades of gray. Visitors can obtain further information from **Tourismusverband, Sächsische Schweiz,** Am Bahnhof 6, 01814 Bad Schandau (tel./fax (035012) 49 50), or **Nationalpark-Verwaltung,** Schandauerstr. 36, 01824 Königstein (tel. (035021) 682 29; fax 684 46).

■ Pirna

Pirna gloats in the fame it gleaned from Canaletto's depiction of its Marktplatz. Once a 16th-century trading town that overshadowed its golden neighbor, Dresden, today Pirna is a toadstool compared to the towns higher on the mountains. The city's greatest significance now lies in its role as "the door to Sächsische Schweiz."

Pirna is the last stop on S-Bahn #1 before entering the region, a mere 30 minutes from Dresden. To see the **Markt** that fills the natives with so much pride, walk straight down Gartenstr. from the train station, turn left on Grohmannstr., and right on Jacobäerstr., which turns into Schuhgasse and leads straight to it. The 16th-century **Marienkirche** on the right of the marketplace is graced by a huge baptismal font once admired by Goethe. At Obere Burgstr. 1, you can see the 16th-century **Teufelserker** (devil's bay window), named for its three evil overhanging figures. At Barbiergasse 10, its Manichean counterpart, the **Engelserker** (angel's bay window) is adorned with a heavenly gold figure. The **Stadtmuseum Pirna,** Klosterhof 2-3 (tel. 52 79 85), provides an explanation of these architectural oddities, as well as a collection of tricks and trinkets that vaguely represents the city's history. You can also see the **Schützenröcklein,** one of the oldest military dresses left in the region. (Open May-Oct. Tu-Su 10am-6pm; Nov.-Apr. Tu-Su 10am-5pm. DM2, students and seniors DM1.)

Pirna's **tourist office,** Dohnaischestr. 31 (tel./fax 52 84 97), just off Jacobäerstr., provides free maps and books rooms (DM20-40) for a DM5 fee (open M-F 9am-6pm, Sa 9:30am-1pm). A private **tourist office** just down the street at Barbiergasse 10 (tel. 44 26 56; fax 44 26 57) offers similar services with better hours (open M-F 9am-6pm, Sa-Su 9:30am-2pm). The **post office** awaits at Gartenstr. 29/30, 01784 Pirna (open M-F 8:30am-noon and 2-6pm, Sa 9:30am-12:30pm). Far from the city, but a shelter from Pirna's otherwise pricey hotel scene, stands the **Jugendherberge-Pirna-Copitz Weltfrieden** (world peace), Birkwitzerstr. 51 (tel. 44 56 01). Take bus line F from the stop on Gartenstr. (direction: "Birkvitzer Str.") to "Sportplatz," then walk in the direction of the phone booth, and turn left. To walk, cross the Elbe, head up Hauptstr., take the first left onto Schillerstr., go under a bridge, and then hang a quick right onto R.-Renner-Str. Take a break and hydrate because from here it's a *long* haul until a left onto Birkvitzer Str. After another brief hike, you will see the phone booth; the hostel will be on your left. This socialist box holds 160 beds and rents **bikes.** (DM21, over 27 DM26. Breakfast included. Reception daily 6am-midnight.) For a meal, scale the 150 steps up to the **Biergarten,** Schloßhof 4, in Schloß Sonnenstein. Treat yourself to some grill fare (DM4-6.50) and a beer. (Open May-Sept. M-Sa 5pm-1am, Su 3pm-1am; Oct.-Apr. Tu-Sa 5pm-midnight, Su noon-midnight.) If you'd like to skip the German food and the steps to the castle, check out **Restaurant Pirnasicher Hof** (tel. 443 80) in the oh-so-posh Pirnasicher Hof hotel (right on the market). There they serve up imaginative, eclectic food, like fried eggplant with wild rice patties (DM14; open daily 11am-midnight). The **telephone code** is 03501.

■ Rathen and Wehlen

Upstream from Pirna, just around the first bend in the Elbe, the magnificent sandstone begins. The first cliffs are called *"Die Bastei"* and were once the roaming grounds of—you guessed it—August the Strong. Closest to Pirna lies **Wehlen,** and on the other end of the Bastei you'll find **Rathen.** To get to Wehlen, hop on S-Bahn #1, and from the *Bahnhof,* take the **ferry** (DM1, children DM.50). A **tourist office** (tel. (035024) 704 14) on the market will find rooms (DM20-25, M-F 9am-6pm, Sa 9am-2pm). There's not much in Wehlen but the trails to Rathen. One of the paths climbs up onto the Bastei and was a favorite of August the Strong's; look for the Höllengrand an Steinern Tisch, his mammoth dining table. The other path—shorter, easier, but much less impressive—is along the Elbe (40min.).

Once in Rathen, you'll find much more to do. Because of its location on the edge of **Sächsische Schweiz National Park,** hiking trails of all lengths and difficulties (well, they're all pretty steep) abound. Rathen also boasts the **Felsenbühne,** one of the most beautiful open air theaters in Europe, with 2000 seats carved into a cliff and stone pillars looming over the stage. Tickets and schedules are available from the **Theaterkasse** (DM6-39; tel. 77 70; fax 77 735). Mateys can hop on board ships headed to the Czech Republic or just back to Wehlen at **Personenschiffahrt Oberelbe** (DM6-24 round-trip, depending on distance). A **tourist office** (tel./fax 704 22) upstairs in the *Gästeamt* helps you out with the hiking options, sells maps, and finds private rooms (open M-F 9am-noon and 2-6pm, Sa 9am-2pm, closed Saturdays in winter). The **telephone code** is 035024.

As the day comes to an end, you have several options. You can stay at the some-what pricey **Gästehaus Bug Altrathen,** up the ramp near the ferry landing (tel. 76 00; fax 760 02), where singles start at DM40. You can also retreat back across the river on a ferry to the S-Bahn station, or you can continue on to **Hohnstein.**

■ Hohnstein

The small village of **Hohnstein** ("high stone" in old Sachsen), with its grand forest vis-tas on all sides, is linked to Rathen by a beautiful hike through one of the national park's most stunning valleys. To get here from Rathen, follow the path of the red stripe (the trail, not a Maoist paramilitary club). Or take the S-Bahn to "Pirna," and then take bus #236 or 237 from the *Bahnhof* to "Hohnstein Eiche" (DM4.10).

The town encircles the **Hohnstein Jugendburg,** Am Markt 1 (tel. 202; fax 203), a fortress that holds a history and nature museum, *Aussichtsturm* (lookout tower), cafe-restaurant, outdoor garden, and youth hostel. The **Museum der Geschichte des Burg Hohnstein** covers the history of the *Burg* with medieval armor, weapons, and an exhibit on anti-fascist resistance in Dresden and Sächsische Schweiz. The museum commemorates Konrad Hahnewald, the beloved father of Hohnstein's *Jugendher-berge* and later the first political refugee of the Hohnstein Concentration Camp. (Open Mar.-Oct. M-F 9am-5pm, Sa-Su 9am-6pm. DM2.) The **Naturfreundehaus Burg Hohnstein** (tel. 812 02; fax 812 03) offers singles, quads, and titanic 6- to 18-bed rooms for the same price per person. (DM26-28, non-HI members DM33-37; DM1.20 tax per day, DM2 per day extra for stays under 3 days. Breakfast and sheets included.) The **tourist office,** Rathausstr. 10 (tel. 194 33; fax 868 10), in the *Rathaus,* doles out information on trails and the *Burg* and finds rooms (open M-W, F 9am-noon and 12:30-5pm, Th 9am-noon and 12:30-4pm). The **telephone code** is 035975.

■ Königstein

The next stop on the Dresden S-Bahn journey into the hills and dales of the Säch-sische Schweiz is **Königstein.** The *Weiße Flotte* boats also alight on these shores. Above the town looms the **fortress,** whose huge walls are built right into the same stone spires that made Sächsische Schweiz famous. (Open daily Apr.–Sept. 9am-8pm; Oct. 9am-6pm; Nov.-Mar. 9am-5pm. DM7, students and seniors DM5. English pam-phlets at the information office within the castle.) Replete with drawbridges and impenetrable stone walls, this castle belongs on the list of legendary royal abodes. An oft-exploited retreat for the kings of Sachsen during times of civil unrest and marital discord (the Sachsen electors tended to flee faster than the French), it was later con-verted into a feared state prison; Nikolai Bakunin and August Bebel were imprisoned here. During the Third Reich, it was used by the Nazis to stash stolen art, and between 1949 and 1955 it served as a juvenile correctional center. Recently, skele-tons were found in the fortress's torture chamber; no one yet knows which of its incarnations produced them. The complex now houses museums on everything from weapons to porcelain. The view from the fortress is worth sweating for—from the city, it's a 30-minute struggle straight up from Hainstr. to Kirchgasse then to Goet-hestr. Around the left side of the rickety movie theater are the stairs, and then the stairs, and then the stairs up to the fortress. The cheesy **Festungs Express** tours Königstein as it drags up walking-weary tourists who are too tired to make the trek (one-way DM4, children DM2; round-trip DM6, children DM3; tickets available on board). Rides leave from Reißigerplatz regularly, just to the right down Bahnhofstr. from the S-Bahn station (Festungs Express runs Apr.-Oct. 9am-6pm). Paths also lead from the town up to the challenging 415m **Lilienstein,** hiked by August the Strong in 1708. The 2km hike takes a steep 30 minutes.

The **tourist office,** Schreiberberg 2 (tel. 682 61; fax 688 87), two blocks uphill from the "Festungs Express" stop, books rooms (DM25-45), but in summer it's wise to call ahead. They have a list of available rooms, vacation houses, and *Pensionen;* prices are in the window when they're closed (open M-Tu and Th-F 9am-noon and 2-6pm, W 2-6pm, Sa 9am-noon; Nov.-Mar. may be open shorter hours). Königstein's **Naturfre-**

unde **Jugendherberge,** Halbestadt 13 (tel. (035022) 424 32), is a lot nicer than most hostels but also more expensive—the stunning one- to four-bed rooms have private showers, and out back an enormous chess board beckons you to play. To get there, cross the river by ferry and turn right. The hostel will emerge on your right in about 10 minutes. (DM38.40, non-members DM46.20. Breakfast included. Reception daily 6am-10pm.) The **campground** (tel. 682 24) is on the banks of the Elbe about 10 minutes upstream from the station in the shadow of the fortress. It has washing facilities, a small supply shop, and a playground (DM6.80 per person, DM4 per tent). The **telephone code** is 035021.

■ Bad Schandau

The biggest town in Sächsische Schweiz, Bad Schandau takes advantage of its location between the two halves of the national park by offering plenty of hiking and tourism opportunities. Bad Schandau is also amply connected to the rest of Sachsen, with the *Weiße Flotte* and S-Bahn to Dresden, and **trains** running to the town of Bautzen in the Zittauer Gebirge every two hours. From the train station, take the **ferry** (7:30am-9:30pm, 1 per hr., DM1) and walk uphill to the *Markt* where you'll find the **tourist office,** Markt 12 (tel. 900 30). They'll find rooms (DM25-30) and hook you up with city tours and trips to the Czech Republic (open M-F 9am-noon and 2-6pm, Sa 9am-noon). **Adler Apotheke,** Dresdnerstr. 2 (tel. 425 08), provides **pharmacy** services (open M-F 8am-12:30pm and 1:30-6pm, Sa 8:30am-noon). Take the solar-powered, eco-friendly *Kirnitzschtalbahn* train (May-Oct. every 30min.; for info call 423 70 or fax 423 33) to the **Lichtenhainer Waterfall,** a favorite starting point for full-day hikes on the **Schrammsteine.** The tourist office can provide suggestions for shorter or longer hikes. To rent a **bike,** try **Fahrradverleih,** Poststr. 14 (tel. 428 83; DM14 per day with ID). Bad Schandau does boast a **Jugendherberge,** Dorfstr. 14 (tel. 424 08), but it is a 40-minute walk uphill from town, in the neighboring town of Ostra. (DM22, over 26 DM26. Reception 7-10am and 4:30-8pm.) In a pinch it'll do, but there are plenty of private rooms to be found, and the rest of Sächsische Schweiz isn't far off at all. The **telephone code** is 035022.

OBERLAUSITZ (UPPER LUSATIA)

Dotted with cows, farmers, and cheery-looking villages, the rolling hills of Oberlausitz border two former Warsaw Pact neighbors, Poland and the Czech Republic. As a result, Oberlausitz remained untouched by Western tourism during the days of the GDR, and the Politburo *apparatchiks* let much of the region's magnificent Medieval, Renaissance, and Baroque architecture decay. As in much of former East Germany, Oberlausitz is currently undergoing extensive restoration in pursuit of its former shine. The area around Bautzen is especially notable, as it is the home of the **Sorbs,** Germany's only national minority, and is rich in customs long abandoned elsewhere.

■ Bautzen (Budysin)

Bautz'ner *Senf* (mustard): sausage in Germany just wouldn't be the same without it. But mustard pilgrims aren't the only folks who flock to Bautzen; with ancient towers on a hill high above the Spree River, a large population of Germany's sole national minority, the Sorbs, and a collection of crumbling Medieval, Baroque, and Art Nouveau architecture, Bautzen has proved itself a stalwart, millennium-old cultural capital worthy of attracting any tourist. During the unique **Easter Riding Event,** lavishly decorated Sorb horses parade through town. Despite the bilingual street signs, Bautzen's character is very German, evolving into the 21st century with Dresden and the rest of Eastern Germany. So slather it thick on your juicy *Wurst* and explore.

PRACTICAL INFORMATION AND ACCOMMODATIONS Bautzen is a one-hour **train** ride from Dresden (1 per hr.). The **tourist office,** Hauptmarkt 1 (tel. 420 16; fax

The Absorbing Sorbs

The Sorbs are a Slav minority stemming from Serbian tribes who streamed into the Niederlausitz and Oberlausitz areas between the Spreewald and Lusatian mountains during the 6th and 7th centuries. Sorbian is similar to Czech and Polish but spoken with two basic dialects: *Niedersorbisch* and *Obersorbisch* (Lower and Upper Sorbian). Niedersorbisch is spoken in and around Cottbus, and Obersorbisch is spoken in the Bautzen region. Since the crystallization of the Sorb nationalist movement in 1848, small Sorbian-speaking communities totalling about 75,000 members have maintained their regional identities. Under Hitler's *Reich,* Sorbian was ruthlessly suppressed in a program of liquidation commenced in 1937; after the war, the *Sorbengesetz* (Sorbs Law) was established to assure the protection and promotion of the culture and language. However, the Sorbs still encountered many barriers as they tried to preserve their culture. After reunification, a special bureau was created to guarantee Sorbian civil rights in the German constitution. The Sorbs are particularly renowned for their ornamental Easter eggs, their Easter rides organized in various towns, and their traditional style of celebrating marriage and weddings. Dance and music abound during the festival of *Zapust,* which lasts from the end of January to the beginning of March.

53 43 09), offers listings of accommodations in hotels, *Pensionen,* and private homes (DM19-30), as well as **city tours.** (Office open daily 10am-6pm; mid-Oct. to Apr. closed on Sundays. Tours May to mid-Oct. W 2pm, Sa-Su 11am.) At the ancient defense-tower-turned **Jugendherberge (HI),** Am Zwinger 1 (tel. 40 34 7), just to the right through the Nikolaiturm, experience real Saxon hospitality (and great *Sächsische* accents) while sleeping in tight triples. If your luck runs out, you'll get put in the 20-bed rooms, but it's usually the school groups who get shafted. To get there, go to the Hauptmarkt, go up Kornstr., and stick with it as it jogs right and turns into Schulerstr. It's to your right after you go through the Schülertor. (DM18, over 26 DM23. Breakfast included. Reception M-F 7am-8pm, Sa-Su 6pm-8pm. No lockout. Curfew 10pm, but you'll get a key.) The **post office,** 02607 Bautzen, is located on Postplatz (open M-F 8am-6pm, Sa 9am-noon). The **telephone code** is 03591.

FOOD Aesthetic: airbrush artwork. Cuisine: Hungarian. Prices: DM15-25 for dinner. If this package sounds appetizing, check out **Zum Mathias,** which serves *Eibauer!* (Open M-F 11:30am-3pm and 5-10pm, Sa-Su 11:30am-midnight. Closed Wednesdays Oct.-Mar.) With a decor heavy on gangsta motifs, **Al Capone's,** Schülerstr. 4, bangs out pizzas (DM7.50-12) and pasta (DM9-14; open M 5pm-midnight, Tu-Su 11:30am-2pm and 5pm-midnight). **Wjelbik,** Kornstr. 7 (tel. 420 60), serves tasty Sorbian specialities. Try the *Sorbische Stulle* (DM13), or relish a hefty veggie dish (DM16-17, open daily 11am-11pm). The Hauptmarkt hosts a fresh food **market** (Tu 8am-1pm, Sa 7-11am). **Optimal,** right around the corner from Rechnerstr. 18 on Ressnerstr., fills all of your grocery needs (open M-F 9am-6pm, Sa 9am-4pm).

SIGHTS To reach the *Altstadt* from the station, walk straight through Rathenauplatz and bear left onto Bahnhofstr., then left at the post office onto Karl-Marx-Str. True comrades follow the Marxist path to the intersection up ahead; on the left is the **Stadt Museum,** Kornmarktstr. 1 (tel. 498 50), specializing in the regional and cultural history of Bautzen. *(Open W-Su 10am-5pm. DM3, children and students DM2.)* The museum also displays a collection of wood carvings and copper engravings from the 15th through 17th centuries. Up Kornmarktstr. from the museum is the leaning tower of Bautzen, the **Reichen Turm,** on Reichenstr. *(Open daily Apr.-Oct. 10am-5pm. Last entrance at 4:30pm. DM1, students and children DM0.50.)* It was built in 1490, with a Baroque top added in 1715. It deviates exactly 1.44m from the perpendicular. The view is marvelous. A block away, at the intersection of Wendische Gasse and Wendischestr., is the **Alte Caserne** (old barracks), an elegant building designed by Dresden master Gottfried Semper that housed unappreciative 19th-century troops and currently houses business offices.

Left from the Reichen Turm down Reichenstr. is the **Hauptmarkt.** The grand yellow building is the **Rathaus** (built in 1213), with the Fleischmarkt behind it alongside the Gothic **Dom St. Petri.** *(Open June-Sept. M-Sa 10am-4pm; May and Oct. M-Sa 10am-3pm.)* Also built in 1213, the Dom has been Eastern Germany's only *Simultankirche* (simultaneously Catholic and Protestant) since 1524. The division of the church was a remarkably peaceful compromise, although until 1952 a 4m-high fence in the middle of the church was what kept it peaceful. Farther along sits the ornate red-and-gold **Domstift,** housing the **Domschatz** (cathedral treasury), a phenomenal collection of jewel-studded gowns, icons, and gold regalia. Ring to get in. *(Open M-F 10am-noon and 1-4pm. Free.)* Follow An der Petrikirche downhill from the cathedral until you see the **Nikolaiturm** down the hill on your right. Crossing under the gate, note the face carved above the entrance. Locals claim that this is a likeness of a former mayor, who was bricked alive into the tower as retribution for opening the city to Hussite attackers in the 16th century.

The Sorbs have had a significant effect on the Bautzen landscape, and much of this history can be experienced again today. If you head back through Nikolaiturm and right onto Schloßstr., you'll find the **Sorbisches Museum,** Ortenburg 3 (tel. 424 03), which details the intriguing history and culture of the Sorbs. *(Museum open Apr.-Oct. daily 10am-12:30pm and 1-5pm; Nov.-Mar. 10am-12:30pm and 1-4pm. DM3, students and children DM2.)* Displays include samples of their writing, life-sized costumes, the area's special Sorbian Easter eggs, and those crazy *Dudelsacks,* which look like psychedelic water-filtration devices. Today the Sorbian language is seldom heard in the city, but buses leave regularly for villages such as **Panschwitz-Kuckau, Neuschwitz,** and **Crostwitz,** which are roughly 80-90% Sorb, and where both the mother tongue and colorful traditional costumes are alive. The **Sorbische Kultur Information Office,** Postpl. 2 (tel. 421 05; fax 428 11), can help facilitate your visit, finding rides and even accommodations in Sorb homes. They also sell Sorb CDs, literature, and Easter eggs. *(Open M-F 10am-6pm.)* If your timing is right, you can catch one of the celebrations held on Catholic holidays. On Easter (April 4 in 1999), the people of Bautzen and neighboring towns gather to ride around on horses, proclaiming the good news. January 25 marks the **Marriage of the Birds** *(Vogelhochzeit),* during which children act like sycophantic peckers dressed in bird costumes. The children run around like overjoyed pigeons to represent local birds' gratefulness for seeds left by their human friends and to celebrate marital merriment. For more info on the Sorbs, see **The Absorbing Sorbs,** p. 159.

From the Nikolaiturm or the Sorbisches Museum, follow the **Osterweg** path around the city walls and along the Spree, taking in the views of the 1480 **Mühlbastei** (mill tower), the 1558 **Alte Wasserkunst** (old water tower), and the spire of the 1429 **Michaeliskirche.** On the way back up the hill, on the other side of the fortress, lies the brown-shingled **Hexenhäusrl** (witches' cottage). This small wooden structure, the oldest house in the area, was the only home in the area to survive two devastating fires. The villagers subsequently shunned the inhabitants as witches, though the fire was actually averted by a well inside the house.

■ Görlitz

The easternmost town in Germany, Görlitz offers an untouristed *Altstadt* that has changed little since Napoleon trudged through it on the way to his unsuccessful invasion of Russia. Many of the elegant pastel Renaissance and Baroque homes of former *Bürgermeister*s still stand. In fact, Görlitz was one of the only German towns to survive WWII completely unharmed. With historic buildings competing for attention on every corner, straightforward rail connections, and easy access to major bus routes, Görlitz is an excellent starting point for exploring Oberlausitz.

Most of Görlitz's central sights are located around the **Obermarkt.** From the train station's main north exit, go straight down **Berliner Straße,** Görlitz's attractive pedestrian zone. The street intersects **Postplatz,** home to a beautiful central fountain surrounded by a motley collection of flowers, the gloomy main **post office,** and the darkly stained **Frauenkirche** (a late Gothic cathedral built in 1431; open M-Tu and Th-

F 2:30-4:30pm, W 12:30-2:30pm). The 5m-thick **Dicker Turm,** a squat gray tower, stands tall and proud at Marienplatz, located right past the Karstadt department store.

Across the *Markt,* you'll see the **Dreifaltigkeitskirche.** Originally a 13th-century Franciscan monastery, the church bears marks of frequent expansion. Walking past it down Brüderstr. you will come to the Untermarkt. Here stands the **Rathaus** (built in 1537, remodeled in 1902-1903). At its top is a clock-face in which a sculptured head yawns with the passing of each minute. On the corner is the **Ratsapotheke,** a Renaissance building from 1550 that still has an astrology and astronomy chart painted on its crumbling surface—the confluence of tweaked clocks is indicative of Görlitz's position on the 15-degree meridian, the center point of the Central European time zone. Feel the synergy, sun baby. Don't miss the **St. Peter and Paul Church** down Peterstr. from the Untermarkt. Its brightly adorned interior, speckled with gilded suns and clocks, is enough to impress even the most jaded of tourists. Enter on the backside (open M-F 10:30am-4pm, Sa 10:30am-5pm, Su 11:30am-5pm). When you get to St. Peter, don't miss the view (or a stroll) across the river to the tower painted with an enormous head.

Trains chug to Bautzen (50min., 1 per hr.), Dresden (2hr., 1 per hr.), and Zittau (50min., 1 per hr.). The **tourist office,** Obermarkt 29 (tel. 475 70; fax 47 57 27), sells maps and finds rooms (DM30-40) in private homes for free (open M-F 10am-6:30pm, Sa 10am-4pm, Su 10am-1pm). For a **taxi,** call 40 68 93. The **telephone code** is 03581.

Görlitz has a sweet, sweet *Jugendstil* **Jugendherberge (HI),** Goethestr. 17 (tel./fax 40 65 10). This villa, poised over beautiful shaded grounds, is one of the coolest hostels for miles around. Take the south exit *(Südausgang)* of the train station, bear left up the hill, turn right onto Zittauerstr., and continue until Goethestr. just past the **Tierpark.** Turn left, and the hostel is ahead on the right (15min.). Enter the gate up the stairs to reach the entrance on the right. The huge stained-glass windows are almost as brilliantly colorful as the comforters (we exaggerate—*nothing* is as colorful as the comforters). Accordions and guitars are supplied for guests' use; you can also rent skis, baby carriages, and grills. Mostly of the rooms have four beds and balconies. (DM21, over 27 DM26. Breakfast included, but they'll jack you for DM1 if you want coffee, *kakao,* or tea. Reception M-F 7am-9:30pm, Sa-Su 7-10am and 4-9:30pm. No lockout. Curfew 10pm, but keys available. Wheelchair accessible.)

Many cost-effective *Imbiß* options line Berliner Str., while the nooks and crannies of the *Altstadt* shelter numerous restaurants (see the beer glass key on the city map at the tourist office). **Destille,** Nikolaistr. 6 (tel. 40 53 02), directly across from the *Nikolaiturm* and down the street from St. Peter, serves *Soljanka* soup with toast (DM5) to the many locals who flock to its wooden tables. They also weigh patrons down with a hefty farmer's omelette, served with ham and potatoes (DM10; open daily 11:30am-3pm and 5:30-11pm). The immaculate seafood restaurant **Gastmahl des Meeres,** Struvestr. 2 (tel. 40 62 29), whips up Alaskan fish for DM11.70 (open M-Sa 11am-9:30pm, Su 11am-3pm). Two **Edeka-Markts** make **supermarket** hunting easy: Steinstr. 1 is in the *Altstadt* (open M-F 8:30am-6pm, Sa 8-11am), and Goethestr. 17 is but a few doors down from the hostel (open M-W 8am-6:30pm, Th-F 8am-7pm, Sa 7:30am-2pm).

ZITTAUER GEBIRGE

In a sliver of Germany that borders Czech Bohemia and Poland rise the rocky cliffs of the Zittauer Gebirge. Once a favored spot of medieval monks, these beehive-shaped mountains are the conquests of choice for skiers, hikers, and landscape lovers. The sublime surroundings were a fountain of inspiration for Romantic artists like Ludwig Richter. But matters have not always been so picture-perfect. In 1491, the Gebirge was the scene of the vicious **Bierkrieg** (beer war), when the citizens of Görlitz protested Zittau's success as a beer-brewing town by destroying barrels of the beverage. The horror! More recently, the local forests and workers of this region have experienced a nasty socialist hangover plaguing much of eastern Germany, as inefficient factories are being shut down, leaving many residents unemployed.

SACHSEN

■ Zittau

Wedged into a junction of three nations—Poland, the Czech Republic, and Germany—Zittau has served as a trading and cultural center for many years. Under the rule of the Bohemian kings in 1238, Zittau took on a dominant role in Oberlausitz; it later came to dominate the textile industry. The more important sights lie in the *Altstadt*. From the train station, follow Bahnhofstr. through Haberkornplatz to Bautzner Str., which will lead you directly to the Johanniskircheplatz. There, you can behold the recently renovated exterior of the **Johanniskirche**, first rebuilt in 1837, and climb to the tower (open May-Sept. M-F noon-6pm, Sa-Su 10am-4pm; DM3, students and seniors DM2). From the church, walk directly down Bautznerstr. to the grand **Marktplatz**. The Renaissance-style **Rathaus** was designed by Prussian architect Friedrich Schinkel in 1843. Heading left down Johannistr., you'll see the late Gothic **Kloster Kirche**, and farther up Klosterstr., the **Stadtmuseum** (tel./fax 51 02 70), housed in a former 13th-century Franciscan monastery. (Open Tu and Th 10am-noon and 1-4pm, W 10am-noon and 1-6pm, F 10am-1pm, Sa 2-4pm, Su 10am-noon and 2-5pm. DM3, students DM2.) A collection of standard medieval torture devices awaits in the cellar.

Trains roll in from Dresden (1½hr., every 2hr.) and Görlitz (1hr., 1 per hr.). The **tourist office**, Markt 1 (tel. 75 21 37; fax 75 21 61), rests in the *Rathaus* on the first floor near the left side entrance. It provides hiking maps and a room-finding service (rooms DM20-40) for a DM5 fee (open M-F 8am-6pm, Sa 9am-1pm; summers also Su 1-4pm). A **pharmacy,** Johannis Apotheke, Johannisstr. 2 (tel. 51 21 64), has night services listed on the door (open M-F 8am-6pm, Sa 8am-noon). The **post office,** 02763 Zittau, is at Haberkornpl. 1 and even sells groceries (open M-F 6am-8pm, Sa 7am-4pm). Head up Johannisstr. from the tourist office for the historic **Kloster Stüb'l,** Johannisstr. 4-6 (tel. 51 25 76). Pictures of merry monks with large glasses of beer grace the entrance of the restaurant, built in 1810. Try the *Abernmanke* "mit Brotwurscht and Sauerkroattch" (DM8.50) or lighter *Soljanka* soup with toast and lemon (DM4). There's also an all-you-can-eat salad bar for DM9 (open M-Th 11am-10pm, F-Sa 11am-midnight). A myriad of cafes and pastry shops in the *Markt* and along Johannesstr. provide tasty delicacies, while the **Rewe Markt,** Bautznerstr. 11, also satisfies **grocery** needs (open M-F 8am-6pm, Sa 8am-noon). The **telephone code** is 03583.

■ Oybin

The neighboring *Kurort* of Oybin is a love-child of beauty and *kitsch* that will make everyone smile. The surrounding scenery is sublime, with pine-forested hills punctuated by imposing mounds of twisted, eroded sandstone. At the top of the cliffs outside the town are the ruins of a high-Gothic fortress and cloister built in the 14th century. In the summer, concerts are held in the halls of the **cathedral.** To get there, start up the stairs (it'll cost DM5 at the top, under 16 DM2) to the left of the church and across from the **tourist office.** There's good hiking and more stone on the other side of Oybin's village. *Kitsch* is king at **Märchenspiele,** a small *Biergarten* next to the train station, which brings fairy tales to life with delightfully cheesy moving miniature dwarves and hikers (open daily 9:30am-6pm; DM2, under 6 DM1). There's more where that came from at the **Schmalspurbahn** (small gauge steam train) **Museum,** where the first tickets ever sold to the adorable train in 1890 are displayed (open M-F 1-4pm, Sa-Su 10am-noon and 1-4pm; DM2, children DM1).

To get to Oybin, hop on that very same *Schmalspurbahn*, just outside the Zittau train station (45min., 3-4 per day, DM5.40 one-way). To sleep over, stop by the **tourist office,** Hauptstr. 15, and get a cheap private room (DM18-22) or an elaborate vacation apartment (DM40-80). They also sell maps. (Open M-F 10am-5pm, Sa noon-4pm, Su 2-4pm; when closed, a list of accommodations is posted next to the door.) In a pinch, the nearby town of *Jonsdorf* is home to the **Jugendherberge Dreilandereck (HI).** From Zittau, you can take the *Schmalspurbahn* to Jonsdorf (the last station) and then turn down Hainstr. From Oybin, you have to take the *Bahn* to Bertsdorf., then switch trains to Jonsdorf, or take the bus (last bus 6:55pm, 6 per day). The office is at Hainstr. 14 (tel. (03 58 44) 702 20, call in advance; DM21, seniors DM26; reception 7am-9pm). The **telephone code** is 035844.

■ Chemnitz

Chemnitz may be the most elusive city in the former East Germany. Always an industrial center, it was bombed extensively during WWII and was subsequently rebuilt in the most monolithic, pre-fab style imaginable. Since the *Wende*, the smaller, more human scale of small business and culture has feverishly tried to push itself into every crack of socialist temples, but with mixed results. There are pockets of energy all over the city, but it seems that Chemnitz has yet to unite into a cohesive urban fabric.

PRACTICAL INFORMATION Across from Marx, in the *Stadthalle,* you'll find the **tourist information office,** Rathausstr. 1 (tel. 194 33; fax 450 87 25), on the other side of the *Halle.* There you can get info and find private rooms (DM25-40, DM3 fee). For a **taxi,** call 44 62 44 or 30 22 51. On the other side of Straße der Nationen looms the **post office,** 09009 Chemnitz (open M-F 9am-6pm, Sa 9am-noon). The **telephone code** is 0371.

ACCOMMODATIONS AND FOOD Accommodations in Chemnitz are relatively expensive, and the youth hostel is way out of town and virtually inaccessible by public transportation. Deciding whether or not it's worth it to stay in Chemnitz is difficult. The (relative) luxury of nearby Augustusburg beckons with a castle youth hostel, but Chemnitz comes right back with a hard-to-miss nightlife. If you do stay, it'll cost you. For a quick bite, swing by the market next to the *Rathaus,* which is always full of *Imbiße.* For something more, stop by the *Brühl,* or **Bogart's,** Hartmannstr. 7d, which serves up a healthy vegetable platter (DM12) as well as tasty blueberry shakes (DM5; open daily 4pm-3am). A good **supermarket** waits in the train station (open M-F 6am-9:45pm, Sa-Su 7am-9:45pm). It's also remarkably easy to find cheap eats of the fast food variety along Straße der Nationen.

SIGHTS To begin your search for that energy, head straight down Georgstr. from the *Hauptbahnhof;* after a block, you'll come to **Straße der Nationen,** the north-south axis of Chemnitz. To your right, on the north end of this axis, you'll find a quiet neighborhood of old houses that centers on the **Brühl,** a serene pedestrian zone. Farther south along Straße der Nationen, the city begins building itself up to its socialist crescendo. Every street corner boasts statues of frolicking children or happily scrubbed workers. But nothing outshines the **bust of Karl Marx,** an enormous concrete chunk that bears the likeness of the city's adopted philosopher—Chemnitz was called Karl-Marx-Stadt from 1953 to 1990, even though Marx never lived here.

After all that bewildering concrete pomposity, it's great to retreat to Chemnitz's two museums. Halfway down Straße der Nationen on the *Theaterplatz* is the **König-Albert-Museumsbau,** with the **Städtische Kunstsammlungen Chemnitz** (City Art Exhibit) and the **Museum für Naturkunde Chemnitz** (Natural History Museum). The art exhibit features a nice sampling of 19th- and 20th-century German art, as well as a huge collection of paintings and woodcuts by local Expressionist Karl Schmidt-Rotluff. *(Open Tu and Th-Su 11am-5pm, W 11am-7:30pm. DM4, students and seniors DM2.)* Farther north, you'll find a peaceful park and the **Schloß Complex.** To reach the complex, at Schloßberg 12, dash to Straße der Nationen from the train station and turn right, and take a left onto Elisenstr., which merges with Müllerstr., which in turn leads to Schloßberg on the right. The castle that stood here was destroyed in the Thirty Years War; the **Schloßbergmuseum** occupies a reconstructed building that approximates the old structure. *(Open Tu-F 10am-5pm, Sa-Su 10am-6pm. DM4, students DM2.)* The goods reside upstairs in the **Stadtgeschichte** (city history) display. A large room documents the history of Chemnitz from its 12th-century foundation. The posters advertising Hitler's *Entartete Kunst* (Degenerate Art) exhibit, on display in Chemnitz at the outset of World War II, and the collections of Communist kitsch from the Karl-Marx-Stadt days are particularly intriguing.

SACHSEN

ENTERTAINMENT AND NIGHTLIFE Nightlife options buzz, including **Chemnitzer Kabarett,** An der Markthalle 1-3 (tel./fax 67 50 90), a hilarious establishment with a huge repertoire and a loyal following. (Performances begin daily at 8pm. M-Th tickets DM12-22, DM5 student discount. F-Su DM15-25, no discount.) You can also try the **Chemnitz Opera** or a play at the **Schauspielhaus.** Schedules and info for both are posted on the *Theaterplatz.* (Opera tickets DM10-30, 50% student discount. Box office open M-F 10am-6pm, Sa 2-6pm.) If high culture's not for you, shake it at **Fuchsbau,** Carolastr. 8 (tel. 67 17 17; grooves W-Su after 9pm), where local cats head for disco, techno, and jazz. Check out Chemnitz magazines *Blitz* and *Stadtstreicher* for more on nightlife.

■ Near Chemnitz: Augustusburg

A night at the lively and beauteous castle in Augustusburg facilitates recovery from the exhaustion of post-industrialist, post-Marxist, monochromatic Chemnitz. The princely mountaintop hamlet can be reached by bus T-244 or T-245 from the Chemnitz *Busbahnhof,* down Georgstr. from the train station to "Schloßberg." (45min., 7am-7pm, DM4.90, check schedules early.) The stop is at the foot of the path leading to the castle. The Renaissance **hunting lodge** of the Sachsen Electors is perched 1500m above town with a mesmerizing 360-degree panorama of the surrounding **Erzgebirge** mountains—look for the Czech Republic on the horizon. (*Schloß* open May-Oct. daily 9am-6pm; Nov.-Apr. 10am-5pm.) A guided tour (required) of the royal playhouse will lead you through the **Brünnenhaus** (well house) and the intimate **Schloßkapelle** (church chapel), the only Renaissance chapel left in Sachsen. The altar is graced by a Lucas Cranach painting, portraying the dour Herzog August, his wife Anna, and their 14 pious children. (Tours every hr. at 30min. past the hr.; DM4, students DM2.50.) Explore the **Motorrad Museum** (Motorcycle Museum), the **Museum für Jagdtier und Vogel kunde des Erzgebirges** (Hunting and Game Museum), or the **Kutschen Museum** (Carriage Museum). A day pass for all museums costs DM10 (students DM6). Tickets for individual museums can also be purchased separately. The real treat of a visit to Augustusburg is the **Jugendherberge (HI),** located inside the castle (tel. (037291) 202 56), with high domed ceilings, animal skins on the walls, and a supreme view of the surrounding mountains. Narrow and crooked stone stairways lead from the spacious bunk-bed rooms to the romantic doubles (2 mattresses tucked together in an alcove). The ambience really is medieval—you are the prince or princess of the castle, and the screaming schoolchildren your lowly serfs. (DM26, students DM21. Breakfast included. Reception 7am-8pm, check-in after 3pm.)

The Greatest Budget Souvenir Ever—Castles for DM1!

Many travelers like to buy postcards of castles and happily shell out a few *Marks* for pretty little pictures of royal abodes. Some travelers, however, prefer to buy their own castle. The state of Sachsen has more royal palaces than it knows what to do with (about 1000), and has begun a novel pilot program to market some of these treasured historical fortifications for a mere DM1. There is, sadly, a slight drawback. Those who purchase the castles must renovate them—40 years of GDR neglect has produced a terrible state of disrepair. The cost of renovation tacks about DM7-20 million onto the purchase costs. Still, the opportunities for those who want to buy something by which to remember their travels in Germany are spectacular. Schloß Gaußig, about 10km from Bautzen, has a newly renovated ballroom with all the posh adornments one could ever hope for. Its dining room provides a *Jägermeister* fantasy, with deer antlers lining the walls. The nearby Schloß Milkel comes with a mausoleum and many remains of ancient royalty. Schloß Lichtenwalde, 10km from Chemnitz, is also up for grabs. Response to the offer has been rather slow, so the opportunity to purchase your very own bit of royalty should endure for a while.

■ Freiberg

A history as one of Germany's most fantastically rich cities during the late Middle Ages and a college-town atmosphere combine to make Freiberg one of the most refreshing cities in Sachsen. *Dom-* and *Altstadt*-weary travelers can check out the compelling silver mines at **Himmelfahrt Fundgrube** or **Freiberger Silberbergwerk.** Mined since the 14th century, the silver deposits have been a major source of wealth for Freiberg and Sachsen. While the first notice of anyone striking silver in the town dates to the Frankish and Thüringer settlers in 1168, the 700m deep mine has been used for educational purposes since 1765, providing geology and mining students with a "laboratory." Today, the mine attracts down 'n' dirty adventure-seeking tourists who want to toss on an old-school uniform, jump into Wellington boots, and strap on a headlamp before descending into the dark bowels of the earth.

To get to the entrance of the **silver mine** from the station, walk along Bahnhofstr., take a left on Poststr., and veer right onto Hornstr., which leads to Himmelfahrtsgasse. After passing the cemetery, turn left on Füchsmuhlenweg, which leads to the mine, the **Reiche Zeche Schacht.** The two-hour **tour** begins when everyone sports the GDR-style *Schutzkleidung* (protective clothing). The guide retells the history of the mine as he leads the group through the dark, wet tunnels, illuminated only by headlamps. (Tours May-Sept. M-F 9:30am, Sa 8, 11am, and 2pm; Sept.-Apr. M-F 9:30am, first Sa every month 8, 11am, and 2pm. DM15, students DM10.) After all that sloppin' around underground, it's especially interesting to re-emerge and see just where all that money went. The spectacular **Freiberger Dom** towers at the edge of the Untermarkt, easily reached from the train station: walk straight on Bahnhofstr., turn left on Poststr., which changes names twice (Erbischestr. and Burgstr.) before it reaches Kirchgasse, and continue straight to the *Dom.* The *Dom* stores some worldclass treasures. The intricately ornate **Goldene Pforte** (Golden Portal) is almost as stunning as the free standing **Tulpen Kanzel** (Tulip Pulpit). The pulpit is an amazing sculpture, more like something you'd see in a Wieronymous Bosch painting than in a German cathedral. The *Dom* may usually only be visited on a tour. (Tours May-Oct. M-Sa 10, 11am, 2, 3, and 4pm, Su 11am, 2, 3, and 4pm; Nov.-Apr. daily 11am, 2, and 3pm. Tours with organ demonstration (their organ, not yours) Th 2 and 8pm, Su 11am. Tours DM4, students DM2; organ tours DM5, students DM3.)

The **tourist office (Freiberg Info),** Burgstr. 1 (tel. 236 02; fax 27 32 60), behind the *Rathaus,* sells tickets and silver trinkets, gives **tours,** and finds **private rooms** (DM30-50) for a small fee (open M-F 9am-6pm, Sa 9am-noon). On the opposite side of the *Rathaus,* the **Rats-Apotheke pharmacy** has been pushing pills since 1539 (open M-Tu and Th 7am-6:30pm, W and F 7am-6pm, Sa 8am-noon). The **post office,** 09599 Freiberg, is at the end of Poststr. on the way to town (open M-F 9am-6pm, Sa 9am-12pm). The **telephone code** is 03731.

For an elegant setting and delicious food, the **Hartmann Café** (tel. 228 07), at the corner of Obermarkt and Peterstr., cooks up breakfast all day (veggie omelette with *Brötchen* DM7.50) and light meals (tasty quiche DM3.50). They specialize in fantastic baked goods—savor some *Kaffee und Kuchen* (open Tu-Sa 8am-6pm, Su 11am-6pm). To see geophysics students get their rocks off as you have a drink, dance at **Das Füllort,** the beer garden **Wolfsschlucht,** and the bar **Abgang**—all located on Petersstr. 5 (tel. 26 24 04 for all; disco and bar open M and Sa 10pm-late; beer garden open daily 2pm-late). For groceries, visit the **E Activ Markt** on the Marktplatz (open M-W 8am-6:30, Th-F 8am-7pm, Sa 7:30am-1pm).

THE ERZGEBIRGE

In the region of Sachsen just south of Chemnitz lie the Erzgebirge, rolling hills dotted by modest villages. Rich in a history of silver-mining and woodworking, the region puts on its best face for Christmas, when every village fills up with wooden angels, nutcracker soldiers, and those weird pyramid things that spin when you light their candles, all Erzgebirge specialties. In fact, they get down so hard here that it's often just referred to as "Christmas-land." If you come in the summer you'll still find plenty of beautiful woods for hiking, and Erzgebirge hospitality that will cure even the worst case of the Eastern-Bloc blues.

■ Annaberg-Buchholz

Formerly two less-than-friendly cities that sat across a kingdom's border, but on top of the same silver deposit, these two towns merged in 1945 and now serve as the center of the Erzgebirge. Although the town functions as a transportation hub for the region, it does boast a few tourist gems of its own. Up Große Kirchgasse from the tourist office resides **St. Annenkirche,** Saxony's most spectacular late gothic church. The interior is awe-inspiring, with every corner filled with an altar or sculpture, all spectacularly preserved. That crazy sculptor Hans Witten surfaces again with his baptismal, complete with piously begging babies. (Open M-F 10am-4pm, Sa 10-11:30am and 2-4pm, Su 2-4pm). Just across the street is the **Erzgebirgemuseum** (tel. 2 34 97), where you can find out about the political and geological history of the region (open Tu-Su 10am-5pm; DM4.50, students DM2.50). The real highlight, though, is in the **mine** out back, where you throw on a poncho and go right to the source of the Erzgebirge treasure. The mine can only be visited by groups of four or more, but if you check ahead, the office will be happy to let you tag along with the next tour (DM7, students DM3.50; combo ticket for mine and museum DM10.50, students DM5.50).

Annaberg-Buchholz is connected to the rest of Saxony by its *Bahnhof.* From here, buses leave for Chemnitz *Omnibusbahnhof* (1hr., DM7.60), Dresden *Hauptbahnhof* (2½hr.), and just about every town in the Erzgebirge. To find out which you'd like to visit, head over to the **tourist office,** Markt 1 (tel. 42 51 39). From the *Busbahnhof,* go down Wolkensteinstr. until it bends right; the office is right in front of you. There the staff gives out info for the whole region and finds private rooms (DM25-40, DM2 fee). They also sell hiking maps and handicrafts (open M-F 9am-7pm, Sa 9am-noon). The **postal code** is 09456. The **telephone code** is 03733.

If you work up a hunger traipsing through the tunnels, head to **Akropolis,** Markt 9 (tel. 229 20), when you emerge. Right in the far corner of the Markt, its huge menu offers everything from pizza to Greek and vegetarian specialties (DM12-15; open daily 8:30am-midnight).

■ Neudorf

If you'd like to spend the night in the Erzgebirge and see a bit of the countryside, your best bet is Neudorf. The **Jugendherberge,** Vierenstr. 26 (tel. (037342) 82 82), is only a 10-minute walk from the bus stop and is right at the head of several trails. To get there from Annenberg-Buchholz, get on the Neudorf bus at the *Busbahnhof,* and go until "Neudorf-Oberdorf" (30min., DM4.70). From there head farther up Karlsbaderstr., Neudorf's main road. Vierenstr. will branch off to your right shortly. (DM24, over 26 DM29. Reception 6am-10pm.) If hunger sets in after the hike, you can head back down Karlsbaderstr., where you'll find a **Spar** and a **bakery and butcher** (15min. past the bus stop; all open until 5pm).

Although Neudorf doesn't have much to offer besides hiking, you can take the **Fichtelbergbahn,** which stops at Vierenstr., up to **Oberwiesental** (30min., DM10) a small town at the base of the **Fichtelberg,** the highest mountain in the former East Germany. In the winter, its a jumpin' ski town, and in the summer you can still find plenty to do, including a hike to the top. If you are lucky enough to be there in the winter, Jugendherberge Neudorf rents skis.

■ Zwickau

Zwickau is best known as the Motor City of Eastern Germany. For over 35 years, the city's Sachsenring-Auto-Union produced the GDR's ubiquitous consumer car, the tiny

Trabant. An ill-engineered, two-cylinder plastic jalopy, the *"Trabi"* was Communist industry's inferior answer to the West's *Volkswagen,* and, like cockroaches, the wheezing little cars persist. Officially, the city would prefer to play up its more genteel distinctions, such as its active artistic tradition, which launched composer Robert Schumann and a couple of members of the *Brücke* painting school into the world. But it may be a losing battle; the tinny whine of a *Trabi* laboring uphill is never far from the ears of a visitor.

The dusky-colored, four-story **Schumann Haus** stands at Hauptmarkt 5 (tel./fax 21 52 69). The museum plays up the Romantic composer's childhood in Zwickau before his life as a "globetrotting" celebrity. The museum also devotes several parts of the display to Schumann's wife, Clara Wieck, one of the most accomplished pianists of her day—today, Clara is eternalized as "the woman on the DM100 bill." No mention here of Schumann's later insanity, although the less than flattering busts of the composer hint that all was not well. Musicians perform both Robert and Clara's works in the *Klavierhalle.* (Open M-Sa 10am-5pm; DM5, students and seniors DM3.)

Amid a smattering of Schumann memorabilia and a dark, imposing, old **cathedral** at the newly-renovated central Platz, Zwickau's unique offering is its **Automobilienmuseum,** W. Rathenau-Str. 51 (tel. 332 22 32). To find it, make your way north from the Ring on Römerstr., which becomes Walther-Rathenau-Str., to an out-of-the-way little building past the auto factory (20min.). Before the days of GDR mediocrity, Zwickau turned out classy cars—its early production days spawned the Audi company, and auto pioneer August Horch designed some roadsters that'll knock your socks off. Over a dozen *Trabant* models are on display, prompting wonder at the design's invulnerability to innovation over the years. The sight of the last *Trabi* ever produced (in 1991) in all of its pink "splendor" and emblazoned with the words, "Trabant: Legend on Wheels," is enough to make even the most ardent Cold Warrior misty-eyed. (Open Tu and Th 9am-noon and 2-5pm, Sa-Su 10am-5pm; DM5, students and seniors DM3.50.)

Located in the middle of the busy Sachsen Thüringen rail network, Zwickau is easily reached by **train** as a daytrip from Leipzig (1½hr., 13 per day), Dresden (2hr., 26 per day), or Altenburg (40min., 17 per day). Its oldest attractions and most beautiful streets are confined to a circular region in the *Altstadt,* bounded by a bustling three-lane roundabout named **Dr.-Friedrichs-Ring.** Zwickau's **tourist office,** Hauptstr. 6 (tel. 29 37 13; fax 29 37 15; email zwickau@lfr-sachsen.imedia.de), lies in the center of the circle; from the station, head along the left fork, which becomes Bahnhofstr., until it ends at Humboldtstr. Turn right, and then quickly left on Schumannstr., which will lead you across the Ring. The street resumes as Innere Plauensche Str., a pedestrian zone, which takes you past the Marienkirche. Hang a right to the *Markt;* the office is right behind the Burger King. The staff provides maps and books rooms, which run DM35 and up (open M-F 9am-6pm, Sa 9am-noon). The main **post office,** Humboldtstr. 3, 08056 Zwickau, is just outside the Ring. The **telephone code** is 0375.

The monthly *Stadtsreicher,* free at the tourist office, lists the major events in the area, ranging from shows to bars to food. Just outside the Ring, **Bistro International,** Schumannstr. 10 (tel. 29 88 09), has Turkish pizzas (DM8-10) that please the palate (open daily 10am-midnight). To imbibe some spirits and GDR nostalgia, head to **Roter Oktober,** at the corner of Leipziger Str. and Kolpingstr. Toast the hammer and sickle if you really feel like getting crazy. The **Markt** serves up food stands (Th-F 8am-6pm). Cheap dining options can be found along the Hauptmarkt and Innere Schneebergerstr. during the day, while the **SPAR supermarket,** across from the Schumann Haus, fills your grocery bags (open M-F 8am-6:30pm, Sa 8am-noon).

■ Plauen

Plauen sits in the middle of the Vogtland, a region of rolling hills and fields that includes all of western Sachsen. The city has spent most of the 20th century clambering to become one of the top German cities. Industrial sectors flourished in the 20s, but bombing sent it right back to square one. Now Plauen is trying to capitalize on its prime location at the corner of no less than five *Bundesländer*. Though progress is slow in the economic sector, Plauen has been able to channel its location's strength into an impressive cultural scene.

PRACTICAL INFORMATION Unlike other German cities, Plauen has no central train station. Trains come into the **Oberer Bahnhof** from most major cities, including Leipzig (the ride is one of the most beautiful train rides in Germany, featuring aqueducts and woods). Trains from Gera and a few other places arrive at the **Unterer Bahnhof**. Luckily, a great **Straßenbahn** system connects the two stations (tickets DM9 for 7, available at *Automaten* at most stops). The **tourist office,** Untergraben 1 (tel. 291 10 27; fax 291 18 09), in the back corner of the *Rathaus,* gives out maps and books rooms (DM35-40) for a DM1-5 fee (open M-F 9am-6pm, Sa 9am-noon). A **post office,** 08523 Plauen, looms over Postplatz, the city's main square (open M-F 8am-6pm, Sa 8am-noon). The **telephone code** is 03741.

ACCOMMODATIONS AND FOOD Plauen's **Jugendherberge**, Reusauer Waldhaus 1 (tel. 47 28 11), sits at the edge of the woods just outside town, with a spectacular view of the rest of the city. Take *Straßenbahn* #4 (direction: Reusa) to "Schloß Reusa," head down the small alley "Am Reusauer Wald" until it hits the woods, then turn right. The hostel will be on your left after a short uphill hike. Call ahead before heading out. (DM24, over 27 DM29. Reception M-F 3-9:30pm, Sa-Su 5-9:30pm.) Closer to the city, try **Ristorante Pizza-Bistro**, Forststr. 25 (tel. 22 25 89). Yes, it is a pizza place, but it also has nice rooms upstairs. (Singles DM45; doubles DM60.)

If you're looking for a quick bite, Postplatz offers a selection of *Imbiß* stands. For pure calories, try **Schweizerstube**, Klostermarkt 4 (tel. 22 00 01), where heavy Swiss specialties like fondue (DM20) and pasta with gorgonzola sauce (DM14) abound (open daily 11:30am-11:30pm). Wannabe artists head to **Café Art,** Brömgaßchen 2 (tel. 22 35 35), just across the *Markt* from the *Rathaus,* to flip through back issues of *Art* and munch light bistro fare for DM10-15 (open Tu-Th 11am-11pm, F and Sa 11am-midnight, Su 3-7pm).

SIGHTS Considering that Allied bombing destroyed over three-quarters of the city, it's understandable that Plauen comes up short on the church-and-castle scene. Most of Plauen's museums focus on the industry that made the city famous: lace. The **Museum Plauener Spitzen** (tel. 22 23 55), in front of the old *Rathaus,* displays examples of lace from throughout Plauen's dainty history. *(Open M-F 10am-5pm, Sa 9am-2pm. DM2.50, students DM1.50.)* Sheer pleasure awaits a little further away. Jump on Straßenbahn #4 to "Vogtland Klinikum" and walk straight ahead up Reusauer Str. The **Schaustickerei,** Obergarten Weg 1 (tel. 44 31 87), is on the right. *(Open M-Sa 10am-5pm. DM3, students DM1.50.)* Inside, a working lace factory showcases machines from every stage in the development of the industry. Check out the transmission on the 1860 machine, used 40 years before it was "discovered" for the automobile.

Besides lace, Plauen boasts beautiful views. To catch a glimpse of scenery, head up to the **Stadtpark,** right next to the *Oberer Bahnhof.* Wander through fields of wildflowers to the **Bärenstein Turm,** a tower with spectacular views. *(Open daily May-Sept. 8am-2am; Oct.-Apr. 9am-7pm.)*

ENTERTAINMENT AND NIGHTLIFE The **Vogtland Theater** (tel. 291 24 38 or 291 24 37) presides over Postplatz near the *Neues Rathaus,* and offers everything from musicals to Chekhov. (Box office open Tu 10am-1pm and 3-6pm, W 10am-3pm, Th 10am-1pm and 3-5pm, F 10am-1pm, Sa 9am-noon, and 1hr. before performances.) Plauen hits it *really* big with the **Malzhaus,** Alter Teich 7-9 (tel. 153 20). A 250-year-old building once used for roasting hops, it now houses an art gallery, a cafe, a film club, and a cabaret. (Film Mondays and Tuesdays, techno Wednesdays, concerts Saturdays and Sundays. Gallery open daily 1-8pm. Cafe and bar open 11am-1am.) In the fall, the Malzhaus sponsors the **Volkherbst,** one of Europe's premier folk music festivals. Different artists play every week, competing for Germany's only European folk music prize. To get there, head down the alley next to Art Café, and take a right.

■ Leipzig

Leipzig jumps out from the calm Eastern German landscape in a fiery blaze of nowNowNOW. The glitzy nightlife and glassy skyscrapers amid concrete blights cast a decidedly cosmopolitan flavor upon the city. The *Uni*-culture spawned by over 20,000 students creates a sense of youthful vitality as it did when Goethe, Nietzsche, and Leibniz stalked these ivory towers. At the same time, Leipzig harbors centuries of cultural importance. The echoes of musical genius emanate from the top-notch *Gewandhaus Orchester,* founded by Felix Mendelssohn in 1850 in the spirit of Bach and Wagner, who both preceded him as residents of this city. Goethe revered Leipzig for its cultivated inhabitants. The city even inspired him to set a pivotal scene from *Faust* in Auerbach's Keller—it was here that Mephisto tricked his student.

Despite such a strong and lofty academic presence, Leipzig has been a site of repeated populist upheaval—first in the "Wars of Liberation," in which the city kicked Napoleon out of Germany in the 1813 Battle of Leipzig, again in the abortive revolutions of 1830 and 1848, and, most recently, in 1989, when Leipzig gained fame as Germany's *Heldenstadt* (city of heroes) for its role as the crucible of *die Wende,* the sudden toppling of the GDR. Leipzig's half-millennium tradition as a *Messe Stadt* (Fair City) continues to impart international verve (and money) into the city. This boom town is bursting with *style* as it charges through the transformations of the *Neue Bundesländer,* resolutely resisting any threats to the student-hipster vibe by self-serving capitalists and specious speculators.

ORIENTATION AND PRACTICAL INFORMATION

Most Leipzig's sights and its entertainment district dwell in the ringed *Innenstadt,* but you'll have to leave the comforting sight of the huge, metal university tower for nightlife and any untouristed underground scenes. It's a 10-minute walk from the main train station on the north edge of the *Innenstadt* to the **Augustusplatz,** the center surrounded by the *Gewandhaus,* the university, and the main post office. The cavernous **Leipziger Hauptbahnhof** is a sight in itself—its curved-beam roofs enclose one of Europe's largest train stations and recall the grander days of rail travel. The station was recently renovated by *Deutsche Bahn* to include a three-story underground shopping center as crassly American as apple pie (most shops open M-Sa 9am-8pm).

Transportation

Flights: Flughafen Leipzig-Halle (info tel. 224 11 55), in Schkendingasse, about 20km from Leipzig. International service throughout central Europe. An **airport city liner bus** leaves Goethestr. next to the tourist office every 30min. M-F 5:30am-10pm, Sa 6:30am-9.30pm, Su 4:30am-10pm. DM9, round-trip DM15.

Trains: (tel. 194 19), Leipzig lies on the Berlin-Munich line, with regular InterCity service to Frankfurt. Trains also zoom you away to Dresden (1hr., 2 per hr., DM31); Halle (20min., 3 per hr., DM9.40); and Berlin (2hr., every 2hr., DM48). Information counter on the platform near track 15, or ask at one of the counters in the huge and hugely helpful new *Reisezentrum* at the entrance of the station.

Public Transportation: Streetcars and buses cover the city; the hub is on Platz der Republik, in front of the *Hauptbahnhof.* Your best bet for tickets is either four 1hr. tickets for DM8 or a day card for DM7. Most major lines run through the night, though usually only 1 per hr. midnight-6am. To transfer at night, go to the *Hauptbahnhof* stop; almost all trains connect there. Tickets are available from the tourist office, vending machines, and drivers.

Taxis: tel. 48 84, 98 22 22, or 42 33.

Car Rental: Sixt-Budget and **Avis** both have counters at the *Bahnhof's Reisezentrum* (open M-F 7am-9pm, Sa-Su 8am-6pm). More offices are at the airport.

Mitfahrzentrale: Goethestr. 7-11 (tel. 194 40), just past the tourist office, organizes ride-shares. Dresden DM16, Berlin DM22. Open daily 8am-8pm. Call ahead.

Hitchhiking: *Let's Go* does not recommend hitchhiking as a safe mode of transportation. Hitchers going to Dresden and Prague take *Straßenbahn* #2, 3, 6, or 8 to "Pounsdorfer Allee," and turn left down Pounsdorfer Allee to the *Autobahn* interchange. To Berlin, take *Straßenbahn* #16 to "Essener Str.," switch to bus F, get out at Sachsenpark, and walk to the *Autobahn*.

Tourist Services

Tourist Office: Leipzig Information, Richard-Wagner-Str. 1 (tel. 710 42 60; fax 710 42 65; email lipsia@aol.com). Walk across Willy-Brandt-Platz in front of the station and turn left at Richard-Wagner-Str. Among the gorgeous brochures, there's a useful free map of the *Innenstadt* and suburbs with a street name index. They book rooms in opulent hotels and *Pensionen* for free and sell tickets. Free magazines *Fritz* and *Blitz* fill you in on nightlife, but the superior *Kreuzer* (also sold at newsstands, DM2.50) puts these to shame. Open M-F 9am-8pm, Sa 9am-4pm, Su 9am-2pm. Room-finding service (tel. 710 42 55) open M-F 9am-6pm, Sa 9:30am-2pm.

Tours: The tourist office leads bus tours (2½hr.) daily at 10am, 1:30pm and 4:30pm. The Sunday 1:30pm tour is in English; the 4:30pm tour is always in English and German. DM28, students DM16, seniors DM20. Walking tours (2hr.), on themes from "the bar mile" to a visit of the fairgrounds, depart daily in the summer at 10am, and 4, 5, 7, and 7:30pm. DM10-15. Shorter tours are also available (Tu-Th 1pm; DM20, students DM15, seniors DM16). Some guides are English-speaking.

Budget Travel: Kilroy Travels Germany, Augustuspl. 9 (tel. 211 42 20), in the university courtyard. Open M-F 10am-7pm, Sa 10am-1pm.

Consulate: U.S. Wilhelm-Seyfferth-Str. 4 (tel. 21 38 40). Entrance on Wächstr. behind the Museum der Bildenden Künste. Available in emergencies M-F 8am-7pm or by appointment. Also home to the **Amerika Haus Bibliothek** (tel. 213 84 25). Open Tu-F 2-5pm.

Currency Exchange: Dresdner Bank, Goethestr. 3-5, just off Augustusplatz. Open M-Th 8:30am-7:30pm, F 8:30am-4pm. Several **ATMs.**

American Express: Bergpl. 2 (tel. 96 70 00), on the 2nd floor of a building just behind the Neues Rathaus. The office acts strictly as a travel agency, and does not exchange money or issue traveler's checks. For that, they have a bureau in the **airport** (tel. 22 41 850). Office open M-F 9:30am-6pm, airport branch open M-F 8am-6pm, Sa-Su 8am-noon.

Local Services

Library: British Council, Lumumbastr. 11-13 (tel. 564 67 12), stocks a reading room with English books a-plenty. Bus to "Nordplatz." Open Tu 1-8pm, W-F 1-5pm.

Gay and Lesbian Information: AIDS-Hilfe, Ossientzkystr. 18 (tel. 232 31 26), features a popular gay cafe on Tu and Th 3-9pm. Also offers the updated **Queer Stadtplan,** a map of gay and lesbian nightlife. Office open M-F 10am-6pm, counseling Tu and Th until 9pm.

Women's Resources: Frauenkultur e.V., Braustr. 17 (tel. 213 00 30), is a center for art, meetings, and cafe relaxation. Office open M-Th 10am-2pm.

Laundromat: Maga Pon, Gottschedstr. 11 (tel. 960 79 22), takes the cake as the jazziest laundromat in Sachsen—it doubles as a hep-cat bar and restaurant, so come in your coolest clothes (unless you want to wash them). Wash DM6, dry DM1. Open daily 9am-3am.

Emergency and Communications

Emergency: Police, tel. 110. **Fire** and **Ambulance,** tel. 112.

Pharmacies: Löwen Apotheke, Grimmaischestr. 19 (tel. 960 50 27). Open M-F 8am-8pm, Sa 9am-4pm. Whenever the shop is closed, push the button by the door for emergency service.

Internet Access: In **Café le bit,** Kohlgartenstr. 2 (tel. 998 20 20; email lebit@wilder.osten.de; see **Food,** p. 172).

Post Office: Hauptpostamt 1, 04109 Leipzig (tel. 212 25 88), across from Augustusplatz on Grimmaischestr. Open M-F 8am-8pm, Sa 9am-4pm.

Telephone Code: 0341.

ACCOMMODATIONS AND CAMPING

The budget accommodation scene in Leipzig is a mess. The development and renovation of the *Innenstadt* has provided a great new hangout, but it has also chased

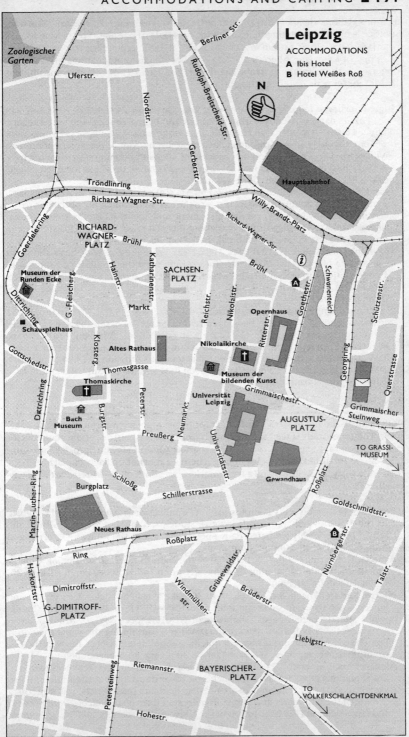

Leipzig
ACCOMMODATIONS
A Ibis Hotel
B Hotel Weißes Roß

accommodations cheaper than DM100 per night way out into the suburbs. The tourist office is no help, with their hefty booking fees (DM10 per night) on private rooms. Your best bet is either a room in a cheap *Pension,* which the office reserves for free, or a copy of **Leipziger Allerlei,** a listing of all of the accommodations in town. For longer stays, the **Mitwohnzentrale,** Goethestr. 7-11 (tel. 194 30), in the same office as the **Mitfahrzentrale,** can help you out.

Jugendherberge Leipzig Centrum (HI), Volksgartenstr. 24 (tel. 245 70 11; fax 245 70 12). Its name is a leftover from an earlier and better location; the hostel is actually a 15min. streetcar ride from the city. Take cars #17, 27, or 57 (direction: Schönefeld) to "Löbanerstr.," and take a right just in front of the supermarket onto Volksgartenstr. This GDR pre-fab apartment keeps the communist party pumpin' straight into the new millenium. DM24, over 26 DM29. Breakfast included. Sheets DM7. Reception until 1am. Curfew 1am.

Hotel Weißes Roß, Roßstr. 20 (tel. 960 59 51). Take the streetcar to Augustusplatz, and walk down Roßplatz until it curves to the left. Go through the portal just to the left of center of the large, curving apartment building; the hotel is 100m straight ahead. Nothing decadent or four-star about this place, but it's very close to the city and has no curfew. Room with breakfast DM60. Reception M-F 2-8pm.

Hotel Ibis, Brühl 69 (tel. 218 60; fax 218 62 22). From the *Bahnhof,* cross the street and head a block down Goethestr. Take a right onto the Brühl. If you run out of budget options, the Ibis is a 2min. walk from the train station, and in summer offers a per-room special price of DM89.90. Rooms normally DM125. Breakfast DM15. 24hr. reception.

Camping: Campingplatz Am Auensee, Gustav-Esche-Str. 5 (tel. 465 16 00), in the nearby suburb of Wahren. A budgetary *deus ex machina* in the absense of hostels. From the station, streetcar #10, 28, or 30 (direction: "Wahren") to "Rathaus Wahren." Turn left at the *Rathaus,* and follow the twisting main road for 10min. DM6-10 for tents, DM12 for caravans. Small tent-huts function as 2-bed bungalows. DM40 per hut, DM45 in winter. Two-person huts with bath DM80. Reception M-Sa 6am-9:30pm, Su 6am-8:30pm.

FOOD

Budget meals are not as hard to find in Leipzig as budget rooms, but it's still no cakewalk. The **Innenstadt** is well supplied with *Imbiß* stands, bistros, and restaurants for consumption on the go. A **Kaiser's supermarket** (open M-F 7am-8pm, Sa 7am-4pm) pops up on the Brühl, near Sachsenplatz. There's a **market** on Sachsenplatz on Tuesdays and Fridays. You'll also find a daily **market** just south of the *Innenstadt* near Bayerischer Platz.

Eck-Café, in the university complex just off Grimmaischestr, across from the *Mensa.* As the *Mensa* is only open to Leipzig U. students, a much better bet is this cafe, which serves freshly prepared daily specials for about DM3. Open Oct.-Feb. and Apr.-Aug. M-Th 9am-10pm, F 11am-3pm.

◉Ashoka, Georgiring 8-9 (tel. 961 48 19) to the right of the *Hauptbahnhof.* Chill to sitar music while consuming orgasmically good Indian food. Dinner DM13-25. Open daily noon-midnight.

Maître, Karl-Liebknecht-Str. 62 (tel. 31 17 30), like Maga Pon (below), treads the fine line between bar, cafe, and restaurant. Streetcar #10, 11, or 28 (direction: "Connewitz," "Markleeberg Ost," or "Markleeberg West," respectively) to "Arndtstr." Also serves breakfast buffet Su 10am-3pm (DM11.80), but during the week they do it French-style with generous slices of quiche and onion tart (DM4). Revel in the bistro hipness of it all. Open M-F 9am-1am, Sa 2pm-1am, Su 10am-midnight.

Alexandrina, Körnerstr. 27 (tel. 213 18 88), a store front on Karl-Liebknecht-Str.; follow directions to Maître and backtrack a bit toward town. An ideal location for satisfying the late-night cravings of patrons at the many nearby bars, but it merits a trip out of the city center anytime. A friendly staff fixes up delectable *Döner* (DM5) and fantastic falafel (DM4.50). You never knew *Imbiß* stands could live so large.

Bagel Brothers, Nikolaistr. 42 (tel. 980 33 30), between the *Hauptbahnhof* and the Nikolaikirche, smears cream cheese on light and fluffy bagels. Bagel with flavored cream cheese DM2.90. Gorge yourself at the Sunday morning all-you-can-eat breakfast. Open M-Th 7am-11pm, F 7am-2pm, Su 10am-9pm.

Café le bit, Kohlgartenstr. 2 (tel. 998 20 00; email le-bit@mediagroup.de), right off Friedrich-List-Platz. Heading toward the train station on Georgiring, turn right on Schützenstr., which becomes Rosa-Luxemburg-Str. and leads straight there (10min. from the station). Cyberfreaks check **email,** or play games, or drink themselves silly in the hyper-cyber-hip surroundings. DM2 per 10min. The bar menu includes great crepes (DM3-8.50). Open M-F 8:30am-3am, Sa 10am-late, Su 10am-1am.

Dreiundzwanzigstunden, corner of Emilienstr. and Petersteinweg. A 5min. walk from the Innenstadt; head down Petersteinweg from Roßplatz. This self-service restaurant heaps on the German food at great prices (*Schnitzel* DM5.50-6.90, breakfasts DM6) 23 hours a day. Open daily 6am-5am.

SIGHTS

Leipzig's historic *Innenstadt* suffered both from WWII bombers and from poorly planned architectural creations of the post-war era. The heart of the city beats on the **Marktplatz,** a colorful, cobblestone square guarded by the slanted 16th-century **Altes Rathaus,** with its elegant **clock tower** showing four bright-blue faces. Inside, a grand festival hall runs above the **Stadtgeschichtliches Museum Leipzig** (tel. 96 51 30), which offers a straightforward look at Leipzig's history and generally entrancing temporary exhibits. *(Open Tu 2-8pm, W-Su 10am-4pm. DM5, students DM2.50.)*

The temporary home of the **Museum der Bildenden Künste Leipzig** (Museum of Fine Arts), Grimmaische Str. 1-7 (tel. 21 69 90), is just behind the Altes Rathaus. *(Open Tu and Th-Su 10am-6pm, W 1-9:30pm. DM5, students DM2.50.)* The museum was housed since WWII in the pre-war Supreme Court building, but the court recently decided to move back, leaving the museum homeless. Until the new building on Sachsenplatz is finished (sometime after 2000), the museum is making do with the 3rd floor of an old trade hall. Although things are a bit jumbled, the core of the collection is still on exhibit, including several interesting Romantic works.

Just a bit farther, on Nikolaistr., the 800-year-old **Nikolaikirche** witnessed the birth of Bach's *Johannes Passion* as well as the GDR's peaceful revolution. *(Open M-Sa 10am-6pm, Su after services. Free.)* The sandstone exterior, an unfortunate product of 19th-century *fin-de-siècle* malaise, hides a truly exceptional interior. The ceilings and columns feature a majestic array of pinks and greens—not your usual flavor for a church, but the late-18th-century renovation was, after all, inspired by the not-so-usual French Baroque school. The attempt to make the columns resemble palms is evocative of the sunny tropics. In 1989, the church became the gathering point for what would become truly revolutionary political engagement. What began as regular Monday meetings at the Nikolaikirche turned into massive weekly demonstrations *(Montagdemos),* in which ever-growing numbers of Leipzigers called for an end to the Communist government's policies. On October 7, 1989, the nerves of the Communist government erupted in a display of police violence against unarmed citizens. Despite the heightened security measures, over 70,000 people showed up at the church for the demonstration on Monday, October 9. For reasons that remain unclear, the armed forces allowed the protest to pass without a response. The following Monday demonstration drew 120,000 emboldened citizens, and on October 18, SED party chief Erich Honecker resigned.

Continuing away from the Marktplatz, take Universitätsstr. to the former Karl Marx University, now rechristened **Universität Leipzig.** Its "Sharp Tooth" tower, a steel and concrete behemoth, displaced the centuries-old Universitätskirche and other popular buildings following a wave of faculty protests in 1968. The university will move out soon, as the tower's design has proven increasingly unstable over the years.

Past the university and down Grimmaischer Steinweg is the **Grassimuseum** (tel. 214 20) on Johannisplatz, an Art Deco home for three small museums. The largest of the three (and we mean *large*), the **Museum für Völker Kunde** (Museum for Anthropology), seems somehow politically incorrect, but the huge collection of clothing, religious objects, artwork, and just about everything else documenting different "peoples" around the world is strangely fascinating, with clay huts and some disturbing anatomically correct decorations. *(Open Tu-F 10am-5:30pm, Sa 10am-4pm.)* The university's **Musikinstrumenten-Museum** contains more than 5000 instruments, some dating back to the 16th century. *(Open Tu-Sa 10am-5pm, Su 10am-2pm.)* Enter the courtyard to find the **Museum des Kunsthandwerk** (handicrafts). The *Jugendstil* pieces are especially attractive. *(Open Tu and Th-Su 10am-6pm, W noon-8pm. Each museum DM5, students DM2. A ticket to all three is DM8, students DM4.)* Also housed in the building is the **Ausstellungsraum,** which features changing, and occasionally fascinating, international art exhibitions. *(Open M and Sa-Su 10am-8pm, Tu and Th-F 10am-6pm. DM6, students DM3.)*

From the *Markt,* head away from the *Rathaus,* and you'll see the **Auerbach's Keller,** Grimmaische Str. 2-4 (tel. 21 61 00), Leipzig's most famous restaurant. *(Open daily 11:30am-midnight.)* Tucked inside the Mädlerpassage, it was here that Mephisto tricked his student in Goethe's *Faust.* The entrees don't quite make the budget range (DM25-30), but it's still worth taking a peek. A little farther down the street is the **Thomaskirche,** the church in which Bach spent the majority of his career. Unfortunately, the church is undergoing massive renovations for the Bach Festival of 2000, so much of the church may be closed, and concerts of the **Thomaschor,** one of Europe's most prestigious boy's choirs, have been cancelled. Across the street, the **Johann-Sebastian-Bach-Museum,** Thomaskirchhof 16, chronicles Bach's work and time in Leipzig from 1723 to 1750. *(Open daily 10am-5pm. Last entry 4:30pm. DM4, students and seniors DM2.50. Tours daily 11am and 3pm; admission-tour combo DM8 and DM5. The Sommersaal hosts 2-3 concerts per week. DM15, students DM8.)*

From behind the Thomaskirche, heading right on Dittrichring, you'll find the **Museum der "Runden Ecke"** (Museum of the Round Corner), Dittrichring 24 (tel. 961 24 43), one of the more fascinating museums in the new *Bundesländer.* *(Open W-Su 2-6pm. Free.)* Housed in the main building of the East German Ministry for State Security, or *Stasi,* regional headquarters, the museum presents a stunningly blunt exhibit on the history, doctrine, and tools of the *Stasi.* While the surveillance equipment is enough to inflict erythmea on any conspiracy theorist, the museum also chronicles the triumph of the resistance that overthrew the *Stasi* terror. The Monday demonstrations in the Nikolaikirche often ended at the *Stasi* headquarters; the wax from candlelight vigils on the front steps can still be seen. On the night of December 4, 1989, the people of Leipzig took over the *Stasi* building. Inside they found some 50,000 letters seized over the last 40 years and entire floors devoted to documentation of the actions of suspected resistors. Even more disturbing, perhaps, are the mountains of paper-pulp which were found outside, indicating that much of what went on inside the building will never be known.

Outside the city-ring, the **Völkerschlachtdenkmal** (tel. 878 04 71), on the *Süd-Friedhof,* remembers the 400,000 soldiers engaged in the 1813 Battle of Nations—a struggle that turned the tide against Napoleon and determined many of Europe's current national boundaries. *(Open May-Oct. daily 10am-5pm; Nov.-Apr. 9am-4pm. To climb to the top DM5, students DM2.50.)* The monument, overlooking a large pool, is an absolutely massive pile of sculpted brown rock that all but conclusively proves that Kaiser Wilhelm had a very small penis. A dizzying 500 steps spiral up in a nearly windowless, one-person-wide passage to the very top of the monument; on clear days, you can see the Harz mountain range. Take *Straßenbahn* #15 or 20 from the *Hauptbahnhof* (direction: "Meusdorf" or "Probstheida") to "Völkerschlachtdenkmal" (20min.).

The **Leipziger Messegelände** (trade grounds) are monumental in another way. The building complex, finished in 1996, consists of five mammoth halls all clustered around an arched, glass main building that resembles the Biosphere. The building hosts trade fairs nearly non-stop throughout the year, but the futuristic buildings themselves are more worth seeing than the *Schicki-Micki* yupsters who convene inside. Ask the tourist office for more information, or take *Straßenbahn* #16 or 21 to "Messegelände," and check it out yourself.

ENTERTAINMENT

The patrons that frequent the super-cool, slightly artsy cafes scattered around Leipzig also support a throbbing theater and music scene. Be forewarned: most theaters, musical and otherwise, take a *Spielpause* in July and August, offering no performances. The musical offerings are top-notch, particularly at the **Gewandhaus Orchestra**, a major international orchestra since 1843. Some concerts are free, but usually only when a guest orchestra is playing; otherwise buy tickets (from DM7; 30% student discount) at the *Gewandhaus* **box office,** Augustuspl. 8 (tel. 127 02 80; fax 127 02 22), next to the university (open M 1-6pm, Tu-F 10am-6pm, Sa 10am-2pm). Leipzig's **Opera** (tel. 126 10) receives wide acclaim and gives Dresden's *Semper* company a run for its money. Tickets run DM11-70, with a DM10-20 student discount (except for premieres). Head to the ticket counter at Augustuspl. 12 for more information. (Ticket by phone daily 8am-8pm. Counter open M-F 10am-8pm, Sa 10am-4pm, and 90min. before shows.) **Bach Festivals** every July and August bring the orchestra and opera to the streets with free performances.

The opera house is also the entry point to Leipzig's diverse **theater** scene. The opera company hosts the experimental **Kellertheater** (tel. 126 10) in its basement. Known for its theater, Leipzig has unleashed a wave of experimental plays in the wake of the revolution. The **Schauspielhaus**, Bosestr. 1 (tel. 126 80), just off Dittrichring, serves up established plays, including offerings from Euripides, Heiner, Müller, and Brecht. The cabaret scene centers around the understated **academixer,** Kupgergassc 6 (tel. 960 48 48), run by the Leipzig student body (open M-F 10am-6pm, Sa 10am-1pm), the more brash **Gohglmohsch**, Markt 9 (tel. 961 51 11), and the **Leipzig Pfeffermühle,** Thomas Kirchhof 16 (tel. 960 32 53). While movie theaters are in abundance, Leipzig also offers documentaries and short films at its annual **film festival** at the end of October (call 980 39 21 for information, or ask at the tourist office).

NIGHTLIFE

Barfußgäschen, a street just off the *Markt,* serves as the see-and-be-seen bar venue for everyone from students to *Schicki-Micki*s. **Markt Neun, Steel, Gohglmohsch** (whose cobblestones are covered in summer with outdoor seating from all sides), and **Spizz** start to fill up between 8 and 10pm, and remain packed into the wee hours.

Karl-Liebknecht-Straße is just as *Szene*-ic without being quite as claustrophobic as Barfußgäschen. Take streetcar #10 or 11 to "Arndtstr." During the day, **Boom Town** and **Mrs. Hippie** fill that extra space in your pack with used or otherwise funked-out clothing. At night, bars along the street pour drinks for Irish lovers (**Killiwilly** at #44), Francophiles and Francophones (**Maître** at #62, see **Food,** p. 172), tough art-house film types (**naTo** at #46), caffeine addicts (**KAHWE** at the corner of Arndtstr. and Karl-Liebknecht-Str.), and everyone else (**Weisses Rössel** right next door). Most are open during the day for food and three-martini lunches, but nighttime revelry kicks off around 8pm. **naTo** shows indy films, usually in original language with subtitles.

Moritzbastei, Universitätsstr. 9 (tel. 702 59 13; tickets tel. 70 25 90), next to the university tower. Leipzig U. students spent two years excavating this series of medieval tunnels so they could get their groove on. A totally rockin' yet chill atmosphere presides over the multiple bars and dance floors, enhanced by frequent concerts. Above ground, **Café Barbakan** (open M-F after 10am, Sa after 2pm), an **open-air movie theater** (screenings June-Aug. M-Tu and Th-Sa at 10pm, weather permitting), and the outdoor terrace and *Biergarten* (open in nice weather M-F 11:30am-midnight, Sa-Su 2pm-midnight) provide respite from the wild music scene. Things kick off after 9pm, with a particularly salacious scene for the jam-packed, Wednesday night *"Papperlapop"* disco. Cover DM4-7 for discos, slightly more for concerts. Bring student ID for discount.

Distillery (tel. 963 82 11), at the corner of Kurt-Eisner-Str. and Loßniger Str. *Straßenbahn* #5 or 16 (direction: "Lößing") to the "K.-Eisner-Str./A.-Hoffman-Str." stop. Distillery is to the left at the dead end on Kurt-Eisner-Str. Fridays bump with hip-hop and funk, and Saturdays come up big with techno, in a setting that's just underground enough to be very cool. Cover DM5-7.

Jam, Große Fleischergasse 12 (tel. 961 74 32). About as commercial and top-ten as discos can get, but with one saving grace: the building it's in was the former *Stasi* headquarters. So get your groove on capitalist-style, and give the *Stasi* the *Stinkfinger.* Open F and Sa at 10. Fridays free for women 'til midnight, cover DM6-10.

RosaLinde, Lindenauer Markt 21 (tel. 484 15 11). Not exactly in the middle of the *Markt,* but it features a hellaciously cool gay and lesbian scene on Friday and Saturday nights in addition to its daily bar. Tuesday amply entertains with "Queer Film Night." Said to be the epicenter of the gay and lesbian scene. Open daily after 8pm.

Kutsche (tel. 211 43 74), on Brandenburger Str., by the station. Gay bar and disco that's not as commercial as RosaLinde, with a darkroom in the basement. Dancing F-Su, with a mad Wednesday pick-up scene dubbed *"Kennen Lernen Party."* Cover DM5. Open daily after 7pm.

■ Near Leipzig: Naumburg

The town of Naumburg squats in the "Tuscany of the North," the beautiful scenery between Leipzig and Weimar, and beckons visitors with its medieval flavor. Naumburg, one of the 12 "model cities" in the former East Germany, has been saved from destruction and blessed with a phenomenal cathedral. Careful restoration has revealed a colorful city center, reminiscent of Naumburg during its medieval days of glory—a trading city, rivaled only by Frankfurt am Main.

ORIENTATION AND PRACTICAL INFORMATION Naumburg, well-situated along the rail network, is an excellent sidelight during a visit to Leipzig (30min. away), Halle (45min.), Weimar (45min., 31 per day), or Erfurt (30min., 31 per day). There are two competing **tourist offices** in Naumburg. One is right on the market square at Markt 6 (tel. 20 16 14; fax 26 60 47; open Mar.-Oct. M-F 9am-1pm and 2-7pm, Sa 10am-4pm; Nov.-Feb. M-F 9am-5pm, Sa 10am-2pm). The other is right near the entrance to the *Dom* at Steinweg 15 (tel./fax 20 25 14; open daily 10am-5pm). Both are stocked full of brochures and books on Naumburg and the area, and the office on the *Markt* arranges private rooms for free (most DM26-40). Several full-service banks are in town, as well as an **ATM** on Markgrafenweg, immediately to the right as you exit the train station. The **telephone code** is 03445.

ACCOMMODATIONS AND FOOD To reach Naumburg's **Jugendgästehaus,** Am Tennispl. 9 (tel./fax 70 34 22), from the Marktplatz, follow Wenzelsstr. out of the old walled city to Bürgergartenstr., which will appear slightly to the right at the end of Wenzelsstr., then go straight until reaching signs for the hostel (15min.). A monument to good ol' eastern youth-hosteling, this hostel is slowly being remodeled out of its current "GDR-Standard." Double rooms with bath attached (and larger dorms without) all come with breakfast. (Dorms DM23 per person, over 26 DM28; doubles DM26, over 26 DM32. Sheets DM6. Reception 8-10am and 5-10pm.) Cheap meals await at the *Markt* and the Holzmarkt areas, within three blocks of each other. For a truly chic cup of coffee or light meal, try **Engelgasse 3** (tel. 20 07 70)—"What's the address?" you might wonder. To get there, face the *Rathaus* from the *Markt,* and walk all the way around the building. A cafe, used book store, and art gallery, it has the retro, feel-good, funky style of renowned Leipzig illustrator Thomas Müller, further enhanced by omnipresent posters, menus, paintings, and postcards featuring the artist's work. The friendly owner, Wieland Führ, happened to know Müller since his Crayola days and was able to get the full-service treatment for his new venture. Almost all of the ingredients on the menu come from small area farms and a *Brötchen* with *Bratwurst* or goat's milk gouda will run DM4.90-DM5.90. (Open M-W 10am-7pm, Th-F 10am-11pm, Sa 10am-4pm.) Another interesting culinary surprise is **China-Garten,** Rosbacher Str. 4 (tel. 30 90), near the cobblestone path. The restaurant flaunts lacquer trim, mirrors, and pseudo-Asian instrumental pop. The lunch specials (DM9-14) are the best deal—tons of food plus a big veggie-stuffed spring roll. (Open daily 11:30am-2:45pm and 5:30-11:30pm.)

SIGHTS A relic from those days, the **Naumburger Dom,** undoubtedly merits a pilgrimage if only to gaze upon the lovely Uto, one of 12 striking stone figures put in place in 1250 as the *Dom* was being completed. *(Open Apr.-Sept. M-Sa 9am-6pm, Su noon-6pm; Nov.-Feb. M-Sa 9am-4pm, Su noon-4pm; Mar. and Oct. M-Sa 9am-5pm, Su noon-5pm. DM6, students and seniors DM3. DM10 for the right to take photos or use video cameras inside.)* Uto is considered to be one of the best examples of realism between Classical times and the Renaissance. Too humble to carve his name in the cathedral's stone, the artist is remembered today simply as the *Naumburger Meister* (the Naumburg Master). The sculptures of the double-chinned Ekkehard and Snow-White-esque bride Uta were nearly taken from the *Dom* as reparations payments to the French after WWII. The removal proved to be effectively impossible, so Naumburg kept its treasures. One of the more overlooked masterpieces of the church is its handrails, whose fanciful figures have very little to do with Christianity, but sure are cool. The helpful staff at the front desk will provide English pamphlets on request. Foreign-language tours are also available. To reach the *Dom,* head down Markgrafenweg from the station, bearing right until you reach the end of the street. To the left is the winding cobblestone path that leads uphill to the town proper. At the top of the path a sign points to the *Dom;* follow it until the cathedral's huge towers poke above the rooftops to guide you.

The rest of Naumburg has recovered amazingly well from its 45 years as a backwater Red Army post. A jaunt past the *Dom* on Steinweg leads to Naumburg's bright, lively **market.** Just off the market square is the **Wenzelskirche,** the *Dom*'s earnest runner-up. *(Open M-Sa 10am-6pm, Su and holidays noon-4pm; last entrance 15min. before closing. Free.)* Its peeling walls provide a solemn backdrop for a few paintings by Cranach the Elder and an impressive 18th-century organ that received Bach's approval. Lest you think Naumburg functions solely as a bastion of religious relics, Nietzsche, Fichte, and even the world-famous founder of Egyptology, Richard Pelsius, all lived in Naumburg for parts of their illustrious lives. In spite of the pious monuments, Nietzsche spent some of his formative years here from 1850 to 1858 (before he sported the bushy mustache) and returned in 1890 to visit his mother, who wouldn't let little Friedrich leave because he was too darn crazy. The **Nietzsche-Haus,** Weingarten 18 (tel. 20 16 38), off Jakobstr., has a well presented display on Nietzsche's life, plus a second floor full of truly esoteric changing exhibits. *(Open Tu-F 2-5pm, Sa-Su 10am-4pm. DM3, students DM1.50.)*

Thüringen (Thuringia)

Affectionately dubbed the "Green Heart of Germany," Thüringen is the hub of a wheel formed by Bayern, Sachsen, Sachsen-Anhalt, Niedersachsen, and Hessen. Certainly the most beautiful of the new Federal States, Thüringen might also be called Germany's Cultural Belt, with Weimar—Europe's "Cultural Capital" in 1999—the shiny brass buckle. Echoes of Thüringen are heard throughout Europe's cultural canon: Bach, Goethe, Schiller, Luther, and Wagner all left their mark on this landscape, which in turn left its mark on their work. The Thüringer Wald is the deep green, hilly nucleus of the *Land*. Around this, a necklace of shining historic cities—among them Jena, Weimar, Erfurt, and Eisenach—is strung together by a direct east-west rail line. South of these cities are the hills and highlands of the forest itself, bisected by the equally historic Rennsteig hiking trail. All this pastoral beauty is set to an inspirational soundtrack, as Thüringen's *Musiksommer* celebrates its history of musical giants with a series of concerts; a schedule is available at most tourist offices. Relatively unknown to foreigners, and thus refreshingly free of mass tourism, Thüringen is the perfect destination for an authentic and dazzling German experience.

🏛 HIGHLIGHTS OF THURINGEN

- This year, **Weimar** is indisputably the most exciting city in Thüringen—indeed, if you listen to the tourist office, the most exciting city in all of Europe—as it celebrates **Goethe's 250th birthday** and its year-long status as **Europe's cultural capital** (see p. 178).
- The memorial and ruins at **Buchenwald,** site of a concentration camp during WWII, display an eerie contrast between the atrocities of Nazi Germany and the beauty of the Thüringen landscape (see p. 185).
- With a beautiful *Altstadt* and lush parks, cosmopolitan **Erfurt** is beginning to attract a tourist population commensurate with its coolness (see p. 192).

■ Weimar

1999 is a hallmark year for Weimar. It's Goethe's 250th birthday, the 80th birthday of the Bauhaus, the 50th birthday of the FRG, and the tenth anniversary of reunification—this all adds up to one huge party. The icing on the cake is just as tasty; Weimar has been designated **Europe's Cultural Capital for 1999,** which basically means that there will be something entertaining or captivating all year long. In this city, rich with the ghosts of the German classical movement and the energy and shadows of modernity, the festivities should be particularly interesting. Weimar is pulling out all the tricks up its sleeve to cap off this tumultuous century, and if there's one thing in Germany not to be missed this year, Weimar is it.

ORIENTATION AND PRACTICAL INFORMATION

Weimar is near the center of Germany, well-situated on the Dresden-Frankfurt and Berlin-Frankfurt rail lines. It also lies on a handy rail route running from Jena in the east to Erfurt (15min., 4 per hr.) and Eisenach in the west; call 33 30 for train information. Weimar's intelligently designed bus system runs through two nerve centers: the train station and the central **Goetheplatz.** To get to Goetheplatz from the station, head straight down Carl-August-Allee (10min.). Walk down the pedestrian **Schiller-straße** to get to the *Markt* and major sights.

Weimar offers several **discount cards,** but unless you know exactly what you are going to be doing you may not save any money with them. The **Weimarcard** (DM25) is offered through the tourist office, and is good for 72 hours of free buses, entry to Weimar's art museums, and discounts on city tours. Most of Weimar's cultural sights

(take in a rock show)

and use **AT&T Direct**℠ Service
to tell everyone about it.

It's all within **AT&T** your reach.

 Exploring lost cultures? You better have an

AT&T Direct^{SM} Service wallet guide.

It's a list of access numbers you need to call home fast and clear from

around the world, using an AT&T Calling Card or credit card.

What an amazing planet we live on.

For a list of **AT&T Access Numbers,**
take the attached wallet guide.

It's all within  **AT&T** your reach.

www.att.com/traveler

For your
calling
convenience
tear off
and take
with you!

 AT&T

Calling From Specially Marked Telephones

Throughout the world, there are specially marked phones that connect you to AT&T Direct℠ Service. Simply look for the AT&T logo. In the following countries, access to AT&T Direct Service is *only* available from these phones: Ethiopia, Mongolia, Nigeria, Seychelles Islands.

Public phones in Europe displaying the red 3C symbol also give you quick and easy access to AT&T Direct Service. Just lift the handset and dial ✱60 (in France dial M60) and you'll be connected to AT&T.

Pay phones in the United Kingdom displaying the New World symbol provide easy access to AT&T. Simply lift the handset and press the pre-programmed button marked AT&T.

 NEW WORLD

Customer Care

If you have any questions, call 800 331-1140, Ext. 707.

When outside the U.S., dial the AT&T Access Number for the country *you are in* and ask the AT&T Operator for Customer Care.

Printed in the U.S.A. on recycled paper.

108-25   © AT&T 6/98

To Call the U.S. and Other Countries Using Your AT&T Calling Card℠ or credit card,* Follow These Steps:

1. Make sure you have an outside line. (From a hotel room, follow the hotel's instructions to get an outside line, as if you were placing a local call.)

2. If you want to call a country other than the U.S., make sure the country *you are in* is highlighted in blue on the chart like this:

3. Enter the AT&T Access Number listed in the chart for the country *you are in.*

4. When prompted, enter the telephone number you are calling as follows:

   • For calls to the U.S., dial the Area Code (no need to dial 1 before the Area Code) + 7-digit number.

   • For calls to other countries, enter 01 + the Country Code, City Code, and Local Number.

5. After the tone, enter your AT&T Calling Card* or credit card number (not the international number). If you need help or wish to call the U.S. collect, hold on for an AT&T Operator.

   * You may also use your AT&T Corporate Card, AT&T Universal Card, or most U.S. local phone company cards.
   † The cost of calls to countries other than the U.S. consists of basic connection rates plus an additional charge based on the country you are calling.
   ∞ Credit card billing subject to availability.

Special Features

Just dial the AT&T Access Number for the country *you are in* and follow the instructions listed below.

● To call U.S. 800 numbers: Enter the 800 number you are calling. (Note: Based upon the 800 number dialed, calls may be toll-free or AT&T Direct℠ Service charges may apply for the duration of the call; some numbers may be restricted.)

● To set up conference calls: Dial AT&T TeleConference Services at 800 232-1234. (Note: One conferee must be in the U.S.)

● To access language interpreters: Dial AT&T Language Line® Services at 408 648-5871.

● To record and deliver messages: Dial #123 if you get a busy signal or no answer, or dial AT&T True Messages® Service at 800 562-6275.

Here's a time-saving tip for placing additional calls: When you finish your conversation, or if there is a busy signal or no answer, don't hang up – press # and wait for the voice prompt or an AT&T Operator.

 AT&T

AT&T Access Numbers

(Refer to footnotes before dialing.) From the countries highlighted in blue below, like this [____], you can make calls to the U.S. location in the world, and from *all* the countries listed, you can make calls to virtually any

Country	Number
Albania ●	00-800-0010
American Samoa	633 2-USA
Angola	0199
Anguilla ♦	1-800-872-2881
Antigua ♦	1-800-872-2881
(Public Card Phones)	#
Argentina	0-800-54-288
Armenia ▲●	8♦10111
Aruba	800-8000
Australia ○	1-800-881-011
Austria ○	022-903-011
Bahamas	1-800-872-2881
Bahrain	800-000
Bahrain ↑	800-000
Barbados ♦	1-800-872-2881
Belarus ✕ —	8♦800101
Belgium ●	0-800-100-10
Belize ●	811
(From Hotels Only)	555
Benin	102
Bermuda ♦	1-800-872-2881
Bolivia ●	0-800-1112

Country	Number
Bosnia ▲	00-800-0010
Brazil	000-8010
British V.I. ♦	1-800-872-2881
Brunei ●	800-1111
Bulgaria ▲.	00-800-0010
Cambodia ✱ #	1-800-881-001
Canada	1 800 CALL ATT
Cape Verde Islands	112
Cayman Islands ♦	1-800-872-2881
Chile	or 800-800-311
	800-800-288
China, PRC ▲	10811
Colombia	980-11-0010
Cook Island	09-111
Costa Rica	0-800-0-114-114
Croatia ▲	99-385-0111
Cyprus ●	080-90010
Czech Rep. ▲	00-42-000-101
Denmark ●	8001-0010
Dominica ♦	1-800-872-2881

Country	Number
Dom. Rep. ★·□	1-800-872-2881
Ecuador ▲	999-119
Egypt ● (Cairo)	510-0200
(Outside Cairo)	02-510-0200
El Salvador ○	800-1785
Estonia	8-00-8001001
Fiji	004-890-1001
Finland ●	9800-100-10
France	0800 99 00 11
France	0800 99 00 11
French Antilles	0800 99 0011
French Guiana	0800 99 00 11
Gabon	00♦001
Gambia ●	00111
Georgia ▲	8♦0288
Germany ●	0130-0010
Ghana	0191
Gibraltar	8800
Greece ●	00-800-1311
Grenada ♦	1-800-872-2881
Guadeloupe ♦·✱ (Marie Galante)	0800 99 00 11

Country	Number
Guam	1 800 CALL ATT
Guantanamo Bay ↑ (Cuba)	935
Guatemala ○.✱	99-99-190
Guyana ★	165
Haiti	183
Honduras	800-0-123
Hong Kong	800-96-1111
Hungary	00♦-800-01111
Iceland	800 9001
India ✕.▷	000-117
Indonesia →	001-801-10
Ireland ✓	1-800-550-000
Israel	1-800-94-94-949
Italy ●	172-1011
Ivory Coast ●	00-111-11
Jamaica □	1-800-872-2881
Jamaica	872
Japan ✕ DDI ▲	005-39-111
Japan IDC ● ▲	0066-55-111
Japan KDD ● ▲	005-59-111
Korea ●✱	00729-11 or 0039-11
Korea ↑	550-HOME or 550-2USA
Netherlands Antilles ●♦	001-800-872-2881

Country	Number
Kuwait	800-288
Latvia (Riga)	8♦27007007
(Outside Riga)	8♦27007007
Lebanon ○ (Beirut)	426-801
(Outside Beirut)	01-426-801
Liechtenstein ●	0-800-89-0011
Lithuania ✕ —	8♦196
Luxembourg‡	0-800-0111
Macao	0800-111
Macedonia, F.Y.R. of ●.○	99-800-4288
Malaysia ○	1800-80-0011
Malta	0800-890-110
Marshall Isl.	1 800 CALL ATT
Mauritius	73120
Mexico ▽'	01-800-288-2872
Micronesia	288
Monaco ●	800-90-288
Montserrat ♦	1-800-872-2881
Morocco	002-11-0011

Country	Number
Netherlands ●	0800-022-9111
New Zealand ●	000-911
Nicaragua	174
Norway ●	800-190-11
Pakistan ▲	00-800-01001
Palau	02288
Panama	109
(Canal Zone)	281-0109
Papua New Guinea	0507-12880
Paraguay ■.▲ (Asuncion City)	008-11-800
Peru ▲	0-800-50000
Philippines ●	105-11
Poland ○♦	0-800-111-1111
Portugal ▲	05017-1-288
Qatar	0800-011-77
Reunion Isl.	0800 99 0011
Romania ▲	01-800-4288
Romania ↑	01-801-0151
Russia ●).▲ (Moscow)	755-5042
(Outside of Moscow)	8-095-755-5042
Suriname △	156

Country	Number
Russia ●).▲ (St. Petersburg)	325-5042
(Outside St. Petersburg)	8-812-325-5042
St. Kitts/Nevis & St. Lucia ♦	1-800-872-2881
St. Pierre & Miquelon	0800 99 0011
St. Vincent △.▲	1-800-872-2881
Saipan ▲	1 800 CALL ATT
San Marino ▲	172-1011
Saudi Arabia ◇	1-800-10
Senegal	3072
Sierra Leone	1100
Singapore ■	800-0111-111
Slovakia ▲	00-42-100-101
Solomon Isl.	0811
So. Africa	0-800-99-0123
Spain ●	900-99-00-11
Sri Lanka ■	430-430
Sudan	800-001

Country	Number
Sweden ●	020-795-611
Switzerland ●	0-800-890011
Syria	0-801
Taiwan	0080-10288-0
Thailand ✓	001-999-111-11
Trinidad/Tob.	0800-872-2881
Turkey ●	00-800-12277
Turks & Caicos ♦ ↑	01-800-872-2881
Uganda	800-001
Ukraine ▲	8♦100-11
U.A. Emirates ●	800-121
U.A.E. ↑ ♦	0800-89-0011 or 0500-89-0011
U.S. ▽	1 800 CALL ATT
Uruguay ■	000-410
Uzbekistan 8 ♦	641-744-0010
Venezuela ●	800-11-120
Vietnam ●	1-201-0288
Yemen	00 800 101
Zambia	00-899
Zimbabwe ▲	110-90990

..., you can make calls to virtually any

● Public phones require coin or card deposit. ✱ Press red button. ↑ Additional charges apply when calling outside of Moscow. ✕ AT&T Direct™ calls cannot be placed to this country from outside the U.S. ✱ Available from public phones.
Phnom Penh and Siem Reap only. ✕ Not available from public phones.
✚ From St. Maarten or phones at Bobby's Marina, use 1-800-872-2881.

◇ From this country, AT&T Direct™ calls terminate to designated countries only.
→ From U.S. Military Bases only. — Not yet all available from all areas. ★ Select hotels.
↑ From U.S. Military Bases only. ▲ May not be available from every phone/public phone. † Collect Calling from public phones. ▷ Available from phones with international calling capabilities or from most phones.
Public Calling Centers. ✓ From Northern Ireland use U.K. access code.

★ Collect calling only. ○ Public phones require local coin payment through the call duration. ▽ Await second dial tone. ▽ When calling from public phones, use phones marked "Lasdatel." If call does not complete, use 001-800-462-4240. ◁ When calling from public phones only. ♦ Public phones marked Lenso.

□ Calling Card calls available from select hotels. → Use phones allowing international access. ▲ Including Puerto Rico and the U.S. Virgin Islands. ⊠ AT&T Direct™ Service only from telephone calling centers in Hanoi and port offices in Da Nang, Ho Chi Minh City and Quang Ninh. ↑ If call does not complete, use 0800-013-0011.

WE GIVE YOU THE WORLD...AT A DISCOUNT

LET'S GO®
TRAVEL

MERCHANDISE CATALOG FOR 1999

LET'S GO®

Euralpass
Euralpass Unlimited travel in and among all 17 countries: **Austria, Belgium, Denmark, Finland, France, Germany, Greece, Holland, Hungary, Italy, Luxembourg, Norway, Portugal, Republic of Ireland, Spain, Sweden, and Switzerland.**

First Class	15 days	21 days	1 month	2 months	3 months	10 days	15 days
	consecutive days					*in two months*	
1 Passenger	$554	$718	$890	$1260	$1558	$654	$862
2 or More Passengers	$470	$610	$756	$1072	$1324	$556	$732
Youthpass (Second Class)							
Passengers under 26	$388	$499	$623	$882	$1089	$458	$599

Europass Travel in the five Europass countries: **France, Germany, Italy, Spain, and Switzerland.** Up to two of the four associate regions (Austria and Hungary; Benelux (Belgium, Netherlands, and Luxembourg); Greece; Portugal) may be added.

First Class	5 days	6 days	8 days	10 days	15 days	first	second
	in two months					*associate country*	
1 Passenger	$348	$368	$448	$528	$728	+$60	+$40
2 to 5 Passengers traveling together	$296	$314	$382	$450	$620	+$52	+$34
Youthpass (Second Class)							
Passengers under 26	$233	$253	$313	$363	$513	+$45	+$33

Pass Protection For an additional $10, insure any railpass against theft or loss.

Discounts *with the purchase of a railpass*
- $30 off a World Journey backpack
- $20 off a Continental Journey backpack
- Any *Let's Go* Guide for 1/2 Price
- Free 2-3 Week Domestic Shipping

Call about Eurostar—the Channel Tunnel Train—and other country-specific passes.

Airfares & Special Promotions

Call for information on and availability of standard airline tickets, student, teacher, and youth discounted airfares, as well as other special promotions.

Publications & More

Let's Go Travel Guides
The Bible of the Budget Traveler

USA • India and Nepal • Southeast Asia...........22.99

Australia • Eastern Europe • Europe..................21.99

Britain & Ireland • Central America • France •
Germany • Israel & Egypt • Italy • Mexico •
Spain & Portugal.....................................19.99

Alaska & The Pacific Northwest • Austria &
Switzerland • California & Hawaii • Ecuador
& The Galapagos Islands • Greece • Ireland.....18.99

South Africa • Turkey.............................17.99

New York City • New Zealand • London •
Paris • Rome • Washington D.C. 15.99

Let's Go Map Guides
*Know your destination inside and out!
Great to accompany your Eurailpass.*

Amsterdam, Berlin, Boston, Chicago, Florence, London, Los Angeles, Madrid, New Orleans, New York, Paris, Rome, San Francisco, Washington D.C. **8.95**

Michelin Maps

Czech/Slovak Republics • Europe •
France • Germany • Germany/Austria
/Benelux • Great Britain & Ireland •
Greece • Italy • Poland • Scandinavia &
Finland • Spain & Portugal **10.95**

LET'S GO Order Form

Last Name*	First Name*	Home and Day Phone Number* (very important)

Street* (Sorry, we cannot ship to Post Office Boxes)

City*	State*	Zip Code*

Citizenship‡§ (Country)   School/College§   Date of Birth‡§   Date of Travel*

Qty	Description	Color	Unit Price	Total Price

Shipping and Handling

2-3 Week Domestic Shipping
Merchandise value under $30	$4
Merchandise value $30-$100	$6
Merchandise value over $100	$8

2-3 Day Domestic Shipping
Merchandise value under $30	$14
Merchandise value $30-$100	$16
Merchandise value over $100	$18

Overnight Domestic Shipping
Merchandise value under $30	$24
Merchandise value $30-$100	$26
Merchandise value over $100	$28
All International Shipping	$30

Total Purchase Price	
Shipping and Handling	+
MA Residents add 5% sales tax on gear and books	+
TOTAL	

☐ Mastercard	☐ Visa
Cardholder name:	
Card number:	
Expiration date:	

When ordering an International ID Card, please include:
1. Proof of birthdate (copy of passport, birth certificate, or driver's license).
2. One picture (1.5" x 2") signed on the reverse side.
3. (ISIC/ITIC only) Proof of current student/teacher status (letter from registrar or administrator, proof of tuition, or copy of student/faculty ID card. FULL-TIME only).

* Required for all orders
‡ Required in addition for each Hostelling Membership
§ Required in addition for each International ID Card
☐ Required in addition for each railpass

Prices are in US dollars and subject to change.

Make check or money order payable to:
Let's Go Travel
17 Holyoke Street
Cambridge, MA 02138
(617) 495-9649

1-800-5LETSGO

Hours: Mon.-Fri., 10am-6pm ET

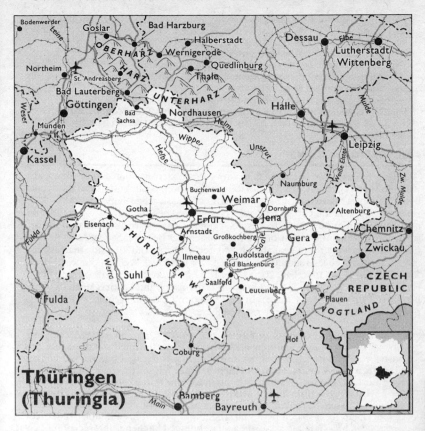

Thüringen
(Thuringia)

are controlled by the **Weimar Classics Foundation,** Frauentorstr. 4 (tel. 54 50). The office has a gift shop with information, and also offers a discount card of its own (DM25, students DM15). This gets you into every museum of the foundation, marked in the guide with "(WC)." No peeing on the paintings! Contact the foundation to arrange tours or get info on the museums.

Trains: DB trains head out to Erfurt (15min.; 3-4 per hr.); Leipzig (1½hr; 1 per hr.); Dresden (3hr.; 1 per hr.); and Frankfurt (3hr.; 1 per hr.).

Public Transportation: Weimar's lack of streetcars is more than compensated for by an extensive **bus network.** If you buy tickets from the driver, you'll pay an inflated price (DM2.50). Instead, buy tickets at the *Hauptbahnhof* (open M-F 5:45am-6pm, Sa 8am-2pm) or at kiosks scattered throughout the city (DM12 for 8 tickets). Most buses run until midnight.

Taxis: tel. 90 36 00 or 90 39 00.

Tourist Office: The seriously modern and efficient **Weimar Information,** Marktstr. 10 (tel. 240 00; fax 24 00 40), is within view of the city's *Rathaus*. It provides maps, brochures, souvenirs, and tickets for the *Deutsches Nationaltheater.* The office also books rooms in private homes, hotels, *Pensionen,* or hostels for a DM5 fee. **Walking tours** leave the office daily at 11am and 2pm (DM12, students DM8). Alternatively, get on with your own bad self with a walking-tour brochure (DM1.50), available in various languages. Open M-F 10am-7pm, Sa-Su 10am-4pm.

Currency Exchange: A number of banks line Schillerstr. and Goetheplatz, but beware—none are open between Saturday afternoon and Monday morning.

Pharmacy: Bahnhof Apotheke, Carl-August-Allee 14 (tel. 614 24), near the station and the *Jugendherberge*. It has evening hours as well as a *Notdienst* (emergency) buzzer and a list of night pharmacies. Open M-F 7:45am-7pm, Sa 9am-noon.

Women's Center: Frauenzentrum, Schopenhauerstr. 21 (tel. 994 25), hosts a **Frauen Café** daily 2-6pm, and serve "women's breakfast" Wednesdays at 10am. Also offers a variety of lesbian-oriented services. Office open daily 2-6pm, usually longer, depending on what's planned.

Emergency: Police, tel. 110. **Fire and Ambulance,** tel. 112.

Post Office: Mail postcards of Goethe and Schiller from the *Hauptpostamt*, Goethepl. 7-8, 99423 Weimar (tel. 23 10). Open M-F 8am-6:30pm, Sa 9am-1pm.

Telephone Code: 03643.

ACCOMMODATIONS

Weimar is home to one of eastern Germany's most extensive tourist industries, and it will shift to high-gear in 1999. Thanks to the city's three youth hostels and the "youth hotel," finding a cheap place to stay should now be easier than in many Eastern cities. However, the Cultural Capital festivities promise to keep the city swamped all summer. Call ahead or be a suck-ah. Private accommodations are also available and are accessible through the tourist office. Remember that prices vary according to location, not comfort; a room near the city center may cost DM50, while many of the nicer rooms in Weimar's southern suburbs go for DM25-30. Weimar's "finest," **Hotel Elephant,** Am Markt 19 (tel. 80 20; fax 653 10), has catered to such discerning travelers as Napoleon, J.S. Bach, Richard Wagner, Leo Tolstoy, and Thomas Mann (who set his novel *Lotte in Weimar* there). In case you don't have the requisite DM155-285 per person, console yourself: Hitler stayed there, too.

🌐**Jugendhotel Hababusch,** Geleitstr. 4 (tel. 85 07 37; email yh@larry.scc.uni-weimar.de; http://www.uni-weimar.de/yh). Smack in the middle of the sights, this hostel, run by a bunch of architecture students, is the best-located and coolest place to stay in Weimar. From Goetheplatz, turn left on Geleitstr. and follow its rightward twist to the clearing with the statue on the left. Absolutely chill, these hip environs just scream for you to kick back and indulge in all of your Eurotrash fantasies. A common room with couches makes most college students feel at home. DM15 for a shared bedroom, DM20 per person for a double. DM20 key deposit. No breakfast, but access to a fully equipped kitchen. 24hr. reception.

Jugendherberge Germania (HI), Carl-August-Allee 13 (tel. 85 04 90; fax 85 04 91). Within spitting distance of the train station, this has convenience written all over it. Walk straight downhill 2min., and a stately foam-gray vision with newly renovated facilities appears before your disbelieving eyes. DM23, over 26 DM27. Breakfast included. Sheets DM7. 24hr. reception.

Jugendherberge Am Poseckschen Garten (HI), Humboldtstr. 17 (tel. 85 07 92), is situated near the city center (although fairly distant from the train station). Bus #6 from the station (direction: "Merketal") to "Poseckschen Garten." Make a right onto Am Poseckschen Garten, then a left onto Humboldtstr.; the hostel is immediately on your left. A big turn-of-the-century brownstone with 8- to 10-bed rooms. The hostel tends to fill with school groups because of its proximity to cultural attractions, so come early. DM23, over 26 DM27. Breakfast included. Lunch and hot dinner DM6-10 each. Reception 7-10am and 3pm-12:30am. Curfew 12:30am.

Jugendgästehaus Maxim Gorki (HI), Zum Wilden Graben 12 (tel. 85 07 50; fax 85 07 45). Bus #8 from the station (direction: "Merketal") to "Wilder Graben." A converted villa in a tranquil Weimar suburb. With only 58 beds, its less than pristine facilities fill quickly. Careful: buses stop running in this direction early, and the walk back from downtown is poorly lit. DM25, over 26 DM30. Sheets DM7. Breakfast included. 24hr. reception. No curfew.

FOOD

The last few years of building in Weimar wreaked havoc with many restaurants, especially those that catered to the proletariat and the budget traveler. If you look hard enough, you can find cheap eats, but look (and look and look) you must. For not-so-expensive delights, try the daily **produce market** at the Marktplatz (open M-F 10am-

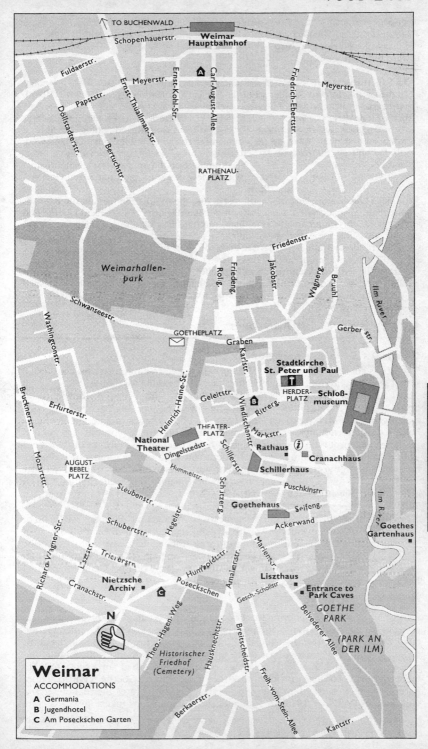

TO BUCHENWALD

Schopenhauerstr.

Weimar Hauptbahnhof

Fuldaerstr.

Meyerstr.

Ernst-Kohl-Str.

Carl-August-Allee

Papststr.

Ernst-Thällmann-Str.

Meyerstr.

Friedrich-Ebertstr.

Döllstädterstr.

Beruchstr.

RATHENAU-PLATZ

Friedenstr.

Jakobstr.

Wagnerg.

Bruhl

Ilm River

Weimarhallen-park

Schwanseestr.

Friedeng.

Rolg.

Gerber str.

Washingtonstr.

GOETHEPLATZ

Graben

Karlstr.

Stadtkirche St. Peter und Paul

HERDER-PLATZ

Schloß-museum

Brucknerstr.

Erfurterstr.

Geleitstr.

Windischenstr.

Ritterg.

Markstr.

Mozartstr.

Heinrich-Heine-Str.

National Theater

THEATER-PLATZ

Dingelstedtstr.

Rathaus

i

Cranachhaus

AUGUST-BEBEL PLATZ

Hummelstr.

Schillerstr.

Schützeg.

Schillerhaus

Puschkinstr.

Steubenstr.

Goethehaus

Seifeng.

Ackerwand

Ilm River

Goethes Gartenhaus

Schubertstr.

Hegelstr.

Richard-Wagner-Str.

Lisztstr.

Trierersrn.

Humboldtstr.

Amalienstr.

Marienstr.

Liszthaus

Cranachstr.

Nietzsche Archiv ■

C

Poseckschen

Gesch-Schollstr.

Entrance to Park Caves

GOETHE PARK

Theo-Hagen-Weg

Hausknechtstr.

Breitscheidstr.

(PARK AN DER ILM)

N

Historischer Friedhof (Cemetery)

Berkaerstr.

Freih-vom-Stein-Allee

Kantstr.

Weimar

ACCOMMODATIONS

A Germania
B Jugendhotel
C Am Poseckschen Garten

THÜRINGEN

6pm, Sa 9am-noon), or the **Rewe grocery store,** in the indoor mall *("Handelhaus zu Weimar")* right of Theaterplatz (open M-F 7am-8pm, Sa 7am-4pm). Another option is the array of **bakeries** and **bistros** ringing the *Markt* and along Karl-Liebknecht-Str. toward the train station.

Da Toni Ristorante Pizzeria, Windsichenstr. 12 (tel. 50 27 19). Delicious, no-foolin' Italian food close to Schiller's house. Pizzas from DM5.50, pastas from DM8.50. Open daily 10am-1am.

Bistro Donecker, Theaterpl. 1 (tel. 51 55 51). A cafeteria-style restaurant that serves German and international foods (DM5-12). Toast Goethe and Schiller (or at least their statues) while enjoying the comforts of sleek chairs that look like they were ripped off from the Bauhaus Museum. Open M-Sa 7am-6pm, Su 7am-4pm.

Anatolia, Frauenplan 15 (tel. 51 71 93). Ruminate on the immortals while nourishing yourself on a *Döner* kebab (DM5) with a view of a giant park statue and Goethe's house. Open daily 10:30am-10pm.

Bauhaus Universität, on Marienstr., just across the footpath in front of the Bauhaus building. Also accessible from Park an der Ilm. Flee the omnipresent Goethe and Schiller in this sanctuary of modernism, and fraternize with the German students in a smoky ambience. Downstairs you can get coffee and pay cheap-ish prices in the cafeteria. Upstairs, in the **Mensa,** grab the grub for DM3-5. Cafeteria open M-F 7:30am-7pm, Mensa opens at 11am. Meals DM2-5.

Gerber III (see **Entertainment and Nightlife**). This ultra-funky bar-like joint almost always has a pot of some filling goody on a back-burner (DM2-3). No bibs, mashed peas, or tiny plastic-coated spoons. Stop by weekdays 12-2pm and daily in the evenings to see what's cookin'.

SIGHTS AND CELEBRATIONS

Cultural Capital Celebration

So much is going on this year that Weimar has created an entire corporation to make sure it goes off without a hitch. **1999 inc.** has been working for four years to get it all straight. It may seem like typical German overkill, but with most of the buildings and nearly all of the streets and sidewalks in the city being renovated and spit-shined, a well-organized effort has proven indispensable. A brand-new structure, the **Weimarhalle,** has also been built to act as the center for the bombastic blow-out. The cultural offerings range from the opening of a new "museum of modernity" to the Universal Couch—a daily five-minute reading of Goethe on a red couch at random and unannounced sites in the city. In short, anything and everything is happening in Weimar this year. For a full bill of the action or any information about the Cultural Capital action, write **Ticket Service Weimar,** 1999 GmbH, Markt 10, D-99423 Weimar (tel. 24 00 24; http://www.weimar1999.de).

Needless to say, all of the commotion means that budget travelers may have a bit of difficulty. Most museum entry prices are scheduled to go up a *Mark* or two, and all of the construction has made it tough for cheaper restaurants to stay open. Especially busy will be New Years 1999, and Goethe's Birthday, August 28. But with four solid hostels and a few cheap places to eat, visiting Weimar won't be totally impossible. Just plan as far in advance as possible, and call ahead.

Goethe and Schiller

If there is one man who is going to sit center-stage for Weimar's 1999 festivities, it is going to be the artist, novelist, and poet **Johann Wolfgang von Goethe.** Such immortality would not surprise the egotistical poet; nor would the numerous sights in his adopted home of Weimar, which dwell upon him and his friend, collaborator, and rival **Friedrich Schiller.** While countless German towns leap at any excuse to build memorial *Goethehäuser* (proclaiming Goethe slept here, Goethe went to school here, Goethe once asked for directions here), Weimar features the real thing. *The* **Goethehaus (WC),** Frauenplan 1, an elegant butter-colored mansion with a commanding view of the central pedestrian zone, shows off the immaculately preserved private chambers where the poet entertained, wrote, studied, and ultimately died after spending 50 years in Weimar. *(Open summer Tu-Su 9am-6pm, winter 10am-4pm. DM8, students and seniors DM5.)* It's jammed to the bursting point with busts, paintings, and sculptures from Goethe's 50,000-piece art collection (not all are on display). The master's tastes were pleasantly Bacchanalian: rampant Neoclassical images dominate the collection, including a bottle-stopper in the shape of the bust of Napoleon (apparently, Goethe felt the need to take revenge for the little general's criticisms of his works). To get the most out of the largely unlabeled exhibits, pick up the handy English guide "Goethe's House on the Frauenplan at Weimar" (DM3) at the desk.

The **Schillerhaus (WC)**, Schillerstr. 12, sits a neighborly distance from Goethe's pad. *(Open summer daily 9am-6pm, winter 10am-4pm. DM5, students DM3.)* This was Schiller's home during the last three years of his life after he resigned from his academic chair at Jena. Showcasing the backgrounds to *The Maid of Orleans* and *William Tell*, both written here, the house offers original drafts and early editions of plays and a detailed biographical chronicle of its owner's life. One block away on Hummelstr., Schiller and Goethe are reconciled in bronze before the **Deutsches Nationaltheater** (tel. 75 53 34; fax 75 53 21), which first breathed life into their stage works. The theater is the epicenter of Weimar's cultural and political spheres—in addition to operating as a first-run venue for their plays, it was also the locale from which the Weimar Constitution emerged in 1919. At the **Wittumpalais (WC)**, across the square at Palais 3, Goethe, Schiller, and Herder sat at the round table of their patron, Duchess Anna Amalia. Under the same roof, the **Wieland Museum** documents the life and works of the extraordinary duchess. *(Open summer Tu-Su 9am-6pm, winter 10am-4pm. DM6, students DM4.)*

The **Park an der Ilm** ("Goethe Park") flanking the river was landscaped by Goethe. It sports numerous 18th-century pavilions and shelters for grazing sheep and goats (or picnickers). Of particular note are the fake ruins built by the Weimar shooting club and the "Kubus," a huge black cube that is used as a theater and as a movie screen, complete with hammer and sickle. Perched on the park's far slopes is Goethe's **Gartenhaus,** on Corona-Schöfer-Str., the poet's first Weimar home and later his retreat from the city. *(Open Mar.-Oct. M and W-Su 9am-noon and 1-5pm; Nov.-Feb. 9am-noon and 1-4pm. DM4, students and seniors DM3.)* It was here that Goethe put the moves on a certain *Fräulein* Christiane Vulpius, who later became *Frau* Goethe. South of the town center, Goethe and Schiller lie in rest together at the **Historischer Friedhof** cemetery, where twisted black metal crosses protrude from a jungle of unkempt wild-flowers and weeds. *(Open Mar.-Sept. 8am-9pm; Oct.-Feb. 8am-6pm.)* Goethe arranged to be sealed in an airtight steel case. Schiller, who died in an epidemic, was originally buried in a mass grave, but Goethe later combed through the remains until he identified Schiller and had him interred in the tomb. Skeptics argued for a long time that Goethe was mistaken, so a couple of "Schillers" were placed side by side for a while. In the 1960s, a team of Russian scientists determined that Goethe was right after all. *(Tomb open daily Mar.-Oct. 9am-1pm and 2-5pm; Nov.-Feb. 9am-1pm and 2-4pm. DM4, students DM3.)*

Other Attractions in Weimar

All of Weimar's sights aren't so stale. Directly across from the theater is the slick **Bauhaus-Museum** (tel. 54 60; fax 54 61 01), featuring, in an appropriately well-designed space, historical artifacts about, and works produced by, the Bauhaus School of Design and Architecture. *(Open summer Tu-Su 10am-6pm, winter 10am-4:30pm. DM5, students and seniors DM3.)* Weavings, sculptures, prints, furniture, books, toys, and other nifty objects bear eloquent testimony to the breadth of the school's philosophy and undertakings. The **Bauhaus Universität,** on Marienstr., ironically offers no exhibits related to the iconoclastic design movement—there is no relation between the two, save the name. Instead, its sleek, prim yellow buildings are the 1911 creation of Henry van de Velde, a pioneer of the *Jugendstil* movement. Steps away is the **Franz**

Liszt Haus (WC), where the composer spent his last years. *(Open summer Tu-Su 9am-1pm and 2-6pm, winter 10am-1pm and 2-4pm. DM4, students and seniors DM3.)* The instruments and furnishings are supposedly original, but given Liszt's torrid love life, the single bed seems improbable.

Back in town, the cobblestone **Marktplatz**, straight down Frauentorstr., spreads out beneath the neo-Gothic **Rathaus** and the colorful Renaissance facade of the **Lucas Cranach Haus**, where the prolific 16th-century painter spent his last days. Both are closed to the public, but the Cranach Haus shelters an **art gallery** of fairly hip modern paintings, photos, and sculptures by still-to-be-discovered talents. *(Gallery open Tu-F 10am-6pm, Sa 11am-3pm.)* Left of the Marktplatz sits the **Schloßmuseum**, at Burgpl. 4. *(Open Tu-Su 10am-6pm. DM6, students and seniors DM3.)* The first floor is a major-league Lucas Cranach fest; the second floor is a minor-league collection of 19th- and 20th-century German works, along with a Rodin sculpture and one of Monet's Rouen cathedral paintings. For the morbid: Cranach himself rests in the churchyard of the **Jakobskirche** on Am Graben. *(Open M-F 11am-3pm, Sa 10am-noon.)* Down Jakobstr., the **Stadtkirche St. Peter und Paul** features Cranach's last triptych altarpiece. *(Open M-Sa 10am-noon and 2-4pm, Su after services are over until noon and 2-3pm. Free.)* The church is also called the **Herderkirche**, in honor of philosopher and linguist Johann Gottfried von Herder, who preached here regularly in the 1780s. Herder's works spurred two later cultural developments: the Romantics embraced his sermons about freedom, and his ground-breaking discussions of the progression of human history pointed directly to Hegel's dialectic of the spirit. Herder was buried in the church in 1803. The church's interior is at odds with its solemn exterior: dazzlingly colorful coats of arms painted on all the balconies give the hall a festive air.

Down Humboldtstr. from the *Jugendherberge* is the **Nietzsche-Archiv (WC)**, Humboldtstr. 36. *(Open Tu-Su summer 1-6pm, winter 1-4pm. DM4, students and seniors DM3.)* Nietzsche spent the last three wacky years (1897-1900) of his life in this house; he was pretty far gone by the end, as is painfully evident from the cross-eyed glares emanating from the myriad pictures and busts. The archive was founded by Nietzsche's sister Elisabeth, a woman whose misunderstandings set the stage for the Nazis' cynical distortion of her brother's philosophy—she gave Hitler a tour of the house in 1932.

ENTERTAINMENT AND NIGHTLIFE

If there's one thing that's going to be hard to come by in 1999, it's going to be tickets to the many prominent cultural offerings. The **Deutsches Nationaltheater** is emerging from more than a year of renovation for a season of some of Germany's best-loved plays. Tickets for the theater, as well as all other cultural capital activities, are available through **1999 inc.** (see **Sights and Celebrations**, above).

Weimar's nightlife is stuck in a pretty hard spot. With the more active rave culture of Erfurt to the west and Jena's *Uni*-culture to the East, Weimar is left with just a few cozy student clubs. When something cool does happen, the Bauhaus Universität's *Mensa* has posters and bulletin boards directing you to what's going down (see **Food**, p. 180). The **Studentenklub Kasserturm** is in an old medieval tower on Goetheplatz opposite the main post office. With a disco up top and a groovy beer cellar below, this is the oldest student club in Germany and a good place simply to chill (cover varies; disco M-Sa after 8pm). The **Studentenklub Schützengasse**, on Schützengassestr., has a disco on Tuesday and Friday nights, and a beer garden outside (open M-Th after 7:30pm, F-Sa after 9pm). **Gerber III**, Gerberstr. 3, is a former squatter house that now houses all things leftist. A cool cafe, club, climbing wall, movie theater, and bicycle repair shop are all under this roof. The building itself is something mom would be proud of...if mom's an anarchist. Weimar also has a growing gay scene. **Jugendclub Nordlich**, on Staufenbergstr., has a gay disco every other Saturday night (10pm-3am). **AIDS-Hilfe** (tel. 614 51), Erfurter Str. 17, holds a popular gay cafe (open Tu-Sa from 8pm).

■ Near Weimar: Buchenwald

"Where is God now?" is a question that echoes throughout Elie Wiesel's autobiography *Night*, and through every inch of Buchenwald. Wiesel himself was a prisoner here, and the knowledge that the horrors he described took place within the same barbed wire, on the same gravel on which you stand, is enough to shake the most devout faith. The weight of Buchenwald's history is so great that no tears, no flowers, and no human response can fully digest it for the unprepared visitor. Perhaps the only solace one can find is in two simple German words: *Nie Wieder*—Never Again.

Buchenwald sits on a hill with a stunning view of Weimar (it was one of Goethe's favorite mountain retreats) in the middle of a peaceful forest that makes for an eerie contrast with its violent past. The best way to reach the camp is by taking bus #6 from the station or from downtown Weimar. Check the bus schedule carefully; half the buses run to Etterburg, a full 5km away. Buses with "B" or "EB" on the schedule are ok; "E" is not. If you're not sure, just look on the front of the bus. If it says "Buchenwald," you're good. Buses leave from the *Bahnhof* (1 per hr., 1 every 2hr. on weekends). From 1937 to 1945, the concentration camp held over 250,000 Jews, political prisoners, gypsies, and gays (after 1942, there was also a large Communist contingent); most did not survive the Holocaust. What remains is the **Nationale Mahn-und Gedenkstätte Buchenwald** (National Buchenwald Memorial; tel. (03643) 43 00). At the memorial, signs will point to two destinations: the **KZ Lager** and the **Gedenkstätte**. (Camp open May-Sept. Tu-Su 9:45am-5:15pm; Oct.-Apr. Tu-Su 8:45am-4:15pm.) The former refers to the remains of the camp, while the latter is a solemn monument overlooking the valley, a 20-minute walk away.

Death claimed members of many groups at Buchenwald. A plaque near the former commandant's horse stable matter-of-factly states that an estimated 8000 Soviet prisoners were executed by firing squad in the little space before the war's end. Many Jews were sent here, but after 1942, most were deported to Auschwitz. For the most part, Buchenwald served to detain and murder political enemies of Nazism and prisoners of war. The Soviet Union used the site from 1945 to 1950 as an internment camp in which over 28,000 Germans, mostly Nazi war criminals and opponents of the Communist regime, were held; 10,000 died of hunger and disease. An exhibit detailing the Soviet abuses opened in 1997. In the woods behind the museum rests a cemetery with the graves of both the victims and perpetrators of the Soviet abuses.

The central camp area, downhill from the reception, is now a vast, flat, gravel plain; gone are the ramshackle wooden *Blocks* that crammed prisoners. The former crematorium building has been preserved with a wrenching suggestion of the terror wrought here; flowers and wreaths are lain at the base of the open-mouthed ovens. Downstairs lurk the dreadful rooms where the corpses were piled before their incineration. In the large storehouse building, a museum documents both the history of Buchenwald (1937-1945) and the general history of Nazism, including German anti-Semitism. The museum sets real documents (most of which are translated into or summarized in English) in wrought-iron boxes visibly riveted together. A moving installation by Polish artist Jòzef Szajna features thousands of photos of inmates pasted onto large silhouettes of human figures. Just outside the museum lies a brutally ironic symbol: the charred stump of the **Goethe-Eiche** (Goethe oak), left standing in the middle of the camp to commemorate Buchenwald's former role as a get-away for Germany's greatest cultural figure. The memorial stones recently embedded in the ground around the former children's barracks read, in English, German, and Hebrew: "So that the generation to come might know, that the children, yet to be born, may rise and declare to their children." Tiny candles and flowers are regularly placed near the stones, just outside the main gate close to the remains of the camp zoo, built for the amusement of the SS officers' children. The camp **archives** are open to anyone searching for records of family and friends between 1938 and 1945. Call ahead to schedule an appointment with the curator (tel. (036431) 43 01 54).

THÜRINGEN

To get to the **memorial bell tower** (*Glockenturm*) from the camp, start by facing the reception at the bus stop and head right. Around the corner of the right-most building is the footpath to the **Mahnmal** (monument). After a short walk through the woods, it emerges at a two-way fork in the street. Head right, and keep walking past a parking lot and a bus stop. Keep going as the street curves left, and soon you'll come to the somber GDR-designed bell tower, with no marking other than an immense "MCMXLV" carved on each side. The plaque inside commemorates the memory of the anti-fascist "resistance fighters of the Republic of Germany." On the great stone plaza behind the tower unfolds a commanding view of the surrounding countryside, overseen by the slightly awkward **Plastikgruppe**, a sculpture of ragged, stern-jawed socialist prisoners claiming their freedom. Like the rest of the grounds outside of the buildings, the memorial can be visited until nightfall.

■ Jena

Once home to the country's premier university, Jena still triggers intellectual fireworks in the German historical consciousness. Under the stewardship of literary greats Schlegel, Novalis, Tieck, and Hölderlin, Jena first transplanted the Romantic movement to German soil. It was here that philosophers Fichte and Schelling argued for a new conception of intellectual and political freedom, and here, in 1806, that a then-unknown junior philosophy professor named Herr Doktor Professor Georg Wilhelm Friedrich Hegel wrote the epoch-making *Phenomenology of Spirit* by candlelight in his ramshackle lodgings by the centuries-old *Collegium Jenense*. Today, the university bears the name of Friedrich Schiller, who, in 1789, graced its halls with his lectures on the ideals of the French Revolution. True to its 19th-century tradition, Jena remains a campus town, albeit an increasingly Westernized one. Students keep this town youthful, left-leaning, and multicultural, so that Jena's dearth of touristy sight-seeing is made up for with its dynamism and forward-looking spirit.

ORIENTATION AND PRACTICAL INFORMATION Jena lies in the Saale Valley, 25km east of Weimar by **train** (1hr., 27 trains per day). Trains between Dresden and Erfurt stop at **Bahnhof Jena West** (45min., 3-4 per hr.) while trains on the Berlin-Munich line stop at the more distant **Jena Saalbahnhof** (15min. north of the center). All stations and most of the city are connected by a bus and streetcar system that uses the *Zentrum* stop on Löbdergraben as its hub. Tickets are DM8.30 for 5 rides, and are available at the tourist office, train stations, and hard-to-find *Automaten*. From the Saalbahnhof, turn left down Saalbahnhofstr. and take a right on Saalstr. to arrive at the center of town. Or take bus #15. From Bahnhof Jena West, head toward Westbahnhofstr. until it becomes Schillerstr. Turn left up the street to the towering university building. Rent **bikes** for DM15 per day (you must pay in advance and present a photo I.D.) at **Kirscht Fahrrad**, Löbdergraben 8 (tel. 44 15 39), near the Zentrum bus stop (open M-F 9am-7pm, Sa 9am-4pm). **Jena-Information**, Johannisstr. 23 (tel. 58 63 20; fax 58 63 22), on the *Eichplatz*, hands out maps and schedules of special events. They also book private and hotel rooms (open M-F 9am-6pm, Sa 9am-2pm). The **Goethe-Apotheke** (tel. 45 45 45) is conveniently located on Weigelstr., just north of the vast concrete Eichplatz; a sign directs you to other **pharmacies** that are open when it's closed (open M-F 8am-8pm, Sa 8am-4pm). The **post office** is at Engelpl. 8, 07743 Jena (open M-F 8am-6:30pm, Sa 8am-1pm). The **telephone code** is 03641.

ACCOMMODATIONS AND FOOD Jena's budget accommodations aren't nearly as robust as its alternative culture. The **IB-Jugendgästehaus**, Am Herrenberge 3 (tel. 68 72 30) is the safest bet, although it's a 10-minute bus ride from town. It caters mostly to construction workers, but the rooms are clean and often available. Take bus #10 or 13 (direction: "Burgau") to "Lichtenhain." Go left on Mühlenstr., which turns into Am Herrenberge. (DM34. Breakfast DM3-4. Reception M-Th 24hr., F until 6pm. Weekends call ahead.) Otherwise, head to the tourist office, which finds rooms (DM30-45).

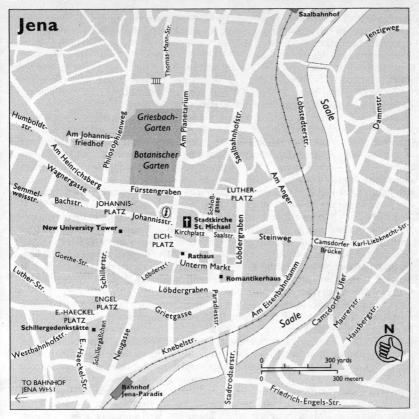

Jena

Saalbahnhof

Jenzigweg

Thomas-Mann-Str.

Humboldt-str.

Am Johannis-friedhof

Philosophenweg

Am Heinrichsberg

Wagnergasse

Semmel-weisstr.

Bachstr.

Griesbach-Garten

Botanischer Garten

Am Planetarium

Saalbahnhofstr.

Löbstedterstr.

Saale

Dammstr.

Fürstengraben

LUTHER-PLATZ

Am Anger

JOHANNIS-PLATZ

Johannisstr. (i)

Schloß-gasse

† **Stadtkirche St. Michael**

New University Tower ■

Goethe-Str.

EICH-PLATZ

Kirchplatz Saalstr.

Löbdergraben

Steinweg

Camsdorfer Karl-Liebknecht-Str. Brücke

Schillerstr.

Löbderstr.

■ **Rathaus**
Unterm Markt

■ **Romantikerhaus**

Camsdorfer Ufer

Luther-Str.

ENGEL PLATZ

E.-HAECKEL PLATZ

Schillergedenkstätte ■

E.-Haeckel-Str.

Schillergäßchen

Neugasse

Löbdergraben

Grietgasse

Paradiesstr.

Am Eisenbahndamm

Saale

Maurerstr.

Hausbergstr.

Knebelstr.

N

Westbahnhofstr.

Stadtrodaerstr.

TO BAHNHOF
JENA WEST
←

Bahnhof
Jena-Paradis

Friedrich-Engels-Str.

0 ___ 300 yards
0 ___ 300 meters

The **Spar Markt,** down Ludwig-Weimar-Gasse to the right of the *Rathaus*, wins the prize for most central **supermarket** (open M-F 8am-6pm, Sa 8am-12:30pm). After five years in India, the owners of **Taj of India,** Wagnergasse 7 (tel. 42 03 33), developed a taste for subcontinental food, and today they invite you to an oasis of authenticity in a sea of Asia-*Imbiße*. Daily specials (DM7-10) are served with Basmati rice, *raita,* and salad, including plenty of vegetarian options. Quench your thirst with Chai. (Open Tu-F 11:30am-11pm, Sa-Su 5:30-11pm.) A crunchier clientele frequents the nuclear-free zone of **Café Immergrün,** Jenergasse 6 (tel. 44 73 13). Hiding just off Fürstengraben, this ultra-eco cafe is all about fresh and friendly. An unofficial environmental center, it proves that green doesn't have to be soft, with modern furniture that would do any eco-cafe proud. Tasty green specialties like veggie pizzas run DM5. (Open M-Sa 11am-1am, Su 3pm-whenever.) Numerous **bakeries** and **butcher shops** cluster around Eichplatz and the St. Michaelkirche, while *Imbiße* of all sorts park at Hochplatz. The **market** on Eichplatz provides a panoply of cheap culinary options (open Tu and Th-F 10am-6:30pm). That huge, round, metal eyesore of a university actually provides its students with very, very cheap meals in the ground floor **Mensa.** Ask one of them to buy you a ticket and partake in the fun. (Full meals DM2.50-4.50. Open M-Th 8am-4pm, F 8am-3pm, Sa 11am-3pm.)

SIGHTS The **Romantikerhaus,** Unterm Markt 12a (tel. 44 32 63), just off the old market square, once bubbled with the raw creative energy of the Romantic period. Owned by philosopher and fiery democrat Johann Fichte, who lectured here, it later hosted the poetry and philosophy parties of the Romantics. It's a curious and small museum where first-edition books and portraits scattered around the interior are interspersed with big stenciled quotes of great thinkers on the walls. Everything is in German. At the center of the museum's strangeness, the **Kritische Guillotine** (critical guillotine) remains frozen in mid-chop of a pile of books. Upstairs resides the **Fine Arts Museum of Jena,** which would be spectacular if nearly its entire collection hadn't been confiscated by the Nazis as "degenerate." *(Open Tu and Th-Sa 10am-1pm and 2-5pm, W 10am-1pm and 2-6pm. DM5, students and seniors DM3.)* Today it cowers with a small bit of GDR art and interesting temporary exhibits.

A few blocks to the southwest sits the **Schillergedenkstätte,** Schiller's swank summer home on Schillergäßchen (tel. 63 03 94), just off (you guessed it!) Schillerstr. *(Open Tu-F 10am-noon and 1-4pm, Sa 11am-4pm. DM2, students and seniors DM1.)* Another museum where the furniture, including a standing desk, looks like it *could* have been used by Schiller—who knows? A helpful information brochure translated into English brings some history to these recently renovated rooms and delightful sculptured garden. Jena's most visible structure is neglected as a tourist sight: the cylindrical, 24-story **new university tower.** A product of the late-GDR architectural imagination, it looks like a Buck Rogers-inspired vision of the future. A competing, more contemporary vision of the future is the **Jenoptik** building, across Leutragraben from the *Uni*-tower. This ultra-slick edifice with an adjacent mall attests to Jena's high-tech corporate aspirations and new-found joy of consumption. The **original university building,** just up Oberlauengasse from the *Romantikerhaus,* dates from the 13th century. It housed a Dominican monastery until Wittenberg University took over, when it temporarily relocated to dodge the plague.

The **Stadtkirche St. Michael,** just off Eichplatz, presides proudly over **Luther's tombstone.** *(Church open M-F 10am-6pm, Sa 10am-2pm.)* He's not resting here, though the stone was intended for him; the folks at the Stadtkirche claim it got held up in shipping during a war, while back at the grave site in Wittenberg, tour guides mutter something under their breath about 17th-century plundering. The 16th-century church is unusually frightening and black outside, but the interior is graceful and light. Up Weigelstr. and left onto Fürstengraben, lies the **Botanischer Garten** (open dawn-dusk), and the row of statues of the university's distinguished faculty—notice that teachers and students of **Marx** are given particularly large statues. But there's one glaring exception—Marx's intellectual godfather and Jena's most famous professor, **Hegel,** has no bust at all. In fact, the only mention of him in the entire city is a piddly plaque on the back of the *Romantikerhaus.* Maybe it's a legacy of Communist *Angst* about Hegel, whose writings inspired Marx's work but themselves propounded a spiritual, bourgeois-centered political vision (to make Hegel's theories right, Marx once wrote, you had to "stand him on his head").

The **Wagnergasse,** which extends from Eichplatz, is shaping up as Jena's funkiest area, chock full o' bars, shops, and little restaurants. Face the university tower, walk around its right side, past the small battlement (the *Pulverturm*) on your right, then bear right at the fork. The university energy has clearly been funneled in this direction. Rave culture invades **Backstage** and the adjacent **Stahlwerkt,** clothing stores on Wagnergasse 3 and 4. *(Both open M-F 11am-6pm, Sa 10am-1pm.)* At the end of the street lies the **Studentenhaus Wagner,** Wagnergasse 26 (tel. 63 63 24), the source of the funk, as it were. *(Open M-F 11am-1am, Sa-Su 7:30pm-1am.)* This university-sponsored bar/hang-out doubles as a performance space for plays, readings, live music, and movie showings. The **Zentrum** area is saturated with swinging saloons. Wednesdays at **Kassablanca,** Felsenkellerstr. 13a (tel. 282 60), are all about "Gay-House" disco, beginning at 10pm.

■ Near Jena: Dornburg

Just a 10-minute train ride north of Jena, one of the more majestic summer estates in Thüringen presides over the *Saale* valley. The **Dornburg Schlößer** (info. tel. 222 91) are three royal palaces, running the gamut from boring to Baroque, lined up along a white chalk cliff. First in line is the **Altes Schloß,** the oldest and homeliest castle, built in 937 when the *Kaiser*s still visited Dornburg. The first German *Reichstag* met here; the building was also used as a prison by both the Nazi and Communist regimes. The interior is closed to the public. The summer residences of the Grand Duke of Sachsen-Weimar-Eisenach, the **Renaissanceschloß** and the **Rokokoschloß,** preside majestically and frivolously (respectively) over the magnificent rose gardens where Goethe practiced his horticultural skills while writing letters to his lover, Charlotte von Stein. (See **Großkochberg,** p. 201, for some juicy details. Open Mar.-Oct. Tu-Su 9am-6pm, Nov.-Feb. Tu-Su 10am-4pm.) Inside the whitewashed, slate-roofed, 16th-century Renaissance castle, the plain royal belongings are spiced up with stories about Goethe's frequent visits to the *Schlößer.* Goethe never actually napped on the big ottoman in the guest bedroom, since he traveled everywhere at great expense with his portable bed (the bed now sits in the Gartenhaus in Weimar, p. 178). One look inside the lush chambers of this 1740 Rococo pleasure palace will reveal why Goethe chose its ornate, luxurious, and window-filled rooms for 19 of his 20 visits to Dornburg. Visitors can partake in the voluptuous pleasure of gliding along the slick surface of the main hall in slippers provided to protect its plum-tree wood. The high-Rococo gilded decorations and large porcelain collection border between priceless treasures and gaudy kitsch. Even the castles themselves seem like background for the formal rose gardens that fill the park all the way up to the cliff.

The castles and the mini-village are a grueling climb up a very steep hill. Fortunately for pedestrians (you can also drive the route), steps lead partway to the summit. Use them or face a hike up a mile of winding, steep highway. From the tiny *Bahnhof,* turn left and then take the first right onto Am Born; the stairs will be immediately to your left. When you reach the main road, turn right and continue upward. When the first houses come into sight, watch on the left for signs to the *Markt* or *Schlößer.*

Dornburg also has a bloomin' lot of roses, which are celebrated during the last weekend in June with the **Dornburg Rose Festival,** marking the anniversary of King Karl August's lavish birthday parties held here a century ago. The townspeople elect a pseudo-queen who hands out food and candy to spectators. Locals don their party hats again during the last week in August to celebrate **Goethe's birthday.** One of the coolest things about Dornburg is that it entertains your fantasies of royalty at borderline budget prices. Right next door to the ticket window in the Renaissanceschloß is a **Café** (tel. 704 19) that also has a *Pension* on the 3rd floor (DM50 per person). You can dine on the patio overlooking the entire valley (DM10-16), stroll through the gardens, then retreat to your room, just like Goethe used to do. To reach Dornburg from Jena, hop on one of the hourly **trains** from either the Jena Saalbahnhof or Bahnhof Jena-Paradies, on Kahlaischestr., a five-minute walk from Bahnhof Jena West. The lockers in the Saalbahnhof are perfect for storing your pack before attempting the steep walk to the castles; Dornburg's train station is too small to have lockers of its own. Dornburg is also an easy and attractive **bike ride** from Jena, though you may want to save your strength for the climb to the castles. The **post office,** right by the castle and on the *Markt,* doubles as the grocery store (open M-F 8am-1pm and 3-5pm, Sa 8-10am). The **telephone code** is 036427.

▨ Gera

Oddly enough, the second-largest city in Thüringen has a very limited plate of attractions. Moving beyond its shortcomings, the city blends the usually less-than-attractive architecture of the GDR with occasional cultural gems to create a happy co-existence between the functionalist aesthetic of the past decades and the rich history of the *Land.* The birthplace of renowned painter Otto Dix, Gera's handful of art museums make the city a fine daytrip from any number of cities in the region.

PRACTICAL INFORMATION Frequent **trains** connect Gera to Erfurt (1¾hr., 38 per day) running through Jena and Weimar. Lines also steam in from Leipzig (80min., 20 per day). The **tourist office,** Ernst-Toller-Str. 14 (tel. 61 93 01; fax 61 93 04), finds private rooms (DM25-45) for a DM5 fee, the only real overnight option in the absence of a youth hostel. The staff also equips patrons with free maps and brochures in English and German. From the *Hauptbahnhof,* head right and then turn left onto Ernst-Toller-Str. (Open M-F 9am-6pm, Sa 9am-1pm.) A **pharmacy,** the **Stadt-Apotheke,** sits right by the *Rathaus* at Markt 8/9 (tel. 83 32 70, open M-F 8am-7pm, Sa 8am-1pm). The **post office,** 07545 Gera, lies at Puschkinplatz on Ernst-Toller-Str. (open M-F 8am-7pm, Sa 8am-1pm). The **telephone code** is 0365.

FOOD Restaurants and food stands are plentiful throughout the center of town, but the real meal deal is at **Gastronom,** close to the Stadtmuseum at the intersection of Reichstr. and Heinrichstr. beneath the Spielpalast in a black building. This self-serve restaurant serves a clientele undaunted by fears of cholesterol, dishing out huge portions of delectable Thüringer home-cooking for DM5.50-6 (open M-F 8am-4pm). A **Kaiser's supermarket,** around Sorge 41 in the basement of the Horton's, fills any remaining gaps (open M-F 9:30am-8pm, Sa 9:30am-4pm).

SIGHTS Gera's main attractions all lie within 10 to 15 minutes of the *Hauptbahnhof.* Like a vein of pure capitalism running through the heart of the town, the **Sorge** is filled with Western brand names in a less glitzy setting than in Köln or Düsseldorf. Heading right from the *Hauptbahnhof* and left onto Ernst-Toller-Str. will bring you to this pedestrian area. Following the Sorge up and then heading right onto Steinweg to Greizerstr. takes you to the **Museum für Angewandte Kunst,** Greizerstr. 37 (tel./fax 287 50). *(Open Tu-Su 10am-5pm. DM4, students and seniors DM1.50; special exhibitions DM9-10, students and seniors DM3.)* A medium-sized collection of Art Deco and functionalist objects (furniture, posters, tableware, etc.) occupies half the space of this mansion. The other half hosts revolving two-month exhibitions ranging from the serious to the downright silly. Heading out from the museum onto Böttchergasse and then right through Kornmarkt to the Marktplatz brings you to the center of historic Gera. The Renaissance **Rathaus** has a 300-year-old fountain of Samson wrestling with a lion; despite his age, Samson looks like he's still going strong. The **Stadtmuseum,** Heinrichstr. 2 (tel. 838 14 70), straight down from the *Markt* on Kloster Kirchstr., houses a small but well-constructed museum documenting Gera's history. *(Open daily 10am-5pm. DM4, students and seniors DM1.50.)*

Gera recently recognized its import as the birthplace of famed *Neue Sachlichkeit* painter Otto Dix in 1991 with the establishment of the **Otto-Dix-Haus,** Mohrenpl. 4 (tel. 832 49 27). *(Open Tu-F 10am-5pm, Sa-Su 10am-6pm. DM4, students and seniors DM1.50; combined admission with Orangerie DM5, DM2.)* The museum documents Dix's life and career with photos, letters, and a tiny collection of his paintings. To get there via a scenic route from the *Hauptbahnhof,* turn right from the station, and take another right under the tracks to Kückengartenallee. Enter the park to the left of the sherbet-colored Neoclassical Theater, head through the Orangerie, cross a bridge, and land directly at the museum. The late-Baroque **Orangerie,** Küchengartenallee 4 (tel. 832 21 47), at the head of the manicured garden park, serves as an exhibition space for a small permanent collection and displays some fairly avant-garde works. *(Open Tu 1-8pm, W-F 10am-5pm, Sa-Su 10am-6pm. DM4, students and seniors DM1.50.)*

■ Altenburg

Altenburg's fame and hilltop castle are literally built upon a house of cards. Famous for its role as the world's only *Skatstadt,* Altenburg revels in its card-playing glory and savors its status as the birthplace of the card-game *Skat.* Not surprisingly, the city is also the home of a centuries-old playing cards manufacturing industry. The city now serves as the fount of inspiration for travel-guide card-game puns.

ORIENTATION AND PRACTICAL INFORMATION A web of rail-lines connects Altenburg with Zwickau (40min.) and Leipzig (45min.). To reach the **tourist office,** Moritzstr. 21 (tel. 59 41 74; fax 59 41 79), turn left from the train station and walk to the end of Wettiner Str., then turn right onto Gabelentzstr.; follow it past the *Schloß* until Burgstr. emerges on your right. Turn left from Burgstr. down Weibermarkt,

No More Hot Dogs

In an effort to dip into the high culture of German cuisine, you will undoubtedly be confronted with the dilemma of whether or not to indulge in a *Wurst*—a German sausage. The staple of the German diet, they're tasty, they're cheap, and dammit—they're German! There can be a severe downside, however, to living the life of a German gourmet. Nietzsche, in *Ecce Homo*, described how the German character, particularly its food, necessarily inflicted him with bad digestion. But for those in search of the quintessential German experience (and who have vicious, carnivorous inclinations), a sausage is a must. The following brief guide is an attempt to help you navigate through both the perils and the delights that define the *Wurst*. You will be hard-pressed not to make the leap of faith into the unknown world of *Würste*. Just remember to proclaim beforehand, *"Das ist mir Wurst!"* (I don't give a damn!)

Thüringer Bratwurst—The direct ancestor of the American "hot dog" comes cupped in a flaky Brötchen, doused in mustard. Also known as a Roster or Thüringer Brat, the zesty sausage puts the sickly pink American frank to shame.

Rheinländer Wurst—Some barbaric Rhinelanders have been known to grab a naked, greasy *Wurst* in their bare hands, alternately biting the meaty mass and a roll. It is not known whether they bathe or observe any social norms.

Bavarian Weißwurst—The ubiquitous meal is sometimes referred to as *Scheißwurst* (shit *Wurst*), owing to its reputation from the era predating refrigeration, when eating a *Weißwurst* after noon guaranteed a stomach-buckling experience. Thanks to modern technology, they can now be enjoyed any time of day.

Frankfurter—This legal title refers only to sausages produced following an official recipe within a certain distance of Frankfurt's city center. A gruesome process yields tasty results: meat extracted from the tender front legs of a pig is mixed with fatty bacon and bunches of spices before being hand-stuffed in sheep intestines. These hearty concoctions make Oscar Mayer look like a wiener.

which becomes Moritzstr. The tourist office books rooms for a DM3 fee, provides free maps with information in English, and leads **tours** in both English and German on Mondays at 10am and 3pm. (Open M-F 9:30am-6pm, Sa 9:30am-noon). When closed, the office posts available rooms in the window. Altenburg's **postal code** is 04600. The **telephone code** is 03447.

ACCOMMODATIONS AND FOOD Altenburg sadly lacks a youth hostel, but booking a private room through the tourist office may cost less than DM30 per person. A novel (and cheap) option is a stay at the **Magdalenenstift,** Stiftsgraben 20 (tel. 31 16 13). The *Stift* is a Lutheran-run home for the elderly partially converted into friendly dormitory-style rooms. It's best to call ahead on weekends to make sure rooms are available. To get there, head left from the *Schloß* on Morstallstr., take a right on Münsterstr.; the *Stift* is to the right as soon as you turn right on Stiftsgraben. The office is on the second floor in entrance G. Heavenly peace reigns under Martin Luther's gaze. (Beds DM20 plus a one-time DM7.50 fee for linens. Breakfast DM6.50.) While the restaurants in the *Markt* are a touch pricey, the food **markets** throughout the town soften the budget sting (most open M-F 8am-6pm, Sa 8am-noon). The less expensive restaurant scene resides close to the *Schloß* driveway. **Eiscafé Angela,** Rosa-Luxemburg-Str. 15 (tel. 26 33), has a menu of daily *Thüringer* specials and homemade ice cream (DM6-8.50; open M-F 10am-10pm, Sa 1-11pm, Su 1-10pm). The *Biergarten* and restaurant **Kulisse,** Theaterpl. 18 (tel. 50 09 39), has a weird cow-themed menu (*Kuh*-lisse) that features moderately interesting bar-fare. (Open M-Th 4pm-1am, F-Sa 4pm-3am, Su 2pm-midnight.)

SIGHTS The wide cobblestone footpath leading up to the looming **Schloß** winds from Theaterplatz in the heart of town. A massive sand-colored enclosure, the castle was begun in the 11th century and expanded over the next 700 years. The architecture ranges from a humbly squatting 11th-century guard tower called the **Flasche**

(bottle) to the dazzlingly Gothic 15th-century **Schloßkirche**. The church organ, the **Trostorgel**, was given a thumbs-up by Bach after a trial performance in 1730. Unfortunately, the only way to view the inside of the church, its organ, and some of the castle's gems is through guided **tours** which leave from the second floor of the museum every hour, on the hour. Adjacent to the church is a museum that cunningly combines Altenburg's two claims to fame in one neat package: the **Schloß-und-Spielkartenmuseum**. *(Castle and playing card museum. Church and museums open daily Apr.-Sept. 9:30am-5:30pm; Oct.-Mar. 9am-5pm. DM5, students DM2.50.)* The *Schloß* amply entertains with its huge, hanging portraits of the Dukes of Sachsen-Gotha-Altenburg. The **Waffenmuseum** (weapons museum) section sports ornately gilded muskets, jagged-edged Bavarian cavalry sabres, and bizarre pointy helmets; the **Stadtgeschichte** (city history) displays, which have yet to recover from their socialist days, place Altenburg in the middle of all rebellious proletarian activities. You'll find a full house in the **Spielkarten** wing, occupying gorgeous, Rococo-ceilinged rooms jammed with excellent giant playing-card displays, representing over 400 years of international gaming history. The most occult elements of the exhibit are the hand-enameled extra-large 15th-century Florentine tarot cards, each the size of a hand. The cards of the former GDR are fascinatingly comical—meant to indoctrinate the incorrigible, frenzied school groups who make life in hostels hell, they come in four suits: the October Revolution, solidarity, anti-Fascism, and the triumph of Communism. Presumably, no kings, queens, or jacks in this set.

Altenburg's ace in the hole is a hidden cultural treasure: the **Lindenau-Museum** at Gabelentzstr. 5. It possesses an unexpectedly sophisticated collection of cutting-edge modern paintings and some representatives of major movements of the past, including many works from the GDR. The museum also boasts an ultra-suave cafe, where you can skat it up at tables surrounded by plaster casts of antique sculpture (museum open Tu-Su 10am-6pm; DM7, students and seniors DM3). Altenburg also has a couple of parties up its sleeve: the highlight of the **Skatbrunnenfest**, during the first weekend in May, is an attempt by four skinny boys to re-enact the statue near the Markt. There are equally lively attractions at the **Schloßfest** in mid-July and the **Altstadtfest** during the first weekend in October.

■ Erfurt

The capital of Thüringen, Erfurt surprises its guests with an exquisitely renovated and quirky *Altstadt*, many cosmopolitan cafes, and an abundance of verdant parks. Hardly a historical cultural powerhouse like Dresden or even Eisenach, the city has gained fame more through political connections. Napoleon based his field camp here for over a year, Konrad Adenauer lived here before WWII, and, more recently, Willy Brandt met here with Erich Honecker, commencing the long and arduous process of German-German reconciliation in 1970. A lot of money has been funneled into Erfurt recently, allowing the cultural offerings to flourish and creating a nearly ideal transportation system. Erfurt also offers a stunning cathedral, a handful of museums, and a civic atmosphere fueled by three educational institutions. For those despairing over the stagnation in the eastern cities, Erfurt is a refreshing and reassuring counterpoint.

ORIENTATION AND PRACTICAL INFORMATION

Erfurt lies in the heart of Thüringen, only 15 minutes from Weimar (4-5 trains per hr.), 1½ hours from Leipzig (29 per day), and three hours from Frankfurt (20 per day). The city is also properly referred to as the gateway to the Thüringer Wald, with numerous connections throughout the forest. The train station stands south of the city center. Head straight down Bahnhofstr. to reach the **Anger**—the main drag—and then the *Altstadt*, which is cut through by the **Gera River**. Take Schlößerstr. across the river to the **Fischmarkt** square, dominated by the neo-Gothic **Rathaus**. Marktstr. then leads left to the **Domhügel** hill, one of Erfurt's oldest districts and site of the **cathedral**.

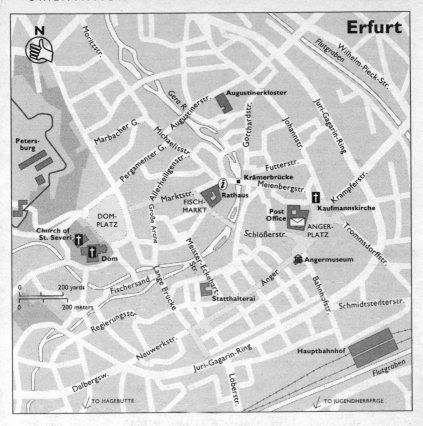

Trains: From the *Hauptbahnhof,* trains go to Dresden (every 2hr.), Würzburg (2½hr., every 3hr.), and Frankfurt am Main (2½hr., every 3hr.).

Public Transportation: An effective combination of **buses** and silent **streetcars** runs through the pedestrian zones. DM2 per trip, or 5 trips for DM7.50. For most purposes, the yellow tariff zone is all that you need. 50% senior discount. Validate your tickets on board. For info call 194 49 or stop by the office at the *Hauptbahnhof.* Most streetcars and buses stop just before 1am.

Taxis: tel. 511 11, or for those with bad memories 555 55, 666 66, or 777 77 77.

Bike rental: Velo-Sport, Juri-Gagarin Ring 72a (tel./fax 56 23 540). From Bahnhofstr., turn left and walk for about 3min. DM10-15 per day, and you must leave a passport. Open M-W and F 10am-6pm, Th 10am-7pm, Sa 9am-1pm.

Tourist Office: Erfurt Fremdenverkehrsamt, Fischmarkt 27 (tel. 664 00; fax 664 02 90) down the street to the *Rathaus's* left. Pick up a copy of the monthly *Erfurter Magazine* with a worthy map in the center, and for nightlife either *In* (hard to get) or *Boulevard.* Maps of the Thüringer Wald are also available. The staff reserves tickets and books rooms in costly hotels and cheap private rooms for a DM5 fee (singles DM30-50). Open M-F 10am-7pm, Sa-Su 10am-4pm. **Tours** of the city are also offered, leaving from the office Sa and Su at 1pm (DM6).

Currency Exchange: Reisebank, in the train station. Offers money transfer, phonecards, and cash advances on credit cards. Nice hours, but somewhat stiff rates. Open Tu-F 8:30am-7:45pm, Sa-Su 10am-4pm. Close to the train station, and with better rates and a 24hr. **ATM,** is the **Deutsche Bank,** on the corner of Bahnhofstr. and Juri-Gagarin-Ring. Open M, W, and F 8am-4pm, Tu and Th 8am-6pm.

Laundry: Jump for joy at the sight of washing machines across the street and to the left as you exit the *Hauptbahnhof.* Open daily 6am-11pm. DM6 per load.

Pharmacy: Bahnhof-Apotheke, on Bahnhofstr. 40 (tel. 55 54 10), has a wide selection and lists the daily all-night pharmacy. Open M-F 8am-6pm, Sa 9am-noon.

Women's Center: Frauenzentrum, Espachstr. 3 (tel. 225 14 73), in the southwest part of the city, has information, counseling, and a cafe. Open M 2-6pm, Tu-Th 9:30am-10pm, F 9:30am-2pm, Sa 2-6pm.

Gay and Lesbian Concerns: At the **AIDS-Hilfe,** Windhorststr. 43a (tel. 7 31 22 33. On the edge of the city park near the *Bahnhof* flies the rainbow flag over a house filled with a library, archive, and cafe. Open 9am-8pm, Café SwiB open W, F, and Su 7pm-midnight. At both locations *Buschlunk* is available, Thüringen's ultra-thorough, ultra-helpful monthly gay and lesbian magazine.

Emergency: Police, tel.110. **Fire and Ambulance,** tel 112.

Post Office: The main post office, 99084 Erfurt, the focal point of the Anger, occupies an ornate beast of a building probably larger than some of the punier European countries. Open M-F 8am-7pm, Sa 9am-1pm.

Internet Access: Internet-Café, Willy-Brandt-Pl. 1, across from the *Bahnhof,* has fast machines DM12 per hr. Open M-F 7am-8:30pm, Sa and Su 10am-6pm.

Telephone Code: 0361.

ACCOMMODATIONS

When you're going for housing in Erfurt, you know what you want to do: keep it chill, save a little money, and enjoy. To do so, check out the tourist office's **Zimmervermittlung,** Schmidstedterstr. 28 (tel./fax 643 09 71), down the road across from the tourist office, which has rooms in private homes for DM36.50 (fee included; open M-F 10am-6pm). Erfurt's two hostels are perfect, but they're both a long walk (or expensive taxi ride) away from the city.

    Jugendherberge Karl Reiman (HI), Hochheimer Str. 12 (tel. 562 67 05; fax 562 67 06). From the station, take streetcar #5 (direction: "Steigerstr.") to the last stop. Backtrack a little, and turn left onto Hochheimer Str.; the pillar-fronted hostel is on the left corner at the first intersection. Check your karma before checking in here. The new building features all new rooms and sparkling showers. But, like Santa, they know who's been naughty or nice, and instead of coal they give out crowded rooms in the more utilitarian old wing of the house. (DM24, over 26 DM28. Breakfast included. Sheets DM7. Reception 6-9am and 3-10pm. Curfew midnight. Wheelchair accessible.) **Haus der Jugend "Hagebutte",** Hagebuttenweg 47 (tel./fax 655 15 32), is nestled deep in the forests of pre-fab apartment buildings that sprouted south of the city in the last 40 years. You wouldn't want to call this place home for long, but the clean rooms and close proximity to a supermarket make the place very livable. Take streetcar #6 (direction: "Wiesenhügel") to "Färberwaidweg." Take a left on Färberwaidweg, a quick right after the tracks, and then a left on the first footpath. Climb 100m uphill, and in you go. (DM15, over 27 DM30. Mandatory one-time DM5 sheet fee. Breakfast DM6. 24hr. reception.)

FOOD

Decent food in Erfurt isn't nearly as rare as a cheap bed. Groceries await at the **Rewe supermarket** on Bahnhofstr., less than 100m from the train station (open M-F 6am-8pm, Sa 8am-4pm), or fill up at the **market** on Domplatz (open M-Sa 6am-2pm). But Erfurt does offer some of the better restaurants in the *neue Bundesländer,* with spicy oases at some of the more exotic Chinese, Italian, or Argentine restaurants. The capital of Thüringen is a good place to discuss the region's wondrous specialty: *Thüringer Bratwurst* (DM2-3), served at stands all over the city (see **No More Hot Dogs!,** p. 191). Many budget meals can be had from the fast- and semi-fast-food restaurants on the **Anger,** several of which have appealing late-night hours.

    Schmalztopf, Dompl. 12-13 (tel. 646 30 73) attracts locals in the know, who come here to dine on native specialties amid the owner's self-congratulatory pictures of hearty customers eating gustily. Dinner specials are around DM6.50, with a good view of the *Dom* at no extra charge. (Open daily noon-midnight.) **Kloster Stube,** next to the *Kloster,* with outdoors seating, is a supreme place to experience the German tradition of *Kaffee und Kuchen.* The *Stube* serves Goliathan mugs of delicious coffee (DM1.50), and sweet freshly baked cake—apple strudel or the daily special (DM1.50). (Open W-Sa and M 10:30am-5:30pm.)

SIGHTS

The mammoth **Marien-Dom** completely dominates the view from the marketplace at its perch on **Domhügel hill,** impressing even the most ardent heathen. *(Open May-Oct. M-F 9am-5pm, Sa 9am-4:30pm, Su 2-4pm; Nov.-Apr. M-Sa 10-11:30am, Su 2-4pm. Su mass 11am and 6pm. Free.)* Today a Gothic extravaganza, the church's Romanesque foundation dates back to 1154. Its rusty green spires explode against the sky, conspiring with the adjacent church to create a fantastical, prickly skyline. Inside, the most impressive part of the cathedral is the 15th-century **Hochchor** in the eastern wing; the **altar** is fully 17m high, embellished with miniature oil paintings and intricate carvings. The 15 **stained glass windows** rise higher than the altar and are currently about halfway through a massive cleaning that will make them brighter than they've been in centuries. Already, the density of adornment in the clean parts is enough to make your eyes cross. While the newer, paler windows—designed and made by Quedlinburg native Charles Crodel in the early 1960s—desperately needs some polishing up, Lucas Cranach the Elder's altar painting is in perfect condition. Luther was invested as a priest here, and word has it that his first mass was disrupted by a visit from…Satan. In mid-liturgy, the doughty Luther hurled his Bible across the altar, which sent the Dark One fleeing but failed to impress the Bishop. The muted sandstone interior of the neighboring **Church of St. Severi** proves less impressive than its turrets would lead one to believe. *(Open May-Oct. M-F 9am-5pm, Sa 9am-4:30pm, Su 2-4pm; Nov.-Apr. M-Sa 10-11:30am, Su 2-4pm. Su mass 11am and 6pm. Free.)* The enormous, wooden, Baroque organ appendages scream with flying golden angels, sunbursts, flames, and a pastel palate of fake marble.

From the Domplatz, Marktstr. leads down to the breezy, open **Fischmarkt,** bordered by restored guild houses with wildly decorated facades. Overlooking the space is the brazenly neo-Gothic **Rathaus,** whose bonanza of **paintings** depicting mythical sequences, including Faust and Tannhäuser portrayals, is open for public gawking. Late-19th-century Thuringians weren't into subtlety. *(Open M and W-Th 9am-4pm, Tu 9am-6pm, F 9am-2pm. Free.)*

Further down Marktstr. flows the quietly babbling **Gera River,** which provides the raison d'être for one of Erfurt's most interesting architectural attractions. The little river is spanned by the **Krämerbrücke,** a medieval bridge completely covered by small shops, some of which date back to the 12th century. In the 1400s, this bridge was part of a great trade-route running from Kiev to Paris. When you're walking on the bridge, it is impossible to see the water; it looks for all the world like a "regular," narrow Central European street. Even more fascinating is the view from underneath— take one of the paths leading off the bridge to get a glance up from the water's edge. The **Brückenmuseum,** Krämerbrücke 20-21, (tel. 562 67 71) in a small house on the far end (away from the *Altstadt*), chronicles the bridge's history as well as medieval period costume. *(Open Tu-Su 10am-6pm. DM2, children DM1.)* On the other side of the river, just beyond the museum, a chalk-written sign announces that the *Turm* (tower) of the St. Aegidii church is open for thrill-seeking stair-climbers. For DM2, the tower gives you another perspective of the Krämerbürcke and evidence that Erfurt suffered very little from modern architecture. *(Tower open sporadically, but always Su noon-6pm.)*

From the far side of the bridge, follow Gotthardtstr. and cut left through Kirchengasse to reach the **Augustinerkloster,** where Martin Luther spent 10 years as a Catholic priest and Augustine monk. *(Hourly tours Apr.-Oct. Tu-Sa 10am-noon and 2-4pm; also on Sundays after morning services, around 10:45am; Nov.-Mar. Tu-Sa 10am, noon, and 2pm. The cloister usually won't lead a tour if fewer than five people show up. You may get bumped back an hour or more. DM4.50, students DM3.)* He got his way, and the cloister now functions as a Protestant college. The **library** here has one of Germany's most priceless collections, including a number of early Bibles with personal notations by Luther himself. During WWII, the books were moved to make room for a bomb shelter. When U.S. bombers destroyed the library in February 1945, 267 people lost their lives, but the books remained unscathed.

From the Krämerbrücke, head down Futterstr. and turn right on Johannesstr. to reach the **Kaufmannskirche,** where Bach's parents tied the knot. *(Open M-Sa 9am-6pm, Su 11am-5pm; service Su 10am.)* In front of the church, feet planted firmly on a pedestal decorated with scenes from his days here, a squat **Martin Luther** casts an indifferent stare over the **Anger,** Erfurt's wide pedestrian promenade. Beautified with numerous statues and fountains, the Anger is one of the most attractive shopping streets in Eastern Germany. No, it's not Milan (or even Dortmund, for that matter), but the street's collection of shops, mega-cafes, fast food joints, and cinemas bring Erfurt solidly into the realm of conspicuous consumption. The architecture lining the street—most of it 19th-century Neoclassical or *Jugendstil*—is for the most part fascinating, though some GDR-era behemoths mar the effect, refusing to let the recent past go unnoticed. Across from the post office lies **House #6,** where Russian Czar Alexander I stayed when he came to Erfurt to meet with Napoleon in 1808.

The **Angermuseum,** Anger 18 (tel. 562 33 11), in an immaculate yellow mansion, is dedicated to displaying a collection of medieval religious art mostly from Erfurt and its vicinity. *(Open Tu-Su 10am-6pm. DM3, students DM1.50; special exhibits add a few Marks to the price.)* Don't miss the room designed and painted by Expressionist Erich Heckel in 1922. The bold colors and primitive style tell the tale of the artist's development in mural form.

Bear right at the end of the Anger and follow Regierungstr. to the abode formerly known as the **Statthalterei,** the massive Baroque building from which the Communists ruled the city. Here, in a small salon on the second floor, Napoleon had breakfast with Goethe in 1808. Goethe later wrote that Napoleon spent the entire time chastising him for his gloomy tragedies, which the French emperor seemed to know inside and out, while Goethe listened passively. Both understood themselves to be immortals—Goethe also realized, however, that Napoleon's immortality was backed by an army. The building is being converted to the Thüringen Minister-President's office and is not open to the public, but the exterior still merits a healthy gawking.

ENTERTAINMENT AND NIGHTLIFE

Erfurt's 220,000 inhabitants manage a fairly indulgent nightlife. The area near the Domplatz and the Krämerbrücke between **Michaelisstraße, Marbachergasse,** and **Allheiligenstraße** glows at night with cafes, candlelit restaurants, and bars. While the Opera House is closed, a victim of stringent German safety regulations, the Theater Erfurt puts on regular shows at the nearby **Schauspielhaus**. The **ticket office** (tel. 223 31 55), Dalbersweg 2, is in the green house just down the street from the Opera House. (Office open Tu-F 10am-1pm and 2-5:30pm, Sa 10am-1pm, Su 10am-noon, and 1hr. before performances, when prices drop 60% on unsold seats; tickets can also be purchased at the tourist office.) Just off the Domplatz, the **Theater Waidspeicher** (tel. 598 29 24) charms all with a marionette and puppet theater; cabaret cooks up on weekend nights. (Box office at Dompl. 2 open Tu-F 10am-2pm and 3-5:30pm; puppet shows DM10-15, cabaret DM15-21. Ask about student discounts.)

The **Double b,** Marbacher Gasse 10 (tel. 642 16 71), near the Domplatz, functions as a hybrid Irish pub, German beer garden, and Amsterdam cafe; all the cool kids in Erfurt show up there to chill in the fiercely cool vibe (open M-F 8am-midnight, Sa-Su 9am-midnight). The **Studentenclub Engelsburg,** Allerheiligenstr. 20/21 (tel. 290 36), just off Marktstr., is down with the disco and moderate punk scene, especially at the frat-like musical grotto within. Live bands from Erfurt and the surrounding area offer their talents as an alternative to the disco in the party room. (Cover DM8, students DM4. Open July-Sept. W and Sa 9pm-1am, Su 10pm-midnight; Oct.-June W-Sa 9pm-1am.) Erfurt also feeds a very healthy electronic music scene. Much of it is underground, but to get the info, stop by **Pure,** Johannesstr. 18a (tel. 643 09 55), a record store that has fliers for every concert going on between Eisenach and Leipzig (open M-F 11am-6:30pm, Sa 11am-2pm). To get a reliable fix of bass, stop by **Joue Joue,** Juri-Gagarin-ring 113-117 (tel. 2 22 56 12), where everybody gets down hard right off of the *Hertie* parking lot (doors open M-F 10pm, Sa midnight; cover around DM10).

THÜRINGER WALD
(THURINGIAN FOREST)

"The area is magnificent, quite magnificent…I am basking in God's world," wrote Goethe from the Thüringer Wald in a letter more than 200 years ago. Goethe's exuberant exclamation is still accurate; the time-worn mountains make for perfect skiing during the winter and excellent hiking, camping, and walking in the summer. The peaceful pine woods of the Thüringer Wald have attracted Germans for generations. Cradled within these mighty but gentle hills, the small towns and villages have cultivated and inspired many German composers, philosophers, and poets. Goethe and Schiller scribed some of their most brilliant poetry on these slopes (and on the walls of huts). The unspoiled forests stretch south of Eisenach, Weimar, and Erfurt to the border with Bayern. Trains and buses trek regularly from larger cities to the smaller, wood-framed villages.

The **Rennsteig,** snaking through this forest, is a famed scenic, antique hiking trail, which was a favorite wilderness trail before the war. While history books date the trail to 1330, locals claim that it was first trodden by prehistoric hunter-gatherers. During the years of East-West division, much of the route was closed because of its potential as an escape route. Now hikers wander all 168km from Hörschel near Eisenach right into Bayern, and veterans of the five-day hike can't stop talking about the route's delights. **Erfurt,** the new state capital, is without question the door to the Thüringer Wald. The **tourist office** (see p. 192) equips you with guides and maps for an extended jaunt. If you're thinking about taking on the Rennsteig, you need to reserve trail-side huts in advance. To find out about the hike, hit up **Gästeinformation Brotterode,** Bad Vibeler Platz 4, 98599 Brotterode (tel. 03 68 40 or 33 33). Keep in mind that foreign tourists and modern conveniences are rare here. English is only understood in larger tourist offices, although an increasing number of brochures are published in English. Get yourself ready for a true, poetic wilderness experience.

■ Arnstadt

The oldest town in Thüringen, stately **Arnstadt** (founded in 704) lies at the fringe of the forest just beyond Erfurt. Still very much a work in progress, much of the funds for restoration have sputtered out. Johann Sebastian Bach began his career here as an organist in **Bachkirche** (closed indefinitely). Before they named holy edifices in honor of him, the local authorities found Bach's license with musical forms as well as local women "shocking to community standards." They politely but firmly asked him to leave town for good. Nevertheless, a statue on the Marktplatz—the young Bach slumped on an organ stool, looking mildly displeased—commemorates the life of the trumpeted composer.

PRACTICAL INFORMATION Next to the town museum, the helpful stall of the **tourist office** (tel. 60 20 49; fax 74 57 48) finds rooms (DM25-40) for a DM3 fee and gives out free maps (open M-F 10am-6pm, Sa 9am-noon). Ask about the **Drei Gleichen,** three matching castles outside of town. The **post office,** 99310 Arnstadt, is right down Ritterstr. from the Neues Schloß (open M-F 8am-6pm, Sa 8am-noon). The **telephone code** is 03628.

ACCOMMODATIONS AND FOOD For a brand spankin' new room, try the **Dickes Hamster,** Kohlenmarkt 10 (tel. 423 90), a bar that has rooms starting at DM40 upstairs. To get there, turn right from Erfurter Str. at Ledermarkt instead of left, and go all the way down Holzmarkt (call after 4pm). Besides that, it's to the tourist office for a private room for you. For sit-down eats, try the **Ried**, a large street formed by Marktstr. curving out of the *Markt* and to the right. **Feinbäckerei und Cafe am Jakobsturm,** Ried 18, bakes the freshest cakes, breads, and pastries for miles around (open M-F 6:30am-6pm, Sa 7-11am and 2-5pm, Su 2-5pm). At the hearty **Hotel-Restaurant Goldene Sonne,** Ried 3 (tel. 60 27 76), you can dine on *Bratwürstchen* (DM8.80) or *Klopse*, the forest's special meatballs (DM7.80). Most meals run DM7.50-14. (Open M-Th 10am-3pm and 6-10pm, F 10am-3pm, Su 11am-3pm.) For typical Thuringian meals (read: hot sausages) hovering around DM10, try the **Ratsklause,** Ledermarkt 3 (tel. 480 73; open M-Th 7:30am-4pm, Sat. 7:30am-2pm).

SIGHTS Almost emblematic of Arnstadt is its **town museum,** housed in the Renaissance-era **Haus Zum Palmbaum,** Markt 3 (tel. 60 29 78). *(Open M-F 8:30am-12:30pm and 1-5pm, Sa-Su 9:30am-5pm. DM4, students DM2.)* Inside, the museum celebrates the rich musical history of the city with a Bach exhibit and then traces the history of the city through the eyes of the proletariat with a fascinating GDR-era exhibit. See how many catastrophes you can blame on capitalism! To get there from the *Bahnhof*, turn left, and then go right on Bahnhofstr. Continue down Erfurter Str., and then walk around the *Bachkirche*. The museum will be at the far end of the *Markt.*

Farther down the hill from the *Markt* is the **Liebfrauenkirche** (tel. 74 09 65). *(Open Mar.-Sept. Tu-Sa 10am-noon and 2-4pm, Su 2-4pm; otherwise, call the tourist office.)* Although multiple restorations have mashed styles in this small-town church, the overall effect remains pleasing, especially the contrast between the dark nave and airy choir. For an even better jumble of architecture, head back toward the train station, but turn right off of Erfurter Str. onto Ritterstr. At the bend you'll find the decadent **Neues Palais** (New Palace), Schloßpl. 1 (tel. 60 29 32), which houses one of Germany's more fascinating doll museums: **Mon Plaisir.** *(Open May-Oct. Tu-Su 8:30am-noon and 1-4:30pm; Nov.-Apr. Tu-Su 9:30am-4pm; last entry 30min. before close. DM3.50, students and seniors DM2.50.)* In the mid-18th century, the local princess whimsically demanded that court employees and craftsmen fashion a miniature panorama of the community. More than 400 wax and wooden dolls are displayed in 24 dollhouses, with a total of 82 furnished rooms decorated with thousands of miniature props from spinning wheels to musical instruments.

Across the street you'll see the ruins of **Schloß Neideck**. It's being restored, but the gardens are open. Their ordered paths, all contained within the palace's former walls, make a perfect place for a walk. Head to the **Theater im Schloßgarten** (tel. 61 86 33) if you'd like to see a play, or even if you'd just like a cup of coffee in a chic ultramodern cafe. *(Cafe open Tu-Su 1-6pm. Box office open Tu and Th 10am-noon and 4-6pm. Tickets DM13-25, students get DM3 discount.)*

■ Ilmenau and the Goethe Trail

The train to Ilmenau blazes through wide verdant valleys, prickled with clusters of red-roofed houses and occasional patches of wild flowers. Closer to Ilmenau, the prefab apartment buildings mar the scenery, providing a bizarre contrast to the mountainous backdrop. The center of this puny university town, however, retains a picturesque, shabby medieval feel. History of a different sort put Ilmenau on the map. Thüringen claims several geniuses, but its favorite offspring by far is Johann Wolfgang von Goethe. Johann's beginnings in the region were tediously bureaucratic. Goethe first worked in Ilmenau reorganizing the region's mining industry while he was a government minister under the Duke of Weimar. Only later did he come back to the area as a poet looking for a place of his own. Today, in turn, the main attractions on the way to the market square are the stunning scenery and a number of his old haunts. South of the city center, parallel to Waldstr., stretches the 18.5km **Goethewanderweg** (Goethe Trail) marked by the author's over-flourished "g" monogram, that leads through the forest to **Stützerbach** (6-8hr. each way).

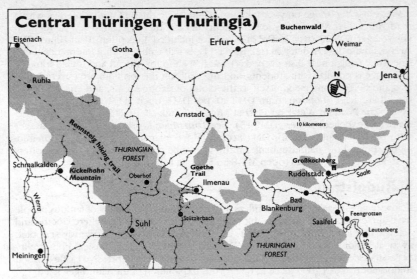

Central Thüringen (Thuringia)

The trail starts from the delightful market area, endowed with pedestrian-friendly fountains and sidewalk cafes, just to the right of the **Amtshaus,** Am Markt 1 (tel. 26 67). (Open May-Oct. daily 9am-noon and 1-4:30 pm; Nov.-Apr. 10am-noon and 1-4pm; DM2, students and seniors DM1). Follow the "g" signs to the **Grab Corona Scröters,** the grave of the first actress to portray Goethe's renowned *Iphigenia.* Next along the trail is the **Schwabenstein,** the rock upon which Goethe wrote Act IV of *Iphigenia.* At this point, practically every rock, stone, and pebble gains fame: Goethe observed this tree in 1779, Goethe reclined on this rocky ledge in 1782, etc. About 4km into the trail (much of which is uphill) is the **Goethehäuschen** on the **Kickelhahn,** where you can read the poetry he scratched on the walls in his youth. Farther along (2hr.) lies the **Jagdhaus Gabelbach** (tel. 20 26 26), often visited by Goethe in summer; it now features a display of his scientific experiments. (Open May-Oct. W-Su 9am-noon and 1-5pm; Nov.-Mar. W-Su 9am-noon and 1-4pm. DM4, students DM3.) The hike ends in **Stützerbach,** where the local glass-works magnate often hosted the poet. The house is now a **Goethe memorial,** but as a nod to the patron there are demonstrations of traditional **glass-blowing.** (Open May-Oct. Tu-Su 9am-noon and 1-5pm, Nov.-Apr. W-Su 9am-noon and 1-4pm; DM4, students DM3.)

Ilmenau can be reached by **train** from Erfurt (1hr.; 17 per day) and Arnstadt (40min.; hourly). Ilmenau also makes a good starting point for a hike along the 168km long **Rennsteig,** reached by taking the train to Schmiedefeld. Cutting across a good section of mid- and southern-Thüringen, the Rennsteig links gorgeous scenery and traditional villages that lie scattered along the path. Pick up a map and ask for tips about day trips at any of the tourist offices along the way. The **tourist office** awaits at Lindenstr. 12 (tel. 20 23 58 or 621 32; fax 20 25 02). From the *Hauptbahnhof,* walk straight ahead on Bahnhofstr. to Wetzlarer Platz, and follow the pedestrian zone until it becomes Lindenstr. (15min.). Staff provides maps and hiking brochures and books private rooms (DM20-35) for a DM2 fee per person (open M-F 9am-6pm, Sa 9am-noon). You can obtain a trail map from the office or the **Goethe-Gedenkstätte im Amtshaus** (see above). The **post office,** Poststr., 98693 Ilmenau, is located just uphill from Wetzlarer Platz (open M-F 8am-12:30pm and 2-5:30pm, Sa 9am-noon). The **telephone code** is 03677.

An ultra-modern but somewhat strict **Jugendherberge** awaits at Am Stollen 49 (tel. 88 46 81; fax 88 46 82). It offers a shower and bathroom for each spacious four-bed room. Leaving the *Hauptbahnhof* to the left, take another left at the dead end, cross the tracks and veer to the right on the path alongside the tracks. After the sharp right

THÜRINGEN

curve, cross the bridge on your left, and continue on the trail until it merges with a road, Am Stollen. Make sure you have plenty of cash: there's a DM20 deposit for each key you get. (DM20, over 26 DM24. Breakfast included. Reception 10am-10pm.) **Die Arche,** Straße-des-Friedens 28 (tel. 89 41 11), is half cafe featuring international cuisine (they cook a new dish every day) and half shop for African and Indian trinkets. The place is popular with students, and the walls on the top floor are covered with teas and herbs. Immerse yourself in the cloud of exotic scents, and enjoy a pot of tea—there are 170 options (cup DM2.50, pot DM3; open M-F 10am-7pm, Sa 10am-6pm). **Zur Post,** on Wetzlarer Platz at Mühltor 6 (tel. 67 10 27), offers regional specialties at excellent prices (DM9-15). Try *Thüringer Rostbrätel* (roasted sausage) with fresh peasant bread for DM10 (open M-F 8:30am-midnight, Sa-Su 11am-midnight). Behind the Raiffeisenbank on the right side of Bahnhofstr., a **market** offers fresh fruits and vegetables (open M-F 8am-5pm, Sa 8am-11am).

■ Rudolstadt

Below Jena, the Saale Valley meanders down to Rudolstadt. A litany of famous people have aimlessly strolled on its cobblestone streets. This is the city where Goethe and Schiller first locked pens (Schillerstr. 25), where Schopenhauer furiously scribbled away at his dissertation, and where Richard Wagner's star of musical immortality began its ascent. With plenty of bus connections and a very impressive castle to boot, Rudolstadt makes a good place to begin your exploration of the Thüringer Wald.

During the 18th century, social life in Rudolstadt centered on the princes of Schwarzburg-Rudolstadt and the dusty-yellow, Baroque-towered **Heidecksburg palace.** From the tourist office, veer right on Allestr. and turn left twice onto the "Schloßaufgang." Look for the steep *Hähner Treppe* (Chicken Steps) on your right, which lead straight to the palace. The **museum** in *Heidecksburg* (tel. 429 00) showcases a frightening weapons collection and an insanely ornate Rococo *Festsaal.* (Open Tu-Su 10am-6pm; last entrance 30min. before closing. DM6, students and children DM3.) The ceiling drips with chandeliers, while the walls suffocate in gold molding and four-colored imitation marble. Rudolstadt also celebrates its more modest history with the **Volkskundemuseum Thüringer Bauernhäuser** (Thuringian Farmhouse Museum; tel. 42 24 65), an open-air display of two regional farmhouses, completely restored and furnished. Go right from the station and cross the bridge into the park. (Open Mar.-Nov. 10am-noon, 1-5pm; DM2, children DM1.) Farther in the park you'll also find the **Stadtfreibad** (city swimming pool) where you can pamper those hiking-weary legs. (Open summers daily 9am-7pm, weather dependent. DM2, students DM1.50, under 16 DM1.)

Trains go through **Scalfeld,** the rail hub of the Thüringer Wald. **Buses** from Weimar (bus #14) and Erfurt (bus #13) take about an hour to reach Rudolstadt, and four of each run per day (for bus info call 42 26 12). To explore town, rent a **bike** from **Kern,** Markt 32 (tel. 42 73 71; DM20 with DM20 deposit). To reach the **tourist office,** Marktstr. 57 (tel. 41 47 43; fax 42 45 43), walk straight ahead from the train station to the right of the park *(Platz der Opfer des Faschismus),* down Bahnhofgasse to Marktstr., and turn left. Look through the free brochures on the information rack to find Rudolstadt maps—the ones they sell cost DM1 and up. They find rooms (DM25-40) for a DM3 fee (open M-F 9am-6pm, Sa 9am-noon). **Exchange money** at Deutsche Bank, Marktstr. 45 (tel. 223 51; open M 9am-4:30pm, Tu 9am-6pm, W and F 9am-4pm, Th 9am-6pm). The **postal code** is 07407. The **telephone code** is 03672.

For accommodations, about the only other option besides the tourist office is the **Hotel Thüringer Hof,** Bahnhofgasse 3 (tel. 42 24 38). A block straight ahead from the *Bahnhof,* the hotel occupies an old building, old enough that there are small, bathroomless rooms on the third floor that they'll give to you for DM50 (single), with an enormous breakfast buffet included. **Zum Brummochsen,** Altestr. 12 (tel. 243 55), serves heavy food of the Thüringer Wald (DM6-7.50) or small *Wurst* meals (DM4-6); its mascot is a big, smiling cow (open Su-Th 11am-10:30pm, Sa 6-10:30pm). For lighter fare, **Café Brömel,** Bahnhofsgasse 1 (tel. 42 20 76), serves pastries, pies, and

"I wish they all could be East German girls ..."

Among the many concerns about the loss of cultural and social identity that would result from reunification, sex was not the least of them. A professor at University of Leipzig performed a study in the wake of the Wall's shattering that found that "the rate of orgasms in the Eastern part of Germany is substantially higher" than the rate in the West, with 37% of East German women regularly achieving orgasm against an average of 26% of women in the West. The findings were greeted with such headlines as "Experts Fear Cooling of East German Sex." While this fact is entirely frivolous, it might say something about the very liberated women of the former East: the GDR's many social programs—daycare, guaranteed maternity leave, and virtually certain employment—produced an image of independence that was one of the few things West German women admired about their Eastern counterparts.

meals (salmon filet and salad DM10) in a 300-year-old locale, with "quick lunch" specials (DM7.50) between 11am and 2pm (open M-Sa 8am-6pm, Su 1-6pm). Stock up on basics at the **Lebensmittel Markt** right next to the tourist office (open M-W 8am-6:30pm, Th 8am-7:30pm, F 8am-6:30pm, Sa 8am-12:30pm). On Wednesdays (6am-6pm) and Saturdays (6am-noon), buy fruits and vegetables at the **farmer's market** on the Marktplatz.

■ Großkochberg

From Rudolstadt, big, comfortable buses and bumpy, serpentine foot trails run the 8km north of Rudolstadt to **Großkochberg** (the bus ride takes 40min.). The moated **Schloß Kochberg,** once the summer home of **Charlotte von Stein,** was the inspiration for many of Goethe's powerful love poems, the proximate source for his sentimental hit novel *The Sorrows of Young Werther,* and in general the *ewig Weibliche* (eternal feminine) of his life—or so he thought. (Open Mar.-Oct. W-Su 9am-6pm, Nov.-Feb. W-Su 10am-4pm; DM6, students DM4.) For 10 years Goethe and Frau von Stein frolicked here in the beautiful English gardens while her husband stayed in Weimar with the kids. Goethe fled to Italy to find himself, came back two years later and took up with a simple factory girl 20 years his junior. Understandably a touch bitter, Frau von Stein promptly returned everything Goethe had ever given her. When he did likewise, she publicly burned her letters to him and composed the nasty tragedy *Dido,* a fictive act of retaliation and character assassination against the poet. The castle lost nothing in the nasty breakup; it did, however, get custody of the children. Just kidding. Today you can wander its 11 furnished rooms to see the first letter Schiller wrote Goethe (June 13, 1794), the first letter Goethe wrote Schiller (June 24, 1794), an odd sketch of Schiller riding a donkey, and sculptures of Goethe's and Charlotte's hands (right or left?). Move on to see the table that supported Goethe's 1700 love letters to her—a man of letters indeed. Behind the castle, the landscaped gardens, soggy with ponds and paths, shelter picnic alcoves. If you have a moment before the bus comes, visit the church just down the hill with a touching **memorial** to the victims of the Franco-Prussian and World Wars. From Monday through Friday seven buses per day make the trip to Großkochberg. Beware; on weekends, the only way back to Rudolstadt is a hiking trail (4hr. each way). A taxi costs about DM30. **Rosas Bauernstübel,** a white farm house down the street from the bus stop and the castle on the left, serves delicious and filling *Bauernfrühstücke* (farmer's breakfast) at dinner time (DM7.40; open Tu-Su 11am-9pm). At **Goetheplatz** (tel. 225 17), on Goetheplatz (surprise), meals range from DM4.50-12 for *Schnitzel,* roasted potatoes, and jellied meats—just the way Goethe liked 'em (open Th-M 11:30am-9pm).

■ Leutenberg

As the Saal valley continues south, it pinches together, yielding steep hills and thick pine forest. In the middle of this sits Leutenberg, surrounded on all sides by high pas-

THÜRINGEN

tures and woods straight out of *The Sound of Music*. The town itself is a sleepy, split-timbered jumble that provides a great retreat for recharging backpacker batteries. For an in-town excursion, a walk up Schloßstr. and up the path of the Schloßberg will, not surprisingly, bring you to Leutenberg's 9th-century **castle** (15min.). **Schloß Friedensburg** is an old-school type of domain that now serves as a hospital, but the view that it offers cures any disappointment at its lack of romance. If you're looking for a more challenging way to break in your boots, the tourist office has a "Top six hikes" pamphlet (DM1) that tells where all the *Wandern* action's at. If R&R translates more into loafing than vigorous hiking for you, stop by Leutenberg's brand-new **swimming pool**, complete with slide and whirlpool. (Open summers 9:30am-8pm. DM5, students DM3.) To get there, go one block farther down Leninstr. than Hauptstr., and turn right.

Trains arrive from Saalfeld (15min.). To get to the **tourist office,** Herrngarten 7 (tel. 222 62), take a right at the station down Bahnhofstr., turn left at the post office onto Am Ilmbach, then make a right onto Hauptstr. The office will be on your right directly off the main street. The staff offers room booking services at no charge (private rooms DM15-20, *Pensionen* DM25-50). (Open M-Th 8am-noon and 1-5pm, F 8am-2pm.) Leutenberg's **telephone code** is 036734.

For tasty eats of the sit-down variety, **Gute Quelle,** Am Ilmbach 17, will provide you with a *Stammer Max* meal (ham and bread with fried eggs; DM7.50); for vegetarians, they serve a *Reispfanne* (rice and veggies in a creamy mushroom sauce; DM9.80; open Tu-Su Lunch served in the Ratskeller, on the *Markt* 11:30am-2pm, and dinner at the restaurant 5-11pm). Grab grub at **E Aktiv supermarket** at the end of Bahnhofstr. (open M-W 8am-6pm, Th-F 8am-7pm, Sa 8am-1pm).

■ Eisenach

Birthplace of Johann Sebastian Bach and home-in-exile for Martin Luther, Eisenach boasts impressive humanist credentials. Yet inside the walls of the town's mammoth Wartburg Fortress, student fraternities convened in 1817 to promote a bizarre agenda of democracy and xenophobic nationalism; they celebrated their dedication to liberal tolerance by burning conservative books. The writings of Marx and Engels were so well received in Eisenach that the duo called the local communist faction "our party." Adolf Hitler is said to have called the idyllic Wartburg "the most German of German castles," and he fought a pitched (and unsuccessful) battle with the local church to replace its tower's cross with a swastika. More recently, the GDR regime tapped into old associations by dubbing its "luxury" automobile the *Wartburg*. It's fitting that Eisenach—this romantic, rationalist, conservative, radical, democratic, despotic bundle of contradictions—should be home to one of the new reunified Germany's most treasured national symbols.

ORIENTATION AND PRACTICAL INFORMATION Frequent **train** connections link Eisenach to Erfurt (1hr., 50 per day) and Weimar (1¼hr., 50 per day) in the east, and Bebra on the IC or IR in the west. Eisenach's **tourist office,** Markt 2 (tel. 67 02 60), smack-dab in the center of the Marktplatz, has plenty of information on the *Wartburg* and books rooms in private homes (DM30-40) for free. From the train station, walk on Bahnhofstr. through the arched tunnel, and angle left until you turn right onto the pedestrian Karlstr. (Open M 10am-6pm, Tu-F 9am-6pm, and Sa 10am-2pm). Eisenach's *Bahnhof* provides a world of services for budget travelers; there's **luggage storage,** an **ATM,** a **grocery store** (open M-F 5:30am-8pm, Sa-Su 8am-8pm), a flower shop, and everything short of a hot tub. For a **taxi,** call 22 02 20. The **Ost-Apotheke,** Bahnhofstr. 29 (tel. 20 32 42), has a list of night **pharmacies** (open M-F 8am-6pm, Sa 8am-noon). Send your *Wartburg* postcard from the **post office** on the *Markt,* 99817 Eisenach (open M-F 8am-6pm, Sa 8am-noon). The **telephone code** is 03691.

ACCOMMODATIONS AND FOOD **Jugendherberge Artur Becker (HI),** Mariental 24 (tel. 74 32 59; fax 74 32 60), fills a comfortable old villa located fairly far from the center, a bit beyond the castle. From the station, take Bahnhofstr. to Wartburger Allee, which runs into Mariental. Here you can walk down the street until the hostel comes up on your right, past the pond (35min.). Alternatively, ride bus #3 (direction: "Mariental") to "Lilienstr." About 100m past the bus stop, signs point the way up the sloping drive to the right. The hostel is a touch worn, and by no means immaculately clean, but it has lots of wood trim and a nice sunny terrace outside, plus it's cheap. (DM22, over 26 DM26. Breakfast included. Sheets DM7. Reception 4-9pm. Curfew 10pm.) Eisenach also offers a couple of very central *Pension* options. **Gasthof Storchenturm**, Georgenstr. 43 (tel. 21 52 50; fax 21 50 82) fills a secluded courtyard next to a park with a restaurant, *Biergarten,* and several rooms. They're clean and quiet and have showers, and the restaurant's red bean soup (DM7.80) will beat any Texas chili. (Singles DM45; doubles DM70. Breakfast DM7.50. Restaurant open 7am-1am.) On a street just off from the Lutherhaus you'll find **Pension und Pub Babylon,** Schmelzerstr. 17 (tel. 21 63 89). Hardly sinful, you'll get a modest room with shower for a do-able DM50. (Reception from 10am.) The nearest **camping** is at **Am Altenberger See** (tel./fax 21 56 37), offering showers, a sauna, and a view of the lake in the hamlet of Eckartshausen. From the Eisenach station, take the **bus** toward Bad Liebenstein (4 departures daily 7:35am-5:35pm) and tell the driver your destination. About 10km from town, the campground offers 13 cabins, with four rooms each. (DM7 per person, DM5 per tent, DM2 per car. Reception until 10pm.)

For large and delicious ice cream cones with a mini-Dickman (a chocolate-covered marshmallow) on top for a mere DM3, pay a visit to **Dänishe Eiscreme.** They also sell a melange of crepes and Danish waffles. From the Marktplatz, walk on Karlstr., and veer right onto Querstr. (Open M-Sa 11am-8pm.) Near the train station, **Café Moritz,** Bahnhofstr. 7 (tel. 72 65 75), raises your daily caloric intake with Thüringer specialities (around DM8), served outside if the weather permits. (Open May-Oct. M-F 8am-10pm, Sa-Su 10am-10pm; Nov.-Apr. M-F 8am-10pm, Sa-Su 10am-8pm.) For a wide array of inexpensive food, head to **Edeka Neukauf supermarket,** on Johannisplatz (open M-F 8am-7pm, Sa 8am-4pm).

SIGHTS High above Eisenach's half-timbered houses, the **Wartburg Fortress** lords over the northwestern slope of the rolling Thüringer Wald. *(Open Mar.-Oct. daily 8:30am-5pm; Nov.-Feb. 9am-3:30pm. Admission to the whole complex DM11, students and children DM6, seniors and people with disabilities DM8. Admission to museum and Luther study DM6, DM4, and DM5 respectively.)* In 1521, this much-hyped castle sheltered Martin Luther after his excommunication. To thwart the search, Luther grew a beard and spent his 10-month stay disguised as a noble named Junker Jörg. Burning the midnight oil working on his landmark German translation of the Bible, the reformer was visited by the devil (the perceptive traveler can't help but marvel at how often the Prince of Darkness and Luther's paths crossed during Luther's travels). By Luther's account, it only took a toss of an ink pot to dispel the Beast. Later pilgrims took the fable literally and mistook a smudge of stove grease for the blessed ink spot, gutting the wall (now a big hole) in their search for a souvenir.

Petty vandalism aside, the Romanesque *Wartburg* is notable for the peaceful character of its history—aside from sheltering Luther, it was a haven for the 12th-century *Minnesänger,* the originators of German choral music. In one of the castle's restored chambers, a wall-sized copy of lyrics from Wagner's *Tannhäuser* is illustrated with ornate murals of the 12th-century battle of musicians that inspired the opera. Like many of the more dazzling chambers in the *Wartburg,* the mural room is a product of 19th-century imagination, not medieval reality. The Romantics' obsession with Wartburg began in 1777 when Goethe fell in love with the place and convinced some backers in the nobility to restore the interior as a museum. As a general rule, anything you see that's frayed and restrained-looking is old; anything shiny and ornate (unfortunately, the vast majority of the castle) is the product of the 19th-century fan club. The castle's **Festsaal** preserves the memory of the 1817 meeting of 500 representatives of university fraternities who threw a party, got inspired, and formed Germany's first bourgeois opposition (ruthlessly crushed two years later); the flag they toasted still hangs in this room. From the walls of Wartburg's courtyard, trace the line of your path through the countryside below. The view is spectacular—if you turn to the side opposite Eisenach, you can see the Thüringer Wald and all the way across the former East-West border to Hesse. The first floor of the tower is a deep dungeon dating from darker days.

The *Wartburg* sits on the south side of Eisenach; the foot of the hill can be reached by a stroll down **Wartburger Allee** from the train station. A multitude of city-sponsored **tourist buses** run between the train station and the castle (Buses run hourly on weekdays, 2 per hr. on weekends. One-way DM1.50, round-trip DM2.50.) Mini-vans shuttle visitors from parking lots near the base (one-way DM4). For the more adventurous, there are a number of well-cleared **footpaths** up the incline—hiking downhill is a blast. Arriving at the medieval stronghold after a 30-minute hike through rich-smelling pines and lilacs, you'll wipe your sweat and feel like a pilgrim. If you weigh 60kg (132 lbs.) or less, you can opt for a donkey ride for the last stretch (DM5). When eastern Germany was East Germany, West Germans were issued special visas that allowed them to visit the castle and nothing else, but those visas were hard to come by. Now, legions of sightseers are making up for lost time. On weekday mornings during the summer, expect crowds of schoolchildren; on weekday afternoons, crowds of German pensioners; on weekends, just be prepared for crowds. The interior of the castle can be visited only with a tour, and the wait may be more than an hour. To kill the time, grab an English-language pamphlet when you buy your ticket. Alternatively, hike around the rich woods and grounds without spending a *Pfennig*.

Back at the base of the mountain, the **Bachhaus,** Frauenplan 21 (tel. 793 40; fax 79 34 24), where Johann Sebastian stormed into the world in 1685, recreates the family's living quarters. *(Open Apr.-Sept. M noon-5:45pm, Tu-Su 9am-5:45pm.; Oct.-Mar. M 1-4:45pm, Tu-Su 9am-4:45pm. DM5, students DM4.)* Downstairs are period instruments such as a harpsichord, a spinet, and a beautifully preserved "house organ" from 1750, about the size of a telephone booth, with a little stool for the player. Roughly every 40 minutes, one of the museum's guides tunes up for a musical tour, including anecdotes about Bach's life, and spellbinding musical interludes—you can join the tour at any stage. Turn off Wartburger Allee down Grimmelgasse to reach the house. The **Reuter-Wagner-Museum,** Reuterweg 2 (tel. 74 32 93; fax 74 32 94), below the Wartburg, is dedicated to the joint memory of writer Fritz and composer Richard. *(Open Tu-Su 10am-5pm. DM4, students and seniors DM2.)* Town life centers on the pastel **Markt,** bounded by the tilting dollhouse of a **Rathaus** and the latticed **Lutherhaus,** Lutherpl. 8 (tel. 298 30), home of young Martin's school days from 1498 to 1501. *(Open daily 9am-5pm. DM5, students DM2.)* Communist performance car is not an oxymoron at the **Automobilbaumuseum,** Rennbahn 6-8 (tel. 772 12), where shiny chitty-chitty-Wartburgs are on glorious display. *(Open Tu-Su 10am-5pm. DM4, students, seniors, and kids DM2.)* Leave from the *Hauptbahnhof's* "Ausgang Nord," and veer left; after a refreshing eight-minute walk, the museum is on the right.

■ Gotha

Like many towns in the former GDR, Gotha suffers from troublesome construction and architectural decay. Standing in Gotha's palatial gardens on the palisade overlooking the Orangerie will tell you a lot about the city. Below you stretches an incredible garden, first planted in 1770, enclosed on three sides by buildings of stunningly beautiful architecture. Get closer, though, and you'll realize that the garden is being tended by unemployed citizens, and that one of the buildings has sunk deep into disrepair. The lively Marktplatz and the extensive castle grounds are both islands of beauty in a sea of industrial filth and dirt. Gotha's past, on the other hand, tells a more pampered story. Prince Albert, one of the Dukes of Sachsen-Coburg-Gotha, married Queen Victoria of England, and hence Queen Elizabeth and Prince Charles are direct descendants of this house—the royal family's name of "Windsor" is a product of a name change during WWI, when Germany was "out of fashion." The birth of the

Social Democratic Party in Gotha made Marx hopping mad, furthering his revolutionary career. When Charlemagne visited the city, he spent only a day—more than enough time to see everything.

ORIENTATION AND PRACTICAL INFORMATION Gotha is connected by frequent **trains** to Erfurt and Eisenach (20min.). The city is built around the four sides of the **Schloß Friedenstein** and its grounds. Coming from the *Bahnhof,* the entrance to the *Schloß* is on the far side of the grounds. From there you'll be looking down on the **Hauptmarkt**, a collection of 17th-century homes and businesses set on a 45-degree incline. At the far end of the Hauptmarkt and to the right you'll find the **Neumarkt**, the most bustling part of town. The wave of renovation scared the **tourist office**, Blumenbachstr. 1-3 (tel. 85 40 36; fax 22 21 34), from the Hauptmarkt to the low-rent district. Facing the *Rathaus* entrance, go left down the narrow Hützelsgasse past the Socialist-era apartment block until you see the welcoming "**i.**" Get information on the *Schloß* and nearby Thüringer Wald (ask about the *Rennsteig* hiking trail), or book a private room (DM35-40 per bed) for free. (Open M-F 10am-5pm, Sa 10am-noon.) City **tours** leave on Wednesday at 11am from the steps of Gotha's *Rathaus,* overlooking the market. The tourist office also sells the Gotha **Touristenticket** (DM9.50) which knocks a mark or two off the price of most attractions and is good for one free trip each on Gotha's bus system and the *Thüringer Waldbahn,* which leads from the train station into hiking country. Unless you plan to use the *Waldbahn,* don't bother; Gotha is small enough to see on foot. The city **postal code** is 99867. The **telephone code** is 03621.

ACCOMMODATIONS AND FOOD The place to stay in Gotha is the **Pension Am Schloß,** Bergallee 3a (tel. 85 32 06). Centrally located, the pension is a small house that boasts beautifully furnished rooms and a small kitchen for guests. Unfortunately, the bargain is so good that it's tough to get a room. Call between 10am-8pm, though, and give it a try. (DM35-48. Breakfast included.) If that fails, Gotha's **Jugendherberge (HI)**, Mozartstr. 1 (tel. 85 40 08), rests on the corner of the Schloßpark. From the station, walk an easy two blocks straight ahead; the beige hostel is on the right. Explore your musical side with accordion (DM5) or acoustic guitar (DM3) rentals. In the hallway, schoolchildren crowd the 80s arcade games, relics from the pre-Nintendo era. (DM15, over 26 DM19. HI members only. Breakfast DM5, lunch DM8, dinner DM6. Sheets DM7. Reception 3-10pm. Curfew 10pm, but guests over 18 can ask for a key.)

Load up on edible booty at the *Markt* (open M-F 8am-6pm, Sa 8am-1pm), which fills the Haupt- and Neumarkt, and picnic in the palace gardens for an aesthetically pleasing bargain. **Bella Italia Eiscafé/Ristorante,** Erfurter Str. 11-13, provides decent Italian food (pizzas and pastas DM6.50-10) at a sidewalk cafe with a great view of the sparkling ice cream monstrosities that people are crazy enough to consume here (open M-Sa 9am-11:30pm, Su 11am-11pm). Another solid option is **Kuhn and Kuhn,** Hühnersdorfstr. 14, a few blocks down from the castle and adjacent to the Buttermarkt. They offer cafe fare as well as German standards (DM7.50-14) until the wee hours. (Open Tu-Th 9am-2am, F 9am-3am, Sa 11am-3am, Su 11am-1am.)

SIGHTS Gotha's city-planning, history and tourist attractions are all dominated by the imposing **Schloß Friedenstein**. *(Castle open Tu-Su 10am-5pm. Tickets to the Schloß and all other museums DM10, students DM5. Tickets just to the Schloß DM8, students DM4.)* Rumored to once have had as many rooms as the years has days, the building is enormous. It served as a center of the Enlightenment in Germany, with Voltaire himself spending quite a bit of time here. Goethe, too, had only good things to say about the castle. Today the **Schloßmuseum** (tel. 823 40) does a good job of capturing the eclectic intellectual curiosity that was the Enlightenment. The men in the castles could see looking in all directions: to Greece, to Egypt, inwards into anatomy, even into mechanics, and the galleries of the museum reflect this.

Upstairs, the splendor of royal apartments contrasts strikingly with the castle's spartan exterior. It's a treat to follow the red carpets that lead through the 16 fully restored, lavishly furnished ducal rooms. The Rococo *Festsaal* (feast hall), decorated with colorful crests from each of the duchy's provinces and cities, houses the original royal silver service. Other highlights include beautifully inlaid walls in the smaller rooms and the royals' bedroom cabinets. It must have been good to be the duke. Also in the palace buildings are the **Museum für Regionalgeschichte,** a small *Waffensammlung* (arms collection) of guns and knives, and the world's first museum of maps, the **Kartographisches Museum.** The Renaissance and early Mercator maps (named for a Flemish cartographer) are especially fascinating: watch the Americas slowly, awkwardly take their correct shape. The palace also provided a place for Konrad Eckhof to flourish. The "Father of German Drama," Eckhof worked at making theater as realistic as possible, a bit of a contradiction, considering that the **Eckhof Theater,** still in use today, is full of optical illusions and tricks to make it seem bigger than it is. *(Theater and small theater museum are part of Schloßmuseum. Tickets for plays are available through the tourist office DM25-60.)* The rest of the palace's splendor resides in its gardens, some of the largest in Europe. The **Orangerie** is especially stunning. Also included in *Schloß* admission is the **Museum der Natur,** a large collection of natural history, located in the gardens.

Much of the rest of Gotha's history has managed to slip out of preservations's hands. The **Haus am Tivoli,** at the intersection of Cosmartstr. and Am Tivoli, was where August Bebel and others got the Social Democratic Party (SPD) together. The modern SPD is the largest political party in Germany and main opposition since the coalition regime, headed by the Christian Democrats, took the reins. The house was the site of an extensive display during the GDR, including the fully preserved room where all the action went down. The bourgeoisie has stormed back, though, and the house is now closed indefinitely due to a leaky roof and lack of funds. A similar story goes with the **Cranach-Haus,** Hauptmarkt 17. The wife of the famous painter was born here, and they lived shortly in the house, but now all to be seen is the exterior.

Sachsen-Anhalt (Saxony-Anhalt)

Sachsen-Anhalt's endless, mesmerizing grass plains offer one of the more tranquil landscapes in Eastern Germany. Once serving as the stronghold of the Holy Roman Empire, the region today suffers from the highest unemployment rates in Germany, and is also the most polluted province of the former GDR. Cities here once belched enough toxic filth into the air to make a smoggy day in Los Angeles seem fresh and healthy. But with the help of Western tourist dollars, Sachsen-Anhalt is rapidly cleaning up its act and gradually creating a stable work force. The region contains a number of worthwhile destinations that include Wittenberg, the city of Martin Luther and crucible of the Protestant Reformation, and Magdeburg, home to a splendid Gothic *Dom* where the first Holy Roman Emperor is buried. The grand cathedrals filling the skyline attest to the region's former importance, and the many construction sites mushrooming across the *Land* point toward the future.

🖐 HIGHLIGHTS OF SACHSEN-ANHALT

- **Martin Luther,** the instigator of the Reformation, posted his *95 Theses* on a church in **Wittenberg**. The city is still in constant celebration of its former Jesus Christ superstar, and will soon be blessed with a **Hundertwasser**-designed high school (see p. 207).
- The original **Bauhaus** demonstrates principles of the merger of form and function, imbuing the city of **Dessau** with design-school hipness (see p. 210).
- The castle-spotted **Harz mountains** offer tons of outdoor fun (see p. 216). Walk in Goethe's footsteps to the top of **Brocken** mountain, or visit the half-timbered towns of **Quedlinburg** (see p. 223) and **Wernigerode** (see p. 220).

■ Wittenberg

Wittenberg does everything in its power to milk Martin Luther for what he's worth; in 1938, the town even went so far as to rename itself **"Lutherstadt Wittenberg."** Luther claimed that Wittenberg was the source and fount of his life's work: he preached, taught, married (a scandal to the Catholic clergy), raised children, and led the Protestant Reformation in this picturesque town. The city's fondest memories are of Luther nailing the *95 Theses* to the **Schloßkirche** (castle church) in 1517 and of his scandalous (and exceptionally contrived) wedding, a made-for-TV event that the town re-enacts every June. The infamous "Luther Year," 1996, witnessed the 450th anniversary of Martin Luther's death—an unparalleled tourist extravaganza. If you missed it, don't worry. Martin's remains still remain; although he died in Eisleben in 1546, his body was buried directly beneath the pulpit of the *Schloßkirche.*

Luther managed to hang onto his celebrity status in the officially atheistic GDR; he was, after all, a harsh critic of Catholic wealth, inciting early bourgeois revolutions. He also had a presence in the civil sphere—for many East Germans the image of Luther risking his life to nail up his *95 Theses* became an emblem of courageous resistance. A successor of Luther at the *Schloßkirche* pulpit, Pastor Friedrich Schorlemmer, was a key player in the 1989 revolution. Since that time, religious pilgrims have returned in full force to Luther's city. The slow shuffle of Scandinavian church groups has pushed up *Schnitzel* prices while giving a fresh gleam to the architectural remnants. The huge new projects planned for the Expo-2000 spearhead an attempt to widen the spectrum of tourist attractions. But whether a concert park/museum/laser shows-island and a technicolor *Gymnasium* designed by **Hundertwasser** will overshadow the Great Reformer is a question for the next millennium.

ORIENTATION AND PRACTICAL INFORMATION Wittenberg is a mere hour and a half by **train** from Berlin, Halle, and Leipzig, making it an excellent daytrip from any of these cities. Rent **bikes** at **M&B Fahrradladen,** Coswiger Str. 21 (tel. 40 28 49), for a measly DM8 per day. Instead of disembarking at the less-than-central *Hauptbahnhof,* get off at *"Haltepunkt Lutherstadt Wittenberg-Elbtor."* Walk straight down Elbstr., hook a left at the second intersection (Schloßstr.), and walk for five minutes to the *Schloß.* Directly across the street, the brand new **Wittenberg Information,** Schloßpl. 2 (tel. 49 86 10; fax 49 86 11), happily caters to all your map, room, postcard, and info needs (open M-F 9am-6pm, Sa 10am-2pm, Su 11am-3pm). Another branch is inside the Stadtkirche St. Marien (open Tu-F 10am-4pm). City tours leave daily at 2pm from the Schloßkirche. The **regional tourist office,** Mittelstr. 33 (tel. 40 26 10; fax 40 58 57), by Lutherhalle, has lots of info about cultural events (call 44 57 65 for schedules and tickets), and the staff is eager to welcome you to scenic Sachsen-Anhalt. Bikers can purchase a great trail map for DM9.80. (Open Apr.-Oct. daily 9:30am-5:30pm; Nov.-Mar. M-F 9:30am-5:30pm.) The **pharmacy** on the Marktplatz, where painter Lucas Cranach pushed drugs to support his art habit, posts a rotating schedule of all-night pharmacies (open M-F 8am-6:30pm, Sa 9am-noon). The **post office,** 06886 Wittenberg, is near Lutherhalle on the corner of Friedrichstr. and Fleischerstr. (open M-F 8am-6pm, Sa 9am-noon). The **telephone code** is 03491.

ACCOMMODATIONS Hotels in the *Altstadt* are overpriced, but **private rooms** provide a reasonable option. The Wittenberg information center finds rooms for a DM3 fee (DM25-75). Alternatively, you can pick up a list of accommodations at the tourist office (DM2). The **Jugendherberge (HI),** located in the castle (tel./fax 40 32 55), is simultaneously haunted by the ghosts of the Reformation and the rabid kids who tear through the place every summer. Cross the street from the tourist office and walk straight into the castle's enclosure, then trek up the spiraling stairs to the right. All rooms sport snazzy new bunkbeds and closets as part of a renovation campaign that has also left the bathrooms immaculate. The staff will wash, dry, and fold your dirty knickers for a mere DM4 per load. There are a few two- to four-bed rooms and a bunch of spacious 10- to 18-bed rooms. (DM20, over 26 DM25. Breakfast included. Sheets DM6. Reception 5-10pm. Lockout 10pm, but keys are available for a DM10 deposit. Reservations recommended, but the hostel offers floor space for a reduced rate if it's full.)

While not centrally located, **Gästehaus Wolter,** Rheinsdorfer Weg 77 (tel. 41 25 78), sings sweet lullabies with its truly homey ambience, complete with playground, family dog, a grill for guests to use, sunny rooms with TV, and spotless bathrooms. Ride bus #302, 314, or 315 to "Elbedruckerei," walk in the direction of the bus, take the first right, and finally veer right on Rheindorfer Weg. If this sounds confusing, call Frau Wolter and she will happily pick you up from town. (Singles DM35; doubles DM85. Breakfast included. 24hr. reception.)

FOOD AND ENTERTAINMENT A number of delectable delights at low cost lie along the Colliegenstr.-Schloßstr. strip, and a **City-Kauf** supermarket waits across from Coswiger Str. 15, about 20m from the tourist office (open M-F 8am-6:30pm, Sa 8am-12:30pm). **Bosphorus,** a Turkish restaurant at Collegienstr. 64 (tel. 454 11 05), cooks up a filling, spicy *Döner Kebab* platter with a cucumber-tomato salad (DM10); tasty vegetarian entrees, such as falafel (DM4), provide a cheap respite from the tyranny of *Schnitzel.* (Open M-F 9am-10pm, Sa-Su 11am-10pm.) Get Guinness on tap and eat pub grub at the **Irish Harp Pub,** Collegienstr. 71 (tel. 41 01 50), where live English and Irish music rumbles on Saturdays (open daily 3pm-3am; cover DM5). Members of Wittenberg's artsy theater crowd occasionally burst into song or soliloquy at **Vis à Vis,** Sternstr. 14 (tel. 40 67 65), a cozy alternative establishment with an almost entirely vegetarian menu (main courses DM10) and beer and tea specialities that add flavor to the lively atmosphere. The staff puts up musical productions, and local bands rock the house on weekends. (Open M-Th 3pm-1am, F-Sa 3pm-2am.) Across the street is the **Central Theater Cinema,** Sternstr. 12-13 (tel. 40 22 21). Theater

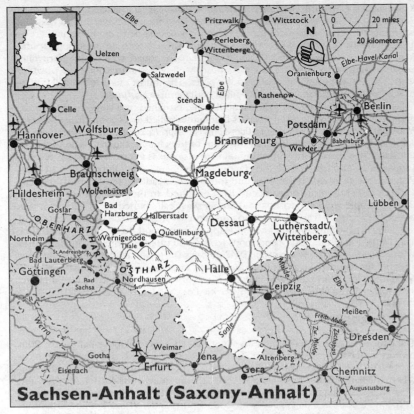

Sachsen-Anhalt (Saxony-Anhalt)

buffs can get their fix at the **Cranachhof,** the painter's former palace of a home. The **Mitteldeutsches Landestheater** puts on everything from the *Frog Prince* to *Hallo, Dolly!* The ticket office is at Collegienstr. 74 (tel. 40 20 85 or 40 20 86; open daily 10am-12:30pm and 1-5:30pm), or buy them at either tourist office.

SIGHTS Wittenberg's sights provide unending adulation of the eminently historical Luther. Plan your sight-seeing around **Collegienstr.;** the street is less than 1.5km long and encompasses all of the major sights. At Collegienstr. 54 lies the **Lutherhalle** (tel. 40 26 71), to which Martin moved in 1508. *(Open Apr.-Sept. Tu-Su 9am-6pm; Oct.-Mar. Tu-Su 10am-5pm. DM7, students DM4.)* Inside the minister's rather posh digs is a museum that chronicles the history of the Reformation and also features lots of paintings analogizing Luther to geese; while the metaphor may seem strained (Luther was a dumpy man, not a goose), the representation is supposed to symbolize Luther's triumph in the face of adversity encountered in the fallout over his *95 Theses.* Nonetheless, you can see Luther's ground-breaking translation of the Bible, considered a model of the German language, an original **Gutenberg Bible,** and many angry responses to the feisty minister's theses. An obnoxious tourist's graffiti has also been preserved: Russian Czar Peter the Great scribbled his name above the door when he stopped by in 1702. Turn right as you leave the Lutherhaus and stroll down Collegienstr. until you reach Lutherstr. to behold the elm tree under which Luther defiantly burned a papal bull (a decree of excommunication, not a Catholic beast).

    Stadtkirche St. Marien, known for its dazzling altar painted by pharmacist and hometown art genius **Lucas Cranach the Elder,** lies at the end of Mittelstr., near Collegienstr. at the Marktplatz. *(Open May-Oct. M-Sa 9am-5pm, Su 11am-5pm; Nov.-Apr. M-Sa 10am-4pm, Su 11am-4pm.)* The interior is a blend of Protestant severity and Catholic adornments—it bears eloquent testimony to the iconoclastic tradition begun here in 1522. Near the church, Wittenberg's **Rathaus** towers with an imposing facade. Matching statues of Luther and Melanchthon share the square with the **Jungfernröhrwasser** (fountain of virginity), a 16th-century well whose refreshing (and potable) waters still flow through original wooden pipes. The tourist office sells small bottles of this "water of innocence," actually filled with German *Schnapps.*

Farther down Collegienstr., the **Schloßkirche,** crowned by a sumptuous Baroque cupola, holds a copy of the complaints that Luther nailed to its doors. *(Open May-Oct. M 2-5pm, Tu-Sa 10am-5pm, Su 11:30am-5pm; Nov.-Apr. M 2-4pm, Tu-Sa 10am-4pm, Su 11:30am-4pm. Services Su at 9am.)* At the front of the church, the man who fought to translate the scriptures into the common man's tongue is interred, ironically, under a Latin plaque. Also featured are the graves of Wittenberg's other important dead folks: Prince Electors Friedrich the Wise and Johann the Steadfast, and Reformation hero Philip Melanchthon the non-adjectivally monikered. In the 1840s, it was arranged that 15 people would check that old Luther was really buried here. The crypt was opened in secret for fear that failure to find Luther would discredit the church (sort of like Geraldo and Al Capone's vaults). Happily they found the remains—or so they said. At the top of the castle's enormous **tower,** you can digest the surrounding lands with pleasure. *(Open daily noon-5pm. DM2, students DM1.)* Should the view excite your appetite for nature, take a bus from Mauerstr. (11 per day, almost 1 per hr. 4:45am-6:15pm) to the **Wörlitzer Park,** built by a local prince who wanted his quaint palace and Gothic house to be surrounded by exotic flora and fauna (open dawn to dusk).

■ Dessau

The Bauhaus is undoubtedly the most significant architectural movement of the 20th century, and it was in Dessau, from 1925 to 1932, that its ideals and practices found a home. The **Bauhaus art school** was (and remains) a school of architecture and design where the Bauhaus *Meisters* Walter Gropius, Hannes Meyer, Laszlo Moholy-Nagy, and their students struggled with aesthetic representations of modernity and attempted to reconcile human living space with 20th-century industrialization and urbanism. Hannes Meyer dubbed an ironic motto for the Bauhaus when he said, "Building is *not* an aesthetic process." What he meant, and as Mies van der Rohe said, is that form follows function, where functionality consists not merely of pragmatic requirements, but also of the body and soul's needs. In short, the Bauhaus sought a unity of the human, the material, and the aesthetic. Though Dessau was not transformed in these short years, the masters did leave behind a number of stunning buildings. Unfortunately, Dessau *was* totally made over by bombing in WWII; many Bauhaus buildings were obliterated, others survived with considerable damage. It is appropriate and fortunate that Dessau has had more success in its post-war reconstruction than other former GDR cities. Though it has its share of run-down, faceless apartment blocks, much of Dessau's residential areas are lush and attractive, and its commercial areas are sleek and modern.

The history of Dessau stretches back into antiquity. Founded as a medieval fortress in 1341, Dessau became one of the first German Renaissance settlements. With the backing of Princess Henrietta Catharina von Oranien, Dessau flourished as a thriving center of cultural and economic importance. Dessau's famed Prince Leopold invented the method of marching in step, and introduced it into his regiment, thus creating a model for the Prussian army and stereotypes about German militarism. Dessau evolved into a factory town during the late-blooming German Industrial Revolution. Dessau prides itself on a unique civic culture and its two major historical offspring. Moses Mendelssohn, one of the greatest German-Jewish philosophers and a fervent proponent of religious tolerance in the 19th century, lived in Dessau, as did the greatly admired modern composer Kurt Weill (1900-1950), whose critical theater encouraged artistic resistance against Nazism. In effect, Weill's *Verfremdungseffekt*

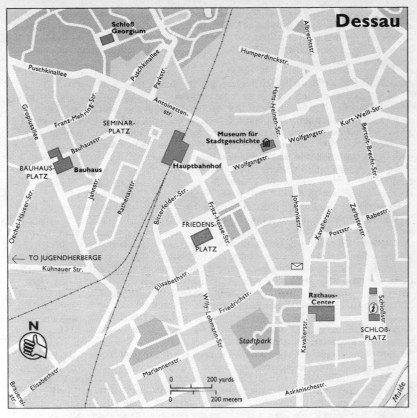

(alienation effect) makes its listeners feel drunk and confused. Every year (Feb. 27-Mar. 8 in 1999), a **Kurt Weill Festival** alienates a new generation of fans with international artists performing his work in media as wide ranging as conventional musicals, big brass bands, chamber concerts, films, and lectures. (Tickets are available at the *Theatricals,* tel. 251 13 33; DM10-60).

ORIENTATION AND PRACTICAL INFORMATION Hourly trains undertake the journey from Wittenburg (35min.) and Berlin (2hr.), while trains from Leipzig depart about every two hours (1hr.). **Bicycle rentals** help navigate the scattered sights of the city and protect you from the perils of pedestrianism. **Fahrradverleih Dieter Becker und Sohn,** Coswiger Str. 47 (tel. 216 01 13), can make you an honorary Sprocket with rentals (4hr. DM6, day DM10-12; open M-F 9am-noon and 2-6pm, Sa 9am-noon). The **Fahrradverleih am Wörlitzer Bahnhof,** Unruhstr. 10 (tel. 221 32 34), rents street bikes, mountain bikes, tandem bikes, and kids bikes, but no unicycles (open M-F 9am-6pm; call for prices). The local **tourist office,** Zerbster Str. 2c (tel. 204 14 42 and 194 33; fax 204 11 42), can be reached by riding streetcar #1 or 2 from the train station's main exit to "Hauptpost." It sits across the street from the huge "Rathaus-Center" signs. Walk toward the center and veer left on Ratsgasse. Take the first right; the office is on your left (open M-F 9am-7pm, Sa 9am-noon). They find private rooms (from DM30) for a DM5 fee and book hotel rooms for free (call 220 30 03 for reservations). They also sell the **Dessau Card,** a three-day ticket that allows up to one adult and one child unlimited access to all buses and streetcars in Dessau, as well as free entry into most of the museums and sights (DM15). Tours are also available (Apr.-Oct.

Sa at 10am; DM7, children DM1.50). In an **emergency,** call 21 44 55. **Internet access** is at the **Cyberb@r** on the top floor of the Karstadt, in the Rathaus-Passage mall (DM5 for 30min.; open M-F 9:30am-8pm, Sa 9:30am-4pm). The **post office,** 06844 Dessau, is at the corner of Friedrichstr. and Kavalierstr. (open M-F 8am-6pm, Sa 8am-noon). The **telephone code** is 0340.

ACCOMMODATIONS AND FOOD The **Jugendherberge (HI),** Waldkaterweg 11 (tel. 61 94 52), is a 25-minute walk from the train station through suburban Dessau. Exit from the smaller *Westausgang* of the station (through the underground tunnel), make a left onto Rathenaustr., and follow it to the end; at the intersection zig-zag across and follow the main street (Kühnauer Str.) for 10 minutes until you cross Kiefern Weg. About 50m farther, a small path to your right (Waldkaterweg), marked by a pedestrian sign, will lead you straight to the woodsy entrance. The hostel remains less than clean while it undergoes renovations, but it's got a common room with comfy couches and a TV. (DM21, over 26 DM26. Breakfast included. Sheets DM6. Reception M-F 8am-4pm and 7:30-9:30pm, Sa-Su 6-9pm. Check-out 9am.)

Affordable restaurants are difficult to come by in Dessau. The stunningly hip **Klub im Bauhaus,** in the *Bauhaus* school basement (tel. 650 84 21), is a delightful place to indulge in angsty pretense over a light meal. To feel like the coolest cat ever, order the *anarchisten Frühstück* (anarchist's breakfast) of a pot of coffee, some bread, and a *Karo* cigarette (DM4). For something less revolutionary, the spaghetti *al pesto spezial* (DM8) with pesto, feta cheese, and fresh tomatoes is enough savory food to make you wish they had doggie bags in Germany. The silver and black *Bauhaus* furniture completes the sensory experience (open M-F 8am-midnight, Sa 10am-1am, Su 10am-5pm). The **Ratskeller,** across the street from the *Rathaus-Center,* serves up Milchreis (DM9.80), the Dessau specialty that is best described as rice pudding with sugar, cinnamon, and (of course) *Bratwurst.* They've also got a tasty veggie and potato dish for DM10.60. (Open daily 11:30am-midnight.) The gleaming expanse of the newly built Rathaus-Center satisfies every craving for mall life, and the bakeries, produce stands, and **Tip** supermarket inside provide an easy end to the harrowing search for cheap eats. (All open M-F 8am-8pm, Sa 8am-4pm.) Just off Kurt-Weill-Str., a 10-minute walk north of the tourist information center (turn right as you are leaving), **Kiez Café,** Bertolt-Brecht-Str. 29a (tel. 21 20 32 or 37; email kiez@misa.uni-magdeburg.de), is a good locale for a nightcap in the company of students. Kiez is a **one-stop-shop** for all your cultural needs, with a photo lab, theater, art studios, a cinema, bike rental, and **Internet access.** Call for info and prices.

SIGHTS The Bauhaus began in Weimar in 1919, but the conservative local oligarchy pressured it to leave. The school toted its theory of constructive and artistic unity to Dessau in 1925; in 1932 the school fled yet again to the more brash Berlin before being exiled from the country in 1933 by the Nazis. Despite the necessity of remaining itinerant to avoid total dissolution, the Bauhaus masters inspired an architectural renaissance that attained its aesthetic zenith with the sleek skyscrapers of America's metropoli. After the war, as Dessau rebuilt, city planners perversely translated the shapely Bauhaus legacy into building-block-shaped monotony. Since 1977, the **Bauhaus,** Gropiusallee 38 (tel. 650 82 51), has housed a design school for international architecture. *(Open Tu-Su 10am-5pm. DM5, students DM3.)* The school currently decorates its sparsely linear walls with the works of legendary *Bauhausmeisters* Gropius, Klee, Kandinsky, Geinger, and Brandt. To get there from the station, turn left and go up the steps, then head left over the railroad tracks. Veer left at the first street onto Kleiststr., then right onto Bauhausstr. Or take bus K or E to "Bauhaus." The building is open for a free self-guided tour daily (24hr.), and there are rotating exhibits on Bauhaus themes in the hallways. There is also a special exhibit in the north space.

Turning left from the Bauhaus entrance, a right on Gropiusallee, and a left on Ebertallee bring you to the **Kurt Weill Zentrum,** Ebertallee 63 (tel./fax 61 95 95), located in the former house of designer and painter Lyonel Feininger. *(Open Tu-F 10am-5pm, Sa-Su noon-5pm. DM5, students DM3.)* The center has been restored to its original splendor, thus providing lucid insight into the school's musings. Occasional concerts celebrate the wacky Weill. It is the first in the row of the three famous Bauhaus *Meisterhäuser;* Georg Muche and Oskar Schlemmer each resided in house number two, and the third served as home to the greats Kandinsky and Klee. Both houses are being restored and should be complete by 2000. Several more spectacular Bauhaus buildings are scattered across town. To find them, pick up a copy of "Bauhaus Bauten in Dessau" at the tourist office or the Weill Center (DM1). It tells you about each building, and includes a map. Carl Fieger's **Kornhaus,** at the end of Elballee, off of Ebertallee, was designed as a modern house-of-fun, with a beer hall, cafe, dance floor, and two terraces. Hop on streetcar #1 (direction: "Dessau Süd") and hop off at "Damaschkestr." to get a peek at the **Laubenganghäuser** on Peterholzstr. These were designed to be efficient, attractive housing tenements. Take a left onto Mittelring and behold an entire residential neighborhood in Bauhaus style. The house at Mittelring 38 is the **Moses Mendelssohn Zentrum** (tel. 850 11 99), which includes a museum about his life and work. *(Open M-F 10am-5pm, Sa-Su noon-5pm. DM3, children DM2.)*

Dessau also has its share of ornate, old-school architecture. From the Bauhaus, make a right on Gropiusallee and you'll reach the garden of the **Schloß Georgium** (tel. 61 38 74), home to the Anhaltische Gemäldegalerie. *(Open Tu-Su 10am-5pm. DM5, students DM3. Gardens open daily 24hr.)* Set in the midst of carefully tended formal gardens, this 17th-century country estate displays a range of lesser-known Old Masters' paintings from the 16th to the 19th century. The tired exterior encases a couple of Lucas Cranach the Elder's star paintings. The **Schloß Mosigkau,** Knobelsdorffallee 3 (tel. 52 11 39), about 20 minutes from central Dessau, is a historic castle built in 1752 as a summer hangout for the Princess Anna Wilhelmine. *(Open May-Sept. Tu-Su 10am-6pm; Apr. and Oct. Tu-Su 10am-5pm; Nov.-Mar. Tu-F 10am-4pm, Sa-Su 11am-4pm.)* Furnished in opulent Baroque style, the castle displays works by such masters as Rubens and van Dyck. For the botanist in all of us, there are 100-year-old plants in the surrounding gardens. Take bus D or L (direction: "Kochstedt") to "Schloß Mosigkau."

If Dessau really floats your boat, visit the **Museum für Stadtgeschichte,** Wolfgangstr 13 (tel. 21 29 13), on the third floor of Dessau's *Volkshochschule. (Open M 9am-4:30pm, Tu-W 9am-6pm, Th 9am-2pm. DM3, students DM1.50.)* A central room hosts exhibitions focusing on Dessau's regional history and contemporary political, historical, and cultural concerns in off-beat ways. On the way up to the museum, traverse the 75-year-old *Volkshochschule* building—catch a glimpse of socialist school life.

▨ Halle

Halle an der Saale, the town saved by Katrin's drumming in the climactic scene of Brecht's *Mother Courage,* emerged from WWII relatively unscathed, although sometimes it's hard to tell in the dull physical landscape. Three months after the war came to a close, occupying Americans swapped Halle for a bit of Berlin under the terms of the Yalta agreement, and in the post-war decades, it served as Sachsen-Anhalt's political and industrial capital. Although several thousand have lost their jobs since reunification, adding a grim edge to the town, efforts are being made to salvage Halle's former beauty from the cascade of modern buildings that dominates its streets. While the *Neustadt,* an immense district of housing projects built under the Communist regime, stands untouched by capitalist evolution, the *Altstadt* boasts a few sites of historic beauty. The Moritzburg Fortress, with its meager but well-chosen offerings of 20th-century avant-garde art, the lively university culture, and the contemporary theater scene all help Halle push toward the future.

ORIENTATION AND PRACTICAL INFORMATION Halle is divided into several town sectors; most significant are the GDR-style Halle **Neustadt** and the historical **Altstadt,** separated by the scenic Saale River. Come nightfall, *Neustadt* is not so secure, as political extremists (both right and left) reportedly roam this area. The train station and major streetcar lines run predominantly through the *Altstadt.* If you haven't come to see the dingy and gray GDR-era housing, stick with the safer, brighter *Altstadt* areas—you'll still get your share.

SACHSEN-ANHALT

Although most of Halle is walkable, the streetcar system efficiently covers the town (single ticket DM2.50, day pass DM7). The streetcar system is easy to use, and all stops are clearly marked. The main street is Große Ulrichstr.; as you move away from the Marktplatz, it becomes Geiststr., then Bernburger Str. With the cold war a thing of the past, Lenin and Honecker Streets and Squares have been replaced by *Freibeit* (Freedom) and *Geist* (Spirit) Boulevards. Capitalism is so liberating! A **Mitfahrzentrale** at R.-Paulick-Str. 5 (tel. 202 44 26) arranges ride shares.

The **tourist office** (tel. 202 33 40; room-finding service tel. 202 83 71; fax 50 27 98) is in the Roter Turm, on the Marktplatz. From the main station, leave from the E.-Karieth-Str. exit and head right to buses, streetcars, and the pedestrian tunnel to town. Follow the pedestrian tunnel to a left onto the pedestrian street Leipziger Str. and past the Leipziger Turm to the Marktplatz (15min.). Or take streetcar #4 (direction: "Heide/Hubertusplatz") or 7 (direction: "Kröllwitz") to "Markt" (four stops). The office hands out city maps, sells tickets, offers a number of pamphlets on cultural events, and finds rooms (DM35-50, with shower from DM50) for a DM5 fee. (Open M-Tu and Th-F 9am-6pm, W 10am-6pm, Sa 9am-1pm; Apr.-Sept. also Su 10am-2pm.) **Tours** leave from the Marktplatz. (Tours offered May-Oct. and Nov.-Apr. M-Sa 2pm. DM8.50, students and seniors DM5.) You can **exchange money** at several banks near the Marktplatz, including **Deutsche Bank,** which has a 24-hour **ATM** (open M, Tu, and Th 9am-6pm, W and F 9am-3pm). The **Weiberwirtschaft women's agency,** Robert-Franz-Ring 22 (tel. 202 43 31), complements the usual meetings and lectures with a help-line and cafe (office and help-line open M-F 10am-4pm; cafe Tu-F 4pm-midnight, Tu women only). For advice on all things queer, contact **AIDS-Hilfe Halle,** Böllberger Weg 189 (tel. 23 09 00 or 194 11). The **post office,** 06108 Halle, is at the corner of Hansering and Große Steinstr., five minutes from the Marktplatz (open M-F 8am-6pm, Sa 9am-noon). The **telephone code** is 0345.

ACCOMMODATIONS Hotels and *Pensionen* are generally far above the budgetary means of simple traveling folk (most singles start at DM100), but the tourist office lists **private rooms.** Halle's **Jugendherberge (HI),** August-Bebel-Str. 48a (tel./fax 202 47 16), rests in a newly restored mansion north of the market. To get there, it's either a five-minute walk straight down August-Bebel-Str. from the *Opernbaus* on Universitätsring or a ride on streetcar #7 (direction: "Kröllwitz") to "Geiststr.," two stops from the *Markt.* Follow Geiststr. one block, turn right onto Puschkinstr., and then right onto August-Bebel-Str. at the Hong Kong restaurant. Walk two blocks down; the hostel is on your left. The quiet residential location and hardwood elegance of the common areas elicit that sublime feeling of youth hostel joy. You know—the tingle. (DM23, over 26 DM28. Breakfast included, dinner DM7. Sheets DM6. Reception 7-10am and 5-11pm, but someone is usually there during the day. Curfew 11pm. Call ahead.)

FOOD Affordable sit-down restaurants are a difficult find in Halle, but coffeehouses, ice cream parlors, and cafes line Leipziger Str. and the Marktplatz. Between the Marktplatz and Moritzburg cafes cater to a lively student crowd. When you get sick of circling the Marktplatz, dive right into its center for one big market and what looks like a little slice of *Imbiß* heaven. (*Markt* vendors sell M-F 9am-6pm, Sa 9am-1pm.) Halle also boasts several outdoor **markets** and cheap **supermarkets. EDEKA-neukauf** is on Leipziger Str., approximately one block from the train station (open M-F 8am-8pm, Sa 8am-4pm). **Cafe Nöö,** Große Klausstr. 11 (tel. 20 21 65 1), at the end of the street facing Domstr., is far töö green-tinted and cööl to say nöö to. Occupying the ground floor of a building filled with social change and environmental groups, the cafe serves cheap breakfast (DM3.90-5.90, with coffee DM8.50) and a daily international menu that allows you to forget the evils of the world for a while. Vote Green! Salad and spaghetti costs DM4-8. Ask here for concert info, and read the newspaper *Queer.* (Open M-Th 8am-1am, F 8am-2am, Su 4:30am-8:30am and 10am-2am.) At **Café Unikum,** Universitätsring 23 (tel. 202 13 03), there's serious hipster *Uni*-action amidst smoke and modern art. On the menu are cheap salads, sandwiches, and daily specials (DM4.50-10), including a baked potato with *tzaziki* sauce and olives. (Open M-F 8am-midnight, Sa 4pm-midnight, Su 10am-2pm.) Local flavor suffers an identity crisis at **Zur Apotheke**, Mühlberg 4a, off Mühlgasse between the *Dom* and Moritzburg Fortress, with Thüringer morsels (DM5.50-10) served in Sachsen-Anhalt (open M-Th 8:30am-1am, F 8:30am-2am, Sa 5pm-2am, Su 5pm-1am).

SIGHTS Central Halle revolves around the **Marktplatz**, which bustles with traffic, vegetable stands, and three-card monte con artists. At its center stands the **Roter Turm**, a 400-year-old bell tower. A number of popular myths surround the origin of the tower's name; some credit the copper roof, while others say the architect was a commie. The most gruesome version relates that after it was built (1418-1506), the blood of the people being executed on the adjoining gallows splattered onto the tower, lending it a grisly tinge (tower interior closed to the public, except for the historically insignificant tourist office). Across from the tower lies the **Marktkirche Unsere Lieben Frauen**, whose altar is adorned with a triptych painted by students under the direction of Lucas Cranach. *(Open M-Tu, Th-F 10am-noon and 3-6pm, W 3-4pm, Sa 9am-noon and 3-5pm. Su services 10am. Free 30min. organ concerts Tu and Th 4:30pm.)* The organ on which Händel began his musical studies swings above the altar—the organ was silent for over 100 years until recent renovations. Just to the right of the church is the red 16th-century **Marktschlößchen**, an unassuming, rather small castle overlooking the Marktplatz. You can find the **Galerie Marktschlößchen**, Markt 13 (tel. 202 91 41), inside. *(Open M-F 10am-7pm, Sa-Su 10am-6pm.)* Wander these galleries free of charge to see the works of lesser-known contemporary European artists. The second floor houses the **Musikinstrumentensammlung des Händel-Hauses** (musical instrument collection of Händel's House), with an impressive collection of keyboard instruments, as well as three majestic music boxes on display. *(Open W-Su 1:30-5:30pm. DM2, students DM1, Th free.)*

An 1859 centennial memorial to composer Georg Friedrich Händel decorates the Marktplatz, but the most important Händel shrine remains his familial home. The outstanding **Händelhaus**, Große Nikolaistr. 5 (tel. 50 09 00), is only a short walk from the market down Kleine Klausstr. *(Open M-W and F-Su 9:30am-5:30pm, Th 9:30am-7pm. DM4, seniors and students DM2, Th free.)* If you call ahead you can also get a cassette tour in one of 20 languages, which covers the composer's career. From Händel's home, the **Dom** is a five-minute walk down Nikolaistr. *(Open irregularly during renovations; check signs outside for hours.)* This ancient complex, begun in 1250, remains a significant repository of religious relics. Today the church's most treasured offerings, renovations permitting, are 17 life-size figures by Peter Schroh from the 16th century. From June 4 to 13, 1999, witness the annual **Händel-Festspiele**, a celebration of Baroque music and one of its masters. Tickets are available from the tourist office.

To reach the white-washed **Moritzburg Fortress**, go around the far side of the *Dom* and head downhill, then turn right on Schloßburgstr. and walk up the hill. The **Staatliche Galerie Moritzburg Halle** (tel. 281 20 10) occupies most of this 15th-century giant. *(Open Tu 11am-8:30pm, W-Su 10am-6pm; last entry 30min. before closing. DM5, students DM3, Tu free.)* The largest art museum in Sachsen-Anhalt, it focuses mostly on 19th- and 20th-century German painters. Halle's once extensive Expressionist collection—including works by Max Beckmann, Paul Klee, and Oskar Kokoschka—offended Hitler, who drew heavily from this museum to furnish the infamous exhibit of "degenerate art" that toured Nazi Germany. Although much of the collection was either burned or sold off by the Nazis, the salvaged works remain an impressive monument to artistic freedom. Lyonel Feininger, Bauhaus headmaster and Expressionist painter, lived part-time in the tower at the entrance from 1929 to 1931 while completing his series of paintings of Halle; two still remain in the museum.

ENTERTAINMENT AND NIGHTLIFE Halle's swiftly growing theater scene produces the classics and German contemporary plays. Near the university and around the **Moritzburg Turm**, you'll find entertainment and gastronomical pleasures. Halle hosts a number of organ concerts in the **Konzerthalle**, Kleine Brauhausstr. 26 (tel. 202 89 36; tickets on sale Tu.-Th 10am-1pm and 3-6pm, W-F 10am-1pm). To remain on top of Halle's groovin' nightlife, pick up free copies of the **city magazines** *Fritz* and *Blitz* at the tourist office or in cafes and bars.

Completed in 1990, the **Neues Theater,** Große Ulrichstr. 50 (tel. 205 02 22), features wide palate of works—everything from Schiller, Shakespeare, Moliere, and Brecht to Halle's own homegrown playwrights. (Orchestra tickets DM15, all others DM10-12.50. Students and seniors 50% off. Call ahead. Box office open on days of performance M-F 8am-8:30pm, Sa 10am-1pm, Su 4-8:30pm; mid-July to Sept. usually no performances.) Halle's satirical theater, **Die Kiebitzensteiner,** in the Moritzburg Turm's South Tower (for tickets tel. 202 39 81), is tucked beneath the fortress and serves as a contemporary forum for criticism, holding spicy and engaging performances, often as benefits for current noble causes. The downstairs restaurant **Kiebitzkeller** offers snacks and spirits for nightly performances. (Theater open Tu-Sa from 7pm. Ticket office open Tu-Sa 5-8pm and 1hr. before shows. Restaurant opens at 6pm on evenings of performances.) **Kleines Thalia Theater,** on Thaliapassage (tel. 20 40 50), off Geiststr., premieres avant-garde theater productions as well as kiddie performances. (Box office open Tu and F 10am-noon and 1-4pm, W 10am-noon, Th 10am-noon and 1-6pm. DM12, children and students DM7.) **Turm** (office tel. 202 51 90, club tel. 202 37 57), in the northeast tower of the Moritzburg Turm, hosts the city's *Studentenklub* for the music-loving and grooving literary set in Halle. The music is a mishmash of disco, punk, funk, blues, techno, and rock performed by local bands. A *Biergarten* and grill are outside (open daily 6-10pm). Foreign students with ID (18 and over) are welcome. (Open Su, Tu, and sometimes Th from 8:30pm; disco W and F-Sa from 9pm.) **Pierrot,** Großer Sandberg 10, just off Leipziger Str., is a popular gay bar and disco. (Cover W DM3, F-Sa DM6. Open daily after 5pm; disco open W and F-Sa after 10pm.) **Zoom,** Rudolf-Breitscheid-Str. 92, is another queer hot spot.

HARZ MOUNTAINS

Heinrich Heine wrote that even Mephistopheles stopped and trembled when he approached the Harz, the devil's dearest mountains. It's easy to see why Heine—as well as Goethe, Bismarck, and a host of others—fell in love with these mist-shrouded woodlands. Germany's 45-year political division allowed the Harz Mountains to flourish in an artificial time warp. Since the region straddled the Iron Curtain, both East and West declared much of it off-limits, sparing it from destructive development.

Now that the armed border guards have gone, visitors have taken their places and multiplied like mosquitoes; hikers and spa-fiends alike incline to these misty, rugged hills in the heart of the restored nation. The range stretches from the northwestern **Oberharz** to the wind-sheltered, mineral-rich valleys of the south and Wernigerode in the east. All through the Harz, historic villages compete with the lush, natural beauty of the mountains and valleys. In summer, the foliage offers great biking and striking hiking. In June, the mountains' famed cherries, *Harzkirschen,* are in season on both sides of the former political division. With the first snow, the terrain becomes a splendid winter playground for skiing, skating, and tobogganing. The **Ostharz,** untouched by the deforming winds of capitalism, are endowed with gorgeous scenery and stubborn, half-abandoned castles. The **Harzquerbahn** and **Brockenbahn,** antique, narrow-gauge railways, steam through gorgeous Harz scenery from Nordhausen to **Wernigerode,** pass through the unfortunately named towns of **Sorge** and **Elend** (Sorrow and Misery), reach a 540m peak on **Drei-Annen-Hohne,** and chug along to Brocken, the Harz's highest peak (1142m). These trains are operated by the Harzer **Schmalspur Bahnen,** which has an office in Wernigerode (see p. 220). These trains run regularly in the summer months, from 8:30am to 8:30pm. Schedules are available at most tourist offices, at http://www.hsb-wr.de, and in the handy monthly pamphlet *Brocken Tips,* which lists events and activities in Wernigerode, Goslar, Bad Harzburg, and Quedlinburg (free). For more on cultural happenings and hiking tips, pick up a free copy of **Harz-Blick 43** at any Harz tourist office.

The easiest means of traveling between the Ostharz and Oberharz is by the new **bus** lines between Bad Harzburg and Wernigerode, which restore the region's common identity. A more strenuous and interesting way involves a little jaunt through the

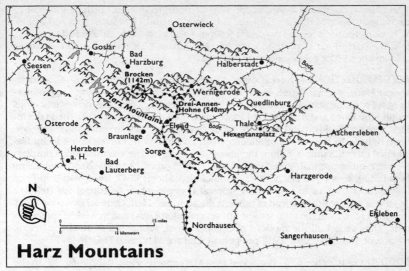

Harz Mountains

woods. Torfhaus, Braunlage, Schierke, Elend, and Drei-Annen-Hohne all lie within a day's hike of one another. The **regional tourist office** in Goslar (see p. 284) and the **regional bus station** in Wernigerode offer a wealth of information for navigating the region. Pick up a copy of the *Fahrplan der Verkehrs und Tarifgemeinsschaft Ostharz* (DM3) to get a comprehensive list of bus and rail lines in the Ostharz. A similar *Fahrplan* is available for the buses in the Goslar Landkreis, which runs all over the *Oberharz*. From the main Wernigerode *Bahnhof*, the end of the *Querbahn*, it is a short trek to the regional bus station, whose routes extend like tentacles throughout the Ostharz and provide a convenient means of reaching small mountain towns. Always be prepared for bad weather here, especially sudden and violent rainstorms. Travelers should call the **Braunlage Wetterstation** at (05520) 13 20 for summertime (Apr.-Oct.) weather conditions (open 5:30am-11pm). During the winter months (Nov.-Mar.), contact the **Schnee Telefon in Goslar** at (05321) 34 04 44 or 200 24.

If possible, dive into the Harz to join in the immense regional celebration of **Walpurgisnacht** (Apr. 30). The hedonistic festivities, immortalized by Goethe, center around legendary **witches** who sweep through the sky on broomsticks to land on **Brocken,** the Harz's highest peak. The legendary witches dance with the devil until midnight, at which point the May King cleans house. For more on regional sorcery, see **Raising Hell! Witchcraft in the Harz,** p. 225.

∎ Bad Harzburg

Bad Harzburg lacks the typical attractions of the German half-timbered towns—no cathedral, no spectacular *Rathaus,* and only the ruins of an imperial castle. Indeed, it may well be the building with some of the worst luck of all time. Built in 1065 by Heinrich IV, a stipulation in the Peace of Gerstugen forced him to destroy it a mere nine years later. In 1215, Kaiser Otto IV hiked up the hill, saw the castle, and died. In 1574, Herzog Julius commenced an ambitious renovation project, but, alas, ran out of *Geld.* Sadly enough, even today Bad Harzburg has little to offer in terms of grandiose monuments. Nevertheless, the quaint town has a lovely **Fußgängerzone** (pedestrian zone), lined with flowers, fountains, and a stream that runs the length of the main street, *Bummelallee.* To reach it, walk straight up Herzog-Wilhelm-Str. from the train station; the pedestrian zone starts right after Schmiedestr.

PRACTICAL INFORMATION The **tourist office** (tel./fax 29 27) to the left of the station will find rooms (from DM30) for a DM5 fee (open M-F 9am-1pm and 3-6pm, Sa

10am-1pm). **Deutsche Bank,** at the start of pedestrian zone, provides **currency exchange.** (Open M 8:30am-1pm and 2-4:30pm, Tu and Th 8:30am-1pm and 2-6pm, W 8:30am-1pm, F 8:30am-1pm and 2-3:30pm.) The **post office,** 38655 Bad Harzburg, is at the start of the pedestrian zone (open M-F 8am-12:30pm and 2:30-5:30pm, Sa 8:30am-noon). The **telephone code** is 05322.

ACCOMMODATIONS A retreat owned by the "Naturfreunde" society, **Braunsch-weiger Haus,** Waldstr. 5 (tel. 45 82; fax 18 67), doubles as Bad Harzburg's **Jugendher-berge.** From the station, take bus #73 to "Lärchenweg" (the bus drives in 2 rings around the town and may not hit Lärchenweg until the 2nd go-round), then take Im Bleichental to Waldstr. and go up the stone steps at the "Naturfreunde" sign. On foot, head right from the station to Silbornstr. and follow its curves uphill to Im Ble-ichental (about 35min.); follow the above directions to the mountainside complex. It's got a quintessential "cabin camp" feel. (DM25, ages 12-18 DM20.50. Non-mem-bers DM29, ages 12-18 DM26. Breakfast included. Sheets DM7. Reception 9am-7pm. Call ahead.) The bus to Goslar only stops at **Campingplatz Göttingerode** (tel. 812 15) if you ask the driver ahead of time. At the stop, head left. Or head down Dr.-Hein-rich-Jasper-Str. from the train station (for several kilometers) and make a left onto Kre-isstr. They've got all the modern necessities: pool, sauna, hot showers, solarium, restaurant. (DM9 per tent, DM7 per person. Call ahead. Closed Dec. 16-26.)

FOOD There is a cheap, well-stocked **Mini Mal supermarket,** Bahnhofspl. 2, to the right of the train station (open M-F 9am-6:30pm, Sa 8am-1pm), and there are lots more along the street that leads to the pedestrian zone. Those heading to Torf-haus and trails beyond should pick up food and camping supplies here or in the pedestrian zone, because none can be found in Torfhaus. A mountain-produce **market** appears in the **Badepark,** at Herzog-Julius-Str. and Schmiedstr. (market Th 8am-1pm). The Badepark's green lawns and fountains make a lovely setting for a picnic. Vegephobic Germans arrive later at the **Biergarten,** also in Badepark (tel. 62 30), to watch the vendors over a *Reichelbräu* (DM3) and a pair of Bavarian *Weißwürstchen* with sweet mustard and potato salad (DM5.50). (Open Apr.-Nov. daily 10:30am-10pm; Nov.-Apr. Tu-Su 10:30am-6pm.) To quench the travel-induced thirst, head right from the *Biergarten* to the 19th-century **Trinkhalle** to guzzle any of a surprising variety of waters from a selection of Bad Harzb urg's fin-est springs (DM0.50 a glass; open M-F 8am-1pm and 1:30-3pm, Sa-Su 8am-noon). You can also relax and do some reading in the Trinkhalle's *Lesesaal* (reading room), or enjoy the music of a jazz group or choir at the Brunnenkonzert (May-Oct. Tu-Su 10-11:30am, Nov.-Apr. Tu-Su 10:30am-noon; DM2).

SIGHTS At the end of Bummelallee is the **Kurpark,** which serves as the gateway to the **Harz National Park,** a 22,000 hectare nature and wildlife preserve that spreads over two of Germany's *Bundesländer.* The park is committed not only to environ-mental protection, but also to minimizing human impact: *"Natur Natur sein zu las-sen"* (to allow nature to be nature). All you could ever want to know about the park and the Harz in general can be learned at the **Haus der Natur** (tel. 17 74) in the Kur-park. Feast your eyes on the piles of pamphlets (a small donation is requested) and exhibitions detailing the park's history and wildlife. Friendly forest rangers will answer your questions and tell you about the various hikes they lead. (*Haus* open M and Tu-Su 10am-5pm. Hikes occur year-round, but most are Apr.-Sept., 2-6hr. A dona-tion of DM5, children DM3 is requested.) The Kurpark's main tourist attraction is the Bergbahn—a cable car that runs a 481m length and gets you 478m above sea level. Take in spectacular treetop scenery as you ascend, and once on top, scope out the defunct castle and the stern black 1877 obelisk (dedicated to Bismarck). Hauling ski-ers in the winter and snap-shooting tourists in the summer, the *Bergbahn* runs up the Burgberg every 15 minutes year-round, minus the second half of November and the first half of December. (DM4 for the ascent, DM3 for the descent, DM6 round-trip.) In case this is all too woodsy and organic, a heaping dose of artifice awaits at the **March-**

enwald (also in the Kurpark), a melancholic "fairy-tale forest" with mechanically animated scenes from the Brothers Grimm's fables and shining, smily gnomes. (Open daily 9am-6pm. DM4, children DM3).

■ Torfhaus

Tourists only come to Torhaus for its near-perfect hiking trails, and to climb the Brocken, at 1142m, the Harz's highest mountain. Since Goethe's first ascent in 1777, bodies have trampled the **Goetheweg**, the 16km round-trip trail to the summit. Though much of the path is littered in parts, it is still lovely and historically interesting—it occasionally follows the old patrol road along the Iron Curtain. To get to the Goetheweg, walk away from the bus stop (toward Braunlage) and at the yellow "Altenau—8km" sign turn left. The Brocken peak (2½hr. from Torfhaus) is now a full-fledged tourist trap. The **Brocken Museum** inside the electronic warfare post of the former East German state security service houses an information counter where you can buy hiking maps (museum open daily 9:30am-5pm in summer; DM3, students DM2). From the top of the Brocken, you can also head to the Ostharz. The trails leading to Schierke and Drei Annen Hohne are well traveled and thoroughly marked. The **Schmalspurbahn,** a train that transports less nimble tourists to and from the Brocken, runs regularly, takes a long time, and costs a lot. (Brocken to Wernigerode 1½hr.; one-way DM26, round-trip DM42). The **Nationalparkhaus Torfhaus,** Torfhaus 21 (tel./fax 263), sells maps of Brocken's trails (DM7.80). The Goetheweg is clearly marked; you won't need a map. Hikes to more distant destinations are worth the map investment. (Open daily 9am-5pm.)

Torfhaus lies at the middlepoint of the bus route (line 63) that connects Bad Harzburg and Braunlage. Buses depart from 7:45am to 8:25pm from both end stations (20min., M-F 13 buses, Sa-Su 11 buses, DM3.80, half-price with BahnCard). **Ski-Verleih,** near the bus stop, rents cross-country skis for DM20 per day (open daily 8am-5pm when snow adorns the ground). Walking away from Bad Harzburg, turn right at the "Altenau 8km" sign for the **Jugendherberge (HI),** Torfhaus 3 (tel. 242; fax 254). The rooms are designated by species of avian rather than by number. (DM22, over 26 DM27. HI members only. Various levels of breakfast available. Ski rentals from DM10 per day. Reception noon-1:30pm and 5-7pm. Curfew 10pm.) The **postal code** is 38667. The **telephone code** is 05320.

■ Braunlage

The ideal stop for hikers working the trails around the fantabulous Brocken mountain, Braunlage provides a needed rest from other excessively cute Harz villages. The town amply compensates for its lack in architectural panache with kilometers and kilometers of excellent trails and the luxury of an ice-skating rink, as well as spas at backpacker prices. Braunlage is also a likely bus stop for those traveling from the Oberharz in the West to the Ostharz.

The **Wurmbergseilbahn** open-air chairlift is an exhilarating way to approach the hiking paths around Braunlage. You can take the lift all the way up (17min.), and from there take a leisurely three-hour hike to the **Brocken,** the Harz's famed peak. You can also disembark at the Mittelstation to reach the **Schierke** (2½hr.). The lift departs from the mountain base at the huge parking lot behind the ice rink; from the tourist office, turn left, then take the first right to its end. (Open May-Oct. 9am-5pm. One-way to the top DM8, round-trip DM13. To Mittelstation DM5, round-trip DM8. Extra for closed cabins.) When winter hits, everyone cowers inside the closed lifts on their way back up the slopes. (Open Dec.-Jan. daily 8:45am-4:15pm; Feb.-Apr. 9am-4:45pm. Day pass for open cabins and other ski lifts DM32, closed cabins and lifts DM35.) **Skis** and **boots** are rented at **Horst Bähr,** Harzburger Str. 23 (tel. 627) for DM20 per day (cross-country skis DM15 per day); skis can also be rented at the **Café Zur Seilbahn** at the chairlift station (tel. 600; open daily 9am-5pm, DM20 per day). An **Eisstadion** (ice rink; tel. 21 91) on Harzburger Str. fulfills the need for winter sports year-round. (2hr.; DM5.50, with *Kurkarte* DM5. Skate rental DM4.50. Open M 10am-noon and 2-4pm, Tu and Th-F also 5-7pm, W and Sa 10am-noon and 2-4pm and 8-10pm, Su 10am-noon, 1:30-3:30, and 4-6pm.) The **Kurmittelhaus**, Ramsenweg 2 (tel. 22 41), and the adjacent **Hallen- und Freizeitbad** (tel. 27 88) soak, steam, massage, and mud-pack the weary into clean, relaxed, well-adjusted personalities. (Kurmittel-haus open M-F 7:30am-noon, 2-5pm. Bath open M-W and F 9am-12:30pm and 2-6:30pm, Th 9am-12:30pm and 2-8:30pm, Sa 9am-6:30pm, Su 9am-5pm; Tu women only, all other days mixed. Sauna DM15, DM13 with *Kurkarte;* pool DM9 for 3hr., DM7 with *Kurkarte.*)

Buses cruise from Bad Harzburg (40min., DM7) and Torfhaus (20min., DM3.60) to Braunlage (half-price with Bahn Card). Disembark at the "Von-Langen-Str." stop to land in the center of town. To get to the **Kurverwaltung,** Elbingeröder Str. 17, which houses Braunlage's **tourist information office** (tel. 194 33), backtrack on Herzog-Wil-helm-Str. and make a right onto Elbingeröderstr. You'll think you're entering a space-ship, but it's actually an enormous interactive electronic board that indicates which hotels and pensions are full (red light) and which have vacancies (green light). A bro-chure of the town with a hotel and pension list (on paper) is also available (DM0.50) for luddites. (Open M-F 7:30am-12:30pm and 2-5pm, Sa 9:30am-noon.) The **postal code** is 38700. The **telephone code** is 05520.

The view through the wall of windows in the dining room of Braunlage's **Jugendherberge (HI),** Von-Langen-Str. 28 (tel. 22 38; fax 15 69), provides reason enough to crash in its ideal location. It's really popular with the kids—the hostel often fills with school groups and single travelers, so call ahead. From the bus stop, follow Von-Langen-Str. uphill for about 15 minutes. (DM20, over 26 DM25. If you stay two nights or more, they slap on a DM3 per night *Kurtaxe,* which gets you the dis-count-laden *Kurkarte.* Breakfast included. Sheets DM6. Reception 5-10pm.) Braun-lage has so many pensions (from DM30) and vacation homes (from DM25 per person) you won't believe your eyes. Check out the electronic board or roam the streets—you're sure to find something. Pick up groceries at the **Penny Markt,** Markt-str. 22 (open M-F 8am-7pm, Sa 8am-2pm), and fresh produce right next door at **Fruchthaus Möller,** Marktstr. 21 (M-F 9am-1pm and 3-8pm, Sa 9am-1pm). **Rhodos,** Elbingeröderstr. 3 (tel. 22 23), heaps your plates with Greek specialties (DM10-15) and pizzas (DM8.50-13.50; open daily 11:30am-3pm and 5pm-midnight).

■ Wernigerode

Wernigerode was one of Goethe's secret spots in the hills, and in some ways, it's still the same small town he visited on trips through the Harz, packed with half-timbered houses and crowned with the cool stone of a magnificent hilltop castle. This *Berg-stadt* (mountain city) is a well-preserved, well-worth-it destination for riders of the **Querbahn.** Wernigerode is the natural crossing-over point from Western to Eastern Harz, establishing it as the region's most-touristed town.

ORIENTATION AND PRACTICAL INFORMATION
To reach Wernigerode from Magdeburg, change trains at Halberstadt (30min., 18 per day); trains also run directly from Halle (2hr., 10 per day), and a bus travels from Bad Harzburg. The town has two **train stations** that serve its 37,000 citizens. **Wernigerode-Westentor** is the next-to-last stop on the *Harzquerbahn* and close to the city center—just head up Mittelstr., and then right on Bahnhofstr. to arrive at the *Markt.* The antique steamer also stops at the main **Bahnhof Wernigerode,** next to the regional **bus terminal** (see p. 216). To get to the Marktplatz and the tourist office from the *Bahnhof,* walk up Albert-Bar-tels-Str., which is right by the *Busbahnhof,* and make a right at the big intersection onto Breite Str., which leads into the pedestrian zone. The **tourist office,** Nicolaipl. 1 (tel. 63 30 35; fax 63 20 40; http://www.harztourist.de), will be on your right at Nico-laiplatz around the corner from the *Rathaus.* The staff books rooms in private homes or hotels (from DM35) for a 10% commission but they'll also sell you a *Gastge-berverzeichnis* that lists most of the rooms in town (DM1). It also sells a small town

guide with an excellent pull-out map (DM3)—but you can also ask for the free map. (Office open May-Oct. M-F 9am-7pm, Sa 10am-4pm, Su 10am-3pm; Oct.-Apr. M-F 9am-6pm, Sa-Su 9am-3pm. **Tours** leave the tourist office Tu at 10:30am, W-Th at 2pm, Sa at 10:30am and 2pm, Su at 2pm). To the left of the *Rathaus* is an office of the **Harzer Schmalspur Bahnen,** Marktstr. 3 (tel. 55 81 43; fax 55 81 48). They are eager to help you navigate through the Harz (especially if you choose to ride on their pricey trains). In addition to selling train tickets, they sell numerous guides and maps of the area, and they rent bikes for DM18 per day. (Open daily 9am-6pm.) There is a **Deutsche Bank** near the tourist office, at the corner of Kohlmarkt and Breite Str. (open M, Tu, and Th 8:30am-1pm and 2-6pm, W 8:30am-1pm, F 8:30am-2pm). **Exchange currency** and mail cards at the **post office,** Marktstr. 14, 38855 Wernigerode (open M-F 8:30am-1pm and 2-5:30pm, Sa 8:30am-12:30pm). The **telephone code** is 03943.

ACCOMMODATIONS AND FOOD To reach Wernigerode's **Jugendgästehaus,** Friedrichstr. 53 (tel. 63 20 61), from the Westerntor station, go right on Unter den Zindeln and turn right on Friedrichstr. (25min.). From the *Hauptbahnhof,* take bus #1, 4, or 5 to "Kirchstr." The hostel is on the corner of Friedrichstr. and Kirchstr. The rooms have recently been refurbished and sport modern facilities. The friendly staff offers up a particularly fresh breakfast buffet. (DM24, over 26 DM29. Breakfast included. Sheets DM6. Reception M-F 6:30am-3pm and 5-7pm, Sa-Su 6:30-10am and 4:30-7pm.) **Frucht-haus Lucke,** Westernstr. 36, a five-minute walk from the Marktplatz, stocks fresh fruits and other groceries (open M-Th 9am-6pm, F 8am-6pm, Sa 8am-1pm). There is a **farmers' market** in the pedestrian zone (Tu and Th 10am-5pm). **Eurogrill,** just off the Markt on Westernstr., serves salads (DM3-6) that are visual and gastronomical feasts. Better yet, they only charge DM4 for a *Döner,* and on Saturday it's a mere DM2.99. The **Kochlöffel,** just a few minutes away at the intersection of Breitestr. and Große Bergstr., fulfills pipe dreams of even *cheaper* eats: after 7pm, hamburgers cost DM1.50. (Open M-F 9am-10pm, Sa 10am-10pm, Su 11am-10pm.) Swim and steam at the **Schwimmhalle** and **Sauna** (respectively), Weinbergstr. 1 (tel. 63 22 03). Opening hours during the week are confusing and sporadic; your best bet is on the weekend. (Pool open Sa 9am-9pm, Su 9am-6pm. Sauna open Sa 9am-8pm, Su 9am-5pm. DM5 for 2hr., students DM3.)

SIGHTS Wernigerode's **Schloß** (tel. 50 03 95), on its looming perch in the wooded mountains above town, is a plush and pompous monument to the Second Reich. *(Open May-Oct. daily 10am-6pm; Nov. Sa-Su 10am-6pm; Dec.-Apr. Tu-Su 10am-6pm. Last entry 5pm. DM8, students DM7; DM1 additional for a tour.)* Though the place was maintained by the GDR as a museum of feudalism, its guiding spirit was much more recent. Graf Otto, one of Bismarck's main flunkies, hosted Kaiser Wilhelm I here for wildly extravagant hunting expeditions. The perfectly preserved **Königszimmer** guest suite, where the *Kaiser* stayed, oozes inbred, masculine luxury down to the deep green and gold brocaded wallpaper in the bedroom. The other regal rooms include a chapel, two drawing rooms, and the jaw-dropping *Festsaal* (dining hall), featuring a sky-high inlaid wooden ceiling, panoramic murals of glorious Teutonic dukes, and the heaped wealth of the ducal table service. Outside on the flower-trimmed terrace, you can see straight to the peak of the **Brocken,** the Harz's highest and supposedly most haunted mountain. Ride up to the *Schloß* on the bumpy **Bimmelbahn,** a train that leaves from the clock at the intersection of Teichdamm and Klintgasse behind the *Rathaus. (May-Oct. daily every 20min. 9:30am-5:30pm; Nov.-Apr. every 45min. 10:30am-4:30pm. One-way DM3, under 10 DM2.)* To walk it, take the gravel *Christiantalweg* path or follow the white brick road marked "Burgberg," and ascend the wooded park to the castle (20min. from town center).

Back in town, the newly renovated **Rathaus** looms over the *Fachwerk* (half-timber) madness. The colorful town hall dominates the Marktplatz with its steep spire and sharply pitched roof. Small figurines of saints, virgins, miners, and other Wernigerode notables decorate the facade of the 500-year-old building. The **Krummelsche Haus,** Breitestr. 72, is so completely covered with ornate wood carvings that the original *Fachwerk* is hardly visible. The **Älteste Haus,** Hinterstr. 48, is the oldest house in the city, having survived fires, bombs, and various acts of God since its construction in the early 15th century. The **Kleinste Haus,** Kochstr. 43, is 2.95m wide, 4.2m to the eaves—and for the diminutive, the door is only 1.7m high. *(Open daily 10am-4pm. DM1.)* The **Normalste Haus,** Witzestr. 13, has no distinguishing traits.

■ Halberstadt

If you plan to travel any farther east than Wernigerode, chances are you'll have to make a connection here. Halberstadt, known before the devastation of World War II as a producer of cigars, gloves, and sausages (everything a gentleman needed), emerges as a grimy town from the moment you enter the train station. En route to Halberstadt's only attraction—a large Romanesque cathedral—your apprehensions are confirmed. Block after block of textbook GDR-depression assault you while meandering on the streets of the stagnant *Stadt.* Follow Bahnhofstr. and turn left on Magdeburgerstr.; things begin to look up as Magdeburger Str. turns into **Breiter Weg.** This pedestrian lane ends at the **Fischmarkt,** currently a construction site. New apartments, walls, and office buildings in the town center promise to make Halberstadt's *Innenstadt* less of an eyesore; construction in the Fischmarkt will probably continue through 2000. For now, the *Markt* is held on Breiter Weg (Tu and F 8am-5pm, Sa 8am-noon). Behind the Fischmarkt stands the **Martinikirche** that, despite its name, is not a shrine to olive-garnishing intoxicants.

The unquestioned focus of the city center is the **Domplatz,** framed by the super-flying buttresses of the 13th-century **Dom St. Stephanus** and the not-so-flyly buttressed Romanesque **Liebfraukirche.** The effect of the former's midnight-sooted spires is heightened by the sheer bulk of the edifice: it's a couple sizes too large for a city center like Halberstadt's. The only way to see the **Dommuseum** and its **treasury,** complete with gilded everything and the oldest known tapestries in the world (dating from 1150), is to take a combined tour of it and the *Dom.* (Open M-F 10am-5pm, Sa 10am-4:30pm, Su 11am-4:30pm. Tours Apr.-Oct. Tu-F 10, 11:30am, 2 and 3:30pm, Sa 10am and 2pm, Su 11:30am and 2:30pm; Nov.-Mar. Tu-Su 11:30am and 2:30pm.) The *Dom*'s enormous **organ** belches out concerts every weekend from June until September (prices and times vary, but there are discounts for students and seniors). In the 1930s, the *Dom* was the sight of several *Hitler-Jugend* rallies. In an act of *Vergangenheitsbewältigung* (coming to terms with the past), a group of quartz-like stones placed in front of the cathedral pay tribute to Halberstadt's once-thriving Jewish community, completely annihilated in the Holocaust. On the night of the dedication in 1992, the memorial was plastered with fascist and neo-Nazi symbols; the *Denkmal* (monument) was fully cleaned the following morning. Bookworms might also enjoy the **Gleimhaus,** Domplatz 31 (tel. 687 10), a collection of books, letters, and paintings that documents the history of the late German enlightenment. (Open May-Oct. M-F 9am-5pm, Sa-Su 10am-4pm; Nov.-Apr. M-F 9am-4pm, Sa-Su 10am-4pm. DM5, students DM2.50.) Johann Gleim was buddy-buddy with guys like Lessing, Wieland, and Herder, so the collection is pretty impressive.

The newly renovated **tourist office,** Düsterngraben 3 (tel. 55 18 15; fax 55 10 89), down an alley just in front of the *Dom,* has information on these sights and more, and will find you a room (from DM30) in one of the three hotels or myriad guest houses for free. To get to the office from the Fischmarkt, make a right onto Hoher Weg and a left onto Lichtengraben; the office will be on your right at the end of the street. Or take streetcar #1 or 2 from the train station to "Am Johannisbrunnen." (Open May-Oct. M-F 9am-1pm and 2-6pm, Sa 10am-2pm, Su 10am-1pm; Nov.-Apr. closed Su.) There's no *Jugendherberge* here, but the futuristic-sounding **Campingplatz SH 200,** Warmholzberg 70 (tel. 60 93 08), will surely lure you to the **Halberstädter See** in the northeast part of town. From the station follow Bahnhofstr., go right on Magdeburger Str., and left on Warmholzberg (30min; reception 10am-8pm; DM7.50 per person; DM8 per tent). Your best bet for cheap food is on Breiter Weg, as well as some food stores on Düsterngraben. **Geiersbach,** on Breiter Weg, takes care of your bakery needs, even on Sundays (open M-F 6am-6pm, Sa 6-11:30am, Su 2-6pm). Adjacent to the Fischmarkt is the super-cheap **Pizza, Pasta, & Co.;** an individual pizza is DM3 (open M-Sa 11am-10pm, Su noon-10pm). The **Museumscafé** in the Domplatz offers light meals for DM5-10. On the street behind the tourist information, the **internet cafe Deja Vu,** Lichtengraben 7 (tel. 57 04 25), sets you surfin' (1hr. DM10, 2hr. DM16, 3hr. DM20; open daily 4pm-1:30am). The **telephone code** is 03941.

■ Quedlinburg

For sheer authenticity, no other destination in the Harz can match Quedlinburg. This town gets medieval on your ass, coming complete with spires, castles, torture chambers, and half-timbered houses that look as though they've been around since 919, when Heinrich I waited in the market square for the news that he'd been chosen as emperor. In addition to being the first king of Germany, Heinrich's claim to fame is his "truce" with the Magyars. The deal was that he'd give them a hefty sum to leave, but instead of paying up, Heinrich flung a dead dog at the feet of the Magyar leader. In 1994, the city was crowned by UNESCO as one of the world's most important cultural treasures. Quedlinburg has been a bit run-down for the past 40 years, but locals are busy painting and patching. Unfortunately, navigational difficulties will no doubt survive the renovations: the tiny alleys, bends, kinks, and crazily oblique intersections are the price of Quedlinburg's historic charm.

ORIENTATION AND PRACTICAL INFORMATION Get a free map from the tourist office as soon as you arrive, and use it. If you have to ask for directions, try to get the person to show you the route to your goal on the map; this is not the place to test your grasp of German prepositions. **Trains** arrive every two hours from Halberstadt (20min.), and every hour from Thale (10min.) and Magdeburg (1hr.). There are also regular **buses** that depart from the train station to most Harz towns. Rent **bikes** at the *Fahrradverleih* at the station (tel. 51 51 18; DM15 per day, mountain bikes DM20 per day). Quedlinburg's **tourist office,** Markt 2 (tel. 90 56 22, fax 28 66), finds private rooms for no fee (from DM25), sells museum tickets, leads tours, and provides everything short of a massage. (Open May-Sept. M-F 9am-8pm, Sa-Su 9am-6pm; Oct. M-F 9am-6pm, Sa-Su 10am-3pm; Nov.-Feb. M-F 9am-5pm; Mar.-Apr. M-F 9am-6pm, Sa-Su 10am-3pm.) **Exchange money** at decent rates or use the ATM in the **Deutsche Bank,** Am Markt 3 (open M 8:30am-4pm, W and F 8:30am-1:30pm, Tu and Th 8.30am-6pm). The main **post office,** 06484 Quedlinburg, stamps 'n' sends at the intersection of Bahnhofstr. and Turnstr. (open M-F 8am-noon and 2-6pm, Sa 8:30am-noon). The **telephone code** is 03946.

FOOD On the way to the castle, grab some local brew at the **Brauhaus Lüdde,** Blasiistr. 14 (tel. 70 52 06). The interior is a high-ceilinged, circular, wooden brewing hall with a bar, filled with shiny copper brewing kettles. You can also elect to sip your tasty, light Pilsner (DM2.90) or the excellent, nutty **Lüdde-Alt** (ale; DM3.30). Tasty snacks and meals at around DM12 may improve that rumbling down under. (Open M-Th 11am-midnight, F-Sa 11am-1am, Su 11am-10pm.) **Pasta Mia,** Steinbrücke 23 (tel. 21 22), faces the Marktplatz and serves up inexpensive Italian meals. Pizzas run DM7.50-15.50, pastas DM8.50-16.50. After 6pm on Monday, Wednesday, or Friday, any pizza is only DM7.50. (Open M-Sa 11am-10pm.) Local **farmers** sell their most treasured foods at the Marktplatz (W 7am-5pm, Sa 7am-noon).

SIGHTS Heinrich I died within the original walls of the **Schloßberg,** an old Saxon stronghold, in 936. The current 13th-century structure has been a favorite residence-in-exile for the ruling family's widows and inconvenient relatives. The castle complex consists of three parts: the museum, the garden, and the church. The **Schloßmuseum** (tel. 27 30) depicts city history from the Paleolithic era until the present, all according to good old Marxist historiography. *(Open May-Sept. Tu-Su 10am-6pm; Oct.-Apr. Tu-Su 9am-5pm. DM5, students DM3.)* Several rooms, decorated according to 17th- and 18th-century fashion, allow you to cruise back in time, while a wooden box with two tiny peepholes cut in the sides—built as a show prison—gives you the creeps. Loiter in the gardens around the *Schloß,* or walk down the castle path past an impressive row of old houses, cramped together on the hillside.

Underneath the castle, the **Lyonel Feininger Museum,** Finkenherd 5a (tel. 22 38), is tucked away in a smart, more modern-looking white house. *(Open Tu-Su 10am-noon and 1-6pm.)* Inside is an *Angst*-heavy selection of works by the artists in the *Die Brücke* artistic circle, including Feininger's own bleak landscapes and portraits vivisected by characteristic fracture-like lines. The unavoidable stone statue of **Roland** guards the ivy-covered **Rathaus** after nearly four centuries underground: the statue was smashed and buried as punishment for the people after a failed insurrection in the mid-14th century. The neighboring **Benediktikirche** graces the Markt with its 13th-century base; the twisting Solomonic columns of the altar are truly exceptional. The **Schreckens-Turm,** at the end of Neuendorf, served as Quedlinburg's 14th-century S&M torture palace; now, it disintegrates amidst ghost-like, virtually abandoned blocks. The **Wipertikirche** (tel. 77 30 12), a squat, mostly rebuilt Romanesque church, a short walk from the *Schloß,* stands guard over the 1000-year-old crypt, resting on the site of Heinrich I's court. *(Open daily 11am-5pm.)*

■ Thale

Above the dramatic front of Thale's flowing rivers, jagged cliffs, and lush mountainside scenery lurks a region of myths, legends, witches, and demons. Like most towns in the Harz, Thale boasts that Goethe fancied its **Bodetal** valley—hence, the *Goetheweg.* The peaks on either side of the valley are the sites around which the regions rich folklore centers—lucky for us that Germany's witches just happened to do their thing in the middle of lush mountain forests with peaks that offer spectacular views.

ORIENTATION AND PRACTICAL INFORMATION Trains leave for Thale from Halberstadt (30min.) and Quedlinburg (10min.) hourly. Buses depart to many Harz towns from the *Busbahnhof,* next to the train station. Across the street from the train station, the **tourist office,** Rathausstr. 1 (tel. 25 97 or 22 77; fax 22 77), can hook you up with a private room (DM25-40 per person) for no charge. You can also purchase spirits in the form of the *Hexen Gesoff* alcohol sold in cute little bottles (DM2.50). (Open May-Oct. M-F 9am-6pm, Sa 9:30am-4:30pm, Su 9:30am-3:30pm; Nov.-Dec. M-F 9am-4pm; Jan.-Apr. M-F 9am-5pm.) A **Sparkasse,** on Bahnhofstr. close to the train station, takes care of your **money-exchanging** needs. The **Hubertus-Apotheke,** Poststr. 15, is easily reached by walking left as you exit the train station (open M-F 8am-6pm, Sa 8am-noon). The **post office,** Poststr. 1, 06502 Thale, lies across from the *Apotheke* (open M-F 9am-6pm, Sa 9am-noon). The **telephone code** is 03947.

FOOD AND ACCOMMODATIONS Thale's **Jugendherberge (HI),** Bodetal-Waldkater (tel./fax 28 81), deserves a lofty laud; its cavernous, eight-bed rooms look out into the mountains and the running river below. The *Jugendherberge* may or may not be haunted; check with the tourist office for more details. Follow the directions to the cable car station, but instead of taking a right over the bridges, keep walking along the river on Hubertusstr. (DM16, over 26 DM 21. Breakfast DM6. Dinner DM7. You are required to buy 1 meal. Sheets DM6. Reception 3-6 and 8-10pm.) The hostel's cafeteria has lunch and dinner specials (DM7-9). Otherwise, the many food stands by Hexentanzplatz can fill your need for cheap eats. Straight ahead of the Sparkasse, Karl-Marx-Str. provides each according to his needs with shops, restaurants, and amusements. The **Wolf and Sohn supermarket** (open M-F 7:30am-1pm and 2:30-6pm, Sa 7:30-11am) and the **J. Goethe bakery** fill the gaps for the needier ones. Left on Bahnhofstr. from the train station, continue until it becomes Eisenbahnstr. Thale goes crazy every year on April 30 for the **Walpurgisnacht,** but only go if you dare commit yourself to an orgy of sin.

Raising Hell! Witchcraft in the Harz

German ritualism is not limited to beer drinking. In prehistoric times, nomadic German tribes who weren't concerned about public infamy would gather atop the highest neighborhood mountain on the eve of April 30 to celebrate the wedding anniversary of Wodan and Freja (Nordic gods who controlled the seasons). In celebrations that would make most decadents blush, shepherds and farmers danced naked around live human and animal sacrifices in hopes of receiving a good harvest. (Ozzy Osborne's bark at the moon doesn't compare.) The pagan rituals persisted into the modern era; Charlemagne and other zealous missionaries weren't enamored of the blasphemous celebrations, so they attempted to usurp the occasion by proclaiming the events of April 30 to May 1 **Walpurgisnacht,** in memory of St. Walpurga. Even Charlemagne's efforts to quiet the madness failed; the festivities later came to celebrate witchcraft and the devil. In 1484, Pope Innocent VIII decided to put a vicious end to the infernal games. A crusade against witchcraft over the next century tortured and slaughtered over 7000 *"Hexen"* (witches). The campaign brought activity to a halt until Goethe's interest in witchcraft and things Faustian inspired historical societies to spring up in this century and spread the myths of devilish delight anew. Today, the most vexing *Hexen* you'll likely encounter will be grumpy *Pension* owners who will curse you with nasty showers and stale *Brötchen.*

SIGHTS Legend dates Thale's cultic history back to prehistoric times, when a sorceress named **Watelinde** led pagan rituals that forced incorrigible youths down a path of destruction in the fast-lane lifestyle of witchery. A few thousand years later a Harz resident named **Hilda** got lost in the woods for a couple of years—her reappearance was, by all accounts, a touch sketchy. Watelinde freaked out at the sight of Hilda and begged God to save her from the frightening countenance before her. Amidst explosive thunder and lightning, a whirlwind threw poor Watelinde into some rocks, which now comprise the nifty attraction **Hexentanzplatz** (witches' dance place). Amidst the celebrated spot of splattering are statues of demonic and ghoulish creatures adorned with parasitic animals. Walk down the hill from the Hexentanzplatz and you'll find the wildly entertaining **Walpurgishalle,** a museum commemorating the Harz history of witchcraft through displays of Thale's cultic ceremonies, as well as animal heads with pentagrams attached (open May-Sept. daily 9am-5pm; Oct.-Apr. 9am-1pm; DM2, students DM1). Right next to the museum is the impressive **Harzer Bergtheater Thale** (tel. 23 24), a huge, outdoor amphitheater vacillating between the sublime and the infernal, the sacred and the profane, with performances ranging from broadway musicals and operas to Goethe's *Faust* and the *Hexenkonzerte* (witches' concerts). (Shows run sporadically May-Sept. Starting times also vary. Tickets DM15-32; 30% discount for students.) One can ascend to the Hexentanzplatz either by following the adventure-filled **Winde** that begins by the hostel (30min.)—on foggy days its teeming life and poor visibility are reminiscent of Yoda's cave in the Dagobah system—or by means of the **Kabinenbahn,** a cable car that crosses the Bodetals to Hexentanzplatz. The Kabinenbahn offers spectacular views of the Bodetal; after the *Goethezeit* was well over, the valley was dubbed the "Grand Canyon of Germany." You can reach the **Roßtrappe,** the rocky peak across the valley from the Hexentanzplatz, by hiking up Präsidentenweg and then up Esselsteig; the trail starts a bit up-river from the chair lift station in the valley. Or take the **Sessellift** (chair lift). (Lift open 9:30am-6pm daily in the summer, Sa-Su 10am-4:30pm in the winter. Round-trip in the Kabinenbahn DM8, kids DM6. Round-trip in the chair lift DM6, kids DM4. Combination ticket gets you a round trip ticket on both DM12, kids DM8.) Both cable cars depart from a station in the valley. From the tourist office, walk diagonally through the park, turn right onto Hubertusstr. and cross the bridges on your right.

SACHSEN-ANHALT

■ Magdeburg

Magdeburg has four claims to fame: it has a spectacular cathedral, it's the birthplace of 18th-century composer Georg Phillipp Telemann, and it was devastated in both the Thirty Years War and World War II. On May 10, 1631, one of the most gruesome battles of the Thirty Years War decimated the city after Protestant town leaders refused to cut a deal with Catholic troops. As a major German industrial center, it was a prime target for the Allied forces in World War II. After the war, Magdeburg was rebuilt GDR-style—blessed with enviably broad boulevards and parks but cursed by concrete, cookie-cutter apartment blocks. In the months before reunification, Magdeburg had the good luck to triumph over Halle, becoming the new capital of Sachsen-Anhalt. Now, the gentrification fairies have arrived. Magdeburg offers its visitors a *Dom* and historical sites, all set in a cosmopolitan shopping district. Yet Magdeburg's increased popularity has brought increased trouble—skinheads congregate here, instigating various problems. Despite some of the bumps of reunification, Magdeburg increasingly resembles its sister-in-*Dom*ness, Köln, with a vibrant university life and cultural *Szene* surrounding the humongous heart of the city.

ORIENTATION AND PRACTICAL INFORMATION The city is conveniently configured for pedestrians: most of the sights and museums are located on Otto-von-Guericke-Str. and Breiter Weg, parallel streets that lie less than 15 minutes away from the train station via Ernst-Reuter-Allee. The *Straßenbahnen* run frequently and shuttle you between the sights and museums. A single ticket, good for 90 minutes, is DM2.40; a day ticket (good for unlimited travel on the day of purchase until 2am) is DM5, for up to two adults and three kids DM7, and for up to five adults DM9.

In the days of the Iron Curtain, Magdeburg was one of the few rail links to West Germany and West Berlin's centrally located Bahnhof Zoo. As a result, travelers en route to Berlin from eastern cities can often save time by traveling through Magdeburg to avoid the Berlin Ostbahnhof (a 20min. S-Bahn ride to the city center) or Bahnhof Lichtenberg (a good 45min. away). ICE bullet trains also connect Magdeburg with Hannover (1½hr., 2 per hr.) and Munich (6-7hr., 2 per hr.). For towns near Magdeburg, the **bus** station is to the right of the train station. For **bicycle rental, Zweirad-Schulz,** Frankefeldel (tel. 631 21 82), charges DM18 per day. Take Bus #53 or 54 to "Am Teich" (open M-Sa 9am-12:30pm and 1:30-6:30pm, Su 9am-1pm). The **tourist office,** Alter Markt 12 (tel. 540 49 03; fax 540 49 10; email mi@magdeburg.de; http://www.magdeburg.de), is on the main market square. From the train station, head straight on Ernst-Reuter-Allee (a bit to the left from the front doors) then left at the second intersection onto Breiter Weg; turn right onto the market. Inquire about tours and maps in English. Pick up a copy of *Dates* magazine, which has an up-to-date schedule of cultural and nightlife activities (free). The **Zimmervermittlung** (tel. 540 49 04), in the same office, finds rooms (DM25-75) for a DM3 fee. The **Kartenvorverkauf** (tel. 540 49 02) sells tickets to shows, concerts, and other cultural events in town. (Office open M-F 10am-6pm, Sa 10am-1pm; the *Zimmervermittlung* and *Kartenvorverkauf* have the same hours, minus a rest period from 1-1:45pm.) **Tours** leave daily from the office at 11am (DM5). There are banks all over the place, and a 24-hour **ATM** with international service right outside of the main doors of the **Karstadt** department store, on Breiter Weg. The **Women's Communication Center, Courage,** is at Porsestr. 14 (tel./fax 404 80 89). **Internet access** is available in **Cyb@r** (see **Food,** below) and **Orbit cyber cafe** (see **Nightlife,** p. 228). The **post office** sits in a sprawling, late Gothic, dark hulk on Breiter Weg, 39104 Magdeburg, toward the *Dom* (open M-F 7am-6pm). The **telephone code** is 0391.

ACCOMMODATIONS AND CAMPING The **Jugendherberge Magdeburger Hof** is a sight for sore eyes: the walls are cracked, pipes show all over the place, and the linoleum floors look like they've been through a lot. However, the ecstatic relief you will experience when you find that the hostel is a mere two-minute walk from the train station, and even closer to the main sights and museums, will shove aside any dissatisfaction with the hostel's aesthetic condition. Follow the streetcar tracks to the right from the main train station, and when they end, walk up the stairs under the cement covering and the hostel is on the right 30m ahead. (DM21, over 26 DM26. Breakfast DM6. Sheets DM6. Reception 2-10pm.) Camp at **Campingplatz Am Barleber See** (tel. 50 32 44). Take streetcar #10 (direction: "Barleber See") to the last stop, continue down the main street, then cross underneath the highway bridge. Bike rental is available for DM5 per day. (DM4 per person; DM2 per tent; DM2.50 for showers, bathroom, and water. Reception 7am-9pm.)

FOOD Many of the cheaper restaurants crowd the streets around the intersection of Breiter Weg and Einsteinstr. in Hasselbachplatz. This was the only section of the downtown area to survive wartime bombing. The **Alter Markt** proffers a bounty of flea market doo-dads and cheap food—half-roasted chickens (DM3.50), cheese, *Bratwurst*, and more (open M-F 8am-5pm, Sa 7am-noon). The **Karstadt Restaurant-Cafe**, Breiter Weg 128, across from the market, offers groceries as well as an international selection of food sold by weight. (100g Asian DM2.40, Italian DM2.75, salad DM2 in the basement level, and a complete self-service cafeteria on the 2nd floor. Open M-F 9am-8pm, Sa 9am-4pm.) Next door, the **Cyberb@r** brings the **Internet** to Magdeburg (30min. DM3; same hours as the restaurant). **Ratskeller** (tel. 568 23 23), in the Alter Markt, is a historical set-up in the basement of the Baroque *Rathaus*. If you play your cards right, this can be the best food deal in Magdeburg: while *à la carte* dinners are prohibitively expensive, the restaurant offers two special deals. Each weekday features a different *Stammessen* (lunch special) from noon to 2pm including an entree, starch, and dessert for a delightful DM8-10. Get there by 1pm if you can. The other sweet deal occurs every day; 5-10pm is "Grillzeit," when a steak costs a mere DM5 and a baked potato DM2.50. (Open M-Sa 11am-11pm, Su 11am-9pm.) Enjoy lighter meals, or a simple cup of coffee (DM2.60) right next door at the **Marietta Kaffee-Haus**, Breiter Weg (open M-F 8am-10pm, Sa 10am-10pm). **Mausefalle**, Breiter Weg 224 (tel. 543 01 35), at the north end of the lively Hasselbachplatz, attracts a young crowd, particularly students. The big wall over the bathroom doors is decorated with old newspaper clippings and vintage car memorabilia. Solid spaghetti dishes run DM10-14, and an extensive liquor and mixed-drink selection awaits (open M-F 8:30am-3am, Sa-Su 11am-3am). A **SPAR supermarket** waits at the corner of Breiter Weg and Julius-Brenner-Str. (open M-F 8am-7pm, Sa 8am-2pm).

SIGHTS Dominated by modern grays and beiges, Magdeburg's urban neutrality offers no challenge to the city's few dazzling sights. The main landmark and city symbol is the sprawling **Magdeburger Dom** (tel. 541 04 36), adjacent to the old square on Breitestr. *(Open in summer M-Sa 10am-6pm, Su 11:30am-6pm; in winter M-Sa 10am-4pm, Su 11:30am-4pm. Tours M-Sa 10am and 2pm, Su 11:30am and 2pm. Free. Tours DM4, students DM2.)* In fact, the *Dom* was famed as the largest cathedral in the nation until reunification forced it to yield that honor to Köln. But there's nothing second-rate about the spectacle of the wide **courtyard** quadrangle within the cathedral's twin dark towers spearing the skies above. At the front of the cathedral lies an inconspicuous tomb, the 973 grave site of Otto I, the second Holy Roman Emperor (after Charlemagne). Local ghost stories credit the *Kaiser's* spectral guardianship with preservation of the *Dom* during the destruction of 1631 (Catholic raiders) and 1945 (B-17 bombers), though the bombs did in fact give the cathedral quite a buzz. Ernst Barlach's famous wooden memorial to the victims of WWI, originally designed for the spot it now occupies, was removed by the Nazis, fortuitously spending the war years stored safely in Berlin's National Gallery.

The ancient **Kloster Unser Lieben Frauen**, Regierungstr. 4/6 (tel. 56 50 20), lies near the *Dom*, between the many faceless apartments. *(Open Tu-Su 10am-6pm. DM4, students and seniors DM2.)* An 11th-century nunnery, it now serves as a museum for visiting exhibitions, and as a concert hall. The grounds around the cloister still shimmer in sheltered tranquility; sit and cogitate on the benches or on the remains of stone walls. Heading away from the *Dom* and crossing Breiter Weg on Danzstr., the **Kul-**

SACHSEN-ANHALT

turhistorisches Museum, Otto-von-Guerike-Str. 68-73 (tel. 53 65 00), will pop up on your left. *(Open Tu-Su 10am-5pm. DM4, students DM2.)* You can view everything from a potato bug model 15 times the bug's actual size to the city's history from the Stone Age (check out the mammoth hairs) to the demonstrations that led to the *Wende* in 1989. The ruins of the **Johanniskirche,** almost on the Elbe behind the Alter Markt, best seen from the walkway along the river, stand as a memorial to the 1945 bombing. The skeletal remains of the central church, including the empty patterned stainglass window frames, are slowly being rebuilt, transforming the church into a cultural center. The statues and the frightening bronze doors juxtapose the terror of the bombings with the image of a **Trümmerfrau** (rubble woman), providing an emblem of the city's efforts to recover from its difficult past. Climb the **tower** for a magnificent view of the city. *(Open Tu-Su 10am-6pm.)* Across from the Johanniskirche rises the clock tower of the elegantly proportioned 17th-century **Rathaus.** On the Marktplatz in front of the *Rathaus* is a replica of the **Magdeburger Reiter** (built in 1240), the oldest free-standing equestrian figure in northern Europe. The original rides into the sunset at the Kulturhistorisches Museum. Giddy-up.

ENTERTAINMENT Magdeburg's cultural scene is packed. The magazine *Dates* and the pamphlet "Stadtpass" provide extensive information about what's going on in theaters, cinemas, and concert halls (both are free and available at the tourist office). The **Theater Magdeburg,** Universitätspl. 9 (tel. 540 64 44 and 540 65 55), is located at the corner of Breiter Weg and Erzbergerstr. Its *Großes Haus* hosts big-name operas, ballets, and plays, whereas the *Podiumbühne* is somewhat more experimental. (Ticket sales Tu-F 10am-7:30pm, Sa 10am-2pm, and 1hr. before the performance. Theater closed mid-July to early Sept.) The **Stadthalle,** Heinrich-Heine-Pl. 1 (tel. 59 34 50), hosts a very wide range of special events, including a live jazz festival every summer in mid-June, and other open-air events in the **Stadtpark Rotehorn.** Tickets available at the tourist office and the Stadthalle. The **Freie Kammerspiele,** Otto-von-Guericke-Str. 64 (tel. 598 82 26), puts on modern interpretations of the classics (tickets available M-Th 4-6pm, F 2-6pm, and 1hr. before performances). The Magdeburger *Kabarett* (cabaret) **Die Kugelblitze,** Breiter Weg 200 (tel. 541 44 26), around the corner from the youth hostel, was well known during the GDR era, and the last eight years have fed its sardonic sensibility. (Performances start around 8pm. Tickets DM20, students and seniors DM10.)

For bars, restaurants, and the inexpensive sport of people-watching, there are three superior areas in Magdeburg: **Hasselbachplatz** (see **Food,** p. 227), **Sudenburg,** along Halberstädterstr. and its cross streets (S-Bahn #1 or 10 or bus #53 or 54 to "Eiskellerplatz" or "Ambrosiusplatz"), and **Diesdorfstr.** (S-Bahn #1 or 6 to "Westring" or "Arndstr."). As well prepared for emergencies as its namesake predecessor, the **Feuerwache** (Fire Station), Halberstädter Str. 140 (tel./fax 60 28 09), answers calls for theater, art exhibits, and concerts while serving as a winter cafe and a casual summer beer garden (garden open daily 7pm-midnight). Heading left from Feuerwache on Halberstädter Str., you will pass the **Scala** movie theatre (tel. 620 19 13), which plays American blockbusters in German, as does the **Cinemaxx** movie complex (tel. 599 00 99) across the street from the train station. Back to Halberstädter Str., after the cinema, take a right on Heidestr., where **Orbit cyber café,** Heidestr. 9 (tel. 609 17 11), offers to beam you up to a land with funky decorations, drinks of all sorts, occasional live DJs, and **Internet access** (open M-F 6pm-1am, Sa-Su 6pm-2am; DM5 per hr.). The clientele at **Layla,** Lessingstr. 66 (tel. 731 70 28), gulp down pints of Guinness in a relaxing setting. *Uni*-students and expatriates gather to indulge in German bar food (daily specials DM7.90, salads DM 5.50) and the weekly English fest Thursdays at 8:30pm. (Open M-Th 11am-1am, F 11am-2am, Sa 10am-2am, Su 10am-1am.)

Mecklenburg-Vorpommern

Over 1700 lakes, the marshy coast of the Baltic Sea, and labyrinthine medieval towns characterize the lonely landscape of Mecklenburg-Vorpommern. Once a favored vacation spot for East Germans, this sparsely populated northernmost province of the former GDR retains the sturdy, raw-boned natural beauty of the *Bundesboonies*. Cyclists and hikers flock to the Mecklenburg lakes and Rügen island, which offer some of Germany's most spectacular scenery. As restoration work in the region's main cities continues, dramatic Hanseatic architecture begins to emerge from the rubble. With an unemployment rate hovering around 25%, Mecklenburg-Vorpommern's cities remain economically and politically troubled, and the presence of neo-Nazis is, unfortunately, palpable.

🗨 HIGHLIGHTS OF MECKLENBURG-VORPOMMERN

- **Rostock,** perched on an inlet of the Baltic, is a dynamic and complicated city. The city's reputation for neo-Nazi violence is strangely contrasted by its beautiful architecture and left-leaning student population (see p. 234).
- Swarms of Germans descend upon the island of **Rügen** every summer—and for good reason. The **spectacular cliffs** and **great beaches,** some protected by a national park, make for a fantastic getaway (see p. 239).
- Unlike many decayed eastern cities, **Schwerin** shines with a fantastic *Altstadt* and a slew of lush gardens (see p. 229).

▓ Schwerin

A keepsake of Heinrich the Lion's 12th-century march through the East, Schwerin is a rejuvenating stop on the way to the swarming Baltic seacoast. With reunification, the city regained its status as capital of Mecklenburg-Vorpommern. Schwerin again administers this *Land* of fallen *Junkers,* rye bread, and brick churches. Surrounded almost entirely by lakes and largely free of Communist "architectural innovations," Schwerin is home to a charming *Altstadt* brimming with well-preserved townhouses and remnants of its past life as an elegant spa town.

ORIENTATION AND PRACTICAL INFORMATION Schwerin lies on the Magdeburg Rostock rail line and is easily accessible from all major cities on the Baltic coast. Hourly **trains** connect Schwerin to Rostock (1¼hr.) and Lübeck (1½hr.). **Schwerin Information,** Am Markt 11 (tel. 592 52 12; fax 55 50 94), sells maps for DM1 and books private rooms (DM30-50) for free; cheap rooms go quickly, so call ahead. From the station, go right on Gründthalplatz, continue as it turns into Wismarsche Str., then left on Arsenal, right on Bischofstr., and left on Schmiedestr. (Open M-F 10am-noon and 1-6pm, Sa 10am-2pm.) The **Apotheke am Markt,** Puschkinstr. 61 (tel. 59 23 50), just off the Marktplatz, has an emergency bell (open M-F 8am-6pm, Sa 8:30am-1pm). At the **SB Münz Wasch Center,** Werderstr. 6, wash 6kg for DM6, soap included; dry for DM1 per 15 minutes. Take bus #10 (direction "Knaudtstr.") to the corner of Werderstr. and Knaudtstr. (Open daily 6am-11pm.) **Goethe Fahrradverleih** (tel. 834 78) rents bikes at the Platz der Jugend, near the train station. The main **post office** resides at Mecklenburgstr. 6, 19053 Schwerin. From the *Markt,* go down Schmiedestr. and turn right. (Open M-F 8am-6pm, Sa 9am-noon.) The **telephone code** is 0385.

ACCOMMODATIONS AND FOOD The **Jugendherberge (HI),** Waldschulenweg 3 (tel. 21 30 05), is located south of town in the woods by the lake. Take bus #15, get off at the end, and walk toward the zoo. It's on the left. With Schwerin's increasing popularity, the friendly hostel frequently fills, so phone first. (DM20, over 26 DM25. Tasty breakfast included. Sheets DM6. Reception 4-10pm. Curfew 10pm.) **Kaiser's,** on Schmiedestr., is the most convenient supermarket (open M-F 8am-8pm, Sa 8am-4pm). The fancy **Friesenhof Restaurant,** on Mecklenburgstr., next door to the post office, parts the seas of edible goodness with 40% discounts from 3 to 5pm daily; steaks and seafood dishes miraculously become a reasonable DM9-12 (open daily 11:30am-10:30pm). **Boomerang** on Mecklenburgstr., across from McDonald's, offers breakfast seven days a week for DM5-8, with more expensive Australian fare later in the day (opens M-F at 8am, Sa-Su at 9am).

SIGHTS Schwerin's **Schloß** (tel. 56 57 38) is just south of the city center, over the bridge at the end of Schloßstr. *(Open Tu-Su 10am-6pm. DM6, students DM3.)* The castle served as the seat of the Dukes of Mecklenburg, who ruled the area until the 1918 upheaval chased the *Kaiser* from power. The castle's gilded Baroque cupolas runneth over with luxury—the red silk wallpaper and mahogany floors pale in comparison to the sumptuous throne room, with its gilt and marble columns. Across from the *Schloß*, the **Alter Garten** square was the site of mass demonstrations preceding the downfall of the GDR in 1989. Atop a cascade of stairs on the right sits the **Staatliches Museum Schwerin,** which houses a good collection of 15th- to 19th-century Dutch and German art, including a few works by Rembrandt, Cranach the Elder, and Rubens. *(Open Tu-Su 10am-5pm. DM7, students DM5.50.)* The striking cream pillared building next door is the **Mecklenburgisches Staatstheater Schwerin** (tel. 530 00), currently in the midst of a dramatic revival (box office open Tu-F 10am-1pm and 2-6pm, Su 10am-1pm; tickets DM15-25, students DM10). Looking uphill, the nearest spire belongs to the 13th-century **Gothic cathedral.** *(Open M-F 11am-noon and 2-3pm, Sa 11am-1pm and 2-4pm, Su noon-3pm. Services 10am.)* For DM2 you can sweat your way up the 110m tower. Schwerin's former **synagogue** reposes silently at Schlachterstr. 3, off the Marktplatz; the temple was destroyed in a pogrom in 1938. The building used to house the region's memorial to its Jewish community, but closed several years ago after an interior looting by local skinheads.

Tamer animals cavort at the **Schweriner Zoo** (tel. 20 80 30), which borders the *Jugendherberge,* adjoining the **Fauler See.** *(Open Apr.-Sept. M-F 9am-5pm, Sa-Su 9am-6pm; Oct.-Mar. M-F 10am-4pm. DM8, students DM5.)* The zoo specializes in waterfowl, but it has its share of ferocious mammals. Another option for nature lovers is the reserve on **Kaninchenwerder Island,** set in the midst of the Schweriner See. In summer, **ferries** leave at least once an hour from the docks to the left of the *Schloß* to visit the island's rabbits. *(One-way DM3, children DM1.)*

MECKLENBURGISCHE SEENPLATTE (MECKLENBURG LAKE REGION)

When things got hectic in Berlin, Otto von Bismarck often found refuge among the reserved but sincere folk of the Mecklenburgische Seenplatte. With the exception of Neubrandenberg, the reminders of the GDR are not as painfully obvious here as in other regions of Eastern Germany, perhaps because the socialist-era architects were wise enough to leave the forests and hills alone. A popular vacation area for more than a century, the Seenplatte attracts summer crowds; consider advance reservations.

■ Waren

Conveniently located within an hour of Rostock and two hours of Berlin, Waren draws many German tourists to the northern edge of the **Müritz,** Germany's largest freshwater lake. Smaller streams weave from the lake into **Müritz National Park,** a unique preserve of rare birds and marshland. The Waren tourist office has tons of info about guided tours of this paradise for hikers or bikers, ranging from early-morning bird-watching jaunts to all-day canoeing, biking, and hiking triathlons.

Since Waren's primary attractions are nature-related, it's not surprising that restoration of the former *Altstadt* is not a top priority. The weather-beaten 14th-century **Altes Rathaus,** the crumbling **Speicher** (granary) that presides over the harbor, and the 290-year-old **Altes Schulhaus** (old schoolhouse), have all seen better days. Next door, the **Georgenkirche** lost its roof to fire in 1699 and received only a modest, flat replacement. Under the Herrenseebrücke lives Müritz's modest **aquarium** and garden. (Open Mar.-Sept. Tu-F 9am-6pm, Sa-Su 9am-noon and 2-5pm; Oct.-Apr. Tu-F 10am-4pm, Sa-Su 10am-noon and 2-5pm. DM4, students DM2).

Warener Schiffahrtsgesellschaft, Kietzstr. 14a (tel. 12 56 24; fax 12 56 93), and **Müritzwind Personenschiffahrt,** Strandstr. (tel. 66 66 64; fax 66 58 79), both offer boat **tours** of the Müritz lake that vary in length from one to four hours (DM7-22, children half-price). **Bikes** can be rented at the train station (tel. 590; open M-F 6am-10pm, Sa-Su 8am-8pm; DM10-12). **Waren Information,** Neuer Markt 21 (tel. 66 61 83; fax 66 43 30), in the town square, has maps of the park, brochures, and a free room-finding service (rooms DM30). The office runs both park and town tours (in German; M-W, F 10am; DM3). From the train station, take the Schweriner Damm exit and walk left, then turn right on Friedenstr. and left on Langestr. (Open M-F 10am-noon and 2-6pm, Sa 10am-noon and 1-4pm; winter M-F 10am-4pm.) A pharmacy (*Löwenapotheke;* tel. 66 61 53) is next to the tourist office (open M-F 8am-6:30pm, Sa 9am-noon). Reach the **post office,** Güstrower Str. 24, 17192 Waren, by turning right as you exit the train station and following the road along the tracks (open M-F 10am-noon and 2-6pm, Sa 10am-noon and 1-4pm). The **telephone code** is 03991.

The **Jugendherberge (HI)**, Auf dem Nesselberg 2 (tel. 66 76 06), dwells in the woods south of town. From the station's Schweriner Damm exit, go left on Schweriner Damm, bear right at the fork in the road, and then walk along the harbor down the successive streets Zur Steinmole, Strandstr., Müritzstr., and Am Seeufer. When you reach the wooded hill on the left, head straight up the path (25min. walk). Or simply go 100m to the left as you leave the train station and take bus #3 from the Schweriner Damm (direction: "Ecktannen") to "Wasserwerk." The 60 beds in barracks book quickly, but the hostel boasts a lovely location, and the friendly management will try to set up tents outside if they're full. (DM15, over 26 DM19.50. Breakfast DM6; lunch or dinner DM7. Sheets DM7. Reception 4-6pm and 8pm, or ring the bell. Members only.) There is regular camping at **Azur**, on Fontanestr. (tel. 26 07). Follow the directions to the youth hostel (above), but keep going on Am Seeufer until you reach Fontanestr. The **City Ristorante**, Friedenstr. 8 (tel. 66 87 03), offers big and small pizzas (DM5-12) and other dishes (open daily 10am-11pm). Waren's dinky **supermarket** lies on Friedenstr. (open M-F 9am-6pm, Sa 9am-1pm).

■ Güstrow

Were it not home to a huge collection of works by the prolific 20th-century artist **Ernst Barlach**, Güstrow would be like most of Mecklenburg-Vorpommern's towns—a mass of crumbling buildings with satellite dishes and *Imbiße* poking out of the brickwork. In addition to filling Güstrow with pacifist sculptures, Barlach fiercely opposed German nationalism and fascism, causing the Nazis to condemn his work as *Entartete Kunst* (Degenerate Art). Güstrow is also the hometown of **Uwe Johnson**, the GDR author subjected to constant surveillance and forced into exile in 1959 for "subversive" writings that criticized the divisions between East and West.

ORIENTATION AND PRACTICAL INFORMATION Central Güstrow lies south of the train station. To get there, follow Eisenbahnstr. until it becomes Lindenstr., then go about 45 meters farther on Lindenstr. before turning left onto Pferdemarkt. **Fahrrad Dräger**, Langestr. 49 (tel. 68 40 10), rents **bikes** for DM8-10 per day. **Güstrow Information**, Domstr. 9 (tel. 68 10 23), finds rooms (DM30 and up) for a DM3 fee (open Mar.-Sept. M-F 9am-6pm, Sa 9:30am-1pm, Su 9:30am-1pm; Oct.-Apr. closed Su). The office offers guided city **tours** (DM4, students DM2) that leave from the Rathaus daily at 11am (June-Sept.). Do laundry across the street at **SB Waschsalon**, Pferdemarkt 35 (wash DM6; dry DM2; open 7am-10pm). The **post office** is at Pferdemarkt 52, 18271 Güstrow (open M-F 8am-6pm, Sa 9am-noon). The **telephone code** is 03843.

ACCOMMODATIONS AND FOOD Güstrow's cute **Jugendherberge (HI)**, Heidberg 33 (tel. 84 00 44), a rather inconvenient a one-hour walk, and serviced only by a bus that comes every three hours. Take the same route as to the Barlach Atelierhaus (see **Sights**, below), but stay on the path until it hits Heidberg, instead of cutting onto Bukower Chausee (DM22, over 26 DM27; curfew 10pm). Also consider using the **Zimmervermittlung** at the tourist office (tel. 84 00 44) to find rooms. **Cafe Küpper**, on Domstr., boasts a 143-year history of serving sweets, sandwiches, and (more recently) pizza (DM7; open M-F 8am-7pm, Sa 11am-7pm, Su 1-7pm).

SIGHTS The Barlach tour of Güstrow begins on the southwest side of town with the **Dom**, which houses Barlach's most famous work, *Der Schwebende Engel* (The Hovering Angel). *(Open Tu-Sa 10am-noon and 2-4pm, Su 2-4pm.)* Created as a testament to the horrors of war, the angel was originally designed to hang above the pews of the *Dom* but is now tucked away in a corner. The statue was originally cast in 1926, but was then publicly melted down and made into bullets by the Nazis in 1941. After World War II, a plaster cast of the statue was found buried in western Germany, and, in 1952, the angel was restored and rededicated to the war's victims.

Walking back to Domstr., the recently renovated **Schloß** towers ahead. A grand example of Renaissance architecture, it is complete with a cute **Schloßgarten** surrounded by an ingenious shrub wall (gates and windows included). The **Schloßmu-**

seum (tel. 75 20) brims with Italian and Dutch paintings from the 15th to the 17th century, as well as works by Barlach. *(Open Apr.-Oct. Tu-Su 10am-6pm; Nov.-Mar. Tu-Su 10am-5pm. DM5, students DM3.)* On the west side of town, the **Gertrudenkapelle,** Gertrudenpl. 1 (tel. 68 30 01), houses a collection of Barlachs in an octagonal white chapel and peaceful garden. *(Open Mar.-Oct. Tu-Su 10am-5pm; Nov.-Feb. Tu-Su 11am-4pm. DM3, students DM2.)* The only church in town neglecting Barlach is the **Pfarrkirche St. Marien.** *(Open Tu-Sa 10am-noon and 2-4pm, Su 2-4pm.)* Sitting in the shadow of the *Dom,* the church displays a recently restored altarpiece from 1522, and over 180 sculpted figures by Brussels artist Jan Borman. Organ music echoes in the church on Wednesdays at 12:15pm.

Barlach's **Atelierhaus** (studio), Heidberg 15 (tel. 822 99), hosts the largest collection of his works in the very house in which they were created. *(Open Tu-Su 10am-5pm.)* It's a one-hour walk from the *Altstadt,* and bus #4a comes here every three to four hours, so renting a bike is the best way to visit. Head down Glevinerstr. from the Marktplatz and follow it as it turns into Planerstr. until you see the bike path signs for "Barlachweg." Follow this path all the way around the lake until you reach the "Boots-Verleih," then head down to the parking lot on the left and cut up to Bükoner Chausee; the museum is 200m to the right.

■ Wismar

Wismar still reels from a vicious one-two combination of war damage and 50 years of neglect. Leprous buildings blackened from the fires of war and scabs of exposed masonry still pepper the *Altstadt.* Although restoration of old buildings was a low priority during the GDR days, the Marktplatz area has been fully cleaned up, and the rebuilding of the two remaining cathedrals progresses, albeit at a sluggish pace. Off the Marktplatz on Sargmacherstr., the 80m tower of the **St. Marienkirche** is the only remaining shred of a beautiful 14th-century *Basilika* that was destroyed in World War II. The **St. Georgenkirche,** west of the St. Marienturm, was once the local church for craftsmen and traders and is now the local construction site during its renovation. The **Nikolaikirche,** nearer the port on Hinter der Chor, with its disproportionately small tower (the original was destroyed in a 1703 hurricane), provides a hint of how Wismar's churches once appeared. Its interior contains one of the oldest organs in Mecklenburg (open daily 1-6pm). Closer to the Marktplatz, the **Heiliger Geist Kirche** contains works of medieval art (open M-Sa 10am-noon and 1-5:30pm, Su 1-5:30pm).

The Marktplatz itself boasts a dizzying juxtaposition of architectural styles. The medieval **Rathaus** was rebuilt in 19th-century Neoclassical style after its roof collapsed in 1807 and destroyed most of the original building. The **Wasserkunst,** a metal mushroom built in Dutch Renaissance style in front of the Alter Schwede pub, was the village spigot for 300 years. Running downhill from the Marktplatz on ABC-Str., the **Schabbelhausmuseum** features the works of local artists and an extensive medical history museum. (Open Tu-Su 10am-8pm. DM3, students DM2.) Its gory centerpiece is a display case full of the most deformed teeth pulled by a local dentist. *Let's Go* recommends brushing your fangs at least twice a day.

Frequent **trains** connect Wismar to Rostock and Schwerin (via Bad Kleinen). From the train station, follow Bahnhofstr. right, make a left on Am Poeler Tor, and follow it past the Nikolaikirche to reach the Marktplatz. Wismar has no youth hostel, so finding a place to sleep requires a visit to the **tourist office,** Stadthaus am Markt 11 (tel. 25 18 15; fax 28 29 58). The staff will find rooms (DM30-50) for a DM5 fee, and provide helpful brochures and maps. Call ahead (open M-Sa 9am-6pm). For a bite to eat, head to **Das Kittchen** (slang for prison), Vor dem Fürstenhof 3 (tel. 259 43 20). It's decorated with cheerfully black humor in a jailhouse motif. Enjoy the *goulash à la gulag* (DM9) while waiting for your parole (open M-Sa from 5pm, Su from 10am. Meals DM6-12). The **Spar** supermarket, Lübschestr 21, off the Heiligenkirche corner of the Marktplatz, sells groceries (open M-F 8am-6pm, Sa 8am-noon). The **post office,** Mecklenburgerstr. 18, 23966, is around the corner from the Marktplatz. The **telephone code** is 03841.

Cheap (DM2), uncrowded beaches stretch around the nearby island of **Poel.** Bus #460 goes from Große Schmiedstr. just off the Alter Schwede corner of the Marktplatz to "Timmendorf Strand" (DM5). Aside from its beaches, Poel has little to offer but views of horses galloping in rolling fields and grassy marshes by the sea.

■ Rostock

East German schoolchildren were always taught to think of Rostock, the largest and most active port in Eastern Germany, as socialist GDR's "gateway to the world." After reunification, Rostock's booming business declined as industrial ships began to shift their home harbors to Hamburg. Then, seven years ago, an event occurred that would change the way the world viewed the city. The tension caused by an immigratory flood finally caused the dam to break. On August 24, 1992, a hostel for foreigners seeking political asylum in Germany was attacked and set ablaze by neo-Nazis youths.

Today, most Rostock natives would like to place this event in the past; many walls spray-painted with swastikas also carry the response, *"Nazis raus!"* ("Nazis out!"), added by a later hand, evidence of the city's considerable left-leaning student population. Both psychologically and physically, the people here have made an effort to move on. Reconstruction and restoration work can be seen in most quarters of the *Altstadt* and the number of tourists flocking to the beaches is once again high. Indeed, what happened in 1992 should not discourage you from a visit to Rostock, but rather leave you aware of continuing problems in the new Germany. You might come to see the old church towers, or pass through on your way to Scandinavia; whatever the case may be, recall Günter Grass's words: "since Rostock, Germany has changed."

ORIENTATION AND PRACTICAL INFORMATION

The majority of Rostock's sights lie in the downtown area, with the exception of **Warnemünde,** a peaceful fishing village and resort town to the northwest. If you spend a night in Rostock, it will be impossible to avoid the newer city suburbs, which consist of huge brick-and-concrete apartment blocks linked by long, wide roads. These areas are not well-lit, and local thugs have been known to be hostile and aggressive toward foreigners. *Single travelers, particularly women, should avoid these areas at night.* Rostock is well served by an extensive network of S-Bahn trains, buses, and trams; they run less frequently during the late hours and at night, so check schedules before you set out.

Trains: Hourly connections to Schwerin (1hr.), Stralsund (1½hr.), and Wismar (1¼hr.). Numerous daily connections to Berlin (2½hr.), Hamburg (3hr.), and Dresden (7½hr.). Call 493 44 54 for information.

Public Transportation: Streetcars #11 and 12 shuttle from the main station to the *Altstadt.* Single ticket DM2. *Tageskarte* (combined 1-day ticket) for streetcar, bus, and S-Bahn DM7.50. The S-Bahn leaves from the main station for Warnemünde and the newer suburbs every 15min. To get to the bus station for lines to smaller towns, exit the station through the Südstadt exit. Bus service peters out at night, leaving only the *Fledermaus* buses connecting a few central stops. Schedules of late night buses have blue circles with pictures of bats on them.

Ferries: Boats for **Scandinavia** leave from the **Überseehafen** docks. **TT-Linie,** Hansakai (tel. 67 07 90; fax 670 79 80) runs to Trelleborg, Sweden (5hr., 6 per day, peak season July-Oct. one-way DM60, students and children DM25). **Scandlines Europa GT Links** (tel. 670 06 67; fax 670 66 71) sails to Gedser, Denmark (2hr., 5 per day, one-way DM8, children DM4). Ferries also leave from the **Warnemünde** docks; the **DFO** (tel. 514 06; fax 514 09) sails to Gedser, Denmark, with special trips to other Scandinavian ports (8 per day; one-way DM10-16, children DM5-8; round-trip DM20-32, children DM10-16).

Bike Rental: Fahrradverleih Strandläufer (tel. 45 28 27), in the InterCity Hotel next to the train station. DM12 per day, DM8 per day for 5 or more days. ID required. Open M-F 9am-6pm, Sa 10am-1pm.

Mitfahrzentrale: Am Kabutzenhof 21 (tel. 493 44 38). Matches riders and drivers. Generally open 9am-1pm, but call ahead. Prices start at DM0.06 per km.
Tourist Office: Schnickmannstr. 13/14 (tel. 194 33; fax 497 99 23). Streetcar #11 or 12 to "Langestr.", then follow the signs to the right. **Room service** finds rooms for a DM5 fee (free if you call or write in advance). Staff also leads 1½hr. **tours** through the town (May-June and Sept. W and F-Su at 2pm; DM7, children DM5). Open M-F 10am-6pm, Sa-Su 10am-2:30pm. Oct.-Apr. closed one hour earlier on weekdays.
Currency Exchange: Citibank, on Kröpelinerstr. near Universitätsplatz, charges a 1% fee for exchanging cash. ATM open 24hr. Bank open M and W 9am-1pm and 2-4:45pm, Tu and Th 9am-1pm and 2-6pm, F 9am-1pm.
Emergency: Police, tel. 110. **Ambulance and Fire,** tel. 112.
Gay and Lesbian Info: AIDS-Hilfe Rostock: tel. 45 31 56.
Women's Hotline: Frauen in Not, Kinderkrippe Lichtenhagen, E. Warnkestr. 10 (tel. 71 11 67).
Pharmacy: Rats-Apotheke, Neuer Markt 13 (tel. 493 47 47). Open M-F 9am-6pm, Sa 9am-1pm.
Post Office: *Hauptpostamt,* Neuer Markt, 18055 Rostock. *Postlagernde Briefe* at counter 8. Open M-F 8am-6pm, Sa 8am-noon.
Telephone Code: 0381.

ACCOMMODATIONS

Rostock has two hostels, both situated in neighborhoods of questionable safety far from the sights of the *Altstadt.* Past travelers have complained of harassment by aggressive hooligans while walking to the *Jugendgästeschiff.* **Zimmervermittlung** at the tourist office (tel. 194 14) finds rooms with better safety and proximity, as does the **Zimmervermittlung** outside the train station (tel. 591 76; rooms run DM30-50).

The **Jugendherberge Rostock-Warnemünde (HI),** Parkstr. 46 (tel. 54 81 70), is fairly new and provides spacious rooms. Take the S-Bahn (direction: "Warnemünde") to the end, cross the bridge, and head straight on Kirchenstr. which becomes Mühlenstr. and then Parkstr. (20-25min.). To avoid the walk, ride the S-Bahn to "Lichtenhagen" and take bus #36 (direction: "Warnemünde-Strand") to the end of Parkstr. Most rooms are doubles. (DM19.50, over 26 DM23. Breakfast and resort tax included. Sheets DM5. 24hr. reception.) The **Jugendgästeschiff Rostock-Schmarl** (tel. 71 62 24; fax 71 40 14), is a massive breakthrough in leisure technology, containing a hostel, a museum, and a bar. Leaving the boat is never necessary, and at night, not advisable, as the harbor neighborhood is dangerous. Take the S-Bahn (direction: "Warnemünde") to "Lütten Klein," then bus #35 to "Schmarl-Fähre." Follow the buoy-lined road across from the bus stop to the end of the street. The bus stops running at 8pm. Alternatively, walk out of the train stop, follow the foot path alongside the off ramp, then go left on Warnower Allee for 30 minutes, and left again on the road full of buoys by the Schmarl-Fähre bus stop. (DM20, over 26 DM25. Breakfast DM6. Sheets included.)

FOOD AND NIGHTLIFE

While no one will ever accuse Rostock of being a gastronome's heaven, eating here doesn't necessarily mean choking on *ein Whopper* and *Pommes Frites.* **Spar** supermarket, Kröpelinerstr. 37 near the Kröpeliner Tor, offers a sizeable selection (open M-W and F 8am-6pm, Th 8am-8pm, Sa 8am-2pm). In Warnemünde, several restaurants along the beach fish up the bounties of the ocean. If you're trying to stay financially afloat, try the fast food joints on Kirchplatz.

Mensa, on the corner of Südring and Albert-Einstein-Str. From the train station or the *Altstadt,* tram #11 (direction: "Neuer Friedhof") to the end and bus #27 (direction: "Biestow") or 39 (direction: "Stadthalle/ZOB") to "Mensa" (one stop). Generous helpings of good food. With college ID DM2-4, others DM4-6. Open M-F 11:15am-2pm. Downstairs a bulletin board advertises all major parties and club shows, while on weekends the *Mensa* holds what students claim is the best **disco** in Rostock. Cover DM5 and up. Open Th-Su after 10pm. Call 459 12 48 for the program.

Studentenkeller, Universitätspl. (tel. 45 59 28). Rostock's students go to unlearn in this Clark Kent *Keller.* A mild mannered cafe by day jumps into its phone booth, emerging as a rock club and disco by night. Cafe open daily 8:45am-5:30pm (closed in Mar. and Aug.). Club open M-Sa after 10pm.

⊛**Mo Mo,** Barnstorfer Weg 36. Tram #11 to "Doberanerplatz." Serves Middle Eastern noodle dishes along with tasty hip-hop. Word. All-you-can-eat brunch every Sunday (DM14.50; 9am-noon). Open daily 9am-2am.

Wespennest, Karlstr. 19 (tel. 492 21 93). A women-only cafe and women's center. Open Tu-Sa 7pm-midnight.

In Warnemünde:

Café 28, Mühlenstr. 28 (tel. 524 67), on the way to the hostel, is a shiny, happy hangout. Soups, salads, and small but tasty dishes run DM4-20. Vodka and coffee served (separately, unfortunately). Open May-Oct. M-Sa 10am-late.

Seehund Warnemünde, Am Strom 110 (tel. 511 93), is a cheerful and cheap oasis of drinks built into the promenade of the *Alter Strom;* you can tread its roof on the upper road. Open daily 10am-late.

SIGHTS

The principal landmark in Rostock is the 13th-century **Marienkirche,** a beast of a brick basilica near the main square at the Steintor end of Kröpelinerstr. *(Open M-Sa 10am-5pm, Su 11am-noon. DM2, students DM1.)* In the final days of the 1989 turmoil, the services here overflowed with political protesters who came to hear the inspiring sermons of Pastor Joachim Gauck. In one of his more heroic gestures, Pastor Gauck began to publicly chastise the secret police by calling out the names of those *Stasi* members whom he could identify from the pulpit; after reunification, Gauck was entrusted with the difficult job of overseeing the fate of the *Stasi* archives. The 12m **astronomical clock** behind the altar dates from 1472. At noon and midnight, mechanical apostles strut in a circular procession.

Relics of Rostock's past as a center of Hanseatic trade still stand. Although half of the city was destroyed in World War II, many of the half-timbered and glazed-brick houses and Gothic churches have been restored. **Kröpelinerstraße** (or simply "Kröpe"), the main pedestrian mall, runs east to the **Kröpeliner Tor,** the former town gate. The main buildings of the **Universität Rostock,** one of the oldest universities in North Central Europe, are just a bit farther down Kröpelinerstr. Next to the university, along the remains of the city wall, sits the **Kloster zum Heiligen Kreuz,** a restored cloister originally built by the Danish Queen Margaret in 1270. *(Open Tu-Su 10am-5pm. DM4, students DM2.)* The museum contains medieval art, sculptures by the omnipresent Ernst Barlach, and special exhibits.

Rostock's Renaissance **Rathaus,** a strawberry-pink eyesore on Neuer Markt, was originally composed of three separate *Bürger* houses visually united by a Gothic wall with seven towers; elaborate detailing can still be seen above some of the portals. The **Steintor, Kuhtor,** and **Lagesbuschturm** sit in close proximity to Steinstr., connected by remnants of the recently renovated town wall. The **Alter Markt,** Rostock's commercial center before the war, now buzzes with the hammering sounds of extensive restoration. Strike a Quasimodo pose as you ascend the tower of the **Petrikirche,** atop which you can see all of Rostock including the ominous cooling towers of its nuclear power plant. *(Open M-F 9am-noon and 2-5pm, Sa-Su 11am-5pm. Tower DM2.)* Rostock's **Zoo** (tram #11 to "Zoo") deserves the adoration of the 800,000 visitors who flock here annually; the animals in residence include polar bears, elephants, and other biggies. *(Open May-Sept. daily 9am-6pm, Oct.-Mar. 9am-4pm. DM9, students DM7, children DM5.)* The **Schiffahrtmuseum der Hansestadt,** August-Bebel-Str. 1 (tel. 492 26 97), tram #11 to "Steintor," tells tales of wild seafaring along the rocky Baltic coast. *(Open Tu-Su 9am-5pm. DM4, students DM2.)*

Rostock was once home to a substantial Jewish population; many American and European Jews still carry the last name "Rostock." Little remains, however, of Rostock's Jewish community. The S.A. razed the synagogue on Augustenstr., and the S.S. began the murders soon after. Only partially destroyed in the war, the **Jewish ceme-**

tery still stands. In the 1970s, the government decided to embed the gravestones face-down into the earth in order to create the city's **Lindenpark**. Pressure from the international Jewish community forced the city to right most of the stones and add a memorial in 1988. Take tram #1, 3, or 11 to "Saarplatz," then go south through the park. The sign outside claims that Rostock began renovating the cemetery in 1945 and finished in 1988—no mention of the detour along the way.

To the north of Rostock and accessible by S-Bahn lies the beach town **Warnemünde**. The **Alter Strom** (old harbor), across the bridge from the train station, rings with the sounds of fishing boats, fish hawkers, and the shattering of teeth on rock candy. Warnemünde's sunny side lies along **Parkstraße**, with tan concrete houses on one side facing the sandy beaches of the Baltic behind the woods. Along the *Alter Strom* toward the sea stands a **watch tower** whose middle platform is accessible during the day (DM3). For a comprehensive survey of those tiny, colorful *Pfister* houses, visit Warnemünde's **Heimatmuseum**, at Alexandrinerstr. 31, just off the Kirchenplatz. *(Open W-Su 9am-12:30pm and 1-5pm. DM3, students DM1.50.)*

▓ Stralsund

Albrecht von Wallenstein, commander of the Catholic army during the Thirty Years War, lusted after Stralsund. "Even if it were chained to heaven, I'd want to have it," he panted, but Stralsund resisted his advances. The beauty that seduced Wallenstein is now unfortunately obscured by dust and rubble; as in so many eastern German medieval towns, restoration is far from complete. Even though it may be crumbling around the edges, the once-spectacular architecture is still a poignant testimony to Stralsund's former wealth. As a free city, Stralsund helped to found the Hanseatic League in 1293, and quickly asserted itself as a trading hub and ship building center. Today the key to Stralsund's charm is its unique geography; the hill of the *Altstadt* is bordered to the south and west by two natural ponds and slopes gently north toward the Strelasund, the strait that separates the mainland from Rügen island.

ORIENTATION AND PRACTICAL INFORMATION

The major sights and attractions are concentrated in the *Altstadt*, where the distinctive spires of the city's three churches make excellent navigational beacons. **Ossenreyerstraße** is the main pedestrian zone; it runs north-south and encompasses a department store, supermarkets, and bakeries. Two of the city's former gates, the **Kutertor** and the **Kniepertor,** sit to the west and north respectively.

Trains: Stralsund is directly connected to Rostock (every hr.), and to Binz and Sassnitz on Rügen; trains also leave several times daily for Hamburg and Berlin.

Buses: Trains are usually cheaper, but intercity buses depart the central bus station at Frankenwall for Rügen and other surrounding areas.

Public Transportation: Bus lines #1-6 circle the Altstadt, serving the outskirts of town. Single fare DM2.

Ferries: Water tours of the harbor and the Strelasund depart daily from the dock behind the conspicuously floating hotel (1hr.; DM6, children DM5). **Reederei Hiddensee** (tel. 28 81 16) runs 3 times per day to the ports of Kloster, Vitte, and Neuendorf on Hiddensee (round-trip DM22-26, children DM12, bikes DM10) and to Schaprode on Rügen's west coast (DM7, children DM3.50).

Bike Rental: (tel. 28 01 55), in the train station. DM11-13 per day. Open M-F 6am-9pm, Sa 7am-2:30pm, Su 9am-4:30pm.

Tourist Office: Stralsund Information, Ossenreyerstr. 1 (tel. 246 90; fax 24 69 49). From the station, head straight on Jungfernstieg, turn right onto the dirt path at the intersection about 300m from the Bahnhof to transverse Knieper Teich, continue straight through the Kütertor, and turn left on Ossenreyerstr. Or bus #4 or 5 to "Kütertor." The office distributes free maps, finds private rooms (DM25-100) for a DM5 fee, and sells tickets for **tours** through the *Altstadt* (DM7). They also offer a **tourist pass** (DM19, students DM9) valid for admission to most of the city's sights and museums. Open M-F 9am-7pm, Sa-Su 9am-2pm; Oct.-May M-F 10am-6pm, Sa

10am-2pm. The office in the **train station** (tel. 29 38 94) books rooms (DM5 fee). Open daily 10am-8pm.

Emergency: Police, tel. 110. **Fire** and **Ambulance,** tel. 112.

Pharmacy: Bahnhofsapotheke, Tribseer Damm 6 (tel. 29 23 28), by the station.

Post Office: Neuer Markt, 18439 Stralsund, in the red-brick building opposite the Marienkirche. **Exchanges currency.** Open M-F 9am-6pm, Sa 9am-1pm.

Telephone Code: 03831.

ACCOMMODATIONS

Jugendherberge Stralsund (HI), Am Kütertor 1 (tel. 29 21 60; fax 29 76 76). The hostel is a gorgeous 15min. walk from the *Bahnhof.* Follow the directions to the tourist office (above), but stop at Küter Tor. Turn right and take the first left onto Heilgeiststr.; the hostel is just before the big gate on the left. Located in a 17th-century town hall with a courtyard, the hostel is convenient, but watch those strange angles and low ceilings. Many school groups in summer. DM20, over 26 DM24. Breakfast buffet included. Sheets DM6.50. Reception 7-9am and 3-10pm. Lockout 9am-3pm. Curfew 10pm, but you can ring the bell until midnight. Closed Jan.

Jugendherberge Stralsund-Devin (HI), Strandstr. 21 (tel. 49 82 89 or 27 03 58). From the station, bus #3 or 60 to "Devin" (25min., DM2.50), then walk straight into the woods. Take the trail on the left side of the dreary-looking Kurhaus-Devin, and left when you hit Strandstr. (5min.). Located in the nearby village of Devin, this place is bigger and more modern than the Stralsund hostel, but much harder to reach. The 20 buildings are close to the beach, and they're sometimes generous even when "full." DM22, over 26 DM26. Breakfast included. Sheets DM7. Bike rentals to guests DM10 per day. Reception 3-8pm. Curfew 10pm. Open Mar.-Oct.

FOOD

Large portions and decent prices rarely keep company in Stralsund these days; even supermarket bills are pretty steep. **Teddy Bär** on Ossenreyerstr. handles the town's need for cheap, fast, and greasy food (open daily 8am-6pm). Stock up on **groceries** at **Lebensmittel-Feinkost,** Ossenreyerstr. 49, in the Ost-West Passage (open M-F 8am-7pm, Sa 8am-1pm).

Stadtbäckerei und Café, Ossenreyerstr. 43 (tel. 29 40 82). A cheap place to indulge in *Kaffee und Kuchen.* Open M-F 7am-6pm, Sa 8am-5pm, Su noon-6pm.

Café Lütt, Alter Markt 12 (tel. 29 23 48), serves brightly iced little cakes (DM3-5), including some Northern German rarities. Open daily 9am-6pm.

Zur Kogge, Tribseerstr. 26 (tel. 29 38 46). Fish and matching maritime interior. Open M-F 10:30am-3:30pm and 6-11pm, Sa-Su 11:30am-11:30pm.

Al Porto, Seestr. 4 (tel. 28 06 20). Stralsund's beautiful people get their noodle fix at this mildly pretentious harbor restaurant and cafe. While much of the food is on the pricey side, the pizza is decently priced (DM10-15). Open daily 11am-11pm.

SIGHTS

Stralsund's compact *Altstadt* island is unpolluted by GDR-era architecture. The **Alter Markt,** to the north, is surrounded by several of the town's oldest buildings. The remarkably well-preserved 14th-century red-brick facade of the Gothic **Rathaus** displays the coats-of-arms of the other major players in the Hanseatic League, such as Rostock and Hamburg, as well as Stralsund's trademark green and gold 12-point stars. Behind the *Rathaus* loom the unmatched towers of the **St. Nikolaikirche,** built in the same French gothic style as Lübeck's Marienkirche. *(Open Tu-F 10am-5pm, Sa 10am-4pm, Su 2-4pm. Services Su 10am.)* After a fire in 1662, one of the towers received a sophisticated Baroque dome while the other kept its flat roof.

From the Alter Markt, Ossenreyerstr. (right at the end) leads to the **Neuer Markt** and the Gothic **Marienkirche.** *(Organ concerts every other Wednesday 8pm; DM7, DM5. Graves open M-Sa 10am-5pm, Su 11am-5pm. Services Su 10am.)* Besides the usual large church attractions like a huge organ, and a rather phallic Soviet Memorial out front, the church also offers the best view of Stralsund from its **tower.** Getting to the top is an adventure; after climbing the narrow, winding staircase, ascend the last 150 feet on a ladder. The third of Stralsund's monumental churches, **St. Jakobi,** on Böttcherstr., was heavily damaged in 1944 and is currently being restored.

Between the Alter and Neuer Markt, Stralsund's two major museums have replaced the monks in the adjoining buildings of the **St. Katharinen** monastery. A good way to use your tourist pass coupon is to visit Stralsund's big aquarium, the **Deutsches Museum für Meereskunde und Fischerei,** Katharinenberg 14 (tel. 29 51 35), which contains many tanks of tropical fish, a shark tank, and the mandatory collection of Baltic Sea fish. *(Open May-Oct. daily 10am-5pm; Nov.-Apr. Tu-Su 10am-5pm. DM7, students DM3.50.)* Bring a camera, as the gift shop doesn't sell any postcards of the five-foot-long whale penis on display.

A stroll along the **Sudpromenade** at sunset reveals rolling green Rügen across the bay. Another beautiful walk runs along **Knieperwall,** the **Knieperteich** (pond), and the remains of the **town wall.** The gates **Kniepertor** and **Kütertor** date back to the 13th century. An alternate route from the Alter Markt follows Külpstr. to Schillstr., ending at the **Johanniskloster,** a Franciscan monastery built in 1254—45 years after Francis of Assisi founded the order. *(Open W-Su 10am-6pm; tours Sa-Su 10am and 1pm.)* The monastery is down by the harbor and is a glory of Gothic hallways, 14th-century mosaics, murals (rescued from 30 layers of peeling paint), roses, and red-brick walls. The former **Johanniskirche,** ruined in 1944, now hosts occasional open-air concerts. *(Church open Tu-Su 10am-6pm. DM3, students DM2, including a tour. Free last Wednesday of every month.)* The quiet courtyard (usually locked, but they'll open it if you ask) contains a dramatic Ernst Barlach *pietà,* as well as a **memorial** to Stralsund's lost Jewish community. The sculpture used to sit on the Apollonienmarkt, near the former site of the synagogue, but was placed in the cloister for safe-keeping after it was vandalized by neo-Nazis in 1992; graffiti marks still remain.

RÜGEN

Bathing in the Baltic Sea northeast of Stralsund, Germany's largest island offers a varied landscape of white beaches, rugged chalk cliffs, farmland, beech forests, heaths, and swamps. Stone Age ruins and megalithic graves (easily identified piles of big stones) are scattered about like enormous paperweights. Teutonic tribes were pushed out by Slavs during 5th-century migrations; 500 years later, the rule of the pagan Slavs was broken by invading Danes, who bestowed the joys of Christianity upon the not-so-eager Slavs. In the 19th century, the island was discovered by the nobility and transformed into a resort stacked with expensive Neoclassical buildings that are now showing their age after decades of neglect.

The most striking architectural achievement of the island is understandably understated in the official tourist literature. An important part of Hitler's racial purification plan was the **Kraft durch Freude** *(KdF;* strength through joy) initiative, intended to cultivate Aryans for the new Germany. As part of this plan, the Nazi authorities designed a 3.5km complex of interconnected five-story buildings at **Prora** (5km north of Binz) that was intended to provide seaside lodging for 20,000 German workers at the negligible cost of three *Reichsmarks* per day. After the war, the nearly finished complex fell into the hands of the GDR, which intended to dynamite the place. But after two unsuccessful attempts at demolition, the durability of the armored-concrete walls proved stronger than the will of East German authorities to purge the past. The buildings lodged the military until 1989. Except for a hotel, a youth hostel (see p. 241), a *Kindergarten,* and a few cafes, the long hallways are now empty.

Today, the tourist industry in Rügen is treading water. Once the prime vacation spot for East Germans, tourism has decreased somewhat as easterners explore western Germany for vacations. Still, summer months are busy. *Let's Go* strongly recommends that you book a room in advance by phone or by writing ahead; be sure to specify for how many people you need lodging, how long you want to stay, and what you're willing to pay. If you don't speak German, write in English. For groups of three

MECK.-VORPOMMERN

or more (sometimes even couples), a *Ferienwohnung* (vacation apartment) can be a surprisingly affordable option (DM20-30 per person). There are only two hostels, one in **Prora** and the other in **Binz,** and the latter is almost constantly booked. The campgrounds peppering Rügen are viable options. A handy helper is the "Wander und Freizeitkarte von Rügen und Hiddensee" map (DM9.90), which includes hiking trails, campgrounds, and sights—you can pick it up at any bookstore. Many tourist offices provide a free brochure of the island's campgrounds as well.

Rügen is so close to Stralsund's coast that you could almost swim there; since **trains** leave hourly for Bergen, Binz, and Sassnitz, however, you can probably leave your water wings at home. It's only an hour from Stralsund to Sassnitz, which makes daytrips feasible, especially if the hostels on Rügen are booked. **Buses** connect Stralsund with Rügen's largest towns, and a **ferry** runs to Schaprode, near Hiddensee, on Rügen's west coast. Major towns on the island include **Bergen** in the center, **Putbus, Binz,** and **Göhren** in the south, and **Sassnitz** in the north.

Once on the island, public transportation gets to be a little tricky—most visitors come with cars. The *Deutsche Bahn* connects Bergen with Stralsund, Binz, Prora, Sassnitz, Putbus, and Lauterbach. To get to Kap Arkona in the north or Göhren in the south, however, you'll have to take an **RPNV** bus (which run every 1-2hr.); check schedules carefully, and make sure you know when the last bus leaves, lest you get stuck. The **Rasender Roland,** a narrow-gauge rail line, runs from Putbus to Göhren with stops in many spa towns—unfortunately, the railway is more of a tourist attraction than a means of practical transportation. Although the island is large, the major points of interest generally lie no more than 20km from one another. The best way to get around is by combining the train and buses with walking, hiking, and biking. Well-marked **trails** cover the entire island.

■ Bergen

With the majority of Rügen's buses and trains passing through it, Bergen serves as the island's waiting room. As a transportation hub, this landlocked town, short on natural beauty and charm, cannot be avoided. Because it lacks a beach—the main reason to visit Rügen—no one really stays long. Marred by pre-fab apartment complexes and a severe economic depression, Bergen is useful only because it usually has a plentiful supply of private rooms when the spa towns are full. In a pinch, contact the friendly staff at the **tourist office,** Markt 11 (tel. 25 60 95), in the *Rathaus,* who can find private rooms (DM25-35) for a DM10 fee. To get there, take a left from the station to Bahnhofstr., then take a left onto the *Markt* (open June-Oct. M-F 10am-8pm, Sa 10am-2pm; winter M-F 10am-6pm). The **telephone code** is 03838.

■ Binz and Prora

"They paved paradise and put up a parking lot." Joni Mitchell's words ring painfully true in describing Binz, the main beach town on Rügen Island. The beat on the street here is the sound of jackhammers working furiously to resurrect Binz as Germany's "other Sylt." Decrepit seaside mansions offer the ghost-like remains of Binz's former incarnation as a fashionable, aristocratic resort along the **Strandpromenade,** and are rapidly opening as spiffed-up luxury hotels. While there isn't much to see in Binz, there is plenty to do, with miles of sandy beach perfect for swimming, sunbathing, windsurfing, or playing badminton with accountants from Düsseldorf. There are also two **nude beaches** tastefully situated at the far ends of the town beach, suitable for just hanging out. Equally gritty fun can be found at the **Kurhaus;** while it undergoes a massive reconstruction, take in the outdoor stage's family entertainment, where crooners and oompah bands dish out tunes that may leave you in tears. Luckily, Binz leaves a better taste in the mouth than in the ears, as it teems with restaurants, bars, and ice cream stands. The **Strandcafé Binz/Pizza Ristorante da Barbara,** Strandpromenade 29, serves pasta and herring specialties. Try the tortellini primavera (DM14.20), or one of a dozen pizzas (DM7-15). (Open daily 11am-midnight.) More

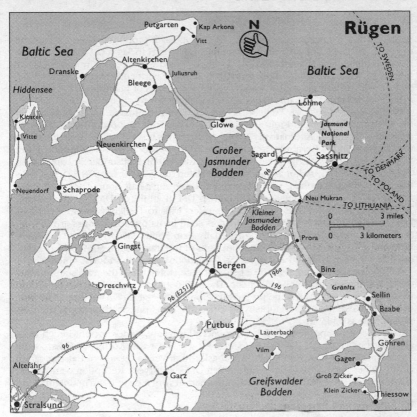

restaurants and a **crazy billiards** game (miniature golf with pool cues, DM2.50 for 18 holes) are in the **Vitarium,** a greenhouse-type building at the north end of the beach.

Accommodations in Binz fill up quickly and are DM10-15 more expensive in other parts of the island. To deal with this, the town abounds with **Zimmervermittlung** offices, many of them charging immodest fees, although the office at Jasmunderstr. 2 (tel. 27 82) finds rooms free of charge (open M-F 9am-5pm, Sa 9am-noon). Equally plentiful in Binz are **tourist offices;** the most convenient is in the *Bahnhof* (tel. 22 15), offering free maps and advice (open M-F 9am-5pm, Sa Su 9am-1pm). The **post office** is at Zeppeliastr. 3, 18609 Binz (open M-F 9am-noon and 2-6pm, Sa 9am-noon). The **telephone code** is 038393.

The scarcity of rooms worsens at the better-located of Rügen's two youth hostels, the **Jugendherberge Binz (HI),** Strandpromenade 35, 18609 Binz (tel. 325 97; fax 325 96), located directly on the beach. (DM24, over 26 DM29.50. Breakfast included. Sheets DM6. Reception 8am-noon and 7:45-9:30pm. Curfew 10:30pm, but you can get an access code.) More dependable but exponentially less attractive accommodations await in the **Jugendherberge Prora (HI)** (tel. 328 44), a 400-bed beast of a hostel. Its bleak, Orwellian hallways have the acoustics of a stethoscope, enabling guests to hear the beating of the tell-tale hearts of school groups that stay here. To its credit, it does have a **bar** on the first floor. To get there, take either the Bergen-Binz train or the Binz-Sassnitz bus to "Prora-Ost" (not "Prora"), cross the tracks and follow the signs. (DM22, over 26 DM26. Reception 7am-9am and 4-10pm. Curfew 11pm. Call ahead or show up by 4pm.) The **Edeka supermarket,** on Schillerstr. and Zeppeliastr., boasts long hours and high prices (open M-F 8am-7pm, Sa 8am-6pm, Su 10am-6pm).

MECK.-VORPOMMERN

■ Sassnitz

Sassnitz was a 19th-century seaside resort so popular it prompted Theodor Fontane to pen in *Effi Briest:* "To travel to Rügen means to travel to Sassnitz." Today, Sassnitz is a crumbling mass of apartment blocks interspersed with recently refurbished seaside villas. While the town is little more than an unpleasant enclave of GDR nostalgia, its proximity to the stark chalk cliffs and bucolic forests of **Jasmund National Park** make it an attractive base for hikers and other nature-lovers.

Ferries leave Sassnitz for Trelleborg, Sweden, Denmark, Russia, and Lithuania from the nearby *Fährhafen* in **Mukran.** Take bus #414b from the *Bahnhof* to "Sassnitz Fährhafen" (15min.). Alternatively, some smaller ships leave from the *Stadthafen* for the Danish island of Bornholm as well as the Polish border town Swinemünde. From the *Bahnhof,* head straight down Bahnhofstr., turn left on Stralsunder Str., and left on Trelleborger Str. The **Arkona-Reederei,** Am Hafen (tel. 578 50; fax 578 52), has ships that leave Sassnitz at 9am, reach Bornholm three-and-a-half hours later, and leave Bornholm at 4:30pm (May-Sept. round-trip DM38, children DM19). **DFO-Linie,** Trelleborger Str. (tel. 641 80; fax 642 00), offers trips to Trelleborg (4hr., 5 per day, DM33, under 11 DM20). Other companies send boats on **water tours** around the *Stubbenkammer* and to Kap Arkona (daily 9am-5pm, DM10-15). Rent a **bike** at Birkenweg 12 (tel. 350 75), about 500m right of the train station (DM10-15 per day; open M-F 9:30am-1pm and 2-5:30pm, Sa 10am-noon). Sassnitz's **tourist office,** Seestr. 1 (tel. 51 60; fax 516 16), is in the 11-story Rügen Hotel. From the train station, walk down Bahnhofstr. and left on Hauptstr. The staff books rooms (DM30-40) for a DM8 fee. (Open Apr.-Oct. M-F 8am-7pm, Sa-Su 3-7pm; Nov.-Mar. M-F 8am-7pm.) The **post office,** 18546 Sassnitz, is at Hauptstr. 34 (open M-F 8am-5pm, Sa 9am-noon). The **telephone code** is 038392.

The closest campground is **Campground Nipmerow,** under ancient beech trees next to the National Park (tel. (038302) 92 44), near the *Königstuhl.* Catch the *Stubbenkammer* bus from Sassnitz and ask the driver to let you out at the camp. (DM7.50 per person. DM3-5 per tent. Wash DM5; no dryers. Reception 6am-10pm.) **Am Kai** fries fish (DM10-15) directly on the harbor (open daily 10am-midnight).

■ Jasmund National Park

The spectacular chalk cliffs rising just north of Sassnitz and culminating in the famous **Großer Stubbenkammer** were forged by massive glaciers 12,000 years ago; despite some erosion, they'll still give you the chills. There are a couple of options for approaching the cliffs. The most direct (but also the least fun) is to take bus #408 to "Stubbenkammer" from the stop outside the Sassnitz train station (DM2.50); it runs hourly during the summer and lets you off about 500m away from the **Königstuhl** (king's chair), the most famous of the cliffs. You can also follow one of the **bike trails** through the forest from Sassnitz to the *Königstuhl* (8km), but these bypass the most dramatic scenery. For the best views, take the **Hochuferweg** (high coastal trail) all the way from Sassnitz to the *Stubbenkammer.* Despite the intimidating name, the 8.5km trail (a 3hr. hike) is fairly easy and runs from one incredible scenic lookout to the next. To pick up the trail, follow the "Stubbenkammer" signs through Sassnitz up the hill until you reach the parking lot, where there's a detailed map of the park showing all of the trails and their corresponding blazes—follow the ones for "Hochuferweg."

The trail takes you first to the **Wissower Klinken** (3km), which you might recognize from Caspar David Friedrich's paintings—these were his favorite chalk cliffs. Even though they've lost about 3m to erosion since he painted them, their beauty still seems almost supernatural. Continuing for another 5km, you'll reach the **Victoria-sicht** lookout, named after a German empress, and then the famous *Königstuhl,* which is anticlimactic after all the beautiful views. If you follow the mob to the **lookout area,** you'll have to pay for the view, which isn't much better than what you've already seen for free (DM2, students DM0.50).

Legend has it that the kings of Röf had to climb up to the top of the 110m *Königstuhl* to be crowned upon the stone chair. If you look up to the left, you'll notice a small guard post once used by GDR authorities to make sure no one escaped by boat to Sweden. For a bit of solitude, walk down the steep and windy paths to the flint-covered beach. Another trail leads from the *Königstuhl* to the lovely **Herthasee,** a lake named after the German harvest goddess Hertha. According to myth, Hertha drowned her mortal servants in this lake, and their spirits supposedly still gather on the banks each night, although we didn't stick around to find out. Nearby, the **Herthaburg,** a U-shaped earth wall built by the Slavs in the 7th century, recalls the less peaceful periods of this violently beautiful landscape.

■ Granitz and Göhren

The **Jagdschloß Granitz** is a cheesy castle-like hunting lodge designed and built in 1836 by Prussian architect Schinkel, whose unmistakable creations can be seen all over the island. Built atop the *Tempelberg* hill, its 38m tower offers a breathtaking panorama of the island. Bambi's family tree is mounted on the walls of the **Jagdmuseum** (hunting museum) inside the "castle" (open Tu-Su 9am-5pm; DM4.50, students DM3.50). The *Roland* stops at the Jagdschloß, as does the **Jagdschloßexpress,** which makes round-trips from the *Kurhaus* in Binz (DM10, children DM6). From the "Jagdschloß" *Roland* stop, head uphill on the trail off to the right to reach the castle. To walk or bike the 5km from Binz, pick up the trail near the "Binz Roland" station. If you head south from the *Roland* "Jagdschloß" stop to the village of Lancken-Granitz, you'll pass a bunch of huge prehistoric graves; one dates back to 2300 BC.

The *Roland's* final stop is **Göhren,** on the easternmost tip of the forested **Mönchgut peninsula,** which looks like a four-fingered glove. The peninsula was settled in the 13th century by monks, who believed in total self-sufficiency. Things move at a noticeably slower pace than in the rest of Rügen. Göhren, like every other town worth its salt on Rügen, has a nice beach; it's also the base of numerous **hiking and biking trails** leading through peaceful beaches, forests, and the rolling hills of the **Zickersche Alpen.** Göhren's main attraction is the **Mönchguter Museum,** composed of four tiny museums scattered about the town. The museums display local history through exhibits housed in an old schoolhouse, a 17th-century cottage, and a thatched-roof barn. (All open May-June and Sept.-Oct. Tu-Su 10am-5pm; July-Aug. daily 10am-6pm. Each museum DM4, students DM3, with *Kurkarte* DM3 and DM2, respectively. Day card for all 4 museums DM14, students DM10, with *Kurkarte* DM10 and DM6, respectively.)

Navigating in Göhren requires little effort, as almost everything lies either on **Strandstraße** or right off it. To get to the center of town from the train station, follow Strandstr. up the hill. **Buses** connect Göhren to Binz, Bergen, Sassnitz to the north and Klein Zicker to the south. **Tilly Fahrräder,** Schulstr. 7 (tel. 22 40), rents sturdy one-speed **bikes** for DM7 and touring bikes for DM9 (open M-F 9am-6pm, Sa-Su 9am-noon and 5-6pm). The **tourist office** *(Kurverwaltung),* Schulstr. 8 (tel./fax 21 50), provides information and helps find rooms for a 10% fee. From the train station, follow Strandstr. up and to the left, then go right on Waldstr., and right again onto Schulstr. (Open M-Th 8am-6pm, F 8am–12:30pm and 4-6pm, Sa-Su 4-6pm.) **Sparkasse Rügen,** on Strandstr., cashes traveler's checks for free and has an **ATM** (open M-Tu and F 8:30am-12:30pm and 2-4pm, W 8:30am-12:30pm, Th 8:30am-12:30pm and 2-6pm). The **post office,** 18586 Göhren, is at Poststr. 9 (open M-F 11am-noon and 3-5pm, Sa 11am-noon). The **telephone code** is 038308.

The **campground** (tel. 21 22) is near the train station and the beach. From the station, turn right and follow the signs. They have **bike rental,** a cinema, restaurants, and a **laundromat.** (DM6 per person; DM3.50-6 per tent. Reception 7am-10pm.) Get groceries at **Edeka** on Strandstr. (open M-F 8am-7pm, Sa 8am-1pm and 4-6pm, Su 8am-noon and 4-6pm). **Ostseeresidenz Göhren** (tel. 912 55), on the beach down the hill from Strandstr., has slightly expensive fish entrees served in a pleasant ballroom overlooking the sea. Try the *Rotbarschfilet* (DM18.50).

■ Kap Arkona and Vitt

At the northern tip of Rügen, Kap Arkona—Germany's only cape, flanked on either side by the villages of Putgarten and Vitt—stretches into the Baltic. **Buses** run hourly from Sassnitz (#419) and Bergen (#110) to Altenkirchen, where you can transfer to bus #403 to Putgarten. Infested with tour buses and gift shops, **Putgarten** serves as the transportation hub and tourist center of Kap Arkona. The two main attractions on the cape are accessible from Putgarten: the **lighthouses** and the town of **Vitt.** The **Arkonabahn,** a cheesy motorized train, connects to Putbus, Vitt, and the lighthouses for a modest cost (DM8, students DM5). **Horse-drawn carts** offer even less efficient transportation between Putgarten and the lighthouses for the same prices as the slightly faster *Arkonabahn.* Before reunification, the two lighthouses on Kap Arkona resided in a restricted area belonging to the GDR's National People's Army. The **Leuchtfener Arkona,** designed by Schinkel, has been open to the public since 1993. Built in 1826, it guarded the GDR's sea borders. Nearby, the **Marinepeilturm** was built in 1927 and rigged with a fancy electronic system that could eavesdrop on British radio communications. Now it houses archaeological finds from the former **Tempelburg Arkana,** a Slavic fortification built in the 8th century and destroyed by the Danes in 1168 (lighthouses open daily 10am-4pm; DM5).

The new **tourist office,** in the parking lot by Kap Arkona (tel. 419; fax 419 17), 300m down the road from Putgarten's bus stop, finds rooms for a DM15 fee (open Jan.-Mar. daily 11am-5pm; Mar.-May 10am-5pm; June-Oct. 10am-7pm). Pick up a free guide or rent a **bike** to wheel around (DM2.50 per hr., DM10 per day). The **Drewoldke campground** (tel. 124 84) is east of Altenkirchen (DM6 per person; DM4-6 per tent; reception 8am-9pm; open Apr.-Oct.). The **telephone code** is 038391.

■ Near Rügen: Hiddensee

West of Rügen lies the slender island of Hiddensee, known in the *Plattdeutsch* dialect as *dat söte Länneken* (the sweet island). Free of youth hostels, campgrounds, motor vehicles, and other sources of pollution, Hiddensee remains the same sliver of untrammeled, unadulterated natural beauty that drew Sigmund Freud, Albert Einstein, and Käthe Kollwitz here. Ferries serve Hiddensee's three towns: Neuedorf, Vitte, and Klöster. Of the three, **Neuendorf** is the least spectacular; like the heath surrounding it, Neuendorf rests silently except during the winter, when local plants are picked for *Sanddorn,* a rust-colored, honey-like drink (DM5 per bottle, DM15-25 for the alcoholic variant). North of Neuendorf lies **Vitte,** the island's main town with the island's sandiest beach. As Hiddensee has neither a hostel nor a campground, visit the **Zimmervermittlung** at the **Vitte tourist office,** Nordereude 1662 (tel. 642 26; fax 642 25; open M-F 7am-5pm, Sa 10am-1pm), which finds rooms for a 10% fee, or the **Stralsund** tourist information (see p. 237), which has a free list of houses with rooms for rent. The island's beauty and action climax in **Klöster,** the northernmost town. The great naturalist author and social dramatist Gerhardt Hauptmann summered in Klöster from 1930 to 1943 and is buried here; there is a memorial to him and his work. The huge wine cellar reveals that Hauptmann loved the bottle nearly as much as the pen.

Klöster's museums and sandy beaches are mere appetizers for the hills above the town which make up the **Dornbusch,** an area so pristine that not even bikes are allowed. Follow the trails (hay-covered to avoid erosion) which run along the grassy hillsides carpeted with wildflowers to reach the **Leuchtturm,** atop which you can see the entire island. Fully enjoying Hiddensee requires renting a **bike,** preferably a burly one with plenty of gears and nice fat tires, as the majority of the island's roads are either muddy country trails or sandy beach paths. Bike rentals *(Fahrradverleih)* are everywhere on the island, with DM10 per day the standard rate for a three-speed.

Provided you get up very early, you can go bombing down the path from the *Dornbusch* to Klöster, a winding 1.6km descent over gnarly, pot-holed cement. At the bottom, buy a thirst-quencher at the **Spar supermarket,** Hatenweg 6 (open M-F 8am-7pm, Sa 8am-6pm).

Ferry connections are available to Hiddensee from Stralsund on the mainland (see Stralsund, p. 237) and Schaprode on Rügen's west coast. Ferries leave Schaprode approximately four times per day (45min.; DM8, children DM6; round-trip DM12, children DM8; bikes DM10). The **telephone code** is 038300.

The Osmonds of Central Europe

Although most of today's young people have had regretfully little exposure to the phenomenon of singing-and-dancing, vaguely Christian, large-littered rock 'n' roll families, **the Kelly Family,** enormously popular in Germany and the rest of central Europe, can provide a quick (and addictive) fix. Composed of nine long-haired gender-neutral siblings, the Family members are American expats who outfit themselves in a weird mixture of 60s hippy headbands and bell-bottoms, medieval robes, and the latest Eurotrash fashions (including some mongo red platforms). Their message is similarly bizarre; their repertoire includes everything from gospel songs to catchy little ditties like "Papa Cool" and "Fell in Love with an Alien." While some may find the family's aesthetics unappealing, Europeans go gaga for the Kelly kids, with their latest album selling a whopping four million copies in all of central Europe. While traveling through Germany, keep your eyes peeled for their colorful posters emblazoned with their bubbly, 60s style logo; if you see one, that means the Family—double-decker bus and all—is coming to town. Buy a ticket if you can; shows sell out fast.

Schleswig-Holstein

The only *Land* to border two seas, Schleswig-Holstein's past and present livelihood is based on the trade generated by its port towns. In between the coasts, verdant plains, populated mainly by sheep, produce much of northern Germany's agricultural output and provide a peaceful backdrop to contrast with the often stormy seascape. Hamburg, the progressive metropolis on the region's southern border, is a politically autonomous *Land*, but looms influentially over the region. Although Schleswig-Holstein became a Prussian province in 1867 following Bismarck's defeat of Denmark, the *Land* retains close cultural and commercial ties with Scandinavia. Linguistically, Schleswig-Holstein is also isolated from its southern neighbors by the various dialects of *Plattdeutsch* and, to a lesser extent, Frisian spoken within its borders. The most noticeable difference is the local greeting "*Moin,*" a *Plattdeutsch* derivation of "*Guten Morgen*" used throughout the day.

🎙 HIGHLIGHTS OF SCHLESWIG-HOLSTEIN

- The second-largest city in Germany, **Hamburg's** cultural offerings are world-class: the **Hamburger Kunsthalle** displays a huge collection of art from medieval times to the present, the **Deichtorhallen** hosts contemporary creations, and the **Museum für Kunst und Gewerbe** boasts bric-a-brac (see p. 255).
- Hamburg is also damn **sexy,** with its **Reeperbahn red-light district** (see p. 247) second only to Amsterdam's, and an **Erotic Art Museum** (see p. 255).
- Overflowing with medieval architecture, **Lübeck** takes visitors back—*way* back—to the days when it was capital of the Hanseatic League (see p. 258). Check out the **largest mechanical organ in the world** and Thomas Mann's former house and literary inspiration, the **Buddenbrookshaus.**

▓ Hamburg

The largest port city in Germany, Hamburg radiates an inimitable recklessness. Calling its atmosphere "liberal" or "alternative" does not do the city justice. With a fiercely activist population of squatters and a thriving sex industry comparable only to Amsterdam's, Hamburg is a crazy coupling of the progressive and the perverse. As a busy port, Hamburg gracefully grew over the centuries into an industrial center of nearly two million inhabitants. After gaining the right to navigate the Elbe in 1189, Hamburg held off pirates and trading rivals, and emerged in the 13th century as a leading power of the Hanseatic League. Straddling several rivers, it was an early hub for overland trade from the Baltic Sea, and the growing profits of the lucrative shipping trade led to dabbling in other financial concerns. The first German stock exchange convened here in 1558, and the Bank of Hamburg dates back to the early 1600s. In 1618 Hamburg gained the status of Free Imperial City, a proud tradition of autonomy that endures to this day, as it wields considerable political power both locally and nationally as one of Germany's sixteen *Länder*.

Poised on the crest of Germany's breakneck industrialization and naval construction drive, Hamburg became one of Europe's wealthiest metropoli by World War I. The *Hamburg-Amerika Linie* ruled the oceans of industry as the largest shipping firm in the world. The city suffered a severe pummeling at the outset of World War II, when it became the first stop for the Royal Air Force's wrath. Because the port was a primary Allied target, a single air raid killed more than 50,000 civilians, many of whom lived in crowded tenements along the waterfront. The conflagration in the streets reached temperatures of 1000°C, leaving nearly half of the city's buildings in ruins. Fortunately, Germany's richest city could afford the reconstruction of much of its copper-roofed brick architecture. Since the late 1960s, an active conservation movement has steadily lobbied for the restoration of historic buildings, including

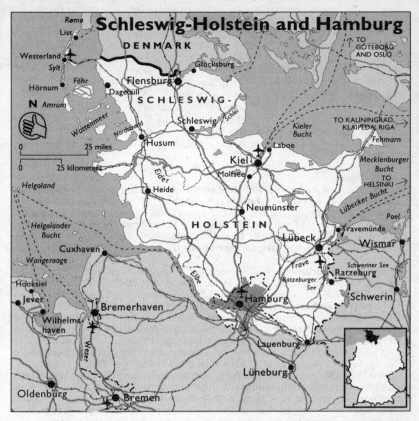

museums, hotels, and houses. In the early 80s, violent riots erupted when police attempted to evacuate warehouses occupied by anarchists and left-wing intellectuals protesting property speculators' acquisition of the real estate. Today, Hamburg expresses its restlessness less violently; instead, it exudes the excitement of a city that has become a center of contemporary artists and intellectuals as well as reveling party-goers who live it up in Germany's self-declared "capital of lust."

ORIENTATION AND PRACTICAL INFORMATION

Hamburg's fame as a North Sea port relies upon its huge harbor 100km inland, on the north bank of the **Elbe River.** The city center is squeezed between the river and the two city lakes, **Außenalster** and **Binnenalster,** formed by the confluence of the Alster and Bille Rivers with the Elbe. Most major sights lie between the **St. Pauli Landungsbrücken** port area in the west and the *Hauptbahnhof* in the east. Both the **Nordbahnhof** and **Südbahnhof** U-Bahn stations exit onto the *Hauptbahnhof.*

The **Hanse Viertel** is a quarter thick with banks, shops, art galleries, and auction houses. The area's glamour turns otherwise humdrum window-shopping into an aesthetic adventure. North of the downtown, the **University of Hamburg** dominates the **Dammtor** area and sustains a vibrant community of students and intellectuals. To the west of the university, the **Sternschanze** neighborhood is a politically active community home to artists, squatters, and a sizeable Turkish population. The **Altona** district, with its own major train station, was once an independent city ruled by Denmark; as Hamburg grew, the Danes were ousted. At the south end of town, an entirely different atmosphere reigns in **St. Pauli,** whose raucous **Fischmarkt** (fish market) is juxtaposed by the equally wild (and no less smelly) **Reeperbahn,** home to Hamburg's infamous sex trade. At the Fischmarkt, veritable anarchy reigns as vendors haul in and hawk huge amounts of fish, produce, and other goods. It fascinates in the morning, as early risers mix with revelers from St. Pauli who rally to keep the night going. Listen for cries of "*Ohne Geld!*" ("No Money!") and keep your head up—to grab attention, the fruit vendors toss free pineapples into the crowd (market open Su 6-10am, off-season 7-10am; U- or S-Bahn to "Landungsbrücken" or S-Bahn to "Königstr."). The **Hamburg Card,** available at the tourist offices, offers a great means of exploring the city. It provides unlimited access to public transportation, admission to most museums, and discounts on bus and boat tours (1 day DM12.50, 3 days DM26, without transportation DM10). An even better deal is the **Group Card,** which provides the same deals for up to five people (1 day DM24, 3 days DM42, without transportation DM21).

Transportation

Flights: For information call 507 50 or contact individual carriers. **Lufthansa** (tel. (01803) 80 38 03) and **Air France** (tel. 50 75 24 59) are the two heavy hitters that fly to Hamburg. **Jasper** (tel. 227 10 60) makes the 25min. trip from the Kirchenallee exit of the *Hauptbahnhof* to **Fuhlsbüttel Airport** every 20min. (daily 5am-9:20pm; DM8, ages 12 and under DM4). Or take U-Bahn #1 or S-Bahn #1 to "Ohlsdorf," then take an express bus to the airport (daily 5:30am-11pm, every 10min., DM3.90).

Trains: The **Hauptbahnhof** handles most traffic with connections to Berlin (2¾hr., hourly 8am-9pm, DM93), Munich (5½hr., 23 per day, DM256), Frankfurt (3¾hr., 27 per day, DM182), Copenhagen (6hr., 7 per day) and Zurich (9½hr., 18 per day). The efficient staff of the **DB Reisezentrum** sells tickets and books vacation packages. Open daily 5:30am-11pm. For **train information** call 194 19. **Dammtor** station is across the Kennedy/Lombards bridge, and **Altona** station is in the west of the city. Most trains to and from Kiel, Schleswig, Flensburg, and Westerland stop only at **Altona.** Frequent trains and the S-Bahn connect the 3 stations. **Lockers** can be rented for a maximum of 72 hrs. (open 24hrs.; DM2-4 per day).

Buses: The **ZOB** (you down with ZOB? Yeah you know me!) is located across Steintorplatz from the Hauptbahnhof. To: Berlin (6 a day, DM40), Paris (3 a week, DM90), Copenhagen (5 a week, DM55). **Polenreisen** has good deals to Poland. Open M-F 9am-8pm, Sa 9:30am-1pm and 4-7:30pm, Su 4-7:30pm. **Lockers** are located in the main hall but cannot be accessed between 9pm and 5:30am (DM2).

Ferries: Scandinavian Seaways, Van-der-Schmissenstr. 4 (tel. 38 90 30; fax 38 90 31 20), about 1km west of the Fischmarkt (U-Bahn to "Königstr."), sets sails to England and Ireland. Overnight ferries run to Harwich, England (20hr.) every other day. The cheapest tickets cost DM183, students DM147; F-Sa DM183, students DM163. Other destinations include Copenhagen, Oslo, and Amsterdam—call for details. Open M-F 10am-4:30pm; phone reservations M-F 10am-6pm, Sa 10am-2pm.

Public Transportation: HVV operates an efficient U-Bahn, S-Bahn, and bus network. Single tickets within the downtown area cost DM1.80. There are also 1- and 3-day tickets (DM9.50 and 23.30 respectively); consider buying a **Hamburg Card** instead (see above). All tickets can be bought at orange Automaten.

Taxis: Taxiruf, tel. 44 10 11.

Car Rental: Hertz has an office in the *Hauptbahnhof*'s ReiseBank (see above; tel. 280 12 01; fax 24 53 78). Rates start at about DM400 per week.

Mitfahrzentrale: City Netz Mitfahrzentrale, Gotenstr. 19 (tel. 194 44). S-Bahn #3 to "Hammerbrook." Ride-sharing deals. To: Berlin DM30, Cologne DM45, Amsterdam DM59, Paris DM89. Open M-F 8:15am-8pm, Sa 8:15am-6pm, Su 9am-8pm.

Bike Rental: O'Niel Bikes, Beethovenstr. 37 (tel. 53 11 77 44), offers German-language bike tours of the city and environs. Prices range from DM49 for 3hr. to DM129 for an all-day extravaganza. They also rent bikes (DM19 per day).

Boat Rental: You can rent sailboats, paddleboats and rowboats on the Außenalster from **Segelschule Kpt. Pieper,** An der Alster (tel. 24 75 78), directly across from the Hotel Atlantic at the foot of the Kennedy bridge. See the directions for **Alster-Touristik** above. Sailboats DM26 per hour for 1-2 people (additional skippers DM2 per person); paddleboats and rowboats DM18 per hour. Sailing license required to rent sailboats.

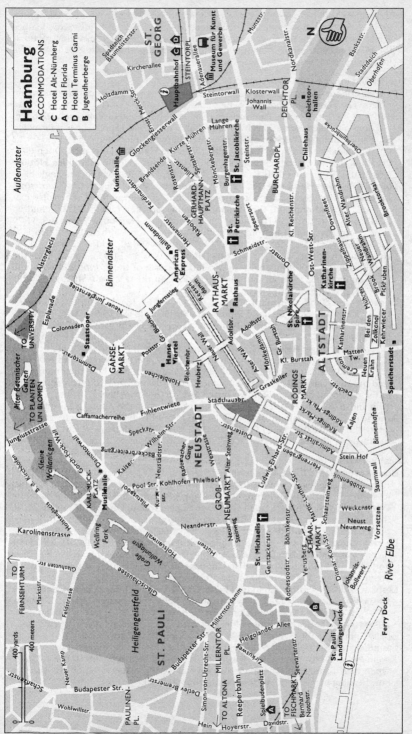

Hitchhiking: *Let's Go* does not recommend hitchhiking as a safe mode of transportation. Those headed to Berlin, Copenhagen, or Lübeck take U-Bahn #3 to "Rauhes Haus" then walk up Hammerstr. to Hamburg Horn (a treacherous traffic rotary at the base of the *Autobahn*). Hitchers aiming for points south take S-Bahn to "Wilhelmsburg" and wait at Raststatte Stillhorn.

Tourist and Financial Services

Tourist Offices: Hamburg's two main tourist offices supply free maps and pamphlets. The **Hauptbahnhof office,** near the Kirchenallee exit (tel. 30 05 12 01; fax 30 05 13 33; http://www.hamburg-tourism.de), books hotel rooms for a DM6 fee, but does not take reservations by phone. Open daily 7am-11pm. The less crowded **St. Pauli Landungsbrücken office** is located between piers 4 and 5 (tel. 30 05 12 00). Open daily 10am-7pm. A third office is in the **Hanse Viertel** mall. Open daily 9am-6pm. For advanced reservations and information, call the **Hamburg Hotline** (tel. 30 05 13 00; open daily 8am-8pm). The staff at all locations speaks English.
Tours: Top-Tour-Hamburg (tel. 227 10 60) operates sight-seeing tours (*Stadtrundfahrten*) leaving every 20 minutes from 9:30am to 5pm from the Kirchenallee exit of the **Hauptbahnhof** and the St. Pauli Landungsbrücken (adults DM22, children DM11; 50% discount with Hamburg Card—see above). **Hamburg Vision** (tel. 31 79 01 27; http://www.city-hopping.de) offers a similar tour with additional stops at the *Rathaus* and Michaeliskirche (DM25, students DM20, under 12 free). Tours last between 75min. and 2hr. **Alster-Touristik** (tel. 34 11 41), across from the Hotel Atlantic on the Außenalster (two blocks north of the *Hauptbahnhof*), will lead you on a 1hr. jaunt around the lakes (daily on the :15 10am-5pm; DM2, children DM1, senior citizens DM1.50).
Consulates: Ireland Feldbrunnenstr. 43 (tel. 44 18 62 13). U-Bahn to "Hallerstr." Open 9am-noon. **New Zealand** Heimhuder Str. 56 (tel. 442 55 50). **U.K.** Harvestehuder 8a (tel./fax 448 03 20) U-Bahn to "Hallerstr." Open 9am-noon and 2-4pm. **U.S.** Alsterufer 27 (tel. 41 17 10), on Außenalster's west side. Open M-F 9am-noon.
Currency Exchange: ReiseBank, on the second floor of the *Hauptbahnhof* near the Kirchenallee exit, arranges money transfers for Western Union, cashes traveler's checks, and exchanges money for a DM3 fee. Amuse yourself with their computerized business card maker (DM2-10). Open daily 7:30am-10pm. Otherwise, try one of the dozens of banks downtown (open M-W, F 9am-1pm and 2:30-4pm, Th 9am-1pm and 2:30-6pm). There's also a ReiseBank branch in the Altona train station.
American Express: Ballindamm 39, 20095 Hamburg (tel. 30 90 80, refund service tel. (0130) 85 31 00; fax 30 90 81 30). Mail held for cardmembers up to 4 weeks (no charge). All banking services. Open M-F 9am-5:30pm, Sa 10am-1pm.

Local Services

Bookstores: Heine Buch, Grindelallee 24-28 (tel. 441 13 30; fax 44 11 33 22; http://www.buchkatalog.de), in the university district, has a superb selection of German literature. It also has an impressively comprehensive English-language section. Open M-F 9:30am-7pm, Sa 10am-4pm. **Der Bücherwurm,** Ottenser Hauptstr. 60, in the pedestrian zone near the Altona train station, has a huge collection of used books, ranging from 19th-century etiquette manuals to the latest best-sellers.
Library: Staats- und Universitätsbibliothek, Von Melle Park 3 (tel. 41 23 22 33; http://www.sub.uni-hamburg.de). Hamburg University's library holds 2.75 million volumes, including a fine English-language collection. Open M-F 9am-9pm, Sa 10am-1pm; Aug. M-F 9am-7:30pm, Sa 10am-1pm.
Lesbian and Gay Center: Hein und Fiete Gay & Lesbian Information Center (tel. 24 03 33), Pulverteich 17-21, across from the Pulverfass cabaret. Open M-F 4-9pm, Sa 4-7pm. **Magnus Hirschfeld Centrum,** Borgweg 8 (tel. 279 00 69). U-Bahn #3 or bus #108 to "Borgweg." Daily films and counseling sessions. Evening cafe open daily 5pm-midnight. Center open M and F 2-6pm, Tu-W 7-10pm.
Laundromat: Schnell und Sauber, Grindelallee 158, in the university district. S-Bahn #21 or 31 to "Dammtor." Wash 6kg DM6, soap included. Dry DM1 for 15min. Open daily 6am-11pm. There are also several laundromats on Simon-von-Utrecht-Str., heading towards the Altona station from St. Pauli.

Emergency and Communications
Emergency: Police, tel. 110. From the Kirchenallee exit of the Hauptbahnhof, turn left and follow the signs for "BGS/Bahnpolizei." There's also a police station on the **Reeperbahn** located at the corner of Davidstr. and Spielbudenplatz. **Ambulance,** tel. 112. Headquarters at the Berliner Tor U-Bahn station. **Fire,** tel. 112.
Rape Crisis Line: tel. 25 55 66, M and Th 9:30am-1pm and 3-7pm, Tu-W 9:30am-1pm and 3-4pm, F 9:30am-1pm.
Pharmacy: Exit the *Hauptbahnhof* on Kirchenallee and turn right. The staff of the **Senator-Apotheke** speaks English. Open M-F 7am-8pm, Sa 8am-4pm.
Post Office: Branch at the Kirchenallee exit of the *Hauptbahnhof*, 20099 Hamburg (open M-F 8am-8pm, Sa 8am-6pm, Su 10am-4pm). **Poste Restante** *(Postlagernde Briefe),* 20097 Hamburg, in the main branch on Gr. Burstah 3. Open M-F 8am-6pm, Sa 8am-12pm.
Fax: Use the credit card-operated fax/phone in the Hauptbahnhof's **ReiseBank** (see above) to send or receive faxes. Open daily 7:30am-10pm.
Internet Access: In the **Staats- und Universitätsbibliothek** (see above). Head to the second floor and look for the "Bibliografien" section. Open M-F 10am-7pm, Sa 10am-1pm. Free. Note that there are only six PCs, and the wait can be long. To avoid the lines, head to the **Cyberb@r,** located on the third floor of the gigantic **Karstadt** department store on Mönckebergstr. For DM5, you get 30min. of superfast digital Internet access.
Telephone Code: 040.

ACCOMMODATIONS AND CAMPING

Hamburg's single rooms, from DM60, reflect the cost of the city's accommodations. Many establishments are tawdry with few comforts. A slew of small, relatively cheap *Pensionen* line **Steindamm, Steintorweg, Bremer Weg,** and **Bremer Reihe,** around the *Hauptbahnhof.* While the area is filled with drug addicts and wannabe-*mafiosi,* the hotels are for the most part safe. The tourist office's *Hotelführer* (DM1) aids in navigating past the filth. For longer stays, try the **Mitwohnzentrale** at Lobuschstr. 22 (tel. 194 45; open M-F 9am-5:30pm, Sa 9am-1:30pm). A passport is required, as well as a deposit of either DM100 cash or DM50 and a bank account number.

Hostels and Camping

Jugendherberge auf dem Stintfang (HI), Alfred-Wegener-Weg 5 (tel. 31 34 88; fax 31 54 07; email jh-stintfang@t-online.de; reservations via internet at http://www.schoelzel.com/jh-hamburg/index.shtml). S-Bahn #1, 2, or 3, or U-Bahn #3 to "Landungsbrücke." A great location near the Reeperbahn and the subway and a beautiful view of the harbor compensate for the regimental house rules. Very clean rooms, showers, and kitchen facilities. All halls are same-sex. The hostel also features a high-tech email, Internet, fax, phone, and word-processing facility. DM24, over 26 DM29, sheets and breakfast included. Non-members pay a DM6 surcharge. Private rooms available for couples and families. Safe-deposit boxes can be rented for DM2 plus a DM40 deposit. Serves lunch at noon and dinner at 6pm (meals DM8.50 each). Reception 12:30pm-1am. Lockout 9:30-11:30am. Curfew 1am.

Jugendgästehaus-und-Gästehaus Horner-Rennbahn (HI), Rennbahnstr. 100 (tel. 651 16 71; fax 655 65 16; email jgh-hamburg@t-online.de), U-Bahn #3 to "Horner-Rennbahn" or bus #160 from Berliner Tor. From the main exit of the station, turn right—the hostel is about 10min. by foot, at the corner of Tribünenweg. Rather far from the center, located next to a horse-racing track. Extremely clean and secure. DM29.50, over 26 DM35. Members only. Double and family rooms available. Reception 7-9:30am and 12:30pm-1am. Curfew 1am, stragglers admitted at 2am.

Camping: Campingplatz Rosemarie Buchholz, Kieler Str. 374 (tel. 540 45 32). From Altona train station, take bus #182 or #183 to "Basselweg," then walk 100 meters in the same direction as traffic. Leafy setting near a very busy access road. DM7 per person. Showers DM1.50. Call ahead. Reception 7am-10pm. Quiet hours 10pm-7am. Check-out time is noon.

Hotels

⊛Schanzenstern Übernachtungs-und-Gasthaus, Bartelsstr. 12 (tel. 439 84 41; fax 439 34 13; http://www.schanzenstern.de). U–Bahn #3, S-Bahn #21 and #3 to "Sternschanze." Left onto Schanzenstr., right on Susannenstr., and left to Bartelsstr. Located in the middle of an electrifying neighborhood of students, working-class Turks, and left-wing dissenters, the Schanzenstern is managed by a politically and ecologically progressive cooperative with great skill. Situated on the upper floors of a renovated fountain pen factory, the hotel's 50 rooms are clean, quiet, bright, and tastefully decorated with Swedish wood furniture, plants, and cheerfully painted walls. Wheelchair accessible. Dorms DM33; singles DM60; doubles DM90; triples DM 110; quadruples DM130; quints DM160. Breakfast buffet DM11. Reservations are a must in the summer and at New Year's.

Hotel Alt Nürnberg, Steintorweg 15 (tel. 24 60 23; fax 280 46 34). From the station, go straight ahead from Kirchenallee, veering off toward Steintorplatz..on the right, then look for Steintorweg on the left. Heidi-themed decor in the heart of Hamburg's somewhat sketchy *Hauptbahnhof* neighborhood. Very convenient to trains. Each clean, safe, and smallish room features a telephone, and some have TVs. Singles DM60, with shower DM90; double DM90, with shower DM130.

Hotel Florida, Spielbudenplatz 22 (tel. 31 43 94). U-Bahn #3 to "St.Pauli," or S-Bahn #1 and #3 to "Reeperbahn." Located in the heart of Hamburg's thriving nightlife and sex-industry, Hotel Florida offers small but clean rooms adjacent to Hamburg's biggest clubs. Singles DM55, doubles DM95, triples DM135. Breakfast included.

Hotel Terminus Garni, Steindamm 5 (tel. 280 31 44; fax 24 15 18). From the *Hauptbahnhof*'s Kirchenallee exit, turn right. Almost always has vacancies. Doubles DM45, with shower DM60; triples with bath DM165. Breakfast included. 24hr. reception. Major credit cards accepted.

Hotel Annerhof, Lange Reihe 23 (tel. 24 34 26). From the station's Kirchenallee exit, take the second left. Singles DM48; doubles DM82. Breakfast DM8. Call ahead.

FOOD

The most interesting part of town from a culinary standpoint is **Sternschanze,** where Turkish fruit stands, Asian *Imbiße*, and avant-garde cafes entice the hungry passersby with good food and (equally important!) atmosphere. Slightly cheaper establishments abound in the **university** area, especially along Rentzelstr., Grindelhof, and Grindelallee. In **Altona,** the *Fußgängerzone* (pedestrian zone) leading up to the train station is packed with ethnic food stands and produce shops. Check out the **Mercado** mall, which includes everything from **sushi** bars to Portuguese fast-food. There's even a **Safeway!** (Open M-F 10am-8pm, Sa 9am-4pm.) In a pinch, the shopping arcade at the **Hauptbahnhof** has about a dozen fast food joints (open daily 6am-11pm).

Mensa, Schlüterstr. 7. S-Bahn to "Dammtor," then head north on Rothenbaumchaussee, left on Moorweidenstr., then right onto Schlüterstr. A place to catch up with students and check bulletin boards for special events. Meals DM1.70-6 with student ID, more for non-students. Serves lunch M-F 11am-2pm and dinner 4-7pm.

Libresso Antiquariat, Binderstr. 24 (tel. 45 16 63). U-Bahn to "Hallerstr.," south on Rothenbaumchaussee, then right onto Binderstr. Bookstore and cafe mix high quality used literature and dark espresso, served up for students at the nearby university. Open M-F 9am-6pm.

Asia Imbiß Bok, Bartelsstr. 29. U-Bahn #3 to "Sternschanze." *Imbiß* is a misnomer here—this joint serves real restaurant food. Try the spicy Thai noodles, or some of the other savory Korean and Chinese options (circa DM6-12). Full Korean dinner DM25. Open daily 10am-8pm.

⊛Noodles, Schanzenstr. 2-4 (tel. 439 28 40). U-Bahn #3 to "Sternschanze." Along with innovative pasta creations, Noodles serves up veggie entrees alongside a full bar. Trippy ambient music provides an appropriate acoustic background for the alternative community of Sternschanze. Try the tortellini with broccoli and ham (DM10.50, small portion DM8) or one of their generous, nationally inspired salads. Beer DM5. Open Su-Th 10am-1am, F-Sa 10am-3am. (It's kiwi.)

Turm-Restaurant, Lagerstr. 2-8 (tel. 43 80 24). Hamburg just wouldn't be a world-class city without a revolving restaurant towering above it. Diners sit in one of half a dozen compartments named after world cities, distinguishable from one another only by the color of the tablecloth. Soak in the faded 1970s elegance along with the spectacular view of the city while enjoying a coffee (DM3.90) or beer (DM6). For DM12, wolf down all the cake and coffee you can (daily 3:30-4:45pm)! Open daily noon-11pm.

Geo Pizza aus dem Holzbackofen, Beim Schlump 27 (tel. 45 79 29). Delectable pizzas (DM8-15), baked in an oven hot enough to make steel glow, highlight the large vegetarian selections. The Inferno Pizza (DM11.80-13.80), topped with an incendiary blend of jalapenos, red peppers, beef, onions, salsa, and corn, transforms humans into fire-belching beasts. Open Su-Th 11am-1am, F-Sa 11am-2am.

Indian Tandoori, Ottenser Hauptstr. 20, in the pedestrian zone near Altona train station. Whether you eat inside or outdoors in the *Fußgängerzone,* Indian Tandoori's food is sure to jump-start your Teutonically impaired taste buds. If you're in a hurry, grab an order of samosas (DM6); otherwise, feast on their namesake tandoori chicken (DM11) or chicken tikka masala (DM10). There are also a number of vegetarian options; try the palak paneer (DM13.50).

Machwitz, Schanzenstr. 121 (tel. 43 81 77). Join the hip student crowd in the funky tangerine angular interior or people-watch outside. Daily menu DM9.80. Occasional concerts from local bands. Open daily from 10am until everyone leaves.

Frauenbuchladen und Café, Bismarckstr. 98 (tel. 420 47 48). U-Bahn to "Hoheluftbr." A women-only establishment. Pick up the *Hamburger Frauenzeitung* (DM6) if you can read German. Open M-F 10am-7:30pm, Sa 10am-2pm.

Falafel-König, Schanzenstr. 113. As the name implies, this Lebanese *Imbiß* is indeed the seat of the "Falafel-King." Basic falafel DM5, with one of half a dozen toppings (mmm...cauliflower!) DM6. Open daily 10am-11pm.

SIGHTS

The **Hamburg Hafen,** the largest port in Germany, lights up at night with ships from all over the world. More than 100,000 dockers and sailors work the ports, and their presence permeates Hamburg. After sailing the East Indies, the 19th-century **Windjammer Rickmer Rickmers** (tel. 35 69 31 19) was docked at Pier 1 and restored as a museum ship. Old navigation equipment, all brass and polish, is juxtaposed with modern nautical technology (open daily 10am-6pm; DM6, students DM5, children under 12 DM4). Numerous companies offer **Hafenrundfahrten** (harbor cruises); **Kapitän Prüsse** (tel. 31 31 30) departs every half hour from Pier 3. **HADAG** (tel. 311 70 70; fax 31 17 07 10) offers more elaborate cruises of outlying areas in many combinations from Pier 2 (every 30min. 9:30am-6pm; DM15, children DM7.50). Inside the building behind Pier 6 resides the elevator to the Old Elbe Tunnel. With all of its machinery exposed, the building looks like a nautilus machine built for the gods. East of the docks near the copper dome of the **St. Katharinenkirche** (open daily 9am-4pm; organ concerts W at 12:30pm) across the river from Zippelhaus, lies the historic warehouse district known as the **Speicherstadt.** These elegant late 19th-century brick storehouses are filled with cargo, spices, and swarms of stevedores.

The copper spires of the **Rathaus,** a richly ornamented, neo-Renaissance monstrosity that serves as the political center of Hamburg, rises above the city center. *(Tours of the Rathaus in German every 30min. M-Th 10am-3pm, F-Su 10am-1pm. Tours in English and French every hr. M-Th 10:15am-3:15pm, F-Su 10:15am-1:15pm. Call 36 81 24 70 for details.)* The *Rathausmarkt* in front of it is the place for constant festivities, ranging from demonstrations to medieval fairs.

To the north of the *Rathaus,* the two **Alster lakes** are bordered by tree-lined paths. Elegant promenades and commercial facades surround **Binnenalster,** while windsurfers, sailboats, and paddleboats dominate the larger **Außenalster.** Ferries, more personal than the bigger Hamburg boats, sail from here (see **Orientation and Practical Information,** p. 247). To the west of the Alster near the university area, the **Planten un Blomen park** provides a bucolic sanctuary on the edge of the downtown. Dozens of obsessively well-planned and -trimmed flower beds surround two lakes and a handful of outdoor cafes. From May to September, daily performances ranging from Irish step-dancing to the police orchestra shake the outdoor **Musikpavillon;** there are also nightly **Wasserlichtkonzerte** (lighted fountain arrangements put to music; May-Aug. 10pm, Sept. 9pm).

After a fire destroyed much of old Hamburg in 1842, the city government launched an ambitious reconstruction project that created the current urban landscape, including its familiar six green copper spires. Just south of the *Rathaus,* off Ost-West-Str., rest the somber ruins of the old **St. Nikolaikirche.** The Allied bombing of 1943 flattened this early example of neo-Gothic architecture. City officials have left the ruins unrestored as a memorial to the horrors of war. In front of its bombed-out hull lies the **Hopfenmarkt,** home to a motley melange of *Imbiße,* book-, and clothes-stands.

The area behind the church is a zig-zagging maze of canals and bridges centered on the **Alte Börse** (old stock market). The buildings along the nearby **Trostbrücke** sport huge copper models of clipper ships on their spires—a reminder of the importance of sea-trade in the making of Hamburg's wealth. The gargantuan 18th-century **Große Michaelskirche** (tel. 37 67 81 00) is the mack daddy of all Hamburg churches. *(Tower and church open Apr.-Sept. M-Sa 9am-6pm, Su 11:30am-5:30pm; Oct.-Mar. M-Sa 10am-4:30pm, Su 11:30am-4:30pm. Church entrance DM1; elevator DM4, students and children DM2; crypt DM2.50 (for the living). Organ music Apr.-Aug. daily at noon and 5pm.)* It is affectionately and somewhat fearfully referred to as *"der Michael."* While the exterior is a bit imposing—the statue of St. Michael above the doorway mischievously grins at the passing tourists—the inside looks like a concert hall with its scalloped walls. *Der Michael's* bulbous Baroque tower is the official emblem of Hamburg; it's also the only one of the city's spires that can be ascended—by foot or by elevator. On weekends, the tower is used to project a multimedia presentation about Hamburg's millennial existence onto a five-meter-high screen (screenings Th-Su at 12:30, 1:30, 2:30, and 3:30pm; DM5, students and Hamburg Card holders DM2.50).

The pedestrian shopping zone, which stretches from the *Rathaus* to the *Hauptbahnhof* along **Mönckebergstraße,** is punctuated by two spires. The first belongs to the **St. Petrikirche,** site of the oldest church in Hamburg. *(Open M-F 9am-6pm, Sa 9am-5pm, Su 9am-noon and 1-5pm. English services first Su of every month at 5pm.)* Free concerts resonate through its Gothic arches every Wednesday evening at 5:15pm. The second church in the area is the **St. Jakobikirche** (tel. 536 60 79), known for its 14th-century **Arp-Schnittger organ** (open daily 10am-5pm).

Below Steinstr., the **Chilehaus** showcases architecture of a different generation. This striking *trompe l'oeil* office building is the work of Expressionist architect Fritz Höger, who also designed the **Sprinkenhof** building across the street. The Great Fire of 1842 consumed many splendid 17th- to 19th-century office buildings, which are carefully restored today. On summer afternoons, locals gather in the sidewalk cafes.

Beyond the city center, various monuments bear testimony to the Holocaust. In 1923, Communist leader Ernst Thälmann led a Mar. on the police headquarters, setting off a riot that resulted in the death of 61 protestors and 17 police officers. Thälmann was later murdered by the Nazis at Buchenwald and subsequently became the first martyr of the GDR. His life and times are chronicled at the **Ernst-Thälmann Gedenkstätte,** on Ernst-Thälmann-Platz (tel. 47 41 84; open Tu-F 10am-5pm, Sa-Su 10am-1pm; donation requested). In the midst of warehouses stands the **Gedenkstätte Janusz-Korczak-Schule,** Bullenhuser Damm 92 (tel. 78 32 95), S-Bahn to "Rothenburgsort." *(Open M-F 9am-4:30pm, Sa 10am-5pm. Free.)* Walk north from the station and make a right onto Bullenhuser Damm; the school is 200m down on the right. It serves as a memorial to 20 Jewish children brought here from Auschwitz for "testing" and murdered by the S.S. only hours before Allied troops arrived. Visitors are invited to plant a rose for the children in the flower garden behind the school. An idyllic agricultural village east of Hamburg provides the backdrop for the heinous **KZ** (concentration camp) **Neuengamme,** Jean-Doldier-Weg (tel. 723 10 31). Take S-Bahn #21 to "Bergdorff," then bus #227 (about 50min. from Hamburg). The bus stops at the base of the road on its way there, so watch for the sign; it makes several stops along Jean-Doldier-Weg on its return trip. Here the Nazis murdered approximately

50,000 prisoners through slave labor. In 1948, Hamburg prison authorities took over the camp and demolished all of the buildings to construct a German prison on the site; the mayor at the time believed that the facility would cleanse Neuengamme's sullied reputation. In 1989, the Hamburg Senate moved the prison in order to build a more appropriate memorial on the site. Banners inscribed with the names and death-dates of the victims hang in the **Haus des Gedenkens.**

MUSEUMS

Hamburg's many museums exhibit everything from erotica and high *Kunst* to history and folk art. The one- or three-day **Hamburg Card** (see p. 247) allows access to most of these museums, with the exception of the Deichtorhallen and the Erotic Art Museum. Hamburg also has a thriving and exciting contemporary art scene; pick up a list of the city's galleries and their current exhibits at either tourist office. Once a week, most museums offer a short presentation or lecture on topics ranging from Cezanne to Korean shamanism; pick up a copy of the brochure "Mittwochs" for details (Wednesdays at noon, DM4).

Hamburger Kunsthalle, Glockengiesserwall 1 (tel. 24 86 26 12), 1 block north of the *Hauptbahnhof.* This first-rate art museum is 3-pronged: the first part of the collection contains a superb exhibition of German and Dutch art, from the medieval era through the 19th century. The next assortment contains works by 19th-century French painters such as Millet, Courbet, Manet, and Monet—hey!. The newly built **Galerie der Gegenwart** displays Warhols, Picassos, and a pair of Levi's nailed to the wall. Open Tu-W and F-Su 10am-6pm, Th 10am-9pm. DM15, students DM10, family pass DM21.

Deichtorhallen Hamburg, Deichtorstr. 1-2 (tel. 32 10 30). U-Bahn to "Steinstr." Follow signs from the subway station; look for two entwined iron circles. Hamburg's contemporary art scene resides here in the former *Hauptbahnhof.* New exhibits each season showcase artists such as Warhol amidst mind-boggling architecture. Open Tu-Su 11am-6pm. DM10, students DM8.

Museum für Kunst und Gewerbe, Steintorpl. 1 (tel. 24 86 26 30), is a large yellow building one block south of the *Hauptbahnhof.* A fantastic, rich collection of handicrafts, china, and furnishings ranging from ancient Egyptian and Roman to Asian and *Jugendstil.* The collection is sure to inspire you to new heights of interior decoration. Open Tu-W and F-Su 10am-6pm, Th 10am-9pm. DM10, students and seniors DM6, Hamburg Card holders DM5, under 16 DM3.

Erotic Art Museum, Nobistor 12 (tel. 317 47 57). S-Bahn #1 and 3 to "Reeperbahn." Follow the silver sperm painted on the floor as they lead you through four floors of tactful iniquity. The first two floors examine postcard-sized sketches of assorted aristocrats and their voluptuous maids, while the top two focus on the art of bondage. The exhibit is in surprisingly good taste, as evidenced by the Haring originals on the 4th floor and the sonorous classical music. The Reeperbahn peep-show crowd tends to head elsewhere. Needless to say, a stimulating collection. Open Tu-Su 10am-midnight. DM15, students DM10.

Hamburgisches Museum für Völkerkunde, Rothenbaumchausee 64 (tel. 44 19 55 24). U-Bahn #1 to "Hallerstr." With two floors of glass cases brimming with weapons, clothing, and cooking utensils, the exhibit is a treasure trove of imperial plunder. Open Tu-W and F-Su 10am-6pm, Th 10am-9pm. DM7, family card DM14, students and seniors DM3.50, under 16 DM2. Half-price on Fridays.

Herzlichen Geburtstag!

Need a place to celebrate your birthday while on vacation? For DM75-100, the **Museum für Kunst und Gewerke** (see **Museums**, above) will lead you and your friends around its hallowed halls on appropriately themed tours. Topics include "amor vincit omnia" (depictions of love) or the indubitably more popular "in vino veritas," which traces the importance of wine and is, of course, followed by ample samplings of the "devil's elixir." *Zum wohl!*

SCHLESWIG-HOLSTEIN

ENTERTAINMENT

As the cultural capital of the North, Hamburg patronizes the arts with money and attention. Federal and municipal subsidies of high culture in Germany lower the ticket prices significantly; in addition, most box offices and concert halls offer generous student discounts. For DM20, the **Kulturkarte** offers steep discounts at theaters, concert halls, museums, and even clubs. Call 30 05 13 00 for details. The **Staatsoper,** Dammtorstr. 28, houses one of the best opera companies in Germany, churning out a steady stream of Bizet and Puccini along with more modern innovations. Tickets start at DM7 and can be bought by calling 35 17 21 (open M-F 11am-6:30pm, Sa 11am-2pm). Take U-Bahn #1 to "Stephansplatz." For the past decade, John Neumeier has directed the associated **ballet company,** transforming it into the acknowledged dance powerhouse of the nation. **Orchestras** abound—the **Philharmonie,** the **Nord-Deutscher-Rundfunk Symphony Orchestra,** and **Hamburg Symphonia,** the big three, all perform at the **Musikhalle** on Karl-Muck-Platz (tel. 34 69 20). Take U-Bahn to "Gänsemarkt" or "Messehallen." The Musikhalle also hosts **chamber music** concerts on a regular basis, as well as the odd jazz performance. Call 41 80 68 for tickets. Hamburg's many churches offer a wide variety of classical concerts (usually free)—see **Sights** above. The German **cabaret** tradition is still alive and kicking at a number of venues, including **Das Schiff,** (tel. 36 47 65) on Holzbrückestr. (take U-Bahn to "Rödeingsmarkt") and the drag theater **Pulverfass,** Pulverteich 12 (tel. 24 97 91; take U- and S-Bahn to "Berliner Tor"). Shows daily at 8:30 and 11:30pm, Friday and Saturday also at 2:30am. DM20 minimum.

The **Deutsches Schauspielhaus,** Kirchenallee 39 (tel. 24 87 13; student tickets 24 87 11 12; current schedule at http://www.is-europe.net/kultur/schauspielhaus.de) is located across from the *Hauptbahnhof.* The theatre presents a full venue—Ibsen, Brecht, Fassbinder—even *A Clockwork Orange.* Box office open 10am-showtime. The **Thalia,** Alstertor 1 (tel. 32 26 66; http://www.thalia-theater.de; take S-Bahn to "Jungfernstieg"), sets up adventurous avant-garde musicals, plays, and staged readings. They also have regular performances in the **Kunsthalle** (see **Museums,** above). Most theaters sell half-price tickets to students at the regular box office as well as at the evening box office, which generally opens one hour before performance times. In July and August, many theaters close down, but only to make way for the **Hamburger Sommer** festival of the arts. Pick up a schedule at any kiosk. The **Theaterkarten Last-Minute** kiosk in the Hanse-Viertel tourist office (see **Tourist and Financial Services,** p. 250) sells tickets for regular and special events. The **English Theater,** Lerchenfeld 14 (tel. 227 70 89; take U-Bahn to "Mundsburg"), entertains both natives and tourists with its English-language productions (performances M-Sa at 7:30pm, matinees Tu and F at 11am).

The movie scene in Hamburg is dauntingly diverse, ranging from the latest American blockbusters to independent film projects by students at the university. The **Kommunales Kino Metropolis,** Dammtorstr. 30a (tel. 34 23 53), a non-profit cinema, features new independent films and revivals from all corners of the globe, focusing on pieces from the U.S., France, Germany, and Italy. **Kino 3001,** Schanzenstr. 75 (tel. 43 76 79; take U-Bahn to "Sternschanze"), also shows artsy alternative flicks.

Live music prospers in Hamburg, satisfying all tastes. Superb traditional jazz for both the amateur and the connoisseur swing at the **Cotton Club** (see **Nightlife,** below) and on Sunday mornings at the Fish Auction Hall of the **Fischmarkt.** Rock groups jam at **Große Freiheit,** Große Freiheit 36 (tel. 31 42 63), and at **Docks,** Spielbudenpl. 19 (tel. 319 43 78). The renowned **Fabrik,** Barnerstr. 36 in Altona (tel. 39 10 70), features everything from funk to punk. Cover runs about DM12. For more info, check the 'zines *Szene, Oxmox,* or *Prinz* (available at newsstands for DM5; hostels keep free copies).

The **Hafengeburtstag,** or "Harbor Birthday," is the city's biggest bash. Hamburg owes its prosperity to May 7, 1189, when Friedrich Barbarossa granted the town the right to open a port. The city still celebrates the anniversary for a weekend in early May, featuring music and other events. In 1999, the 810th birthday party will run May

7-9. For a month, three times every year, the **Heiligengeistfeld Square** just north of the Reeperbahn metamorphoses into the **Dom,** a titanic amusement park with fun-booths, kiosks, and merry-go-rounds. The **Frühlingsmarkt** (Spring Fair) is held from the end of Apr. until the end of May; the **Hummelfest** throughout August; and the **Dommarkt** throughout November. This festival's offerings of beer and wild parties have submerged its historical connection to the church.

NIGHTLIFE

The Sternschanze, St. Pauli, and Altona areas virtually monopolize Hamburg's crazy nightlife scene. The infamous **Reeperbahn,** a long boulevard, is the spinal cord of St. Pauli; sex shops, strip joints, peep shows, and other establishments seeking to satisfy any libidinal desires compete for space along the sidewalks. Crowds meander up and down the Reeperbahn like ants, occasionally crossing the street to curiously peek into a shop window or dodge one of the many greaseballs who beckon passersby to enter the "erotic" interiors of their stripclubs. Though the Reeperbahn is reasonably safe for both men and women, it is not recommended to walk alone or, if a woman, venture to the adjacent streets. Herbertstr., Hamburg's only remaining legalized prostitution strip, runs parallel to the Reeperbahn, and is open only to men over 18. The prostitutes flaunting their flesh behind large windows on Herbertstr. are licensed professionals required to undergo health inspections, while the streetwalkers are venereal roulette wheels. Needless to say, men (mostly) and women flock to this district to revel all night long in an atmosphere simmering with sultry energy. Although the sleaze peddlers commodify women, they have failed to stifle the vital spark of the many clubs that cater to those not seeking sex for sale. Indeed, St. Pauli houses many of Hamburg's best bars and clubs.

Students trying to avoid the debauchery of the Reeperbahn head north to the spiffy streets of **Sternschanze** and **Altona.** Unlike St. Pauli, these areas are centered around cafes and weekend extravaganzas of an alternative flavor. The sheer artistic quality of the posters and the graffiti adorning the exterior and interior of the cafes bespeak an intensity and coherence that far surpasses the Reeperbahn's superficiality. Much of the Hamburg gay scene is located in the **St. Georg** area of the city, near Berliner Tor. Gay and straight bars in this area are more welcoming and classier than those in the Reeperbahn. In general, clubs open late and close late, with some techno and trance clubs remaining open until noon the following day. *Szene, Oxmox,* and *Prinz* list events and parties. The *Dorn Rosa* journal lists lesbian and gay events.

⊛**Rote Flora,** Schulterblatt 71 (tel. 439 54 13). Held together both figuratively and literally by the graffiti and posters which cover all of its vertical surfaces, this venue serves as the nucleus of the Sternschanze scene. A cafe (and motorbike repair shop!) during the week, the Flora lights up on weekends, with huge club and drum 'n' bass parties inside the spooky and decrepit shell of an old mansion; political films, such as the wittily titled "Trainstopping" (about efforts to stop the shipment of nuclear waste via Germany's railway), are also shown in this squatter's community center. Cafe open M-F 5-10pm; weekend cover DM8+, opening times vary (call ahead for a schedule).

Große Freiheit 36/Kaiser Keller, Große Freiheit 36 (tel. 31 42 63). U-Bahn to "St. Pauli"; S-Bahn to "Reeperbahn." The Beatles played on the small stage downstairs during their early years. Today the Wu-Tang Clan stomp about on the big stage upstairs. Go figure. Call for show times and ticket prices. Open daily.

Molotow, Spielbudenpl. 5 (tel. 31 08 45), parallel to the Reeperbahn. This basement lives at the fringes of Hamburg's club scene. While mildly committed to funk with "Der Motor Booty Club" playing every Sunday, the club's DJ spins an eclectic mix of hip-hop, garage, salsa, and industrial Th-Sa from 10pm onwards. Cover DM10.

Mojo Club, Reeperbahn 1 (tel. 319 19 99), has more attitude than it knows what to do with. Called the best club in Germany by MTV. Go Mojo. The attached **Jazz Café** attracts the trendy. Features dance-floor jazz and acid-jazz. DM10 cover on weekends. Open W-Th 10pm-4am, F-Su 11pm-4am.

Insults for Sale

The concept of free speech in Germany does not imply *cost-free* speech. While doling out compliments requires no budget, dropping insults will unload your wallet in no time. Public humiliation in Germany carries such destructive force that officials have created an insult price list. Angry, offended, or drunk budget travelers should beware. The heaviest fines are incurred by mouth-flappers who put down a female police officer's respectability: belting out *Trottel in Uniform* (fool in uniform) costs DM3000, while the lesser insult *Dumme Kuh* (dumb cow) requires a mere DM1200 payoff. Call any uniformed official *Idiot* (idiot), and you'll be out a whopping DM3000. The budget traveler's insult, *Holzkopf* (wood-headed), goes for DM1500. Equivalent insults in English are not exempt; stories abound of policemen who've doled out thousands of *Marks* in fines to tourists who think that Germans don't understand what "asshole" means. We tell you this merely as a warning—and prices, of course, are subject to change, you idiot.

Cave, Reeperbahn 6. Hamburg's house for "house" (meta-house!), Cave spins nothing but wild, raving techno at a hundred beats per minute with enough bass to turn your eardrums inside out. More than a great club, Cave is also one of Hamburg's best accommodation deals. In exchange for a DM15 cover charge, you can stay from opening time at 1am until the close at noon without having to worry about any curfew. Breakfast not included.

Cotton Club, Alter Steinweg 10 (tel. 34 38 78; fax 348 01 23); U-bahn to "Rödingsmarkt." Gives a different jazz, swing, or skittle band a chance every night. Smoky atmosphere, mostly older crowd. Great jazz. Cover varies, usually DM10. Open M-Sa 8pm-midnight. Shows start at 8:30.

Logo, Grindelallee 5 (tel. 410 56 58). If you can play it live, you can play it at Logo. Nightly live music at this smoky club near the university gives locals a chance to be rock stars. Cover varies. Open nightly from 9:30pm.

Front, Heidencampsweg 32 (tel. 23 25 23), U-Bahn #3 to "Berliner Tor." House and jungle for Hamburg's gay and lesbian scene interspersed with straight people just trying to stay hip. Cover DM10-12. Open W and F-Sa 11pm.

Frauenkneipe, Stresemannstr. 60 (tel. 43 63 77), S-Bahn #21 or #3 to "Holstenstr.," or bus #11. A bar and meeting place for women. Visitors who are disconcerted by the Reeperbahn and drunken-sailor scene will discover here that red-lighters do not represent the whole of Hamburg. Primarily a place for women, gay or straight. Open M-F and Su 8pm-1am, Sa 9pm-3am.

■ Lübeck

With a skyline of neo-classical townhouses punctuated by 13th-century copper spires, Lübeck is easily Schleswig-Holstein's most beautiful city. Amidst the medieval cobblestone streets and tree-lined river promenades of the *Altstadt,* one would hardly guess that the entire city was almost razed to the ground in World War II, yet Lübeck's present appearance is thanks to a painstaking reconstruction effort undertaken in the 1950s. As a result, the *Altstadt* has successfully staved off inroads by modern architecture, giving it a slightly anachronistic feeling. In its heyday, Lübeck was the capital of the Hanseatic League, wielding a considerable amount of power through its control of goods across Northern Europe. More recently, the city was home to literary giants Heinrich and Thomas Mann. While no longer a center of political and commercial influence, Lübeck today retains the pulse and energy of a bustling business city beyond the bubble-gum and ice-cream tourist industry.

ORIENTATION AND PRACTICAL INFORMATION

Because water surrounds Lübeck, getting into serious navigational trouble requires getting wet first. However, getting around Lübeck can be a very Kafka-esque experience, particularly at night when everything looks the same and you're never sure

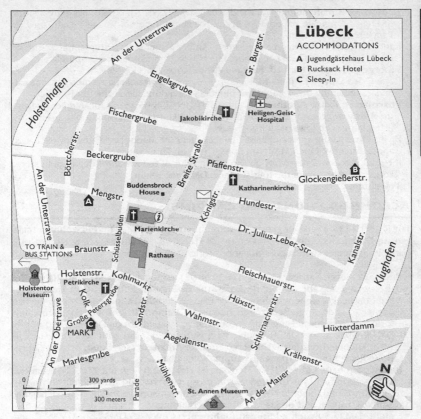

Lübeck
ACCOMMODATIONS
A Jugendgästehaus Lübeck
B Rucksack Hotel
C Sleep-In

where you are or whether you've been there before. When lost, a good rule of thumb is to head uphill, returning to Königstr. and Breitestr., the two main streets.

Trains: Lübeck is a main transfer point for crossing the former East/West border. Frequent departures for Hamburg (40min.), Schwerin (1½hr.), Rostock (2hr.), and Berlin (4hr.).

Public Transportation: Although the *Altstadt* is easily seen on foot, Lübeck has an excellent bus network. The **ZOB** (central bus station) is across from the train station. A single ride costs DM2.80, children DM1.50. **Mehrfahrkarten,** books of 6 tickets, cost DM14. The best value is the **Lübeck Card**—it's valid on all local buses, including those going to Travemünde, and also offers significant discounts at most museums (1 day DM9, 3 days DM18).

Ferries: Quandt Linie (tel. 777 79) has cruises around the *Altstadt* and harbor every 30min. from 10am to 6pm daily from the bridge in front of the *Holstentor* (DM10, students DM8). Best deals to Scandinavia are found in Travemünde (see p. 262).

Taxi: tel. 811 22. Available 24hr., but best to call at least 30min. ahead.

Car Rental: Hertz, Willy-Brandt-Allee 1 (tel. 717 47), by the train station, next to the Mövenpick hotel. Open M-F 7am-6pm, Sa 7am-1pm, Su 9-10am.

Bike Rental: Buy Cycle, Mühlenbrücke 1 (tel. 757 57), *rents* bikes, despite the name. DM12 per day. ID required. Open M-Sa 10am-6:30pm.

Tourist Office: Avoid the tourist office in the train station; they charge DM4 for maps and rob you blind for booking a room (DM5 plus 10% of your hotel bill!). Instead, head for the helpful office in the *Altstadt* at Breitestr. 62 (tel. 122 54 13 or 122 54 14; fax 122 54 19). They don't book rooms, but staff can point you in the right direction and give you a free map. Open M-F 9:30am-6pm, Sa-Su 10am-2pm.

Bookstore: Buchhandlung Weiland, Königstr. 67a (tel. 16 00 60), has a great stock of English-language paperbacks in the basement. Open M-W and F 9am-7pm, Th 9am-8pm, Sa 9am-4pm.

Laundromat: McWash, on the corner of An der Mauer and Hüxterdamm. Wash 7kg DM7. Dry 10kg DM1.20 per 15min. Open M-Sa 6am-11pm. No Hamburglars.

Emergency: Police, tel. 110. **Fire** and **Ambulance,** tel. 112.

Rape Crisis Line: tel. 70 46 40. Pick up a copy of **Zimtzicke,** a women's events calendar containing other important numbers and addresses, at the tourist office.

Pharmacies: Adler Apotheke, Breitestr. 71 (tel. 798 85 15), is located across from the *Marienkirche.* Open M-F 8am-7pm, Sa 8:30am-4pm. Late-night pharmacies are listed in the windows of all *Apotheken.*

Post Office: Königstr. 44-46, 23552 Lübeck, near the Marktplatz. Currency exchange and 24hr. ATM. Open M-W 8am-6pm, Th-F 8am-7pm, Sa 8am-2pm.

Internet Access: Cyberb@r, on the fourth floor of the *Karstadt* department store, across the street from the tourist office. DM5 per 30min.

Telephone Code: 0451.

ACCOMMODATIONS AND CAMPING

For longer stays, consider renting a room in an apartment. The **Mitwohnzentrale Home Company,** Glockengießerstr. 28 (tel. 194 45; http://www.HomeCompany.de), arranges such accommodations (open M-F 9am-1pm).

⊛**Rucksack Hotel,** Kanalstr. 70 (tel./fax 70 68 92), on the north side of the *Altstadt* by the canal. From the station, walk past the *Holstentor,* left on An der Untertrave, right on Beckergrube which becomes Pfaffstr. and then Glockengießerstr. On the corner of Glockengießerstr. and Kanalstr. (20min.). Bright, cheery rooms in a former factory-turned-alternative cooperative. 10-bed dorms DM24, 6-bed dorms DM26, 4-bed dorms DM28; double with bath DM80, quad with bath DM136. Self-serve kitchen. Breakfast DM8, served in Café Affenbrot (see **Food,** below). Sheets DM6. Reception 9am-1pm and 3-10pm. Wheelchair access.

Jugendgästehaus Lübeck (HI), Mengstr. 33 (tel. 702 03 99; fax 770 12). From the train station head for the *Holstentor,* cross the river and make a left on An der Untertrave, and then right on Mengstr. This superb hostel is ideally located, hosting doubles, triples, and quads in its historic building. 3- or 4-bed dorms DM29 first night, DM26.50 each additional night, guests over 26 DM37.50, DM35; 2-bed dorms DM31, DM28.50, over 26 DM40, DM37.50. Breakfast included. Lockout midnight, but guests over 18 can get a key. Call ahead.

Sleep-In (CVJM), Große Petersgrube 11 (tel. 789 82; fax 789 97), near the *Petrikirche,* in the *Altstadt,* 10min. from the station. Walk past the *Holstentor,* turn right on An der Obertrave, left on Große Petersgrube, look to the right for the sign. Germany's answer to the YMCA comes complete with pub and *Fußball.* In the old town, 10min. from the station. Whip up some slop in the guest kitchen. 10-bed dorms DM15; doubles DM40. Apartment-style accommodation DM30 per person. Breakfast DM5. Sheets DM5. Reception M-F 8am-5pm, Sa-Su 8am-noon.

Baltic Hotel Priebe, Hansestr. 11 (tel. 855 75 or 812 71), across the street from the *ZOB.* Small but clean rooms located 2min. from the train station and 5min. from the *Altstadt.* Telephone and TV in every room. DM50-110, filling breakfast buffet included. Reception 8am-10pm.

Camping: Campingplatz Lübeck-Schönböcken, Steinraderdamm 12 (tel. 89 30 90 or 89 22 87), on a somewhat distant grassy site northwest of the city. Showers, washing machines, and cooking facilities available. From the *ZOB,* bus #8 (direction: "Bauernweg") to the end; then walk 300m along Steinraderdamm toward the city. DM7 per person, DM6 per tent.

FOOD

While the rest of Germany swims in beer, Lübeck drowns in coffee, with no point more than a saucer's throw away from a caffeine fix. Of course this is still Germany, so Lübeck's cafes function as the nightlife venue of choice by staying open until the wee hours serving beer. Hipper, more popular cafes lie along **Mühlenstr.** in the eastern part of the city. A local specialty is *Lübecker Marzipan,* a delectable candy made with sugar and almonds. The confectionery **I.G. Niederegger,** Breitestr. 89 (tel. 530 11 26), across from the *Rathaus,* is renowned for its beautifully shaped marzipan. The **Mädchen und Frauencafé,** on the second floor of the women's center at An der Untertrave 97 (tel. 122 57 46), is a friendly women-only cafe that serves coffee, tea, and cake, and hosts a "women's breakfast" (W-Th 10am-1pm; also open Su 3-8pm). The **Co-op** supermarket is at the corner of Sand- and Schmiedstr. (open M-F 8:30am-7pm, Sa 9am-4pm).

Tipasa, Schlumacherstr. 12-14 (tel. 706 04 51). The hip waitstaff leisurely delivers pizza, pasta, and vegetarian dishes to a hungry students. Try the Tipasa-Topf, a spicy stew of tomatoes, beef, mushrooms, and peppers (DM11). Pizza DM6.50-11. Open Su-Th noon-1am, F-Sa noon-2am; kitchen closes 30min. before closing time.

Café Affenbrot, Kanalstr. 70 (tel. 721 93), on the corner of Glockengießerstr., is a popular vegetarian cafe. Dine on *Salattasche* (salad in pita bread; DM6) at tables made from old-fashioned sewing machines. Vegetarian meals DM8-11. Open daily 9am-midnight, but the kitchen closes at 11:30pm.

Café Amadeus, Königstr. 26 (tel. 70 53 57). If the name conjures up images of a sophisticated cafe in Vienna, think again—the decor is as cheesy as the pizza. Good Italian meals for DM6-14. Open Su-Th 8am-12:30am, F-Sa 8am-2am.

SIGHTS

On the eve of Palm Sunday, 1942, Allied bombers flattened most of Lübeck. After the war, the city used Marshall Plan funds to begin the daunting task of renovating the leveled *Altstadt.* The core of the *Altstadt* is the **Rathaus,** a striking 13th-century structure of glazed black and red bricks. *(DM4, students DM2. Rathaus tours leave M-F at 11am and noon.)* Behind the Marktplatz towers the schizophrenic **Marienkirche,** begun in the Romanesque style around 1200 but finished as a Gothic cathedral in 1350. *(Open daily 10am-6pm; winter 10am-4pm. Services Su at 10am and 6pm.)* Completely gutted in the 1942 raid, the church's interior has been carefully restored. The church's music comes from the **largest mechanical organ in the world.** Free 10-minute soundbites of world-famous organ concerts occur daily at noon; prices vary for Saturday evening organ concerts (6:30pm). The saints literally come marching in, also at noon, on the church's newly restored **astronomical clock.** The famous medieval **Totentanzbild** (death-dance mural) used to encircle the chapel opposite the astronomical clock, but it was destroyed in 1942; all that remains is a reproduction, including the *Kaiser* holding hands with skeletons representing the plague.

Opposite the Marienkirche is the **Buddenbrookshaus,** Mengstr. 4 (tel. 122 41 92), where literary giants Heinrich and Thomas Mann lived as children, and from which Thomas Mann's 1911 novel took its name. *(Open daily 10am-5pm. DM7, students DM4.)* The house is now a museum dedicated to the life and works of both brothers. Thomas's works expressed his fierce opposition to Nazism and a profound ambivalence about German culture. While Thomas received the Nobel Prize for Literature in 1929, his brother also wrote a number of important works including *Professor Unrat,* on which the famous Marlene Dietrich film *Der Blaue Engel* (The Blue Angel) is based. The house holds special summer events, including a "literary walk" through Lübeck on weekends from June to September (DM12, students DM10); pick up a schedule of events at the museum.

The medieval **Jacobikirche,** farther north on Breitestr., traditionally a church for seafarers, contains a beautifully ornamented organ. *(Open daily 10am-6pm; services Su at 9:40am.)* Behind the Jacobikirche stands the **Heiligen-Geist-Hospital,** Am Koberg 9. The long corridor of tiny cabins was built as a hospital in 1280 and served as an old-age home from 1518 to 1970. The neighboring **cloister** contains a small medieval mural. *(Open Tu-Su 10am-5pm; Oct.-Apr. Tu-Su 10am-4pm. Free.)* Heading south on Königstr., the **Katharinenkirche,** a 14th-century church that served as a Franciscan monastery, now houses modern art exhibitions including terracotta sculptures by Barlach. Note the cheerfully ornate depictions of misery and death. At the nearby **Behnhaus** and **Drägerhaus** museums (Königstr. 11, tel. 122 41 48), modern art clashes beauti-fully with the neo-classical architecture of an 18th-century townhouse. *(Open Tu-Su 10am-5pm; Oct.-Mar. 10am-4pm. DM5, students DM3. Free first Friday of every month.)* The first floor features works by contemporary Lübeck artists, while the second houses a nifty collection featuring Edvard Munch, Max Liebermann, and Max Beckmann.

Between the inner city and the station is the massive **Holstentor**, one of the four gates built in the 15th century and the symbol of Lübeck. Inside, the **Museum Hol-stentor** (tel. 122 41 29) displays exhibits on ship construction, trade, and quaint local implements of torture. *(Open Apr.-Sept. Tu-Su 10am-5pm; Oct.-Mar. 10am-4pm. DM5, stu-dents DM3, under 19 DM1.)* The **Petrikirche**, east on Schmiederstr., is about 750 years old. An elevator climbs to the top of the steeple for a sweeping view. *(Church open daily noon-7pm. Tower open Apr.-Oct. 9am-7pm. Admission DM3.50, students DM2, Lübeck Card-holders DM2.50.)* At the southern end of the inner island lies the **Dom**, on Domkirch-hof (tel. 747 04), founded by Heinrich the Lion in 1173 as evidenced by his trademark lion statue. *(Open Apr.-Sept. 10am-6pm; Mar. and Oct. 10am-5pm; Nov. 10am-4pm; Dec.-Feb. 10am-3pm. Services Sa at 6pm and Su at 10:40am. Free.)*

The **Museum für Puppentheater**, Kleine Petersgrube 4-6 (tel. 786 26), just below the Petrikirche, has 13 rooms filled with more than 700 puppets. *(Open daily 10am-6pm. DM6, students DM5, children DM3.)* The **St. Annen-Museum**, St.-Annen-Str. 15 (tel. 122 41 37), off Mühlenstr., displays crosses, tablets, and other paraphernalia of the opiate of the masses, as well as an exhibit recounting Lübeck's cultural history. *(Open Tu-Su 10am-5pm. DM5, students, under 19 DM1. Free first Friday of every month).*

ENTERTAINMENT AND NIGHTLIFE

Lübeck is world-famous for its **organ concerts**. The **Marienkirche** offers several per week from April to December, mostly on Thursdays and Saturdays (DM9, students DM6). From June to September, the **Jacobikirche** and the **Dom** offer a joint program of concerts every Friday at 8pm (DM10, students DM6). The smaller **Propsteikirche Herz Jesy**, Parade 4, has free concerts Wednesdays at 8pm; call 328 58 for details. For entertainment listings, pick up *Piste, Szene, Zentrum*, or (for women) *Zimtzicke* from the tourist office. Lübeck's two major theaters offer generous student discounts: the huge **Theater Lübeck** puts on operas, symphonies, and mainstream German and American plays, while the smaller **Theater Combinale**, Hüxstr. 115 (tel. 788 17), gets down with avant-garde works (tickets DM15-20).

Finnegan, Mengstr. 42 (tel. 711 10), an Irish pub, serves Guinness and other dark, yeasty beers guaranteed to make you go Bragh the next morning. Very popular with the locals (most drinks DM4; open weekdays 4pm-1am, weekends 4pm-whenever). While most Lübeckers shun clubs like the plague, **Bad Taste**, an der Untertrave 3a, draws healthy crowds to watch local bands rock out under camouflage netting and disco balls. There's something obnoxious every night, with weekends reserved for particularly vicious events like tattooing and piercing. Times and cover vary.

■ Near Lübeck: Travemünde

Travemünde, 15km north of Lübeck, is an attractive spa town known for its beaches and casinos. Boutiques line the town streets, *Strandkorben* (wicker chairs) clutter the stretch of beach near the north pier, and the monolithic Hotel Maritim towers above it all. The **Aqua-Top**, Strandpromenade 1b (tel. 804 42), a fun-filled glass com-plex of spas and swimming pools, will pamper you with saunas, massages, and water-slides. (Open daily 10am-9pm. Day pass DM16, children DM8; with sauna DM22, children DM16; massage extra.) Across the inlet in Priwall, the four-mast trade ship **Passat** is moored (open May-Sept. 18 daily 10am-4:30pm; admission DM4, students and children DM2). To get there, take the ferry that leaves from near the corner of the *Strandpromenade* and *Travepromenade* (every 15min., DM0.60). From the deck, look back on the 16th-century **lighthouse** situated on Trelleborg Allee (tours Mar.-Sept. W at 5pm; admission DM2). **Travemündewoche** takes place every year in the last week of July and includes outdoor concerts and sailing activities.

Travemünde is easily accessible from Lübeck by **train** (25min., every hr.) or by **bus** #30 or 31 from the *ZOB* (45min., day pass valid); both the train and bus cost DM2.80 each way. Trains also run from Hamburg (1¼hr., every hr.). There are three main train/bus stops: **Skandinavienkai** accesses the Scandinavia-bound ferries, **Travemünde-Hafen** is close to the town center, and **Travemünde-Strand** leads directly to the beach. **Quandt Linie** (tel. (0451) 777 99) runs harbor tours every hour from the Travepromenade (DM14, children DM12). Another option is to go on a **duty-free cruise:** for DM1 or DM2, several companies will chauffeur you around the Baltic for an hour or two, all the while enticing you with tax-free shopping. **TT-Line** runs to Trelleborg, Sweden for as low as DM69 return (departures Su-Th at 10am and 10pm). For more information, contact **TT-Line** in Hamburg (tel. (040) 360 14 42), or **Nordische Touristik Information** in Travemünde (tel. 66 88; open M-F 9am-5pm). The **tourist office,** Strandpromenade 1b (tel. 804 30; fax 804 60), is located in the Aqua-Top building that faces the beach. Walk from the Travemünde-Strand station down Bertlingstr. and turn right on Strandpromenade. Staff finds rooms free of charge or gives you an accommodations list (open M-Sa 10am-6pm, Su 10am-1pm). The **post office** on Rose has a 24hr. **ATM** (post office open M-F 8:30am-12:30pm and 2:30-6pm, Sa 8:30am-noon). Travemünde's **telephone code** is 04502.

The **Jugend-Freizeitstätte Priwall,** Mecklenberger Landstr. 69 (tel. 25 76; fax 46 20), is right across the inlet. Take the ferry to Priwall, walk along the beach path for 300m; it's on your right. Surrounded by a standing army of green tents, the hostel makes you feel like a member of the *Bundeswehr.* They also rent bikes to guests for DM8 per day. (DM14, over 26 DM19. Kurtax DM2-5. Breakfast DM6. Sheets DM5. Reception 2-10pm. Curfew Su-Th 10pm, F-Sa midnight. Open Apr. to mid-Oct. Call ahead.) Pitch your tent next door at **Strandcamping-Priwall,** Dünenweg 3 (tel. 28 35; DM9 per tent, DM7 per person; reception 9am-noon and 3-7pm; open Apr.-Sept.). Decent fast food and bakeries decorate the downtown beach path; similar options lie along Düneweg on the Priwall.

■ Ratzeburg

The island town of Ratzeburg, founded in the 11th century by Heinrich the Lion, lies 24km from Lübeck in the middle of the Ratzeburger See. The natural beauty of the town and the surrounding area hypnotically draws bicyclists and hikers, along with the German Olympic crew team, which trains daily on the huge lake surrounding the island. Other than the scenery, Ratzeburg's main attraction is its art culture—two small but significant museums offer unique collections by 20th-century artists A. Paul Weber and Ernst Barlach, who lived in the town, as well as Günter Grass, who resided in the nearby town of Behlendorf.

Weber's astounding, satirical lithographs and watercolors are on permanent display at the **A.-Paul-Weber-Haus,** Domhof 5 (tel. 80 83 26; open Tu-Su 10am-1pm and 2-5pm; admission DM3, students DM1). Ratzeburg's **Dom,** built by Heinrich the Lion soon after he colonized Schleswig-Holstein, houses galleries containing religious works. (Open Apr.-Sept. daily 10am-noon and 2-6pm; Oct.-Mar. Tu-Su 10am-noon and 2-4pm; services Su at 10:15am.) Between the Weber-Haus and the Dom lies the **Kreismuseum** (regional museum; tel. 123 25), filled with a random mishmash of Biedermeier furniture, art by Weber, Grass, and Barlach, and the obligatory pointy Prussian helmet display (open Tu-Su 10am-1pm and 2-5pm; DM2, students DM1). A larger collection of Barlach's work sits across the Marktplatz in the **Ernst-Barlach-Gedenkstätte,** Barlachpl. 3 (tel. 37 89); haunting, meditative bronzes and manuscripts are on display (open Tu-Su 10am-1pm and 2-5pm; DM3, students DM1.50; closed Dec.-Feb.).

The **train station** is a 30-minute walk from the Marktplatz; alternatively, take bus #2 to "Marktplatz." Hourly trains connect Ratzeburg with Lübeck (20min.) and, via Lüneburg, with Hamburg (1hr.). Join the hordes of nature-lovers by renting a **bike** from the **Fahrrad Verleih Schloßwiese** (tel. 44 66) on the lake, just past the tourist office (DM8 per 3hr., DM15 per day; open daily 10am-6pm). A combined bike rental and ferry ticket (DM12) will take you to the other side of the lake, where there are additional bike paths. The **tourist office**, Schloßwiese 7 (tel. 80 00 80; fax 53 27), is between the train station and the Marktplatz. From the station, head down Bahnhof-sallee until it becomes Lüneburger Damm (15min.); it's in a huge parking lot on the left. They book **private rooms** (DM30-40) for free (open M-W and F 9am-5pm, Th 9am-6pm, Sa-Su 10am-4pm). The **post office** is at Herrenstr. 12 (open M-F 8am-noon and 2-6pm, Sa 8am-noon). The **telephone code** is 04541.

To reach Ratzeburg's **Jugendherberge (HI)**, Fischerstr. 20 (tel. 37 07; fax 847 80), take any bus from the train station to the Marktplatz, or embark on a 45-minute journey along Bahnhofsallee as it becomes Lüneburger Damm, Unter den Linden, Herrenstr., and finally empties out into the main square. Continuing straight, turn right onto Große Wallstr. and follow it until it becomes Fischerstr.; it's at the end of the street. (DM20, over 26 DM25. Sheets DM6. Laundry DM6, soap included. Reception 7am-10pm. Curfew 10pm, but you can ring the bell until 11:30pm.) Groceries await at the **Edeka Aktiv Markt** on the corner of Herrenstr. and Barlachstr. (open M-F 8am-7pm, Sa 7:30am-4pm).

■ Lauenburg

A geographic anomaly, Lauenburg is located at the intersection of three *Bundesländer:* its native Schleswig-Holstein; Niedersachsen; and Mecklenburg-Vorpommern, formerly part of East Germany. Once a minor light of the Hanseatic League, 800-year-old Lauenburg still shines quietly, with picture-book ferry docks, half-timbered houses painted with posies, and winding cobblestone streets. Easy transport to Lauenburg is one of many remnants of the town's past; the town earned its bread as a stop on the great medieval canals connecting the mines of Lüneburger Heide to the salt-starved towns of the Baltic coast. Lauenburg is still on the train route from Lüneburg to Lübeck, with connections to Hamburg and Berlin at either end. Lüneburg is a mere 15 minutes away, while the journey to Lübeck takes just under an hour (hourly trains in both directions, 5am-11pm).

The Lauenburg *Altstadt* consists of two halves—the **Unterstadt** (lower city) down by the river, and the **Oberstadt** up above, joined by pathways of narrow steps. The apartment buildings of modern Lauenburg loom above. Most of the sights are located in the *Unterstadt*, an uninterrupted half-timbered strip built over a stone embankment (the *Sperrmauer*). The **Uferpromenade** runs along the river's edge, and is ideal for walking or biking. Lauenburg's houses, many of which date back to the 16th century, are distinctive for their elaborately painted wood-and-brick framework. The **Mensingschehaus**, Elbstr. 49, off the Kirchplatz, is one of very few survivors of a catastrophic 1616 fire that charred the Duke, his young wife, and most of the posher houses in town. The former **Rathaus**, Elbstr. 59, stands tall and now houses the **Elb-schiffahrts museum** (tel. 512 51), which documents the town's shipping industry (open Mar.-Oct. daily 10am-1pm and 2-5pm; Nov.-Feb. W and F-Su 10am-1pm and 2-4:30pm). The house at Elbstr. 97, only about 6 ft. wide, is one of the smallest in Germany; if you've ever wondered what a house would look like in a fun-house mirror, look no further. You can even rent it if you really want to live out your Grimms' fairy tale fantasies; call 522 20 for details.

In the center of the *Altstadt*, the **Maria-Magdalena Kirche**, Kirchpl. 1, stands tall and solid over the city; the church tower was a signal to returning sailors that they were home at long last. (Open Th-Tu 9am-5pm; services Sa 5pm, Su 10am.) The 13th-century building was commandeered by the French for a celebration in May 1804 on the day Napoleon crowned himself Emperor. To the left of the church is a pretty 17th-century square, filled with sagging *Fachwerk* houses whose beams are inscribed with religious messages.

Above the church in the Oberstadt's Amtsplatz is the **Schloßturm,** built between 1457 and 1477. After the town burned down in 1616, the tower served as a state-of-the-art vantage point from which vigilant watchdogs observed the town burning down six more times. Recognizing the observation post's uselessness, the town has closed the tower. Nothing remains from the **Schloß** except one wing, now used to house municipal offices.

To reach the town from the train station, cross the bridge and turn left; the *Altstadt* will appear about 20m after you pass the giant **Hitzler** (don't forget the z!) **wharfs.** Alternatively, bus #138 makes the 15-minute trip from the train station to the ZOB (bus station) in the Oberstadt (every hr., M-F 6am-8pm, Sa 8am-3pm). The **tourist office** (tel. 59 09 81) sits across from the *Schloßturm* on Amtsplatz. (Open M-Tu and F8:30am-12:30pm and 1:30-4:30pm; W 8:30am-12:30pm and 1-3pm; Th 8:30am-12:30pm and 1:30-6pm—got that?) The **Jugendherberge Lauenburg (HI),** Am Sportpl. 7 (tel. 25 98), is a pleasant hike—if a long one (20min.)—from the *Altstadt.* At the fork in the road at Elbstr. 20, follow the "Radweg zur Jugendherberge" sign left to the *Uferpromenade* (river path). After about 10 minutes the paved promenade will end; make a right here onto Kuhgrund (unmarked). Turn left at the *Jugendherberge* sign and take the dirt path through the woods (5min.). The hostel is the big brick building at the top of the hill. The brightly colored hostel, packed with school groups, offers game rooms with ping pong and a TV. (DM19, over 26 DM23.50. Breakfast included. Sheets DM6. Closed Dec. 15-Jan. 15. Call ahead. The hostel also plays host to a summer cooking school; DM7 to test the budding talents of young chefs.) *Pensionen* abound in the *Altstadt,* mostly closer to the train station; look for "Fremdenzimmer" or "Zimmer frei" signs. The tourist office puts out a **guide** (DM1) listing all accommodations, available at the blue *Automaten* scattered around the town. Private rooms run DM25-55.

The outdoor cafés on the waterfront tend to cater to the wealthier tourists who frequent the river cruises (fish dishes DM16-25). Cheaper eats can be had in the Oberstadt's pedestrian zone. There is also an **Aldi** supermarket there (open M-F 8am-6pm, Sa 8am-1pm). There is an **ATM** in the Oberstadt at the corner of Askanierring and Berliner Str. The **telephone code** is 04153.

■ Kiel

Site of the 1936 and 1972 **Olympic sailing events,** the waters around Kiel swim ceaselessly with brightly colored sails. These multiply in the last full week of June, when the annual **Kieler Woche** takes place. An internationally renowned regatta, the festival enlivens the harbor and floods the town with music, food, and beer. Outside of this festival, Kiel offers little for the traveler besides ferry connections to Scandinavia and access to the world's busiest artificial waterway, the **Nord-Ostsee-Kanal** (North-Baltic Sea Canal). Allied bombings here were unsurprisingly ruthless, destroying 80% of the city. Unfortunately, Kiel retained little of its historic beauty.

The sights and sounds of the harbor, the city's focal point, are omnipresent in stolid, modern Kiel. The highlight is the largest team of **canal locks** in the world. The view of the canal and the harbor is amazing. Take bus #4 north to "Kanal," then the ferry that runs every 15 minutes (free). Walk right 10 minutes along Kanalstr. from the ferry dock to the *Schleuseninsel,* or Lock Island. Alternatively, landlubbers can take bus #1 or #41 to "Schleuse." (30min. Obligatory tours daily 9am-3pm, every 2hr. DM3, 50% off with *Kieler Karte,* students DM1.) Hugging the west coast of the **Kieler Förde** (Kiel Harbor), the **Schiffahrtsmuseum** (Navigation Museum; tel. 98 10) displays authentic-looking model ships. (Open mid-Apr. to mid-Oct. daily 10am-6pm; mid-Oct. to mid-Apr. Tu-Su 10am-5pm. Free.) North of the ship museum is the **aquarium** (tel. 597 38 57), home to a smallish collection of marine life. (Open daily Apr.-Sept. 9am-7pm; Oct.-Mar. 9am-5pm; DM2.50, students DM1, children DM0.50.) At the end of the Holstenstr. shopping district stands the 13th-century **St. Nikolaikirche** (tel. 929 37; open M-F 10am-1pm and 2-6pm, Sa 10am-1pm). The church is frequently the site of free concerts, occasionally of Gregorian chant.

All **ferries** except those bound for Norway and the Baltics leave from the piers on the west side of the harbor. **Baltic Line** (tel. 98 20 00) will take you to Sweden (1 per week; DM430); **Color Line** (tel. 97 40 90) sails to Oslo (1 per day; DM150, students 50% off on selected sailings); and **Langeland-Kiel** (tel. 97 41 50; fax 945 15) will ship

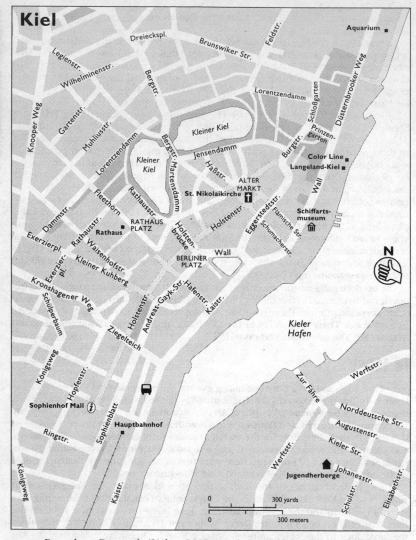

Kiel

you to Bagenkop, Denmark (2½hr.; DM7, in July DM9). Boats bound for Denmark leave from the Ostseekai; for Sweden and St. Petersburg, Schwedenkai; for Kalinin-grad and the Baltics, Ostuferkai; for Oslo, Norwegenkai. The **Mitfahrzentrale,** Sophienblatt 54 (tel. 194 40), two blocks south of the train station, matches riders and drivers for a fee of DM0.10 per km, paid to the driver (open M-W and F 9am-7pm, Th 9am-8pm, Sa 10am-3pm, Su 11am-3pm). At DM3.10 per ride, Kiel's extensive pub-lic transportation system will quickly result in a massive cash hemorrhage. Avoid the fiscal bloodletting by investing in a **Kieler Karte,** which comes with coupons for sights and restaurants (1-day DM12, 3-day DM17); it's available in hostels, the tourist booth, and the KVAG (Kiel Transit Authority) office at the *Bahnhof.* Most of Kiel's buses pass through the rows of stops outside the train station; the ones on the train station side of the street *generally* head north, while the ones on the *Sophienhof* side go south. Kiel's **tourist office** (tel. 76 09 01; fax 760 54 39) is located in the *Sophien-hof* mall across from the train station. It finds rooms for a DM3.50 fee; maps are

DM0.80. (Open May-Sept. M-Sa 9am-6:30pm; also open June-July Su 9am-1pm; Oct.-Apr. M-F 9am-6:30pm, Sa 9am-1pm.) The **post office**, Stresemannpl. 1-3, 24044 Kiel, is on the other side of the *ZOB* from the train station (open M-F 8am-7pm, Sa 8:30am-2pm). **Exchange money** at the adjacent **Postbank** (same hours as the post office; closes at 1pm on Saturdays). The **telephone code** is 0431.

Kiel's boss hostel, **Jugendherberge Kiel (HI)**, Johannesstr. 1 (tel. 73 14 88; fax 73 57 23), has uncrowded four-person bedrooms, each with its own shower and bathroom. A bus stop nearby motors passengers to the *Hauptbahnhof* every 15 minutes. Take bus #4 from the train station on the *Sophienhof* side to "Kielerstr.," and backtrack one block, then turn right on Johannesstr. (DM24, over 26 DM29. Sheets and breakfast included. Reception 7am-1am. Curfew 1am.) Camping is distant at **Campingplatz Falckenstein**, Palisadenweg 171 (tel. 39 20 78), about 10km north of the city center. Take bus #44 (direction: "Strand") to "Seekamp." Backtrack to Scheidekoppel and hike for 20 minutes through wheat fields until Palisadenweg, then turn left down toward the beach (DM8-12 per tent, DM7 per person). Get groceries at the **Kaiser's** supermarket on the ground floor of the *Sophienhof* (open M-F 9am-8pm, Sa 8:30am-4pm). Holstenstr. and the *Markt* are the best places in town for a meal. **Sandwich**, Holstenstr. 92, counts on tourists' thirst for expensive Coca-Cola, but if you fight the power by bringing your own drink, you can enjoy the yummy little sandwiches noted in the appellation (DM2.50-3.50 each; open M-F 6:30am-6pm, Sa 7am-2pm).

■ Near Kiel: Laboe

While some choose to mix it up with the crowds and swim in the **Kieler Förde**, warmer water awaits in nearby **Laboe**. Use of the beaches requires a **Strandkarte** (DM4 June-Sept., DM2 in May), which must be purchased at the *Automaten* to avoid a DM10 fine. Bus #100, from the *Sophienhof* side of the bus stop (direction: Laboe), will take you on a tour through the 'burbs to the beach (50min., DM5.40, *Kieler Karte* valid). A much more attractive way to get there is to take the **ferry**, which costs the same as the bus and offers a spectacular tour of the *Förde*. From the *Hauptbahnhof*, walk toward the water and follow the signs for *FSK*. Laboe's harbor, which on weekends hops to the sound of jazz, is at the head of the **Strandstraße**, a bucolic boardwalk lined with ice cream shops, fish restaurants, and the occasional flea market. The crowds thin out considerably about 300m down at the non-smoking section of the beach. A bit farther, **U-Boot 995**, with eight-person rooms the size of phone booths, is a tourist attraction, not a hostel. Used in the Nazi campaign of submarine warfare during World War II, U-Boot 995 is now open to tourists. (Open daily Apr. 15-Oct. 15 9:30am-6pm, Oct. 16-Apr. 14 9:30am-4pm. DM3.50, under 18 DM2.50, free for German soldiers in uniform. *Let's Go* does not recommend enlisting in the German army as a means of obtaining discounts.) Across the street, winning no awards for architectural subtlety, stands the **Marine-Ehrenmal** (tel. (04343) 87 55), a 72m concrete erection commemorating "the sailors of all nations who died on the seas." The exhibits chronicle, in a somewhat disturbingly unapologetic manner, the maritime successes of the World Wars. Take the elevator to the 57m-high observation deck for an incredible view of the *Förde* and Baltic Sea. (Same hours as the U-Boot. DM5, under 18 DM3.) Laboe's **tourist office**, Strandstr. 25 (tel. (04343) 42 75 73), on the boardwalk, will hook you up with a room (DM30-40, breakfast included) for a 10% fee. (Open May-Aug. M-F 10am-noon and 1-4:30pm, Sa-Su 10am-3:30pm. For room reservations, call (04343) 79 36 or come in person M-F 11am-2pm.) **Bikes** can be rented down the street at the Fahrradverleih, Strandstr. 14.

■ Schleswig

At the southernmost point of the **Schlei inlet**, Schleswig bills itself as the "friendly city of culture," a title its picture-perfect fishing settlements, 16th-century castle, and extensive museum collections rightly deserve. Once a major Viking settlement, Schleswig became an important fishing and trade center in the Middle Ages. The city subsequently became the seat of the Gottorfer dukes, lesser German nobles who built a grandiose castle on the Schlei banks. Today Schleswig is a quiet town whose laid-back pace and beautiful surroundings and millennium-long history make it an attractive place to visit.

ORIENTATION AND PRACTICAL INFORMATION Schleswig's **train station** is located quite a distance from the city center; take bus #1, 2, 4, or 5 from the stop outside the *ZOB*, which is close to the *Altstadt* (15min., DM1.80). Trains head hourly to Kiel, Flensburg, Husum, and Hamburg (via Neumünster). The **tourist office**, Plessenstr. 7 (tel. 248 78 or 207 03), is up the street from the harbor; from the *ZOB*, walk down Plessenstr. towards the water. The staff books private and hotel rooms (DM25-60) for a DM10 fee if calling ahead or DM2 on the spot. (Open May-Sept. M-F 9:30am-12:30pm and 1:30-5pm, Sa 9am-noon; Oct.-Apr. M-Th 9am-12:30pm and 1:30-5pm, F 9am-12:30pm.) **Schnell und Sauber**, Stadtweg 70 at the edge of the *Altstadt*, will wash 12kg of laundry for DM12 (detergent included; open M-Sa 6am-10pm). The **post office**, Poststr. 1, **exchanges money** at counter 5 (open M-F 9am-12:30pm and 2:30-6pm, Sa 9am-12:30pm). The **postal code** is 24837. The **telephone code** is 04621.

ACCOMMODATIONS AND FOOD The **Jugendherberge (HI)**, Spielkoppel 1 (tel. 238 93), lies close to the center of town. Take bus #2 (direction: "Hühnhauser-Schwimmhalle") from either the train station or the *ZOB* to "Schwimmhalle"; the hostel is across the street. It's on the right across from the school. Great location and a view of the Schlei inlet. (DM20, over 26 DM25. Sheets DM7. Breakfast included. Reception 7am-1pm and 5-11pm. Curfew 11pm.) For a night in a former *Fischerhaus* overlooking the water (or for the TV in every room), try **Pension Schleiblick**, Hafengang 4 (tel. 234 68). To get there from the *ZOB*, follow Plessenstr. toward the harbor. Continue as it turns into Am Hafen, then bear left onto Hafengang. (Singles DM65; doubles DM120. All have showers. Breakfast included.) **Da Paolo**, Stadtweg 65 (tel. 298 97), serves up traditional pizza and pasta on red-checkered tablecloths (DM9-15; open daily noon-3pm and 5:30pm-midnight). For German food, **Panorama**, up the street from the *ZOB* at Plessenstr. 15 (tel. 239 46), has lunch specials for DM9. Also try the seafood—fresh and cheap—at the *Imbiße* down by the *Stadthafen*.

SIGHTS Schleswig's *Altstadt*, located a few blocks up from the harbor, is stuffed to the gills with meandering cobblestone streets leading along Schleswig's unusually hilly terrain. **Stadtweg**, the main pedestrian zone, is lined with smart shops and a department store. Towering over it all is the copper steeple of the 12th-century **St. Petri-Dom**, renowned for its successful combination of Romanesque and high Gothic architecture, as well as for its intricately carved wooden altarpiece by Brüggemann (1514-1521). Climb the tower for DM2. *(Open M-Th and Sa 9am-5pm, F 9am-3pm, Su 1-5pm.)* In the summer the church offers a choral and organ concert series on Wednesday evenings. *(DM10-15, students DM5-8.)* Two blocks beyond the Dom, the narrow alleys unfold onto the **Rathausmarkt**, a quiet square adjacent to the 15th-century **Rathaus**. From the square, follow Töpferstr. and turn right on Fischbrückestr. Beyond Knud-Laward-Str. begins the **Holm**, a small fishing village with a tiny church in the main square, which doubles as Holm's cemetery.

A 20-minute walk along the harbor from the *Altstadt*, 16th-century **Schloß Gottorf** and its surrounding buildings house the **Landesmuseen**, a treasure trove of artwork and artifacts in six museums. The castle itself is home to most of the exhibits; the first floor consists of 16th- and 17th-century Dutch and Danish artwork, alongside tapestries, suits of armor, and the Gottorfs' apartments. Upstairs the path leads into the incredibly ornate **Kapelle** (chapel), built in 1591. The grand finale is the appropriately named **Hirschsaal**, whose deer-endowed walls feature real antlers. The room itself houses an oddly out-of-place collection of Ottoman and Persian artifacts. The second floor is also home to the excellent **Jugendstilmuseum**, a collection of art deco paintings and furniture. Wipe your shoes before going in—even the carpets are part of the exhibit! One floor up houses the main exhibits of the **Archäologisches Landesmuseum**. The rest of the museum is in the **Nydamhalle** adjacent to the castle, including a 4th-century fishing boat and an exhibit on the Saxon migration to England. On the other side of the castle, the **Kreuzstall** and the adjacent buildings house the **Museum des 20. Jahrhunderts,** an extensive collection devoted to the artists of the Brücke school, including Emil Nolde, Max Pechstein, and Ernst Ludwig Kirchner, as well as a well-rounded presentation of adherents to the *Neue Sachlichkeit*. Finally, the park surrounding the castle is also an **outdoor sculpture museum,** featuring contemporary German sculptors. *(All museums open daily Mar.-Oct. 9am-5pm; Nov.-Feb. 9:30am-4pm. DM7, students DM3.)*

If you find yourself longing for breast plates and horned helmets, ferries travel from the Stadthafen port near the *Dom* to the **Wikinger Museum Haithabu.** The museum, next to an archaeological dig of a former **Viking settlement,** covers all aspects of Viking life. *(Open daily Apr.-Oct. 9am-5pm; Nov.-Mar. Tu-Su 9am-4pm. Admission DM2, students DM1. Ferry DM3.50, round-trip DM6.)* About five minutes up the road heading to the train, the **Städtisches Museum,** Friedrichstr. 9-11 (tel. 936 80), houses documents and *objets trouvés* from Schleswig's history.

■ Flensburg

Flensburg is Germany's northernmost city, with the Danish border lying only a hop, skip, and a stumble away. The presence of a large international student population and lots of locally brewed alcohol injects some pulse into the staid northern German atmosphere. You can't go anywhere in northern Germany without encountering **Flensburger Pilsner** on tap, and the town itself is swimming in it. Flensburg is located around the perfect harbor that forms the tip of the **Flensburger Förde;** the streets run along the water to wind into the hills.

Heading straight down Bahnhofstr. from the station and zigzagging across Friedrich-Ebert-Str. will lead you to the lively *Altstadt* and Flensburg's huge pedestrian zone along **Holm** and **Großestr.** Along the way you'll pass the **Deutsches Haus,** a *Bauhaus*-style concert hall donated to Flensburg in recognition of the city's loyalty in the 1920 referendum. In the **Südermarkt,** the beautiful 14th-century **Nikolaikirche** boasts a gargantuan organ, the *Organ Maximus.* (Open Tu-F 9am-5pm, Sa 10am-1pm. Free.) The church underwent tremendous renovations in 1998 and is scheduled to reopen in 1999. Just beyond the **Nordermarkt** stands the **Marienkirche,** with its rather bizarre 1950s-era stained-glass windows (open Tu and Th-F 10am-4pm, W and Sa 10am-1pm; free). The church has an extensive program of choral and organ concerts. At Norderstr. 50, next to the Danish library, is the **Marientreppe,** which offers a glimpse of Denmark from atop its 146 stairs. At Schiffbrücke 39, a 150-year-old customs house has become the **Schiffahrtsmuseum** (Navigation Museum; tel. 85 29 70), documenting Flensburg's nautical history and role in Denmark's once-thriving Caribbean trade (open Tu-Sa 10am-5pm; DM5, students DM2.50). The rum exhibit is impressive. *Ahhrr!* What's the booty? The last weekend of May sees the **Rum Regatta,** an event for traditional boats and sober sailors only.

Trains link the city to Hamburg via Neumünster (2½hr.) and Kiel (1½hr.) at least every other hour, while others head north to Copenhagen (5hr.) and many other Danish cities. **Buses** from the *ZOB* also cross the border to the Danish towns of Sønderborg (1¼hr.) and Aabenrá (50min.) from gate D1. From the west bank of the harbor, **ferries** country-hop between Flensburg and Glücksburg in Germany and Gravenstein and Kollund in Denmark (DM3). Flensburg's high-tech bus system saves a lot of uphill walking; practically all buses circulate through the *ZOB* (central bus station) two blocks from Holm below the harbor (one-way fare DM2.30, 24hr. *Tageskarte* DM6). The **tourist office,** Speicherlinie 40 (tel. 230 90; fax 173 52), lies off Großestr.; follow the signs through the courtyard (open M-F 9am-6pm). They'll find a room (DM20-35) without a fee and can arrange summer tours of the brewery for DM5. The main **post office,** near the train station at Bahnhofstr. 40, 24939 Flensburg, **exchanges currency** (open M-F 8am-6pm, Sa 8am-1pm). The **telephone code** is 0461.

Flensburg's **Jugendherberge (HI),** Fichtestr. 16 (tel. 377 42; fax 31 29 52), offers no escape from exercise, whether it be running laps on the nearby track or making the long walk into town. From the train station, take bus #1 (direction: "Lachsbach") or 4 (direction: "Klueshof") to *"ZOB"* and change to #3 or 7 (direction: "Twedter Plack") to "Stadion," then follow the signs. (DM20, over 26 DM25. Sheets DM7. Reception 8-8:45am, 5-6pm, and 9:30-10pm.) The **Nordermarkt** simmers with a slew of cafes and bars. For those itching to see what a metric hangover feels like, **Hansen's Brauerei,** Großestr. 83 (tel. 222 10), serves home-brewed beer by the meter for DM26 (12 drinks for the price of 10!) and German food in equally absurd quantities. Their whopping Sunday special bloats you with 1kg of ribs for DM13.90.

Just 10km away from Flensburg, **Glücksburg** boasts beautiful beaches (DM4) and a fairy tale **Schloß** (tel. (04631) 22 13) surrounded by a looking-glass lake. Unlike Wonderland, Glücksburg can be reached by bus from gate B6 of the *ZOB* (35min., DM3.50) or by ferry via Kollund, Denmark (50min., 6 per day, DM3, passport necessary). From the Glücksburg *ZOB*, walk down towards the post office and follow the signs left to the *Schloß*, or get off at the beach (one stop earlier) and follow the signs around the lake (2.5km). Skate around the floor in the slippers provided while discovering just how inbred 19th-century royals were. On the third floor, Gobelin tapestries depict scenes from Ovid's *Metamorphoses*. Don't miss the "corpses" in the dungeon. (Open Apr.-Oct. 10am-5pm, Nov.-Mar. 10am-4:30pm. DM7, students DM5.)

■ Husum

A laid-back fishing town on Schleswig-Holstein's west coast, Husum's big claim to fame is the 19th-century novelist and hometown hero **Theodor Storm** (who dismissed the city as "the grey town by the sea"). The hamlet on the Wattenmeer now successfully resists both modernization and the construction of a tourist trap, offering a genteel flavor and low-key pace that attract tourists from all over Germany. While the town itself is no great cultural attraction, its proximity to the Wattenmeer makes it the perfect base for the budget traveler.

Husum's quiet, tree-lined streets converge on the pedestrian zone in and around the **Marktplatz.** At one end of the square stands the solemn and plain **Marienkirche,** built between 1827 and 1832 from the designs of Danish master Christian Frederik Hansen. Across the square is the 17th-century **Rathaus.** The **Schloß vor Husum** (tel. 25 45), one block north of the Marktplatz, was built by the Gottdorfer dukes at the end of the 16th century. (Open Mar. 12-Oct. 31 Tu-Su 11am-5pm. DM4, students DM2. Guided tours DM30.) Instead of the usual diet of swords, crests, and other medieval party favors, the *Schloß* offers kinder and gentler exhibits in its special art exhibitions. The castle also hosts summer evening concerts and free choral concerts on the first Friday evening of every month.

Everywhere in Husum statues, paintings, and restaurants are dedicated to **Theodor Storm**. He cried and wet his diaper for the first time on September 14, 1817 at Marktplatz 9, next to the *Rathaus*. The building is now a bank. The **Theodor-Storm-Haus,** Wasserreihe 31 (tel. 66 62 70), was the writer's residence from 1866 to 1880 and is now a museum with original furnishings and manuscripts. (Open Apr.-Oct. Tu-F 10am-noon and 2-5pm, M, Sa, and Su 2-5pm; Nov.-Mar. Tu, Th, and Sa 2-5pm. DM3, students DM2.) Completing our tour of the three ages of Man, Storm is buried in the *Klosterkirchhof* in Osterendestr., east of the Marktplatz. The **Nissenhaus,** Herzog-Adolf-Str. 25 by the *ZOB*, houses the **North Frisian Museum** (tel. 25 45). (Open daily Apr.-Oct. 10am-5pm; Nov.-Mar. Tu-F and Su 10am-4pm. DM5, students and seniors DM2.) Its collection focuses on dike building, dike breaking, and offers part of a real medieval dike as a *coup de grace*.

Husum has hourly rail connections to Hamburg (2hr., one-way DM40), Kiel (1½hr.), and Sylt (1hr.). To reach the town from the train and bus stations, follow Herzog-Adolf-Straße until it ends; then turn left on Norderstr. and you'll be in the Marktplatz. Rent **bikes** from **Koch Fahrrad-Center,** Schulstr. 4 (tel. 44 65; DM10 and a photo ID). The **tourist office** (tel. 89 87 30; fax 89 87 90) in the *Rathaus* books rooms in private homes for a 10% fee. Singles start at DM30, doubles at DM55. Call ahead in the summer (open July-Aug. 9am-6pm; Sept.-June 9am-noon and 2-4pm).

Husum's gorgeous **swimming pool**, Flensburger Chaussee 28 (tel. 899 71 55), the center of the town's weekday nightlife, has two heated pools, a waterslide, and a sauna (pool open Tu-F 2-10pm, Sa 8am-5pm, Su 8am-6pm; DM6, under 19 DM4). The **post office**, Großstr. 5, 25813 Husum, is off the Marktplatz (open M-F 9am-6pm, Sa 9am-12:30pm). The **telephone code** is 04841.

To reach the **Jugendherberge Theodor Storm (HI)**, Schobüllerstr. 34 (tel. 27 14; fax 815 68), head left from the tourist office and make a right onto Neustadtstr., which turns into Marktstr. Make a left at Adolf-Brütte-Str. and bear right as it turns into Schobüllerstr. Or take bus #51 from the *ZOB* just down the street from the train station to "Westercampweg" (DM2). The farmhouse exterior suggests rural charm, while German *Schulkinder* bark and whine like farm animals. Still, the ample kitchen facilities provide some sanity. (DM22, over 26 DM26. Breakfast included. Reception open intermittently 4:30-10pm. Curfew 10pm. Closed Jan.15-Feb.15. Call ahead.) The area around the harbor is filled with restaurants and *Imbiß* stands, while a **Plus** grocery store is in the Marktplatz (open M-F 8:30am-7pm, Sa 8am-4pm). Sustain yourself with a crab sandwich, the local specialty (DM15). Feast on cheap eats at **Porto Bello**, Hafenstr. 3, which serves 30cm pizzas for DM8.50-15 (open daily 11am-11pm). Thursday is **farmer's market** day—from 8am to 1pm stands sell the weekly harvest of fruits, vegetables, fish, and leather wear in the Marktplatz.

■ Sylt

The sandy, windswept island of **Sylt** stretches far into the North Sea, culminating in Germany's northernmost point. The 10km-long *Hindenburgdamm* connects Sylt—traditionally a favorite spot for government luminaries and other wealthy vacationers, but now a more democratic affair—to the mainland. The beauty of Sylt's undulating dunes and fragrant pine forests attracts large crowds, especially to **Westerland**. The mother of all Kurtowns and the largest town on the island, Westerland is abuzz with bourgeois types traipsing down the *Strandpromenade* (boardwalk).

From Westerland, the best way to explore the island is by bicycle. The main **bike path** follows the highway, making it good for intertown travel, while the smaller dirt and gravel paths meander through the dunes, affording stunning views of the ocean. Outside the recreational chaos of the main town, however, Sylt offers sparsely populated beaches, including the (in)famous **Bühne 16**, whose nude bathers reveal that water wings do not a swimsuit make. Sylt's beaches also provide the only locale in Germany where surfing is possible. While they're no Waikiki, the beaches of **Wallingstedt**, **Hörnum**, and **Strandhalle** all produce rideable surf.

While Westerland is a convenient base for exploring the island, its rows of designer shops and overpriced restaurants can become claustrophobic in the high season. To avoid (most of) the crowds, head either north or south; beyond Westerland's city limits, unpopulated dune trails and small vacation villages await. North of **Kampen**, the main road leads through rolling grass-covered dunes and fields sparsely inhabited by cows and horses. **List**, Sylt's northernmost town, is an excellent base for hikers and bikers wishing to explore the trails leading into the remote dunes of **Ellenbogen**, the northernmost point in Germany.

Trains from Hamburg **Altona** travel to Westerland via Husum (2½hr., about 18 per day). **Public transportation** on the island is quite expensive (DM6.20 to reach either hostel from Westerland, day card DM20). Buses leave from the *ZOB* terminal to the left of the Westerland station. **Rent a bike** from **Fahrrad am Bahnhof** at the Westerland train station, across from track 1 (DM9 per day, DM49 per week; open daily 8:30am-6:30pm). Sylt imposes a levy called a *Kurtaxe* on any easy riders hoping to hit the beaches (all 1-day visitors DM6; May-Oct. DM5.50 per day; Nov.-Apr. DM3; under 18 free). Ferries run 7 to 11 times a day from List harbor to **Havneby** on the Danish island of **Rømø** (55min., round-trip DM8). Call **Rømø-Sylt Linie** (tel. 87 04 75) in List for reservations and information. **Adler-Schiffe**, Boysenstr. 13 (tel. 987 00), runs daytrips to Amrum, Föhr, and the Halligen (see below). The **tourist office** (tel. 99 88; fax 99 81 00) in the train station reserves rooms (DM35 and up) for a DM10 fee and gives you a super-beachin' island map for DM4.90 (open daily in the summer 9am–8pm). For rooms in List, call 952 00; in Hörnum call 96 26 26. The **post office,** Kjeirstr. 5, 25992 Sylt, is around the corner from the train station (open M-F 8am-6pm, Sa 8am-noon). The **telephone code** is 04651.

Sylt offers two youth hostels. Those neither wayward nor lucky enough to earn a spot in Hörnum's reform school will have to settle for the adjacent **Jugendherberge Hörnum (HI),** Friesenpl. 2 (tel. 88 02 94; fax 88 13 92). The hostel offers a convenient location next to a bus stop and a **SPAR grocery store** (open M-F 8am-noon and 2:30-6pm, Sa 8am-1pm). From the *ZOB* take bus #2 (direction: "Hörnum Hafen") to "Hörnum-Nord" and continue along Rantumerstr., turning left at the *Jugendherberge* sign. Behind the hostel, a sheltered, secluded beach stretches for miles. (DM22, over 26 DM27. Sheets DM7. Reception noon-1pm and 5-10pm. Curfew 11pm. Reservations strongly recommended.) List's **Jugendherberge Mövenberg** (tel. 87 03 97; fax 87 10 39) lies near the northern tip of the island amid the dune trails. Catch bus #1 (direction: "List Hafen") from the Westerland *ZOB* and take it to the end of the line (DM6.20). If you're lucky you can change for the infrequent Weststrand bus to "Mövenberg"; otherwise, return to the intersection, turn right and follow the *Jugendherberge* sign 3km, past the sheep and dunes. Be aware that school groups covet the hostel's proximity to the *Jugendstrand* (youth beach). (DM22, over 26 DM27. Breakfast included. Reception 7-9am, noon-2:30pm, and 4-10pm. Curfew 11pm. Written reservations strongly advised: write to Jugendherberge Mövenberg, 25992 List/Sylt. Definitely call ahead. Closed Nov. to mid-Mar.)

■ Near Sylt: Amrum

The closest island to Sylt, **Amrum** draws (mostly wealthy) visitors with its towering dunes, fragrant pine forests, and miles of sandy beaches. Getting there provides its own excitement as folks can run to Amrum at low tide. The path connecting the two islands contains a few **quicksand** pits, making it advisable to take a guided tour (tel. 14 85; DM6). For the less adventurous, **Adler-Schiffe** (tel. (04842) 268; fax 264) runs boats to Wittdün from Hörnum on Sylt (50min., 2 per day, DM32 round-trip, children DM16) and Nordstrand near Husum (2hr., 2 per day, DM29.50 round-trip, children DM18). **Wittdün,** the main town, has a pleasant main street (Hauptstr.), as well as a pretty Strandpromenade (boardwalk). But the island's main attraction is the **Kniepsand**—ten square kilometers of the whitest sand bordering the North Sea. Between the *Kniepsand* and the towns lies a narrow strip of grassy dunes interspersed with lakes and hiking trails, crowned by the **Amrumer Leuchtturm,** the tallest lighthouse on Germany's North seacoast (open Apr.-Oct. M-F 8:30am-noon).

The **tourist office** (tel. (04682) 94 03 11; fax 94 03 94), one block from the ferry station, has extensive maps and brochures and books rooms for DM15 per person plus *Kurtaxe.* The **Jugendherberge Wittdün,** Mittelstr. 1, has large, clean rooms, some with beach views. (DM22, over 26 DM27 plus *Kurtaxe.* Members only. Reception 11:30am-1pm and 4:30-9:30pm. Closed in Dec.; Jan.-Mar. stays only by reservation.) Restaurants tend to be fairly expensive, but fortunately there are two **SPAR** supermarkets on Hauptstr. Several shops around the tourist office rent **bikes.** The **post office** is also on Hauptstr. (open M-F 9am-noon and 2:30-5pm, Sa 9am-noon). Amrum's **telephone code** is 04682.

Niedersachsen (Lower Saxony)

Extending from the Ems River to the Harz Mountains and from the North Sea to the hills of central Germany, Niedersachsen has two distinct flavors. Along the northern coast, descendants of the Frisians run their fishing boats from ports built on foggy marshland. The vast remainder of the *Land* is a broad plain which supports agricultural communities. Since the Middle Ages, the region has been the seat of intense individualism and unbridled innovation. Christianity found a foothold here in the wake of Charlemagne's march through the fringe of the deep-purple Lüneburger Heide. Niedersachsen still treasures its autonomy, harkening back to the Hanseatic traders who made the region's fortune. A pocket of its area belongs to Bremen and Bremerhaven, two seafaring cities united in a unique case of state federalism to form Germany's smallest *Land*.

👆 HIGHLIGHTS OF NIEDERSACHSEN

- **Hannover** is Niedersachsen's metropolis, boasting a cookin' cultural scene. The **Sprengel Museum** houses a great modern art collection, and the city maintains a respectable nightlife (see p. 273).
- Surrounded by rolling hills and filled with tons of young folks amid superb old architecture, **Göttingen** is the college town *par excellence* (see p. 280).
- It's no surprise that the city of **Bremen** is also its own small state within Niedersachsen—the residents are feisty, the political climate is especially liberal, and the collection of museums and nightlife cannot be contained (see p. 301).
- A respite from the German city circuit can be found along the coast of the **North Sea,** where the **East Frisian Islands** offer barren beauty and a long string of **superb beaches** (see p. 313).

■ Hannover (Hanover)

Despite its relatively small size, Hannover puts on a magical display of culture and cosmopolitan charm, rivaling that of cities twice as large. As the most important railway center in Northwest Germany, the city's myriad attractions easily lure in travelers moving through the Berlin-Hamburg-Köln triangle. But Hannover has seen darker times. Because of an unusual marriage that bound the Hannoverian royalty to the United Kingdom, the city found itself repeatedly attacked by foreign powers striking at the British throne. Later, under Prussian domination, Hannover thrived under the prosperity of a unified empire. World War II saw the end of that, as 60% of the city was flattened. Yet resilient Hannover, accustomed to severe poundings, emerged like a jack-in-the-box, leaping joyfully from the ashes. Today, with great economic vigor, a wealth of museums, a supreme opera hall, and a tradition of outdoor festivals, Hannover reigns proudly as the political and cultural capital of Niedersachsen.

ORIENTATION AND PRACTICAL INFORMATION

The old Sachsen *"Hon overe"* means "High Bank," referring to the city's position on the river Leine. In the heart of Hannover lies the *Hauptbahnhof*, where a statue of Ernst August, first king of Hannover, beams from the saddle of his horse, surveying the city he founded. **Bahnhofstraße** extends from the horse's hooves, leading to the landmark **Kröpcke Café.** Below the statue's feet sprawls the underground **Passerelle,** a bizarre conglomeration of cheap diners and souvenir shops. Behind the station is the **Raschplatz,** home to a disco and club scene. A pedestrian zone connects most of the middle city, including the shopping districts along **Georgstraße,** and the *Altstadt.*

Available at youth hostels and **ÜSTRA** offices, the **Hannover Card** provides public transportation within the city and to the airport, as well as free admission or discounts for several museums. (DM14 for 1 day, DM23 for 3 days; group ticket for up to 5 people DM30 for one day, DM50 for 3 days.) Plan ahead: the card is only valid from 7pm on the day of purchase, so you must buy your ticket one day ahead of time.

Flights: The Hannover airport is 15-20min. from the *Altstadt. Schnellbuslinie* (express bus line) #60 runs from the *Hauptbahnhof* to the airport (M-F 5am-10pm, every 20min.; Sa-Su every 30min.; DM9). Flights depart to Berlin, Dresden, Frankfurt, Leipzig, Munich, Nürnberg, and Stuttgart, as well as other European cities. For flight information, call 977 12 23.

Trains: Hannover is well connected to cities in Northern Europe, especially within Germany. Trains to Munich (4-4½hr.), Hamburg (1½hr.), and Berlin (3hr.).

Public Transportation: ÜSTRA, Hannover's mass-transit system, is extremely thorough and fast. As soon as you arrive, walk to the lime-green stand in front of the King or at the "Raschpl." bus stop behind the station, and pick up the free map of the U-Bahn and bus lines. Single-ride tickets DM3, ages 4-11 DM1.50. Blocks of 6 tickets can be purchased at discount rates, but the best deal for travelers is either a **24hr. Pass** (DM7.50) or a **Schuler-Wochen** card, which opens up the magical world of public transportation to students for 1 week; you'll need a student ID and a passport-sized photo to hand over (DM17.50). All tickets can be purchased from drivers or in vending machines at stations. For more info and maps, call the **ÜSTRA Customer Service Office** in the Kröpcke station (tel. 16 68 22 38). Open

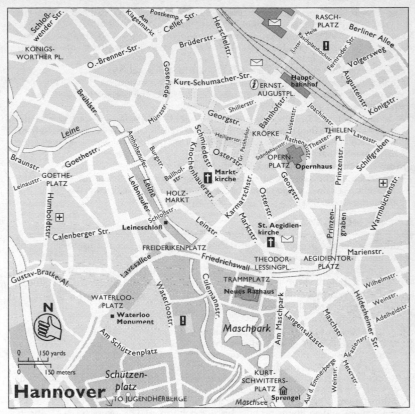

NIEDERSACHSEN

M-W and F 8am-6pm, Th 8am-7pm, Sa 9am-2pm. The **Hannover Card** provides more comprehensive savings (see above).

Bike Rental: Radgeber Linden, Kötnerholzweg 43 (tel. 210 97 60). Take U-Bahn #10 to "Leinaustr." DM10 per day. Open M-Tu, Th-F 10am-1pm and 3-6pm, W and Sa 10am-1pm.

Mitfahrzentrale: Citynetz, Weißekreuzerstr. 18 (tel. 194 44), matches drivers with riders. Open M-F 9am-6pm, Sa 9am-1pm, Su 11am-2pm.

Tourist Office: Hannover Information, Ernst-August-Pl. 2 (tel. 30 14 20 or 30 14 21; fax 30 14 14). Outside the main entrance of the train station, facing the large rear of the king's splendid steed, turn right. In the same building as the post office. The superb staff finds rooms for any budget for a steep DM10 fee, provides maps and information on cultural events, sells tickets to concerts and exhibits, and runs a full travel agency. Free hotel list available. Open M-F 9am-7pm, Sa 9:30am-3pm.

Tours: The tourist office offers 16 different tours. DM10-20, students DM7.50-15.

Student Travel Office: RDS, Fortunastr. 28, off of Limmerstr. (tel. 44 60 37). The basics for the budget traveler. Flights and train packages. Open M-F 9am-6pm.

Consulate: U.K. Berliner Allee 5 (tel. 388 38 08). Behind the train station, across Raschplatz, inside the DG-Bank building.

Currency Exchange: Reise Bank, in the train station, is the most convenient with the longest hours and decent commissions. Open M-F 7:30am-7pm, Sa 7:30am-5pm, Su 9am-12:45pm and 1:30-4:30pm.

American Express: Georgstr. 54, (tel. 36 34 28), across from the Opera House. Travel agency and full cardmember services. Mail held for a maximum of 4 weeks for cardmembers, traveler's check clients, and travel agency customers. Open M-F 9am-6pm, Sa 10am-1pm.

Bookstores: Schmorl und von Seefeld, Bahnhofstr. (tel. 367 50), has English-language novels downstairs. Open M-F 9:30am-8pm, Sa 9:30am-4pm.

Laundromat: Wasch Center, at the corner of Hildesheimer Str. and Siemensstr. Take U-Bahn #1, 2, or 8 to "Geibelstr." Wash DM6 (including detergent), dry DM1 per 15min. Open daily 6am-11pm.

Emergency: Police, tel. 110. **Fire,** tel. 112. **Ambulance,** tel. 192 22.

Medical Assistance: EMS, tel. 31 40 44. **Medical Information,** tel. 31 40 44.

Women's Resources: Rape Crisis Line, tel. 33 21 12. **Shelter,** tel. 66 44 77.

AIDS-Hilfe: tel. 194 11.

Pharmacy: Europa Apotheke, Georgstr. 16 (tel. 32 66 18; fax 363 24 63), near the train station. 14 languages spoken, including English. Open M-F 8am-8pm, Sa 8am-4pm. Info about emergency service *(Notdienst)* posted when closed, or call the **Emergency Pharmacy Service** (tel. 011 41).

Internet Access: In Daily Planet (see **Nightlife,** p. 279).

Post Office: In the same building as the tourist office, 30159 Hannover. Open M-F 9am-8pm, Sa 9am-4pm, Su noon-3pm. Mail held, currency exchanged.

Telephone Code: 0511.

ACCOMMODATIONS

Finding budget accommodations in Hannover is difficult but not impossible. The youth hostel and two *Naturfreundehäuser* (similar to hostels, but not part of HI) provide affordable respites, as do private accommodations through the tourist office. Call the **reservation hotline** (tel. 811 35 00; fax 811 35 41). Should all else fail, traveling to the hostels in nearby Braunschweig or Celle may be cheaper than bedding down in one of Hannover's royally priced hotels.

Jugendherberge Hannover (HI), Ferdinand-Wilhelm-Fricke-Weg 1 (tel. 131 76 74; fax 185 55). U-Bahn #3 or 7 (direction: "Mühlenberg") to "Fischerhof/Fachhochschule." Cross the tracks and walk on the path through the school's parking lot; follow the path as it curves, and cross the street. When you see an enormous red footbridge, cross the bridge and turn right. The hostel is 50m down on the right (15min.), within walking distance of the Maschsee and the Schützenfestplatz. The walk at night is poorly lit—take care. The 6- to 12-bed rooms are a bit tight. Major renovations and additions promise greater comfort. DM22, over 26 DM27. Sheets DM5.70. Reception 7:30-9am and 2-11:30pm. Curfew 11:30pm.

Naturfreundehaus Misburg, Am Fahrhorstfelde 50 (tel. 58 05 37; fax 958 58 36). U-Bahn #4 (direction: "Roderbruch") to "Misburgerstr.," then bus #631 to "Misburg Waltfriedhof." Stroll up am Fahrhorstfelde to the very end. Go 10m straight ahead on the trail and follow the sign. On a beautiful lake brimming with ducks. 4- to 6-bed rooms decked out in homey brown. DM30. Breakfast DM8.50. Sheets DM7.50 Reception Tu-Su 2-8pm. No curfew. The *Haus*'s 30 beds fill quickly—reservations are necessary.

Naturfreundehaus Stadtheim, Hermann-Bahlsen-Allee 8 (tel. 69 14 93; fax 69 06 52). U-Bahn #3 or 7 (direction: "Lahe" or "Fasanenkrug") to "Spannhagengarten." Walk 15m back to the intersection and follow Hermann-Bahlsen-Allee to the left for about 5min.; follow the sign to your right down the paved road 200m to the hostel. Tiny rooms, with a superior breakfast. Prices vary, but it's around DM34.80 per night. Breakfast included. Reception 8am-10:30pm. No curfew.

Hotel am Thielenplatz, Thielenpl. 2, (tel. 32 76 91; fax 32 51 88). Luxurious furnishings in the lobby and 150 beds in well-maintained rooms, all with TV. Singles with shower DM88-190; doubles with shower DM140-300. Breakfast included. Check-out 11:30am.

FOOD

Kröpcke, the world-renowned food court/cafe at the center of the pedestrian zone, can hook you up with small snacks (from DM2.50) or nice sit-down meals (from DM13.50). The **Cliccadou/Mövenpick restaurant** has reasonably-priced sandwiches (DM3.20-6.50), and delicious ice cream treats (DM3-10.80). The Lister Meile area behind the train station also offers an interesting selection of cafes with pleasant seating options. A **Spar supermarket** sits by the Lister Meile U-Bahn stop (open M-F 8am-7pm, Sa 8am-2pm). An **Edeka Activ Markt,** at the corner of Pfarrlandstr. and Limmerstr. (U-Bahn #10 to "Leinaustr."), gets in on the grocery action (open M-F 8am-8pm, Sa 8am-4pm). For a more international flavor, ride on down to the **Markthalle,** where a wide variety of snacks, meals, and booze awaits (open M-F 7am-6pm, Sa 7am-1pm).

Hauptmensa, Calinstr. 23 (tel. 768 80 35). U-Bahn #4 or 5 to "Schneiderberg." Take a right up Schneiderbergstr., just past the small bridge in the green-trimmed building. DM3 gets you the card on which you can deposit however much you wanna spend. Meals DM2.20-3.70, DM6-8.50 for guests. Open M-F 11:40am-2:30pm.

Nudel Holz, Kötnerholzweg 25 (tel. 21 21 22). U-Bahn #10 to "Leinaustr." Award-winning Italian restaurant. Huge pasta dishes (from DM10) and 11 potato dishes (DM11.90-12.90). 28 wines, from French to Californian. Open daily noon-1am.

Jalda, Limmerstr. 97 (tel. 21 23 26), serves a delightful combination of Italian and Arabic dishes. Lunch specials (M-F noon-4pm, DM10-11). Pizzas DM6-13, veggie fare DM9-15, meaty chow DM13-18. Open Su-Th noon-midnight, F-Sa noon-1am.

⊛**Uwe's Hannen Faß Hannover,** Knochenhauerstr. 36 (tel. 326 16). Located in the center of the *Altstadt,* in the timber-framed house where the master brewer of Hannover once lived. The steaming *Niedersachsenschmaus* (DM7.50), a potato casserole, steadies the stomach while a *Bowle* of the house-brewed *Hannen Alt* lightens the head (DM5.40). Also a popular. Foot-long sandwiches DM9.50. Salad bar DM5.50. Daily specials served noon-3:30pm. Open M-Sa noon-2am, Su 3pm-2am.

Peach Pit, Lister Meile 5 (tel. 34 34 32). A late night/early morning haven for the drunk, tired, and hungry. Although you won't run into Brenda or Brandon, you will likely see happy inebriates (Hi, Dillon!) looking for a sandwich (DM2.80-7), milk-shake (DM3.50), or more beer. Open W 8pm-2am, Th 6am-2am, and F 6am until Su at 2pm—that's 56 continuous hours of 90210 antics!

SIGHTS

In 1714, the son of Electoral Princess Sophie ascended the throne of the United Kingdom as George I, and his descendents continued as the rulers of Hannover and the United Kingdom until 1837, when the Hannoverians refused to accept a queen—Sophie's great-great-great-great-granddaughter Victoria. The city owes much to Sophie, who furnished the three paradisiacal **Herrenhausen Gardens.** The Baroque landscaping is wild and ambitious. Take U-Bahn #4 (direction: "Garbsen") or 5 (direction: Stöcken") to "Herrenhausengarten." The centerpiece is the **Großegarten** (Great Garden). Its **Herrenhausen Palace,** built in the 18th century, hosts frequent concerts and ballets; snap up advance tickets from DM16 at the tourist office, or buy tickets at the door on the evening of the performance. During the "illuminations," geyser-like fountains shoot from the ground to glow in the warm backlighting—gushing in their midst is Europe's highest garden fountain, the **Große Fontäne.** Originally 32m high, it has been gradually built up to 80m. Adjacent to the Großegarten, the smaller **Georgengarten** and **Berggarten** offer equally bewitching vegetation. Various *Feuerwerkswettbewerbe* (fireworks contests), held during the summer, provide dazzling displays. *(Georgengarten open 24hr. Free. Großegarten and Berggarten open Apr.-Oct. M-Tu 8am-8pm, W-Su 8am-11pm; daily Nov.-Mar. 8am-dusk. DM3. Light show W 5-7:30pm. DM5. Fountains M-F 11am-noon and 3-5pm, Sa-Su 11am-noon and 2-5pm. DM3.)*

The *Altstadt,* almost totally reconstructed since WWII, is a 15-minute walk from the train station. Walk down Bahnhofstr. and continue along as it becomes Karmarschstr.; take a right on Knochenhauer Str. and the 14th-century **Marktkirche,** Hans-Lilje-Pl., will be on your left. *(Open daily 10am-4pm; check for concerts.)* The large construction site next to the church is the **Altes Rathaus.** Though the city government has not used the Old Town Hall for official purposes since 1913, it has decided to restore the building to its original glory. Turn down Krämerstr. from Knochenhauerstr. and you will reach Holzmarkt and the **Leibnizhaus,** Holzmarkt 5 (tel. 62 44 50). *(Open Su 10am-1pm and 1:30-6pm.)* A beautifully restored Baroque mansion, the house was home to brilliant mathematician, philosopher, man of letters, and royal advisor Gottfried Wilhelm Leibniz until his death in 1716. Tread carefully—this site cost DM22 million to restore. A jog down Leinstr. brings you past the magnificent **Leineschloß,** seat of the Diet of Niedersachsen, to the ivy-covered shell of the crumbling **St. Aegidienkirche.** The massive damage suffered during WWII was intentionally left untouched as a grim reminder of the folly of war.

Against the ruined remains of Hannover's medieval fortifications, the **Friedrichswall,** down Marktstr. from the *Altstadt,* rises the more modern, spectacular **Neues Rathaus.** *(Open Apr.-Oct. M-F 9:30am-5:30pm, Sa-Su 10am-5pm. DM3, students DM2.)* Hannoverians painstakingly recreated this palatial turn-of-the-century complex after World War II. Step inside to see models of the city in 1689, 1939, 1945, and today. Take the slanted elevator up the tower to gawk at the real thing. From up high, you can scout out Hannover's many parks, including the woods around the **Maschsee.** This artificial 2km long lake just south of the *Rathaus* is covered with sailboats and rowboats during the summer and ice skaters in winter. Hannover's links with Britain are espoused in the **Waterloo Monument** (from the *Neues Rathaus,* cross the Leine River bridge or walk through the tunnel near the subway), a high column commemorating the Niedersachsen citizens who fought with the Brits, Russians, Austrians, and Prussians against Napoleon. To fully experience Hannover, follow the **Red Thread,** a 4km walking tour guided by a painted red line connecting all the major sites. The accompanying *Red Thread Guide* (DM3) details the tour in English—available from the tourist office. Enjoy your very own Freedom Trail in Germany!

MUSEUMS

Sprengel Museum, Kurt-Schwitters-Pl. (tel. 16 84 38 75), at the corner of the *Maschsee* and *Maschpark* (near the *Neues Rathaus*). A modern art lover's dream: James Turrell, Henry Moore, Dalí, Picasso, Magritte, and Horst Antes. Check out the light experiments by Turrell—the results will amaze you. Open Tu 10am-8pm, W-Su 10am-6pm. Permanent collection DM8.50; special exhibit DM4.50.

Wilhelm-Busch Museum, Georgengarten 1 (tel. 71 40 76). U-Bahn #4 or 5 (direction: "Stöcken") to "Schneiderberg." See wit and sarcasm channeled onto paper in vivid colors. Just as fun are the art books and postcards from past exhibitions—don't miss the Sebastian Krüger pieces or the history of Max and Moritz. Open Tu-Sa 10am-5pm, Su 10am-6pm. DM4, students and kiddies DM2.

Historisches Museum am Hohen Ufer, Burgstr. (tel. 16 84 21 20), next to the Leibnizhaus, sits in a 1960s replica of a 10th-century fortress. A very thorough exposition of Hannover's history and its cultural links with Britain. Also houses a huge collection of dioramas depicting scenes from battlefields. Open Tu 10am-8pm, W-F 10am-4pm, Sa-Su 10am-6pm. DM5, students and children DM3.

Kestner-Museum, Trammpl. 3 (tel. 16 84 21 20), through the park behind the *Rathaus.* Numismatics will go dizzy over the ancient coin collection. The centerpiece is the Greco-Roman and Egyptian art. Open Tu and Th-Su 11am-6pm, W 11am-8pm. DM5, students DM3. Free on Wednesdays.

Kubus Museum, Theodor-Lessing-Pl. 2 (tel. 16 84 57 90), an der Aegidienkirche. A gallery organized around the alphabet. TE*x*T aS I**M**AgE. Open Tu-F 11am-6pm, Sa-Su 11am-4pm. Free.

ENTERTAINMENT

If you're within a 100km radius of Hannover between July 3 and July 12, detour to its **Schützenfest** (marksmanship festival), the largest such *fête* in the world. Every summer since 1539, Hannoverians have congregated—weapons in hand—to test their marksmanship and retreat to the beer gardens to get *Schützen*-faced. In that order. The 10-day festival comes complete with parade, fireworks, chintzy stuffed animals, and rickety amusement park rides, but its main attraction is the *Lüttje Lage,* a feisty traditional drink. Without spilling, you must down the contents of two shot glasses simultaneously, holding them side by side in one hand; one glass contains *Weißbier,* the other *Schnapps.* And if this isn't enough fun for you, Hannover delivers a nifty one-two punch. After giving the liver a brief respite, the **Maschseefest** (July 28-Aug. 15, 1999) hits you with another wild combination of concerts, masked balls, and street performances. For anyone left standing, the knockout blow falls with the **Altstadtfest** in the first or second weekend in August. All the big *Kneipen* and cafes convene for one last hurrah until next year. The **Flohmarkt** (flea market) on the **Leibnizufer** hits town every Saturday from 7am to 2pm.

Over 20 theaters make their homes in Hannover, supplying ballet, opera, dramas, and Broadway musicals. The **Opera House,** Opernpl. 1, the **Ballhof,** Ballhofstr. 5, the **Schauspielhaus** at Theaterplatz (U-Bahn #10), and the **Theater am Aegi,** on Aegidientorplatz, are the four largest. Tickets for most of the theaters (from DM12) are sold at the tourist office; call their ticket line at 31 24 33. (Advance tickets for the Opera house and the *Schauspielhaus* are also sold at the Opera House M-F 11am-7:30pm, Sa 11am-1pm, or by calling 16 84 61 40 for the opera or 16 84 67 10 for the *Schauspielhaus* 1 hr. after the box office opens.) Most theaters offer student tickets 30 minutes before each show. For the official line on theater listings, festival dates, and other items of interest, pick up the monthly *Hannover Vorschau* from the tourist office (DM3) or the free *Hannover Live,* available at the Kubus Museum among other places. The **Kino am Thielenplatz,** Lauesstr. 2 (tel. 32 18 79), shows movies in English. The enormous **Cinemaxx,** Nicolaistr. 8 (tel. 130 93), and the **Palast Filmtheater,** Bahnhofstr. 5 (tel. 32 28 73), show dubbed American blockbusters.

NIGHTLIFE

When the sun goes down, Hannover lets 'em rip with an impressive array of packed cafes and pumping discos. Kröpcke buzzes with an alternative scene in the small plazas. The happening university crowds swarm the area of Linden North, between Goetheplatz and Leinaustr., filling the cafes and *Kneipen.* For parties, snoop around the **Mensa** for signs, or check either *Prinz* (DM4.50) or *Schädelspalter* (DM5), outstanding guides to nightlife in the city. The free *MagaScene* lists dance clubs and concerts. Each university *Fach* (department) throws monthly parties, and the best ones, believe it or not, are held by the *chemistry* students. For live music, check out **The Capitol** (see below) or **Altro Mondo,** Bahnhofstr. 8 in the "City Passage" (tel. 32 33 27). Tickets are available by phone at 41 99 99 40.

The Capitol, Schwarzer Bär 2 (tel. 44 40 66), sets the floor thumping with dance hits. Loosen up in a sea of bumping bodies. Next to the bar, a smaller floor for hard rock gets heads banging. Cover around DM8. Opens F-Sa 10pm. Also houses the **Balou Music Club,** open W-Sa at 9pm. Call for a schedule.

Daily Planet, Aegidientorpl. 1 (tel. 32 30 02). Jump out of your phone booth and stop the friggin' presses. A cool news bar with **Internet access,** burgers, and beers (DM3.30). Open M-Sa 10am-midnight.

The Loft, Georgstr. 50b (tel. 363 13 76). Right near Kröpke, this hip joint is packed with students and smoke on the weekends. Open M-Th 9pm-2am, F-Sa 9pm-5am, Su 8pm-2am. Go through the back door to enter the alternative bistro-bar **Masa.** Enjoy falafel (DM6.50) and milkshakes (DM5.50) by candlelight. Masa open Sa-Su noon-5am, M-F noon-2am.

Finnegan's Wake, Theaterstr. 6 (tel. 32 97 11). A place to chill with real Dubliners, where everybody knows Ulysses's name. Daily happy hour (4-6pm) and live Irish music (F-Su 9pm) liven the scene. Open M-F 4pm-late, Sa-Su noon-late.

Osho Disco, Raschpl. 7L (tel. 34 22 17), caters to a similar crowd as The Capitol. A lounge area surrounding the dance floor is a great place to meet (read: pick up) folks. Every Wednesday is "over 30-night"—no cover for survivors of the "Stayin' Alive" years. Cover W-Th and Su DM5, F-Sa DM8. Open W-Su at 10pm.

Schwule Sau, Schaufeldstr. 29 (tel. 700 05 25). U-Bahn #6 or 11: "Kopernikusstr." Don't even try to translate the name; we'll do it for you (it means "gay pig"). One of the most popular gay and lesbian bars in Hannover, located in the university district. On good nights, the 3-person sofa in the corner seats 15. Tu ladies only. W men only. Open F-Sa 8pm-late; other days, call ahead for times.

■ Göttingen

Contemporary Göttingen remains a college town to the core, serving as home to Europe's first free university. The Georg-August-Universität boasts Otto von Bismarck as an alumnus and the Brothers Grimm as faculty members, but its real fame comes from its spectacular track record in hard science. Forty-one Nobel laureates have been students or faculty members, including Max Planck (the father of quantum mechanics) and Werner Heisenberg (the brilliant but eccentric head of the German A-bomb project). Heisenberg may have been one of World War II's unsung heroes, reputedly disclosing information to Allied scientists while leading his research teams down fruitless paths to keep the Bomb out of Hitler's hands. Such anti-authoritarianism is a Göttingen tradition—in the years after its founding in 1737, the university was one of the most liberal in the German lands. By the 1920s, however, it degenerated into a hotbed of reactionary nationalism. After World War II, the pendulum briefly swung the other way as Göttingen earned a reputation as a *"rote Uni"* (red university). The ideological sparks have now subsided as the town exudes a serene yet cosmopolitan air for its students and visitors.

ORIENTATION AND PRACTICAL INFORMATION

Göttingen's *Altstadt* lies within the confines of the horseshoe-shaped Ernst-Hönigwall. At its center you can find the old **Rathaus** and the **Great Hall** at **Wilhelmsplatz,** which served as the sole university building when it was founded in 1734.

Trains: Göttingen is easily reached by trains from Frankfurt (2½hr.), Hamburg (2hr.), and Hannover (1hr.).

Public Transportation: Almost all city buses depart from "Markt" and "Kornmarkt." A bus ride will cost you DM2.70, with one transfer included.

Taxis: Hallo Taxi, "Göttingen's friendly taxis." Call 340 34 and say hallo.

Car Rental: Sixt-Budget, Groner Landstr. 33B (tel. 54 75 70). Open M-F 7:30am-6pm, Sa 8am-1pm.

Mitfahrzentrale: Citynetz Mitfahr-Zentrale, Burgstr. 7 (tel. 194 44), hooks up riders and drivers. Cheap fares to cities within and outside Germany. Open M-F 9:30am-1pm and 2-6pm, Sa-Su 10am-1pm.

Bike Rental: The youth hostel (see below) rents bikes to guests for DM9 per day, DM18 for 3 days. DM50 deposit or ID required.

Tourist Office: Tourist-Information, *Altes Rathaus*, Markt 9, 37073 Göttingen (tel. 540 00; fax 400 29 98; email tourismus@goettingen.de). From the station, cross busy Berliner Str. to pick up the perpendicular Goetheallee. Follow it for several blocks as it becomes Prinzenstr., and turn right onto Weenderstr., which runs into the market square. From there, the *Rathaus* will be visible. You can purchase a handy guide to the city that includes a hotel and restaurant list, a map, and a schedule of events for the month (DM1). The staff will also book a private room (from DM45) for free. Open Apr.-Oct. M-F 9:30am-6pm, Sa-Su 10am-4pm; Nov.-Mar. M-F 9am-6pm, Sa 10am-1pm. A smaller **Tourist-Center,** Bahnhofspl. 5 (tel. 560 00; fax 531 29 28), is located at the train station. Open M-F 9am-6pm, Sa 9am-1pm.

Tours: Leave from the main hall of the *Rathaus* daily at 2:30pm if 5 or more people attend. DM5, students DM3. Tours in English available for large groups only.

Currency Exchange: Commerzbank, Prinzenstr. 2 (tel. 40 80), has the best rates in town. Open M-W 8:30am-4pm, Th 8:30am-6pm, F 8:30am-3:30pm. The **Postamt** in the *Bahnhof* exchanges currency on weekends.

American Express: Goetheallee 4a (tel. 52 20 70). Open M-F 9am-6pm, Sa 9:30am-12:30pm.

Bookstore: Deuerlich, Weenderstr. 33 (tel. 49 50 00), is the main store. Smaller, specialized branches at Weender Landstr. 6 and Theaterstr. 25. Open M-W and F 9am-7pm, Th 9am-8pm, Sa 9am-4pm.

Laundromat: Wasch-Salon, Ritterplan 4, opposite the Städtisches Museum. Wash DM5, soap included. Dry DM1 per 12min. Open M-Sa 7am-10pm.

NIEDERSACHSEN

Göttingen

ACCOMMODATIONS
A Hotel Zum Schwan
B Hotel-Gaststätte Berliner Hof
C Jugendherberge

Emergency: tel. 110. **Fire:** tel. 112. **Police,** Am Steinsgraben 19 (tel. 49 11). **Ambulance:** Krankentransport Göttingen, tel. 192 22.
Women's Concerns: Frauenhaus (tel. 483 20). Open daily 24hr.
AIDS-Hilfe/Gay Information: AIDS-Beratung, tel. 400 48 31.
Post Office: Heinrich-von-Stephan-Str. 1, 37073 Göttingen (tel. 498 61 50), to the left of the train station. Open M-F 8am 6:30pm, Sa 8am-1pm.
Telephone Code: 0551.

ACCOMMODATIONS

The abundance of students and visitors in Göttingen makes the long-term housing market tight but not unreasonable. Fortunately, the hostel is excellent and generally has available rooms, while those wishing to stay a few days or even a few months can check the **Mitwohnzentrale,** Rasenweg 8a (tel. 194 22), which matches up potential roomies (open Su-F 10am-5pm).

Jugendherberge (HI), Habichtsweg 2 (tel. 576 22; fax 438 87). From the station, turn left onto Berliner Str., which becomes Nikolausberger Weg; it's a long trek down this street, but you'll eventually see Habichtsweg on your left (45min.). Or, bus #8, 10, 11, 15, or 18 to "Kornmarkt;" and then bus #6 (direction: "Theaterpl./ Klausberg") to "Jugendherberge." This place puts most *hotels* to shame with immaculate rooms, many singles, and new sinks and furnishings. DM22, over 26 DM27. Room keys require DM20 deposit. Breakfast included. Sheets DM5.70. Bikes for rent. Reception 6:30am-11:30pm. Curfew at midnight, but get a key with a DM50 deposit.

Hotel "Zum Schwan," Weender Landstr. 23 (tel. 448 63). Make a left from the station onto Berliner Str. and another left onto Weender Landstr. (10min.). Cool tie-like patterns cover the walls of some pretty darned big rooms. Singles DM49, with shower DM69; doubles DM79, with shower DM89. Breakfast included. Reception M-F 7am-10pm, Sa 7am-2pm, Su 7am-2pm and 7-10pm.

Hotel-Gaststätte Berliner Hof, Weender Landstr. 43 (tel. 38 33 20; fax 383 32 32). Down the street from Hotel "Zum Schwan" and neatly tucked up next to the university. Can also be reached from the train station with bus #20 or 24 to "Kreuzbergring." Floral comforters will put you to sleep on the spot...and your little dog, too. "The poppies! The poppies..." Singles DM58, with shower DM70; doubles with the works DM98. Reception 3-11pm.

FOOD

Göttingen is blessed with a high quality **Mensa** and vegetable **Markt,** two great budget-food institutions. An impressive array of farm-fresh peddlers haggle in the area between Lange and Kurze Geismarstr., including at a fruit market adjacent to the Deutsches Junges Theater (Tu, Th, and Sa 7am-1pm) and in the square in front of the *Rathaus* (Th 2-8pm). The most central **supermarket** is **Plus,** Prinzenstr. 13, across from the library (open M-F 8am-6:30pm, Sa 8am-2pm). **Goetheallee,** running from the station to the city center, has late-night Greek, Italian, and Turkish restaurants.

Zentral Mensa, Platz der Göttinger Sieben 4 (tel. 39 51 51). Follow Weender Landstr. onto Platz der Göttinger Sieben, turn right into the university complex, and walk through the dusty central plain to the cavernous *Studentenwerk* building off to the left. Swarming with people and plastered with events listings, the cafeteria serves meals for DM2.50-5, guests (non-students) DM4.80-5.80. Meal tickets sold downstairs—buy one or you can't eat. Food served M-F 11:30am-2:15pm, Sa 11:30am-2pm. The **Central Café** sells baguettes and snacks (open M-Th 9am-8pm, F 9am-7pm).

Nudelhaus, Rotestr. 13 (tel. 442 63). Oodles of noodles, with a fully stocked international menu (most DM8-13). A beer garden in back facilitates merry slurping. Open daily noon-11:30pm.

⊛Shucan, Weenderstr. 11 (tel. 48 62 44). Just follow your nose to the giant toucan out front. A hip cafe and bar with hundreds of outdoor seats overlooking the Marktplatz behind the Rathaus. Baguettes (DM5-7) are an afterthought; their over-ornate, neo-Gothic/Baroque ice cream concoctions tower over the central city (from DM5). No Fruit Loops. Open Su-Th 9am-2am, F-Sa 10am-3am.

Asia-Imbiss, Goetheallee 16 (tel. 479 24), serves up *gebranntes Reis* (fried rice) and your favorite Chinese dishes, á la Deutschland. Most entrees DM10-15; lunch specials daily 11am-3pm (most are DM8-12). Open M-Sa 9am-3am, Su 10am-3am.

Pizzeria Sorrento, Jüdenstr. 13a (tel. 550 20). With Göttingen's plethora of gyro-joints, how does one choose? This one is popular with the locals—great selection, dirt cheap. Gyros DM6, pizzas DM6.50-12.50, lasagna DM8.50. They deliver! Open Su-Th 11am-2am, F-Sa 11am-3am.

SIGHTS

The courtyard of the **Altes Rathaus** serves as the meeting place for the whole town: punker, professor, and panhandler alike. The little 1m-high **Gänseliesel** (goose-girl) on the fountain in front of the *Rathaus* is Göttingen's symbol, edging out Ginger Spice as "the most-kissed girl in the world"; graduating students, particularly budding doctors, line up to kiss the promiscuous bronze beauty after receiving their diplomas. The repressed city council imposed a "kissing ban" in 1926, prompting one incensed (or perhaps just, uh, frustrated) student to sue. He lost, but town officials now turn a blind eye to extracurricular fountain activities. The bronze lion-head doorknob on the south portal of the **Rathaus** was crafted in 1300, making it the oldest town hall door knob in Germany. (So it's not the Pyramids. Deal.) Inside, elaborate murals depict 19th-century working-day life in Göttingen. Tours of the city depart from the *Gänseliesel* (see **Practical Information,** p. 280). The renowned **university** lies outside the Ernst-Hönig-Wall. The campus fills an area bounded by Weender Landstr. and

Nikolausberger Weg. Göttingen's student body is diverse, representing many styles, outlooks, and nationalities; still, you won't meet the cast from *Animal House* here. The **Bismarckhäuschen** (tel. 48 62 47), outside the city wall, is a tiny stone cottage built in 1459 where 17-year-old law student Otto von Bismarck took up residence after authorities expelled him from the inner city for boozing it up. *(Open Tu 10am-1pm, Th and Sa 3-5pm. Free.)* A **Bismarckturm**, im Hainberg (tel. 561 28), in the *Stadtforest*, commemorates the larger-scale trouble-making of his later career (see **Bismarck and the Second Reich**, p. 60). *(Open Sa-Su 11am-6pm. Free.)* From the top of the old stone tower, there's a Göttingen-wide view. Take bus A to "Bismarckstr./Reitsall." Göttingen also flaunts a few notable medieval churches. At the corner of Prinzenstr. and Weenderstr., **St. Jacobi's** (tel. 575 96) 72m tower rises up next to the stone lambada sculpture called "Der Tanz." *(Open daily 10am-5pm. Free organ concerts F at 6pm.)* Inside, it's fun to play with the miniature model of the impressive 1402 altar triptych. Down Weenderstr. behind the *Altes Rathaus* stands the fortress-like **St. Johanniskirche** (tel. 48 62 41). The interior is unexceptional, but the tower in which students have lived since 1921 is more interesting. *(Open daily 10:30am-12:30pm. Tower open Sa 2-4pm.)* On Untere Maschstr. stands a spiraling pyramid erected as a **memorial** to the Göttingen synagogue that was razed in 1938. Viewed from above, the structure spirals into a monumental Star of David. Elsewhere, venerable *Fachwerk* mark the town's zenith, constructed when Göttingen was a member of the **Hanseatic League** (1351-1572).

The **Städtisches Museum**, Ritterplan 7 (tel. 400 28 43), one block north on Jüdenstr. from the Jacobikirche, gives a detailed examination of the city over the last several millennia or so, with stuff on Captain Caveman and friends. *(Open Tu-F 10am-5pm, Sa-Su 10am-1pm. DM3, students DM2.)* The third floor holds the compelling **Göttingen History** wing; the limited scope tells the story well. Hostel-sleepers will get a strange chill from a display of *Hitlerjugend* memorabilia which includes a number of *Deutsche Jugendherbergswerk* pins complete with swastikas on them. There's also a display of dozens of cover pages from Göttingen's Nazi-run local newspaper that presents a rather distorted view of history. Much is made of Göttingen's intellectual distinction and liberal sentiments: in 1837, on the 100th anniversary of the university's founding, a group of professors known as the **Göttingen Seven** made German history by sending a public letter of protest to King Ernst August, who had revoked the liberal constitution established four years earlier by his predecessor. Courageous signers included the Brothers Grimm, then well-known professors of literature; as expected, the Seven were all removed from office.

ENTERTAINMENT AND NIGHTLIFE

Göttingen's entertainment industry covers the entirety of the theatrical spectrum. For world-class performances, the renowned **Deutsches Theater**, Theaterpl. 11 (tel. 49 69 11), puts on the classics with tickets as low as DM11. Check out the slick **DT** catalog for the schedule, available at the box office (open M-F 10am-1:30pm and 5-7pm, Sa 10am-noon, and 1hr. before shows). To sample the youthful perspective, head down to the **Junges Theater**, Hospitalstr. 6 (tel. 551 23), which presents both the classic and the innovative (DM19, students DM12). They show films on Tuesday nights (DM9, students DM6). **All theaters close for the summer from July to mid-September.** Otherwise shows run daily Wednesday to Sunday. (Box office open M-Sa 11am-1pm and 6-8:30pm, Su 6-8:30pm, and 1hr. before shows begin.) The Junges Theater also houses the **KAZ-Keller**, which serves occasionally as a concert hall or dance club, and hosts other neat cultural events. Call 471 45 for schedules and more info. Film buffs can indulge in the perverse pleasure of ruthlessly dubbed blockbusters and German-language flicks at **Capitol 3 Cinema**, Prinzenstr. 13 (tel. 48 48 84), or at the nine screens of the gigantic **Cinemaxx** (tel. 521 22 00) complex behind the *Bahnhof*. The artsy **Lumière**, Geismar Landstr. 19 (tel. 48 45 23), is more cosmopolitan and foreign-language friendly (DM9, students DM8). For cheaper film options, check out the university's **clubkino**. They screen films on Mondays at 7:30pm, in Hörsaal 011 of the *Studentenwerk* building (see **Food, Zentral Mensa**).

Although Göttingen's disco and pub scene primarily occupies the *Altstadt*, a few popular clubs perch on the outskirts of the university. The aptly named **Outpost,** Königsallee 243 (tel. 662 51), reputedly the best dance club in the city, keeps gettin' jiggy until 1am (open Tu, F-Sa 9pm-1am). Within the *Altstadt*, the best place to hear music and hang with students is the **Blue Note,** Wilhelmpl. 3 (tel. 469 07), under the *Alte Mensa* in Wilhelmsplatz. There's a different musical theme each day of the week, and live bands at least once a week. Jazz, reggae, and African pop are well represented. (Open M-F 6pm-2am, Sa-Su 8pm-3am. When big-name DJs hop into the fray, cover DM12, students DM8.) **Nörgelbuff Musik-Kneipe,** Groner Str. 23 (tel. 438 85), has an impressive venue and live music—including the occasional "rock concert"—several times a week. (Located next to the "Kornmarkt" bus stop. Happy hour M-Sa 7-9pm. Opens M-Sa at 7pm, Su at 8pm.) **Irish Pub,** Mühlenstr. 4 (tel. 456 64), is one of the most popular student watering holes with a seemingly infinite supply of Guinness and a ton of Gaelic *Gemütlichkeit* (open daily 6pm-2am). **Club Kiss,** Jüdenstr. 13 (tel. 531 25 13), is the local gay and lesbian dance club. Call for hours and cover prices.

■ Goslar

Goslar flaunts a winning hand. The *Altstadt* is congested with immaculate half-timbered houses and winding narrow streets, and encircled by the divinely lush, green Harz Mountains. Exciting museums and provocative sculptures, designed and crafted by artists such as Henry Moore and Botero, are scattered throughout the village, enchanting the most jaded aesthete. In addition, as the hub of an extensive bus network, Goslar can spin you to any part of the region. Goslar's postcard perfection, and its perch at the edge of the peaceful and popular Harz mountains, has, however, turned it into something of a tourist trap. Beware.

During the 11th century, Heinrich II governed Goslar from the solemn **Kaiserpfalz** (Imperial Palace). However, when the Swabians deposed Kaiser Heinrich IV in 1077, Goslar's good fortune went with him. In the 13th century, the town hit the jackpot again: the **Rammelsberg,** a tall hill at the southern edge of town, turned out to be loaded with high-quality silver ore. Soon, prosperity hit Goslar broadside, and a powerful guild class took control of the city council. The mines sustained the boom until the 16th century, when Free Goslar began to spend all of its time and money fighting off the covetous dukes of Braunschweig. Finally, in 1552, Goslar lost its luck again: it was occupied and forced to cede its mine-mountain to Braunschweig.

This loss 450 years ago now creates an extraordinary windfall for tourists: all building halted after the occupation, and Goslar's immense 16th-century *Altstadt* was effectively frozen in time. During World War II, Goslar's citizens proclaimed it neutral and free of soldiers, painting red crosses atop the pointy *Fachwerke*. Under the Geneva convention, this act rendered the town a non-target for bombing, saving it from destruction. UNESCO recognized Goslar's unique character by declaring virtually the entire town a historic site, beckoning tourists and Diva Fortuna back.

ORIENTATION AND PRACTICAL INFORMATION Trains from Hannover (16 per day) and Göttingen (14 per day) stop at Goslar. Perched near the defunct border with the East, Goslar is a good base for a bus or hiking tour of the Harz Mountains. **Harz Bike,** Bornhardtstr. 3-5 (tel. 820 11), rents bikes for DM35 per day (open M-F 9:30am-6pm, Sa 9am-2pm). The **tourist office,** Markt 7 (tel. 780 60; fax 230 05), across from the *Rathaus*, finds rooms (from DM30) for no fee and offers numerous guides and maps to the Harz Mountains. Tours depart regularly from the Marktplatz (DM7-8). (Open May-Oct. M-F 9:15am-6pm, Sa 9:30am-4pm, Su 9:30am-2pm; Nov.-Apr. M-F 9:15am-5pm, Sa 9:30am-2pm.) There is also a **Harz regional tourist office** in Goslar: the **Harzer Verkehrsverband,** Marktstr. 45 (tel. 340 40; fax 34 94 66), inside the Industrie und Handels Kammer building. (Open M-F 8am-4pm.) Their indispensable "Grüner Faden für den Harz-Gast" pamphlet (DM5) lists every attraction from ski schools to tours on horseback. Unfortunately, the most recent edition of the "Grüner Faden" is from 1994. The office also sells detailed guides on the hostels, public transportation, attractions, and hiking and biking in the region. The **Frauenzentrum Goslar,** Breitestr. 15a (tel. 422 55), provides counseling for women. The entrance is on Bolzenstr. (open M 9am-noon and 3-5pm, W and F 9am-noon). The **post office** is at Klubgartenstr. 10, 38640 Goslar (open M-F 8am-5:30pm, Sa 9am-noon). The **telephone code** is 05321.

> **Note:** While the Oberharz Mountains loom over Niedersachsen and Thüringen, information about the entire Harz region can be found in Sachsen-Anhalt (see **Harz Mountains,** p. 216).

ACCOMMODATIONS AND CAMPING The half-timbered Goslar **Jugendherberge (HI),** Rammelsbergerstr. 25 (tel. 222 40; fax 413 76), wins the prize for being the most confusingly located hostel in the book. Non-locals try to reach the hostel via the streets and suffer. There's a **shortcut:** from the Marktplatz, take twisty Bergstr. southwest until it ends at the large east-west Clausthalerstr. Directly across the street, between the trees, a stairway marked with a "Wanderweg" sign awaits. Take this pleasant path through the pines, head right at the fork at the path's midpoint, and you'll find yourself in the hostel's backyard (20min.). Or, take bus C from the train station (direction: "Bergbaumuseum") to "Theresienwall"; continue along in the same direction as the bus, and at the big white sign that says "Jugendherberge," take a sharp left up the hill (10 min). The path is poorly lit at night. The hostel features smallish 2- and 6-bed rooms with new furniture and newly equipped bathrooms. (DM20, over 26 DM25. Members only. Breakfast included. Vegetarian meals available. Reception 9:30am-10pm. Check-in after 3pm. Curfew midnight.) **Campingplatz Sennhütte,** Clausthalerstr. 28 (tel. 224 98), 3km from town along the B241, has a restaurant (tel. 225 02) and sauna (DM5.50 per person; DM4 per tent; showers DM1).

If you've a bit more money to spare, Goslar proffers several excellent *Pensionen.* Next to the *Markt* is the impressive **Gästehaus Schmitz,** Kornstr. 1 (tel. 234 45). While Schmitz has all of the quirky architectural details of an authentic half-timbered house, the place is nicely decorated and comfortably modern, complete with a fully equipped kitchen, sauna, solarium, whirlpool, and sunny breakfast area. From the *Markt,* turn left on Kornstr. (Singles DM55; doubles DM70. Apartments for 1 or 2 people available at DM55-80. Reception 9am-7pm.) **Gästehaus Elisabeth Möller,** Schieferweg 6 (tel. 230 98), comes with a large, shady garden (3000sq. m) and a patio that invites afternoon lounging. From the station, make a right onto Klubgartenstr., which becomes Am Heiligen Grabe; cross Von-Garssen-Str., and turn right on Schieferweg. (Singles with shower DM45, with full bath DM55; doubles DM80, DM100.)

FOOD AND ENTERTAINMENT The town's mountain **Markt** yodels every Tuesday and Friday (open 8am-1pm). The beautiful market square is ringed with cafes and restaurants; unfortunately, most are of the DM5-per-beer variety. Cheaper bistros and cafes can be found along Hokenstr., where *Imbiß* stands provide meals for DM4-8. If for no other reason than its great name and special sauce, grab a bite to eat at **Mac Döner,** Marktstr. 36 (tel. 12 30). Fast food, under 5 billion served. (Open M-Th 11am-11pm, F-Su 11am-1pm). If you're craving something slightly more exotic (no, gyros don't count), dine at **Hindustan,** Hoher Weg 3 (tel. 186 36), the local Indian restaurant. The regular menu is a bit pricey, but lunch specials (served M-Sa noon-3pm) like lamb masala and curry chicken are only DM9-10. (Open M-Sa noon-3pm and 6-11pm, Su noon-11pm). Music, beer, and the local crowd are served up at the **Kö Musik-Kneipe,** Marktstr. 30 (tel. 268 10; open Su-Th 4pm-2am, F-Sa 4pm-3am).

SIGHTS Guarded by a pair of bronze Braunschweig lions, the austere **Kaiserpfalz,** Kaiserbleek 6 (tel. 70 43 58), is a massive Romanesque palace that served as the ruling seat for 11th- and 12th-century emperors. The palace fell into sad decay by the 19th century but was extensively restored by nationalistic 1870s Prussian aristocrats. The interior of the **great hall** is plastered with 19th-century murals; the huge paintings display carefully selected historical incidents in the mythic, pompous manner that only 19th-century Germans could properly pull off. In the palace's **Ulrichs-kapelle,** Heinrich III's heart lies tucked away inside a massive sarcophagus. *(Museum and tomb open Apr.-Oct. daily 10am-5pm; Nov.-Mar. 10am-4pm. Last entry 30min. before closing. DM3.50, children DM2.)* Below the palace at Kaiserbleek 10 is the **Domvorhalle,** Kaiserbleek 10 (Cathedral Foyer), the sad remains of a 12th-century imperial cathedral destroyed 170 years ago. The plaque on the wall is the engraved equivalent of a scrawled "Heinrich Heine wuz here."

The central **Marktplatz** is delightful with its rush of ornate woodwork and trellises. The **Hotel Kaiserworth,** a former guild house, was for many years an eccentric, but striking addition to the square, with its superb tapering gable spires and copious wooden statues of emperors gracing the facade. Recently, however, its elegant white front has been repainted a vulgar red. The hotel's statues have been painted up, too, in full comic-book color; it's now easier to see the coarsely humorous smaller figures on the corners. Each day in the market square, small **Glocken- und Figurenspiel** figures of court nobles and the miners whose work made the region prosperous dance to the chime on the treasury roof (9am, noon, 3, and 6pm). The *Rathaus's* **Huldi-gungssaal** is coated with early 16th- century depictions of the prophesying of Christ's return. Renovations were supposed to be complete by 1999, but who knows…for now, the *Rathaus* is off-limits.

The twin towers of the reconstructed 12th-century **Marktkirche** (tel. 229 22) poke up from right behind the *Rathaus*. *(Open Apr.-Sept. Tu-Th and Sa 10:30am-3:30pm, F 10:30am-2pm, Su noon-3:30pm; Oct.-Mar. Sa 10:30am-3:30pm.)* Inside, see the stained-glass saga of St. Cosmas and St. Damian, third-century twin doctors and martyrs. In a classic instance of the Roman empire's overkill, the saints were disciplined and punished by drowning, burning at the stake, stoning, and crucifixion. The **Mönchehaus,** Mönchestr. 3, exhibits a grand modern art collection, including Anselm Kiefer, Calder, Miró, and Joseph Beuys. *(Open Tu-Sa 10am-1pm and 3-5pm, Su 10am-1pm; free, but donation requested.)* Long before he wrapped the *Reichstag,* Christo came to Goslar to wrap the last wagon of coal from the now-closed mine. On the way back from the *Kaiserpfalz,* the fantastic **Musikinstrumente- und Puppenmuseum,** Hoher Weg 5 (tel. 269 45), is not to be missed. *(Open daily from 11am-5pm; DM4, children DM2.)* The owner has spent more than 40 years assembling the largest private instrument collection in Germany, including one of the **world's first accordions** and a 50s Wurlitzer jukebox. Visit the museum tucked inside, billed as the "smallest musical instrument museum in the world." Your ticket will also get you into the antique doll and toy exhibit, and the racier "Beauty" porcelain exhibit of naked women, hidden in the basement. Goslar gets funky every year from August 30 to September 1 with its **Altstadtfest**—a kind of watered-down *Oktoberfest.*

■ Hameln (Hamelin)

In the 700 years since the Pied Piper first strolled out of town, Hameln has transformed from a rat trap to a tourist trap. The original story was sordid enough: after Hameln failed to pay the piper his rat-removal fee, he walked off with 130 children in thrall. But today the legend of the *Rattenfänger,* as he is known in Germany, draws tourists as mysteriously as his flute drew rodents in 1284. What do people find so attractive about this legend? Its allegorical link to the settlement of the eastern regions (the so-called *"Drang nach Osten"*), to which many of medieval Hameln's citizens were lured? The cynical delight of comparing children to rabid rodents? Whatever the case may be, the appeal of the dancing rats is a certainty upon which Hameln has built a good deal of prosperity. Along the souvenir-choked streets today, you can almost hear the town mayor consoling grieving parents, "You haven't lost a child, you've gained a lucrative tourist industry."

ORIENTATION AND PRACTICAL INFORMATION Hameln bridges the Weser River, 45 minutes from Hannover by **train** (daily 4:23am-10:23pm, 26 per day). When riding **buses** in Hameln, check the schedule carefully. If there is a little picture of a telephone next to the time, a bus does not come. Instead, you must call 194 19 and tell the operator at least 45 minutes prior to departure that you would like a **taxi;** a Mercedes will then roll up and take you along the bus route (DM2-4). **Oberweser-Dampfschiffahrt,** Inselstr. 3 (tel. 93 99 90), runs **ferries** up and down the Weser River (Mar.-Oct.), offering a complete package of tours (1hr. expeditions DM7.50, students DM5; call for a schedule and prices). **Rent a bike** (DM20 per 24hr.) from the **Fahrradverleih Troche,** Kreuzstr. 7 (tel. 136 70; open M-F 9:30am-1pm and 2:30-6pm, Sa 9:30am-12:30pm). The hostel (see below) also has a few old bikes to rent to guests (DM8 per day). The **tourist office,** on the Bürgergarten at Deisterallee 3 (tel. 20 26 17 or 20 26 19; fax 20 25 00), tracks down rooms (from DM25) for a DM2 fee. (Open May-Sept. M-F 9am-1pm and 2-6pm, Sa 9:30am-12:30pm and 2-4pm, Su 9:30am-12:30pm; Oct.-Apr. M-F 9am-1pm and 2-5pm.) They also give out a very comprehensive list of hotels and *Pensionen*. From the station, cross Bahnhofplatz, make a right onto Bahnhofstr., and turn left onto Deisterstr., which becomes Deisterallee. A smaller booth in the **Hochzeithaus** has summertime **information** (open mid-Apr. to Oct. Tu-F 11am-2pm and 2:30-4:30pm, Sa-Su 10am-2pm). City **tours** take off from the Bürgergarten (May-Sept. M-Sa 3pm, Su 10am and 3pm; DM5, children DM3). **Buchhandlung Matthias,** Bäckerstr. 56 (tel. 947 00), has a decent selection of English paperbacks (open M-F 9-6:30pm, Sa 9am-4pm; May-Sept. also open Su 11am-4pm.) The **post office** is at Am Posthof 1, 31785 Hameln (open M-F 8am-6pm, Sa 8am-1pm). The **telephone code** is 05151.

ACCOMMODATIONS AND CAMPING
The beautifully located but regrettably Piper-festooned **Jugendherberge (HI),** Fischbeckerstr. 33 (tel. 34 25; fax 423 16), sits on a dreamy bend in the Weser. From the station, ride bus #2 to "Wehler Weg," and turn right onto Fischbeckerstr. By foot, cross Bahnhofplatz, make a right onto Bahnhofstr., turn left on Deisterallee, and then go right around 164-er Ring (along the Hamel rivulet) to Erichstr. as it bends into Fischbeckerstr. (40 min.). German school kids *love* dreamy bends in rivers, so call a couple of months in advance if possible. Crowded rooms, but there's a sweet view from the outdoor patio. (DM20, over 26 DM25. Breakfast included, magic flute to lure away schoolkids is not. Sheets DM5.70. Reception 12:30-1:30pm and 5-10pm. Curfew 10pm, but key available with DM30 deposit.)

Hameln's tourist boom has resulted in a large number of *Pensionen*. Close to the center is **Pension Wiese,** Alte Marktstr. 44 (tel. 39 72), directly across the street from the *Redenhof*. Ask Wiese to tell you how he escaped from the Russians in 1942 by faking nature's call. (DM40. Reception until 10pm. Reservations highly recommended.) The **Gästehaus "Alte Post,"** Hummenstr. 23 (tel. 434 44; fax 414 89) is centrally located and kid-friendly (DM34.50-55). Southeast of the city center, on the Tonebon Lake, lies **Campground Jugendzeltplatz,** Tonebonweg 8 (tel. 262 23), equipped with a sauna. Take bus #44 or 51 to "Südbad." (DM5 per person; reception M-F until 10pm, Sa-Su until 11pm; open May-Sept.)

FOOD
The streets of the *Altstadt* around Osterstr. and Pferdemarkt are lined with restaurants and cafes, but the chances of finding a bargain are slim. A few good deals loom along Bäckerstr. near the *Münster*. Duck into **Julia's Restaurant,** Bäckerstr. 57 (tel. 73 37), which serves spaghetti (DM8.50) and various sorts of *Schnitzel* and *Würste* (open daily 11am-2:30pm and 5:30-7pm). **Mexcal,** Osterstr. 15 (tel. 428 06), serves excellent Mexican meals, and the lunch offers are a good deal (burritos DM9.90; lunch M-Sa noon-3pm). Daily happy hour gets you cheap drinks 'til 6:30pm. (Open daily noon-midnight.) *Hamelners* flock for fruit, vegetables, and other treats to the open-air **market** on the Bürgergarten (open W and Sa 8am-1pm). Hameln boasts an impressive array of edible rodents (if you swallow them whole, the fur will tickle your throat...Mmm!). To catch these rats, pay to the tune of DM0.35 for tiny marzipan critters and up to DM6 for a jumbo pastry rat. Little crusty bread-rats cost DM3 at **Schnelz Reformhaus,** Osterstr. 18 in the *Altstadt*. The *Haus* also sells all-natural foodstuffs of every sort, a delight for the vegetarian with some cooking equipment (open M-W 8:30am-6pm, Th-F 8:30am-6:30pm, Sa 8:30am-2pm). **Plus supermarket,** Bahnhofstr. 34-36, sells the basics (open M-F 8am-7pm, Sa 8am-2pm).

SIGHTS If you cringe at the thought of small rodents or little flute players in motley capes, Hameln is probably not the best vacation spot; the Piper motif is inescapable. One of the few buildings unadorned by Pied Piper paraphernalia is the modern **Rathaus** (did we say RAT Haus?). In the courtyard out front, however, several elfin children hang suspended in mid-air, following a piper statue to the **Rattenfänger-Brunnen.** The **Bürgergarten,** right down the street, lends small but soothing relief to the tourist rat race. *(Open daily 7am-10pm; fountains run daily Apr.-Oct. 11am-noon, 3-4pm, and 7:30-8:30pm.)* Chess players will enjoy the massive game board and 3-foot-high pieces. Walk back down Kastanienwall and turn right into the massive auto-free *Altstadt.* Off to the left, the **Rattenfängerhaus** (built in 1602) is decked out with startled-looking figureheads recalling the sudden surge in the average age of townsfolk. Trek down another 100m to the 1589 **Leiesthaus,** Osterstr. 8-9 (tel. 20 22 15), where the **Museum Hameln** exhibits the Piper in 20 poses and 20,000 books. *(Open Tu-Su 10am-4:30pm. DM2, students and children DM1.)* The grim *Rattenfänger* tale is re-enacted each Sunday at noon (May-Sept., weather permitting) in a **Freilichtspiel** (open-air show) at the 1610 **Hochzeithaus** (free). Small children dressed as rats chase a man with a large wooden instrument in his mouth wearing a multicolored suit and tight pants; it's simply saucy. At 9:35am, the **Glockenspiel** on the *Hochzeithaus* plays the *Rattenfänger-lied* (Pied Piper Song); at 11:45am you're serenaded by the *Weserlied;* and, at 1:05, 3:35, and 5:35pm, a tiny stage emerges from the *Hochzeithaus,* and "rats" circle around a peculiar wooden flautist.

■ Hannoversch Münden

Hannoversch Münden, known to all as "Hann. Münden," lies between forested hills where the Fulda and the Werra combine—with the newborn Weser River popping out as a result of the consummation. Alexander von Humboldt called it "one of the seven most beautifully located cities in the world." With over 700 preserved *Fachwerkhäuser,* this is one of the most attractive of Germany's six zillion half-timbered towns. The impeccable *Altstadt* remains refreshingly free of tourists despite its picture-book setting at the foot of the *Deutsche Märchenstraße* (German fairy tale route). To taste the flavor of the town, strolling aimlessly through the *Altstadt* might offer a richer palate than dragging yourself between sights. Either way, Hann. Münden offers a tiny world of architectural beauty and authenticity.

ORIENTATION AND PRACTICAL INFORMATION: Hann. Münden is easily accessible by **train** from Göttingen (40min.) or Kassel (20min.). **Ferries** navigate the Fulda and Weser rivers with water tours of Hann. Münden (DM7.50-10). Ask for information at the tourist office (see below), or walk to the **Weserstein** at the tip of the island "Unterer Tanzwerder" and hop on a ferry. Get hiking maps and Weg & Fähre, a free and complete guide with information for the town and its environs, from the **tourist office** (tel. 753 13; fax 754 04) in the Rathaus. The staff will book you a room (from DM40) for free. (Open June-Sept. M-F 9am-6pm, Sa 9am-1pm, Su 10am-1pm; Oct.-May Su-F 9am-4pm.) Help is also on hand from the Auskunftschalter (information counter; tel. 750), in the same building, after the office closes (open daily May-Sept. until 9pm; Oct.-Apr. until 8pm). Walking **tours** of the Altstadt are available (June-Sept. M-Sa 10:30am, Su 2pm; DM4, children DM2). Rent bikes and boats at **Busch Freizeit,** located at **Campingplatz Münden** (see below; open 8am-6pm; DM15 per day). Paths along the Weser River lead to the Tillyschanze and continue on toward the **Reinhardswald forest** area. **Hiking** and **biking maps** are available at the tourist office and the hostel (free, but bigger and better ones are DM7.80). The **telephone code** is 05541.

ACCOMMODATIONS AND FOOD The **Jugendherberge (HI),** Prof.-Oelkers-Str. 10 (tel. 88 53; fax 734 39), sits just outside the town limits on the banks of the Weser. From the station, walk down Beethovenstr., turn left at Wallstr., cross the Pionier-brücke, turn right along Veckerhägerstr., and when the road makes a left turn, turn with it (40min.); or take bus #135 from the train station (direction: "Veckerhäger/Kasselerstr.") to "Jugendherberge" (DM2.70). (Hostel DM20, over 26 DM25. Breakfast included. Sheets DM5.70. Reception 5-7pm and 9:45-10pm. Curfew 10pm, but a key to the front door is available. Call ahead. Closed 2 random weekends per month June-Sept.) Pitch your tent in view of the city walls at **Campingplatz Münden,** Oberer Tanzwerder (tel. 122 57; fax 66 07 78), 10 minutes from the train station on an island in the Fulda River off Pionierbrücke. Follow Kasseler Schlagd along the city walls, and turn left onto Tanzwerder. A bridge will lead you over to the island. (DM8.50 per person, DM5 per child. DM5.50 and up per tent. Reception 7am-10pm.)

The cheapest eats can be found at bakeries along Langestr. or at the **Markt** behind the *Rathaus* (W and Sa 7am-1pm). For some historic action, dine at the **Tillyhaus,** Marktstr. 15, where the infamous French general lived for five years during the town's occupation: the restaurant is called **Café-Bistro Caruso** (tel. 730 42). Beer starts at DM1.90 (open Su-Th 5pm-midnight, F-Sa 5pm-2am). For cheap eats to top off the beers, **Pizza Eck,** Rosenstr. 14 (tel. 20 94), serves hefty pizza and pasta plates (DM6-9; open M-Sa 11am-11pm, Su 5-11pm). **Plus,** Marktplatz 5, satisfies grocery needs (open M-F 8am-7pm, Sa 8am-2pm).

SIGHTS Weave through the angled side streets to admire the 14th-century *Fachwerkhäuser;* some of the oldest and most impressive are tucked away on **Ziegelstraße.** The 16th-century **Hinter der Stadtmauer 23,** a Jewish school since 1796, was gutted in 1938. A plaque stands outside in memoriam. Recent owners restored it and uncovered a *Mikwe* (ritual bath) in the basement. The ornate **Rathaus** is a prime example of the Weser-Renaissance style that originated in the area around 1550. To reach the **Rathaus** from the train station, cross the street and walk down Beethovenstr.; make a right onto Burg-Str., then a left onto Marktstr.; the *Rathaus* will be on your left immediately after Lange Str. Centuries-old markings of Weser flood heights mark the *Rathaus* corner walls, and coloring book scenes from the city's past line the walls inside. Figurines appear in the upper windows of the *Rathaus* and dance to the ringing of the bells daily at noon, 3, and 5pm. Also outside is the wagon of Hann. Münden's former resident and favorite tourist gimmick, **Doctor Eisenbart,** an 18th-century traveling physician whose ability to treat many illnesses was overshadowed by his reputation as a quack and a swindler. The comic story of his life is played out at 11:15am every Sunday June-Aug. on the stage in front of the *Rathaus* (DM4, children DM2). The striking **St. Blasiuskirche,** opposite the *Rathaus,* is decked out in periwinkle and emerald, with ornate Solomonic columns surrounding the altar, a somber *Rittergrabmal,* and a 15th-century crucifix. *(Open M-F 11am-12:30pm and 2-5pm, Sa 11am-12:30pm, Su 2-6pm.)*

Hann. Münden's three islands—**Doktorwerder, Unterer Tanzwerder,** and **Oberer Tanzwerder**—are all easily accessible by small, historic bridges on the outskirts of the *Altstadt.* Kasseler Schlagd and Bremer Schlagd are the streets that will lead you to them. The U.K.'s hired guns, the famed Hessian mercenaries, took off from the islet's former pier to face off against the upstart American colonists. The best view of the valley is from across the Fulda atop the **Tillyschanze** tower (tel. 18 90), built in 1882 to commemorate May 30, 1626. On this day during the Thirty Years War, General Tilly stormed through Hann Münden, slaughtering over 2000 citizens. *(Open daily 9am-dusk. DM1.50, children DM1.)* To get there, cross the Pionierbrücke and hang a left. Make another left onto Tillyschanzenweg and follow it to the tower. On the banks of the Werra, the austere **Welfenschloß** proves that not all Weser Renaissance buildings look like over-iced birthday cakes. The gray parts of the building are remnants of the original Gothic structure that burned down in 1560. The interior can only be admired on a guided tour (Sa 2:30 pm; meet in front of the *Rathaus*), but it's not worth your DM4. It also houses the **Städtisches Museum,** which boasts a sizable antique fayence collection (18-19th centuries) and several of Gustav Eberlein's neo-Baroque sculptures. *(Open W-F 10am-noon and 2:30-5pm, Sa 10am-noon and 2:30-4pm, Su 10am-12:30pm. DM2, students DM1.)* The city walls still show seven of the original defense towers, as well as the **Alte Werrabrücke,** built in 1329, and the **St. Aegiden Kirche,** built in the 12th century. Another victim of Tilly, a nearby *Pulverturm* (gun powder tower) exploded and ignited the church. You can also see Doctor Eisenbart's gravestone there; shed a tear for the poor old quack.

■ Hildesheim

The **Tausend Jähriger Rosenstock** (The Thousand-Year-Old Rose Bush) symbolizes the prosperity of the town of Hildesheim. According to legend, Emperor Ludwig der Fromme (the Pious) lost his way after a hunt and fastened his Marian relic to the branch of a conspicuous rose bush. He managed to find his way home, and the next day, remembering his relic, returned to find it still clinging to the branch. He interpreted this as a divine sign and erected a chapel on the site, around which grew the majestic **Dom** and the town of Hildesheim. As long as the bush flourishes, so will Hildesheim. On March 22, 1945, Allied bombers flattened the town, yet the remarkable bush survived. The collapsed ruins of the *Dom* sheltered the roots from the flames. Eight weeks later, 25 buds were growing strong.

ORIENTATION AND PRACTICAL INFORMATION Hildesheim is 45km southeast of Hannover, with good *Autobahn* connections and almost hourly **trains**. **Bus** tickets cost DM2.20 and are good for one hour of unlimited rides. **Rent bikes** at **Räder-Emmel,** Dingworthstr. 20-22, Moritzberg (tel. 438 22); it's on your way down the mountain from the *Jugendherberge* (open M-F 9am-1pm and 3-6pm, Sa 9am-1pm; DM5-10 per day). The **tourist office,** Am Ratsbauhof 1c (tel. 179 80; fax 17 98 88), two blocks from the *Rathaus,* offers brochures and also books rooms for free. From the *Hauptbahnhof,* walk straight up Bernwardstr. which becomes Almsstr., turn left onto Rathausstr., and turn right down Ratsbauhof. (Open M-F 9am-6pm, Sa 9am-1pm.) There is also a **branch office** in the **Kirchturm** of St. Andreas Church that passes out maps and city guides (open M-Sa 11am-4pm, Su noon-5pm). Enjoy the two-hour city **tours** (Apr.-Oct. Su-F 2pm, Sa 10am and 2pm; DM5). **Die Gerstenbergsche,** Hoher Weg 10, Rathausstr. 20 (tel. 10 66), offers **English language books** and chairs to lounge in (open M-F 9am-6pm, Sa 9am-4pm). **Internet access** awaits in the **Internet-Café,** Judenstr. 3 (open M-Sa 10am-11pm; 30min. connection DM5). The **post office,** 31134 Hildesheim, sits next to the *Hauptbahnhof* (open M-F 8am-6pm, Sa 8am-1pm). The **telephone code** is 05121.

ACCOMMODATIONS Although its four- to six-bed rooms are cramped, Hildesheim's pastoral **Jugendherberge (HI),** Schirrmanweg 4 (tel. 427 17; fax 478 47), perches on the edge of a bucolic farm with a beautiful view of the city. Breakfasts are ample and there's a backyard disco, so shake your booty onto bus #1 (direction: "Himmelsthür"), and don't yank it off until "Dammtor." There, bust a move to bus #4 (direction: "Bockfeld") to "Triftstr." Cross the street and climb uphill (10min.) to the hostel. (DM22, over 26 DM27. Breakfast included. Sheets DM5.70. Reception M-Sa 8-9:30am, 5-7pm, and 9:45-10pm, Su 6-7pm and 9:45-10pm. Curfew 10pm, but key available for DM50 deposit.) A little farther out, but well worth the extra trouble, rests **Maria Schröder's Pension,** Bleckenstedterstr. 2 (tel. 434 21; fax 227 67). From the train station, take bus #3 (direction: "Hildesheimer Wald") to "Schützenwiese"; cross the street and you'll find Bleckenstedterstr. right across from the *Polizei.* Frau Schröder has got to be one of the nicest ladies in all of Germany, and, amazingly enough, her rooms are as big as her heart. Plush sofas will have you feeling like a million *Marks,* but you'll only spend DM35.

FOOD AND ENTERTAINMENT Hildesheim has a diverse culinary scene, with plenty of variety and reasonable prices. The **Amsthausstuben** in *Knochenhauer-amtshaus,* Markt 7 (tel. 323 23), serves German dishes from DM10 (open daily 11am-1am). If you're looking for some fresh vegetarian eats, check out **Scheidemann's Salad & Toast Bar,** Osterstr. 18 (tel. 390 04). Sandwiches cost DM4-7, pizzas DM5-8. Meat dishes are available, too. (Open M-F 10am-9pm, Sa 10am-2pm and 6-9pm.) **Paulaner im Kniep,** Marktstr. 4 (tel. 360 13), offers a piece of Munich in Hildesheim. Lunch dishes *(Bratwurst, Schnitzel)* start at DM6.80, but the real draw is the beer—sweet *Münchener* Paulaner (0.5L DM5.80; *Maß* DM10.50). (Open daily 10am-midnight). The students in the area get down at **Vier Linden,** Alfelder Str. 55b (tel. 252 55), a hip dance-mecca with a popular bar (club open M and Th 10pm-3am; bar open

W-Su 6pm-1am). More relaxing but just as fun is the Irish *Kneipe* **Limerick**, Klaperhagen 6 (tel. 13 38 76; open M-Th 11am-1am, F-Sa 11am-2am, Su 11am-midnight).

SIGHTS Ludwig's favorite chapel, the **Annenkapelle**, and the famous *Tausend-Jähriger Rosenstock* bush are featured in the *Dom*'s courtyard. *(Open M-Sa 9:30am-5pm, Su noon-5pm. DM0.50, children and students DM0.30.)* The **Dom-Museum** and **Domschutz** (tel. 17 91 63), around to your left as you exit the *Dom*, showcases the Marian relic of old Ludwig—it's #8 on the "Schlacht bei Dinklar" exhibit—and other ecclesiastical goodies. *(Dom open M-F 9:30am-5pm, Sa 9:30am-2pm, Su noon-5pm. Museum open Tu-Sa 10am-5pm, Su noon-5pm. DM4, students DM1.50.)* The **Marktplatz** is a plaza of reconstructed half-timber buildings and archways featuring the majestic **Knochenhauer-Amtshaus** (Butcher's Guild House), reputed to be the "most beautiful wooden structure in the world." The facade is lavishly decorated with colorful paintings and German proverbs (e.g., *"arm oder reich, der Tod macht alles gleich"*—"poor or rich, death treats all the same"). South of the city center at the intersection of Gelber Stern (Yellow Star) and Lappenberg, lie the remains of Hildesheim's **synagogue**. The temple itself was torched on *Kristallnacht* in 1938, and a memorial has been erected on the site. The warped facade of the 1606 **Wernerhaus** (down from Gelber Stern to Brühl) rests untouched by bombs or modernization.

Looping back around the western tip of the city, drop in at the **Römer- und Pelizaeus-Museum**, Am Steine 1 (tel. 936 90), featuring a colorful collection of Egyptian art and artifacts (including mummies), as well as frequent and extensive special exhibits, ranging from "The World of the Whale" (presented by Greenpeace) to the history of ancient Persia. *(Renovations and special exhibits mean prices and hours are in constant flux; call for info. Generally open Tu-Su 9am-4:30pm. DM12, students DM5.)*

■ Bodenwerder

In the land of **Baron von Münchhausen**, the King of Liars, you might not be sure what to believe. Here on the banks of the Weser, the Baron first told his hunting buddies his fabulous adventure stories of flying to the Moon and sailing through a sea of milk to an island of cheese. But is this Baroque Jon Lovitz himself a fabrication of Bodenwerder's tourist industry, an attempt to out-fable Hameln? Verily not: the little town's church ledgers have birth and death listings for Baron Hieronymus Carolus Friedericus von Münchhausen. More useful truths can be found on the carved wooden signs which point out the various sights of Bodenwerder.

On Münchhausplatz, the mansion-turned-**Rathaus**, the Baron's birthplace, holds the **Münchhausenzimmer Museum** (tel. 405 41). Inside, you'll find color illustrations of his exploits along with the legendary pistol with which he shot his horse off a steeple (DM2, children DM1.20). The streets lining the **Fußgängerzone** (pedestrian zone) are riddled with 114 half-timbered houses; the oldest dot Königstr, Homburgstr., and Grossestr. Farther up the pedestrian zone is a beautiful fountain depicting three of the Baron's most outrageous adventures.

Bodenwerder is best reached by bus from Stadtoldendorf, a town on the Altenbeken-Braunschweig train line. Take bus #520 (direction: "Bodenwerder/Hameln") or #523 (direction: "Kemnade") to "Weserbrücke, Bodenwerder." From Hameln take bus #520 (direction: "Stadtoldendorf"). BahnCards get you a 50% discount on these routes. Rent **bikes** from **Karl-Heinz-Greef**, Danziger Str. 20 (tel. 33 34), for DM10 per day (open Mar.-Oct. daily 8:30am-6pm). The **tourist office**, Weserstr. 3 (tel. 405 41; fax 61 52) has *Weg und Fähre*, which lists events. (Open M-F 9am-12:30pm and 2:30-6pm, Sa 9am-1pm; closed Sa Nov.-Mar.) City **tours** start at 3pm every Wednesday May-Sept. out front (DM3). The **post office**, 37619 Bodenwerder, is located across the street from the *Rathaus* (open M-F 8:30am-noon and 2:30-5pm, Sa 8:30-11:30am). The **telephone code** is 05533.

The tourist office will give you a list of hotels, pensions, and private rooms available for rent (from DM25). Bodenwerder's **Jugendherberge (HI)**, Richard-Schirmann-Weg (tel. 26 85; fax 62 03), is a 15-minute walk from the *Fußgängerzone*, but the last

100m is steep, steep, steep. Walk across the Weser River (via bridge, that is) and turn left, then right on Siemensstr., and follow the signs up Unter dem Berge. The institutional exterior conceals a fun-filled interior brimming with *Fußball* and ping-pong. (6-bed dorms DM20, over 26 DM25. Breakfast included. Lunch DM8.70, dinner DM6.80. Sheets DM5.70. Reception 4-7pm and 9:30-10pm. Curfew 10pm, but you can get a key to the side door.) **Campingplatz "Rühler Schweiz,"** Großes Tal (tel. 24 86), is located on the Weser, south of the *Altstadt* on the opposite side of the river. Cross the *Weserbrücke* and make a right on the path by the river. (Open Mar.-Oct.)

Bodenwerder's culinary offerings are nothing shocking: pizza, baked goodies, ice cream. **Café König,** Große Str. 32 (tel. 4855), serves it up with style and a great view of the pedestrian zone. Most entrees run DM6-10, beer DM2.20-5. (Open M-Tu and Th-Su 10am-6pm). For good deals on groceries check out the **Rewe Supermarkt,** just across the Weserbrücke from the post office (open M-F 8am-8pm, Sa 8am-4pm). On the first Sunday of each month at 3pm, from May to October, a **free play** in the Spa Gardens reenacts Münchhausen's exploits. On the second Saturday of August, Bodenwerder sets the Weser ablaze with its pyrotechnic **Festival of Lights.**

■ Braunschweig

Now that Braunschweig's Cold War border town duties are over, this middleweight city is pumping up its cultural attractions. The history of Braunschweig (sometimes called "Brunswick" in English) began in 1166, when Heinrich the Lion settled here. After hanging up his hat, Heinrich set about building a kingdom: he erected the famous Braunschweig lion statue (the city's emblem) and inaugurated Braunschweig's metamorphosis into a thriving religious and commercial center. The town is saturated with gargantuan cathedrals and other monuments that once marked the free city's economic importance to the Holy Roman Empire. Later a member of the Hanseatic League, Braunschweig now boasts a robust economy, which, combined with its brash bids for tourism, make it one of Niedersachsen's most vital cities.

ORIENTATION AND PRACTICAL INFORMATION

Braunschweig crouches between the Lüneburger Heide and the Harz Mountains. It serves as the crossing point for high-speed trains connecting Frankfurt and Hannover to Berlin and other lines. The *Hauptbahnhof* lies southeast of the city center, essentially an island ringed by the Oker River. Walking straight from the *Bahnhof* brings you across Berliner Platz to the wide **Kurt-Schumacher-Str.** This curves to the left to meet **John-F.-Kennedy-Platz,** a major crossroad at the southeast corner of the central city. Following Auguststr. northwest from JFK-Platz leads to Aegidienmarkt, which brings you to Bohlweg, the wide street that is the eastern boundary of the pedestrian zone. Turn left at Langer Hof to get to the *Rathaus.* Braunschweig's downtown attractions are mostly within the great circle formed by the branching Oker River. Streetcars and buses criss-cross the city; most lines pass through either the "Rathaus"/ "Bohlweg" stops (downtown) or "JFK-Platz"/"K.-Schumacher-Str." stops (a 10min. walk from the *Bahnhof*). Streetcars #1 and 2 from the train station bring you to all those stops.

Public Transportation: A thorough system of **streetcars** and **buses** laces Braunschweig and its environs. A 90-min. ticket, valid for any number of line changes, costs DM2.80; buy two at once and pay DM5. A 24hr. ticket costs DM7, and a family day ticket (valid for up to 2 adults and 3 kids) costs DM9. Pick up a network **map** (*Liniennetzplan*) at the booth in front of the train station or at the tourist offices.

Taxis: call 555 55 or 25 62 50. Call 444 44 for **Frauennacht-Taxi** (women's taxi).

Car Rental: Hertz, Berlinerpl. 1D (tel. 710 55), near the station. Turn left from the *Bahnhof,* and you'll see the office. Open M-F 7am-6pm, Sa 8am-noon.

Bike Rental: Hahne, im Hause Eisenvater, Neustadtring 9-11 (tel. 507 802). DM8 per day. Open M-F 9am-5pm.

Mitfahrbüro, Wollmarkt 3 (tel. 194 40), Walk to the northern tip of the pedestrian zone and then up Alte Waage, which turns into Wollmarkt. Open M-F 10am-6pm, Sa 10am-2pm.

Tourist Office: There are 2 tourist offices in town; one is inside the train station (open M-F 8:30am-5pm, Sa 9am-noon), and the other sits a block from the *Rathaus,* on Bohlweg (tel. 273 55 30 or 273 55 31; fax 273 55 19; open M-F 9:30am-6pm, Sa 9:30am-12:30pm). An excellent free map of the bus and streetcar system is available from the ticket booth outside the station. A range of tours (DM4-27) depart from the Bohlweg branch; both offices find rooms in hotels and *Pensionen* for free (DM39 and up), but you can also just get a free copy of the hotel list from them.

Mitwohnbüro: Wollmarkt 3 (tel. 130 00; fax 152 52). In the same office as the Mitfahrbüro (see above). Open M-F 10am-6pm, Sa 10am-2pm.

Currency Exchange: Dresdner Bank, at the corner of Neue Str. and Gördelingerstr., near the *Altstadtmarkt.* Their ATMs have international services. Open M and F 8:30am-4pm, Tu and Th 8:30am-6pm, W 8:30am-1pm.

Bookstore: Pressezentrum Salzman, in the Burgpassage Galerie mall, sells paperback pulp novels, as well as a limited selection of English and American magazines and newspapers. Open M-F 9:30am-8pm, Sa 9am-4pm.

Library: Öffentliche Bücherei, Hintern Brüdern 23 (tel. 470 68 38), right off Langestr. Main building open M-Tu and Th-F 10am-7pm, Sa 10am-2pm, but the **foreign language library** is only open Tu noon-6pm and F 11am-4pm.

Emergency: Police, tel. 110. **Ambulance and Fire,** tel. 112.

Pharmacy: Apotheke am Kennedy Platz, Auguststr. 19 (tel. 439 55). Open M-F 8:30am-6:30pm, Sa 9am-1pm. **Emergency service** *(Notdienst)* info posted on the door.

Post Office: The main office, 38106 Braunschweig (tel. 709 27 96), is in the 16-story building to the right of the train station. Open M-F 8am-6pm, Sa 8am-1pm.

Telephone Code: 0531.

ACCOMMODATIONS

Considering the city's size, Braunschweig's budget accommodation cupboard is pretty bare. Little that is inexpensive can be found within walking distance; most affordable *Pensionen* and private rooms require a 10- to 15-minute bus or streetcar ride. Pick up a free copy of *Hotels und Gaststätten* at the tourist office. It includes a listing of accommodations and cafes with prices, phone numbers, and city maps.

Jugendgästehaus (HI), Salzdahlumerstr. 170 (tel. 26 43 20; fax 264 32 70). From the station, bus #11 (direction: "Mascherode") to "Klinikum," or bus #19 (direction "Lieferdestr.") to "Klinikum Salzdahlumerstr." By foot, walk left from the station on Berliner Platz to H.-Büssing-Ring, turn left on Salzdahlumerstr. and go under the overpass. Continue for 20min. Far from town, these antiseptic buildings contain bright, spacious rooms, a huge backyard, and kitchen facilities. DM18.50-37, depending on number of roomies and bathroom facilities; over 26 DM22.50-37. Members only. Breakfast DM7. Sheets included. Key deposit DM30. Reception 7am-10pm.

Hotel-Pension Wienecke, Kuhstr. 14 (tel. 464 76; fax 464 64). From the station, walk up Kurt-Schumacher-Str. to JFK Platz, bear right onto Auguststr. and then Kuhstr. (15min.). Quiet, comfortable rooms with big windows, private bathrooms, and TVs. Singles DM69-75, with bath DM89-99; doubles with bath DM125-145; apartments for 1-4 people DM85-170 per day. Breakfast included. AmEx, MC, Visa.

Pension Friedrich, Am Magnitor 5 (tel. 417 28, fax 34 67 77). In the Magni Quarter, right by the Städtisches Museum. Cozy, and there's a swimming pool! DM50-80.

FOOD

A plethora of *Kneipen* (bars) and *Imbiß* kiosks along **Bohlweg,** the eastern boundary of the *Innenstadt,* proffer pizzas, salads, soups, and small sandwiches at reasonable prices. There's a produce market in the *Altstadt* every Wednesday and Saturday 8am-1:30pm. The **Kohlmarkt** area, southeast of the *Altstadt Markt* in the city center, is a bustling, open space with many pleasant (though not terribly cheap) cafes and restaurants. The **Magni Quarter's** winding streets, boutiques, and half-timbers provide a great setting for a meal or drink. Several malls—the *Burgpassage Galerie,* the *Weltenhof,* and *City Point*—also have excellent food stands. **Atlantik's Früchtchen,** in the Burgpassage Galerie mall, is a fruit stand with frequent sales and unbelievably low prices (open M-F 10am-8pm, Sa 10am-4pm); and **Gemüse Paradies,** in City Point, has delicious salads (DM2-5) and baked potatoes (DM4.90-5.90; open M-F 9am-8pm, Sa 9am-4pm, Su 11am-6pm).

Delicato, Münzstr. 9 (tel. 40 07 16), 3 blocks from Burgplatz, protruding from the corner of Münzstr. and Kattreppeln. A top-notch Turkish specialty deli with colorful salads and fresh-baked lasagna. Specials like a fat half of warm eggplant with spiced lamb and tomatoes, plus potato salad (DM7.90). Open M-F 9am-8pm, Sa 9am-4pm.

⊛**Tolle Knolle,** Stobenstr. 15-16 (tel. 437 44), near the "Bohlweg/Damm" stop. Potato soups (DM3.50-5.50), potato omelettes (DM8-9), potato salads (DM4-8), baked potatoes (DM4-14)...get it? They like their tubers. Open Su-F 11:30am-3pm and 5:30-10pm.

Vegetarisches Vollwert-Restaurant Brodocz, Stephanstr. 1 (tel. 422 36), across from the Karstadt perfume department, will help clear clogged arteries with vegetarian meals. Serves a delectable daily menu with salad, main course, and dessert (DM15). Daily specials (DM8.50). Open M-Sa 11am-11pm, Su 3-10pm.

Cafe MM, Kuhstr. 6 (tel. 422 44), near Hotel-Pension Wienecke, offers omelettes, salads, and pastas (DM6.80-10.50). The ritzy sidewalk cafe has antipasto specials and many other tasty morsels. Open Su-Th 9am-midnight, F-Sa 9am-2am.

SIGHTS

All of Braunschweig was once crowded on a small island surrounded by offshoots of the Oker River; the streams now form a moat-like line around the *Altstadt.* Braunschweig's medieval sights encircle the cobbled **Burgplatz,** over which the city's (and Heinrich's) emblem, a **bronze lion,** stands guard. First cast in 1166 as a symbol of Heinrich's regional dominance, the lion is challenged by the **St. Blasius Cathedral,** which towers over the city center. The 12th-century **Dom,** erected on the spot of another church, shows only one telltale sign of its inheritance: a wooden crucifix pendant above the Nave. The faded, motley paintings adorning the far end of the church are remnants of 13th-century murals, illustrating the lives of John the Baptist, Thomas of Canterbury, Christ, Mary, and St. Blaze. The first level looks like an elegant, eerie meeting ground for vampires. A couple of steps below in the gloomy granite **crypt** rest the sarcophagi of Heinrich the Lion and his consort Mathilde (*Dom* open daily 10am-5pm; crypt DM2). The original Braunschweiger lion has retreated to the confines of the **Dankwarderode Castle,** also on the Burgplatz. Originally Heinrich's 12th-century den, it now keeps a modest trove of saints' relics (see **Museums,** below). Just across the Domplatz is the **Neues Rathaus,** a textbook example of the neo-Gothic style. The 1900 edifice boasts jutting spires, golden sandstone walls, russet roof tiles—the works. To reach the historic center, take streetcar #1 or 2 to "Rathaus" from the train station; or walk (15min.) along Kurt-Schumacher-Str., then bear right at JFK-Platz. through Ägidienmarkt onto Bohlweg.

The *Burg* and *Dom* lie at the eastern border of the pedestrian zone; at the western end is the *Altstadtmarkt,* dominated by the *Altstadt Rathaus.* Its facade is covered with statuettes of Saxony's sovereigns, standing guard over the marketplace. Right next door to the old town hall is **St. Martini's Cathedral,** built concurrently with the St. Blasius Cathedral. *(Open Tu-F 10am-1pm and 3-5pm, Sa 10am-1pm, Su 10am-noon. Free.)* Its magnificently ornamented interior includes sculptures of the Wise and Foolish Virgins, who look like they carry larger than life Martini glasses. The story says that they were waiting for their grooms; the smarter bunch had enough lamp oil, and the less cerebrally gifted, well, didn't, and will thus continue to practice the safest form of safe sex.

If your ecclesiastical hunger is not yet satiated, check out the spectacular **Aegidienkirche** and the neighboring monastery, just up the street from JFK–Platz. The church of the former Benedictine Monastery was built in the 11th century and was conse-crated in 1150—about 50 years before Heinrich the Lion strolled into town. Some years later, his great-grandmother had the relics of St. Aegidius, the patron saint of the monastery, and St. Autor, the patron saint of Braunschweig, transferred to Braunsch-weig. The things money can buy....

Possibly the most relaxing place in Braunschweig is the **Löwenwall,** an oval-shaped park in the eastern part of the Innenstadt Island, near the Städtisches Museum. The obelisk, flanked by lions between two splashing fountains, is a monument to the city nobles who died in the Napoleonic Wars. As you walk up Kurt-Schumacher-Str. from the *Bahnhof,* the Löwenwall will be on your right just before you reach JFK-Platz. From the park, walk up Steintorwall and make a left onto Am Magnitor to reach the Magni Quarter, where you will find well-restored medieval houses.

MUSEUMS

Herzog Anton Ulrich-Museum, Museumstr. 1 (tel. 484 24 00; http://www.dhm.de/ museen/haum). From the pedestrian zone, walk across Bohlweg and down Georg-Eckert-Str., which turns into Museumstr.; or ride streetcar #5 to "Museumstr." This was the first European museum to open its doors to the general public. Its galleries are papered with Dutch masterpieces, including works by van Dyck, Vermeer, and Rubens. A special room sets aside a group of 5 Rembrandts, charting the artist's sty-listic development over the decades. Open Tu and Th-Su 10am-5pm, W 1-8pm. DM5, students DM3.

The Dankwarderode Castle, Burgpl., holds a museum which houses medieval goodies from Ulrich's collection and the original bronze lion (see p. 294). The newly renovated **Rittersaal** dazzles with its golden technicolor paintings. Museum open Tu and Th-Su 11am-5pm, W 1-2:30pm and 4-8pm. Rittersaal open Tu and Th-Su 10-11am, W 2:30-4pm. DM5, students DM2.50.

◉Landesmuseum Braunschweig (tel. 484 26 02). This museum has several branches in town, and one in neighboring Wolfenbüttel. The main collection is in the Vieweg-Haus, Burgpl. 1. Among its treasures are another copy of the bronze lion (surprise!), an entire room full of Bieder Maier furniture, love letters from the 1880s, little Nazi toy soldiers (including an angry man with a puny dark mustache), and a 1960s living room rimmed with avocados. Open Tu-W and F-Su 10am-5pm, Th 10am-8pm. DM5, students DM2.50. The branch at Hinter Ägidien is devoted to **Jewish culture** (tel. 484 25 59). A reconstruction of the main room of the old syna-gogue hauntingly complements memorials to victims of the Holocaust. The furni-ture is all authentic, rescued from the deteriorating synagogue. Open Tu-W and F-Su 10am-5pm, Th 10am-8pm. DM5, students DM3.50.

Städtisches Museum, Löwenwall 16 (tel. 470 45 05), is a specialized "domestic museum"; holdings include historical originals of furniture, appliances, living room bric-a-brac, and the world's first motorcycle. Open Tu-F and Su 10am-1pm. The branch at Am Löwenwall (tel. 470 45 05) is devoted to Braunschweig's artistic and cultural history. Open Tu-W and F-Su 10am-5pm, Th 10am-8pm. Both free.

Museum for Photography, Helmstedter Str. 1 (tel. 750 00), just down Museumstr. from the Ulrich museum (or bus #13 or 43 to "Steintor"). The collection of photo-graphs is small, but diverse, and changes often. Nifty old cameras and photo albums are also on display. Open Tu-F 1-6pm, Sa-Su 2-6pm. DM5, students DM3.

ENTERTAINMENT AND NIGHTLIFE

The high-water marks of Braunschweig's theatrical scene were stained in 1772, with the first performance of Lessing's *Emilia Galotti,* and in 1829, with the premiere of Goethe's *Faust* at the Court Theater on Hagenmarkt. The monumental **Staatsthe-ater,** built in the Florentine Renaissance style, was erected in 1861 to replace the old theater hall. This building, the **Großes Haus,** Am Theater (tel. 484 28 00) is only one of three stages run by the state theater; the other two are the **Kleines Haus,** Magnitor-wall 18 (tel. 484 28 00), and the **Theaterspielplatz,** Hinter der Magnikirche 6a (tel. 484 27 97). The Großes Haus plays big-name operas, ballets and musicals (DM8-51), and orchestral concerts (DM19-45); the Kleines Haus and Theaterspielplatz have everything from Goethe to David Mamet to modern dance (DM6-35). Their info number is 500 01 41. (Tickets at the *Großes Haus* available M-F 10am-6:30pm, Sa 10am-1pm. Tickets are also sold at the tourist offices.) The **Lot Theater,** Kaffeetwete 4a (tel. 173 03), is the home of the local avant-garde theater company. Walk up Gördelingerstr. from the Altstadtmarkt. (Tickets DM13-20; available at the theater M-F 11am-2pm.) Pick up a copy of the free magazine *Filmtips* for a movie schedule. There are a lot of movie theaters in Braunschweig; Lupe, Gördelinger Str. 7 (tel. 493 11), and Broadway, Kalenwall 3 (tel. 455 42), show more artsy films.

Braunschweig has several free monthly magazines that provide the skinny on local events: *Subway, Da Capo,* and *Cocktail*. It's telling that these magazines sometimes direct readers to cities as far away as Hamburg. Still, the Braunschweig scene heats up to a steady simmer on the weekends. The most lively area is the square formed by the intersection of Sack, Vor der Burg, and Schuhstr., as well as the nearby Neuestr. The **Magni Quarter,** around the St. Magni church, south of the Ulrich Museum, brims with restaurants, bars, and genuine Braunschweig charm.

Movie, Neuestr. 2 (tel. 437 26), will not serve you buttered popcorn. Lots of beer on tap, cheap bar food (2 *Wieners* DM4.50), and rock and blues constitute the "feature presentation." Open daily 9am-2am.

⊛**Pupasch Kneipe,** Neue Str. 10-12 (tel. 445 61), just down the street from Movie. They're "die total verrückte Kneipe" ("the totally crazy bar"). Friendly service, lots of beer, and they *will* serve you popcorn—a movie-style box of it awaits you at your table. Open Su-Th noon-midnight, F-Sa noon-4am.

The Jolly Joker, Broitzemerstr. 220 (tel. 281 46 60). Bus #5, 6, or 19 to "Broitzemerstr." This titanic joint holds a large dance floor (which also hosts live concerts), six bars, a *Biergarten,* a cheap restaurant (fast-food meals DM5), and a Brechtian movie theater that offers a bar and pop flicks. Cover DM3; movies free. Open M 9:30pm-2am, Tu and Th 9:30pm-2:30am, F-Sa 9pm-4am.

The Pink Cadillac, Breitestr. 23 (tel. 416 61), just off the Altstadt Markt, has pool tables and sporadic **Internet access** (DM15 per hr.). Open M-Th 6pm-midnight, F-Sa 6pm-2am, Su 4pm-midnight.

■ Wolfenbüttel

Just a few kilometers from Braunschweig lies Wolfenbüttel, its pretty little sister city (bus #21 from the *Hauptbahnhof,* or a 10min. train ride). Most of Wolfenbüttel's meticulous Baroque-era urban planning remains intact. Though a few of the city's old half-timbers show their age, the dominant aura is one of well-kept prosperity; the good vibes swell from the **Schloßplatz,** the riverside enclave within the city that features shady lawns and a bevy of brightly colored historical attractions. Wolfenbüttel's medieval streets, red-tiled houses, and the occasional canal provide the quintessential German experience. Although the town attracts plenty of visitors, it retains a feeling of authenticity.

The sights of Wolfenbüttel capture the atmosphere of Candyland—the pink **Trinitatiskirche** in the Holzmarkt (open Tu 11am-1pm, W 11am-1pm and 2-4pm, Th 3-5pm, Sa 11am-4pm), the wildly tilting half-timbered houses of the inner city, and the **Kanzlei** (Royal Chancellery) look like the results of architects fighting over the gingerbread man. The Kanzlei, Kanzleistr., which extends from the Stadtmarkt, can only be described as an absurd mini-castle, with red walls and a bizarre metal statue perched outside defying architectural jargon. The Kanzlei houses the pre-history collection of the **Braunschweig Landesmuseum**—rocks, fossils, primitive tools, and the like (open Tu-F and Su 10am-5pm; DM3, students DM1.50). Walking from the Schloßplatz down Löwerstr., keeping left, you will see a sign for "Kleiner Venedig." Two more bits of craziness lurk through the entryway: at #15 humbly rests a house a mere 1.7m wide, and a little farther up, on Schiffwall, porches hover over canal remnants.

Once a stately, pure-white vision, the ducal **Schloß** (tel. 57 13) has been repainted in crimson with white trim. The cheery castle has its roots in a 13th-century fortress of the Guelphs, but its current appearance is pure Baroque with a beautifully proportioned 17th-century clock tower. A **Schloßmuseum** displays restored rooms from the ducal living quarters; be sure to indulge in a view of the ceilings. (Museum and castle interior open Tu-Sa 10am-5pm, Su 10am-1pm. Museum DM3.) You can also learn all about the town's political and cultural history—including funky lamps and rugs from the 70s. Those funky Wolfenbüttelers. Open-air performances take place in the Schloß's enclosed courtyard nearly every day from mid-June to mid-July. Musicals, choral performances, chamber music concerts, jazz shows, and ballets are performed. Tickets are available at the *Braunschweiger Zeitung* office in Wolfenbüttel, Löwenstr. 6 (tel. 800 10), for DM40 and less.

Across the street from the *Schloß* is the C-shaped **Lessinghaus** (tel. 80 80), a compact mansion that was the local duke's gift to big-time *litérateur* Gotthold Ephraim Lessing, the court librarian of the nearby August-Bibliothek. The **museum** inside recalls Lessing's life and work through manuscripts, letters, and paintings (open Tu-Su 10am-5pm). Across a tree-dotted lawn from the Lessinghaus, the stern **Herzog-August-Bibliothek** (tel. 80 82 14) guards a priceless collection of medieval and Renaissance books. Under the loving care of bookworm Duke August (who reigned 1634-1666), the library became the largest in Europe. A series of medieval manuscripts culminates with a facsimile of the famous **Braunschweiger Evangelier**, a kaleidoscopically illuminated gospel drawn up in the late 12th century at the request of Heinrich the Lion; Lower Saxony shelled out millions of *Marks* for the manuscript in 1983. The original is locked safely away. Across from the castle is the 17th-century **Zeughaus**; the high-gabled facade belies its former role as an armory. (Open Tu-Su 10am-5pm. The two libraries and the Lessinghaus each sell admission tickets for DM6, students DM4, family DM12; a ticket from one attraction is good for the other two.) It now serves as a library annex holding the other half of the Herzog-August collection. The city's other major sight, the **Hauptkirche Beate Mariae Virgins**, raises its spires across town in the Heinrichstadt section. An aggressive stone-gray edifice, a jutting four-faced clock tower, and full-sized statues of saints grace the church's exterior. (Open Tu-Sa 10am-noon and 2-4pm. Free, but they encourage a donation of DM1 for the pamphlet.)

The Wolfenbüttel **tourist office**, Rosenwall 1 (tel. 29 83 46; fax 29 83 47), hides in the "little Venice" part of town. From the station, head left on Bahnhofstr., and make a left onto Schulwall. Turn right onto Löwenstr., and bear left on Krambuden, going over the little bridge; the street straight ahead is Rosenwall, and the tourist office is around the corner, on the right. They lack a room-finding service, but they book rooms in hotels for no fee and lead **tours** from the Schloßplatz for DM5. (Office open M-F 9am-12:30pm and 2-4pm, Apr.-Oct. also Sa 10am-1pm. Tours Apr.-Dec. Sa 2:30pm and Su 11am; Oct.-Mar. Su 11am.) Wolfenbüttel's **postal code** is 38300. The **telephone code** is 05331.

Wolfenbüttel has a first-rate **Jugendgästehaus**, Jägerstr. 17 (tel. 271 89; fax 90 24 45). Head left on Bahnhofstr. and take a left at Schulwall; continue on the same street when you reach Schloßplatz; you'll cross a little river and end up on Dr.-Heinrich-Jasper-Str.; make a left at Jägerstr. The *Haus* has stellar rooms with lots of space, new furniture, and pictures on the walls, as well as free access to **laundry machines** and **dryers**. (DM24, over 24 DM30; full pension DM33, over 24 DM46. Breakfast included. One-time sheets fee DM3. Bikes DM5 per day or DM10 per week. Free canoe rental.) The **market** displays its bounty every Wednesday and Saturday with fresh fruit stands (8am-1pm). Krambuden and Lange Herzogstr., just off the center of the *Stadtmarkt*, have many fruit stands and bakeries. The **Altstadt Bistro**, Okerstr. 8 (tel. 1088) serves lasagna (DM6), "Hawaii-Pizza" (DM4), and lots of other goodies. They deliver, too. (Open M-Sa 10am-10pm, Su 11am-10pm.) Down the street, a **Kaiser's** supermarket sells inexpensive foodstuffs (open M-W 8:30am-7pm, Th-F 8:30am-8pm, Sa 8am-4pm). While in Wolfenbüttel, don't miss the delicious coconut macaroons (DM1.20) served in the bakeries around town.

LÜNEBURGER HEIDE (LUNEBURG HEATH)

Between the Elbe and Aller rivers stretches the shrub-covered Lüneburger Heide. The symbolic power of the *Heide* is evidenced by many German literary greats: the delicate *Heideröslein* (wild rose) found a role in one of Goethe's *Lieder* while Heine charmingly compared one lady's bosom to the "flat and bleakly desolate" landscape of the *Heide*. Morning journeys by bicycle or horseback from one mist-shrouded town to the next provide a tranquil escape from the worries of backpacking. The undulating countryside moves quickly back and forth from farm to forest; green gives way to purple from July to September, when the bushes flower. Tiny sheep farms and dairies dot the countryside, and many farmers often "allow" tourists to help out with farm chores, for small fees.

If you want to see the grassy *Heide* during the flowering season, but would prefer not to sleep on it, put down the book and make reservations now. All of Germany comes here to bike, hike, motor, and otherwise frolic in the late summer. The most important regional towns are Lüneburg and Celle. In Lüneburg, the **Fremdenverkehrsverband Lüneburger Heide,** Barckhausenstr. 35 on the 2nd floor (tel. (04131) 737 30; fax 426 06), finds rooms in remote hamlets barely on the map. Of particular interest to budget travelers are the Heide's *Hen-Hotels* (Hay Hotels), real-life functional barns with rooms that farmers rent out to travelers for nominal fees (around DM20). They're called hay hotels because that's where you sleep (bring a sleeping bag). But all have showers and toilets, and many are surprisingly luxurious. Their list even tells you which animals you can expect to encounter. Extensive and detailed maps, available from the *Fremdenverkehrsverband,* outline the *Heide's* 10 major bike tours. Tour 5, the 350km **Heide-Rundtour,** is the most comprehensive; it passes through both Celle and Lüneburg; just follow the purple, green, and white signs. (Office open M-Th 7:30am-5pm, F 7:30am-1pm.) For those without a bike, rentals abound. Hiking through the area is not as popular as biking; hikers are welcome to follow the bike tours, but should be aware that *bikers have the right-of-way.* **Trains** along the Hannover-Hamburg line run frequently but provide access to only a handful of towns. Most other towns are serviced by occasional **buses.**

■ Lüneburg

Perhaps because there is no salt-god, or perhaps because the name Salzburg was already taken, Lüneburg derives its name from the moon-goddess Luna. Regardless, this is a city built, literally and figuratively, on salt. The city made a 13th-century fortune with its stores of "white gold." The citizens' salt monopoly held Northern Europe in an iron grip until granny blew it all in a high stakes poker game, and the plague and the war that struck the town in the 1620s. Although "salt shocks" no longer pose a threat to the world economy, and Lüneburg's wealth and power have faded, neither the salt nor the town are obsolete. The former is channeled into the city's famed rejuvenating baths, and the latter, with its Gothic brick *Altstadt* and elegant half-timbered houses, retains its ancient grace. It was in Lüneburg that native poet Heinrich Heine penned Germany's greatest and most melancholic Romantic *Lied* (epic song), the *Lorelei.*

ORIENTATION AND PRACTICAL INFORMATION Lüneburg serves as the main transportation axis for the *Heide.* The 60,000-strong city lies between Hamburg (30min.) and Hannover (1hr.). For a **bike,** try **Laden 25,** Am Weder 25 (tel. 379 60) (DM12 per day, DM60 per week; DM50 deposit and ID required. Open M-F 9am-noon and 1-5:30pm, Sa 9am-12:30pm.) The **tourist office,** Am Markt in the *Rathaus* (tel. 30 95 93 or 322 00; fax 30 95 98), books rooms for a DM5 fee. From the station, head downhill away from the post office, take a left onto Lünertorstr., and then turn left onto Bardowickerstr. at the end. (Open M-F 9am-6pm, Sa-Su 9am-1pm. Daily **tours** of the *Altstadt* leave M-F at 11am and Sa-Su 2pm. Adults DM5, children DM2.50.) A separate **regional tourist office** serves the entire *Heide* area (see above). The main **post office,** 21332 Lüneburg, is on the corner of Soltauerstr. and Saltztorstr. (open M-F 8am-6pm, Sa 8am-noon). The **telephone code** is 04131.

ACCOMMODATIONS Hotels fill up rather quickly when the *Heide* blooms in July, August, and September. At **Jugendherberge Lüneburg (HI),** Soltauerstr. 133 (tel. 418 64; fax 457 47), cheap and charming go hand in hand. During the week and Saturday morning until 1pm, bus #11 (direction: "Rettmer/Hecklingen") runs from the train station to the hostel stop, "Scharnhorststr./DJH." During other hours, take bus #7 from "Auf dem Klosterhof" behind the *Rathaus* to "Ginsterweg," and walk 200m farther along Soltauerstr. Or, brace yourself for a long haul from the station (30min.)—turn left on Bahnhofstr., right at the bottom onto Altenbrückerstr, then left onto the very long Berliner Str. Follow the street as it turns into Uelzenarstr., make a right at Scharnhorststr., and continue until you meet Soltauerstr. (DM20, over 26 DM25. Breakfast included. Sheets DM5.70. Laundry DM5. Reception until 10pm. Curfew 10pm, but pocket a house key with DM10 deposit. Call ahead.) **Hotel "Stadt Hamburg,"** Am Sande 25 (tel. 444 38), will put a grin on your face, unlike the dour visages of famous Lüneburgers whose portraits line the staircase. (Singles DM50, with shower DM55; doubles DM80, with shower DM90. Call ahead.)

FOOD AND NIGHTLIFE Although salt is plentiful in restaurants here, the real staple in town is another of mankind's ancient preservatives: beer. At **Kronen-Brauerei,** Heiligengeiststr. 39-41 (tel. 71 32 00), you can imbibe a fresh brew (from DM3.50) in a late 15th-century beer hall (open daily noon-10pm). For cheap food, try the local college **cafeteria** and the **Café Vamos.** The cafeteria, Building 9, serves the Pizza Diablo (*Dio Mia!* DM8.50; open M-Th 10am-6pm, F 10am-3pm). The cafe, Building 26, features live music. From #9, walk away from the street and turn left. The cafe is in the building with the funky windows. (Open M-Th 10am-7pm, F 10am-7pm and from 8pm, Sa only if there's a party, Su 11am-3pm.) **Café Central,** Schröderstr. 1 (tel. 40 50 99) serves several entrees and delicious daily specials (DM10-18) like *tortiglione* with *tun* (say that five times fast) and German potato pancakes. The extensive drink list, boisterous and young clientele, and loud music also make this a great place to chill at night. During the week, nightlife piles up around the Lüner Bridge, while locals pack the cafes along Am Stintmarkt. The patios offer cheap food and beer. Strike it up at **Garage,** Auf der Hude 76-80 (tel. 358 79). Frequent live acts, raves, and theme parties complement the regular dance scene. (Open W and F-Sa after 10pm. Cover W DM2; F DM2 before 11pm, DM6 after; Sa DM2 and DM8.)

SIGHTS Legend has it that Lüneburg's salt stores were discovered when a wild boar fell into a pit and, clawing his way out, shook salt loose from his bristles. At the **Deutsches Salz Museum,** Sülfmeisterstr. 1 (tel. 450 65), you can see, touch, taste, smell, mine, melt, and generally be one with salt. *(Open May-Sept. M-F 9am-5pm, Sa-Su 10am-5pm; Oct.-Apr. daily 10am-5pm. 1hr. tours M-F at 11am, 12:30pm and 3pm, Sa-Su at 11:30am and 3pm. DM6, students DM4, children DM3.50. With the tour, tack on DM1.50 for adults, DM1 for students and children.)* From the *Rathaus,* take Neue Sülze to Salzstr.; at Lambertiplatz, take the path behind the supermarket. The piquant museum features exhibits on salt production, ancient salt ships, salt use, and a medieval salt mill.

The **Kloster Lüne** (cloister; tel. 523 18), on Dömänehof, just over the Lünetor bridge, proudly displays its 15th-century face. *(Open Apr.-Oct. M-Sa 10am-12:30pm and 2:30-5pm, Su 11:30am-12:30pm and 2-5pm. DM5.)* Side streets with old, ivy-covered houses and boutiques lead to the Gothic **Michaeliskirche** (tel. 314 00), on Johann-Sebastian-Bach-Platz in the *Altstadt. (Open M-Sa 10am-noon and 2-5pm.)* This imposing brick, wood, and ceramic church was built in 1418 on a foundation of salt; the massive pillars have warped somewhat since then. The **Johanniskirche** spire, Am Sande (tel. 445 42), soars over the gables of the streets. *(Open daily 10am-5pm.)* Late 13th-century walls protect a Gothic altar and Baroque organ.

Lüneberg's other offbeat museums should be taken with a grain of...never mind. The **Brauereimuseum** (Brewery Museum), Heiligengeiststr. 39-41 (tel. 410 21), was a working brewery for 500 years until its copper vats became museum pieces in 1985. The museum shows you exactly how hops, malt barley, and a few extras make the magic potion that keeps Germany going, going, and going. *(Going daily 10am-noon and 3-5pm. Free.)*

■ Celle

The powerful prince electors of Lüneburg moved to Celle in 1398 after the Lüneberger War of Succession and remained here until 1705 when the last duke croaked. During those 307 years, the royalty spent lavishly on their residence, building a massive castle and promoting the city's growth. Celle celebrates this rich cultural past with its cobblestone streets lined with half-timbered houses (*Fachwerkhäuser*). In the heyday of *Fachwerk,* residents were taxed by the number of crossed diagonal beams on their houses; they quickly became coveted status symbols—until the advent of the Mercedes-Benz logo.

ORIENTATION AND PRACTICAL INFORMATION Celle is 40km northeast of Hannover, 35 minutes by frequent **trains** (DM11.20). Rent a **bike** from **2-Rad-Meier,** Neustadt 42a (tel. 413 69). Follow Neustadt behind the train station for 10 minutes. (DM15 per day, ID required. Open M-F 8am-1pm and 2:30-6pm, Sa 8am-1pm.) The **tourist office,** Markt 6 (tel. 12 12; fax 124 59), reserves rooms for free and distributes the *Jahresveranstaltungen,* a list of concerts and musical productions, as well as "The Wonderful Nine," a huge, full-color English brochure, describing Niedersachsen's historical highlights. From the train station, walk up Bahnhofstr. as it becomes Westcellertorstr., turn left onto Schloßplatz, then take the second right onto Stechbahn, and finally take the second left onto Markt. Or bus #2 or 3 to "Schloßpl." and follow the signs. (Open Apr.-Oct. M-F 9am-7pm, Sa 10am-4pm, Su 11am-2pm; Nov.-Mar. M-F 9am-5pm, Sa 10am-1pm.) City **tours** start from the bridge in front of the *Schloß* (Apr.-Oct. M, W, and Sa 2:30pm, Su 11am; DM3). The **post office,** 03100 Celle, is on Schloßplatz (open M-F 8am-6pm, Sa 8am-1pm). The **telephone code** is 05141.

ACCOMMODATIONS AND FOOD The **Jugendherberge (HI),** Weghausstr. (tel. 532 08, fax 530 05), offers cozy 6-bed rooms with lacy curtains—sex-ay! Smells wafting from the nearby farm nearly complete the home-on-the-range feeling. From the train station, take bus #3 (direction: "Boye") to "Jugendherberge." Turn left out of the station, walk up the pedestrian/bike path as it becomes Biermannstr., turn left on Bremer Weg, and turn up the first right onto Petersburgstr. (DM20, over 26 DM24.50. Breakfast included. Sheets DM5.70. Reception until 10pm, but best time for check-in is 5-7pm. Curfew 10pm; house keys available with a DM50 deposit.) At **Pension Luhmanns Hof,** Dorfstr. 8 (tel. 530 94), a little chocolate on each bed adds the touch of elegance. From Petersburgstr., it's the first building on the right after you pass Weghausstr. (Singles DM70; doubles DM110. Breakfast included. Reception until 9pm, reservations recommended.) **Hotel Blühende Schiffahrt,** Fritzenwiese 39 (tel. 227 61), is considerably closer to the *Altstadt* (DM65 per person; breakfast included; call ahead). **Campingplatz Silbersee** (tel. 312 23) lies 7km northeast of the town proper; take bus #6 (direction: "Vorwerk") to "Silbersee" (DM5.50 per person; showers included).

Café Fricke, Neuestr. 14 (tel. 21 49 18), at the intersection with Brandplatz, sets a merry table with artsy decorations and cooks up crepes from DM5 (open daily 10:30am-6pm). The young and bad break bread at **Alex's Antik Cafe,** Schuhstr. 6 (tel. 21 75 40), and it's easy to see why—cheap, simple food (soup and sandwich combo DM10), a spectrum of alcohol and coffee drinks, and smoky surroundings. Even Bohemians need food. (Open M-Sa 9am-2am, Su 9am-9:30pm.) During Celle's **market** (W and Sa 7am-1pm), the *Altstadt* fills with people carrying cloth-lined baskets in search of bargains on meats, fruits, vegetables, socks, and flowers.

SIGHTS Some of the city's finest *Fachwerk* houses are tucked away on side streets; to find them, wander down any of the smaller streets radiating from Schloßplatz or Großerplatz in the *Altstadt*. The **oldest house** in the area is at Am Heiligen Kreuz 26. The **Stadtkirche** stands just outside the massive pedestrian zone that dominates the *Altstadt*. The climb up the church tower rewards with a view of red- and brown-shingled roofs fading into the countryside. *(Tower open Apr.-Oct. Tu-Sa 10am-noon and 3-4pm. DM2, students and children DM1.)* In the *Altstadt*, the **Rathaus** is richly wrought in the *Weserrenaissance* style. Directly across the road, fine figures out of Celle's colorful history mark the hour on the **Glockenspiel**. *(Daily at 10, 11am, noon, 3, 4, and 5pm.)* The **Herzogschloß**, Schloßpl. 13 (tel. 123 73), just west of the *Altstadt*, flaunts foundations that date back to 1292. *(Tours of the ducal staterooms Tu-Su hourly from 10am; last tour starts at 4pm; Oct.-Apr. tours at 11am and 3pm. DM5, students and children DM2.50. Castle open M-F 10am-1pm, Sa-Su 10am-noon.)* One of the most renowned residents of the castle was Caroline-Mathilde; she was granted asylum here in 1772 after her politically expedient marriage to the King of Denmark collapsed and her affair with the King's minister was exposed. *(Caroline-Mathilde's personal rooms open Tu-Su 10am-4pm.)* Caroline-Mathilde's weeping likeness is found in the **Französischer Garten**, south of the *Altstadt*; guess why she's crying, Mr. "I've got a headache" King of Denmark. The 1740 Baroque **synagogue**, Kriese 27, survived even the Nazi cruelties, and persists as a memorial to Celle's once thriving Jewish community. *(Open Tu-Th 3-5pm, F 9-11am, Su 11am-1pm. Free.)*

■ Bergen-Belsen Concentration Camp

Visitors to the Lüneburger Heide have a moral obligation to visit the site of the **Bergen-Belsen concentration camp**. The camp was founded in 1940 as a "labor camp" for prisoners-of-war. For five years, about 20,000 Soviet prisoners were held there, performing futile, torturous "labor" like rolling heavy stones up and down hills, or digging ditches only to refill them. In January 1945, the POW camp was dissolved and the SS took over, bringing in thousands of Jews, homosexuals, and political dissidents who were evacuated from Auschwitz and other concentration camps. For four gruesome, unimaginable months, tens of thousands of people lived in cramped conditions and suffered the mindless torture of their Nazi imprisoners. Over 35,000 died of hunger and typhoid fever, including **Anne Frank** and her family. In total, Bergen-Belsen claimed more than 100,000 lives. Human capacity for evil is on full display, whether through the film taken by the British liberation forces, or the countless mass graves at the memorial erected in memory of Soviet prisoners of War. A somber stone obelisk commemorates the 30,000 Jewish victims. The camp buildings were razed by the British troops in 1945 to reduce the spread of disease, and the expansive cemetery, with mound upon mound marking mass graves, would be peaceful today if it weren't for the sound of explosions and artillery fire from the nearby NATO military training grounds. A visit to Bergen-Belsen can be extremely troubling and disturbing, but it firmly ingrains that which must not be forgotten. The **Bergen-Belsen Memorial** (tel. (05051) 60 11) is open daily from 9am to 6pm. Take bus #9 from the Celle train station to "Belsen Gedenkstätte" (55min., daily 11:55am and 2:55pm, return at 4:50pm, DM8). Contact the tourist office in Celle for further details.

■ Bremen

Much like Hamburg, its Hanseatic sister city to the North, Bremen has given over its once famed medieval ambience to a thriving cosmopolitan swirl in which internationalism and mass consumerism displace *"echtes"* German culture. The donkey, dog, cat, and rooster of the Brothers Grimm's fairy tale *Die Bremer Stadtmusikanten* (The Musicians of Bremen) were en route to Bremen when they terrified a band of robbers with their singing. The transients singing for attention at the city's train station maintain the tradition. Closer to the *Altstadt*, more talented artists ply their crafts, creating beautiful murals with charcoal and spray paint as musicians provide accompaniment on a mind-boggling array of instruments.

NIEDERSACHSEN

The most enduring *Bremisch* trait is a strong desire for independence: despite continuing struggles, Bremen and its daughter city Bremerhaven remain their own tiny, autonomous *Land* in the middle of Lower Saxony. This feisty streak has helped foster a decidedly liberal political climate that erupted into violent battles between police and demonstrators in 1980. People here flaunt high-flying, don't-tread-on-me, bad-ass, mo-fo attitudes—Bremen is one of the few places in Germany where jaywalkers will feel at home.

ORIENTATION AND PRACTICAL INFORMATION

Bremen lies south of the portal of the Weser River at the North Sea. The city is perfect for meandering, but beware of the blocks surrounding Ostertorsteinweg and Am Dobben; as you move out of the *Altstadt*, bong shops replace bakeries for several blocks, and sirens drown out singers on the streets.

A **Tourist Card Bremen,** available at the tourist office, provides free travel on city transportation, 20% discounts to theater shows and city tours, and 50% off the cost of admission at many of Bremen's museums. (2-day card for 1 adult and 1 child DM19.50, 3-day card DM26; 2-day group card for up to 5 folks DM35, 3-day DM46.)

Flights: Bremen's international airport (tel. 559 51) is only 3.5km from the city center; take S-Bahn #5 (20min.). Frequent flights to major German cities, the East Frisian Islands, and other European countries.

Trains: DB rolls 'em out to Hannover (1hr., 2 per hr.), Hamburg (1hr., 2 per hr.), Osnabrück (1hr., 2-3 per hr.), and Bremerhaven (45min., 2-3 per hr.).

Public Transportation: An integrated system of streetcars and buses covers the city and suburbs. Information and the hub of the main connections in front of the train station. The best deal by far is the **Bremer Kärtchen** (Little Bremen Card), with unlimited rides for 2 adults for 1 calendar day (*not* 24hr. from time of purchase), DM8. Single rides DM3.20, children under 16 DM1.60. 4-ride ticket DM9.60.

Ferries: Ferries from **Schreiber Reederei** (tel. 32 12 29) shuttle to the suburbs and towns along the Weser, ending up at Bremerhaven. (May 16-Sept. 14 W-Th and Sa at 8:30am. One-way to Bremerhaven DM21, round-trip DM34.) From Bremerhaven, ferries are available to Helgoland, high-seas shopping paradise.

Taxi: Frauen Nachtaxi operates a women's taxi service daily 7pm-4am. Call 133 34.

Car Rental: Avis, Kirchbachstr. 200 (tel. 21 10 77). Open M-F 7am-6pm, Sa 8am-1pm.

Bike Rental: Leave a DM50 security deposit and a photo ID, and pedal away from the **Fahrrad Station** (tel. 30 21 14), a bright red stand with colorful bikes, on your left as you exit the station. DM15 per day, children DM9; DM60 per week, children DM45. Biker's city map DM9.80. Open June-Sept. M and W-F 10am-5pm, Sa-Su 10am-noon and 5-5:30pm; Mar.-May and Oct.-Dec. M-F 10am-5pm.

Tourist Office: The souvenir-jammed central office (tel. 308 00 51; fax 308 00 30), across from the *Hauptbahnhof*, books rooms for DM3 plus a DM10-20 deposit. It also offers guides to museum exhibits and theater schedules, and sells tickets for concerts and festivals. A smaller kiosk next to the *Liebfrauenkirche* and *Dom* performs the same tasks during the same hours. Open M-W 9:30am-6:30pm, Th-F 9:30am-8pm, Sa-Su 9:30am-4pm.

Consulate: U.K., Herrlichkeit 6 (tel. 590 90). Open M-Th 8:30am-12:30pm and 2:30-3:30pm, F 8:30am-12:30pm.

Currency Exchange: DVB, in the train station, exchanges currency and cashes traveler's checks for a 1% commission, minimum DM10. Open M-F 7:30am-7pm, Sa 8am-4pm.

American Express: Am Wall 138 (tel. 17 46 00). Get off at Schüssel Korb and walk away from the Deutsche Bank. Follow the curve to the right and then go left onto Am Wall; it's 30m to the left. Open M-F 9am-5:30pm, Sa 9am-noon.

Bookstores: Storm, Langenstr. 10 (tel. 32 15 23). Impressive selection of English books, dictionaries, and travel guides. Open M-F 9am-7pm, Sa 10am-3pm.

Gay Information Line: (tel. 70 41 70), provides information about gay events and services. Open M-W and F 10am-1pm, Th 4-5pm.

Bremen
ACCOMMODATIONS
B Hotel Enzensperger
A Jugendgästehaus Bremen
C Pension Weidmann

Women's Center: The offices at Am Hulsberg 11 (Streetcar: "Am Hulsberg"). Info pertinent to travelers is available in the lobby. **Frauenbuchladen Hagazussa,** Friesenstr. 12 (tel. 741 40), stocks over 3000 books of particular interest to women. Only women are admitted. Open M 10am-2pm, Tu-F 10am-6pm, Sa 10am-2pm.

Laundromat: Wasch Center, Vor dem Steintor. Streetcar #2, 3, or 10 to "Brunnenstr." Continue down the streetcar line 30m. DM6 for wash, soap, and spin dry; another DM1 per 10min. to dry in a standard machine. Open daily 6am-11pm.

Pharmacy: Päs Apotheke, Bahnhofpl. 5-7 (tel. 144 15). Pick up a map of the city's pharmacies with their rotating schedule of late and emergency openings. Open M-F 8am-6:30pm, Sa 8am-2pm.

Emergency: Police, tel. 110. **Fire and Ambulance,** tel. 112.

Post Office: Main office at Domsheide 15, 28195 Bremen (tel. 367 33 66), near the *Markt.* Open M-F 8am-6pm, Sa 9am-1pm. Another office is on Bahnhofpl. 21, by the train station. Open M-F 8am-8pm, Sa 8am-2pm, Su 9am-2pm.

Internet Access: in all local libraries (*Bibliotheken*).

Telephone Code: 0421.

ACCOMMODATIONS AND CAMPING

The key phrase is "call ahead." Inexpensive hotels exist, but they fill fast. The tourist office's *Hotel-Liste* (free) lists a few rooms in the DM20-40 range, but prices quickly rocket into the DM100 range. New bus connections have made direct links with the somewhat distant campsite possible.

Jugendgästehaus Bremen (HI), Kalkstr. 6 (tel. 17 13 69; fax 17 11 02). Bus #26 or streetcar #1 or 6 to "Am Brill," then walk along Bürgermeister-Smidt-Str. to the river, turn right, and walk 2 blocks. From the train station, take Bahnhofstr. to Herdentorsteinweg, go right at Am Wall, then turn left on to Bürgermeister-Smidt-Str. and right along the water to the 162-bed hostel. The linen is clean, the ping pong is fun, and the glowing Beck's brewery sign across the Weser lulls you to sleep with visions of malt dancing in your head. DM27, over 26 DM32. Breakfast and sheets included. 24hr. reception. Check-out 10am. No curfew.

Hotel Enzensperger, Brautstr. 9 (tel. 50 32 24). Bus #24 to "Am Neuenmarkt," then right on Brautstr. Or, from the *Markt,* cross the Wilhelm-Kaisen Bridge over the Weser, turn right on Osterstr., and right on Brautstr. Clean, no-frills accommodations. Singles DM48, with shower DM49; doubles DM70, with shower DM92. Breakfast included. Call a few days ahead.

⊛**Hotel-Pension Garni Weidmann,** Am Schwarzen Meer 35 (tel. 498 44 55). Streetcar #10 to "St.-Jürgen-Str." and continue down the streetcar line 300m. The plush comforters and cavernous rooms complete with coffee-makers are fit for royalty. Such pampering at bargain prices is in demand. Singles from DM40; doubles from DM80. 2-week advance reservations are recommended.

Hotel Weltevreden, Am Dobben 62 (tel. 780 15; fax 70 40 91), just off Ostertorsteinweg. Comfortable rooms, good prices, close to Bremen nightlife. Singles DM60; doubles DM100, with shower DM120. Breakfast included. Reception M-Sa 7am-10pm, Su 7:30am-1pm and 5-10pm. Call a few days ahead.

Camping: Am Stadtwaldsee I (tel. 21 20 02). Bus #26 to "Hemmstr.," then #28 to the door. DM7.50 per person, DM4.50 per child; 2-person tent DM5, bigger tent DM9.50. Washers and dryers DM4 each. Free showers and electrical hookup. Open from one week before Easter until Nov. 1.

FOOD

In the *Rathaus,* Bremen's renowned **Ratskeller** (tel. 32 16 76) is worth a visit. Dating back to 1405, it's one of the oldest wine bars in Germany. Settle in a cozy leather-and-wood booth or among huge barrels to enjoy one of 600 German wines; most are reasonably priced (from DM4.60 per 0.2L glass), but the elegant beef and fish meals run around DM40 (always open, kitchen open noon-2:30pm and 6-11pm). A cheaper way to eat well is in the open-air **market** daily from 8am to 2pm. The restaurants that pack the **Schnoorviertel** are silly, charming, and exceedingly pricey, so shop around. Bronze pigs herd pedestrians into shops and take-out cafes on **Sögerstraße,** where shops sell everything from chocolate truffles to *Fischbrötchen.* Student pubs proliferate farther east in the **Viertel** (the Quarter), and on and around **Ostertorsteinweg** (see **Nightlife,** p. 306). **Comet,** at the corner of Vor dem Steintor and Friesenstr., brings grocery shopping to the heart of the ultra-hip Viertel. Posters for parties and concerts line the walls.

⊛**Engel,** Ostertorsteinweg 31-33 (tel. 766 15). Simple, elegant dining, and prime people-watching facilities in both the Art-Nouveau interior and the leafy terrace outside. Prime *Viertel* location. Lunch specials (DM10.50) even include dessert. Other artful entrees cost DM10-15. Concerts on the terrace on summer weekends. Open Su-Th 7am-2am, F-Sa 7am-3am.

Café Torno, Am Dobben 71 (tel. 70 06 11). Relax nerves to Western showdown music. Their hefty gyros (DM6-10) will scare hunger from your stomach. Pasta dinners DM9-12. *Cheap* drinks from DM1.50. Open M-Th noon-2am, F-Sa noon-4am, Su noon-1am.

Alex Brasserie, Pelzerstr. 8, (tel. 173 57 70). This bistro in the *Altstadt* is where locals meet for lunch. And coffee. And dinner. And drinks. Baguette platters from DM7.50. Open Su-Th 8am-1am, F-Sa 8am-3am.

Café Harlekin Bookshop, Lahnstr. 65b (tel. 50 19 11). Bus #5 to "Theater am Leibnizpl." Walk in the direction away from the *Hauptbahnhof,* past the centaur; take the second right and cross the street. Bremen's best breakfast selection (served all day) is flanked by an alternative bookstore (few trashy namesakes, unfortunately). The generous *Türkisches Frühstück* ("Turkish Breakfast"; *Fladenbrot,* feta, olives, and cucumbers for DM7.50) makes a filling lunch. Cafe open daily 10am-6:30pm.

Ada, Ostertorsteinweg 99 (tel. 783 57). Subtitle: "Ardor." Try a *tzatziki* pizza (DM4) and chase it down with a Turkish mocha (DM3). Always open.

Becks in'n Schnoor, Schnoor 35-37 (tel. 32 31 30). Cozy, warm-hearth atmosphere, a tradition-rich Schnoor locale, Beck's brew on tap. Open daily 11am-late.

SIGHTS

Bremen's *Altstadt* revolves around the **Rathaus,** its 15th-century base decorated by a startlingly ornate Renaissance facade. It survived WWII only because the English pilot who bombed the area deliberately missed this target. *(Tours occasionally available M-F at 10, 11am, and noon; Sa-Su at 11am and noon. The tourist office can provide more details.)* Just left of the town hall is the 1951 sculpture by Gerhard Marcks, *Die Musikanten,* which shows the Grimms' donkey, dog, cat, and rooster in their model-mugging, robber-foiling stance. Also a war survivor, the **St. Petri Dom,** Sandstr. 10-12 (tel. 36 50 40), next to the *Rathaus,* has a mosaic interior of orange, gold, and gray stone arches. The foundation dates to 798, when Charlemagne had the first stone placed there. If gilded chandeliers and artwork are too overwhelming, descend into the subterranean crypts at the front and rear of the church. *(Cathedral open M-F 10am-5pm, Sa 10am-1:45pm, Su 2-5pm. Free. Tower, all 265 steps, open May-Oct. M-F 10-11:20am and 12:20-4:20pm, Sa 10am-noon, Su 2-5pm. DM1.)* In a corner of the cathedral is the **Dom Museum** (tel. 365 04 75), housed in part of the original foundation with frescoes dating back 500 years. *(Open May-Oct. M-F 10am-5pm, Sa 10am-noon, Su 2-5pm; Nov.-Apr. M-F 1-4:30pm, Sa 10am-noon, Su 2-5pm. DM3, students and children DM2.)* Your museum ticket is good for a DM1 discount on an entrance to the macabre **Bleikeller,** in the basement of the *Dom.* *(Open May-Oct. M-F 10am-5pm, Sa 10am-2pm, Su 2-5pm; Nov.-Apr. daily 1-5pm. DM2, children DM1. Admission ticket likewise good for DM1 discount at museum above.)* The mummified corpses of workers who fell from the roof of the cathedral were discovered here in 1695 and have been on exhibit for three centuries.

Just past the *Domshof,* turn left on Domsheide for the medieval **Schnoorviertel,** a district of red-roofed gingerbread houses, dainty shops, and dog salons. Between the Marktplatz and the Weser lies the narrow red brick and cobblestone **Bottcherstr.** Once a crowded artisans' quarter, the street offers a winding labyrinth of gilded archways, stained-glass windows, boutiques, and craft shops. It's worth standing with all the tourists at noon, 3, or 6pm for the magic of the Böttcherstr. **Glockenspiel.** Bells ring and part of the building swings open to deliver a performance by mechanical figures, re-enacting wild sea and air exploits from the building's early memory. Come early—the prime gawking spots fill up quickly. Modern offices are now housed in some of the city's beautiful Renaissance structures; look for the **Gerichtsgebäude** (municipal court), Domsheide 16. The smell of brewing beer lures the helpless lush across the Weser to the **Beck's Brewery** (tel. 50 94 55 55). Pilgrims can visit the inner sanctum for a paltry DM5. Unlike its exported counterparts, *bremisch* Beck's offers the famous full bouquet expected in a German beer. *(Hourly tours Tu-Sa 10am-5pm, Su 10am-3pm. English tours at 1:30pm.)*

MUSEUMS

Neues Museum Weserburg Bremen, Teerhof 20 (tel. 59 83 90), across the Wilhelm Kaiser Bridge, then right on Herrlichkeit on the small island that splits the Weser River. Savor the irony of works by Assig, Darboven, and Warhol, and just enjoy the bounty of smart modern works. Open Tu-F 10am-6pm, Sa-Su 11am-6pm. DM8, students and children DM4.

Übersee Museum, Bahnhofplatz 13 (tel. 361 91 76), next to the train station. With the motto "the world under one roof," this collection brings a fifth-grade social studies textbook to life. Exhibits ranging from a Shinto garden to a South Seas fishing village attempt to show the wonders of the world outside Germany's borders. Open Tu-Su 10am-6pm. DM6, students and children DM3.

Gerhard Marcks Haus, Am Wall 208 (tel. 32 72 00), next to the Kunsthalle. An indoor and outdoor sculpture garden of works by the sculptor of *Die Musikanten.*

7 display rooms and an outdoor area house changing exhibitions of modern sculpture and graphic art. Open Tu-Su 10am-6pm. Tours Th at 5pm. DM6.

Rundfunkmuseum, Findorffstr. 85 (tel. 35 74 06 or 35 37 97). A large-scale center depicts the progress of telecommunications with exhibits that light up and whirl when touched—whee! Open M-Tu and Th-F 9:30am-5pm. DM2, children DM1.

Kunsthalle, Am Wall 207 (tel. 32 90 80). Bremen's main collection includes some Expressionism and contemporary pop art. Open Tu 10am-9pm, W-Su 10am-5pm. DM8, students DM4.

ENTERTAINMENT AND NIGHTLIFE

You want singing barnyard animals? Bremen delivers. Plus there's opera in the **Theater am Goetheplatz,** Am Goethepl. 1-3 (tel. 365 33 33), new drama in the **Schauspielhaus,** Ostertorsteinweg 57a (tel. 365 33 33), and auldies but goodies in the **Bremer Shakespeare Company,** Theater am Leipnizplatz (tel. 50 03 33). The **Theater im Schoor,** Wüste Stätte 11 (tel. 32 60 54), does cabarets and revues, from postmodern Shakespeare (nothing is sacred) to parodies of the *Wehrmacht*. Summertime brings performances to parks around the city. Discount tickets are usually held for students. Check the tourist office, the theaters, or *Bremer Umschau* (DM3) for schedules and prices, as well as information on free performances. *Belladonna* lists cultural events of special interest to women. *Prinz*, a monthly entertainment mag, has comprehensive nightlife listing and the full scoop on the Bremen *Szene* (DM4.50 at the tourist office and newsstands). *Partysan*, a zine based in Hamburg, also lists big parties in Bremen (free at Engel and other cafes).

During the last two weeks of October, Bremen drinks beer and eats tubs of yummy lard cakes in honor of its trading heritage and freedom as a *Land* with the colorful **Freimarkt** fair, an annual event since 1095. And Bremen rocks—big concerts are often held in the **Weserstadion** (tel. 43 45 00) behind the train station. Tickets and information for small- and large-scale events are available at the tourist office. Many clubs host live music nights that feature American bands making their European debuts. **Modernes Complex,** Neustadtswall 28 (tel 50 55 53), hosts cinema, theater, concerts, and dancing (times and cover charges vary).

Bremen offers a well-developed and raucous pub culture. The long and densely populated **Ostertorsteinweg** is the place to find the true pulse of the nightlife. A lively gay and lesbian nightlife scene is scattered throughout the city.

Litfass, Ostertorsteinweg 22 (tel. 70 32 92). An all-day, all-night bastion of alternative chic that poses as a bar. As the eyes of the supermodel on the wall cast flirting glances toward you, coolly take down one of their piping hot coffees from DM4. The extensive outdoor terrace and open facade make it the place to see and be seen. Open Su-Th 10am-2am, F-Sa 10am-4am.

⊛**Moments,** Vor dem Steintor 65 (tel. 780 07). A wildly popular disco with well-advertised and well-attended parties. The music invariably improves during happy hour (10-11pm) with half-price drinks. Open daily 10pm-late.

Café Engel, Ostertorsteinweg 31-33 (tel. 766 15). A hip indoor/outdoor bar and restaurant whose patrons lack nothing in style, sophistication, or libations. Open Su-Th 11am-1am, F-Sa 11am-4am.

Aladin, Hannoversche Str. 11 (tel. 41 23 04). A bar that hosts live music and popular disco events. Open W 9pm-2am, F-Sa 9pm-7am, sporadically for other performances. Cover DM7.

Confession, Humboldtstr. 156 (tel. 738 22). A swingin', swank gay and lesbian club featuring live blues, jazz, and alternative bands. Open Su-Th 7pm-2am, F-Sa 9pm-late. Saturday women-only.

TheaLit, Im Krummen Arm 1 (tel. 70 16 32). An evening club and center for women's and lesbian events. Also contains a bar. Women only. Information office open Tu 10am-noon, W-F 4-6pm. Bar open M-F and Su 5pm-late.

■ Bremerhaven

ARRR, matey! Founded in 1827 as a port for land-locked Bremen, Bremerhaven is a younger and saltier version of its bigger sister city. The harbor, once the city's commercial *raison d'être*, serves as a tourist hub. The city itself has added a modern architectural veneer to its maritime foundations. Ferries sail daily for Helgoland, Germany's own Fantasy Island, at 9:45am (see **Helgoland**, p. 308). The harbor also houses the **Deutsches Schiffahrts-Museum** (German Maritime Museum; tel. 48 20 78), which pays tribute to boats, boats, and more boats, with models and relics inside the building and real full-scale *Museumschiffe* (museum ships) outside. (Open Apr.-Oct. daily 10am-6pm; Nov.-Mar. Tu-Su 10am-6pm. Admission DM5, students, seniors and children DM2.50.) Docked nearby, but with separate admission, is the **U-Boot Wilhelm Bauer,** one of the only German submarines (U-Boats) from WWII that was neither sunk nor scrapped (open Apr.-Oct. daily 10am-6pm; DM3, under 18 DM2). At the **Zoo am Meer,** farther up the harbor, German schoolchildren hoot and dash about frantically, while animals on the other side of the bars (polar bears, sea lions, monkeys) sit calmly and watch. (Open May-Aug. daily 8am-7pm; Apr. and Sept. 8am-6:30pm; Oct.-Mar. 8am-5pm. DM4, students and children DM2; free tours available with prior reservation.) Annual festivals abound; in 1999, the Bremerhaven **Fest Woche** (Festival Week) will be held the last week of July.

Bremerhaven is 30 minutes from Bremen by **trains** that leave and arrive at least hourly; a **ferry** leaves Bremen each morning at 8:30am (see Bremen, p. 301). To **rent a bike,** visit the **BBU** (tel. 860 23), in a train car at the entrance to the harbor, near the zoo. (DM10 per day, DM42 per week; children DM6 per day, DM30 per week. Open Apr.-Sept. Tu-Su 10am-6pm.) The **tourist office,** in the Columbus Center, finds rooms gratis (tel. 430 00; open M-W 9:30am-6pm, Th-F 9:30am-8pm, Sa 9:30am-4pm). Take bus #2, 5, 9, or 12 to "Große Kirche," then take the escalators to the second floor. The office is in the back on the left side. The **Verkehrsamt,** Van-Ronzelenstr. 2 (tel. 94 64 60; fax 460 65), does the same with different hours (open M-F 8am-4pm). The **post office,** 27570 Bremerhaven, directly to the left as you leave the *Hauptbahnhof,* offers **currency exchange** and cashes traveler's checks for a DM6 fee all without going postal (open M-F 8am-6pm, Sa 8am-1pm). The **telephone code** is 0471.

Bremerhaven's number one combo platter, the **Jugendgästehaus-Jugendherberge (HI)** two-for-one, at Gaußstr. 54-56 (tel. 856 52; fax 874 26), offers a dazzling array of conveniences. Take bus #2 or 9 to "Gesundheitsamt." As your clothes whirl in the washer and dryer (DM2.50 each), you can borrow one of the management's TVs or clock-radios for free. For a few *Marks* extra, work out in the mini-gym followed by a trip to the sun lamp and a Volkswagen-sized spa (for *Jugendgästehaus* guests only). Incidentally, the hostel also offers beds to sleep in. (Hostel DM28, over 26 DM31.50. *Jugendgästehaus* DM29.90. Breakfast and sheets included. Reception 7am-6am.)

■ Cuxhaven

In German, Cuxhaven's motto, "more than a feeling," is actually a clever wordplay. In German that would be *"mehr als ein Gefühl,"* but salty Cuxhaven emphasizes *"Meer"* (the German word for 'sea') *als ein Gefühl.* Sneaky bastards. But it's not an inaccurate motto: much more than just another beach town, Cuxhaven offers tourists the chance to watch huge international freighters pass by on a heavily traveled trade line, indulge in a kitschy, bright-neon beach-party culture, and explore the North Sea's singular sand-marsh **Watt** landscape—all in one town. The huge *Watt* area here, in combination with the equally large tourist following, fortunately means that *Watt*-information is centralized: the tourist office's *Watt Wangdorn* guide has a comprehensive list of tide tables, wild-life tours, and walking expeditions to nearby **Neuwerk Island** (most tours around DM5). *Never cross without a guide*—the tide comes in much faster than you can run. For those too unmotivated to make the 11km trek by foot, the horse-drawn **Wattwagen** cart accesses all that wet sand (DM25, ages 10 and under DM12.50). If you find yourself hindered by tons of water during high tide, the

MS Flipper makes several daily trips to the island (DM20, round-trip DM28; ages 4-17 DM21, round-trip DM15). Once on the island, it's possible to tour with a guide (DM3, children DM2).

Trains run frequently from Cuxhaven to Bremerhaven (50min.). Ferries run to Helgoland daily at 10:30am. For intra-Cuxhaven cruising, try renting a **bike** from **Zwei-rad-Paulsen,** Schillerstr. 47 (tel. 362 66), for DM9 per day with ID (open M-F 10am-5pm). Take bus #1, 5, or 21 to "Kasernenstr." Walk away from Kasernenstr. on Marienstr., then veer right onto Schillerplatz, and left on Schillerstr. Pick up a schedule of high and low tide times at the **tourist office** (tel. 360 46; fax 525 64), at Lichtenbergplatz (bus #1, 4, or 21, direction: "Duhnen"; open July-Aug. M-F 9am-5pm, Sa 9am-1pm and 2-4pm; Sept.-June M-F 10am-5pm). The **post office,** which cashes traveler's checks, lies at Rohdestr., 27472 Cuxhaven. The **telephone code** is 04721.

Cuxhaven's **Jugendherberge (HI)** (tel. 485 52; fax 457 94) is 1½ blocks from the deep, blue sea. From the station take bus #1, 2, or 4 (direction "Döse-Duhnen") to "Seelust," and backtrack to the *Jugendherberge* sign. The rooms are clean and cheery. Save your room receipt to get onto the beach for free; otherwise you'll pay DM5.50. You can wash your laundry (DM5 with soap) and hang it to dry. (DM16, over 26 DM23.70. Breakfast DM6. Sheets DM6. Reception 12:30-1pm and after 7pm. Curfew 11:30pm but key available upon request. Partial wheelchair access. Call 1 week ahead.) **Camping** is available just down the street at **Nordsee Campingplatz,** Cuxhavenstr. 17 (tel. 489 51; DM7.50 per tent, DM6 per person). The shopping center around the dunes (bus #1,2, or 4 to "Duhnen") offers several beachy dives with an authentic under-the-boardwalk feel. **Hansagrill,** 14a Nordersteinstr. (tel. 252 70), offers grilled and fishy food (not to be confused with fish food) for DM9-13 (open daily 10am-10pm).

■ Helgoland

The German tourists who flock to the island of Helgoland every day take the slogan "Shop 'til you drop" to an almost revolting extreme. Tempted by duty-free prices, they endure an often harrowing two to four-hour ferry ride, jump into tiny skiffs to row to shore, and then run all over the island, snatching up as many cartons of cigarettes, meter-tall bottles of liquor, and cheese as they can legally carry before the ship departs at 4pm. A different kind of mayhem reigned at the conclusion of World War II, when the British navy evacuated the strategically valuable island and attempted to obliterate it with thousands of tons of dynamite. The island bears heavy and multiple battle scars, including long concrete docks that protrude far into the ocean and a fair amount of stark, military-style architecture, but the glitz and glam of the duty-free shops and the swarms of die-hard shoppers gild most of the historical blight with the flashy veneer of consumerism.

If you have only one day to visit Helgoland, don't go. Getting there is *not* half the fun—they don't call these the high seas for nothing—and you can't really get beyond the shopping district in the three hours you'd have on the island. An open-ended ticket (DM13 more than a daytrip) will give you time to push through the throngs and enjoy the view. The extra time will also allow you to find tiny trails and quiet corners to admire the red cliffs that give Helgoland poetic cachet equal to that of its pale English cousin Dover. Even Goethe was inspired by tales of the high seas island, which he described in 1827 as "still fresh evidence for the survival and work of the eternal spirit of the age." The tiny sandy island next to Helgoland, **Dünne,** is essentially one big beach (without stores). Ferries from the dock run frequently. Today's tourists are the latest incarnation of an age-old imperialist assault on the island, previously led by pirates, Frisians, the Hanseatic League, Danes, and Britons. The small **Museumswerkstatt Nordseehalle,** located between the Nordost-Bohlwerk and the Northeast harbor, documents this legacy of plunder (hours vary).

The cheapest and most reliable way to get to Helgoland is through Cuxhaven, Norddeich, or Bremerhaven; ferries also leave from some of the Frisian Islands (including Norderney and Langeoog), but their schedules are erratic. The **MS Wappen von**

Hamburg, which sails from Cuxhaven's *Fährhafen* harbor, is probably your best bet. The ride is relatively short (2hr.), the boat is as large and as luxurious as a small cruise ship, and the price is competitive. (Departs May-Sept. daily 10:30am. Daytrips DM55, ages 12-18 DM36; open-ended return DM68, ages 12-18 DM40.) The **MS Frisia III,** operating from Norddeich, offers a lower fare but a longer ride (4hr.) and a skimpier schedule. (Departs May-June Tu 8am; July-Aug. Tu and F 8am. Daytrips DM43, under 13 DM27.) Ferry company **Reederei Warrimp** (tel. (04464) 949 50) sends the **MS Helgoland** and the **MS Wilhelmshaven** from Wilhelmshaven (daytrip DM57, open-ended return DM70). The **telephone code** is 04725.

With thousands of visitors each year, Helgoland's **tourist office** (tel. 813 70; fax 81 37 25) greets travelers as they step off the skiff. Their free prospectus offers a wealth of information, including a list of accommodations. (Open Apr.-Oct. M-F 9am-4pm, Sa-Su 11am-3pm; Nov.-Mar. M-F 9-11:30am and 1-4pm, Sa-Su 1-2pm.) Helgoland's **Jugendherberge (HI)**, Postfach 580 (tel./fax 341), sits right on the beach, a short 15-minute walk from the ferry dock. Follow the signs. (DM22, over 26 DM27. 3 meals included. Sheets DM10. Reception Apr.-Oct. 10am-2pm and 5-7pm. Curfew 10pm. Call 4-6 weeks ahead.)

▒ Oldenburg

The city of Oldenburg, founded in 1108, was spared the destruction of the Thirty Years War largely because its head honcho at the time, Count Anton Günther, raised the most beautiful horses in all of Germany. Today's Oldenburg is much more than a one-trick pony. The unique Frisian culture runs deep in this city, but the city's position on major rail lines and strong ties to sister cities in Denmark, France, Russia, the Netherlands, and Israel give the city a dynamic international flavor.

ORIENTATION AND PRACTICAL INFORMATION Oldenburg is easily accessible from Bremen (35min.). The old, moated city lies along an off-shoot of the Weser River, opening the way to East Frisia, and it serves as the take-off point for most excursions. The **tourist office,** Wallstr. 14 (tel. 157 44), finds rooms for a DM4 fee (from DM35; call ahead) and piles visitors with numerous North Sea brochures (open M-F 9am-6pm, Sa 9am-noon). You can also visit the **Fremdenverkehrsverband Nordsee-Niedersachsen-Bremen,** Bahnhofstr. 19-20 (tel. 92 17 10), for invaluable information on the East Frisian islands as well as regional information for the area between Holland and Hamburg (open M-Th 8am-5pm, F 8am-4pm). **Rent bikes** at the **Fahrradstation** (tel. 163 45) on Neuesstr., right across the street from the tourist office on Wallstr. (Open M-Th 7am-11pm, F 7am-3pm, Sa 8am-3pm. DM12 per day, DM42 per week. Passport or other personal ID required.) **AIDS-Hilfe** (tel. 194 11) offers information on AIDS and gay concerns, with a separate line (tel. 122 39) for lesbian concerns. Oldenburg's **postal code** is 26123. The **telephone code** is 0441.

ACCOMMODATIONS AND FOOD The city's modern **Jugendherberge (HI),** Alexanderstr. 65 (tel. 871 35), is 1.5km from the station. Go down Moslestr. and turn right on Am Stadtmuseum; as Am Stadtmuseum disintegrates into an impossible jumble of intersecting streets, head in the general direction in which you were previously moving until you reach the greens of the Gertruden-Friedhof cemetery, with Alexanderstr. veering to your left. Or take bus #7, 9, or 12 to "Lappen," and then #2 or 3 to "Von Finckstr." (DM22, over 26 DM26. Breakfast included. Reception 5-10pm. Curfew 10pm. The hostel fills quickly, so call several weeks ahead.) The **Hotel Hegeler,** Donnerschweerstr. 27 (tel./fax 875 61), has clean rooms and a bowling alley—really! From the station, cross the pedestrian bridge over the tracks (near the post office) and follow the road to Donnerschweerstr., then turn left and walk 150m. They've got clean, spacious rooms with wooden desks and down comforters. (Singles DM45, with bath DM75; doubles DM90, with shower DM130. Call ahead.)

Picknick, Markt 6 (tel. 273 76), serves up regional specialties like potato pancakes with apple sauce (DM9) and baguettes (from DM7; open M-Th 11am-midnight, F-Sa

11am-1am). **Marvin's Biergarten,** Rosenstr. 8, is as laid-back as it gets. Their beer garden is a perfect place to relax in the sun. Head up Bahnhofstr. and go left on Rosenstr. (open M-Th and Su 7pm-2am, F-Sa 8pm-3am). Modernity-induced *ennui* is alleviated at **Zauberkessel,** Kurwickstr. 6 (parallel to Wallstr.), where patrons get medieval with live bards and not-so-medieval with an ample vegetarian menu (open Su-Th noon-1am; F-Sa noon-3am).

SIGHTS AND ENTERTAINMENT Every morning, the city's residents jockey for position with hundreds of tourists as daily markets bustle in two different squares: one on the **Pferdemarkt,** an erstwhile horse-showing arena near the yellow brick state library, the other on the main square surrounding the 1888 **Rathaus.** The adjacent 13th-century **Lambertikirche** has gracefully endured Baroque and Neoclassical additions to its Gothic structure. *(Open Tu-F 11am-12:30pm and 2:30-5pm, Sa 11am-12:30pm. Free.)* The **Landesmuseum,** Schloßpl. 26, housed in the yellow-and-white *Schloß* with gingerbread trim, exhibits an extensive painting collection with special emphasis on Goethe's friend and fan, Johann Tischbein. *(Open Tu-F 9am-5pm, Sa-Su 10am-5pm. DM4, students, seniors, and children DM2.)* The **Augusteum,** Elisabethstr. 1 (tel. 220 26 00), is an extension of the *Landesmuseum* with two floors of groggy Surrealist dreamscapes and Kirchner's Expressionist street scenes. *(Open Tu-F 9am-5pm, Sa-Su 10am-5pm. DM4, students, children, and seniors DM2.)* For slightly less esoteric action, walk another 300m to the **Naturkunde and Vorgeschichte Museum** (Natural and Prehistory Museum), Damm 40-44 (tel. 924 43 00), and meet some real-life bogeymen, whose macabre appearances persist through the millennia. *(Open Tu-Th 9am-5pm, Sa-Su 10am-5pm. DM3, students and children DM1.50.)* Where Wallstr. turns into Lappan, **Alte Schmiede am Lappan,** an old-style blacksmith shop, offers a glimpse of craftspeople at work. *(Open M-F 9:30am-6pm, Sa 10am-1:30pm.)* Farther down Lappan and crossing to Am Stadtmuseum 4-8, the **Stadtmuseum** holds everything from period-based studies of Oldenburg's long history to the naturalist and expressionist collections of local notable Theodor Francksen. *(Open Tu-F 9am-5pm, Sa 9am-noon, Su 10am-5pm. Free.)*

Oldenburg's nightlife centers around a curious man named "Popeye" who runs the club **JFK's** on Wallstr. Despite the campy and strangely morbid motif, Popeye injects some pulse into Oldenburg after hours. He organizes numerous raves, dance parties, and beach parties (no pajama-jammy-jams or Olive Oil wrestling). Just ask him what's goin' on. Oldenburg also offers **Pulverfass,** Kaiserstr. 24 (tel. 126 01), a popular men-only gay disco. *(Open Tu-Th 10pm-2am, F-Sa 11pm-5am. Cover F-Sa DM5.)*

■ Wilhelmshaven

Crazy Kaiser Wilhelm II, spurred by megalomaniacal dreams of creating a "place in the sun" for Germany, built the modestly named Wilhelmshaven in an attempt to lay the groundwork for German military and naval expansionism. Today, the somber statue of the Kaiser on **Friedrich Wilhelm Platz** oversees a less-than-lively seaport and empty town. The city's location on the **Jadebusen,** the protected North Sea inlet on which Wilhelmshaven was built, and its well-located harbor enable the town to pursue its three passions—eating, drinking, and boating—in close proximity. The **Südstrand** beach is accessible by taking Ebertstr. east from the *Hauptbahnhof* and crossing the **Kaiser-Wilhelm-Brücke** (beach open May-Sept. daily 8am-6pm; DM4, children DM1). Right by the Kaiser-Wilhelm Brücke floats the bright red **Feuerschiff,** used until 1981 to fight boat fires (open Tu-Su 11am-10pm; free). The boat houses a bar and grill (open daily 11:30am-3pm and 6-10pm). For more active *Schiffvergnügen* (ship pleasure), rent a sail, paddle, or rowboat at the **Bootverleih** (tel. 20 26 22; open Apr.-Sept. daily 11:30am-9pm, boats DM18 per hour). The adjacent *Gaststätte* serves *Bockwurst* and beer. From the Pumpwerk stop, go south on Jadestr. then right onto Ems for 10 minutes, follow the signs left onto Henschelstr., then walk 200m.

For something completely different, visit the **Pumpwerk Kulturzentrum,** An der Deichbrücke (tel. 438 77). Witness the decline of Western civilization daily with some of Germany's most egregious pop bands, get down at a Schlager Party, or revel in the death of theater. Times, prices, and quality of entertainment vary. A *Pumpwerk* program is available at the ticket office and at the youth hostel. A few rungs higher on the hipness ladder stands the **Hotel Kling Klang**, Böxsenstr. 73 (tel. 133 22), just up the street from the tourist center. By day, it's a pleasant, unassuming cafe with spray-painted stools. By night, the small stage showcases acts ranging from a KISS revival to original hip-hop and DJs, with live music on Fridays (open daily 10am-late). No one can rock all night on an empty stomach; that's why there's *Auflauf* at **Pumpwerk I** (not to be confused with the Kulturzentrum), Ahrstr. 24 (tel. 445 90). Take line 3 (or line A after hours) to "Kaiser-Wilhelm-Brücke." Choose ingredients from broccoli to salami to add to the starchy mash that is *Auflauf* (DM11.80; open daily from 6pm).

Conveniently located down Gökerstr. from the hostel is **Oeltermann's**, Holtermanstr. 2 (tel. 321 54), where you can rent a **bicycle** for DM9 per day (open M-F 8am-1pm and 3-6pm, Sa 8am-1pm). From the train, walk straight through the brand-new Nordsee-Passage and out the front door to get to the **tourist office**, Börsenstr. 55b (tel. 92 79 30), which can find you a private room (open M-F 9am-6pm, Sa 9am-1pm). Wilhelmshaven's **postal code** is 26382. The **telephone code** is 04421.

The **Wilhelmshaven Jugendherberge (HI)**, Freiligrathstr. 131 (tel. 600 48; fax 647 16), sits on the city outskirts by the botanical gardens. Take bus #1 (or bus A after hours) to Friedenstr. and follow the sign (200m). This is a warm, friendly place with lots of tourist information. (DM20, over 26 DM24. Breakfast included. Sheets DM5. 24hr. reception. Curfew 11:30pm, but you get a house key. Closed Nov.). There are a number of inexpensive *Pensionen*, but **Privat-Pension Heine Lübben**, Rheinstr. 25 (tel. 434 19), is close to the beach and the city. From the station, walk along Virchowstr. toward the water and turn left on Rheinstr. Go down three blocks and look to your left. If you find yourself standing in the Jadebusen, you've gone too far. (Singles DM40; doubles DM80. Reception daily 10am-10pm.) From Wilhelmshaven you can sail to the sun and surf of the German vacation paradise **Helgoland** (see p. 308).

■ Jever

Jever is the small town equivalent of a happy drunk—often charming, occasionally vulgar, and wholly kept afloat by beer. The astute observer can't help but notice, next to the town water pump in the city center, a sculpture of a dog answering nature's call on the pump. To uncover the town's frothy foundations, follow your nose to the **Jever Brewery** (tel. 137 11) for a **tour** of the complex that puts Jever on the map—and on tap—all over northern Germany. (Tours Apr.-Oct. every 30min. M-F 9:30am-12:30pm; Nov.-Mar. Tu-Th 10:30am only. DM10, including a souvenir mug, pretzel, and glass of beer. Call ahead.)

Like most lushes in denial, Jeverians dismiss their barley fetish, claiming that their finest offering is the castle located across from the tourist office at Alter Markt 18. The rose-colored, 15th-century **Schloß** houses an engaging museum filled with art and trinkets dating back 500 years. (Open Mar. to mid-Jan. Tu-Su 10am-6pm. DM4, students DM2, children DM1.) The beautiful Renaissance **Rathaus** towers in the main square. The **Stadtkirche**, on Kirchplatz, is Jever's monument to persistence; after being burned down and reconstructed nine (!) times, it is fully modernized. Teetotalers take the bus to Hooksiel, a small coastal port northwest of Jever, to indulge in its beaches and cozy camping grounds.

The **tourist office**, Alter Markt 18 (tel. 710 10; fax 93 92 99), across from the *Schloß*, books rooms for free and directs the smell-impaired to the brewery. (Open May-Sept. M-F 10am-6pm, Sa 10am-2pm, Su 10am-noon; Oct.-Apr. M-Th 10am-5pm, F 9am-1pm.) The **telephone code** is 04461. The **Jugendherberge Jever (HI)**, Mooshütterweg 12 (tel. 35 90), idles on a small street behind the *Schloß*. Rooms and facilities are standard. Unlike most other hostels in the region, rooms are generally available. (DM18, over 26 DM24. Breakfast included. Sheets DM5. Reception 5-9:45pm. Curfew 10pm. Open Apr.-Oct.)

■ Osnabrück

Three-hundred and fifty-one years ago, Osnabrück provided a negotiating table for the fighting factions of the Thirty Years War. The city works for peace and tranquility even today and moves at a pace more relaxed than most cities of comparable size. Osnabrück's stunning **Rathaus** hides inside the perfectly preserved **Friedenssaal.** (Open M-F 8:30am-6pm, Sa-Su 10am-1pm. Tours Su 10:30am. Free.) Next to the *Rathaus* stands the **Marienkirche,** completely destroyed during the war, but now fully rebuilt (open M-Sa 10am-noon and 3-5pm; Oct.-Mar. M-Sa 10:30am-noon and 2:30-4pm). The **tower** can be toured Sundays from 11:30am to 1pm (DM2, children DM1). The immense **Dom,** Kleine Domsfreiheit 24, has been collecting priceless religious relics for nine centuries (open Tu-F 10am-1pm and 3-5pm, Sa-Su 11am-2pm; DM2, children DM1).

The warm afterglow of Westphalia quickly fades amidst the permanent **Felix Nussbaum** (1904-1944) exhibit at the **Museum of Cultural History;** Nussbaum's paintings depict the tragedy of the Holocaust with heart-wrenching symbolism (open M-F 8:30am-6pm, Sa-Su 10am-1pm; DM3, students and children DM1.50). Osnabrück's most famous son is **Erich Maria Remarque,** the acclaimed author of *Im Westen nichts Neues* (All Quiet on the Western Front). Though Allied bombing completely destroyed his house on Hafenstr., literary travelers (that's you, sport!) can tour the new **Erich Maria Zentrum,** Am Markt 6 (tel. 969 45 11), which documents his life and times. (Open Tu-F 10am-1pm and 3-5pm, Sa 10am-1pm, 1st Sunday of the month 11am-5pm.) The Osnabrück **Zoo,** Am Wald Zoo 2/3 (tel. 95 10 50), is fantastic. (Open Apr.-Oct. daily 8am-6:30pm; Nov-Mar. 9am-5pm, last entrance 4pm.) Take bus #25 to "Zoo." Watch the tigers and bears frolic. Squeal with pleasure.

The **bus** travels around the city center (DM2) and to the outer zones (DM2.50), but the best deal is a *Tagesticket* (DM6), good for a day of unlimited travel after 9am. The **Fahrradverleih** (tel. 25 91 31), in the train station, rents bikes. (DM8 per day, DM35 per week. Open M-F 6am-8pm, Sa 7am-2pm. ID and DM20 deposit required.) The **tourist office,** Krahnstr. 58 (tel. 323 22 02; fax 323 42 13), is just off the *Rathaus.* Facing the *Rathaus,* look left; or, from the station, walk up Möserstr. as it turns into Herrenteichsstr., follow the curve around, and turn onto Krahnstr. The staff books rooms (from DM30 per person) for free. (Open M-F 9:30am-6pm, Sa 9:30am-1pm.) Launder your duds at **Wasch Center,** on the corner of Kommenderiestr. and Petersburger-Wall (wash DM7, dry DM1; open daily 6am-11pm). The **telephone code** is 0541.

South of the city center is the newly outfitted **Jugendgästehaus Osnabrück,** Iurgerstr. 183a (tel. 542 84; fax 542 94). From the station, ride bus #13, 15, 62, or 83 to "Neumarkt," then change to #23, 25, or 27 to "Kinderhospital"; turn left and follow the signs up a tree-lined path. (DM26, over 26 DM31. Breakfast and sheets included. Reception 5-10pm. Wheelchair accessible. Call ahead.) Clean rooms fill the **Hotel Jägerheim,** Johannistor-Wall 19a (tel. 216 35). From the station, turn left on Konrad-Adenauer-Ring, which becomes Petersburger-Wall and then Johannistor-Wall. (Singles DM40, with bath DM64; doubles DM80, with bath DM104. Reception until 9pm.) For **camping,** try **Freizeitpark Attersee,** Zum Attersee 50 (tel. 12 41 47). From the station, take bus #22 to "Attersee." (DM5.50 per person. No tent rentals. Showers included.) In a pinch, rooms are almost always available at the **Bad Essen Jugendherberge** (tel. (05472) 21 23), easily accessible by bus #302 (DM22, over 26 DM25; *Kurtaxe* DM2.50; breakfast included; reception 5-10pm).

Café Extrablatt, Jürgensort 4 (tel. 26 06 39), is Osnabrück's cafe *du jour;* its light cafe fare (baguettes and small entrees from DM7) and spacious sidewalk terrace attract what seems like all of the town's youth all the time. (Open M-Th 8am-1am, F-Sa 8pm-3am, Su 10am-1am.) **Lagerhalle,** Rolandsmaner 26 (tel. 33 87 40), is the town's one-stop nightlife center, with a popular *Kneipe,* a restaurant with international and vegetarian specials from DM5, an art-house film theater, and frequent rock concerts and dance parties. (Open Tu-Th 6pm-1am, F 6pm-2am, Sa 7pm-2am, Su 7pm-1am.) Liberace has nuthin' on the **Pink Piano,** Lotterstr. 99 (tel. 428 23), which offers live blues every Monday night (open daily 4pm-late).

EAST FRISIAN ISLANDS

Germany's North Sea shoreline and the seven sandy islands that bracelet the coast may as well belong to an entirely different country. The unbelievably flat landscape ringed with windmills, the vaulting, dramatic cloud scenes, and the bizarre, apocalyptic seascapes of the area known as *Ostfriesland* seem to bear no relationship to the rest of the country's cheerful river valleys and bustling cities. Amidst such dramatic and engrossing scenery, it's easy to forget that people actually live here, but the Frisian culture is worth looking into. That Frisians are sea-farers is clear from the popularity of vaguely Dutch clothing, especially the omnipresent blue sailor's hat worn by almost every man in sight. Frisians treasure their delicious **tea,** which is often served with sugar candies called *Kluntje* in elaborate porcelain tea sets. The Frisian dialect is actually English's closest linguistic relative; this musical accent is nearly incomprehensible to Germans, but makes it easier on Anglophilic tourists whose English accent is better understood here. Frisians constantly greet each other by saying *"Moin! Moin!,"* the North German phrase for hello. You can even hear them yelling it to the sea lions flapping their tails on nearby sand banks.

When the tide goes out on the Frisian coast, all of the water goes with it, exposing the ocean floor—called the *Watt*—between the mainland and Baltrum, Norderney, Spiekeroog, and Langeoog. *Never venture onto the Watt without a guide*—quicksand pits abound, and the tide's quick return is *extremely* dangerous. Guides, called *Wattführer,* are plentiful and well advertised; check at the tourist office or on any number of posters for a schedule of *Watt* tours.

Finding a cheap place to stay on the islands is a difficult task. Even though six of the islands—Borkum, Juist, Norderney (2), Langeoog, Spiekeroog, and Wangerooge—have **HI youth hostels,** don't expect to stay there unless you have a reservation. The islands are as popular with school groups as with tourists. The best bet for the budget traveler is a **private room,** booked through a tourist office. If you plan on staying longer than a few days, and especially if you're traveling with a group, renting a **vacation apartment** (*Ferienwohnung*) is, surprisingly, the best option. These apartments usually include a kitchen and start at about DM80 per night. Both private rooms and vacation apartments are widely available—it's not necessary to call more than a few days ahead. Fortunately, miles of breathtaking barren beaches and rolling dunes more than compensate for all of the annoying pre-planning.

■ Port Towns

Only two mainland ports are accessible by train: **Emden,** the ferry port for Borkum, and **Norddeich,** ferry port for Norderney and Juist. The departure points for all other islands lie in a string of tiny ports on the coast—all connected by the free **Bäderbus,** which runs from Norden. The ferry companies servicing **Baltrum, Langeoog,** and **Wanderooge** all run separate buses from area train stations to the ports. Keep your eye peeled for new ferry services and specials; companies often run inter-island trips or excursions to the high seas island of Helgoland. Trains run from Bremen to Emden (2hr., 1 per hr., DM34), Norden (2-2½hr., every 2hr., DM42), and Norddeich (2½hr., 1 per hr., DM43); and from Oldenburg to Emden (1¼hr., 1 per hr., DM22), Norden (1½-2hr., every 2 hr., DM30), and Norddeich (1½-2hr., 1 per hr., DM31).

■ Emden

A large seaport, **Emden** has a history as a thriving trading center. Today, the town is pleasant but unremarkable; it is important chiefly because of its Volkswagen plant and the ferry port that sees travelers off to the island of Borkum. The **Landesmuseum** in the *Rathaus* offers a menacing display of 16th- and 17th-century weapons (open daily 10am-5pm). The **Kunsthalle,** Hinter dem Rahmen 13 (tel. 209 95), is a perfect afternoon outing; the permanent collection includes Picasso, Franz Marc, and an impressive gathering of *Neue Sachlichkeit* works. (Open Tu 10am-8pm, W-F 10am-5pm, Sa-Su 11am-5pm. DM7, students and seniors DM4.) It also hosts great special exhibits. Rooms atop the museum's spiral staircases offer crash courses in 20th-century art. The highly-acclaimed **Bunker Museum** (tel. 271 06) is the newest museum in town. (Open May-Oct. Tu-F 10am-1pm and 3-5pm, Sa-Su 10am-3pm. DM3, students DM1.) Explore six floors of an old air-raid shelter stocked with memorabilia tracing the sad fate of Emden's population from 1941 to 1944, when the city was firebombed and 85% of its buildings were destroyed. For a more light-hearted experience, a visit to the charming **Dat Otto Huus** is in order. The three-story edifice is a shrine to comedian, children's entertainer, and **living legend Otto Waalkes,** a native Emdener. The first floor is free; see kissing elephants (Otto's symbol) and buy images of Otto on everything from rubber to silicon. To see the second and third floors, featuring photos of Otto clowning with Boris Becker and Steffi Graf and other madcap antics, pilgrims must pay. (Open Apr.-Oct. M-F 9:30am-6pm, Sa 9:30am-1pm and 3-6pm, Su 10am-4pm; Nov.-Mar. M-F 9:30am-1pm and 3-6pm. Admission to floors 2 and 3 DM4, children DM1.50.) Call 86 23 90 to tour the town's mammoth **Volkswagen plant** (open M-Th 9:30am-1:30pm).

Emden is located near the island of Borkum. Ferries leave daily from the Emden *Außenhaven;* for more info on getting there, see **Borkum,** p. 315. To get to town from the *Hauptbahnhof,* head to the *Innenstadt* by taking bus #3001 to "Rathaus" or by walking 15 minutes along Grossestr. The **tourist office** (tel. 974 00; fax 974 09), at Am Stadtgarten across from the *Rathaus,* gives out brochures and sells a bargain ticket that lets you into four of the city's museums. (DM9, under 18 DM4.50. Open May-Sept. M-F 9am-6pm, Sa 10am-1pm, Su 11am-1pm; Jan.-Apr. M-F 9am-1pm and 3-5:30pm, Sa 10am-1pm.) The **telephone code** is 04921.

Jugendherberge Emden (HI), An der Kesselschleuse 5 (tel. 237 97; fax 321 61), overlooks a small stream and offers bikes and canoes for rent. If you miss Bus #3003 to Herrentor (M-Sa every hr.), it's a 20-minute walk from the *Rathaus* along am Herrentor. The hostel caters to the kiddies, with comical paintings of cartoon animals in some of the bedrooms. (DM20, over 26 DM24. Breakfast included. Sheets DM6. Reception 5-10pm. Curfew 10pm.)

■ Norden and Norddeich

Norden is the transportation polestar for any excursion around Frisia. By train, it connects to Emden and Norddeich (every hr., DM3-5), and as the anchor of the **Bäderbus** and the only public link to Neßmersiel, it provides easy access to every other port town. Call or visit the **tourist office** (*Kurverwaltung;* tel. 98 62 01; fax 98 62 90), next to the *Rathaus* for specific transportation info or to book rooms (from DM25) for no fee (open M-F 8:30am-4pm, Sa 9am-4pm).

From the *Rathaus,* it is impossible to miss the gigantic steeple on the other side of the market. The spire belongs to the 15th-century **Ludgerkirche,** famed for its exquisite organ, just like Marky Mark. (Open Apr.-Sept. M 10am-12:30pm, Tu-Sa 10am-12:30pm and 3-5pm. Organ concerts mid-June to mid-Sept. W 8pm.) The great East Frisian fascination with tea is explained at the **East Frisian Tea Museum** (tel. 121 00), am Markt in the town square (open Mar.-Oct. Tu-Sa 10am-4pm; DM4, children DM1.50). For DM1 on Wednesdays (May-Aug. only), participate in an East Frisian **tea ceremony,** which resembles its Japanese counterpart only in its placid atmosphere. The ceremony takes place at tea time (2 and 3pm), of course. In the same building is the **Heimat Museum,** which shows the early culture of *Ostfriesland,* including dike construction and shoemaking (same admission and hours as tea museum).

Often passed through only en route to Norderney or Juist, suburban port **Norddeich** actually offers spectacular land and seascapes well worth an extra look. The town's **Jugendherberge (HI),** Sandstr. 1 (tel. 80 64; fax 818 28), is an excellent base for exploring Friesland. From the station, with your back to the sea, walk behind the dike 30m past the Hotel Regina Maris, and go left on Sandstr. The main hostel compound is almost always filled with schoolchildren, but the newly built pine cabins

(Hüttchen) in the backyard allow you to escape the shrill *Schulkinder* and the 10pm curfew. They're cheaper, too! (DM23, over 26 DM28. DM14 for a bed in a cabin. DM15 to pitch your own tent in the backyard. Sheets DM5. Reception 5-8pm.) **Nord-see-Camp,** Deichstr. 21 (tel. 80 73; fax 80 74), is 20 minutes farther down Badestr., which turns into Deichstr. It has impressive views, but dike-side camping gets chilly (DM5 per day, DM8.25 per person; *Kurtaxe* DM3; open mid-Mar. to Oct.).

Ferries leave Norddeich daily for Norderney and for Juist. The Norddeich **tourist office,** Dörperweg 22 (tel. 98 62 00), finds rooms in *Pensionen* (DM23-35) and doles out ferry schedules and **Watt** tours. From the train station, head down Badestr. and turn left on Dörperweg. (Open M-Th 8:30am-1pm and 2-4:30pm, F 8:30am-4pm, Sa 10am-4pm.) The **postal code** is 26506. The **telephone code** for both cities is 04931.

■ Islands

Because they're remote and still extremely popular, the Frisian islands present several problems to the spontaneous traveler. No transportation hub exists; the ferries for each island are almost all operated by separate, private companies, and all depart from separate mainland ports. Island-hopping is virtually impossible—you always have to return to the mainland. However, with good planning these obstacles should not prevent you from passing peaceful vacation days on the Frisian Islands.

■ Borkum

Lodged in an inlet halfway between Germany and Holland, Borkum is where the ever-industrious Germans go to do *nothing.* The island has a festive, laid-back atmosphere; witness the tiny, brightly painted train that carts vacationers through a serene, flower-filled landscape to the shiny happy town at the far end of the island. The town itself centers on a century-old **lighthouse,** a lovely structure that provides all the aforementioned brightness and a great view of the island from its top.

AG EMS operates the ferry service from Emden's **Außenhaven.** To get to the *Außenhaven* from the train station, take bus #3004 to "Emden Außenhaven," the infrequent train, or a taxi (DM14). The ferry runs several times daily (2hr., daytrip ticket DM25, open-ended return DM47). For DM15 more, you can get to the island in half the time on the wicked cool **catamaran.** For info, call 89 07 22. The ferry service also runs ferries to Dutch shopping town **Eemshaven.** Rent bikes at **Fahrrad Verleih,** also at the train station. (DM3 per hr., DM8 per day. Open M-F 7am-6pm, Sa 7-8am, 9am-noon, 1-2, and 3-5pm, Su 7-8am, 9am-noon, 1-2, and 4-6pm.) Borkum's **tourist office,** Am-Georg-Schütte-Pl. 5 (tel. 93 30; fax 93 31 04), at the train station in town, books rooms for free, and hands out maps and a gorgeous prospectus (open M-F 9am-6pm, Sa 10am-noon). The **telephone code** is 04922.

Borkum's **Jugendherberge (HI),** Jann-Berghaus-Str. 63 (tel. 579; fax 71 24), a five-minute walk from the dock, fills up quickly. To get a room, a written request one month in advance is necessary. (DM34.70, over 26 DM38.55. 3 meals included. Curfew 10:30pm, but house keys are available.) **Insel-Camping,** at Hindenburgstr. 114 (tel. 10 88), is 15 minutes from the train station by foot. (DM20 per person, tent included. Open mid-Mar. to Oct.)

■ Norderney

As Germany's oldest North Sea spa, the island of **Norderney** has served as a retreat for illustrious luminaries like the Hannoverian monarchs, Otto von Bismarck, and Heinrich Heine. The town and over-run beaches on the west tip of the island are a little kitschy, but the desolate dunes and endless beaches that cover the eastern two-thirds of the island are free from the hustling hordes of bourg-ee ("BU-zhee") German tourists. **Ferry company Frisia** (tel. 913 13) runs ferries to Norderney from the same dock that houses the Norddeich train station. (55min., day-trip DM25, open-ended return DM37. Call for information and schedules.) The **Fahrradverleih am Hafen** (tel. 13

26), 300m down Hafenstr. as you step off the ferry, rents **bikes** at an unbeatable location. (DM9 for 4hr., DM12 per day, children DM6 and DM9. Open daily 9am-6pm.) If you want to spend the night, the friendly folks at the **tourist office,** Bülowallee 5 (tel. 918 50; fax 824 94), sniff out rooms in *Pensionen* (DM40) or private homes (longer stays only, DM30) for a DM7.50 fee. (Open M-F 9am-6pm, Sa 10am-12:30pm and 2-4pm, Su 10am-12:30pm.) The **telephone code** is 04932.

Norderney's two **Jugendherbergen (HI)** are both excruciatingly crowded and expensive; they require you to pay for full pension (3 meals) for the duration of your stay. However, the owner of the hostel at **Südstraße** (tel. 24 51; fax 836 00) takes pains to provide a haven for stranded travelers. Follow Zum Fähranleger to Deichstr., then onto Südstr. (DM37.50, including both the *Kurtaxe* and full board. Members only. Sheets DM5. Reception 8:30-9am, 5:15-6pm, and 9:45pm. Open Mar.-Oct.) Somewhat less inviting, due to its inconvenient location, is the hostel **Am Dünensender 3** (tel. 25 74; fax 832 66); if you miss the bus to "Leuchtturm" (1 per hr.), you'll have to rent a **bike** in town or suffer the 90-minute to two-hour walk. Follow Deichstr. to its end, and head left on Karl Reger Weg, where signs point you to the hostel. (DM35.50, over 26 DM43.50. Full board included. Reception 8:30-10am. Open Mar.-Oct.) **Camping** is available in summer for HI members only (DM11 per person with breakfast). **Haus Westend,** Friedrichstr. 40 (tel. 26 85; fax 832 61), offers elegant rooms across the street from the beach for surprisingly low prices. Rooms on the top floor have ocean views. (Singles from DM55; doubles from DM60.) **Camping Booken,** Waldweg 2 (tel. 448), is expensive, but the next best thing to the hostels. Call ahead. (DM12 per person; DM12 per tent. Warm showers included. Wash DM6, dry DM5. Reception 10am-noon.)

■ Juist and Baltrum

Juist is 17km long, 500m wide, and famous for its birds. First settled in 1398, it's a bit tough to settle there now unless your "tent" is made of twigs and dried leaves. **Ferries** leave from the port at Norddeich at odd times, depending on tides and season; call ferry service **Frisia** at (04931) 98 70 in Norden or (04935) 910 10 on Juist. (Ferries June-Oct. roughly 2 per day. Day excursion DM28.50, round-trip DM40, ages 4-11 half-price.) You can also walk there across the *Watt* from Norddeich, but *only with a guide.* Check with the tourist office for schedules. The rental shop **Germania,** Wilhelmstr. 17 (tel. 297), has over 600 **bikes** to lease (from DM12 per day, ID required; open daily 9am-6pm). The **tourist office,** Friesenstr. 18 (*Kurverwaltung;* tel. 80 92 22; fax 80 92 23; email juist@t-online.de), has maps and a free room-finding service. (Rooms DM30-60 per person. Open May-Sept. M-F 8:30am-noon and 3-5pm, Sa 10am-noon; Oct.-Apr. M-F 3-6pm.) There is even a **Jugendherberge,** Loogster Pad 20 (tel. 929 10; fax 82 94), on this tiny island. (DM29.20, over 26 DM34.20. Breakfast and dinner included. Reception 8-10pm or whenever a boat arrives. Open Mar.-Dec.) The **telephone code** is 04935.

The smallest of the Frisian Islands, with a population of 500, **Baltrum** is the ideal escape from civilization. Anything but modern, Baltrum maintains a Luddite ambience, supported by a total ban on cars and the absence of bike rentals. To reach **Baltrum,** take the bus from the Norden train station (1 short stop from Norddeich) to **Neßmersiel** to meet the ferry (open-ended return DM36, children DM17; daytrip DM22, DM11). Train, bus, and boat are all timed for a convenient rendezvous (June-Nov. 2-3 per day; last ferry to the island does not have a corresponding ferry back). For more information, check the schedule, call the ferry company at 235, or visit the **tourist office,** Rathausstr. 130 (tel. 800; for rooms call 80 48; fax 80 27) in the *Rathaus.* The office also offers hotel information and books private accommodations for a 5% commission. (Open Mar.-Oct. M-F 8:30am-noon and 2-5pm; Nov.-Feb. M-F 9am-noon). The **telephone code** is 04939.

■ Langeoog, Spiekeroog, and Wangerooge

The bus from Norden (DM7.50) or from **Esens** (DM3.50) travels to Bensersiel, the departure point for ferries to **Langeoog,** which served as a base for 18th-century pirates. (May-Sept. 7 departures per day, Oct.-Apr. 4 per day, open-ended return DM34, children DM17; daytrip DM28.) Call ferry service **Schiffahrt der Inselgemeinde Langeoog** on Langeoog at (04971) 928 90. Rent a bike on Hauptstr. at **Fahrrad Verleih** (tel. 64 74; open daily 9am-12:30pm and 1:30-6pm). For more info or to book a room (DM30 and up), visit the **tourist office** in front of the *Bahnhof,* at Hauptstr. 28 (tel. 69 32 01; fax 65 28; open in summer M-Sa 9am-7pm, Su 10am-2pm; in winter M-F 9am-5pm). The **telephone code** is 04972.

Langeoog's **Jugendherberge Domäne Melkhörn (HI)** is smack-dab in the middle of the island (tel. 276; fax 66 94). One can only reach the hostel by foot, bike, or horse and buggy—motor vehicles are prohibited. (DM33.55, over 26 DM35.55. Members only. Full board included.) The hostel also runs a **campground.** (DM28.35, over 26 DM29.75. Members only. Full board included. Reservation required. Curfew 10pm, but if you're 18 or older, you can get a key. Open Apr.-Sept.)

"No festivals celebrated here," brags the official brochure for **Speikeroog,** the island that takes pride in its natural silence and shipwrecks. The **Bäderbus** out of Norden travels to Neuharlingersiel, the departure point for Spiekeroog. Its **tourist office,** Noorderpad 25 (tel. 919 30; for rooms call 919 25), has information on ferries, rooms for as little as DM16, and dune paths (open Apr.-Sept. M-F 9am-noon and 2-5pm, Sa 9am-noon; Jan.-Mar. M-F 9am-noon). Spickeroog's **Jugendherberge,** Bid Utkiek 1 (tel. 329), is a trifling 10-minute walk from either the port or the beach. (DM35.50 per person. Full board included. Written reservations are required 1 year in advance! Open Apr.-Oct.) The **telephone code** is 04976.

The journey to **Wangerooge** is a Herculean labor, but worth it if you're desperate to avoid the crowds that plague the other islands. From Norden, take a 90-minute ride on the *Bäderbus* to the town of **Harlesiel.** Boats leave the dock two to five times daily from April to October and once or twice daily the rest of the year; exact times vary widely with the season. (Open-ended return DM44, children 4-11 DM22; daytrip DM29.) Wangerooge's **tourist office** on the Strandpromenade (tel. 990; for rooms call 948 80; fax 991 14) has ferry information (open M-F 9am-noon and 2-5pm, Sa-Su whenever a ferry arrives). They can also direct you to the haunting **Westturm,** a landmark that's been converted into a striking **Jugendherberge (HI)** (tel. 439), a 20-minute walk from the station. Look for the stone tower. (DM34.10, over 26 DM38.10. Full board included. Reception 7-9am, 1-3, and 5-7pm. Curfew 10pm for those under 18. Open May-Sept. Call weeks in advance.) The **telephone code** is 04469.

Matjes

Matjes (MAH-ches), the Scandinavian word for herring, is all the rage in northern Germany during the first few weeks of June, which are officially dubbed the *"Matjes-Wochen"* (Herring Weeks). Several varieties exist: *nederlandisch* (Dutch), with cream sauce and vegetables; *hausfrau* (housewife), in sour cream with onion and apple; and sweet and sour, doused in sugared vinegar—but any restaurant worth its salt has its own secret recipe. Look for *Matjes* advertised everywhere, from the dives in the train station to the hip Schanzenstr. cafes in Hamburg. The fish has a very strong, sweet taste that is not acquired—you'll either love it or hate it. Wash it down with a glass of *Alsterwasser*—literally "water from the Alster" (one of Hamburg's lakes), but actually a gentle mix of beer and Sprite that tastes a lot better than it sounds.

Nordrhein-Westfalen (North Rhine-Westphalia)

In 1946, the victorious Allies attempted to speed Germany's recovery by merging the traditionally distinct regions of Westphalia, Lippe, and the Rhineland to unify the economic nucleus of post-war Germany. The resulting *Land,* Nordrhein-Westfalen, meets no typical German stereotype, a fact which has unfairly tarnished its image. True, the avant-garde multiculturalism of Berlin, the *Lederhosen* and beer halls of Bavaria, and the unspoiled natural beauty of the Black Forest are all far from here, but the region's dense concentration of highways, rail lines, and people connect and unite the diverse traditions. With its 17 million inhabitants and the mighty Ruhr Valley, North Rhine-Westphalia is the most heavily populated and economically powerful area in Germany. But industry has brought strife to the region in the past: the industrial boom of the late 19th century sparked social democracy, trade unionism, and revolutionary communism—the popular moniker "Red Ruhr" didn't refer to the color of the water. Despite downturns in heavy industry and persistently high unemployment, the great industrial wealth of the region continues to support a multitude of cultural offerings for the citizens and visitors of its lively towns and beautiful river valleys. And while the region's industrial squalor may have inspired the philosophy of Karl Marx and Friedrich Engels, the natural beauty of the Teutoburg and Eifel and the cultural and intellectual energy of Köln and Düsseldorf have spurred the muses of writers from Goethe to Heine to Böll.

🖐 HIGHLIGHTS OF NORDRHEIN-WESTFALEN

- The crowning glory of German piety, **Köln's Dom** (cathedral) is the largest example of High Gothic architecture in the world. Köln shines beyond its cathedral, however, with a collection of **world-class museums** on Heinrich-Böll-Platz, a **great nightlife,** including a burgeoning gay scene, and a fountain that gushes forth **perfume** (see p. 318).
- **Düsseldorf** is a wealthy, wealthy city, with a glitzy strip of designer boutiques **(the "Kö")** and a palpably cosmopolitan air (see p. 341). Budget travelers can have fun, too; enjoy the exceptional **Kunstsammlung Nordrhein-Westfalen,** or visit the city's shrine to hometown writer-hero Heinrich Heine.
- Bordering Belgium and the Netherlands, beautiful **Aachen** exudes internationalism in an atmosphere of **college-kid coolness** (see p. 337).
- See Germany's current capital, **Bonn,** while you can; it will soon be emptied as governmental bureaus and bureaucrats begin to colonize Berlin (see p. 329).

▪ Köln (Cologne)

Founded as a Roman colony (*colonia,* hence Köln) in AD 48, Köln was Petrarch's "city of dreams" when the rest of Germany was just wilderness. The city's location at the intersection of several international trade routes ushered in a Golden Age during the Middle Ages and the Renaissance; this position has helped establish Köln's present status as Germany's commercial, technical, and communications center *par excellence.* Today, almost a million citizens call the city home.

Köln's major attraction is the majestic and legendary *Dom.* Designed to exceed all other churches in splendor, the Gothic structure took an amazing 632 years to build. During World War II, at least 14 bombs struck the *Dom.* It somehow survived and has since become a powerful symbol of Köln's miraculous recovery from the allied raids, which left 90% of the city center in ruins. Today, Köln is the largest city in Nordrhein-Westfalen and the most important culturally, with a full plate of world-class museums

Nordrhein-Westfalen
(North Rhine-Westphalia)

NETHERLANDS

Enschede
Arnhem
Kleve
Xanten
Duisburg
Krefeld
Düsseldorf
Mönchengladbach
Maastricht
Liege
Aachen
Monschau
Altenahr
Koblenz
Burg Eltz
Cochem
Beilstein

Osnabrück
Münster
Dortmund
Essen Bochum
Wuppertal
Solingen
Köln
Bonn

Hanover
Hameln
Lemgo
Detmold
Bodenwerder
Lügde
Horn
Paderborn
Lippe
Münden
Kassel
Fritzlar
Frankenberg
Siegen
Marburg
Wetzlar
Gießen
Fulda
Weilburg
Limburg
Loreley
Bad Homburg
Frankfurt am Main

EIFEL RANGE
TAUNUS RANGE

NORDRHEIN-WESTFALEN

and theatrical offerings. It is a prosperous, modern city with a penchant for bibulous celebrations, such as the annual *Karneval* (like *Mardi Gras,* but with more drinking).

Modern Köln is also the city of Nobel Prize-winning novelist Heinrich Böll, who set *The Lost Honor of Katharina Blum* and the scandalous *Clown* here. The novels concern the venom of press slander and the violation of civil liberties—topics appropriate to a city steeped in literary and journalistic tradition. Köln is the base for many national media networks, just as it was during the days of Karl Marx, who began his revolutionary career here as a local newspaper editor (although Karl did not get to host a TV program when orchestrating the Gotha program). Although Köln's citizens conduct their own communications in the impenetrable "Kölsch" dialect, a locally brewed *Kölsch* beer offers a savory experience that can bring to all visitors' taste buds the kind of experience that the heavenly *Dom* delivers to their eyes.

ORIENTATION AND PRACTICAL INFORMATION

Eight bridges carry Köln across the Rhine, but nearly all sights can be found on the western side. The *Hauptbahnhof* is in the northern part of the *Innenstadt.* The *Altstadt* is split into two districts; the *Altstadt-Nord* is near the station, and the *Altstadt-Süd* is just south of the Severinsbrücke.

Many high-end hotels in the center city, including the **Dom Hotel,** across from the *Dom,* sell the simply delectable **Köln Bonbon,** a packet of vouchers entitling the holder to a print of the 1531 town panorama woodcut, discounts on Rhine cruises, reduced admission to area attractions, and a three-day pass for free entry into all of the city's museums (DM15; with voucher for 2hr. **city bus tour** DM26).

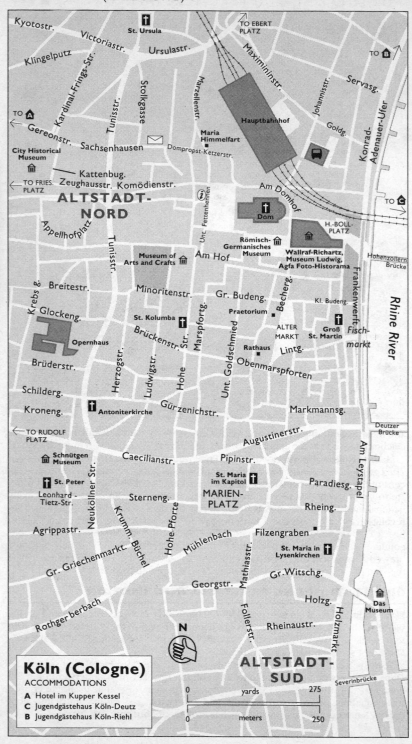

NORDRHEIN-WESTFAIEN

Kyotostr.
Victoriastr.
Klingelputz
Kardinal-Frings-Str.
Tunisstr.
Stolkgasse
Marcellenstr.
Ursulastr.
St. Ursula

TO EBERT PLATZ
Maximininstr.
Johannistr.
Servasg.
TO B
Goldg.

TO A
Gereonstr.
Sachsenhausen
Maria Himmelfart
Dompropst-Ketzerstr.
Hauptbahnhof
Konrad-Adenauer-Ufer

City Historical Museum
Kattenbug.
TO FRIES. PLATZ
Zeughausstr.
Komödienstr.
Am Domhof
TO C

ALTSTADT-NORD
Appellhofplatz
Tunisstr.
Unt. Fettenhennen
Dom
H.-BOLL-PLATZ

Museum of Arts and Crafts
Am Hof
Römisch-Germanisches Museum
Wallraf-Richartz, Museum Ludwig, Agfa Foto-Historama
Hohenzollern Brücke

Krebs g.
Breitestr.
Minoritenstr.
Gr. Budeng.
Becherg.
Kl. Budeng.
Frankenwerft
Rhine River

Glockeng.
St. Kolumba
Marspfortg.
Praetorium
ALTER MARKT
Groß St. Martin
Fisch-markt

Opernhaus
Brückenstr.
Herzogstr.
Hohe Str.
Ludwigstr.
Unt. Goldschmied
Rathaus
Lintg.
Obenmarspforten

Brüderstr.
Schilderg.
Kroneng.
Antoniterkirche
Gürzenichstr.
Markmannsg.
Deutzer Brücke

TO RUDOLF PLATZ
Augustinerstr.
Am Leystapel

Schnütgen Museum
Caecilianstr.
Pipinstr.
St. Maria im Kapitol
Paradiesg.

St. Peter
Leonhard - Tietz-Str.
Neuköllner Str.
Sterneng.
MARIEN-PLATZ
Rheing.

Agrippastr.
Krumm. Büchel
Hohe Pforte
Mühlenbach
Filzengraben
St. Maria in Lysenkirchen

Gr. Griechenmarkt.
Georgstr.
Mathiasstr.
Gr. Witschg.
Holzg.
Das Museum

Rothger berbach
Follerstr.
Rheinaustr.
Holzmarkt

N

ALTSTADT-SUD
Severinbrücke

Köln (Cologne)
ACCOMMODATIONS
A Hotel im Kupper Kessel
C Jugendgästehaus Köln-Deutz
B Jugendgästehaus Köln-Riehl

0   yards   275
0   meters   250

Transportation

Flights: Flights depart from **Köln-Bonn Flughafen** for 50 destinations non-stop; a shuttle to Berlin leaves 24 times per day. Call (02203) 40 25 38 for more information. Bus #170 leaves stop #4 of the *Hauptbahnhof* daily at 5:40, 6, and 6:30am, and then every 15min. 7am-8pm, and every 30min. 8-11pm; it stops at Köln-Deutz 5min. later, then proceeds to the airport (15min., DM8.20, children DM4.50).

Trains: Direct train lines connect Köln with Düsseldorf (30min., 5 per hr.), Frankfurt (2½hr., 1 per hr.), Munich (6-8hr., 2 per hr.), Hamburg (4hr., 1-2 per hr.), and Berlin (5½-7½hr., 1 per hr.).

Ferries: Köln-Düsseldorfer (tel. 258 30 11; fax 208 82 38) begins its ever-popular Rhine cruises here. Sail upstream to Koblenz and fairy-tale castle-land in the Rhine Gorge. Connections to Mosel River ferries. Seniors half-price on M and F. Students and children ages 4-12 half-price. Most trips (excluding the hydrofoils) covered by Eurail and German rail passes. Ask about the unadvertised student discount.

Public Transportation: Any **VRS** *(Verkehrsverbund Rhein-Sieg)* office has maps of the S- and U-Bahn lines throughout the Köln-Bonn area, as well as maps of city bus and streetcar lines. One is downstairs in the train station near the U-Bahn. Major convergence points include the *Hauptbahnhof,* Köln-Deutz, Appellhofpl., and Barbarossapl. Tickets priced by distance: 1-ride tickets DM1.55-13.50; day cards DM11-33; the DM11 card gets you anywhere in Köln. Determine the zone you want (A-D), as prices vary widely.

Gondola: Rheinseilbahn (tel. 76 20 06), U-bahn #16 or 18 (Direction: "Ebertpl./Mülheim") to "Zoo/Flora." Float over the Rhine from the Zoo to the Rheinpark. DM6.50, kids DM3.50; round-trip DM9.50, DM5. Times change daily.

Taxi: Funkzentrale (tel. 28 82). Cold medinas not available.

Car Rental: Avis, Clemensstr. 29 (tel. 23 43 33); **Hertz,** Bismarckstr. 19-21 (tel. 51 50 84).

Bike Rental: Kölner Fahrradverliehservice, Sedanstr. 27 (tel. 72 36 27). From the station, walk along the shore toward Deutzer Bridge. Go right at the spiral staircase. DM4.50 per hr., DM21 per day. Open M-Sa 8am-8pm, Su 11am-8pm.

Mitfahrzentrale: Citynetz Mitfahrzentrale, Maximinstr. 2 (tel. 194 40), to the left of the train station, lists rides. Open M-F 9am-6pm, Sa 9am-2pm.

Hitchhiking: *Let's Go* does not recommend hitchhiking. For all destinations, hitchers say to take bus #132 to the last stop.

Tourist and Financial Services

Tourist Office: Verkehrsamt, Unter Fettenhennen 19 (tel. 221 33 45; fax for hotel reservations 221 33 20; http://www.koeln.org/koelntourismus), across from the main entrance to the *Dom,* provides a free city map (you must pay for most other brochures), books rooms in advance for DM6 (written requests only), or for DM5 in person. Ask about English **tours** of the city and *Dom.* Pick up the *Monatsvorschau* (DM2), a booklet with essential info and a complete monthly schedule of events. Open May-Oct. M-Sa 8am-10:30pm, Su 9am-10:30pm; Nov.-Apr. M-Sa 8am-9pm, Su 9:30am-7pm.

Budget Travel: STA Travel, Zülpicherstr. 178 (tel. 44 20 11).

Currency Exchange: There's an office at the **train station** (open daily 7am-9pm), but the service charges are lower at the **post office.**

American Express: Burgmauerstr. 14 (tel. 925 90 10), near the *Dom.* ATM. Cardmembers' mail held free for 4 weeks. Open M-F 9am-5:30pm, Sa 9am-noon.

Local Services

Bookstore: Mayerische Buchhandlungs, Hohestr. 68-82 (tel. 257 57 85), has a fabulous paperback selection, including English language books. Open M-F 10am-8pm, Sa 9:30am-4pm.

Cultural Centers: Amerika Haus, Apostelnkloster 13-15 (tel. 20 90 10; fax 24 45 43), offers English cultural activities. English language **library** open Tu-F 2-5pm. The **British Council,** Hahnenstr. 6 (tel. 20 64 40), on Neumarkt, offers the same services with a British accent and a better Monty Python collection. Open M-W and F 1-5pm, Th 1-7pm (closed for 6 weeks in July and Aug.).

AIDS-Hilfe: Beethovenstr. 1 (tel. 194 11). **Hotline,** tel. 20 20 30.

NORDRHEIN-WESTFALEN

Women's Resources: The municipal **Frauenamt,** Markmansgasse 7 (tel. 221 64 82), fields questions on cultural opportunities and services. Open M-Th 8:30am-1pm and 2-4pm, F 8:30am-12:30pm, but it's best to call for an appointment. **Women's crisis hotline,** tel. 420 16 20.

Laundry: Öko-Express, Neue Weyerstr. 1, is ökey-dökey. Wash DM6. Dry DM1 per 10min. Soap included. Open M-Sa 6am-11pm. Also available at Zülpicher Wall 2 and at the Köln-Deutz hostel (same times and prices).

Emergency and Communications

Emergency: Police, tel. 110. **Fire** and **Ambulance,** tel. 112.

Pharmacy: Dom Apotheke, Komodienstr. 5 (tel. 257 67 54), near the station. Their *Pharmacie-Internationale* advises in English, and has a list of other after-hours pharmacies posted outside. Open M-F 8am-6:30pm, Sa 8:30am-4pm.

Post Office: Main office, WDR Arkaden, 50667 Köln. From the *Dom* exits of the train station, head down Breitestr. and then An den Ruhr. Open M-F 8am-6pm, Sa 8am-6pm, Su 8am-1pm. Limited service M-F 6-8pm, Su 1-6pm.

Internet Access: In **FuturePoint** (see p. 324).

Telephone Code: 0221.

ACCOMMODATIONS AND CAMPING

The brisk convention and tour business in Köln produces a wealth of rooms; the trick is pinning one down. Hotels fill up (and prices set sail) in the spring and fall when trade winds blow conventioneers into town. Summer is high season for Köln's two hostels, both of which brim to the beams from June to September. The main hotel haven centers around Brandenburger Str., on the less interesting side of the *Bahnhof.* The **Mitwohnzentrale,** An der Bottmühle 16 (tel. 32 70 84), is a matching service for longer stays (open M-Th 8:30am-1pm and 2-4pm, F 8:30am-12:30pm). Scrounging for a last minute room during *Karneval* is futile—most people book a year or more in advance for the festivities. If all else fails, schlepp to Bonn; remember to calculate the time and transportation cost if you go there, as a round-trip generally consumes 1-1½ hours and DM8-15.

Jugendherberge Köln-Deutz (HI), Siegesstr. 5a (tel. 81 47 11; fax 88 44 25), just over the Hohenzollern Bridge. From the main exit of the train station, walk down Neuhöfferstr., the first street to the left of the mirrored building, and take the first right; the hostel is tucked behind the courtyard with big trees (2min.). Or S-Bahn #6, 11, or 12 to "Köln-Deutz" (1 stop). Small, but clean rooms in a good location, with two pinball machines and free access to washing machines (soap DM1). The 374 beds fill quickly and the staff is overworked. DM32, over 26 DM37. Breakfast buffet DM8. Sheets included. Best check-in is 6-9am. Later is riskier, but reception opens again 12:30pm-12:30am. Curfew 12:30am.

Jugendgästehaus Köln-Riehl (HI), An der Schanz 14 (tel. 76 70 81; fax 76 15 55), on the Rhine north of the zoo. U-Bahn #16 or 18 (direction: "Ebertpl./Mülheim") to "Boltensternstr.," or walk along the Rhine on Konrad-Adenauer-Ufer until it becomes Niederländer-Ufer and finally An der Schanz (40min.). Big common areas, with plush sofas, 4-6-bed rooms, and lockers big enough to hide in. DM38.50, singles DM63.50. Breakfast and sheets included. Reception 24hr. No curfew. The **Bistro Backpackers Inn** sells beer, baguettes, and fries (open 8pm-12:30am).

Hotel Im Kupferkessel, Probsteigasse 6 (tel. 13 53 38; fax 12 51 21). From the station bear right; follow the street as it changes from Dompropost-Ketzer-Str. to An den Dominikern to Unter Sachsenhausen to Gereonstr. and on and on and on and on as it becomes Christophstr., then turn right on Probsteigasse. Comfortable, clean rooms, but this hotel is far from all points of interest. Singles from DM54, doubles from DM120. Breakfast included. Call ahead.

⑨Jansen Pension, Richard-Wagner-Str. 18 (tel. 25 18 75). U-Bahn #1, 2, 6, 15, or 19 to "Rudolfpl." and head west out of the U-bahn (2-3 blocks). Infinitely charming rooms in this Victorian row-house make this a Grand Hotel style *Pension* in an equally grand neighborhood. Singles DM45-60, doubles DM95. Breakfast included.

Hotel Heinzelmännchen, Köln-Riehl, Hohe Pforte 5-7 (tel. 21 12 17; fax 21 57 12). Bus #132 (direction: "der Frankenstr.") to "Waidmarkt," or walk down the Hohestr. shopping zone until it becomes Hohe Pforte. Bright hallways and firm mattresses. Reception until 10:30pm. Singles DM62, with bath DM70; doubles DM95, with bath DM110; triples DM135. Less for stays over 2 days. Breakfast included.

Hotel Hubertus Hof, Mühlenbach 30 (tel. 912 91 62; fax 21 55 89). Follow above directions to Hohe Pforte, then turn left onto Mühlenbach. Monster-size rooms and fuzzy carpets. Showers and toilets are off the hall. Reception 7am-9pm. Singles DM60; doubles DM80-85. Breakfast included.

Hotel Berg, Brandenburgerstr. 6 (tel. 12 11 24; fax 139 00 11). Bear left onto Johannisstr. from the back exit of the train station and take the third left onto Brandenburgerstr. A stand-out for its well-kept rooms and down-home breakfast room. Reception 24hr. Singles start at DM60, with shower DM90; doubles DM85, with shower DM160. Breakfast included. AmEx, Diners, MC, Visa.

Am Rathaus, Burgstr. 6 (tel. 257 76 24; 258 28 29). Standing on the front porch of the *Rathaus,* Am Rathaus is immediately on your right. Across the street from the Scion Kölsch brewhouse. This place is all about location. Singles DM75, doubles DM120. Private showers and breakfast included.

Das Kleine Stapelhäuschen, Fischmarkt 1-3 (tel. 257 78 62; fax 257 42 32). Beware the jaws-of-death elevator, but avoid nothing else in this perfectly elegant *Rheinisch* inn replete with classic oak furnishings and a stunning circular staircase. For huge medieval oaken mill wheels suspended above your bed, ask for the *historisches Turmzimmer* (DM220). Singles DM70-80, with shower DM102, with bath DM110; doubles DM105, with shower DM165, with bath DM185. Breakfast buffet included. AmEx, Eurocard, Visa.

Camping: Campingplatz Poll, Weidenweg (tel. 83 19 66), on the Rhine, southeast of the *Altstadt.* U-Bahn #16 to "Marienburg" and cross the Roddenkirchener Bridge. Reception 8am-noon and 3-10pm (later in the summer). DM6 per person, DM5 per tent, DM5 per car.

NORDRHEIN-WESTFALEN

FOOD

Small cafes packed with students and cheap restaurants offering quick meals line **Zülpicherstraße** all the way to the university complex. Take U-Bahn #12, 14, 16, or 18 to "Neumarkt," then U-Bahn #7 or 9 to "Zülpicherpl." Mid-priced restaurants with a fine selection of ethnic cuisine are concentrated around the perimeter of the *Altstadt,* particularly from Hohenzollernring to Hohenstaufenring. For glitzy cafes, the city's wealthy patrons head to **Neumarkt.** Don't pass through Köln without sampling the city's extraordinarily smooth **Kölsch beer,** served in little glasses (0.2L—Munich this is not). Local brews of the delightful stuff include *Sion, Küppers, Früh,* and the devout *Dom.* Köln offers hungry visitors scrumptious *Rievekoochen* (potato pancakes), slabs of fried potato dunked in *Apfelmuß* (apple sauce). A number of authentic German-style places, generally well priced, surround the Dompl. The city's best inexpensive eats are found in the Turkish district on Weidengasse. An open-air **Markt** on Wilhelmspl. takes over the northern Nippes neighborhood to offer farm-fresh joys (open M-Sa 7-11:30am). **HL Deutsche Supermarkt,** Hohenzollernring 20 (tel. 25 47 74), is a good grocery store (open M-F 8am-8pm, Sa-Su 9am-4pm).

Café Rendezvous, Heinsberg 11a (tel. 23 34 98), at the corner of Heinsberg and Zülpicherstr, capitalizes on silver-screen glitz with classic Hollywood decor and starving actor prices (all under DM10). Breakfast spreads served all day. Open Su-Th 8am-1am, F-Sa 8am-3am.

Schlotzky's Deli (tel. 920 13 20), at the corner of Hohenzollern Ring and Edro Palmstr. It's difficult to get a decent pastrami sandwich in Germany, but this burgeoning chain has all the classics, including a large vegetarian selection (DM6.50-9.50). Open Su-Th 11am-midnight, F-Sa 11am-1am.

Café Waschsalon, Friesenstr. 80 (tel. 13 33 78), is filled with washers; turn on the spin cycle in your head with their fine assortment of drinks. Breakfast (DM6.50 and up) served until 4pm. No dryers—let the balmy breezes take it from here. Open M-Th 8am-1am, F 8am-3am, Sa 10am-3am, Su 10am-1am.

Taco Loco, 40 Zülpicher Str. (tel. 240 15 16), serves up good Mexican food in a friendly, relaxed environment. Slip back to the *Biergarten* and grab one of Köln's only Coronas. The tacos here are crazy. Just plain loony. Open Su-Th 11am-2am, F-Sa 11am-3am.

FuturePoint, Richmodstr. 13 (tel. 206 72 06), gives Köln's sleekest clientele just what they want: a huge drink menu, esoteric snacks, and cheap **Internet access** (DM3 per 30min., DM10 per 2hr., DM20 per day) in a chic cafe straight out of the *Jetsons*. Open daily 9:30am-1am.

Brauhaus Früh am Dom, Am Hof 12-14 (tel. 258 03 97). This *echtes* establishment arguably offers the best *Kölsch* in town. An excellent place to eat, patrons enjoy a number of Kölner and German specialties (*Schnitzel, Brats, Kartoffeln,* it's all here) while basking in the warm glow of a lit *Dom* and "lit" Germans in the outdoor *Biergarten.* Most dishes DM9-22. Open daily 8am-midnight (later for drinks).

SIGHTS

The Dom

Directly across from the Bahnhof. Tel. 52 19 77. **Open** *daily 6am-7pm. Free admission. Free* **tours** *in German M-Sa 10 and 11am, 2 and 3pm, Su 2 and 3pm. English tours Su-F 2pm, Sa 10:30am; DM6, children DM4. Free* **organ concerts** *mid-June to Sept. Tu 8pm.* **Tower** *open May-Sept. 9am-6pm; Mar.-Apr. and Oct. 9am-5pm; Nov.-Feb. 9am-4pm. DM3, students DM1.50.* **Domschatzkammer** *open Apr.-Oct. M-Sa 9am-5pm, Su 12:30-5pm; Nov.-Mar. M-Sa 9am-4pm, Su 1-4pm. DM3, under 18 and students DM1.50.* **Diözesan Museum** *open F-W 10am-5pm. Free.*

When sight-seeing in Köln, it's impossible to save the best for last. Most train stations offer only drunks, beggars, and transients, but visitors exiting Köln's *Bahnhof* are immediately treated to the beauty, power, and sorrow that emanate from the colossal **Dom,** Germany's greatest cathedral. Dedicated to St. Peter and St. Mary, visually overwhelming in intricacy and scale, the edifice took six centuries to build before reaching completion in 1880. Moreover, Köln's *Dom* is a pure example of High Gothic style, the largest of its kind in the world. For 500 years, the giant wooden crane, now kept inside, was as much Köln's trademark as the two massive towers. The stunning stained glass windows—enough to cover the floor twice—cast a harlequin display of colored light over the interior. Moving toward the front, the section to the right of the center altar bears the **Dombild triptych,** a masterful painting and gilded altarpiece from the 15th-century Kölner School. The enormous sculpture shining brilliantly in the dim light is the **Shrine of the Magi,** a reliquary of the Three Kings in blinding gold, brought to the city in 1164. The Three Kings are the town's holy patrons; they stand behind the altar in a magnificent 1531 woodcut of the town by Anton Woensam, and their three crowns grace Köln's official heraldic shield. Tapestries of Rubens' *Triumph of the Eucharist* line the central nave. While in the *Dom,* look for the 976 **Gero Crucifix,** the oldest intact sculpture of **Christus patiens** (depicting a crucified Christ with closed eyes) in the world.

Five hundred and nine steps and 15 minutes are all it takes to top the **Südturm** (south tower) and peer down at the river below. Catch your breath at the *Glockenstube* (400 steps up), a chamber for the tower's nine bells. Four of the *Glocken* date from the Middle Ages, but the 19th-century upstart known affectionately as **Der große Peter** (at 24 tons, the world's heaviest swinging bell) rings loudest. Hailed as "Germany's Bell on the Rhine," it bears an engraved call for national unity. The **Domschatzkammer** in a corner of the cathedral holds the requisite clerical artwork and reliquaries: thorn, cross, and nail bits as well as pieces of 18 saints. Find more ecclesiastical favors in the **Diözesan Museum,** Roncallipl. 2, just outside the south portal in the red building.

The allure of the cathedral illuminated from dusk until midnight is irresistible, drawing natives and tourists alike to the expansive **Domvorplatz** for a daily carnival of relaxation, art, and activism. Since time and acid rain have corroded much of the *Dom's* original detail, every piece is gradually being reproduced and replaced with new, treated stone. To expedite this task, you can play the *"Dom* lottery" at posts around the plaza and save a statue's fingernail (DM1-2).

Central City

In the shadow of the cathedral, the **Hohenzollern Brücke** crosses the Rhine. The majestic bridge empties out onto a promenade guarded by equestrian statues of the imperial family. A monumental flight of stairs leads to the **Heinrich Böll Cultural Center** (see p. 326), a piece of modern architecture that succeeds in complementing the *Dom*. Farther on, the squares and crooked streets of the old **Fischmarkt** district open onto paths along the Rhine; the cafe patios give way to a wide expanse of grass along the river, perfect for a picnic serenaded by musicians.

The **Rathaus** (Town Hall), partially bombed in World War II, has been reconstructed in its original mongrel style. *(Open M-Th 7:30am-4:45pm, F 7:30am-2pm. Tours W at 3pm.)* The Gothic **tower** stands guard over Baroque cherubs flying around an ornate 1570 Renaissance arcade called the *loggia*, the only section to survive the war. The tower is adorned with a diverse array of historical and cultural figures; Marx and Rubens loom above rows of popes and emperors. On the *Rathaus* facade, a **Glockenspiel** offers a titillatingly tintinnabulary experience daily at noon and 5pm. Classical historians and *Ben Hur* fans will be more impressed by the **Römisches Praetorium und Kanal,** the excavated ruins of the former Roman military headquarters from the province of Niedergermania (Lower Germany). *(Open Tu-F 10am-4pm, Sa-Su 11am-4pm. Admission DM3, students DM1.50.)* To get there from the *Rathaus* porch, take a right towards the swarm of hotels and then a left onto Kleinen Budengasse. Looking like an abandoned set from a gladiator movie, the museum displays the remains of various Roman gods and a befuddling array of rocks left by the city's early inhabitants. The glass pyramid visible to your left as you exit the *Rathaus* shelters the **Mikwe Judenbad,** a 12th-century Jewish ritual bath that burrows 15m down to groundwater. *(Open M-Th 8am-4pm, F-Sa 8am-2pm. Free.)* Medieval bathers generally went in naked, but you'll need at least a passport (ooohh...sexy moneybelt, stud) to obtain a key from the *Rathaus*.

Goethe, the original 18th-century *grenouille*, noted "how grateful the women are for the fragrance of **Eau de Köln.**" This magic water, once prescribed as a drinkable curative, made the town (via the oft-mimicked export) a household name. If you're after the authentic article, be sure your bottle says *"Echt kölnisch Wasser"* (real Köln water); or look for the world-renowned "4711" label. Its name comes from the Mühlens family house, labeled **House #4711** by the Napoleonic system that abolished street names. *(Open M-F 9am-6:30pm, Sa 9am-2pm.)* It has been converted into a perfect boutique, with a small fountain continually dispensing the famous scented water. Visit regularly and you'll be torn apart by worshipful throngs. The house is on Glockengasse, at the intersection with Tunisstr.; from Hohestr., turn right on Brückenstr., which becomes Glockengasse.

The **Rheinseilbahn** (gondola; see p. 321) touts a terminus near Köln-Riehl's **zoo** (open daily 9am-6pm; in winter 9am-5pm), **aquarium** (open daily 9:30am-6pm), and **botanical garden** (open daily 8am-dusk). Take U-Bahn #16 or 18 to "Zoo/Flora." *(Combined admission DM15, students DM8.50, children DM7.50.)* Köln-Bayenthal, south of the city center, hosts the **Historische Braustätte der Küppers-Kölsch-Brauerei,** Alteburgerstr. 157, the brewery where *Küppers* beer is made as it has been for 100 years; take bus #132 to "Bonntor" (open Sa 11am-4pm).

Churches

Köln's success in building awe-inspiring churches began hundreds of years before the idea for the *Dom* was even conceived. The Romanesque period from the 10th to mid-13th century saw the construction of 12 churches roughly in the shape of a semicircle around the *Altstadt,* using the holy bones of the saints to protect the city. The churches attest to the sacred glory and tremendous wealth of what was, at the time, the most important city north of the Alps. The city's piety even received poetic embodiment in a Samuel Taylor Coleridge poem: "In Köln, a town of monks and bones/And pavements fanged with murderous stones/And rags, and hags, and hideous wenches/I counted two-and-seventy stenches...." Probably the perfume.

One of the first medieval structures to use the unique decagon layout, **St. Gereon** (tel. 13 49 22) houses a floor mosaic of David hacking off Goliath's head. *(Open M-Sa 9am-noon and 1:30-6pm, Su 1:30-6pm.)* Along with the *Dom,* **Groß St. Martin** (tel. 257 79 24) defines the legendary Rhine panorama of Köln. *(Open M-F 10:15am-6pm, Sa 10am-12:30pm and 1:30-6pm, Su 2-4pm. Church free; crypt DM1, students and children DM0.50.)* The renovated church was reopened in 1985 after near destruction in World War II. Crypts downstairs house an esoteric collection of stones and diagrams. Visitors to the **St. Maria im Kapitol** (tel. 21 46 15) are treated to amazingly ornate carved wooden panels detailing the life of Christ. *(Open daily 9:30am-6pm.)* On the portal behind **St. Cäecilian** (tel. 221 23 10) stands "Death"—the masterpiece of a professional sprayer, not drunken vandals. *(Open Tu-F 10am-4pm, Sa-Su 11am-4pm.)*

The **St. Ursula** church (tel. 13 34 00), north of the *Dom,* commemorates Ursula's attempts to maintain celibacy despite her betrothal. She and 11 virgins under her tutelage were mistaken for Roman legionnaires and burned at sea. The Latin record of the tale indicated "11M," meaning 11 martyrs, but was later misread as 11 *thousand* virgins. Over 700 human skulls and innumerable reliquaries line the walls of the **Goldene Kammer.** *(Church and Goldene Kammer open M 9am-noon and 1-5pm, W-Sa 9:30am-noon and 1-5pm. Chamber DM2, children DM1.)*

St. Peter's church, a tiny construction by St. Cäecilien (entrance on Leonard-Tietz-Str.), provides a rare opportunity to see a masterwork in its original position. Rubens's **The Crucifixion of St. Peter,** above the main altar, beautifully illuminates the tiny church. *(Open Tu-Su 11am-6pm. Closed for renovations until Dec. 1998; meanwhile, the Rubens is on display in the Dom.)* Behind the *Rathaus,* inside the overgrown ruins of the bombed **Alt St. Alban** church, parents mourn the lost children of war in a statue created by Käthe Kollwitz.

MUSEUMS

Köln's cultural, religious and economic significance in Europe stocks this rich city's museums with a vast and impressive array of holdings. The main museums are free with the **Köln Bonbon** (see p. 319). Many smaller, more specialized "museums" stretch the definition of the word to its limit.

Near the Cathedral

Römische-Germanisches Museum, Roncallipl. 4 (tel. 221 44 38), built over the ruins of a Roman villa. The displays include the world-famous Dionysus Mosaic, the tomb of Publicus, an intimidating six-breasted sphinx, and some naughty candleholders—score! Open Tu-Su 10am-5pm. Call about tours (usually Su 11:30am). DM7, students and children DM4.

Heinrich-Böll-Platz, Bischofsgartenstr. 1, behind the Römische-Germanisches Museum (tel. 221 48 02). This unusual building, designed to maximize the natural lighting, houses 3 complementary collections. The **Wallraf-Richartz Museum** (tel. 221 23 72) features crackly masterpieces from the 13th to the 19th century, from the Italian Renaissance through the Flemish and Dutch masters, and up to Renoir and Manet. The **Museum Ludwig** (tel. 221 23 70) travels from Impressionism through Picasso, Dalí, and Roy Lichtenstein, to art where the glue and paint have yet to dry. The **Agfa Foto-Historama** (tel. 221 24 11) chronicles chemical art of the last 150 years, including a rotating display of Man Ray's works. All open Tu 10am-8pm, W-F 10am-6pm, Sa-Su 11am-6pm. A dazzling array of tours; tours for Wallraf and Ludwig W 4:30pm, Sa-Su 11:30am. Comprehensive admission DM10, students DM5. Free with the *Bonbon.*

Museum für Andgewandte Kunst (Museum of Applied Art), An der Rechtschule (tel. 221 67 14), west of the *Dom* across Wallrafpl. A giant arts and crafts fair spanning 7 centuries with a fabulous 20th-century design display. Lots of English captions. Open Tu and Th-F 11am-5pm, W 11am-8pm, Sa-Su noon-5pm. Tours Tu 6:30pm, Su 11:30am. DM5, students and children DM2.50. Free with the *Bonbon.*

Elsewhere in Köln

⊛**Das Museum (Imhoff-Stollwerk Museum),** Rheinauhafen 1a (tel. 931 88 80), near the Severins bridge. Better than Willy Wonka's Chocolate Factory. Salivate at every step of chocolate production from the rainforests to the gold fountain that spurts streams of silky, heavenly, creamy.... As you view the provocative photos, resist the urge to slobber uncontrollably on yourself. Free petite samples. Exhibits in German. Open M-F 10am-6pm (last entry 5pm), Sa-Su 11am-7pm (last entry 6pm). Tours (DM3) Sa at 2 and 4pm, Su at 11:30am, 2, and 4pm. DM10, students, seniors, and children DM5.

NS-Dokumentations-Zentrum, Am Appellhofpl. 23/25 (tel. 43 40). From the side of the Stadtmuseum, follow the angel's wing, which points down Appellhofpl. Once a citadel for perpetrators of Nazi terror, the museum now houses a shrine to its victims and 1200 wall inscriptions by political prisoners. Open Tu-F 10am-4pm, Sa-Su 11am-4pm. Tours first Sa of each month at 2pm. Free.

Beatles Museum, Heinsbergstr. 13 (tel. 21 25 98), off Zülpicherstr. U-Bahn #12, 16, or 18 to "Barbarossapl." Crammed with Fab Four nostalgia. With new 60s-style cafe, it's bigger—bigger than Jesus? Not in Köln (see the *Dom,* p. 324). Open Sept.-July W-Sa 10am-7pm. Free coffee and souvenir sack with admission (DM5).

Käthe Kollwitz Museum, Neumarkt 18-24 (tel. 227 23 63), in the Neumarkt-Passage. U-Bahn #9, 12, 14, 16, or 18 to "Neumarkt." The world's largest collection of sketches, sculptures, and prints by the brilliant artist and activist. Her images chronicle the sadness of early 20th-century Berlin in stark black-and-white. Open Tu-W and F-Su 10am-5pm, Th 10am-8pm. Tours Su at 11am. DM5, students DM2.

Schnütgen Museum, Cäecilienstr. 29 (tel. 221 36 20), in St. Cecilia Church. U-Bahn to "Neumarkt." Ecclesiastical art from the Middle Ages to the Baroque, notably tapestry and priestly fashion displays. Open Tu-F 10am-5pm, Sa-Su 11am-4pm. Tours Su at 11am, W at 2:30pm. DM5, students DM2.50. Free with the *Bonbon.*

ENTERTAINMENT

Köln explodes in celebration during **Karneval,** a week-long pre-Lenten festival. Celebrated in the hedonistic spirit of the city's Roman past, *Karneval* is made up of 50 major and minor neighborhood processions in the weeks before Ash Wednesday. **Weiberfastnacht,** on the Thursday before Ash Wednesday (Feb. 11 in 1999), is the first major to-do; the mayor mounts the platform at Alter Markt and abdicates leadership of the city to a trio of fools. For the rest of the day, the city's *Weiber* (an archaic and not too politically correct term for women) are given rule of the roost. In the afternoon, the first of the big parades begins at Severinstor. The weekend builds up to the out-of-control, dancing-in-the-streets parade on **Rosenmontag,** the last Monday before Lent (Feb. 15, 1999). Everyone's in costume and gets and gives a couple dozen *Bützchen* (Kölsch dialect for a kiss on a stranger's cheek). Arrive early, get a map of the route, and don't stand anywhere near the station or cathedral—you'll be pulverized by the lollapaloozian crowds. While most revelers nurse their hangovers on Shrove Tuesday, pubs and restaurants set fire to the straw scarecrows hanging out their windows. For more information on the festival and tickets to events, inquire at the **Festkomitee des Kölner Karnevals,** Antwerpenerstr. 55 (tel. 57 40 00). Also pick up the *Köln, Karneval* booklet at the tourist office (available in December).

Köln's traditional entertainment offers fierce competition, with over 30 theaters including the **Oper der Stadt Köln** and the **Kölner Schauspielhaus** near Schildergasse on Offenbachpl. The **box office** (tel. 84 00) for the Schauspielhaus sells tickets for both (open M-Sa 9am-2pm). **Köln Ticket** (tel. 28 01), a ticket agent located in the same building as the Römische Germanisches Museum, sells tickets for everything else—Köln's world-class **Philharmonic,** open-air rock concerts, and everything in between (open daily 10am-6pm). For more on Köln's theaters, check the *Monatsvorschau.* The **Cinemanthek** (tel. 257 59 21) entrance is on the ground floor of the three-museum building in Heinrich-Böll-Platz; current movies show almost daily, with most films in the original English. The **Metropolitan,** Ebertpl., shows movies exclusively in English and offers a selection of gay and lesbian pieces. Once a train station, the 3000-seat **Cinedom** (tel. 95 19 51 95 98), with 13 screens, is part of the **Media Park.** From April to October, catch the **craft market** the last weekend of every month in the *Altstadt,* around Groß St. Martin church.

NIGHTLIFE

Celebrating life with lavish festivities has long been a tradition in Köln. Roman mosaics dating back to AD 3 record the wild excesses of the city's early residents. But instead of grape-feeding and fig-wearing, modern life in Köln now focuses on house music and a more sophisticated bump-and-grind. The closer to the Rhine or the *Dom* you venture, the more quickly your wallet gets emptied. Students congregate in the **Quartier Lateng**, a.k.a. the *Bermuda Dreieck* (triangle). The area is bounded by Zülpicherstr., Zülpicherpl., Roonstr., and Luxemburgstr. The center of gay nightlife runs up **Matthiasstraße** to Mühlenbach, Hohe Pforte, Marienpl., and up to Heumarkt in the area by the Deutzer Brücke. Radiating westward from Friesenpl., the **Belgisches Viertel** is spiced with slightly more sophisticated and expensive bars and cafes.

The worshippers of Dionysus boozed themselves into stupors here, and the tradition of getting plastered is still highly respected in Köln. At the various *Brauhäuser*, where the original *Kölsch* is brewed and served in-house, the *Köbes* will bring one glass after another until you fall under the table unless you place your coaster over your glass. Saying *"Ich bin nicht zum Spaß hier"* ("I'm not here to fool around") informs the *Köbes* of your serious intentions; just watch that the lines on your coaster correspond to the number of beers you actually drank—it's said they might count on the fact that you won't be able to count.

Papa Joe's Jazzlokal, Buttermarkt 37 (tel. 257 79 31), defines Köln's jazz scene with traditional, high-caliber live jazz and oodles of New Orleans atmosphere. For die-hards, "Non-Stop Jazz" starts every Su at 3:30pm and goes for 8 hours. No cover! Open M-Sa 7pm-2am, Su 3:30pm-1am.

Museum, Zülpicherpl. 9 (tel. 23 20 98). No temple of science is complete without a two-story **dinosaur** looking out over blood alcohol experiments. Order your own 10 liter mini keg of *Kölsch*. RRRRAWR! Popular Köln University field trip. Open Su-Th 7pm-1am, F-Sa 7pm-3am.

MTC, Zülpicherstr. 10 (tel. 240 41 88). A veritable smörgasbord of olfactory and ol' factory fun. The musical offerings are schizophrenic, alternating between techno/house, punk/grunge, live concerts, and recorded bar music. *"Sheiss Montag* (Shit Monday) Crash Club" convenes Monday nights with drink specials. Cover, including one drink, DM6. Open M-Th and Su 9pm-2am, F-Sa 9pm-3am.

Café Magnus, Zülpicherstr. 48 (tel. 24 16 69). This smooth cafe and sometimes disco brims with students getting down to booty jams. Open daily 8am-3am.

The Corkonian, Alter Markt 51 (tel. 257 69 31). Not a *Biergarten,* a *Bierstube,* or a *Kneipe,* this authentic Irish corner is pure pub. Trade your lager for some dark beer, topped with a clover. Open Su-Th noon-1am, F-Sa noon-3am.

Päffgen Brauhaus, Friesenstr. 64-66 (tel. 13 54 61). A local favorite since 1883. Legendary *Kölsch* is brewed on the premises and consumed in cavernous halls or in the *Biergarten* (0.2L shot DM2.20). Follow *Brauhaus* rules as enumerated above. Open 10am-midnight. Kitchen open 11am-11pm.

Das Ding, Hohenstaufenring 25-27 (tel. 24 79 71). Popular, smoky, and very *noir.* All flavors of techno. No severed hands. Cover DM7. Open daily 9pm-3am.

Star-Treff, Alte Wallgasse (tel. 25 50 63), at the corner of Ehrenstr. This shmaltzy gay friendly cabaret shines with lavish drag shows in an ocean of cigarette smoke and red velvet. Showtimes W-Th and Su 8pm, F-Sa 7pm and 10:10pm.

Café Stövchen, Ursula Kloster 4-6 (tel. 13 17 12), in the shadow of the St. Ursula church. Sink into a swank couch, beer in hand, and dish out a schoolin' to some suckas at Monopoly. Local flavor. Open M-F 11am-1am, Su 10am-1am.

Joe Champs, Hohenzollernring 1-3 (tel. 257 61 65). A 2-story sports bar serving huge burgers and motley cocktails. Shows major U.S. sporting events—the Superbowl, World Series, NBA finals, and more. Open Su-Th noon-1am, F-Sa noon-3pm.

Oxygenia, Hohenstaufenring 78 (tel. 9 23 46 67; http://www.oxygenia.com). If the climb up the *Dom's* tower has left you gasping for breath, Köln's premier oxygen bar will fill your lungs with goodness. 18-min. DM27. Open M-F 9am-11pm, Sa-Su 11am-6pm.

Broadway, Ehrenstr. 11 (tel. 25 52 14). Appropriately located in a gutted theater box-office, this funky cafe is haunted by Köln's hippest artists and intellectuals. Open daily 10am-1am.

🏷**Gloria,** Apostelnstr. 11 (tel. 25 44 33). Crowded, popular, and plastered with cellophane wall-coverings, this cafe and occasional club is at the nexus of Köln's trendy gay and lesbian scene. Call for a schedule. Cover averages DM10. Cafe open Su-Th 9am-1am, F-Sa 9am-3am.

■ Bonn

Derisively called the *"Hauptdorf"* (capital village) by Germans, Bonn has been the whipping boy of Germany for 50 years simply because it's not Berlin. Founded by the Romans, Bonn remained a non-entity for most of its 2000-year history before arriving in the limelight by chance. Konrad Adenauer, the Federal Republic's first chancellor, resided in the stumbling suburbs, and the ever-considerate occupying powers made Bonn the "provisional capital" of the Western Occupation Zone before they baptized it as the *Hauptstadt* (capital) of the fledgling Republic. The summer of 1991 brought headlines of "Chaos in Bonn" as Berlin fought for the right to reclaim the seat of government in a political catfight that cleaved every party from the CDU to the Greens. By the narrowest of margins, Berlin won; the *Bundestag* will pack up and move sometime within the next few years (reportedly the date has finally been set as September,1999). Bonners have taken the loss well. Although Berliners joke that Bonn is "half the size of a Chicago cemetery and twice as dead," the sparkling streets of the *Altstadt* bustle with notable energy and eclecticism. The well-respected university and excellent museums bolster a thriving cultural scene.

PRACTICAL INFORMATION

The **Bonncard,** available in the tourist office for DM12 per day, covers transportation costs after 9am (all day Sa-Su) and admission to the city's museums.

Flights: International departures from the **Köln-Bonn Flughafen.** Bus #670 runs there from the train station (5am-10pm, every 20min.; DM7.70, children DM3.90).

Public Transportation: Bonn is linked to Cologne and other riverside cities by the massive **VRS** (Verkehrsverbund Rhein-Sieg) S-Bahn, U-Bahn, and Bundesbahn network. Areas are divided into **Tarifzonen;** the farther you go, the more you pay. Single tickets (DM2-13.50), 4-ride tickets (DM7.60-49.60), and day tickets (DM11-33) are available at *Automaten* and designated vending stations. With the *Minigruppenkarte* (DM9 per day), 5 people can ride M-F after 9am, and all day on weekends. Stop by the **Kundenzentrum** under the *Hauptbahnhof* for network maps and more information. Open M-F 7am-8pm.

Taxi: Funkzentrale (tel. 55 55 55). The funk never grows old. (But this joke might.)

Car Rental: Hertz, Avis, InterRent Europcar, and **Budget** have airport offices.

Mitfahrzentrale: Herwarthstr. 11 (tel. 69 30 30), behind the *Bahnhof.* Open M-F 10am-6:30pm, Sa 10am-2pm, Su for phone calls only 11am-2pm.

Bike Rental: Kurscheid, Römerstr. 4 (tel. 63 14 33), charges DM16 per day and offers a DM20 weekend special (Saturday morning to Sunday night). Cars rented here as well. ID required for both. Open M-Sa 7am-7pm, Su 9am-1pm and 5-7pm.

Tourist Office: Münsterstr. 20 (tel. 77 34 66 or 19 44 33; fax 77 31 00), in a passageway near the train station in the pedestrian zone. Take the "Stadtmitte" exit from the station, walk 60m up Poststr. to Münsterstr., and turn left; the office is to the right. The helpful staff doles out fantastic maps (DM1), makes same-day hotel reservations (DM3-5) and can answer any questions you have about Bonn. Inquire about the variety of tours. Open M-F 9am-6:30pm, Sa 9am-5pm, Su 10am-2pm.

Budget Travel: STA Travel, Nassestr. 11, inside the Mensa building. Open M-F 10:30am-4pm.

Embassies and Consulates: The tourist office has a 140-page list. **Australia,** Godesberger Allee 105-107 (tel. 810 30; fax 810 31 30). U-Bahn #16 or 63 to "Max-Löbne." Open M-Th 8:30am-1pm and 2-5pm, F 8:30am-1pm and 2-4:15 pm. **Can-**

ada, Friedrich-Wilhelm-Str. 18 (tel. 96 80; fax 968 39 03). Open M-F 8am-noon and 1-4pm. **Ireland,** Godesberger Allee 119 (tel. 81 00 06; fax 37 57 39). Open M-F 9am-1pm and 2:30-5:30pm. **New Zealand,** Bundeskanzlerpl. 2-10 (tel. 22 80 70; fax 22 16 87). U-Bahn #16 or 63 to "Heussallee." Open M-Th 9am-1pm and 2-5:30pm, F 9am-1pm and 2-4:30pm. **South Africa,** Auf der Hostert 3 (tel. 820 10; fax 820 11 48). Open M-F 8am-4:30pm. **U.K.,** Friedrich-Ebert-Allee 77 (tel. 916 70; fax 916 72 00). Open M-F 9am-5:30pm. **U.S.,** Deichmanns Aue. 29 (tel. 33 91; fax 339 20 53). U-Bahn #16 or 63 to "Rhineallee," then bus #613 to "Deichmanns Aue." Open M-F 8:30am-5:30pm.

Bookstore: The mammoth **Bouvier,** Am Hof 28 (tel. 729 01 64), across from the University *Schloß*, has a wide range of foreign books on the top floor. **Tickets** for local concerts and events sold here. Open M-F 9:30am-8pm, Sa 9:30am-4pm.

Women's Resources: The **Gesamtvertrauensfrau,** Bachstr. 21 (tel. 77 34 76). Open M and Th 9am-1pm, W and F 10am-noon.

Gay and Lesbian Center: Schwul & Lesben Zentrum (tel. 63 00 39) is located in a Mobil Autoöle parking lot. For counseling call 194 46; **gay assault hotline** 192 28. From bus stop "Kunsthalle," cross the street and go towards the Kunst Forum. In its Cafe "Z," Monday gay night, Tuesday lesbian night, and Wednesday and Thursday mixed. Open M-Tu and Th 8pm-midnight, W 9pm-midnight.

Laundromat: Wasch Center, on the corner of Breitestr. and Kölnstr. Wash DM7, soap included. Dry DM1 per 10min. Open M-Sa 7am-11pm.

Emergency: Police, tel. 110. **Fire** and **Ambulance,** tel. 112.

Rape Crisis Line: tel. 63 55 24.

Pharmacy: Bahnhofs Apotheke dispenses the goods right next to the tourist office. Open M-W and F 8am-7pm, Th 8am-8pm, Sa 9am-4pm.

Post Office: Münsterpl. 17, 53111 Bonn. Big. Yellow. Different. Walk down Poststr. from the station. Open M-F 8am-8pm, Sa 8am-4pm.

Telephone Code: 0228.

ACCOMMODATIONS AND CAMPING

National capitals attract visitors, and Bonn has responded with a fine stock of hotels to take them in. Most hotel prices are suited to wealthy tax-subsidized politicians. With one *Jugendgästehaus* but no *Jugendherberge*, even hosteling gets financially taxing in Bonn.

Jugendgästehaus Bonn-Venusberg (HI), Haager Weg 42 (tel. 28 99 70; fax 289 97 14), is far from the center of town. Bus #626 (direction: "Ippendorf Altenheim") to "Jugendgästehaus" (runs *very* infrequently) or Bus #620 (direction "Venusberg") to "Sertürnerstr.," turn left on Haager Weg and walk for 10min. A sparkling, supermodern place in the suburbs; it even has glass doors that slide open automatically (*á la* your local supermarket) and a bar open nightly. DM37. Breakfast and sheets included. Laundry DM10. Reception 9am-1am. Curfew 1am. Wheelchair access.

Hotel Mozart, Mozartstr. 1 (tel. 65 90 71; fax 65 90 75). From the south exit of the station, turn right onto Herwarthstr., left on Bachstr., then right on Mozartstr. Around the corner from Beethovenpl. Just the kind of Viennese elegance you'd expect in such a classical neighborhood. Large, trim rooms. Conveniently located. Singles DM65-75, with bath DM110-135; doubles DM110, with bath DM195.

Hotel Bergmann, Kasernenstr. 13 (tel. 63 38 91; fax 63 50 57). From the station, follow Poststr., turn left at Münsterpl. onto Vivatgasse, then right on Kasernenstr.; after 10min., the hotel is on the left. Cozy, elegant rooms. *Very* pink bathrooms in the hall. Singles DM60; doubles DM95. Reception hours sporadic—call ahead.

Hotel Virneburg, Sandkaule 3a (tel. 63 63 66). U-Bahn #62, 64, or 66 to "Bertha-von-Suttner-Platz" or walk up Poststr. and bear right on Acherstr. at the north end of Münsterpl. Turn left on Rathausgasse and left again onto Belderberg, which runs into Sandkaule. Functional rooms, unbeatable price and location. Singles DM35-45, with shower DM55-65; doubles DM65-70, with shower DM90. Breakfast included.

Hotel Haus Hofgarten, Fritz-Tillman-Str. 7 (tel. 22 34 82; fax 21 39 02). From the station, turn right onto Maximilianstr., continue on Kaiserstr., and then turn left on Fritz-Tillman-Str. Live like an ambassador in this stately hotel. A fabulous splurge. Singles DM75-135; doubles DM110-175. Breakfast included. Call ahead.

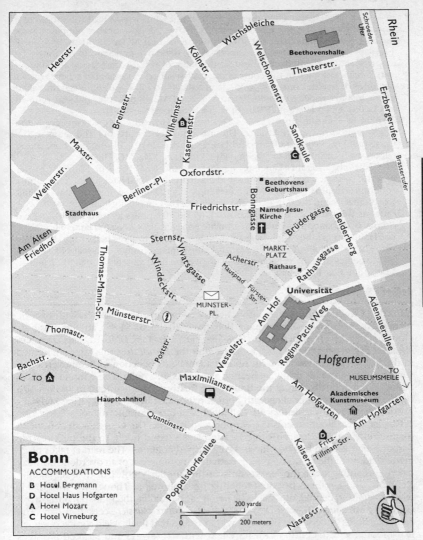

Bonn

ACCOMMODATIONS

B Hotel Bergmann
D Hotel Haus Hofgarten
A Hotel Mozart
C Hotel Virneburg

0   200 yards

0   200 meters

N

Camping: Campingplatz Genienaue, Im Frankenkeller 49 (tel. 34 49 49). U-Bahn #16 or 63 to "Rhein Allee," then bus #613 (direction: Giselherstr.) to "Gunterstr." Turn left on Guntherstr. for 120m and right on Frankenkeller for 300m until you reach the site. Rhine-side camping in the Mehlem suburb. DM8 per person; DM5-8 per tent. Reception 9am-noon and 3-10pm.

FOOD

The market on **Münsterplatz** teems with haggling vendors and determined customers trying to get the best meat, fruit, and vegetables at the lowest prices. At the end of the day voices rise and prices plummet (M-Sa 9am-6pm). Further from the pedestrian zone, along Max and Dorothenstr., ethnic restaurants sustain high quality at low cost.

Mensa, Nassestr. 11, a 15min. walk from the train station along Kaiserstr. In Bonn's glory days it swung with cosmopolitan flair. Reagan would sip *Dom Perignon* out of Maggie Thatcher's stilleto heels, and Helmut Kohl would lead the crowd in a round of bawdy German drinking songs. Now, it's just another *Mensa*. Cheap meals DM2-4. DM1 extra for non-students. Lunch M-Th 11:30am-2:15pm, F 11:30am-2pm, Sa noon-1:45pm. Dinner M-F 5:30-8pm. Open Sept. to mid-July.

ⓋCassius Garten, Maximilianstr. 28d, at the edge of the *Altstadt* facing the station, with a back entrance in the court of the tourist office. A veggie bar where zealous disciples of health consume 50 kinds of salads, noodles, and whole-grain baked goods in a futuristic, white-glossed atrium. Pay DM2.58 per 100g and seat yourself at a booth. Open M-W and F 9am-8pm, Th 8am-9pm, Sa 9am-4pm.

Pizzeria la Piccola, Bonngasse 4 (tel. 63 78 16), only a few steps from the *Beethovenhaus* and Marktplatz. The insidious scent curls out and drags in the unsuspecting. Pizzas a-plenty and large salads (DM10). Ubiquitous dark wood decor and hilarious waiters. Open daily 11am-1am. Visa, MC, Diners.

Café Göttlich, an Franziskanerstr. across from the *Uni*. The *Uni*'s hippest gather here for a huge variety of coffee and a surprisingly laid-back intellectual atmosphere. *Haus Musik* played in the evenings. Beer DM3.50-6, desserts DM5-8, light foods (snacks and breakfast cereals) under DM10. Open daily 9am-1am.

Brauhaus Bönnsch, Sterntorbrücke 4 (tel. 65 06 10), pours its own highly civilized *Bönnsch*, the smooth-as-butter illegitimate son of Köln's *Kölsch* (DM2.30 for 0.2L). For DM6 you can buy their beer glasses—contoured to your hand for easy imbibing. Their delicious *Bönnsche Flammkuchen* made from a 250-year-old Alsatian recipe comes in many vegetarian (and non-vegetarian) varieties. Open M-Th and Su 11am-1am, F-Sa 11am-3am.

SIGHTS

Bonn's old town center winds into a lively pedestrian zone puddled with historic niches. The **Beethoven Geburtshaus,** Bonngasse 20 (tel. 63 51 88), attracts music aficionados of all sorts. *(Open M-Sa 10am-5pm, Su 11am-4pm. DM8, students DM4. Call ahead for English tours.)* Bonn's biggest draw after the *Bundestag*, this museum located in the house of Beethoven's birth houses a fantastic collection of Beethoven's personal effects—from his primitive hearing aids to his first violin. The symphonic ghost haunts Bonn annually during the **Beethoven Festival.** The first fête, in 1845, was a riot, with Franz Liszt brawling with French nationalist Berlioz while King Ludwig's mistress Lola Montez table-danced. Call the tourist office for information.

Farther down Bonngasse is the **Namen-Jesu Kirche.** The church suffers from an identity crisis; the primary Gothic facade plays second fiddle to the pink marble Baroque altar hidden behind blue-and-gold striped columns. The market takes place in the shadow of the voluptuous pink **Rathaus**—reminiscent of an overdone birthday cake—presiding over the Marktplatz; in the similarly colorful 60s, de Gaulle, Kennedy, and Elizabeth II visited together for a photo-op. Though the *Rathaus* is indeed a sight to behold, one might be better off beholding the **Münster Basilika,** on (surprise) Münsterpl. *(Cloister open daily 9:30am-5:30pm. Münster sleeps 7pm-7am.)* The cathedral holds three stories of arches within arches that finally yield a gorgeous goldleaf mosaic; a 12th-century cloister laced with crossways and latticed passages branches off. Keep an eye out for the incongruous blue-red Expressionist windows.

The castles, palaces, and museums that lend the area its cultural wealth lie just outside the city center. Forty thousand students study within the **Kurfürstliches Schloß,** the huge 18th-century palace now serving as the center of Bonn's **Friedrich-Wilhelms-Universität.** The *Schloß* is the gateway to the refreshing **Hofgarten** and **Stadtgarten,** forever filled with students and punks. To uncover Bonn's "other" palace, stroll down Poppelsdorfer Allee to the 18th-century **Poppelsdorfer Schloß.** This castle touts a French facade and an Italian courtyard, plus beautifully manicured **Botanical Gardens.** *(Gardens open May-Sept. M-F 9am-6pm, Su 9am-1pm; Oct.-Apr. M-F 9am-4pm. Greenhouses open M-F 10:30am-noon and 2-4pm. Free.)*

No visit to Bonn is complete without the obligatory governmental romp. The vaguely *Bauhaus* **Bundestag,** Bundeshaus, Eingang V (tel. 16 21 52), has earned the coveted title of "Least Prepossessing Parliament Building" in the world. Take U-Bahn #16, 63, or 66 to "Heussallee/Bundeshaus" or bus #610 from the main station to "Bundeshaus." Alas, you can't just stroll in and exercise the ol' pocket veto; you must take a less than thrilling tour which begins on the hour at Hermann-Ehlers-Str. 29, opposite the Hochhaus. *(Tours mid-Mar. to Dec. M-F 9am-4pm, Sa-Su 10am-4pm; Jan. to mid-Mar. M-F 9am-4pm. Bring your passport.)* For those hungry for more functional buildings, the **Bundeshaus** (Germany's Parliament) is visible on Görresstr. from the bank of the Rhine. The postwar architectural mandate to turn this small city into a world-class capital has produced goofy results. A wacky example is the old **Post Ministry,** at Zweite Fahrgasse on the river. The Rhine-side face sports the interpretive relief *Tier-Symbole der Fünf Kontinente* (Animal Symbols of the 5 Continents), with a megalithic eagle (America), bull (Europe), elephant (Africa), kangaroo (Australia), and a big friendly wildcat (Asia). An elaborate joke, you think? No, this is what happens when you give people money and tell them to build a national capital.

On Adenauerallee, south of the city center, rest the **Villa Hammerschmidt,** home of the German chancellor, and **Palais Schaumburg,** home of the German president. The less majestic **Denkmal** (monument) outside the Palais was erected in honor of Konrad Adenauer, one of Germany's and Bonn's most prominent personas. Nick-named *"der Alte"* (the old guy), the postwar chancellor was Bonn's guiding light, but the 3m hollow-cheeked bust at Adenauerallee 135-141 looks like a skull lifted from a pirate flag. Engraved into his cranium are allegorical figures—various animals, a pair of bound hands, and two French cathedrals. Mind you, this is how Bonners commemorate their *heroes.* Don't get on their bad side.

MUSEUMS

While the parliamentary side of Bonn sight-seeing leaves something to be desired, the museums are superb. Bonn has enjoyed nearly 50 years of generous federal funding, and much of the public wealth was channeled into the expansion of the town's museums. The **"Museum Mile"** begins at the **Museum Alexander Koenig.** To get there, take U-Bahn #16, 63, or 66 to "Museum Koenig." A **Bonncard** provides free admission to seven museums (see p. 329).

Museum Mile

Kunstmuseum Bonn, Friedrich-Ebert Allee 2 (tel. 77 62 60). U-Bahn #16, 63, or 66 to "Heussallee." A stunning contemporary building houses this superb selection of Expressionist and modern German art. Open Tu-Su 10am-6pm. DM5, students DM3.

⊛**Haus der Geschichte,** 1 block from the Kunstmuseum Bonn (tel. 916 50). A futuristic museum dedicated to critical and "interactive" German history. Well-designed, thoughtful exhibits are highlighted by some antique VWs and a black enclosure with the scrolling names of Holocaust victims. Open Tu-Su 9am-7pm. Free.

Kunst-und Ausstellungshalle der BRD, Friedrich-Ebert Allee 4 (tel. 917 12 00), takes you to utopia. U-Bahn #16, 63, or 66 to "Heussallee." The art here is so new you can smell the paint; check out the ultra-modern media-art room. The 16 columns flanking the *Ausstellungshalle* represent the 16 *Bundesländer* of united Germany. Open Tu-W 10am-9pm, Th-Su 10am-7pm. DM8, students DM4.

Museum Alexander Koenig (tel. 912 22 11), south of the city. U-Bahn #16, 63, or 66 to "Museum Koenig." If taxidermy has a Louvre, this is it. People who dislike animals will take pleasure in the stuffed, sterilized, glass-encased exhibits. Snakes and lizards crawl in the basement. Open Tu-F 9am-5pm, Sa 9am-12:30pm, Su 9:30am-5pm. DM4, students DM2.

Elsewhere in Bonn

Frauenmuseum (tel. 69 13 44). The vast galleries glitter with interactive, modern art pieces by women. U-Bahn #61 to "Rosental/Herrstr." (Herrstr.?) The 2nd floor covers medieval art. Peculiar pieces on the roof and a Yoko Ono room provide more thought-provoking works. Open Tu-W and F-Sa 2-5pm, Th 2-8pm, Su 11am-5pm.

Akademisches Kunstmuseum (tel. 72 77 38) on the far side of the *Hofgarten.* Lazy sculpture fans can forget about going abroad to see the masterpieces because they're all here, in the largest collection of plaster casts in Germany. Exhibits include Venus de Milo, the Colossus of Samos, and Laocöon. Better than the real thing. Open Su-W and F 10am-1pm, Th 10am-1pm and 4-6pm. DM1, students free.

NIGHTLIFE

Bonn's bombastic and versatile nightlife forcefully debunks myths suggesting that Bonn is boring. Savvy students, hip journalists, and diverse visitors more than compensate for the city's conservative civil servants (70% of Bonn's population). Of Bonn's monthly glossies, **Schnüss** is unbeatable when it comes to "who, what, when, and where"; it is more complete than the free *Bonner Gästeführer* and *Szene Bonn.*

Bubbles, Bornheimerstr. 20-22. Quirkiest club in Bonn. Themed evenings (different every night) range from Brit pop parties to gothic-industrial "funerals." Opens Tu and Th 11pm, W 9pm, F-Sa 10:30pm, Su 7am and 9pm. Stays open late.

🍸**Spitz,** Sterntorbrücke 10, at the corner of Sterntorbrücke and Oxfordstr. (tel. 69 29 66; fax 69 29 82). Animated conversation drowns out the recorded music in this trendy watering hole where young, hip journalists and the rising stars of Bonn's political arena come to dish the dirt. Open 9am-late. Kitchen closes at midnight, but the bar is open much, much later.

The Jazz Galerie, Oxfordstr. 24 (tel. 65 06 62), becomes a hub for jazz and rock concerts nearly every night. Call ahead for a schedule. Cover for concerts DM10-20, for discos DM5. On concert nights opens at 8pm, but the show begins around 9:15pm. Open daily 9pm-3am.

Sharon, Oxfordstr. 20-21, is a soul discotheque for those who haven't quite had enough. "What's missin' we got it" is their slogan. If the only things missin' are strobe lights and a disco ball, then that's good advertising. 21 and over. Clean clothes required. Cover DM10. Soul and funk F-Sa 10pm-5am.

The Pantheon, Bundeskanzlerpl. (tel. 21 25 21). Even though it's dangerously close to the *Bundeshaus,* the clientele of this popular disco, which also hosts concerts, stand-up comedy, and art exhibits, tends to be younger, hipper, and more attractive than your average politician. Pick up their monthly schedule at the door. Cover DM10. Open M-Sa 8pm-3am.

■ Near Bonn: Königswinter and Drachenfels

"The castled crag of Drachenfels frowns o'er the wide and winding Rhine," wrote Lord Byron in "Childe Harold's Pilgrimage." According to the *Nibelungenlied* and to local lore, epic hero Siegfried slew a dragon who once haunted the now-castled crag. Siegfried then bathed in the dragon's blood and would have been invincible if not for the bare spot left by a leaf on his back. The ruins and the incredible view can be reached by U-Bahn #66 from Bonn and from **Königswinter,** the town in the valley below the ruins. Simply follow Drachensfelsstr. It's officially a 45-minute walk, but Siegfried wanna-bes hustle up in under 25 minutes. The less heroic take the **Drachenfelsbahn,** Drachenfelsstr. 53 (tel. (02223) 920 90), a railway leading to the top. (DM10 up, DM9 down, DM13 round-trip.; ages 4-13 DM6 up and DM5 down; dogs DM1.) There are also donkey and carriage rides to the top. The **Nibelungshalle,** where the dragon once munched on tasty young virgins, is now a **reptile zoo** and **museum** (tel. (02223) 241 50) with over 150 live reptiles. Not surprisingly, it's the largest of its kind in the world. (DM5, children DM4. Open May 15-Nov. 15 daily 10am-7pm.) Drachenfels' little brother **Schloß Drachenburg** (tel. 261 55) raises its ornate turrets halfway between the museum and the ruin. Guided tours through the castle's fine interior are given hourly (Apr.-Oct. Tu-Su 11am-6pm; DM3, rugrats DM2).

The Königswinter **tourist office** is at Drachenfelsstr. 11 (open M-F 9am-5pm, Sa 10am-2pm). Bad Honnef's **Jugendherberge,** Selhoferstr. 106 (tel. (02224) 713 00; fax 792 26), provides a base to explore the mythical surroundings. From the Bad Honnef train station, head up and left, following the "Stadtmitte" signs onto Menzenbergerstr.; when this ends, go left on Linzerstr., and Selhoferstr. will be the first (unmarked) right. From the U-Bahn, walk under the pedestrian overpass and over the next bridge to the left to Menzenbergerstr. Either way, it's almost a half-hour walk; keep on truckin'. (DM25, over 26 DM30. Breakfast included. Sheets DM7. Reception 9am-10pm. Curfew 11:30pm.) Also in Bad Honnef is the **Bundeskanzler-Adenauer-Haus,** Konrad-Adenauer-Str. 8c, where Herr Adenauer, then mayor of Köln, retired in 1937 after being driven from office by local Nazis. The exhibits tell the story of his personal and political survival. (Open Tu-Su 10am-4:30pm. Last entry 4pm.)

Europe's greatest monument to sexual frustration, **Rolandsbogen,** stands just across the Rhine from Königswinter and Bad Honnef. Legendary hero Roland returned from the battle at Roncevalles to find that his wife, upon the news of his death, had taken a vow of chastity and retreated to the convent on **Nonnenwerth Island.** He channeled his sexual energy into building the **Rolandsbogen** in hopes of catching a glimpse of her. Today, too late for Roland but convenient for modern convent peepers, ferries depart from Königswinter, running from the east to west banks, and from the west bank to the island (1½hr.). Call (0228) 63 63 68 for more info.

■ Near Bonn: Remagen

What is perhaps the Rhine valley's most vivid reminder of WWII is found in **Remagen,** a town just upstream from the confluence of the Rhine and Ahr rivers. In March 1945, as Nazi engineers demolished most of the bridges over the Rhine, G.I. Joes preparing to cross the river found the celebrated steel bridge at Remagen intact. Under heavy fire, the Allied troops crossed the bridge on March 7, 1945, and held off a German couterattack until the crossing was secured. The bridge collapsed from the heavy weight 10 days later. Remagen Mayor Hans Kuerten sold souvenir-sized chunks of the now-demolished bridge to fund the **Friedensmuseum** (Museum of Peace; tel. 218 63) that inhabits the restored bridge tower. (Open May-Oct. daily. DM2.50, students DM1.) To reach the museum, take any street down to the Rhine, turn right on the promenade, and keep going. Poems, letters, pictures, and artifacts inhabit the many rooms and tell the bridge's history. There is also a permanent exhibit on the Nobel Peace Prize. Despite Kuerten's efforts, the grimly blackened bridge ruins remain the most potent warning against war.

The jewel of Remagen remains the gorgeous mountainside **Apollinariskirche,** whose distinctive Gothic spires can be seen both from the Rhine and the town center. Shining frescoes cover nearly every surface; hike uphill on Bergstr. to visit the serene crypt. On the way, admire the quiet **St. Peter and Paul** church and nearby 12th-century Romanesque gate.

To get to the Marktplatz from the train station, follow Drususstr. and turn right onto Bachstr. The **tourist office,** on the Marktplatz at Kirchstr. 6 (tel. 20 10), hands out maps and books rooms (starting at DM30) for a 10% fee (open M-Th 8:30am-noon and 2-4pm, F 8:30am-noon). You can also check their comprehensive list of Remagen hotels across the street on the Marktplatz. To reach the **Campingplatz Goldene Meile** (tel. 222 22) head east (right as you face the Rhine) on Marktstr. As it becomes Altestr. and Goethestr., turn left at the sign. (15min. DM7.50, ages 6-16 DM6.50; per tent DM6-13. Reception 7:30am-noon and 2-6pm.) If you're feeling too sweaty, head to the swimming pool and aspiring water park, **Allwetterbad Remagen,** up the road toward Goethestr. The **telephone code** is 02642.

EIFEL MASSIF

Germans flock to the Eifel for the wonderful hiking opportunities provided by these wooded hills. Bordered by the Mosel Valley on the south and Aachen at the north, the Eifel stretches across the Belgian border on the west where it becomes the Ardennes, commonly remembered as the site of the Battle of the Bulge, the last German offensive of World War II. Now, unobtrusive Germans in hiking knickers and thick socks come to ramble over and through the peaceful hills, drink the delicious wine, and eat the still-ubiquitous Roman specialty *Schinken* (ham). Infrequent transportation makes many parts of the Eifel nearly inaccessible. Transportation is regular to the **Ahrtal,** south of Bonn and most scenic around the town of Altenahr. The **Hohe Eifel** in the center of the Massif features crater lakes and rock formations formed by volcanoes produced as recently as 10,000 years ago. The **Nordeifel** is home to the **Siebengebirge** (Seven Lakes), popular venues for fishing and water sports.

■ Monschau

The tiny town of Monschau subtly blends the French with the *Rheinisch*, assuming a hybrid character. In the 17th century, a deluge of Huguenots fleeing Catholic persecution settled in this region, plying their traditional skills to stimulate a thriving cloth industry. In 1794, Napoleon captured the town, kicking off 12 years of occupation. After some international horse-trading, Monschau again became part of Germany; yet many residents still have French names, and the local cuisine offers many delicious treats from Germany's friendly neighbor to the west. However, Monschau still *looks* distinctly North Rhine-Westphalian. In a narrow, secluded valley cut by the swift-flowing Ruhr about 30km south of Aachen, the town is a visual compendium of gray slate roofs, cobblestones, and brickwork. The surrounding hills are filled with hiking trails. In the city proper, the Ahr winds around tall, stone houses with small, flowered balconies, and the streets are lined with lovely cafes and terraces.

The serene beauty of the landscape is juxtaposed with the gloomy **Burg**, the ruins of a massive castle perched above Monschau. A steep set of stairs leads to the castle from the town center. Midway up, the elegiac gray 1649 **Alte Katherine Pfarrkirche** stands with its shingled onion-turret. The fragile **Glashütte** (glassworks museum), Burgaustr. 15 (tel. 32 16), has demonstrations every hour on the half-hour between 10:30am and 5:30pm (open daily 10am-6pm; DM3, students and children DM2). On the path leading down from the *Burg*, the **Rotes Haus**, Laufenstr. 10 (tel. 50 71), opens its bright pink doors into a stunningly well-preserved 18th-century cloth merchant's house. (Tours Easter-Nov. Tu-Su 10 and 11am, 2, 3, and 4 pm. DM5, students and children DM3.) Across the bridge stands the **Evangelische Pfarrkirche,** another of the town's delicately-cut churches. On the other end of town, the authentic 19th-century **Senfmühle** (mustard mill), Laufenstr. 18 (tel. 22 45), can leave you delirious. Monschau is famous for its mustard. (Open for demonstrations Mar.-Oct. W 11am and 2pm. DM4, students and children DM2.)

Monschau is accessible from Aachen by bus #163 that leaves hourly from the *Hauptbahnhof* on weekdays, but less frequently on weekends. The **tourist office**, Stadtstr. 1 (tel. 33 00; fax 45 34), reposes across from the steps leading to the *Burg*. (Open M-F 9am-noon and 1-4pm, Sa 11am-3pm, Su 11am-2pm; Oct.-Easter M-F 9am-noon and 1-4pm.) To help you recover from the mustard shock, the amicable staff book rooms (from DM25) for a DM5 fee and sell hiking maps for the whole Eifel region. The **Jugendherberge Monschen (HI),** Auf dem Schloß 4 (tel. 23 14; fax 43 91), in the *Burg*, teems with rebellious school children who shriek in German, French, and Flemish. (DM24, over 26 DM29. Breakfast included. Sheets DM6. Reception 8:30-9am, 12:30-1pm, and 6:30-7pm. Curfew 10pm, but keys are available.) A calmer haven, the larger, more modern **Jugendherberge "Monschau-Hargard" (HI),** Hargarasgasse 5 (tel. 21 80; fax 45 27), lies outside of town. Take bus #163 or 166 (direction: "Hargard") from in front of the post office to "Hargard," backtrack 100m, and follow the sign. (DM25, over 26 DM30. Breakfast included. Sheets DM6. Reception until 9pm. Curfew 10pm.) **Hotel Zum Stern**, Eschenbachstr. 21, offers gorgeous, brook-side rooms just off the Marktplatz. The antique furniture and charmingly curving floors attest to the house's 360 years (singles from DM60; doubles from DM115). To satisfy the royal appetite without emptying the royal treasury, feast on pizzas (DM4.50-9) at **Tavola**, Stadtstr. 42 (tel. 72 17 63; open daily 10am-9pm). The **telephone code** is 02472.

■ The Ahrtal

The string of tiny hamlets that dots the serene Ahr River refers to itself as *"Rotwein Paradies Deutschlands"* (Germany's red wine paradise). Unlike most cheesy tourist bureau slogans, the Ahrtal lives up to its claims; in many picturesque places the vineyards climb up and *over* the area's craggy hills, continuing straight down the other side. Wine cellars and itty-bitty family-owned wineries abound, and the bulk of information in the valley's tourist offices helps guide those in search of vinic pleasures (the *"Erlebnis Ahrwein"* pamphlet is the boozehound's bible).

Trains travel into the region from **Remagen** (see p. 335), halfway between Bonn and Koblenz. Trains depart approximately once every hour; the *"Linie 42"* pamphlet in Remagen's *Reisezentrum* explains it all. As the train chugs west, the hills become more rocky and steep, culminating in the violent, craggy peaks that surround the town of **Altenahr.** Developed to supply peasants for the royalty of the local castle, **Burg Ahr** (reached by a trail beginning at the *Rathaus*), the town today caters to a different ruling force—the tourist industry. The **Sommer-Rodelbahn** (tel. 23 21) resembles a luge, without the cold, snow, or embarrassingly tight suits. Cables pull your sled to the summit and then let you rip down a 500m slippery steel track. A brake is provided for the meek. At DM3.50 per ride, DM5 for two (cheaper for more rides or more people), it's a cheap kick. The 4km hike from Altenahr (follow *Autobahn* 357 towards Bonn) doesn't seem to dissuade crowds, especially on Sundays. (Open Apr.-Oct. Su-F 10am-6pm, Sa 10am-sundown; Nov.-Mar. Sa afternoons and Su.) Lazy and well-heeled blue-bloods take the taxi from the station (DM2.50 per person, 4-person min.). Another example of the strange interaction between cheesy technology and mountainsides is the **Seilbahn** (tel. 83 83), an 8-minute walk to the left from the train station (follow the signs). The lift will haul you up to mountaintop trails (DM3.50, children DM2; round-trip DM6, DM3). For less mechanical pleasures, sample the sweet juices of the Ahr through a *Weinprobe* (local wine tasting) at **Mayschoß-Altenahr,** on Tunnelstr. (tel. 936 00). Probe each delicate *Ahrtal* vintage, inhale the aromatic flavor, or just chug 'em (open M-Sa 8am-noon and 1-6pm, Su 10am-6pm).

Information on hikes, lodgings, and train tickets is available at the **tourist office,** Altenburger 1a (tel. 33 00; fax 45 34), located in the station. (Open M-W 10am-4pm, Th-F 10am-6pm, Sa 11am-6pm, Su 11am-4pm.) The 24km *Rottweinwanderweg* begins here; follow the red grapes for a comprehensive tour of the valley. The **Jugendherberge Altenahr,** Langfigtal 8 (tel. 18 80), is in a nature reserve 20 minutes from town by foot. From the station, cross the bridge and turn right on Brückenstr., which becomes Tunnelstr. Don't go through the tunnel; as if on your way to grandmother's house, just go over the river and through the woods. Really. (DM19.50. Breakfast included. Sheets DM5. Reception daily 8am-10pm. Curfew 10pm. Call ahead.) On the Ahr, the **Camping Schulz campground** (tel. 85 03) offers its bosom to your tired sole. Head right as you face the tracks, follow them on the footpath, and take a left when you reach Altenburgerstr. The campground is on your right across the river. (DM6 per adult, DM4 per child. DM5 per tent. Reception 8am-10pm.) Altenahr is a virtual paradise for the wine imbiber and traditional food *bon vivant.* To stay within your budget without using a plastic *Imbiß* fork, visit **Im Weinhäuschen,** Brückenstr. 27 (tel. 31 15). This homely restaurant serves savory specials for less than DM10, and potato pancakes with ambrosial apple sauce for a mere DM7. At night, loud locals populate the bar (open daily 11am until bedtime). The **telephone code** is 02643.

■ Aachen

Aachen jives day and night in four different languages, exuding a youthful internationalism that belies its old age. Charlemagne sang the mantra of multiculturalism when he made the city the capital of his Frankish empire in the 8th century, and the tunes are still heard today—a flux of students and international travelers continually renew the vibrant atmosphere. Despite this dynamism, the city maintains strong ties to its Roman, medieval, and Renaissance past.

ORIENTATION AND PRACTICAL INFORMATION

Aachen is at the crossroads between Germany, Belgium, and the Netherlands. Many travelers cross the Dutch border (a 15min. bike ride) to stock up on cheese.

NORDRHEIN-WESTFALEN

Trains: To: Köln (1 hr. 2-3 per hr.), Brussels (2hr., every hr.), and Amsterdam (4hr., 1-2 per hr.).

Public Transportation: Tickets are priced by distance with one-way trips running DM2.30-9.30. *24-Stunden* tickets provide a full day of unlimited travel for DM8-20, but the DM8 kind gets you anywhere in Aachen. For those under 21, a weekend pass for all buses can be purchased on Saturdays for DM5. Some hotels also offer a DM7 *Hotelgastkarte* good for 2 days of unlimited travel. Call for details.

Mitfahrzentrale: Roesmonderstr. 4 (tel. 194 40). Matches riders and drivers. After hours, call 15 20 17. Open M-Th 10am-6pm, Sa 10am-4pm.

Bike Rental: Park & Bike, Parkhaus Wirichsbongardstr. 47 (tel. 312 43). Go up the street directly across from the tourist office; it's in the blue parking garage. Prices start at DM8 per 3r., DM20 per day. Open 24hr.

Tourist Office: Aachen's central tourist office, **Atrium Elisenbrunnen** (tel. 180 29 60; fax 180 29 31) on Friedrich-Wilhelm-Pl., dispenses literature and finds rooms (from DM35). From the station, cross the street and head up Bahnhofstr., turn left onto Theaterstr., which becomes Theaterpl., then right onto Kapuzinergraben, which becomes Friedrich-Wilhelm-Pl.; the atrium is on your left. Check here for city **tours.** Open M-F 9am-6pm, Sa 9am-2pm.

Currency Exchange: At the post office in the train station. Open M-F 9am-6pm, Sa 9am-1pm, Su 10am-noon. Also at the *Hauptpostamt*, near the tourist office.

Bookstore: Mayersche Buchhandlung, at Ursulinerstr. 17-19 (tel. 477 70), at the corner of Buchkremerstr. A fantastic English section. Open M-W and F 9:30am-6:30pm, Th 9:30am-8:30pm, Sa 9:30am-2pm.

Laundromat: Waschcenter, Heinrichsallee 30. Wash DM6, soap included. Dry DM1 per 15min. Open M-Sa 6:30am-11pm; last call at 10pm.

Emergency: Police, tel. 110. **Fire** and **Ambulance,** tel. 112.

Post Office: The *Hauptpostamt*, Kapuzinergraben, 52064 Aachen, is to the left of the station. Walk down Lagerhausstr., right down Franzstr., and then right on Kapuzinergraben. Open M-F 9am-6pm, Sa 9am-1pm.

Telephone Code: 0241.

ACCOMMODATIONS AND CAMPING

Aachen has too much history for a town of its size, and the oodles of visitors push the lodging prices up. Call ahead. The **Mitwohnzentrale,** Süsterfeldstr. 24 (tel. 87 53 46), sets up lodging for longer stays. Take bus #7 (direction: "Siedlung Schönau") or 33 (direction: "Vaals") to "Westbahnhof" (open M-F 9am-1pm and 3-6pm).

Jugendherberge (HI), Maria-Theresia-Allee 260 (tel. 711 01; fax 70 82 19). Two buses go to the hostel leaving from the "Finanzamt" bus stop. To get to this departure point from the station, walk left on Lagerhausstr. until it intersects Kareliterstr. and Mozartstr.; the bus stop will be on the other side of the street. Bus #2 (direction: "Preusswald") to "Ronheide" or 12 (direction: "Diepenbendem") to "Colynshof." DM25, over 26 DM30. Reception until 10pm. Curfew 11:30pm.

⊛**Hotel Marx,** Hubertusstr. 33-35 (tel. 375 41; fax 267 05). Just a hop, skip, and jump from the station. Hop left on Lagerhausstr. which becomes Boxgraben, skip right on Stephanstr., and jump left on Hubertusstr. Clean and charming rooms. Friendly hotel in a great location 2 blocks from the *Altstadt*. Singles without any shower DM60, with bath DM85; doubles DM100, with bath DM130. Breakfast included.

ETAP-Hotel, Strangenhäuschen 15 (tel. 91 19 29; fax 15 53 04). From the *Bushof*, bus #5 to "Strangenhäuschen." This hotel is far from the center of town, but offers standard rooms at a great price. F-Su all rooms only DM60. M-Th singles with shower DM60; doubles with shower DM70. Breakfast DM8.50. Reception 6:30-10am and 5-11pm.

Hotel Cortis, Krefelderstr. 52 (tel. 15 60 11; fax 15 60 12). From the central bus station (*Bushof*), bus #51 to "Tivoli." Backtrack down Krefelderstr. about 300m. Located outside Aachen proper, this hotel offers bright, comfortable rooms. Singles from DM50, with shower DM67; doubles DM75-89, with shower DM110-114. Breakfast included. Reception 24hr.

Aachen

ACCOMMODATIONS
A ETAP Hotel
B Hotel Am Tivoli
C Hotel Cortis
D Hotel Marx

Hotel Am Tivoli, Krefelderstr. 86 (tel./fax 91 95 20 21). Bus #51 to "Tivoli"; the hotel is 100m down Krefelderstr. on the right. A small inn with dark-wood local flavor. Singles with bath DM65; doubles with bath DM100. Breakfast included.

FOOD

The hungry mouths of the book- and beer-laden are fed by a dense concentration of student restaurants and pubs that line **Pontstr.** from the edge of the pedestrian zone to the medieval Pont Tor. But beware—this region is also the prowling ground of the *Bahkauv,* a fearsome mythical blend of dog, puma, and dragon, which pounces on the throats of drunken revelers, inducing head-splitting hangovers. While in Aachen, be sure to try the *Printen,* a tremendously appetizing spicy gingerbread biscuit refined from an old Belgian recipe. It's now a world-famous snack with an annual production of 4500 tons—try it at any bakery. For the budget traveler, **Kaiser's,** Markt 24-31 (tel. 332 21), provides a well stocked **supermarket** (open daily 9am-10pm).

Mensa, in the green-trimmed building on Pontwall (tel. 80 37 92), near the Pont Tor. Meals DM3-3.80. Guest meals DM6.20-7.50. Open M-Th 11:30am-2:15pm, F 11:30am-2:15pm.

Katakomben Studentenzentrum, Pontstr. 74-76 (tel. 470 01 41), encloses **Café Chico Mendes,** a vegetarian co-op cafe of the Catholic College. DM7 or DM10 for the larger portion. Half-off a very long list of drinks during Happy Hour (Su 8:30-9:30pm). Open M-F 4:30pm-1am, Sa 6pm-1am.

Tam-phat, Pontstr. 100 (tel. 250 80), offers primarily Thai and Chinese dishes. Even slim budgets can afford their phat meals, including numerous vegetarian options (DM7-14). Open M-F 11am-3pm and 5-11pm, Sa-Su noon-11pm.

Egmont, Pontstr. 1 (tel. 40 60 44). Just off the *Rathaus.* This trendy bar/cafe attracts droves of students, who come to wine and dine in the updated dark-wood-and-mirrors decor. Bring student ID for discounts. Open daily 9am-3am.

Van Den Daele, Büchel 18 (tel. 357 24), just off the Markt. The finest selection of baked goods in Aachen's oldest house. Built in 1655, this *Printen* factory was made famous by artist/baker Leo van den Daele. The atmosphere is pure 18th-century, and the house speciality is *Reisfladden* (rice pudding)—DM4 buys you one huge slice. Open M-W 9am-6:30pm, Th-Sa 9am-9pm, Su noon-6pm.

SIGHTS

In 765, the Frankish King Pepin the Short took a dip in the hot springs north of Aachen's present city center. When his son, **Charlemagne** (Karl der Große), assumed power, he made the family's former vacation spot the capital of the rapidly expanding kingdom, and later of the Holy Roman Empire. The emperor's presence still dominates the city and local legends claim that in WWII, a bomb aimed at the **cathedral** was deflected by a statue of Charlemagne. *(Cathedral open daily 7am-7pm. Individual tours M 11am and noon; Tu-F 11am, noon, 2:30, and 3:30pm; Sa-Su 12:30, 2:30, and 3:30pm. DM3. For group tours or English-speaking guides, call 47 70 91 27. The gateway to the throne and shrine open for tours only.)* The 8th-century dome at its center tops three tiers of marble arches that separate the gilded roof from the mosaic floor. The neo-Byzantine structure demonstrates Charlemagne's attempt to transplant the grandeur of Constantinople into his own capital. His throne on the second level is a simple chair of marble slabs. Stained glass rings the 15th-century Gothic choir, and beneath the chancel lie the bones of the big guy himself in a sparkling gold and jewelled casket.

Old Karl cuts more of a figure in the **Schatzkammer,** around the corner to the right from the *Dom* exit, tucked into the Klostergasse. *(Open M 10am-1pm, Tu-W and F-Su 10am-6:30pm, Th 10am-9pm. Last entrance 30min. before closing. DM5, students, seniors, and children DM3.)* The most famous likeness of the emperor, a solid gold bust *(die Karlsbüste)* shines in this exceptionally rich treasury. Not bad-looking. Among the other golden tidbits of Chuck, you'll find Christ's alleged belt and scourge rope as well as the Imperial Crown Jewels. Groupies shouldn't miss Charlemagne's wall-size "Missionary Man" tour map.

The 14th-century stone **Rathaus** (tel. 432 73 10), built on the ruins of Charlemagne's palace, looms over the wide Marktplatz beside the cathedral. *(Open daily 10am-1pm and 2-5pm. DM3, students and children DM1.50.)* Seventeenth-century citizens with a decorative obsession added Baroque flourishes to the facade. On the northern face stand 50 statues of former German sovereigns, 31 of whom were crowned in Aachen (not to mention the 12 queens who were also coronated here, but didn't make the *Rathaus* cut). A copy of the famed **Charlemagne statue** draws a picnicking, multi-colored-hair crowd to the fountain on the square. The **Puppenbrunnen,** a fountain whose lovable characters represent Aachen's clever townspeople, is at the intersection of Krämerstr. and Hofstr.

MUSEUMS

Although the range of museums in Aachen is limited, the streets, especially in the *Altstadt,* shelter numerous little galleries worth browsing.

Ludwig Forum für Internationale Kunst, Jülicherstr. 97-109 (tel. 180 70). Look for the large clown in drag. The *Forum* scorns the title "museum"; it's more of a works-in-progress arena. The converted *Bauhaus* umbrella factory is a perfectly stark setting for this rich collection which includes a huge dose of American pop art, an ironic Eastern European collection, and a French/German Poetry-in-Motion board guaranteed to leave you cross-eyed. Free tour W 8pm. Open Tu and Th

10am-5pm, W and F 10am-8pm, Sa-Su 11am-5pm. Last entrance 30min. before closing. DM6, students DM3.

Internationales Zeitungsmuseum, Pontstr. 13 (tel. 432 45 08), just up from the Markt. "What's black and white and re(a)d all over?" This classy museum houses over 120,000 different international newspapers, including press from the revolutions of 1848, World War I, World War II, and the day Hitler died. Open Tu-F 9:30am-1pm and 2:30-5pm, Sa 9:30am-1pm. Last entry 30min. before closing. Free.

Suermondt-Ludwig-Museum, Wilhelmstr. 18 (tel. 47 98 00), a recently expanded museum, holds 44 galleries of sculptures, paintings, engravings, and crafts, commencing with the modern and ending with the medieval. Open Tu and Th-F 11am-7pm, W 11am-9pm, Sa-Su 11am-5pm. Last entry 30min. before closing. DM6, students and children DM3.

ENTERTAINMENT AND NIGHTLIFE

Aachen has a lively theater scene, beginning with the **Stadttheater,** on Theaterpl. (tel. 478 42 44), in the central city (box office open M-Sa 9am-1pm, 5-7pm, and 30min. before performances). A small strip of newer, unconventional theaters line Gasbornstr., spearheaded by the **Aachener Kultur und Theater Initiative,** at Gasborn 9-11 (tel. 274 58). At night, the streets come alive as swarms of students hit the cafes and pubs for a study break with the *Bahkauv* (see **Food,** p. 339). **Klenkes Magazine** (DM3.50), available at most newsstands, offers readers movies and music listings galore. **Stonewall TAC,** available in most cafes near the University and some newsstands, has a thorough listing of gay and lesbian events.

⊛**Atlantis,** Pontstr. 141 (tel. 242 41), fills *all* entertainment needs with a multi-screen cinema that shows popular releases (many in English), a mellow terrace cafe, a space-age underground *Kneipe,* and a grab-and-go bar right outside the cinema for the requisite pre-movie beer run. Cafe and *Kneipe* open Su-Th 10am-1am, F-Sa 10am-3am. Movie times vary—check out their weekly or monthly schedule.

B9, Blondelstr. 9. This popular club fills nightly with students and Gen-Xers getting down to a diverse selection of music. Check any of the multi-colored party posters all over town (open daily 10pm-5am).

Till Eulenspiegel, Pontstr. 114 (tel. 373 97). Named after the mischievous German elf, this bar is proud of its laminated Ted Nugent album adorning the wall. On Thursday nights locals and tourists alike revel in *Kölsch* (DM2), Hofewerzen (DM3), and Guinness (DM3). What a bargain! Open daily 6pm-3am (or later).

Café Kittel, 39 Pontstr. (tel. 365 60). Posters smother the walls with announcements for live music, parties, and special events. Enjoy bowls of coffee in the outdoor *Biergarten* or in the greenhouse. Vegetable quiches DM4.50. Daily menu DM5-10. Take it down with the house specialty, milk coffee (DM4.80). Open M-Th 10am-2am, F-Sa 10am-3am, Su 11am-2am.

■ Düsseldorf

As Germany's mod-ish fashion hub, advertising center, and multinational corporation base, as well as capital of the densely populated province of Nordrhein-Westfalen, Düsseldorf runneth over with German patricians and wanna be aristocrats. Founded in the 13th century, the city has endured a series of terrific pummelings. After suffering calamitous destruction during the Thirty Years War, the War of Spanish Succession, and World War II, Düsseldorf rebounded each time with an indefatigable resilience and renewed independence that translates into fierce pride among the city's residents. Set on the majestic Rhine, Germany's "Hautstadt" (a pun on *Hauptstadt,* the French *haute* meaning superior, and the German *Haut* meaning skin) is a stately, modern metropolis. Residents claim that Düsseldorf is not on the Rhine, but on the Königsallee (the central promenade, a.k.a. "the Kö"), a kilometer-long catwalk that sweeps down both sides of the old town moat. At night, propriety (and sobriety) are cast aside as thousands of Düsseldorfers flock to the 500 pubs in the *Altstadt,* trading their monacles and Rolexes for beer goggles and a damn good time.

ORIENTATION AND PRACTICAL INFORMATION

Flights: Frequent S-Bahn trains and a Lufthansa shuttle travel from the station to the international **Flughafen Düsseldorf.** Call 421 22 23 for flight information. Open 5am-12:30am. 24hr. emergency service tel. 421 66 37.

Trains: All trains arrive at **Düsseldorf Hauptbahnhof** (tel. 194 19).

Public Transportation: The *Rheinbahn* includes subways, streetcars, buses, and the S-Bahn. Single tickets, DM1.90-11.70, depending on distance traveled. The *Tagesticket* (DM10; higher prices for longer distances) is the best value—groups of up to 5 people and one dog can travel 24hr. on any line. Tickets are sold mostly by vending machine; pick up the *Fahrausweis* brochure in the tourist office for instructions. Düsseldorf's S-Bahn is integrated into the mammoth regional **VRR** *(Verkehrsverbund Rhein-Ruhr)* system, which connects Bochum, Dortmund, Duisburg, Essen, Hagen, Krefeld, Mönchengladbach, Mühlheim, Oberhausen, Solingen, and Wuppertal. **Schedule Information,** tel. 582 28.

Boat Tours: The **Köln-Düsseldorfer Deutscher Rheinschiffahrt A6** (tel. (02212) 208 83 18) gives tours Mar.-Oct. Times and prices vary from month to month.

Taxi: tel. 21 21 21.

Car Rental: Hertz, Immermannstr. 65 (tel. 35 70 25). Open M-F 7am-6pm, Sa 8am-noon.

Mitfahrzentrale: Konrad-Adenauer-Pl. 13 (tel. 37 60 81), to the left as you exit the station, and upstairs over a tiny travel office. Open M-F 9am-6:30pm, Sa-Su 11am-3pm. **City-Netz Mitfahrzentrale,** Kruppstr. 102 (tel. 194 44), is a chain with slightly higher prices. Open M-F 9am-7pm, Sa 10am-2pm, Su noon-3pm.

Bike Rental: Zweirad Egert, Ackerstr. 143 (tel. 66 21 34). S-Bahn #6 (direction: "Essen") to "Wehrbahn" and walk 10min. Call ahead to check availability. Bikes DM18.50 per day, DM42 per week. DM50 deposit and ID required. Open M-F 9:30am-6:30pm, Sa 9am-2pm.

Tourist Office: Main office, Konrad-Adenauer-Pl. (tel. 17 20 20; fax 35 04 04). Walk up and to the right from the station and look for the towering Immermanhof building. This shiny office with friendly staff is a bastion of information, and its free monthly *Düsseldorfer Monatsprogram* details all goings-on about town. Open for concert and theater ticket sales (12% fee) and general services M-F 8:30am-6pm, Sa 9am-noon; hotel reservations (DM55 and up) M-Sa 8am-8pm, Su 4-10pm. The **branch office,** Heinrich-Heine-Allee 24 (tel. 899 23 46), specializes in cultural listings. Open M-F 9am-5pm.

Budget Travel: Council Travel, Graf-Adolf-Str. 64 (tel. 36 30 30). Open M-F 9am-1pm, Sa 10am-1pm.

Consulates: Canada and **U.K.,** Yorckstr. 19 (tel. 944 80). Open M-F 8am-noon. **U.S.,** Kennedydamm 15-17 (tel. 47 06 10).

Currency Exchange: Deutsche Verkehrs Credit Bank, in the *Hauptbahnhof* or at the airport. Open M-Sa 7am-9pm, Su 8am-9pm.

American Express: Neusserstr. 111 (tel. 90 13 50). Mail held up to 4 weeks for card members. All financial services. Open M-F 9am-5:30pm, Sa 8:30am-noon.

Bookstore: Stern-Verlag, Friedrichstr. 24-26 (tel. 388 10). A good selection of English paperbacks. Open M-F 9am-6:30pm, Sa 9am-2pm.

Women's Agency: Any questions or concerns regarding women's issues can be directed to the **Frauenbüro,** Mühlenstr. 29, 2nd floor (tel. 899 36 03), at the municipal office. Walk-ins M-Th 8am-4pm, F 8am-1pm.

AIDS-Hilfe: Oberblicker Allee 310 (tel. 726 05 26). Open M-Th 10am-1pm and 2-6pm, F 10am-1pm and 2-4pm. Advice and assistance hotline tel. 194 11.

Laundromat: Wasch Center, Friedrichstr. 92, down the street from the Kirchpl. S-Bahn. Wash DM6. Dry DM1 per 15min. Soap included. Open daily 6am-11pm.

Emergency: Police, tel. 110. **Ambulance** and **Fire,** tel. 112.

Pharmacy: In the *Hauptbahnhof.* Closed pharmacies post lists of nearby open ones. **Emergency pharmacy,** tel. 115 00. **Emergency doctor,** tel. 192 92.

Post Office: Hauptpostamt, Konrad-Adenauer-Platz, 40210 Düsseldorf, a stone's throw to the right of the tourist office. Open M-F 8am-6pm, Sa 9am-2pm, Su noon-1pm. Limited service M-F 6pm-8pm, Su 10am-2pm. **Branch office** in *Hauptbahnhof* open M-F 8am-6pm, Sa-Su 2pm-midnight.

Internet Access: See g@rden, p. 347.

Telephone Code: 0211.

Düsseldorf

ACCOMMODATIONS

C CVJM Hotel
B Hotel Amsterdam
D Hotel Diana
A Jugendgästehaus

Hauptbahnhof

KONRAD-ADENAUER-PLATZ

Worringer Str.

Kölner Str.

Bagelstr.

St. Rochus

Stiftung Ernst Schneider

Vagedesstr.

Goethe Museum

Dumont-Lindemann Archiv

Jägerhofstr.

Schadowstr.

Kölnerstr.

Friedrich-Ebert-Str.

Bismarckstr.

Charlottenstr.

Graf-Adolf-Str.

Karlstr.

Immermannstr.

Klosterstr.

Feldstr.

Schauspielhaus

Thyssen-Haus

Kaiserstr.

Kreuzstr.

Oststr.

Stresemannstr.

Komodie

Berliner Allee

TO C

TO D

TO PUPPENTHEATER

Hofgarten

Johannes Kirche

Steinstr.

Grünstr.

Königs-allee

Königs-allee

Städtische Kunsthalle

Opera

Heinrich-Heine-Allee

Junges Theater

Breite Str.

Kaserenstr.

Hohe Str.

Kunstmuseum

Lancesmuseum Volk und Wirschaft

Tonhalle

Hofgarten

Ratinger Tor

Max-Weye-Allee

Fritz-Roebber-Str.

Kunstakademie

Kunstsammlung N.-Westfalen

Kreuzherrenkirche

St. Andreas

Hunsruckenstr.

Grabenstr.

Berger Str.

Flinger Str.

Benrather Str.

Heinrich-Heine Institut

Bilker Su...

Südstr.

Poststr.

Scheibenstr.

Kapelstr.

Schlossufer

Ratterstr.

ALTSTADT

Mahn-und Gedenkstätte

Mählenstr.

Marktstr.

Neanderkirche

Rathaus

Berger Kirche

Schulstr.

Hotjens Museum

St. Maximilian Kirche

KARL PLATZ

Marionatten-theater

Berger Allee

Harlstr.

Landtag

St. Lambertus Kirche

Hofgarten-ufer

Hofgarten-ufer

Oberkasseler Br.cke

Rhine

Rathaus-ufer

Rheinkniebrücke

Rhine

Kaiser-Friedrich-King

San-Remo-Str.

Theater an der Luegallee

Ring

Kaiser-Wilhelm-Ring

Markgrafenstr.

Brendamourstr.

Sallerstr.

Lueg-allee

Oberkasseler Str.

Düsseldorfer Str.

Rhine

1/2 mile

1/2 kilometer

N

0

ACCOMMODATIONS AND CAMPING

Call ahead, at least a month ahead if possible. Düsseldorf is a convention city where corporate crowds make rooms scarce and costly; it's not unusual for hotels to double their prices during a convention. For a budget hotel stay, try calling the tourist office for trade fair *(Messe)* dates and show up during a lull. Most spots go for at least DM50 per person even in the off season. Check around the train station or consider the hostels in Duisberg, Mönchengladbach, Neuss, or Ratingen (all within 30min. by S-Bahn). Most hotels accept major credit cards.

Jugendgästehaus Düsseldorf (HI), Düsseldorferstr. 1 (tel. 55 73 10; fax 57 25 13), is conveniently located in the Oberkassel part of town, just over the Rheinknie-brücke from the Altstadt. U-Bahn #70, 74, 75, 76, or 77 to "Luegpl.," then walk 500m down Kaiser-Wilhelm-Ring. Clean, modern facilities, private lockers, and an unbeatable location. DM33.50, over 26 DM37. Laundry DM9; free soap and drying. Reception 7am-1am. Curfew 1am, but doors opened every hour on the hour 2-6am.

Jugendherberge Duisburg-Wedau, Kalkweg 148E (tel. (0203) 72 41 64; fax 72 08 34). S-Bahn #1 or 21 to "Duisburg Hauptbahnhof," then bus #934 to "Jugendher-berge." Neighboring town Duisberg is accessible by many buses and trains, but public transportation closes by 1am and the hostel is too far for a taxi. Old but clean rooms. DM22.50, over 26 DM27.50. Laundry DM2.50 each for wash and dry. Reception 8:30-9am, 12:30-1pm, and 6:30-7pm. Open mid-Jan. to mid-Dec.

Hotel Amsterdam, Stresemannstr. 20 (tel. 84 05 89; fax 840 50), between Oststr. and Berliner Allee. From the station, start up Graf-Adolf-Str. and turn right at Strese-mannpl. Baroque rooms and princess-style furniture. No-frills single DM70, with shower, TV, and breakfast DM90; doubles from DM120. Reception 7am-midnight.

Hotel Diana, Jahnstr. 31 (tel. 37 50 71; fax 36 49 43), 5 blocks from the station. Head left down Graf-Adolf-Str., left on Hüttenstr., and then a quick jog to the right on Jahnstr. Small, comfy rooms with phone and TV. Singles DM60; doubles DM85, with bath DM125. Breakfast included. 24hr. reception.

Hotel Bristol, Aderstr. 8 (tel. 37 07 50; fax 37 37 54), 1 block south of Graf-Adolf-Str. at the bottom tip of the Königsallee. The well-appointed hotel offers elegance in profusion—even by the Kö's standards. Singles DM75, with shower DM95, with bath DM130. Breakfast included.

Hotel Manhattan, Graf-Adolf-Str. 39 (tel. 37 71 38; fax 37 02 47), 2 blocks from the station. The spacious, comfortable rooms are a convenient respite from a hard day's shopping, but if the mirror-plated, Coca-Cola-postered decor represents Germany's view of America, America is in trouble. Singles DM68-120; doubles DM100-180, depending on ritziness and whether it's convention time. Breakfast buffet included. 24hr. reception.

CVJM-Hotel, Graf-Adolf-Str. 102 (tel. 17 28 50; fax 361 31 60), down the street to the left of the train station. Clean, modern rooms in a convenient location. Singles DM70; doubles DM117. 24hr. reception. No credit cards.

Camping: Kleiner Torfbruch (tel. 899 20 38). S-Bahn to "Düsseldorf Geresheim," then bus #735 (direction: "Stamesberg") to "Seeweg." Pitch your palace and live like a *König,* li'l scout. DM6 per person; DM9 per tent.

FOOD

For a cheap meal, the conglomeration of dives in the **Altstadt** can't be beat. Endless rows of pizzerias, *Döner Kebabs,* and Chinese diners reach from Heinrich-Heine-Allee to the banks of the Rhine. The **Markt** on Karlspl. offers shoppers lots of foreign fruits and a local favorite, *Sauerbraten* (pickled beef). For *trés chic* cafes that provide the beautiful people with abundant atmosphere and high prices, hit the **Kö. Olto Mess** (tel. 200 10), a popular grocery chain, should satisfy all your DIY needs. The most convenient location is at the eastern corner of Karlspl. in the *Altstadt* (open M-F 8am-8pm, Sa 8am-4pm).

◉Galerie Burghof, Burgallee 1-3 (tel. 40 14 23), in Kaiserwerth next to Friedrich's Rhine ruins. U-Bahn #79 to "Klemenspl." Walk down Kaiserwerthermarkt and turn left on the Rhine promenade. Enjoy very delicious pancakes in the funky, multi-level restaurant, or drink in a view of the Rhine at the **Biergarten.** Open daily 11am-1am, but pancakes served only M-F 6-10:45pm, Sa 2-10:45pm, Su 2-11pm.

Marché, Königsallee 60 (tel. 32 06 81), in the Kö-Galerie mall. The only way to dine on the Kö and keep your savings intact: it's the swankiest cafeteria you'll ever see. Entrees start at DM6.80, including generous portions of fried chicken, fish, and noodles with zany sauces. Cafe-bar open daily 7:30am-11pm, restaurant 8am-11pm.

Linanon Express, Bergerstr. 21 (tel. 32 95 93). Düsseldorf's *Altstadt* is probably the last place you would expect to find Lebanese food, but this hip cafe serves up great falafel (DM4.50), in the heart of *Kneipe*-land. Open daily noon-midnight.

La Copa, Bergerstr. 4 (tel. 323 84 58). Sammy, Deano, and Barry Manilow have left the building, but not without bequeathing their beloved Copa with 50 tasty dishes (DM8-15). Hep cats wash it down with a glass of sangria. Open daily noon-1am.

Zum Uerige, Bergerstr. 1 (tel. 86 69 90). Some pheromone in the air draws cool Germans here. Try house specialties of *Blutwurst* (blood sausage) for DM3.50 and *Mainzer* (Mainz cheese) for DM4. When you're finished eating, settle down with a *Schlossor Alt* beer and soak up the crisp *Rheinisch* zephyrs. Open daily 10am-midnight. Kitchen open M-F 6-9pm, Sa 11am-4pm.

SIGHTS

The glitzy **Kö** located just outside the *Altstadt* embodies the vitality and glamour of Düsseldorf. No bargains here, but the Kö sports the best of everything; you, too, can window-shop at Armani or ogle the Lotus parked outside. To get there, head down Graf-Adolf-Str. from the station (10min.). Properly called the Königsallee, the *belle époque* expanse was laid out over a century ago. Stone bridges span the little river that runs down the middle to trickle at the toes of a decadent statue of the sea god Triton. Three shopping guides for the Kö are printed by the tourist office. Midway up is the awesome **Kö-Galerie**—in Nietzschean terms, an *Übermall* (with *über*-prices). Items *start* at US$100 here, and even the mannequins have attitude. At the upper end of the Kö, the **Hofgarten** park is an oasis of green and culture inside urban Düsseldorf. **Schloß Jägerhof,** at the eastern end, houses the **Goethe Museum** behind its pink facade and white iron gates. The Hofgarten meets the Rhine at the **Ehrenhof,** a plaza of museums (see below). The **Deutsches Oper am Rhein** (opera house) is here, as is the Neoclassical Napoleonic **Ratinger Tor** gate house. Twilight walks along the east bank of the Rhine are breathtaking.

Düsseldorf has had mixed luck with its cultural heroes. Famed composer **Robert Schumann** was so miserable here that he tried to drown his sorrows by jumping off a town bridge. Beloved poet **Heinrich Heine** is a more popular, if equally melancholic, son. His birthplace and homestead are marked by plaques, and every third restaurant and fast-food stand on his Bolkerstr. block bears his name. **The Heinrich Heine Institut,** Bilkerstr. 12-14 (tel. 899 55 71), is the official shrine with a collection of manuscripts and an unsettling death mask. *(Open Tu-F und Su 11am-5pm, Sa 1-5pm. DM4, students DM2.)* In addition to many works of contemporary artists honoring Heine, the institute holds a vast array of the author's correspondence, which shows the intellectual and artistic development of the literary master. Farther up the *Altstadt*, the **Burgpl.** used to be the site of a glorious castle, but tired citizens have saved only a single tower. The castle was built in 1324, burnt in 1490, rebuilt in 1559, razed in 1794, rebuilt in 1851, and flattened in 1872, at which point the townsfolk gave up—only the tower was reconstructed in 1900, and *that* was bombed to rubble in World War II. The pessimistic citizens waited until 1984 to rebuild the tower. Tread carefully—rumor has it that the cartwheel was invented in Düsseldorf, and the *Radschlager,* the legendary Düsseldorf "somersaulting boys," grace every manhole cover and top a fountain on Burgpl.

North on the Rhine but still within Düsseldorf dwell the **ruins** of Emperor Friedrich's palace in the tiny town of **Kaiserwerth.** *(Open daily 8am-12:30pm. Free.)* Built in 1184, the palace was destroyed in 1702 in the War of Spanish Succession, but the gloomy *Kaiserpfalz* frame remains. Take U-Bahn #79 to "Klemenspl.," then follow Kaiserwerther Markt to the Rhine, and walk left another 150m. Just in case

NORDRHEIN-WESTFALEN

you're curious, the seemingly out-of-place **tower** with the blinking lights visible from the Rhine at night is actually a clock called the **Rheinturm**. From bottom to top, the dots represent 1 second, 10 seconds, 1 minute, 10 minutes, 1 hour, and 10 hours.

Schloß Benrath, in the suburbs of Düsseldorf (S-Bahn #6 (direction: "Köln") to "Benrath"), is a large 18th-century castle with an excess of pink paint. *(Castle open Tu-Su 10am-5pm; tours every half hour. DM7, students and children DM3.50.)* In nearby **Zons, Schloß Friedestrom** is accessible by ferry (tel. (012133) 421 49). The real attraction is the summer production of plays based on Grimm's Fairy Tales. For more information, call the **Freilichtbühne Zons** (tel. 422 74).

MUSEUMS

Düsseldorf is a city of museums. Most cluster around the Hofgarten. Internationally important holdings abound in the string of museums along Grabbepl. and Ehrenhof. These museums are expensive, so choose carefully. The **ArtTicket** (DM20) includes entrance to all museums, and can be purchased at the tourist office or any museum.

Grabbeplatz

⊛**Kunstsammlung Nordrhein-Westfalen,** Grabbepl. 5 (tel. 838 10), is the black, reflecting, glass thing west of the Hofgarten. U-Bahn #70, 75, 76, 78, or 79 to "Heinrich-Heine-Allee" and walk north 2 blocks, or bus #725 to "Grabbepl." Skylights lavish sunshine on the exhibits—Matisse, Picasso, Surrealists, and Expressionists. The collection of works by hometown boy Paul Klee is one of the most extensive in the world. Open Tu-Th and Sa-Su 10am-6pm, F 10am-8pm. Tours Su 11am and W 3:30pm. DM5, students DM3. Special exhibits DM10, students DM8.

Kunsthalle, Grabbepl. 4 (tel. 889 62 40), across the square from the Kunstsammlung Nordrhein-Westfalen. Not a museum, mind you, but a forum for modern exhibits of every shape and size—and nearly all bizarre. Admission depends on the exhibit; usually DM10, students and children DM7. Open Tu-Su 11am-6pm.

Ehrenhof—Hofgarten

Kunstmuseum Düsseldorf, Ehrenhof 5 (tel. 899 62 40; fax 899 24 60), surrounding the fountain. A spectacular collection of sculpture, painting, prints, weaving, and crafts spanning 2 stories and 11 centuries. Stunning glassware and the Baroque and Renaissance drawings are some highlights. Open Tu-Su 11am-6pm. DM5, students and children DM2.50. The **Kunstpalast** is an extension of the Kunstmuseum across the fountain at Ehrenhof 5, devoted to rotating contemporary exhibits.

Landesmuseum Volk und Wirtschaft, Ehrenhof 2 (tel. 492 11 08), dissects every nugget of the area's development, including a mini-mineshaft, with a side order of economic and social history. Open M-Tu and Th-F 9am-5pm, W 9am-8pm, Su 10am-6pm. DM2, students DM1.

Goethe Museum, Jakobistr. 2 (tel. 899 62 62), in Schloß Jägerhof, at the east end of the garden. Streetcar #707 or bus #752 to "Schloß Jägerhof." The museum makes up for its lack of hometown advantage with the extent of its collection—30,000 souvenirs of the poet and his friends. Goethe was Heine's idol, and in Germany, that is ground enough to claim a connection—he is the German Shakespeare, after all. Everything in the mini-palace is furnished as Goethe would have wished it: to evoke his character. Open Tu-F and Su 11am-5pm, Sa 1-5pm. Library open Tu-F 10am-noon and 2-4pm. DM4, students and children DM2.

Elsewhere in Düsseldorf

Film Museum/Hetjens Museum, Schulstr. 4 (tel. 899 42 00), south of the *Schloßturm* on Rheinuferstr. Hetjens provides a comprehensive history of ceramics, while the film museum showcases 4 floors of costumes, photos, and even clips of classics (all dubbed in German). Both open Tu and Th-Su 11am-5pm, W 11am-9pm. Admission to each DM6, students and children DM3. The **Black Box** theater, a cinema specializing in art-house flicks, is in the same complex. See **Entertainment.**

Stadtmuseum, at Berger Allee 2 (tel. 899 61 70), by the Rheinkniebrücke. The new building clashes with its 18th-century surroundings, but the exhibits summarize Düsseldorf's culturally rich consumer history perfectly. Open Tu and Th-Su 11am-5pm, W 11am-9pm. DM5, students DM2.50.

Mahn- und Gedenkstätte, Mühlenstr. 29 (tel. 899 62 06). Stark museum and document collection commemorating victims of the Third Reich. Open Tu-F and Su 11am-6pm, Sa 1-5pm. Free.

Neanderthal Museum, Thekhauser Quall (tel. (02104) 311 49), in the suburb of Erkrath. S-Bahn #8 to "Hochdahl," then bus #741 to "Neanderthal." A museum where low-brows, thick-skulls, and knuckle-draggers can feel comfortable. The first remains of an entity identified as "Neanderthal Man" were found here; the museum allows you to meet his 60,000-year-old relatives. Open Tu-Sa 10am-5pm, Su 11am-6pm. DM2, students DM1.

ENTERTAINMENT AND NIGHTLIFE

Folklore holds that Düsseldorf's 500 pubs make up *"die längste Theke der Welt"* (the longest bar in the world). Pubs in the *Altstadt* are standing-room-only by 6pm, and foot traffic is shoulder-to-shoulder by nightfall. **Bolkerstr.** is jam-packed nightly with street performers of the musical and beer-olympic varieties. *Prinz* magazine (DM4.50) is Düsseldorf's fashion cop and scene detective; it's often given out free at the youth hostel. *Facolte* is the gay and lesbian nightlife magazine and is available at most newsstands. The free cultural guides *Coolibri* and *Biograph* are less complete but more than sufficient to keep your thang jiggin' all night long. **Das Kommödchen** ("The Little Commode"; tel. 32 94 43) is a tiny, extraordinarily popular theater behind the Kunsthalle at Grabbepl. (Box office open M-Sa 1-8pm, Su 3-8pm. Tickets DM33, students and children DM23; call at least 2 days ahead.) Ballet and opera tickets are best bought (without service charge) at the **Opernhaus** (tel. 890 82 11), on Heinrich-Heine-Allee (box office open M-F 11am-6:30pm, Sa 11am-1pm, and 1hr. before performances). Tickets can be purchased by phone (M-F 9am-5pm). **Black Box,** Schulstr. 4 (tel. 899 24 90), off Rathaus-Ufer along the Rhine, serves the art-film aficionado with unadulterated foreign flicks (DM8, students DM6).

Stahlwerk, Ronsdorfer Str. 134 (tel. 73 03 50). U-Bahn #75 to "Ronsdorferstr." Facing away from downtown, turn right onto Ronsdorferstr. This classic factory-turned-disco in one of Düsseldorf's grittier neighborhoods packs in 1500(!) of the city's most divine. Cover DM10. Opens F-Sa and last Su of every month at 10pm.

Tor 3, Ronsdorfer Str. 143 (tel. 733 64 97). More techno and younger than Stahlwerk, Tor 3 rocks around the clock. Arrange alternate transport home from this disco—the S Bahn stops running far too early. Cover DM15. Open F-Sa 10pm-5am.

Café Rosa, Oberbilker-Allee 310. The socio-cultural mecca of Düsseldorf's queer community, this do-it-all *Kulturzentrum* offers self-defense classes and activities and throws killer parties. Tuesday, Thursday, and most Saturdays mixed; Friday lesbians only; last Saturday of each month gays only. Call 77 52 42 for gay programs and 54 42 for lesbian events. Daytime hours vary (call hotlines); evenings Tu-Sa 8pm-1am, sometimes later on weekends.

g@rden, Rathansufer 8 (tel. 86 61 60; email gsg@garden.de; http://www.garden.de). In addition to **Internet access** and loads of mellow atmosphere, this futuristic cafe and bar is also one of Düsseldorf's best jazz scenes; gigs here tend much more toward progressive jazz than in most German clubs. Open daily 11am-1am.

Engelchen, Kurzestr. 11 (tel. 32 73 56). This mellow oasis papered with posters and emanating Seattle grunge offers Gen X types an atmosphere a lot less bombastic than the 300 or so *Altstadt* bars around the corner. Open M-F 9am-1am, Sa 10am-3am, Su 10am-3am.

McLaughlin's Irish Pub, Kurzestr. 11, loads up on live bands while Anglophiles load up. No German spoken here—practice your brogue instead. Open Su-Th 11am-1am, F-Sa 11am-3am.

Zum Uel, Rattinger 16 (tel. 32 53 69). At the crossroads of the *Altstadt's* busiest streets, this classic pub fills with students who stop by for house favorite *Schlösser Alt* (DM2.30 for 0.2L). Open Su-Tu and Th 10am-1am, W and F 10am-3am.

Brauerei Schumacher, Bolkerstr. 44 (tel. 32 60 07), is Düsseldorf's oldest house brewery. This cross-generational *Treffpunkt* fills every night with a mellow crowd. Open M-Th, Su 10am-midnight, F-Sa 10am-1am.

Fire Club, Grupollostr. 8 (tel. 369 48 16), in the city center. A sleek, trendy magnet for a young, gay crowd that works it nightly. Open daily from 5pm until late.

NORDRHEIN-WESTFALEN

■ Near Düsseldorf: Mönchengladbach

Mönchengladbach, known to all as MG (em-gay), has always stayed way ahead of the times. Their pre-Neanderthal ancestors set up one of the largest communities in the region over 300,000 years ago. In 974, Archbishop Gero founded a prominent Benedictine monastery and intellectual center, **Abteiberg,** a structure that still dominates the skyline. About 800 years later, the French kicked the monks out, and since then the deserted building has served as the **Rathaus.** Next door towers the 11th-century **Münster,** whose ecclesiastical treasures include a portable altar and a bust of the Saxon St. Vitus, the city's guardian. (Church open M-Sa 8am-6pm, Su noon-6pm. Museum open Tu-Sa 2-6pm, Su noon-6pm.) Around the corner, the mirrored **Städtisches Museum Abteiberg,** Abteistr. 27 (tel. 25 26 37), just beyond the *Rathaus,* houses a cool-ass collection of 20th-century art including pieces by Andy Warhol, Roy Lichtenstein, and George Segal (open Tu-Su 10am-6pm; DM5, students and children DM2.50). Also at the top of the Abteiberg is the **Alter Markt,** an old cobblestone square now studded by small diners and craft shops. Gaze down at the residential district, a dense blanket of pastel decorated houses with flowers spilling out of windows. To reach the Alter Markt, turn left out of the train station and head up Hindenburgstr. past the snazzy new stores, or take bus #13 or 23 up the hill. Five **parks**—Geropark, Brundespark, Kaiserpark, Hardtor Wald, and Volksgarten—lie within MG proper, but most affecting is the **Bunter Garten** (Garden of Colors), in the center of town, three blocks northwest of the Alter Markt on Kaldenkirchenorstr.

Just outside of town stands the majestic **Schloß Rheydt** (tel. 66 92 89 00). From the station, take bus #6 to "Bonnenbroich" and then bus #16 to "Sparkasse" (30min., but worth it). This pristine Renaissance palace is upstaged only by its own beautiful grounds, prize peacocks, and a tranquil, Monet-esque lily-padded moat. The museum inside houses rotating art and historical exhibits. (Open Oct.-Mar. Tu-Sa 11am-4pm, Su 11am-6pm; Apr.-Sept. Tu-Su 11am-7pm. DM5, kids DM2.50.)

Mönchengladbach is best seen as a day trip from Düsseldorf. Nevertheless, the **tourist office,** Bismarckstr. 23-27, located in the *First Reisebüro* (travel agency) one block to the left of the train station (tel. 220 01; fax 27 42 22) finds rooms (from DM45) for free (open M-F 9:30am-6pm, Sa 9:30am-12:30pm). The **Jugendherberge Hardter Wald,** Brahmstr. 156 (tel. (02461) 55 95 12; fax 55 64 64), lies at the boundary of a wheat field and a forest. From the station, take bus #13 or 23 to "Hardtmarkt" (20min.), walk straight and make a left at the *Jugendherberge* sign onto Brahmstr. (1.2km). The facilities are excellent but the hostel's bucolic location far from Mönchengladbach and really, really far from Düsseldorf rules out nasty nightlife action. (DM22.50, over 26 DM27.50. Breakfast included. Sheets DM6. Reception noon-10pm.) The **telephone code** is 02161.

RUHRGEBIET (RUHR REGION)

Germany's modern wealth and working class were forged from the coal and steel of the Ruhr Valley. After 1850, the Ruhr was the source of railroad expansion and the immense manufacturing demands of a newly unified (and bellicose) Germany, quickly becoming the foremost industrial region in Europe. Not everything was ticky-boo in this era, however; the growing proletarianization and exploitation of the workers led to numerous strikes and strong socialist leanings. Nevertheless, the workers remained loyal to the government, and the Ruhr was torn apart not by Marxist revolution but by Allied bombers in World War II. The reconstruction program in the following years yielded numerous parks and gardens to brighten the region's smoggy visage; travelers weary of the bleak landscape can get their aesthetic fix at many of the region's excellent museums and cultural centers. At the same time, the Ruhr's sprawling conglomeration of the streetcar, S-Bahn, bus, and U-Bahn systems, linking many of the region's cities, offers the densest concentration of rail lines in the world, providing a snapshot of the industrial past.

NORDRHEIN-WESTFAIEN

■ Essen

For a millennium, Essen was just another German cathedral town. By the eve of World War I, however, Essen had advanced to become the industrial capital of Germany, thanks to its seemingly limitless deposits of coal and iron. After its destruction in World War II, the city reformed its image as a soot-belching monstrosity by returning to an emphasis on its religious and cultural faces. At the same time, Essen's high-tech factories remain the industrial cornerstone of the Ruhr.

PRACTICAL INFORMATION AND ACCOMMODATIONS Essen's **U-Bahn** and **streetcar** lines cost DM3.10 per ride. Essen's **Mitfahrzentrale**, Freiheit 4 (tel. 194 40), pairs riders with drivers (open daily 9am-7pm). Essen's spiffy new **tourist office** (Touristikzentrale Essen), Am Hauptbahnhof 2 (tel. 451 27), across the street from the station, makes reservations and doles out a *lot* of brochures (open M-F 9am-5:30pm, Sa 10am-1pm). The **Jugendherberge (HI)**, Pastoratsberg 2 (tel. 49 11 63; fax 49 25 05), resides in Werden, a suburb notable for its 8th-century **Abtei Kirche** and **Lucius Kirche**, the oldest parish churches north of the Alps. Take S-Bahn #6 to "Werden" (25min.) and bus #190 to "Jugendherberge." If you feel like playing Alpine mountain climber, cross the bridge, take the second right onto Bungerstr., and follow Kemensborn uphill as it winds all over the map to a sharp right at Pastoratsberg. Rooms are standard and only marginally clean. (DM24, over 26 DM29. Breakfast included. Sheets DM6. Reception 7am-11:30pm. Curfew 11:30pm.) The basic, comfortable **Hotel Kessing**, Hachestr. 30 (tel. 23 99 88; fax 23 02 89), is close to the train station; turn left on Hachestr. (Singles DM59, with bath DM85; doubles DM118, with bath DM138. Breakfast included. Prices go up when conferences are in town—call ahead.) Camp at **"Stadt-Camping" Essen-Werden**, Im Löwental 67 (tel. 49 29 78), on the west bank of the Ruhr. Take the S-Bahn to "Essen-Werden" and continue south along the river. (DM7.50 per adult, DM5 per child, DM15 per tent. Reception 9am-1pm and 3-9:45pm.) The **telephone code** is 0201.

FOOD Grocery store **Drospa** meets basic food needs in the train station (open M-Sa 6:30am-9:30pm, Su 9am-9:30pm). The maze of stairs and escalators at **Porscheplatz,** near the *Rathaus,* is Cheap Food Central. Take the U-Bahn to "Porschepl." The **Mensa** (tel. 18 31) is in the green-rimmed building at the university. Take the U-Bahn to "Universität" and follow the signs to the building (open M-F 7:30am-4pm, Sa 7:30am-3:30pm). Just across the street from the *Mensa,* **Beaulongerie,** on Segeroth-str. (tel. 32 62 12), offers huge (30cm), freshly baked baguettes (DM4.50) with a variety of fillings and sauces (open M-Th 11am-11pm, F-Sa 11am-1pm). **Salzmarkt 1,** same address, offers an enormous drink menu, stylin' atmosphere, and a sidewalk terrace perfect for catching the live jazz that goes down every Wednesday on the Salzmarkt, to the left of Kennedypl. (open M-Th noon-1am, F Sa noon-3am).

SIGHTS Infamous 19th-century arms and railroad mogul **Alfred Krupp** perfected steelcasting in industrial Essen. **Villa Hügel** (tel. 48 37), the Krupp family home for decades, was given to the city in the 1950s in order to brighten the company's image, which was tarnished by its Nazi affiliation. (*Grounds open daily 8am-8pm. Villa open Tu-Su 10am-6pm. Special exhibits open M and W-Su 10am-7pm, Tu 10am-9pm. DM1.50, students and seniors DM0.50.*) While exhibits and concerts showcase the villa's magnificent mahogany halls, the house itself reflects Krupp's gaudy arrogance. Take S-Bahn #6 to "Essen-Hügel." Essen's **Münster Kirche,** close to the city center on Burgpl., is an ancient, cloistered string of flowering courtyards and hexagonal crypts. (*Open daily 7:30am-6:30pm. DM2, students DM1.*) The 1000-year-old doll-like *Goldene Madonna* stands beside the nave. Although Nazis gutted Essen's **Alte Synagoge** (tel. 452 80) in 1938, it stands today as the largest synagogue north of the Alps. (*Open Tu-Su 10am-6pm. Free. Tours DM1, free for students with a call one day in advance.*) Inside, slides, pictures, and objects from the Third Reich era make up the *Dokumentationsforum,* a monument to the Jews of Essen. Take the U-Bahn to "Porschepl." and follow the signs to the Schützenbahn; as you head south on the Schützenbahn, the synagogue is on your left.

NORDRHEIN-WESTFALEN

The **Deutsches Plakat Museum** (German Poster Museum), on the third floor of the shopping mall at the intersection of Rathenaustr. and Am Glockenspiel, features everything from the unusual (a one-eyed nude) to the downright bizarre (two pig heads eating a human heart). Exhibits rotate every two months. *(Open Tu-Su noon-8pm. DM2, students, handicapped, and children free.)* The **Design Zentrum Nordrhein West-falen,** Hindenburgstr. 25-27 (tel. 82 02 10), is a haven for design aficionados, or any-one who is *Bauhaus*-ed out by the Ruhrgebiet. *(Open Tu-F 10am-6pm, Sa 10am-2pm. Free.)* Take U-Bahn #17 or 18 to "Bismarckpl." **Museum Folkwang,** in the *Museum-szentrum* at Goethestr. 41 (tel. 884 53 00), drops all the big names in modern art, and hosts superstar special exhibits. The Folkwang's **Fotographische Sammlung,** in the same complex, takes on camerawork from the early days. Take streetcar #101, 107, or 127, or U-Bahn #11 to "Rüttenscheider Stern." Follow signs to the Museumzen-trum and continue (north) on Rüttenscheiderstr., then turn left on Kuhrstr., and right onto Goethestr. *(Both open Tu-W and F-Su 10am-6pm, Th 10am-9pm. The photography col-lection is closed during summer holidays. Combined admission DM5, students and children DM3.)* The **Ruhrland Museum,** Goethestr. 41 (tel. 884 51 28), exhibits the Ruhr in its indus-trial heyday. *(Open Tu-W and F-Su 10am-6pm, Th 10am-9pm. DM5, students DM3.)* Expe-rience the life of a miner in the Weimar Republic without getting your hands dirty.

■ Dortmund

With the exception of its American soul-twin, Milwaukee, Dortmund annually pro-duces more beer than any other city in the world: 1000L for each of its 600,000 citi-zens (you do the math). The best known of Dortmund's sudsy brood is the ubiquitous *Dortmunder Union* beer. As part of Germany's industrial backbone, Dort-mund was a tempting target for Allied bombers, and 93% of the city center was lev-eled in WWII. Today, the city is still largely industrial. But there is more to this town than brewing and drunken bowling—Dortmund nurtures significant cultural offer-ings, and the post-war greening outside the city center has added a new face to this classic *Hendelstadt.* The city gleefully follows its soccer team, **BVB09** (among the best in Europe) with a passion: walk down any street, and when you hear gnashing of teeth, the BVB has just given up a rare goal.

Museum am Ostwall, Ostwall 7 (tel. 502 32 47), was built in 1947 over the ruins of the *Altstadt* in order to make room for modern art, especially the kind suppressed by the Third Reich. (Open Tu-Su 10am-5pm. DM4, seniors, students, and children DM1.) The plastic-fruit-and-wooden-grass exhibit makes the museum's Picasso look down-right conventional. The Lennies and Squiggies of the world will be more comfortable in the **Brauerei-Museum,** Märkischestr. 81 (tel. 541 32 89), located in the Kronen Beer Works, southeast of the city center. (Open Tu-Su 10am-5pm. Free, but no sam-ples.) It's four floors of German art in the form of kegs, steins, and 5000 years of brew-ing history. Take U-Bahn #41, 45, or 47 to "Markgrafenstr." and walk along Landgrafenstr. in the direction of the tower. The white-washed **Adlerturm,** at Klep-pingstr. and Südwall, near the *Rathaus,* is the last remaining section of the old city walls (open Tu-Su 10am-5pm; DM2, seniors, students, and children DM1). The tower has been bisected to show the layers of foundation. Dortmund's 12th-century **Marienkirche,** also in the city center, has an artistically brilliant altar and an enthroned figure of Christ (open Tu-F 10am-noon and 2-4pm, Sa 10am-5pm). The **Dortmunder Tierpark** houses over 2500 animals, including a special South Ameri-can exhibit in the three-tiered (err, many-*Tier*ed) Amazon House. (Open daily 9am-5pm. DM8, children DM4.) Take U-Bahn #49 to "Hacheney."

Dortmund is on the eastern edge of the tangle of cities in the Ruhr River area. The S-Bahn (#1 and 21) connects it to Essen and Düsseldorf. **ADFC,** Hausmannstr. 22 (tel. 13 66 85), **rents bikes** for DM9 per day (open W-M 10am-6pm). The **tourist office,** Königswall 20 (tel. 502 56 66, room booking 14 03 41; fax 16 35 93), across from the station, will book rooms (DM55 and up) for a DM3 fee (open M-F 9am-6pm, Sa 9am-1pm, Su 10am-noon). The **post office,** 44137 Dortmund (tel. 98 40), is located out-side the north entrance of the *Hauptbahnhof* (open M-F 8am-6pm, Sa 8am-1pm, Su 10am-11am). The **telephone code** is 0231.

Hotel prices in Dortmund are high (singles from DM50), and there is no hostel or campground, but hostelers can easily jump the train to nearby Essen (see p. 349). Close to the station, **Hotel-Garni Carlton,** Lütge Brückstr. 5-7 (tel. 52 50 30; fax 52 50 20), has big, comfy rooms. Head left on Königswall as you exit the station, take a right on Gnadenort and then another right on Lütge Brückstr. (Singles DM50, with bath DM70; doubles DM90, with bath DM110. Breakfast included. Reception M-F 7am-4am, Sa 7am-2pm and 6:30pm-4am, Su 6:30pm-4am.) After satisfying your curiosity about beer mechanics at the Brauerei Museum, go for some interactive experience at **Hövels Hausbrauerei** (tel. 914 54 70), whose light brew is a town favorite (open daily 11am-1am; kitchen open 11am-12:30am). **Alex,** Am Ringoldikirche, serves up delicious sandwiches (from DM6.50) in a colorful, rad atmosphere that will make you feel like a character in a Dr. Seuss book (open daily 8am-1am).

■ Wuppertal

The **Schwebebahn,** a renowned suspension rail that was likened to a "flying milli-pede" when its tracks were laid in 1929, was the glue that cemented together the mill towns that now form Wuppertal, and it remains its number-one tourist attraction today. Enthusiasm for the miraculous contraption boiled over when Tuffi, a circus elephant on a promotional tour, shocked (and later delighted) everyone by jumping out of his train into the river. The *Schwebebahn* makes the full run several times daily, and on Sundays you can do it in style with coffee and *Kuchen* in the **Kaiser-wagen,** a turn-of-the-century car once occupied by Kaiser Wilhelm I himself.

A statue of stone proletarians sits in front of the slate **Engels-Haus,** Engelsstr. 10, where Marx's co-author and pamphleteer Friedrich Engels grew up. Works of this most famous Commie sidekick saturate the house, while multilingual devotions fill the guest book. The **Museum für Frühindustrialisierung** (early industrialization), in an old textile mill to the rear of the house, explains some of Fred's political ire, docu-menting inhumane working conditions. (Open Tu-Su 10am-1pm and 3-5pm. Admis-sion DM3. Ring the doorbell to enter.) Guides operate the old machinery, explaining every whirr. The **Historisches Zentrum** (tel. 563 64 98), a house and a mill, is easily accessible from the Schwebebahn "Adlerbrücke" stop, the Wuppertal-Barmen train station (go down Flügelstr. and right past the Opera), or bus #610. **Friedrichstraße,** lined with bars, pubs, and cafes, ends at the copper tower of the Elberfeld *Rathaus* and a huge, flamboyant fountain of Neptune. Follow the sea-king's imperious gaze through Kirstenpl. as it curves to Poststr. 11, where a *Glockenspiel* chimes (M-Sa at 10am, noon, 4, and 6pm, Su at noon, 4, and 6pm). In the heart of the pedestrian zone, the **Von der Heydt-Museum,** Turmhof 8 (tel. 563 22 23), houses an exciting array of works by artists from the Dutch masters to the French Impressionists (including Degas) and moderns (Dalí, Kokoschka, and Picasso, among others; open Tu-W, F-Su 10am-5pm, Th 10am-9pm; DM6, students and children DM4.)

You can get a hotel reservation (from DM35) from the folks at the **tourist office,** in the Döppersberg Pavillon (tel. 563 21 80; fax 563 80 52), at the foot of the *"Haupt-bahnhof Schwebebahn"* stop. Take the tunnel from the station to the pedestrian zone, and turn right upon exiting (open M-F 9am-6pm, Sa 9am-1pm). Wuppertal's **Jugendherberge (HI),** Obere Lichtenplatzerstr. 70 (tel. 55 23 72; fax 55 73 54), is in a park in Barmen, south of the city center. From the Barmen station, take bus #640 to "Jugendherberge," or walk right on Winklerstr., turn right on Fischertal, walk up the hill, and make a right on Amalienstr. Turn left on the path opposite Fischerstr.—the hostel is up the dirt path on the right. The six-bed rooms have sinks and new wood furnishings. (DM22.50, over 26 DM27.50. Members only. Breakfast included. Sheets DM6. Reception until 10pm. Curfew 11:30pm.) Take the *Schwebebahn* or any num-ber of buses to transportation hub *Altermarkt* to reach **Café Moritz,** Am Altermarkt (tel. 57 33 49). Popular among students, this cafe offers large bowls of pasta (from DM8), vegetarian specials, a gargantuan drink menu, and **Internet access** (DM3.50 per 30min.) in a mellow blue atmosphere. Gather mass quantities at **Akzenta,** the region's largest grocery store. Veer off Friedrichstr. at the sign. (Open M-W 9am-6:30pm, Th 9am-8:30pm, F 8am-8:30pm, Sa 8am-2pm.) The **telephone code** is 0202.

NORDRHEIN-WESTFALEN

■ Solingen

Cutlery from Solingen has been a tradition for six centuries, prized throughout the world for quality of the highest caliber. Surviving even the harsh Treaty of Versailles, which barred the production of bladed weapons, the Solingen tradition persists to this day—look for the city's name or the ubiquitous "Zwilling" emblem (two stock figures walking like Egyptians) on a pair of scissors near you. In recent times, the people of Solingen have emphasized the good deeds of businessman **Hermann Friedrich Grähe,** the Solinger "Schindler," whose actions saved many Jews from Auschwitz.

The **Kotten at Balkhausen** (tel. 452 36), just outside of Solingen, has been preserved as a monument to early knife-grinders. (Open Tu-Su 10am-5pm, or by appointment. Workshop and Grinder's Museum open Sa-Su 10am-5pm.) From the Solingen station, take bus #681 to "Hästen," then go left on Balkhauser Weg (400m). Learn how to grind (but not bump) for free. The **Klingenmuseum,** Klosterhof 4 (tel. 258 36 10), exhibits very big and bad cutlery, including baguette-sized pocketknives and exotic African swords. (Open Tu-Th, Sa-Su 10am-5pm, F 2-5pm. DM5, students and children DM2.50.) Take bus #683 to "Täppken," then follow the signs. Look for the 20 ft. pair of silver scissors rooted in the courtyard.

The **tourist office,** in the *Rathaus* on Cronenbergerstr., Room 24 (tel. 290 23 33; fax 290 24 79), happily delivers information on the town and the surrounding area including **Burg an der Wupper,** which has no tourist office (open M-Tu and Th 7:30am-5pm, W 7:30am-4pm, F 7:30am-1pm). The **Jugendherberge Solingen-Gräfrath,** Flockertsholzerweg 10 (tel. 59 11 98; fax 59 41 79), labels its rooms with cute pictures of animals. Take bus #695 (direction: "Abteiweg") to "Eugen-Maurer-Heim," then walk uphill, and turn right onto Flockertholzerweg. Inside, the 2-, 4-, 6-, and 8-bed rooms are extremely clean. (DM21.60, over 26 DM26.60. Sheets DM6. Reception until 10pm. Curfew midnight.) For accommodations closer to the scenic Burg an der Wupper, consider the **Hotel-Landhaus Arnz,** Burger Landstr. (mmm…burgerland) 249 (tel. 440 00; fax 479 14). Take bus #683 (direction: "Burg" to "Jagenberg" and get off right at the door. (Singles DM45, with bath DM65; doubles DM80, with bath DM110. Reception Su-Th 5-10pm.) An impressive array of cheap cafes and grocery stores line **Konrad-Adenauer-Straße** between Kronprinzstr. and Kölnerstr. The **telephone code** is 0212.

■ Burg an der Wupper

In a setting straight out of a Grimms' fairy tale, the Burg an der Wupper perches majestically 110m above the softly flowing waters of the Wupper. The castle, erected in the 12th century by **Count Englebert II of Berg,** Archbishop of Köln, is surrounded by a lush forest in a valley untouched by time. The little town below touts *Fachwerk* houses with blossoming *Blümchen* billowing out of the windows. Wander the cobblestone streets along the river and pick a little bakery to sample the local *Brezeln.* To reach the **castle,** walk up the gently sloping paths through the forest or ride the **Seilbahn Burg** to experience the bizarre feeling of riding a chair lift without skis. (Open daily 10am-6pm. One-way DM3, children DM1.50; round-trip DM4.50, children DM2.50.) From Solingen, take bus #683 to "Burg Brücke" and then cross the street and follow Schloßbergstr. up the mountain. As you approach the peak, the ivy-covered *Schloß* turrets will appear. Look back for a full view of the lush Wupper Valley. The castle is now a museum detailing many aspects of castle life from the cool defensive arrow slits in the battlements to the medieval privies. (Open Tu-Su 10am-6pm, M 1-6pm; Nov.-Feb. Tu-Su 11am-5pm. DM6, students DM4.50.)

Burg an der Wupper does not have a tourist office, but the office in **Solingen** provides plenty of info on the area. To get to Burg an der Wupper from Solingen, take bus #681 to "Graf Wilhelm Platz" and transfer to #683 to "Burg." Transportation can be tricky on weekends and holidays. There's a hostel here: **Jugendherberge Burg an der Wupper,** An der Jugendherberge 11 (tel. 410 25; fax 494 49). Take bus #266 from behind the castle to "Jugendherberge," or trudge up the hill, turn left on Jorgensfeld, left again onto Graf-Adolf-Str., and follow the street as it curves (10min. from the castle). You'll find standard rooms with two beds and a sink. (DM21.60, over 26 DM26.60. Sheets DM6. Reception 2-6pm. Curfew 10pm). Eat like a king at **Café-Restaurant Burghof,** Wermelskirchenstr. (tel. 410 24), behind the castle. As you sit on a tapestry chair inside the 17th-century house, gaze on the rolling hills and indulge in a waffle made from a secret *Burg* recipe (DM4; open Tu-Su 8:30am-7pm).

Detmold

Worlds away from the industry of the Ruhrgebiet crouches **Detmold,** the premier city of the Teutoburger Wald. Towering over the dense forest, the striking **Hermannsdenkmal** commemorates the Teutonic chief Hermann, proclaiming him liberator of the German people. (Open Mar.-Oct. daily 9am-6:30pm; Nov.-Feb. 9:30am-4pm; DM2.50, children DM1.) Over-eager nationalists erected Hermann's monolithic likeness on an old encampment in 1875, and Kaiser Wilhelm I came to cut the ribbon. Complete with winged helmet, the statue wields a 7m sword with the disconcerting inscription, "German unity is my power, my power is Germany's might." The memorial also serves as a source of Germanic historical confusion: research continually re-locates the battle to other hills. The only consensus reached is that the colossus does *not* mark the spot of the battle. The hike is beautiful but rather steep for the inexperienced (or lazy) hiker. Bus #792, which leaves from the train station, makes the ascent easier. (Apr.-Oct. M-F 8:10, 9:10am, 3:10pm, Sa 9:10am and 3:10pm; Su and holidays 10:30am and 2:30pm.)

No less impressive and far more exhilarating is the **Adlerwarte** (Eagle's Watch; tel. 471 71), featuring over 80 birds of prey. Time your arrival with bus #701 from Detmold (direction: "Weidmüller") to "Adlerwarte" to catch a free flight exhibition. The falcons strafe the crowd, passing inches above startled faces and causing children and adults alike to shriek. (Park open mid-Mar. to Oct. 9:30am-5:30pm; displays at 11am, 3, and 4:30pm; Nov. to mid-Mar. park open 10am-4pm; displays at 11am and 2:30pm. DM7, kids DM3.50.) You can save money with the tourist office's new combination ticket: **Der Fliegende Hermann.** The ticket gets you into the Hermannsdenkmal, Adlerwarte, and the **Vogel- und Blumenpark** (Bird and Flower park; tel. 474 39; open Apr.-Nov. daily 9am-6pm.) On weekends, the ticket also lets you ride the shuttle connecting these three sights for free (ticket DM11, children DM4.50).

Detmold's **Westfälisches Freilichtmuseum,** (tel. 706 105) is less touristy, more original, and just plain cooler. (Open Apr.-Oct. Tu-Su 9am-6pm. DM7, kids DM3.) This outdoor museum, spread over 80 hectare, consists of over 100 houses, barns, windmills, and furry animal friends that tell the story of a rural German community. A horse-drawn carriage will take you from the entrance to the far end of the museum, where the central village is located (DM3, kids DM2). Take bus #701 (direction: Weidmüller) to "Freilichtmuseum." In the *Altstadt,* cannons still arm the courtyard of the **Fürstliches Residenzschloß** (tel. 700 20), a Renaissance castle in the town's central park. (Hourly tours Apr.-Oct. daily on the hr. 10am-5pm; Nov.-Mar. tours available on request. Written English translations available. DM6, children DM3.)

Detmold's unbeatable location makes it an ideal base for exploring the Teutoburger Wald. To make the best use of the outstanding **bus** connections, swing by the **SVD** office, Langestr. 70 (tel. 97 77 44), at the "Rosental" bus stop, and pick up a schedule for each bus line (open M-F 9am-6pm, Sa 9am-1pm). From the tourist office, walk north on Langestr. and then onto Richthofenstr. 14, where **Fahrradbüro Detmold** (tel. 97 74 01; fax 30 02 01) rents out old **bikes.** (DM6 per day, DM30 per week. Passport or ID and DM50 deposit required. Open Apr.-Oct. Tu and Th 5-7pm, Sa 10am-1pm.) It might be a good idea to pick up a bike in neighboring Lemgo or Horn and bring it here on the bus. For in-depth info on biking, pick up the "Lipperland" map (DM14.80) at the **tourist office,** Rathaus am Markt (tel. 97 73 28; fax 97 74 47), which is stocked with everything you need. (Open M-Th 9am-noon and 1-5pm, F 9am-4pm, Sa 10am-noon; Nov.-Mar. M-Th 9am-noon and 1-5pm, F 9am-noon.) From the station, head left on Bahnhofstr., turn right on Paulinenstr., then left on Bruchstr.

into the pedestrian zone; walk another five minutes to the *Rathaus*. The tourist office is on the right side of the building. The city brochure is excellent, with a map thorough enough for hikes to the *Denkmal* and the surrounding area (DM1). Rooms in town start at DM35, but the tourist office doesn't make reservations. **City tours** of the *Altstadt* take off from the main entrance of the Residenzschloß (Apr.-Oct. Sa at 10am, Su at 11am; DM4, students DM2). The **telephone code** is 05231.

In addition to the regular pack of wild school children, the **Jugendherberge "Schanze" (HI)**, Schirrmannstr. 49 (tel. 247 39; fax 289 27), features its own mule in a bucolic setting with standard rooms. From *Bussteig* 3 at the train station, take bus #704 (direction: "Hiddesen") to "Auf den Klippen," and walk 10 minutes down the trail. By foot from the station, make a right onto Paulinenstr., and then a right onto Freiligrathstr. (which becomes Bandelstr.), and then a left on Bülowstr., followed by a right onto Schützenberg. (45min. DM22.20, over 26 DM27.20. Breakfast included. Lunch DM7.40. Dinner DM6.40. Reception until 10pm. Curfew 10pm, but guests are provided with keys.) Enjoy delicious crepes (DM3-6), baked potatoes (DM2-7), and salads (DM5) at **Knollchen**, Lange Str. 21 (tel. 283 99), just up the street from the *Rathaus* (open M-F 11am-7pm, Sa 10am-4pm). A **Kaiser's supermarket,** Bruchstr. 18-20, provides raw materials (open M-F 8am-7pm, Sa 8am-2pm).

■ Near Detmold: Lemgo

From the Detmold *Hauptbahnhof,* hike, bike, or take bus #790 or 791 (DM4.90) along the 12km trail to Lemgo, where the Weser Renaissance lives again. Those wondering what a Weser Renaissance is and why it should occur here could do no better than to visit the aptly-named **Weserrenaissance Museum,** Schloßstr. 18 (tel. 945 00), right inside **Schloß Brake.** (Open Tu-Su 10am-6pm. DM4, children DM2, under 6 free.) As you enter the pedestrian zone, make a right onto Mittelstr., which turns into Bismarckstr.; when the road forks, bear right onto Pagenhelle, and Schloßstr. will be on your left (20 min.); or take bus #790 to "Schloß Brake." The current castle was built under Graf Simon VI zur Lippe from 1584 to 1592; his chambers and other period rooms are on display in the seven-story castle tower. If you're more interested in burning people alive, head down to the **Hexenbürgermeisterhaus Lemgo,** Breitestr. 19 (tel. 21 32 76), a collection of historical odds and ends focusing on the **witch-trial** era. Watch it, Goody. (Open Tu-Su 10am-12:30pm and 1:30-5pm. DM1.50, children DM1.) Nearby, the 800-year-old **St. Nicolai Kirche** dominates the Marktplatz with twin towers. Check out the cross over the bronze doorknob—it's made from wood from the wreckage of England's Coventry Cathedral.

Contact the **tourist office,** at Papenstr. 7 (tel. 21 33 47; fax 21 34 92), for room-finding assistance (from DM35 per person). (Open Mar.-Oct. M-F 10am-5pm, Sa 10am-1pm; Nov.-Feb. M-Th 10am-5pm, F 10am-2pm.) City tours leave every Saturday at 11am (Apr.-Oct.) from the main portal of the *Nicolaikirche* (DM4, children DM2). From the *Bahnhof,* make a right onto Paulinenstr., and then a right onto Papenstr. Continue straight on Breite Str. until Mittelstr., the main street in the pedestrian zone. Accommodations can be found (as long as you bring them yourself) at the **Campingplatz,** Regenstorstr. 10b (tel. 148 58; fax 18 83 24). From Breitestr., turn right onto Orpingstr.; when Orpingstr. becomes Regenstorstr., the camp is on the left 100m ahead. (DM7 per person, DM3 per child; DM3-9 per tent.) Enjoy sizable portions of pizza, pasta, and salad (DM7-12), or a simple cup of coffee (DM2) at **Café Meffert,** Mittelstr. 128 (tel. 18 87 16). (Open M-F 7am-6pm, Sa 8am-1pm; pizza delivery M-Sa 6-10pm, Su 5-10pm.) The **postal code** is 32657. The **telephone code** is 05261.

▒ Münster

Perhaps even more than other tranquil, medium-sized German cities, Münster maintains a level of repose and dignity that reflects its history as a place of peaceful reconciliation. As the capital of the old Kingdom of Westphalia, Münster presided over the 1648 Peace that brought the Thirty Years War to an end, defining the borders of scores of German mini-states for centuries and casting the city as a place for peaceful resolution. But the Münster of today offers much more than conscientious objection and historic checkpoints: the 55,000 students of the **Wilhelmsuniversität** know how to put those 9th-century reveling monks to shame. Still, the monks do their damnedest to keep the students in line, with the sporadically enforced 1am curfew providing a powerful reminder of the ecclesiastic legacy.

ORIENTATION AND PRACTICAL INFORMATION

Münster is located at the confluence of the lower channels of the Ems River, in the midst of the Münsterland plain. Frequent trains stop in Münster, running from Düsseldorf (1½hr.) and Köln (2¼hr.) to the southwest, and from Bremen to the northeast.

Flights: Flughafen Münster-Osnabrück, located to the northeast of the city, has flights daily to Berlin, Frankfurt, Munich, and Zurich, Su-F to London, and M-F to Paris and Amsterdam. Bus #S50 shuttles between the train station and the airport (board to the right of the station); the schedule is posted in the station. For **flight information,** call (02571) 940.

Car Rental: Hertz, Hammerstr. 186 (tel. 773 78). ID required. Open M-F 7:30am-7pm, Sa 7:30am-2pm, Su 9:30-11:30am.

Bike Rental: Münster's train station has an impressive bike rental service (tel. 69 13 20), with 300 bikes up for grabs. DM11, DM7 for DB customers. You can reserve your wheels by phone. Open daily 7:30am-9:30pm.

Boat Rental: Soverschmidt Yachtschule Aasee (tel. 803 03) rents sailboats (DM15) as well as rowboats and paddleboats (DM13) and offers lessons. Bus #4 to "Goldene Brücke." Open daily 9am-6pm.

Mitfahrzentrale: des AStA, Schloßpl. 1 (tel. 405 05). Open M-F 8:30am-4pm.

Tourist Office: Klemensstr. 10 (tel. 492 27 10; fax 492 77 43). Just off the Marktplatz. From the station, cross Bahnhofstr. and head left, taking a sharp right onto Windthorststr., and veer right onto Stubengasse; the office is on your left as Stubengasse crosses Klemenstr. and becomes H.-Bruning-Str. Staff books rooms (from DM50 per person) for free, and offers tours and theater tickets. Open M-F 9am-6pm, Sa 9am-1pm.

Laundromat: Wasch Center, Moltekestr. 5-7. Wash DM7. Dry DM1 per 15min. Open M-F 6am-11pm. Another branch at Wolbeckerstr. 81 has the same prices and hours. Bus #11, 320, 330, 311, or 313 to "Sophienstr." Or take the rear exit of the train station, turn left on Bremerstr., and right onto Wolbeckerstr. (15min.)

Emergency: Police, tel. 110. **Fire** and **Ambulance,** tel. 112.

Post Office: Berliner Str. 37, 48001 Münster. Located directly to the left of the train station. Open M-F 8am-6pm, Sa 8am-5pm.

Telephone Code: 0251.

ACCOMMODATIONS AND CAMPING

Münster's accommodations are less than adequate. The shiny *Jugendgästehaus* is no steal, and hotels fill up quickly, so be sure to call days ahead. In a pinch, there's a hostel in **Nottuln,** a 50-minute bus ride away (tel. (02502) 78 78; fax 96 19). Take bus #560 or 561 to "Rodepl.," then follow the signs. (DM22, over 26 DM27. Breakfast included. Sheets DM6. Reception until 10pm.) Some travelers have been known to simply hit up local students for a place to sleep.

Jugendgästehaus Aasee, Bismarckallee 31 (tel. 53 24 70; fax 52 12 71). Bus #10 or 34 to "Hoppendamm." An Orwellian vision of our hosteling future: huge brick and mirror-glass compound with security cameras. Toilet and bath in each room and flowers galore in the lobby. 4-bed room DM39 per person; 2-bed room DM48. Breakfast buffet and sheets included. Reception 7am-1am. Lockout 1am.

Haus vom Guten Hirten, Mauritz-Lindenweg 61 (tel. 378 70; fax 37 45 44). Bus #14 to "Mauritz Friedhof." Or, take a long (40min.) walk—from the rear entrance of the train station, turn left on Bremer Str., right on Wolbeckerstr., left onto Hohenzollern-Ring, right on Manfred-von-Richthofen-Str., and finally left on Maurits-Lindenweg. Run by the church, this hotel offers huge, comfy suites that debunk the myth that monks and nuns mustn't indulge. But you'll feel naughty anyway. Singles DM55; doubles DM94; triples DM129. Breakfast included. Reception 6am-9pm.

Hotel Bockhorn, Bremer Str. 24 (tel. 655 10), a 5min. walk from the train. From the rear exit of the train station, walk right on Bremer Str. 400m. Tidy, no-frills rooms are convenient to the *Altstadt* and to the train. Singles DM55; doubles DM110. Full-service breakfast included. 24hr. reception.

Hotel An'n Schlagbaum, Woselerstr. 269 (tel. 79 21 80). Bus #7, 15, or 16 to "Kappenburger Damm." 11 affordable rooms. Singles DM50-60. Breakfast included.

Camping: Campingplatz Münster, auf der Laer 7 (tel. 31 19 82). Bus #320 to "Wersewinkel." DM4 per person; DM4 per tent. Showers DM0.50. Reception 8am-1pm and 3-6pm.

FOOD

On Wednesdays and Saturdays, a farmer's **market** takes over the plaza in front of the *Dom,* vending fresh fruit, fresh meat, and not-so-"fresh" clothes (open daily 7am-2pm). The student district, **Kuhviertel** (literally, "cow quarter"—gives you an idea of how much Münster loves its students), is lined with *Kneipen* and fairly inexpensive eateries. A **grocery store** sits on Bahnhofstr. 15 (open M-Sa 8am-8pm, Su 8am-4pm).

⊛**Diesel,** Harsewinkelgasse 1-4 (tel. 57 96), in the *Altstadt,* at the intersection of Windhorsterstr., Stubengasse, and Loerstr. Fuel pumps, Keith Haring artwork, a red neon shrine filled with plastic flowers, and funky bossa nova music combine to create a smart, *chic* student hangout. Daily specials DM6-12. Pool, darts, and an extensive magazine collection. Breakfast served daily 10am-4pm, dinner 7-11pm. Bar open 11am-1am, F-Sa 11am-3am.

Cavete Akademische Bieranstalt, Kreuzstr. 38 (tel. 457 00). Founded by students for students in 1959, this first student pub in Westphalia serves dark, carnivalesque decor and delicious homemade spinach noodles (DM8-10). Open daily 7pm-1am; kitchen closes M-Th and Su 11pm, F-Sa midnight.

Pfefferkorn, Am Prinzipalmarkt, offers delicious tapas and baked potatoes (from DM7.50) in a prime people-watching locale on the main market. Open M-Sa 10am-11pm, Su noon-11pm.

John Doe's Diner, Spiekerhoff 44 (tel. 51 84 06). This nostalgic, kitschy diner looks like a hyper-real Hopper painting. Burgers, buffalo wings, and exotic, imported American beer. Open M-F 5:30pm-1am, Sa 10:30am-1am, Su 10:30am-midnight.

SIGHTS

When Goethe's carriage turned onto the tree-lined **Promenade** encircling the Münster *Altstadt,* he would slow it and smell the flowers. The Promenade is idyllic all the way around, but the **Botanical Gardens,** on the campus of the **Wilhelmsuniversität,** are especially inspiring. *(Open Mar.-Oct. daily 8am-7pm; Nov.-Feb. 8am-4pm.)*

The heartbeat of Münster's religious life echoes through the huge **St. Paulus-Dom** on Dompl. in the center of the *Altstadt. (Open M-Sa 6am-6pm, Su 6:30am-7:30pm.)* Though bombed in WWII, this cathedral has been beautifully restored. The peaceful Bishop's inner courtyard is open to the public. *(Open Tu-Sa 10am-noon and 2-6pm, Su 2-6pm.)* A stone from the similarly bombed Cathedral of Coventry stands in the entrance-way, carrying a wish for mutual forgiveness between Britain and Germany. From his pulpit in the cathedral, Bishop Clemens von Galen delivered a courageous sermon against the Nazi program of **euthanasia** for so-called "incurables." After wide distribution of the sermon, pressure from the church prompted a rare partial retreat by Hitler. The speech can be read in the **Domkammer.** *(Open Tu-Sa 10am-noon and 2-6pm, Su 2-6pm. DM1.)* Inside, a statue of St. Christopher points its massive toes to the 16th-century **astronomical clock,** which recreates the movements of the planets and plays a merry *Glockenspiel* tune. *(M-Sa noon, Su 12:30pm.)*

Münster's ever-present religious grandiloquence takes a turn to the macabre at the **Marktkirche St. Lamberti,** off the Prinzipalemarkt, where three cages hang above the clockface. In the 16th century, rebel Anabaptists took over the town, led by the self-styled Prophet Jan van Leiden. He had 16 wives, and killed all who refused to surrender their property to his "New Zion" in Münster. After a bloodbath of episcopal reconquest, van Leiden and his two cohorts were executed, their bodies then hung in cages on the steeple. The authorities finally cleaned the cages out but left them hanging as a "reminder." Also suspended here is Germany's only free-hanging organ. Free concerts are given the first Saturday of every month at noon. Next door to the church is the **Friedenssaal** (Hall of Peace), which kept one unknown woodcarver very busy for a very long time. *(Open M-F 9am-5pm, Sa 9am-4pm, Su 10am-1pm. DM1.50, children and students DM0.80.)* The treaty that ended the Thirty Years War was sworn here. Among the many elaborate carvings are a mysterious withered human hand and the Golden Cock, a ceremonial carafe used to honor distinguished visitors. Pick up a guide in English from the front desk; call 83 25 80 for group rates.

MUSEUMS

Münster treasures its historical and cultural artifacts in a well-maintained **Landesmuseum**, but its real gems are the small collections that celebrate the random. Ask the tourist office for information about all of the city's offerings, including a **Railway Museum**, a **Carnival Museum**, and a **Museum of Organs** (unrelated to the Leprosy Museum) located in the suburbs.

Landesmuseum für Kunst und Kultur, Dompl. 10 (tel. 59 07 01). Contains modern sculptures and ancient paintings, arranged on 3 floors around a central atrium. Call ahead to find out about special exhibits. Open Tu-Su 10am-6pm. DM5, students and children DM2. Free on Fridays.

⊛Museum of Leprosy, Kinderhaus 15 (tel. 285 10), to the northwest of the *Altstadt*, is a little far away, but you should definitely drop by. The exhibits, including playful little leper-puppets, are strictly hands-off. Open Su 3-5pm. Free. Call for an appointment on other days.

Mühlenhof-Freilichtmuseum, Sentruperstr. 223 (tel. 820 74), is a completely restored industrial village with a bonus *Don Quixote*-style windmill, which sells pointy wooden shoes for DM20. Get cloggin'! Open Apr.-Oct. daily 10am-5pm; Nov.-Mar. 11am-4pm. DM5, students and seniors DM3, children DM2.

Museum für Lackkunst, Windthorstr. 26 (tel. 41 85 10), just off the Promenade. The world's only exhibition of all things lacquered. Videos and extensive descriptions tell you how to make your living room the shiniest on the block. Visiting modern exhibits in the basement. Open Tu noon-8pm, W-Su noon-6pm. DM3, students and children DM1.50. Free on Tuesdays.

NIGHTLIFE

Kneipen line the streets across from the *Schloß* in the student quarter, and discos abound farther southwest between the train station and the harbor. **Ultimo** provides bi-weekly print coverage of nightlife and art openings in Münster and the surrounding area (free at the AStA and Diesel; DM3 at newsstands).

Blechtrommel, Hansaring 26 (tel. 651 19), features live music and a menu that changes weekly. The name refers to the famous post-war Günter Grass novel, "The Tin Drum." Evade adulthood with *Fußball* tournaments on Monday and darts on Saturday. Pizza DM11-17.50. Open daily 6pm-1am. Kitchen open 7-11:30pm.

C.u.b.a., Achtermannstr. 10-12 (tel. 582 17). This culture center, disco, and *Kneipe* throws a massive Cuba-*fête* every 1st, 3rd, and 4th Saturday of the month. Open daily 6pm-1am, but a young, crazycool crowd doesn't come until 11pm.

The Pilgrims Irish Pub, Nienberger Kirchpl. 2-4 (tel. 41 24). Pilgrims flock here to pay homage to the god of Guinness and then pray to the porcelain Providence. Live blues and jazz, darts, and billiards. Open daily 6pm-1am.

Gaststätte Pinkus Müller, Kreuzstr. 7 (tel. 451 51). About as hip as an elbow, but one of Germany's most acute joys is drinking beer in the house where it's brewed; the *Pinkus Alt* (DM5) here is a fine beer with a fine name. Peruse the genealogy of

the Müllers, including Doug and Carl "Pinkus" Müller himself, as you steel yourself for the *Szene*. Open M-F 11:30am-2pm and 5pm-midnight, Sa 11:30am-midnight.
Le Différent, Hörsterstr. 10 (tel. 51 12 39), is the center of Münster's gay nightlife. Techno and charts on 2 dance floors. Open F-Sa 10pm-5am.

LOWER RHINE

■ Kleve (Cleves)

The town of **Cleves** is famed for its daughter, **Anne of Cleves,** the local princess whom Henry VIII *didn't* make the happiest woman in the world. Henry's third wife had just died, so he sent Hans Holbein out to bring back paintings of eligible princesses. Henry chose Anne, but when she arrived in England, he decided he'd been misled. Henry insulted her looks until she left and banished Holbein from court.

The 11th-century **Schwanenburg** (Swan's Castle) bears testimony to another of the town's unhappy endings. (Open Apr.-Oct. daily 11am-5pm; Nov.-Mar. Sa-Su 11am-5pm. DM2, students DM1, children DM0.50.) The founders of the castle traced their lineage to the Knight of the Swan. The Knight successfully wooed local Princess Elsa and promised to marry her on the condition that she never ask his name. Curiosity got the better of Elsa, though, and a large swan dragged the knight away from her. The story is immortalized in Wagner's opera *Lohengrin* and in the poignant and strangely unromantic bronze fountain in the center of town. Kleve's recently opened **Museum Kurhaus,** Tiergartenstr. 41 (tel. 750 10), offers a fascinating collection of modern art, including a special exhibit of the Rhineland's modernist *Ewald Mataré* movement. (Open Apr.-Sept. Tu-F 10am-6pm; Oct.-Mar. Tu-F 10am-5pm. DM6, students and seniors DM3, under 14 free.) To get there from the castle, turn right on Großestr. then left on Minoritenstr., which turns into Tiergartenstr. Close to the hostel, the **Reichswald nature preserve** is ideal for hiking or chilling.

Kleve is accessible by **train** from Düsseldorf (1hr. 15min.) and Krefeld (50min.). The nearby town of Emmerisch makes the Dutch connection for Kleve with hourly trains to Amsterdam (2hr.) and more frequent trains to Arnheim, whose great museums make it an attractive day-trip. Bus #56 from the Kleve Station goes to Emmerisch once an hour. The **Sport & Reise Animation** (tel. 201 10) rents **bikes** with reservations only (DM10 per day, DM12.50 on weekends). The **tourist office,** on Kavarinerstr. in room 217 of the *Rathaus* (tel. 842 67; fax 237 59), gives out city maps, gossip about Anne and Henry, and a list of rooms (DM30 and up) in the city (open M and W-Sa 8:30am-12:45pm and 2-5pm, Tu and Th 8:30am-12:45pm and 2-3:30pm, F 8:30am-12:45pm). The **Jugendherberge Kleve (HI),** St. Annaberg 2 (tel. 236 71; fax 247 78), resides in the west end of town, next to the naughty Netherlands. From the station, take bus #57 (direction: Haus Ida) to "Annabergstr." and walk uphill. After 6:30pm, you've gotta hike it (30min.): follow Großestr. as it becomes Hagschestr. and eventually Hoffmannallee. Turn right on Römerstr. and follow it straight to the hostel. (DM24. Sheets DM6. Reception 4-4:45pm, 7:15-7:30pm, and 9:45-10pm. Curfew 10pm. Call ahead.) **Fellini's,** Große Str. 88 (tel. 233 85, fax 141 49) is *really* good at tasty, cheap food. Fresh, hot baguettes with gobs of filling start at DM6 (open daily 10am-midnight). The **telephone code** is 02821.

■ Xanten

If all of the cities of the lower Rhine Valley were to become people, Xanten would be the granddaddy of them all. Founded by Roman Emperor Augustus in 15 BC, Xanten's ancient settlement served as the mythical birthplace of Siegfried after the Romans skipped town in the fourth century. The city weathered the centuries until Canadians decided that "X" marked the spot and flattened the city in World War II. Despite the raid, the Roman ground plan remains intact at the creatively named **Archäologischer Park** (tel. 29 99), which offers visitors a rare glimpse of the living past; the enormous structures demonstrate the skill of the Roman architects and the park's big budget. (Open Mar.-Nov. daily 9am-6pm; Dec.-Feb. daily 10am-4pm. DM7, students DM4, children DM2.50.) Every summer, the park hosts live concerts and musicals (but no gladiator fights) in grand Roman style. The tourist office can provide details.

During the Middle Ages, Xanten flourished as a satellite of Köln. To build the fortifications, the townspeople cleverly carted the walls of the Roman ruins down the street. Medieval times are still alive at the **Klever Tor** in the southwest corner of town, and at the **Markt.** Towering above is the 12th-century **Dom St. Viktor** (tel. 71 31 34), whose two Romanesque towers and vast Gothic cathedral were built on the grave site of an early Christian martyr (open M-Sa 10am-6pm, Su 12:30-6pm; closed Jan.-Feb. noon-2pm). Next door, the **Regionalmuseum,** Kurfürstenstr. 7-9 (tel. 77 22 98), exhibits artifacts recovered from the archaeological dig, including wild Roman helmets. (Open May-Sept. Tu-F 9am-5pm, Sa-Su 11am-6pm; Oct.-Apr. Tu-F 10am-5pm, Sa-Su 11am-6pm. DM3, students and children DM1.50.)

Xanten is a 50-minute bus ride from Kleve (every hour, DM5.50). From the bus stop at the train station, walk up Bahnhofstr. to the *Markt.* **Rent bikes** from **Reineke,** Marsstr. 19 (tel. 14 74), just off the *Markt,* for DM12 per day or DM8 after 3pm. The **tourist office,** at the far end of the square (tel. 372 38; http://www.nissy.com/xanten), is in the *Rathaus.* There is no hostel, but the friendly staff at the tourist office books hotel rooms (from DM60) with a 12% deposit (open M-Sa 10am-4:30pm, Sa-Su 10am-4pm). If the office is closed, have fun with the computer outside. **Dom Stübchen,** Kleverstr. 14 (tel. 907 88), serves cheap gyros and pizzas (DM6-8.50; open daily noon-10pm). The **telephone code** is 02801.

NORDRHEIN-WESTFALEN

Hessen (Hesse)

Prior to the 20th century, Hesse was known for exporting mercenary soldiers to rulers such as King George III, who sent them off to put down an unruly gang of colonial hicks on the other side of the Atlantic in 1776. Absorbed by Bismarck's Prussia in 1866, Hesse ceased to exist as a political entity until the Allies resurrected it in 1945. Somewhere along the line, the Hessians made an ostensible collective decision to exchange their guns for briefcases. Today, Hesse is the busiest commercial center in the country, led by the banking metropolis of Frankfurt. Overshadowed by Frankfurt, the rest of Hesse attracts little attention from tourists, leaving the medieval delights of Marburg's *Uni*-culture and the fascination of Kassel blessedly off the beaten path.

🐌 HIGHLIGHTS OF HESSEN

- With its historical **Römerberg,** happenin' nightlife scene, and museums galore, **Frankfurt** is a truly multicultural city, respectable for much more than its central high-traffic airport and train station (see p. 360).
- The **Lahn Valley** abounds with hiking, cycling, and water activities (see p. 373). **Weilburg's** 14th-century *Schloß* and **crystal caves** are not to be missed (see p. 374), while **Wetzlar** is a mecca for die-hard Goethe fans (see p. 375).
- The university town of **Marburg** influenced the writings of the **Brothers Grimm** and has provided bountiful beer-drinking opportunities for tourists and Nobel-prize winning scientists alike (see p. 375).
- The fairy-tale castles and waterfalls of **Wilhelmshöhe Park** and the cutting-edge **documenta** modern art exhibitions successfully merge in the curiously cosmopolitan city of **Kassel** (see p. 381).

▓ Frankfurt am Main

Skyscrapers loom over crowded streets, investment bankers scurry to and fro—it's not hard to see how Frankfurt acquired the derisive nicknames "Bankfurt" and "Main-hattan." Many visitors view Frankfurt as the most Americanized city in Europe, a claim quickly verified by the flashy McDonald's on every street corner. It may be the big daddy of German crime, but compared to New York City, it's *Kindergarten.*

Frankfurt made its first appearance in the annals of history way back in 794, and since then hordes of Frankfurters have gone on to influence western culture. Anne Frank and Goethe lived here, families such as the Oppenheims and Rothschilds influenced Frankfurt's economic development, and Erich Fromm and Frankfurt School members Theodor Adorno, Max Horkheimer, and Walter Benjamin elaborated their theories of art and society.

Martin Luther once remarked that Frankfurt resembles a pot of silver and gold, and today the city government spends more on cultural attractions and tourism than any other German city. The *Kulturszene* is also rich—nearly one third of the Frankfurters you pass on the street are likely to speak Turkish or English as they munch on cuisine of an international flavor. Frankfurt manages to retain an aura of hipness, gravity, and agelessness all at once. If all this isn't enough to make you visit, the likelihood of arriving in Germany at Frankfurt's Rhein-Main Airport probably is.

ORIENTATION AND PRACTICAL INFORMATION

A sprawling conglomeration of steel, concrete, glass, and scaffolding, Germany's fifth-largest city bridges the **Main River** 35km east of its confluence with the Rhine. Frankfurt's airport and *Hauptbahnhof* are among the busiest in Europe. The train station lies at the end of Frankfurt's red-light district, which in typical Frankfurt fashion brings together sex bars, international airline offices, and banks. From the station, the town center is a 20-minute walk down Kaiserstr. or Münchenerstr., crossing from the

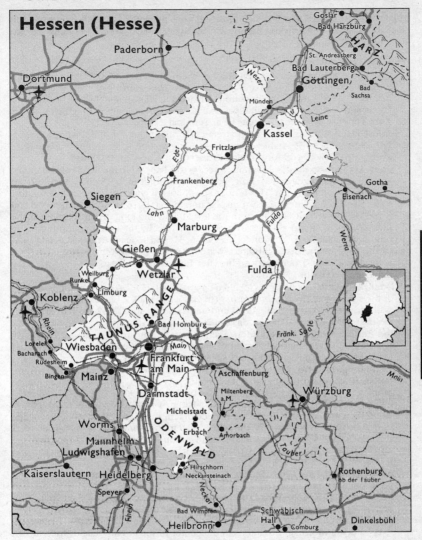

Hessen (Hesse)

newer part of the city to the *Altstadt*. Located just north of the Main, the *Altstadt* contains the historical **Römerberg**, the well-touristed domain of old German kitsch. Take U-Bahn #4 (direction: Seckbacher Landstr.) to "Römer." A few blocks north lies the commercial heart of the city, an expanse of department stores and ice cream vendors that stretches along Zeil from **Hauptwache** (S-Bahn #1-6 or 8, 2 stops from the Hauptbahnhof) to **Konstablerwache** (one stop farther). Students, student cafes, stores, and services cluster in **Bockenheim**, as does the very angry graffiti demanding *Aktion, Solidarität*, and *Freiheit*. Take U-Bahn #6 or 7 to "Bockenheimer Warte." Across the Main, **Sachsenhausen** draws the *Ebbelwei*-lovers, the pub-crawlers, and the museum-goers (U-Bahn #1, 2, or 3 to "Schweizerpl."). On a nice day, Sachsenhausen is a delightful walk directly across the bridge.

The **Frankfurt Card** (available at tourist offices and in most travel agencies; one day DM10, two days DM15) allows unlimited travel on all trains and buses, including the airport line; it also gets you 50% off admission to 15 museums, the *Palmengarten*, the zoo, and that veritable carnival funhouse, the airport visitors' terrace. Eurailpasses are valid on all S-Bahn trains.

Transportation

Flights: The Frankfurt airport, **Flughafen Rhein-Main** (tel. 69 01), is a major hub. From the airport, S-Bahn #5 and 8 travel to the *Hauptbahnhof* every 15min. Buy tickets (DM5.80) from a green automat marked *"Fahrkarten"* before boarding or face a stiff fee (DM20-80); Eurailpass valid. Most public transport vehicles depart from Terminal 1; a free tram runs from Terminal 2 to Terminal 1.

Trains: Trains from most of Europe frequently roll in and out of Frankfurt's *Hauptbahnhof*. Munich (3½-4½hr., every hour), Berlin (5-6hr., every hour), Paris (6-8hr., every 2hr.). Call 194 19 for schedules, reservations, and information.

Public Transportation: For unlimited access to S-Bahn, U-Bahn, Straßenbahn trams, and buses, the *Tageskarte* 24hr. pass (DM8, children DM5) is available from machines in every station. This is not to be confused with the 24 or 48hr. Frankfurt Card. Some hotels offer a 2-day transportation pass (DM10) as well. S-Bahn #1-6 and 8 and U-Bahn vehicles depart from the level below the long distance trains. At the *Hauptbahnhof*, trams #10, 11, 16, 19, and 21 pass by the island platform directly outside the main (west) entrance; buses #35, 37, and 46 leave from just outside and to the right of the main entrance. Watch out: the public transportation system shuts down around 1am every night. After 1am, walk or take a. . .

Taxi: Call 23 00 01 or 25 00 01.

Mitfahrzentrale: Baselerstr. 7 (tel. 23 64 44 or 23 61 27). Take a right on Baselerstr. at the side exit of the *Hauptbahnhof* (track 1), and walk 2 blocks. Connects riders with drivers for a fee. Call ahead and get to Berlin for DM32, or Barcelona for DM88. Open M-F 8am-6:30pm, Sa 8am-2pm.

Bike Rental: Holger's Rad-Laden, Eschersheimer Landstr. 470 (tel. 52 20 04). U-Bahn #1, 2, or 3 to "Lindenbaum." DM15 per day. Bikes are allowed on the subway. Open M-Tu and Th-F 9am-1pm and 3-6:30pm, Sa 9am-1pm.

Hitchhiking: *Let's Go* does not recommend hitchhiking as a safe mode of transportation. Hitching on the highway itself is strictly forbidden. Masochists heading to Munich from Konstablerwache south take buses #36 or 960 to the *Autobahn* interchange; to Cologne or Düsseldorf, take S-Bahn #1 or 8 to Wiesbaden *Hauptbahnhof,* then a local train to Auringen-Medenbach, turn right, walk 800m, proceed under the *Autobahn,* and take the access road to the *Autobahn* rest stop; all other directions, take S-Bahn #19 or bus #61 and continue along Mörfelder-Landstr.

Tourist and Financial Services

Tourist Office: In the *Hauptbahnhof,* on the right side of the Reception Hall as you go through the main exit (tel. 21 23 88 49). Maps, brochures, souvenirs, tours, and lots more. Books rooms for a DM5 fee (tel. 21 23 08 08). Open M-F 8am-9pm, Sa-Su and holidays 9am-6pm. **Another branch** borders Römerplatz at Römerberg 27 (tel. 21 23 87 08); no room reservations. Open M-F 9:30am-5:30pm, Sa-Su 10am-4pm. **City-Info,** an information stand, is in the center of the commercial district, at Zeil 94a. Open M-F 10am-6pm, Sa-Su 10am-4pm.

Consulates: Australia, Gutleutstr. 85 (tel. 273 90 90; fax 23 26 31). Open M-Th 8:30am-1pm and 2-5pm, F 8:30am-1pm and 2-4:15pm. **South Africa,** Ulmenstr. 37 (tel. 719 11 30). Open M-F 8am-noon. **U.K.,** Bockenheimer Landstr. 42 (tel. 170 00 20; fax 72 95 53). Open M-F 9am-noon and 2-4pm; phone hours M-Th 8:30am-1pm and 2-5pm, F 8:30am-1pm and 2-4:30pm. **U.S.,** Siesmayerstr. 21 (tel. 753 50; fax 74 89 38). Open to the public M-F 8-11am; phone hours M-F 8am-4pm.

Currency Exchange: In Airport Hall B (open daily 7:30am-9pm) or the *Hauptbahnhof* (open daily 6:30am-10pm). Better rates at the post office or any of the banks.

American Express: Kaiserstr. 8 (tel. 21 05 01 11, 24hr. hotline (0130) 85 31 00; fax 28 33 98). Holds mail for 4 weeks. Exchanges foreign money, handles traveler's checks, and arranges hotel reservations and car rentals. Services are free for cardholders or traveler's check customers. Open M-F 9:30am-6pm, Sa 9:30am-12:30pm.

Local Services

Bookstores: Süssman's Presse und Buch, Zeil 127 (tel. 131 07 51). Mostly English titles for those who need their Shakespeare or Clancy. Open M-W and F 9am-7pm,

Frankfurt am Main

ACCOMMODATIONS

B Jugendherberge
A Pension Brüns,
Pension Backer,
Pension Gölz

HESSEN

SACHSENHAUSEN

WESTEND

ROTHSCHILD PARK

ALTE OPER

OPERNPLATZ

THEATERPL.

TAUNUSANLAGE

Zoologischer Garten

ALFRED-BREHM-PL.

ZOO

OSTENDSTR.

KONSTABLER WACHE

KONSTABLERWACHE

ESCHENHEIMER TOR

HAUPTWACHE

Museum für Moderne Kunst

Katharinenkirche

Paulskirche

Dom

Schirn Kunsthalle

RÖMER

Römerberg

Nikolaikirche

Historisches Museum

Goethe Haus

American Express

Städtische Bühnen

Museum für Kunsthandwerk

Museum für Völkerkunde

Deutsches Filmmuseum

Architektur Museum

Städel

SCHWEIZER PL.

FRANKENSTEINER PLATZ

Eiserner Steg

Untermain Brücke

Alte Br.

Obermainbr.

Flösser Brücke

Sachsenhäuser Ufer

Schöne Aussicht

Main

Commercial Train Station

Haupt-Güterbahnhof

Hauptbahnhof

PLATZ DER REPUBLIK

TO PALMENGARTEN, NATURMUSEUM, AND

Universität

Senckenberganlage

0   ½ mile

0   ½ kilometer

N

Windeckstr.

Am Tiergarten

Uhlandstr.

Hanauer Landstr.

Friedberger Anlage

Obermain anlage

Langestr.

Oskar-von-Miller-Str.

Sonnemannstr.

Deutschherrnufer

Seehofstr.

Dreieichstr.

Paradiesgasse

Große Rittergasse

Walter-Kolb-Str.

Oppenheimer Str.

Schweizerstr.

Wallstr.

Brückenstr.

Schaumainkai

Untermainkai

Wilhelm Leuschner Str.

Gutleutstr.

Münchener Str.

Kaiserstr.

Düsseldorfer Str.

Baseler Str.

Mannheimerstr.

Karlstr.

Taunusstr.

Weserstr.

Elbestr.

Gallusanl.

Neue Mainzerstr.

Kornmarkt

Braubachstr.

Berliner Str.

Bleidenstr.

Fahrgasse

Battonnstr.

Allerheiligenstr.

Rechneigrabenstr.

Kurt-Schumacherstr.

Reineckstr.

Fahrgasse

Hasengasse

Zeil

Stephanstr.

Brönnerstr.

Stiftstr.

Schäfer gasse

Bleichstr.

Seilerstr.

Anlage

Eschenheimer Anlage

Oederweg

Gr. Eschenheimer-str.

Hochstr.

Schillerstr.

Taubenstr.

Bockenheimer Anlage

Gärtnerweg

Schillerstr.

Goethestr.

Große Bockenheimer

Freßg.

Junghofstr.

Taunusanlage

Gallusanlage

Beethovenstr.

Hochstr.

Bockenheimer Landstr.

Mainzer Landstr.

Mendelssohnstr.

Westendstr.

Liebigstr.

Kettenhofweg

Guiolettstr.

Niddastr.

Zimmerweg

Westendstr.

Rheinstr.

Berthaweg

Grüneburgweg

TOR

Saalgasse

Seckbächerg.

Kleine Friedbergerstr.

Kleine Hochstr.

Münchener Str.

Weißfrauenstr.

Stiftstr.

Zeil

Th 9am-8pm, Sa 9am-4pm. **British Book Shop,** Börsenstr. 17 (tel. 28 04 92). Classics and popular novels in English. Open M-F 9:30am-7pm, Sa 9:30am-4pm.
Laundromat: Schnell & Sauber, Wallstr. 8, in Sachsenhausen near the hostel. Wash DM6, dry DM1 per 15min., soap included. Change machine. Open daily 6am-11pm. **SB Wasch Center,** Große Seestr. 46 (tel. 77 35 80). U-Bahn #6 or 7 to "Bockenheimer Warte." From the station, go down Adalbertstr. and right on Große Seestr. Wash DM8, dry DM1 per 10min., soap included. Open daily 6:30am-11pm.

Emergency and Communications

Emergency: tel. 110. **Fire** and **Ambulance:** tel. 112.
Rape/Battered Women's Hotline: tel. 70 94 94.
Pharmacy: In the basement of the train station by the subway entrances (tel. 23 30 47; fax 24 27 19 16). Open M-F 6:30am-9pm, Sa 8am-9pm, Su and holidays 9am-8pm. If pharmacies are closed, call 192 92 for emergency prescriptions.
Post Office: Main branch, Zeil 90, 60313 Frankfurt (tel. 21 11; fax 29 68 84). Recently relocated, it's now inside Hertie's department store. Follow the yellow "Post" signs. U- or S-Bahn to "Hauptwache." Send and be sent. Fax and be faxed. Open M-F 9:30am-8pm, Sa 9am-4pm. Branch office also on the upper level of the *Hauptbahnhof.* Open M-F 6:30am-9pm, Sa 8am-6pm, Su 11am-6pm.
Internet Access: CybeRyder Internet Cafe, Töngesgasse 31 (tel. 92 08 40 10; email info@cyberyder.de; http://www.cyberyder.de). DM6 per 30min. Open M-F 10am-9pm, Sa 10am-10pm. More access in **Cyber's: the Inter-n-Active Cafe,** Zeil 112-114 (tel. 29 49 64; cybers@internet.de). DM6 per 30min. Open M-F 11am-1am, Sa 10am-1am, Su noon-midnight.
Telephone Code: 069.

ACCOMMODATIONS

The cheapest options are the hostels and *Pensionen* in the Westend/University area. If all else fails, there are four other hostels less than 45 minutes away: Bad Homburg (S-Bahn #5, direction: Friedrichsdorf); Darmstadt (S-Bahn #12), Mainz (S-Bahn #14, direction: Wiesbaden), and Wiesbaden (S-Bahn #1 or 14).

Jugendherberge (HI), Deutschherrnufer 12 (tel. 61 90 58; fax 61 82 57). Bus #46 from the main bus station (DM2.90, rush hours DM3.30) to "Frankensteinerpl." Turn left along the river; the hostel sits at the end of the block. After 7:30pm, S-Bahn #2-6 or tram #16 to "Lokalbahnof" (DM1.90) then turn right on Darmstädter Landstr., which becomes Dreieichstr. (bear right), then turn left on Deutschherrnufer. In the midst of the Sachsenhausen pub and museum district, the hostel tends to be lively and loud. Breakfast on the veranda is free if unfilling, while lunch and dinner come in big portions (lunch 12:15-2pm, dinner 6-7:30pm; DM8.70; vegetarian meals available). DM25, over 20 DM32; singles DM52 and doubles DM42 per person, but they are *very rarely* available. Required sheet deposit DM10. 24hr. reception. Check-out 9am. Lockout 9am-1pm. Official curfew is midnight—beg to extend it. Written reservations only for single and double rooms.

Pension Brüns, Mendelssohnstr. 42 (tel. 74 88 96; fax 74 88 46). From the *Hauptbahnhof,* take a left onto Düsseldorferstr., and walk north. After 2 blocks veer right on Beethovenstr. At the circle, go right on Mendelssohnstr. (10-15min.). Located in the Westend near *Palmengarten* and the university. Ring the bell—it's on the 2nd floor. Homey, with sunny rooms and high ceilings. All rooms have TV and phone. Doubles DM79; triples DM105. Free breakfast in bed! Showers DM2. Call ahead.

Hotel an der Galluswarte, Hufnagelstr. 4 (tel. 73 39 93; fax 73 05 33). Run by the same folks as the Pension Brüns. Offers rooms at comparable prices available only to *Let's Go*-reading backpackers; mention the guide! S-Bahn #3, 4, 5, 6 to "Galluswarte." Singles DM70; doubles DM90; includes private shower, TV, and phone.

Pension Backer, Mendelssohnstr. 92 (tel. 74 79 92), up the street from Pension Brüns. U-Bahn #6 (direction: "Heerstr.") or 7 (direction: "Hausen") to "Westend." Smaller rooms are bright, clean, and cheap. Singles DM50; doubles DM60; triples DM68. Breakfast included. Showers 7am-10pm (DM3). Reservations with deposit.

Hotel Wiesbaden, Baselerstr. 52 (tel. 23 23 47 or 23 23 48; fax 25 28 45). Turn right as you leave the *Hauptbahnhof* and follow Baselerstr. towards the river.

Upscale, with spacious rooms, all with TV and phone. Singles DM65, with shower DM95; doubles with shower DM125; triples with shower DM150. 24hr. reception. **Hotel-Pension Gölz**, Beethovenstr. 44 (tel. 74 67 35; fax 74 61 42). One street north of Pensions Backer and Brüns. Quiet and beautiful, and all rooms have TV and phone. Singles DM65, with shower DM79-94; doubles with shower DM135-158; triples with shower DM165-188. Big breakfast included.

FOOD

While cheap eats in Frankfurt are not nearly as rare as cheap beds, light eats may prove harder to come by, especially if you stick to the local culinary gems. Traditional German *Würste* and beers are popular in Frankfurt, but the region also treasures some dishes of its own: *Handkäse mit Musik* (cheese curd with raw onions), *grüne Sosse* (a green sauce with various herbs, usually served over boiled eggs or potatoes), and *Ebbelwei*. Ah, *Ebbelwei*. Large mugs of this apple wine (also called *Ebbelwoi*, or *Äpfelwein* up north) should never top DM3. Don't expect anything akin to the sharp sweetness of cider or the dryness of chardonnay; this ain't no sippin' wine. Non-German foods abound; tasty crepes and even T-bone steaks are right at your fingertips, as are samosas, lo mein, and those omnipresent *Döner* (less than DM6).

For those seriously looking to economize, supermarkets are nearby. Just a few blocks from the youth hostel is a fully-stocked **HL Markt**, Dreieichstr. 56 (tel. 59 56 44), while a **Tengelmann**, Münchenerstr. 37 (tel. 23 13 60), is close to the *Hauptbahnhof* (Tengelmann open M-F 8:30am-7:30pm, Su 8am-2pm). The most reasonably priced kitchens surround the university in Bockenheim and nearby parts of Westend (U-Bahn #6 or 7 to "Bockenheimer Warte"), and many of the pubs in the Sachsenhausen and Alt Sachsenhausen districts serve food at a decent price (U-Bahn #1, 2, or 3 to "Schweizerpl."). Bockenheim, the Zeil, and Römerplatz attract carts and stands.

Zum Gemalten Haus, Schweizerstr. 67 (tel. 61 45 59; fax 603 14 57). One of the most famous joints in Sachsenhausen, it drips with *gemütlich* greasiness. Sit in the rustic *Gartenlokal* (garden restaurant) while waiters bring you the full range of regional specialties (DM5-23) and promptly replace your spent glasses of home-brewed *Ebbelwei* (DM2.50 for 0.3L). Open W-Su 10am-midnight.

Adolf Wagner, Schweizerstr. 71 (tel. 61 25 65; fax 61 14 45). Another famous Sachsenhausen haunt, 4 doors down from Zum Gemalten Haus. Owned and operated by the same family since 1931. Proffers *Ebbelwei* (DM2.50 for 0.3L), hot meals, *Würste*, and all the Frankfurt specialties in heart-warming and heart-burning portions (DM8-26). Open daily 11am-midnight.

The Kleinmarkthalle, on Hasengasse between Berlinerstr. and Töngesgasse, is a 3-story warehouse with several countershops: bakeries, butchers, fruit and vegetable stands, and more. Cutthroat competition between the many vendors pushes prices way down. Innumerable varieties of cheese for sale, as well as skinned rabbits ("Kill da wabbit!"). Open M-F 7:30am-6pm, Sa 7:30am-3pm.

Lorsbacher Taf, Große Rittergasse 49-51 (tel. 61 64 59), in the cobblestone area of Sachsenhausen. A hang-out for tourists and local families alike. Distinctive ivy overhang creates a cozy feel. Entrees DM8-25, *Ebbelwei* (DM2.50) in abundance. Open M-F 4pm-midnight, Su noon-11pm. Beer garden open until 11pm.

Shamrock Pub, Kleine Rittergasse 4-8 (tel. 62 77 36). No escape from potato concoctions here, but the traditional Irish cuisine (DM5-15) and Guinness (DM6) testify merrily to that wee bit o' Erin that has crept its way into Germany. Pool tables available, as are Irish breakfasts on Sundays. Open M-Th 5pm-2am, F-Sa 3pm-4am, Su 12pm-2am; open daily in winter 6pm-3am.

Die Wallnuss, Wallstr. 6 (tel. 61 99 10 95), a mere block from the cobblestone area of Sachsenhausen. The Walnut's candlelit interior is adorned with original artwork, while an eclectic, somewhat pricey menu features everything from pasta to Indian samosas to grilled goat cheese (DM5-28). Open M-Th 6pm-2am, F-Sa 6pm-3am.

SIGHTS

"Everywhere one looks," wrote 18th-century author Johann Kaspar Riesbeck, "everything exceeds the bourgeois and borders on the most unimaginable splendor." Things have gone downhill a bit since then, as Frankfurt's glamorous glitziness was crumbled by allied forces during World War II. However, industrious Frankfurters have dedicated themselves to renovating their churches and restoring their city's former brilliance. And, to a large extent, they've succeeded.

In this city of conspicuous consumption, the most logical starting point to begin devouring the sights is the **Römerberg,** the cluster of surviving historical buildings in the city center. This is the place that graces most postcards of Frankfurt, and, indeed, the half-timbered architecture and medieval fountain define the city's central tourist district. Just east of the Römerberg stand the spires of the **Dom** (tel. 29 70 32 36), a huge red sandstone Gothic cathedral with several splendidly elaborate altarpieces. *(Open Sa-Th 9am-noon and 2:30-6pm, F 2:30-6pm.)* It served as the site of coronation ceremonies for German emperors between 1562 and 1792. The view of the Main valley and the city's bustling vitality is well worth the punishing climb (round and round you go) to the top. *(Tower open daily Nov.-Mar. 9am-6pm. DM3, children DM1.)* The **Dom Museum** inside the main entrance contains architectural studies of the *Dom,* intricate chalices, and venerated robes of the imperial electors. *(Open Tu-F 10am-5pm, Sa-Su 11am-5pm. DM2, students DM1.)* Between the *Dom* and the rest of the Römerberg lies the Schirn Kunsthalle (see **Museums,** p. 367) and the **Historischer Garten,** a plantless "garden" with ruins from Roman to medieval times, discovered when workers were digging a sewer line. Ahhhh, the miasma of history.

In the main part of the *Römerberg,* the **Römer** stands at the west end, its distinctively red sandstone gables demarcating the site of Frankfurt's city hall since 1405. *(Open daily 10am-1pm and 2-5pm. Obligatory hourly tour DM3, students DM1.)* Only the upper floors (not the council chambers) are open to the public. These include the **Kaisersaal,** a former imperial banquet hall adorned with portraits of the 52 German emperors from Charlemagne to Franz II, 13 of whom were coronated here. To the south, the **Alte Nikolaikirche,** also made of pinkish sandstone, raises its considerably more modest spires. *(Open daily Apr.-Sept. 10am-8pm; Oct.-Mar. 10am-6pm. Free.)* Its minimalist interior is home to occasional fits of organ music. The **Paulskirche** (St. Paul's Church) stands directly across Braubachstr. from the *Römerberg. (Open daily 10am-5pm.)* Now used as a political memorial and conference venue, this unusually round church served as the gathering place for Germany's first democratic National Assembly, when it convened to draw up a constitution for a fledgling German republic in the wake of the waves of revolution that swept through Europe in 1848-49. Cognizant that Germany could not unify without the assent of powerful Prussia, the assembly attempted to cajole Prussia's Friedrich Wilhelm IV into accepting the crown of a constitutional monarchy. The king replied that he ruled by the grace of God, and the whole episode ended with the bloody repression of the democratic movement.

Of the half-dozen or so German cities that claim Goethe as their native son, Frankfurt legitimately possesses his early years. The master was born in Frankfurt in 1749, found his first love (a girl named Gretchen, said to be the inspiration for Marguerite in *Faust*), and penned some of his best-known works here, including *The Sorrows of Young Werther.* The aptly named **Goethe Haus,** Großer Hirschgraben 23-25 (tel. 13 88 00), a few blocks northwest of the Römer, was the icon's birthplace and family home. *(Open Apr.-Sept. M-F 9am-6pm, Sa-Su 10am-4pm; Oct.-Mar. M-F 9am-4pm, Sa-Su 10am-4pm. Tours daily 10:30am and 2pm. DM7, students DM3.)* Unless you're a huge Goethe fan, the house is little more than a well-preserved, well-furnished pad.

The **Museumsufer** is home to a number of high-powered museums (see **Museums,** below), Frankfurt's weekly **flea market** (open Sa 9am-2pm during the warm months), and the **Museumsuferfest,** a huge cultural jamboree that draws more than a million visitors over three days in late August. Tourists, children, businesspeople, and an extensive variety of native and exotic birds take refuge in the sprawling, lush **Palmengarten,** Siesmayerstr. 61 (tel. 21 23 39 39; http://www.stadt-frankfurt.de/Palmengarten), in the northwest part of town. *(Open daily Mar.-Oct. 9am-6pm; Nov.-Jan.*

9am-4pm; Feb. 9am-5pm. Admission DM7, students DM3.) Take U-Bahn #6 or 7 to "Bock-enheimer Warte." Rent a wooden boat and pretend you're rowing on the Main (DM4 per 30min.). The garden's greenhouses contain seven different "worlds," from the tropics to the plains. In summer, the grounds host a number of performances and exhibitions. For animal lovers, over 650 species ranging from the commonplace to the exotic are represented at the **Zoo**, Alfred-Brehm-Platz (tel. 21 23 37 35), on the eastern side of town. *(Open mid-Mar. to Sept. M-F 9am-7pm, Sa-Su 8am-7pm; Oct. to mid-Mar. daily 9am-5pm. DM11, under 18 and students DM5; with U-Bahn ticket DM9 and DM4, respectively. Last Saturday of every month DM5.50, students DM2.50; with U-Bahn ticket DM4, DM2.)* Take U-Bahn #6 or 7. The feeding of the apes (daily at 4:30pm; winter 4pm) and the piranhas (Su and W at 11am) excites a certain blood-thirsty pleasure.

MUSEUMS

On the south bank of the Main, between the *Eiserner Stag* and the Friedensbrücke, sits an eclectic collection of museums: the **Museumsufer** on the Schaumainkai. Once envisioned as a massive institution to culturally pump up the city of Frankfurt, these seven museums have since atrophied a bit with recent funding cuts. Admission is no longer always free, but an extensive range of exhibits is still offered. Frankfurt also has spectacular commercial art galleries—nearly 50, many of which are in the Braub-achstr./Saalgasse area. Pick up a Frankfurt Card for big savings. Expect Goethe-themed exhibits to fill Frankfurt's museums; it's his 250th birthday in 1999.

Museumsufer
  Museum für Kunsthandwerk, Schaumainkai 17 (tel. 21 23 40 37 or 21 23 85 30). Arts and crafts from Europe (the Middle Ages to the present), the Near East (9th to 19th centuries), and the Far East (Neolithic to the present). One division is devoted entirely to icons. Open Tu and Th-Su 10am-5pm, W 10am-8pm. DM8, students DM4. Free on Wednesdays.
  Galerie 37, Schaumainkai 37 (tel. 212 57 55). The only portion of the **Museum für Völkerkunde** (Museum of Ethnology) left open during renovations of the large site at Schaumainkai 29, scheduled for completion sometime over the next 3 years. Bra-zilian, Aboriginal, and Kenyan art from the 1980s and 90s. Interesting, but very small. Open Tu-Su 10am-5pm, W 10am-8pm. Free.
  Deutsches Filmmuseum, Schaumainkai 41 (tel. 21 23 88 30). Exhibits on the development of filmmaking. Old movies shown on the 3rd floor. Film yourself fly-ing on a carpet above the Frankfurt skyline. **Cafe Kino** adjoins the museum. Museum open Tu, Th-F, and Su 10am-5pm, W 10am-8pm, Sa 2-8pm. Tours Su 3pm. DM5, students DM2.50; free on Wednesdays. Films DM8, students DM6.
  Architektur Museum, Schaumainkai 43 (tel. 21 23 88 44). A 3-floor survey of the last 10 years in European architecture in a beautifully designed space of white sur-faces and right angles. Open Tu and Th-Su 10am-5pm, W 10am-8pm. Tours Su 3pm. DM8, students DM4.
  Deutschespostmuseum, Schaumainkai 53 (tel. 606 00; http://www.museumsstif-tung.de). A history of German travel and communication in an innovatively designed building. Interactive video displays in German, with English audio transla-tion tours available. Special exhibits in 1999 will include a study of anti-semitic postcards and forms of secret communication. Open Tu-Su 10am-5pm. An amateur radio booth (ask for *Funkstation*) on the top floor is open W 10am-5pm, Th 10am-1pm, and the first Sunday of each month 1-5pm. Museum and radio booth free.
  Städel, Schaumainkai 63 (tel. 605 09 80), between Dürerstr. and Holbeinstr. One of Germany's leading art museums with an excellent collection of Old Masters, housed in a stately mansion. Renovations should be completed by 1999; until then, access to limited special exhibits varies, as do hours and admission fees. Use the side entrances. Open Tu and Th-Su 10am-5pm, W 10am-8pm. DM8, students DM4.
  Liebieghaus, Schaumainkai 71 (tel. 21 21 86 17). This castle-like building and its gar-dens contain a fine collection of Asian and Egyptian art and sculptures from the Medieval, Renaissance, Baroque, Rococo, and Classical periods. Hungry art-lovers can enjoy the cafe on the patio. Open Tu and Th-Su 10am-5pm, W 10am-8pm. Tours W 6:30pm and Su 11am. DM5, students DM2.50, free on Wednesdays.

HESSEN

Elsewhere in Frankfurt

Museum für Moderne Kunst, Domstr. 10 (tel. 21 23 04 47; email: mmk@stadt-frankfurt.de; http://www.frankfurt-business.de/mmk). Not to be missed. Just a few blocks up the street from the *Dom,* the triangular building's interior (the "slice of cake") is an ideal setting for the stunning modern art housed within, including impressive works by Claes Oldenburg, Roy Liechtenstein, and Jasper Johns. Art in every medium imaginable, guaranteed to push the borders of your mind. The basement shows films and slides. Open Tu and Th-Su 10am-5pm, W 10am-8pm. DM7, students DM3.50, free on Wednesdays.

Schirn Kunsthalle, next to the *Dom,* entrance in a narrow alley (tel. 299 88 20). A postmodern art gallery hosting visiting exhibits with self-satisfied titles like 1999's "Between Art and Life: From Abstract Expressionism to Pop Art." Open Tu and F-Su 10am-7pm, W-Th 10am-10pm. DM9, students DM7. DM6 and DM4 on Sundays.

Historisches Museum, Saalgasse 19 (tel. 21 23 55 99), back toward the river from the *Römer.* A series of exhibitions on the history of Frankfurt, including a permanent "Äpfelwein Museum," an exhibit of Frankfurt porcelain, and a comparative display of the city before and after the bombing of WWII. 1999 special exhibits on Robert Schumann and Goethe. Open Tu and Th-Su 10am-5pm, W 10am-8pm. DM6, students DM2.50, free on Wednesdays.

Naturmuseum, Senckenberganlage 25 (tel. 754 20; http://www.senckenberg.uni-frankfurt.de). U-Bahn #6 or 7 to "Bockenheimer Warte." Features several fully-mounted dinosaur skeletons, impressive works of taxidermy, and some big whales thrown in for kicks. The largest natural history museum in Germany attracts the largest school groups in Frankfurt. Open M-Tu and Th-F 9am-5pm, W 9am-8pm, Sa-Su 9am-6pm. DM7, students DM3, free on Wednesdays.

ENTERTAINMENT AND NIGHTLIFE

Frankfurt wields a nightlife commensurate with its size. There are two major theaters, the **Alte Oper** (not just opera) and the **Städtisches Theater,** in addition to many smaller venues. Shows and schedules of the city's stages are detailed in several publications, including *Fritz* and *Strandgut* (free at the tourist office), and the *Journal Frankfurt* (DM2.80, available at any newsstand). Students can often buy leftover tickets at reduced prices one hour before a performance. Regular prices for these events range from DM10 for a youth orchestra performance to DM210 for a prime opera seat. For information, call 21 23 79 99, or fax 21 23 72 22. Kleine Bockenheimerstr., known as **Jazzgasse** (Jazz Alley), is the historical center of Frankfurt's jazz scene, which once earned the city the distinction of being the jazz capital of Europe.

If you're looking for a drinking night, the **Alt Sachsenhausen** district, between Brückenstr. and Dreieichstr., is home to a huge number of rowdy pubs and taverns specializing in *Äpfelwein,* the local drink of choice. The complex of narrow cobblestone streets centering on **Grosse** and **Kleine Rittergasse** teems with canopied cafes, bars, and restaurants, buzzing with natives and tourists alike, especially during the summer. Gregarious Irish pubs also abound.

Frankfurt has a number of thriving discos and a hyped-up techno scene, most happening between Zeil and Bleichstr. in the commercial district. Wear something dressier than jeans—unless they're *really* hip jeans—if you plan to try your luck with the neurotic bouncers. Most clubs are for folks 18 or older; drinks range from the DM5 Pilsner to the DM15 Long Island iced tea, cover charges run DM10-15. Don't think you'll escape these, either—most clubs make you pay upon exiting.

Nachtleben, Kurt-Schumacher-Str. 45 (tel. 206 50). On the corner of Kurt-Schumacher-Str. and Zeil, this hoppin' place serves as a postmodern cafe during the day, and hosts hordes of rocking 20-somethings on its red-velour-draped basement dance floor at night. Live acts during the week; house Th 11pm-5am, "Black music" F 11pm-4am, and punk-alternative Sa 11pm-4am. Cover Th DM6, F-Sa DM7. Cafe open M-W 11:30am-2am, Th-Sa 11:30am-4am, Su 7pm-2am.

Sinkkasten, Brönnerstr. 5 (tel. 28 03 85). A traditional nightclub: smoke, nifty lighting, clientele in their 20s-30s. Large, with a dancefloor pumping Euro-alternative, several bars, the obligatory pool table, and a late-night cafe. Various live bands, with covers ranging from DM10-30, but Saturday is always DM8.

Opium, Am Salzhaus 6 (tel. 13 37 60 72). Off Goetheplatz, Opium is another cafe-by-day, dance-club-by-night. Like its namesake, it promises the exotic and the sensuous, aided by the Oriental decor and gold dragon lanterns, but the music is largely house, and the young crowd is largely white and well-dressed. Cover DM10-15. Open Th-Sa until 4am, M-W until 2am.

Cooky's, Am Salzhaus 4 (tel. 28 76 62), off Goetheplatz next to Opium. Not quite as chic as its newer neighbor, Cooky's hosts a less sophisticated, slightly older crowd in a basement pumped up by mirrors, a hyperactive fog machine, and flashing lights. Cover DM8-10. Open Su-Th 11pm-4am, F-Sa 10pm-6am.

Omen, Junghofstr. 14 (tel. 28 22 33). With a boomin' techno line-up and a monstrous sweat-soaked dancefloor, Omen is *the* place to shake what your mamma gave ya. You'll hear the bass beat for days. Cover DM18. Open F-Sa 11pm-7am

Dorian Gray, Terminal 1 at the airport, right outside the U-Bahn exit (tel. 69 02 21 21). Don't plan on coming here until 1am. The far-out location can help explain the late hours of this expansive, sumptuous club. Young crowd, techno galore; Brian Eno can't compete. Cover DM15. Open Th 10pm-4am, F-Sa 10pm-8am.

Der Jazzkeller, Kleine Bockenheimerstr. 18a (tel. 28 85 37). An older crowd swings and swigs in this grotto-like mainstay of the Frankfurt jazz scene. Live music Thursday and Saturday. Cover DM8 W, DM10 F, otherwise varies. Open Tu-Su 9pm-3am.

⊛**Blue Angel,** Brönnerstr. 17 (tel. 28 27 72). One of the liveliest gay men's clubs around, Euro-techno music, flashing lights and police whistles dominate the interior. Cover DM10, including drinks Friday and Saturday. Open daily 11pm-late.

▨ Wiesbaden

Wiesbaden is a city Edith Wharton would have understood. While most German cities flaunt their castles and cathedrals, Wiesbaden's center of gravity is a ritzy Monte-Carlo-esque casino. The city's designer boutiques and *über*-hip citizens still pay homage to the heady years of the 19th century when Europe's aristocracy came to frolic away its time and money. And despite the large American presence due to the nearby military base (from which the Berlin airlift was launched), a bit of the old Wiesbaden is here for the taking; you can still test the curative waters of the thermal baths and, provided that you're formally attired, gamble away your life's savings at the casino.

The **casino** *(Spielbank)* clings and clangs within a large, posh compound *(Kurhaus)* alternately used for business conferences, old-style parades, and local art exhibitions as well as gambling. Situated off Wilhelmstr., the complex is bordered on two sides by the expansive and serene **Kurpark,** where locals unwind under century-old willow trees during the summer. Take bus #1 or 8 to "Kurhaus/Theater." The casino is inside the *Kurhaus* (tel. 53 61 00). Compulsive gambler Fyodor Dostoevsky squandered the last 30 rubles that stood between him and destitution while visiting Wiesbaden, and so can you (coat and tie rental DM10; open daily 3pm-3am; 21 and over). Or flout the dress code and get down and dirty with the slots next door at **Kleines Spiel** (open daily 2pm-2am; admission DM2; 21 and over). Opposite Kleines Spiel, on the other side of the *Kurhaus* is the stately **Staatstheater** (tel. 13 23 25), inscribed with the ominous instruction "*Der Menscheit Würde ist in Eure Hand gegeben, bewahret Sie*" ("the dignity of mankind is in your hands, preserve it"). The Staatstheater and neighboring **Kleines Haus** present traditional and modern ballets, operas, and plays; tickets occasionally sell for as little as DM9-15 (box office serving Staatstheater and Kleines Haus open Tu-F 11am-6pm, Sa-Su 11am-1pm; tickets can be purchased 1hr. before show). On Burgstr. west of the Staatstheater warbles the **world's biggest cuckoo clock,** which is topped by an unexpected giant moosehead. The birdies strut their fluffy stuff every half hour from 8am to 8pm. Toward the *Bahnhof* on Friedrich-Ebert-Allee, the **Museum Wiesbaden,** reminiscent of a train station, houses temporary exhibits of modern German art (open Tu noon-8pm, W-F 10am-4pm, Sa-Su 11am-5pm; admission DM5, students, seniors, and children DM2.50).

The **Neroberg,** a low hill at the north end of town, provides an alternative to Wiesbaden's hustle and bustle. The hill is crowned by the **Russische-Griechische Kapelle,** easily the most impressive monument in the city. (Open daily Apr.-Oct. 11am-4pm. Admission DM0.50.) This painstakingly decorated Greek Orthodox chapel was built in 1855 as a mausoleum for Princess Elizabeth of Nassau, the niece of a Russian Czar who was married to a local duke and died in childbirth at age 19. Her tear-jerking tomb dominates the chapel's inspiring interior. Take bus #1 to "Nerotal," and from there walk or take the **hydraulic funicular** to the summit of the 254m hill. (Funicular open May-Aug. daily 10am-7pm; Apr. and Sept. W and Sa noon-7pm, Su 10am-7pm; Oct. W, Sa, and Su noon-6pm. DM2; round-trip DM3.) Take a dip in the *Bauhaus*-style **swimming pool** (open 9am-8pm; DM8).

Wiesbaden's **tourist office** is conveniently located in the main train station. It books rooms (singles DM70 and up) for a DM6 fee and distributes handy transportation schedules and glossy brochures. (Open M-F 9am-6pm, Sa-Su 10am-4pm.) The **DB Service Desk,** in the train station next to the tracks, gives great directions and terrific maps. Wiesbaden makes a natural destination for a day-trip from Mainz (see p. 397), as the two cities share a **public transportation** system. The **Mitfahrzentrale,** located in a camper on Bahnhofstr. 9 (tel. 33 35 55 or 194 40), halfway between the pedestrian zone and the train station, connects riders with drivers (open M-F 7:30am-6pm, Sa 7:30am-noon). In emergencies, call the **International Help Line** (tel. 194 33). The **post office,** Kaiser-Friedrich-Ring 81, to the left as you come out of the *Bahnhof,* changes money and sells traveler's checks (open M-F 8am-6pm, Sa 8am-noon). The **telephone code** is 0611.

Wiesbaden's plate of inexpensive accommodations offers slim pickings. The **Jugendherberge (HI),** Blucherstr. 66 (tel. 486 57; fax 44 11 19), provides cheap beds, high-quality facilities, and a friendly staff. Take bus #14 to "Gneisenanstr." The bus lets you off on Blucherstr. Turn left, cross Gneisenanstr. and continue to the end of the street. (DM24, over 26 DM29. Breakfast included. Lockers DM10 deposit. Sheets DM6. Reception until midnight. Check-in after 2pm. Lockout midnight-6:30am.) The *Fußgängerzone* (pedestrian zone) west of the *Kurhaus* is brimming with pubs and restaurants, and spice abounds in the ethnic joints around Schwalbacherstr. between the Platz der Deutschen Einheit and Einserstr. The **Kebab House,** Schwalbacherstr. 61 (tel. 30 63 45), dishes out gigantic servings of ready-made Turkish food for unbeatable prices (DM5-8; open daily 10am-1am). **The Irish Pub,** Michelsbergstr. 17 (tel. 30 08 49), serves dinner nightly (6-10pm), rocks with live music every evening, offers enormous Irish breakfasts on Sundays (11am-3pm; DM14), and serves beer, wine, and coffee (DM3.50-7) until the wee hours. Victuals can be obtained at the **supermarket** on the second floor of the *Kaufhalle* on the corner of Langgasse and Mittestr.

■ Darmstadt

Home to the venerable German Academy of Language and Literature, which annually awards the most prestigious honor in German letters, one would expect Darmstadt to be staid and reserved. But its other great distinction—its collection of superb pieces of late 19th-century *Jugendstil* architecture—graces the city with its light-hearted, colorful appearance. Lush gardens and a great big *Schloß* smack-dab in the center of town complicate the city further, making it a surprisingly diverse, largely untouristed little place that's a short trip from Frankfurt.

ORIENTATION AND PRACTICAL INFORMATION Darmstadt is accessible from Frankfurt by frequent **trains** (25min.) or by S-Bahn #12 (DM5.80). **S-Bahn** and **bus** tickets cost DM2, DM7 for 24 hours, or DM17 for a 7-day ticket (students DM13). For a **taxi,** call **Funk** (tel. 194 10) any time of the day or night. **Bike rental** *(Fahrradverleih)* is available at **Prinz-Emil-Garten,** Heidelberger Str. 56. Take S-Bahn #1 to "Prinz-Emil-Garten." Rent either at the *Nachtbarschaftsheim* (tel. 632 78) up the hill (open 8am-8pm), or at the *Minigolfplatz* (tel. 66 48 90), up the hill and to the left (open 1-8pm; both locations DM7 per day; ID required). The **tourist office,** in front of the main train station (tel. 13 27 82), provides good city maps and hotel guides, and finds rooms (open M-F 9am-6pm, Sa 9am-noon); a **branch office**, at Luisenpl. 5 (tel. 13 27 80 or 13 27 81), is located in the Luisencenter (open M-F 9am-6pm, Sa 10am-1pm). **AIDS-Hilfe Darmstadt**, Saalbraustr. 27 (tel. 280 73), in addition to providing an array of AIDS-related services, also deals with gay and lesbian concerns. The **post office**, 64293 Darmstadt, **exchanges currency**, sells traveler's checks, and sends telegrams and faxes. There are two branches: Postamt 1, to your left as you exit the main train station, and Postamt 11, at Louisenpl. 3 (both open M-F 9am-6pm, Sa 9am-noon). The **telephone code** is 06151.

ACCOMMODATIONS, FOOD, AND ENTERTAINMENT The **Jugendherberge (HI)**, Landgraf-Georg-Str. 119 (tel. 452 93; fax 42 25 35), maintains spotless facilities, friendly service, and bright but tight rooms. Take Bus D to "Großer Woog." (DM24, over 26 DM29. Breakfast included, or bag lunch upon request. Reception until 10pm. Lockout 1-6am. Members only.) The Jugendherberge overlooks **Großer Woog** (tel. 13 23 93), an artificial lake and swimming hole. (Open daily mid-May to mid-Sept. 8am-8pm. DM3.50, students DM2. Boats DM6 per hr.) **Zentral Hotel**, Schuchardstr. 6 (tel. 264 11; fax 268 58), offers fine small rooms. (Singles DM60, with shower DM90; doubles DM120, with shower DM150.) From Luisenplatz, walk south along Luisenstr. past the Neues Rathaus before turning left onto Schuchardstr.

Eating in Darmstadt can be pricey. Try **Plus,** the grocery store across from the *Schloß* (open M-Th 8:30am-7pm, Sa 8am-4pm). Most of the city's inexpensive dining can be found in the two student areas: the *Cohannesviertel*, northwest of the city center, and the *Martinsviertel*, northeast of the city center. The university **Mensa** dishes out cheap meals. With your back to the northern side of the *Schloß*, cross Alexanderstr., then walk along the street with the yellow *Staatarchiv* and concrete five-story building to your left. Once past these, turn left down the stairs, then right into the University's Otto-Bernd Halle. Follow the signs. A decent selection of sandwiches and light fare runs DM3-6. (Open M-Th 9am-5pm, F 9am-3:45pm. Kitchen open 11:45am-2pm.) **Efendi's,** 13 Landgraf-Georg-Str. (tel. 29 38 09), has generous, spicy portions of Mediterranean fare, including vegetarian options and large salads (DM3-9; open daily 10am-1am). Pool action can be found at **Kuckucksnest,** a happening after-hours establishment a little farther up Landgraf-Georg-Str. The music is loud and the beers are DM3-7. (Cover M-Tu DM0.55, W-Su DM5.99. Open daily 8pm-3am.)

SIGHTS The mecca of Darmstadt's *Jugendstil* architecture is **Mathildenhöhe**, an artists' colony on a hill west of the city center founded by Grand Duke Ernst Ludwig in 1899. The Duke fell in love with *Jugendstil* and spent huge amounts of money to transform the urban landscape with this nature-friendly predecessor to Art Deco. The result was this startling architectural complex, heavy on flowered trellises and somber fountains. Though the seven original artists of the colony have since passed away, their masterpieces remain, such as the five-fingered **Hochzeitsturm** (wedding tower), the city's wedding present to Grand Duke Ernst Ludwig in 1908. *(Open Mar.-Oct. Tu-Su 10am-6pm. DM3, students DM1.)* Rising like a monstrous jukebox against the German sky, the 48m tower offers a scenic view of Darmstadt. To reach the tower and all of Mathildenhöhe, walk east from the Luisenplatz along Erich-Ollenhauer-Promenade, or take bus F to "Lucas," and walk south on Lucasweg. The Mathildenhöhe also hosts two art museums, the **Austellungsgebäude**, Sabaispl. 1 (tel. 13 27 78; open Tu-Su 10am-5pm; DM6, students DM3), and the **Museum der Künstlerkolonie**, Alexandraweg 26 (tel. 13 27 78; open Tu-Su 10am-5pm, tours 11am on the first Sunday of each month; DM5, students DM3), both of which house rotating exhibits of modern art. A gilded, three-domed Russian Orthodox Church, the **Russische Kapelle** (Russian Chapel), Nikolai Weg 18 (tel. 42 42 35), rests on the Matildenhöhe. *(Open Apr.-Sept. 9am-6pm, Oct.-Mar. 9:30am-5pm. DM1.50, students DM1.)* The chapel was imported stone by stone from Russia at the behest of Czar Nicholas II upon his marriage to Darmstadt's Princess Alexandra.

Just south of the Mathildenhöhe, the **Institut für Neue Technische Form,** Eugen-Bracht-Weg 6 (tel. 480 08), enshrines the Braun Design collection, which showcases the evolution of the company's renowned electrical appliances since 1955—everything from Aunt Sally's prized blender to Uncle Jörg's cutting-edge electric razor. *(Open Tu-Sa 10am-6pm, Su 10am-1pm. Free.)* A few blocks farther east at the corner of Seitersweg and Wolfskehlstr. lies the entrance to the **Rosenhöhe,** a verdant park that houses a rose garden and a mausoleum of the city's deceased dukes. The garden was planted in 1810 at the request of Grand Duchess Wilhelmine, who wanted a garden that breathed "the free, noble Spirit of Nature." With its overgrown lawns, hulking evergreens, and cemetery-like serenity, it seems to fulfill Wilhelmine's wish.

The gigantic coral and white **Schloß** is smack-dab in the middle of the city. Built between 1716 and 1727, it was modeled by a wistful Frenchman after his voluptuous Versailles. Since World War II, the *Schloß* has served as a public university library-*cum*-police station. A small **Schloßmuseum** (tel. 240 35) tucked in the eastern wing holds 17th- to 19th-century ducal clothing and furniture. *(Open M-Th 10am-1pm and 2-5pm, Sa-Su 10am-1pm. Obligatory 1hr. guided tour; last tour begins 1hr. before closing. DM3.50, students DM2.)* And what's a *Schloß* without a *Garten?* **Herrngarten,** a lush expanse of well-maintained greenery north of the *Schloß,* provides space for loafing students, gamboling dogs, and ducks (which you can't feed). Even more exquisite is the **Prinz Georg Garten,** arranged in Rococo style and maintained by a brigade of six gardeners. *(Open Apr.-Sept. 7am-7:30pm; Oct.-Mar. 8am-dark.)* Next to it, the recently renovated **Porzellanschlößchen** (little porcelain castle; tel. 78 85 47) flaunts an extensive collection of porcelain. *(Open M-Th 10am-1pm and 2-5pm, Sa-Su 10am-1pm.)* Those with a geological, paleontological, or zoological bent will appreciate the **Landesmuseum** (tel. 16 57 03), at the southern end of the Herrngarten across from the *Schloß. (Open Tu-Sa 10am-5pm, also W 7-9pm, Su 11am-5pm. DM5, students DM2.50.)*

■ Erbach and Michelstadt (Odenwald)

In the heart of the densely forested Odenwald rest Erbach and Michelstadt, two tiny villages that have perfected the art of being cute. In fact, strolling through the postage-stamp *Marktplatz,* one half expects to see everyone's favorite large-eared cartoon mouse saunter by, toting *Lederhosen,* a feathered cap, and a frothy mug of Pilsner. Even the German word for the region's star tourist attraction seems too cute to be believable: *Elfenbein* (ivory; literally, "elf bone"). And the seclusion of the two towns ensures that tourist populations remain quite small.

Erbach is the more appealing of the two towns, mainly because it is home to the spectacular **Elfenbeinmuseum,** Otto-Glen-Str. 1 (tel. 64 64), which boasts over 1000 ivory works. (Open daily Mar.-Oct. 10am-5pm; Nov.-Feb. Tu-Su 10am-5pm. DM8, students DM5.) Walk uphill on Hauptstr. and continue straight on Obere Marktstr. (15min.); the museum appears on your left. The ivory exhibits range from a 30,000-year-old carving of a girl's head made from mammoth ivory to complex Asian masterpieces. Demonstrations feature masters creating new works. The ethical and ecological problems of ivory carving were legally recognized in 1989 with a ban on hunted ivory. However, the workshops at the museum received special permission to use hunted ivory already in storage at the time of the ban, and they can provide permits for those wishing to bring such goods through customs. Next to the town's *Rathaus* lies the **Erbacher Schloß** (tel. 943 30), where you can see an actual chastity belt and wonders of medieval armor and weaponry. The tour includes the **African Hunting Museum.** (Obligatory tours daily 10 and 11am, 2, 3, and 4pm. DM8, students DM5. English tours available for an extra DM3).

Erbach is linked by train to Darmstadt and Heilbronn (over Eberbach). From the train station, turn right on Bahnhofstr., then left on (careful!) Bahnstr. to reach the Marktplatz. The elaborate **tourist office,** Marktplatz 1 (tel. 94 39; fax 94 33 47), doles out free city maps. Bring your German phrasebook—not much English spoken (open M-F 9am-6pm, Sa-Su 10am-5pm). The **post office,** 64711 Erbach, across from the Sportplatz on Michelstädterstr., has **currency exchange** and sells traveler's checks (open M-F 8:30am-noon and 2:30-6pm, Sa 9am-noon). The **telephone code** is 06062.

If you intend to spend several days in the region, the tourist office can help find very cheap lodging on local **Bauernhöfe** (farms). Live with a family and partake in a number of pastoral duties: milk cows, brush horses, bake bread. No experience required; language skills are preferred. If farms aren't your thang, try the local **Jugendherberge (HI)**, Eulbacherstr. 3 (tel. 35 15; fax 628 48). From the Marktplatz, take a left after the bridge and follow Hauptstr. uphill to the right; take a left onto Michelstädterstr., and about 300m later turn right on Eulbachestr. Or take the itty-bitty CityBus #4 towards "Michelstadt" and get off at "Jugendherberge." (DM15.50, over 27 DM20.50; singles DM20.50. Breakfast DM8. Reception until 5pm. Check-out 9am. Call ahead; lots of young ones.) The central **Hotel Gebhardt**, at Jahnstr. 32 (tel. 32 86), is over the bridge and one or two blocks to the right. (Singles with shower DM52; doubles with shower DM96. More than 2 nights DM48, DM88. Breakfast included.) For reasonably priced Italian food (DM6-22), try **Schmucker Stube** just off the Marktplatz on Bahnstr. 7-9 (tel 74 23). For historic dining, cross the bridge from the Marktplatz to **Restaurant Erbacher Brauhaus**, Jahnstr. 1 (tel 57 32), with its own *Biergarten*. Regional specials for DM9.50-16 (open daily 10am-midnight).

Within walking distance of Erbach (45min.), the town of Michelstadt joins the cute-fest. The oldest city in the Odenwald, Michelstadt features a picturesque *Rathaus*. To get to the *Marktplatz*, walk south along Bahnhofstr., make a right onto Große Gasse, and keep going until you hit the tourists. The **tourist office** is located right at the corner of the Marktplatz, on the left (open M-F 9am-noon and 2-4pm). Also in town is the quaint **Odenwald Museum** and a **Spielzeug (Toy) Museum**. Buses from Erbach roll into town every hour Monday through Friday from 7am to 6pm and Saturday 10am to 1pm. The Darmstadt-Heilbronn trains that stop in Erbach also stop here.

THE LAHN VALLEY

The peaceful Lahn River flows through verdant hills, bounteous vineyards, and dinky *Dörfer*. The valley itself breathes with a refreshing absence of tourists. It is, however, a very popular destination for German families wishing to enjoy the great outdoors; every spring and summer, campgrounds and hostels fill with people who have come to take advantage of the hiking, biking, and kayaking along the Lahn. Rail service runs regularly between Koblenz in the West and Gießen at the eastern extremity of the valley, as well as between Frankfurt and Limburg.

■ Limburg an der Lahn

Limburg an der Lahn flourished during the Middle Ages as a bridge for merchants and journeymen traveling from Köln to Frankfurt. Today, it serves much the same function, but for a different region—as the most important train station between Koblenz and Gießen, Limburg is an excellent base from which to explore the Upper Lahn Valley. Often confused with a notoriously cheesy Dutch city of the same name, Limburg an der Lahn, or "L.L." (no Bean here), is known for the **St. Georg-Dom**, a majestic cathedral that rests on the peak of the *Altstadt*. In addition to serving as the seat for the bishop of the Limburg diocese, this architectural hybrid of Romanesque and Gothic styles shelters a series of galleries and carefully restored frescoes. Next to the *Dom*, in a beautifully renovated building from 1544, the **Diözesan-museum/Dom-schatz**, Domstr. 12 (tel. 29 53 27), displays a small but significant collection of medieval religious artifacts dating back to the 12th century. The *Staurothek* is a Byzantine reliquary cross that a local knight spirited away from Constantinople during the Crusades. (Open mid-Mar. to mid-Nov. Tu-Sa 10am-1pm and 2-5pm, Su 11am-5pm. DM3, students DM1.) Limburg, left largely unscathed by WWII, prides itself on its well-preserved *Burgmannenhöfe* (medieval town houses) scattered throughout the *Altstadt*.

The **tourist office** *(Verkehrsverein)*, Hospitalstr. 2 (tel. 61 66; fax 32 93), finds rooms (from DM30) for free. Turn left on the street in front of the station, then make a quick right onto Hospitalstr. Ask about guided tours of the town. The office can also provide details about the local **Oktoberfest,** which begins the third week in October. (Open Apr.-Oct. M-F 8am-12:30pm and 2-6pm, Sa 10am-noon; Nov.-Mar. M-Th 8am-12:30pm and 2-5pm, F 8am-1pm.) The **Jugendherberge (HI),** Auf dem Guckucksberg (tel. 414 93; fax 438 73), in Eduard-Horn-Park, has fuzzy green beds and a really friendly staff. Walk through the tunnel to the right of the station exit. When you emerge from the tunnel, make an immediate right onto Eisenbahnstr., and then a right onto Frankfurterstr., which will curve around to the left; proceed for 15 minutes until you see signs for the *Jugendherberge.* Or take bus #3 from "Hospitalstr." (direction: "Am Hammerberg") to "Jugendherberge." (DM23.50, over 26 DM28. Breakfast included. Sheets DM6. Reception 5-10pm. Curfew 11:30pm but a key is available with a deposit.) There's a **Campingplatz** (tel. 226 10) in a riverside location on the far side of the Lahn. From the station, take Bahnhofstr. into the city. When it ends in the *Altstadt,* turn left on Salzgasse and take the first right over the Alte Lahnbrücke; turn right onto Schleusenweg (not Inselweg) and walk down for 10 minutes; follow the Lahn up to the *Campingplatz.* (DM5.80 per person. DM4.50 per tent. Reception open 8am-7pm. Open May to mid-Oct.) The **telephone code** is 06431.

■ Weilburg

As the Lahn crosses through the Taunus hills and the Wester Forest, the river bends itself around Weilburg into a shape resembling Gumby's head. Sprawled across a high ridge, the town's 14th-century **Schloß** and its terraced surroundings dominate the valley below. The residence of the counts and dukes of Nassau from 1355 to 1816, the castle now houses the **Schloßmuseum** (tel. 22 36), which flaunts a 10th-century Frankish foundation, a Romanesque interior, and a princely Baroque garden. To reach the *Schloß* from Mauerstr., walk up Neugasse to the *Schloßplatz.* (Open May-Sept. M-F 10am-5pm, Sa-Su 10am-6pm; Mar.-Apr. and Oct. Tu-Su 10am-5pm; Nov.-Feb. Tu-Su 10am-4pm. DM6, children DM4, includes a 1hr. guided tour. Free access to courtyard 10am-5pm.) Across the *Schloßplatz* you'll find the **Bergbau-und Stadtmuseum,** Schloßpl. 1 (tel. 314 59), where you can gawk at the Weilburg mineshafts (active until the 1950s) and speed through the city's economic and social history. (Open Apr.-Oct. Tu-Su 10am-noon and 2-5pm; Nov.-Mar. M-F 10am-noon and 2-5pm; DM4, students DM2.) The **Weilburger Schlosskonzerte** bring a dizzying array of international musicians to Weilburg every June and July. For schedules and tickets call 410 42. Weilburg is very proud of its magnificent crystal caves, actually located in Kubach, 4km away. Even if castles and churches a few centuries old do not impress you, the 350 million year-old limestone chunks of the **Kubacher Kristallhöhle** (tel. 940 00), Germany's highest crystal caves, might do the trick. To reach the caves, take bus #660 from the Weilburg/Denkmal bus stop at the corner of Neugasse and Mauerstr. to the stop "Kubach/Abzw. Edelsb. (Kristallh.)." (Open M-F 2-4pm, Sa-Su 10am-5pm. DM4.50, students DM3.)

The **tourist office,** Mauerstr. 10 (tel. 76 71; fax 76 75), rents **bikes** (DM12 per day) and reserves rooms (from DM30) for free. From the *Busbahnhof* in front of the train station, take bus #671 (direction: "Oberbrechen") to "Landtor," and then walk uphill along Vorstadtstr., which becomes Mauerstr. From the train station, walk left along the tracks and over the bridge, then veer right at the yellow restaurant. When you reach the 18th-century Landtor gate, turn right and walk up Vorstadtstr. (Open M-F 9am-noon and 2-4:30pm, Sa 10am-noon.) The newly-renovated **Jugendherberge Weilburg-Odersbach (HI),** Am Steinbühl (tel. 71 16; fax 15 42), is comfortable, spacious, and clean. From the *Busbahnhof,* take bus #656 (direction: "Waldernbach") to the stop "Am Steinbuhl," and then walk up the path. (DM23.50, over 26 DM28. Breakfast included. Sheets DM6. Reception 5-10pm.) Inexpensive gyro and pizza joints rest across the street from the *Bahnhof* (DM6-8), but for a real Hessian meal, the **Weilburgerhof,** Schwanengasse 14 (tel. 71 53), right of the *Markt* behind the *Schloß,* serves regional délicacies (DM12-29; open daily 11am-2:30pm and 5pm-1am). The **telephone code** is 06471. **There is no bus service in Weilburg on Sundays.**

■ Wetzlar

Wetzlar peaked in political stature at the end of the 17th century when the imperial legal court of the Holy Roman Empire established itself here. This, in turn, led to the city's even bigger cultural claim to fame when, in 1772, Goethe came to study at the court. The young author found the court dull and decided to pursue a more exciting interest—a woman named Charlotte Buff. She was already engaged to Goethe's friend Kestner, so finally unable to continue the fruitless *Spiel*, Goethe left for Frankfurt where he learned that his good friend Jerusalem had just committed suicide. Goethe intertwined this and his own tale of woe into the enormously popular novel *The Sorrows of Young Werther*, dissolving the real Lotte Buff into literary legend and setting off a wave of suicides referred to as "Young Werther syndrome." The **Lottehaus,** Lottestr. 8-10 (tel. 992 21), enshrines numerous *Werther* first editions in the brown-trimmed home where Lotte lived with her parents. Although the actual house is undergoing renovations and will be closed until May 1999, for now you can view its contents in an exhibit at the **Stadt- und Industriemuseum,** Lottestr. 8-10 (tel. 992 21), which is located right next to the *Lottehaus*. Reach both sights by walking up *Pfaffengasse* from the top of the *Domplatz*. (Open Tu-Su 10am-1pm and 2-5 pm. Free.) Literary die-hards might also dig the **Jerusalemhaus,** Schillerpl. 5 (tel. 992 69), where Goethe's poor friend shot himself. Descend from Domplatz to Eiseu and follow the sign to the Jerusalemhaus. When you reach Schillerplatz turn left. (Open Tu-Su 10am-1pm and 2-5pm; access to library Fri. 3-4:30pm. Free.) If you want a peek at how the filthy rich lived during the Renaissance, walk up Kornblumengasse from Schillerplatz to find the **Dr. Irmgard von Lemmers-Danforth Collection,** Kornblumengasse 1 (tel. 993 66). From Kornblumengasse, make a left onto Hofstatt and you'll find the **Reichskammergerichtsmuseum,** Hofstatt 19 (tel. 996 12), which showcases original documents, and explains the clockwork of the most complex, inefficient, and Byzantine legal system of all time; most documents are accompanied by English translations (open Tu-Su 10am-1pm and 2-5pm). Trek back up the alleys and staircases to reach the **Dom.** Begun in 897 and repeatedly altered and enlarged over the centuries (by Friedrich Barbarossa, among others), the *Dom* was never actually finished; it remains a perpetual architectural history lesson (open until dusk).

Wetzlar's **tourist office** *(Verkehrsamt),* Dompl. 8 (tel. 993 38; fax 993 39), in the pre-1350 *Rathaus,* is itself an aesthetic and historical attraction. Take bus #18 from the station to "Dompl.," or trudge uphill for half of the steep 25-minute walk: exit the station, walk through the passageway, and continue on Bahnhofstr. to Buderusplatz. Turn left on Brückenstr., cross the bridge, and take the first right, the first left, and then the first right again. The Domplatz is just over the crest of the hill. Signs lead you all the way from the bridge. The tourist office is behind the left face of the *Dom* (tourist office open M-F 9am-1pm and 2-4:30pm, Sa 10am-noon). When the office is closed, you can find maps and brochures at the *Stadt- und Industriemuseum.* The spacious rooms of the **Jugendherberge (HI),** Richard-Schirmann-Str. 3 (tel. 710 68; fax 758 26), offer superb views of the valley. Some rooms have their own shower. From the station, take bus #12 (direction: "Krankenhaus") to the *second* "Sturzkopf"—the correct one is a 25-minute ride. Walk in the same direction as the curve. (DM24.50, over 26 DM29. Breakfast included. Sheets DM6. Reception 8am-1pm and 2pm-12:30am. Curfew 12:30am.) The **telephone code** is 06441.

■ Marburg

Almost two centuries ago, the Brothers Grimm spun their tales around these rolling hills, and from a distance, Marburg an der Lahn seems more of their world than ours. The city's isolation in the Lahn Valley allowed Landgrave Philipp to found the first Protestant university here in 1527. Its alumni list now reads like a syllabus for an intellectual history course: Martin Heidegger, Boris Pasternak, T.S. Eliot, Richard Bunsen (of burner fame), and the Spanish philosopher José Ortega y Gasset, to name a few. Those less familiar with Nobel Prize winners will recognize graduates **Jakob and Wil-**

HESSEN

helm Grimm, who briefly attended the university from 1802 to 1805; their philological studies led them to collect the fairy tales that brought them fame. Today, 15,000 students pore over books, conversation, and each other on the banks of the Lahn. The rest of Marburg enjoys a slightly less academic but no less intoxicating activity— beer-drinking. Not that those hard-working intellectuals are committed exclusively to their studies—the father of Otto Hahn, the Nobel Prize-winning atomic physicist, is known to have said: "My son is in Marburg drinking beer." Things get hopping on the first Sunday in July, when costumed citizens parade onto the *Markt* for the rowdy **Frühschoppenfest** (Early Beer Festival). Drinking officially kicks off at 11am when the brass rooster on top of the 1851 **Rathaus** flaps its wings. Unofficially, however, the kegs of *Alt Marburger Pils* are tapped at 10am when the ribald old Marburger *Trinklieder* (drinking ballads) commence.

ORIENTATION AND PRACTICAL INFORMATION

Built around a bend in the river, Marburg is served by frequent **trains** from Frankfurt (1hr.) and Kassel (1hr.); it also serves as the starting point for trips to Frankenberg, and from there to the Waldecker *Land*. Rudolphsplatz lies at the foot of the elevated *Oberstadt*, which is the heart of the city. To reach Rudolphsplatz from the train station, take buses #1-6. Rudolphsplatz forms the intersection of Pilgrimsteinstr. and Biegenstr. Along Pilgrimsteinstr. narrow staircases and steep alleys will lead you to the Oberstadt, and they'll work those calves, too. If a few beers have dulled the athletic nerve, you might want to take the Oberstadt-Aufzug (elevator to the upper city) from Pilgrimstein to Reitgasse, in the Oberstadt (operates daily 7am-11:30pm, free).

Trains: Information office across from the ticket counters. Open M-F 8:10am-5:45pm. Trains go to Frankfurt (1hr., departs every hr.), Hamburg (4hr., departs every 2hr.), and Kassel (1hr., departs every 30min.).

Public Transportation: Single tickets (DM2.20) get you anywhere in the city.

Taxi: Funkzentrale (tel. 477 77). Funk is long, life is short.

Bike Rental: Velociped, Auf dem Wehr 3 (tel. 245 11), just over the bridge from Rudolphsplatz, off the riverside path. DM15 per day. Open daily 10am-4pm.

Tourist Office: Pilgrimsteinstr. 26 (tel. 991 20; fax 99 12 12), a mere 150m from Rudolphsplatz. Bus #1-6 to "Rudolphspl.," and exit to the north along Pilgrimsteinstr.; the office is on your left. Sells maps and hotel lists for DM0.50-1.50, and books rooms (from DM35) for free. Ask for a schedule of cultural and musical events. Open M-F 9am-6pm, Sa 10am-2pm. If the office is closed you can call **hotel information** at 194 14.

Bookstore: N.G. Elwert, Pilgrimstein 30 (tel. 17 09 34; http://www.elwert.de), one block from Rudolphsplatz, has a selection of English books. There is an annex of the store above it at Reitgasse 7. Open M-F 9:30am-7pm, Sa 9:30am-4pm.

Laundromat: Wasch Center, at the corner of Gutenbergstr. and Jägerstr. Sip a beer (DM2.80-5.50) in its adjacent **Bistro Waschbrett** during the rinse cycle. Wash DM6. Dry DM1 per 12min. Open M-Sa 8am-10pm, Su 1-10pm.

Women's Concerns: Autonomes Frauenhaus, Alter Kirchainer Weg 5 (tel. 16 15 16). Open M and W 10am-1pm, Th 4-7pm. Otherwise, call and leave a message.

AIDS-Hilfe: Bahnhofstr. 27 (tel. 645 23). Drop-in times M 2-4pm and Th. 8-9pm; otherwise, call.

Emergency: Police, tel. 110. **Fire,** tel. 112. **Ambulance,** tel. 192 92.

Post Office: *Hauptpostamt,* Bahnhofstr. 6, 35037 Marburg, a 5min. walk from the train station and on the right. Open M-F 9am-6pm, Sa 9am-noon.

Telephone Code: 06421.

ACCOMMODATIONS AND CAMPING

Although small, Marburg boasts more than 30 hotels and *Pensionen;* however, competition hasn't done too much to keep prices down. Plan ahead if you intend to spend under DM60.

Jugendherberge (HI), Jahnstr. 1 (tel. 234 61; fax 121 91). From Rudolphsplatz, cross the bridge and immediately turn right onto the riverside path. Continue until reaching the small wooden bridge. From the station, walk all the way down Bahnhofstr. and make a left onto Elizabethstr., which will become Pilgrimsteinstr. after the church. This will lead to Rudolphsplatz (20min.). Clean, spacious rooms, some with bath. The *Jugendherberge* catches the nighttime music of the *Altstadt* from across the Lahn. DM24.50, over 27 DM29.50. Breakfast included. Sheets DM6. Reception 9am-noon and 1:30-11:30pm, but house keys available with ID or DM50 deposit.

⊗**Tusculum-Gästehaus,** Gutenbergstr. 25 (tel. 227 78; fax 153 04). Follow Universitätstr. from Rudolphsplatz and take the first left onto Gutenbergstr. You might confuse this bright, well-kept hotel with an art gallery—each room is individually designed in the style of a modern artist (e.g., a blue Picasso room and a Joan Miró washroom). Recently renovated. Singles DM55-70, with shower DM75-90; doubles DM100-120, with shower DM125-140. Reception 10am-6pm. Kitchen open 24hr.

Hotel Garni, Bahnhofstr. 14 (tel. 656 44), a 5min. walk from the station. Tastefully furnished and fastidiously kept rooms in a homey atmosphere, though the rooms overlooking Bahnhofstr. can be noisy. Singles DM65-72, with shower DM77-85; doubles DM130, with bath DM140-165. Breakfast included. Reception 7am-9pm. Closed for Christmas. AmEx, MC, Visa.

Camping: Camping Lahnaue, Trojedamm 47 (tel. 213 31), on the Lahn River. Follow directions to the *Jugendherberge* and continue down-river for another 5min. Person DM7, tent DM5. Open Apr.-Oct. Call ahead.

FOOD

Marburg's cuisine caters to its large student population. Most establishments offer *Würste* or hefty pots of pasta. See **Nightlife** (p. 378) for cafes with food as sidelights to drinks. The streets surrounding the **Markt** are replete with *Steh-Cafes* (bread and sandwich shops with standing room only; salami sandwich DM4.50) and pizza and *Döner* joints (pizza slice DM3.50, *Döner* DM5). **ALDI Markt,** Gutenbergstr. 19, will cater to your grocery needs (open M-F 9am-6:30pm, Sa 8am-2pm).

Mensa, Erlenring 5. Cross the bridge at Rudolphsplatz and make the second left onto Erlenring. Satisfy your hearty appetite with the university crowd. Three-course meals DM2.90-4.60. Open during the semester M-F 8am-10:30pm, Sa 11:45am-2:30pm; during breaks M-F 8am-8pm, Sa 11:45am-2:30pm.

Bistro-Cafe Phönix, Am Grün 1 (tel. 16 49 69). Tucked in a short alley between Rudolphsplatz and Universitätstr., the Bistro serves traditional dishes as well as some lighter fare. An ice-cold piña colada (DM9) serves as a nice break from the omnipresent *Marburger Bier.* Open Su-Th 10am-2am, F-Sa 10am-3am.

Cafe Barfuß, Barfüßerstr. 33 (tel. 253 49), gets packed every day with locals. Big breakfast menu (DM5.50-12.50) served until 3pm. Amusing menu with very funny cartoons helps digest any of the 5 beers on tap (DM2-5.50). Open daily 10am-1am.

Café Vetter, Reitgasse 4 (tel. 258 88), is a traditional cafe, quite proud of its terrace on the edge of the Oberstadt. *Kaffee und Kuchen* (coffee and cake)—Germany's 4pm sugar rush—costs DM8-15. A town favorite for 90 years. Open M and W-Sa 8:30am-6:30pm, Tu 11am-6:30pm, Su 9:30am-6:30pm.

SIGHTS

Marburg Tourism (tel. 99 12 23) will gladly lead you through the *Altstadt* to the historic sights, but you can find them on your own. Various tours are available from April to December (DM3-5). To reach the exalted **Landgrafenschloß,** former haunt of the infamous Teutonic knights, take bus #16 (direction: "Schloß") from Rudolphsplatz or Markt, or hike up the more than 250 steps from the *Markt. (Open Apr.-Oct. Tu-Su 10am-6pm; Nov.-Mar. Tu-Su 11am-5pm; DM3, students DM2.)* The *Schloß,* begun in the year 1228, looks today nearly as it did in 1500. Count Philip brought rival Protestant reformers Martin Luther and Ulrich Zwingli to his court in 1529 to convince them to kiss and make up; he verged on success when an epidemic made everyone grumpy and uncooperative. Towering over Marburg, the castle is illuminated until 11pm. It houses the university's **Museum für Kulturgeschichte** (Museum of Cultural History), which exhibits Hessian history and religious art, as well as the recently unearthed wall remnants in the *Westflügel* (West Wing) that move the castle's construction date back to the 9th century. Occasional performances are given in the open-air theater of the **Schloßpark,** the gardens stretching to the west of the fortress; contact the **Stadthalle,** Biegenstr. 15 (tel. 20 13 33), for times and tickets.

Past a strikingly ugly boar's head, down the 140 steps of the "Ludwig-Bickell-Treppe" stairway, rests the 13th-century **Lutherische Pfarrkirche St. Marien,** Lutherische Kirchhof 1 (tel. 252 43), with amber-colored stained glass and an elaborate organ (open daily 9am-5pm; free organ concerts Oct.-July Sa at 6:30pm). Down Kugelgasse the 15th-century **Kugelkirche** (sphere church) owes its peculiar name not to its shape but to the hats *(cuculla)* worn by the religious order that founded it. As you descend onto the *Markt,* the **Rathaus** will be directly in front of you; greeting you is a horseman slaying a figure that tragically resembles Puff the Magic Dragon. Walk around the left of the *Rathaus* and you will find the **Aula der Alten Universität,** Reitgasse (tel. 991 20). Today's university building was erected in 1871, but the original **Alte Universität** on Rudolphsplatz was built on the rubble of a monastery conveniently vacated when Reformation-minded Marburgers ejected the resident monks. The nearby houses with technicolor flags are former **fraternities.**

Save some ecclesiastical awe for the oldest Gothic church in Germany, modeled on France's cathedrals in Rheims and Amiens (c. 1235-83): the **Elisabethkirche,** Elisabethstr. 3 (tel. 655 73). The name of the church honors the town patroness, a widowed child-bride (engaged at four, married at 14) who took refuge in Marburg, founded a hospital, and snagged sainthood four years after she died. The **reliquary** for her bones in the *Kunstschätze* is so overdone, it's glorious. With your back to the train station, walk down Bahnhofstr. for about five minutes then turn left onto Elisabethstr. *(Church open daily Apr.-Sept. 9am-6pm; Oct. 9am-5pm; Nov.-Mar. 10am-4pm, Su after 11am. Church free; reliquary admission DM3, students DM2. Wheelchair accessible. For information about music in the church call 68 62 73.)* Walk up the stairs across from the Elisabethkirche (Friedrich-Siebert-Weg) to the 13th-century **St. Michaelskapelle** surrounded by a medieval pilgrim cemetery that looks like a time-forsaken oasis.

The university's impressive collection of 19th-and 20th-century painting and sculpture is housed in a banal-looking building surrounded by parking lots and a mini-mall. You can find the **Universitätsmuseum für Bildende Kunst** (Museum of Fine Art), Biegenstr. 11 (tel. 28 23 55), by walking down Pilgrimstein and making a left onto Biegenstr. *(Open Tu-Su 11am-1pm and 2-5pm. Free.)* The variety of paintings includes masterpieces by Cranach, Picasso, and Kandinsky. The section on Expressive Realism depicts the lost generation of talented artists who matured during the Nazi period. For a glance at some really modern art, check out the **Kunstverein,** Markt 16 (tel. 258 82). *(Open Tu-Sa 10am-1pm and 2-5pm, Su 11am-1pm. Free.)* Exhibits of artwork by Heather Betts, Sibylle Prange, Max Neumann, and others in 1999. In August, the museum displays pieces by local Marburger artists.

ENTERTAINMENT AND NIGHTLIFE

Because of the student population, bars and pubs in Marburg breed faster than bunny rabbits. In the **Oberstadt** there are over 60 such establishments, giving Marburg the proud distinction of having the densest concentration of *Kneipen* in Germany. Live music, concert, theater, and movie options are listed in the weekly *Marburger Express,* available at hotels and the hostel.

Diskothek Kult, Temmlerstr. 7 (tel. 941 83). Bus A1 (direction: "Pommernweg") or A2 (direction: "Cappeler Gleiche") to "Frauenbergstr." The only disco in town, this place gets 'em all, bringing in DJs from England and the U.S. with mad skillz. Cover DM3 weekdays, DM5 on weekends. Open Tu-W 9pm-3am, F-Sa 9pm-4am.

@**Barfly/Café News/Hemingway's/Down Under Dance Club,** Reitgasse 5 (tel. 212 05 or 25). **Barfly** is a bistro and terrace cafe. **Café News** is a trendy meeting spot with a mesmerizing view of the Lahn Valley. Open daily 9am-1am. **Hemingway's,** down the spiral staircase, serves special drinks and American fare. Happy hour daily 6-7:30pm; open daily 6pm-1am. **Down Under** raves on the weekends—a dance mecca. Work it out! Open F-Sa 9pm-1am.

Bolschoi Café, Ketzerbachstr. (tel. 622 24). From Rudolfsplatz, walk up Pilgrimstein until you reach the Elizabethkirche, and turn left onto Ketzerbachstr. You'll find it on the left side of the street. Then prepare for the *real* Left—the Communist kitsch here will warm the cockles of any Cold Warrior's heart with its red candles, red walls, a red foil ceiling, and 19 brands of domestic and imported vodka (DM3-5.80). Lenin's bust is stenciled on the wall. The *Rollmops* (raw pickled herring; DM1) may boost your tolerance. Open Su-W 8pm-1am, F-Sa 8pm-2am.

Hinkelstein, Markt 18 (tel. 242 10), a classic hangout for locals and students, was built when Columbus discovered America. While listening to Hendrix and Jackson Brown, the patrons enjoy a game of darts. This traditional club provides a respite from Germany's omnipresent techno scene. Open daily 7pm-1am.

Kulturladen KFZ *(Kommunication Freizeit Zentrum),* Schulstr. 6 (tel. 138 98; http://www.bop.de/kfz), hosts an impressive schedule of multicultural events, including concerts, theater, cabaret, parties, and gay/lesbian events. Cover varies from free to DM15. Call for a schedule.

■ Near Marburg: Fritzlar

The birth of the town of Fritzlar as *Frideslar* (Place of Peace) dates to a not-so-peaceful act of St. Boniface, who, in 723, chopped down the huge **Donar's Oak,** the pagan religious symbol of the tribal Chats. The "Apostle of the Germans" used the timber to build his own wooden church, which today is the beautiful St. Peter *Dom.* It was also here that Heinrich I was proclaimed king in 915, inaugurating the medieval incarnation of the Holy Roman Empire. Since then this diminutive medieval town has become isolated from the main routes of buzzing commerce and affluence. Nevertheless, Fritzlar is content with its role as a postcard friendly *Fachwerkstadt* (a town of half-timbered houses) sitting on the **Märchenstraße,** the German fairy tale road.

The gem of Fritzlar is the 12th-century **St. Peter Dom,** with its two massive red sandstone towers and sizeable *Domschatz* (cathedral treasury), which includes the diamond and pearl-covered **Heinrich Cross** (created around 1020) as well as numerous precious robes and relics (Open May-Oct. M-Sa 10am-noon and 2-5pm, Su 2-4pm; Nov.-Apr. M-Sa 10am-noon and 2-4pm, Su 2-4pm. DM4, students DM2. Tours DM5, children DM2.) On the western extremity of the still-standing medieval city wall, the 39m **Grauer Turm** (grey tower) is the tallest defense tower in Germany. It was built in 1274, a few years after Fritzlar had been leveled for the third time by enemy attacks. Though it no longer serves its original purpose, you can still climb it and enjoy the spectacular view (DM0.50). The **Hochzeitshaus** (tel. 98 86 28), on Burggrabenstr., has hosted weddings and festivals since the 16th century. It also houses the **Regional Museum,** which does its best to reflect all aspects and stages of Fritzlar's bumpy history. (Open Mar.-Nov. Su-F 10am-noon and 3-5pm; Dec.-Feb. M-F 10am-noon and 3-5pm; DM3, children DM1.)

Fritzlar is an ideal daytrip. It can be reached from either of the main train stations in Kassel by rail (direction: Bad Wildungen) or bus (40min.). The **tourist office,** Zwischen den Krämen 5 (tel. 98 86 43; fax 98 86 38), sits in the *Rathaus*—the oldest official building in Germany, built in 1109. To get there, make a left out of the train station, and a quick right onto Gießenerstr. After the bridge, make a left onto Fraumünsterstr., and then a right onto Nikolausstr. At the top of the hill you'll find Gießenerstr. (again). Hang a left, walk through the Marktplatz, and make a left onto Zwischen den Krämen. The office has lists of rooms (from DM25), but makes no reservations. (Open M 10am-6pm, Tu-Th 10am-5pm, F 10am-4pm, Sa-Su 10am-noon.) City **tours** leave from the *Rathaus,* but only if there is a minimum of five people (May-Sept. M-Sa 10am, Su 11am; DM5). **Dom-Grill,** Gießenerstr. 2 (tel. 26 55), just off the Marktplatz on the way to town, is the place to catch up on local gossip (if you can decipher Hessian accents) and fill up on greasy kebabs, burgers, *Würste,* and fries

(DM2.20-8.30; open M-F 10am-8pm, Sa 10am-1:30pm). Little towns spawn big festivals, and Fritzlar's *Wunderkinder* are no exception: the **Pferdemarkt** (2nd weekend in July) and the **Altstadtfest** (mid-Aug.) draw out *Lederhosen*, traditional music, and beer goggles. The **telephone code** is 05622.

■ Frankenberg

Frankenberg an der Eden offers travelers a surprisingly big bag of goodies for a town of its small size. Dominating the skyline is the 13th-century **Liebfrauenkirche** ("Church of Our Lady"), modeled on the *Elizabethkirche* in Marburg. Make a left out of the train station and follow Bahnhofstr. as it leads into the pedestrian zone to Neustädterstr.; continue trudging uphill as Neustädter becomes Ritterstr. Take the first right onto Neue Gasse, and make a right onto Kirchberg at the top of the hill. The church is graced by 14th-century glass panels depicting the life of Christ and a 6.5m high statue of the Virgin Mary. Upon exiting, head directly onto Obermarkt to the 1509 **Rathaus.** With its whopping 10 towers, it ranks as one of the most attractive townhouses in Germany. Despite the entrancing exterior, the inside is disappointingly empty except for a sobering plaque dedicated to the Jews of Frankenberg. Ask at the tourist office about **free city tours** that depart from here. At the far end of *Obermarkt* you will find the faded red **Steinhaus** ("Stone House"), Pferdemarkt 27, which dates from 1240; as the oldest house in Frankenberg, it now shelters the city's library (open M and W 10am-1pm and 2-5pm, Tu and F 2-5pm, Th noon-2pm). The ominous 13th-century **Hexenturm** (Witches' Tower), the sole survivor of an original 20 towers and five gates, stands out sharply against the residential houses and blossoming flowers. Peek inside at the walls to see where *very* unlucky crooks did their time. To get there, walk through the passage to the right of the *Steinhaus,* and take a left on Auf der Heide; then take a right and then another right onto Gadengasse. To enter the tower, you have to arrange a 15-person tour with the tourist office.

The **tourist office,** Obermarkt 11-13 (tel. 50 51 13 or 50 50; fax 50 51 00; email frankenberg-eder@t-online.de), passes out nifty maps and brochures (open M-Th 8:30am-noon and 2-4pm; F 8:30am-12:30pm). There is no hostel in Frankenberg, but Marburg is only 40 minutes away. Trains run regularly between these cities; the last train out of Frankenberg is at 5:40pm Monday through Friday, 6:40pm on Saturday, and 7:30pm on Sunday. Be sure to leave your luggage in Marburg, because Frankenberg's train station has no lockers. But before you leave Frankenberg, you might want to check out the town's newest addition: **Cafe Online,** Neue Gasse 1 (tel. 63 08). Thirty minutes of surfing time will cost you DM5, and you can get a slice of homemade cake to go with that (DM3; open W-Sa 11am-10pm, Su 11am-5pm). The **telephone code** is 06541.

■ Fulda

In the grim old days of the East-West division, Fulda earned a dubious distinction as the most likely target for a Warsaw Pact invasion, gaining the undesirable nickname of the "Fulda Gap." The city's central location between Hamburg, Berlin, Munich, and Köln changed from burden to asset as reunification turned Fulda into a transportation hub. Today Fulda is rich in culture and serves as the economic and political center of eastern Hesse. The result of this unsteady evolution is a strange contrast: in startling proximity to the marvelous historical treasures are rows of fast-food restaurants, boutiques, and mini-malls which maintain a steady flow of trendy local teens.

The Fulda Prince-Abbots who dominated the city's spiritual and secular life for almost 700 years commissioned the construction of the compact Baroque quarter. Inside the **Stadtschloß,** built as the centerpiece of the quarter and the residence of the Prince-Abbots, the white **Kaisersaal** displays the portraits of 16 Habsburg emperors, while its **Historischen Raümen** (festivity hall) and the famous collection of Fulda porcelain. (Open daily 10am-6pm. DM4, students DM3, DM0.50 extra for a guided tour. Tours in German Apr.-Oct. daily at 10:30am and 2:30pm; Nov.-Mar. Sa-Su and holidays 10:30 am and 2:30pm.) To reach this sprawling yellow behemoth from the main train station, head down Bahnhofstr. and turn right in front of the church onto Friedrichstr. Climb the **Schloßturm** (tower) to admire the lush greenery carpeting Fulda. Behind the palace lies a luxurious **park** lined with terraces and home to the 18th-century **Orangerie** (built 1722 to 1725), a striking piece of architecture originally built to house the royal garden of imported orange and lemon trees, but now home to a ritzy cafe and a convention center. The **Floravase,** one of the most treasured baroque sculptures in Germany, graces the front steps of the *Orangerie.* Directly to the right of the *Dom* is **St. Michaelskirche** (open daily Apr. to mid-Oct. 10am-6pm; mid-Oct. to Mar. 2-4pm; free).

Across the street from the **Schloß** stands the enormous and magnificent 18th-century **Dom,** which houses the tomb of St. Boniface. (Open Apr.-Oct. M-F 10am-6pm, Sa 10am-3pm, Su and holidays 1-6pm; Nov.-Mar. M-F 10am-5pm, Sa 10am-3pm, Su and holidays 1-6pm. Free. Organ concerts May-June and Sept.-Oct. Sa noon. Free.) An 8th-century English monk and missionary known as "the apostle of Germany," Boniface founded the Fulda abbey. An alabaster Baroque memorial edged with black marble supposedly depicts St. Boniface surrounded by angels lifting his coffin lid on Judgment Day, though it looks more like the cherubs are trying to stuff him back in. The **Dommuseum,** accessible through the courtyard, displays the dagger with which the head of St. Boniface was severed in 754, as well as Lucas Cranach's *Christ and the Adulteress.* (Open Apr.-Oct. Tu-Sa 10am-5:30pm, Su 12:30-5:30pm; Nov.-Mar. Tu-Sa 10am-12:30pm and 1:30-4pm, Su 12:30-4pm; closed in January. DM4, students DM2.50.) Visitors can purchase a **Museum Passport** from tourist information good for admission to the Historical Rooms, Cathedral Museum, German Fire-Brigade Museum, and Vonderau Museum (which puts Fulda's cultural history on exhibit) for DM12, students and children for DM8 (DM10 and DM7, respectively, if you take public transportation).

Due to its strategic location, Fulda offers good rail connections. Many of the departing trains are ICE—super-fast but expensive. **Trains** go from Fulda to Hamburg (3hr., every hr.), Nuremburg (1hr., every hr.), and Frankfurt (1hr., 2-3 every hr.). The main **tourist office** (*Verkehrsbüro;* tel. 10 23 45; fax 10 27 75; email verkehrs-buero@fulda.de; http://www.fulda.de) 36037 Fulda, lies through the courtyard of the *Schloß.* The office offers free maps and books rooms for free, by telephone or internet (open M-W and F 8:30am-4:30pm, Th 8:30am-5:30pm, Sa 9:30am-2pm). The staff offers guided walks through the city. (Apr.-Oct. daily 11:30am and 2pm; Nov.-Mar. Sa-Su and holidays 11:30am and 2pm. DM5-7, students DM2.50-5.) There is also a **Deutsche Bahn Service Point** at the train station, which has tons of maps, though they don't book rooms. The **telephone code** is 0661.

Fulda's **Jugendherberge (HI),** Schirmannstr. 31 (tel. 733 89; fax 748 11) can be reached with bus #1B or bus line 5052 from the train station. Get off at "Stadion" and proceed two minutes up the hill—it will be on your left. Pleasant vistas, purple hallways, a friendly staff, and clean rooms make for an overall pleasant experience. The front door closes at 11:30pm, but you can get the combination if you want to come in later. (DM23.50, over 27 DM28.50. Breakfast included. Sheets DM6.) Frau Kremer runs a spartan but delightfully inexpensive ship at the **Gasthaus Zum Kronhof,** Am Kronhof 2 (tel. 741 47), behind the *Dom* just outside the old city walls. From the *Schloß,* cross the street and walk downhill on Kastanian-Allee, which becomes Wilhelmstr. after the *Dom.* Take a right along the city wall on Kronhofstr. and look for a raspberry-pink building three blocks down on the left. (Singles DM35; doubles DM70, with shower DM90. Breakfast included.)

▓ Kassel

After Napoleon III and his soldiers were trounced by Prussian troops at the Battle of Sedan in 1870, the unlucky French emperor was captured. While crossing the Franco-German border on his way to the Schloß Wilhelmshöhe prison, Aacheners jeered *"Ab nach Kassel"* ("off to Kassel") at the crestfallen Frog. The slogan echoed throughout Germany. Today, hordes of travelers still answer the call, coming to see the many treasures the ultra-sophisticated metropolis of Kassel has to offer. The city's eclecticism produces both contemporaneous and historical delights which gain vibrancy through their intermingling. The steeped traditions of Wilhelmshöhe, the grand hillside parks, and the fairy-tale atmosphere that inspired the Grimm Brothers to create their famous **Kinder- und Hausmärchen** complement the cutting-edge thinking of the **documenta** modern art exhibitions and a pulsating *Uni*-setting.

ORIENTATION AND PRACTICAL INFORMATION

Kassel is a diffuse city, the product of a nightmarish building boom that followed the postwar housing shortage. Somehow the boom never stopped. The *Deutsche Bahn* powers-that-be chose Kassel to be an InterCity Express connection and have rebuilt the **Bahnhof Wilhelmshöhe-Kassel** with streamlined contemporary specs. The Wilhelmshöhe station is the point of entry to Kassel's ancient castles and immense parklands on the west side; the older **Hauptbahnhof** is the gateway to the tightly packed and entirely modernized *Altstadt*. The *Hauptbahnhof* is now a model of extravagant hipness; its remodeling in the past year saturated it with (post)modern adornments and one of the *documenta* exhibitions, the **caricatura**. IC, ICE, and most IR trains only stop at Wilhelmshöhe. Frequent trains, city buses, and streetcars shuttle between the stations; you can catch most other bus and streetcar lines at either the "Rathaus" or "Am Stern" stops. From the *Hauptbahnhof*, take streetcar #7 or 9 to "Rathaus," and streetcar #4, 7, or 9 to "Am Stern"; from Wilhelmshöhe take streetcar #1, 4, or 6 to "Rathaus" or "Am Stern." The underground walkway in front of the *Hauptbahnhof* is often full of shady-looking folks; don't walk there alone after dark. Instead, explore around **Treppenstraße**, Kassel's original pedestrian zone and the first in all of Germany, or around **Königsstraße,** the current pedestrian zone.

Trains: To and from Frankfurt (2hr.), Hamburg (2hr. with ICE), Düsseldorf (3½hr.), Berlin (3½hr. with ICE), and Munich (5hr. with ICE).

Ferries: Personenschiffahrt Söllner, Die Schlagd/Rondell (tel. 77 46 70; fax 77 77 76), at the *Fuldabrücke* near the *Altmarkt*, offers Fulda Valley tours (3hr.) mid-June to Aug. daily 2pm, May to mid-June and Sept. W and Sa-Su 2pm. One-way DM10, round-trip DM16, children half-price. You can also sail to the junction of the Fulda and Werra rivers (May to mid-Sept. Su and W at 9:30am). One-way DM20, round-trip DM30, children half-price.

Public Transportation: Kassel's ultra-sophisticated system of buses and streetcars is integrated into the **NVV** (Nordhessischer Verkehrsverbund). Tickets priced by distance; **one-ride cards** range from DM2.40 (short trips) to DM4.30 (anywhere in the area). The **Multiticket** (DM8.50) is valid for 2 adults and 3 kids for a weekday or a weekend. Ask questions at the NVV-Center at Königsplatz 366 (tel. 70 75 80).

Taxi Service: tel. 881 11.

Car Rental: City-rent Autofairmietung, Kurt-Schumacherstr. 25 (tel. 77 08 21). DM49-260 per day.

Bike Rental: FahrradHof, Wilhelmshöher Allee 253, in the Wilhelmshöhe train station (tel. 31 30 83). Bikes from DM20 for 24hr., DM80 for 5 days. Open M-F 9am-1pm and 2-6pm, Sa 9am-1pm.

Tourist Office: Kassel-Service, Königspl. 53, 2nd floor (tel. 707 71˙07; fax 707 71 69), sells maps (DM0.50), a hotel list (DM0.50; rooms DM45 and up), and brochures in English (from DM1.50). City tours leave from Königsplatz (May-Oct. Sa 2pm; 2hr.; DM18, children DM12). Ask about "Kassel Service Cards," which give access to public transportation and other discounts. Office open M-Th 9:15am-6pm, F 9:15am-4:30pm. **Branch office** in the Wilhelmshöhe *Bahnhof* (tel. 340 54; fax 31 52 16). As super-modern as the rest of the station. Doles out catalogs and maps and finds rooms for a DM5 fee. Open M-F 9am-1pm and 2-6pm, Sa 9am-1pm.

Bookstore: Buchladung Vaternahm, Obere Königsstr. 7 (tel. 78 98 40; email vaternahm-kassel@t-online.de). Broad selection of paperbacks in English from Hobbes to *Calvin and Hobbes.* Open M-F 9:30am-8pm, Su 9am-4pm.

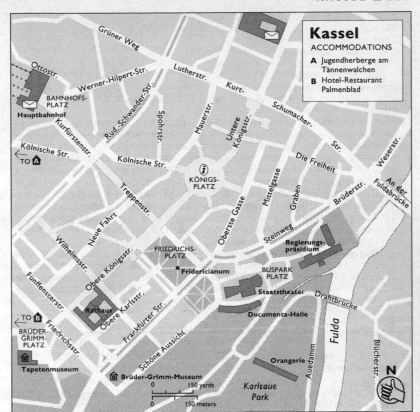

Kassel
ACCOMMODATIONS

A Jugendherberge am Tännenwalchen
B Hotel-Restaurant Palmenblad

[Map labels: Grüner Weg, Ottostr., Werner-Hilpert-Str., Lutherstr., Kurt-, BAHNHOFS-PLATZ, Hauptbahnhof, Rud. Schwander-Str., Spohrstr., Mauerstr., Untere Königsstr., Schumacher-, Str., Kölnische Str., TO A, Kurfürstenstr., Kölnische Str., KÖNIGS-PLATZ, Die Freiheit, Wesertstr., An der Fuldabrücke, Treppenstr., Neue Fahrt, Oberste Gasse, Mittelgasse, Graben, Brüderstr., Wilhelmsstr., FRIEDRICHS-PLATZ, Steinweg, Regierungs-präsidium, Fünffenscerstr., Obere Königsstr., Fridericianum, BUSPARK PLATZ, TO B, Rathaus, Obere Karlsstr., Staatstheater, Drahtbrücke, BRÜDER-GRIMM-PLATZ, Friedrichsstr., Frankfurter Str., Documenta-Halle, Schöne Aussicht, Fulda, Blücherstr., Tapetenmuseum, Brüder-Grimm-Museum, Orangerie, Auedamm, Karlsaue Park, N, 0 150 yards, 0 150 meters]

Laundromat: **Schnell & Sauber,** Friedrich-Ebert-Str. 83, near the hostel, is ecologically friendly and computerized—one *great* quickie...without the mess! Wash DM6. Dry DM1 per 11min. Open M-Sa 5am-midnight.

Women's Concerns: Frauenhaus Kassel, Frankfurterstr. 65 (tel. 89 88 89). **Beratungsstelle Schwarze Winkel,** Goethestr. 44 (tel. 10 70 25).

AIDS-Hilfe: Frankfurterstr. 65 (tel. 28 39 07). Open daily 10am-1pm.

Emergency: Police, tel. 110. **Fire** and **Ambulance,** tel. 112.

Hospital: Städtische Klinik, Möncherbergstr. 41-43 (tel. 98 00).

Post Office: Hauptpostamt, Untere Königsstr. 95, 34117 Kassel (tel. 700 63 00), between Königsplatz and the university. Open M-F 8am-6pm, Sa 8am-noon.

Internet Access: In **New York** (see **Entertainment and Nightlife,** p. 387).

Telephone Code: 0561.

ACCOMMODATIONS AND CAMPING

Hotels in Kassel actively seek conventioneers and business crowds, but the large accommodations industry generally has a surplus of moderately priced rooms.

Jugendherberge am Tannenwäldchen (HI), Schenkendorfstr. 18 (tel. 77 64 55; fax 77 68 32). Streetcar #4 or 6 from the Rathaus or the Wilhelmshöhe Station (direction: "Ottostr." or "Lindenberg") to "Annastr." Continue walking up Friedrich-Ebert-Str., and make a right on Schenkendorf. Or walk from the *Hauptbahnhof;* leave from the *Südausgang,* turn right on Kölnische Str., and turn right again onto Schenkendorfstr. Your window might overlook train tracks, but you might get your own bathroom. The disco (for little stinkers) and bar (for tipsy drinkers) downstairs don't help the noise level either. DM24.50, over 26 DM29.50. Sheets DM6. Breakfast included. Reception until 11pm. Sunday and winter curfew 12:30am. No phone reservations.

⊛**Hotel-Restaurant Palmenbad,** Kurhausstr. 27 (tel./fax 326 91). Streetcar #3 (direction: "Ihringshäuserstr.") to "Wigandstr.," then 5min. uphill on An den Eichen. Or walk from the Wilhelmshöhe *Bahnhof* up Wilhelmshöher Allee (towards Herkules), left on Baunsbergstr., right on Kurhausstr. Cozy quarters, friendly folks. Singles DM49; doubles DM90, with shower DM95. Reception M-F 5:30-11pm, Sa 10am-11pm, Su 10am-3pm.

Hotel-Restaurant Lenz, Frankfurterstr. 176 (tel. 433 73; fax 411 88), is too far to reach by foot from either main station, but the Niederzwehren station right around the corner is serviced by bus #24 (from Wilhelmshöhe) and streetcar #9 from the *Hauptbahnhof*. Sharp-looking rooms and bathrooms big enough for Herkules. Singles DM49.50, with bath DM90; doubles DM90, with bath DM130. Breakfast included. Reception 4-10pm.

Hotel Am Rathaus, Wilhelmsstr. 29 (tel. 97 88 50; fax 978 85 30). From the *Rathaus,* make a left onto Fünffensterstr., a left down Obere Karlstr., and another left where the statue of Langraf Karl is striking a pose. Snug rooms and a central location. Singles DM61, with shower DM75; doubles with shower DM110. Breakfast included. Reception until 9pm.

Camping: Kurhessen-Kassel, Giesenallee 7 (tel. 224 33). Bus #16 (direction: "Auestadion") or bus #25 (direction: "Bebelplatz") to "Damaschkebrücke." The campground boasts a stunning spot right on the Fulda and is pleasantly close to the "Island of Flowers" in the Karlsaue park. DM5 per adult, DM2 per child; DM10 and up per tent. Reception 8am-1pm and 3-10pm. Open Mar.-Oct.

FOOD

Many of Kassel's culinary offerings take a bite out of ye olde budget. Friedrich-Ebert-Str., the upper part of Wilhelmshöher Allee, and the area around Königsplatz have supermarkets and cafes sprinkled among department stores and fashion boutiques. The **okay! supermarkts** (one is at the Wilhelmshöhe station, the other at 27 Friedrich-Ebert-Str.) function as grocery stores, fruit stands, and bakeries rolled into one (open M-F 8:30am-8pm, Sa 8am-2pm). Or pick through goodies at the **Markt,** on Königsplatz. Inexpensive meals await in the university complex. From Wilhelmshöhe train station, take streetcar #1 to "Holländischerpl.," cross through the underground passage, and continue in the same direction; walk along the left side of the university to the back and hang a right onto Arnold-Bode-Str. As in most large German cities, Kassel's *Altstadt* has numerous food stands, bakeries, and fast food restaurants.

documenta

Hordes of art-lovers, didactic dilettantes, and camera-toting curiosity seekers descended upon Kassel in the summer of 1997 to take part in the world's preeminent exhibition of contemporary art, *documenta* X. As the world careens toward a new millennium, artists of the exhibition struggle to critique art's modern political function. Viewing contemporary art as a means of "social regulation or indeed control through the aestheticization of information and forms of debate that paralyze any act of judgment in the immediacy of raw seduction or emotion (what might be called 'the Benetton effect')," the contributors to *documenta* emphasized the soul-searching and democratic potential of new media that subvert traditional notions of artistic form. Amid collections of giant Chia Pets and ironic images of "ideal" cityscapes, the show included a bevy of internet pieces which were broadcast worldwide in real-time (http://www.documenta.de). While the political posturing could be both enrapturing and excruciating, the exhibit represented the ultimate postmodern dream (evidenced by the insistence of the organizers that no label could describe the event) whose influence will resonate in the art world for decades, or millennia, to come. Documenta XI will take place in Kassel from June 8 to September 15, 2002.

Mensa (tel. 804 25 87), on Arnold-Bode-Str. in the back left corner of the University, 100m across a gorge from the big red brick tower. Look for the "Mensa" sign—it's the only way to tell this brick building from the 50-odd others. Students with ID DM2.90-4.50, others tack on DM2. Lunch M-F 11:45am-2:15pm. The **Moritz-Restaurant** in the same building serves a slightly more elaborate lunch with much shorter lines. Students DM4.70, others DM6.90. Open M-F 11am-2:30pm. Just around the corner the **Studentwerke-Pavillion,** Diagonale 13, slaps together meals later in the day for the same prices (open M-F 5-9pm). The cafe downstairs sells the cheapest ice cream around (DM0.80 per *Kugel,* or scoop).

@**Lohmann Biergarten,** Königstor 8 (tel. 122 90). From the Rathaus, walk up Fünffensterstr. and make a left onto Königstor. Lohmann Biergarten is the only outdoor *Biergarten* in Kassel that is open until 2am. As it is surrounded only by office buildings, it can serve until 2am on weekdays and until 1am on Fridays and Saturdays. One of Kassel's oldest and largest beer gardens. Traditional and tasty entrees (Spaghetti Bolognese DM9), washed down with *Apfelwein* (DM3). Opens at noon.

Bistro & Restaurant Eckstein, corner of Obere Königsstr. and Fünffensterstr. (tel. 71 33 00). The selection here is as large as the portions. Vegetarians, dig in. (Pizzas DM5.90-13, vegetarian dishes around DM10.50, other entrees DM10-18). Lunch specials M-F 11:30am-5pm (DM8.90). Open F-Sa 11am-2am, Su-Th 11am-1am.

Wok, Kölnischerstr. 124 (tel. 71 11 44), on the way to the youth hostel. Surprisingly good and spicy Thai food awaits those who have had their fill of *Schnitzel* and *Wurst.* Lunch entrees available Tu-F (DM7.50-12.50). Dinner entrees are more pricy (DM12.80-25). Beer DM3.80-4.90. You can also order to go. Open Tu-F and Su noon-3pm and 6pm-midnight, Sa 6pm-midnight.

SIGHTS

Kassel's sights fall into three categories: those associated with *documenta,* those at Wilhelmshöhe, and those near the *Rathaus.* The museums and galleries of *documenta* are scattered downhill of Königsstr. between the *Rathaus* and Königsplatz towards the Fulda River. The sights at Wilhelmshöhe Park lie at one end of the long Wilhelmshöher Allee. At the other end stands the *Rathaus,* just after Wilhelmshöher Allee becomes Obere Königsstr. This latter road runs through Königsplatz to the *Uni.* Most of the museums—Schloß Wilhelmshöhe, Ballhaus, Hessisches Landesmuseum, Neue Galerie, and Orangerie—belong to **Staatliche Museen Kassel** and are covered by a package deal: the **Verbundkarte** (combination ticket) lets you visit all of these attractions and is for sale at any of them (DM15, students DM10).

documenta

The concept behind the **documenta** is to confront and address the controversies behind expression. In 1997, the city hosted the exhibition for the 10th straight time since 1955. Several of the past *documentas* have become permanent exhibitions: you can visit Claes Oldenburg's "Pick-axe" on the banks of the Fulda near the Orangery *(documenta 7, 1982),* and Joseph Beuy's "7,000 oak trees" *(documenta 7, 1982).* You can even count them. Even the *Hauptbahnhof* has gotten in on the *documenta* action—it houses a collection, the **caricatura** (tel. 77 64 99), which is a self-proclaimed "gallery for bizarre art." *(Open Tu-F 2-8pm, Sa-Su noon-8pm.)* The enormous **Museum Fridericianum,** Friedrichspl. 18 (tel. 70 72 70), the oldest museum building on the continent, contains the lion's share of *documenta*-related exhibitions. *(Open W-Su 10am-6pm, Th 10am-8pm. DM8, students DM5; free admission Th 6-8pm.)* Kassel's newest tribute to the growing world of *documenta* is a super-modern gallery of changing exhibitions: the **documenta-Halle,** Friedrichspl. (tel. 10 75 21; DM6, students DM4). If you are still thirsting for more, you can visit the **documenta-Archives,** Untere Karlsstr. 41 (tel. 787 40 22; open M-F 10am-2pm). The future holds still more! Kassel will host *documenta* 11 in June 2002.

Wilhelmshöhe Park

Wilhelmshöhe is a hillside park with one giant Greek hero, two castles, three museums, and five waterfalls, punctuated with rock gardens, mountain streams, and innumerable hiking trails. The whole park experience—a cross between the halls of Montezuma and a Baroque theme park—takes up half a day in itself; approach it with humor, cynicism, or a bicycle (see **Bike Rentals,** p. 382). From the Wilhelmshöhe station, take bus #43 (direction: "Herkules") to the last stop. This brings you to the northern tip of the park, and from here you can work your way downhill. The structure before you will be the monumental **Riesenschloß** (giant's castle), a massive octagonal amphitheater topped by the figure of **Herkules**—Kassel's emblem. The mighty Herkules jeers at his conquered foe, the giant Encelades, whose head pokes out of the rocks at the top of the cascades. An English author traveling in the 18th century described it as "one of the most splendid structures in all of Europe, not excluding those in Versailles, Frascati, or Tivoli." You can climb up onto Herkules's pedestal, and if you're brave enough, into his club. *(Access to the base of the statue free; extra altitude available mid-Mar. to mid-Nov. Tu-Su 10am-5pm. DM3, students DM2.)* Climb down the right-hand side steps along the **cascades**—some are for humans and some are for giants. But be warned, when there isn't enough water, the cascades aren't quite "cascading." If you arrive at the top of Herkules on a Sunday or Wednesday, you'll see the **fountain displays** *(Wasserspiele)* that start at 2:30pm; they're timed so that a walk down the clearly designated path lands you at the next waterfall as the show begins (Easter-Sept. only). The grand finale comes at 3:45pm in the Palace Lake when the *Wasserspiele* end in a grand gush—a 52m-high geyser. Stake out a vantage point early. At the bottom, veer off on the path to your right to get to the **Steinhöfer Wasserfall.** When the path and road split, stay on the path. At the waterfall, turn onto the path to your left. When you reach the road, make a right onto it and follow it to the **Schloß Löwenburg,** or take bus #23 there.

The **Schloß Löwenburg** is an amazing piece of architectural fantasy. *(Open Mar.-Oct. Tu-Su 10am-5pm; Nov.-Feb. Tu-Su 10am-4pm. Tours almost every hour. DM6, students DM4.)* It was built by Wilhelm in the 18th century with stones deliberately missing to achieve the effect of a crumbling medieval castle; to add to the ancient look, the material used was a rapidly deteriorating basalt. For some reason this Teutonic Don Quixote was obsessed with the year 1495 and fancied himself a time-displaced knight. In order to supplement the credibility of this pretense, he even built a Catholic chapel on the *Schloß* to date it before the Reformation, even though he himself was Protestant. Despite his claims of chivalry, the castle was built as a boinking bungalow for his favorite concubine, who bore him 15 children—13 more than his wife.

Exit Löwenburg on the same road that led you to it, and you'll see a footpath to your right. It's a 20-minute walk to the **Schloß Wilhelmshöhe** along this path, but you can stop, rest, and soak your footsies along the way. The *Schloß* is the mammoth former home of the rulers of Kassel. Napoleon III was imprisoned here after being captured in the Battle of Sedan. The **Schloß Museum** (tel. 935 70), records the extravagant royal lifestyle. *(Open Mar.-Oct. Tu-Su 10am-5pm; Nov.-Feb. Tu-Su 10am-4pm. Tours of private suites leave when there are "enough" people. DM6, students DM4.)* Although the **Gallery of Old Masters** is closed for renovations until 2000, some of its famous works can be seen at the **Neue Galerie,** the **Hessisches Landesmuseum,** and the **documenta-Halle.** All done with *Wilhelmshöhe*? Go down the steps behind the *Schloß,* and continue along the lakeside path. When you reach the windy road (Mulangstr.), make a left and then a right onto Wilhelmshöher Allee. Hop on *Straßenbahn* #1 (direction: "Holländische Straße") and take it to the Wilhelmshöhe *Bahnhof,* the *Rathaus,* or "Am Stern."

Near the Rathaus

The English Garden of **Karlsaue Park** sprawls along the Fulda. At its north end, the bright yellow **Orangerie** manor house, built in 1701, is home to the **Museum of Astronomy and Technological History** (tel. 715 43), crammed full of mechanical and optical marvels as well as a planetarium. *(Open Tu-Su 10am-5pm. Museum DM5, students DM3. Free on Fridays. Daily planetarium shows DM5, students DM3.)* At the southern tip of the park is the "Insel Siebenbergen"—Karslane's unique "Island of Flowers." You can take a one-hour hike there, or hop on bus #16 (direction: "Auestadion") from Königsplatz to "Siebenbergen." Lavishly illustrated, the

Brüder Grimm Museum in Palais Bellevue, Schöne Aussicht 2 (tel. 787 20 33) near the Orangerie, exhibits the brothers' handwritten copy of *Kinder- und Hausmärchen,* their fabled collection of fairy tales, and translations into dozens of languages. *(Open daily 10am-5pm. DM3, students DM2.)* To get there, walk toward the Fulda from Friedrichspl. and make a right onto Schöne Aussicht. Nothing quite matches the **Deutsches Tapeten Museum** (German Wallpaper Museum), Brüder-Grimm-Platz 5 (tel. 784 60), in the yellow **Hessiches Landesmuseum** close to the *Rathaus. (Open Tu-Su 10am-5pm. DM5, students DM3.)* The only museum of its kind in the world, this place is wall-to-wall, floor-to-ceiling fun! Surprises include 16th-century embossed leather-and-gold Spanish hangings, a rare depiction of the battle of Austerlitz, a six-color wallpaper printer, and a letter from Goethe to Schiller mentioning an order of wallpaper. Shadow box scenes display the fascinating development of styles from the Middle Ages to the 1930s.

ENTERTAINMENT AND NIGHTLIFE

Dozens of music bars, pubs, cafes, and discos spice up the *Altstadt.* The stretch along Ebertstr. and Goethestr. between Bebelplatz and Königsplatz, and extending south along Rathenau-Allee toward the *Rathaus,* packs in the party *Geist.* The free magazine *INFOTIP,* available at the hostel or tourist office, details the *Szene.* It contains a useful schedule of "parties" at each of the city's clubs; hours change often, so be sure to check out this calendar. Also available is *Kasselaktuell,* the free culture and information magazine.

The city fosters a lively film culture. Theaters cluster the *Altstadt;* **Capitol** (tel. 729 09 66) on Wilhelmstr. screens films in English (F-Sa). Kassel hosts an **open-air film fest** every summer at the theater **dock 4** (tel. 787 20 67). Take Streetcar #1 or 3 to "Friedrichpl." Shows range from the artsy pretense of Godard to pure blockbuster mayhem (e.g. *Star Wars* and *das Imperium schlägt zurück;* tickets DM10). The **Staatstheater** at Friedrichpl. hosts plays, concerts, operas, and ballet performances; everything from *Grease* to *Romeo and Juliet.* (Season is mid-Sept. to early July; tickets DM21-42; call 109 42 22 for info and tickets.)

Salzmanns Factory, Sandershäuserstr. 36 (tel. 57 25 42), pumps it up with the phattest house and techno tracks in *Action Club.* Their brand new addition is *Labor Ost*—an experimental theater and dance room. Dieter? Is that you? Cover DM-10. Open F-Sa 10pm-3am.

Mr. Jones, Goethestr. 31 (tel. 71 08 18; http.//www.Mr-Jones.de). An ultra-hip, ultra-modern bar and restaurant flaunting giant fluorescent insects. Excellent food of the Tex-Mex and grilled varieties (sandwiches DM8-12). Open Su-Th 10am-1am, F-Sa 10am-midnight.

Musiktheater, Angersbachstr. 10 (tel. 840 44). A disco-party mecca located on the other side of the tracks (from the hostel, bus #27 to "Angersbachstr."). Three humongous dance floors—1 for techno, 1 for house and hip-hop, 1 for rock/pop—occupy 2 city blocks. Cover DM5. Open W and F-Sa after 10:30pm.

Knösel, Goethestr. 25 (tel. 354 11). Genuine Kassel townies hang out in this classic beer-drinking environment. They love their beer and their *Fußball.* Open M-Th 4pm-1am, F-Sa 4pm-3am, Su 5pm-1am.

Café Suspekt, Fünffensterstr. 14 (tel. 10 45 22). Popular gay and lesbian pub belies its name with a laid-back and friendly ambience. Open Tu-F 10pm-1am, Sa-Su 10pm-2am.

Rheinland-Pfalz
(Rhineland-Palatinate)

A trip to the Rheinland-Pfalz to see the castles and wine towns along the Rhine is an obligatory tourist tromp. The region is a visual feast—the Mosel River curls downstream to the Rhine Gorge, a soft shore of castle-backed hills. But it also provides a literal feast; a rich agricultural tradition keeps fresh fruits and vegetables in abundance, and the many vineyards in the Rhine and Mosel Valleys produce sweet and delicious wines. Trier is a millennia-old collage of sights, while the medieval towns of Mainz, Worms, and Speyer bow down around glorious cathedrals. Politically potent since the days when its electors were the king-makers of the Holy Roman Empire, the Rheinland-Pfalz is now the home of the Federal Republic's large leader, Chancellor Helmut Kohl.

🖐 HIGHLIGHTS OF RHEINLAND-PFALZ

- The **Rhine Gorge** is a poet's dream come true. From its mystical **Lorelei cliffs** to its majestic castles and famous wineries, the **Gorge** cannot fail to impress (see p. 393).
- Tiny hamlets with half-timbered houses abound in the **Moseltal.** The many well-touristed towns in the region keep up the German tradition of gorgeous, ubiquitous castles and are surrounded by endless hills of vineyards (see p. 399).
- At the confluence of the Rhine and the Mosel, **Koblenz** busts out with beautiful churches and German spirit. Wave "Hi!" to Beethoven's mom (see p. 388).
- **Mainz** was once home to **Johannes Gutenberg,** inventor of the printing press. Copies of his famous **Bibles** are on display at the Gutenberg Museum, while the fantastic **Dom** draws the devout (see p. 397).

■ Koblenz

The etymology of "Koblenz," a corruption of the Latin word for "confluence," illuminates the city's volatile history. Over the past 2000 years, Rome, France, Prussia, and Germany all fought to control this beautiful city where the Rhine and Mosel rivers converge. Although wars of conquest have died down in recent years, the frenetic activity has not. Trains rattle along both sides of the Rhine, and barges ringed by flirtatious speedboats plow through the water. For tourists, the rivers may be shining paths of history and legend, but they also serve as the conduits of modern German industry. Before reunification, the city served as the *Bundesrepublik's* largest munitions dump; today, the pyrotechnics that light up the city are decorative, not destructive. During the annual **Rhein in Flammen** (Rhine in Flames), held in August, the city is transformed into one fabulous flaming fiesta.

ORIENTATION AND PRACTICAL INFORMATION

Sites of interest cluster in the cone-shaped *Altstadt* fanning out from the Deutsches Eck; the *Hauptbahnhof* rests farther to the south. Löhrstr., Koblenz's shop-lined avenue of capitalism, connects the two. To the east, the Pfaffendorfer Brücke spans the Rhine, while the Europabrücke and the Balduinbrücke cross the Mosel in the north.

Trains: Koblenz lies along the line that connects Frankfurt to Köln and points north via the Rhine valley. Trains go to Köln (1hr., 3-4 per hr.), Mainz (50min., 3 per hr.), Frankfurt (2½hr., 2-3 per hr.), and Trier (1½hr., 2 per hr.).

Public Transportation: 10 main lines bus you around the city and into the 'burbs for DM1.80-5 per ride. Children's discount 50%. Day pass DM9. Tickets available from the driver. Bus hub **Zentralplatz** offers the most convenient access to the *Altstadt.*

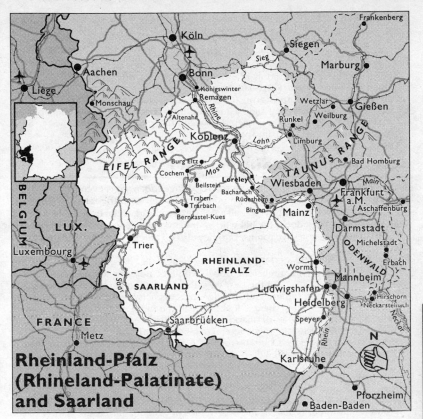

Frankenberg

Köln

Siegen

Aachen Bonn Marburg

Sieg

Liège Königswinter
Monschau Remagen Wetzlar Gießen

Altenahr Runkel Weilburg

Koblenz Lahn Limburg

Burg Eltz Bad Homburg

Cochem Mosel TAUNUS RANGE

Beilstein Loreley Wiesbaden Frankfurt Main
Traben- Bacharach a.M. Aschaffenburg
Trarbach Rüdesheim Bingen Mainz

Bernkastel-Kues

EIFEL RANGE

Darmstadt

Trier Michelstadt

LUX. Erbach

Luxembourg RHEINLAND- Worms ODENWALD
PFALZ

SAARLAND Mannheim

Ludwigshafen Hirschorn
Heidelberg Neckarsteinach

FRANCE Saarbrücken Speyer

Metz N

**Rheinland-Pfalz
(Rhineland-Palatinate)
and Saarland**

Karlsruhe

Pforzheim
Baden-Baden

BELGIUM

Taxi: Funk Taxi (tel. 330 55). Bring in da noise, bring in da...taxi.

Bike Rental: Biking the Rhine and Mosel is more satisfying (and wetter) than travel by boat or train. See the tourist office pamphlet *Rund ums Rad.* **Radschlag Fahrrad,** the cheapest option, has a selection that ranges from one-gear cycles (DM7 per day) to mountain bikes (DM18 per day), tandems, and the *Rikscha,* a 3-wheeled Laff Mobile (DM35 per day). Passport and deposit required. Open Apr.-Jan. 10 M-F 8:30am-noon and 2-6pm, Sa 9am-1pm; otherwise by appointment. **Fahrrad Franz,** Hohenfelderstr. 7 (tel. 323 63), has full service. Open M-W and F 9:30am-6:30pm, Th 9:30am-8pm, Sa 9am-2pm. **Vélo,** on Konrad-Adenauer-Ufer 1 (tel. 151 02), and **Campingplatz Rhein Mosel** will outfit you for DM10-13 per day.

Tourist Offices: The **main office** (tel. 313 04 or 331 34; fax 129 38 00), across the street from the train station, hands out boat schedules and city maps with hotel, restaurant, and pub listings. They find rooms for a DM2 fee (they'll give you the same list for free if you ask). Open May-Sept. M-F 9am-8pm, Sa-Su 10am-8pm. The **Konrad-Adenauer-Ufer** branch (tel. 129 16 30), next to the docks, has the same services. Open June-Sept. Tu-Su noon-6pm. A **walking tour** leaves from this office June-Oct. Sa at 2:30pm. Call ahead for groups or foreign language tours. **Rheinland-Pfalz information office,** Löhrstr. 103-105 (tel. 915 20 40), on the 3rd floor of an office building, has enough glossy brochures to outrage a *Grüne.* Open M-Tu and Th 8am-5pm, W and F 8am-3:30pm.

Bookstore: Reuffel, Löhrstr. 92 (tel. 30 30 70), has bunches of English paperbacks. Open M-W and F 9am-7pm, Th 9am-8pm, Sa 9am-4pm.

Laundromat: Wash that stink right out of your clothes at **Wasch Center,** on the corner of Rizzastr. and Löhrstr. Wash DM6, soap included. Dry DM2 per 15min. Open M-Sa 6am-midnight, last wash 11pm.

Emergency: Police, tel. 110. **Fire** and **Ambulance,** tel. 112.

Pharmacy: Posen Apotheke, up Löhrstr. to the left when leaving the train station, posts a list in its front window of other pharmacies providing emergency services. Open M-F 8am-6:30pm, Sa 8:30am-1pm.

Post Office: The **Hauptpostamt,** 65068 Koblenz, to the right of the train station exit, **exchanges currency** and cashes traveler's checks. Open M-F 8am-6pm, Sa 8am-noon. Limited services rendered M-W and F 7-8am and 6-8pm, Th 7-8am, Sa 7-8am and noon-4pm, Su 10am-1pm.

Telephone Code: 0261.

ACCOMMODATIONS AND CAMPING

Wake up with Koblenz at your feet in the regal *Jugendherberge;* even folks who can afford to stay elsewhere want to sleep here. The hostel sits at the zenith of Koblenz, but the difficult trek deters few, so call a day or two ahead. If the hostel is full, they'll send you straight back down the hill with your heavy pack. Some of the hotels nearer the station offer inexpensive rooms, but they also go quickly—always call ahead.

⊛Jugendherberge Koblenz (HI), in the castle (tel. 97 28 70; fax 972 87 30). Mailing address: Festung Ehrenbreitstein, 56077 Koblenz. Boasting a sparkling hostel, a museum, several cafes, and the best view this side of the *Lorelei,* the *Festung* is a worthy destination for any visitor. Since inaccessibility was the fortress's *raison d'être,* however, getting there is less than half the fun. First, get to the bottom of the hill: take bus #8, 9, or 10 (marked by "Jugendherberge" signs at the *Hauptbahnhof*) to "Ehrenbreitstein" if you intend to hike uphill. To ride the chairlift, take the bus one stop further to "Obertal" (rides daily Mar.-Sept. 9am-6pm; DM4, round-trip DM6). Hardier souls can hike up the hill from this stop. Fortunately, the hostel is friendly, super-clean, and well worth the hike. DM23.50. Breakfast included, dinner DM9. Reception 7am-11pm. Curfew 11:30pm (and you *don't* want to cut it close—the fortress is not lit at night!).

Hotel Jan-van-Werth, Van-Werth-Str. 9 (tel. 365 00; fax 365 06). This classy family-run establishment is among the best values in Koblenz. From the station, walk through Bahnhofplatz to Emil-Schuller-Str. up on your left. At the end take a left onto Hohenzollernstr. and then left (5min.) onto Van-Werth-Str. Singles DM35, with shower and toilet DM65; doubles DM85, with shower and toilet DM100-120. Gummi bears and breakfast included. Reception 6:30am-10pm.

Zur Kaul, Heffensteinstr. 64, (tel. 752 56; fax 768 72), at the bottom of the *Festung* hill, at the corner of Charlottenstr. and Heffensteinstr. Utility is key here; they may not be elegant, but these rooms provide what's really important—a bed. DM35 per person.

Camping: Campingplatz Rhein-Mosel, Am Neuendorfer Eck (tel. 827 19), across the Mosel from the Deutsches Eck. A ferry journeys across the river during the day (DM0.60). Reception 8am-noon and 2-8pm. DM5.50 per person, DM4.50-6 per tent. Open Apr.-Oct. 15.

FOOD AND NIGHTLIFE

⊛Marktstübchen, Am Markt 220 (tel. 755 65), is down at the very bottom of the hill from the hostel, though this restaurant's clientele seem to have never seen a hosteler. Authenticity's last stand, this hole-in-the-wall serves up *real* German food for *real* budget prices (most entrees under DM11). Open daily 9am-midnight.

Salat Garten (tel. 13 64 55), where Casinostr. becomes Gymnasiumstr. in the *Altstadt* just off Zentralplatz. Arteries (and taste buds) cry out for the vegetarian wonders that crop up here. Good salad bar. Self-service keeps prices low (daily specials DM8). Open M-W and F 11am-7pm, Th 11am-9pm, Sa 11am-3pm.

Altes Brauhaus, Braugasse 4 (tel. 15 10 01). Wildly popular with locals and tourists alike, this pub dishes out German food (around DM15) and home brew. Open M-Sa 10:30am-10pm. Kitchen open 11:30am-2:30pm and 5:30-10pm.

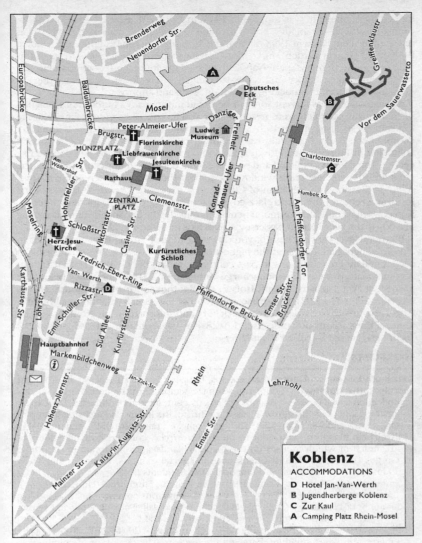

Koblenz

ACCOMMODATIONS

D Hotel Jan-Van-Werth
B Jugendherberge Koblenz
C Zur Kaul
A Camping Platz Rhein-Mosel

Tatort, Münzpl. 15 (tel. 42 19). This grungy rock and roll bar occasionally usurps Münzplatz as a stage for local bands and always brings a young twist to the *Altstadt*. Open daily 4pm-late.

SIGHTS

German nationalism, along with Germany's two greatest rivers, converges at the **Deutsches Eck** (German Corner). A peninsula at the confluence of the Rhine and Mosel, it purportedly witnessed the birth of the German nation in 1216 when the Teutonic Order of Knights settled here. Today, the **Mahnmal der Deutschen Einheit** (Monument to German Unity) stands on the right, commemorating a rather different sort of union. Erected in 1897, it stands in tribute to Kaiser Wilhelm I for forcibly reconciling the internal conflicts of the German Empire (though the *Kaiser* played second fiddle to Bismarck). The 14m high equestrian statue of the *Kaiser* that once topped the monument was toppled in 1945. In a move that raised questions about German aesthetic sensibilities, not to mention resurgent nationalism, the statue was replaced by a duplicate in 1993. Behind the *Mahnmal*, in the beautiful, unassuming **Blumenhof** (flower garden), lurks more blatant national *braggadocio*, though this time not on the Germans' part. Napoleon erected the **fountain** to commemorate the "certain impending victory" in his Russian campaign. The Russians, after routing the French army, added the mocking inscription "seen and approved."

Attractions of a less fervent sort can be found in the many churches of Koblenz's *Altstadt*, many of which were restored after WWII. The 12th-century **Florinskirche** lost some of its luster in the 19th-century wars when Napoleon used it as a military encampment. Today, beautifully restored frescoes and windows illuminate a fantastic collection of liturgical art. The oval Baroque towers of the **Liebfrauenkirche** rise nearby. The church's emerald and sapphire stained glass and intricate ceiling lattice-work are stunning; the choir windows document the role of women in the *Heilsgeschichte* (Passion and Salvation of Christ). The masterful *Rheinisch* facade of the **Jesuitenkirche** on the Marktplatz conceals a startlingly bright, modern interior. Koblenz's most mischievous monument lurks outside; the **Schängelbrunnen**, a statue of a boy that spits water on passersby, drives kids into frenzied glee.

If ground-level viewing has got you down, head for **Festung Ehrenbreitstein**, an old Brobdingnagian fortress at the highest point in the city. The Prussians used it to accommodate French troops in past centuries; today, the German state uses it to accommodate *you* (see **Jugendherberge Koblenz**, p. 390). In the valley below the fortress, at Wambachstr. 204, off Hofstr., sits **Beethoven's mother's house.** Now a museum (tel. 129 25 02), the sparse collection of letters will disappoint all but die-hard Ludwig van Groupies. **Theater tickets** and information on Koblenz can be found at the *Rathaus* box office (tel. 129 28 40). Ask about student discounts. *(Open Tu-F 11am-1pm and 2-4pm, Sa 11am-1pm.)*

MUSEUMS

Museum Ludwig im Deutschherrenhaus, Danziger Freiheit 1 (tel. 30 40 40), right behind the *Mahnmal*. The hilarious bronze sculpture in the courtyard gives this collection a well-deserved thumbs up! Mostly contemporary French art, but expect anything and everything from Picasso to Christo, the infamous *Reichstag* Wrapper. Open Tu-W and F-Sa 11am-5pm, Th 11am-7pm, Su 11am-6pm. DM5, students DM3.

Mittelrhein Museum, next door to the *Florinskirche*, contains 4 diverse floors of art, much of which focuses on the painterly landscapes upstream in the Rhine Gorge. They've got Klimt! Check out the special exhibits. Open Tu and Th-Sa 11am-5pm, W 11am-7pm, Su 11am-6am. DM5, students DM3.

Landesmuseum Koblenz, Hohe Ostfront, in Festung Ehrenbreitstein (tel. 970 30). Lots of cannons, wine, tobacco, and guns. A dangerous combination. Alas, no live ammo or tasty samples. Open mid-Mar. to mid-Nov. daily 9am-12:30pm and 1-5pm, last entrance 15min. before closing. DM3, students DM2.

Mittelrheinisches Postmuseum, Friedrich-Ebert-Ring 14-20 (tel. 128 20 60), in the Oberpostdirektion building. Enter on Friedrichstr. The evolution of communication from the days when mailmen carried sabers and bugles. Also documents the unholy alliance between the German post and telephone systems, and Mucho, Mucho Maas. Open through rain, hail, sleet, and snow M-Th 10am-4pm. Free.

Rhein Museum Koblenz, Charlottenstr. 53a (tel. 70 34 50). Bus #9 or 10 to "Charlottenstr." A private museum devoted to all things *Rheinisch,* including old boats, engines, fish (dead), and even an old captain's seat. Four floors of maritime history. A good double-header with Beethoven's mother's house. Open daily 10am-5pm. DM4, children DM3.

THE RHINE GORGE

> At present, the sun and moon alone cast their light upon these old buildings famed in story and gnawed by time, whose walls are falling stone by stone into the Rhine, and whose history is fast fading into oblivion. O noble tower! O poor, paralyzed giants! A steamboat packed with travelers now spews its smoke in your faces!
>
> —Victor Hugo

Though the Rhine River runs all the way from Switzerland to the North Sea, the Rhine of the imagination exists only in the 80km of the gorge stretching from Bonn to north of Mainz. As the river rolls out to the sea, treacherous whirlpools and craggy shores surround the castles of aristocrats. This is the Rhine of sailors' nightmares, poets' dreams, and the rhetorical storms of nationalism. From the famed Lorelei Cliffs, legendary sirens lured passing sailors to their deaths on the sharp rocks below. Heinrich Heine immortalized the spot with his 1823 poem *"Die Lorelei,"* but he can hardly take sole credit for the literary resonance felt all along this river. The renown of Rhine wines from the hillside vineyards have inspired many a lesser illusion. Two different train lines (one on each bank) traverse this fabled stretch; the line on the west bank that runs between Koblenz and Mainz sticks closer to the water and provides superior views. If you're willing to put up with lots of tourists, the best way to see the sights is probably by **boat**. The **Köln-Düsseldorfer (KD) Line** makes the complete Mainz-Koblenz cruise three times per day during the summer, while more frequent excursions travel along shorter stretches of the river (see **Köln: Orientation and Practical Information**, p. 319).

■ Lorelei Cliffs and Castles

The mythic distortion of the Rhine explodes into rocky frenzy along the **Cliffs of the Lorelei**. This section of the river, with its switchbacks and boulders, was so difficult to navigate that a sailors' song, immortalized by Heinrich Heine, developed about a siren *(Lorelei)* who seduced sailors with her intoxicating song, disastrously distracting them. Protected by the plush interiors and tinted windows of the gigantic and ubiquitous "Loreley Express" tourbuses, most of today's Rhine travelers avoid such grim fates. If you'd like to press your luck with a more direct encounter, a marked path climbs to the top of the cliffs 10 minutes south of **St. Goarshausen.**

Directly above St. Goarshausen the fierce **Burg Katz** (Castle Cat) eternally stalks its prey, the smaller **Burg Maus** (Castle Mouse). Fortunately, the mouse escapes the Kafka-esque little fable by hiding away upstream in the Wellmich district of Goarshausen. About an hour by foot from the station, the smaller castle keeps eternally vigilant, sometimes with hour-long displays of eagles, falcons and other scary carnivorous birds, which circle and sometimes land on tourists' shoulders. Two minutes away from the Lorelei Cliffs the hostel **Tuner- und Jugendheim Loreley** (tel. 26 19; fax 81 89) lures travelers in with friendly little ditties of hip hostelers, only to drown them in crashing waves of school children. It boasts a picnic area, sports facilities, and an open-air stage nearby. (DM23.50. Breakfast included. Curfew 10pm.) Turn left and hug the Rhine to reach the **Campingplatz Loreleystadt** (tel. 25 92; fax (02137) 49 98), an eight-minute walk from the *Bahnhof* (DM7, children DM4, dogs DM3). The **telephone code** is 06771.

Across the river, the town of **St. Goar** provides a pleasant home base for Lorelei explorations. The view from the cliffs on the eastern side is spectacular, and the castle **Burg Rheinfels** is dazzling. You can tour this sprawling, half-ruined castle and its underground passageways by candlelight—it doesn't get more *romantisch* than this. (Open daily 9am-6pm, last entrance 5pm. DM5, children DM3. Candle rental DM1.) St. Goar's **tourist office** (tel. 383; fax 72 09) is located in the *Fußgängerzone* at Heerstr. 86. The town has a convenient **Jugendherberge (HI)**, Bismarckberg 17 (tel. 388; fax 28 69) 10 minutes from the train station. (DM19.50. Breakfast included. Sheets DM5. Reception open 5-6pm and 7-8pm. Curfew 10pm.) On the **Marktplatz, Hotel Hauser** (tel. 333; fax 14 64) offers spotless, relaxing rooms at cheap prices. (Singles DM44, with bath DM55-75; doubles DM100-110. Breakfast included.) St. Goar's **postal code** is 56329. The **telephone code** is 06741.

■ Bacharach

Bounded by the high security walls of a lush park on the river, a resilient town wall, and dramatically sloping vineyards, Bacharach maintains the kind of low-profile coveted by glamour queens, B-movie has-beens, and royalty. All the sequestering has paid off—this hidden gem retains an irrepressible sense of identity in the face of increasing (return-visiting) tourist traffic. Once home to an altar stone to Bacchus (Roman god of wine and revelry), this village's name means Altar to Bacchus. And, like any holy city, Bacharach fills with pilgrims who come from near and far to worship dutifully at the town's numerous **Weinkeller** and **Weinstuben** (wine cellars and pubs), scattered throughout the impeccably preserved original *Fachwerkhäuser* (half-timbered houses). Locals and tourists alike swear by **Die Weinstube,** located right behind the stunning **Altes Haus** (an original half-timbered house) in the center of town on Oberstr. You can view the source of that precious potable from the **Wernerkapelle,** ghost-like remains of a red sandstone chapel that took 140 years to build (1294-1434) but only a few hours to destroy in the War of Palatine Succession in 1689. It's a short climb up the steps next to the late-Romanesque **Peterskirche** on Oberstr.

The **tourist office,** Oberstr. 1 (tel. 12 97; fax 31 55) in the *Rathaus,* a three-minute walk up to the right from the station, provides maps of hiking trails (open M-F 9am-12:30pm and 1:30-5pm, Sa 10am-1pm). Hostels get *no* better than the unbelievable **Jugendherberge Stahleck (HI)** (tel. 12 66; fax 26 84), a gorgeous 12th-century castle that provides an unbeatable panoramic view of the Rhine Gorge for its 40,000 yearly visitors. Painstaking thought has gone into the minutest details of the hostel, from the individually-named rooms (you might stay in *Falcon's Nest* or *Castle View*) to the great selection of Bacharacher wines in the bar downstairs and the cheerful plaid sheets on your bed. The steep, exhausting 20-minute hike to the hostel is worth every painful footstep. Call ahead; they're usually full by 6pm. To reach the hostel from the station, turn left at *Peterskirche* and take any of the marked paths leading up the hill. (DM23.50. Breakfast included, all-you-can-eat dinner with vegetarian option DM9. Laundry, with soap DM5. Curfew 10pm.) For those weary of uphill treks, the dynamic mother and son Dettmar duo run two centrally located pensions. Frau Dettmar runs clean **Haus Dettmar,** on Oberstr. 8. (tel. 26 61 or 29 79). Son Jürgen operates wonderful **Pension Ferienwohnungen** (tel. 17 15; fax 29 79) in an even better location. (It's all in the family; rates are the same at both Dettmar outposts. Singles DM45; doubles DM60.) Turn right immediately after leaving the station (heading downhill towards the river), then walk south for 10 minutes to reach **Campingplatz Bacharach** (tel. 17 52), where you can camp directly on the Rhine for DM5 per tent and DM7.50 per person. The price is right at the uniquely named **Cafe Restaurant,** on Oberstr. 40, where three-course meals go for DM11-17.50. The city's **telephone code** is 06743.

■ Rüdesheim

Seen from the other side of the Rhine, Rüdesheim is a romantic's dream come true. Terraced vineyards stretch steeply up from the tiny town framed by two stone castles. Across the river, however, the cruel ogre of commercialism has found a home. Rüdesheim's location in the heart of the Rheingau wine-producing region has made the town a formidable tourist magnet, and you can now almost set your watches by the fleets of tour buses that pour into the valley when they roll out the first barrels at 9am. The picturesque 12th-century **Brömserburg Fortress,** Rheinstr. 2, like the rest of Rüdesheim, now succumbs to Bacchanalian indulgence—it's a **wine museum** (tel. 23 48) just five minutes from the train station and the ferry docks toward town along Rheinstr. (Open daily mid-Mar. to mid-Nov. 9am-6pm. Last admission 5:15pm. DM5, students and children DM3.) The fortress boasts all important styles of architecture, from the Middle Ages through the Renaissance, Baroque, Rococo, Empire, Biedermeyer, *Jugendstil,* and Art Deco periods. Servings are available along the nearby **Drosselgasse,** a tiny alley where merchants peddle fake cuckoo clocks, lots of wine, and plenty of "authenticity." Up Drosselgasse to the left are signs for **Siegfrieds Mechanisches Musikkabinett,** Oberstr. 29 (tel. 492 17; fax 45 87), a museum of automatic musical instruments with one of the largest collections of music boxes and player pianos in the world. (Open mid-Mar. to mid-Nov. 10am-10pm. Obligatory tours leave every 15min.; English tours available. DM9, students DM5.) The **Mittelalterliches Foltermuseum** (medieval torture museum), Grabenstr. 13 (tel. 475 10), displays devices prisoners endured to "salvage" their souls. (Open daily Apr.-Nov. 10am-6pm. DM6, children DM3.) Eighty instruments (including a *Sage,* a saw used to slice victims in half while they dangled upside down, still alive), as well as paintings, drawings, and etchings provide a delightfully grisly exhibition.

The **Niederwalddenkmal,** a 38m monument crowned by the unnervingly nationalistic figure of *Germania* wielding a 1400kg sword, looms high above the town. Erected to commemorate the establishment of the Second Reich in 1871, the central frieze features legions of 19th-century aristocrats pledging loyalty to the *Kaiser* flanked by winged emblems of war and peace. For the heavy of foot and purse, the bronze piece of allegorical extremism is best reached by the **chairlift** *(Seilbahn),* which runs from the top of Christofelstr. and can carry 1200 people every hour. (Open mid-Mar. to mid-Nov. daily 9:30am-5pm. DM5.50, children, large dogs, and luggage DM3.50, round-trip DM10.) To reach the chairlift, take a left directly before the tourist office (10min.). To reach the monument by foot, take Oberstr. from the station to the footpath leading uphill.

The **tourist office,** Rheinstr. 16 (tel. 29 62; fax 34 85), is perched along the river. It offers walking-tour pamphlets and a room-finding service (10% fee; cheapest rooms DM40-50). It also exchanges money and cashes traveler's checks (no commission).

The **post office,** towards Brömserburg on Rheinstr., also has an ATM and exchanges money (open M-F 8:30am-noon and 2:30-5pm, Sa 8:30-11:30am). The **telephone code** is 06722.

The **Jugendherberge (HI),** am Kreuzberg (tel. 27 11; fax 482 84), is in the vineyards high above the town, but the 25-minute walk through flowers, vines, and silence proves aesthetically rewarding. Call ahead—they're often booked solid. From the train station, walk down Rheinstr. and make a left on any street that catches your fancy, up to and including Löhrstr. At Oberstr., turn right and bear left at the fork onto Germaniastr. and follow it to Kuhweg and the "Jugendherberge" signs. (Members only. DM21.50, over 26 DM26. Breakfast included. Sheets DM6. Reception 8-9am, 1-2pm, and 5-11pm. Curfew 11:30pm.) **Campingplatz am Rhein** (tel. 25 28) has prime riverside real estate for those with portable roofs. From the train station, walk past town while hugging the Rhine, past the **Asbachbad** (swimming pool), and you'll run into the campsite. (DM6.40 per person, children DM4.20, tents DM6.10-8.20. Reception 8am-10pm. Open May-Sept.)

■ Bingen

Caught at the junction between the Nahe and the Rhine, this little hillside town has long been overshadowed by Rüdesheim. Onetime home of cult-figure **Hildegard von Bingen,** and less trafficked than neighbor Rüdesheim, Bingen has taken a turn for the swingin'. On an island near the village of Bingen, downstream from Rüdesheim, the **Mäuseturm** (Mouse Tower) leans over the winding Rhine. According to legend, Archbishop (and arch-villain) **Hatto II** of Mainz was challenged during a famine by starving peasants demanding the food he hoarded. He proceeded to lock them up in a barn and set it on fire. Hearing their shrieks of pain, the sadistic Hatto cackled, "listen to my mice squeaking." Suddenly, a horde of mice rushed out of the barn, chased him into the tower, and ate him alive. Unfortunately, the tower can be visited only twice per year on a tour announced in the local newspaper. The town's main daytime attraction, **Burg Klopp** (tel. 149 86), is five minutes from the **tourist office** through maze-like streets (follow red mice signs). Besides the castle cafe, affordable only for royalty (entrees start at DM22.50), Burg Klopp features the **Heimatmuseum,** displaying third-century Roman milestones and a view from the top of its tower (museum open Apr.-Oct. Tu-Su 9am-noon and 2-5pm; DM1, students and children DM0.50).

The **tourist office,** Rheinkai 21 (tel. 18 42 05; fax 162 75), finds rooms for a DM3 fee (singles start at DM31) and offers a wealth of information on the 20km of hiking through the surrounding *Bingerwald.* From the *Hauptbahnhof,* stick by the tracks as they head east to Rheinkaistr. or get off at the Bingen station and head toward town for five minutes (open Apr.-Nov. M-F 9am-6pm, Sa 9am-12:30pm; Dec.-Mar. M-F 9am-4pm). Bingen offers the best access to the Rhine Gorge, with two **train** stations, good connections to Frankfurt and Koblenz, and docks from which several brands of **ferries** depart; ferries cross the river to Rüdesheim (every 40min.; DM1.60 one-way, DM2.80 round-trip, bikes, dogs, and strollers DM0.80). The ubiquitous **Kölner-Düsseldorfer** ferry sails to Koblenz (DM66.20) and Bacharach (DM22). The **Bingen-Rüdesheimer** ferry service offers the best buy on Rhine cruises to Bacharach (one-way DM12) and St. Goar (one-way DM18). Ask about the unadvertised student rate. They also offer evening trips with live music, dance, and plenty of *Rheinwein* (during May, Saturday; June-Sept. Wednesday and Saturday; DM14). For a **taxi,** call 356 49 or 145 00. The **Rettungsdienst** (ambulance) can be reached by dialing 437 37. The **telephone code** is 06721.

To get to the **Jugendherberge Bingen-Bingerbrück,** Herterstr. 51 (tel. 321 63; fax 340 12), follow the signs from the *Hauptbahnhof* across the bridge and bear left (15min.). The hostel perches high on a hill and offers *very* spartan bedrooms and few amenities. Still, it has a great view. (DM19.50, with 2 meals DM28.20, with 3 meals DM32.50. Breakfast included. Sheets DM5. Check-in 5-10pm. Curfew 10pm.) **Hotel Hans Clara,** Rhein Kai 3 (tel./fax 92 18 80) offers clean, lovely rooms in the middle of

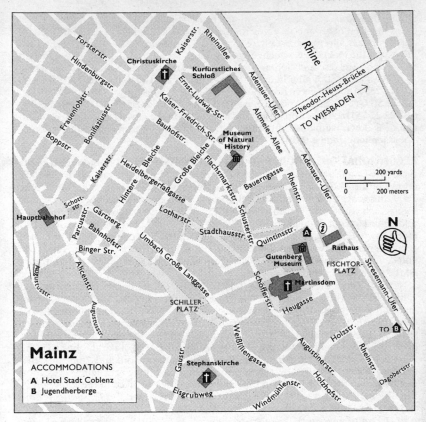

Mainz
ACCOMMODATIONS
A Hotel Stadt Coblenz
B Jugendherberge

town (singles without shower DM50 and up). **Prina's Pizzeria,** Fruchtmarktstr. 8, serves up plenty of pizza and pasta for under DM10. **Pallazzo,** Rheinufer (tel. 100 32), Bingen's renowned **mega-disco,** resembles a pink train station, attracting hostelers from all along the Gorge. Hours often change, but the party's always pumpin' Friday and Saturday from 9pm to 7am. The disco is right on the river—you can't miss it.

■ Mainz

As the capital of the Rheinland-Pfalz, Mainz has metamorphosed into a modern metropolis, but the monumental *Dom* and the maze of minuscule streets in the *Altstadt* are still the center of the city. Mainz successfully combines modernity and antiquity as concrete and cobblestone seamlessly mesh to carry people of every stamp through the vibrant city. Mainz has been at the center of Germany's media industry since the 1450s when native son Johannes Gutenberg invented the printing press.

ORIENTATION AND PRACTICAL INFORMATION To maneuver in the Mainz maze, streets running parallel to the Rhine sport blue nameplates, while streets running perpendicular to the river bear red ones. Mainz's well-developed transportation system makes it user-friendly and offers easy daytrips to Wiesbaden (S-Bahn #6). The **Köln-Düsseldorf Ferries** (tel. 22 45 11; fax 23 69 36) dock in Mainz and depart from the nearby docks on the other side of the *Rathaus*. **Bike rentals** are available at **City-Port,** a stone's throw away from the *Hauptbahnhof* toward the university at the "Hallenbad/CityPort" bus stop. Recently moved into a swanky new office on the ultramodern *Rathaus*'s *Brückenturm*, the **tourist office** (tel. 28 62 10; fax 286 21 55) doles out free maps and reserves rooms for DM5, but singles start at DM50 and quickly rocket into the stratosphere (open M-F 9am-6pm, Sa 9am-1pm). The tourist office sells the **Mainzcard,** which offers free museum admission, free public transportation, and hotel discounts for one day. At DM10 for one person and DM20 for a family, it pays for itself within hours. Purchase tickets to dance, theater, and concerts (DM12-25) at the **Mainzer Kammerspiele,** Emmerich-Joseph-Str. 13 (tel. 22 50 02; fax 22 50 04), off Schillerplatz (open Tu-F noon-6pm). Mainz's **AIDS-Hilfe** hotline (tel. 22 22 75) has the scoop on gay and lesbian life in the city. The **post office,** 55116 Mainz, is down Bahnhofstr. from the station (open M-Tu 8am-6pm, Sa 8am-noon). The **telephone code** is 06131.

ACCOMMODATIONS, FOOD, AND ENTERTAINMENT Mainz's **Jugendgästehaus (HI),** Otto-Brunfels-Schneise 4 (tel. 853 32; fax 824 22), is in Weisenau at the far right corner of the *Volkspark.* Take bus #22 to "Jugendherberge/Viktorstift." As of May 1999, this is scheduled to be a model hostel with clean, well-furnished, and secure rooms each with a private bath. (Doubles DM26.80; quads DM26.80. Reception 7am-midnight. Lockout midnight-6:30am. Closed Oct. 1998-Apr. 1999 for renovations.) **Hotel Stadt Coblenz,** Rheinstr. 49 (tel. 22 76 02), has inexpensive, finely furnished rooms across the street from the *Rathaus* and within sight of the *Dom.* Take your choice of several buses to "Rheingoldhalle."(Singles DM80; doubles DM140; triples DM180. Breakfast included.)

Near the *Dom,* the **Central Café** (tel. 22 56 66), on the corner of Rheinstr. and Heugasse, cooks up a wide variety of *Essen,* from burgers to traditional German fare and vegetarian dishes, with almost everything on the menu under DM10 (open Su-Th 10am-midnight, F-Sa 10am-1am). **Taverne Academica,** the university's so-called "friendly bar," lives up to its slogan, serving good, cheap eats and drinks to the student crowd. All entrees are under DM10. Take the bus to "Universität" and make a left (open M-F 10am-late, Sa noon-3pm and 7pm-late). **Bistrorante D'angelo,** staffed by a stylin', surprisingly attentive waitstaff, serves good quality Italian food for less than DM12. Behind the *Dom,* face in the direction of the Rhine and take a right; walk four to five blocks down the *Fußgängerzone.* (Open M-Sa 11am-midnight, Su noon-midnight.)

KUZ *(Kulturzentrum),* Dagobertstr. 20b (tel. 28 68 60), is Mainz's standard, eternally hip disco. Take bus #1 or 37 to "Holzturm/Furt-Malakoff Park," face the shopping center across the street and turn right. Walk one and a half blocks and turn left on Dagobertstr. (open W 9pm-3am and F 9pm-4am; Sept.-June also Sa 9pm-4am). **Lindenbaum,** Holzstr. 32 (tel. 22 71 31), pleases with diverse dance tunes for the multi-aged crowd. Oldies and classic rock on Mondays and Wednesdays attract disco-dinosaurs, while the younger divas make appearances on all other days. Take bus #1 or 37 to "Holztärm/Fort-Malakoff-Park." Turn right on Holzstr. (Open Su-W 8pm-3am, Th 8pm-4am, F-Sa 8pm-5am.) After the city holiday of *Johannistag* during the third weekend in June, Mainz celebrates **Johannisnacht**—three days of old-fashioned revelry dedicated to Gutenberg. Movable type and Bacchanalian revelry do not easily combine, but Mainz manages it in high style.

SIGHTS At the heart of Mainz lies the colossal sandstone **Martinsdom,** the resting place of the archbishops of Mainz, whose extravagant tombs line the walls. *(Open Apr.-Sept. M-F 9am-6:30pm, Sa 9am-4pm, Su 12:45-3pm and 4-6:30pm; Oct.-Mar. M-F 9am-5pm, Sa 9am-4pm, Su 12:45-3pm. Free.)* The adjacent **Dom-and Diözesanmuseum Mainz** houses changing exhibitions. *(Open Tu-Su 10am-7pm, Th-F 10am-9pm. Prices vary with the exhibition.)* A bustling, cosmopolitan shopping area with winding streets and sunny fountains surrounds the *Dom.*

Behind the *Dom,* the *Altstadt* stretches for a few blocks in and around Augustiner-str. On a hill several blocks south, moving away from the river, stands the Gothic **Stephanskirche,** notable for its stunning stained-glass windows created by Russian artist-in-exile **Marc Chagall** in the eight years prior to his 1984 death. On sunny days (sweepin' the clouds away), the windows bathe the church in an eerie blue light.

(Open daily 10am-noon and 2-5pm.) Favorite son Johannes Gutenberg, the father of movable type, is immortalized at the **Gutenberg Museum,** Liebfrauenpl. 5 (tel. 12 26 44). *(Open Tu-Sa 10am-6pm, Su 10am-1pm. Admission DM5, students and children DM2.50; Su free.)* Located conveniently near the *Dom,* the museum contains several **Gutenberg Bibles,** a replica of his original press, an impressive collection of text art, early Asian calligraphy, and several other relics of the early printing industry. Near the museum, the **Experimental Print Shop,** at Fischtorstr. 2 (tel. 12 26 86), lets visitors try their luck at Gutenberg's craft by setting and printing their own designs. *(Open M-F 10am-5pm. Free, but call ahead to make sure that Schulkinder haven't taken over.)* North of the Gutenberg Museum, on Rheinstr., is the **Brückenturm-Galerie der Stadt Mainz**—a city-funded modern art museum that displays the works of regional artists. *(Open Tu-F 11am-6pm, Sa-Su 11am-2pm.)*

North of the Marktplatz, along Schusterstr. from the *Dom* and right on Christophstr., is the **Pfarrkirche St. Cristoph,** a half-ruined church that brings a poignant reminder of war to an otherwise gilded city. The site of Gutenberg's baptism, the church was seriously damaged in WWII; the former tower is still used for services, but the main body is in ruins. Along the river near the Theodor-Heuss-Brücke rests the **Kurfürstliches Schloß,** former palace of the archbishopric. A comprehensive collection of art and archaeology, including a Judaica division and enormous Roman arches, awaits in the **Landesmuseum,** up the street at Große Bleiche 49-51. *(Open Tu 10am-8pm, W-Su 10am-5pm. DM5, Sa free.)* To the northwest of the *Schloß* stands the commanding **Christuskirche.** *(Open Th-F 3-5pm, Sa-Su 3-6pm.)* Flanked by fountains and a flower-filled promenade, the gray-brick church looks more like a government building than a place of worship. If you have time to spare when you've exhausted Mainz, Wiesbaden (see p. 369) conveniently commends itself across the Rhine.

MOSELTAL (MOSEL VALLEY)

Trying to avoid its inevitable surrender to the Rhine at Koblenz, the Mosel River slowly meanders past the sun-drenched hills, pretty towns, and ancient castles of the softly cut Moseltal. The headwaters of the Mosel flow from the Vosges Mountains of France, following a northeasterly course that winds over 200km of German territory from Trier to Koblenz. The slopes aren't quite as steep as the Rhine's narrow gorge, but the countless, less-touristed vineyards of the gentle hillsides have been pressing quality vintages since the Romans first cultivated the vines 2000 years ago. The only local complaints heard about the region is that the summers are too dry (the least of worries for a visitor) and the winters too wet. Periodically, the mellow Mosel goes berserk, flooding and making the valley Venetian for a few days. In December 1993, many of the towns were buried under 2m of water.

The best way to view the valley's scenery is by boat, bus, or bicycle; the train line between Koblenz and Trier strays frequently from the course of the river, cutting through the unremarkable countryside. Although passenger **boats** no longer make the complete Koblenz-Trier run, several companies run daily trips along shorter stretches through the summer; local tourist offices can provide details. Some train stations will rent you a rugged three-speed **bike** for DM11 per day (bring or buy a ticket or railpass, otherwise rental prices double).

■ Cochem

Like so many German wine-making villages, the hamlet of Cochem has become a repository of German nostalgia, its quintessential quaintness eaten up voraciously by busloads of elderly German city-dwellers. But despite this presence, Cochem's impressive vineyard-covered hills and sparkling **Reichsburg castle** (tel. 255) simply can't be cheapened into run-of-the-mill tourist fodder. Perched high atop a hill adjacent to the village, the castle is visible from afar, with its majestic and elaborately painted turrets lending the town a pleasant fairytale quality enhanced by gnarled streets lined with clapboard houses.

RHEINLAND-PFALZ

Originally built in the 11th century, the castle was destroyed in 1689 (like much of the Palatinate) by French troops under Louis XIV. In 1868, a wealthy Berlin merchant rebuilt it in neo-Gothic style. The view from the castle grounds alone warrants the 15-minute climb along Schloßstr. from the Marktplatz. Unfortunately, a peek into the castle's opulent interior can be taken today only as part of a guided tour. (Open daily Mar. 15-Oct. 9am-5pm. Frequent 40min. tours; written English translations available. DM6, students DM5, children DM3.) The tiny lane to the **Peterskapelle** (left as you walk down from the castle), built in 1422, is enclosed by high walls and the ubiquitous vine-covered trellises. The other popular hillside attraction in town is the **Sesselbahn** (chair-lift; tel. 98 90 63) on Edenstr., which runs to the **Pinnerkreuz**, a lone cross standing on a high peak. (Lift runs daily June-Oct. 9:30am-7pm; Nov.-May 10am-6pm. One-way DM6.90, round-trip DM8.90; DM3.20 and DM4.50 for children, respectively). For even more theme-park style thrills 'n' spills, head across the river and follow the signs for the *Freizeitzentrum* to reach the gigantic **Moselbad** (tel. 979 90), a sprawling complex of pools, saunas, jacuzzis, and waterslides located five minutes north of the Nordbrücke (the bridge near the train station). (Open M 2-10pm, Tu and Th 9am-10pm, W and F 10am-10pm, Sa-Su 10am-7pm. All-inclusive day ticket DM16, ages 12-17 DM9, ages 6-11 DM6, younger kids free. Outdoor pool only DM5, DM3, DM3.) They've even got a wavepool that lets 'em loose for five minutes every hour. Hang ten, Big Kahuna.

Unlike much of the Mosel Valley, Cochem is easily accessible by **train** from Koblenz and Trier. Although Cochem is equidistant to the two cities, the route to Koblenz hugs the Mosel, making for some spectacular views; the trip to Trier traverses serene but non-fantastic countryside. The *Moselbahn* links DB trains to the rest of the Mosel Valley in **Bullay,** a town one stop away from Cochem (10min.; Trier from Cochem; DM4.60). The **tourist office,** on Endertpl. 1 (tel. 39 71 or 39 72; fax 84 10) next to the bridge, makes same-day room reservations for free and doles out brochures. From the train station, go to the river and turn right. (Open May-Nov. 15 M-F 10am-5pm, Sa 10am-3pm.) Along the way, you'll pass **Fahrrad-Shop Kreutz** (tel. 911 31), tucked in behind the Shell gas station along the river, which leases an array of two-wheeled chrome beauties. (DM14 per day, DM70 per week. Open M-F 9am-6pm, Sa 9am-1pm, Su 10-11am and 5-6pm. Passport required.) The **post office** is at the corner of Ravenestr. and Josefstr., one block from Endenplatz. They cash traveler's checks and exchange money. (Open M-F 8am-noon and 2-5pm, Sa 8am-noon.) The **telephone code** is 02671.

Cochem's friendly, basic **Jugendherberge (HI),** Klottenerstr. 9 (tel. 86 33; fax 85 68), is 10 to 15 minutes from the station on the opposite shore. Cross the Nordbrücke (to the left as you exit the station); the youth hostel is next to the bridge on the right. Beware of the wicked echoes that make the schoolchildren seem much louder than usual. (DM21, with dinner DM29.20. Breakfast included. Sheets DM5. Reception daily noon-1pm and 5-10pm, but someone's always around. Curfew 10pm.) There are also plenty of rooms available in town; look for the *"Zimmer Frei"* signs, or use the tourist office's Lite-Brite-esque hotel finder. If you've got your own portable party palace, walk down the path below the hostel to the **Campingplatz am Freizeitzentrum** (tel. 44 09) on Stadionstr. (DM6.50 per person, DM6-12 per tent. 4min. shower DM1.50. Washing machine and dryer DM2; bike rental DM14 per day. Reception 8am-9pm. Open Easter-Oct.) Indulge in food and divine Mosel wine at the cheesy, good-hearted **Weinhexenkeller** (wine witches' cellar), on Hafenstr., across the Moselbrücke. Local legend says that guests who imbibe too much fall under a witch's spell. Modern science says they become drunk. Either way, you'll have a perfect excuse to go nuts when the live music kicks in at 7pm. (Open daily noon-1am.) The **Mosel-Wein-Woche** begins a week and a half after Pentecostal Monday and features some of the Mosel's finest vintages (DM1-2 per 100ml taste). During the last weekend in August, the **Heimat-und-Weinfest** culminates in a dramatic Saturday night fireworks display.

■ Beilstein

Beilstein, 10km upstream from Cochem, is a life-size embodiment of a child's fairy-tale dreams. A tiny hamlet with half-timbered houses, crooked cobblestone streets, and about 170 residents, Beilstein takes pride in being the smallest official town in Germany (it received town rights in 1319). Spared in WWII, Beilstein's untarnished beauty has made it the idyllic backdrop of several movies and political summits. Once upon a time, Adenauer and DeGespari created the European Economic Community (now the European Union) here. By day, Beilstein's natural charm draws a tourist crowd that exponentially increases its population, yet after 6pm, the spell breaks, and the peaceful town is yours! **Burg Metternich** is the resident castle; the French sacked it in 1689, but the view is still spectacular (open daily Apr.-Oct. 9am-5pm; DM2, students DM1.50, children DM0.50). Also worth a look is the Baroque **Karmeliten-kirche**, with its intricately carved wooden altar and the famous **Schwarze Madonna von Beilstein** (black Madonna), a 16th-century Montserrat sculpture left behind by Spanish troops reintroducing Catholicism to the region.

The town can be reached by public buses that depart approximately once an hour from both Endertplatz and the station in Cochem (DM3.50 each way) or by a private bus line that makes five trips per day. The boats of **Personnenschiffahrt Kolb** (tel. 15 15) also float there (1hr., 4 per day May-Oct., one-way DM12, round-trip DM19). **Cafe Klapperburg**, uphill a block on the left from the bus stop, is the home of Beilsteins's **tourist office** (basically a friendly manager with a couple of brochures). Lay down your sleepy head at the comfy **Pension Erna Burg**, Moselstr. 2 (tel. 14 24), next to the highway along the river. It offers the softest down comforters you'll ever find and a wallpaper scheme that would make Matisse's head spin. (DM32 per person. Breakfast included.) The **Kloster Café** outside the church (tel. 16 53) serves up outstanding traditional food, fantastic Mosel wine, and a view that beats them both (open M-Sa 10am-6pm). The **telephone code** is 02673.

■ Bernkastel-Kues

Yet another contender in *Let's Go's* Beautiful *Dörfer* of the Mosel River Valley Pageant is the dynamite duo of Bernkastel-Kues. Our esteemed panel of judges is not alone in recognizing the beauty here—the towns are a favorite stop for huge German motorcruisers. The **Bernkastel Marktplatz,** located one block from the bridge, is a 400-year-old half-timbered beauty. Around the corner, the narrow, steep-roofed edifice of the **Spitzhäuschen** leans to one side; it looks like it came straight out of a children's cartoon. A scenic but grueling 20-minute climb along a vine-laden path leads to the ruins of **Burg Landshut** above the town and valley. A summer home for the archbishops of Trier until it was gutted by fire in 1693, the ruins have since been rudely usurped by an outdoor cafe-restaurant. The gorgeous view remains the same (and DM0.50 augments it by allowing you to climb the tower). Back in town, walk north from the Marktplatz onto Graacherstr. to reach the **Graacher Tor,** the only preserved gate from the city wall of 1300.

Across the river lounges **Kues.** A few stately 19th-century mansions tower along the river and the **Cusanusstift** reposes next to the bridge. Also known as the **St.-Nikolaus-Hospital,** this home for the aged and destitute was founded in the 15th century by a local philanthropist and includes an elaborately decorated chapel. The number of boarders is kept at a constant 33 in honor of the life expectancy of itinerant messianic Nazarene carpenters. Next door, the **Moselweinmuseum,** at Cusanusstr. 1, pays tribute to the tools of the wine-making trade (open Apr.16-Oct. daily 10am-5pm; Nov.-Apr. 14 2-5pm; DM2.50, students DM1.50).

Rail service no longer connects Bernkastel-Kues to the world; instead, *Moselbahn* operates a **bus service** from Bullay to Trier, stopping in Bernkastel-Kues about once every hour (DM7.50 to the DB-linked Mosel town of Traben-Trarbach; bus stop in Bernkastel-Kues across the street from the defunct train station). By some freak of nature (or provincial engineering), the road connecting Traben-Trarbach and Bernkastel-Kues curls around the Mosel for some 24km, but a footpath makes a bee-line between the two towns in 6.5km. The path is too steep to trek with a heavy backpack, but it's otherwise an easy and gorgeous hike. **Personen-Schiffahrt Gebr. Kolb OHG** (tel. 47 19) makes the trip to and from Traben-Trarbach twice a day. The **tourist office, Am Gestade 5** (tel. 40 23; fax 79 53), across the street from the bus stop in Bernkastel, finds rooms for a DM3 fee. (Open May-Oct. M-F 8:30am-12:30pm and 1-5pm, Sa 10am-4pm; closed Sa Nov.-April.) The **telephone code** is 06531.

Bernkastel's **Jugendherberge,** Jugendherbergstr. 1 (tel. 23 95; fax 15 29), is actually better positioned to defend the valley than its neighbor **Burg Landshut**—the hostel is actually *uphill* from the castle! Despite the traumatic 30-minute hike, the hostel offers classy, clean facilities and an incredible view. (DM20.50, over 26 DM24.50. Breakfast included. Sheets DM5. Reception 7:30-9am, noon-1pm, and 5-7pm. Curfew 10pm.) Otherwise, snuggle in at **Campingplatz Kueser Werth,** Am Hafen 2 (tel. 82 00), on the Kues side of the river. From the bridge, turn left and follow the road along the river for 1.5km. (DM6 per person, DM5 per tent. Reception 8am-noon and 3-7pm. Open Apr.-Oct.) **Kapuzinerstübchen,** Römerstr. 35 (tel. 23 53), serves traditional Ger-man meals without traditional tourist trap prices. (Soups DM2.50, entrees DM8-17. Open Tu-Sa 11:30am-2pm and 5:45-8:45pm.) Thousands arrive in town for Bernkas-tel-Kues's **Weinfest** the first week of September.

■ Trier

Older than any other German town and, in fact, older than Germany itself, Trier has weathered two millennia in the western end of the Mosel Valley, stubbornly refusing to act its age. Founded by the Romans during the reign of Augustus, Trier reached the height of its prominence in the early 4th century as the capital of the western Roman Empire. Having lived through many epochs, Trier is a patchwork quilt of uncommon design and grace. The vitality of its visitors and students blends harmoniously with the dignity and beauty of its Roman ruins and well-preserved *Altstadt.* The birthplace and boyhood home of Karl Marx, Trier is one of the few places in united Germany that refuses to give up its "Karl-Marx-Straße."

ORIENTATION AND PRACTICAL INFORMATION

Trier lies less than 50km from the Luxembourg border on the Mosel River. Most of the sights sit in the vicinity of the compact *Altstadt.* The gate to the *Altstadt,* **Porta Nigra,** is a 10-minute walk from the train station down Theodor-Heuss-Allee or Chris-tophstr. Although most sights are within walking distance, the bus system can carry you anywhere for DM2.40. A **Trier Card,** available at the tourist office, offers admis-sion to 7 museums and reduced rates on theater performances and tours (among other things) over a 3-day period (single DM17, family (2 adults, 3 children) DM32). A **Trier Card Plus** also includes free public transportation (single DM25, family DM44).

Trains: Frequent trains to Koblenz (1½hr.), rosy Luxembourg (45min., approxi-mately 1 per hr.; day excursion DM12.80), and Saarbrücken (1½hr.).

Ferries: Personen-Schiffahrt (tel. 15 15) sails to Bernkastel-Kues from the Kaiser-Wilhelm Brücke. May-Oct. daily at 9:15am. Round-trip DM44, under 13 DM22.

Taxi: Taxi-Funk (tel. 330 30). Whoever smelt the funk dealt the funk.

Mitfahrzentrale: Mitwohn- und Mitfahrzentrale, Kaiserstr. 13 (tel. 474 47; fax 492 32). The double whammy: rides and room rental hooked up in one office. Open M-Tu 10am-1pm, W-F 10am-1pm and 4:30-7pm, Sa 10am-1pm.

Bike Rental: Lasso yourself a two-wheeled filly at the station (tel. 200 25 18). DM10 per day with railpass or ticket. Bike rental open M-F 7am-7pm. Or strap on some style with **in-line skates** from **Skate Away** (tel. 30 90 82), on the riverside bike path at Schotterpl./Messpark. 1hr. DM8, 2hr. DM15, 3hr. DM21, each additional hour DM4. DM20 deposit and ID required. Open Tu-F 3pm-dusk, Sa-Su 10am-dusk.

MCI Spoken Here

Worldwide Calling Made Simple

For more information or to apply for a Card call: **1-800-955-0925**

Outside the U.S., call MCI collect (reverse charge) at: **1-916-567-5151**

International Calling As Easy As Possible.

Calling Card

123 456 7890 1234
J.D. SMITH

WorldPhone

The MCI Card with WorldPhone Service is designed specifically to keep you in touch with the people that matter the most to you.

The MCI Card with WorldPhone Service....

- Provides access to the US and other countries worldwide.
- Gives you customer service 24 hours a day
- Connects you to operators who speak your language
- Provides you with MCI's low rates and no sign-up fees

For more information or to apply for a Card call:
1-800-955-0925

Outside the U.S., call MCI collect (reverse charge) at:
1-916-567-5151

Pick Up the Phone, Pick Up the Miles.

Please cut out and save this reference guide for convenient U.S. and worldwide calling with the MCI Card with WorldPhone Service.

You earn frequent flyer miles when you travel internationally, why not when you call internationally? Callers can earn frequent flyer miles if they sign up with one of MCI's airline partners:

- American Airlines
- Continental Airlines
- Delta Airlines
- Hawaiian Airlines
- Midwest Express Airlines
- Northwest Airlines
- Southwest Airlines
- United Airlines
- USAirways

Your MCI Worldphone Access Numbers

COUNTRY		WORLDPHONE TOLL-FREE ACCESS #
#Singapore		8000-112-112
#Slovak Republic (CC)		0421-00112
#Slovenia		080-8808
#South Africa (CC)		0800-99-0011
#Spain (CC)		900-99-0014
#Sri Lanka	(Outside of Colombo, dial 01 first)	440100
#St. Lucia ÷		1-800-888-8000
#St. Vincent		1-800-888-8000
#Sweden (CC) ♦		020-795-922
#Switzerland (CC) ♦		0800-89-0222
#Syria		0800
#Taiwan (CC) ♦		0080-13-4567
#Thailand ★		001-999-1-2001
#Trinidad & Tobago ÷		1-800-888-8000
#Turkey (CC) ♦		00-8001-1177
#Turks and Caicos ÷		1-800-888-8000
#Ukraine (CC) ÷		8▼10-013
#United Arab Emirates ♦		800-111
#United Kingdom (CC) To call using BT ■		0800-89-0222
	To call using C&W ■	0500-89-0222
#United States (CC)		1-800-888-8000
#Uruguay		000-412
#U.S. Virgin Islands (CC)		1-800-888-8000
#Vatican City (CC)		172-1022
#Venezuela (CC) ÷♦		800-1114-0
♥ietnam		1201-1022
★Yemen		008-00-102

▲ Automation available from most locations.
(CC) Country-to-country calling available to/from most international locations.
♦ Limited availability.
► Wait for second dial tone.
◄ When calling from public phones, use phones marked LADATEL.
■ International communications carrier
★ Not available from public pay phone.
♦ Public phones may require deposit of coin or phone card for dial tone.
● Local service fee in U.S. currency required to complete call.
▲ Regulation does not permit Intra-Japan calls.
÷ Available from most major cities

And, it's simple to call home.

1. Dial the WorldPhone toll-free access number of the country you're calling from (listed inside).

2. Follow the voice instructions in your language of choice or hold for a WorldPhone operator.
   - Enter or give the operator your MCI Card number or call collect.

3. Enter or give the WorldPhone operator your home number.

4. Share your adventures with your family!

MCI

The MCI Card with WorldPhone Service... The easy way to call when traveling worldwide.

Calling Card

123 456 7890 1234
J.D. SMITH

WorldPhone

For more information or to apply for a Card call:
1-800-955-0925

Outside the U.S., call MCI collect (reverse charge) at:
1-916-567-5151

Please cut out and save this reference guide for convenient U.S. and worldwide calling with the MCI Card with WorldPhone Service.

COUNTRY	WORLDPHONE TOLL-FREE ACCESS #
American Samoa	633-2MCI (633-2624)
#Antigua (available from public card phones only)	1-800-888-8000
#Argentina (CC)	#2
#Aruba ÷	800-888-8
#Australia (CC) ♦ To call using OPTUS ■	1-800-551-111
To call using TELSTRA ■	1-800-881-100
#Austria (CC) ♦	022-903-012
#Bahamas	1-800-888-8000
#Bahrain	800-002
#Barbados	1-800-888-8000
#Belarus (CC) From Brest, Vitebsk, Grodno, Minsk	8-800-103
From Gomel and Mogilev	8-10-800-103
#Belgium (CC) ♦	0800-10012
#Belize From Hotels	557
From Payphones	815
#Bermuda ÷	1-800-888-8000
#Bolivia (CC) ♦	0-800-2222
#Brazil (CC)	000-8012
#British Virgin Islands ÷	1-800-888-8000
#Brunei	800-0011
#Bulgaria	00800-0001
#Canada (CC)	1-800-888-8000
#Cayman Islands	1-800-888-8000
#Chile (CC) To call using CTC ■	800-207-300
To call using ENTEL ■	800-360-180
#China ✦	108-17
For a Mandarin-speaking Operator	108-12
#Colombia (CC) ♦	980-16-0001
Collect Access in Spanish	980-16-1000
#Costa Rica	0800-012-2222
#Cote D'Ivoire	1001
#Croatia (CC) ★	0800-22-0112
#Cyprus ♦	080-90000
#Czech Republic (CC) ♦	00-42-000112
#Denmark (CC) ♦	8001-0022
#Dominica	1-800-888-8000
#Dominican Republic	1-800-888-8000
Collect Access	1121
Collect Access in Spanish	1-800-888-8000
#Ecuador (CC) ÷	999-170
#Egypt (CC) ♦ (Outside of Cairo, dial 02 first)	355-5770
El Salvador	800-1767

FOLD

COUNTRY	WORLDPHONE TOLL-FREE ACCESS #
#Federated States of Micronesia	624
#Fiji	004-890-1002
#Finland (CC) ♦	08001-102-80
#France (CC) ♦	0800-99-0019
#French Antilles (CC) (includes Martinique, Guadeloupe)	0800-99-0019
French Guiana (CC)	0-800-99-0019
#Gabon	00-005
#Gambia	00-1-99
#Germany (CC)	0800-888-8000
#Greece (CC) ♦	00-800-1211
#Grenada ÷	1-800-888-8000
#Guam (CC)	1-800-888-8000
Guatemala (CC) ♦	99-99-189
Guyana	177
#Haiti ÷	193
Collect Access in French/Creole	190
Honduras ÷	8000-122
#Hong Kong (CC)	800-96-1121
#Hungary (CC) ♦	00▼800-01411
#Iceland (CC) ♦	800-9002
#India (CC) ÷	000-127
Collect Access	000-126
#Indonesia (CC)	001-801-11
Iran ✦	(SPECIAL PHONES ONLY)
#Ireland (CC)	1-800-55-1001
#Israel (CC)	1-800-940-2727
#Italy (CC) ♦	172-1022
#Jamaica ÷	1-800-888-8000
Collect Access (From Special Hotels only)	873
(From payphones)	*2
#Japan (CC) ♦ To call using KDD ■	00539-121▼
To call using IDC ■	0066-55-121
To call using ITJ ■	0044-11-121
#Jordan	18-800-001
#Kazakhstan (CC)	8-800-131-4321
#Kenya ✦	080011
#Korea (CC) ✦ To call using KT ■	00309-14
To call using DACOM ■	00369-14
Phone Booths✦	Press red button, 03, then ✳
Military Bases	550-2255
#Kuwait	800-MCI (800-624)

FOLD

COUNTRY	WORLDPHONE TOLL-FREE ACCESS #
Lebanon Collect Access	600-MCI (600-624)
#Liechtenstein (CC) ♦	0800-89-0222
#Luxembourg (CC)	0800-0112
#Macao	0800-131
#Macedonia (CC)	99800-4266
#Malaysia (CC) ♦	1-800-80-0012
#Malta	0800-89-0120
#Marshall Islands	1-800-888-8000
#Mexico (CC) Avantel	01-800-021-8000
Telmex ▲	001-800-674-7000
Collect Access in Spanish	01-800-021-1000
#Monaco (CC) ♦	800-90-019
#Montserrat	1-800-888-8000
#Morocco	00-211-0012
#Netherlands (CC) ♦	0800-022-9122
#Netherlands Antilles (CC) ÷	001-800-888-8000
#New Zealand (CC)	000-912
Nicaragua (CC) (Outside of Managua, dial 02 first)	166
Collect Access in Spanish	
From any public payphone	*2
#Norway (CC) ♦	800-19912
Pakistan	00-800-12-001
#Panama	108
#Papua New Guinea (CC)	05-07-19140
#Paraguay ÷	00-812-800
#Peru	0-800-500-10
#Philippines (CC) ♦ To call using PLDT ■	105-14
To call using PHILCOM	1026-14
Collect Access via PLDT in Filipino	1237-77
Collect Access via ICC in Filipino	105-15
#Poland (CC) ÷	00-800-111-21-22
#Portugal (CC) ÷	05-017-1234
#Puerto Rico (CC)	1-800-888-8000
#Qatar ★	0800-012-77
#Romania (CC) ÷	01-800-1800
#Russia (CC) ♦ ÷ To call using ROSTELCOM ■ (For Russian speaking operator)	747-3322
To call using SOVINTEL ■	747-3320
#Saipan (CC) ÷	960-2222
#San Marino (CC) ♦	950-1022
#Saudi Arabia (CC) ÷	172-1022
	1-800-11

STUDENT TRAVEL
This ain't your parents travel agency.

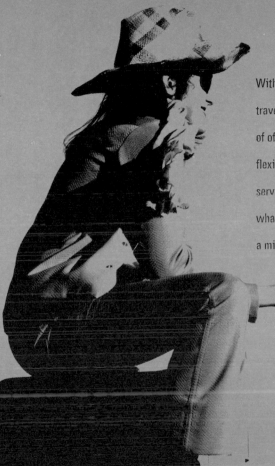

With our staff of experienced travelers, a global network of offices, great prices, ticket flexibility and a ton of travel services, we know firsthand what it takes to put together a mind-blowing trip...

...just remember to thank mom for packing your suitcase.

STA TRAVEL
We've been there.

800-777-0112

CST #1017560-60

OR CONTACT YOUR NEAREST STA TRAVEL OFFICE

AUSTIN	CAMBRIDGE	MADISON	ORLANDO	SEATTLE
BATON ROUGE	CHICAGO	MIAMI	PHILADELPHIA	TAMPA
BERKELEY	GAINESVILLE	MINNEAPOLIS	SAN FRANCISCO	WASHINGTON DC
BOSTON	LOS ANGELES	NEW YORK	SANTA MONICA	WESTWOOD

BOOK YOUR TICKET ONLINE: WWW.STATRAVEL.COM

If you're stuck for cash on your travels, don't panic. Millions of people trust Western Union to transfer money in minutes to 153 countries and over 45,000 locations worldwide. Our record of safety and reliability is second to none. So when you need money in a hurry, call Western Union.

WESTERN UNION | MONEY TRANSFER®

The fastest way to send money worldwide.®

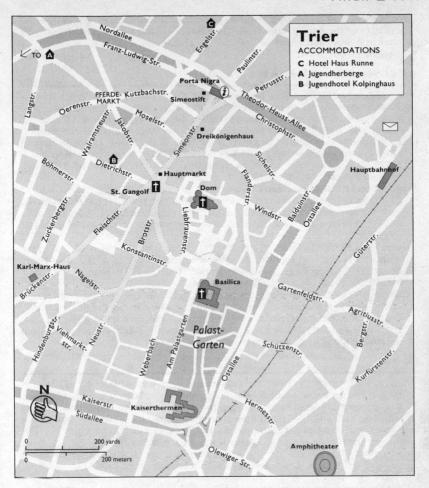

Trier
ACCOMMODATIONS
C Hotel Haus Runne
A Jugendherberge
B Jugendhotel Kolpinghaus

Tourist Office: Tourist-Information (tel. 97 80 80; fax 447 59) in the shadow of the *Porta Nigra*, offers daily **tours** in English at 1:30pm (DM9). Open Jan.-Feb. M-Sa 9am-5pm; Mar. M-Sa 9am-6pm, Su 9am-1pm; Apr.-Nov. M-Sa 9am-6:30pm, Su 9am 3:30pm; Nov.-Dec. M-Sa 9am-6pm, Su 9am-3:30pm. Whew! During these constantly fluctuating hours, the staff hands out free maps and books rooms for free (advance, written requests only).

Bookstore: Akademische Buchhandlung, Fleischstr. 62 (tel. 97 99 01). Small selection of English paperbacks. Open M-F 9am-7pm, Sa 9am-4pm.

Wine Information: Konstantinpl. 11 (tel. 736 90), near the Basilika. Staff and computers help you make decisions about **wine tasting** in the Mosel region (and in the amply stocked office). Open M-F 10:15am-6:30pm, Sa 10am-4pm, Su 1-5pm.

Laundry: Wasch Center, Brückenstr. 19-21, down the street from Karl Marx's old house. Contemplate your relationship to the means of production as you wash (DM8) according to your abilities, dry (DM3 per 25min.) according to your needs. Although there will be a need for proletarian leaders, there's no need to bring your own soap—it's included! Open M-Sa 8am-10pm.

Gay and Lesbian Concerns: Lesbentelefon (tel. 491 33) for the ladies, **Schwule Männerinitiative** (tel. 425 14) for the gents.

Post Office: Most convenient is the branch office on Bahnhofplatz, 45292 Trier, to the right of the train station. Open M-F 8am-6pm, Sa 8am-noon. Limited services open M-F 7-8am and 6-8pm, Sa 7am-2pm, Su 11am-noon. **Telephone Code:** 0651.

ACCOMMODATIONS AND CAMPING

Jugendgästehaus (HI), An der Jugendherberge 4 (tel. 14 66 20; fax 146 62 30). Bus #2 or 8 (direction: "Trierweilerweg" or "Pfalzel/Quint") to "Moselbrücke," and walk 10min. downstream on the path along the river embankment. Or take the 30min. walk from the station. Follow Theodor-Heuss-Allee as it becomes Nordallee, forks right onto Lindenstr., and ends at the bank of the Mosel. Extensive array of ping-pong tables and vending machines. Singles DM50 or 60; doubles DM36; quads DM26.80. All with toilet and shower. Breakfast and sheets included. Reception open sporadically 7am-midnight. Loose midnight curfew.

⊛Jugendhotel Kolpinghaus/Hotel Kolpinghaus, Dietrichstr. 42 (tel. 97 52 50; fax 975 25 40), offers spotless rooms in an ideal location one block off the *Hauptmarkt.* Beds in the dorm housing DM27; singles DM37; doubles DM74; four-bed dorms DM25 per person. Breakfast included. Reception 8am-11pm. Key available for late returns. Call as far ahead as possible.

Hotel Haus Runne, Engelstr. 35 (tel. 289 22). Follow Theodor-Heuss-Allee from the train station and turn right on Engelstr. after the *Porta Nigra.* Did Mike Brady design the interior? Large rooms with shower, toilet, and TV. Singles DM45; doubles DM90; quads DM160. Breakfast included.

Camping: Trier City Campingplatz, Luxemburgerstr. 81 (tel. 869 21). From Hauptmarkt, follow Fleischstr. to Bruckenstr. to Karl-Marx-Str. to the Römerbrücke. Cross the bridge, head left on Luxemburgerstr., and then left at camping sign. DM7, ages 4-12 DM3, under 4 free, dogs DM2. Reception daily 8-11am and 6-10pm in Gortätle Kranich, up from the river.

FOOD

⊛Astarix, Karl-Marx-Str. 11 (tel. 722 39), is squeezed in a passageway next to Miss Marple's. If you get to the dreadfully tasteful sex shops, you've gone too far. A cool student hangout, Astarix combines cheap food, a hip waitstaff, and 120 varieties of whiskey. Tortellini DM6.90. Gorgonzola-tomato garlic toast DM5.90. Open M-Th 11am-1am, F-Sa 11am-2am, Su 6pm-1am. Kitchen closes daily at 11:30pm.

Warsberger Hof, in the Kolpinghaus Hotel, Dietrichstr. 42 (tel. 97 52 50). Walk from *Porta Nigra* to the Hauptmarkt and turn right. Lunch specials and vegetarian fare for DM12.50. Evening menus available in English. Open daily 11am-midnight. Kitchen closes at 11:30pm. Visa, MC, Diners.

Zum Domstein, Am Hauptmarkt 5 (tel. 744 90), across from the cathedral's main entrance. Traditional German food (DM8-22) and a great wine tasting opportunity (DM8-10.50). If you see two *Doms,* you've had enough. Open daily 9am-11pm.

Bierakademie, Bahnhofstr. 28 (tel. 729 22), half a block down from the train station. Today's geography lesson: around the world in 100 beers! For those who foolishly insist that man cannot live on beer alone, simple combinations of meat, cheese, and bread are available for under DM10. An array of specialty coffee served in the mornings. Open M-F 10am-1am, Sa 11am-1am.

SIGHTS AND ENTERTAINMENT

Trier is fraught with reminders of its Roman past, the most impressive of which is the **Porta Nigra** (Black Gate). *(Open daily Palm Sunday-Sept. 9am-6pm; Oct.-Nov. and Jan.-Palm Sunday 9am-5pm; Dec. 10am-4pm. Admission DM4, students DM2, children DM1.50. One-day ticket for admission to all Roman monuments DM9, DM4.50, and DM4 each season, respectively.)* Built in the 2nd century, the massive stone gate gained its name from the centuries of grime that metamorphosed its originally light yellow sandstone face into uneven sallow shades of gray. In the past, the gate served as the strongest line of defense against attacks on the city; now, throngs of tourists penetrate the barrier every day. The **Simeonstift,** an 11th-century monastery, enveloped by the courtyard, now holds the **Städtisches Museum** (tel. 718 24 40). *(Open Apr.-Oct. daily 9am-5pm; Nov.-Mar. M-F 9am-5pm, Sa-Su 9am-3pm; admission DM6, students DM5).*

Fruit stalls, florists, and ice-cream vendors crowd the **Hauptmarkt** in central Trier. The colorful Gothic **Dreikönigshaus** (House of the Three Magi), on the left hand side of the *Hauptmarkt* as you walk away from the *Porta Nigra*, bears eloquent testimony to class antagonisms in old Europe. The front door of this medieval merchant's home is located on the second story above street level, accessible only by a ladder, and was pulled inside when angry *Lumpenproletariat* besieged the lavishly adorned house. Growing up in such a neighborhood, it's no surprise that young Karl Marx was inspired to write his theory of class conflict. The **Karl-Marx-Haus,** where young Karl first walked, talked, and dreamed of labor alienation, still stands at Brückenstr. 10 (tel. 430 11), and is a must-see for indefatigable Marxists. *(Open Apr.-Oct. M 1-6pm, Tu-Su 10am-6pm; Nov.-Mar. M 3-6pm, Tu-Su 10am-1pm and 3-6pm. Admission DM3, students DM2.)* Busts and copies of the *Manifesto* abound. For the next leg of *Let's Go's* "Fathers of Communism" Tour, see **Wuppertal** (birthplace of Friedrich Engels), p. 351. On Nagelstr., around the corner from the Karl-Marx-Haus, placate your inner child at the **Spielzeug Museum** (toy museum) with two centuries of dolls, teddy bears, and automata. *(Open Apr.-Oct. daily 11am-5pm; Nov.-Mar. Tu-Su noon-4pm. Admission DM7.50, ages 10-18 DM4, under 10 DM3.)*

A left turn onto Sternstr. from the produce stands of the Hauptmarkt brings you to the 11th-century **Dom,** whose interior design is delightfully impressive. *(Open daily 6:30am-6pm; Nov.-Mar. 6:30am-5:30pm. Daily tours at 2pm. Free.)* Its many nooks and crannies shelter the tombs of archbishops. What is reputedly the **Tunica Christi** (Holy Robe of Christ) is enshrined at the eastern end of the cathedral. Tradition holds that this relic was brought from Jerusalem to Trier around 300 by St. Helena, mother of Emperor Constantine. It was last shown to the public in 1996. If you didn't see it, don't worry; it's *so* two millennia ago. Also in the *Dom,* the **Schatzkammer** touts a treasury of religious artifacts. *(Open Apr.-Oct. M-Sa 10am-5pm, S. 2-5pm; Nov.-Mar. M-Sa 10am-noon and 2-4pm. Admission DM2, students and children DM1.)* Adjacent to the *Dom* is the magnificent Gothic **Liebfrauenkirche.** Its stained glass windows turn the interior of the cathedral a dark red and splash the floor with color. Also next to the *Dom* is the **Bischöfliches Dom-und Diözesanmuseum,** Windstr. 6-8 (tel. 710 52 55), a surprisingly modern building which showcases holy art of all types. *(Open M-Sa 9am-1pm and 2-5pm, Su 1-5pm. DM2, students DM1.)* The museum also boasts one of the largest archaeological collections of any diocesan museum.

Liebfrauenstr. leads to the **Konstantin Basilika,** originally the location of Emperor Constantine's throne room. *(Open M-Sa 9am-6pm, Su 11am-6pm. Free.)* Next door lies the bubble-gum pink **Kurfürstliches Palais,** a former residence of the archbishop-electors of Trier that today houses municipal government offices. It overlooks the well-kept **Palastgarten** where the statues have abnormally elongated toes…yummy. Along the eastern edge of the garden lies the **Landesmuseum,** Ostallee 44, an impressive collection of Roman stonework, sculpture, and mosaics, as well as a few other random relics, including a 2700 year-old Egyptian casket complete with mummy (open Tu-F 9:30am-5pm, Sa-Su 10:30am-5pm; admission DM5, children DM3). At the southeast end of the park are the **Kaiserthermen,** the ruins of the Roman baths where Constantine once scrubbed his grubby tummy, with long dark underground passages make it easy to get lost (same hours and admission as *Porta Nigra*). It's a 5-minute walk uphill from here along Olewigerstr. to the remains of the 2nd-century **Amphitheater.** *(Open Apr.-Sept. daily 9am-5:30pm; Oct.-Mar. 9am-4:30pm. Admission DM4, students DM2, children DM1.50.)* Had the Rolling Stones toured in 169, this 20,000-seat venue (one of the largest in the Roman Empire) certainly would have been on the itinerary. Instead, it hosted a spectacle even more appalling than an aged Mick Jagger: the theater hosted demonstrations of the most spectacular and gruesome ways of inflicting pain (and death) on humans and animals. If you're simply not impressed, ride the **Kabinen Schwebelbahn** (gondola; tel. 14 72 30) across the Mosel to the Stadtwald and admire the forest primeval, the murmuring pines, and the hemlocks. *(Open M-F 9am-6pm, Sa-Su 9am-7pm. Round-trip DM8, kids DM4; one-way DM4.50, DM3.)*

Karl Marx Streets

Immediately after reunification, East Germany experienced a rush to change street names that commemorated Communist heroes of the GDR. But now a backlash to the revisionist movement is gaining strength. In many Western cities, left-wing parties such as the SPD and Greens are agitating to preserve street names honoring 20th-century socialist and communist reformers, including Ernst Thälmann and Rosa Luxemburg, who lost their lives for their ideals. In Berlin, the question of street-name reform was a hot issue in the 1996 local elections. But in Trier, where it all began, **Karl-Marx-Straße** is here to stay.

Several annual festivals spice up Trier's atmosphere. Every fourth weekend of June **Altstadtfest** brings live music, wine, and beer to the streets. The second weekend in July welcomes the **Moselfest,** with Saturday night fireworks over the water. The first weekend in August brings on the **Weinfest,** kicked off by Friday fireworks.

NIGHTLIFE

Pubs, clubs, and *Kneipen* of all flavors fan out from the Hauptmarkt, with dense collections on the *Judengasse* off the Hauptmarkt and at the northwesternly Pferdemarkt. Check posters and free weekly *Der Kleine Dicke* for parties and concerts.

Blaues Blut, Pferdemarkt (tel. 412 53). Mellow blue lighting and tiles on the tables make you feel like you're drinking on the floor of a swimming pool. Instead of getting an eyeful of chlorine, you can gawk at the sleek crowd and enjoy the house and techno music. Open M-Th 9am-1am, F-Sa 9am-2am, Su 10am-1am.

Exil, Zurmainer Str. 114 (tel. 251 91). Huge, graffiti-adorned complex with a *Biergarten.* A bewildering array of dance parties, as well as Trier's best concert venue. Hours and cover vary. Check posters or call for info.

Palais Walderdorff, across from the *Dom* (tel. 410 62). By day, a mellow cafe, by night a disco with creative and beautifully advertised themes. Open M-F 10am-6:30pm, Sa 11am-3pm. Party times vary, but posters are everywhere.

The Dive, Judengasse 21 (tel. 444 24). Descending into the first subterranean bar, you feel like you're in a hyper-real beach bar, replete with plastic bamboo and wooden parrots. Keep going–the disco downstairs caters to a happy crowd with high-intensity techno.

■ Saarbrücken

Once again, Saarbrücken is in shambles. For centuries, the city's proximity to the French border has made it a center of one violent conflict after another, leaving virtually none of the *Altstadt* intact and clearing the way for rampant industrial development. Fortunately, today's destructive forces are much less pernicious—legions of bulldozers and jackhammer-wielding construction workers are tearing the city's streets apart to build a slick new DM500-million rail transit system, scheduled for completion by the year 2000. Focus on the future is found everywhere in Saarbrücken—postmodern architecture, countless factories and power plants, a downtown area that beats with a cosmopolitan pulse. If you're looking for history, Saarbrücken isn't the place, but with a surprisingly urban atmosphere and a plethora of punks and other young progressives, Saarbrücken may be one of the least touristed centers of the modern European cultural scene.

ORIENTATION AND PRACTICAL INFORMATION Saarbrücken is connected by train to Trier (1-1½hr., 2 per hr.). **Der Fahrradladen,** Nauweiserstr. 19 (tel. 370 98), rents bikes (open Tu-F 10am-7pm, Sa 10am-2pm, M 2-7pm). **Mitfahrzentrale,** Großherzog-Friedrich-Str. 59 (tel. 631 91), will hook you up with a chauffeur (open M-F 10am-6pm, Sa 10am-2pm, Su noon-3pm). The handy **Saarbrücken Card** (DM13 for 2 days) provides transportation, free entrance to several sights, and theater discounts. The **tourist office,** Am Hauptbahnhof 4 (tel. 365 15; fax 905 33 00; http://

www.saarbruecken.de), lies to the left of the station. The staff finds rooms for DM3 and provides free brochures and maps. (Open M-F 9am-6pm, Sa 9am-3pm.) Do your **laundry** at Eisenbahnstr. 8, across the bridge and a block behind the Ludwigskirche. (Wash DM6, soap included. Dry DM1 per 10min. Open M-Sa 7am-10pm. Last wash 8:30pm.) Check your email at the **inter@ctive cafe,** Uferg. 2 (tel. 320 80). It's off Bahnhofstr. near the Wilhelm-Heinrich-Brücke, on the 4th floor (DM4.50 per 30min; open M-Th 2pm-midnight, F-Sa 'til 1am, Su 4-10pm). The **post office,** 66111 Saarbrücken, is to the right of the station (open M-F 7am-6:30pm, Sa 7am-2pm, Su 9am-3pm). The **telephone code** is 0681.

ACCOMMODATIONS AND CAMPING Although Saarbrücken is on few foreign tourists' itineraries, its hostels and hotels do brisk business; it's always good to call ahead. The **Jugendgästehaus Europa (HI),** Meerwiesertalweg 31 (tel. 330 40; fax 37 49 11), is a 25-minute walk from the station. Head downhill and left, at the intersection veer left onto Ursulinenstr., take a left at the huge Hela supermarket, and cross the parking lot. The eastern exit flows to Meerwiesertalweg. Or take bus #19 to "Prinzenweiher" and backtrack to the hostel. Mad modern and hopping with young folks, especially with the bar downstairs. (Quads DM26.80 per person; doubles DM36 per person. Breakfast and sheets included. Reception 7:30am-1am. Curfew 1am.) **Gästehaus Weller,** Neugrabenweg 8 (tel. 37 19 03; fax 37 55 65), offers huge rooms with bath, phone, TV, and amazing color coordination. Go down Ursulinenstr., right on Mozartstr., carry on to Schumannstr., left on Fichtestr., and cross the bridge to Neugrabenweg. (Singles DM59-79; doubles DM89-105. Reception M-Sa 8am-11pm, Su 6-11pm. Call ahead.) **Hotel Schlosskrug,** Schmollerstr. 14 (tel. 354 48; fax 37 50 22), at the corner with Bruchwiesenstr., is 10-15 minutes from the station in a quiet, yet hip, location. Go left onto Ursulinenstr., right on Richard-Wagner-Str., and right on Schmollerstr. (Singles with shower DM55, with bath DM65; doubles with shower DM108, with bath DM145; triples with bath DM170.) **Campingplatz Saarbrücken,** Am Spicherer Berg (tel. 517 80), is far from the station. Take bus #42 to "Spicherer Weg," then cross Untertürkheimstr., and head right uphill on Spicherer Weg. (DM6 per person. DM8 per tent. Reception 7am-1pm and 3-10pm. Open Apr.-Sept.)

FOOD The streets around **St. Johannis Markt** brim with bistros, beer gardens, and ethnic restaurants. Walk down Reichstr. and turn left on Bahnhofstr. The buzzing **Schnokeloch,** Kappenstr. 6 (tel. 333 97), serves pizza and pasta for DM8.50-10.80 (open M-F noon-3pm and 6pm-1am, Sa noon-1am, Su 6pm-1am). Traditional German food (DM8-15) is served at the mellower **Spaten am Alten Brunnen,** Türkenstr., right before the church (open M-F noon-2pm and 5pm-midnight, Sa-Su 5pm-midnight). **Blue Moon** (tel. 317 80), on the corner of Schmollerstr. and Martin-Luther-Str., serves up eclectic entrees (DM9-14) and boasts a funky ambience (open M-F 10am-3pm and 6pm-1am, Sa 6pm-1am, Su 10am-1am). Come nightfall, students fill *Kneipen* in the *Chinesenviertel* a few blocks further, between Rotenbergstr., Richard-Wagner-Str., Dudweilerstr., and Großherzog Friedrichstr. **Hela,** at the end of Ursulinenstr., is a monstrous supermarket-drugstore-hair salon (open M-F 8am-8pm, Sa 8am-4pm).

SIGHTS AND ENTERTAINMENT While Saarbrücken is mainly remarkable for its super-modern commercial district, its **St. Johannis Markt** does boast some pretty pieces of old Europe. Since the details on the bronze doors of the **Basilika St. Johann** have faded since its 1754 construction, it's difficult to tell whether the engraved figures are writhing in hell-fire or heavenly ecstatic bliss. *(Open M, W, and F at 8:30am; Tu, Th, and Su 9:30am-evening mass; Sa 9am-evening mass.)* To get there, take Kappenstr. from the market and then turn right at the intersection with Katherinen-Kirche-Str.; the *Basilika* will be on your left. The massive mustard **Staatstheater** stands south of the market next to the Alte Brücke; it was presented to Hitler after the Saarland was re-integrated into Germany in 1935. A walk along Am Stadtgarten with the river on the right leads you to one of three parts of the **Saarland Museum** saga, the **Moderne Galerie,** Bismarckstr. 11-19 (tel. 996 40). Scheduled to be reopened in June 1999, the gallery features such superstar modern art mofos as Picasso, Matisse, and Beckmann.

Part two, the **Alte Sammlung,** Karlstr. 1, is across the street; medieval Madonnas, French porcelain, and antique jewelry are all here. Attached is the **Landesgalerie,** introducing some of the more promising regional artists. *(Both museums open Tu and Th-Su 10am-6pm, W noon-8pm. Joint admission DM3, students and children DM1.50; extra for special exhibits.)* Part three, the hipster's favorite, is the **Graphisches Kabinett,** Bismarckstr. 17, next to the Moderne Galerie. *(Open M-F 10am-5pm. Free.)*

The **Saarbrücker Schloß** (tel. 50 62 47), on the other side of the Saar river, has morphed many times since the 9th century and now has tall sparkling glass columns on either side of its entrance. *(Tours in German given Sa-Su at 4pm. Free.)* Its plaza (the Schloßplatz) is officially the **Platz des unsichtbaren Mahnmals** (Place of the Invisible Reminder) and home to one of the most interesting monuments you'll never see. In 1990, students at a nearby art school, under cover of darkness, dug up 2196 stones in the plaza and carved the names of former Jewish cemeteries on their undersides. Three museums surround Schloßplatz. To the south, adjacent to the *Schloß,* the **Historisches Museum** (tel. 50 65 49) includes cars, chairs from the 70s, and a disturbing collection of war propaganda. *(Open Tu, W, F, and Su 10am-6pm, Sa noon-6pm, Th 10am-8pm. DM4, students DM2, Th after 5pm free.)* To the north, the **Museum für Vor-und Frühgeschichte** (pre- and early history), at Schloßpl. 16 (tel. 95 40 50), has finds that include a Celtic countess's grave and jewelry from the 4th century BC. *(Open Tu-Sa 9am-5pm, Su 10am-6pm. Free, though special exhibits occasionally cost some.)* The 1498 **Rathaus** west of the *Schloß* hosts the wacky **Abenteuer-Museum** (tel. 517 47), which crams lots of anthropological loot into a few rooms, all of it collected by the original globe trotter Heinz Rox Schulz on his rampages through Asia, New Guinea, Africa, and South America. *(Open Tu-W 9am-1pm, Th-F 3-7pm. DM3, children DM2.)* The **Ludwigskirche** is an architectural gem only five minutes down Schloßstr. and to the right. Its bright white interior is a refreshing departure from the usual gothic gloom. *(Open Tu 3-5pm, W 10am-noon, Sa 4-6pm, Su 11am-noon.)* Watch for its high-powered concert series. Saarbrücken is the proud birthplace of renowned filmmaker Max Ophüls, and the town honors him annually with the **Max Ophüls Preis** film festival in late January. The *Kakadu* is Saarbrücken's free culture calendar. Ask for it by name (heh-heh!) at the tourist office.

■ Worms

Of course you've heard of Worms. It was in European history class, when an unfortunate student (maybe it was you) raised his hand and asked what the whole class was thinking: "What's a diet of worms?" The teacher chuckled for a little longer than necessary and replied with characteristic wit, "I don't know what a diet of worms is, but the DEET of VOHRMS *(the Diet of Worms)* was the imperial council that sent Martin Luther into exile for refusing to renounce his heretical doctrines." Remember how funny that was? No? No matter—a visit to Worms will certainly refresh your memory, especially since little else of importance has happened here in the centuries since the famous gathering. Today's Worms is a fairly modern conglomerate of businesses with several fantastic historical and architectural sites scattered throughout. Although the city lacks any sort of core (no jam-packed *Altstadt* here), the many churches, monuments, and puny museums warrant a daytrip for anyone in the area.

PRACTICAL INFORMATION Worms is 45 minutes from Mainz by train (2 per hr.). The **tourist office,** Neumarkt 14 (tel. 250 45; fax 263 28; http://www.worms.de), is in a small shopping complex across the street from the *Dom St. Peter* (office open M-F 9am-6pm, Sa 9am-noon; Nov.-Mar. closed Sa). Guided German walking **tours** meet at the south portal of the *Dom* (2hr., Apr.-Oct. Sa at 10am and Su at 3pm, DM5). **Exchange money** at the *Deutsche Bank* down Wilhelm-Leuschner-Str. from the station (open M-W 8:30am-12:30pm and 2-4pm, Th until 6pm, F until 3:30pm). The **main post office,** Kämmerstr. 44, 67547 Worms, is at the northern end of the pedestrian zone (open M-F 8am-6pm, Sa 8:30am-12:30pm). The **telephone code** is 06241.

ACCOMMODATIONS AND FOOD To walk to the **Jugendgästehaus (HI),** Dechanei-gasse 1 (tel. 257 80; fax 273 94), follow Bahnhofstr. right from the main train station to Andreasstr., turn left and walk until the *Dom* is on your left; the hostel is on your right. This well-equipped, very comfy hostel has bright two-, four-, and six-bed rooms, each with private bath. (DM26.80. Sheets and a great breakfast included. Reception 7am-11:30pm. Strict curfew 11:30pm.) A relaxed staff runs **Weinhaus Weis** (a *Pension,* not a drinking establishment), Färbergasse 19 (tel. 235 00), supplying soft beds in spacious rooms. (Singles DM38; doubles DM68. Breakfast included. Reception generally opens whenever you call them.)

The Worms University **Mensa** is your ticket to cheap food—tastier than the notorious diet of worms. Travelers technically need an ID, but they often get by with language ability. To reach the campus, turn right as you exit the station, go right across the bridge, walk down Friedrich-Ebert-Str., and turn left on Erenburgerstr. It's a block and a half up on your right, past the U.S. Army barbed-wire barracks. Lots of posters about impending events cover the walls. (Open Mar.-July and Oct.-Jan. M-F 11:45am-1:45pm; July and Sept. noon-1:30pm; cafeteria open M-Th 9am-4:30pm, F until 4pm.) In the basement of the building opposite the *Mensa* is the **Taberna,** a groovy *Studenten Kneipe* with a weekly **disco.** (Often closed July-Sept. Taberna open M-Th 3pm-1am. Disco open Th 9pm-1am or later. Any student ID will suffice.) A swank young crowd swims in colorful tropical drinks at **Ohne Gleich,** Kriemhildenstr. 11 (tel. 41 11 77), down Bahnhofstr. to the right of the station. You'll feel like you've stepped into a Magritte painting (Wednesday all cocktails DM7; open Su-Th 9am-1am, F-Sa 9am-2am). The sounds of intense haggling at the **farmer's produce market** echo across the Marktplatz on Monday, Thursday, and Saturday mornings.

SIGHTS AND ENTERTAINMENT The site of Luther's confrontation with the *Diet,* during which he shocked the membership by declaring, *"Ich stehe hier. Ich kann kein anders"* (Here I stand, I can do no other), is memorialized at the **Lutherdenkmal,** a larger-than-life statue erected in 1868 three blocks southeast of the station along Wilhelm-Leuschner-Str. Across the southeast intersection stands the **Kunsthaus Heylshof** art museum, which showcases a small collection of late Gothic and Renaissance art, including Rubens's *Madonna with Child (Open May-Sept. Tu-Sa 11am-5pm, Su 10am-5pm; Oct.-Apr. Tu-Sa 2-4pm, Su 10am-noon and 2-4pm. Closed Jan. DM3, students DM2.)* The lush, inviting greenery and deserted paths of the **Heylshofgarten** surround the museum, providing a welcome bit of solitude amid Worms's day to day clamor.

Chief among Worms's architectural treasures is the **Dom St. Peter,** a magnificent Romanesque cathedral with a spooky crypt. *(Open daily 9am-5:45pm. Free, but a usurious DM0.50 donation, students DM0.20, is requested.)* Let your vampire fantasies run wild or stand and face the hounds of hell. According to the *Nibelungenlied,* Siegfried's wife Kriemhilde had a spat with her sister-in-law Brunhilde in the square in front of the *Dom.* Not as heavenly, but of great historical importance, is the tiny, 1200-year-old **Magnuskirche,** the oldest Protestant church in Germany and the starting point for the Reformation in Worms. *(Open daily Mar.-Nov. 10am-6pm.)* Just beyond, in the Gothic *Andreas-Stift,* stands the **Museum der Stadt Worms,** (tel. 946 39 11), with a bevy of Wormser artifacts dating from the Stone Age on, as well as changing exhibits. *(Open Tu-Su 10am-5pm. DM4, students DM2.)* The late-Gothic **Liebfrauenkirche,** Liebfrauen-ring 21 (tel. 442 67), several blocks north of the *Altstadt off Mainzer Str.,* is gorgeous. *(Open daily 9am-6pm; Nov.-Mar. 9am-5pm.)* The vineyards around the church produce the lush, lingering *Liebfraumilch* (known in its export variety as "Blue Nun").

The 900-year-old **Heiliger Sand** (Holy Sand), the oldest Jewish cemetery in Europe, is the resting ground for sundry rabbis, martyrs, and celebrities. Enter the cemetery through the gate on Willy-Brandt-Ring, just south of Andreasstr. and the main train station. On the opposite end of the *Altstadt,* the area around the **Judengasse** stands witness to the thousand-year legacy of Worms's substantial Jewish community (once known as "Little Jerusalem"), which prospered during the Middle Ages but was wiped out in the Holocaust. The **synagogue,** just off Judengasse, houses the *yeshiva* of the famous Talmudic commentator Rabbi Shlomo Ben-Yitzhak, better known as

Rashi. *(Open daily 10am-noon and 2-5pm.)* Behind the synagogue is the **Judisches Museum** (tel. 85 33 45 and 85 33 70) in the *Raschi-Haus*. A modest collection traces the history of Worms's Jews. *(Open Tu-Su 10am-noon and 2-5pm. DM3, students DM1.50.)* The Worms open-air **jazz festival** takes place every year in the beginning of July. The **Backfischfest** brings a *vino*-drenched party of 70,000 people to Worms for nine days beginning the last weekend in August.

■ Speyer

Speyer's political star rose and fell early. During the reign of the mighty Salian emperors in the 11th century, the town served as a principal meeting place for the Imperial Diets. As the emperors' power waned, Speyer slipped in significance until ultimately the entire city was burned to the ground during the Palatinate War of Succession. By the time the two World Wars rolled around, Speyer didn't merit destruction; its gracefully ramshackle **Altstadt** and several glorious churches, until recently well off the beaten path of mass tourism, were spared from the bombings.

ORIENTATION AND PRACTICAL INFORMATION Speyer is easily reached by **train** from Mannheim (15-30min.) and Heidelberg (1-1½hr.). Also, bus #7007 from Heidelberg (1½hr.) deposits passengers at the steps of the cathedral. The helpful **tourist office,** Maximilianstr. 11 (tel. 14 23 92; fax 14 23 32; http://www.speyer.de), two blocks before the cathedral's main entrance, distributes maps and lists of *Pensionen*. From the train station, take the city shuttle to "Maximilianstr." (Open May-Oct. M-F 9am-5pm, Sa 10am-4pm, Su 11am-3pm; Nov.-Apr. closed Su.) **Tours** of the city depart from in front of the tourist office (Apr.-Oct. Sa-Su 11am; DM5). The **shuttle bus** runs the length of the city every 10 minutes (1-day ticket DM1). The **post office,** 67346 Speyer, is on Postplatz, next to the Altpörtal. It **exchanges money** and cashes traveler's checks (open M-F 8am-6pm, Sa 8am-12:30pm). The **telephone code** is 06232.

ACCOMMODATIONS AND FOOD With all its well-preserved churches, Speyer deserved to be blessed with its incredible new **Jugendgästehaus Speyer (HI),** Geibstr. 5 (tel. 615 97; fax 615 96). Fun is guaranteed by the nearby *Schwimmbad* and the hostel's very own indoor ball pit. (DM26.80; doubles DM35.50; singles DM49.80. Members only. Reception 5-7pm and 9:30-10pm. Lockout 9-11am. Curfew 10pm.) Affordable housing is not common in Speyer. **Pension Grüne Au,** Grüner Winkel 28 (tel./fax 721 96), has comfortable rooms with gleaming sinks. From Maximilianstr., go left on Salzgasse, continue to St. Georggasse, left through Fischmarkt, and right onto Grüner Winkel (singles DM50-75; doubles DM70-90). The side streets of Korngasse and Große Himmelsgasse, just north of Maximilianstr., shelter excellent restaurants. The **Gaststätte "Zum Goldenen Hirsch,"** Maximilianstr. 90a (tel. 726 94), offers Czech specialties and German fare (DM10.50-16.50; open M-Tu, Th-F 11am-1am, Sa 11am-2am, Su 11am-11pm).

On the second weekend in July (Friday to Tuesday), Speyer celebrates its **Bretzelfest** (pretzel festival). The festivities involve all sorts of music, parades, and special events. In early August, the **Kaisertafel Speyer** takes place—tables are set up along the streets and visitors are herded along and stuffed full of regional specialties.

SIGHTS Since its construction in the 12th century, the **Kaiserdom** (Imperial Cathedral) has been the symbol of Speyer. *(Open daily 9am-7pm; Nov.-Mar. 9am-5pm; services at 7, 9, 10:30am, and 6pm on Sundays and holidays.)* The immense Romanesque cathedral is noted for its main portals flanked by seven statues on each side, recounting the tale of Christ's crucifixion. The crypt under the east end coddles the remains of eight Holy Roman Emperors and their wives. Just south of the *Dom*, the excellent **Historisches Museum der Pfalz,** Dompl. D (tel. 132 50), offers a comprehensive presentation on Palatinate history and hosts highly-touted special exhibits on anything from pop art to Napoleon. *(Open Tu, Th-Su 10am-6pm, W 10am-8pm. DM8, students and children DM5, more for visiting exhibitions; Tu after 4pm free. Free tours Su at 11am.)* Also included are the exquisite **Domschatzkammer** (Treasury of the Cathedral) and the

oldest bottle of wine in the world—a slimy leftover from some wild Roman blowout in the 3rd century. A left on Große Pfaffeng. and a right down the Judengasse alley lead to the **Judenbad,** a Jewish ritual bathhouse *(mikwe)* from the 12th century. *(Open Apr.-Oct. M-F 10am-noon and 2-5pm, Sa-Su 10am-5pm. DM1.50.*

Maximilianstr., Speyer's main thoroughfare, spreads westward from the *Dom*, culminating in the medieval **Altpörtel,** an exquisitely preserved four-story village gate. *(Tower open Apr.-Oct. M-F 10am-noon and 2-4pm, Sa-Su 10am-5pm. DM1.50.)* Climb it (from the inside) for a great view. From the *Altpörtel*, a southward jaunt (not a 3hr. tour) on Gilgenstr. leads to the **Church of St. Joseph** and its sister across the street, the **Gedächtniskirche.** *(Both open M-Sa 10am-noon and 2-6pm, Su 2-6pm.)* For those seeking something slightly more up-to-the-minute, the **Technik-Museum-Speyer,** Geibstr. 2 (tel. 670 80; fax 67 08 20), fills a gigantic warehouse with 30,000 cubic meters of trains, planes, and automobiles, as well as an **IMAX theater** (program hotline tel. 67 08 50) and the "Adventure-simulator." *(Museum open daily 9am-6pm. Admission DM12, children DM8; IMAX DM12, children DM10; combination ticket DM22, children DM15.)* Take the city shuttle to "Technik Museum."

Baden-Württemberg

Once upon a time, Baden, Württemberg-Hohenzollern, and Württemberg-Baden were three distinct states. When the Federal Republic was founded in 1951, the Allies masterminded a shotgun wedding, and the three became one: Baden-Württemburg. However, the threesome did not live quite so happily ever after. The Badeners and the Swabians (*never* "Württembergers") still proudly proclaim their distinct identities. Today, two powerful German stereotypes—the brooding romantic of the Brothers Grimm and the modern *homo economicus* exemplified by Mercedes-Benz— battle it out in Baden-Württemberg. Pretzels, cuckoo clocks, and cars were all invented here, and the region is as diverse as its homegrown products. Rural custom and tradition live on in the lush hinterlands of the Schwarzwald and the Schwäbische Alb, while the modern capital city of Stuttgart celebrates the latter-day ascendancy of the German industrial machine. The province also hosts the ritzy millionaires' resort of Baden-Baden, the lovely vacation getaways of the exquisite Bodensee, and the exuberant, historic university towns of Freiburg, Tübingen, and Heidelberg.

🖐 HIGHLIGHTS OF BADEN-WÜRTTEMBERG

- **Heidelberg's** cobblestone streets, literary past, historic buildings, and hopping nightlife draw oodles of tourists. Ride the **cablecar** up to the crumbling *Schloß* or indulge in contemplative thought as you stroll the **Philosophenweg** (see p. 412).
- A modern, corporate culture lies among luscious greenery in **Stuttgart.** The **Schloßgarten** beautifies the city with fountains and flower gardens, while **mineral baths** provide hours of indulgent relaxation (see p. 429).
- Red-roofed **Tübingen** is known for its university and its **half-timbered houses.** The intricate, untouristed **Altstadt** displays medieval German architecture at its finest (see p. 439).
- Hikers live out their fantasies in the **Schwarzwald** (see p. 455). Stretches of pine forest and serene lakes cover the slopes of towering mountains from **Freiburg** (see p. 448) in the south to **Baden-Baden** (see p. 446) in the north.
- About as tropical as Germany gets, the **Bodensee** boast beautiful beaches with turquoise waters (see p. 463). Gaze at the **Swiss and Austrian Alps** from a boat or roam amid the animals made from flowers in the manicured gardens of the **Island of Mainau** (p. 467).

BADEN-WÜRTTEMBURG

■ Heidelberg

One of the countless German cities that flaunt their ancient architecture in glossy tourist propaganda, Heidelberg is surrounded by magnificence that truly shines. From the crumbling walls of the once-majestic *Schloß* to the historic, gabled buildings and the hodge-podge of cobblestone streets in the *Altstadt*, Heidelberg has retained the spirit that once lured numerous writers and artists—including Mark Twain, Wolfgang von Goethe, Friedrich Hölderlin, Victor Hugo, and Robert Schumann—to the woodsy idyll. Today, during the high season (June-Aug.), roughly 32,000 tourists *per day* also answer the call. Even in the most "off" of seasons, legions of camera-toting fannypackers fill the length of Hauptstr., where postcards and t-shirts sell like hotcakes and every sign is in four languages. However, the incessant buzz of mass tourism is worth enduring, as Heidelberg's beautiful hillside setting, endless list of attractions, and lively nightlife actually live up to its well-known reputation.

ORIENTATION AND PRACTICAL INFORMATION

About 20km east of the Neckar's confluence with the Rhine, Heidelberg stretches along the river's shores for several kilometers, with almost all of the city's attractions

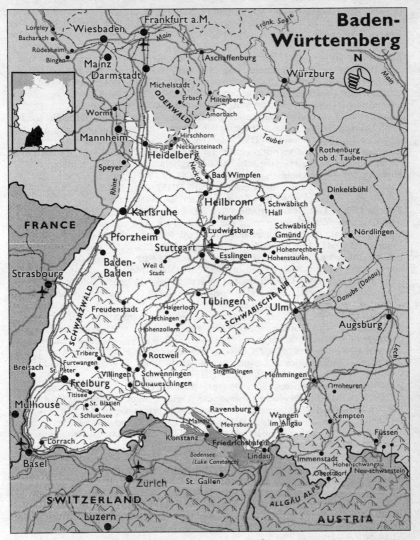

Baden-Württemberg

clustered in the eastern quadrant on the southern shore. To get to the *Altstadt* from the train station, take almost any bus or street car to "Bismarckplatz," where **Haupt-straße** leads into the city's heart. Known as the longest shopping street in Germany, Hauptstr. is undoubtedly the city's backbone—an unending stream of tourists, locals, and the businesses that keep them happy.

Trains: Frequent trains run from Stuttgart (45min.) and Frankfurt (1hr.); Mannheim is less than 10min. away. Other trains run regularly to towns in the Neckar Valley. Call 52 54 74 for information on times and fares.

Public Transportation: To get into, out of, and around Heidelberg, buy a **24hr. pass** that's good on all streetcars and buses (DM10). Passes are available at the tourist office or at the HSB Kiosk, located halfway across the street on Gneisenaustr. (the street that runs by the side entrance to the train station). Or, more simply, buy a pass on any bus or streetcar. Single-ride tickets DM3.30.

Ferries: Rhein-Neckar-Fahrgastschiffahrt, down at the southern bank in front of the *Kongresshaus* (tel. 201 81), runs Neckar cruises. A popular destination is **Neckarsteinach** (1¼hr.; runs Easter-late Oct.; 7 per day 9:30am-3:30pm; round-trip DM16.50).

Taxi: tel. 30 20 30.

Bike Rental: Per Bike, Bergheimer Str. 125 (tel. 16 11 48; fax 16 11 09), has city, mountain, and children's bikes. Half-day DM15, full day DM25, additional days DM20. DM55 Friday-Monday weekend special. DM120 per week. DM50 deposit or ID required. Open M-F 9am-6pm; Apr.-Oct. also open Sa 9am-1pm.

Boat Rental: Rent **paddleboats** and **rowboats** on the north shore of the Neckar by the Theodor-Heuss-Brücke at **Bootverleih Simon.** Three-person boat 30min. DM9, 1hr. DM15. Four-person boat DM12, DM18. Open daily 10am-sundown.

Hitchhiking: *Let's Go* does not recommend hitchhiking as a safe mode of transportation. Hitchers walk to the western end of Bergheimerstr. for all directions.

Mitfahrzentrale: Bergheimerstr. 125 (tel. 246 46 or 194 44; fax 14 59 59), matches riders and drivers in an orderly fashion. Paris DM51, Köln DM28, Hamburg DM54, Freiburg DM24. Open M-F 9am-5pm; Apr.-Oct. also Sa 9am-noon.

Tourist Office: Tourist Information (tel. 142 20; fax 14 22 22; http://www.heidelberg.de/cvb), directly in front of the station. Pick up a copy of the mags *Meier* (DM2) or *Fritz* (free) to figure out what's up. Rooms reserved (7% deposit) and maps sold (DM1). You may want to call lodgings yourself as the tourist office steers guests toward more expensive places. Open M-Sa 9am-7pm, Su 10am-6pm; Jan.-Feb. M-Sa 9am-7pm. Additional tourist offices at the **Schloß** (tel. 211 44; open daily 9am-5pm) and at **Neckarmünsplatz** (open daily 9am-6:30pm; closed in winter).

Currency Exchange: If banks and the post office are closed, try the *Hauptbahnhof.* Its exchange office is open M-Sa 8am-8pm, Su 9am-1pm. On holidays, one can change cash at the *Sparkassen* on Universitätsplatz and Bismarckplatz.

American Express: Brückenkopfstr. 1 (tel. 450 50; fax 41 03 33), at the north end of the Theodor-Heuss-Brücke (bridge) is also a travel agency. They hold mail for card members and owners of AmEx traveler's checks. Open M-F 10am-6pm, Sa 10am-1pm. A secondary office at Kornmarkt (tel. 60 18 16; fax 60 18 60) deals only with traveler's checks. Open M-F 10:30am-4:30 pm, Sa 10am-2pm.

Bookstores: Potter Books, Plöck 93 (tel. 18 30 01; fax 18 30 06), is a hardwood-floored English-only bookstore that stocks a wide variety of new and used titles, from classics to trashy romances, all at reasonable prices. Open M-F 10am-8pm, Sa 10am-4pm. **Old Bridge Books,** Kettengasse 1 (tel. 61 63 33; fax 61 63 34), buys and sells new and used English books. Open M-F 10am-6:30pm, Sa 10am-4pm.

Laundromat: Wasch Salon SB, Poststr. 49 (tel. 450 03), next to Kurfürst Hotel. Wash DM7. Dry DM1 per 20min. Beware: the machines do not give change—you could be forced to dry your clothes for hours. Open daily 6am-3am.

Emergency: tel. 110. **Police:** Römerstr. 2-4 (tel. 990). **Fire** and **Ambulance,** tel. 112.

Women's Resources: Frauennotruf (women's emergency hotline), tel. 18 36 43. **Buchhandlung Himmelheber,** Theaterstr. 16 (tel. 222 01; fax 230 52), stocks books by, for, and about women, and also hosts readings. Open M-W and F 9am-6:30pm, Th 9am-8pm, Sa 9am-2pm.

AIDS-Hilfe: tel. 194 11.

Post Office: *Hauptpostamt,* Belfortstr., 69115 Heidelberg, diagonally to the right across from the front of the station. Held mail can be picked up at counters 15-17. Open M-F 8am-6pm, Sa 8am-noon.

Telephone Code: 06221.

ACCOMMODATIONS AND CAMPING

Finding a bed in Heidelberg can be extremely taxing. During the summer, save yourself a major headache by arriving early in the day or, better yet, calling ahead. Possible options for those with some ingenuity and a railpass are the countless little towns and villages scattered around Heidelberg. There are **Jugendherbergen** in: Neckargmünd (10min. away; tel. (06223) 21 33); Eberbach (25min.; (06271) 25 93); and Zwingenberg (35min.; tel. (06251) 759 38). All these Neckar Valley towns lie along the Heidelberg-Heilbronn railroad; train service is reliable and regular between them. Better yet,

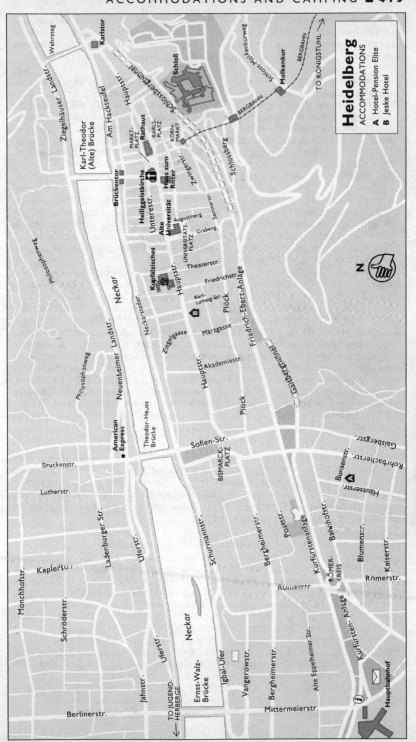

Heidelberg
ACCOMMODATIONS
A Hotel-Pension Elite
B Jeske Hotel

the **Mannheim Jugendherberge** is only five minutes from Mannheim's *Hauptbahnhof,* 15-20 minutes from Heidelberg, and is close to an array of goings-on right in Mannheim (see p. 419). Best of all, a single room in a **private home** in these outlying areas can cost only a fraction of an impersonal place in one of Heidelberg's hotels.

Jugendherberge (HI), Tiergartenstr. 5 (tel. 41 20 66; fax 40 25 59). From Bismarckplatz or the train station, bus #33 (direction: "Zoo-Sportzentrum") to "Jugendherberge" (first stop after Zoo; 10min.). "The Jugendherberge is full today" sign on the tourist office door is practically permanent. Calling less than a week ahead rarely works. Become one of the lucky to stay in this hostel by faxing your reservation. Crowded and noisy, but its small **disco** can be fun (open nightly). DM22, over 26 DM27. Members only. Sheets DM5.50. Reception until 11:30pm. Lockout 9am-1pm. Curfew 11:30pm (negotiable). Partial wheelchair access.

Jeske Hotel, Mittelbadgasse 2 (tel. 237 33). From the train station, bus #33 (direction: "Köpfel") or 11 (direction: "Karlstor") to "Bergbahn," then follow Zwingerstr. west back towards the *Hauptbahnhof* (don't go back up the hill). Mittelbachgasse is the first right after Oberbadgasse. English-speaking Euro-roamers galore fill this delightfully antiquated *Altstadt* facility, and for good reason—it's the best value in Heidelberg. Truly unbeatable location for just a few more marks than the hostel. Reservations only accepted an hour ahead of time. Arrive early! Call for updated prices. Open Feb. to mid-Nov. Other times call ahead.

Hotel-Pension Elite, Bunsenstr. 15 (tel. 257 33). From Bismarckplatz, follow Rohrbacherstr. away from the river and turn right onto Bunsenstr.; the *Pension* is on the left. Nice rooms with high ceilings, Victorian decor, and pastoral views. Bath and TV in each room. Single DM75; doubles for one person DM85; doubles for two DM95-100; DM15 per extra person. Breakfast included. DM5 credit card surcharge.

Camping: Haide (tel. (06223) 21 11; email camping.haide@t-online.de; http://atexcom.com/camping.haide), between Ziegelhäuser and Kleingmünd. Bus #35 to "Orthopedisches Klinik," then cross the river and turn right; the campground is on the right 10min. away. "No-flood" guarantee. DM14.50-20 per person; DM6-12 per tent; DM2 per car. Cabins DM14.50-20. Reception 8am-noon and 4:30-7:30pm. Open Apr.-Oct. If this side of the river doesn't float your boat, head to **Camping Heidelberg-Schlierbach,** located on the other bank (tel. 80 25 06), near the Clinic. Bus #35 (direction: "Neckargmünd") to "Im Grund." DM10 per person; DM4-12 per tent; DM2 per car.

FOOD

Eating out tends to be depressingly expensive in Heidelberg; most of the restaurants on and around Hauptstr. are exorbitantly priced. However, just outside this central area are historic student pubs that offer better values. Fill up a picnic basket at **Handelshof supermarket,** Kurfürsten-Anlage 60, 200m in front of the train station on the right (open M-F 7:30am-8pm, Sa 7:30am-4pm).

Mensa, in the *Marstall,* on Marstallstr. Bus #35 to "Marstallstr." Or, from the Alte Brücke, take a left along the river; it's the huge stone installation on the left. State-subsidized cafeteria turns into a cafe in the afternoon. Cheap food, beer, and cheesecake. Forgot your student ID? Ask one of the students on the green in front to buy you *Mensa Marks* (DM5 each; sold in fives). Open M-F 11:30am-2pm, Sa 11:30am-1:30pm. During vacations, it alternates with the *Mensa* on Universitätsplatz. A popular cafe next door serves coffee, snacks, and beer (DM2.70-3) amidst foozball and World Cup viewings. Open M-F 9am-12:30am, Sa 11am-1am.

Thanner, Bergheimerstr. 71 (tel. 252 34), is a swanky cafe with an eclectic international menu (ratatouille, anyone?), original artwork on the walls, and the only *Biergarten* in Heidelberg allowed to play music. The daily lunch is a bargain at DM7.90, available M-F noon-2:30pm. Open daily 11am-1am.

⬤Zum Schwarzen Wal, Bahnhofstr. 27 (tel. 201 85), at the corner of Landhausstr. *The* place in Heidelberg for big, delicious breakfasts. Each meal is given a nationality (the *Amerikanisches Frühstück* inexplicably includes a crepe). Also serves lunch and dinner (DM10-20). Full breakfast DM6-15. Open M-F 7:30am-1am, Sa 8:30am-1am, Su 9am-1am.

Hemmingways Bar-Cafe-Meeting Point, Fahrtgasse 1 (tel. 16 50 53) at the corner of Neckarstaden. As the name implies, this place is a veritable shrine to the laconic writer. Fishing rods, hunting trophies, and black-and-white memorabilia cram the walls as adventure-seekers munch on pseudo-American fare (DM7-16.50) over red-checked tablecloths. Six breakfasts are available any time. Open daily 9am-1am.

SIGHTS

American author Mark Twain's description of Heidelberg is the highlight of his 19th-century travelogue *A Tramp Abroad.* Twain recorded, with rare respect, his impressions of this university town's beauty. In the ensuing years, Heidelberg has lost none of the stateliness captured so well in Twain's description; its streets still bustle with an energy that would do a much younger city proud. Presiding over all the majestic elegance are the ramparts of the **Heidelberger Schloß** (tel. 53 84 14 or 538 40; fax 16 77 32), the jewel in the crown of an already striking city. (*Grounds open daily 8am-dusk. DM3, students DM1.50, charged 8am-5:30pm only.*) Its construction began early in the 13th century and lasted over 400 years. The conglomeration of styles ranges from Gothic to High Renaissance. Thrice destroyed, first by war (1622 and 1693) and later by nature (lightning in 1764), the castle's regal state of disrepair is best viewed from the **Philosophenweg** (Philosopher's Way) high above the northern bank of the Neckar. On June 5, July 10, and September 4, 1999, fireworks will illuminate the surrounding sky in the **Schloßbeleuchtung.** The *Schloß* is easily accessible by foot or by the **Bergbahn** (the world's oldest cable car), which runs from the "Bergbahn/Rathaus" bus stop to the castle (round-trip DM4.70) and continues on to the Königstuhl TV tower (round trip DM7). Trams take off from the Kornmarkt parking lot next to the bus stop every 10 minutes from 9am to 7:45pm. Take bus #11 towards "Köpfel" or 33 towards "Karlstor." Getting inside the *Schloß* is possible only with a **tour.** (*Tours DM4, students DM2. English tours daily at 11:30 am, 2, and 3:45pm.*) Those not on a tour can still visit the musty wine cellar and its *Faß,* a brutally large wine barrel. Local lore tells of a court jester and *Faß* guardian who drank nearly 18 bottles per day and finally perished after accidentally drinking a glass of water. The **Apothekenmuseum** (tel. 258 80), also in the castle, stopped dishing out the goods in 1693 but still features all sorts of creepy displays on pre-modern drugs, pharmacy, and alchemy. (*Open daily 10am-5:30pm. Free with entrance to castle grounds.*)

The *Altstadt* centers on the **Marktplatz,** a cobbled square where **Hercules' Fountain** stands, and where, in the 15th century, accused witches and heretics were burned at the stake; now tourists recline on a legion of plastic chairs while a **market** purveys fruit on Wednesdays and Saturdays. The two oldest structures in Heidelberg border the Marktplatz. The 14th-century **Heiliggeistkirche** (Church of the Holy Ghost) is the largest Gothic church in the Palatinate and contains the tomb of Ruprecht I, founder of the University. (*Open to visitors M-Th and Sa 11am-5pm, F 1-5pm, Su 1:30-5pm. Free.*) Climb the church tower for only DM1 (students DM0.50). Across from the church's southern face, the ornate facade of the swanky **Haus zum Ritter** dates from the 16th century. The stately **Rathaus** overlooks the entire spectacle from the far end of the square.

Walking west from the Marktplatz down Hauptstr. yields views of trendy shops and cafes, while history hides behind them; five blocks down, the **Universitätsplatz,** centered about a stone-lion fountain, is the former headquarters of the **Alte Universität** (Old University). In the aristocratic tradition, students were exempt from prosecution by civil authorities; instead, the crimes of naughty youths were tried and punished by the university faculty. Guilty students were jailed in the **Studentenkarzer,** Augustinergasse 2 (tel. 54 23 34) between 1778 and 1914. (*Open Apr.-Oct. Tu-Sa 10am-12:30pm and 2-5pm; Nov.-Mar. Tu-F 10am-12:30pm and 2-5pm, Sa 10am-1pm. DM1.50, students DM1.*) Covered with graffiti, the wall tells of a group of honest students who were unjustly imprisoned for returning a loose cobblestone to its rightful owner—through a window. Nearby, the **University Museum,** Grabengasse 1 (tel. 54 21 52), offers some erudite exhibits. *(Open Tu-F 10am-4pm.)* The same can be said of the huge **University Library,** Plöck 107-109 (tel. 54 23 80; fax 54 26 23), with its collection of illegible medieval manuscripts. *(Open M-Sa 10am-7pm. Free.)* The **Kurpfälzisches Museum,** Hauptstr. 97 (tel. 58 34 02 or 58 34 00; fax 58 34 90), is crammed with artifacts such as the jawbone of an unfortunate *homo Heidelbergensis*, a.k.a. "Heidelberg man," one of the oldest humans yet discovered. *(Open Tu and Th-Su 10am-5pm, W 10am-9pm. DM5, students DM3; Su DM3, students DM2.)* Elsewhere in the museum stand well-preserved works of art by Dürer, and a spectacular archaeology exhibit.

No trip to Heidelberg would be complete without a visit to the northern bank of the Neckar. Walk across the modern **Karl-Theodor-Brücke;** on the south side of the bridge stands a plump statue of the Prince-Elector himself, which he commissioned as a symbol of his modesty. On the left side of the bridge, the **Zoo,** Tiergartenstr. 3 (tel. 48 00 41), lies beyond a perfect picnic park. *(Zoo open Apr.-Sept. daily 9am-7pm; Oct.-Mar. 9am-5pm.)* Or take bus #33 towards "Sportzentrum Nord" to "Tiergarten." To the right of the bridge, in the direction of the Marktplatz, lies the shining path to enlightenment: the **Philosophenweg.** Contemplate the Nietzschean *Übermensch* as you gaze upon the masses of peons in the city, or bring your sweetheart and smooch 'til sunrise. Either way, the view is one of the best in the city.

Atop the **Heiligenberg,** the mountain traversed by the *Philosophenweg,* lie ruins of the 9th-century **St. Michael Basilika,** the 13th-century **St. Stephen Kloster,** and an amphitheater built under Hitler in 1934 on the site of an ancient Celtic gathering place. Take *Straßenbahn* #1 or 3 to **Tiefburg,** a moated castle in neighboring Handschuhsheim, where you can begin the hike upwards.

Heidelberg is home to a number of merry festivals. The **Faschings Parade (Carnival)** struts through the city on Shrove Tuesday. The **Spring Festival** spices up the last few days of May. The **Handschuhsheim Fest** lures revelers across the river on the third weekend in June, while the **Schloßfestspiele Heidelberg** features a series of concerts and plays at the castle for five weeks, beginning in late July (call 583 52 for info and tickets). On September 30th, the **Heidelberger Herbst** brings a medieval market to the Altstadt, which later witnesses the **Weihnachtsmarkt** (Christmas Market) from Dec. 1-23.

NIGHTLIFE

Even at night, Heidelberg's Marktplatz is the heart of the city's action; most popular nightspots fan out from here. **Unterestraße,** on the Neckar side of the Heiliggeistkirche, boasts the most prolific—and often congested—conglomeration of bars in the city. During fair weather, drunken revelers fill the narrow way until 1 or 2am. **Hauptstraße** also harbors a fair number of venues, and a few dot the north side of the river as well.

Roter Ochsen, Hauptstr. 217 (tel. 209 77). A popular student hangout since 1703. Bismarck and Mark Twain used to get plastered here; so can you for DM4.30. Just don't let the beer foam stick to your walrus mustache. The pervasive antiquity is even visible in the clientele. Meals DM14-30. Open Apr.-Oct. M-Sa 11:30am-2pm and 5pm-midnight; Nov.-Mar. M-Sa 5pm-midnight.

Zum Sepp'l, Hauptstr. 213 (tel. 230 85). Next door to Roter Ochsen with a similarly loud crowd that's been partying since 1634. Look for the (yes, it's true!) "Adolf-Hitler-Platz" sign on the wall. Meals DM12-25. Beer DM4.80, "the Boot" (2L of beer) DM6.20. The Boot can kick yer butt. Open daily 11am-midnight.

Reichsapfel, Unterestr. 35 (tel. 279 50), is a popular bar, filled with a fairly diverse crowd of locals. *Pils* DM4.60. Open daily 6pm-1am.

Cave 54, Krämergasse 2 (tel. 278 40), keeps a somewhat older crowd jumping with live music every Tuesday and Sunday. Beer DM5. Cover DM5, Tu and Su DM12. Open daily 10pm-3am.

O'Reilly's, on the corner of Brückenkopfstr. and Uferstr. (tel. 411 01 40). Cross Theodor-Heuss-Brücke, turn right, and follow the noise to this hoppin' Irish pub, where a young crowd drinks Guinness (DM5) and eats smoked salmon salad (meals DM7-24). Open M-F 4pm-1am, Sa-Su noon-1am.

Schwimmbad Musik Club, Tiergartenstr. 13 (tel. 47 02 01; http://www.smc.rhein-necker.de), across the river. Conveniently located up the street from the hostel, but a trek otherwise, it's the city's main catwalk for bands with names like "Fatal Function" or "Mr. Hate and Crossroad Edge." Every Wednesday is independent alternative; every Thursday is "Deutschrock." Open W-Th 8pm-3am; F-Sa 8pm-4am.

Little Heaven, Fahrtgasse 18 (tel. 226 61). Heidelberg's local outpost of Euro-dance music culture. Tuesday salsa and merengue, Wednesday hip-hop. Thursday all-you-can-guzzle beer for DM12-15. Cover DM5-15. Open daily 10pm-3am.

VaterRhein, Untere Neckarstr. 20-22 (tel. 213 71; fax 062 21), close by the river, near the *Stadthall.* College students converge after midnight to chill here, among the vintage 1950s American ads that decorate the dark wood-paneled walls. Cheap food and drinks, plenty of smoke. Goulash DM6, pizza DM11.50. *Pilsner* DM4.40. Open daily 8pm-3am.

Mata Hari, on Zwingerstr. near Oberbadgasse (tel. 18 18 08). Cramped, subdued gay and lesbian bar. Tuesday men only. Beer DM4. Open daily 11pm-3am.

■ Mannheim

For nearly a thousand years, Mannheim existed merely as a simple fishing village. In 1720, however, history took a step forward, when Elector Karl Phillipp made the city the capital of the Rheinland-Pfalz. Mannheim's heady days as capital came to an end a mere 57 years later when the court packed up and marched off to Munich, as Elector Karl Theodor bid farewell—*Auf Wiedersehen,* baby. The desertion appears to have had little effect on the city; today's Mannheim is one of the most urbanized locales in southwest Germany. Besides the many grand buildings which the nobility left behind, Mannheim flaunts a substantial cultural scene and a virtual shoppers' paradise. The easily navigated streets and almost nonexistent tourist population make Mannheim a worthy destination for city-loving independent travelers.

ORIENTATION Mannheim perches on a peninsula partitioned by the **Kaiserringstr.** (directly in front of the *Hauptbahnhof*); the **Innenstadt** lies to the west and the rest of the city lies to the east. The *Innenstadt* is divided into a grid of 144 blocks along a central axis, the **Kurpfalzstraße,** which runs from the center of the *Residenzschloß* northward to the *Kurpfalzbrücke* (bridge) on the Neckar River. Each block is designated by a letter and a number. Streets to the west of Kurpfalzstr. are designated by the letters **A** through **K** (from A blocks in the south to K blocks in the north) while streets to the east are similarly lettered **L** through **U**. The blocks on the central axis are numbered 1; the number of the block increases as you move away from Kurp-falzstr. The giant grid is bounded by Bismarckstr. to the south, Parkring to the west, Luisenring to the north, and Friedrichsring and Kaiserring to the east. East of Kaiser-ringstr., streets assume regular names; perhaps the Pfalz electors discovered a more poetic side, or saw that they were running out of letters. The **A** and **M** streets will keep you well oriented.

PRACTICAL INFORMATION Mannheim's **train station** is large and busy with ICE and international trains making frequent stops. It's only a 15-minute ride from Heidelberg, 45 minutes from Frankfurt, and 1 hour from Stuttgart. **Transportation** via Mannheim's streetcars costs DM1 per ride within the *Innenstadt,* and DM3.20 for rides beyond that. A day card, **Ticket 24 Plus,** costs DM9. The **tourist office,** Willy-Brandt Platz 3 (tel. (0180) 521 44 99; fax (0621) 241 41; http://www.tourist-mannheim.de), a block from the *Hauptbahnhof,* distributes maps (necessary despite, or, rather, because of, the weirdo street arrangement), information on accommodations, and tickets to upcoming events (open M-F 9am-7pm, Sa 9am-noon). The office also offers a **Mitfahrzentrale** ride-share service. While you're here, pick up a free copy of *Scala* for local cultural events, or *T5* for nightlife. Tickets for upcoming events can also be bought by calling 10 10 11. A **laundromat** waits for you on block G7 on the Luisen-ring side. (Wash DM6, soap included. Dry DM1 per 15min. Open daily 6am-11pm, last entry 10pm.) A **pharmacy,** Bahnhof Apotheke (tel. 12 01 80), dispenses therapeutic goods at block L15, across from the station and to the left (open M-F 6am-8pm, Sa 7:30am-4pm). The **post office**, 68161 Mannheim, is one block east of the main station, easily within sight. *Postlagernde Briefe* are at counters 10 and 11. (Open M-F 8am-8pm, Sa 8am-noon.) The **telephone code** is 0621.

ACCOMMODATIONS Mannheim's **Jugendherberge (HI)**, Rheinpromenade 21 (tel. 82 27 18; fax 82 40 73), provides somewhat cramped rooms. But its delectable deluxe breakfast (they even have cheesecake!) and super-convenient location, 10 minutes from the train station, more than make up for the aging facilities. Walk through the underground passage (toward *Gleis* 10) and exit at the back of the train station, then take a right. Follow Joseph-Kellner-Str., cross the tracks, continue down the street with the park on your right for about a block, and enter at the first official entrance, by the mailbox. (DM20, over 26 DM25. Members only. Make sure you pay DM2 more for the incredible breakfast buffet. Sheets DM6. Reception 1-2pm, 4-6pm, 7-10pm. Curfew 12:30am.) The next best value is the spotless and conveniently located **Pension Arabella**, block M2, #12 (tel. 230 50; fax 156 45 27), two blocks north of the *Schloß* (singles DM40-45; doubles DM70-80; triples DM100; breakfast DM7.50). **Goldene Gans**, Tattersallstr. 19 (tel. 10 52 77; fax 422 02 60), two blocks northwest of the train station, has its entrance around the corner. Friendly and efficient service in pleasant rooms with phones and sinks is marred only by traffic noise, audible in street-side suites. (Singles from DM55; doubles from DM100. Breakfast included. Reception M-Sa 6am-midnight, Su 7am-8pm.)

FOOD AND NIGHTLIFE The cheapest meals in town are at the government-subsidized **Studentenwerk Mannheim Mensa** (open M-F 11:30am-2pm and 5-7pm) and the adjacent, slightly more expensive **cafeteria** (open M-Th 8:30am-4pm, F 8:30am-3:45pm). The *Mensa* is located behind the *Residenzschloß* in the southwest corner. An old piano, theater posters, and antique bicycles and clocks fill **Harlekin**, Kaiserring 40 (tel. 10 33 54), on the corner of Moltkestr. Sandwiches, pasta, and *Maltauschen* are all yummy, and most cost less than DM16. (Open M-F 9am-1am, Su 5pm-1am.) **Max und Moritz,** S4, #17-22 (tel. 273 48), boasts an even wackier interior: fake palm trees and a big boat accompany salads, soups, and generous entrees (DM10-18). They have frequent foreign theme weeks and cocktail parties every Friday and Saturday (Open daily 9am-midnight; kitchen open 10:30am-11pm.) Folks of all ages congregate at the newly opened **Stonehenge Irish Pub,** M4, #8-9 (tel. 122 39 49), which offers live Irish music a few times a week and Irish breakfasts every Sunday for DM11. All cocktails DM9 on Thursdays; students get beer o' the week for half price on Wednesdays. (Open Su-Th 12:30pm-1am, F-Sa 'til 3am.) Blocks G7 and H7 teem with lots of busy bars. Email and caffeine (and alcohol) cravings can be slaked at the **Neworld Internetcafé,** S3, #11 (tel. 12 95 00), a 30-computer techno-playing cyber-everything two-floor complex that claims to be Europe's largest Internet cafe. (Open daily 10am-5am. DM2.50 per 30min. before 4pm, DM3 after 4pm. Th nights all drinks and computer access for a DM25 cover fee.) Butchers, bakers, and grocers gather at the **market** in the square at the intersection of Kurpfalzstr. and Kirchstr. at the center of the city grid (open Tu, Th, and Sa 7am-2:30pm). Most large department stores in the shopping district sell **groceries** in the basement.

SIGHTS Mannheim's real attraction is its bustling commercial area, which centers around the **Paradeplatz** at block O1 and extends for several teeming blocks in all directions, though most densely north and east. Restaurants, department stores, cafes, movie theaters, and lots and lots of people combine with the city's funky layout to form an urban space of an intensity rarely found in gnarled European roads. If the milieu of metropolitan Mannheim leaves you feeling guilty for not taking in enough Old Europe, the city has several substantial offerings, beginning with its emblematic masterpiece, the **Wasserturm** (water tower) and surrounding gardens of **Friedrichs-platz**. Restored to its original glory in 1956, the elegant sandstone tower topped by a statue of Amphitrite almost lives up to its billing as "the most beautiful water tower in the world." On the south side of the manicured foliage and crystalline fountains of

Friedrichsplatz crouches the **Kunsthalle**, a museum surveying art from the mid-19th century to modern times. *(Open Tu-W and F-Su 10am-5pm, Th noon-5pm. DM4, students DM2.)* To reach Friedrichsplatz from the station, walk north on Kaiserring (10min.).

Along with a bizarre street-naming scheme, the Palatinate left the giant **Residenzschloß**. The largest palace of the Baroque period, it now houses the **Universität Mannheim**. In the oddly gaudy **Schloßkirche** (tel. 292 28 90), the sleek coffer of the crypt holds Karl Phillip's third wife, Violante von Thurn und Taxis. *(Tours Tu-Su 10am-1pm and 2-5pm; Nov.-Mar. Sa-Su 10am-1pm and 2-5pm. DM4, students DM2.50.)* Even odder, a Masonic symbol and a post horn decorate the altar, suggesting a bizarre link between efficient mail and eventual Masonic world domination—Mucho, Mucho Maas cometh. The extensive **Reiß Museum** (tel. 293 31 50) consists of three buildings located around C5, northwest of the *Schloß*, which contain exhibits on archaeology, ethnology, and natural science. *(Open Tu-W and F-Su 10am-5pm, Th noon-5pm. DM4, students DM2, free on Thursday afternoons; special exhibitions extra.)* Between the museum and the *Schloß* at block A4 stands the **Jesuit Church**, built as a symbol of the Pfalz court's reconversion to Catholicism. *(Open daily 8am-noon and 2-6:30pm.)* The poet Friedrich Hölderlin called it "the most splendid building I have encountered during my travels." This is perhaps poetically licentious, but the church is fantastic.

On the other side of the *Innenstadt*, several blocks northeast of the *Wasserturm*, the 100-acre **Luisenpark** (tel. 41 00 50) sprouts away. *(Open daily 9am-dusk; May-Aug. closes at 9pm. DM5, students DM4.)* The greenhouses, flower gardens, aviary, zoo, water sports, mini-golf, and frequent afternoon concerts offer something for everyone. South of Luisenpark, due east of Friedrichsplatz on the *Augustanlage*, lies the terrific **Landesmuseum der Technik und Arbeit** (State Museum of Technology and Labor), Museumstr. 1 (tel. 429 89), which displays the inner workings of big, creaky, rusty things through fun-as-hell hands-on exhibits. *(Open Tu and Th-F 9am-5pm, W 9am-8pm, Sa 10am-5pm, Su 10am-6pm. DM5, students DM3, families DM7; more for special exhibits.)* Take streetcar #6 (direction: "Neuostheim") to "Landesmuseum." In its six stories connected by tunnels and ramps, the museum covers "250 years of technical and social change and industrialization in southwest Germany." Get a tetanus shot. There's a working waterwheel, printing presses, and BMWs galore. Right nearby is the **world's first Planetarium** (tel. 41 56 92), still projecting spacey visions. *(Shows Tu 10am and 3pm, W and F 3pm and 8pm, Th 3pm, Sa-Su 5 and 7pm. DM8, students DM6.50.)* The **Museumsschiff "Mannheim"** (tel. 156 57 56) floats in the Neckar, just by the Kurpfalz Bridge. Once the paddle steamer **Mainz**, which sank in 1956, it has since been retrieved from the Rhine's murky depths and now offers a history of navigation. *(Open Tu-Su 10am-4pm. DM2.)*

NECKARTAL (NECKAR VALLEY)

The **Neckartal**—a scenic stretch of narrow, thickly wooded ridges—embraces the Neckar River as it meanders from Heilbronn to Heidelberg. Centuries ago, a series of enterprising royalty decided to build castles for the lofty goal of protecting merchant vessels from pirates—as well as the not-so-lofty goal of charging exorbitant tolls for their generous services. Today, their trail of medieval castles dot the hilltops of the Neckartal and form part of the Burgenstraße (the German Castle Road) that stretches all the way to Nürnberg in the heart of Bayern. Largely unspoiled by tourism, the Neckartal is an excellent daytrip from Heidelberg.

Two train lines connect Heidelberg and Heilbronn hourly, with stops in the many smaller towns along both sides of the valley. One of the best ways to explore the valley is by biking along the well-maintained 85km route. **Bike rentals** are available at the **train station** in Neckargmünd, 12 minutes by train from Heidelberg (DM13 per day, DM9 with a train ticket). In Hirschhorn (see p. 422), **Josef Riedel**, Hainbrunnerstr. 6 (tel. (06272) 20 17), has 'em for DM5 per half-day, DM10 per day. Finally, there's the **train station** in Eberbach (tel. (06271) 22 20), 30 minutes from Heidelberg. Also check **Per Bike** in Heidelberg (see p. 412). The **Rhein-Neckar Fahr-**

gastschiffahrt runs **boat tours** from Easter through late October between Heidelberg (departing from the *Stadthalle*), Neckargemünd, Neckarsteinach, Hirschhorn, and Eberbach. All round-trips cost DM4-19.50. For information and departure times, call (06221) 201 81 or (06229) 526.

■ Neckarsteinach

At the north end of the valley, 14km upstream from Heidelberg, lies Neckarsteinach, notable for its four medieval **castles** all within three kilometers of one another along the north bank of the Neckar River. They were built by the same ruling clan, the Steinachs, during the 12th and 13th centuries. The two westernmost castles stand in ruins, while the two to the east tower and shine in their splendor; they are privately occupied, however, and visitors are not allowed inside. All can be reached by foot via the **Burgenweg** (castle path)—a journey of 30 minutes to several hours, depending on the strength of your legs and the weight of your backpack. Tourists may visit all but the first castle on the path. From the train station, turn right on Bahnhofstr., and follow it until you reach Hauptstr. Turn left and follow the bend in the road to the Pizzeria Castello; the *Schloßsteige* begins at the brick path leading upward to the right and connects to the Burgenweg, whose trees are studded with identifying plaques (open Mar.-Oct. M-Sa 9am-8pm). Fireworks emblazon the sky above the town on the last Saturday in July during the **Vierburgenbeleuchtung** (four-castle lighting). *Rhein-Neckar-Fahrgastschiffahrt* organizes trips for the fiery festivities, and also makes daily trips from Heidelberg (see p. 412) all summer long.

Neckarsteinach's **tourist office,** Hauptstr. 7 (tel. 920 00; fax 318), inside the *Rathaus,* is one block down from Bahnhofstr. in the same direction as the *Schloß-steige.* The office lists hotels, *Pensionen,* and private homes offering inexpensive rooms (open M-W 8am-noon and 1:30-3:30pm, Th 8am-noon and 1:30-5pm, F 8am-noon). A mile or so from town, the hostel-like **Hoher Darsberg,** Außerhalb 1 (tel. 96 00 50; fax 96 00 99) offers vegetarian meals and a night's lodging for DM29. Directly across the river from town lies the **Unterm Dislberg campground** (tel. 725 85; DM6 per person; open Apr.-Sept.). **Bistro Stadtgarten am Neckar,** Schiedweg 22 (tel. 24 34), serves pizza and *Pommes Frites* with an outstanding view of the valley (food DM4-14; open M-Sa noon-10pm, Su 11am-10pm). The **postal code** is 69239. The **telephone code** is 06229.

■ Hirschhorn and Burg Guttenberg

Just south of Neckarsteinach lounges Hirschhorn am Neckar, ruled for centuries by the Knights of Hirschhorn. In 1200, the knights built their castle on Stockelberg Mountain, cruelly displacing a happy herd of reindeer from its favorite grazing spot. History repeated itself many hundreds of years later, when an enterprising young capitalist bought the knights out; the mountain is now a posh hotel/restaurant complex. Nevertheless, the surrounding countryside is excellent for hiking, and the former **castle of the knights of Hirschhorn** is still worth a peek. By foot, follow the gray brick of Schloßstr. upward from the *Bürgerhaus* intersection (15min.). Unless you are in a car, do not follow the road signs. The castle's terraces offer a fine panorama, and an even better one can be had at the top of the tower for a mere DM0.30. Stone stairs curl from the castle down into the *Altstadt;* along the way, they pass the 15th-century **Karmeliter Klosterkirche,** with its Gothic interior and graceful altar. Some days, monks' chants echo softly through the church, mesmerizing passersby.

Detailed maps of the local hiking trails are available at the **tourist office,** Alleeweg 2 (tel. 17 42 or 92 31 40), which books rooms for free. From the station, turn left on Neckarsteinacherstr. and follow it to the intersection as it curves to the right. Turn right and walk downhill toward the river, just past the hotel. The office is in the rear of the yellow building on the right. (Open M-F 8am-noon and 2-5pm; Apr.-Oct. also Sa 9am-noon.) The office's home, the **Haus des Gastes,** also houses the **Langben Museum,** an art and natural history museum with a collection of 17th- and 18th-century wooden statues, weaponry, and a truly terrifying diorama that crams over 100 native fauna into a space the size of a king-size bed (open Tu and Th-F 2-4pm, Su 10am-noon and 2-4pm; DM1, children DM0.50). The **post office**, Alleeweg 4, 96434 Hirschhorn, is to the left of the tourist office (open M-F 8:30am-noon and 2-5pm, Sa 8:30am-noon). The **telephone code** is 06272.

For overnight accommodations, check the hotels and *Pensionen* along Hauptstr. and the board outside the tourist office. **Haus La Belle,** Hauptstr. 38 (tel. 14 00), has cushy rooms (with bath and TV) from DM30 per person, including breakfast. Camp between April and mid-October at **Odenwald Camping,** Langenthalerstr. (tel. 809; fax 36 58), one kilometer outside of town in the direction of the castle; follow signs from the tourist office (DM7 per person).

Thirty kilometers south of Hirschhorn along the *Burgenstraße* towers **Burg Guttenberg.** The castle houses a **museum** detailing its 800-year history (open Apr.-Oct. daily 10am-6pm). Also within the castle walls is an aviary for **birds of prey,** maintained by prominent ornithologist Claus Fentzloff. Twice per day (at 11am and 3pm Apr.-Nov.; Mar. and Nov. at 3pm only), Fentzloff sends eagles and vultures flying inches above the heads of the crowds, plucking poor little chickens out of the sky, while he launches into lengthy scientific diatribes. (Admission for museum and castle DM5, for bird show DM12, for all DM15.) To reach Burg Guttenberg by rail, get off at Gundelsheim (along the Heidelberg-Heilbronn run), cross the big bridge past the camping site, and walk 2km following the signs along the road, past wheatfields and terraced hillsides (25min.).

■ Bad Wimpfen

Just downstream from Heilbronn along an alternative rail route on the road to Heidelberg reposes the village of **Bad Wimpfen,** long one of the best-kept secrets in southwest Germany. In the past few years, however, the infamous megabuses have infiltrated the area. Although this seems to be just one more innocuous village set against the sweeping backdrop of fields, the town opens unexpectedly into four gnarled bumpy streets and rough-worked, half-timbered houses built atop the ruins of a Roman imperial castle on a ridge high above the Neckar.

From the ornately Gothic train station, the immaculately preserved *Altstadt* is a 10-minute walk. Go straight ahead and follow Karl-Ulrich-Str. as it bends right. Or, if your calves need toning, take the steep hiking trail to the right of the station. Up we go. Laid out along the northern side of the old castle walls, easily accessible points on the ancient battlements offer incredible views of the valley and surrounding countryside. Just beside the *Roterturm* (Red Tower; open Sa-Su 10am-noon and 2-5pm), along Burgviertel, is the **Pfalzkapelle,** with the **Kirchenhistorisches Museum,** which exhibits ecclesiastical artifacts from the town's monastery and churches. (Open Apr.-Oct. Tu-Su 10am-noon and 2-4:30pm; DM2, students DM1.) Along the castle ruins between the Marktplatz and the train station are the **Blauer Turm** (Blue Tower) and the **Steinhaus.** The former, on Burgviertel 9 (tel. 89 08), offers another view to those willing to climb the 169 steps (open Tu-Su 10am-6pm; DM2). The tower's dramatic 1984 decapitation by lightning is documented on the way up the stairs. Next door, the sandstone *Steinhaus* contains the **Historisches Museum,** a somewhat sparse collection of artifacts both ancient and medieval (open Apr.-Oct. Tu-Su 10am-noon and 2-4:30pm; DM2, students DM1). The **Kulturamt,** Hauptstr. 45 (tel. 95 00 73), distributes information on cultural events in town. The **Galerie der Stadt** features a small exhibit on contemporary artwork, while the **Reichstädtisches Museum** carefully displays the history of Bad Wimpfen. (Both open M-F 10am-noon and 2-5pm. Admission to the Galerie is free; to the museum DM3, students DM2. An inclusive ticket for the Historisches, Kirchenhistorisches, and Reichstädtisches museums can be bought for DM5, students DM3.) This does not, unfortunately, include the world's only **Pig Museum,** Kronengäßchen 2 (tel. 66 89; email schweinemuseum@marena.com), off Hauptstr. near the *Kulturamt,* which details the history of swine (considered a good luck symbol in Germany) with collector's items and lucky charms. (Open daily 10am-5pm. DM5, students DM2.50, children under 1m DM1.)

The friendly **tourist office** in the train station (tel. 972 00; fax 97 20 20) hands out a number of glossy brochures on Bad Wimpfen. The staff will also help find lodging (including private rooms DM25-30; open M-F 9am-1pm and 2-5pm, Sa-Su 10am-noon and 2-4pm). The **telephone code** is 07063.

Hotel Garni Neckarblick, Erich-Salier-Str. 48 (tel. 96 16 20; fax 85 48), offers affordable luxury with a capital "L," very hospitable management, and a stunning view of the valley. From the Marktplatz, follow Mathildenbadstr. from the pedestrian zone out to the street, then hang a right. Proceed for 15 minutes along Erich-Salier-Str. as it curves around the hillside (past the park); the hotel is on the right. All rooms include TV, telephone, and bath. (Singles DM80; doubles DM115-140; triples DM175. Discounts available for longer stays. Call ahead or fax reservations.) Much closer to the *Bahnhof,* **Pension zur Traube,** Hauptstr. 1 (tel. 65 21), offers less cushy but still comfy rooms with showers (singles DM55; doubles DM105; breakfast included). For traditional German fare, try **Dobel's Maultaschen,** Hauptstr. 61 (tel. 82 12), where *Maultaschen* (Swabian pasta pockets) are the house specialty (DM9-16). Their salad bar (DM7) is a rare source of green fiber in the Neckar Valley (open M-Sa 10am-midnight, Su 10am-10pm). **Grocery stores** are located on the other side of the *Altstadt* along Rappenamerstr.

SCHWÄBISCHE ALB (SWABIAN JURA)

The limestone plateaus, sharp ridges, and pine-forested valleys that stretch from Tübingen in the north to the tropical Bodensee in the south are collectively known as the Schwäbische Alb, a region often considered an ugly cousin of the adjacent Schwarzwald. But the periphery is colored by the brush of the exotic and a bit of the uncanny. Its rough-hewn landscape is scenic yet stubborn, with a harsh climate that often vents its wrath on travelers. The powerful medieval dynasties that held the area found the Swabian peaks perfect sites for fortification, as they command panoramic views of the surrounding valleys. Big-time families like the Hohenstaufens filled the region with castles and abbeys. Now some placid herds of sheep, lofty castle ruins, and the region's name—Staufenland—are all that remain of the Hohenstaufen legacy. The **Schwäbische Albstraße** (Swabian Jura Road) bisects the plateau, intersecting the Romantische Straße at Nördlingen. A web of trails serves hikers; maps are available at regional tourist offices in major towns. These towns have a tranquil aura ideal for rest and rejuvenation; nightlife doesn't have much of a place in the *Alb.* Train service to many points is roundabout and often incomplete, but bus routes pick up the slack.

■ Schwäbisch Hall

Riding into the Schwäbisch Hall station on one of the hourly trains from Heilbronn is like entering the Twilight Zone. After nearly an hour of monotonous German countryside, the windows suddenly fill with hundreds of red-tiled roofs, soaring cathedral towers, and crumbling stone walls. Virtually ignored during the world wars, Schwäbisch Hall's steeply sloping *Altstadt* is one of the most expansive and well-preserved in Germany. Although tourism is present, it has yet to reach large proportions, leaving the city almost entirely to its residents and the few independent travelers who wander the ancient streets. From the ominously named landmarks to its uncannily quiet Sunday mornings, Swäbisch Hall evokes an aura of surreal timelessness.

ORIENTATION AND PRACTICAL INFORMATION Schwäbisch Hall has two **train** stations. The *Hauptbahnhof* is close to town, but the larger and more important station is in **Schwäbisch Hall-Hessental,** which lies on the main rail line to Stuttgart. If you're coming from the south, you'll probably end up arriving here. Although you will be 3km from the salty pleasures of the *Altstadt,* do not panic—buses #1 and 4B frequently connect the Hessental station to Schwäbisch Hall proper (DM2; Sa-Su DM1; every 20-30min.). To **rent a bike,** useful in navigating this very steep city, try **2-**

Rad Zügel, Johanniferstr. 55 (tel. 97 14 00), or closer to the Hessental area, **Radsport Fiedler,** Kirchestr. 4 (tel. 93 02 40). Prices start at DM10 a day. **For a taxi,** dial 61 17. Schwäbisch Hall's **tourist office,** Am Markt 9 (tel. 75 12 46; fax 75 13 75), next to St. Michael's Church, has maps and finds rooms for free (open May-Sept. M-F 9am-6pm, Sa-Su 10am-3pm; Oct.-Apr. M-F 9am-5pm). All Stadtbus lines can be accessed from the main bus station at Am Spitalbach just one block west and a few blocks down from the tourist office. For **police,** dial 40 00. The **post office,** Hafenmarkt 2, 74523 Schwäbisch Hall, hides behind the *Rathaus* (open M-F 8:30am-12:30pm and 2:30-5:30pm, Sa 8:30am-noon). The **telephone code** is 0791.

ACCOMMODATIONS AND FOOD Schwäbisch Hall's **Jugendherberge (HI),** Langenfelder Weg 5 (tel. 410 50; fax 479 98), is past the Marktplatz on the *Galgenberg* ("Gallows Mountain"). Follow Crailsheimerstr. up to take a left onto Langenfelderstr. A legion of couches decks the halls of a clean and homey (if sporadically occupied) hostel. (DM22, over 26 DM27. Members only. Breakfast included. Sheets DM5.50. Reception 4:30-7pm. Curfew 10pm.) **Bahnhofgastätte mit Hotelbetrieb,** Karl-Kurz-Str. 24 (tel. 25 84), offers decent rooms at a convenient price, and at an even more convenient location—right across the street from the Hessental *Bahnhof.* (Singles DM40; doubles DM80. All with private bath, TV. Breakfast included. Check-out noon.) There is a **Campingplatz** (tel. 29 84) at Steinbacher See. Take bus #4 to "Steinbach/Mitte," then backtrack slightly and follow the signs (DM7 per person, under 16 DM9; DM9 per tent; shower DM1). **Taverne bei Vangeli,** Bahnhofstr. 15 (tel. 67 43), serves a bewildering array of Grecian specialities with a sizable vegetarian section (entrees DM8.50-15; open daily 11:30am-2pm and 5pm-midnight). **Ilge,** Im Weiler 2 (tel. 716 84) is where twentysomethings go to drink delicious yogurt shakes (DM4-6).

SIGHTS Architecture is the reason for coming to Swabisch Hall, and nowhere is this more evident than in the marvelously preserved *Altstadt.* From the Schwäbisch Hall train station, cross Bahnhofstr. and head down the stone steps and footpath toward the river. Turn left on Mauerstr. and cross the wooden footbridges that connect the islands in the Kocher. Finally, follow the winding cobblestone streets to the **Marktplatz.** Use the church tower as a beacon. From the Schwäbisch Hall-Hessental train station, take bus #1 to "Spitalbach Ost," the last stop (20min.; DM2). The restrained Baroque *Rathaus* confronts the **Kirche St. Michael,** which perches precariously atop a steep set of stone stairs. *(Open Mar. to mid-Nov. M 2-5pm, Tu-Sa 9am-noon and 2-5pm, Su 11am-noon and 2-5pm; mid-Nov. to Feb. Tu-Sa 11am-noon and 2-5pm, Su 11am-noon. No visits during church services. Entrance to church free, tower DM1.)* The church's high altar is a Dutch-influenced series of painted panels; one of the paving stones behind the altar has been removed to reveal a medieval **ossuary** (a room full of human bones and skulls). The **Turmzimmer** (tower room) atop the church's tower provides an incredible view of the red-tiled roofs sloping down into the valley.

A number of narrow, *Fachwerk*-lined alleys wind their way outwards from the Marktplatz. To the east, Obere Herrngasse leads to the eight-story Romanesque **Keckenturm,** on Keckenhof, which houses the **Hällisch-Fränkisches Museum** (tel. 75 12 89). Located in the medieval tower, this museum contains a smashing Baroque room and extensive exhibits on the natural and human history of Schwäbisch Hall. *(Open Tu and Th-Su 10am-5pm, W 10am-8pm. Tours W 6:30pm and Su 11am. Free with varying fees for special exhibits.)* The covered **Henkersbrücke** (Hangman's Bridge), down Neuestr. from the Marktplatz, delivers a view of Schwäbisch Hall's bubbling brook of a river. A few blocks farther into the lower city is the **Henkersturm** (Hangman's Tower—sense a trend here?), with a disappointingly less than grisly appearance. In the northern part of the *Altstadt,* the old **Gelbinger Gasse** is the town's most beautiful section. For a relaxing walk along the river, the gardens of the **Ackeranlage** back the tremendous architectural vista with tall, shady trees.

Above town on an adjacent hill, the **Kloster Großcomburg** (tel. 93 81 85)—monastery, castle, and institute for teacher training—dates to the 11th century. The fully preserved wall provides peep holes for views of the valley, but you must take a tour (in German only) to see the museum and 18th-century Baroque church. Take bus #4 to "Steinbach/Mitte," cross the street, and head left around and up Bildersteige. *(Tours Apr.-Oct. Tu-F at 10, 11am, 2, 3, and 4pm, Sa-Su at 2, 3, and 4pm. Nov.-Mar. call ahead. DM4.)* The **Hohenloher Freilandmuseum** (open-air museum) in Museumsdorf Wackershofen (tel. 97 10 10) packages a tiny 50-building village into a delectable morsel of *Vergangenheit*, with all sorts of animals and vegetables (including humans and pigs) reenacting the life of an old German agricultural village. *(Open Mar. 14-Apr. Tu-Su 10am-5pm; May-Nov. 8 Tu-Su 9am-6pm; also July-Sept. M 9am-6pm. DM9, students DM5.)* Watch Schnapps being made. *Prost!* Touch a cow. Take bus #7 to "Wackershofen."

ENTERTAINMENT On summer evenings between mid-June and mid-August the **Freilichtspiele**, a series of old and modern plays running from Shakespeare to Brecht, are performed on the steps of the Kirche St. Michael. For schedules and tickets (DM20-45, student discounts DM6-10; some concerts run only DM7-10), contact **Freilichtspiele Schwäbisch Hall**, Am Markt 8 (tel. 75 13 11; fax 75 14 56; open M-F 9am-noon and 2-5pm; during the season open M-F 9am-noon and 3-8:30pm, Su 3-8:30pm). You can watch the directors do their thing for free during the frequent open rehearsals. On the Saturday, Sunday, and Monday of Pentecost (May 22-24, 1999), Schwäbisch Hall celebrates the **Kuchen- und Brunnenfest** (salt simmerer's cake and fountain festival), during which locals don 16th-century salt-simmerers' costumes to dance traditional jigs. During **Sommernachtsfest** (August 22, 1999), 30,000 little candles light patterns along the Akeranlage.

■ Schwäbisch Gmünd

Schwäbisch Gmünd, located on the northern cusp of the range, provides a base for excursions into the region. Billed as the oldest town of the Staufenland, it's also been a center for gold and silversmithing since the 14th century. Beautifully wrought jewelry and ornaments can be found in many shops in the town center, which bristles with Baroque plaster facades and *Fachwerk* buildings dating from the 15th and 16th centuries. More recently, Swäbisch Gmünd took on a less pacific role when an American military base stationed itself in the Mutlagen suburb. Here protests erupted in the early 80s over the stationing of U.S. Pershing missiles in Germany, drawing brilliant writer and political activist Günter Grass to the town. However, the GIs left after the fall of East Germany, and the former barracks have now transformed into a campus for the University of Maryland. Go Terps.

The lengthy Marktplatz can be reached from the train station by turning left onto Lorchenstr., which becomes Ledergasse and eventually leads to the major bus stop hub labelled "Marktplatz" (10min.). Farther southwest, Münsterplatz hosts the 14th-century **Heligkreuzmünster** (Holy Cross Cathedral), one of the most compellingly freakish churches every built. The roof was too weak to support any towers, and the boxy compromise renders the building decidedly nonecclesiastic in appearance. Perhaps to compensate for this shortcoming, the powers-that-be have covered the exterior in frightening and amusing statues that protrude horizontally in every direction. The bizarre collection ranges from screaming, tortured human figures to large-fanged beasts of all varieties to one bright green frog. The **Silberwaren- und Bijouteriemuseum** (Silver and Jewelry Museum), across from the tourist office (tel. 389 10), features real silversmiths tooling silver in the traditional style. Exhibits cover the history of the silver trade, the Silver Age, and silver arts (open W and Sa 2-5pm, Su 10am-noon and 2-5pm; DM5, students DM2).

The 16th-century **Kornhaus**, an old grain storage building right off the Marktplatz, two blocks behind the *Rathaus*, now houses a **tourist office** (tel. 60 34 55; fax 60 34 59). They book rooms for a 5% fee and offer a large selection of maps. (Open M-F 9am-5:30pm, Sa 8am-noon.) The **police** can be reached at 35 80. The **post office**, 73525 Swäbisch Gmünd, is across from the train station (open M-F 8am-noon and 2:30-5:30pm). The **telephone code** is 07171.

Schwäbisch Gmünd's **Jugendherberge (HI)**, Taubalentalstr. 46/1 (tel. 22 60), is located on the edge of an idyllically forested region criss-crossed by footpaths, only 10 minutes from the train station. Turn left and pass underneath the railroad tracks; follow the road, then veer left onto Taubentalstr. and keep on truckin' uphill. At the end of the street, immediately before the recreational park parking lot, turn right up the path toward the large cream-colored building obscured by trees. This is the *Jugendherberge*, which has an understandably rustic feel and a neverending stream of shouting *Schulkinder*. (DM20, over 26 DM25. Breakfast included. Sheets DM5.50. Reception 5-8pm. Curfew 10pm. Call ahead.) **Gasthof Weißer Ochsen**, Parlerstr. 47 (tel. 28 12), has discreet singles (DM38) and one double (DM70). Another accommodation option is the hostel in Hohenstaufen (see below). **Gasthaus "Zum Lamm,"** Rinderbachgasse 19 (tel 26 61), has a daily menu of Swabian specialties (DM8.50-20. Open M 5pm-midnight, Tu-Sa 10am-2pm and 5:30pm-midnight, Su 11am-2pm.) An open-air **market** fills the Münsterplatz every Wednesday and Saturday (7am-noon) while "closed-air" **supermarkets** are a block north, along Bocksgasse.

■ The Kaiserberge

Just south of Schwäbisch Gmünd lie the three conical peaks, **Hohenstaufen, Hohen-rechberg**, and **Stuifen**, which make up the **Dreikaiserberge**. This curtain of mountains marks the beginning of the Schwäbische Alb. Hohenstaufen was named after the castle that once graced its summit, built by the Hohenstaufen family. The castle is gone, but the view of the other two Kaiserberge peaks and of the Schwäbische Alb in the distance is spectacular. To reach Hohenstaufen from Swäbisch Gmünd, take bus #12 to the "Göppingen ZOB", then transfer to bus #13, and get off at "Hohenstaufen: Jugendherberge" (every 1½hr., last bus leaves at 7pm). Bus #13 goes directly there on Sundays and holidays, but alas—the second and final bus rolls away at noon. Or, take bus #13 to "Juhe" and put yourself right in the middle of hill action around **Jugendherberge Hohenstaufen**, Schottengasse 45 (tel. (07165) 438; fax 14 18), which has six- and eight-bed rooms on a gently sloping plain (DM22, over 26 DM27; breakfast included; sheets DM5.50; call ahead).

Another prime hiking trail winds around **Hohenrechberg** to the east, and boasts a mysterious **castle ruin** and a Baroque **Wallfahrtskirche** (pilgrimage church) at its summit. The **Burgruine** are halfway up; pay DM1 to catch a breathtaking glimpse of the Schwäbische Alb from the castle's crumbled walls. The old castle wall now functions as the foundation for a footpath. To reach Hohenrechberg, take bus #4 (direction: "Wißgoblingen") to "Rechberg: Gasthof Rad." Walk straight up Hohenstaufenstr., and the trail starts between the Volksbank and Jägerhof. It's about a one-hour climb from there. The last bus to Swäbisch Gmünd leaves before 5pm. The **tourist office** in Schwäbisch Gmünd (see p. 426) has a number of hiking maps with routes (some are free). All buses to the Kaiserberge depart from Schwäbisch Gmünd at the ZOB at the train station, though most also stop at the "Marktplatz."

▓ Ulm

The flagship city of the surrounding Schwäbische Alb, Ulm is perhaps best known as the birthplace of **Albert Einstein** (though he lived here only a year). However, history often overlooks another local scientific genius: the ill-fated "**Tailor of Ulm.**" Albrecht Ludwig Berblinger, tailor by day, inventor by night, made one of the earliest serious attempts at human flight in 1811, when he tried to cross the Danube on his "kite-wings." He nearly drowned. Banished irrevocably from intelligent society for the remaining 16 years of his life, the unappreciated Berblinger took up residence in the destination he never quite reached—Neu Ulm. Though this half of the city split off when Napoleon designated the Danube the border between Bayern and Württemberg, the *alt* and the *neu* have operated as one for the past 800 years. Home to the **world's tallest church steeple,** which soars where Berblinger only dreamed to soar, present-day Ulm treats its rich past with a forward-looking, good-natured pride, mocking Berblinger's feats on tourist postcards and seamlessly blending new and old.

ORIENTATION AND PRACTICAL INFORMATION Ulm is connected by **train** to all of southern Germany; hourly trains head to Munich and Stuttgart, and several trains travel daily to Berlin, Hamburg, and most other big German cities. **Rent bikes** for DM15 per day from **Ralf Reich,** Frauenstr. 34 (tel. 211 79; DM30 per weekend, DM80 per week; 15% discount with BahnCard). The contrast between the strikingly voluptuous white building that houses the **tourist office,** Münsterpl. 50 (tel. 161 28 30; fax 161 16 41), and the towering ornate spire of the adjacent *Münster* epitomizes Ulm's strange unity of past and present. The office sells maps (DM0.50), the comprehensive and helpful *Gästemagazin* (DM2), and a do-it-yourself cardboard *Münster* sculpture kit (DM54.80). They also find rooms at no charge. (Open M-F 9am-6pm, Sa 9am-12:30pm.) The *Automat* outside vends a list of accommodations (DM1). Satisfy pharmaceutical fancies at the **Neue Apotheke,** Bahnhofstr. 13 (tel. 600 74), or check the posted list there to find out which pharmacies in town are open after hours (open M-F 8am-7pm, Sa 8am-2pm). The **post office,** Bahnhofpl. 2, 89073 Ulm, is left of the station (open M-F 8am-6pm, Sa 8am-1pm). The **telephone code** is 0731.

ACCOMMODATIONS AND FOOD Ulm's **Jugendherberge "Geschwister Scholl" (HI),** Grimmelfinger Weg 45 (tel. 38 44 55; fax 38 45 11), looks like a high school with sparkling facilities, communal showers, and four- to eight-bed rooms. Take any bus from the train station to "Ehinger Tor," and change to bus #4 or 8 ("Kuhlberg"). Walk through the underpass just up the road, and follow the signs for the "Sport Gaststätte" to a set of stairs on the right side of the building. Descend. Cut through the grass to the right of the tennis courts, and turn left on the paved path. Follow the lone *Jugendherberge* sign. The hostel is named in memory of a brother and sister who were executed in 1943 for conspiring against Hitler. (DM22.50, over 26 DM27.50. Breakfast included. Sheets DM5.50. Reception 5-9:45pm. Curfew 10pm.) **Münster-Hotel,** Münsterpl. 14 (tel./fax 641 62), is located (surprise!) to the left of the *Münster.* Spotless, smallish rooms with maps of Europe on every desk. (Singles DM45, with shower DM65; doubles with shower DM90, with bath DM110.) Across the river in Neu Ulm, **Gasthof Rose,** Kasernstr. 42a (tel. 778 03), has lovely rooms in a quiet district (singles DM40, doubles DM80; breakfast included).

Ulm's restaurants reflect the culinary influences of both Swabia and Bayern, including the unusual *Schupfnudel,* a half-potato, half-wheat noodle. For cheap and greasy *Imbiß* fare, wander around Bahnhofstr. and Hirschstr. on the way to the *Münster.* For the largest variety and the densest collection of restaurants, the territory between Neuestr. and the river is prime grazing ground. Across from the *Rathaus,* the **Erstes Ulmer Weizenbierhaus,** Kronengasse 12 (tel. 624 96), pours more than 20 varieties of *Weizenbier* and serves up a number of decent dishes (DM5.50-12.80). An interesting ambience is created by a synthetic tree and red-tiled roofs inside the restaurant. (Open daily 4pm-3am.) Inside the *Rathaus,* **Dinea Restaurant,** Marktpl. 1 (tel. 66 11 26), offers a dazzling self-service buffet of fresh salads, pasta, and fish. (Daily specials DM6-12. Local brews from the tap DM2.90. Open M-Sa 8am-10pm, Su 10am-9pm. In winter daily until 9pm.) Both Swabian and Bavarian dishes are served up in an inviting local-joint atmosphere at **Restaurant "Zur Zill,"** Schwörhausgasse 19 (tel. 659 77). Meals cost DM9-14, *Gold Ochsen Bier* (the local brew) runs DM4.40 per 0.5L. (Open M-F 11am-2pm and 5pm-midnight, Sa 11am-2pm and 5pm-1am.) A **farmer's market** springs up on Münsterplatz on Wednesday and Saturday mornings.

SIGHTS At 161m, the steeple topping the **Ulm Münster** (tel. 15 11 39) is the tallest in the world, and the soaring ceilings of the chapel are almost as astonishing. *(Open daily Apr.-June 8am-6:45pm; July-Aug. 8am-7:45pm; Sept. 8am-4:45pm; Oct. 8am-5:45pm; Nov.-Jan. 9am-4:45pm; Mar. 9am-5:45pm. Tower closes 1hr. earlier. Church free. In the summer, free organ concerts Su at 11:30am and Sa at 7pm. Spire DM3.50, children DM2.50.)* Next to the front portal of the cathedral is *The Man of Sorrows,* a famous representation of Christ by 15th-century sculptor Hans Multscher. Inside the Gothic walls, extravagantly carved choir stalls (by Jörg Syrlin the Elder) contain a community of busts: the lowest tier depicts Greek and Roman philosophers. Climb the 768 dizzying cork-screw steps of the spire on a clear day to see the Alps. Nearby, the white building that houses the tourist office is also home to the **Stadthaus**. *(Open M-W and F-Sa 9am-6pm, Th 9am-8pm and Su 11am-6pm.)* The basement has interesting archaeological and historical exhibits on the Münsterplatz and the painstakingly slow construction of the *Münster* itself, begun in the 14th century and finally completed in 1892 to become the towering behemoth it is today. Towards the river on Neuestr., the **Rathaus**, built in 1370, is decorated with brilliantly colored murals and an elaborate astronomical clock, both from 1540. The old **Fischerviertel** (Fishermen's Quarter), down Kronen-gasse from the *Rathaus*, has classical half-timbered houses, narrow cobblestone streets, and canal-spanning footbridges. Don't miss the **Schiefeshaus** (Crooked House) at Schwörhausgasse 6. One of the oldest houses in Ulm, it's now a tiny hotel for tourists as it slowly slides into the nearby canal.

On the other side of the *Rathaus* in a former *Patrizierhaus* is the **Ulmer Museum**, Marktplatz 9 (tel. 161 43 00), which features outstanding exhibits on both contemporary art and the archaeological past of the region. *(Open Tu-Su 10am-5pm, Th 10am-8pm. DM5, students DM3. Free on F. Special exhibits DM8; students, children, and seniors DM5.)* The **Deutsches Brotmuseum** (German Bread Museum), Salzstadelgasse 10, (tel. 699 55) documents 6000 years of bread-making and waxes philosophical about "the *Leitmotiv* of Man and Bread." *(Open Tu and Th-Su 10am-5pm, W 10am-8:30pm. Free tours W at 7pm. DM5, students DM3.50.)* Very well put together, it's a cultural history fan's dream come true. Don't miss "Cake—the pride of the housewife," or "Corn and bread in arts and crafts." One can easily overlook the tiny monument marking **Albert Einstein's birthplace**, donated to Ulm by India. It's in front of the train station, next to the McDonald's. The house itself has long since given way to a glass-and-chrome sav-ings-and-loan establishment. Every year on the penultimate Monday of July, the mayor of Ulm takes the stand at the **Schwörhaus** (Oath House) to carry on a centuries-old tradition by swearing allegiance to the town's 1397 constitution. The whole affair is accompanied by excessive drinking—that is, merrymaking.

■ Stuttgart

Visiting Stuttgart is like stepping into a little piece of Utopia. Blown to bits in WWII, the city had nowhere to aim but the future, to which it heads with vibrant optimism. Despite the rampant modernization, Stuttgart boasts one of the most verdant settings of any major German city. Surrounded by green hills, criss-crossed by leafy parks, and laced by a vineyard that stretches to the *Hauptbahnhof*, the city swathes all traces of urban blight in a cloak of lush green. The ground also proved fertile for the seeds of a number of small start-ups, which quickly bloomed into highly successful businesses; Porsche, Daimler-Benz, and a host of other corporate thoroughbreds graze here. As the capital of Baden-Württemberg, Stuttgart maintains a thriving cultural scene, promoting an aura of tranquility and repose in a very livable metropolis.

ORIENTATION AND PRACTICAL INFORMATION

At the heart of Stuttgart lies an enormous pedestrian zone where shops and restau-rants stretch as far as the eye can see. **Königstraße** and **Calwerstraße** are the main pedestrian thoroughfares; from the train station, both are accessible through the underground **Arnulf-Klett-Passage**. To the left lies the tranquil *Schloßgarten*, to the right the thriving business sector. Stuttgart sells itself as a compact and dynamic city, and it sells itself well. A number of sweet discount packages and passes are available. Among these is the **Stuttgart City Pass**, which offers three free days of inner city transportation, free admission to two state museums, and bargains for guided tours, theaters, the zoo, mineral baths, and other sights. Young folks 16 to 26 are entitled to the above perks, plus a night's bed and breakfast and a **Stuttgart Night Pass** (see **Entertainment and Nightlife**, p. 435) for DM88. Call 222 82 53 for more information.

Transportation

Flights: Flughafen Stuttgart (tel. 948 33 88 from 6am-11pm for schedule info). S-Bahn #2 or 3 goes to the city (30min.; one-way DM4.60).

Trains: The transportation hub of southwestern Germany, Stuttgart has direct rail links to most major German cities. Trains roll to Frankfurt (1½hr., every hr.), Munich (2½hr., 30 per day), Berlin (6hr., 12 per day), and Paris (6hr., 3 direct trains per day). Call 194 19 for 24hr. schedule information.

Ferries: Neckar-Personen-Schiffahrt (tel. 54 99 70 60). Boats cruise to little towns along the Neckar (1-2 per day) from May to late-Oct. Round-trip DM9.80-49.80. Watch out for older folks dancing the polka on board; bring your accordion or your earplugs. **Harbor tours** daily 9am and 11am (2hr., DM15.60). Boats leave from the Bad Cannstatt dock, by Wilhelmina zoo. U-Bahn #13 or 14 to "Rosensteinbrücke."

Public Transportation: Information office, Arnulf-Klett-Passage (tel. 250 53 03), next to the escalator up to Königstr. Look for the *"Kundenberatung"* sign. Bus, streetcar, U-Bahn, and S-Bahn maps and schedules, along with needed map-and-schedule deciphering. Open M-F 9am-6pm, Sa 9am-noon. A **single-ride ticket** runs DM3.20-9.60. Four-ride *Mehrfahrkarten* range DM10.20-33.20; they save 10% off single ride rates. *Tageskarten*—day passes for trains and buses (except night buses)— are DM12 or DM20 for longer distances. Weekend passes (DM35) are available, valid from F midnight to M at 2am. A *Kurzstrecke* pass (DM1.70) covers short distances. Railpasses are valid *only* on the S-Bahn. **Nachtbus** (night bus) stops are marked with purple-and-yellow signs. The tourist office has schedules. Those staying in city accommodations are eligible for a **great deal—DM12 for 3 days of U-Bahn travel, DM19 for 3 days of travel on the entire transportation system.

Car Rental: An office at the *Hauptbahnhof* near track 16 is Stuttgart's home to **Hertz** (tel. 226 29 21), which rents 'em at DM97-217 per day (open M-F 7:30am-9pm, Sa 8am-5pm, Su 11am-7pm). In the same space are offices for: **Europacar** (tel. 224 46 30; open M-Sa 7:30am-9pm, Su 8:30am-9pm), **Sixt/Budget** (tel. 223 78 22; open M-F 7:30am-9pm, Sa 8am-5pm, Su 10am-6pm), and **Avis** (tel. 223 72 58; open M-F 7am-9pm, Sa 8am-4pm).

Bike Rental: Rent a Bike, Kronenstr. 17 (tel. 209 90). Prices range from DM8 per hr. to DM25 per day. Bikes are allowed on the S- and U-Bahn all day Sa-Su and M-F 8:30am-4pm and 6:30pm until closing; they're forbidden on buses and streetcars.

Mitfahrzentrale: There are two: **Stuttgart West,** Lerchenstr. 65 (tel. 636 80 36). Bus #42 (direction: "Schreiberstr.") to "Rosenberg/Johannesstr." **Hauptstätterstr. 154** (tel. 60 36 06). U-Bahn #14 (direction: "Heslach/Vogelrain") to "Marienplatz." Both open M-F 9am-6pm, Sa 9am-2pm, Su 11am-2pm.

Tourist Services

Tourist Offices:

I-Punkt, Königstr. 1 (tel. 222 80; fax 222 82 53; http://www.stuttgart-tourist.de), directly in front of the escalator down into the Klett-Passage. They may be busy, but they book rooms for free, sell excellent maps (DM1), distribute bus and train schedules, and speak English. Their *Monatsspiegel* (in German; DM3.50) lists museum hours, cultural events, and musical performances, and includes a guide to food and nightlife. Open May-Oct. M-F 9:30am-8:30pm, Sa 9:30am-6pm, Su and public holidays 11am-6pm; Nov.-Apr. same hours but Su and holidays 1-6pm.

Tips 'n' Trips, Rotebühlpl. 26/27 (tel. 222 27 30; fax 222 27 33; email jugendinformation@tips-n-trips.shuttle.de; http://www.shuttle.de/tips-n-trips), in the underground U-Bahn passage at Theodor-Heuss-Str. and Fritz-Elsas-Str. The with-it, ultra-helpful staff hands out reams of youth-oriented pamphlets (in German and English) about travel and the Stuttgart scene. A great resource. Open M-F noon-7pm, Sa 10am-4pm.

Consulates: South Africa, Erich-Herion-Str. 27 (tel. 58 64 41). **U.K.,** Breitestr. 2 (tel. 16 26 90).

American Express: Schillerpl. 4 (tel. 162 49 20; fax 162 49 22), by the Schloßplatz. Holds mail, cashes traveler's checks, and doubles as a travel agency for members. A **2nd branch,** Lautenschlagerstr. 3 (tel. 187 51 00; fax 187 51 32), does much the same. Both open M-F 10am-6:30pm, Sa 9:30am-12:30pm.

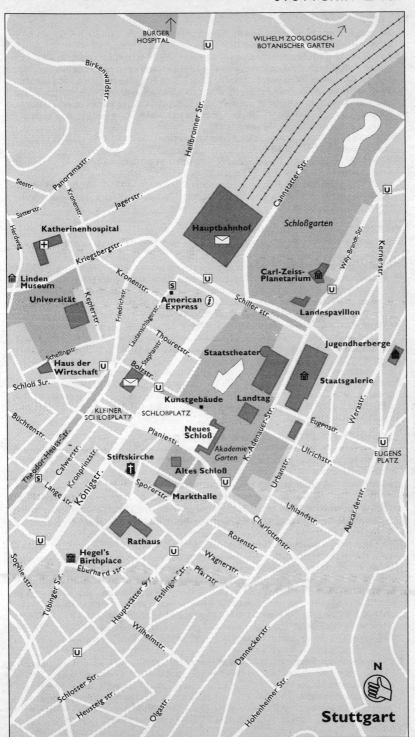

BÜRGER
HOSPITAL

WILHELM ZOOLOGISCH-
BOTANISCHER GARTEN

Birkenwaldstr.

Heilbronner Str.

Cannstatter Str.

Panoramastr.

Seestr.

Kronenstr.

Jagerstr.

Schloßgarten

Satterstr.

Hardweg

Katherinenhospital

Kriegsbergstr.

Kronenstr.

Hauptbahnhof

Kernerstr.

Willy-Brandt-Str.

**Carl-Zeiss-
Planetarium**

■ **Linden
Museum**

Friedrichstr.

**American
Express**

Keplerstr.

Universität

Schellingstr.

**Haus der
Wirtschaft**

Schloß Str.

Büchsenstr.

Theodor-Heuss-Str.

Schiller str.

Landespavillon

Thouretstr.

Stephanstr.

Lautenschlagerstr.

Bolzstr.

Staatstheater

Jugendherberge

Staatsgalerie

Kunstgebäude

KLEINER
SCHLOßPLATZ

SCHLOßPLATZ

Landtag

Werastr.

Planiestr.

**Neues
Schloß**

Akademie
Garten

K.-Adenauer-Str.

Eugenstr.

Ulrichstr.

**EUGENS
PLATZ**

Calwerstr.

Kronprinzstr.

Stiftskirche

Königstr.

Altes Schloß

Urbanstr.

Lange str.

Sporerstr.

Markthalle

Uhlandstr.

Alexanderstr.

Charlottenstr.

Sophiestr.

Rathaus

Rosenstr.

**Hegel's
Birthplace**

Eberhard str.

Wagnerstr.

Tübinger Str.

Hauptstätter Str.

Essinger str.

Pfarrstr.

Wilhelmstr.

Danneckerstr.

Schlosser Str.

Heusteig str.

Olgastr.

Hohenheimer Str.

N

Stuttgart

Local Services

Lost and Found: Fundsachenstelle, Eberhardstr. 61f (tel. 216 20 16). Open M-W 8:30am-1pm, Th 8:30am-3:30pm, F 8:30am-12:30pm.

Bookstore: English Shop, Schellingstr. 11 (tel. 226 09 02), specializing in all things British, offers both classics and current bestsellers, and even rents English language videos. **Buchhaus Wittwer,** Königstr. 30 (tel. 250 70), also has books in English.

Gay Resources: Weissenburg, Weißenburgstr. 28a (tel. 640 44 94) is Stuttgart's gay and lesbian center. Office open M-F 7:30-9:30pm, cafe open 3-10pm. **Erlkönig,** Nesenbachstr. 52 (tel. 63 91 39), is a popular gay and lesbian bookstore. Open M-F 10am-1:30pm and 3-8pm, Sa until 4pm.

Women's Resources: Fraueninformationzentrum (Women's Information Center), Landhausstr. 62 (tel. 26 18 91).

AIDS-Hilfe: Hölderlinpl. 5a (tel. 224 69 00), open M-F 10am-noon and M-Th 2-5pm. Anonymous hotline (tel. 194 11) open M and Th-F 6:30-9:30pm.

Laundromat: SB Wasch Salon, Kienbachstr. 16 (tel. 52 30 08). S-Bahn #13 (direction: "Giebel-Hedelfingen") to "Kienbachstr." Wash DM8, dry DM2 per 10min. Open daily 8am-10pm.

Emergency and Communications

Emergency: tel. 110. **Police,** Hahnemannstr. 1 (tel. 899 01). **Fire** and **Ambulance,** tel. 112.

Hospital: Bürgerhospital, Tunzhoferstr. 14-16 (tel. 253 00).

Pharmacies: For a schedule of 24hr. pharmacies, buy *Amstblatt* (DM1.20) from the tourist office, or have a look at the copy posted at the *Rathaus*. **Internationale,** Königstr. 70 (tel. 22 47 80), is a centrally-located pharmacy. Open M-W and F 8:30am-6:30pm, Th 8:30am-8:30pm, Sa 8:30am-2pm.

Internet Access: Tips 'n' Trips offers the best deal in town at DM5 per hour (See **Tourist Office**). If you don't want to stand in line for their lone computer, check out the top floor of the **Kaufhof** near the train station (DM3 per 30min.; open M-F 9:30am-9pm, Sa 9am-4pm), or the 3rd floor of the **Karstadt** department store, across the way (DM5 per 30min.; open M-F 9am-8pm, Sa 9am-4pm).

Post Office: At the *Hauptbahnhof*, 70001 Stuttgart (tel. 226 03 30). Open M-F 8am-8pm, Sa 8am-2pm, Su 10am-2pm. The post office at Bolzstr. 3, 18750 Stuttgart (tel. 225 43 31), mails parcels but does not hold mail. Open M-F 9am-8pm, Sa 9am-2pm.

Telephone Code: 0711.

ACCOMMODATIONS AND CAMPING

Most of Stuttgart's budget beds are located on the two ridges surrounding the downtown area and are easily accessible by streetcar. Accommodations around the pedestrian zone and train station cater to customers used to paying top *Mark* for creature comforts. Make "call ahead" your mantra. Contact Tips 'n' Trips (see **Tourist Office,** above) for information on cheap overnighting in Stuttgart. Though a commute away, the *Jugendherbergen* in Esslingen and Ludwigsburg are good alternatives.

Jugendherberge Stuttgart (HI), Haußmannstr. 27 (tel. 24 15 83; fax 236 10 41). Take the "ZOB" exit of the Klett-Passage, continue through the Schloßgarten, and follow the signs leading uphill via the paved path. Or U-Bahn #15 (direction: "Heumaden") to "Eugensplatz" and go down the hill past the *Apotheke,* bearing left down Kernerstr. Entrance on Kernerstr. A lively mix of nationalities shacks up in slightly crowded 6-bed rooms, most offering spectacular city views. The 220 beds are often full; *always* call ahead. DM22, over 26 DM27. Breakfast included. Sheets DM5.50. Reception 7-9am and noon-11pm. Lockout 9am-noon. Strict curfew 11:30pm. The doors re-open briefly at 1am and then at 5am for hard-core children of the nightlife.

Jugendgästehaus Stuttgart, Richard-Wagner-Str. 2 (tel. 24 11 32 and 248 97 30). Straßenbahn #15 (direction: "Heumaden") to "Bubenbad." Continue in direction of the *Straßenbahn* on the right side of the street and veer right immediately; the place is on the right. An excellent hostel situated in a quiet residential neighborhood. Spotless rooms with a great view, but a distant location. Singles DM30, with bath DM40, with bath and shower DM50; DM35 per additional person, with bath and shower DM10 more. Breakfast and lockers included. Dinner DM8. Key deposit DM20. Reception M-F 9am-8pm, Sa-Su 11am-8pm. No curfew.

Pension Märklin, Friedrichstr. 39 (tel. 29 13 15). Convenient, period. Take a right from the station, and turn left on Friedrichstr. Singles DM45-50; doubles DM80-90. No breakfast, but you can avail yourself of the showers and the bathtub. No lockout, few rules—get your keys and kick back. Call 2 weeks ahead if you can.

Tramper Point Stuttgart, Wiener Str. 317 (tel./fax 817 74 76). U-Bahn #6 (direction: "Gehrlingen") to "Sportpark Feuerbach," then cross the tracks, walking toward the sport park. Despite its name, this bizarre mural-covered wooden structure is not a gathering place for women of ill repute, but the funkiest and cheapest alternative accommodations in town; shack up here on one of 25 cots in a crescent-shaped room, or an *Iso-matte* in case of overflow. DM13. Breakfast and shower included. Wool blanket DM1.50, or bring your own sleeping bag. Cooking facilities. Reception 5-11pm. Ages 16+ only. Open late June to early Sept. for individuals, Apr.-Nov. for reserved groups.

Camping: Campingplatz Cannstatter Wasen, Mercedesstr. 40 (tel. 55 66 96; fax 48 69 47), on the river in Bad Cannstatt. S-Bahn #1, 2, or 3 to "Bad Cannstatt." Exit through the back of the station, and follow the signs for "Wasen." After the tunnel, head diagonally left across the never-ending parking lot. Reception 7am-noon and 2-10pm. DM8 per person; DM4 per child. DM6-8 per tent. DM4 per car.

FOOD

Due to a sizable contingent of *Gastarbeiter* (guest workers), Stuttgart's restaurant scene is heartily spiced with Greek, Turkish, African, and Asian eateries as well as an astounding variety of snack bars. But the cuisine of the *Schwaben* region is itself one of the most appealing forms of German food. *Spätzle* (thick noodles) and *Maultaschen* (pasta pockets filled with meat and spinach) are especially prevalent. For basic fruits and veggies as well as staples like bread and cheese, the **Wochenmarkt** is on Marktplatz and Schillerplatz (Open Th and Sa 8am-3pm). For groceries, try the basement of **Kaufhof,** two blocks from the station (open M-F 9am-8pm, Sa 9am-4pm).

University Mensa, Holzgartenstr. 11. From the *Bahnhof,* take Kriegsbergstr. to Holzgartenstr., turn left, and go down the right side of the street over the underpass; the restaurant is on the right. A plain but functional place where quantity compensates for quality (meals DM4-5). Open during school M-F 11·15am-2:30pm.; the rest of the year M-F 11:15am-1:30pm. The **Mensastüble** downstairs offers restaurant fare at slightly higher prices. Open M-F 11:15am-1:45pm.

Iden, Eberhardstr. 1 (tel. 23 59 89). U-Bahn to "Rathaus." Good vegetarian fare served cafeteria-style. Fifty kinds of salads (DM2.68 per 100g, which adds up quickly), noodles, and potatoes, served in a bright atmosphere with lots of Nordic furniture. More desserts than you can imagine. Open M-F 11am-9pm, Sa 10am-5pm.

Akademie der Schönsten Künste, Charlottenstr. 5 (tel. 24 24 36). U-Bahn to "Charlottenplatz." High ceilings, art-covered walls, a garden, and fewer seats than necessary at such a paragon of European sophistication. Considered the perfect date restaurant among trendy Stuttgarters; you'll understand why. Light fare may not be the cheapest (DM4-15), but the ambience more than makes up for it. Open M-F 7am-midnight, Sa-Su 9am-4pm.

Weinhaus Stetter, Rosenstr. 32 (tel. 24 01 63). U-Bahn to "Charlottenplatz," walk down Esslinger Str., and take a left onto Rosenstr. This local favorite offers intriguing Swabian specialties (DM7-9), all to be washed down with an incredible wine selection (DM5-7). Open M-F 3-11pm, Sa 10am-3pm.

Waschsalon, Charlottenstr. 27 (tel. 236 98 96), at the corner of Charlottenstr. and Alexanderstr. U-Bahn to "Olgaeck." A *Kneipe* with an identity crisis (it thinks it's a laundromat). Schwabian specialities and crepes adorn the tables, while metallic pants grace the walls. Wild potatoes (like home fries with veggies and special sauce) DM6.90. Open Su-F 10am-1am, Sa 4pm-2am.

UDO-Snack, Calwerstr. 23. Bills itself as "Stuttgart's Kult-Imbiß for over 20 years." Strolling through the *Fußgängerzone* late at night, appease your growling stomach with cheap, greasy favorites like *Pommes Frites* and *Currywurst* (DM2.80-5.80). Open M-Tu 11am-11pm, W-Th 11am-midnight, F-Sa 11am-1am, Su 3-11pm.

SIGHTS

Though there's little *Gemütlichkeit* to be found in Stuttgart, this sparkling modern metropolis offers much more than the average half-timbered town of *Lederhosen*-wearing grandpas. Almost 20% of Stuttgart is under a land preservation order, resulting in something known as "the green U," much of which contains the **Schloßgarten,** Stuttgart's main municipal park. Running from the station southward to the *Neues Schloß* and northeast to the Neckar, the *Schloßgarten* is crammed with fountains and beautifully tended flower gardens. The north end of the park contains the expansive **Rosensteinpark,** which also holds the **Wilhelma** (tel. 540 20), a large zoological and botanical garden with over 1000 species of animals and plants. *(Open Mar.-Oct. daily 8:15am-5:30pm; Nov.-Feb. 8:15am-4pm. DM14, students DM7; after 4pm and from Nov.-Feb. DM9, DM4.50.)* The *Schloßgarten* runs to the **Schloßplatz,** off Königstr., upon which reposes the elegant, Baroque **Neues Schloß,** now home to stodgy bureaucrats and the 40 or so mythological statues that vogue on its roof. The 16th-century **Altes Schloß** (across the street on Schillerplatz) offers a graceful, colonnaded Renaissance courtyard.

To interface with the *Weltgeist* (world-spirit), head to **Hegel's birthplace,** Eberhardstr. 53 (tel. 216 67 33), a couple blocks east from the end of Königstr., and a few doors down from a busy porn shop. *(Open Tu and F 10am-5:30pm, Th 10am-6:30pm.)* The house provides a thorough exegesis of the philosopher's life through letters, manuscripts, and notes.

Stargazers feast their eyes at the **Karl-Zeiss-Planetarium,** Willy-Brandt-Str. 25 (tel. 162 92 15). U-Bahn #1, 4, 9, or 14, or streetcar #2 to "Staatsgalerie," or simply walk from the south exit of the main train station into the Schloßgarten for about 200m. *(Shows Tu and Th 10am and 3pm, W and F 10am, 3, and 8pm, Sa-Su 2, 4, and 6pm. DM9, students DM5.)* You can attend one of the shows with informative German voice-overs, cool visual effects (comets shooting, black holes sucking), and clichéd background music ("2001," Pachabel's "Canon"). To see Stuttgart from on high, ascend the newly-reopened 58m high **clock tower** in the *Hauptbahnhof.* *(Open daily until 7pm. Free.)*

Stuttgart harbors amazing **mineral baths,** which originate from the most productive mineral springs in Western Europe. The 22 million liters of spring water that pump out *every day* contain chemical combinations with curative capabilities. Loll in the **Mineralbad Leuze,** Am Leuzebad 2-6 (tel. 216 42 10), an official health care facility. *(Open daily 6am-9pm. Day card DM15.50, students DM10.50; 2½hr. soak DM9.50, DM6.50; 1¼hr. DM8, DM5.50. Massage DM36.)* Take U-Bahn #1, 2, or 14 to "Mineralbäder," then walk towards the river and the volcano-like fountains. Directly across from the U-Bahn "Mineralbäder" station, **Mineral Bad Berg** (tel. 26 10 60) is a little less posh. *(Open M-F 6am-8pm, Sa 6am-7pm, Su 6am-1pm. Day card DM10. Massage DM30.)* A bit farther away, **MineralBad Cannstatt,** Sulzerrainstr. 2 (tel. 216 92 41), is better-outfitted. *(Open M-F 9am-9:30pm, Sa 9am-9pm, Su 9am-5pm.)* Ride U-Bahn #2 to "Kursaal." All offer spectacular arrays of pools, saunas, and showers—the perfect remedy for budget traveler exhaustion.

MUSEUMS

A plethora of outstanding and diverse museums compensates for Stuttgart's paucity of visible history. In addition to the magnificent art galleries and archaeology exhibits, the city offers funky displays on some of the more hedonistic aspects of everyday life: beer, cars, and playing cards. For once, drinking and driving mix quite well. The monthly *Monatsspiegel* (see **Tourist Office,** p. 430) gives info on all museums.

> **Staatsgalerie Stuttgart,** Konrad-Adenauer-Str. 30-32 (tel. 212 40 50), across from the Schloßgarten. An absolutely superb collection housed in 2 separate parts: the stately paintings in the **old wing** date from the Middle Ages to the 19th century; the **new wing,** a beautiful stroke of colorful postmodern architecture, contains an essential collection of moderns including Picasso, Kandinsky, Beckmann, and Dalí.

Open W and F-Su 10am-5pm, Tu and Th 10am-8pm. DM5, students DM3. Visiting exhibits extra.

⊕Württembergisches Landesmuseum, Schillerpl. 6 (tel. 279 34 00), in the Altes Schloß, details the Swabian region and people, with an emphasis on the abundant local archaeology. Excellent exhibits on Bronze Age Celtic metalwork, along with a multitude of fascinating skulls, crown jewels, and Roman pillars. Open Tu 10am-1pm, W-Su 10am-5pm. DM5, students DM3. Wheelchair accessible.

Linden-Museum Stuttgart, Hegelpl. 6 (tel. 202 23), 10 min. west of the train station along Kriegsbergstr. This State Museum for Ethnology features in-depth collections from America, the South Seas, Africa, and Asia. Western hegemonists can satisfy their curiosity about the exotic Other with accompanying films, lectures, and discussions. Open Tu, Th, and Sa-Su 10am-5pm, W 10am-8pm, F 10am-1pm. Free, except for special exhibits.

Mercedes-Benz Museum, Mercedesstr. 137, Stuttgart-Bad Cannstatt (tel. 172 25 78; fax 175 11 73). S-Bahn #1 to "Neckarstadion"; walk left under the bridge and turn left at the next intersection. A must for car-lovers. The original workshop, where Herr Daimler built the 1st generation of Mercedes-Benzes, now houses an elaborately modern exhibit; visitors can ooh and aah at a century's worth of gleaming Benzes. Hold high-tech "soundsticks" to your ear, and learn all about the little German engine that could. Tight security weeds out BMW spies; you even need to take a special bus from the parking lot to the entrance. Open Tu-Su 9am-5pm. Free.

Porsche Museum, Porschestr. 42, Stuttgart-Zuffauhausen (tel. 827 56 85). S-Bahn #6 (direction: "Weil-der-Stadt") to "Neuwirtshaus"; exit the station to the right (don't go under the tracks). Tells much the same story as the Mercedes museum, but with sexier curves and an even greater *Schicki-Micki* factor. Vroom! Open M-F 9am-4pm, Sa-Su 9am-5pm. Free.

Kunstgebäude, Schloßpl. 2 (tel. 22 33 70; fax 29 36 17), directly across from the *Altes Schloß.* Houses both the Württembergischer Kunstverein and the Galerie der Stadt. Both concern themselves with ultra modern art in a variety of media. Every year, 8-10 intriguing exhibits concentrate on contemporary artists both local and international. Open Tu and Th-Su 11am-6pm, W 11am-8pm. Free, but special exhibits usually DM8, students DM5.

Schwäbisches Brauereimuseum Stuttgart, Robert-Koch-Str. 12, Stuttgart-Vaihingen (tel. 737 02 01). U-Bahn #1, 3, or 6, or S-Bahn #1-3 to "Vaihinger Bahnhof." Walk along Vollmoellerstr. and then turn right onto Robert-Koch-Str. Only in Germany could an entire museum be devoted to beer. Five millennia of the beverage's history culminate in a brew-it-yourself exhibit of current beer production. Everything's free but the samples (DM3.50-4 per beer). Open Th-Su 10:30am-5.30pm.

Deutsches Spielkarten-Museum, Schönbuschstr. 32 (tel. 756 01 20). U-Bahn #5 to "Leinfelden." From the train station, walk down Marktstr. and take a left onto Stuttgartstr. which becomes Schönbuchstr. It's in the basement of the grammar school. The most thorough of its kind in Europe, it reveals only select specimens of its 400,000 card collection (from over 6 centuries and 5 continents) in a series of small but fascinating exhibits. 1999's exhibits examine card-playing in the Third Reich, among other topics. Open Th-Sa 2-5pm, Su 11am-4pm.

ENTERTAINMENT AND NIGHTLIFE

The **Staatstheater** (24hr. ticket information tel. 197 03 or 01 15 17; to order tickets tel. 20 20 90), just across the plaza from the Neues Schloß, is Stuttgart's most famous theater, with opera, ballet, plays, and concerts by the dozen. (Box office open M-F 10am-6pm, Sa 9am-1pm, and 1hr. before performances. DM16-90; student discounts available.) There are 25 other local theaters, and tickets for them are usually much cheaper (DM10-25, students DM5-15). The tourist office provides schedules and sells tickets, which can also be purchased at the **Kartenhäusle,** Geißstr. 4 at Hans-im-Glück Brunnen (tel. 210 40 12; open M-F 9am-6pm, Sa 9am-2pm; order by phone 9am-noon and 2-5pm). Also check out a *Lift* brochure from the tourist office.

Corso Kino, Hauptstr. 6 (tel. 73 49 16), shows primarily original versions of movies—not dubbed into German—with frequent special festivals and revivals. Make sure you're not paying to see a Japanese movie with German subtitles. *"O.m.U."*

means the movie is original with subtitles; *"O.V."* means it's the original version. Take U-Bahn #1 to "Schillerpl." or the S-Bahn to "Vaihingen Bahnhof." Schedules in English are available at the tourist office.

Stuttgart also offers a vibrant selection of yearly festivals to please camera-toting tourists and liquored-up locals alike. The **Stuttgarter Weindorf** (Wine Village) is the largest wine festival in Germany. For 10 days starting on August 26, 1999, wine lovers will descend upon Schillerplatz and Marktplatz to sample over 350 kinds of wine and scrumptious Swabian specialties. Beer gets 16 days of its own worship in the **Cannstatter Volksfest** (Sept. 25-Oct. 10 1999), in Cannstatter Wassen.

From pleasant chats over fine Italian coffee to hypnotic, hyperspeed, techno-fueled hysteria, Stuttgart offers a full spectrum of nightlife nastiness. Serious prowlers should pick up either *Prinz* (DM5) or *Stuttgart Lift* (DM4.50) at any city newsstand; both contain detailed indices to happenings. Tips 'n' Trips (see **Tourist Offices,** p. 430) also publishes up-to-date, dual language guides to the evening scene. Be assured, Dionysus never sleeps in this city. The area along Königstr. and Calverstr. is stayin' alive in the early evenings with lazy chatter (and beers) spilling from numerous cafes. Later on, the nightlife clusters around Eberhardstr., Rotebühlplatz, and the Kleines Schloßplatz. To appease sin-seeking tourists, there's the **Stuttgart Night Pass,** good for three nights' free admission and free second drinks at various clubs, bars, and discotheques; check the tourist office for details.

> **Palast der Republik,** Friedrichstr. 27 (tel. 226 48 87). This wooden bungalow exudes loud music as stylish after-hours aficionados congregate outside to down reasonably priced drinks (beer DM4-6). There's food, too. Open M-W 11am-2am, Th-Sa 11am-3am, Su 3pm-2am; in winter Su-W until 1am, Th-Sa until 2am.
>
> **Radio Bar,** Rotebühlpl. Popular among a young preppy crowd, this place offers drinks (DM4-10), a lively dance floor, and pulsating house music 'til late. No cover.
>
> **Oblomow,** Torstr. 20 (tel. 236 79 24). A cafe that throws open its doors late at night so passersby can hear its upbeat music. Foozball and pinball games. Vegetarian creatures of the night accommodated. Food DM4-8. Open daily 4pm-4am.
>
> **Café Stella,** Hauptstätterstr. 57 (tel. 640 25 83). Polished post-modern cafe where a mellow crowd smokes and reads tarot cards. Occasional jazz performances, pool table upstairs. M-Th 9am-1am, F 9am-2am, Sa 10am-2am, Su 10am-1am.
>
> **Zap,** Hauptstätlerstr. 40, in the Schwabenzentrum (tel. 23 52 27). Formerly the Buddha, this glitzy social mecca is a thriving cesspool of fun. Hiphop, house, and soul. Cover DM8-15. Open Tu and Th 11pm-3am; W and Su 9pm-4am; F-Sa 10pm-6am.
>
> **Laura,** Kronprinzstr. This recently relocated gay and lesbian club blasts house and techno while S&M mannequins pose in cages. No cover. Open Th-Su 10pm-6am. Saturdays men only.
>
> **Kings,** Calwerstr. 21 (tel. 226 45 58). Gays and lesbians groove to spiced-up 80s music beneath black lights and red velvet walls. Private, but open to non-members. Cover F DM10 and Sa DM15; includes 2 drinks. Open F-Sa 10pm-6am.

■ Near Stuttgart: Esslingen am Neckar

Though Esslingen's primary role is as a night-home for thousands of Stuttgart's commuters, it does not scream suburbia. Bounded by steep, terraced vineyards on one side and the Neckar River on the other, Esslingen nurtures an *Altstadt* surrounded by the remnants of the original town fortifications. Though it has a population of over 100,000 and lies within Stuttgart's hegemonic industrial sprawl, Esslingen is a cozy town that defiantly celebrates its independence with many festivals, including the fearsome **Zwiebelfest** (Onion Festival), with its own eye-wateringly delicious mascot—the **Esslingen Zwiebel.**

To reach the *Altstadt* from the train station, walk down Berliner Str. over the bridge and to the right. The blazing mauve Renaissance facade of the **Altes Rathaus** looks out over one corner of the square. The **Glockenspiel** sitting atop it has a repertoire of more than 200 songs (including "Yankee Doodle"), which it flaunts every day at 8am, noon, 3, 6, and 7:30pm. The asymmetrical towers of the **Stadtkirche St.**

Dionys, connected by a small footbridge, guard the other corner of the Marktplatz. (Open daily 8am-6pm; enter through door 4.) The church holds a gorgeous 15th-century rood screen. Up on the hill rises the Gothic stone spire of the much more elegant **Liebfrauenkirche,** which contains luminous 14th-century stained glass, as well as the tomb of its architect, who also designed the famous *Münster* in Ulm. (Open daily from sunrise to sunset.) In the 1530s, the Esslingen town council voted to ride the wave of the Reformation and turn the Liebfrauenkirche into a Protestant place of worship. Farther up the ridge among the vineyards stands the **Burg.** The squat, round, half-timbered tower at the right of the *Burg,* appropriately named **Dicker Turm** (fat tower), has a restaurant that can make you round and squat (adjectives, not verbs), too. A romantic view of the town superimposed on the Swabian Jura backdrop greets those who want to explore the footpaths which criss-cross the *Weinberge.* Free maps identifying the grape-type for each section of the vineyard are available at the tourist office.

Esslingen is on the **train** line between Stuttgart and Ulm, and can also be reached by S-Bahn #1 (direction: "Plochingen") from Stuttgart (20min.; every 15-20min.; DM4.30, railpasses valid). The **tourist office,** in the Neues Rathaus (tel. 35 12 24 41; fax 35 12 29 39), provides maps and books rooms for free (open M-F 8am-12:30pm and 1:30-5pm, Th until 6pm). Esslingen's clean **Jugendherberge (HI),** Neuffenstr. 65 (tel. 38 18 48; fax 38 88 86), is in the Zollberg section of town, reachable by a grueling 30-minute uphill trek; sane people take bus #118, 119, or 120 to "Zollbergstr." (2-3 per hr.), then cross the street and follow the signs (10min.); overflow from Stuttgart's hostel is usually sent here. (DM20, over 26 DM25. Members only. Breakfast included. Sheets DM5.50. Reception 3:30-5pm, 6:45-7:30pm, and 8:30-9:45pm. Curfew 10pm, but keys available with DM20 deposit.) **Gasthof Falken,** Bahnhofstr. 4 (tel. 35 72 88; fax 537 719 90), has good clean rooms at good clean prices. Go right from the station until Bahnhofstr. (Singles DM30, doubles DM50. No breakfast.) Esslingen's cup runneth over with *Weinstuben.* A mosey down Herrgasse takes you past numerous notable eating and drinking establishments. **Weinkeller Einhorn,** Heugasse 17 (tel. 35 35 90), serves Swabian specialties (DM8.50-16.50) and cool wine (DM5.80-6.80) from a 700-year-old cellar (open daily 5pm-midnight) Of the many sociable young folk who populate Esslingen, the stylish ones hang out in the stylish chairs at **Café Mayer,** Unterer Metzgerbach 18/1 (tel. 35 69 60). Beer flows for DM2.50-4.50. (Open M 10am-6pm, Tu-F and Su 10am-midnight, Sa 10am-1am.) **Krokodil,** Rossmarkt 9 (tel. 35 66 23), universally known as "Krok," is a popular bar. If Old Blue Eyes lived in Esslingen, he would've come here for his martinis. (Open M-Sa 11am-1am, Su 2pm-1am.) The **postal code** is 73728. The **telephone code** is 0711.

■ Near Stuttgart: Ludwigsburg

Ludwigsburg popped out of the blue in the early 18th century, the narcissistic love child of Duke Eberhard of Ludwig. His modest idea: to erect a residential castle in the Duchy's new capital bearing his own name. Unfortunately, Ludwig died before his playground was born, and although his successors finished decorating the castle, they preferred to live in Stuttgart. Even without the aristocratic element, Ludwigsburg lived on to become a lively Baroque city with a luxurious trio of palaces.

The opulent Baroque **Residenzschloß** is definitely worth seeing, even if you find yourself lost among German office fieldtrips. (Open mid-Mar. to Nov. daily 9am-noon and 1-5pm. Tours in English at 1:30pm; German tours Nov. to mid-Mar. M-F 10:30am and 3pm. DM8, students DM4). The 1¼-hour guided journey is the only way to see Ludwig's 3m long bed (he was larger than life: almost 7 ft. tall) and the rest of the lavish gold, marble, and velvet interior. This "Suburban Versailles" is situated in an expansive 30-hectare garden that earned Ludwig's complex the tourist brochure epithet **Blühendes Barock,** or "Blooming Baroque." (Open mid-Mar. to early Dec. daily 7:30am-8:30pm. Main entrance on Schondorferstr. open 9am-6pm.) Inside, a perennial **Märchen Garten** recreates scenes of major fairy tales in a large park of wild vegetation. (Open 9am-6pm. Adults DM12, students DM5.) Join 100 kids yelling,

"Rapunzel, Rapunzel, laß deinen Zopf herunter." The **Favoritschloß** (tel. 18 64 40) is an excellent destination for a stroll or picnic. (Open mid-Mar. to Oct. daily 9am-noon and 1:30-5pm; Nov. to mid-Mar. 10am-noon and 1:30-4pm. Frequent guided tours mid-Mar. to Nov. daily 9am-noon and 1:30-5pm; Nov. to mid-Mar. Tu-Su 10am-noon and 1-4pm. DM4.) This smaller Baroque gem was built as a hunting lodge and big-time party venue for Duke Carl Engler. If you're not all *Schloßed*-out by this point, continue for 30 minutes up the alley through the **Favoriten Park** and marvel at the third of the Ludwig palaces—the Rococo **Monrepos** (tel. 225 50). Unfortunately, the castle is now a luxury hotel and is closed to visitors, but you can calm your frustrations by renting a **boat** and rowing on the peaceful lake by the Schloß (boat rides Apr.-Sept.; call 327 96).

All three palace grounds comprise the site of the annual **Ludwigsburger Schloßfestspiele**, a series of open-air concerts and performances that runs from early June to late September. For information on Schloßfestspiele tickets and specifics, call the Forum am Schloßpark (tel. 91 71 00; lines open M-F 8:30am-6:30pm, Sa 9am-1pm). Even without renowned musicians in the neighborhood, Ludwigsburg offers a sense of refined and classy tranquility. No bumpy medieval cobblestone to be found here: the pastel *Marktplatz* is smooth and spacious, with cotton-candy Baroque churches contemplating each other across an aristocratic divide.

To reach this quiet niche from Stuttgart, Ride S-Bahn #4 or 5 towards Marbach or Bietigheim (20min.; DM4.30). Or take a **boat** run by Neckar-Personen-Schiffahrt (see p. 430). The **tourist office**, across from the *Rathaus* at Wilhelmstr. 10 (tel. 910 26 36 or 910 22 52), books rooms for free (open M-F 9am-6pm, Sa 9am-2pm). The only cheap lodging in town is the **Jugendherberge Ludwigsburg (HI)**, Gemsenbergstr. 21 (tel. 515 64; fax 594 40). Take bus #422 to "Schlößlesfeld" (DM2.80). It's quite far from town, but the hostel's pastoral setting and nice balconies lend it an almost resort-like peace. (DM21, over 26 DM27. Huge breakfast DM5. Members only. Cold meal DM7.50, warm meal DM9. Reception 9am-1pm and 5-7pm. Curfew 10pm.) There are several restaurants on or near the Holzmarkt (just by the Marktplatz). **Corfu**, Holzmarktstr. 2 (tel. 92 08 24), serves daily Greek specials, including a giant bean salad (DM6) and vegetarian entrees (DM8.50-20; open daily 11:30am-2:30pm and 5pm-midnight). Grocery stores and bakeries run rampant along Myluisstr. and Arsenalstr. The **telephone code** is 07141.

■ Near Stuttgart: Marbach

Friedrich Schiller was born in Marbach, a fact that is difficult to ignore; from drugstores to hair salons, the name of the prominent and prominently-nosed poet is ubiquitous. The stately **Schiller-National Museum**, Schillerhöhe 8-10 (tel. 60 61) offers a detailed account of Schiller's life and work, and teaches something about his Swabian contemporaries. (Open daily 9am-5pm, except Dec. 25 and Jan. 1. DM4, students DM2.) The audio-visual room at the end of the first floor plays the authentic voice of Bertolt Brecht singing *"Mackie Messer,"* his wicked German song known to English-speakers as "Mack the Knife"— swing it, Louie, swing it! Follow the signs from the train station. Adjacent to the museum is the **German Literature Archive** (tel. 60 61), one of the largest of its kind in the country. Call ahead if you plan on visiting. Diehard Schiller devotees might also want to visit the **Schiller Geburtshaus**, Niklastorstr. 31 (tel. 175 67), where Schiller was born in 1759. (Open daily 9am-5pm, except Dec. 25-26. DM3, students DM1.50.) Not an astounding amount to see here, except some Schiller artifacts and an animated, first-person-narrated video on the man himself. To get there, follow signs through the tiny town. From the Schiller-Museum, you'll pass under the half-timbered **Bürgerturm** and the Marktplatz. The nearby **Rathaus**, Marktstr. 23, has materials on walking tours, hotels, and restaurants (open M 9-11am and 4-6pm, Tu and Th-F 9-11am, W 2-4pm). The city's **telephone code** is 07144. For **food**, head to Marktstr., where most of the restaurants in Marbach are located. To reach Marbach from Stuttgart, take S-Bahn #4 until the very end. Buh-bye!

■ Tübingen

Tübingen is a bookish city and proud of it. With nearly half of its residents affiliated with its 500-year-old university, Tübingen is sincerely academic, a place for relaxed contemplation from which literary giant Hermann Hesse launched his book-dealing career. Things have not always been so peaceful in the forests of academe. The university has been a source of unpredictability from the Middle Ages to the student uprisings of the late 60s and beyond; students have boycotted classes to protest everything from the educational system and the Nazi past of many politicians to American involvement in the Vietnam War. The compact *Altstadt*, a snail shell sheltering a lively student life by day and night, has successfully avoided the fate of over-touristed Heidelberg, allowing independent travelers a chance for solo exploration.

ORIENTATION AND PRACTICAL INFORMATION

30km south of Stuttgart, Tübingen stands guard over the Neckar River, on the edge of the Schwarzwald. Easily reached by rail, it is one of the larger cities in the area, and it is connected by bus and train to many small towns in the Schwäbische Alb.

Trains: Stuttgart is the only major city with a direct link (1hr., every 30-45min.).

Taxis: Taxi Centrale, tel. 243 01.

Bike Rental: RADlager, Lazarettgasse 19-21 (tel. 55 16 51; fax 55 17 51), in the *Altstadt*. DM14 per day; less for each additional day. Open M-Tu and Th-F 9:30am-1pm and 2-6:30pm, W 2-6pm, Sa 9:30am-2:30pm.

Boat Rental: Bootsverleih Märkle (tel. 31 52 29), on the river under the tourist office. Boats DM3.50-4 per person per hr. Open Apr.-Sept. daily 11am-8pm.

Mitfahrzentrale: Münzgasse 6 (tel. 267 89 or 50 81). Rides to Munich DM24 (including gas); Frankfurt DM24; Berlin DM62; Köln DM39. Open M-F 10am-7pm, Sa-Su 11am-5pm. Call 1-2 days in advance.

Tourist Office: Verkehrsverein (tel. 913 60; fax 350 70; http://www.tuebingen.de), on Neckarbrücke. From the front of the train station, turn right and walk to Karlstr., turn left and walk to the river. The office books hotel and private rooms (DM30-100) for a DM5 fee, sells maps (DM1-10), and acts as a box office. Open M-F 9am-7pm, Sa 9am-5pm, Su 2-5pm; Oct.-Apr. closed Su.

Tours: Ask at the tourist office for the comprehensive pamphlet listing all tour offerings. **City tours** (DM5, in English DM10) leave from the tourist office Apr.-Oct. W 10am, Sa-Su 2:30pm. Just show up.

Mitwohnzentrale: Wilhelmstr. 2-3 (tel. 194 45; fax 55 10 70). For stays of 1 month or longer. Open M-Th 10am-noon and 2-5pm, F 10am-3pm, Sa 10am-1pm. Also check the bulletin boards in the *Mensa*.

Bookstores: The venerable, 400-year-old **Osiandersche Buchhandlung,** Wilhelmstr. 12 (tel. 920 10), carries a large selection of English and American literature. Open M-F 9am-8pm, Sa 9am-4pm. **Bücherkabinett Antiquariat,** Bachgasse 13 (tel. 55 12 23), houses 20,000 used books in towering stacks that threaten to overwhelm the proprietor. Open M-F 10am-6:30pm, Sa 10am-3pm.

Cultural Center: German-American Institute, Karlstr. 3 (tel. 340 71).

Women's Resources: Women's cafe (*Frauencafé*), Karlstr. 13 (tel. 328 62), is a hopping, women-only night spot/safe zone. In the magenta house a block from the train station. Open Sept.-June M-F 8pm-midnight. **Frauenbuchladen Thalestris,** a women's bookstore at Bursagasse 2 (tel. 265 90 or 511 90—also the number for **women's information**). Open M-F 10am-7pm, Sa 10am-2pm.

Gay and Lesbian Events: Gay and lesbian bar every Wednesday night in the Sudhaus (see **Nightlife**); **gay afternoons** on Sunday at the **Luscht Cafe,** Herrenbergerstr. 9; **women's disco** on Saturday nights at **Club Voltaire,** Haaggasse 266.

Laundromat: Student Waschsalon, Rumelnstr. 8 in the cellar. Wash and dry DM5. Buy tokens at the **Maquardtei** restaurant (see **Food**). Open until 10pm.

Emergency: Police, tel. 110. **Fire and Ambulance,** tel. 112.

Rape Hotline: Frauenhaus, tel. 666 04.

Post Office: Europapl. 2, 72072 Tübingen, 100m right of the train station. Open M-F 7:30am-6:30pm, Sa 7:30am-12:30pm.

BADEN-WÜRTTEMBURG

Telephone Code: 07071.

ACCOMMODATIONS AND CAMPING

Most of the lodgings in the city are not priced to please, yet rooms rented out by **private families,** listed at the tourist office, are usually economical. Call ahead.

Jugendherberge (HI), Gartenstr. 22/2 (tel. 230 02; fax 250 61), is a 12min. walk from the station. Cross the bridge past the tourist office and make a right. Recently renovated with a terrace offering a shorefront view of the Neckar. DM23, over 26 DM28. Members only. Breakfast included. Reception 5-8 and 10-10:15pm. Lockout 9am-5pm. Curfew 10pm. Lockers DM5 deposit. Wheelchair access.

Hotel am Schloß, Burgsteige 18 (tel. 929 40; fax 92 94 10), on the hill leading to the *Schloß*. Royal lodgings in a great location, with a picturesque view. The sign above the bench outside is exaggerated *Schwäbisch* dialect for "here sit those who always sit here" *(dohoggeddiadiaemmerdohogged)*. Singles DM55, with shower DM72, with bath DM99-130; doubles with bath DM124-148. Breakfast included. All rooms with cable TV and telephone. Send a fax.

Hotel Kürner, Weizsäckerstr. 1 (tel. 227 35; fax 279 20), near the *Uni* but 20min. from the *Altstadt*. Follow Wilhelmstr. past the university and go right on Weizsäckerstr. Or bus #1, 2, 6, 7, or 15 to "Lothar-Meyer-Bau." Friendly management, fun 70s decor, and a restaurant. Singles DM58-68; doubles DM108. Breakfast included.

Camping: Rappernberghalde, on the river (tel./fax 431 45). Go upstream from the *Altstadt* or left from the station, cross the river at the Alleenbrücke, and turn left (20-25min.). Follow the blue signs. Or take bus #9 to "Rappenberg" and keep going with the river to your left. DM9.50 per person; DM5.50-7 per tent. Bike rental DM15 per day. Laundry DM7.50. Reception daily 8am-12:30pm and 2:30-10pm.

FOOD

With the smell of pungent herbs and fresh bread in the air, Tübingen entices students into keeping a number of superb restaurants busy. Most inexpensive eating establishments cluster around the Metzergasse/Am Lutznauer Tor area. Buy bread and Nutella at **Pfannkuch,** Karlstr. 3, next to the tourist office on the Neckarbrücke (open M-F 8:30am-7:30pm, Sa 8am-2pm). The *Altstadt* bristles with grocery stores and bakeries.

◉Marquardtei, Herrenbergerstr. 34 (tel. 433 86). Bus #8, 16, or 30 to "Rappstr." Run by a gang of enterprising students, this place serves pizzas, *Schwäbisch* specialties, and various vegetarian dishes to an equally varied student clientele. Entrees DM9.50-14.30. 1m beer DM18.50. Open M-Sa 11:30am-1am, Su 10am-1am.

Mensa, on Wilhelmstr. between Gmelinstr. and Keplerstr. (on the left with teal trimming). Offers generic fare at low prices. Meals DM3.80 for Tübingen students, DM8.70 for guests. Salad bar DM0.85 for 100g. Open M-Th 11am-2pm and 6-8:15pm, F noon-2pm, Sa 11:45am-1:15pm. Equally cheap is the ID-less **cafeteria** downstairs with cold food and big chunks o' cheesecake all under DM5. Open M-Th 8am-8pm, F 8am-7pm. Both closed the middle 2 weeks of August.

Da Pino, Mühlstr 20 (tel. 55 10 86), is a small but eminently delicious eatery. Crust 'n' cheese in all shapes and sizes. Pizzas DM7-10. Take out or stand at the counter. Open daily 11:30am-2:30pm and 4:30pm-12:30am.

Die Wurstküche, Am Lustnauer Tor 8 (tel. 927 50). Dishes up regional specialties in a gorgeous dining room, with plenty of high *Schwäbisch* camp and friendly service. Entrees DM13-27. Vegetarian dishes DM13-15. Open daily 11am-midnight.

SIGHTS

Atop the hill that rudely isolates the university from the rest of the city stands the **Schloß Hohentübingen,** a castle dating from 1078 that commands the best view of Tübingen's picturesque red roofs. *(Castle grounds open daily 7am-8pm. Free.)* Today primarily occupied by various university institutes, the *Schloß* is also home to the excellent **Museum Schloß Hohentübingen,** Burgsteigell (tel. 297 73 84; fax 29 56 59), the largest university museum in Germany, which features an extensive collection of eth-

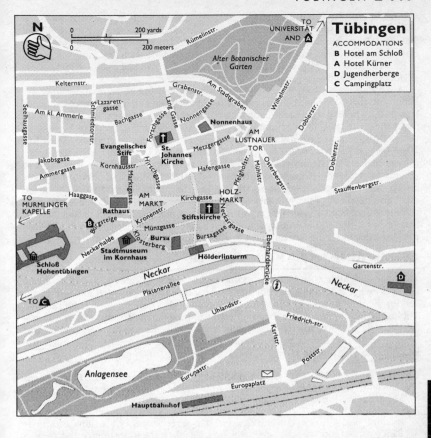

Tübingen

ACCOMMODATIONS
B Hotel am Schloß
A Hotel Kürner
D Jugendherberge
C Campingplatz

nographic and archaeological artifacts ranging from ancient Egyptian to present-day South Pacific—and everything in between. *(Open May-Sept. W-Su 10am-6pm; Oct.-Apr. W-Su 10am-5pm. Tours Su at 3pm. DM4, students DM2.)* Don't miss what is purported to be the **oldest surviving example of handwork** (an ivory horse sculpture that's 35,000 years old) or the ethereal hall that houses countless plaster casts of classical sculptures. If you get to the *Schloß* when the museum's closed, fret not. Just remember to explore the dark tunnel and the staircase on the far side of the courtyard. Both lead through the castle wall to breathtaking views of the surrounding valleys. To soak up even more spectacular scenery, follow the signs to the trail to the **Wurmlinger Kapelle** (red blazes; a few kilometers away). This simple but beautiful chapel sits atop an idyllic pastoral hill, worlds away from Tübingen's crunchy academia.

The 15th-century **Stiftskirche**, on the other side of the magnificent *Altstadt*, serves as the focal point of the winding alleys and gabled houses. *(Church open daily 9am-5pm. Chancel and tower open Apr.-July and Oct. F-Su 10:30am-5pm; Aug.-Sept. daily 10:30am-5pm. DM2, students DM1. Summer organ concerts July-Aug. Th at 6pm, Sept. Sa at 8pm.)* In the chancel lie the tombs of 14 members of the House of Württemberg. Life-size stone sculptures of the deceased top the tombs—men in their finest suits of armor. The church tower offers a rewarding view for those who survive the climb. On the square is **Buchhandlung Heckenhauer Antiquariat**, Holzmarkt 5 (tel. 230 18), where Hermann Hesse worked from 1895 until 1899. It's still selling rare books. Down the street from Kirchgasse, any day of the week, a mind-boggling array of vendors sets up shop beneath the *Rathaus*'s incredibly ornate facade. Just north, the **Kornhaus** (Old Granary) contains the **Tübingen Stadtmuseum**, Kornhausstr. 10 (tel. 20 43 82), with exhibits on the city's history and several rotating art exhibits. *(Open Tu-Sa 3-6pm, Su 11am-1pm and 3-6pm.)* A few blocks below the Marktplatz, on Kronenstr. dwells the **Tübingen Evangelisches Stift,** Klosterberg 2 (tel. 56 10). Once a medieval monastery, now a dormitory for theology students, its alumni include such academic luminaries as Kepler, Hölderlin, Hegel, Schelling, and Mörike. Buy yourself a guide (DM3) at the adjacent *Pforte* and take yourself on a tour of the house.

Down Bursagasse from the Evangelisches Stift is the **Bursa,** an unappealing pink behemoth that serves as a dorm and philosophy lecture hall. Here, *Stift* roommates Hegel and Schelling used to doze through boring theology lectures. Their third roommate, the great 18th- and 19th-century poet Friedrich Hölderlin, lived out the final 36 years of his life in the nearby **Hölerlinturm,** in a state of clinical insanity. *(Open Tu-F 10am-noon and 3-5pm, Sa-Su 2-5pm. Tours Sa-Su 5pm. DM3, students DM2.)* The tower now contains a museum dedicated to his life. Hardcore Hölderlinists may want to contact the **Hölderlin-Gesellschaft,** Bursagasse 6 (tel. 220 40), a society and support group dedicated to helping those addicted to the poet's life and work. All these charming buildings of the **Neckarfront** are best viewed from the **Platanenallee,** the summery, tree-lined avenue that runs the length of man-made island on the Neckar. Rumor has it that the university fraternities located on the riverfront will give free punting trips down the Neckar to those who ask—no keg-stands required.

ENTERTAINMENT AND NIGHTLIFE

Tübingen's nightlife is laid-back. It mostly revolves around cafes in the *Altstadt* that begin brewing quiet cups of coffee at 10am and remain open well into the night, serving beer to groups of students. The *Altstadt* also houses some sublime bars. Tübingen also has two major theaters: the small progressive **Zimmertheater,** Bursagasse 16 (tel. 927 30), and the larger, more conservative **Landestheater,** Eberhardstr. 8 (tel. 931 31 49). Tickets and schedules are available at the tourist office and at the box office at Eberhardstr. 6 (open Tu-F 3:30-7pm, Sa 10am-1pm).

Jazzkeller, Haaggasse 15/2 (tel. 55 09 06; fax 221 63), moves from jazz to funk to salsa (often live) and back again. Open from 7pm daily, Monday until 2am, Sunday and Tuesday-Thursday until 1am, Friday-Saturday until 3am.

Sudhaus, Hechinger Str. 203 (tel. 746 96). Take bus #3 or 5 to "Fuchsstr.," or Nachtbus line N9. A "Socio-cultural Center" that screens wacky art films and hosts dance parties and live acts. Schedules are available at the tourist office and are also plastered all over town. Cover DM10-25.

Tangente-Night, Pfleghofstr. 10 (tel. 230 07), by the Lustnauer Tor corner. A premier Tübingen student hangout for beer and company at night or a book and cappuccino in the morning (0.3L *Pils* DM3.50; coffee DM3). Most fun Sept.-Apr. Th-Su, when a DJ spins house, acid jazz, and techno. Sunday is cocktail night, Monday is Karaoke night, Thursday is happy hour (10pm-midnight), and there's live music or a theme party each week. Open daily 10am-3am.

Neckarmüller, Gartenstr. 4, (tel. 278 48), is close to the youth hostel. Young and old alike drink and schmooze at picnic tables under big shady trees by the banks of the river. The only way to get closer to the Neckar is to rent your own boat. They serve their own amazing brew; light or dark DM3.90 for 0.3L. Wow. In case you want to send some to Uncle Jack, a 5L oaken cask is DM45. Open daily 10am-1am.

O'Donovan's Irish Pub, Burgstraße 7 (tel. 236 98), near the *Schloß*. With occasional live music acts and bar quizzes, this bit o' Erin keeps the students flushed and happy, especially in the winter. Guinness on tap DM4.50 per glass. Irish breakfast on Sundays. Open M-Sa 5pm-1am, Su 11am-1am.

Marktschenke, Am Markt 11 (tel. 220 35). Tipsy students spill out onto Tübingen's largest square. If they don't amuse you, the cartoons on the walls surely will. *Hefe Weizen* (wheat beer) DM5.20 for 0.5L. Coffee DM3.30. Open daily 9am-1am.

■ Near Tübingen: The Hohenzollernstraße

The Staufens may have been big, but the Zollerns were a whole lot bigger. Of the two medieval dynasties that dominated the Schwäbische Alb in their heyday, it was the Zollern family that went on to become the real Mack-Daddy of the German political scene: from 1871 to 1918 they ruled a unified Germany under Kaisers Wilhelm I and II. Today, as evidence of the family's former power in the region, the **Hohenzollernstraße** stretches south of Tübingen, connecting three magnificent castles that served as strongholds for the Zollerns.

The first **Schloß**, in the town of **Haigerloch**, juts upward on a ridge high above the town's center—the *Unterstadt*. Occupied by a group of young artists, the castle bedazzles the town with exhibits of its occupants' works and a series of jazz and classical performances (tickets DM10-50; info available at the tourist office). Between the *Schloß* and the *Unterstadt*, along the stone stairway that leads up from the Marktplatz, lurks the deceptive **Schloßkirche**. (Open daily 9am-6pm.) The 18th-century artist Meinrad von Au is responsible for this Baroque monstrosity—a flashy cacophony of pastel and gold ornaments. Mmm…tastes like birthday cake.

Omnibus #10 connects Haigerloch to the rest of the world only a few times per day, via Horb to the northwest (30min., DM5.50), and Hechingen to the east (35min., DM6.50). The easiest place to catch the bus from either town is at the train station (next to the phone booth in Hechingen and at *Steig* 6 in Horb). Buses drop passengers off in Haigerloch at the Marktplatz in the *Unterstadt* and the *Obere Apotheke* on the outskirts of the *Oberstadt*. Watch out for the "S" on bus schedules; it indicates buses that run only on school days. The **tourist office**, Oberstadtstr. 11 (tel. 697 26; fax 60 68; http://www.haigerloch.de), inside the *Rathaus*, has town guides in English, free hiking maps, and a list of accommodations (open M-F 9am-noon, M-W 2-5pm, Th 2-6:30pm, F 2-5pm; closed F Sept.-Apr.). To reach the tourist office from the Marktplatz, cross the bridge, turn right onto Oberstadtstr. From the *Obere Apotheke*, follow Oberstadtstr.'s curvy descent for 10-15 minutes. The **telephone code** is 07474.

In trying to get to or from Haigerloch, you will probably end up in **Hechingen**, a town that lacks the quirky character of its cousin, but boasts the far more extraordinary second castle of the tour. **Burg Hohenzollern** (tel. 24 28; fax 68 12) rises majestically above a carpet of trees in the distance, often ringed by mist. (Open daily 9am-5:30pm; mid-Oct. to mid-Mar. 9am-4:30pm; entrance to the castle proper only with a tour DM9, students DM6; entrance to the castle grounds DM4, although free after 5:30pm until closing at around 10pm.) A tremendous conglomeration of spiraling trees and imposing battlements, it shines with an interior that is just as opulent as the exterior is fantastical, while the bastions offer an incredible panoramic view that extends to the Swiss Alps on clear days. Don't miss the divine sunset view. Unfortunately, no public transportation connects Hechingen to the castle. Split a taxi (DM15), or better yet, hike; it's is a beautiful journey. Some travlers have had luck hitching. Just follow the blue triangles. From the *Rathaus* (see below) walk down Heiligkreuzstr., take a right at the Heilig-Kreuz-Frischof (cemetery), go under the railroad bridge, and take the first right towards the woods. There are a myriad of trails through the woods to the castle. For more information and city maps, visit the **tourist office**, Marktplatz 1 (tel. 94 01 14; fax 94 01 08), in the *Rathaus*. From the *Bahnhof*, go straight into town and keep walking up. A golden ball tops the *Rathaus* (open M-Th 8am-12:30pm and 2-4pm, F 8am-12:30pm). The **telephone code** is 07471.

In the hamlet of **Sigmaringen** stands the third castle on the Hohenzollernstraße. This breathtakingly dramatic palace, home to the Zollern-Sigmaringen line since the 16th century, remains surprisingly undiscovered on the edges of the Schwäbische Alb. It's worlds away from Heidelberg and Neuschwanstein, yet on par with their architectural magnificence. Thankfully, **Schloß Sigmaringen** (tel. 72 92 30) is also a whole lot more accessible than its absence of tourists would imply. (Open daily May-Oct. 9am-4:45pm, Nov. and Feb.-Apr. 9:30am-4:30pm, Dec. and Jan. only until 4pm by advance calling. DM7, students DM6.) While the Danube-side of the castle is indeed dramatic, on the other side, the tiny *Altstadt* curls right up to the *Schloß's* walls. Enter directly from the Rathausplatz. To get there, hang a right from the train station down Bahnhofstr., then take a left onto Fürst-Wilhelm-Str., then make another right. Tours allow you to see the opulent interior, including lots of amazing Rococo furniture and the heavily-secured Hall of Hubertus, which contains one of the largest private collections of weaponry in Europe.

The surrounding Swabian countryside also offers some enjoyable hiking trails, many leading to castle ruins, narrow caverns, or spectacular look-out points. For a particularly nifty view of the **Schloß** and its village, take the 12km hike that begins at the **Stadthalle** parking lot. Numerous other hiking and outdoors possibilities can be learned via the **tourist office**, Schwabstr. 1 (tel. 10 62 23; fax 10 61 66), on the corner of the **Rathausplatz**. You can pick up a hiking map here and free posters of the *Schloß*. (Open Tu-F 11am-4:30pm, Sa 10am-7pm.) For lodging, the hillside **Jugendherberge Sigmaringen (HI)**, Hohenzollernstr. 31 (tel. 132 77; fax 611 59), offers adequate facilities and a great view of the town. Take bus #2 from Leopoldplatz (from the train station, walk straight through the lush Prinzengarten) to "Hohenzollernstr." Then cross the street and walk downhill to the left. It'll appear on your right shortly. Bus #3 takes you and your pack back to the train station. (DM21, over 26 DM26. Breakfast included. Sheets DM5.50. Reception until 9:15pm. Curfew 10pm.) The **telephone code** is 07571.

■ Karlsruhe

By European standards, Karlsruhe was born yesterday. In 1715, nobleman Margrave Karl Wilhelm built a castle retreat for himself and his mistresses (hence the name, meaning "Karl's Rest"). He then designed a planned city radiating out from the castle in the shape of a fan. It has been an architectural sensation ever since, perhaps due to the refreshingly spacious and navigable streets. Karlsruhe is the home to Germany's two highest courts, the Federal Supreme Court and the Federal Constitutional Court. Relatively overlooked by tourists, modern Karlsruhe is an honest portrayal of modern German society without a quaint little *Altstadt* to conceal the day-to-day doings of its citizens. For travelers, the city offers an impressive selection of museums and a break from the burden of antiquity. For residents, Karlsruhe offers something even better— over 1700 hours of sun per year, earning the title of "Sun City."

ORIENTATION AND PRACTICAL INFORMATION From the station, the town center is a 25-minute walk away from the train tracks on Ettlinger Str. and Karl-Friedrich-Str., or you can take any of the streetcar lines to "Marktplatz" or "Europaplatz." The **Straßenbahn** costs DM3 per ride within the city, DM8 for a 24-hour ticket. If staying in the city for at least one night, you are entitled to a 35% discount on your train ticket (but *not* on the S-Bahn); call the tourist office to make arrangements. For a **taxi**, call 94 41 44. The **tourist office**, Bahnhofpl. 6 (tel. 355 30; fax 35 53 43 99; http://www.karlsruhe.de), located across the street from the train station, finds rooms for free. The staff has lots of events information and gives out the amazing *Karlsruhe Extra*, an annually updated city bulletin and site guide (in English) with great maps. They also arrange a number of cheesy weekend package stays, many timed to coincide with Karlsruhe events and festivals. Though generally pricey, the "Karlsruher Weekend" package runs as low as DM48 per person. The *Karlsruhe Programm* has info on upcoming events. (Office open M-F 9am-6pm, Sa 9am-1pm.) **Braunsche Universitäts Buchhandlung**, Kaiserstr. 120 (tel. 232 96; fax 291 16), has a small, top-notch selection of English-language books (open M-F 8:30am-8pm, Sa 9am-5pm). The **post office**, 76133 Karlsruhe, sprawls at Europaplatz. (Open M-F 8:30am-6:30pm, Sa 8:30am-1pm.) The **telephone code** is 0721.

ACCOMMODATIONS If looking for a bed in Karlsruhe, ask the tourist office for their thorough guide to accommodations. Karlsruhe's **Jugendherberge (HI)**, Moltkestr. 24 (tel. 282 48; fax 276 47), is convenient to the *Schloß* and university, although it's far from the train station. Take nearly any S-Bahn to "Europaplatz," then follow Karlstr. until it ends. Turn left onto Seminarstr. and turn left again on Moltkestr.; it's on the right. (DM23, over 26 DM28. Members only. Breakfast included. Reception briefly at 5, 7, and 9:30pm. Strict curfew 11:30pm. Lockout 9am-5pm.) The tiny **Pension am Zoo,** Ettlinger Str. 33 (tel. 336 78), is a couple blocks from the station and a camel chip's throw from the zoo. It features spacious, well-furnished rooms with TV. Turn right from the train station and then left at the end of Poststr. (Singles DM55-65; doubles DM100, with bath DM120.) **Camping** is at **Türmbergblick,** Tiengererstr. 40 (tel. 49 72 36; fax 49 72 37), in nearby Durlach. Take S-Bahn #3 to "Durlacher Tor," then S-Bahn #1 or 2 to "Durlach." (DM7-10 per person, DM5-7 per child; DM5-7 per tent. Prices vary with season. Reception 8am-1pm and 3-9pm. Open Mar.-Sept.)

FOOD AND NIGHTLIFE Karlsruhe is home to a very large *Fachhochschule* (trade school) that brims with students. The **Mensa** is located near the youth hostel. From the hostel's front door, walk straight ahead across the lawn between two buildings to the very large nondescript building (open M-Th 8:30am-4pm, F 8:30am-2pm). The hangout **Krokodil,** Waldstr. 63 (tel. 273 31), offers salads, *Schnitzel,* breakfasts, and pastas (DM5-17) along with a spacious, hopping mirrored bar and beer garden (open daily 8am-1am). For traditional German fare, try **Goldenes Kreuz,** Karlstr. 21a (tel. 220 54), around the corner from Ludwigspl, where entrees go for DM10-20 (open daily 11am-10pm). On a lazy afternoon, **Eiscafé Pierod,** Kasierstr. 133 (tel. 937 73 37), offers up ice cream confections (DM1.50-12) and rad interior design (open Su-Th 10am-11pm; F-Sa 10am-midnight). The **market** at Marktplatz caters to Durlach campers (open M-Sa 7:30am-12:30pm). Many cafes on Ludwigsplatz stay open until 1am, and the tourist office has a list of all nightlife venues. **Harmonie,** Kaiserstr. 57 (tel. 37 42 09), is a rad student pub that offers cheap eats (sausages and pasta DM7-12; beer DM3.50-6) and live music (open M-F 8am-1am, Sa 10am-1am, Su 9:30am-1am).

Die Kur

In Germany, "The Cure" is not a British rock band, but a venerated excuse for going to the beach. The well-funded German health care system subsidizes trips to spa towns for those over 50, which might explain why more than six million Germans take spa vacations every year. Yet German doctors are divided about the value of the *Kur.* Some believe it to be mostly psychological therapy, while others lend it more credence. The *Kurschatten* (spa romance) has become such a tradition that it's not always admissible as grounds for divorce in Germany, and probably invigorates vacationers more than anything else. This might explain why so many spa towns have at least one *"FKK"* ("Freie Körper Kultur") sunbathing area, better known to English speakers as a nude beach.

SIGHTS The most spectacular sight in Karlsruhe is the locus of the city—all roads literally lead to the classical yellow **Schloß.** The *Schloßgarten,* with its impeccably maintained swathes of green and inviting benches, stretches out behind the castle for nearly 0.5km. Hop a ride on the miniature train. *(Open until 10pm daily. Free, but mini train costs DM3.)* The *Schloß* houses the **Landesmuseum** (tel. 926 65 14), with elaborate special exhibits and a permanent collection of antiques including the flashy **Türkenbeute** (Turkish booty) *(Open Tu and Th-Su 10am-5pm, W 10am-8pm. DM5, students DM3, more for special exhibits.)* In early June, the **Museum Festival** draws 30,000 onlookers. The same entry fee allows you admission to two other museums. The **Museum beim Markt,** Karl-Friedrich-Str. 6 (tel. 926 64 94), dedicated to design and illustration, has a particularly fascinating Art Deco and *Jugendstil* collection. *(Open Tu and Th-Su 10am-5pm, W 1:30-8pm.)* Around the corner are the **Kunsthalle,** Hans-Thomas-Str. 2, and **Kunsthalle Orangerie,** Hans-Thomas-Str. 6, two top-notch art museums (tel. 926 33 55; fax 26 67 88). *(Both open Tu-F 10am-5pm, Sa-Su 10am-6pm. DM8, students DM5.)* European masterpieces from the 15th to the 19th centuries adorn the Kunsthalle—don't miss Grünewald's *Crucifixion*—while the Orangerie contains a smaller collection of modern art. In May-July 1999 the Kunsthalle's special exhibit will feature illustrations of German fairytales. The **Kunstverein,** Waldstr. 3, exhibits a smaller, more modern collection and an artsy cafe. *(Open Tu and Th-Su 10am-5pm, W 10am-7pm. DM4, students DM2.)*

Occupying the upper floors of a former mansion, the recently renovated **Prinz Max Palais** museum, Karlstr. 10 (tel. 133 44 01 or 133 42 30), has a local history display that includes the purported **first bicycle in the world** and bathrooms coolly lit by black lights. Check with the tourist office for current exhibits. *(Open Tu and Th-Su 10am-5pm, W 11am-8pm. DM5, students DM3.50.)* The quirkiest of Karlsruhe's museums is indisputably the **Oberrheinisches Dichtermuseum** (Upper Rhine Poets' Museum; tel. 84 38 18), located in the same building and dedicated to lyrical legends such as von Scheffel, Hebel, and Flake. Flake? *(Open Tu and Th-F 11am-5pm, W 11am-9pm. Free.)* More accessible is Karlsruhe's **Zoo,** in the *Stadtgarten* across the street from the train station. *(Open daily 8am-6:30pm. DM5, students DM4.)* Catch a free glimpse of llamas, goats, and elephants during feeding times (10:30am and 3pm). Between the zoo and the *Schloß* and flanked on the west by the **vigorous shopping district** stretches the placid **Marktplatz.** To one side stands the rose-colored **Rathaus;** to the other, the imposing columns of the **Stadtkirche.** The red sandstone pyramid in the center of the Marktplatz is the symbol of the city and Karl's final resting place.

The visually unremarkable **Bundesverfassungsgericht** (Federal Constitutional Court) stands next to the *Schloß.* It may be ugly, but give it some respect: it houses Germany's strongest legal safeguard against the return of totalitarian rule. Near Friedrichsplatz, the **Bundesgerichtshof** (Federal Supreme Court) is pumped with a formidable security apparatus. Germany's most sensational postwar criminal trials were held here, including those of the infamous Baader-Meinhof terrorist gang.

Perhaps to balance all this heavy-duty legal responsibility, Karlsruhe parties hard, with a number of huge cultural festivals. Every year in mid- to late-February, Karlsruhe hosts the **Händel-Festspiele,** a 10-day series of concerts of Händel's works. The appetizing **Brigande-Feschd** takes place in late May and brings with it a huge display of dishes from local specialty restaurants. And in early September, cyclists burn their calves on their way through Karlsruhe in the annual **Breitling Cup,** the **World Cup for team cycling.** Of course, the local breweries always play an essential role in the reveling **Unifest** (known as *Das Fest*) in late July. The 10-day orgy of live music, food stands, and roaming students clutching mugs of beer takes place at the end of Günther-Klatz-Anlage and is the **biggest free open-air concert in Germany.**

▓ Baden-Baden

You don't have to be fabulously wealthy to have a good time in Baden-Baden, but it sure helps. In its 19th-century heyday, Baden-Baden's guest list read like a *Who's Who* of European aristocracy. Although its status has declined, this spa town on the northern fringes of the Schwarzwald remains primarily a playground for the well-to-do; minor royalty, *Wirtschaftswunderkinder,* and the like gather here year-round to bathe in the mineral spas and drop fat sums of money in the elegant casino. In fact, slightly scruffy backpackers often draw stares from the blazer-wearing wannabe aristocrats who strut from one exclusive shop to another. Still, the *hochnäsig* (high-nosed) atmosphere is worth tolerating—if only for the chance to experience the incredible baths and soak in the chic downtown area.

ORIENTATION AND PRACTICAL INFORMATION Baden-Baden's **train station** is inconveniently located 7km from town. If you're not up for the 90-minute walk along the park path, take bus #201 (direction: "Lichtental/Oberbeuren") to "Augustaplatz" (one-way DM3; 24hr. pass DM8; 4-trips DM9.60). **TaxiFunk** (tel. 621 10) provides taxi service. Even bourgeoisie need the funk. A branch of the **tourist office** is located at the city entrance at Schwarzwaldstr. 52, a few blocks from the train station toward town. The main office, however, is at Augustapl. 8 (tel. 27 52 00; fax 27 52 02), in the painfully postmodern building next to the Kongresshaus. For uncomfortable prices, they offer maps (DM6), city guides (up to DM24!), and a hotel list. (Open daily 9:30am-6pm.) Check your **email** right next door at the **Medici Cafe** (tel. 20 06; open until 1am). The **main post office,** 76486 Baden-Baden, is located in the Wagener department store in the pedestrian zone below the *Rathaus.* It also **exchanges money** (open M-F 9am-7pm, Sa 9am-4pm). The **telephone code** is 07221.

ACCOMMODATIONS AND FOOD The cheapest bed in town is at the modern, five-floor **Jugendherberge (HI),** Hardbergstr. 34 (tel. 522 23; fax 600 12), halfway between the station and the town center. Take bus #201, 205, or 216 to "Grosse-Dollen-Str." (6th stop) and follow the signs uphill. A peaceful climb, indeed; travelers are rewarded the next morning by the luscious breakfast buffet. The hostel's strange lack of showers is perhaps explained by the overabundance of bathing facilities in town and the large public swimming pool next door (see **Sights and Spas,** below). (DM23, over 26 DM28. Members only. Sheets DM6. Reception 5-11pm. Curfew 11:30pm. Wheelchair accessible. Call ahead.) Rooms in the center of the town are, as expected, ritzy and expensive, with a few exceptions. **Hotel am Markt,** Marktplatz 18 (tel. 270 40; fax 27 04 44), is next to the Friedrichsbad and the Stiftskirche. Smack in the middle of the pedestrian zone, it has lovely views of the city and a restaurant downstairs for guests. (Singles DM52-55, with shower DM75-90; doubles DM95-105, DM125-140. Breakfast included. Dinner DM8-15. Reception 7am-10pm. Restaurant open for guests only 6-9pm.) The unassuming **Hotel Löhr,** Adlerstr. 2 (tel. 30 09 60; fax 39 28 09), has its reception a block and a half away at **Café Löhr,** Lichtentalerstr. 19, across the street and back toward the *Bahnhof* from the "Augustaplatz" bus stop. The rooms are spotless but small. (Singles DM40-60; doubles DM80-110.)

Most restaurant prices in Baden-Baden aren't compatible with budget travel, but **daily specials** often run under DM12. **Pizzeria Roma,** Gernsbacherstr. 14, offers affordable pasta (DM10-15) in a prime location below the *Rathaus*. Pizza pizza. Another option is to fill up a picnic basket at a supermarket. **Pfannkucht,** at Augustaplatz (open M-F 8:30am-7pm, Sa 8am-1pm); or **Pennymarkt,** at the Grosse-Dollen-Str. bus stop near the hostel (open M-W 8:30am-6:30pm, Th-F 8:30am-7pm, Sa 8:30am-2pm). While **nightlife** in Baden-Baden is designed for the rich, there's nothing morally offensive about hanging out at **Leo's** (tel. 380 81), on Leopoldplatz, a loud, young bar that keeps it movin' and groovin' until 2am. They've got live music occasionally, and breakfast (DM3-15) is served all day. Also popular are the pricier **Amadeus Bistroant** across Leopoldplatz and the mellower **Le Bistro** closer to the casino with its own strawberry menu. *Schicki-micki?* Never. If you're in search of young, rich, available Europeans, look no farther than **Griffin's** (tel. 296 66), in the basement of the *Kurhaus* under the casino, which sports interesting Americana decor in a clashing interior. There's no cover on Sunday, and Friday or Saturday until 11pm. After that it's DM10. Hipsters don't arrive until 1am. (Drinks from DM5. Open F-Su 10pm-5am.)

SIGHTS AND SPAS Baden-Baden's history as a resort goes back nearly two millennia, to the time when the Romans started soaking themselves in the first **thermal baths** here. Early attempts at hedonism are visible behind a glass wall, in the parking garage underneath the Friedrichsbad. The **Friedrichsbad,** Römerpl. 1 (tel. 27 59 20), is a beautiful 19th-century bathing palace where visitors are parched, steamed, soaked, scrubbed, doused, and pummeled by trained professionals for three hours. It's a marvelous experience, and not a stitch of clothing is permitted. *(Open M-Sa 9am-10pm, Su noon-8pm. Last entry 3hr. before closing. Baths are co-ed Tu and F 4-10pm, all day W, Sa, and Su. Standard Roman-Irish Bath DM36, with soap and brush massage DM48. DM6 discount with hotel coupon. Credit cards accepted, of course.)* More modest or budget-minded cure-seekers should try next door at the also astounding **Caracalla-Thermen,** Römerpl. 11 (tel. 27 59 40), which is cheaper and more public and allows bathing suits, except in the saunas upstairs. *(Open daily 8am-10pm. July-Sept. 3hr. DM19, 4hr. DM25, 5hr. DM29. Oct.-June 1hr. less for the same price. Discount with hotel or hostel coupon.)* Indoor and outdoor pools, whirlpools, and solariums of varying sizes and temperatures allow the weary traveler to be pampered at a very reasonable price. Whichever bath you choose, the experience will be unforgettable. The large public **swimming pool** next to the hostel has a curvy slide and is the cheapest way to take to the waters in Baden-Baden. *(Open 10am-8pm in good weather, last entry 7pm. DM4.50, students DM3; after 5:30pm DM3, students DM2. Hot shower DM1, deck chair DM4.50.)*

When they're not busy pruning themselves at the baths, Baden-Baden's affluent guests head to the **oldest casino in Germany** (tel. 212 60), which, according to Marlene Dietrich, is also the "most beautiful casino in the world." *(Open Su-Th 2pm-2am, F-*

Sa 2pm-3am. DM5.) Modeled after the palace at Versailles, this place prompts oohs and aahs from even the most well-traveled aristocrat. (Tours Apr.-Sept. 9:30am-noon, Oct.-Mar. 10am-noon. Last tour leaves at 11:45am. English language tours by special arrangement. DM6.) In earlier days, neither students nor bank workers were allowed into the casino. These rules no longer apply, but a slew of others still do: in order to gamble here, you must be 21, and you must wear appropriate dress—coat and tie for men, dress or suit for women. The minimum bet is DM5, maximum bet DM20,000. No dress code is required for the **slot machine wing,** located in the Alter Bahnhof on Langestr. (Open Su-Th 2pm-midnight, F-Sa 2pm-1am. DM2.) Next to the casino is the massive Neoclassical **Trinkhalle** (Pump Room), which contains a gold-plated fountain, a huge souvenir shop, and a gallery of murals immortalizing local folktales. (Open daily 10am-6pm. Free.) The free *Heilwasser* (healing water) tastes like it's good for you: warm and saline. Bring it on. A few blocks in the opposite direction, down the paths of the verdant **Lichtentaler Allee,** the **Kunsthalle** (tel. 232 50) houses visiting exhibits of modern art. (Open Tu 1-6pm, W-Th 11am-8pm, F-Su 11am-6pm. Admission varies, but usually DM8, students DM4.) In an attempt to reaffirm its name as a sophisticated city of High *Kultur,* Baden-Baden just last year inaugurated its much-touted **Festspielhaus** on Langestr. near the *Alter Bahnhof* (old train station). One of the largest festival halls in Europe, it hosted Baden-Baden's first ever **Internationale Festspiele** in 1998, a glitzy parade of musical and cultural celebrities, among them the Hasselhoffish David Copperfield. For more information on upcoming events, call 27 53 33.

To rise above it all, escape to the nearby hills. The **Schwarzwaldhochstraße** (see p. 461) begins in Baden-Baden, but the best place for immediate hiking is at the 68m **Merkur** peak east of town. Take bus #204 or 205 from Leopoldplatz to "Merkurwald," then ride the *Bergbahn* to the top, where a slew of trails plunge into the Schwarzwald. (Bergbahn runs daily 10am-10pm, every 15min. DM7 round-trip, DM4 one-way.) The *Bergbahn* station at the bottom is also crossed by the **Panoramaweg.** Marked by easy-to-spot white signs with a green circle, the Panoramaweg connects the best look-out points near Baden-Baden. You don't have to hike the whole thing, of course: pick up a Panoramaweg map at the tourist office (DM3).

More accessible, via the steep stairs from the pedestrian zone, is the ivy-covered **Neues Schloß,** occupied by a museum of the town's history. (Open Tu-Su 10am-12:30pm and 2-5pm. Tours M-F 3pm. DM2, students DM1.) Baden-Baden lies at your feet from the neighboring garden. The view from the 12th-century **Altes Schloß** (tel. 269 48), however, extends all the way to France. (Open Tu-Su 10am-10pm. Free.) Its magestic ruins, the *Ruine Hohenbaden,* are a long and baffling mile hike behind the Neues Schloß. Prepare to venture cluelessly through the Schwarzwald hills. (In general, follow signs that point to "Kellerskreuz" and, of course, "Altes Schloß"). The view is undeniably worth it. If you want to wait, bus #15 makes two loops on Sundays and holidays at 1:15pm and 4:15pm between Augustaplatz and the *Schloß.*

■ Freiburg im Breisgau

When German Luftwaffe pilots mistakenly bombed their own city of Freiburg in May 1940, it was not that difficult to see why. Freiburg, tucked in the far southwest corner of Germany, enjoys a persistent Austro-French influence, which has helped its genial, humor-loving citizens to escape the dour German stereotype. Similarly, this "metropolis" of the Schwarzwald has yet to succumb to the hectic rhythms of city life. The surrounding hills brim with greenery and fantastic hiking trails, paths link the medieval Schwabentor directly to the entire German trail network, and all traces of urbanity dissolve into serene countryside a few kilometers from the city center. The relaxing atmosphere is correspondingly crunchy, with many student-populated cafes and used CD stores scattered throughout cobblestone streets filled with Birkenstocked bicyclists.

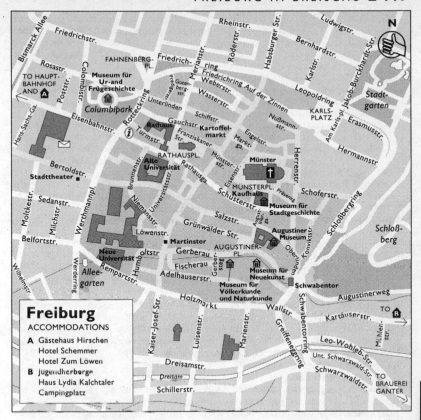

Freiburg
ACCOMMODATIONS

A Gästehaus Hirschen
  Hotel Schemmer
  Hotel Zum Löwen
B Jugendherberge
  Haus Lydia Kalchtaler
  Campingplatz

ORIENTATION AND PRACTICAL INFORMATION

Most of the city's sights and restaurants lie within walking distance from one another in the *Altstadt*, a 15-minute walk from the main train station, which, unfortunately, is under massive reconstruction for the next few years. A dinky *Hauptbahnhof* does the job, temporarily.

Trains: To Karlsruhe (1hr., 2 per hr.) and Basel, Switzerland (45min., 1-2 per hr.). Local trains and buses leave regularly for scattered Schwarzwald towns.

Public Transportation: Single fares on Freiburg's many bus and streetcar lines are DM3.30, 24hr. adult ticket DM8, 2 adults DM10. Get the scoop on regional travel at **PlusPunkt,** Salzstr. 3 (tel. 451 15 00), in the *Altstadt*, which serves your every transportation need. Open M-F 8am-7pm, Sa 8am-2pm. Another branch is below the *Straßenbahn* platform at the station. Most public transportation stops running around 12:30am, but a system of Nachtbusse (named after the planets) covers most major stops throughout the wee hours (DM7 per ride; DM4 with Day-Card).

Taxis: tel. 444 44. Four you.

Mitfahrzentrale: Belfortstr. 55 (tel. 194 44), south of the station, just off Schnewlingstr. You're going to vacation in Germany without riding on the *Autobahn?* No, no. Get a chauffeur. Paris DM46, Zurich DM17, Munich DM38. Open M-F 9am-7pm, Sa 9am-1pm, Su 10am-1pm.

Bike Rental: Velo Doctor, Eschholzstr. 64 (tel. 27 64 77), DM15 per day, DM25 per weekend, DM48 per week. Open M-F 9am-7pm, Sa 9am-2pm.

Hitchhiking: *Let's Go* does not recommend hitchhiking as a safe means of transportation. Hitchers take public transit to departure points. **North:** S-Bahn #5 (direction: "Zähringen") to "Reutebachgasse" and walk back 50m. **West:** S-Bahn #1 to "Padua-Allee," then bus #31 or 32 to "Hauptstr." **East:** S-Bahn #1 (direction: "Littenweiler") to "Lassbergstr.," then bus #18 (direction: "Langmatten") to "Strombad."

Tourist Office: Rotteckring 14 (tel. 388 18 82; fax 388 18 87), 2 blocks down Eisenbahnstr. from the station. Staff finds rooms for DM5, and has free maps, but prefers to sell the comprehensive *Freiburg Official Guide* (in German or English) for DM6 or a small guide for DM1. The entire desk on the left side of the office is devoted to the Schwarzwald: hiking maps, flashy color brochures, and an amazing trilingual regional expert. 24hr. automated displays in front of the office and the train station can help you find accommodations if the staff is too busy (which it often is). Open June-Sept. M-F 9:30am-9pm, Sa 9:30am-5pm, Su 10am-noon; Oct.-May M-F 9:30am-6pm, Sa 9:30am-2pm, Su 10am-noon.

Currency Exchange: The closest to the main train station is now the Volksbank across the street and to the right. Open M-F 9am-6:30pm and Sa 9:30am-2pm. There is also a 24hr. automated currency exchange machine.

American Express: Located inside the tourist office (tel. 224 46; fax 241 40), it offers money transfers, emergency cash checking, held mail, and currency exchange, all for a DM1-5 fee. Open M-W 10am-1pm and 1:30-6pm, Th-F 10am-1pm and 1:30pm-7pm, Sa 10am-2pm.

Bookstore: Walthari, Bertoldstr. 28 (tel. 38 77 70). A fairly large collection of English-language paperbacks. Carries guides to the Schwarzwald region. Yay! Open M-F 9:30am-7pm, Sa 9am-4pm.

Laundromat: Café Fleck, Predigerstr. 3 (tel. 268 29). Laundro-cafe—the truly efficient get a sandwich while they wash. Wash DM7, soap included. Dry DM1 per 10min. Laundromat open M-Sa 7am-1am. Cafe open M-F 7am-6:30pm, Sa 7am-5pm. S-Bahn #5 or 6 (direction: "Reutenbachg.") to "Siegesdenkmal."

Emergency: Police, tel. 110. **Fire and Ambulance,** tel. 112.

Rape Crisis Hotline: tel. 333 39.

Gay Hotline: Rosa Hilfe, tel. 251 61.

Internet Access: WebSPIDERcafe, Molketstr. 28 (tel. 292 37 45). DM10 per hr.; send and receive faxes. Open M-F 10am-8pm, Sa 10am-4pm.

Post Office: Eisenbahnstr. 60, 79098 Freiburg, 1 block straight ahead of the train station. Open M-F 8:30am-6:30pm, Sa 8:30am-2pm.

Telephone Code: 0761

ACCOMMODATIONS AND CAMPING

Most of Freiburg's hotels and *Pensionen* are expensive and are often located outside of the city center. The tourist office books cheaper rooms (DM25-45 for singles; DM45-80 for doubles) in private homes, but a stay of at least three nights is usually required. Unfortunately, Freiburg's youth hostel is large, nondescript, and far from the *Altstadt.* If your accommodation is far away, purchasing the 24-hour ticket for buses and streetcars will ultimately save money (see **Public Transportation,** above).

Jugendherberge (HI), Kartäuserstr. 151 (tel. 676 56; fax 603 67). S-Bahn #1 (direction: "Littenweiler") to "Römerhof," cross the tracks and backtrack 20m, then walk down Fritz-Geiges-Str., cross the stream, and follow the footpath to the right. Rampant schoolchildren sleep in packed rooms amidst bright colors and trees. Feels more like a dorm than most hostels. DM23, over 26 DM28. Sheets DM6. *Gästehaus* DM37, sheets included. Members only. Reception 7am-11:30pm. Curfew 11:30pm.

🏵️**Haus Lydia Kalchtaler,** Peterhof 11 (tel. 671 19). S-Bahn #1 (direction: "Littenweiler") to "Lassbergstr.," then bus #17 (direction: "Kappel") to "Kleintalstr." Turn around and follow Peterhof up and to the left to the large wooden farmhouse with the water trough in front. Operated by the tireless and loquacious Lydia Kalchtaler, this *Pension* is a rest from institutional living at an unbeatable price. A rustic, idyllic atmosphere and usable **kitchen** are definitely worth the 30min. commute to the town center. DM15-21 per person.

⊛**Hotel Zum Löwen,** Breisgauer Str. 62 (tel. 80 97 220; fax 840 23), up the street from Gästehaus Hirschen (see below). An *awesome* deal. Friendly management and large sunny rooms, some with TV. Pretend you're in California with the marble floors and white stucco walls—it sure don't feel like budget travel. A brand-spanking new wing has just been added. Enter in the parking lot; the front door of the building is also labeled "Löwen" but leads into a more expensive place. Singles DM45, with shower DM60; doubles DM80, DM100-130. Breakfast included.

Gästehaus Hirschen, Breisgauer Str. 47 (tel. 821 18). S-Bahn #1 to "Padua-Allee," backtrack 30m along the tracks, and walk down Breisgauer Str. for 5min. Be careful: this *Gästehaus* is on the other side of town from the hotel of the same name; also, it isn't the same as Hirschengarten-Hotel, which is right next door. Old house in a quiet farm neighborhood with rooms as cozy as the exterior would lead you to believe. Spotless pink tile bathroom. Singles DM40, with shower DM56; doubles DM70, DM90; triples DM110. Reception M-W and F-Su.

Hotel Schemmer, Eschholzstr. 63 (tel. 27 24 24; fax 220 10). From the train station, take the overpass that crosses the tracks, then go past the church and turn left. Friendly management and superb location. Looks like grandpa's den circa 1965 in bright blue and orange. Singles DM55, with bath DM65; doubles DM85, DM95. Breakfast included.

Pension Gisela, Am Vogelbach 27 (tel. 824 72; fax 811 52). Bus #10 (direction: "Padua-Allee") to "Hofackerstr.," then double back 1 block and turn left, walk 250m, and turn right on Hasenweg before the train tracks. The tacky Schwarzwald-themed mural on the outside wall conceals large, hotel-quality rooms in a quiet residential neighborhood. Singles DM48-55; doubles DM85-105. Breakfast included. Apartments available for longer-term guests.

Camping: Hirzberg, Kartauserstr. 99 (tel. 350 54; fax 28 92 12), has sparkling new camping facilities and is only 20min. from the *Altstadt* by foot. Endlessly helpful English-speaking staff. S-Bahn #1 to "Stadthalle," then cross the street to the left via the underpass and walk straight (north) on Hirzbergstr. Cross the river at Max-Miller-Steg, keep going till you reach the busy street, then go 30m to the left. Near a quiet residential area. DM8 per person, DM5 per child. DM5-7 per tent. Summer tent rentals DM10-15 per day. Bikes DM15 per day. Laundry DM5. Reception 9am-10pm. **Mosle Park,** Waldeseestr. 77 (tel. 729 38; fax 775 78). S-Bahn #1 to "Hasemannstr.," then a 15min. walk, as follows: backtrack to Jahnstr. and then turn left. Follow Jahnstr. until it ends, then go left on Hammerschmiedstr. Follow that, cross the train tracks, then turn right on Littenweilerstr. Beautiful forested location, ideally situated for hiking. DM8 per person; DM5 per child. DM4 per tent. DM9 per car. Laundry facilities available: wash and dry DM13. Reception 8am-noon and 3-10pm. Open Apr.-Oct.

FOOD

In the early 15th century, the humanist Dietrich von Nieheim noted admiringly that in Freiburg "the supply of victuals is good and readily available." With more than 23,000 university students to feed, Freiburg's budget eateries carry on the fine tradition. During the daytime, the **Freiburger Markthalle** (tel. 38 11 11), next to the Martinstor, is home to food stands serving ethnic specialties for under DM15 (open M-F 7am-5pm, Sa 9am-2pm). At the open-air market on Münsterplatz, you can find everything from fresh radishes to folks who'll scratch your name onto a grain of rice (open M-Sa 7am-1pm). You can get your groceries at the **Edeka ActivMarkt,** Eisenbahnstr. 39, across from the post office (open M-F 8am-8pm, Sa 8am-4pm).

Mensa: Two university *Mensen*—the blue-trimmed building on **Rempartstraße** in the *Altstadt* (serves only lunch) and **Hebelstraße** on the main campus north of the city center (lunch and dinner). It's true you need a Freiburg student ID to buy *Menukarten* (5 for DM19.50; each gets you a hot meal) and *Eintopfkarten* (5 for DM13.50; each gets you a bowl of stew or fries), but local students are willing to help out. One flavor fits all. Rempartstr. location open M-F 11:30am-2pm, Sa 11:30am-1:30pm. Hebelstr. location open M-F 11am-2pm and 5:30-7:30pm.

⊕**Brennessel,** Eschholzstr. 17 (tel. 28 11 87). A plucky student tavern that fills the student gullet without emptying the student wallet. Funk and jazz abound. Don't miss spaghetti bolognese at DM3.50 from 6-8pm, or *Pfannkuchen* at DM5. Open M-Sa 6pm-1am, Su from 5pm. Kitchen open until 12:30am.

Milano, Schusterstr. 7 (tel. 337 35), with its salmon-leather interior and prime location, feels more high-brow than the prices might indicate. Pizza (DM7-18) and pasta (DM7.50-15.50). Try the pasta marinara...mmm. Only a block from the Münsterplatz. Service with Italian flair. Open daily 11am-midnight.

Freiburger Salatstuben, Löwenstr. 1 (tel. 351 55), near Martinstor. A health-food haven with an array of imaginatively smart salads belies the absence of vegetarian pretension (100g DM2.20). Even the desserts (DM4-5) are smart. Open M-F 11am-8pm, Sa 11am-4pm, 1st Saturday of the month 11am-6pm.

Hausbrauerei Feierling, Gerberau 46 (tel. 266 78). 2 gleaming copper vats form the centerpiece of this airy Freiburg institution. Across the way, the *Biergarten* sports thick-shade chestnut trees. Excellent beer (*Inselhof* DM5.80 for 0.5L) and traditional German fare (DM10-26). Open Su-F 11am-midnight, Sa 11am-1am. Kitchen noon-2pm and 6-10pm.

Papalapub, Moltkestr. 30. Near the *Stadttheater.* A place to be for the ever-alternative students of Freiburg. Beer (of course), rock 'n' roll on the radio, and the rise and fall of conversation accompany the excellent pastas and pizzas (DM6-10). Open M-Sa noon-1am, Su 10am-1am.

SIGHTS

Freiburg's pride and joy is its majestic **Münster,** which towers 116m above camera-wielding hordes of tourists. *(Open M-Sa 10am-6pm, Su 1-6pm. Tower open M-F 9:30am-5pm, Su 1-5pm; Nov.-Apr. Tu-Sa 9:30am-5pm, Su 1-5pm. DM2, students DM1. Free summer organ concerts Tu at 8:15pm. Call 20 27 90 for more info.)* With sections constructed between the 13th and 16th centuries, this architectural melange immortalizes in stained glass the different medieval guilds that financed its own construction. Stumble up more than 300 steps to ascend the tower, from which you can watch the **oldest bell in Germany** (her name's Hosanna) and 26 others swing into motion. (Protect your eardrums when the hour strikes.) A breathtaking, 360-degree panorama of the city awaits as well. "One cannot conceive of a more beautiful view than the blue heaven peeking through the thousand openings of this cupola." So said philosopher Wilhelm von Humboldt after the harrowingly claustrophobic climb upwards.

What buildings the errant *Luftwaffe* bombers didn't hit, the Allies decisively finished off one night in 1944, obliterating most of the old city. Since then, the citizens of Freiburg have painstakingly recreated the city's architecture and public spaces. On the south side of Münsterplatz wobbles the pink-tinted **Kaufhaus,** a merchants' hall dating from the 1500s. Two medieval gates—the **Schwabentor** and the **Martinstor**—stand within blocks of each other in the southeast corner of the *Altstadt.* The Martinstor, which served as a revolutionary barricade in the politically tumultuous year of 1848, has since been indelibly profaned by a set of golden arches (boo Ronald!).

From the Schwabentor, you can take the pedestrian overpass across the heavily trafficked Schloßbergring and climb up the glorified **Schloßberg** (castle mountain) for a superb view of the city. From there, a number of hiking trails explore the forested hills. Try the Langbuckweg or its alternate, the Waldfahrtstr.-Hirzberg-St. Ottilien trail. Tucked away in the blocks between the *Münster* and the tourist office is the **Rathaus,** an amalgam of older buildings whose bells chime daily at noon, and the oddly named **Haus zum Walfisch** (House of the Whale), where Erasmus of Rotterdam lived in exile from Basel for two years following the Reformation. This gold-trimmed wonder is a careful recreation of the original, which was destroyed in WWII.

Freiburg's museum circuit is limited but diverse. The **Augustiner Museum,** Salzstr. 32 (tel. 201 25 31), Am Augustinerplatz, housed in a former monastery two blocks south of the *Münster,* has lots of medieval religious artwork, and—better yet—heartwarming artistic depictions of Schwarzwald life. Included is admission to the **Wentzingerhaus Museum für Stadtgeschichte** (tel. 201 25 15), on Münsterplatz, which displays paraphernalia related to Freiburg's colorful history. *(Both open Tu-Su 10am-*

5pm. DM4, students DM2; free 1st Sunday of every month.) Farther south is the **Museum für Neuekunst** (Museum of Modern Art), Marienstr. 10a (tel. 201 25 81), which displays the works of 20th-century German artists such as Otto Dix in a clean-lined, modern building. *(Open Tu-Su 10am-5pm; tours Sa 3pm and Su 11am. Free.)* Borrow the extremely helpful English language guide for an enlightening lesson on the development of modern German art. Along Eisenbahnstr. between the station and the tourist office stands an immaculate, early Victorian *Schloß* atop a hill of vineyards and wildflowers; the **Museum für Ur- und Frühgeschichte** (tel. 201 25 71) is inside. *(Open Tu-Su 10am-5pm. Technically free, but DM3.50 donation requested, students DM2.)* Lots of ancient, crumbling odds and ends focus on the fascinating prehistory of the South Baden region. At Geberau 32, the **Adelhausermuseum Naturkunde und Völkerkunde** (tel. 201 25 66) satisfies dinosaur and other fixations, respectively. *(Open Tu-Su 10am-5pm. Free, but special exhibits often DM5, students DM3.)* Look for the 1999 exhibit on Tibetan art. Conveniently located at the same-name stop of streetcar #1, **Brauerei Ganter**, Schwarzwaldstr. 43 (tel. 218 51 81), conducts tours tracking the production process of the malt beverage. The grand finale of the one-hour tour consists of a portion of *Fleisch-Käse*, bread, potato salad, and **lots of beer** atop one of the factory buildings. The view of the factory, the food finale, and the beer bash are all free (hint, hint). Call the above phone number ahead of time to get in on the group tours (Tu and Th 1:30pm). Unique to Freiburg is a system of narrow streams—known as **Bächle**—that run through the city. During medieval times, these swift-flowing gutters served as open-air sewers. Today they are the bane of any tourist studying his map *too* hard. But there are compensations for sudden footwear; legend has it that any visitor whose feet are wetted by them will one day marry a resident of Freiburg.

ENTERTAINMENT AND NIGHTLIFE

Freiburg proclaims itself to be a city of wine and music. True to its word, it is awash with *Weinstuben* and *Kneipen*, though club offerings are less abundant. For the current events in town, pick up a free copy of *Freiburg Aktuell* (DM5.50) at the tourist office or drop by the *Badische Zeitung* office (tel. 49 6467) at Martinstor, where you can buy tickets for upcoming shin-digs. (Open M-Th 9am-5:30pm, F 9am-4:30pm, Sa 9am-1pm.) The **Freiburger Weinfest** is a weekend-long festival held on Münsterplatz in late June or early July. You can stagger around and sample some 300 different vintages (DM3-6 per glass) while a swing band plays. The annual three-week **Zeltmusikfestival** (Tent Music Festival), held in July, brings big-name classical, rock, and jazz performers to two circus tents pitched at the city's edge. Tickets (DM15-40) sell surprisingly fast and can be bought by calling 50 40 30 or at the *Badische Zeitung* office. Check out http://www.zmf.de, though publicity is enormous. Take S-Bahn #5 to "Bisserstr." and catch the free shuttle bus to the site. In addition, the **Narrenfest** (Fools' Festival) is held the weekend before Ash Wednesday, and the **Weihnachtsmarkt** (Christmas Market) runs from late November until just a few days before Christmas.

Freiburg's nightlife keeps pace with the city's students—afternoon cafes transform into pubs and discos at night. The streets around the university (Niemenstr., Löwenstr., Humboldtstr., and the accompanying alleyways) form the hub of the city's scene. Here, around the Martinstor, pubs and clubs keep things thumping until morning.

zum Schlappen, Löwenstr. 2 (tel. 334 94), near Martinstor. Serious beer drinkers head here. For DM15 you can flex your mettle by polishing off the 2L *Stiefel*, a fearsome vessel known to English-speakers as "The Boot" (DM23-32). Lots of posters, rather on the alternative side. Pizza DM6-10. Pasta DM7-12. Open M-Th 11:30am-1am, F-Sa 11:30am-2am, Su 3pm-1am.

Jazzhaus, Schnewlingstr. 1 (tel. 349 73), across from the *Bahnhof* and to the right. This spacious underground grotto, featuring live performance almost every night, has become a mainstay of the Freiburg cultural scene. Cover under DM10 for small acts, DM10-25 for more well-known performers. Open Su-Th 8pm-2am, F-Sa 8pm-3am. Call for tickets or show up after 6pm.

Dampfross, Löwenstr. 7 (tel. 259 39). Tiny student bar, with dark wood and American movie posters. *Pils* DM3.60 for 0.3L. Salads and pasta DM7-13. The most popular dish is *Pommes mit Kräutercreme* (fries with herb cream; DM5.50). Divine. Connected through the back door to the cafe **Savo,** Löwenstr. 3-5 (same tel.), which plays stylish and mod to Dampfross's earthy and traditional. Drinks and food a bit more upscale. More room, too. Both open M-F 10am-2am, Sa from 11am, Su 5pm-1am. Food until 11pm, F and Sa until midnight.

⊗**Cafe Atlantik,** Schwabentorring 7 (tel. 330 33). Spacious pub that grooves to American alternative tunes, amidst pinball machines and Christmas lights. Daily happy "hour" noon-8pm. Packed in the winter, when the beer gardens close and live music acts abound. Cover DM15-25 for live music. No cover otherwise. Cheap spaghetti DM5-8.50. Guinness on tap. Open daily noon-1am.

Agar, Löwenstr. 8 (tel. 38 06 50), next to Martinstor. Get down with Flower Power and the 80s. Tuesday is student night—free with student ID. Lots of attitude. See or be seen, pick up or be picked up. Open Su, Tu, and Th 10pm-2:30am, F-Sa 10pm-4am. Last entry 2hr. before closing.

Greiffenegg-Schlößle, Schloßbergring 3 (tel. 327 28). Drink, eat, and look down over Freiburg from a terrace above the city. This mellow, chatty restaurant boasts a faaabulous view. Seats 800 and fills up when the weather cooperates. Beer DM5-7. Half-price salad buffet, happy hour on weekdays 11am-1pm. Entrance through the Schwabentor. Open year-round daily 11am-midnight.

■ Near Freiburg: Breisach and the Kaiserstuhl

The town of Breisach am Rhein is so close to France, one could practically spit across the border, given a good set of mouth muscles. The one thing that might get in the way is the wide Rhine River, which separates the French province of Alsace from the German Schwarzwald, 30km west of Freiburg. Breisach's exquisite location comes replete with a beautiful *Altstadt* surrounded by unending hills of vineyards. But the town's most prominent landmark (and its best spitting place for French-directed frustrations) is the **Cathedral of St. Stephen,** which dramatically crowns a steep riverfront promontory crowded with clapboard houses. For its imposing setting, however, this is a rather modest *Münster,* both inside and out. The 12th-century building is almost minimalist compared to the Gothic decoration and Baroque absurdity of other nearby German cathedrals. Only the writhing, twisting wooden altar, the work of the mysterious 16th-century artist known only as Master H.L., comes close to this typical extravagance. From the church's promenade, the view stretches east and south to the rolling hills of the Schwarzwald and westward into France. Be sure to view this at night as well, when the sleepy Rhine breathes tranquility betwixt both French and German borderlands.

Continuing northward along Radbrunnenallee, the walled hilltop fortress boasts well-preserved medieval gates and excellent views of the countryside, culminating in the garden atop the **Schloßberg.** Every summer, this garden becomes a theater for the annual **Festspiele Breisach.** Every last weekend in August, Breisach also witnesses the **Bezirksweinfest,** where local wines are sampled, sprayed, and supped on the banks of the Rhine. Close by, in the 17th-century Rheintor, the **Museum für Stadtgeschichte,** Rheintorpl. 1 (tel. 832 65), contains a large collection of city artifacts, including 3000-year-old ceramics and chain-link undergarments from the 15th century—kinky stuff (open Tu-F 2-5pm, Sa 11:30am-5pm, Su 11:30am-6pm; free).

Connoisseurs should register for a tour of the largest wine cellar in Germany, **Badischer Winzerkeller** (tel. 90 00); English speakers should call the tourist office in advance (3-7 samples DM5-9.50). It's a 1km walk east of town. Go right from the train station on Bahnhofstr. and keep truckin' on Im Gelbstein. Closer by is the **Graflich von Kageneck'sche Wein & Sektkellerei,** Kupfertorstr. 35 (tel. 90 11 37; fax 90 11 99), specializing in sparkling wine *(Sekt).* Buy yourself a crate (closed Su; call tourist office for tour times). Jaunts along the Rhine in big white ships are available through **Breisacher Fahrgastschiffahrt,** on the Marktplatz (tel. 94 20 20; fax 94 20 30). Two-hour joyrides are DM15, and the company also runs ships to Strasbourg and Basel that can be used for one-way travel when not fully booked.

Near Breisach is the **Kaiserstuhl,** a clump of lush green hills that were volcanoes in their heyday. Now they attract hikers and bikers who come to see the flora and fauna, many of which are normally found only in much warmer climes. The Freiburg-Breisach **train** stops at the towns of Ihringen and Wasenweiler, both located on the range's southern fringes. **Buses** handle the route straight into the hills; check the schedule at the Breisach *Hauptbahnhof.* **Rent bikes** at **Firma Schweizer,** Neutorstr. 31 (tel. 76 01), on the main pedestrian thoroughfare (DM15 per day; open M-F 9am-12:30pm and 2-6:30pm). Most famous of the Kaiserstuhl trails is the **Kaiserstuhl Nord-Südweg,** which braves the densely vegetated hills and valleys, forging 16km from Ihringen north to Endingen. From the Ihringen train station, walk straight down Eisenbahnstr. for 5 minutes; once past the church, turn right; the trail begins a block later at an alley on your left. The Nord-Südweg is marked by a blue diamond on a yellow field. Countless other trails depart in the same area. For hiking maps and suggestions, see the Breisach **tourist office** (tel. 94 01 55; fax 94 01 58), on the Marktplatz. They find rooms for a DM1 fee, and also offer guides to the nearby French towns of Colmar and Neuf-Breisach. From the train station, turn left onto Bahnhofstr. and continue going; keep the fountain with the huge spinning globe on your right, and go down Rheinstr. into the Marktplatz. (Open M-F 9am-1pm and 1:30-5pm, Sa 9:30am-noon.) The **post office** is one block from the train station (open M-F 8am-noon and 2:30-5:30pm, Sa 8:30am-noon). The **telephone code** is 07667.

Breisach's superb, modern **Jugendherberge,** Rheinuferstr. 12 (tel. 76 65; fax 18 47), boasts a stunning Rhine-front location. From the train station, take a left and then left again at the intersection. After 20m, take the path leading under the main road. Cross the bridge to turn right, then walk along the river. A hostel sign is on the left, facing away from you; turn left when you see it. (20min. DM23, over 26 DM28. Members only. Meals DM8.70. Sheets DM6. Reception 5-10pm. Curfew 11:30pm.) There is a **market** next door to the tourist office (open Sa 8am-noon). **Futterkrippe,** Rheinstr. 18 (tel. 86 82), offers greasy international food at affordable prices (daily specials DM4-8; open daily 9am-11pm).

SCHWARZWALD (BLACK FOREST)

It might be a bit of an overstatement to say that the Germans are obsessed with the dark, but from the earliest fairy tales to Franz Kafka's disturbing fiction, a sense of the uncanny and the sinister has long lurked in the German cultural consciousness. Nowhere is this collective dream of the dark more at home than in the Schwarzwald, a tangled expanse of evergreen covering the southwest corner of Baden-Württemberg. While the Schwarzwald owes its foreboding name to the eerie darkness that prevails under its canopy of vegetation, it is also the source of inspiration for the most quintessential German fairy tales, including the adventures of Hänsel and Gretel, as well as a slew of poetry and folk traditions. Many of these regional quirks are now exploited at the pervasive cuckoo clock-*Lederhosen-Bratwurst*-keychain-and-ice cream kiosks, which conspire, along with the devastating effects of acid rain, to erode the region's authenticity. The hordes of tourists are easily avoided, however, as innumerable trails wind through the region, leading willing hikers onto the dense forest in mere minutes. Skiing is also available in the area; the longest slope is at Feldberg (near Titisee), and smaller hills smatter the Schwarzwald Hochstraße.

The main entry points to the Schwarzwald are Freiburg, in the center; Baden-Baden to the northwest; Stuttgart to the east; and Basel, Switzerland, to the southwest. Most visitors cruise around in (or on) their own set of wheels, as public transportation is sparse. Rail lines encircle the perimeter, with only one main **train** actually penetrating the region (from Donaueschingen in the southeast to Offenburg in the northwest). The **bus** service is more thorough, albeit slow and less frequent. The best source of public transportation information is the **Südbaden public transport office** at the Freiburg *Hauptbahnhof* (a copy of the indispensable *Fahrplan* costs DM1). The **Freiburg tourist office** (see p. 449) is the best place to gather information about the Schwarzwald before your trip. The most scenic route through the Schwarzwald is the stretch from northern Waldkirch to southeastern Hinterzarten, where the vistas extend to the Alps in the south and the Rhine Valley in the west.

▓ Hochschwarzwald (High Black Forest)

Arguably the most enthralling neck of the woods, the Hochschwarzwald is so named for its high, rounded mountain tops, thickly carpeted with pines and towering dramatically above lonely lakes. The remote villages, isolated for centuries, are home to hospitable and traditional folk who will confound you with their dialect and impress you with their generosity. The best source of general information about the area is probably the **Freiburg tourist office,** Rotteckring 14 (tel. (0761) 368 90 90; fax 37 00 37). The tourist offices of all the individual towns also provide maps and information.

At 1493m, **Feldberg** is the Schwarzwald's highest mountain. The ski lift runs in summer and winter (round-trip DM5). Call or fax the **tourist office** (tel. (07655) 80 19; fax 801 43; http://www.feldberg-schwarzwald.de) for information about Feldberg and 16 other ski slopes in the area (open M-Tu and Th-F 10am-noon and 3-5pm, W 10am-noon). At 1234m above sea level, Feldberg's **Jugendherberge Hebelhof (HI)**, Passhöhe 14 (tel. (07676) 221; fax 12 32), may be the highest in Germany. Take the Titisee-Schluchsee train to Feldberg-Bärental, then the bus to the Hebelhof stop. (DM25.10, over 26 DM30.10. Members only. Reception 8am-10pm. Curfew 10:45pm. Make reservations for winter.) For a **ski report,** call (07676) 12 14.

■ Titisee and Schluchsee

For visual splendor in the Hochschwarzwald, the mountain lakes of Titisee and Schluchsee take the cake. The more touristed Titisee (say it: TEE-tee-zay) unfortunately finds itself mobbed by Germans on hot summer days. Consequently, the lakeside pedestrian zone has become a cheesy strip of souvenir shops and *Imbiß* stands, reachable from Freiburg by hourly trains. The 30-minute train ride chugs through the stunningly scenic Höllental (Hell's Valley). Keep your eyes peeled for the Hirschsprung, the regal statue of a stag that crowns the cliff in a harrowingly narrow part of the valley. According to legend, this was where a deer once narrowly escaped a hunter's arrow by making the impossible leap across the chasm. Today a well-placed cross stands atop the facing cliff.

Once in Titisee, the **tourist office,** Strandbadstr. 4 (tel. 980 40; fax 98 04 40; http://www.titisee.de), will satisfy your basic needs, booking rooms for a suggested DM3 fee, renting bikes at DM15 per day, and arranging horse and carriage rides (1½hr. trip DM80). For DM1-15 they also dispense maps of the 130km of nearby hiking trails. It's in the *Kurhaus;* hang a right from the train station and continue walking in that general direction without turning onto the pedestrian zone. (Open May-Oct. M-F 8am-5:30pm, Sa 10am-noon and 3-5pm, Su 10am-noon; Nov.-Apr. M-F 8am-noon and 1:30-5:30pm.) A hiking trail sign stands in front of the *Kurhaus*. Consider the easy and scenic *Seeweg,* or keep going along Strandbadstr. and turn right onto Alte Poststr. for more challenging trails including the Pforzheim-Basel *Westweg* red diamonds. Rent **paddleboats** from vendors along Seestr. (DM7 per 30min.). Guided boat tours of the lake depart from the same area, run by **Bootsverleih Winterhalder** (tel. 82 14; 25min., DM6). Titisee's **telephone code** is 07651.

If the tourist density in Titisee is too great, go south to the much more serene and picturesque **Schluchsee.** Schluchsee is home to a slew of first-rate hiking trails. The simple Seerundweg follows the lake's shore for all 18km (about 4hr.). Signs and red dots abound. More difficult and rewarding trails depart from the Sportplatz parking lot, a 15-minute walk up Dresselbacher Str. past the huge hillside resort hotel. For an 18km, 6-hour odyssey, follow TK6 to *Vogelhaus* (which houses a folklife museum; open Tu and Su after 2pm). Then follow signs for Hingerhäuser, Fischbach, Bildstein,

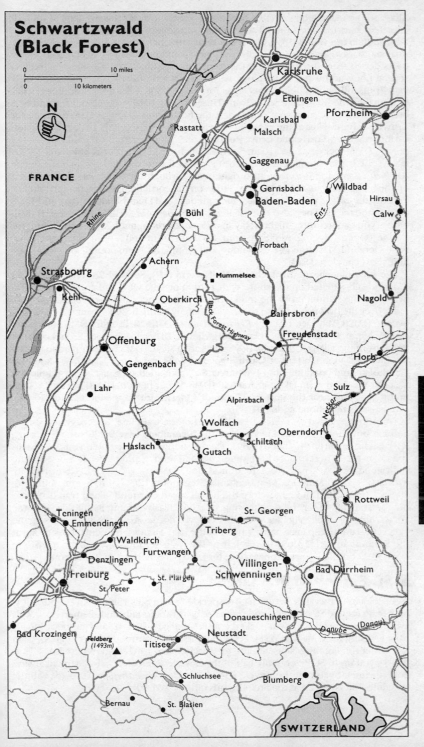

Schwartzwald (Black Forest)

0 ————— 10 miles
0 ————— 10 kilometers

N

FRANCE

Karlsruhe

Ettlingen

Pforzheim

Karlsbad
Malsch

Rastatt

Gaggenau

Gernsbach
Baden-Baden

Wildbad

Hirsau
Calw

Bühl

Rhine

Forbach

Achern

Strasbourg

Mummelsee

Kehl

Oberkirch

Black Forest Highway

Nagold

Baiersbron

Offenburg

Freudenstadt

Gengenbach

Horb

Lahr

Alpirsbach

Sulz

Wolfach

Oberndorf

Neckar

Haslach

Schiltach

Gutach

St. Georgen

Rottweil

Teningen
Emmendingen

Triberg

Waldkirch

Furtwangen

Denzlingen

Freiburg

St. Margen

Villingen-
Schwenningen

Bad Dürrheim

St. Peter

Donaueschingen

Bad Krozingen

Feldberg
(1493m)

Neustadt

Danube (Donau)

Titisee

Schluchsee

Blumberg

Bernau

St. Blasien

SWITZERLAND

BADEN-WÜRTTEMBURG

Aha, and then take it on to Schluchsee again. Fantastic vistas reward dogged souls. If your feet start to ache from all that hiking, cruise around the lake on the **G. Isele Seerundfahrten** (tel. 449), which runs **boat trips** between Schluchsee, Seebrugg, Aha, and Blasiwald (June-Sept. daily every hr. 10am-5pm, DM4-7). In Schluchsee, the boats depart from the **beach** near the **Aqua Fun Spaßbad** (tel. 77 38), which offers several pools and water slides along with a sandy strip (DM6; open May-Sept. daily 9am-7pm; follow the ubiquitous signs for "Strandbad.") An hourly double-decker train makes the 30-minute jaunt from Titisee to the towns of Schluchsee and Seebrugg, both on the lake. **Boat rental** near the hostel runs as low as DM6 per hour for a rowboat. **Rent bikes** at the gas station on Freiburger Str. towards Titisee. Rent **windsurfboards** from **Surfschule Ernst Pohl** in Aha-Schluchsee (tel. (07656) 366; DM15 per hr., DM60 per day; open 10am-5pm). Schluchsee's eager **tourist office** (tel. 77 32; fax 77 59; http://www.schluchsee.de) is a block into the pedestrian zone in the *Kurhaus*. From the *Bahnhof*, turn right, walk through the underpass, and turn left up the brick sidewalk of Kirchsteige. Sitting on the corner of Fischbacher Str. and Lindenstr., the office provides sight-seeing guides (DM1) and hiking maps and finds accommodations. They also offer a *Wanderwochenende* (Hiking Weekend) deal, where you can get three nights' stay in a *Privatzimmer* and hiking maps galore for DM99. (Open July-Aug. M-F 8am-6pm, Sa 10am-noon and 4-6pm, Su 10am-noon; Sept.-Oct. and May-June M-F 8am-noon and 2-6pm, Sa 10am-noon; Nov.-Apr. same hours, except closed Sa.)

The **Jugendherberge Schluchsee-Wolfsgrund (HI)**, Seeweg 28 (tel. 329; fax 92 37), is ideally situated on the shore with a stunning lake view and comfortable facilities; from the station, cross the tracks and hop the fence, and then follow the path right, over the bridge parallel to the tracks, directly to the hostel's front door. (DM23, over 26 DM28. May-Oct. DM2.50 *Kurtaxe*. Dinner DM8.20. Laundry DM6. Reception closed 2-5pm. Curfew 11pm.) **Haus Bergfrieden**, Dresselbacher Str. 23 (tel. 309), is uphill from the village center. Its tidy rooms are a steal. (DM25-28 per person. Breakfast included.) Pitch a tent at **Campingplatz Wolfsgrund** (tel. 77 39). Walk left up Bahnhofstr. and continue onto Freiburger Str., take a left on Sägackerweg, follow it past Am Waldrain, then take another left. (DM8.50 per person; DM10 per tent.) Stock up on groceries near the hostel at **Schmidt's Markt**, Im Rappennest 2 (tel. 15 54). Schluchsee's **telephone code** is 07656.

Three kilometers down the lake at the end of the train line, **Seebrugg** consists of nothing but a train station, a beach, and the **Jugendherberge Schluchsee-Seebrugg (HI)**, Seebrugg 9 (tel. 494; fax 18 89). Then again, what more could you want? This splendid, recently retouched building couched among pine trees is a five-minute walk along the paved path from the train station. (DM23, over 26 DM28. Sheets DM6. *Kurtaxe* DM1.60 May-Oct. Members only. Reception 12:30-1pm, 5-6pm, and 6:30-10pm. Curfew 10pm.) Right before the hostel, a **red diamond hiking trail** darts into the forest, heading for the neighboring village of Blasiwald and its hillside *Althütte*. For a while, this trail coincides with the easier red dot *Seerundweg*, both crossing the excellent dam that spans a narrow neck of the lake. Debut your dental floss thong at the **Strandbad** (tel. 13 65) to the left of the train station (open daily May-Sept.; DM2.50). You can also **rent boats** here for DM6 per 30 min., DM10 per hour.

■ St. Peter and St. Märgen

Sunk deep into the valley between cow-speckled green hills 15km from Freiburg, itty-bitty St. Peter and St. Märgen exude an air of balmy tranquility and seem to be worlds away from the hectic, student-packed cobblestone core. **Bus** #7216 runs occasionally from Freiburg to St. Märgen via St. Peter, but the more common route requires a **train** ride along the Freiburg-Neustadt line to "Kirchzarten" (3rd stop), where bus #7216 whisks you up to St. Peter. Only half of the buses continue on to St. Märgen; always double check by asking the driver. The *"Südbadenbus Fahrplan"* provides all the schedules; pick one up at the Freiburg bus office (DM1.50).

St. Peter, closer to Freiburg and surrounded by cherry orchards, juts high in the curative air, where a halo of green farmland breaks through the dark crust of pine. Its **Klosterkirche** (tel. (07660) 910 10) is yet another contender in the contest for gaudiest church in southern Germany: a Baroque whirlwind of gold, mauve, and tasteless turquoise swathe ethereal beings. **Tours** of the church, cloister, and library are offered (Su at 11:30am, Tu at 11am, Th at 2:30pm; July-Sept. also W at 11am; DM5). For more information, see the **tourist office** (tel. (07660) 91 02 24; fax 91 02 44) at Klosterhof. Get off the bus at "Zähringer Eck"; it's right in front of the church. The office has a list of affordable accommodations starting at DM20 (but it does not book rooms), and only one hiking map. More maps can be found at the frighteningly cheesy tourist shop next door (tourist office open M-F 8am-noon and 2-5pm; June-Oct. Sat. 11am-1pm). Many paths—most of them well marked—begin at the tourist office and abbey. A relatively easy, but **very scenic 8km path** takes you over to St. Märgen; follow the blue diamonds of the Panoramaweg. From the front of the abbey, cut a sharp right alongside the Klosterkirche (do not cross the stream and the main road), heading for *Jägerhaus.* Then cross the highway.

Once in **St. Märgen,** the hiking does not end. Most visitors who come to this hilltop hamlet congregate around the hiking trail head beside the busstop. With links to all the major Schwarzwald trails and a cluster of gorgeous day hikes, this place rightfully calls itself a *Wanderparadies* (hiking paradise). One of the more challenging local trails spirits dedicated wayfarers to the **Zweibach waterfall.** It's 16km in total (at least four hours) and marked by a black dot on a yellow field. From the town center, walk downhill along Feldbergstr. and turn left onto Landfeldweg. Keep going, following signs for Rankmühle. The **tourist office** (tel. (07669) 91 18 17; fax 91 18 40) sits 100m from the St. Märgen "Post" bus stop in the *Rathaus.* (Open M-F 8am-noon and 2-5pm; June-Aug. also Sa 10am-noon; Nov.-Dec. closed afternoons). The staff provides good hiking and biking maps (DM5) and find rooms for free.

■ Central Black Forest

More than hiking and biking, the thing that makes the Central Black Forest tick is clocks. In 1667, the first wooden **Waaguhr** came into existence in Waldau. Since then the Black Forest has become a connoisseur of ticking timepieces with 12,000 clockmakers churning out 60 million clocks a year. The **Deutsche Uhrenstraße** (German Clock Route) winds its way through a number of towns here, connecting glitzy clock museums and historic clock factories with tourist-hungry shops. Along the way, hikers haul past the Neckar and Danube rivers, and the famed **Schwarzwaldbahn** (Black Forest Train) chugs through tunnels and over steep pre-forested chasms.

■ Donaueschingen

A ten-year-old kid named Wolfgang Amadeus Mozart stopped in Donaueschingen on his way from Vienna to Paris and played three concerts in the castle. Since that time, a variety of other famous personalities has passed through Donaueschingen; most, like Mozart, were on their way somewhere else. Located on the Baar Plateau between the Schwarzwald and the Schwäbische Alb, Donaueschingen actually flaunts its status as a rest-stop. Although the city boasts only a few noteworthy sites, its location makes it an ideal starting place for forays into the **Schwarzwald,** the **Lake Constance** region, and the **Wutach Schlucht** (Wutach Gorge) 15km to the south.

Donaueschingen's other claim to fame is its spurious status as the "source" of the 2840km Danube River, the second-longest river in Europe and the only major one to flow west to east. Actually, the Danube begins where the Brigach and Brey Rivers converge, but the townsfolk decided to overlook this minor detail and build a monument to the river anyway. The **Donauquelle** (Source of the Danube) is a shallow, rock-bottomed basin encased by mossy 19th-century stonework in the garden of the **Fürstenberg Schloß,** located (by some inexplicable coincidence) right next to the Fürstenberg Souvenir Booth. The tapestries in the *Schloß* are spectacular, as is the bathroom—a shining marble cave with a massage-shower (no, you don't get to try it). The obligatory tour departs hourly. (Open Easter-Sept. W-M 9am-noon and 2-4:30pm. DM5, students DM4. Garden always open.) Across the street from the Schloß muses the **Fürstenberg Sammlungen,** Karlspl. 7 (tel. 865 63), a museum crammed to the max with former possessions of the princes of Fürstenberg. Diversity is the key with a room of clocks, the oldest known medieval manuscript of the **Nibelunglied,** and the thoroughly horrifying skeletons of infant Siamese twins. (Open Apr.-Sept. Tu-Su 9am-noon and 1:30-5pm; Oct. and Dec.-Feb. 10am-noon and 1:30-4pm; Mar. 10am-5pm. DM5, students DM4.) The museum, the *Schloß,* and the adjacent puddle are all within a 10-minute walk of the train station; take a right in front of the station and walk one block before turning left at Josefstr., then cross the bridge and walk a few hundred meters more.

Get royally smashed on free samples of the Fürstenberg family beer at the **Fürstliche Fürstenberger Brauerei,** between Haldenstr. and Poststr (tel. 862 06). (Tours DM7; arrange in advance.) Bike fiends rejoice: Donaueschingen is one terminus of the **Danube bicycle trail,** which skirts the river all the way to Vienna. The tourist office sells a map-guide for DM18.80. Take Josefstr. from the station and turn right on Prinz-Fritzi-Allee into the **Fürstenberg Park,** where bicycle trails abound. Hikers can also take heart: parts of the Schwarzwald ring the western edge of town. Follow Karlstr. left to the blue **Rathaus,** then take Villinger Str. up away from town, making a left at the signs for **Jägerhaus.** From there, a few trails venture into the forest.

Rent bikes at **Zweiradhaus Rottweiler,** Max-Egon-Str. 11 (tel. 131 48; fax 127 95) for DM10-20 per day, depending on the length of your cycling trip. (10% discount per additional week. Open Mar.-Sept. M-Tu and Th-F 9:30am-12:30pm and 2:30-6pm, Sa 9:30am-1pm.) The **tourist office,** Karlstr. 58 (tel. 85 72 21; fax 85 72 28; http://www.donaueschingen.de), books rooms for free. Veer right up the hill past the *Schloß* and turn left at Karlstr. (Open June-Aug. M-F 8am-5pm, Sa 9am-noon; Sept.-May M-F 8am-noon and 2-5pm.) The office provides information about Donaueschingen's annual **Musiktage** (Oct. 15-17 in 1999), a modern music festival. The **post office,** on Bahnhofstr., 78166 Donaueschingen, is across the street and to the left of the station (open M-F 8am-noon and 2:15pm-5:45pm, Sa 8:30am-noon). The **telephone code** is 0771.

Rest your weary feet at **Hotel Bären,** Josefstr. 7-9 (tel. 25 18; singles DM35, DM45 with breakfast; doubles DM90, with private bath DM120). Donaueschingen is well supplied with pricey restaurants (especially along Josefstr.), although most have specials running DM10-14. **Pizzeria da Alfredo,** Villingen Str. 6 near the *Rathaus,* satisfies Italian cravings, even vegetarian ones, for DM6-20. (Open M-F 11am-3pm and 5:30pm-midnight, Sa until 1am, Su from 10am.)

■ Triberg and Furtwangen

Tucked in a lofty valley 800m above sea level, the touristy whistle stop of **Triberg** has attitude about its altitude. The inhabitants brag in superlatives about the highest **waterfalls** in Germany, a series of bright white cascades tumbling over moss-covered rocks for 163 vertical meters. Swarming with over 400,000 visitors every year, these falls are tame by Niagara standards; however, the idyllic hike through the lush, towering pine trees makes up for the unimpressive trickle. The somewhat steep climb dissuades the less-than-fit from ascending (park admission DM2.50, students DM2). The signs within the park for the **Wallfahrtskirche** point to a trail leading to the small **Pilgrim Church,** where pious ones have, according to legend, been miraculously cured since the 17th century. Keep going along Kroneckweg and follow the signs for Panoramaweg for some hiking with an excellent view of the Schwarzwald valley. Back in town, directly across the street from the waterfalls, is the **Schwarzwald Museum,** Wallfahrtsstr. 4 (tel. 44 34). (Open daily 9am-6pm; Nov.-Apr. 10am-5pm; mid-Nov. to mid-Dec. weekends only. DM5, students DM3.) It is packed with Schwarzwald paraphernalia of every imaginable variety, from re-enactments of the daily life of the *Schwarzwald Volk* (complete with slimy wax people) to a Schwarzwald model railroad that chugs away among a highly detailed cardboard landscape (DM1 to watch it go). In June 1999, a new wing of the museum will feature Europe's biggest organ collection. Beyond these attractions, the region's splendid natural surroundings promise some scrumptious hiking. Numerous **trail signs** on the outskirts of town point the way to a portion of the Pforzheim-Basel *Westweg.* The tourist office (see below) sells hiking maps for DM5.50, and more detailed guides are available at the town's bookstores, souvenir shops, and *Schnitzel* stands.

Triberg's **tourist office** (tel. 95 32 30; fax 95 32 36; http://www.sbo.de/triberg) hides on the ground floor of the local *Kurhaus.* They dish out brochures, sell town maps (DM1), and dispense a mammoth catalog of all hotels, *Pensionen,* and private rooms in the region. From the train station, cross the bridge, then go under it, and charge tirelessly up the hill along Hauptstr. It's past the Marktplatz (open M-F 9am-5pm; May-Sept. also Sa 10am-noon). The town's sparkling, modern **Jugendherberge (HI),** Rohrbacherstr. 35 (tel. 41 10; fax 66 62), requires a masochistic 30-minute climb up Friedrichstr. (which turns into Rohrbacherstr.) from the tourist office. Once there, the sleek facilities and amazing view are quite luxurious. (DM22, over 26 DM27. Sheets DM5.50. Reception 5-7pm and at 9:45pm. Call ahead.) For those apprehensive about the climb, the **Hotel Zum Bären,** Hauptstr. 10 (tel. 44 93), offers worn-in rooms, most with showers, closer to the town center. The jolly staff has been dealing with students for decades (singles DM45; doubles DM84). For decidedly Italian food and music in a decidedly German setting, visit **Heimatkeller** on Hauptstr., across and a little down from the Marktplatz. They cook up damn good pasta (DM6-12)—try the spicy "Triberger" sauce. (Open daily 11am-3pm and 5:30pm-midnight.) The **telephone code** is 07722.

Bus #7270 makes an hourly run between Triberg and the less idyllic town of **Furtwangen.** Here ticks the **Deutsches Uhrenmuseum,** Gerwigstr. 11 (tel. 92 01 17; fax 92 01 20), the granddaddy of all Schwarzwald shrines to time-keeping. Over 4000 clocks are on display, from decrepit 18th-century cuckoos to gaudy Victorian contraptions to hyper-modern timepieces that double as postmodern art (open Apr.-Oct. daily 9am-6pm, Nov.-Mar. 10am-5pm; DM5, students DM4). Catch some Zs at the ultra-comfortable and unbeatably cheap **Don Bosco Jugendgästehaus,** Am Engelgrund 2 (tel. 65 08 46; fax 65 08 11). Although the hostel is officially only for groups and families, the gracious staff often lets weary stragglers stick around if there are empty beds. Dig the mod sheet-metal decor and awesome bedrooms with private sinks. (DM14, after one night DM13. Breakfast DM5. Curfew midnight.) For both the museum and the Jugendgästehaus, take bus #7270 to "Rößleplatz." Furtwangen's **telephone code** is 07723.

■ Schwarzwaldhochstraße (Black Forest Highway)

The dark, meandering valleys of the **Nördlicher Schwarzwald** may lack the remote mountain strongholds of the Hochschwarzwald or the clock-saturated culture of the Mittlererschwarzwald, but they still make for inarguably wonderful hiking. The region's extensive network of trails is easily accessible from the north: direct trains make the 1½-hour trip from Baden-Baden to Freudenstadt every hour, and the final 45-minute stretch is a gorgeous trip through deep valleys and heavily forested hills. The **Schwarzwaldhochstraße** (Black Forest Highway) links the two cities via a slightly different route. It contains some of Germany's most stunning scenery, as well as parts of the two *Bundesstraßen* (federal highways) B28 and B500. Even more arresting, however, is the accompanying footpath **(the Westweg),** which spans the spine of the mountains overlooking the Rhine Valley and the Vosges Mountains of France. Among these is the **Hornisgrinde,** at 1164m the highest peak in the region. Nearby, the **Mummelsee,** with its forested shores and blue waters, is unfortunately also a popular tourist destination. Bus #245 departs daily from Augustaplatz in Baden-Baden at around 9am and 11am (50min.; DM4), returning to Baden-Baden around 2pm and 5:30pm. And down the hill after a rigorous hike rests the **Wildsee,** a more attractive lake devoid of cars and Europabuses.

For a place to rest your weary feet, seek out the **Jugendherberge Zuflucht (HI)** (tel. (07804) 611; fax 13 23), one of Germany's most comfortable youth hostels, which stands along the Westweg, 17km northwest of Freudenstadt and 2km from the cross-roads at Alexanderschanze. A large, converted hotel built in the style of a Schwarzwald farmhouse, it lets lodgers bask in spotless, carpeted six-bed dorm rooms; it also rents ski equipment and bikes. Bus #12 leaves from the Freudenstadt ZOB at the *Stadtbahnhof* twice daily at 9:35am and 1:35pm. (DM23, over 26 DM28. Members only. Sheets DM6. Curfew 10pm or by prior arrangement.)

■ Rottweil

Rottweil bears the distinction of being the oldest city in Baden-Württemberg. A free and independent city under the Holy Roman Empire, Rottweil's contributions to the world's well-being have included both flameless gunpowder (the unfortunate brain-child of one Herr Duttenhofer) and certain pernicious canines. It comes as no surprise that the city itself is a bustling, ferocious little village that knows how to party. Chief among its swingin' shindigs is Rottweil's famous **Fasnet** celebration, which draws gawkers from all over Germany to watch 4000 *Rottweil Narren* (fools) storm through town in wooden masks and expensive costumes in a festive attempt to expel winter (the next outbreak is February 15-16, 1999). The **Fronleichnam** ceremony (June 3, 1999) reignites old Protestant-Catholic feuds in an innocent re-enactment.

ORIENTATION AND PRACTICAL INFORMATION Lying on the Stuttgart-Zurich rail line, Rottweil is easily accessible by hourly regional trains connecting the city with Stuttgart in the north and Singen in the south. The train station lies in the valley below the town center, which translates into an unfortunate 20-minute uphill climb. Turn right upon leaving the station and head upward. When you reach the bridge, take another right to cross it. Hauptstr., the cross-street at the second block on your left, is the center of the town's action. Halfway up the street on the right-hand side is the **tourist office,** Hauptstr. 23 (tel. 49 42 80 or 49 42 81; fax 49 43 73). The office books rooms for free and offers maps, an English guide to the city, and *Freizeit Spiegel*—a free publication detailing artistic, theatrical, and musical offerings (open M-F 9am-12:30pm and 2-5pm; May-Sept. also open Sa 10am-noon). Free 90-minute **city tours** are also available every Saturday at 2:30pm from the tourist office and culminate, if the group is in a sudsy mood, in a round of pub-crawling (May-Oct. only). **Alfred Kaiser, Balingerstr.** 9 (tel. 89 19), at the end of the bridge leading out of town from Hauptstr., will cater to all your **bike rental** desires (DM20 per day, mountain bikes DM30; DM100 per week). The **post office** is on Königstr. 12 (open M-F 8am-noon and 2:30pm-6pm, Sa 8am-noon). The **telephone code** is 0741.

ACCOMMODATIONS AND FOOD Inexpensive accommodations are difficult to find in the summer months. Call early and often. To find the small and homey **Jugendherberge (HI),** Lorenzgasse 8 (tel. 76 64), walk left on Lorenzgasse (while walking down-hill on Hauptstr.), go right at the ivy-covered building, and left at the "Jugendherberge" sign. Many of the cramped six- to eight-bed rooms in this half-timbered house face out onto the terrifically steep plunge into the Neckar. (DM21, over 26 DM25. Breakfast included. Sheets DM4. Reception 5-10:30pm. Open Mar.15-Nov.15 and during Fasnet.) The *Pension* **Goldenes Rad,** Hauptstr. 38 (tel. 74 12), is often booked solid several weeks in advance. (Singles DM40; doubles DM72. Reception M-Tu and Th-Su 11:30am-2pm and from 5pm.) For traditional regional cooking, head to **Zum Goldenen Becher,** Hochbrücktorstr. 17 (tel. 76 85), a family restaurant where meals run DM12-30 (open Tu-Su 11am-midnight). At **Rotuvilla,** Hauptstr. 63 (tel. 416 95), feast on many incarnations of wood-oven pizza (DM9-16) in a half-timbered dining room (open M and W-Su 11:30am-2pm and 5pm-midnight).

SIGHTS Rottweil's fanatic adherence to old traditions is not limited to celebrations. The town is a living architecture museum, its buildings graced with historic murals and meticulously crafted oriel windows. At the summit of the hill looms the 13th-century **Schwarzes Tor** (Black Gate), built in 1289 and enlarged in 1571 and 1650. Higher yet stands the ancient **Hochturm,** which offers a stunning view of the **Schwäbische Alb** from its top. To scale it, pick up the key to the tower from the tourist office in exchange for DM2 and an ID. (On weekends, the key is available next door at Café Schädle.) Across Hauptstr. from the tourist office and the Gothic **Altes Rathaus** stands the **Stadtmuseum,** Hauptstr. 20 (tel. 49 42 56), which houses a 15th-century treaty between Rottweil and nine Swiss cantons—still valid to this day—and a collection of wooden masks from the *Fasnet* celebrations. *(Open Tu-Sa 10am-noon and 2-5pm, Su 10am-noon. DM1.)*

Behind the Altes Rathaus, the Gothic **Heilig-Kreuz-Münster** (Cathedral of the Holy Cross) houses an interesting array of guild lanterns that are carried through town annually in the **Corpus Christi** procession. Subject to the winds of architectural fashion, this cathedral flip-flopped from 12th-century Romanesque to 15th-century Gothic to 17th-century Baroque and back to 19th-century Gothic revivalism. The refreshingly modern **Dominikanermuseum,** on Kriegsdamm (tel. 49 43 30; fax 49 43 77), is home to a bunch of medieval sculptures of saints and, more importantly, an excellent exhibit on Rottweil's Roman past, highlighted by a 570,000 tile 2nd-century mosaic. *(Open Tu-Su 10am-1pm and 2-5pm. DM3.)* For medieval stone sculptures, drop by the neighboring art collection in the **Lorenzkapelle,** Lorenzgasse 17 (tel. 49 42 98; open Tu-Su 2-5pm; DM1).

BODENSEE (LAKE CONSTANCE)

Nearly land-locked Germany has long suffered from something of a Mediterranean complex. For this cold grey country, there are no white sand beaches of the Riviera, no sparkling waters of the Greek islands, none of the sun-bleached stucco of Italy—except for a strip of land on the **Bodensee.** This stretch of southern Baden-Württemberg, bordering the exquisite "Floor Lake," provides an outlet for pent-up *Mittelmeerlust,* an opportunity for Italian fantasies to be enacted and Grecian longings (you know the kind) to be satisfied. Potted palms line the streets, public beaches are filled with sunbathers tanning to a melanomic crisp, and daily business is conducted with a thoroughly un-German casualness. Looking out across the lake, one easily sees how the deception works so smoothly, as the surprisingly warm waters glow an intense turquoise blue more typically found in the Caribbean than in European lakes. With the snow-capped Swiss and Austrian Alps soaring beyond the sparkling *See,* the Bodensee is one of Germany's most stunning destinations.

Getting to the region by **train** is easy; the cities of Konstanz and Friedrichshafen have direct connections to many major German cities. Transport within the region can require long rides and tricky connections due to the absence of a single route that fully encircles the lake. In many instances, the bright white boats of the **BSB** (Bodensee-Schiffsbetriebe) and other smaller lines, known collectively as the *Weiße Flotte* (White Fleet), are a quicker and more therapeutic alternative. Ships leave hourly from Konstanz and Friedrichshafen for all ports around the lake, departing every 1-3 hours. A detailed schedule *(Schiffsfahrplan)* is available free at every ticket counter. Those who plan to spend at least a week here should seriously consider the 7-day **Bodensee-Pass,** which includes one day of free ship travel and a 50% discount on all rail, bus, and gondola-lift tickets (DM57, available at all ship ticket counters). A **15-day card** for 50% off ship, rail, bus, and even cable-car travel runs DM48. For all ship related information, contact the BSB office in Konstanz (tel. 28 13 98; fax 28 13 73).

■ Konstanz (Constance)

Spanning the Rhine's exit from the Bodensee, the elegant university city of Konstanz has never been bombed. Part of the city extends into neighboring Switzerland, and the Allies were leery of accidentally striking neutral territory. The proximity of Switzerland and Austria gives the city an open, international flair. Its narrow streets wind around beautifully painted Baroque and Renaissance facades in the central part of town, while along the river promenades, gabled and turreted 19th-century houses gleam with a confident gentility. The waters of the Bodensee lap the beaches and harbors, and a palpable jubilation fills the streets.

ORIENTATION AND PRACTICAL INFORMATION Tickets for the **Weiße Flotte** are on sale in the building behind the train station (open Su-F 7:40am-6:15pm, Sa 7:40am-8:30pm). Otherwise, buy your tickets on the ship. The tourist office offers a two-day pass (DM34) including transportation on buses, the ferry, the *Weiße Flotte* ship line to Meersburg and Mainau, a city tour, and admission to Mainau (see p. 467). **Giess Personenschiffahrt** (tel. (07533) 21 77; fax (07533) 986 66) runs private boats hourly from behind the train station to **Freizeitbad Jakob** and **Freibad Horn** and leads tours of the Bodensee. (45min.; June-Aug. daily 10:50am-5:50pm; May and Sept. Su only; DM8, children half-price.) **Buses** in Konstanz cost DM2.40 per ride, DM10 for a five-ride ticket, and DM7 for a one-day ticket for two adults and three children. The **Gästekarte**, available at any accommodation in the city, including the youth hostel, costs DM1.50 *Kurtax* per day and gives you bus fare within Konstanz and free or discounted admission to some sights. **Paddleboats and rowboats** can be rented at Am Gondelhafen (tel. 218 81) for DM12-16 per hr. (Apr.-Oct. daily 10am-dusk). Try a solar-powered boat at DM28 per 30min. **Rent bikes** from **Velotours**, Mainaustr. 34 (tel. 982 80; day DM20, week DM100; open Mar.-Oct. daily 9am-5:30pm). The tiny but spunky **Mitfahrzentrale**, Münzgasse 22 (tel. 214 44; fax 166 60), can help find you a ride. (Munich DM23, Freiburg DM16, Stuttgart DM20. Open M 2-6pm, Tu-F 9:30am-12:30pm and 2-6pm, Sa 10am-2pm.)

The **tourist office**, Bahnhofspl. 13 (tel. 13 30 30; fax 13 30 60; email info@tourist information.stadt.konstanz.de), in the arcade to the right of the train station, provides an excellent walking map (DM0.50) and lots of information about the area. The staff finds rooms for a DM5 fee in private homes for a three-night minimum stay, or in hotels for shorter. (Open May-Sept. M-F 9am-6:30pm, Sa 9am-1pm; Oct.-Apr. M-F 9am-12:30pm and 2-6pm; Apr. and Oct. also Sa 9am-1pm.) **City tours** (DM10) depart from here (Apr.-Oct. M-Sa at 10:30am and Su at 2:30pm). The **post office**, 78421 Konstanz, is across the street from the train station at Bahnhofpl. 2 (open M-F 8:30am-6pm, Sa 8:30am-noon). Check your **email** at **Schauzer & Schauzer Internet Cafe**, Pfauengasse 11 (tel. 152 74), near the Schnetztor in the southwest corner of the *Altstadt* (DM5 per 20min., DM15 per hr.; open 'til 1am). Remove your disgusting body odor from your rank and stanky clothing at **Waschsalon und Mehr**, Hofhalde 3 (tel. 160 27; wash DM7, dry DM5 per 10min.; open M-F 10am-7pm, Sa 10am-4pm). The **telephone code** is 07531.

ACCOMMODATIONS Finding lodging in popular Konstanz can induce some massive migraines. Two words: call ahead! Maybe that way you can secure a place at the marvelous **Jugendherberge Kreuzlingen (HI)**, Promenadenstr. 7 (tel. from Germany (00 41) 716 88 26 63, from Switzerland (071) 688 26 63; fax 688 47 61). South of the border in Kreuzlingen, Switzerland, but actually closer to downtown Konstanz than the official Konstanz hostel, it commands the tip of a small lakefront hill. It also offers cushy leather furniture and a multilingual staff practically breaking their necks to serve you. The best way there is by foot (20min.); leaving the *Bahnhof,* turn left, cross the metal bridge over the tracks, turn right, and go through the parking lot to the checkpoint "Klein Venedig." Keep walking along Seestr. until the sharp right curve. Instead of following the street, continue straight ahead on the gravel path through the gate, past the billy goats, right through the Seeburg castle parking lot, and right up the hill to the building with a flag on top. (First night SFr21.20 (about DM26.50—they also accept *Deutschmarks*), subsequent nights SFr18.70 (DM23.40). SFr2.50 cheaper in Mar.-Apr. and Oct.-Nov. Breakfast and sheets included. Rents mountain bikes for SFr12.50 per day, kayaks for SFr10 per 2hr. Reception 8-9am and 5-9pm. Curfew 11pm. Open Mar.-Nov.)

BADEN-WÜRTTEMBURG

Bodensee (Lake Constance)

N

GERMANY

AUSTRIA

SWITZERLAND

10 miles

10 kilometers

Leutkirch

Isny

Bad Wurzach

Wangen im Allgäu

Lindenberg

Bregenz

Dornbirn

Baienfurt

Weingarten

Ravensburg

Meckenbeuren

Tettnang

Kressbronn

Nonnenhorn

Lustenau

Lindau

Wasserburg

Rheineck

Rorschach

Markdorf

Friedrichshafen

Langenargen

Arbon

Meersburg

Hagnau

Immenstaad

Bodensee (Lake Constance)

Salem

Uhldingen

St. Gallen

Überlingen

Konstanz

Romanshorn

Amriswil

Ludwigshafen

Sipplingen

Überlinger See

Dingelsdorf

Mainau

Kreuzlingen

Weinfelden

Bodman

Radolfzell

Mettnau

Reichenau

Wil

Singen

Rielasingen

Izmang

Worblingen

Zeller See

Rhein

Stein am Rhein

Frauenfeld

Engen

Winterthurk

Rhein

Jugendherberge "Otto-Moericke-Turm" (HI), zur Allmannshöhe 18 (tel. 322 60; fax 311 63), is considerably less luxurious, with cramped rooms in a former water tower next to a graveyard. However, it has a terrific view. Take bus #4 from the **Hauptbahnhof** to "Jugendherberge" (7th stop); backtrack and head straight up the hill. (DM21.50, over 26 DM26.50. Members only. Breakfast included. Sheets DM5.50. Reception Apr.-Oct. 3-10pm; Nov.-Mar. 5-10pm. Curfew 10pm. Lock-out 9:30am-noon. Call ahead.) **Jugendwohnheim Don Bosco**, Salesianerweg 5 (tel. 622 52; fax 606 88), is also cheap. From the station, take bus #1 to "Salzberg." Walk toward the intersection along Mainaustr. and keep on going. Or take bus #4, 9B, or 15; same stop, but cross Mainaustr. at the intersection and turn left. Everyone should walk two hundred meters past the intersection, then follow the sign down the path to the right. Choose from 39 channels in the lively dayroom. (DM26 per person. Breakfast included. Sheets DM6.50. Curfew 10pm). **Campingplatz Konstanz-Bruderhofer**, Fohrenbühlweg 50 (tel. 313 88 or 313 92), is even cheaper. Take bus #1 to "Staad." The campground is along the waterfront. Call ahead, as it also fills up fast (DM6.50 per person; DM5.50-8.50 per tent).

FOOD The **University Mensa** dishes out Konstanz's cheapest food. Lunches, including dessert and a view of the lake, cost DM8-9 (open M-F 11:15am-1:30pm). The **cafeteria** on floor K6 has lighter fare, such as sandwiches and desserts, with no ID required (DM2-5; open M-Th 7:45am-6:30pm, F 7:45am-5pm; Aug. M-F 11am-2pm). Take bus #9 from the station to "Universität." The **Fachhochschule Mensa** also comes with a view. You need an international student ID to get yourself a changecard; ask the attendant. The hassle is worth it—meals cost DM4.40 (open M-F 8:30am-4pm). Stroll through the small streets surrounding the *Münster's* northern side: it is the oldest part of Konstanz, and now the center of its vibrant alternative scene, with health-food stores, left-wing graffiti, and student cafes. There is a **Tengelmann grocery store** at the corner of Münzgasse and Brotlaube (open M-F 8:30am-8pm, Sa 8am-4pm). **Sedir**, Hofhaldestr. 11 (tel. 293 52), serves bowls of delectable vegetarian noodles for DM9.50, and lots of other meat and non-meat dishes for under DM12. The photographs on the wall take you to Turkey, the music to vintage 1970 America. (Open M-F 11:30am-2pm and 6pm-1am, Sa noon-3pm and 6pm-1am, Su 6pm-1am; kitchen open until 1:45pm and 11:30pm.)

SIGHTS Konstanz's **Münster**, built over the course of 600 years, has a 76m soaring Gothic spire and a display of ancient religious objects. *(Church open daily 10am-5pm. Free.)* Alas, the tower is subject to renovation until 2003. The **Rathaus** tells the tale of Konstanz's history with its elaborate frescoes. Wander down **Seestraße**, near the yacht harbor on the lake, or down **Rheinsteig** along the Rhine, to two picturesque waterside promenades. The tree-filled **Stadtgarten**, next to Konstanz's main harbor, provides an unbroken view of the Bodensee, and the statue of voluptuous "Imperia" who guards the harbor. Across the Rhine from the *Altstadt*, near the "Sternenplatz" bus stop, is the great **Archäologisches Landesmuseum**, Benediktinerpl. 5 (tel. 510 38 39; fax 684 52), a three-floor assemblage of all things ancient from Baden-Württemberg—jewels, spearheads, and re-assembled skeletons. *(Open Tu-Su 10am-6pm. DM4, students DM3.)* Get your fill of fossils, minerals, and ecological enlightenment at the **Bodensee-Naturmuseum**, Katzgasse 5-7 (tel. 91 42 58; fax 258 64; open Tu-Th 10am-5pm, F-Su 10am-4pm; DM3, students DM1.50).

Konstanz boasts a number of **public beaches;** all are free and open May to September. **Strandbad Horn** (tel. 635 50; bus #5), the largest and most crowded, sports a section for nude sunbathing modestly enclosed by hedges. In inclement weather, head next door to **Freizeitbad Jakob**, Wilhelm-von-Scholz-Weg 2 (tel. 611 63), a modern indoor-outdoor pool complex with thermal baths and sun lamps. Walk 30 minutes along the waterfront from the train station, or take bus #5 to "Freizeitbad Jakob." *(Open daily 9am-9pm. DM8, students DM5.)* **Strandbad Konstanz-Litzelstetten** and **Strandbad Konstanz-Wallhausen** can both be reached via bus #4. The twentysomething set frolics on the beach at the university. Take bus #4 to "Egg" and walk past the *Sporthalle* and playing fields, or take a 10-minute walk down through the fields from the Konstanz youth hostel.

■ Near Konstanz: Mainau

The **Island of Mainau** (info tel. (07531) 30 30; fax 30 32 48), a 15-minute bus ride from Konstanz, is a rich and magnificently manicured garden, the result of the horticultural prowess of generations of Baden princes and the Swedish royal family. A lush arboretum, exotic birds, and huge animals made of flowers surround the pink Baroque palace built by the Knights of the Teutonic Order, who lived here from the 13th to the 18th century. Now thousands of happy little tourists scamper across the foot bridge from Konstanz to pose with the blooming elephants and take in the unparalleled view of the Bodensee, amidst thirty different varieties of butterflies and a near-tropical setting. Amazingly, dozens of palm trees thrive here year-round, thanks to the lake's moderating effect on the climate and the magic green fingers of the island's massive gardening army. In summer, preserve your rapidly diminishing D-marks by waiting until after 6pm, when students get in for free and the island is tranquil and swathed with sunsets. From the Konstanz *Hauptbahnhof,* take bus #4 to "Mainau." Or take a romantic boat trip (one-way DM5.40, round-trip DM9) from behind the train station. (Island open mid-Mar. to Oct. 7am-8pm; Nov. to mid-Mar. 9am-5pm. DM17, students DM9, seniors DM13.50, kids DM5.50; after 6pm and Nov. to mid-Mar. DM9, students and children free.)

■ Meersburg

Overlooking the Bodensee, the massive medieval fortress of the **Burg Meersburg** (tel. 800 00) towers above the gorgeous town of **Meersburg.** Begun in the 7th century, Germany's oldest inhabited castle now houses deer antlers, rusting armor, and a very deep dungeon. (Open Mar.-Oct. daily 9am-6:30pm; Nov.-Feb. 10am-5pm. DM9, students DM8, children DM5.50.) In the 18th century, a prince bishop had declared the **Altes Schloß** unfit to house his regal self, so he commissioned the sherbet pink Baroque **Neues Schloß** (tel. 41 40 71). Elaborately frescoed, it now houses the town's art collection, a **Schloßmuseum,** and the **Dornier Museum,** with models of Dornier airplanes (open Apr.-Oct. daily 10am-1pm and 2-6pm; DM5, students DM4). Meersburg's quirky and packed **Zeppelin Museum,** Schloßpl. (tel 79 09), between the two castles, presents anything remotely connected with zeppelins, including two full-sized zeppelin flight attendant mannequins and a 30-minute film on the history of the flying cigars (open Apr.-Oct. daily 10am-6pm, DM4.50, students DM3.50). To catch a view of the Bodensee against an alpine backdrop, trek up past the *Altstadt,* cross the intersection at Stettenerstr., and turn left onto Droste-Hülshoff Weg, just before the orange house. Follow the signs for "Alpenblick." Or stroll the leisurely **Uferpromenade** along the harbor.

Meersburg is 30 minutes from Konstanz by **boat** (DM4.80 one way). It has no train station but the nearest accessible one is in **Überlingen,** 30 minutes away via bus #7395 (DM5; every 30min.). The **tourist office,** Kirchstr. 4 (tel. 43 11 10; fax 43 11 20; http://www.meersburg.de), provides free city maps, useful for the tangled **Altstadt,** and a list of accommodations. Climb the stairs from the sea-level Unterstadtstr., past the castle and the half-timbered houses, and continue through the Marktplatz towards the Church It's on the right. (Open May-Sept. M-F 9am 6:30pm, Sa 10am-2pm; Oct.-Apr. M-F 9am-noon and 2-5pm.) The office also offers **city tours** every Saturday at 2pm (summer only) and Wednesday at 10:30am (DM5). To reserve rooms, consult the **Zimmervermittlung Office,** Unterstadtstr. 13 (tel. 804 40; fax 804 48), at the bottom of the stairs (DM2 fee; open M-F 8:30am-noon and 2-6pm, Sa 9am-12:30pm). **Haus Mayer Bartsch,** Stettenerstr. 53 (tel./fax 60 50), has balcony rooms with TVs. From the Marktplatz, go up Obertorstr. through the gate, then head straight and bear right onto Stettenerstr. Keep on truckin'; it's on the left past the gas station. (Singles DM45, with bath DM60; doubles DM85, with bath DM135.) For tasty and honestly priced pizza and spaghetti (DM9-16.50, slices DM3) in this city of sky-high prices, **Da Nico,** Unterstadtstr. 39 (tel. 64 48), across the street from the harbor, offers organic Italian food (open daily 11am-11:30pm). The **telephone code** is 07532.

■ Friedrichshafen

A former construction base for Zeppelins, Friedrichshafen was almost entirely leveled by Allied bombing in 1944. The current town was rebuilt with sweeping, wide promenades and tree-lined boulevards that open up onto breathtaking panoramas of the Alps across the water. The city's flagship attraction is the superb **Graf-Zeppelin-Museum**, Hafenbahnhof, Seestr. 2 (tel. 380 10), which details the history of the flying dirigibles and their inventor. The fleet of 16 scale models is overshadowed by an original-size (38m) reconstruction of a section of the unfortunate Hindenburg, which went up in flames in New Jersey in 1936. Climb aboard and check out the recreated passenger cabins. (Open May-Oct. Tu-Su 10am-6pm; Nov.-Apr. 10am-5pm. Last admission 1hr. before closing. DM10, students DM5.) **Schulmuseum Friedrichshafen**, Friedrichstr. 14 (tel. 326 22), documents school life in Germany over the last five centuries and includes hordes of schoolchildren from this century. Don't miss the "punishment" exhibit or the Third Reich room. (Open Apr.-Oct. daily 10am-5pm; Nov.-Mar. Tu-Su 2-5pm. DM2.) The 17th-century **Schloßkirche**, on Friedrichstr. to the right of the station, was practically burned to the ground in 1944. Today it stands in its rebuilt glory, despite the imitation marble high altar. (Open Su-Th 9am-6pm, F 10am-6pm.) The beach is at the **Strandbad**, Königsweg 11 (tel. 280 78); take the hedged path to the right of the Schloßkirche entrance (15min.; open daily mid-May to mid-Sept. 9am-8pm; DM2.50).

Popular among avid cyclists, Friedrichshafen provides direct access to a number of wonderful **biking paths,** including the much-beloved **Bodensee-Radweg,** which whisks spandex-clad cyclists 240km around the entire Bodensee. The *Bodensee-Radweg* is marked by signs with a cyclist whose back tire is filled in blue (for the lake, get it?). Less hard-core folks can follow any of the other clearly marked routes, accessible from the main drag of Friedrichstr.

There are actually two train stations in Friedrichshafen: the larger Friedrichshafen Stadt Bahnhof and the easterly Friedrichshafen Hafenbahnhof, behind the Zeppelin Museum and near the harbor and commercial Buchhornplatz. **Trains** connect the two stations (2-4 times per hr). Hourly trains run east to Munich and west to Radolfzell, which connects to Konstanz. Friedrichshafen is also connected by frequent **buses** and **boats** to Lindau and Meersburg. The boat from Konstanz (1½hr.) costs DM12. Buy boat tickets at the DB Reisezentrum next to the Zeppelin Museum. (Open M-F 8:10am-5:45pm, Sa-Su 9am-5:45pm.) Rent your own boats (though don't attempt to get to Konstanz with 'em) at the Gondelhafen by Seestr. (tel. 217 46; open May-Sept. daily 9am-8pm; rowboats and paddleboats DM7-11 per 30min., motor boats DM28-30). Rent **bikes** from the *Fahrkartenausgabe* counter of the *Stadt* train station (DM13 per day). The **tourist office,** Bahnhofpl. 2 (tel. 300 10; fax 725 88), across the square to the left of the city train station, provides free town maps, details biking routes, and reserves rooms for a DM5 fee. (Open M-F 8am-noon and 2-5pm; May-Sept. M-F 9am-5pm, Sa 10am-2pm; brochures available at the Schulmuseum if the office is closed.) The **telephone code** is 07541.

Friedrichshafen's quality **Jugendherberge "Graf Zeppelin" (HI),** Lindauer Str. 3 (tel. 724 04; fax 749 86), is clean, renovated, and 50m from the water's edge. Call ahead; this place fills up fast, especially in summer. From the *Hafenbahnhof,* walk down Eckenerstr. away from Buchhornplatz (5min.). From the *Stadt Bahnhof,* walk left down Friedrichstr., then turn down Eckenerstr. (20min.) Or take bus #7587 (direction: "Kressbronn") to "Jugendherberge." (DM 24.50, over 26 DM29.50. Breakfast included. Sheets DM5.50. Laundry facilities. Reception 2-7:30pm, 8:30-9:30pm, and 9:45-10pm. Curfew 10pm. Lockout 9am-noon.) Well-touristed Friedrichshafen has virtually no affordable restaurants, so *Imbiß* stands, located along Friedrichstr., are your best bet. The **Naturkost am Buchhornplatz,** Buchhornpl. 1 (tel. 243 35), serves up home-cooked vegetarian food and offers a brisk take-out business (spinach pizza DM4.50). A **Lebensmittel Fehl supermarket** is located on Seestr. promenade and offers weekday lunch specials (DM7-9; open M-F 8am-6:30pm, Sa 8am-2pm).

■ Lindau im Bodensee

When geological forces crunched their way through southern Germany millennia ago, Mother Nature obviously intended for Lindau to be a resort. Connected to the lakeshore by a narrow causeway, this pseudo-island sits cupped in aquamarine waters, enjoying a view of the Alps that's almost the same as the one you see on good chocolates. Tourists come to soak in the balmy climate and stroll among the captivating half-timbered houses of **Maximilianstr.**, which forms the central part of town. Halfway along Maximilianstr., the **Altes Rathaus** is a fruity blend of frescoes. The **Cavazzen-Haus** in the Marktplatz houses the **Stadtmuseum** (tel. 94 40 73), which displays a collection of musical instruments and art ranging from fine French porcelain to 17th-century portraits of ugly German bluebloods (open Apr.-Oct. Tu-Su 10am-noon and 2-5pm; DM4, students DM1). A walk down the less touristed equivalent of Maximilianstr.—In der Grube—will lead you to the ivy-covered **Diebstahl Turm** (robbery tower), which looks more like Rapunzel's tower than the prison it once was. For properly-dressed adults, the **casino** *(Spielbank)* by the Seebrücke offers the regular spinning of roulette wheels and thinning of wallets. The bet ceiling is DM12,000, so don't worry about losing too much money (open 3pm-4am; 21 and over admitted; admission DM5 and a passport—please daaarling, no jeans).

Ferries link Lindau with Konstanz, stopping at Meersburg, Mainau, and Friedrichshafen (3hr., 3-6 per day; one-way DM18.40, under 24 DM11.20). The **train** takes two hours (one-way DM13). Crazy kids can rent **boats** 50m to the left of the casino, next to the bridge (tel. 55 14; open mid.-Mar. to mid.-Sept. daily 9am-9pm; rowboats DM10-18; paddleboats DM14-18 per hr.; motor boat DM45). One-hour excursions (tel./fax 781 94) on a small boat leave from the dock behind the casino at 11:30am, 1, 2:30, and 6pm (DM12, children DM6). **Rent bikes** (tel. 212 61) at the train station (DM15 per day, DM13.50 for hostel guests; open May-Sept. M-F 9am-1pm and 2:30-6pm, Sa 9:30am-12:30pm, Su 9am-noon) or from heavenly **Fahrradies,** In der Grub 5 (tel. 235 39; DM12 per day, mountain bikes DM20; open M-F 9:30am-1pm and 2:30-6pm, Sa 9:30am-1pm). **Bus rides** cost DM2.50 each, although day cards are DM6. The **tourist office,** across from the train station at Ludwigstr. 68 (tel. 26 00 30; fax 26 00 26), finds rooms for a DM5 fee. (Open mid-June to early Sept. M-Sa 9am-1pm and 2-7pm; May to mid-June and Sept. M-F 9am-1pm and 2-6pm, Sa 9am-1pm; Apr. and Oct. M-F 9am-1pm and 2-5pm, Sa 9am-1pm; Nov.-Mar. M-F 9am-noon and 2-5pm.) **Tours** leave from the office at 10am. (Tu and F in German, M in English. DM5, students and overnight guests DM3.) The **post office,** 88101 Lindau im Bodensee (tel. 277 70), is 50m to the right from the train station (open M-F 8am-6pm, Sa 8:30am-noon). The **telephone code** is 08382.

Lindau has three beaches. (All open June to mid-Aug. daily and weekends year-round 10am-8pm; all other times 10:30am-7:30pm; last entrance 1hr. before closing.) **Römerbad** (tel. 68 30) is the smallest and most familial, located left of the harbor on the island (admission DM4, students DM3). To reach the quieter **Lindenhofbad** (tel. 66 37), take bus #1 or 2 to "Anheggerstr." and then bus #4 to "Alwind" (admission DM4, students DM3). Lindau's biggest beach is **Eichwald** (tel. 55 39), about a 30-minute walk away to the right facing the harbor along Uferweg. Alternatively, take bus #1 or 2 to "Anheggerstr.," then bus #3 to "Karmelbuckel" (admission DM5, students DM3). Sit down for Greek at **Taverna Pita Gyros,** Paradiespl. 16 (tel. 237 02), which offers big platters (DM6-19) on the sidewalk or inside (open daily 10am-9pm). There is a **Plus grocery store** in the basement of the department store at the conjunction of In der Grub and Cramergasse (open M-F 8:30am-6:30pm, Sa 8am-1pm).

The spectacular **Jugendherberge,** Herbergsweg 11 (tel. 967 10; fax 496 71 50), lies across the Seebrücke off Bregenzer Str. Walk (20min.) or take bus #1 or 2 from the train station to "Anheggerstrasse," then transfer to Bus #3 (direction: "Zech") and get off at "Jugendherberge." This sleek and modern hostel is very often full; call as early as possible. (DM29. Under 27 and families with small children only. Breakfast, sheets, and *Kurtaxe* included. Reception 7am-midnight. Curfew midnight.) You could eat off the floor in the fine rooms at **Gästehaus Holdereggen,** Näherweg 4 (tel. 65 74).

Follow the railroad tracks across the causeway to the mainland (after the bridge, the path continues to the left of the tracks); turn right onto Holdereggengasse and left onto Jungfernburgstr. Näherweg is on the left (20min.). (Singles DM38; doubles DM70. DM3 *Kurtaxe* per person for one-night stands. Showers DM2.) **Campingplatz Lindau-Zech,** Frauenhoferstr. 20 (tel. 722 36; fax 26 00 26), is 3km south of the island on the mainland. It's within spitting range of the Austrian border and a beach. Take bus #1 or 2 to "Anheggerstr.," then bus #3 (direction: "Zech"). (DM9.50 per person; DM4 per tent. *Kurtaxe* DM1.50. Showers included. Open May-Oct.)

No Bread Crumbs This Time

The Schwarzwald may be a hiker's paradise, but with its labyrinth of twisting trails, it can easily become a tangled hell for novices. Even the trail markers are baffling: red diamonds, blue dots, green circles...purple horseshoes, anyone? Thankfully, the **Schwarzwaldverein** (Black Forest Association) has set up a system of markers for the major trails in the area. These trails are always marked by a diamond and are at least 10km of intense hiking. These odysseys include the Freiburg-Bodensee Querweg (half-red, half-white diamond on a yellow field) and the 280km Pforzheim-Basel Westweg (always marked by a red diamond). Blue diamonds often mark trails with lots of uphill climbing and rewarding panoramas. "Terrain-Kurweg" (Terrain Short Path), or TK, are generally well-marked trails that explore the local territory and are rarely longer than 10km. They are numbered in order of difficulty. A Rundweg is a connect-the-dots loop; a Seerundweg, which follows the shoreline of a lake, tend to be less taxing. A Panoramaweg offers stunning views of the surrounding landscape, and tend to be the most popular with tourists. The local tourist office should provide hiking suggestions and ever-useful *Wanderkarten* (hiking maps).

Bayern (Bavaria)

Bayern is the Germany of Teutonic myth, Wagnerian opera, and fairy tales. From the tiny villages of the Bayerischer Wald and the Baroque cities along the Danube to Mad King Ludwig's castles perched high in the Alps, the region beckons to more tourists than any other part of the country. Indeed, when most foreigners conjure up images of Germany, they are imagining Bayern, land of beer gardens, smoked sausage, and trendy *Lederhosen*. This is in part a relic of Germany's 45-year division, which shifted Western perceptions southward and prevented avant-garde Berlin from acting as a counterweight to more strait-laced Bavarian cities. Though mostly rural, Catholic, and conservative (save Munich), this largest of Germany's federal states nurtures flourishing commerce and industry, including such renowned companies as the Bayerische Motor Werke (BMW).

However, these popular images of Bavaria present a somewhat inaccurate image of the whole of Germany, as the region's independent residents have always been Bavarians first and Germans second. It took wars with France and Austria to pull the Kingdom of Bayern into Bismarck's orbit, and it remained a kingdom until 1918; local authorities still insist upon using the *Land*'s proper name: *Freistaat Bayern* (Free State of Bayern). In a plebiscite, Bayern was the only state to refuse to ratify the Federal Republic's Basic Law, and the ruling CDU still abides by a long-standing agreement not to compete in Bavarian elections (instead, a related party, the Christian Social Union, represents the Right). The insistent preservation of its unique tradition and history, amply demonstrated by the impenetrable dialect used throughout the region, animates the wildest stereotypes about *echtes* German culture.

> **Reminder:** HI-affiliated hostels in Bayern generally do not admit guests over age 26, although families and groups of adults with young children are usually allowed even if adults are over 26.

🖐 HIGHLIGHTS OF BAYERN

- Brimming with bubbly brewskis, swathed with lush green parks, loaded with museums, and blessed with Germany's most well-oiled tourist industry, **Munich** deserves its great reputation among budget travelers. Make reservations early for **Oktoberfest** (Sept. 18-Oct. 3 in 1999), or try out one of the city's dozens of outdoor **beer gardens** (see p. 494). Enough alcohol? Stuff yourself at the city's great **restaurants** (see p. 485) or take a sobering day trip to the site of the first Nazi concentration camp at **Dachau** (see p. 497).
- Like all great visionaries, **King Ludwig II** was a nut. But he was a nut with power, and his vision—the construction of enormous getaway castles in the Bavarian Alps—became reality. These **Königsschlösser** (royal castles) now perch in the mountains near Füssen (see p. 508).
- The South of Bayern borders the spectacular **Alps**. For mountain fun, head to either the Bavarian Alps (see p. 199) or the **Allgäu Alps** (see p. 510).
- Haunted by its many associations with Germany's Nazi past, **Nürnberg** is captivating and solemn, with many Nazi-era ruins still visible (see p. 552).
- The **Romantische Straße** (Romantic Road) snakes through western Bavaria, linking **Würzburg** to **Füssen** by way of well-touristed towns (see p. 543).

■ Munich (München)

Munich is Germany's Second City. The capital and cultural center of Bayern, it is a sprawling, relatively liberal metropolis in the midst of solidly conservative southern Germany. The two cities of Munich and Berlin are emblematic of the two poles of the German character. Munich, exuding a traditional air of merriment with seductive flair, stands in sharp contrast to Berlin, which thrives on its sense of the fragmented avant-garde and is characterized by its dizzying reconstruction.

Munich shines unabashedly with Western German postwar economic glory. World-class museums, handsome parks and architecture, a rambunctious arts scene, and an urbane population collide to create a city of astonishing vitality. Even in the depths of winter, citizens meet in outdoor beer gardens to discuss art, politics, and (of course) *Fußball.* An ebullient mixture of sophistication and earthy Bavarian *Gemütlichkeit* keeps the city awake at (almost) all hours. *Müncheners* (never "Munchkins") party zealously during *Fasching,* Germany's equivalent of Mardi Gras, and during the legendary *Oktoberfest* (Sept. 18-Oct. 3 in 1999). Before reunification, Munich was the shadow capital of West Germany; since the Wall fell, its popularity has been eclipsed by the cutting-edge energy of Berlin and eastern cities like Prague and Budapest. Though it may no longer be the beginning and end of the line, Munich continues to reel in visitors; the fascinating character of the city has its gaze fixed firmly on the future and its consciousness focused on the past.

■ History

Though Munich revels in its cushy Southern German location, the city was actually founded by a northerner, Heinrich the Lion, in 1158. Named after the city's famous monk residents, Munich soon became ruled by one of Europe's most stalwart dynasties—the Wittelsbachs—who controlled the city under strict Catholic piety from 1180 until the 18th century, when Napoleon's romp through Europe turned the city into a Napoleonic kingdom and ushered in the Bavarian Golden Age. At this time, "enlightened" absolutists rationalized state administration, promoted commerce, and patronized the arts. Ludwig I and Maximilian I contributed immensely to the expansion and evolution of the city, while its most famous king, Ludwig II, began his flight toward head-in-the-clouds extravagance. In 1871, after Bismarck's successful wars solidified Prussian dominance of Germany, Ludwig presided over the absorption of Bayern into the greater *Reich;* the process was made smooth by Bismarck's generous funding of Ludwig's loony architectural projects. Munich rose to become a cultural powerhouse rivalling hated Berlin (a city that *Müncheners* regarded as a glorified garrison town), with avant-garde artists and others flocking to its burgeoning scene.

The Golden Age came to an abrupt end with Germany's defeat in World War I. Weimar Munich was something of an incubator for reactionary and anti-Semitic movements: **Adolf Hitler** found the city such a fertile recruiting ground for the new National Socialist German Workers Party (Nazis) that he later called Munich "the capital of our movement." In 1923, Hitler attempted to overthrow the municipal government and lead a march on Berlin to topple the Weimar Republic. His **Beer Hall Putsch** was quickly quashed and its leaders arrested, but evidence of his movement's eventual success still haunts the city: Neville Chamberlain's attempted appeasement of Hitler over the Sudetenland is remembered as the **Munich Agreement,** and the Nazis' first concentration camp was constructed just outside the city at Dachau.

Despite Munich's fortuitous location deep inside the German air defenses, Allied bombings destroyed the city. By 1944, less than 3% of the city center remained intact; since then, much of it has been rebuilt in the original style. When Munich hosted the **1972 Olympics,** it was hoped that the city's tattered image would at last be restored. The city went to great lengths to revolutionize itself: it pedestrianized big chunks of the city center, extended the underground subway system, and brought the city's resources to their current status. But a tragic attack by the Palestinian terrorist group *Black September* during the Games led to the death of 11 Israeli athletes in a police shoot-out and dashed Munich's hopes.

Though Munich's history would appear to speak otherwise, the city is now and always has been—throughout all of its tumult—an indulgent, celebratory place. Thus, today's riotous upheavals are of a much less frightening variety. Consider a recent protest, 20,000 citizens strong, over—what else?—beer. The issue at hand in this first-time "Bavarian Beer Garden Revolution" was the **Waldwirtschaft beer gar-**

Bayern (Bavaria)

(Map labels, reading across the map:)

THURINGIAN FOREST · Ilmenau · Zwickau · Suhl · Plauen · N · Prague (Praha) · Hof · CZECH REPUBLIC · Frankfurt a.M. · Coburg · Aschaffenburg · Bamberg · Bayreuth · Miltenberg a.M. · Würzburg · Plzen · Michelstadt · Erbach · Main · Amorbach · Erlangen · Regnitz · Hirschhorn · Neckarsteinach · Röthenburg ob d. Tauber · Nürnberg · Heidelberg · BAYERISCHE WALD · Heilbronn · Bad Wimpfen · Regen · Bodenmais · Marbach a.N. · Dinkelsbühl · Regensburg · Zwiesel · Ludwigsburg · Schwäbisch Hall · Weltenburg · Frauenau · Pforzheim · SchwäbischGmünd · Nördlingen · Eichstätt · Straubing · Esslingen · Hohenrechberg · Donau · Deggendorf · Weil d. Stadt · Stuttgart · Hohenstaufen · Donau · Ingolstadt · Inn · Tübingen · Neckar · SCHWABIAN JURA · Ulm · Landshut · Passau · Haigerloch · Augsburg · Dachau · Hohenzollern · Lech · München · Wasserburg a.l. · Burghausen · Memmingen · Ammersee · Herrsching · Herreninsel · Ottobeuren · Andechs · Chiemsee · Salzburg · Ravensburg · Starnberger See · Tegernsee · Prien · Grabenstätt · Lake Constance (Bodensee) · Wangen im Allgäu · Kempten · Wieskirche · BAYERISCHE ALPEN · Aschau · Bad Reichenhall · Mainau · Meersburg · Füssen · Oberammergau · Sachrang · Berchtesgaden · Friedrichshafen · Lindau · Ettal · Linderhof · St. Gallen · Immenstadt · Hohenschwangau · Neuschwanstein · Garmisch-Partenkirchen · Ramsau · SWITZ. · ALLGÄU ALPS · Innsbruck · AUSTRIA

den, which can accommodate 2000 customers but has only 100 parking places. Numerous neighborhood complaints had finally led to a draconian court decision mandating a 9:30pm closing time for the beer garden. After *Müncheners* marched on Marienplatz in good revolutionary spirit a few years back, the court reversed its decision and they won back a half hour—enough time to chug at least one more *Muß*.

■ Orientation

Munich rests on the banks of the Isar River in the middle of south-central Bayern. Mad King Ludwig's castles, the Bayerische Alpen, and the weekend paradises of the Lake Region are only a short trip through the squalor of Munich's industrial outskirts.

A map of Munich's center looks like a skewed circle quartered by one horizontal and one vertical line. The circle is the main traffic **Ring,** which changes its name again and again as it bounds the city center. Within it lies the lion's share of Munich's sights. The east-west and north-south thoroughfares, in turn, cross at Munich's epicenter, the **Marienplatz** (home to the **Neues Rathaus**), and meet the traffic ring at **Karlsplatz** (called **Stachus** by locals) in the west, **Isartorplatz** in the east, **Odeonsplatz** in the north, and **Sendlinger Tor** in the south. The **Hauptbahnhof** is just beyond Karlsplatz outside the Ring in the west. In the east beyond the Isartor, the **Isar River** flows by the city center, south to north. To get to Marienplatz from the station, go straight on Schützenstr. to the yellow buildings of Karlsplatz. Continue straight through Karlstor to Neuhauserstr., which becomes Kaufingerstr. before it reaches Marienplatz (15-20min.). Or take S-Bahn #1-8 (two stops from the *Hauptbahnhof*) to "Marienpl."

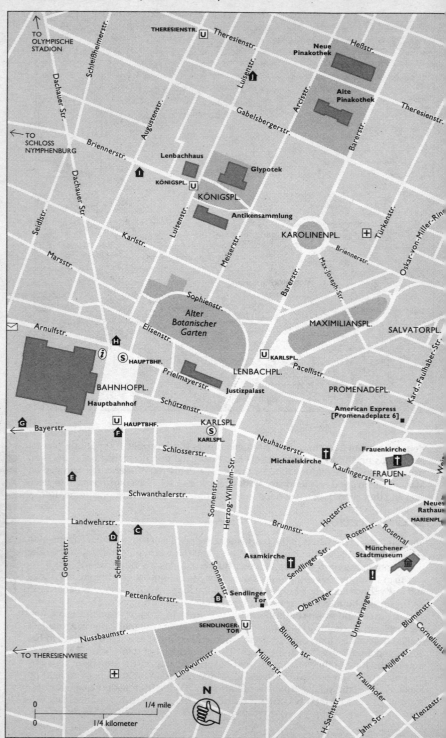

TO
OLYMPISCHE
STADION

THERESIENSTR. Theresienstr.

Luisenstr.

Neue
Pinakothek

Heßstr.

Alte
Pinakothek

Arcisstr.

Barerstr.

Theresienstr.

Dachauer Str.

Schleißheimerstr.

Augustenstr.

Gabelsbergerstr.

TO
SCHLOSS
NYMPHENBURG

Brienerstr.

Lenbachhaus

Glypotek

KÖNIGSPL.

KÖNIGSPL.

Dachauer Str.

Seidlstr.

Karlstr.

Luisenstr.

Meiserstr.

Antikensammlung

KAROLINENPL.

Türkenstr.

Brienerstr.

Oskar-von-Miller-Ring

Marsstr.

Sophienstr.

Alter
Botanischer
Garten

Barerstr.

Max-Joseph-Str.

MAXIMILIANSPL.

SALVATORPL.

Arnulfstr.

Elisenstr.

H

HAUPTBHF.

S

Prielmayerstr.

LENBACHPL.

KARLSPL.

Pacellistr.

Kard.-Faulhaber-Str.

BAHNHOFPL.

Hauptbahnhof

Schützenstr.

Justizpalast

PROMENADEPL.

American Express
[Promenadeplatz 6]

G

Bayerstr.

HAUPTBHF.

KARLSPL.

KARLSPL.

Schlosserstr.

Neuhauserstr.

Michaelskirche

Kaufingerstr.

Frauenkirche

FRAUEN-
PL.

Weis

E

Schwanthalerstr.

Sonnenstr.

Herzog-Wilhelm-Str.

Brunnstr.

Hotterstr.

Rosenstr.

Rosental

Neues
Rathaus

MARIENPL.

Landwehrstr.

Goethestr.

Schillerstr.

D

C

Asamkirche

Sendlinger Str.

Münchener
Stadtmuseum

Untereranger

Blumenstr.

Cornelius

Pettenkoferstr.

B

Sendlinger
Tor

Oberanger

SENDLINGER-
TOR

Blumen str.

Müllerstr.

Fraunhofer

Klenzestr.

Nussbaumstr.

Lindwurmstr.

TO THERESIENWIESE

Müllerstr.

H.-Sachsstr.

Jahn Str.

0   1/4 mile

0   1/4 kilometer

N

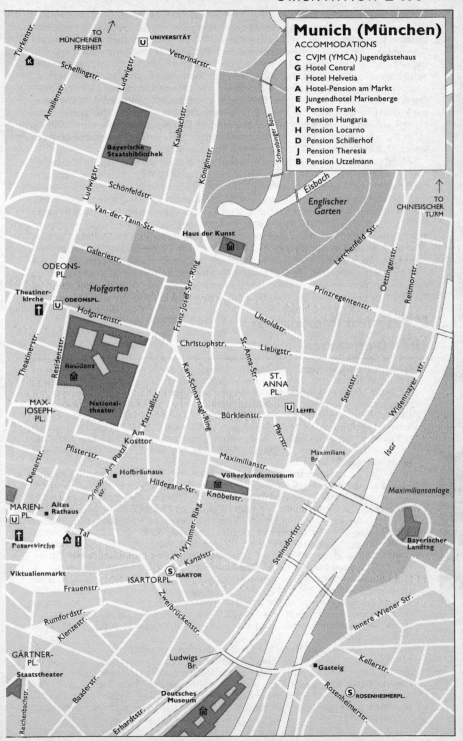

Munich (München)

ACCOMMODATIONS

C CVJM (YMCA) Jugendgästehaus
G Hotel Central
F Hotel Helvetia
A Hotel-Pension am Markt
E Jungendhotel Marienberge
K Pension Frank
I Pension Hungaria
H Pension Locarno
D Pension Schillerhof
J Pension Theresia
B Pension Utzelmann

To the north, at Odeonsplatz, the giant **Residenz** palace sprawls over a hefty piece of downtown land; **Ludwigstraße** stretches north from there toward the university district. **Leopoldstraße,** the continuation of Ludwigstr., reaches farther toward **Schwabing.** This district, also known as "Schwabylon," is student country; it lies to the west of the maddeningly mobbed Leopoldstr. Here Türkenstr., Amalienstr., Schellingstr., and Barerstr. meander through the funk. To the east of Schwabing sprawls the **Englischer Garten;** to the west is the **Olympiazentrum,** the hyper-modern complex constructed for the 1972 games, surrounded by the verdant **Olympiapark.** Farther west sits the posh **Nymphenburg,** built around the eponymous **Nymphenburg Palace.** Southwest of Marienplatz, **Sendlingerstraße** leads past shops to the Sendlinger Tor. From there, Lindwurmstr. proceeds to Goetheplatz, from which Mozartstr. leads to **Theresienwiese,** the site of the *Oktoberfest.*

Several publications can help you find your way around Munich. The most comprehensive one (in English) is the monthly *Munich Found* (DM4), available at the "Internationale Presse" booth in the center of the station across from track 24, at the Anglia English Bookshop (see p. 480), and elsewhere; it provides a list of services, events, and museums. The tourist office distributes the encyclopedic *Monatsprogramm* (DM2.50), with a list of city events in chronological order. The bi-weekly *in München* (free) gives a more intensive insider's look at the Munich *Szene* in German, providing detailed movie, theater, and concert schedules. *Prinz* (DM5) is the hip and hefty monthly with endless tips on shopping, art, music, film, concerts, and food. EurAide's free publication *Inside Track* provides updated information in English on train connections as well as basic tips on getting started in Munich; it's available at EurAide (see below) or at the train-ticket *Reisezentrum* in the main hall of the station.

■ Practical Information

TRANSPORTATION

Flights: The ultramodern **Flughafen München** is accessible from the train station by S-Bahn #8, running to and from the *Hauptbahnhof* daily every 20min. (3:35am-12:35am; DM14 or 8 stripes on the *Streifenkarte;* Eurail, InterRail, and German railpasses valid). Alternatively, a Lufthansa shuttle bus runs between the *Hauptbahnhof* and the airport (45min.), with a pickup at the "Nordfriedhof" U-Bahn stop in Schwabing. Buses leave from Arnulfstr., on the northern side of the train station 6:50am-7:50pm, every 20min. Buses return from Terminal A *(Zentralbereich)* and Terminal D every 20min., 7:55am-8:55pm. One-way DM15, round-trip DM25. For flight info, call 97 52 13 13.

Trains: Can be found at the *Hauptbahnhof* (tel. 22 33 12 56). The transportation hub of Southern Germany, Munich has connections to all major cities in Germany and throughout Europe several times per day. To: Füssen (2hr., 7 direct per day, 14 via Buchloe, or Kaufbeuren); Frankfurt (3½hr., every hr., ICE only); Zürich (4-5hr., 6 per day); Vienna (4-5hr., 1 per hr.); Köln (6hr., every hr.); Hamburg (6hr., 18 per day); Prague (6-8½hr., 6 per day, 3 direct: 6:51am, 2:08, and 11:06pm); Berlin (7½hr., every hr.); Amsterdam (9hr., 17 per day); Paris (9½-10hr., 14 per day, 2 direct: 7:46am and 9pm). Call for **schedules, fare information, and reservations** (tel. 194 19; open 6am-10:30pm). **EurAide** (see **Tourist Offices,** p. 476), in the station, provides free train information in English. Otherwise, the best source is a **destination booklet** *(Städteverbindungen)* available at the counters in the *Reisezentrum.* These list all the possible connections between Munich and scores of other cities. Station open daily 4am-12:30am. Use entrance on Arnulfstr. to reach trains. **Reisezentrum** information counters open daily 6am-11:30pm. Reservation desk open 7am-9pm.

Public Transportation: Munich's public transport system **(MVV)** runs M-F 5am-12:30am, Sa-Su 5am-2:30am. Eurail, InterRail, and German railpasses are valid on any S-Bahn (commuter rail) but *not* on the U-Bahn (subway), *Straßenbahn* (streetcars), or buses. Buy tickets at the blue *"MVV-Fahrausweise"* vending machines and be sure to stamp your ticket in the boxes marked with an "E" **before you go to the platform** (except on the bus; cancel after you board). Payment is made on an honor system, but disguised agents check for tickets sporadically; if you plan to jump the fare or don't validate correctly, bring along an extra DM60 for the fine. **Transit maps** and **maps of wheelchair accessible stations** can be picked up in the tourist office or EurAide, and at MVV counters near the subway entrance in the train station. The U-Bahn is safe, clean, and punctual; most trains run every 10min. during the day. *"Bitte Zurückbleiben"* means "please stand back."

Prices: Einzelfahrkarten (single ride tickets), which cost DM3.50 if you stay within the *Innenraum* (city center), are valid for 3hr. as long as you don't backtrack. **Kurzstrecke** (short trip) tickets cost DM1.80 and can be used for 2 stops on the U-Bahn or S-Bahn, or for 4 stops on a streetcar or bus. Buying rides in bulk will save you money; a *Streifenkarte* (11-strip ticket) costs DM15 and can be used by more than 1 person. Cancel 2 strips per person for a normal ride, or 1 strip per person for a *Kurzstrecke*. Beyond the city center, cancel 2 strips per additional "zone"—these 5 *Außenraum* zones appear as concentric rings around the *Innenraum,* and the entire area together constitutes the *Gesamtnetz*. Most places you will probably want to go (and all of the places listed in the Munich section of *Let's Go* unless otherwise noted) will be covered by an *Innenraum* ticket. **Single-Tages-Karten** (single-day tickets) give 1 person unlimited travel until 6am the next day (*Innenraum* DM8.50, *Außenraum*—only the outer 4 green zones—DM8.50, *Gesamtnetz* DM17). A **Partner-Tages-Karte** (DM12.50 and DM25 respectively) can be used by 2 adults, 3 children under 18, and a dog. If you plan on using public transportation over a longer period of time, the *Innenraum* **3-Day Pass** (DM21) is a great deal. Passes can be purchased at the MVV office behind tracks 31 and 32 in the *Hauptbahnhof.* Children under 15 pay reduced fares, and children under 4 ride free. Whew!

Taxis: Taxi-Zentrale (tel. 216 11 or 194 10) has large **stands** in front of the train station and every 5-10 blocks in the central city. Each piece of luggage DM2.50. Train station to airport costs about DM100. Women can request a female driver.

Car Rental: Flach's Leihwagen, Landsbergerstr. 289 (tel. 56 60 56), rents cars for DM60-112 per day with no mileage charges. Open M-F 8am-8pm, Sa 9am-noon. **Swing,** Schellingstr. 139 (tel. 523 20 05), rents from DM45 per day. **Avis** (tel. 550 12 12), **Europcar/National** (tel. (0180) 52 21 22), **Hertz** (tel. 550 22 56), and **Sixt Budget** (tel. (0180) 525 25 25) have offices upstairs in the *Hauptbahnhof.*

Bike Rental: Radius Bikes (tel. 59 61 13), at the far end of the *Hauptbahnhof,* behind the lockers opposite tracks 30-31. Chat it up with Patrick Holder, the gregarious owner. DM10 per 2hr. 10am-6pm DM25. DM30 per 24hr. DM45 per 48hr. DM75 for a week. Mountain bikes 20% more. Deposit DM100; passport or a credit card also acceptable. Students and Eurailpass holders receive a 10% discount. Also gives daily 2½hr. guided bike tours of the city. Tours meet in front of shop Apr.-May 15 10:15am, May 16-Sept. 6 10:15am and 2:15pm, Sept. 7-Oct. 4 10:15am. DM19 (including a mountain or trekking bike), DM12 if you already have a bike. Self-guided tour info DM5. Open Apr. to early Oct. daily 10am-6pm. **Aktiv-Rad,** Hans-Sachs-Str. 7 (tel. 26 65 06), rents 'em at DM18 per day. U-Bahn #1 or 2 to "Fraunhoferstr." Open M-F 9am-1pm and 2-6:30pm, Sa 9am-1pm.

Mitfahrzentrale: McShare Treffpunkt Zentrale, Klenzestr. 57b and Lämmerstr. 4 (tel. 59 45 61), near the train station matches McDrivers and McRiders (Frankfurt DM41, Berlin DM54, Heidelberg DM34, additional insurance DM2.15). Open daily 8am-8pm. **Frauenmitfahrzentrale,** Klenzestr. 57b, is *for women only.* U-Bahn #1 or 2 to "Fraunhoferstr.," then walk up Fraunhoferstr. away from the river, and turn right. Open M-F 8am-8pm. **Känguruh,** Amalienstr. 87 (tel. 194 44), is in the Amalienpassage near the university (to Frankfurt DM40). Open M-F 9am-6:30pm, Sa 9am-3pm, Su 10am-7pm.

Hitchhiking: *Let's Go* does not recommend hitchhiking as a safe mode of transportation. Those looking to share rides scan the bulletin boards in the **Mensa,** on Leopoldstr. 13. Otherwise, hitchers try *Autobahn* on-ramps; *those who stand behind the blue sign with the white auto may be fined.* Hitchers who've gotta get to *Autobahn Salzburg* (E11; direction: "Salzburg-Wien-Italian") take U-Bahn #1 or 2 to "Karl-Preis-Platz." For *Autobahn Stuttgart* (E11; direction: "Stuttgart-Frankreich"), take streetcar #17 to "Amalienburgstr." or take S-Bahn #2 to "Obermenzing," then bus #73 or 75 to "Blutenburg." Thumbers who want to get to the *Autobahn*

Nürnberg (E6) interchange north to Berlin take U-Bahn #6 to "Studentenstadt" and walk 500m to the Frankfurter Ring. For *Autobahn* A96/E54 to Bodensee and Switzerland, take U-Bahn #4 or 5 to "Heimeranpl.," then bus #33 to "Siegenburger Str."

TOURIST OFFICES

Main Office: The Munich **Fremdenverkehrsamt** (tel. 23 33 02 56 or 23 33 02 57; fax 23 33 02 33; email Munich_Tourist_Office@compuserve.com; http:// www.munich-tourist.de) is located on the front (east) side of the station, next to ABR Travel on Bahnhofplatz. Although friendly and helpful, this office is usually inundated with tourists—have your questions ready, and don't expect to schmooze. The staff speaks English, but for more in-depth questions, EurAide (see below) will probably better suit your needs. The tourist office books rooms for free with a 10-15% deposit, sells accommodations lists (DM1) and excellent English city maps (DM0.50). The English/German young people's guide *München Infopool* (DM1) lists beer gardens, *Mensas,* cinemas, and gives tips on cycling, sightseeing, and navigating the confusing public transportation system. Call for recorded information in English on museums and galleries (tel. 23 91 62) or sights and castles (tel. 23 91 72). Open M-Sa 9am-10pm, Su 10am-6pm. A **branch office** lies at the airport, **Flughafen Munich** (tel. 233 03 00), in the *Zentralgebäude.* Provides general information, but no room booking service. Open M-Sa 8:30am-10pm, Su 1-9pm. An **even smaller office** roosts just inside the entranceway to the *Neues Rathaus,* Marienpl. (tel. 23 33 02 72 or 23 33 02 73), which offers free brochures, friendly smiles, and city maps (DM0.50). A counter on the opposite side of the room sells tickets for concerts and performances. Open M-F 10am-8pm, Sa 10am-4pm.

⍟**EurAide in English:** (tel. 59 38 89; fax 550 39 65; email euraide@compuserve.com; http://www.cube.net/kmu/euraide.html), along track 11 (room 3) of the *Hauptbahnhof,* near the Bayerstr. exit. This is the magic mushroom of *Wunderland*—delve into the intricacies of Munich with one (sound) byte from EurAide's Mad Hatter, Alan R. Wissenberg; a solace for frazzled English-speaking tourists, he's a nearly omniscient American who points you (free of charge) in the right direction, and make room reservations for a DM7 fee. *Inside Track* available (free), English city maps (DM1), Thomas Cook Timetables (DM38) and train tickets sold, and Eurail-passes validated. EurAide also offers an outing to the *Königsschlösser* called the "Two Castle Tour" (see **Tours,** below). AmEx, Diners, MC, Visa accepted for services. Open June-*Oktoberfest* daily 7:45am-noon and 1-6pm; Oct.-Apr. M-F 7:45am-noon and 1-4pm, Sa 7:45am-noon; May daily 7:45am-noon and 1-4:30pm.

TOURS

Munich Walks: (tel. (0177) 227 59 01; email 106513.3461@compuserve.com). Native English speakers give guided historical walking tours of the city with 2 different slants: the comprehensive introductory tour of the *Altstadt* hits all the major sights (Apr.-Oct. daily 10:30am; May-Aug. also M-Sa 2:30pm; Nov. to late Dec. daily 10am), while a more specialized tour visits haunting Nazi sites (Apr. Sa 2:30pm; May-Aug. Tu, Th, Sa 10:30am; Sept.-Oct. Tu, Th, Sa 2:30pm). The 2½hr. tours cost DM15, under 26 DM10, under 14 free with an adult. Both tours leave from outside the EurAide office in the train station. No reservations necessary.

Mike's Bike Tours: (tel. 651 42 75; email Mike@bavaria.com). Ponder the "Eunuch of Munich," "hunt" lions, have lunch at a *Biergarten* in the *Englischer Garten,* and see the sights of the city. The eponymous American emigré Mike and his loyal disciples herd small groups of English-speaking bikers through Munich's cycling paths. Tours leave (rain or shine) from the *Altes Rathaus* by the Spielzeugmuseum; the 4hr. 6.5km Standard City Tour includes a lunch break and runs Apr. to early Oct. daily 11:30am and 4pm; Mar. and late Oct. daily 12:30pm. DM31. The 6hr. 16km. all-day "greener" cycling tour includes 2 beer garden breaks and a frisbee and hacky-sack break. This tour runs June-Aug. daily 12:30pm. DM45. All prices include bike rental and rain gear.

Spurwechsel Bike Tours: (tel. 692 46 99). Entertaining German tour guides lead a 15km cycling spree around the *Altstadt, Schwabing,* and *Englischer Garten,* with

a pause at the *Chinesischer Turm* beer garden for a pretzel and *Weißbier* feast. 3hr. DM26. Call for tour hours and meeting locations.
Panorama Tours: Arnulfstr. 8 (tel. 54 90 75 60 for day excursions, tel. 55 02 89 95 for city excursions; email GLMUC@aol.com). Offers staid bilingual **bus** tours that leave from the train station's main entrance, on Bahnhofplatz. 1hr. tour in an open-topped double-decker bus May-Oct. daily 10, 11:30am, 2:30, and 4pm (DM17, children DM8). A 2½hr. tour leaves daily at 10am and 2:30pm; on Tu-Su, the 10am tour goes to the *Residenz* or the Olympic Park, while the 2:30pm tour visits the Peters-kirche, the Olympic Park, or the Nymphenburg Palace (DM30, children DM15). Six other trips leave from the Neptune Fountain on Elisenstr. Tickets sold on the bus, in some hotels, or in advance. Hotel pick-up available. 10% off day excursions with Eurailpass. Open M-F 7:30am-6pm, Sa 7:30am-noon, Su 7:30-10am.
Two Castle Tour: For those who want to enter the magical realm of Mad King Lud-wig II, two options await: **Panorama Tours** offers a 10½hr. bus excursion (in English) to Schloß Linderhof leaving Apr.-Oct. daily 8:30am; Nov.-Mar. Tu, Th, and Sa-Su 8:30am. DM78, with Eurailpass, Europass, InterRail, or German Railpass DM68, with ISIC DM59; *Schloß* admission not included. Book in advance. **EurAide** leads an English-speaking half-bus, half-train *Schloß*-schlepp that includes Neus-chwanstein and an extra stop at the Rococo Wieskirche. Meet June-July Wednes-day at 7:30am by track 11 in front of EurAide. DM70, with Eurailpass, InterRail, or flexipass DM55, admission not included, but EurAide will get you a DM1 discount. For those who'd like to catch an extra 45min. of sleep, a tour to *Schloß Linderhof* and *Neuschwanstein* leaves June-July Wednesdays at 8:15am in front of EurAide. DM79. Or drop by EurAide for train and public bus schedules and see the castles on your own (see **Hypertravel to the Castles**, p. 510).

CONSULATES

Canada: Tal 29 (tel. 219 95 70). S-Bahn to "Isartor." Open M-Th 9am-noon and 2-5pm, F 9am-noon and 2-3:30pm.
Ireland: Mauerkircherstr. 1a (tel. 98 57 23). Streetcar #20 or bus #54 or 87. Open M-F 9am-noon and 1-4pm.
South Africa: Sendlinger-Tor-Platz 5 (tel. 231 16 30). U-Bahn #1-3 or 6 to "Sendlinger Tor." Open M-F 9am-noon.
U.K.: Bürkleinstr. 10, 4th floor (tel. 21 10 90). U-Bahn #4 or 5 to "Lehel." Consular section open M-F 8:45-11:30am and 1-3:15pm.
U.S.: Königinstr. 5 (tel. 288 80). Bus #53. Open M-F 8-11am. No longer handles visas. For a recording on visa information, call (0190) 27 07 89; to speak to an official, call (0190) 91 50 00) M-F 7am-8pm.

LOCAL SERVICES

Budget Travel: Council Travel, Adalbertstr. 32 (tel. 39 50 22), near the university, sells ISICs. Open M-F 10am-1pm and 2-6:30pm. **abr Reisebüro** (tel. 12 04 46) is located in the train station and at 16 other locations city-wide. Sells train tickets and railpasses. Open M-F 9am-6pm and Sa 10am-1pm.
Currency Exchange: The cheapest way to change money is to head to American Express; otherwise pick up a copy of EurAide's free publication *Inside Track* and take it to the **Reise Bank** (tel. 55 10 80). 2 locations: in front of the main entrance to the main station on Bahnhofplatz (open daily 6am-11pm); and around the corner from EurAide at track 11 (open M-Sa 7:30am-7:15pm, Su 9:30am-12:30pm and 1-4:45pm). Those with *Inside Track* (available at Euraide) get a 50% discount on commission if cashing US$50 or more in U.S. traveler's checks. Otherwise, pay reg-ular DVB traveler's check commissions. No fee for transactions under DM20 or over DM1000. All cash transactions DM3. Western Union services. Credit card operated phone and fax.
American Express: Promenadepl. 6 (tel. 29 09 00; 24hr. hotline (0130) 85 31 00), in the Hotel Bayerischer Hof. Holds mail, cashes traveler's checks, no *Kiquebaque*. Open M-F 9am-5:30pm, Sa 9:30am-12:30pm. **Branch** office also at Kaufingerstr. 24 (tel. 22 80 13 87), by the Frauenkirche. Open M-F 9am-5:30pm, Sa 10am-1pm.

Luggage Storage: At the **train station** (tel. 13 08 50 47) and **airport** (tel. 97 52 13 75). Staffed storage room *(Gepäckaufbewahrung)* in the main hall of the train station. Open daily 6am-11pm. DM4 per piece per calendar day. No credit cards accepted. Lockers opposite tracks 16, 24, and 28-36 DM2-4 per 24hr.

Lost and Found: Fundamt, Otztalerstr. 17 (tel. 23 34 59 00). U-Bahn #6 to "Partnachpl." Open M and W-F 8:30am-noon, Tu 8:30am-noon and 2-5:30pm. For items lost on S-Bahn/local trains, see **Fundstelle im Ostbahnhof** (tel. 12 88 44 09). Open M-F 8am-5:30pm, Sa 8am-11:45pm. Or try the **Deutsche Bahn Fundbüro,** Landsbergerstr. 472 (tel. 13 08 58 59), S-Bahn to "Passing." Open M and W-F 8am-noon, Tu 8am-noon and 12:30-3pm. For the airport, call 97 52 13 70. Open 24hr.

Mitwohnzentrale: An der Uni (tel. 286 60 66), in tunnel passage of U-Bahn #3 or 6 at the "Universität" stop, has apartments available for 1 month or more. Open M-F 10am-6pm, Sa 11am-1pm. **City Mitwohnzentrale,** Klenzestr. 57b (tel. 194 40), has apartments and houses throughout Germany.

⊛**Bookstores: Anglia English Bookshop,** Schellingstr. 3 (tel. 28 36 42), offers reams of English-language books in a gloriously chaotic atmosphere. U-Bahn #3 or 6 to "Universität." Open M-F 9am-6:30pm, Sa 10am-2pm. **Words' Worth,** Schellingstr. 21a (tel. 280 91 41), a bit farther down, carries obscure English novels as well as a full range of literature from the greats. Open M-Tu and F 9am-6:30pm, W-Th 9am-8pm, Sa 10am-2pm. **Lillemor's Frauenbuchladen,** Arcisstr. 57 (tel. 272 12 05), is a women's bookstore/center for women's events. U-Bahn #2 to "Max-Joseph-Platz." Open M-F 10am-6:30pm, Sa 10am-2pm.

Libraries: Many of Munich's city libraries have a hefty English section. Anyone with ID can get a library card. **Bayerische Staatsbibliothek,** Ludwigstr. 16 (tel. 28 63 80), the largest university library in all German-speaking countries, has 6.5 million books and endless magazines and newspapers. Open M-F 9am-7:30pm, Sa 9am-4:30pm. **Universitätsbibliothek der Universität,** Geschwister-Scholl-Platz 1 (tel. 21 80 24 28). Open Dec.-July M-Th 9am-8pm, F 9am-4pm; Aug.-Nov. M-Th 9am-7pm, F 9am-noon. **The Bookshelf e.V.,** Blumenstr. 36 (tel. 61 62 27), in the *Alt-Katholische Kirche,* is an English lending library. U-Bahn #1 or 2 to "Sendlinger Tor." Open M, W, F 3-6pm, Sa 11am-1pm.

Cultural Centers: Amerika Haus, Karolinenpl. 3 (tel. 552 53 70), is the cultural extension of the consulate. U-Bahn #2 to "Königspl." Cultural resources and advice for Americans wishing to teach, a library for reading and research, and language courses. Open Tu-F 1-5pm. **Deutsch-Australischer Stammtisch München** (tel. 928 22). **British Council,** Rosenheimerstr. 116b, Haus 93 (tel. 290 08 60). For Canadians, **Deutsch-Kanadische-Gesellschaft,** Hildeboldstr. 5 (tel. 307 33 45). **Deutsch-Irischer Freundeskreis** (tel. 679 24 81). **Munich Scottish Association,** Keferstr. 246 (tel. 39 12 53).

Women's Resources: Kofra *(Kommunikationszentrum für Frauen),* Baaderstr. 30 (tel. 201 04 50). Job advice, *Kaffeetrinken,* tons of magazines, lesbian politics, and books. Open M-F 4-10pm. **Frauentreffpunkt Neuperlach,** Oskar-Maria-Graf-Ring 20-22 (tel. 670 64 63). An environmentally-conscious women's cafe and shop. Open Tu and Th-F 10am-1pm, W 10am-1pm and 3-6pm. **Fraueninfothek,** Johannispl. 12 (tel. 48 48 90). Open M 10am-1pm, Tu 10am-1pm and 2-5pm, Th 2-5pm.

Gay and Lesbian Organizations: Gay services info tel. 260 30 56. **Lesbian info** (tel. 725 42 72. Open F 6-10pm. Also for lesbians, **Lesbentraum LeTra,** Dreimühlenstr. 23 tel. 725 42 72. Open Th 1:30-4pm; telephones open Th 7-10pm. See **Gay and Lesbian Munich,** p. 496.

Disabled Concerns: Info Center für Behinderte, Schellingstr. 31, has a list of Munich resources for disabled persons. Open M-W 8am-noon and 2-6pm, Th 8am-noon and 2-4pm, F 8am-noon.

Ticket Agencies: Advance tickets for concerts in the Olympiapark and soccer games are available at the **Kaufhof** department store either on Marienplatz, 3rd floor (tel. 260 32 49) or at Karlsplatz, ground floor (tel. 512 52 48). Both open M-W and F 11am-6:30pm, Th 11am-8:30pm, Sa 9am-2pm. To order tickets by phone call **München Ticket** (tel. 54 81 81 81). **Hertie Schwabing,** Leopoldstr. 82, 4th floor (tel. 33 66 59), sells tickets for smaller rock, pop, and theater events. Open M-F 9am-6:30pm, Sa 9am-2pm.

Laundromat: The **City SB-Waschcenter,** Paul-Heyse-Str. 21, is close to the station; right on Bayerstr., then left on Paul-Heyse-Str. for 1½ blocks. Wash DM6, soap included. Dry DM1 per 10min. Open daily 7am-11pm. **Münz Waschsalon,** Amalienstr. 61, near the university. Wash DM6.20, soap DM1. Dry DM1 per 10min. Open M-F 8am-6:30pm, Sa 8am-1pm. **Waschcenter,** Landshüter Allee 77. U-Bahn #1 to "Rotkreuzpl." Wash DM6. Dry DM1 per 15min. Open 24hr. *Bring your own change for laundromats.*

Swimming Pools: Pool season is May to mid-Sept. Choose among 16 local dives. **Michaelibad,** Heinrich-Wieland-Str. 24 (tel. 40 76 91), is a huge pool complex with slides and 5 swimming areas. U-Bahn #2 or 5 to "Michaelibad." Open M 10am-6pm, Tu-Su 7am-9pm. **Müllerisches Volksbad,** Rosenheimerstr. 1 (tel. 23 61 34 29), has Art Nouveau indoor pools and Irish-Roman steam baths. S-Bahn #1-8 to "Isartor." Open M 10am-5pm, Tu and Th 8am-7:30pm, W 6:45am-7:30pm, F 8am-8:45pm, Sa 8am-5:30pm, Su 9am-6pm. The outdoor, heated **Dantebad,** Dantestr. 6 (tel. 15 28 74), in Neuhausen, is excellent and much less crowded—hardly hellish. Streetcar #20 or 21 to "Baldurstr." Open daily 8am-7:30pm.

EMERGENCY AND COMMUNICATIONS

Emergency: Police, tel. 110. **Ambulance,** tel. 192 22. **Emergency medical service,** tel. 55 17 71. **Fire,** tel. 112. **Poison Control,** tel. 192 40.

Rape Crisis: Frauennotruf München, Güllstr. 3 (tel. 76 37 37).

AIDS Hotline: tel. 520 73 87 or 520 74 12 (M-Th 8am-3pm, F 8am-noon). Or 194 11 (M-Sa 7-10pm).

Pharmacy: Bahnhof Apotheke, Bahnhofpl. 2 (tel. 59 41 19 or 59 81 19), on the corner outside the station. Open M-F 8am-6:30pm, Sa 8am-2pm. The hours of all other pharmacies posted in the window. 24hr. service rotates among the city's pharmacies—call 59 44 75 for recorded information (German only). The tourist office and EurAide also have free monthly schedules.

Medical Assistance: Klinikum Rechts d. Isar, clinic across the river on Ismaningerstr. U-Bahn #4 or 5 to "Max-Weber-Platz." STD/AIDS tests are free and anonymous at the **Gesundheitshaus,** Dachauerstr. 90 (tel. 520 71). Open M-Th 8-11am and 1-2pm, F 8-11am. U.K. and U.S. consulates carry lists of English-speaking doctors.

Internet Access: In **Hotel Kurpfalz** (see **Accommodations,** p. 484) and the 2 **Internet Cafes** (see **Food,** p. 487).

Post Office: Post/Telegrafenamt, Arnulfstr. 32, 80074 München (tel. 54 54 23 36). *Poste Restante* and money exchange (DM6 per $20 traveler's check—it's cheaper at AmEx). Go out of the train station and turn left onto Arnulfstr.; the post office will be on your right. Open M-F 8am-8pm, Sa 8am-noon. **Postamt 31** (tel. 552 26 20) up the escalator in the train station, sells stamps and phone cards and mails letters, but doesn't mail packages or exchange money. Open M-F 7am-8pm, Sa 8am-4pm, Su 9am-3pm.

Telephone Code: 089.

■ Accommodations and Camping

Munich's accommodations usually fall into one of three categories: seedy, expensive, or booked solid. During times like *Oktoberfest*, there is only the last category. During summer, the best strategy is to start calling before noon or to book a few weeks in advance. Most singles (without private bath) range DM55-85, doubles DM80-120. If you're planning an extended stay in Munich, call the *Mitwohnzentrale* (see p. 480) or try bargaining with a *Pension* owner. Remember: **Bavarian HI hostels do not accept guests over age 26.** The enforcement of this rule varies. At most of Munich's hostels you can check in all day, but try to start your search well before 5pm.

Don't even think of sleeping in any public area, including the *Hauptbahnhof;* police patrol frequently all night long. A few options for the roomless do exist: the Augsburg youth hostel (tel. (0821) 339 09) is 30 to 45 minutes away by train (until 11pm, 2-3 per hr.; DM10), but be mindful of the 1am curfew. The Ebersberg youth hostel, Attenberger-Schillingerstr. 1 (tel. (08092) 225 23), is 30 minutes away, just outside the city center. Take S-Bahn #5 to "Ebersberg" (last stop; DM10.50 each way, or 6 strips), but the doors lock at 10pm. Or, you can throw your luggage into a locker and party until 5am, and return to re-evaluate the hotel lists afterward.

HOSTELS

⊛Jugendlager Kapuzinerhölzl ("The Tent"), In den Kirschen 30 (tel. 141 43 00; fax 17 50 90). Streetcar #17 from the *Hauptbahnhof* (direction: "Amalienburgstr.") to "Botanischer Garten" (15min.), straight on Franz-Schrank-Str., left at In den Kirschen. The Tent is on the right. Night streetcars run at least once an hour all night. Sleep with 400 fellow "campers" under a big circus tent on a wooden floor. DM13 gets a foam pad, multiple wool blankets, bathrooms, a shower (not necessarily warm), a rudimentary breakfast, and enthusiastic management. Actual "beds" DM17. Camping available for DM5 per tent plus DM5 per person. Includes a super deal on public transportation—rent a *Grüne Karte* that covers everything in the *Innenraum* (DM4 per day), or the *Gesamtnetz* (DM6). Spontaneous merrymaking around a bonfire at night. Bike rental DM10 per day (daily 8-10am), free city tours (W 9am), volleyball, ping-pong, free kitchen facilities, and yes—a beer garden. Laundry DM4, no dryers. Lockers provided. 24hr. reception—register before sleeping passport required as deposit). Reservations only for groups over 10, but rarely full. Open mid-June to early Sept.

⊛4 you münchen *(ökologisches Jugendgästehaus)*, Hirtenstr. 18 (tel. 55 21 660; fax 55 21 66 66), 200m from the *Hauptbahnhof.* Exit at Arnulfstr., go left, quickly turn right onto Pfefferstr., then hang a left onto Hirtenstr. Beautiful ecological youth hostel with restaurant/bar, hang-out areas, a playroom, and wheelchair-accessible everything. 12-bed dorms DM24; 4-, 6-, or 8-bed dorms DM29; singles DM54; doubles DM76. Over 27 15% surcharge. Key deposit DM20. Breakfast buffet DM7.50. Sheets DM5. In their adjoining hotel, singles with bath DM79; doubles with bath DM110, extra bed DM49 (for children 6-18 years old, DM29; under 6 free). Breakfast included. Reception 7am-1:30pm, 3-7pm, and 7:30-10pm. Reserve be4 you arrive—without good 4tune, acquiring a bed is a 4midable task.

Jugendherberge Pullach Burg Schwaneck (HI), Burgweg 4-6 (tel. 793 06 43; fax 793 79 22), in a castle 12km outside the city center. S-Bahn #7 (direction: "Wolfratshausen") to "Pullach" (20min.). From the station, head straight down Bahnhofstr., swing a left onto Münchnerstr., veer right onto Margarethenstr., and then follow the signs (8min.). Unmajestic rooms quiet and well-kept. Romantic surroundings swarm with schoolchildren. 6- to 8-bed rooms DM19.50; 4-bed rooms DM22.50; singles DM34; doubles DM65. Breakfast included. Dinner DM8. Sheets DM5. Reception 4-11pm. Curfew 11:30pm. Try to make reservations 7:30-10am.

Jugendherberge München (HI), Wendl-Dietrich-Str. 20. (tel. 13 11 56; fax 167 87 45). U-Bahn #1 to "Rotkreuzpl." Cross Rotkreuzplatz heading toward the Kaufhof department store, then go down Wendl-Dietrich-Str. The entrance is ahead on the right. The most "central" of the HI hostels (3km from the city center). Safes in the reception area—*use them,* and keep keys with you at *all* times. Big dorm (37 beds) for men only DM23; 4- to 6-bed coed rooms DM25.50. Breakfast and sheets included. Mandatory DM20 key deposit. DM50 deposit for use of safes. Check-in starts at 11am, but the lines form before 9am. 24hr. reception. Reservations only accepted a week in advance; if you get one, arrive by 6pm or call first.

Jugendgästehaus Thalkirchen, Miesingstr. 4 (tel. 723 65 50 or 723 65 60; fax 724 25 67; email BineMunich@aol.com). U-Bahn #1 or 2 to "Sendlinger Tor," then #3 (direction: "Fürstenrieder West") to "Thalkirchen" (Zoo). Take Thalkirchnerplatz exit and follow Schäftlarnstr. toward Innsbruck and bear right around the curve, then follow Frauenbergstr. and head left on Münchnerstr.; take the street as it curves left. Crowded and distant, but the rooms are colorful and comfortable. 8- to 15-bed rooms DM27; singles DM35.50; doubles DM63; triples DM88.50; quads DM118. Sheets and breakfast included. Bike rental DM22 per day, DM90 per week. Reception 7am-1am. Check-in 2-6pm, or call if you'll arrive later. Curfew 1am.

Jump In, Hochstr. 51 (tel. 48 95 34 37), a new, small, private place founded by a brother and Pointer Sister team tired of impersonal hostels. S-Bahn #1-8 to "Rosenheimerpl.," then take the Gasteig exit to the left and walk left on Hochstr. (10min.). Or streetcar #27 or bus #51 to "Ostfriedhof." A little disorganized, but supremely amicable and delightfully informal. Easily accessible location, but rather spartan rooms. Funky thin mattresses DM29, thick mattresses DM35; doubles

DM78. Includes rudimentary breakfast and free kitchen facilities. Try to bargain for longer-term arrangements. Reception 10am-1pm and 5-10pm. No curfew.

Jugendhotel Marienberge, Goethestr. 9 (tel. 55 58 05), less than a block from the train station, staffed by merry nuns. The rooms in this Catholic hostel are spacious, cheery, and spotless. **Open only to women under 26.** 6-bed dorms DM30; singles DM40; doubles DM70; triples DM105. Breakfast included. Kitchen and laundry facilities. Wash DM2, dry DM2. Reception 8am-midnight. Curfew midnight, before you turn into a pumpkin.

CVJM (YMCA) Jugendgästehaus, Landwehrstr. 13 (tel. 552 14 10; fax 550 42 82; email muenchen@cvjm.org). Take the Bayerstr. exit from the station, head straight down Goethestr. or Schillerstr., and take the 2nd left onto Landwehrstr.; it's on the right. Central location with modern, newly renovated rooms and showers in the hall. Singles DM50; doubles DM86; triples DM120. Co-ed rooms for married couples only. Over 27 15% surcharge. Breakfast included. Reception 8am-12:30am. Curfew 12:30am. Reservations by mail, phone, fax, or email must arrive before 4pm. Nifty 50s-decorated restaurant offers dinner (DM6-10), soups, and salads Tu-F 6:30-10pm. Closed during Easter and Dec. 20-Jan. 7.

Haus International, Elisabethstr. 87 (tel. 12 00 60; fax 12 00 62 51). U-Bahn #2 (direction: "Feldmoching") to "Hohenzollernpl.," then streetcar #12 (direction: "Romanpl.") or bus #33 (direction: "Aidenbachstr.") to "Barbarastr." It's the 5-story beige building behind the BP gas station. Pleasantly clean dorm rooms overlook a busy street. Singles DM55, with bath DM85; doubles DM104, with shower DM144; triples DM138; quads DM170; quints DM200. Lunch and dinner available (DM10-14). Free indoor pool (score!), small beer garden, TV room, and newly renovated disco. 24hr. reception. Reservations recommended in summer; depending on room availability, groups of 10 or more may be required to reserve with half-pension (add DM14 per person for dinner).

Euro Youth Hotel, Senefelderstr. 5 (tel. 599 08 80; fax 59 90 88 77), just opened in June 1998. From the Bahnhofsplatz exit of the *Hauptbahnhof,* make a right on Bayerstr. then a left on Senefelderstr. The hotel will be on the left. DM29; doubles and triples DM36, with shower DM45. Breakfast buffet DM6.90. 24hr. reception. No curfew or lockout.

CAMPING

All three Munich campgrounds are open from mid-March to late October.

Campingplatz Thalkirchen, Zentralländstr. 49, 81379 München (tel. 723 17 07; fax 724 31 77), in the Isar River Valley Conservation Area. U-Bahn #1 or 2 to "Sendlinger Tor," then #3 to "Thalkirchen," and change to bus #57 (20min.). From the bus stop, cross the busy street on the left and take a right onto the footpath next to the road. The entrance to the campground is down the tree lined path on the left. Well-run, crowded grounds with jogging and cycling paths and access to a nearby river. TV lounge, grocery store, and a restaurant (meals DM3-8). DM7.90 per person; DM 2.50 per child under 14. DM5.50-7 per tent. DM8.50 per car. Showers DM2. Laundry facilities (wash DM7, dry DM0.5 per 6min.). Curfew 11pm.

Obermenzing, Lochhausener Str. 59, 81247 München (tel. 811 22 35; fax 814 48 07). S-Bahn #3-6 or 8 to "Passing," then exit toward track 8 and take bus #76 to "Lochhausener Str." Head up the street (5min.); it's on the left. On the noisy *Autobahn,* but friendly and well-kept. DM7.50 per person; DM4 per child under 14. DM7.50 per tent. DM5 per car. Showers DM2. Reception 7:30am-noon and 3-8pm.

Langwieder See, Eschenriederstr. 119, 81249 München (tel. 864 15 66; fax 863 23 42). Located near a nice lake, and accessible by car. Go right off the Augsburg *Autobahn* A8, and exit at Lochhausen/Eschenried. The nearest train station is München-Lochhausen, but it's a 2km schlepp toward Eschenried.

HOTELS AND PENSIONEN

While Munich, reputedly a city of 80,000 guest beds, has a surplus of dirt-cheap (and often dirty!) accommodations, it is often a better idea to crash in a hostel. A clean room in a safe area costs at least DM55-65 for a single or DM80-100 for a double. Always call ahead. For Oktoberfest rooms you should call a few months in advance, as some hotels are booked for the entire two weeks by early summer. The tourist office provides a free room-finding service (with a 10-15% deposit) and sells hotel lists for DM0.50. The EurAide staff (at the train station) may better suit your English-speaking needs and will help you for a DM7 fee. Carefully consider the location of the hotels/*Pensionen.* Since transportation is ridiculously expensive in Munich, a hasty decision may end up costing you big bucks.

Near the Hauptbahnhof

Hotel Helvetia, Schillerstr. 6 (tel. 590 68 50; fax 59 06 85 70), at the corner of Bahnhofsplatz, next to the Vereinsbank, to the right as you exit the station. Recently renovated and delicately redecorated. Most rooms have phones. Singles DM53-62; doubles DM68-90, with shower DM115; triples DM99-120. Breakfast included. Also caters to backpackers with new hostel-like dorms: 10-bed DM19, 4- to 6-bed DM24. Rates rise 10-15% during *Oktoberfest.* Breakfast DM7. Sheets DM4. Laundry service (17lb. per 8kg) DM8.50. 24hr. reception.

Pension Utzelmann, Pettenkoferstr. 6 (tel. 59 48 89; fax 59 62 28). From the *Bahnhof* walk 4 blocks down Schillerstr. and go left on Pettenkofer; it's at the end on the left (10min.). Nostalgic, elegant rooms with upholstered furniture and oriental rugs. Singles DM50, with shower DM95, with bath DM125; doubles DM90, with shower DM110, with bath DM145; triples DM125, with shower DM150, with bath DM175; quads DM160, with shower DM180. DM5 for hall showers. Breakfast included. No credit cards. Reception 7am-10pm.

Hotel Kurpfalz, Schwanthalerstr. 121 (tel. 540 98 60; fax 54 09 88 11; email hotel-kurpfalz@munich-online.de; http://www.munich-hotels.com). Exit on Bayerstr. from the station, turn right and walk 5 to 6 blocks down Bayerstr., veer left onto Holzapfelstr., and make a right onto Schwanthalerstr. (10min.). Or streetcar #18 or 19 to "Holzapfelstr." (3 stops) and walk from there. The hotel's Sevdas brothers will win you over with their smiley proficiency in Americana. Satellite TVs, phones, and hardwood furniture in all rooms. Singles DM89; doubles DM129; triples (doubles with cots) DM165. All rooms have private bath. All-you-can-eat breakfast buffet included. Free **Internet access.** Credit cards accepted. 24hr. reception.

Pension Locarno, Bahnhofpl. 5 (tel. 55 51 64; fax 59 50 45), under the AGFA sign at the intersection with Arnulfstr. right outside the train station. Plain rooms, redecorated in 1998, all with TV and phone. Helpful owners. Singles DM55-75; doubles DM85; triples DM125; quads DM140. Breakfast included. DM5 less if you arrange for no breakfast. AmEx, Eurocard, MC, Visa. Mention *Let's Go* for DM5 discount. Reception 7:30am-midnight; locked at 10pm, but your key opens the door 24hr.

Pension Schillerhof, Schillerstr. 21 (tel. 59 42 70; fax 550 18 35). From the "Bahnhofspl." train station exit, turn right and walk 2 blocks. Unpretentious, tidy rooms amid a sea of neighborhood sex shops and *Kinos.* In-room TVs. Singles DM50-65, with shower DM60-75; doubles DM80-95, with shower DM95-110. Extra bed DM20. *Oktoberfest* surcharge DM25-40 per person. Breakfast included. Eurocard, MC, Visa. Reception 6am-10pm.

Pension Hungaria, Briennerstr. 42 (tel. 52 15 58). From the *Hauptbahnhof,* go left onto Dachauerstr., right on Augustenstr., and right onto Briennerstr. (10min.). Or U-Bahn #1 to "Stiglmaierpl."; take the Briennerstr./Volkstheater exit, and it's on the next corner at Augustenstr. Oriental rugs, comfortable furnishings, and small travel library. Singles DM55; doubles DM75-85; triples DM105; quads DM120. Lovely breakfasts included. Showers DM3. *Oktoberfest* surcharge DM10 per room. 24hr. reception 2 floors up.

Hotel Central, Bayerstr. 55 (tel. 543 98 46; fax 543 98 47), 5min. from the Bayerstr. exit of the train station on the right. The unattractive exterior belies the qualities within—just like Quasimodo. Singles DM50-60, with bath DM70-85; doubles DM85-115, with bath DM120-130. Ask for inexpensive group prices (3 or more people) from DM35-45 per person. 24hr. reception. AmEx, MC, Visa.

Schwabing/University/City Center

⚛Pension Frank, Schellingstr. 24 (tel. 28 14 51; fax 280 09 10; http://www.city-netz.com/pensionfrank). From the *Hauptbahnhof*, U-Bahn #4 or 5 to "Odeonspl.," then U-Bahn #3 or 6 to "Universität." Take the Schellingstr. exit, then the first right onto Schellingstr.; it's 2 blocks down on the right. Curious combination of scruffy backpackers, student groups, and dolled-up (second-rate) fashion models. Fabulous location for cafe and bookstore aficionados. 3- to 6-bed rooms DM35 per person. Singles DM55-65; doubles DM78-85. Single beds in shared rooms almost always available. *Oktoberfest* prices no more than DM5 higher. Hearty breakfast and fridge access included. Reception 7:30am-10pm.

Pension am Kaiserplatz, Kaiserpl. 12 (tel. 34 91 90), is located a few blocks from nightlife central—good location if you doubt your own sense of direction after a couple of bubbling brewskis. U-Bahn #3 or 6 to "Münchener Freiheit." Take the escalator to Herzogstr., then left onto Viktoriastr. Walk down Viktoriastr. past the church; it's at the end of the street on the right (10min.). Sweet owner offers elegantly decorated, high-ceilinged rooms. Singles DM49-59; doubles DM82, with shower DM89; triples DM105; quads DM120-130; quints DM150-160; 6-bed rooms DM160-170. Breakfast (room service) included. DM3 to shower more than once per day—hygiene comes at a price! Reception 7am-9pm.

Pension Geiger, Steinheilstr. 1 (tel. 52 15 56; fax 52 31 54 71). U-Bahn #2 to "Theresienstr." Take the Augustenstr. S.O. exit, and then walk straight down Theresienstr. towards Kopierladen München. Take a right onto Enhuberstr. and a left onto Steinheilstr.; enter through the double doors on the right. Family-run *Pension* decorated like a Midwestern living-room, brimming with bric-a-brac and soft sofas. Singles DM50, with shower DM70; doubles DM90, with shower DM98. Hall showers DM2. Reception (2 floors up) 8am-9pm. Arrive by 6pm or call. Closed Dec. 24-Jan. 31.

Pension Theresia, Luisenstr. 51 (tel. 52 12 50; fax 542 06 33). U-Bahn #2 to "Theresienstr.," take the Augustenstr./Technische Univ. exit, head straight down Theresienstr., and take the second right onto Luisenstr.; the entrance is in the passageway left of the Dahlke store. Cheery red carpets and an elegant dining room complement the well-maintained rooms. Singles DM52-69; doubles DM88-115, with shower DM95-125; triples DM123-150; quads DM144-184. Breakfast included. Hall showers DM3. Reception (2nd floor) 6:30am-10pm. Reservations by phone or fax. AmEx, MC, Visa.

Hotel-Pension am Markt, Heiliggeiststr. 6 (tel. 22 50 14; fax 22 40 17), smack dab in the city center. S-Bahn #1-8 to "Marienpl.," then walk through the *Altes Rathaus*, and turn right behind the Heiliggeist Church. Aging photographs recall celebrities who graced the hotel's small but shipshape rooms—recognize anyone? Singles DM62-64, with shower DM110; doubles DM110-116, DM150-160; triples DM165, DM205. Breakfast included. Reserve at least 3-4 weeks in advance.

■ Food

The vibrant **Viktualienmarkt,** two minutes south of Marienplatz, is Munich's gastronomic center, rumbling with a colorful cornucopia of sights, smells, and tastes, offering both basic and exotic foods and ingredients—lots of fun to browse through, but don't plan to do budget grocery shopping here (open M-F 9am-6:30pm, Sa 9am-2pm). Located on every corner, the ubiquitous **beer gardens** (see **Beer, Beer, and More Beer,** p. 487) serve savory snacks along with the booze, yet since the time of King Ludwig I skinflints have been permitted to bring their own food to many of the gardens. To make sure that your fixings are welcome, ask a server or check for tables without tablecloths, as bare tables usually indicate self-service *(Selbstbedienung)*. To stick your fangs into an authentic Bavarian lunch, grab a *Brez'n* (pretzel; pronounced "Braaayzin" by the *Müncheners*) and spread it with *Leberwurst* or cheese (DM4-5). *Weißwürste* (white veal sausages) are another native bargain, served in a pot of hot water with sweet mustard and a soft pretzel on the side. Don't eat the skin of the sausage; instead, slice it open and devour the tender meat. Traditionally, *Weißwürste* are consumed before noon during *Frühschoppen*, but you can find it any time. *Leberkäs*, also a *Müncheners* lunch, is a slice of a pinkish, meatloaf-like compound of ground beef and bacon which, despite its name and dubious appearance, contains neither liver nor cheese. *Leberknödel* are liver dumplings, usually served in soup or with *Kraut; Kartoffelknödel* (potato dumplings) and *Semmelknödel* (made from white bread, egg, and parsley) are eaten along with a hearty chunk of German meat. Those not interested in chowing down on all things meaty can head to Munich's scrumptious and healthy vegetarian cafes.

Tengelmann, Bayerstr. 5, straight ahead from the main station, is most convenient for grocery needs (open M-F 8:30am-8pm, Sa 8am-4pm). The **supermarket HL Markt,** at Rotkreuzplatz is larger and provides a little more variety. Take U-Bahn #1 to "Rotkreuzpl." (open M-F 8:30am-8pm, Sa 8am-4pm). *Munich Found* (DM4) lists a few restaurants, while *Prinz* (DM5) proffers a fairly complete listing of restaurants, cafes, and bars in Munich. Countless fruit and vegetable **markets** are held throughout the city, with many on Bayerstr. just a few blocks from the train station.

University Mensas

Mensas serve large portions of cheap food (DM3-5.50), and offer at least one vegetarian dish. Student ID is required. Buy your token from booths in the lobby *before* getting your meal. These *Mensen* are open year-round.

Technical University, Arcisstr. 17, to the left of the Pinakothek Museums just below Gabelsbregstr. on Arcisstr. U-Bahn #2 to "Königspl." Open M-Th 8:30am-4:15pm, F 8:30am-2:30pm. During vacations open M-F 8am-4pm.

University of Science and Medicine (Fachbereich Medizin Universität), Schillerstr. 43, 4 blocks from the station, behind Hotel Kraft, hidden by a row of trees. A telltale bounty of bicycles parked in front. Open M-Th 9am-4:15pm, F 9am-2:30pm.

Near the University

The university district off **Ludwigstraße** is Munich's best source of filling meals in a lively, unpretentious (but hip) atmosphere. Many restaurants and cafes cluster on Schellingstr., Amalienstr., and Türkenstr.; the nightlife scene trickles away from the city center down Leopoldstr. Ride U-Bahn #3 or 6 to "Universität" to reach these restaurants. **Plus supermarket,** Schellingstr. 38, provides cheap groceries (open M-F 8:30am-7pm, Sa 8am-3pm).

Türkenhof, Türkenstr. 78 (tel. 280 02 35), has a pseudo-Turkish menu. Immortally popular with the low-key student population. Smoky and buzzing from noon 'til night. Variable daily menu with numerous veggie options. Creative entrees (*Schnitzel,* omelettes, soups) DM7-14. Open Su-Th 11am-1am, F-Sa 11am-3am.

Schelling Salon, Schellingstr. 54 (tel. 272 07 88). Bavarian *Knödel* and billiard balls. Founded in 1872 on the philosophy that billiards is the game *"der schweigenden Männer"* (of silent men), this pool joint has racked the balls of Lenin, Rilke, and Hitler. Breakfast DM5-9; *Wurst* DM6-7; *Russ'n Maß* DM9.40. A free **billiard museum** displays a 200-year-old Polish noble's table and the history of pool back to the Pharaohs. Restaurant and museum open M-Tu and Th-Su 6:30am-1pm.

News Bar, Amalienstr. 55 (tel. 28 17 87), at the corner of Schellingstr. Trendy new cafe, teeming with younguns. Crepes DM7-11, granola with yogurt DM7.80, pasta with pesto DM11.90, freshly pressed juice DM4.90. Open daily 7:30am-2am.

In the Center

Munich's touristy interior suffers from an overabundance of high-priced eateries, but there are some good options, even for the budget traveler.

Shoya, Orlandostr. 5 (tel. 29 27 72), across from the Hofbräuhaus. The most reasonable Japanese restaurant in town. Fill up on rice dishes (DM13-19), *teriyaki* (DM8-16), sushi (DM5-30), and meat and veggie dishes (DM4-16) before strolling down Marienplatz. Take-out available. Open daily 10:30am-midnight.

La Fiorentia Trattoria Pizzeria Café, Goethestr. 41 (tel. 53 41 85), a few blocks from the train station, specializes in generating exquisite, mouth-watering fragrances. Salivating pizza-lovers from the nearby medical university transform this cafe into a mini Italian culinary festival every weekday afternoon. Calzones DM11.50, pizza DM7-12.50, *Maß DM8.60.*

Beim Sendlmayr, Westenriederstr. 6 (tel. 22 62 19), off the Viktualienmarkt. Anyone craving a *Weißwurst* will love this slice of Little Bayern. Specials DM7-25. Beer DM5.60 for 0.5L. Open daily 11am-11pm. Kitchen open M-F 11am-9pm, Sa 11am-4pm. For an exotic fruit drink, duck into the **Sama-Sama** fruit and flower shop directly across the street.

⊕**Valentin Musäum Café** (tel. 22 32 66), in the Valentin Museum in Isartorturm. S-Bahn #1-8 or Streetcar #18 or 20 to "Isartor." This curious nook in the bowels of the city's western tower serves up thick mugs of hot milk with honey (DM4.20) and savory *Apfelstrudel* with vanilla ice cream (DM9.40) in a comical and characteristically Valentin atmosphere. Must pay entrance fee for museum to get in. Open M-Tu and F-Sa 11am-5:30pm, Su 10am-5:30pm.

Elsewhere in Munich

Internet-Café, Nymphenburgerstr. 145 (tel. 129 11 20; http://www.icafe.spacenet.de), on the corner of Landshuter Allee. U-Bahn #1 to "Rotkreuzpl." With the addition of 12 terminals, this is an average Italian joint cum hopping, glowing electronic haven—a Neuromancer's paradise. Unlimited free Internet access as long as you order pasta (DM9.50), pizza (DM7.50-10), or beer (DM4.90 for 0.5L). Open daily 11am-4am. **Another location,** Altheimer Eck 12 (tel. 260 78 15), sits in the city center between Marienplatz and Karlsplatz in the pedestrian zone through "Arcade-Passage." Same stuff, different hours—daily 11am-1am.

Schwimmkrabbe, Ickstattstr. 13 (tel. 201 00 80). U-Bahn #1 or 2 to "Fraunhoferstr.," then walk 1 block down Baaderstr. to Ickstattstr. Locals flock to this family-run Turkish restaurant. Try the delicious *Etli Pide* (lamb and veggies wrapped in a footlong bread with salad; DM16). Filling appetizers DM6-14. Hearty dishes DM15-20. Belly-dancing darlings on Friday and Saturday nights add some *exotica* to your trip. Open daily 5pm-1am. Reserve on weekends.

Vegetarian Restaurants

Gollier, Gollierstr. 83 (tel. 50 16 73). U-Bahn #4 or 5 or S-Bahn #7 or 27 to "Heimeranpl." Serves delicious homemade pizzas, casseroles, and crepes (DM6-19). Lunch buffet DM13. Open M-F noon-3pm and 5pm-midnight, Sa 5pm-midnight, Su noon-midnight.

Café Ignaz, Georgenstr. 67 (tel. 271 60 93). U-Bahn #2 to Joesephsplatz. Ecologically sound, romantic cafe with a nutritious and rapturously inexpensive menu. Yogurt with fresh fruit DM6.50. Carrot juice DM4.90. All dinners (pasta, quiche, or stir-fry dishes) DM11. English menu available. Open M-F 7am-10pm, Sa-Su 9am-10pm.

buxs, Frauenstr. 9 (tel. 22 94 82), on the southern edge of the Viktualienmarkt on the corner of Westernederstr. Tasty, artful pastas, salads (100g DM3), soups, and hearty bread. Open M-F 11am-8:30pm, Sa 11am-3:30pm.

BEER, BEER, AND MORE BEER

The six great Munich labels are *Augustiner, Hacker-Pschorr, Hofbräu, Löwenbräu, Paulaner,* and *Spaten-Franziskaner,* yet most restaurants and *Gaststätte* will pick a side by only serving one brewery's beer. There are four main types of beer served in Munich. **Helles** and **Dunkles,** standard but delicious light and dark beers, **Weißbier,** a cloudy blond beer made from wheat instead of barley; and **Radler** (literally "cyclist's brew"), which is half beer and half lemon soda. Munich's beer typically has an alcohol content of 3.5%, though in *Starkbierzeit* (which runs 2 weeks, beginning with Lent), *Müncheners* traditionally drink *Salvator,* a strong, dark beer that is 5.5% alcohol. In May, art folk clean their palates with *Marbock,* a blond Bockbeer. *Frühschoppen* is morning beer and sausage consumption. *Prost! "Ein Bier, bitte"* will get you a liter, known to those in the know as a *Maß* (DM8-11). If you want a half-*Maß* (DM4-6), you must specify it, though many establishments will only serve *Weißbier* in 0.5L sizes. Though some beer gardens offer non-meaty dishes, vegetarians may wish to eat elsewhere before proceeding to a beer garden for a post-meal swig. For an online guide to Munich's beer gardens, visit http://www.biergarten.com.

Beer Garden History 101

The official coat-of-arms of Munich depicts a monk holding a Bible in his right hand. Unofficially, the monk's left hand firmly clenches a large, frothy brewski, raising it high and, with a twinkle in the eye, saying *"Prost."* Sacrilege? Not at all. In 1328, the Augustiner monks introduced *Bier* to unsuspecting *Müncheners,* who have since continued the 600-year-old trend. Bayern proudly holds the title as the largest producer *and* consumer of beer in Germany—in a mighty big way. Local breweries produce 123 million gallons of "liquid bread" per annum, 150,000 seats in Munich **beer gardens** beckon the thirsty, and every year, the average local imbibes over 220 liters of this amber dew of gods, more than twice the average drunk in the rest of Germany (though the figure does include the mighty *Oktoberfest,* during which locals and visitors together swig six million liters). The tradition of beer gardens in Bavaria is said to have begun with King Ludwig I, who allowed brewers to sell beer, but not food, in an outdoor restaurant setting. All citizens could afford to indulge in this yummy beverage by bringing their own meals to the gardens. Many of Munich's beer gardens today are shaded by large-leafed chestnut trees, planted before the invention of refrigeration to keep the ground above the storage cellars cool. Proudly honoring the Beer Purity Law *(Reinheitsgebot)* of 1516 (see p. 82), Bavarians reaffirm their exalted and earned reputation as the ultimate, tried-and-true beer connoisseurs.

The biggest keg party in the world, Munich's **Oktoberfest** finishes on the first Sunday of October and starts 16 days earlier (Sept. 18-Oct. 3 in 1999). The site of this uncontrolled revelry is known as **Theresienwiese** (Therese's meadow)—or *"Wies'n"* (shortened perhaps after one *Maß* too many). Ride U-Bahn #4 or 5 to "Theresienwiese." The festivities began in 1810 when Prince Ludwig married Princess Therese von Sachsen-Hildburghausen; ironically, no alcohol was served at the original reception. The party was so much fun that *Müncheners* repeated the revelry the next year, and every year following that, unable to resist a revival. The party kicks off with speeches, a parade of horse-drawn beer wagons, and the mayor's tapping of the ceremonial first keg. The touristy *Hofbräu* tent is the rowdiest; fights break out often. Arrive early (by 4:30pm) to get a table—you must be seated to be served at *Oktoberfest.*

Within Munich

Augustiner Keller, Arnulfstr. 52 (tel. 59 43 93), at Zirkus-Krone-Str. S-Bahn #1-8 to "Hackerbrücke." Founded in 1824, Augustiner is viewed by most *Müncheners* as the finest beer garden in town. Lush grounds and dim lighting beneath 100-year-old chestnut trees and tasty, enormous *Brez'n* (pretzels; DM5.20) support their cause. The real attraction is the delicious, sharp Augustiner beer (*Maß* DM11), which entices locals, smart tourists, and scads of students. Food DM10-28. Open daily 10am-1am; hot food until 10pm. Beer garden open daily 10:30am-midnight.

Hofbräuhaus, Am Platzl 9 (tel. 22 16 76), 2 blocks from Marienplatz. Established in 1589, Munich's world-famous beer hall was originally reserved for royalty and invited guests (the name means "court brewery house"). Now it seems reserved for American frat boys and drunken tourists. 15,000-30,000L of beer are sold per day. It's a rite of passage to introduce backpackers from around the world to the joys of the Munich beer world. It was in the *Festsaal* that Hitler was proclaimed the first Nazi party chair. Small beer garden out back under chestnut trees. *Maß* DM10.40. *Leberkäs* with spinach and potatoes DM9.90. Open daily 9:30am-midnight.

☻**Hirschgarten,** Hirschgartenallee 1 (tel. 17 25 91). U-Bahn #1 to "Rotkreuzpl.," then streetcar #12 to "Romanpl." Walk straight to the end of Guntherstr. and enter the Hirschgarten—literally, "deer garden." The largest beer garden in Europe is boisterous and verdant, but somewhat remote (in the vicinity of *Schloß Nymphenburg*). Families head here for the grassy park and carousel. *Maß* DM8.60. Open daily 11am-11pm. Restaurant closed Mondays Nov.-Feb. Entrees DM7-25.

Augustiner Bräustuben, Landsbergerstr. 19 (tel. 50 70 47). S-Bahn #1-8 to "Hackerbrücke." A relatively new beer hall in the Augustiner Brewery's former horse stalls.

Shh, it's a local secret. DM4 for 0.5L. For the hungry horse, try the *Bräustüberl* (duck, two types of pork, *Kraut*, and two types of dumplings) for DM14.60. Other delicious heaps of Bavarian food at excellent prices (DM6-20). Especially popular in winter. Open daily until 11pm.

Chinesischer Turm, in the *Englischer Garten* next to the pagoda (tel. 39 50 28). U-Bahn #3 or 6 to "Giselastr." or bus #54 from *Südbahnhof* to "Chinesischer Turm." A fair-weather tourist favorite; lots of kids. *Maß (Weißbier)* DM9.50. Salads DM7-13.50. Pretzels DM5. Open daily in balmy weather 10:30am-11pm.

Augustiner, Neuhauserstr. 16 (tel. 55 19 92 57). Smaller manifestation of the *Keller* of the same name. Beer hall and sidewalk tables on the pedestrian zone between the station and Marienplatz. The restaurant (on the right) is pricier than the beer hall. Bavarian meals DM9-28. Beer hall *Maß* DM9.80; restaurant *Maß* DM10.90. Beer hall and restaurant open daily 10am-midnight. Hot meals until 11pm.

Am Seehaus, Kleinhesselohe 3 (tel. 381 61 30). U-Bahn #6 to "Dietlindenstr.," then bus #44 to "Osterwaldgarten." Directly on the lovely Kleinhesseloher See in the *Englischer Garten*, and beloved by locals for the lack of tourists. *Maß* DM9.80. Open daily 10am-1am. Beer garden closes at 11pm.

Taxisgarten, Taxisstr. 12 (tel. 15 68 27). U-Bahn #1 to "Rotkreuzpl.," then bus #83 or 177 to "Klugstr." This beer garden is a gem—its small size has hidden it from tourists and kept it a favorite of locals and students. Almost always full. Spare ribs, jumbo pretzels DM4.50. *Maß* DM9.50, *Weißbier* DM5. Open daily 10am-10pm.

Löwenbräukeller, Nymphenburgerstr. 2 (tel. 52 60 21). U-Bahn #1 to "Stiglmaierpl." Castle-like entrance, festive and loud cellar. Come here to taste the real *Löwenbräu*, if you dare: the bitter taste has a loyal core of local followers, despite general disapproval—it's considered by some to be the Budweiser of Munich beers. Ribs DM15, *Maß* DM7.80. Hot meals 11am-midnight. Open daily 9am-1am.

Paulaner Keller, Hochstr. 77 (tel. 459 91 30). Also known as Salvator Keller and Nockherberg. It's big, old, and has strong beer. U-Bahn #1 or 2 to "Silberhornstr.," then bus #51 to "Ostfriedhof." Walk back down Bonifaziusstr. over the bridge and to the right. Remotely located on Nockherberg Hill, which is part of its charm; crowd mostly comprised of thirtysomethings. *Maß* DM10.80, "Salvator" (0.5L) DM6.10. *Brez'n* and *Knödel* DM11.80. Open daily 9am-11pm.

Pschorr-Keller, Theresienhöhe 7 (tel. 50 10 88). U-Bahn #4 or 5 to "Theresienwiese." Along with the Hackerkeller down the street, an outpost of the Hacker-Pschorr brewery. Good stuff. Come here for your breakfast beer, mostly with locals. *Maß* DM10.80. Meals DM9.50-20. Open daily 8am-midnight.

Parkrestaurant Tarock, Sophienstr. 7, in the Alter Botanischer Garten, a block to the left from the train station (part of the **Park Café** nightclub). This peaceful outdoor beer garden, secluded from the cars and trains by oodles of greenery, is good for a train layover. *Löwenbräu* DM8.50 per *Maß*. Most meals DM6-12.

Just Outside Munich

Waldwirtschaft Großhesselohe, Georg-Kalb-Str. 3 (tel. 79 50 88). S-Bahn #7 to "Großhesselohe Isartalbahnhof." From the station, go down the stairs and turn right; head down Sollnerstr. after passing Kreuzeckstr., then follow the signs. A 15-min. walk from the station. Relaxed beer garden with live music (daily from noon, no cover) and the site of Munich's recent "Beer Garden Revolution." Classic and international jazz starts on Sunday at noon. On a sunny day, schedule a *Frühschoppen* session for 11am or so. *Maß* DM9.80. Open daily 11am-10pm.

Forschungsbräuerei, Unterhachingerstr. 76 (tel. 670 11 69). Serves up some very strange brew—the name means "research brewery." Pleasant, comfortable tables under arching trees. Paradise for the connoisseur of obscure beers. *Maß* DM9-10. Open Tu-Sa 11am-11pm, Su 10am-10pm.

■ Sights

Munich's Catholic past has left many marks on the city's architecture. Numerous, often mightily impressive, sacred stone edifices prickle the area around the **Marienplatz.** The name of this square, a major S-Bahn and U-Bahn junction as well as the social nexus of the city, originates in the **Mariensäule,** an ornate 17th-century monument dedicated to the Virgin Mary. It was built to commemorate the fact that the amazing and powerful Swedes did not destroy the city during the Thirty Years War. Thanks, Thor. The onion-domed towers of the 15th-century **Frauenkirche** are one (well, maybe two) of Munich's most notable landmarks. *(Towers open Apr.-Oct. M-Sa 10am-5pm. DM4, students DM2, under 6 free.)* At the neo-Gothic **Neues Rathaus,** the **Glockenspiel** chimes with a display of jousting knights and dancing coopers. According to legend, the barrel-makers coaxed townspeople out of their homes, singing and dancing, to prove that the Great Plague had passed (daily 11am, noon, 5, and 9pm). At bedtime (9pm), a mechanical watchman marches out and the Guardian Angel escorts the *Münchner Kindl* ("Munich Child," the town's symbol) to bed. *(Tower open M-F 9am-7pm, Sa 9am-7pm, Su 10am-7pm. DM2.50, under 15 DM1.50, under 6 free.)* Don't miss the rooster perched above the knights; he crows three times after the bells stop tolling. On the face of the **Altes Rathaus** tower, to the right of the *Neues Rathaus,* are all of Munich's coats of arms since its inception as a city—except for one glaring decade-long gap. When the tower was rebuilt after its destruction in WWII, the local government refused to include the swastika-bearing coat of arms from the Nazi era.

Munich's ritual past is represented by the 11th-century **Peterskirche** at Rindermarkt and Petersplatz; its golden interior was Baroquified in the 18th century. *(Open M-Sa 9am-7pm, Su 10am-7pm. DM2.50, students DM1.50, children DM0.50.)* Over 300 steps scale the tower, christened *Alter Peter* (Old Peter) by locals. Ludwig II of Bayern (of crazy castle fame) rests peacefully with 40-odd other Wittelsbachs entombed in the crypt of the 16th-century Jesuit **Michaelskirche,** on Neuhauserstr. *(Crypt open M-F 9:15am-4:45pm. DM2, students and children under 16 DM1.)* The construction of the church, designed to emphasize the city's loyalty to Catholicism during the Reformation, almost bankrupted the state treasury. Father Rupert Mayer, one of the few German clerics who spoke out against Hitler, preached here. A Bavarian Rococo masterpiece, the **Asamkirche,** Sendlingerstr. 32, is named after its creators, the Asam brothers, who promised God that they would build a church if they survived the wreckage of their ship. The rocks at the bottom of the facade represent the rapids, the church's literal and metaphorical foundation.

The richly decorated rooms built from the 14th to the 19th centuries in the magnificent **Residenz,** Max-Joseph-Pl. 3 (tel. 29 06 71), form the material vestiges of the Wittelsbach dynasty. The grounds now house several museums. The beautifully landscaped *Hofgarten* behind the *Residenz* houses the lovely temple of Diana. Take U-Bahn #3-6 to "Odeonspl." The **Schatzkammer** (treasury) contains jeweled baubles, crowns, swords, china, ivorywork, and other trinkets from the 10th century on. *(Open Tu-Su 10am-4:30pm; last admission 4pm. DM6, students with ID, seniors, and group members DM4, children under 15 with adult free.)* The **Residenzmuseum** comprises the former Wittelsbach apartments and State Rooms, a collection of European porcelain, and a 17th-century court chapel. German tours of the Residenzmuseum meet just outside the museum entrance. *(Su and W 11am, Tu and Sa 2pm. Su tour DM10, other days DM8.)* The walls of the **Ahnengalerie** (Gallery of Ancestors), hung with 120 "family portraits," trace the royal lineage in an unusual manner. Charlemagne would be surprised to find himself being held accountable for the genesis of the Wittelsbach family. *(Hours and admission same as Schatzkammer. A combo ticket for the Schatzkammer and Ahnengalerie costs DM10, students and seniors DM8.)*

After 10 years of trying for an heir, Ludwig I celebrated the birth of his son Maximilian in 1662 by erecting an elaborate summer playroom. **Schloß Nymphenburg,** in the northwest of town, is a handsome architectural offspring of Ludwig's dogged desire to copy King Louis XIV of France. *(Open Apr.-Sept. Tu-Su 9am-noon and 1-5pm; Oct.-Mar. 10am-12:30pm and 1:30-4pm. DM6, students DM4.)* Ride streetcar #17 (direction: "Amalienburgstr.") to "Schloß Nymphenburg." A Baroque wonder set in a winsome park, the palace hides a number of treasures, including a two-story granite marble hall seasoned with stucco, frescoes, and a Chinese lacquer cabinet. Check out King Ludwig's "Gallery of Beauties"—whenever a woman caught his fancy, he would have her portrait painted (a scandalous hobby, considering that many of the women were commoners; an ironic one, given that Ludwig grappled with an affection for men throughout his life). The palace contains a wonderful collection of antique porcelain and a modern porcelain studio's manufacturing gallery *(Schönheitgalerie)*, as well as the strange **Marstallmuseum** (Carriage Museum). *(Museum open Tu-Su 9am-noon and 1-5pm. Amalienburg open daily 9am-12:30pm and 1:30-5pm; Badenburg, Pagodenburg, and Magdalenen hermitage open Tu-Su 10am-12:30pm and 1:30-5pm. Entire complex DM8, students DM5, children under 15 with adult free. Grounds open until 9:30pm. Free.)*

Just next door, the greenhouses of the immense **Botanischer Garten** (tel. 17 86 13 10) shelter rare and wonderful growths from around the world. *(Open daily 9am-8pm. Greenhouses open 9-11:45am and 1-7:30pm. DM4, students DM2, under 15 DM0.50.)* Check out the Indian and Bolivian water lily room, the eight foot high, 100-year-old cycadee, and the prickly cactus alcove. Abutting the city center is the vast **Englischer Garten,** one of Europe's oldest landscaped public parks. On sunny days, all of Munich turns out to bike, play badminton, ride horseback, or sunbathe. Nude sunbathing areas are designated "FKK" *(Freikörperkultur)* on signs and park maps. Consider yourself warned (or clued in, rather). *Müncheners* with aquatic daring-do surf the white-water rapids of the *Eisbach,* which flows artificially through the park. An excellent vantage point for witnessing these aquatic stunts is from the stone bridge on Prinzregenten-str., close to the Staatsgalerie Moderner Kunst.

Mixed with Munich's Baroque elegance are visible traces of Germany's Nazi past. Buildings erected by Hitler and his cronies that survived the bombings of 1945 stand as grim memorials. The **Haus der Kunst,** built to enshrine Nazi principles of art, serves as a modern art museum; swastika patterns have been left on its porch as reminders of its origins (see **Museums,** below). The gloomy limestone building now housing the **Music School** was built under Hitler's auspices and functioned as his Munich headquarters. From its balcony, he viewed the city's military parades; it was also here that Chamberlain signed away the Sudetenland in 1938.

■ Museums

Munich is a supreme museum city, and many of the city's offerings would independently require days for exhaustive perusal. Several museums inhabit the gilded grounds of the *Residenz* and *Schloß Nymphenburg* (see **Sights,** p. 489). The *Münchner Volkschule* (tel. 48 00 63 30) offers tours of many city museums for DM8. A day pass that allows entry into all of Munich's museums is sold at the tourist office and at many of the larger museums (DM30).

Museumsinsel-Isartor

Deutsches Museum (tel. 217 91 or for recording in German 217 94 33), on the *Museumsinsel* (Museum Island) in the Isar River. S-Bahn #1-8 to "Isartor." Considered the world's largest and best museum of science and technology. Fascinating exhibits of original models include the first telephone (built in 1863) and the work bench upon which Otto Hahn split his first atom. Don't miss the mining exhibit, which winds through a labyrinth of recreated subterranean mining tunnels. A walk through the museum's 46 departments covers over 10km; better grab an English guidebook (DM6). The planetarium (DM3) and electrical show will warm any physicist's heart. DM10, seniors and disabled persons DM7, students and children under 15 DM4, children under 5 free. Open daily 9am-5pm.

Königsplatz

Alte Pinakothek, Barerstr. 27 (tel. 23 80 52 15), contains Munich's most precious artistic jewels. U-Bahn #2 to "Theresienstr." Built in 1826 under King Ludwig I, the last of the passionate Wittelsbacher art collectors, this world-renowned hall houses works by Titian, da Vinci, Raphael, Dürer, Rembrandt, and Rubens. Open Tu and Th 10am-8pm, W and F-Su 10am-5pm. DM7, students DM4.

Neue Pinakothek, Barerstr. 29 (tel. 23 80 51 95), next to Alte Pinakothek. Sleek space for the 18th to 20th centuries: Van Gogh, Klimt, Cézanne, Manet, etc. Hours and prices same as Alte Pinakothek.

Lenbachhaus, Luisenstr. 33 (tel. 23 33 20 00; recorded German info tel. 23 33 20 02). U-Bahn #2 to "Königspl." Munich cityscapes (useful if it's raining), along with works by Kandinsky, Klee, and the *Blaue Reiter* school (Münter, Marc, Macke, etc.), which disdained perfumed Impressionism, forging the aesthetic of abstraction. Open Tu-Su 10am-6pm. DM8, students DM4.

Glyptohek, Königspl. 3 (tel. 28 61 00), around the corner from the Lenbachhaus. U-Bahn #2 to "Königspl." Assembled by Ludwig I in 1825 in pursuit of his Greek dream to turn Munich into a "cultural work of such sheer perfection as only few Germans have experienced." Features 2400-year-old pediment figures from the Temple of Aphaea on Aegina as well as Etruscan and Roman sculptures. Open Tu-W and F-Su 10am-5pm, Th 10am-8pm. DM6, students DM3.50.

Antikensammlung, Königspl. 1 (tel. 59 83 59), across Königspl. from Glyptothek. U-Bahn #2 to "Königspl." Flaunts a first-rate flock of vases and the other half of Munich's finest collection of ancient art; features Ancient Greek and Etruscan pottery and jewelry. Open Tu and Th-Su 10am-5pm, W 10am-8pm. DM6, students DM3.50. Joint admission with Glyptothek DM10, students DM5.

Elsewhere in Munich

⊛Staatsgalerie moderner Kunst, Prinzregentenstr. 1 (tel. 21 12 71 37), in the **Haus der Kunst** (tel. 21 12 70) at the southern tip of the Englischer Garten. U-Bahn #4 or 5 to "Lehel," then streetcar #17. This sterling gallery celebrates the vitality of 20th-century art, from the colorful palettes of the Expressionists to the spare canvases of the Minimalists. Showcases Beckmann, Kandinsky, Klee, Picasso, and Dalí. Constructed by the Nazis as the Museum of German Art, it opened with the famous *Entartete Kunst* (degenerate art) exhibit that included works of the Expressionists and Dadaists. Excellent visiting exhibits (DM4-6 extra). Open Tu-W and F-Su 10am-5pm, Th 10am-8pm. DM6, students DM3.50.

Münchener Stadtmuseum, St.-Jakobs-Platz 1 (tel. 23 32 23 70). U-Bahn #3 or 6 or S-Bahn #1-8 to "Marienpl." A collection of whimsical museums, all with a Bavarian touch: film, fashion, musical instruments, weapons, and more. The Puppet and Marionette museum offers the opportunity to let those creative juices flow and build your own sweet *Ding*. **Classic films** (DM8) roll every evening at 8pm. Foreign films shown with subtitles; call 23 32 55 86 for a program. Open Tu and Th-Su 10am-5pm, W 10am-8:30pm. Open M 5pm-midnight, Tu-Su 11am-midnight. Museum DM5, students, seniors, and children DM2.50, under 6 free.

⊛ZAM: Zentrum für Außergewöhnliche Museen (Center for Unusual Museums), Westenriederstr. 41 (tel. 290 41 21). S-Bahn #1-8 to "Isartor" or streetcar #17 or 18. A brilliant place that brazenly corrals under one roof such treasures as the Corkscrew Museum, the Museum of Easter Rabbits, and the Chamberpot Museum. Fan of Empress Elizabeth of Austria? Sass on over to the Sisi Museum, sweety. Open daily 10am-6pm. DM8, students, seniors, and children DM5.

Museum für Erotische Kunst (Museum of Erotic Art), Odeonspl. 8 (tel. 228 35 44), in same building as the Filmcasino. U-Bahn #3-6 to "Odeonspl." or bus #53. For those lonely days when you're 5000km away from your beloved (and those uninspired days when you're right next to your beloved), this museum covers all 4 bases around the world and through time. Features a French book of sex-gags entitled *The Circus,* hot and heavy chess pieces, and a set of juicy Japanese illustrations. Open Tu-Su 11am-7pm. DM8, students DM6.

BMW Museum, Petuelring 130 (tel. 38 22 33 07). U-Bahn #3 to "Olympiazentrum." The ultimate driving museum features a fetching display of past, present, and future products of Bavaria's second-favorite export. Open daily 9am-5pm. Last entry 4pm. DM5.50, students DM4.

Valentin Musäum, Isartorturm (tel. 22 32 66). S-Bahn #1-8 or streetcar #18 or 20 to "Isartor." Decidedly esoteric peek at the comical life of Karl Valentin, the German counterpart of Charlie Chaplin, and his partner Liesl Karlstadt. Valentin was Munich's quintessential comedian and social commentator. Curiosities include sham skeletons encased in the stone wall and a nail in the wall upon which Valentin hung up his first career as a carpenter. Open M-Tu and F-Sa 11:01am-5:29pm, Su 10:01am-5:29pm. 299*Pfennig,* students 149*Pfennig.* Wacky Bavarians.

Spielzeugmuseum, Altes Rathaus, Marienpl. (tel 29 40 01). 2 centuries of toys—compare the "futuristic" WWI figurines to the slim, *schicki-micki* Barbie. Open daily 10am-5:30pm. DM5, children DM1, families DM10.

■ Entertainment

THEATER AND OPERA

Munich's cultural cachet rivals the world's best. The Müncheners are great funlovers and hedonists, yet they reserve a place for folksy kitsch, cultivating a supreme and diverse *Szene* with something for everyone. Sixty theaters of various sizes are scattered throughout the city. Styles range from dramatic classics at the **Residenztheater** and **Volkstheater** to comic opera at the **Staatstheater am Gärtnerplatz** to experimental works at the **Theater im Marstall** in Nymphenburg. Standing tickets run around DM10. Munich's **Opera Festival** (in July) is held in the Bayerische Staatsoper (below) accompanied by a concert series in the Nymphenburg and Schleissheim palaces. Write for tickets, or call early that night (tel. 26 46 20) for leftover tickets (around DM15). The *Monatsprogramm* (DM2.50) lists schedules for all of Munich's stages, museums, and festivals.

In the **Schwabing district,** Munich shows its more bohemian face with scores of small fringe theaters, cabaret stages, art cinemas, and artsy pubs. The **Leopoldstraße,** the main avenue leading up from the university, can be magical on a warm summer night in its own gaudy way—milling youthful crowds, art students hawking their work, and terrace-cafes create an exciting swarm. At the turn of the century this area was a distinguished center of European cultural and intellectual life, housing luminaries such as Brecht, Mann, Klee, Georgi, Kandinsky, Spengler, and Trotsky.

Gasteig Kulturzentrum, Rosenheimerstr. 5 (tel. 48 09 80). S-Bahn #1-8 to "Rosenheimerpl." or streetcar #18 to "Am Gasteig." The most modern concert hall in Germany, the *Kulturzentrum* hosts musical performances ranging from classical to non-Western in its 3 concert halls and visual arts center. The hall rests on the former site of the *Bürgerbräukeller* where Adolf Hitler launched his abortive Beer Hall Putsch. Features the **Munich Philharmonic** and a wide range of events such as public readings and ballet. Box office in the Glashalle (tel. 54 89 89) open M-F 10:30am-2pm and 3-6pm, Sa 10:30am-2pm, and 1hr. before showtime.

⊛**Bayerische Staatsoper** (Bavarian State Opera), Max-Joseph-Platz 2 (tickets tel. 21 85 19 20; recorded info tel. 21 85 19 19). U-Bahn #3-6 to "Odeonspl." or streetcar #19 to "National Theater." Standing-room and reduced-rate student tickets (DM6-20) to the numerous operas and ballets are sold at Maximilianstr. 11 (tel. 21 85 19 20), behind the Opera House, or 1hr. before the performance at the side entrance on Maximilianstr. Tickets can also be ordered by phone at the above number with an AmEx, Diners, Eurocard, or Visa card (DM3 processing fee). Box office open M-F 10am-6pm, Sa 10am-1pm. No performances Aug. to mid-Sept.

Staatstheater, Gärtnerpl. 3 (tel. 32 01 67 67). U-Bahn #1 or 2 to "Fraunhoferstr." and then follow Reichenbachstr. to Gärtnerplatz; or bus #52 or 56 to "Gärtnerpl." Stages comic opera and musicals. Tickets available 4 weeks before each performance at the Staatstheater box office (tel. 20 24 11). Open M-F 10am-6pm, Sa 10am-1pm, and 1hr. before performance at the night counter, or at the Bavarian State Opera counter (see above). Standing room tickets start at DM19.

Drohleier, Balanstr. 23 (tel. 48 43 37). S-Bahn #1-8 or bus #51 to "Rosenheimerpl." A mixture of theater, cabaret, and performance art romps across this offbeat stage. One of the best cabaret scenes in Munich. Kitchen serves inexpensive salads and noodle dishes (DM6-15) until 10pm. Reservations required. Open Tu-Sa 6:30pm-1am. Performances Tu-Sa 10:30pm. Tickets DM20-30.

Münchner Kammerspiele, Maximilianstr. 26-28 (tickets tel. 23 72 13 28; recorded info tel. 23 72 13 26). Streetcar #19 to "Maxmonument." Exceptional modern theater and classics grace its two stages. **Schauspielhaus,** Maximilianstr. 26, shows Goethe and Shakespeare (DM10.50-58.50). Buy advance tickets at Münchner Kammerspiele. The **Werkraum,** Hildegardstr. 1, features avant-garde and critical leftist pieces. Standing room tickets DM1.50. Tickets available 1 week in advance. Box office open M-F 10am-6pm, Sa 10am-1pm.

FILM

Newspapers and magazines like *in München* (free) list **movie** showings. English films are often dubbed; search for the initials "OF" (original language) or "OmU" (subtitled) on the poster before buying your popcorn. Munich's **film festival** generally runs for a week in late June or early July. For schedules and information, contact **Internationale Filmwoche**, Türkenstr. 93, 80799 Munich (tel. 381 90 40).

Museum Lichtspiele, Lilienstr. 2 (tel. 48 24 03), by the Ludwigsbrücke and part of the Deutsches Museum (S-Bahn #1-6 or streetcar #18 to "Isator"), holds the world's record for most consecutive daily screenings of the Rocky Horror Picture Show. They do the Time Warp again and again daily at midnight. Non-dubbed English-language films screened daily (DM11-13).

Türkendolch, Türkenstr. 74 (tel. 28 99 66 99), in the middle of the student district, has mini-film festivals dedicated to a particular director or theme.

Forum der Technik, Museumsinsel 1 (tel. 21 12 51 80; http://www.fdt.de), next to the Deutsches Museum, maxes out on magnificent 3-D **IMAX** movies and laser shows (DM15.50, students, seniors, disabled persons, and children under 14 DM12.90). Subtitled foreign films (DM11.90).

Cinema, Nymphenburgerstr. 31 (tel. 55 52 55), screens non-dubbed, English-language flicks daily. U-Bahn #1 to "Stiglmaierpl."

FLEA MARKETS

Fleamarket: Arnulfstr., to the left of the Hackerbrücke, in a former train station. S-Bahn #1-8 to "Hackerbrücke." Knick-knacks, clothing, and stuff you'll never use but have been searching for forever. Open F-Sa 7am-6pm.

Antikmarkt (tel. 49 91 87 87), in Kunstpark Ost at the Ostbahnhof. Auction block, antiques, and regular flea markets. Check a Kunstpark Ost program (see **Nightlife**, p. 494, for details). Open W-Th 1pm-8pm, F 8am-8pm, Sa 7am-6pm.

Auer Dult: Mariahilfpl. U-Bahn #1 or 2 to "Fraunhoferstr.," then streetcar #27 to "Mariahilfpl." Munich's most famous fleamarket. Since 1799, all the pots, pans, china, second-hand clothes, and antiques you can mail home. Three times per year for 9 days.

■ Nightlife

Munich's nightlife is a curious collision of Bavarian *Gemütlichkeit* and trendy cliquishness. Representatives of the latter trait are often referred to as *"Schicki-Mickis,"* loosely defined as club-going German yuppies (expensively dressed, coiffed and sprayed, beautiful, shapely, blonde specimens of both sexes). With a healthy mix of students and other less pretentious locals, the streets bustle with raucous beer halls, loud discos, and exclusive cafes every night of the week; some places are as likely to be packed on a weeknight as on a Saturday. The locals tend to tackle their nightlife as an epic voyage. The odyssey begins at one of Munich's beer gardens or beer halls (see **Beer, Beer, and More Beer,** p. 487), which generally close before midnight and are most crowded in the early evening. The alcohol keeps flowing at cafes and bars, which, except for Friday and Saturday nights, shut off their taps at 1am. Then the discos and dance clubs, sedate before midnight, suddenly spark and throb relentlessly until 4am. The trendy bars, cafes, cabarets, and discos plugged into Leopoldstr. in **Schwabing** attract tourists from all over Europe (see **Entertainment,** p. 493). For easy access, dig the jaded hipster-wear out of your pack, or at least leave the white baseball hat and college T-shirt at home. A few more tips: no tennis shoes, no shorts, and no sandals (no, not even Birkenstocks—or haven't you noticed yet that you're the only person in Germany wearing them?). On weekends, though, you'll have to look like more money than your railpass cost.

The **Muffathalle**, Zellerstr. 4 (tel. 45 87 50 00), in Haidhausen, is a former power plant that generates hip student energy with ethno, hip-hop, jazz, and dance performances (cover up to DM30; open M-Sa 6pm-4am, Su 4pm-1am). Take S-Bahn #1-8 to

"Rosenheimerpl." or streetcar #18 to "Deutsches Museum." Munich's alternative concert scene goes on at **Feierwerk,** Hansastr. 39-41 (tel. 769 36 00), which has seven stages and huge tents. Take S-Bahn #7 or U-Bahn #4 or 5 to "Heimeranpl.," then walk left down Hansastr. (10min.). In summer, there's lots of independent music, comedy, beer gardens, *Imbiß* stands, blues, and rock. Beer gardens open at 6pm; usually doors open at 8:30pm and concerts begin at 9pm. Check out http://db.allmusic.de/live/feierwerk for the word on impending shows. **Münchener Freiheit** is the most famous (and the most touristy) bar/cafe district; more low-key is the southwestern section of Schwabing, directly behind the university on Amalienstr. and Türkenstr. (see **Food,** p. 485). When they close, hangers-on head for the late-night/early-morning cafes to nurse a last *Maß* of beer or first cup of coffee.

Scads of culture and nightlife guides are available to help you sort out Munich's scene. Pick up *Munich Found* (DM4), *in München* (free), or *Prinz* (monthly for DM5; the hippest) at any newsstand to find out what's up. For smaller rock clubs, scope bulletin boards around the university. Big-name pop artists often perform at the **Olympia Halle,** while the **Olympia Stadion** on the northern edge of town hosts mega-concerts. Check listings for dates and ticket information or call 30 67 24 24.

BARS

Many of the charming cafes (see **Food,** p. 485) double as hip nightly haunts of *Müncheners.* A few stalwarts only open the doors for drink after 5pm, and by 1am many places squeeze revelers out into more late-night joints. Also see **Beer, Beer, and More Beer,** p. 494.

Günther Murphy's, Nikolaistr. 9a (tel. 39 89 11; http://www.gunther-murphys.com). U-Bahn #3 or 6 to "Giselastr." Cozy up in the quote-unquote snuggle-box with a Guinness (DM6). Good ol' Irish cheer accompanies each serving of scrumptious British and American food (DM8-15). You won't be able to find a seat, but it's more fun to mingle with the English-speaking crowd. All-you-can-eat, all-day brunch served on Sunday (DM15). "Limp in and leap out!" Karaoke every night at 9pm. Open M-F 5pm-1am, Sa 2pm-3am, Su noon-1am.

Reitschule, Konigstr. 34. U-Bahn #3 or 6 to "Giselastr." Above a club, with windows overlooking a horseback-riding school. Marble tables and a sleek bar. Also a cafe with a beer garden out back—very relaxed. Rumor has it this is where Boris Becker met his wife ("Mrs. Becker"). *Weißbier* DM6. Breakfast served all day.

Master's Home, Frauenstr. 11 (tel. 22 99 09). U-Bahn #3 or 6 or S Bahn #1-8 to "Marienpl." A tremendous stuffed peacock greets visitors as they descend the gold painted staircase to the subterranean bar and *faux* private house. Lounge in the elegant living room with books and dusty velvet furniture, relax in the bedroom, or chill in the tub with a beer in hand. Eat gourmet Italian with the *Schicki-Mickis* in the restaurant (meals DM15-30), or chill with the more relaxed crowd in the bar. Mixed drinks DM11.50, other drinks similarly high-brow in price. Weekdays comfortable; weekends mobbed. Open daily 6pm-3am.

Treznjewski, Theresienstr. 72 (tel. 22 23 49). U-Bahn #2 to "Theresienstr." Handsome dark-wooded bar with stylish frescoes. Good cocktails and chatty crowds until way late. Near the university. Breakfast DM7.50-13.50. Entrees DM11-14.50. Beer DM5. Open Su-Th 8pm-3am, F-Sa 8pm-4am.

MUSIC BARS

Shamrock, Trautenwolfstr. 6 (tel. 33 10 81). U-Bahn #3 or 6 to "Giselastr." Live music runs the gamut from blues and soul to Irish fiddling to rock in this cozy Irish pub. You can pick up a comprehensive music program for all the city's Irish pubs at any one of them. Irish soccer highlights on Sundays. Guinness DM7.50. Pizza DM9.50-12. Open M-Th 5pm-1am, F-Sa 5pm-3am, Su 2pm-1am.

Nachtcafé, Maximilianspl. 5 (tel. 59 59 00). U-Bahn #4 or 5 or S-Bahn #1-8 to "Karlspl." Live jazz, funk, soul, and blues until the wee hours. The chic and the wannabes rub shoulders in this modern jet-black bar. Things don't get rolling until 2am. Very *schicki-micki.* Breakfast served after 2am. No cover, but outrageous prices and a bouncer—easy-going weekdays, very picky on weekends when you'll have to look the part. On warm summer evenings the porch cafe is packed with elegant Müncheners drinking cocktails by moonlight. Karaoke on Sunday. Beer DM8 (0.3L). *Milchkaffee* DM6.50.

Unterfahrt, Kirchenstr. 96 (tel. 448 27 94). S-Bahn #1-8 or U-Bahn #5 to "Ostbahnhof." For the serious jazz lover. The crowd is usually a little older. Groovy rhythms (DM5). Jam session starts every Sunday at 9pm; arrive early for a table. Professional performances from DM10. Open Tu-Su 8pm-1am.

DANCE CLUBS

◉**Kunstpark Ost,** Grafingerstr. 6 (tel. 490 43 50). U-Bahn #5 or S-Bahn #1-8 to "Ostbahnhof." The newest and biggest addition to the Munich nightlife scene. A cultural "city within the city," this huge complex with 27 different venues swarms with young people hitting clubs, concerts, and bars—but most of all, dancing the night away. Try the psychedelic **Natray Temple** (open W and F-Sa), the alternative cocktail and disco joint **K41** (open Tu-Su), the stage/club **Babylon** (open W and F-Su), or concert hall **Incognito** (open M-Sa). Hours, cover, and themes vary—call 49 00 29 28 for info and tickets, or pick up a program in other nightlife spots.

Nachtwerk and Club, Landesbergerstr. 185 (tel. 578 38 00). Streetcar #18 or 19 or bus #83 to "Lautensackstr." The older, larger **Nachtwerk** spins mainstream dance tunes for sweaty mainstream crowds in a packed warehouse. Saturday is the beloved "Best of the 50s to the 90s" night. Its little sister **Club** offers a bi-level dance floor, just as tight and swinging as its next-door neighbor. Mixtures of rock, hip-hop, trip-hop, and house; Friday is "cosmic"; Saturday acid jazz and rare grooves. Avoid Sunday night rehashing of German oldies-but-crappies. Beer DM6 at both places. Cover DM10 for both. Open daily 10pm-4am.

Reactor, Domagkstr. 33 (tel. 324 44 23), in the Alabamahalle. U-Bahn #6 to "Alte Heide." Situated along with **Alabama** next door on a former military base in Schwabing. Techno, house, and German oldies. Open daily 10:30pm-4am.

Oly Disco, Helene-Mayer-Ring 9 (tel. 351 77 33). U-Bahn #3 to "Olympiazentrum." This all-night joint's wide mix of music makes this *the* place to rock out cheap after midnight. Student ID needed to get in.

Backstage, Helmholtzstr. 18 (tel. 18 33 30). S-Bahn #1-8 to "Donnersbergerbrücke." Wide range of music, but lots of "little Seattle," hip-hop, and techno-type nights. Friday "Gathering of the Tribes"; Saturday "Freak Out." Mixed crowd, with lots of nose rings and green hair. Open W-Th 9pm-3am, F 10pm-5am, Sa 9pm-5am.

Pulverturm, Harthof-Schleißheimer-Str. 393 (tel. 351 99 99). U-Bahn #2 to "Harthof"; it's 15min. from the stop. A bit far out (geographically and otherwise), this dance club with beer garden lacks the pretension of Munich's other venues. Anything from psychedelic to grunge; Friday is indie rock and Sunday kicks back with reggae. Cover DM10. Open daily 10pm-4am.

Tilt, Helmholtzstr. 12 (tel. 129 79 69). S-Bahn #1-8 or 27 to "Donnersbergerbrücke." A wacky warehouse disco. Saturday fun acid jazz (cover DM7); Monday "spicy sounds from the swamps"—Swampy Spice? Tell me what you want. Bring ID if you look young. Open W 9pm-1am, Th 9:30pm-1am, F-Sa 10pm-3am.

■ Gay and Lesbian Munich

Although Bayern has the reputation of being intolerant of homosexuality, Munich sustains a respectably vibrant gay nightlife. The center of Munich's homosexual scene lies within the **"Golden Triangle"** defined by Sendlinger Tor, the Viktualienmarkt/Gärtnerplatz area, and Isartor. Bars, cafes, and clubs of all atmospheres abound. Pick up the free, extensive booklet *Rosa Seiten* (pink pages) at **Max und Milian Bookstore,** Ickstattstr. 2 (tel. 260 33 20; open M-F 10:30am-2pm, Sa 11am-4pm), or at any other gay locale for extensive listings of gay nightlife hotspots and services. The **Zentrum schwuler Männer** (gay men's center) offers an array of telephone services (for general information tel. 260 30 56; for violence hotline tel. 192 28; for counseling tel. 194 46; http://www.altmann.de/sub); some English is spoken, depending on the staff (open Su-Th 7-11pm, F-Sa 7pm-midnight). For lesbian information, call **Lesbentelefon** (tel. 725 42 72; open Tu 10:30am-1pm, W 2:30-5pm, Th 7-10pm). **Sapphovision,** a lesbian film center at the **Frauenzentrum Treibhaus,** Güllstr. 3 (tel. 77 40 41), shows films every second Friday of the month. **Lillemor's Frauenbuchladen** (see **Bookstores,** p. 480) provides information for lesbians.

Club Morizz, Klenzestr. 43 (tel. 201 67 76). U-Bahn #1 or 2 to "Fraunhoferstr." Reminiscent of certain Casablanca scenes, this relaxed cafe and bar is frequented by mostly gay men and a few lesbians. Settle into the low red sofa chairs while savoring a delectable shot of espresso (DM7). European and Thai dishes available until 12:30am; Thai curry DM19, pasta and other entrees DM15-27. Open Su-Th 7pm-2am, F-Sa 7pm-3am.

New York, Sonnenstr. 25 (tel. 59 10 56). U-Bahn #1-3 or 6 to "Sendlinger Tor." Fashionable gay men dance the night away. Laser shows F-Su 11:30pm and 7am; cover DM10 (includes drinks). No cover other nights, but no "free" drinks. Beer DM6.50. Open daily 11pm-4am.

Café Nil, Hans-Sach-Str. 2 (tel. 26 55 45). U-Bahn #1 or 2 to "Fraunhoferstr." Sleek cafe that's a day- and nighttime meeting place for gay men of all ages. Mobbed on weekends. Beer DM5 (0.4L), pasta DM13.50. Open M-F 5pm-4am, Sa-Su 3pm-4am.

Soul City, Maximilianspl. 5 (tel. 59 52 72), at the intersection with Max-Joseph-Str. Purportedly the biggest gay disco in Bayern. Beer DM7.50 (0.3L), coffee DM6. Open Su-Th 10pm-4am, F-Sa 10pm-late.

Fortuna Musikbar, Maximilianspl. 5, Reginahaus (tel. 55 40 70). U-Bahn #4 or 5 or S-Bahn #1-8 to "Karlspl.," then walk northeast along the Ring until you hit Maximilianspl. A hip and popular disco for lesbians. *The* place on Thursday evenings with shakin' salsa parties. Open M and W-Su 10pm-4am.

■ Near Munich: Dachau

"Once they burn books, they will end up burning people," wrote German poet Heinrich Heine in 1820. This eerie statement is posted at the **Konzentrations-Lager-Gedenkstätte,** the Dachau concentration camp, next to a photograph of a Nazi book burning. The walls, gates, gas chamber, and crematorium have been restored since 1962 in a chillingly sparse memorial to the victims of Dachau, the first German concentration camp and model for the entire network of 3000 work and concentration camps erected in Nazi-occupied Europe. Once tightly packed barracks are now for the most part only foundations; survivors ensured, however, that at least two barracks would be reconstructed to teach future generations about the 206,000 prisoners who were interned here from 1933 to 1945. German school groups are increasingly coming to visit the memorial, learning about the persecution of homosexuals, Jews, foreigners, and gypsies during the Holocaust. German schoolchildren, as well as residents of the city of Dachau—and it is important to remember that there *is* a town here, which lives in the shadow of the camp every day and with every tourist who brushes by the town on his or her way to the memorial—watch visitors with uncertainty, and even insecurity. Visitors should realize that while the *KZ-Gedenkstätte* is treated as a tourist attraction by many, it is first and foremost a memorial; Jews and gentiles alike come here for personal reasons, to grieve over the horrors of the Holocaust. Take a moment to read the sign-in log at the end of the exhibit; you'll find that visitors from all over the world come here to remember lost relatives or to pay respects to those who perished. Interwoven with the multitude of names and addresses from different countries are statements of resilience and hope. Respectful behavior by those with only a historical interest is in order.

The museum, located in the former administrative buildings, examines pre-1930 anti-Semitism, the rise of Nazism, the establishment of the concentration camp system, and the lives of prisoners through photographs, documents, and artifacts. The thick guide (DM25; available in English) translates the propaganda posters, SS files, documents, and letters; most exhibits are accompanied by short captions in English. A display copy of the English guide is available for perusal in the center of the exhibit. Also on display are texts of the letters from prisoners to their families as well as internal SS memos. A small, annotated map is available for DM0.30. A short film (22min.) is screened in English at 11:30am and 3:30pm (and on some days at 2pm).

The state offers excellent two-hour **tours** in English leaving from the museum (June-Sept. daily at 12:30pm, Oct.-May Sa-Su at 12:30pm; DM5 donation is encouraged). Call (08131) 17 41 for more info. The wrought-iron gate at the *Jourhaus,* formerly the only entrance to the camp, reads *"Arbeit Macht Frei"* ("Work Sets One Free"). It was the first sight as prisoners entered the camp. There is also a Jewish memorial, a Protestant commemorative chapel, and the Catholic *Todesangst Christi-Kapelle* (Christ in Agony Church) on the grounds. (For more discussion about the issues surrounding concentration camps, see **History: The Holocaust,** p. 64.) To get there from Munich, take S-Bahn #2 (direction: "Petershausen") to "Dachau" (20min., DM14 round-trip), then bus #724 (direction: "Kraütgarten") or 726 (direction: "Kopernikusstr.") from in front of the station to *KZ-Gedenkstätte* (20min., DM1.80, grounds open Tu-Su 9am-5pm).

In the mid-19th century, painters such as Carl Spitzweg and Max Liebermann traveled to Dachau. A 16th-century castle and a parish church built in the year 920 tops the *Altstadt.* Tours in German of the castle and the church leave from in front of the modern *Rathaus,* across the street from the tourist office (May-Oct. Sa 10:30am; DM6, children and students DM3). The tiny **tourist office,** Konrad-Adenauer-Str. 1 (tel. 845 66; fax 845 29), has information on the city of Dachau and sells maps for DM1 (open M-F 9am-1pm and 3-6pm, Sa 9am-noon). The **telephone code** is 08131.

LAKE REGION

Müncheners frequently get away to the nearby glacial lakes, particularly the beloved **Starnbergersee** and the **Ammersee.** Called the **Five Lakes** *(Fünf Seen),* this region comprises an aquatic complex of Starnbergersee, Ammersee, Pilsensee, Wörthsee, and Wesslingersee. Ride S-Bahn #6 (direction: "Tutzing") out to the beautiful lakeside promenade of **Starnberg,** an old resort town (DM7 one-way, or 4 strips on the *Streifenkarte).* The castle where Mad King Ludwig II was confined after he was deposed is just around the tip of the lake in **Berg.** His body was found shortly thereafter, mysteriously drowned in the Starnbergersee—a cross in the water now marks the spot. For more information, inquire at the main **Five Sea tourist office** in Starnberg, Wittelsbacherstr. 9 (tel. (08151) 130 07; fax 132 89), at Am Kirchplatz. The **Starnberg tourist office** (tel. 130 08) offers a free central room finding service (open June-Sept. M-F 8am-6pm, Sa 9am-1pm).

■ Herrsching and Ammersee

Herrsching is the start of one of the many *Wanderwege* (hiking paths) established by the transit system in connection with the S-Bahn. Take Munich S-Bahn #5 to "Herrsching" (last stop; DM10.50 each way, or 6 strips) on the Ammersee (40min., every 20min.). To get to the Ammersee from the Herrsching train station, follow Zum Landungssteg right and make a right at the end; continue until you come to the touristy beach area. If you don't mind pebbly beaches, the Ammersee is for you; dodge the ducks and sailboats and take a nippy dip in the refreshing body of water.

Down the path along the sea to the right is a whimsical red-tiled villa with pagoda toppings. It's the **Kurpark Schlößchen** built by Ludwig Scheuermann in 1888 as a summer escape from a Munich infested with beer-drinking tourists (the more things change…). Bear right through the Kurpark to cross a tiny bridge. Here you'll find **Strandbad Seewinkel** (tel. 405 71), Herrsching's public beach (no sand, but lots of grass and pleasantly uncrowded on summer afternoons). In its pleasant terrace beer garden, a *Bier* is DM4.50 and a meal is around DM10. Hop off the dock for a swim (beach area open May-Sept. daily 9am-10pm). The restaurant inside the Seewinkel is separate from the self-service beer garden (open W-M 5-10pm). The **Bayerische Schiffahrt,** a steamship-like tugboat, travels the northern Ammersee route to

Holzhausen and Stegen for DM18 one way (50min.). Southward, chug by Riederau and Diessen for DM15.50 (30min.). Round-trips cost DM23, with under 15 50% off, and under 6 free (boats leave almost once per hr. 9am-7pm). Play **miniature golf** back up Zum Landungssteg. (Open M-F 11am-9:30pm, Sa-Su 10am-9:30pm; last entrance 9pm. DM6, under 14 DM4.)

The **tourist office,** Bahnhofpl. 2 (tel. 52 52 27; fax 405 19), across from the train station, can help you find a room in Herrsching. They also provide information on the 11 paths that leave town for the forest and sea areas. (Open Apr.-Oct. M-F 8:30am-noon and 2-5pm, Sa 10am-12:30pm; Nov.-Mar. M-F 8:30am-noon.) Most hotel singles run DM100-150, doubles DM140-200, and private rooms DM30-50, plus a DM1.50 *Kurtaxe* for those over 18. The nearest **Campingplatz** (tel. 12 06) is in Herrsching-Mühlfeld. (DM6, under 6 DM3. Tent DM4-8. Car DM3. Caravan DM7. DM1 *Kurtaxe* if over 18. Open Apr.-Sept.) Five other camping sites serve the area: one on the Wörth-see, one on Pilsensee, and three on the Starnberger See. **Norma supermarket** is at 11 Zum Landungssteg (open M-F 8am-6pm, Sa 8am-2pm). The **post office,** 82211 Herrsching, is on Bahnhofstr. one block to the left of the station (open M-Th 8am-noon and 3-6pm, F 8am-noon and 3-5:30pm, Sa 8am-noon). The **telephone code** is 08152.

■ Andechs

The monastery at **Andechs** fuses Bayern's two most acclaimed attributes—Catholicism and beer—on a gorgeous mountaintop. The monks here brew up a pale beer and a rocking **Bockbier** that is piously not served on Saturdays or Sundays from Easter to October—young firebrands used to come up the mountain for weekend debauchery, swilling *Bock* and causing too much ruckus for the monk-waiters. The beer garden, **Klosterbrauerei** (tel. (08152) 37 60), now serves *Bockbier* on weekdays, and other beers every day, even holy ones. From the scenic beer garden, admire the fireflies and the blooming hydrangeas in the valley below as you groove to delightful Bavarian zither music (F and Sa 6-10pm). The secular brewing industry is currently up in arms over what it considers an unfair competitive advantage: as a religious institution, the monastery is exempt from the beer tax. (*Maß* Doppelbock Dunkel DM9, Spezial Hell (for special sinners) DM8, *Weißbier* DM9. Open daily 10am-9pm.)

Pagan thoughts aside, you can tour the monastery and church to admire its ornate gold altar. Its framework and interior were originally built in 1430 under the direction of Duke Ernst of Bayern, but the church was redone in the Rococo style to celebrate its 300th anniversary (completed in 1451). The mortal remains of composer **Carl Orff** rest in the building. To reach the monastery, take S-Bahn #5 to "Herrsching," then switch to the private bus line **Omnibusverkehr Rauner** (9-13 per day) or to the public **MVV** bus #956 (M-F 7:55 and 11:15am only, return at 10:57am or 12:37pm) for the 10-minute trip to Andechs. Bus schedules are erratic; check with the tourist office in Herrsching for departure times. (The last return times are M-F 6:45pm, Sa 5:39pm, Su 6:39pm.) Alternatively, huff and puff for a slowly sloping 3km up a picturesque wide footpath through the forest and earn your *Bockbier*. On the way up to the top, stop to explore the mysterious caves in the cliffs to the right of the path and to marvel at the tree whose roots have miraculously formed around a large boulder. Follow the signs marked *Fußweg nach Andechs*, which start on Kientalstr. To get there, head left from the train station down Bahnhofstr. as it turns into Luitpoldstr.; Kientalstr. will be on the right (50min. to Andechs). Be sure to stick to the trail; 11 people have died recently short-cutting down the precipitous slope. The trail is clearly marked except for two three-way intersections. Whether you are headed toward Herrsching or Andechs, hang a left on the first and a right on the second.

BAYERISCHE ALPEN (BAVARIAN ALPS)

Visible on a clear day from the top of the Glockenspiel tower in Munich are a series of snow-covered peaks and forested slopes spanning from southeast Germany across

Austria and into Italy. It was in this rugged and magical terrain that Ludwig II of Bavaria, the certifiably batty "Fairy Tale King," chose to build his theatrical palaces. Mountain villages, glacial lakes, icy waterfalls, and world-class ski resorts lend color to the jagged gray cliffs and thickly forested valleys. The rhythmic beat of cowbells ceases only at dusk, and, after a few days, cow dung no longer smells pungent and foul, but rather fresh and springy (well, almost). The nearly hidden small towns are occupied by possibly the friendliest villagers in all of Germany. This is also the region where people authentically, even nonchalantly, wear *Lederhosen,* and everyone seems to be either going or coming back from a hike. Rail lines are sparse; buses cover the gaps (bus drivers sell timetables for DM0.50). For regional info, contact the **Fremdenverkehrsverband Oberbayern,** Bodenseestr. 113 (tel. (089) 829 21 80), in Munich (open M-F 9am-4:30pm, Sa 9am-noon).

▓ Garmisch-Partenkirchen

Once upon a time, the 1100-year-old hamlets of Garmisch and Partenkirchen were beautiful but unassuming Bavarian villages whose location at the foot of the Zugspitze—Germany's tallest peak—ensured their tranquil isolation. Once the 19th-century nature movement discovered the mountains, the two towns quickly became renowned throughout Germany for their spectacular alpine ski slopes and magnificent hiking and rock climbing routes. Hitler persuaded the Garmisch and Partenkirchen mayors to unite the two villages in 1935 in anticipation of the 1936 Winter Olympic Games. To this day, however, the towns remain geographically distinct—Garmisch in the west and Partenkirchen in the east—and their inhabitants assert their individuality. Both sides of the 30,000-person town staunchly maintain that they speak different dialects, and their cows don't socialize in public.

PRACTICAL INFORMATION Garmisch-Partenkirchen can be reached easily from Füssen by **bus** (2hr., 5-7 per day, DM13, no railpasses valid), or from Innsbruck in Austria by **train** (1½hr., 1-2 per hour DM15.40). **Public transportation** costs DM2, but it's free with a *Kurkarte* (see below). Rent **bikes** at **Werdenfelser Sportagentur,** Marienpl. 18 (tel. 14 25; open M-F 9am-noon and 2-5pm; DM30 per day), or **Mountain-Bike Center Stefan Leiner,** Ludwigstr. 42 (tel. 795 28; open M-F 9am-6pm, Sa 9am-1pm; DM32 per day). Pick up maps of hiking trails (DM8) and city maps (free) at the **tourist office** (Verkehrsamt der Kurverwaltung), on Richard-Strauss-Pl. (tel. 18 06; fax 18 07 55; email tourist-info@garmisch-partenkirchen.de; http://www.garmisch-partenkirchen.de). From the station, turn left on Bahnhofstr. and after 200m turn left again onto Von-Brug-Str.; it faces the fountain on the square. An information board in front will help you locate a room even if the office is closed, or call 194 12 (open M-Sa 8am-6pm, Su 10am-noon). For **lost property** contact the *Fundbüro* in the *Rathaus* (tel. 91 00); for property lost on local buses (tel. 75 33 23). For a **snow** and **weather report** for the Zugspitze or Alpspitze call 79 79 79; for the Wank area, call 75 33 33. For the **police,** call 110. **Bahnhof Apotheke,** Bahnhofstr. 36 (tel. 24 50), to the right as you face the station, has a list in its window of opening times and addresses of all other **pharmacies** (open M-F 8:30am-noon and 2-6pm, Sa 8:30am-noon). The **post office,** 82467 Garmisch-Partenkirchen, is across the street and to the right of the station (open M-F 8am-6pm, Sa 8am-12:30pm). The **telephone code** is 08821.

ACCOMMODATIONS Reasonable rooms exist in Garmisch-Partenkirchen, but you'll have to do a bit of detective work to find one. The tourist office will help you find *Gasthäuser* and *Pensionen* (DM25-45). Alternatively, request a list of private rooms and make calls yourself from the free hotel phone; most rooms require a three-night minimum stay (DM30 per night). No matter where you wind up, there's a **Kurtax** levied on tourists (DM3, ages 6-16 DM1.90). The compensation for paying is a green card entitling you to free rides on the bus system and one free admission to the Alpspitz-Wellenbad, the casino, the Kurpark, and concerts (see below). At the pleasant **Jugendherberge (HI),** Jochstr. 10 (tel. 29 80; fax 585 36), awake to the tolling of church bells. Cross the street from the train station and walk 25m to your left and take bus #3 (direction: "Burgain") or 4 or 5 (direction: "Farchant") to "Burgrain." Walk straight down Am Lahne Wiesgraben, then turn right after two blocks onto Jochstr. Clean, somewhat institutional 6- to 10-bed rooms. (DM21. Ages 18-27 only. Sheets DM5.50. Reception 7-9am and 5pm-midnight. Lockout 9am-3:30pm. Curfew 11:30pm. Open Jan.-Oct.) The **Naturfreundehaus,** Schalmeiweg 21 (tel 43 22), is an independent hostel, more intimate than the *Jugendherberge,* on the edge of the forest at the east end of Partenkirchen. From the station, walk straight on Bahnhofstr. as it becomes Ludwigstr., follow the rightward bend in Ludwigstr., and turn left on Sonnenbergstr. Continue straight as this first becomes Prof.-Michael-Sachs-Str. and then Schalmeiweg (20min.). Sleep in an immaculate and comfortable private room or in a humongous attic loft with 19 other scruffy yet smiling backpackers. (DM14. Breakfast DM8. Quiet after 10pm, but no curfew. Call ahead.) **Camping Zugspitze,** Griesenerstr. 4 in Grainau (tel. 31 80), is on highway B24 at the base of the Zugspitze; take the blue-and-white bus from the station to "Schmölzabzweigung." Campground open year-round. (Person with tent DM16, 2 people DM31.)

FOOD Garmisch's restaurants cater to a range of tastes and tax brackets. The best value in town is probably the friendly Italian **La Baita,** at Zugspitzstr. 16 (tel. 787 77), 100m from Marienplatz, which offers delightful pasta dishes (DM8-16), omelettes (DM9), and pizza (DM8-14; open Th-Tu 11:30am-2:30pm and 5:30-11:30pm). In the heart of Partenkirchen, grab a giant *Schnitzel* (DM9-11) at **Gasthof Fraudorfer,** Ludwigstr. 24 (tel. 21 76), where traditional Bavarian dishes are supplemented with traditional Bavarian folk dances and songs after 6:30pm (open M and Th-Su 7am-1am, W 7am-5pm). **Aldi supermarket,** at the corner of Enzianstr. and Bahnhofstr., stocks the cheapest eats in town (open M-F 8:30am-6pm, Sa 8am-1pm). The **HL Markt,** at the intersection of Bahnhofstr. and Von-Brug-Str. (tel. 500 70), has slightly better hours (open M-F 8am-8pm, Sa 7:30am-4pm).

SIGHTS The mountains are the main attraction in town—marvelous views in the summer, and snowy Alpine antics in the winter. There are three ways to conquer the **Zugspitze,** the highest peak in Germany, though they should only be attempted in fair weather. **Option 1:** Take the cog railway from the *Zugspitzbahnhof* (50m behind the Garmisch main station) via Grainau to Hotel Schneefernerhaus, then a cable car, the *Gipfelseilbahn,* to the outlook, the Zugspitzplatt. *(75min.; 60min. to the ski area. Round-trip DM75, children 16-17 DM52, children 5-15 DM44, under 5 free.)* Continue with the *Gletscherbahn* cable car. **Option 2:** Get off the railway at Eibsee and take the Eibseeseilbahn, one of the steepest cable car runs in the world, all the way to the top. *(80min.; 10min. to Zugspitze. Same prices as option 1.)* A **combo ticket** including the train from Munich/Augsburg and the Zugspitze tour costs DM90, children 16-17 DM65, 4-15 DM51, under 4 free. **Option 3:** Hike it—the cheapest way to get atop the 2964m monster is to climb for about 10hr., usually as part of a two-day trip. **Only attempt this ascent if you are an experienced climber.** Get a good map from the tourist office and check the weather report.

For other Alpine views at lower prices, take the **Alpspitzbahn** to Osterfelderkopf peak (2050m; 9min.; round-trip DM37), the **Kreuzeck** cable car to Kreuzeck (1650m; 8min.; round-trip DM27), or the **Wankbahn** (1780m; 18min.; round-trip DM26). Most trips depart hourly (May-June 8:30am-5pm; July-Sept. 8am-5pm; Oct.-Nov. 8:30am-4:30pm). A neat daytrip includes biking to the **Eibsee,** about 10km from Garmisch. The calm, crystal waters of a mountain lake against the soaring, snow-capped monumentality of the *Zugspitze* will remind you of a movie backdrop. To avoid the 14% uphill of the last 300m, take the blue-and-white Eibsee bus from Garmisch (round-trip DM5, half-off for German *Bahncard* holders). One of the most popular trails leads to the dramatic, 100m deep **Partnachklamm** gorge (DM3). Hikers walk up to the gorge from behind the Olympic ski stadium (35min.) and then meander for another 35 minutes in the narrow darkish tunnels dug in the rocks, extremely close to the foaming water. **WN Alpine,** Zugspitzstr. 51 (tel. 503 40), and **Conrad Outdoors,** Rathauspl. 2 (tel. 563 61), specialize in mountaineering gear and also **rent hiking and climbing equipment.** For general alpine information about hiking trails, rock climbing routes, and mountain lodges, contact the **German Alpine Association** in Munich (tel. (089) 29 49 40). The ski season runs from October to mid-May in all its Alpine glory. Of the six area ski schools, the cheapest **equipment rental** is at **Ski-Schule,** Am Hausberg 8 (tel. 49 31 or 742 60), next to the *Hausbergbahn.* **Ski passes** in the *Zugspitzgebiet* cost DM58 per day, DM44 with railpass. More advanced leg-breakers ski in the **Verbundgebiet,** home of the World Cup Kandehar run, for DM47 per day. A week pass costs DM277, two weeks DM439. If the weather is nice, the **Alpspitz-Wellenbad,** Klammstr. 47, next to the Olympic stadium (tel. 75 33 13), lets you soak your weary feet in hot water or display your athletic prowess from the 5m high jumpboard. *(Open M-F 9am-9pm, Sa-Su 9am-7pm. DM7.50 for 3hr., DM10 for unlimited time; children under 16 DM4.50, DM6. First entry free with Kurkarte, then DM7, DM9. M-F entry after 6pm DM5, children DM3.)* The six-pool complex features artificial waves, saunas, restaurants, and paragliders hovering overhead.

■ Berchtesgaden

Poised at the easternmost point of the Bavarian Alps, Berchtesgaden profits from a sinister and much-touristed attraction: Hitler's **Kehlsteinhaus**—a mountaintop retreat christened "Eagle's Nest" by occupying American troops. A disconcerting horde of tourists, many of them American soldiers, besieges this Bavarian town every year to catch a glimpse of where the Eagle landed on vacation. Despite the connection to German history, Berchtesgaden belongs more properly to Austria and the Archbishophric of Salzburg than to Germany, but Bavaria usurped it in 1809 for its salt deposits. Over the mountains in the northeast, *The Sound of Music*'s Julie Andrews, her arms outstretched, spun round and round in alpine ecstasy—so can you.

ORIENTATION AND PRACTICAL INFORMATION Crouched in the southeastern corner of Germany, Berchtesgaden is a German peninsula in a sea of Austrian mountains. Hourly **trains** run to Munich (2½hr.; change at Freilassing), Salzburg (1hr.; change at Freilassing; DM12), and Bad Reichenhall (30min.; DM5.60). For train-related questions call the Bahnhof (tel. 50 74; open M-Sa 6:05am-7:35pm, Su 7am-7:35pm). The fare for a **bus** ride ranges from DM2 for **public transportation** in Berchtesgaden proper to DM5-8 for trips in the region (Bad Reichenhall DM7.60, Königssee DM3.40, Salzburg DM7.20). For questions about buses call the bus office in the train station (tel. 54 73; open M-F 8am-noon and 2-4pm). Rent **bikes** at **Full Stall Beierl,** Königsseerstr. 15 (tel. 94 84 50), just down the street from the tourist office, or **motorbikes** from **Horst Wagner,** Am Zellerbach 6 (tel. 621 01; DM34-59 per day). You can also rent a **car** at **AVIS,** BP fuel station, Königsseerstr. 47 (tel. 691 07), or grab a **rowboat** at the Königssee dock.

The Berchtesgaden **tourist office,** Königsseerstr. 2 (tel. 96 71 50; fax 633 00; email berchtesgadener_land@t-online.de; http://www.berchtesgadener_land.com), is opposite the train station in an off-white building with blue shutters. Ask the *Lederhosen*-wearing staff—without giggling—for the Berchtesgadener Land general information pamphlet, which lists sights, concerts, and other activities in English. The office's *Wanderpass* brochure (DM5) includes tips on walking trails and climbs in Berchtesgaden National Park, as well as descriptions and locations of overnight mountain shelters (DM 15-35). It comes free with the **Kurkarte,** a tourist card given to overnighters who pay the obligatory *Kurtax* (DM3). The staff at the "Berchtesgaden Mini Bus Tours" desk (across from the counter in the tourist office) speaks fluent English and generously answers tourists' questions. There is no room-finding service, but there is an extensive list of rooms and an automatic hotel finder in front of the office. (Open M-F 8am-5pm, Sa 9am-noon.) Call 194 12 for a recording of **hotel information.**

Most establishments also accept Austrian *Schillings;* you can **exchange currency** at the Salzburg train station post office if arriving from Austria. There are weekly **tennis competitions** among Berchtesgaden tourists at the tennis courts next to the **Hallenbad** (indoor swimming pool), Bergwerkstr. (June-Sept. W 9:30am). The **post office,** Bahnhofspl. 4, 83471 Berchtesgaden (tel. 95 60 23), is adjacent to the train station (open M-F 8am-noon and 2-5:30pm, Sa 8am-noon). The **telephone code** is 08652.

ACCOMMODATIONS AND FOOD The rowdy **Jugendherberge (HI),** Gebirgsjägerstr. 52, 83489 Strub (tel. 943 70; fax 94 37 37), is an uphill 30-minute walk from the station. Turn right from the station and follow the highly trafficked Ramsauerstr. on the left for 15 minutes, then take the first right on Gmundbrücke, and follow the signs up the steep (unnamed) gravel path on the left. Or take bus #9539 (direction: "Strub Kaserne") to "Jugendherberge" (Bus DM2.40. 10-bed dorm DM20, plus DM3 *Kurtax.* All-you-can-eat breakfast included. Sheets DM5.50. Reception 8am-noon and 5-7pm, but you can check in until 10pm. Curfew midnight. Open Dec. 27-Oct.) Most private rooms and *Pensionen* cost DM28-35, with shower DM35-50; hotels run DM80-100. **Gästehaus Hansererhäusl,** Hansererweg 8 (tel. 25 23), is just behind the tourist office. Follow Rossötzweg, bear left onto Hansererweg and look for the flower boxes under the windowsills (DM40 per person; breakfast included). If all four rooms in this *Gästehaus* are full, don't despair—almost every house on this street has a room for rent (look for *Zimmer Frei* signs). The campsite **Campingplatz Allweglehen,** at Untersalzberg (tel. 23 96), is more than an hour's walk downstream from the station (DM34 with tent, children 6-16 years DM6.50). Berchtesgaden is rife with restaurants for wealthy tourists. Pick up a *Wurst* sandwich from a vendor or groceries at the **Edeka Markt,** on Dr.-Imhof-Str., in town near Griesstätterstr. (open M-F 8am-6pm, Sa 8am-noon). The relaxed **Martinklause,** Ludwig-Ganghoferstr. 20, offers *Gulaschsuppe* (DM5.50), *Wurst* dishes (DM7.50-11), and its special red *Weinschorle* (DM3.80), as well as pinball (open daily 10am-2pm and 5pm-midnight).

SIGHTS The **Kehlsteinhaus** (also called "Eagle's Nest") was built for the *Führer*'s 50th birthday as a refuge of entertainment. *(Open daily May-Oct. except on days of heavy snow.)* While Hitler merely visited the mountaintop retreat 14 times, tourists bombard it constantly with their Hawaiian-shirt presence. The stone resort house is now a priccy restaurant (tel. 29 69; meals DM9-20) with no museum in sight. In fact, the best reason for visiting the Kehlsteinhaus is on the way to the spectacular 360° view from the 1834m mountain peak. The 6.5km road is something of an engineering marvel, hewn into solid rock by an army of 3000 men excused from conscription for health reasons—health reasons?! On the way back down, inspect what little remains of another Nazi retreat: bombed by the Allies on April 25, 1945, the **Berghof** in Obersalzburg was used by Hitler to entertain foreign dignitaries. On February 12, 1938, it was here that he browbeat Austrian Chancellor Kurt von Schuschnigg into relinquishing control of the Austrian police to the Nazis, paving the way for the *Anschluß.* Seven months later, British Prime Minister Neville Chamberlain visited Hitler to hammer out the "Munich Agreement" that Chamberlain claimed would guarantee "peace in our time"—so much for Appeasement.

To get to the Kehlsteinhaus first take the "Obersalzburg, Kehlstein" bus (#9538), from the covered platform to the right as you exit the station, to "Obersalzburg, Hintereck." *(June-Oct. roughly every 45min.; off-season much less regularly. Check with the tourist office for schedules. Round-trip DM6.80.)* At Hintereck, while you're waiting for bus #9549 to "Kehlstein Parkpl., Eagle's Nest," buy your dual ticket for both the second leg of the bus ride and the elevator ride you'll take at the *Kasse* on the other end. *(Every 30min. 9:30am-4pm. DM20, with Kurkarte DM19; children DM13, DM12.)* At Kehlstein, reserve your spot on a return bus (we mean it) at the booth when you get off. Reserving a place on a bus leaving one hour after the time of your Kehlstein arrival will give you enough time to explore the mountaintop if you don't plan to stop for lunch at the top (buses return to Hintereck every 30min., last one at 5:05pm). From Kehlstein Parkpl., go through the tunnel and up with the elevator to the Kehlsteinhaus; the elevator's golden mirrors are original, installed to quell Hitler's claustrophobia. Alternatively, climb up the serpentine footpath on the right as you face the mountain (20min.). You will probably want to pack a jacket for the cool weather on the peak. A short English-language **tour** of the Eagle's Nest is available daily at 10:30 and 11:30am (35min.; DM6, children free; meet at the tunnel entrance to the elevator). To catch the 10:30 tour, take the 9am bus to Hintereck, which departs from the main post office, then the 9:40am connection to Kehlstein; for the 11:30 tour, hop the 10 and 10:40am buses, respectively. A 3¾-hour English-language tour must be reserved one day in advance from **Berchtesgaden Mini Bus Tours** (tel. 649 71 or 621 72) in the tourist office. *(DM50, under 13 DM25, under 6 free; includes a tour of Obersalzberg, the second Eagle's Nest mountain bus and the elevator fare to Eagle's Nest. Meet at the tourist office M-Sa 1:30pm.)* The Bavarian hills are alive with the sound of minibuses; the same company also operates *Sound of Music* tours. Join English-speaking tour guides on a walk through the old city of Salzburg and a bus tour of the locations used in the film *The Sound of Music*. On the return to Berchtesgaden, sit back, relax, and listen to the "real-life" tale of the von Trapp family. *(Tours leave M-Sa 8:30am from the Berchtesgaden tourist office; 4hr.; passports and reservations required; DM40, children under 12 DM25, children under 6 free).*

The Berchtesgaden Royal **Schloß** (tel. 20 85) was a monastic priory until Bavarian rulers took over the area and appropriated the property. *(Open Su-F 10am-noon and 2-4pm; Oct.-Easter M-F 10am-1pm and 2-5pm; last entry 4pm; DM7, with Kurkarte DM6, students DM3.50, under 16 DM3.)* It now houses a collection of art and weaponry. To reach the castle and the rest of the *Altstadt*, walk right from the *Bahnhof,* through the overhang labeled "Zentrum" on the right, and go up the covered staircase. Cross over the train tracks on the footbridge behind the station and follow the "zum Markt" signs to Bahnhofweg. Follow Bahnhofweg to Maximillianstr. and continue straight ahead; veer right at the cylindrical yellow parking garage, veer left by Gasthof Triembacher and then veer no more— follow the signs around the corner to the Schloß.

Wedged into extraordinary Alpine cliffs, the **Königssee** calmly mirrors the landscape on its blue-green surface (whither Narcissus?); a bus from Berchtesgaden costs DM6.40 round-trip. Ships operated by **Schiffahrt Königssee** (tel. 96 36 13) glide across the lake irregularly *(Round-trip to St. Bartholomä 1hr., DM17.50; to Obersee 50min., DM22.50. Children 50% off.)* In summer, boats leave roughly every 10 to 20 minutes starting at 7:15am; in the winter, boats go to St. Bartholomä only, every 45 minutes starting at 9:45am. The best lake view is at the **Malerwinkel** (Painter's Outlook), around to the left of the lake, and the best aerial view is serviced by the Jenner cable car (tel. 958 10)—1170m above sea-level. *(Open in summer 8am-5:30pm, in winter 9am-4:30pm. One-way 30min. Uphill DM24, round-trip DM31.)* Take bus #9541 (direction: "Königssee") from the main train station to the end of the line (1 per hr.; DM3.30). At the **Salzbergwerke** (salt mines) near town (tel. 600 20), you can dress up in an old miner's outfit, toboggan down snaking passages in the dark, and go on a raft ride on a salt lake. *(Open May to mid-Oct. daily 9am-5pm; mid-Oct. to Apr. M-Sa 12:30-3:30pm. DM19.50, children 10 and under DM9.50.)* From the station, take bus #9548 to "Salzbergwerke" (1-2 per hr.; 8:37am-7:40pm; DM2) or make the 30-minute walk. To go **moonlight rafting,** call the Berchtesgaden Outdoor Club, Ludwig-Ganghofer-Str. 20½ (tel. 50 01).

■ Near Berchtesgaden: Ramsau

Hiding among the alps just 20km southwest of Berchtesgaden is the tiny village of Ramsau, a humble haven for hikers, white-water kayakers, and cyclists. Dominated by the magnificent, snow-capped Waltzmann and Hochkalter mountains, Ramsau provides an ideal starting point for walks and mountain hikes in the **Berchtesgaden National Park.** In the winter, knicker-clad tourists take advantage of cross-country ski trails, natural sled runs, and ice skating on Lake Hintersee. The world-famous 16th-century **Pfarrkirche** (parish church), Im Tal 82 (tel. 988 60), dwells on a hill a couple sheep pastures down the road from the tourist office. To clear your sinuses, follow the white gravel-lined path across the road from the *Pfarrkirche* to the **Kleingradier-werk Ramsau,** a small "outdoor brine inhalatorium" constructed out of hundreds of branches of mountain brier bush from Berchtesgadener Land. For best results, one visits the inhalatorium twice a week (for a period of about 15min.) to rest on the wooden park benches and to turn nostrils upward to inhale the saltwater mist trickling from the branches above. Even if your aches and pains don't subside, a soothing 15 minutes of cool tranquility is never a bad idea.

Those wishing to stretch their legs and feast their eyes upon some spectacular alpine scenery need only set out upon the vast network of well-marked hiking trails. One short but excellent hike leads from the center of town, following the Ramsauer Ache, through the **Zauberwald** (magical forest) to the sparkling-clear green **Hintersee.** Hitch up your *Lederhosen* and follow Im Tal from the tourist office past the Pfarrkirche, taking a left on Fendtenweg by Cafe Brotzeitstation; cross the narrow foot bridge and, keeping the river on your right, follow the white-gravel trail to Zauberwald and then on to Hintersee (about 1hr.). Weary legs can make the return trip back to Ramsau by bus (leaving from Hintersee Busplatz, 10min., 1-2 per hr., DM1.80).

Ramsau can be reached by bike, by foot, or by bus from Berchtesgaden; Bus #9546 runs hourly from the Berchtesgaden *Busbahnhof,* to the right of the train station (16min.; DM3.80 one-way, DM6.50 round-trip). **Mountain bikes** can be rented at **Sport Brandner,** Im Tal 64 (tel. 790). The friendly staff at the Ramsau **tourist office,** Im Tal 22 (tel. 98 89 20; fax 772), will shower you with trail maps, free brochures, and hiking information, and can assist your search for a room in a *Pension* or *Gästehaus* (open M-F 8am-noon and 1:15-5pm, Sa 9am-noon). American Express traveler's checks can be exchanged at **Raiffeisenbank,** Im Tal 89 (tel. 390; open M-Tu and Th-F 8:30am-noon and 2-4:30pm, W 8:30am-noon and 2-3:30pm). The **post office,** 83486 Ramsau, is located at Im Tal 87 (tel. 275), across from Gasthof Oberwirt (open M-F 8:30-11:30am and 2:30-5pm, Sa 8:30-11:30am). The **telephone code** is 08657.

Although there is no Jugendherberge, Ramsau sports a wide selection of fairly inexpensive *Pensionen* and *Gästehäuser* (DM20-40). **Gästehaus Marxen,** Hinterseerstr. 22 (tel. 213), is a quiet, friendly cottage only two minutes from the "Marxenbrücke" bus stop (DM20-25, includes breakfast, shower, and refrigerator). **Campingplatz Simonhof,** Am Taubensee 19 (tel. 284), has a beautiful location right on the Lattenbach river; it is a five-minute walk from the "Taubensee" bus stop (open all year; 56 sites; DM8 per person, DM8 per car and tent, DM4 for children 3-16). The colorful **Cafe Waldquelle,** Im Tal 62, right next door to the **Berg Kurgarten,** offers seating on an outdoor patio with great opportunities for people-watching. Slurp down a half liter of homemade buttermilk (DM3.40) while filling up on a large plate of bratwurst with sauerkraut and potatoes (DM10.80). To satisfy that sweet tooth, nibble on a large slice of homemade *Mohnstreußel-Kuchen* (DM3.50). The **Bäckerei/Konditorei,** Im Tal 3, across the street from the tourist office, serves up freshly baked bread perfect for a mountain picnic.

■ Oberammergau and Ettal Abbey

Situated in a wide valley surrounded by mountains, meadows, and forests, the tiny Alpine town of Oberammergau is home to world-famous **Passion Plays.** After the town was spared from a plague that swept through Europe in 1633, the inhabitants promised to re-enact the crucifixion and resurrection of Christ every 10 years. The cast is composed of about 1000 locals who begin rehearsing long in advance, often growing long hair and beards. The plays last all day, with a short break for pretzels, *Wurst,* and beer around mid-day. The next Passion Plays will be presented in 2000. By the time this book is published, it will probably already be too late to get tickets. Try *immediately* if you'd like to go. While the plays are not being performed, the most exciting things to do in Oberammergau are hiking along scenic alpine ridges, visiting nearby Ettal Abbey (see below), and watching the beards grow.

Information and tickets can be obtained from the **tourist office,** Eugen-Papst-Str. 9a (tel. 923 10; fax 923 31 90). The staff will provide you with a map and help you find a room (DM20-40) for free. (Open M-F 8:30am-6pm, Sa 8:30am-noon.) If the tourist office is closed, there is an information board with accommodations listings and a free hotel phone directly in front of the office. Turn left from the station and right at the town center onto Eugen-Papst-Str. Currency can be exchanged at the **post office,** Oberammergau 82488 (tel. 30 61), across the street from the train station (open M-F 9am-noon and 2-5:30pm, Sa 9am-noon). Oberammergau's **Jugendherberge (HI),** Malensteinweg 10 (tel. 41 14; fax 16 95), hunches over the gently flowing Ammer river seven minutes upstream from the train station. Head left up Bahnhofstr. for 100m, then take a right on the gravel foot path just before the bridge; follow the path past the farm, keeping the river on your left—the hostel is ahead on the right. The four to six bed dorm rooms are simple and spotless. (DM22.50. Sheets DM5.50. Reception 7-11:30am and 4-10pm. Curfew 10pm. Closed Nov.12-Dec.25.) For an Oberammergau *Schnitzel* speciality, try the inexpensive **Ammergauer Schnitzel-stube,** to the left of the train station. With the exception of steak, every meal DM13. (Open Th-Tu 10:30am-10pm). The **telephone code** is 08822.

In 1330, Ludwig I of Bavaria—not to be confused with the *crazy* Ludwig of Walt Disney castle fame—founded the enormous, domed **Abbey Church** in the tiny village of **Ettal,** about 4km south of Oberammergau (a 45min. hike). Since then, the abbey has conducted a brisk business in house-fermented beer and spirits. The **Kloster-laden,** to the right as you face the church, sells divine six-packs of *Kloster*-brewed beer (DM14.50); there are multiple other "licensed" *Kloster Ettal* pushers in the vicinity. Beautifully stuccoed and richly ornamented with gold and precious stones, this double-domed Baroque sanctuary assumed its present shape after 18th-century renovations. English guides to the history and architecture of the abbey are available (DM4). Be careful not to drown in the human flood of visitors (open 7:45am-7:45pm; winter 7:45am-noon and 1pm-dusk).

Buses to Ettal from Oberammergau leave hourly from the train station (round-trip DM5.20). To **hike** to the abbey from the Oberammergau tourist office, swing a left onto Eugen-Papst-Str. and shimmy down the sidewalk until the road forks at the bridge. Select the gravel bike path straight ahead and follow the signs to Ettal (stopping to take a quick ankle-high dip in the frigid river along the way). The **tourist office,** Ammergauerstr. 8 (tel. 35 34; fax 63 99), gives out free info, including accommodations listings (rooms DM42-70) and a map of hiking trails in the surrounding area (open M-F 8am-noon).

■ Füssen

A brightly painted toenail at the tip of the Alpine foothills, Füssen has captivated visitors ever since the time of mad King Ludwig. Füssen's plethora of scenic hiking trails, access to fabulous alpine ski resorts, and extreme proximity to Ludwig's famed *Königsschlösser* (Royal Castles; see p. 498) lures legions here every month of the year. Under Henry VII, this town found itself a reluctant player in the game of European intrigue and politics. To help finance his Italian campaign, Henry put up the town as collateral against a loan of 400 silver Marks from the prince-bishop of Augsburg. Henry died indebted, so the town was forfeited to the prince-bishop from 1313 until the great German Secularization of 1802. The *Altstadt's* lively cafe-laden pedestrian zone winds between ancient cemeteries, beneath Romanesque archways, and directly into the *Hohes Schloß's* imposing castle walls. The pristine landscape invites tourists to wander among cow pastures, bike the imperial Roman road, or take a refreshing dip in a mountain lake.

Reminders of the prince-bishop's medieval reign linger in Füssen's architectural wonders. The inner walls of the **Hohes Schloß** courtyard scream royalty with their arresting *trompe l'oeil* windows and towers. The **Staatsgalerie** (tel. 90 31 64) resides inside the castle walls, in the dens of late-medieval bishops and knights. (Open Tu-Su 11am-4pm; Nov.-Mar. Tu-Su 2-4pm. DM3, students and seniors DM2.) The museum shelters a collection of regional late Gothic and Renaissance art. Just below the castle rests the 8th-century Baroque basilica **St. Mangkirche** and its abbey. (Tours July-Sept.

Tu and Th 4pm, Sa 10:30am; May-June and Oct. Tu 4pm and Sa 10:30am; Jan.-Apr. Sa 10:30am. Call 48 44 for more info.) An ancient fresco discovered during renovations in 1950 lights up the church's 10th-century subterranean crypt. Also in the abbey is the gaudy 18th-century Baroque library. The **Museum of Füssen,** in the monastery (tel. 90 31 45), details the history, art, and culture of the Füssen region in four distinct departments, including one room devoted solely to the history of lutes and violins (tours Tu and Th 2:30pm). Inside the **Chapel of St. Anne,** macabre skeleton-decked panels depict the *Totentanz* (death dance), a public frenzy of despair that overtook Europe during the plague. (Open Apr.-Oct. Tu-Su 11am-4pm; Nov.-Mar. Tu-Su 2-4pm. Chapel free, library DM3, students DM2.) The purpose of the painting is to show that death conquers all—hurrah!

Trains run to Munich (2hr., every 2hr., DM35) and Augsburg (2hr., every 2hr., DM21). (Station open M-F 6:45am-7:15pm, Sa 6:45am-11:30am and 12:30-6:15pm, Su 7:45-11:30am and 12:30-7:15pm.) Füssen can be reached by **bus** from Oberammergau (1½hr., 5 times per day, DM12). Along the Füssen-Schwangau county line, 80km of cycling paths make Füssen a haven for bicyclists. One of the most scenic daytrips is the 32km Forgensee Cycle Route, which follows along the grassy shoreline of the alpine lake Forgensee. To **rent bikes,** head to **Radsport Zacherl,** Rupprechtstr. 8½ (tel. 32 92; 3-5 gear bike DM14 per day, 7-gear bike DM16). From the station, turn left on Rupprechtstr.; it's 100m down on the right. (Open M-F 9am-noon and 2-6pm, Sa 9am-noon.) The **tourist office** is on Kaiser-Maximilian-Pl. 1 (tel. 938 50; fax 93 85 20; http://www.fuessen.de). From the *Bahnhof,* walk the length of Bahnhofstr., then straight on Luitpoldstr. to the big yellow building. The staff finds rooms for free and proffers bike maps (DM7, DM3 with *Kurkarte*), hiking maps (DM7.80), and city maps (free). They organize guided hikes of the area (DM4; ask about times) and expeditions to the *Königsschlösser* (office open M-F 8am-6pm, Sa 9am-noon). The **Bahnhof Apotheke,** Bahnhofstr. 8 (tel. 918 10), has a bell for night pharmacy service (open M-F 8:30am-1pm and 2-6:30pm, Sa 8:30am-12:30pm). The **post office,** 87629 Füssen, at the corner of Bahnhofstr. and Rupprechtstr., exchanges money and cashes traveler's checks (DM6 per check; open M-F 8am-5:30pm, Sa 8am-noon). The **telephone code** is 08362.

Budget singles in *Gasthäuser* run DM35-40; in *Pensionen,* DM45 and up. During high season, don't expect to find a cheap room. If worse comes to worst, head to the information pavilion in front of the *Kurverwaltung,* where you can buy an information pamphlet (DM1) or peruse a computerized database of hotels (free; open 7am-12:30am). Keep your eyes open for *"Zimmer frei"* signs in private homes; prices fall dramatically as you walk away from the pedestrian zones. Füssen's **Jugendherberge (HI),** Mariahilferstr. 5 (tel. 77 54; fax 27 70), is blessed by a lovely location and friendly staff. Turn right from the station and follow the railroad tracks (10min.). It's often packed, so make a reservation at least one day in advance; if you've made a reservation, they're obligated to find a spot for you. Remember to show up before 6pm or call to let them know you will be coming later, or your precious reservation will suddenly disappear. (DM20.50, plus DM1.40 resort tax. Meals DM8.50. Sheets DM5.50. Basement lockers, DM1 deposit. Wash DM3, dry DM3, soap DM1. Reception 7-9am, 5-7pm, and 8-10pm. Curfew 10pm, but you can get the access code. Open Dec.-Oct.) **Pizza Blitz,** Luitpoldstr. 4 (tel. 383 54), offers gargantuan lip-smacking pizzas and calzones (DM6-13), making it a favorite local hangout (open M-Th 11am-11pm, F-Sa 11am-midnight, Su noon-11pm). **Plus,** on the corner of Bahnhofstr. and Luitpoldstr., is the cheapest grocery store around (open M-F 8:30am-7pm, Sa 8am-2pm).

Near Füssen: Wieskirche (Church in the Meadows)

Tel. (08861) 81 73. Open daily 8am-7pm. The best way to get there is by bus from the Füssen station (Daily 12:25, 3:25, and 4:35pm); return on the daily 3:15 or 3:50pm bus from the church (50min. each way, round-trip DM15.20).

Any daytrip from Füssen (45-75min.) or Oberammergau (45-55min.) to the Ammergau Alps ought to include the **Wieskirche** (Church in the Meadows), a splendid Rococo pilgrimage church. Torrents of light bathe the church in astonishing brightness, and the effect is particularly riveting in the morning and evening when the sun shines directly through the arching windows. The central dome's fresco appears to arch into the sky, a glowing "Gate to Paradise." One of the earliest optical illusions created, the "vaulted" ceiling is actually completely flat, rising directly from the cornice for only 3m before flattening out entirely. The painter and sculptor collaborated to skillfully blend the gold-guilded ornaments into the frescoed walls and ceiling, eliminating the boundary between the two- and three-dimensional world. Dominikus Zimmermann, the architect who built this church in 1746-1754, could not bear to leave Wies, his most beautiful and accomplished masterpiece, and until his death he lived in a tiny house just below the church.

■ Königsschlösser (The Royal Castles)

After Queen Marie bore Maximilian II two healthy sons, there was no reason to expect the fall of the Bavarian royal family—but it was soon to come. Otto, the younger son, developed schizophrenia as a young adult, leaving Ludwig to carry on the family name. In 1864, he assumed the throne at the tender age of 18 as a shockingly handsome lad who was extremely naive about politics. A zany visionary and a fervent Wagner fan, Ludwig used his cash to craft his dreams into reality. He spent his private fortune creating fantastic castles that soar into the Alpine skies, hoping to realize his fantasyland in an ugly and evil world. In 1886, a band of upstart nobles and bureaucrats deposed of Ludwig in a coup d'etat and imprisoned him in Schloß Berg on the Starnbergersee. Three days later, the King and a loyal advisor were discovered dead in the lake under mysterious circumstances—possibly a failed escape attempt, some hypothesize, even though Ludwig was a first-class swimmer. Even today, the enigma of Ludwig's life, death, and dreamworld linger, captivating the imagination.

Hohenschwangau & Neuschwanstein

Hohenschwangau is open mid-Mar. to mid-Oct. daily 8:30am-5:30pm; mid-Oct. to mid-Mar. 9:30am-4:30pm. DM11, students, seniors, and disabled persons DM8, children 6-15 DM8, under 6 free. Neuschwanstein is open Apr.-Sept. daily 9am-5:30pm; Oct.-Mar. 10am-4pm. Same prices as Hohenschwangau except children under 15 free when accompanied by an adult. Tegelbergbahn cable car, tel. 983 60. Open daily 8:30am-5pm; in winter 8:45am-4:30pm. One-way DM15, students and disabled persons DM14.50; round-trip DM25, DM24.

Ludwig II grew up in **Schloß Hohenschwangau,** the bright yellow neo-Gothic castle rebuilt by his father. It was no doubt here that he acquired his taste for the romantic German mythologies of the Middle Ages. Atop a humble hill and forest, this palace is a bit less touristed than its cousin, but also more authentic—the rooms actually appear to have been lived in. After Maximilian II died, Ludwig ordered the servants to paint a dreamy night sky upon the royal bedroom ceiling. The vast constellation of stars would shine brightly down upon the sleeping Ludwig when lit with oil lamps from above. This castle also features Wagner's maple-wood piano and a loaf of bread from the 1830s—it's the nast. German tours run frequently; English-speakers need to herd 20 people for a 30-minute tour in their native tongue.

Ludwig's desperate building spree across Upper Bavaria peaked with the construction of the glitzy **Schloß Neuschwanstein,** now Germany's most clichéd tourist attraction and the inspiration for Disney World's Cinderella Castle. The first sketches of the castle were reportedly drawn by a set designer, not an architect, which explains a lot. The young Ludwig II lived a mere 173 days within the extravagant edifice, in which 63 rooms remained unfinished. The completed chambers include a Byzantine throne-room, a small artificial grotto, and an immense *Sängersaal* (Singer's Hall)—an acoustic masterpiece, built expressly for Wagner opera performances, but never used. A wood carving of a familiar but unidentifiable city skyline tops the king's bed; it depicts most of the famous towers of the world. The lines for the brisk **tours**

(30min.) may seem endless, but they are the only way to get in; the best time to arrive is early in the morning. Like a horde of ants descending upon a singularly spectacular patch of spilled ice cream, tourists abound.

Consider spending the rest of the day hiking around the spectacular environs. For the fairy godmother of all views, hike up to the **Marienbrücke**, spanning the **Pöllat Gorge** behind the castle (10min.). Those with stout hearts and legs can continue uphill from here (about 1hr.) for a knockout overview of the castle and nearby lake. In the opposite direction, descend the mountain from Schloß Hohenschwangau to the lily-pad topped Schwansee lake (trail #49). Follow the Schwansee-Bundweg path #13 through fields of wild flowers to a swan-visited beach area and a secluded swimming hole. Sane people and insane hang-gliders ride the **Tegelbergbahn** cable car for a glimpse of—or a dive into—the same panorama.

From Füssen, hop the bus marked "Königsschlösser," which departs from the train station (1 per hr., DM2.40). It will dump you at the base of a number of surrounding hills in front of the **information booth**. Separate paths lead up to both Hohenschwangau and Neuschwanstein. A less touristed path to Hohenschwangau is path #17, which starts from the left side of the information booth and meanders through the moss-covered forest (10min.). To Neuschwanstein, take path #32, from Car Park D ("Parkpl. Königsschlösser," across the street from the bus stop); it's the shortest but steepest trail to the top (25min.). Alternately, clip-clop your way to the near-tippy-top in a horse-drawn carriage (uphill DM8, downhill DM4; daily 9am-5pm) from Car Park D or Hotel Müller. Consider trekking path #33 from Neuschwanstein back to the base of the hill (20min.; open only in summer). Virtually untouristed, this route winds its way down through the dramatic **Pöllat Gorge**. Private buses run from Hotel Lisl to a beautiful vantage point 650 steep meters uphill from Neuschwanstein (DM3.50 uphill, DM2 downhill, DM5 round trip). For hiking maps (DM7.80) or more information on trails, check out the **information booth** (Schlossverwaltung Hohenschwangau; tel. 811 27; open daily 9am-5pm). The bus to the castles (direction: Hohenschwangau Village) stops here. **Buses** depart from the Garmisch-Partenkirchen train station and stop directly in the Hohenschwangau village (2hr.; daily at 8.05am, 1:05, 4:15, and 5:05pm and M-F at 9:35 and 11:15am; return daily at 8:13, 9:43am, 12:38, 1:13, 3:33, 4, and 5:23pm). Buses also run from the Füssen train station to the Hohenschwangau village (10min., 1-2 per hour, daily from 8:05am-5:15pm; last returning bus leaves Hohenschwangau village M-Sa 7:06pm, Su 7:35pm; round-trip DM4.80). A *Tagesticket* (DM13) entitles castle-hoppers to unlimited bus travel on the regional Alps buses (including the ride to Linderhof); buy it from the bus driver. From Munich, take a **train** to Buchloe and transfer for the train to Füssen (2hr.; DM30).

Schloß Linderhof

Open Apr.-Sept. daily 9am-12:15pm and 12:45-5:30pm; Oct.-Mar. 10am-12:15pm and 12:45-4pm. Apr.-Sept. DM9, students and seniors DM6; Oct.-Mar. DM7 and DM4. Park is free and open to the public.

Halfway between Garmisch-Partenkirchen and Oberammergau lies the exquisite **Schloß Linderhof**, Ludwig II's compact hunting palace, surrounded by a meticulously manicured park. With this edifice Ludwig paid homage to the French Bourbon kings, in particular Louis XIV (the Sun King), just as he did with his Herrenchiemsee palace (see p. 516). Although it lacks Neuschwanstein's pristine exterior, the palace is bathed in gold, creating a remarkable experience of decadence. The royal bedchamber, the largest room in the castle, is unbelievably lush, with gold leaf and a colossal crystal chandelier that weighs half a ton. Dark blue velvet (the king's favorite color) encases the king-size bed; though he topped 195cm (6' 5"), Ludwig had no trouble fitting in between the hand-carved head and foot boards. Across the ceiling stretches the affirmation *"Nec pluribus impar,"* which roughly translates as "I am the MackDaddy of the DaddyMacks." The two malachite tables were gifts from Russian Czarina Marie Alexandrovna, who tried to match Ludwig (a bachelor to his death) with one of her daughters. Ludwig just kept the tables.

More impressive than the palace itself is the magnificent **park** surrounding the palace. The sheer force of water cascading down steps behind the palace powers the fountain in front. On the hour, the dam is opened and water shoots higher than the top of the palace. Paths originating at the swan lake at the park entrance weave through the ornately landscaped grounds. To the right of the palace and up the slope is an enormous, artificial **grotto**; red and blue floodlights illuminate a "subterranean" lake and floating shell-boat. Tacky, tacky, tacky. At least it's refreshingly cool inside. Farther along, brilliant red and blue stained-glass windows richly illuminate the **Maurischer Kiosk** (Moorish Pavilion), an elaborate, mosque-inspired building, and the only sight on the grounds not built expressly for Ludwig. He saw it at the 1867 World Exposition in Paris and liked it so much that he brought it home. Within these walls, Ludwig would smoke his water pipe and implore his servants to dress up in period costumes and read him tales from *1001 Nights*. Following the path down the hill to the left (20min.) is the newly reconstructed **Hunding-Hütte,** another of Ludwig's flights of fancy, modeled after a scene in Wagner's *Die Walküre* from *The Ring of the Nibelungen*. Bearskin-covered log benches surround an artificial tree.

Bus #9606 runs between Oberammergau and the park (9:45am-6:15pm). The last bus leaves Linderhof at 6:45pm. (20min., 1 per hr., DM9.20 round-trip). Hikers or cyclists can follow the well-kept gravel path along the river to Linderhof (10km). From the Oberammergau tourist office head left on Eugen-Papst-Str.; when the road forks at the bridge select the gravel bike path straight ahead and follow the signs to Linderhof. Reach Oberammergau by bus from Garmisch-Partenkirchen (40min., 1 per hr., DM5.40), Schongau (50min.), or Füssen (90min.). **Trains** run from Munich to Oberammergau, switching at Murnau (1¾hr., 1-2 per hr., DM24).

Hypertravel to the Castles

Seeing all three of the **royal castles** (*Königsschlösser*) during a daytrip from Munich requires some fancy footwork and luck with connections (and can only be done M-F). Take the 6:50am train from Munich to Buchloe, and transfer here onto the 7:46am to Füssen. Arriving in Füssen at 8:57am, hop on the 9:35am bus to the *Königsschlösser*. Arriving at 9:43am, you'll have three and a half hours to fight through the lines at Hohenschwangau and Neuschwanstein before you catch bus #1084 at 1:13pm to Schloß Linderhof (changing in Steingaden and Oberammergau). Until 5:05pm you can indulge in the surrounding opulence, but then it'll be time to mount bus #9606 (direction: "Füssen") to "Oberammergau Post/Bahnhof." At 5:25pm you'll get to the Oberammergau train station with plenty of time to catch the 6:07pm train to Murnau, where you'll change trains at 6:58pm and hopefully grab a *Löwenbräu* at 7:55pm back in Munich. Double check your schedule with a timetable before departing. A simpler and more advisable option, particularly if you don't have a railpass, is to sign on with **EurAide** for a charter bus ride to Neuschwanstein, Linderhof, and Wieskirche (see p. 478).

ALLGÄU ALPS

Marketing offices have a ball with the Allgäu Alps; this region's spectacular lakes and snow-laced mountainscapes have "Glossy Brochure Material" written all over them. But there's no way to cheapen the natural grandeur of the landscape. Gazing down on the pine-forested hillsides, how could one be anything but *umweltfreundlich?* Immenstadt, Bühl am Alpsee, and Obertsdorf are all tucked deep within these enchanting mountains, while Kempten lies on the region's edge.

■ Kempten

A surprisingly urban little city in a decidedly rural area of Germany, Kempten makes an ideal base for excursions into the neighboring mountains. Though its *Altstadt* has long been overpowered by department stores and *Döner* stands, a few treasures can still be found, despite the city's uncanny resemblance to American suburbia. The elegant baroque **Fürstäbtliche Residenz** (Prince Abbot's Residence) is a sizable former Benedictine cloister that has served the town as everything from a barracks to a courthouse. Behind the *Residenz* stretches the terraced **Hofgarten**, webbed by paths leading to the 18th-century **Orangerie**, which houses a library (guided tours May-Dec. Tu-Su 10, 11am, 2, and 3pm; Nov.-Apr. Sa 2pm). To reach the town center from the distant train station, ride bus #4, 6, 8, or 9 to "Residenz" (DM2.20), or walk along Bahnhofstr. (a.k.a. Weißstr.) until you reach the pedestrian zone. Continue until you see the trees in the park. Klostersteige leads from the *Residenz* to the pedestrian zone.

Across from the basilica on Residenzplatz, the **Römische Sammlung Cambodunum** (Roman Museum of Kempten) and the **Naturkunde Museum** (Museum of the Natural History of the Allgäu) dwell in the elegant patrician **Zumsteinhaus**, Residenzpl. 31 (tel. 123 67; both open Tu-Su 10am-4pm; DM4, students and seniors DM2). Three blocks down Herrenstr. stands the **Marshall**, Landwehrstr. 4 (tel. 54 01 80), which houses the **Alpinmuseum**, with exhibits on the natural and cultural history of the Allgäu Alps, and the **Alpenländische Galerie**, featuring local religious art of the late Gothic period (Marshall open Tu-Su 10am-4pm; DM4, students DM2). The oldest part of the city, the forested park along Burgstr. boasts a late Roman fortification with a Gothic tower, as well as an amphitheater that features German disco stars in the summer months. *"Ich liebe dich,* Kelly Family!" (See **The Osmonds of Central Europe**, p. 245.) Meanwhile the **Archaeological Park Cambodunum** (the Roman name from which "Kempten" is derived) reveals excavated Roman thermal baths. (Open May-Oct. 10am-5pm, Nov.-Apr. 10am-4:30pm. DM6, students DM3.) In mid-August, Kempten perks up with the **Allgäu Festival Week**, which features a regional trade fair, cultural and athletic events, and a country life exhibition. Nearby **Ottobeuren** is a little town, but it has the **largest Baroque church in Germany**. From Kempten, take the train to Memmingen (20min.) and catch a bus to Ottobeuren (15min.)

Built at a bend in the Iller River, Kempten can be reached by **train** from Lindau, Ulm, or Munich (70min., 3 per hr.). Kempten's **tourist office**, Rathauspl. 24 in the city center (tel. 252 52 37; fax 252 54 27; http://www.kempten.de), a few blocks from Residenzplatz, provides city and hiking maps (DM3-11), accommodations listings, and 1½- to 2-hour city tours for free. (Open May-Oct. M-F 8am-noon and 1:30-5pm, Sa 10am-1pm; Nov.-Apr. M-F 8:30am-noon and 1:30-5pm. Tours in German every Saturday at 11am. Meet at the *Burghalde*.) The **telephone code** is 0831.

The standard facilities of the noisy **Jugendherberge (HI)**, Saarlandstr. 1 (tel. 736 63; fax 77 03 81), are usually packed with school groups, but it offers a spectacular view of the Alps. You'll have plenty of time to enjoy the scenery on your way there by choosing from a number of unattractive options. From the station, catch bus #4, 6, 8, or 9 to "ZUM," and then switch to bus #1 ("direction: "Ostbahnhof") to "Unzfrieder-str./Altersheim" (2 every 30min.). Take a left at the intersection; the gray structure surrounded by a wire fence on top of the hill is the hostel. Alternatively, tighten your backpack for a 45-minute trek. Take the small Wiesstr. behind the post office by the station to Schumacherring, then turn right and follow this never-ending street until you ascend a set of stairs to the right after the intersection with Lenzfriedenstr. Follow the signs to the *Jugendherberge*. (DM18. Breakfast included. Sheets DM5.50. Reception 5-11pm. Curfew 11pm. Open mid-Dec. to Oct.) To reach **Camping Oeschlesee** (tel. (08376) 930 40; fax 930 41), take the bus from the *Altbahnhof* at Sulzberg (20min.; DM6) and walk to the lake (DM5 per person; DM4-7 per tent). The Marktplatz in front of the *Rathaus* offers the usual selection of pleasant cafes. Among them, the **Metro Bar Café**, Rathauspl. 19 (tel. 165 54), has a lively social atmosphere and Swabian noodles from DM10 (open daily 11am-1am).

■ Immenstadt and Bühl am Alpsee

The small, misleadingly named town of **Immenstadt** and the even smaller hamlet of **Bühl am Alpsee** huddle deep in the gorgeous mountains of the Allgäu south of

Kempten, a world away from the resorts to the south. Streams flowing down from the Alps feed two lakes, the **Großer Alpsee** and the **Kleiner Alpsee** (Large and Small Alpine Lakes), whose cool, clear waters are unimaginably refreshing after a hike into the surrounding hills.

The Kleiner Alpsee, a 15-minute walk down Badeweg toward Bühl, offers an extensive park speckled with small, unofficial swimming holes. The Großer Alpsee has *Größer* wet and wild opportunities, but certain stretches are off-limits to swimmers. **Boat and windsurf-board rental** on the Großer Alpsee is rather expensive (DM20-40 per hr.). You can go for a dip at the **Freibad Kleiner Alpsee,** Am Kleiner Alpsee (tel. 87 20), on the other side of the lake (open daily 9am-7pm, in case of bad weather 9:30-1pm; DM5). Immenstadt is also close to two immense skiing areas: **Alpsee Skizirkus** (tel. (08325) 252) and **Mittag Ski-Center** (tel. 61 49). The season runs roughly from December to March. Day passes cost about DM26 in each area, while week-long passes are DM130. Chairlifts and cable cars run summer-long for dedicated wanderers (call 61 49 for more info). Hiking trails are innumerable here. To trek to the lofty **Schloß Rauhenzell** and the Catholic **Church of St. Otmar,** head down Grüntenstr. east of the St. Niklaus Church. Continue behind the school and turn left down the quiet path (Wiedachweg), following the signs for *Sportzentrum.* The trail extends past Auwaldsee and the Iller River on its way upwards.

Immenstadt can be reached by **train** from Kempten along the Munich-Zürich route, or from Ulm along the Stuttgart-Oberstdorf route. The friendly Immenstadt **tourist office,** Marienpl. 3 (tel. 91 41 76; fax 91 41 95; email immenstadt@allgaeu.org; http://www.touristik.de/immenstadt), has loads of hiking maps (DM6.80-9.90) and suggested routes. The staff also finds accommodations (private rooms DM18-32). Wave hi to their mascot, Immi. (Open mid-July to Sept. M-Sa 8am-6pm; Oct. to mid-July M-F 8:30am-noon and 2-5:30pm, Sa 10am-noon.) From the station, turn right on Bahnhofstr. and follow it around the corner to the town square. Every Thursday morning, fruit vendors gather there under the onion-domed Church of St. Niklaus.

Next door to Immenstadt, tiny **Bühl** is accessible by bus (5min., every hr., DM2) and by the exquisite **Hornweg** trail, which begins at the cemetery trailhead. From Immenstadt, it's an hour-and-a-half walk along the steep mountainside. Lazier folks can amble down the pleasant Badeweg path (30-40min.). Bühl's **tourist office,** Seestr. 5 (tel. 91 41 78), has many of the same maps and brochures as its Immenstadt sibling, but no "Immi loves you all!" stickers. (Open M-F 8:30am-noon and 2-5pm, Sa 10am-noon; Nov.-May M-F 8:30am-noon and 2-5pm.) Camp on the Großer Alpsee at **Bucher's Camping,** Seestr. 25 (tel. 77 26 or 48 28), in Bühl. (DM7 per person. DM5-6.50 per tent. DM2.50 per car. DM1.50 *Kurtaxe* per person. Open Easter to early-Oct.) The **telephone code** for both towns is 08323.

■ Oberstdorf

Oberstdorf is heaven for hard-core hikers. Right in the middle of the snow-layered Allgäu Alps, this mecca of outdoorsiness combines solitary forest paths with a refreshing sense of nature-oriented tourism. Its large pedestrian zone deceives with its plethora of sporting goods stores, but beyond the commercial streets, narrow dirt trails taper enticingly toward alpine lakes and desolate hillsides. Foreign tourists are few and far between, as Oberstdorf remains a health resort populated by Germans seeking to enjoy their native *Landschaft.*

Two **Bergbahnen** (cable cars) whisk hikers to the heady heights of the Alps. The closer one delivers folks to the top of **Nebelhorn** (tel. 96 00 96), the highest accessible mountain in the Allgäu Alps (2242m; mid-May to Oct. daily 8:30am-4:50pm). The **Fellhornbahn** (tel. 30 35) climbs 2037m for an equally thrilling view (mid-May to Oct. daily 8:20am-4:50pm). Unfortunately, the prices are as eye-popping as the panoramas. (DM41 to the top of Nebelhorn; DM16 to the lowest station.) On the mountain, gravel trails wind among flowery meadows and patches of snow. Come winter (mid-Dec. to mid-Apr.), the Bergbahn transport skiers and snowboarders ready to hit the slopes. (Winter prices from DM41 for half a day.) To reach the Nebelhornbahn sta-

tion, walk down Nebelhornstr. from Hauptstr. To reach Fellhorn, ride the "Fellhorn" bus from the *Bahnhof.*
  Splash around in the **Moorbad** (tel. 48 63) or **Freiberg lake** (tel. 82 66) against a mountain backdrop. To reach the Moorbad from the Marktplatz, turn onto Oststr. and walk to the end. Follow the sign to the trail that leads to the Moorbad. One prime hiking route leads to the **Breitachklamm**, a vertical chasm in a rock face carved out by a frothing river. It's most easily approachable from Kornau, a sub-village of Oberstdorf. From the train station, take the bus (direction: "Klein Walsertal") to "Reute" (every 20min.; DM2). Walk up the hill and hang a right after House #22. The road becomes a hiking trail over the Breitach River. (45min.-2hr. to the Klamm.)
  Trains link Oberstdorf to Immenstadt (30min., 2 per hr.). Rent a **bike** at the **Zweirad Center,** Hauptstr. 7 (tel. 44 67) for DM15 per day, mountain bikes for DM25 (open M-F 9am-noon and 2:30-6pm, Sa 9am-noon). The Oberstdorf **tourist office** across from the train station of Bahnhofpl. 3 (tel. 70 00; fax 70 02 36; email info@oberstdorf.de; http://www.oberstdorf.de) doles out loads of brochures on hiking possibilities and accommodations (open M-F 8:30am-noon and 2-6pm, Sa 9:30am-noon). A second branch is at Marktpl. 7 with the same hours and contact information. The **post office** is across from the train station (open M-F 7am-7pm, Sa 7am-2pm).
  Closer to Oberstdorf, Kornau is home to the excellent **Oberstadt Jugendherberge (HI)**, Kornau Haus 8 (tel. 22 25; fax 804 46), in a gorgeous setting overlooking the Alps. Its spacious facilities include laundry and a rudimentary bar. (DM24, including *Kurtaxe.* Breakfast included. Ski rentals DM30 per day. Reception 8am-noon, 5-8pm, and 9:30-10pm. Open Dec. 27-Oct. 31.) Take the bus from Oberstdorf to "Reute," but be forewarned: the last bus leaves town by 8pm. Otherwise, you will have to suffer a DM15 taxi-ride or an hour-long climb uphill in the dark. Oberstdorf proper is full of cozy *Ferienwohnungen* and guesthouses. Rates start at DM30 per person. Seek the tourist office for guidance. Restaurants close early and charge seriously, but consider the self-serve **Cafe Felixar** at Nebelhornstr. 48 (noodles, wursts DM5-16) or try the **grocery stores** near Hauptstr.

■ Wasserburg am Inn

A town of red-roofed houses and lively street cafes, Wasserburg floats dramatically atop a promontory on a bend in the Inn River between Munich and Salzburg. Due to its favorable location, the city prospered in the 16th century with the growth of its salt-trade and shipping industries. Remnants of the past, **medieval cobblestone paths** starting at the Innbrücke bridge curl around the ancient half-island, winding between crooked old houses and church steeples. From the *Stadt Bahnhof* train station, make a left up Im Hag and then a right on Hoffstatt down Salzsenderzeile to penetrate the *Altstadt.* If your train doesn't go as far as the city train station, you'll need to take a bus from the *Hauptbahnhof,* which lies outside the town itself. (Though it's only 4km, walking is not recommended, as it involves crossing high-speed interchanges and tangling with restless German drivers.) The buses run regularly and cost DM1.50. The late-Gothic **Rathaus**, built in 1250, is back at Salzsenderzeile; inside, the **Kleiner Rathaussaal** and the **Tanzhaus** host many Wasserburg weddings (tours Tu-F 10 and 11am, 2, 3, and 4pm, Sa-Su 10 and 11am; DM1 50, children DM0.50). The **Erstes Imaginäres Museum** (First Imaginary Museum), Bruckgasse 2 (tel. 43 58) on Marienplatz, around the corner from the *Rathaus* at the foot of the bridge, is a private and eclectic collection of German Old Masters and French Impressionists, as well as primitive and pop art. (Open May-Sept. Tu-Su 11am-5pm; Oct.-Apr. Tu-Su 1-5pm. DM3, students and seniors DM2, under 16 DM1.) Recognize them? These famous works are all painstakingly produced copies by the replication master Günter Dietz.
  Wasserburg can be reached by **train** from Munich (1¼hr., 8 per day). The **tourist office** (tel. 105 22) in the *Rathaus* offers free maps and lists of rooms (DM20-30) for rent. (Open May-Sept. M-F 9am-12:30pm and 3:30-5:30pm; Oct.-Apr. M-F 9am-12:30pm.) Rundfahrten offers daily **river tours** starting at the Innbrücke. (40min. trip daily at 2:30pm, DM10; 80min. trip daily at 11am and 3pm, DM16; 2hr. trip Tu and F

7pm, DM20; children under 15 50% off, under 5 free.) **Badria,** Alkorstr. 14 (tel. 81 33), Wasserburg's amazing recreation center, comes complete with miniature golf, saunas, solariums, outdoor and indoor swimming pools, and the **largest water slide in Germany.** (Recreation center open M-F 10am-9pm, Sa-Su 8:30am-7pm. Admission to pool DM12. Admission to pool and sauna DM20. Discounts for students and children.) To get there from the train station, take the Wasserburg city bus to "Badria" (DM1.50). The **telephone code** is 08071.

The nearest **Jugendherberge,** Schillingerstr. 1 (tel. (08092) 225 23), in Ebersberg, is 30 minutes away by train or bus. From the Ebersberg *Bahnhof,* facing the MiniMal across the street, take a right on Rosenheimerstr., which curves right and dips under the train overpass. Take the first street on the left, Hindenbergallee, and look for the Jugendherberge sign. (DM16.50, breakfast included. Sheets DM5.50. Open Feb.-Nov.) **Gasthof Huberwirt,** Salzburgerstr. 25 (tel. 74 33), across the Innbrücke, is a simple and affordable motel on the hill overlooking the town. Cross the Innbrücke from Marienplatz and take the steps up to Kellerbergweg on the left just before the gas station. Follow this footpath through the woods up to the motel. (Singles DM34-54; doubles DM62, with shower DM90; triples DM90-111. Breakfast included.) The closest **camping** is 6km away in Soyen at **Werner Huthm,** Soyen am See (tel. 38 60), a manageable walk (open Apr. to mid-Oct.). The popular **Brasserie im Stechl Keller,** Marienpl. 6 (tel. 56 53), serves tall glasses of beer (DM4.20 for 0.5L) as well as many tasty meals (DM9-18; open daily 8am-1am; kitchen open 11am-2pm and 6-11pm).

■ Bad Reichenhall

In Bad Reichenhall, it is considered normal to sit in front of a salt water fountain daily, cover oneself in mud, and then inhale oxygen from an intimidating apparatus. But even if you don't come for the facials and cucumber eyepatches, the city's breathtaking views of the Austrian Alps and its "White Gold" salt deposits are just as pleasurable. Because of its proximity to Austria, the Viennese and Salzburger influences are strong in the architecture, dialect, and gastronomy. The **Salz Museum,** Alte Saline (tel. 70 02 51), travels into the 16th-century salty underworld, peppered with exhibits on the history and process of salt-making in the area. The obligatory tour in German winds through the damp underground passageways where brine (salt water) is pumped out of the mountain. (Tours Apr.-Oct. daily 10-11:30am and 2-4pm; Nov.-Mar. Tu and Th 2-4pm. Last tour at 4pm. DM8, with *Kurkarte* DM7, children DM4.) At the **Glashütte** (tel. 697 38), also in the museum, you can experience the beauty of glass-making and glass-buying (tours M-F 9:30am-6pm, Sa 9am-1pm). The **Glasofenwirtshaus** hosts a musical *Weißwurstfrühschoppen* (a Bavarian practice of getting plastered in the morning) every Saturday from 9am to 1pm (restaurant open M-F 9:30am-6pm, Sa 9am-1pm; live music W-F 2:30-5pm).

Walk right from the Alte Saline on Salinenstr. until it becomes Ludwigstr. and follow the cafe-laden pedestrian promenade until you reach the palatial 1870 **Kurgarten** on the left. (Open Apr.-Oct. daily 7am-10pm; Nov.-Mar. 7am-6pm. Free except for 1-1½hr. long concerts. Concerts Apr.-Oct. Tu 4 and 8pm, W 4pm, Th 8pm, F and Sa 4pm, Su 10:45am and 4pm. Concerts DM10, children DM5.) The *Altes Kurhaus* in the garden offers a therapeutic blue theater, a restful music pavilion, and a rejuvenating chess set. At the salt spring fountain, buy a *Becher* (cup) to drink from the *Trinksole* fountain (DM0.20; open M-Sa 8am-12:30pm and 3-5pm, Su 10am-12:30pm). The 170m **Gradierwerk** out front is a bizarre wall known as an "open air inhalatorium." Built in 1912, it's covered with 250,000 bundles of *"Dornbündel"* (branches, briars, and thorns) through which salt-water mist trickles from April to October. For best results, those visiting the wall sit and inhale through their nostrils for 30 minutes. Didn't do much for us, but obviously someone thinks it works, because the city spends DM100,000 on its annual upkeep—there's your *Kurtaxe* at work. The **Predigstuhl,** the oldest cable car of its kind in the world (1928), runs up 1614m of skier's paradise. (1 per hr. May-Sept. 9am-9pm; Oct.-Apr. 9am-5pm. Round-trip

DM24, under 16 DM16, under 6 free. For info call 21 27; weather info tel. 17 19.) In summer you can hike the *Höhenkurweg* trail to the *Almhütte* resthouse.

Trains run hourly to Munich (2½hr., 1 per hr.) and Salzburg (20min., 1 per hr., DM7.40) with a change in Freilassing; both trains and buses run to and from Berchtesgaden (40-45min., 1 per hr., DM5.45). Rent a **bike** at **Sport Müller**, Spitalgasse 3 (tel. 37 76), for DM12 for half a day, DM15 for a whole day, children 20% off (open M-F 9am-6:30pm; Sa 9am-1:30pm). The **tourist office**, Wittelsbacherstr. 15 (tel. 30 03; fax 24 27), is to the right on the same road as the station, across from the Sparkasse. The staff provide maps, hiking advice (mountain tours and hikes up to 500km), guest information, and tips on discounts with the *Kurkarte*. (Open M-F 8am-5:30pm, Sa 9am-noon.) From the tourist office, cross Wittelsbacherstr. over to Kurstr. to the main pedestrian zone (leading up on the right) or to the lush *Kurgarten* and *Kurhaus* on the left. Call **Club Aktiv** (tel. 672 38) to go **rafting** or **canyoning**. The **post office**, Bahnhofstr. 35, 83435 Bad Reichenhall (tel. 77 80), is to the right as you exit the station (open M-F 8am-5:30pm, Sa 8am-noon). The **telephone code** is 08651.

There is no *Jugendherberge* in Bad Reichenhall and unfortunately most hotels are expensive (DM40-150). A small but very pleasant hotel is **Gästehaus Villa Fischer**, Adolf-Schmid-Straße 4 (tel. 57 64), a short walk from the *Kurgarten* (DM32-35, English and French spoken). Along the pedestrian zones of Salzburger and Ludwigstr., you'll find endless cafes where you can try delectable *Mozart Kugeln* (marzipan/chocolate balls) and *Torte mit Sahne* (cake with cream). At **Gasthof Bürgerbräu**, Waaggasse 2 (tel. 60 89), on Rathausplatz, traditionally dressed waiters serve the local beer direct from the in-house brewery (DM4.40 for 0.5L). Bavarian dishes run DM11-17 (open daily 11am-11pm, F-Su dancing after 7pm). **Restaurant Fuchsbau**, Innsbruckerstr. 19, serves pizza and Bavarian meals (DM12-20), including *Weißwürste* (DM11.20; open Tu-Su 7pm-3am). For basics, head to the **grocery store HL Markt**, Bahnhofstr. 20, to the right of the station (open M-F 8am-6pm, Sa 7:30am-1pm).

THE CHIEMSEE

For almost 2000 years, artists, architects, and musicians have chosen the Chiemsee as the setting for their artistic masterpieces. With its picturesque islands, meadows, pastures, forests, marshland, and dramatic crescent of mountains, the region first lured the 9th-century builders of the cloisters on **Fraueninsel**. Later, the wobbly King Ludwig II arrived to build **Herrenchiemsee**, his third and last fairy-tale castle, on the Herreninsel. The poet Maximilian Haushofer lived and died on the Chiemsee shores in **Prien**, and 11-year-old Mozart composed a mass in Seeon while on holiday. Most modern visitors to "The Bavarian Ocean" are artists of leisure, and the area has been overrun by resorts and prices have risen. But don't expect to find very many foreigners—Chiemsee is where the *nouveaux riches* of Munich and Northern Germany vacation. Summer weekends are sheer madness. Prien, the largest lake town, offers easy access to ski areas in the **Kampenwand**, the surrounding curtain of mountains, and resort paradises in **Aschau** and **Sachrang**. For information on white-water **rafting**, call (08649) 243. The **Trachtenfest**, with parades, folklore, and pilgrimages, takes place each year in a different town on the last Sunday in July.

■ Prien am Chiemsee

Without question, the best things about Prien are its idyllic Chiemsee coast and its highly frequented train station, which facilitates the use of the town as a base for the real sights elsewhere on the lake. If lugging around heavy packs wears you down, store your luggage in the lockers at the train station (DM 1-4). To soothe that sore back, wade in the cold water of Prien's *Kneipp Water Cure* and then jump into a 90°F (32°C) thermal bath—it works wonders for some German football players.

Located on the northwestern corner of the Chiemsee, Prien has a convenient and direct **train** link to Munich (1½hr., 1 per hr., DM22) and Salzburg, Austria (50min.,1-

2 per hr., DM16.20). Call 28 74 for train information. You can rent a **bike** at **Radsport Reischonböck,** Hochriesstr. 17 (tel. 46 31), 100m to your left after exiting the train station (DM 13-17; open M-F 8am-12:30pm, Sa 8am-noon). To paddle the Chiemsee, rent a **boat** from **Bootsverleih Stöffl** (tel. 20 00), at the red and white umbrella stand at the end of the footpath to the Chiemsee (DM 17 per boat; open daily Apr.-Oct.). The train station is a few blocks from the city center and a 20-minute walk north of the lake. To reach the *Altstadt,* turn right as you exit the station and then turn left on Seestr., which becomes Alte Rathausstr. The large, modern **tourist office,** Alte Rathausstr. 11 (tel. 690 50 or 69 05 55; fax 69 05 40), five minutes away on the left, is full of free maps and English brochures. The tourist office finds rooms (DM20-40 with breakfast) in private houses for free. (Open M-F 8:30am-6pm, Sa 9am-noon.) If the **information booth** (tel. 690 50) at the train station is closed (open July-Sept. M-F 12:45-5:45pm), head out the main exit to find a city map 10 paces to your right. Try your golf putt at **Minigolf Prien,** Seestr. 100 (DM 4.30, students DM4, children under 16 DM3), or enjoy an evening of dancing and entertainment with **Chiemsee Schiffahrt river cruises** (tel. 690 50), leaving every Friday at 7:30pm from the Prien am Chiemsee dock (DM 23). Phone 10 37 to find out which **pharmacy** is open on any given night. The **telephone code** is 08051.

The cheapest bed in town is at the raucous **Jugendherberge (HI),** Carl-Braun-Str. 66 (tel. 687 70; fax 68 77 15), a 15-minute walk from the station and 10 minutes from the lake. From the station, go right on Seestr. and under the train overpass. After two blocks, take a left on Staudenstr., which curves right and turns into Carl-Braun-Str. (DM25. Showers, lockers, and breakfast included. Sheets DM5.50. Reception 8-9am, 5-7pm, and 9:30-10pm. 6-bed rooms. Lockout 9am-1pm. Curfew 10pm. Open early Feb.-Nov.) **Campingplatz Hofbauer,** Bernauerstr. 110 (tel. 41 36; fax 626 57), is about a 15-minute stroll from the center of town. Walk right from the station, turn left at Seestr., and left again at the next intersection, and follow Bernauerstr. out of town past the gas station and McDonald's. (DM10.50 per person, children 14 and under DM 5.50, DM10 per tent and car. Showers included. Open Apr.-Oct.) Most of the restaurants in Prien cater to the vacationing bourgeoisie. Try **Scherer SB Restaurant,** Alte Rathausstr. 1 (tel. 45 91), on the corner of Alte Rathausstr. and Bernauerstr. This self-serve restaurant cooks up hearty meals and filling salads (DM9-20; open M-F 8am-9pm, Sa 8am-3pm). For a delicious Italian meal, descend into the green candlelight ambience of **La Piazzo,** Seestr. 7 (tel. 56 52). The lively waitstaff serves savory pasta dishes (DM 11-13) and large, thin-crust pizzas (DM 9.80). Gather groceries from **HL Markt,** Seestr. 11, close to the station (open M-F 8am-8pm, Sa 8am-4pm).

■ Herreninsel and Fraueninsel

Ferries float across the waters of the Chiemsee from the port in Prien to the **Herreninsel** (Gentlemen's Island), the **Fraueninsel** (Ladies' Island), and towns on the other side of the lake. (Round-trip to Herreninsel DM10, to Fraueninsel or to both islands DM12, children under 15 DM5, DM6; you can hop on and off various round-trips to visit the islands.) Both islands are co-ed, although this wasn't always the case—a monastery on Herreninsel once complemented the still-extant nunnery on Fraueninsel in religious chastity and isolation. Supposedly, mischievous members of the cloth (of both sexes) met up on *Krautinsel* (Vegetable Island) and practiced the eyebrow-raising act of gardening; nowadays, the island remains uninhabited and unferried. For more information on passage to the islands, call Chiemsee-Schiffahrt (tel. 629 43). To get to the dock, hang a right from the Prien train station's main entrance and follow Seestr. (the major thoroughfare on the right) for about 20 minutes. Alternatively, a slow 19th-century **green steam train** takes visitors from the train station to the dock roughly hourly, departing 9:40am-6:15pm (8min.). To get there, follow the *Chiemseebahn* sign. (One-way DM3.50, round-trip DM5.50; children under 15 DM 1.50, DM 2.50. Total package, including train shuttle and ship passage, DM17.) The train station **information booth,** though central, has very limited hours (open July to mid-Sept. M-F 12:45-5:45pm). Be sure to read the schedules to avoid getting stranded.

Schloß Herrenchiemsee on the Herreninsel

"Never can as unsuitable a location have been chosen for something as tasteless as this unfortunate copy of the palace at Versailles," Bavarian poet Ludwig Thomas pouted. Although some join Thomas in scowling at the Königsschloß's extravagance, year after year thousands of tourists faithfully flock to Herreninsel to stroll the halls of this excessively furnished palace. To get to the palace from the Herreninsel ferry landing, either walk along the paved footpath (20min.) or take one of the horse-drawn carriages that run every 15 minutes (DM4, children DM2.50). The architecture of **Königsschloß Herrenchiemsee** (tel. 30 69) is fabulously overwrought as only King Ludwig II could manage. (Open Apr.-Sept. daily 9am-5pm; Oct.-Mar. 10am-4pm. Admission and obligatory tour DM8, seniors, students, and disabled persons DM5, under 16 free with adult. German tours every 10min.; English tours 10:30 and 11:30am, 2, 3, and 4pm.) Ludwig bankrupted Bayern while building the palace, thus leaving barren rooms with naked white walls in stark contrast to the 20 overadorned chambers which were completed. The entire U-shaped palace is a shameless attempt to be larger, better, and more expensive than Versailles. Ludwig II was so obsessed with the "Sun King" that he commissioned exact replicas of Versailles originals to grace the walls of his palace. Surprisingly, not a single painting of Ludwig is to be found on the palace walls, though a tiny bust of him cowers in the far back of the palace. There's even a **Hall of Mirrors,** only Ludwig's is longer than Louis's; it took 25 people half an hour to light the more than 500 candles in this room when Ludwig decided to tour his palace. Candle-lit concerts are hosted here throughout the summer. While lacking Neuschwanstein's pristine exterior and Linderhof's almost completely gold-laden interior, Herrenchiemsee provides a better glimpse into Ludwig's mind—no other *Königsschloß* so well reflects Ludwig's obsessive qualities or his relentless insistence on creating a world he could never have. A **museum** documenting Ludwig's life lies just inside the castle entrance (DM4, students DM2). If you must wait for an English tour, the cafeteria in the lobby serves up *Frische Weißwürste mit frischer Brezeln und süßem Senf* (white sausage with pretzels and sweet mustard; DM10.50) as well as coffee or hot chocolate (DM5). For Herrenchiemsee **tourist information,** call (08051) 30 69.

Fraueninsel

Despite dwelling so close to Ludwig's material world, Fraueninsel is no material girl. In fact, Fraueninsel is quite the opposite: a small realm of hard-working nuns and old-school fishermen that shuns the most material of all possessions—the automobile. Only footpaths wind through this subdued village. From the boat dock, a marked path curls toward the **island cloister,** passing its medicinal herb garden. (Open mid-June to Sept. daily 11am-6pm; Oct. to mid-June M-Sa 11am-6pm. DM4, students DM1.50.) The nuns make their own marzipan, beeswax candles, and liqueurs, for sale in the convent shop (DM8.50 for 0.2L *Klosterlikör*). The abbey dates back to at least 866. St. Irmengard, the great-granddaughter of Charlemagne and earliest known abbess of the cloister, has a **memorial chapel** behind the main altar of the church. Her sarcophagus was exhumed in the 17th century, and in 1928 her remains were encased in glass within the altar. They're not very interesting—that's what 1000 years will do to you. More entertaining are the countless messages written to Irmengard on the opposite wall in thanks for deliverance after prayer. The **Torhalle** (gate) is the oldest surviving part of the cloister. Various artifacts, including the 8th-century Merovingian **Cross of Bischofhofen,** are displayed in the room above the gate. The entire island can be circumnavigated on foot in 45 minutes. There are quite a few *Gaststätte* scattered all over the island, but prices are high because owners know they have hungry tourists trapped. Bring some food or be prepared to splurge. For **tourist information** call (08054) 511 or 603 or fax 12 72.

■ Elsewhere near the Chiemsee

While Prien is considered the "metropolis of the Bavarian sea," countless other idyllic towns melt into the landscape, offering resort luxuries, nature rambles, and historical attractions galore. **Übersee,** a haven for biking, sailing, and windsurfing, lies on the Chiemsee just past Prien on the Munich-Salzburg train line. Contact their **tourist office** (tel. (08642) 89 89 50; fax 621 14). Just northwest of Chiemsee lies **Bad Endorf,** famed for its thermal baths; call its *Kurverwaltung* for more information (tel. (08053) 30 08 22; fax 30 08 30). Bad Endorf also has a **hostel (HI)** (tel. (08053) 509; fax 32 92) located 3km from the *Bahnhof* on Rankhamer Weg 11. It is quiet, cheery, and super cheap. (DM16.50. Open early-Feb. to Nov.) Little villages curl up at the foothills of the mountains: **Grassau Verkehrsamt** (tel. (08641) 23 40; fax 40 08 41), **Rimsting Verkehrsamt** (tel. (08051) 44 61; fax 616 94), and **Riedering Verkehrsamt** (tel. (08036) 34 48; fax 37 58) can supply more information. **Rottau,** just south of the Chiemsee, nestles in a mountain ridge; call its **Verkehrsamt,** at Grassauerstr. 9 (tel. (08641) 27 73; fax 14 19).

Sachrang is an exquisite Alpine village on the Tyrolean border. For excellent skiing, mountain climbing, and walking tours, call the tourist office, **Sachrang Verkehrsamt,** Dorfstr. 20 (tel. (08057) 378; fax 10 51; open M-Tu and Th-F 8am-noon and 2-5pm, W 8am-noon, Sa 9am-noon). **Aschau** lies near Sachrang, with skiing and hiking trails connecting the two. The panorama is perfect, and the town touts solariums, tobogganing, sailing, and skiing. The **tourist office** is located at Kampenwandstr. 38 (tel. (08052) 90 49 37; fax 47 17; open May-Sept. M-F 8am-noon and 2-6pm, Sa 9am-noon; Oct.-Dec. M-F 8am-noon and 2-5pm; Jan.-Apr. M-F 8am-noon and 2-5pm, Sa 9am-noon). Aschau and Sachrang are easily reached by **train** from the Munich-Salzburg route; at Prien, switch to trains headed for your destination (2hr.). **Buses** link Aschau to Munich. Affordable **accommodations,** like bungalows and vacation homes, run DM20-40 per person. The tourist office in Prien (see p. 515) distributes information about neighboring towns.

■ Burghausen

The proverbial castle-on-the-hill overshadows everything else in Burghausen, a tiny town separated from Austria by the Salzach River. Burghausen and its surrounding towns lie in the ice age sediment deposited from the Salzach glacier. The Salzach river slowly eroded the sediment, carving a deep valley separated from the uppermost layer of sedimentary rock by a steep cliff. Sturdily built high upon the steepest face of this cliff in the 13th century, the 1034m **Burg,** the longest medieval fortress in Europe, was considered impregnable—and indeed, it was only breached once. (*Burg* open Apr.-Sept. M-F 9am-noon and 1-5pm; Oct.-Mar. Tu-Su 9am-noon and 1-4pm. DM4, students DM2. Historical museum open May-Sept. daily 9am-6:30pm; mid-Mar. to Apr. and Oct.-Nov. 10am-4:30pm. DM2.50, children DM1.) In 1742, the Habsburg Empire, eager to extend its borders into Bayern, fell upon the border town of Burghausen. Cowed by the Austrian show of arms and lacking outside reinforcements, Burghausen opened its gates without a fight. Days later, on October 16, 1742, Burghausen's moment of glory came: the brash 26-year-old *Hofkaminkehrermeister* (Master Chimney Sweep) Karl Franz Cura recruited 40 grenadiers for the seemingly impossible task of breaking through the castle walls. In one fell swoop, Cura brilliantly freed the castle and the city. Until the Habsburgs return, Burghausen will remain a distinguished fortress town akin to Heidelberg and Rothenburg in its medieval glory, only much less trafficked.

These days, the **castle ramparts** can be walked without violent reprisals, and the town's **historical museum** (tel. 651 98) is in the upper halls. For the price of lugging your picnic basket up the steep footpath, the castle offers a grassy park area with a ravishing view of the *Altstadt's* roofs of red tiles and colorful gables, perfect for enjoying an afternoon nap or a picnic luncheon. The footpath starts behind **St. Jakob's Kirche,** which is across from the *Rathaus* and dates back to 1140. The castle's old and eerie **torture chamber** (tel. 615 34) was used until 1918. (Open mid-Mar. to Oct. daily 9am-6pm; Nov. to mid-Mar. Sa-Su 9am-6pm; DM2.50, children DM1.) A peek out of an upper story window affords a view of the grassy banks of the Wöhrsee far below, a popular swimming hole in the hot summer months. The **Hexenturm** across the way imprisoned accused witches until 1751. Below the castle, the rows of pastel facades lining the **Stadtplatz** shimmer with such soft medieval splendor that you may suspect that only toys live in this doll house city. At the far end of the Stadtplatz looms the magnificent Baroque **Studienkirche St. Joseph,** a 1630 Jesuit convent.

Burghausen is most easily reached by **train** from Munich (2hr., 1 per hr. via Mühldorf until 8:30pm), though **buses** run from Mühldorf, the transportation hub for eastern Bayern. Stepping off the train, you'll find yourself smack in the middle of suburbia. Don't panic. One hundred meters to your left at the end of the parking lot is a city map. Follow Marktlerstr. (directly in front of you) to the right; it's a 30-minute hike to the *Altstadt* at Stadtplatz. Or take the bus on Marktlerstr. around the corner of the train station (every 30min. 8:12am-7pm; fewer on weekends). It's four stops to "Stadtpl." (DM2). For a **taxi** call 22 33. The **tourist office** *(Fremdenverkehrsamt),* Stadtpl. 112-114 (tel. 24 35; fax 88 71 55), is located in the peppermint green **Rathaus** at the far end of the Stadtplatz. (Open M-W and F 8am-noon and 1:30-5pm, Th 8am-noon and 1:30-6pm, Sa 10am-1pm.) To explore the Burghausen area by boat, join **Plätten-fahrten** (tel. 24 35) on a 1½ hour tour down the Salzach River on an ancient open-air salt gondola. (Tours leave from the dock at Tittmoning, 18km south of Burghausen, and land at the Salzach boat launching dock in Burghausen. Tours leave May-Oct. daily 2pm. DM12, children and disabled persons DM6.) To your left as you exit the *Rathaus* is an archway that opens onto In den Grüben, a narrow cobblestone street; a **post office,** 162 In den Grüben, 84489 Burghausen (tel. 45 80), is one block down on the left (open M-F 2:30-5pm). The **telephone code** is 08677.

The **Jugendherberge Burghausen (HI),** Kapuzinergasse 235 (tel. 41 87; fax 91 13 18), is a schlepp from the train station but close to the cafe-heavy In den Grüben. From the station, take the city bus at Marktlerstr. through Stadtplatz to "Hl.-Geist-Spital," walk ahead, and turn left onto Kapuzinergasse. Or from Stadtplatz, continue through the arch at the far side of the square onto In den Grüben. At the end, cross the intersection to the left of the church onto Spitalgasse and turn right onto Kapuzinergasse. Immaculate, spacious four-bed dorms with private showers and an impressive view of the castle. The staff speaks fluent English. (45min. from the station. DM20. Delicious breakfast (with wide cereal selection) included. Sheets DM5.50. Reception M-F 8-10am and 5-7pm, Sa-Su 8-9am and 5-7pm.) The tourist office finds quieter accommodations for no fee; *Pensionen* and *Gasthöfe* in Burghausen start at DM30, breakfast included. If you're after Bavarian dishes, try **Hotel Post,** Stadtpl. 39 (tel. 30 43). After 450 years, it knows its *Würstchen* (most meals DM13.50-18, beer DM4, *Apfelkuchen* DM3.50). For A-plus "I" cuisine, try **Taj Mahal,** In den Grüben 166, which serves a unique mix of Indian and Italian dishes (open Tu-Sa 11:30am-2pm and 5:30-11:30pm, Su 11:30am-11:00pm; vegetarian Indian dishes DM13.50, pasta DM9, beer DM4). Head to Austria for a *Mozart Kugel* and *Torte.* Follow Bruckgasse from the middle of Stadtplatz over the Alte Brücke spanning the Salzach River (2min.). Buy supplies at the **Edeka Markt,** In den Grüben, across from the post office (open M-F 8am-6pm, Sa 7am-noon).

■ Passau

Baroque arches cast deep shadows across the narrow cobblestone alleyways of Passau, a two millenia-old city uniquely situated at the confluence of the Danube, the Inn, and the Ilz Rivers. Napoleon once remarked of this "Bavarian Venice": "I have not seen a city as beautiful as Passau in all of Germany." A heavily fortified medieval castle, a musty Gothic *Rathaus,* and a row of residential palaces of erstwhile opulent bishops bear witness to the fact that this *"Dreiflüssestadt"* (three-river city) was once a center of administrative, commercial, and religious power. In 739, the church awarded Passau with the seat of a diocese. Centuries later the *Stephansdom,* Passau's pink marble-columned Baroque cathedral, was erected, inspiring the construction of an offspring cathedral of the same name in Vienna. In the 13th century, enterprising local merchants monopolized the central European salt trade—a very profitable achievement, considering that the average salt consumption of this period was six times more than that of modern-day cholesterol-conscious Europe. Today *Eis Cafés* and monasteries, shoe stores and peculiar art galleries line the streets of this ancient city, shaped like the pretentious tip of a bishop's pointy nose.

ORIENTATION AND PRACTICAL INFORMATION

Close to the Austrian border, Passau is directly accessible by rail from both Munich (2hr., every 2hr.) and Vienna (3hr., 6 per day). Buses duplicate most rail routes and are often less expensive, but they almost double travel time. To reach the city center from the train station, follow Bahnhofstr. to the right until you reach Ludwigsplatz. Walk downhill across Ludwigsplatz to Ludwigstr., the beginning of the pedestrian zone, which becomes Rindermarkt, Steinweg, and finally Große Messergasse. If you continue straight onto Schustergasse when the street ends, you will soon reach the *Altstadt;* if you hang a left on Schrottgasse, you will stumble upon the **Rathausplatz,** where the tourist office will be on the left by the riverbank. From there, a glance up from your map yields a picturesque view of the Danube and the steep hill, beyond which lies the **Schloß.** Heading farther east on the tip of the peninsula leads to the point where the three rivers converge. A little blue **City-Bus** can bop you around town (DM0.50); one stop is directly to the right of the station as you exit.

Trains: Station located west of downtown on Bahnhofstr. (tel. 194 19). Trains to Regensburg (1-2hr., every hr.); Nürnberg (2hr., every 2hr.); Munich (2hr., every 2hr.); Vienna (3½hr., 6 per day); and Frankfurt (4½hr., every 2 hr.). The Information Counter at the train station has officials who will answer questions and provide information about train transportation. Open M-Sa 6am-9pm, Su 7am-9pm.

Buses: To various towns on the outskirts of Passau with a number of stops within the city (DM4-7). For schedules call 56 02 72. The **City-Bus** runs from the station to the *Rathaus* (M-F 6:30am-10:10pm, Sa 7:30am-4:15pm; every 10-30min.; DM0.50).

Ferries: Donau Schiffahrt (tel. 92 92 92) steamers chug along the Danube to **Linz,** Austria, from May to Oct. daily at 9am (5hr.). To daytrip it, take the morning steamer to Linz and return to Passau by bus or train in the afternoon (round-trip bus DM44; train DM46). Or stay overnight in Linz and return with the steamer the next day at 2:15pm (returns to Passau at 8:40pm; round-trip DM40). The "Three Rivers" tour of the city runs daily from Mar. to early Nov. (40min., every 30min., 10am-4:30pm, DM10, under 15 DM5). For an elegant evening of live music and dancing, take an evening river cruise on the *"Tanzfahrten ab Passau"* steamer (4¾hr., Apr.-Oct. every Saturday at 7pm, DM26). All ships depart from the docks along the Fritz-Schäffer-Promenade by the *Rathaus.*

Bike Rental: At the *Hauptbahnhof,* prices depend on whether you came to Passau by train. The stunning **Donau Radweg** (bike path) begins in Donaueschingen and continues through Passau into Austria; ask at the tourist office for the "Raderlebnis Zwischen Donau, Inn & Salzach" brochure and for other cycling maps of the area.

Tourist Office: Tourist Information, Rathauspl. 3 (tel. 95 59 80; fax 351 07). On the banks of the Danube next to the *Rathaus* (see directions above). Healthy assortment of free brochures, schedules, and tour information as well as cycling maps and guides. Room-finding for a DM5 fee; also provides information on cheaper hotels and *Pensionen* in the surrounding area (DM35-60). *Aktuell,* a free monthly guide, chronicles everything going down in Passau. An **Automat** in front of the tourist office gives maps and a brochure for DM1. Open Apr.-Oct. M-F 8:30am-6pm, Sa-Su 10am-2pm; Nov.-Mar. M-Th 8:30am-5pm, F 8:30am-4pm. A smaller **branch,** directly across from the train station, at Bahnhofstr. 36 (tel. 955 80; fax 572 98), has free maps and brochures stocked outside in case you get into town after hours. Open mid-Oct. to Easter M-Th 9am-5pm, F 9am-4pm, Sa-Su 10am-2pm.

Tours: German-language walking tours of the city meet at the *Königsdenkmal* (monument) in front of the church at Domplatz. Apr.-Oct. M-F 10:30am and 2:30pm, Sa-Su 2:30pm. 1hr. DM4.50, children DM2.

Budget Travel: ITO Reisebüro, Bahnhofstr. 28 (tel. 540 48), across the street from the train station in the *Donau Passage,* a mall-type establishment. Open M-W and F 8am-6pm, Th 9am-8pm, Sa 9am-4pm.

Currency Exchange: At the **post office** next to the train station; cashes traveler's checks for a steep DM6 per check. Or try **Deutsche Bank,** Ludwigspl. 5, right across the street from the McDonald's. Open M and W 8:30am-noon and 1:30-3:30pm, Tu and Th 8:30am-noon and 1:30-6pm, F 8:30am-3pm.

Laundromat: Rent-Wash, Neuburgerstr. 19. From Ludwigsplatz, walk up Dr.-Hans-Kapfinger-Str. and bear left on Neuburgerstr. Wash DM6, soap DM1. Dry DM3. Fabric softener DM0.30. Open daily 7am-midnight.

Emergency: tel. 110. **Police:** Nibelungenstr. 17. **Fire** and **Ambulance,** tel. 112.

Hospital: Klinikum Passau, Bischof-Pilgrim-Str. 1 (tel. 530 00).

Pharmacy: 24hr. service rotates among the city's pharmacies; check the listings in the notices section of the daily newspapers, either the *Tagespresse* or the *Passauer Neue Presse,* or in the window of **Bahnhof Apotheke,** Bahnhofstr. 17, just to the right of the station. Open M-F 8am-6pm, Sa 9am-1pm.

Post Office: Bahnhofstr. 27, 94032 Passau (tel. 50 50), to the right of the train station as you exit. **Changes money** and cashes traveler's checks for DM6 per check. Open M-F 8am-6pm, Sa 8am-noon. Extra window open M-F 7am-6:30pm.

Telephone Code: 0851.

ACCOMMODATIONS AND CAMPING

Most pensions run DM35-60, while vacation houses (2-6 beds) run DM30-75. The only youth hostel in town is usually swarming with German schoolchildren (especially during June and July).

Jugendherberge (HI), Veste Oberhaus 125, 94034 Passau (tel. 413 51; fax 437 09), in the sentinel guard's living quarters above the main gate to the medieval castle perched high above the Danube. A 35-45min. walk from the train station and a 20-30min. uphill climb from the *Rathouse.* Cross the suspension bridge downstream from the *Rathaus,* then **ignore** the misplaced sign pointing up the steps straight ahead, instead continuing right along the curve, through the lefthand tunnel. (Skeptics who follow the signs will get there, too—they'll just pay an extra 20min. of steep hell for their disbelief.) On your left will be a steep (but more direct) cobblestone driveway leading up to the hostel. Or you can hop the shuttle (*Pendelbus*) from Rathausplatz bound for the museum adjacent to the hostel (runs Easter to mid.-Oct. every 30min. M-F 10:30am-5pm, Sa-Su 11:30am-6pm; DM3, round-trip DM4). Although it has a fantastic location, the youth hostel itself is slightly run-down and the 8-bed rooms feel very cramped. DM16.50. Breakfast included. Sheets DM5.50. Reception 7-11:30am and 4-11:30pm. New arrivals after 6pm only. Curfew 11:30pm. Reservations recommended.

Rotel Inn, 94012 Passau (tel. 951 60; fax 951 61 00). From the train station, walk straight ahead down the steps and through the tunnel to this outlandish hotel. Built in 1993 in the shape of a sleeping man to protest Europe's decade-long economic slumber, this self-proclaimed "Hotel of the Future" packs travelers into tight rooms bedecked with primary-color plastics. Inside, passionate graffiti depicts a monstrous Japanese auto industry trampling America and squashing Europe. Claustrophobes beware; each room has only three feet of walking space before your shins smash against the 4-by-8 foot wall-to-wall bed. Singles DM30; doubles DM50. Breakfast DM8. 24hr. reception.

Pension Rößner, Bräugasse 19 (tel. 93 13 50; fax 931 35 55). From the *Rathaus,* walk downstream along the Danube. Right on the Danube, these homey rooms are among the cheapest in the *Altstadt.* Call upstairs if no one's at reception. Singles DM60-85; doubles DM80-100. All rooms come with bath. Breakfast included.

Gasthof-Pension "Zur Brücke," Landrichterstr. 13 (tel. 434 75), on the Ilz river, 20min. from the *Veste Oberhaus.* From the *Rathaus* cross the *Luitpoldbrücke* bridge and continue right along the curve, through the left-hand tunnel. Follow Halser Str., which turns into Grafenleite, along the Ilz river for about 10min., then turn right on Landrichterstr. Quiet, sunny rooms are bargains for the idyllic location. Singles with bath DM32; doubles with bath DM30. Breakfast buffet included.

Camping: Zeltplatz Ilzstadt, Halserstr. 34, 94034 Passau (tel. 414 57). Downhill from the youth hostel, 10min. from the *Rathaus.* Cross the Luitpold bridge to the castle side, follow Angerstr. to the right, walk left through the tunnel onto F.-Wagner-Str., veer left up the hill, and take the right fork at the "Kahn/Camping" sign. Or bus #1-4 from Exerzierplatz. DM9. Under 18 DM7. Under 6 free. Showers included. Reception 8-10am and 3-10pm. No camping vehicles. Open May-Oct.

FOOD AND NIGHTLIFE

The student district centers on **Innstraße** near the university. From Ludwigsplatz, head down Nikolastr. and turn right on Innstr., which runs parallel to the Inn River. The street is lined with good, cheap places to eat and, more importantly, drink; the night-time action kicks off as early as 7pm. **Tengelmann,** on Ludwigstr. at Grabengasse (open M-F 8am-8pm, Sa 7:30am-4pm), and **Spar,** Residenzpl. 13 (open M 7:30am-6:30pm, Tu-F 7:30am-6pm, Sa 7:30am-1pm), provide **supermarket** eats.

> **Mensa,** Innstr. 29 (email mensa@uni-passau.de), offers cafeteria meals (DM2.40-4.50). From Ludwigsplatz, follow Nikolastr., turn right onto Innstr., head under the bridge, and at #29 take the stairs up and turn right. Then head for the farthest entrance on the left (15min.). Or take bus #3 to "Universität" (every 20min. from Exerzierplatz). *Currywurst* with fries DM2.40, salad buffet DM 1.25 per 100 grams. Any student ID will do. The *Mensa* (downstairs) is open M-Th 8am-4pm, F 8:15am-2:30pm. A snack-filled **cafeteria** upstairs (no ID required) is open similar hours.
>
> **Innsteg: Cafe Kneipe,** Innstr. 13 (tel. 355 03), one block from Nikolastr. and popular with students from morning 'til nite. Black-painted interior, and as inviting to Mozart devotees as to body-pierced revolutionaries. Nurse a beer (*Maß* DM7.80) on the balcony over the riverbank. Daily menu DM5-21. Salads DM5-17. Every Tuesday afternoon, specialty one-eighth liter wine DM1.50. Open daily 10am-1am.
>
> **Café Duft,** Theresienstr. 22. Folksy indoor and outdoor cafe with little lighted trees and an aquatic theme. Lip-smackin' good fruit-topped mueslix DM4.50; breakfast combos DM9-19. Soups DM5-6. Salads DM10-16. Entrees DM9-14. Open M-F 9am-1am, Sa-Su 10am-1am. Kitchen open until 11pm.
>
> **Ratskeller,** Rathauspl. 2 (tel. 26 30). A bustling restaurant in the back of the *Rathaus* with picturesque outdoor seating overlooking the Danube. Salads DM4. Daily "local cuisine" specials DM8-17. Open daily 10am-11pm.
>
> ⊛**Wirtshaus Bayersche Löwe,** Dr.-Hans-Kapfinger-Str. 3 (tel. 958 01 11). Authentic—or at least that's what the waves of tourists believe. For big German food and appetites, try either *Ofenkartoffel gefüllt mit Schinken, Röstwiebeln und Kräuterbutter* (baked potato filled with ham, roasted onions, and herb butter; DM9.80) or their daily lunch specialty (DM10.80). Wolf your meal down with a *Brez'n* (DM1.50), or soup or salad (DM6-10). Beer DM3.60-4. Open daily 9am-1am.
>
> **Camera,** on Frauengasse, around the corner from the McDonald's on Ludwigsplatz. The city center's grooviest dance lair's stark black exterior foreshadows an underground pit of student angst and inebriation. Beer DM4.50. Open daily 10pm-2am.

SIGHTS

Passau's beautiful Baroque architecture achieves its zenith in the sublime **Stephansdom.** *(Open M-Sa 8am-11am and 12:30-6pm. Free.)* Hundreds of cherubs, sprawled across the ceiling, purse their lips as the **world's largest church organ** stands erect above the choir. *(Organ concerts May-Oct. M-Sa noon. DM4, students and seniors DM2. Th at 7:30pm. DM10, students and seniors DM5. No concerts on holidays.)* Its 17,774 pipes can accommodate five organists at once. Behind the cathedral is the **Residenzplatz,** lined with former patrician dwellings, as well as the **Residenz,** erstwhile home of Passau's bishops. The **Domschatz** (cathedral treasury) within the *Residenz* houses an extravagant collection of gold and tapestries purchased by the bishops with the wealth they tithed from their flocks in the 12th through 16th centuries. *(Open May-Oct. M-Sa 10am-4pm. DM2, students and children DM1.)* Tours of the cathedral (in German) are given daily. *(May-Oct. M-F 12:30pm, meet in front of the side aisle; Jan.-Apr. and Nov.-Dec. M-F noon, meet underneath the main organ. DM2.)*

Nearby stands the Baroque church of **St. Michael,** built and gilded by the Jesuits. *(Open Feb. and Apr.-Oct. Tu-Su 9am-5pm; Nov.-Jan. and Mar. 10am-4pm. DM3, students DM1.50.)* The less opulent, 13th-century Gothic **Rathaus** was appropriated from a wealthy merchant in 1298 to house the city government. *(Open Easter-May 15 10am-4pm; May 16-Sept. 30 10am-5pm; Oct. M-F 10am-4pm. DM2, students DM1.)* The *Rathaus Trunksaal* (Great Hall) is a masterpiece showcasing rich, wooden paneling and dark marble. The renowned **Passauer Glasmuseum** (tel. 350 71), next to the *Rathaus* in the Wilder Mann hotel, houses 30,000 pieces of glasswork documenting the last 300 years of glass-making. *(Open daily 10am-4pm. DM5, students DM3, children under 10 free.)*

Over the *Luitpoldbrücke*, across the river and up the footpath, is the **Veste Oberhaus,** former palace of the bishopric. *(Open early Apr.-Oct. Tu-Su 11:30am-5pm.)* Once a place of refuge for the bishop and a prison for various enemies of the cloth, the stronghold now contains the magnificently placed and proud-looking **Cultural History Museum** (tel. 49 33 50), in which 54 rooms of art and artifacts span the last 2000 years. *(Open Mar.-Jan. Tu-F 9am-5pm, Sa-Su 10am-6pm. DM6, students DM3.)* The same bus that goes to the hostel also stops in front of the Veste Oberhaus *(every 30min. from the Rathausplatz; last bus leaves the Oberhaus at 5:15pm).* In the heart of the *Altstadt,* bright, arched skylights shelter the **Museum Moderner Kunst,** Bräugasse 17 (tel. 38 37 90). *(Open Tu-Su 10am-6pm. DM10, students and children DM6.)*

■ Landshut

Residents of Landshut are quick to point out that the House of Wittelsbach did not always call Munich or any of the *Königsschloßer* home. Landshut served as the main seat of government for Max and Ludwig's ancestors until 1255, and even after that it remained the capital of Lower Bayern. The city, just half an hour by train from Munich, straddles the swiftly moving Isar River. Red-roofed houses, flower gardens, and pedestrian walkways frame the wide river, which is a popular stomping ground for cyclists, dog walkers, and landscape artists. The city frolics with style during the **Landshuter Hochzeit,** a three-week medieval orgy with authentic (read: excessive) feasting, jousting, dancing, and period plays. First celebrated in 1475 and resurrected in 1903, the festival, re-enacting the magnificent *Hochzeit* (wedding) that Duke Ludwig arranged for his son Georg and his bride Hedwig, takes place every four years. Modern-day knights and ladies will put on their best boots and wedding dresses, respectively, from June 28 to July 20 in 2001; information and tickets are available from the tourist office.

ORIENTATION AND PRACTICAL INFORMATION Landshut is best reached by **train** from Munich (45min.-1hr., 2-3 per hr., DM19.40) or Regensburg (45min., 2 per hr., DM16.20). The information counter at the train station has a free timetable of all train connections out of Landshut. (Open M 5:20am-7:45pm, Tu-F 6am-7.45pm, Sa 6:45am-5:45pm, Su 8:05am-7:45pm.) From the station, it's a 25-minute walk into town. Walk straight on Luitpoldstr. for about 10 minutes; follow the curve left and cross the bridge. Go through the town gates to your left, then continue straight ahead on Theaterstr. to Altstadtstr. and turn left at the end, and the *Rathaus* will be ahead on the right. Or use **public transportation;** all buses that stop at the station run to the center of town (one-way DM2; day card DM2.70). The **RBO bus information** counter, where you can reserve and purchase tickets, is located at the train station (open M-Th 7:30am-noon and 2:30-4:20pm, F 7:30am-noon). The **tourist office** *(Verkehrsrein),* Altstadtstr. 315 (tel. 92 20 50; fax 892 75), in the *Rathaus,* has primitive city maps for free and better ones for DM2. There's no room-finding service, but they will provide a list of available rooms; prices plummet beyond the magical "20-minute radius" from the city center. Pick up the *"Monatsprogramm,"* a pamphlet listing all concerts, art shows, dances, and films showing in any given month. For the latest on the dance/disco scene in the Straubing/Landshut/Regensburg area, pick up a copy of *bagpipes.* The office also has a free encyclopedia of Landshut's women's groups and help centers for those planning a longer stay in the city. (Open M-F 9am-noon and 1:30-5pm, Sa 9am-noon.) **St. Michael's Apotheke,** Luitpoldstr. 58, lists on-call **pharmacies** (Open M-Tu 8:30am-6:30pm, Th 8:30am-7pm, W and F 8:30am-6pm, Sa 8:30am-12:30pm). The **post office,** 84028 Landshut, is just to the left of the station as you exit (open M-F 7:30am-6pm, Sa 8am-noon). The **telephone code** is 0871.

ACCOMMODATIONS The **Jugendherberge (HI)** is at Richard-Schirrmann-Weg 6 (tel. 234 49; fax 27 49 47). From the tourist office, walk to the left up Altstadtstr. and turn left onto Altebergstr. at the "Burg Trausnitz" sign. Pass the stairs leading to the *Burg*, and a few steps farther on your right follow Richard-Schirrmann-Weg to the end. The elegant modern villa sits on quiet, green grounds overlooking town. Spend the night in comfortable but simple 4-bed dorm rooms with private showers. (DM17.50. Breakfast DM6. Sheets DM5.50. Reception M-F 9am-noon and 5-8pm, Sa-Su 5-8pm. Closed Dec. 23-Jan. 7.) One of the more affordable places in town is the **Pfälzer Weinstube Heigl,** Herrngasse 385 (tel. 891 32; fax 67 01 56), in the city center. Walk right from the *Rathaus* and take the fourth right onto Herrngasse. The rooms are drab, but after an exceedingly cheery day in the colorful *Altstadt,* you'll be thankful. (Singles DM59, with bath DM69; doubles DM94, with bath DM104.) Halfway between the *Haupt-bahnhof* and the *Altstadt,* **Hotel Park Café,** Papierstr. 36 (tel. 693 39; fax 63 03 07), offers the bare necessities of a room. From the station, walk straight on Luitpoldstr., take a left on Stethaimerstr., and a right onto Papierstr. (15min.; singles DM55-95, doubles DM95-160; breakfast included). **Campingplatz Landshut/Mitterwöhr,** Breslauer Str. 122 (tel. 533 66), is located just outside of town along the banks of the Isar River. Minigolf, table tennis, and laundry machines are available. (DM9 per site, DM5 per tent, DM6 per person, children under 13 DM4. Showers DM1. Open Apr.-Sept.)

FOOD Café Cappuccino, Altstadtstr. 337 (tel. 270 92), back through the passageway, has tasty daily specials (DM7.90), salads (DM7-14), pasta (DM12-13), and, of course, cappuccino (DM4; open M-Th 9am-midnight, F-Sa 9am-1am, Su 2-11pm). The more expensive **Wittman,** off Altebergstr. to the right of the footpath to *Burg Trausnitz,* offers noodle soup (DM4) as well as three-course German meals (DM13.80) and beer (DM4.40). A fruit and vegetable **market** appears Monday through Thursday and Saturday (7am-noon) in the *Altstadt,* and Friday on Am alten Viehmarkt (6am-1pm). **HL Markt,** Dreisaltigkeitspl. 177, provides **groceries** (open M-F 8am-8pm, Sa 7am-4pm).

SIGHTS The Landshut *Altstadt* features rows of colorful gabled Gothic and Baroque houses filled with glitzy shops and restaurants. The proud, light greenish-beige **Rathaus** (tel. 88 12 16) stands at the center bearing Renaissance and neo-Gothic architectural facades. Fantastic murals inside the *Prunksaal* (main hall) upstairs capture the original wedding. *(Open M-F 2-3pm. Free.)* Across from the *Rathaus* stands the **Stadtresidenz,** the first Renaissance-style palace to be built in Germany (1533-37). Its gleaming white classical facade conceals a spacious courtyard with arcades of distinct Italian influence. The **Stadtresidenz Museum** (tel. 226 38) upstairs grants peeks at gloriously decadent palace rooms from the 16th to the 18th century and also houses a regional collection of art with works from the 16th and 17th centuries. *(45min. tours Apr.-Sept. daily 9-11am and 1-5pm, last tour 4:30pm; Oct.-Mar. daily 9-11am and 1-4pm, last tour 3:30pm. DM3, students DM2, children under 15 free.)* Geometrically intriguing bricks zig-zag the 130m spire of **St. Martin's Kirche,** the world's highest church tower of its kind. Inside you can see the tasteful features, including the wide-open halls with slender columns, 16th-century choir stalls, and the late-Gothic **Madonna and Child** elaborately carved by Hans Leinberger in 1518. *(Open Apr.-Sept. daily 7:30am-6:30pm; Oct.-Mar. 7:30am-5pm.)* Farther up the main street, a sign points to **Burg Trausnitz** (tel. 226 38). To the left and up the crooked brick stairway (5-10min.) sits a hefty brick and red-tiled fortress built in 1204. The hard, seemingly impenetrable exterior conceals a soft yellow courtyard with tiers of delicate arches. The castle was the luxurious abode of the Wittelsbacher Princes of Bavaria-Landshut until 1503. The amusing "Narrentreppe" (Fool's staircase) inside displays frescoed scenes from the famous Italian folk plays, the **Commedia dell'Arte.** The castle interior can only be seen with a German-language tour, but you can borrow an English translation of the guide's words.

(Same times and tours as Stadtresidenz Museum. DM4, students and seniors DM3.) A free shuttle runs from the *Burg* to the *Altstadt. (Sa-Su 1:20-6:50pm, every 30min.)* The new **Skulpturenmuseum im Hofberg** (tel. 890 21) exhibits the modern sculptures and charcoal sketches of Fritz Koenig (1942-1997). *(Open Tu-Su 10am-1pm and 2-5pm; DM6, students and children DM4.)*

■ Straubing

Perched on the fringe of the Bayerischer Wald near the Danube, Straubing lets down its hair for the annual 10-day **Gäubodenvolksfest** (Aug. 7-17 in 1999). The festival, which started as an agricultural fair in 1812 under King Max, has since evolved into a massive beer-guzzling phenomenon second in size only to *Oktoberfest.* Seven enormous beer tents welcome over a million revelers, who, after imbibing a few liters of the local brews, spend their week's earnings on a bevy of amusement park rides. Adjoining the *Volksfest* is the **Ostbayernschau** (East Bavarian Show), a regional trade and industry exhibition (read: more beer; Aug. 8-16 in 1999). Both are held in "Am Hagen," the *Fest* area 10 minutes north of the *Markt*. During the rest of the year, Straubing serves as a convenient entrance to the Bayerischer Wald. For more information and tips about hiking in the scenic Bayerischer Wald, call the **Straubing Bayerischen Waldverein** (tel. 412 39).

ORIENTATION AND PRACTICAL INFORMATION Straubing is easily reached by train from Regensburg (30min., 1-2 per hr., DM12) or Passau (40min., 7 per day, DM19.40). The information counter (tel. 194 19) is at the **train station** (open M 5:30am-6:15pm, Tu-F- 6am-6:15pm, Sa 7:30am-2:30pm, Su 9:45am-6:30pm). **Lockers** (DM2-4) are located just outside the train station lobby. **Rent bikes at Bund Naturschutz,** Ludwigspl. 14, first floor (tel. 25 12), for DM8 with a DM50 deposit (open M-F 9am-noon and 1-5pm). The Altstadt lies northwest of the train station, five minutes away on foot. Cross the street in front of the station, and follow it straight past the post office as it curves right and turns into Bahnhofstr. Cross the foot bridge and continue down Steinergasse to the pastel green turreted tower. On your left after you pass through the clock tower arch is the **tourist office,** Theresienpl. 20 (tel. 94 43 07; fax 94 41 03), which has free maps and extensive brochures on Straubing and neighboring towns. It finds rooms (DM25-30 per person) for a DM3 fee (open M-W, F 9am-5pm, Th 9am-6pm; May-Sept. also Sa 9am-noon). A public restroom is in the small tunnel just to the left of the tourist office. The tourist office staff give German tours of the Altstadt. (1½hr. May 9-Oct. 3 W and Sa 2pm. DM5, students and seniors DM3, under 6 free. Tours leave from the tourist office. English tours by appointment DM60.) For the **weather,** call 011 64. The city's **pharmacies** rotate 24-hour service; check the listing in the window of **Agnes Bernauer Apotheke,** Bahnhofstr. 16 (tel. 806 75; open M-F 8am-6pm, Sa 8am-noon). The **post office,** Bahnhofspl. 1, 94315 Straubing (tel. 86 10), is across the road and to the left of the train station (open M-F 8am-noon and 1-5:30pm, Sa 8:30am-noon). The **telephone code** is 09421.

ACCOMMODATIONS The **Jugendherberge (HI),** Friedhofstr. 12 (tel. 804 36; fax 120 94), is 15 minutes from the train station. Turn right from the front entrance of the station and follow the curve of the main road left. Turn immediately right onto Schildhauerstr. as it curves into Äußere-Passauer-Str., by the "Passau" sign. A crosswalk and a *Jugendherberge* sign pointing left up Friedhofstr. follows; the hostel is on your right. This old building has a distinct character, with creaking hardwood floors, comfortable leather sofas in the hallways, and a bumbling, affectionate house dog. Informality and cleanliness reign supreme. Doubles are available if you're lucky, but most rooms are 4-, 6-, or 8-beds. (DM16.50, over 27 DM21.50. Breakfast included. Sheets DM5.50. Reception 7-9am and 5-10pm. New arrivals after 5pm only. Lockout 9am-5pm. 10pm curfew, but keys available with DM10 deposit. Showers between 6-8am and 5-10pm. Open Apr.-Oct.) A **Campingplatz** is located on Wundermühlweg 9 (tel. 897 94; DM15-DM40; open May-Oct. 15).

The cheapest and most convenient beds can be found at **Pension Fürst**, Theresienpl. 32 (tel. 107 92). Follow the directions to the *Altstadt*, turning left at the tourist office; it's on the left just past the gold figure. It may not be the most aesthetically pleasing locale, but it's central and cheap. (Singles DM30; doubles DM60; no breakfast.) The sweet staff at the **Weißes Rößl**, Landshuterstr. 65 (tel. 325 81), runs a pacific ship (singles DM35; doubles DM65; breakfast included).

FOOD The restaurant in the **Hotel Bischershof**, Frauenhofer 16, just past the main pedestrian area, serves salads (DM3-9), grill specialties (DM13-21), and super cheap beer (*Maß* DM5.80.) There's a *Biergarten* out back. (Open M-Sa 11am-2:30pm and 5:30pm-1am, Su 11am-1am). **Metzgerei Königsbauer**, Ludwigspl. 6 (tel. 815 94), near the *Stadtturm*, serves a hefty lunch crowd at its *Stehcafé* (standing cafe); every entree is also available for take-out, including *Wienerschnitzel, Wurst, Knödel,* and every other German meat specialty (DM2-10; open M-F 7:30am-6pm, Sa 7:30am-4pm). Fresh fruits and vegetables are sold at the **market** on Ludwigsplatz (open M-Th and Sa 7am-noon, F 7am-5pm). A **farmer's market** is held on Saturdays at Theresienplatz. **Norma**, Bahnhofstr. 14, on the left as you walk into town, has cheap groceries (open M-F 8:30am-6pm, Sa 8am-1pm).

SIGHTS The five-turreted gothic **watchtower** in the middle of the market square is the city symbol. *(1hr. tours in German Mar. 28-Oct. 25 Th 2pm, Sa-Su 10:30am. Th and Sa tours leave from the tourist office; Su tours leave from the entrance to the watchtower. DM5, students DM3, under 6 free.)* Erected in the 14th century, the teal-green structure with an inset gold figure of Mary splits the Marktplatz. To the right, Ludwigsplatz hosts the daily fruit and vegetable market (see above). The **St. Peter's** complex houses a medieval graveyard with wrought-iron crosses and gravestones from as far back as the 13th century, a Romanesque basilica from roughly 1180, and three Gothic chapels, including one with a red marble epitaph devoted to the memory of Agnes Bernauer (see below). Tours of St. Peter's depart from the tourist office. *(1½hr. Su 2pm, except June 14, July 12, Aug. 23, Oct. 18. DM5, students DM3, under 6 free.)* Tall, slender white columns and graceful sculptures of saints clothed in gold give the **Basilika St. Jakob**, Pfarrplatz 1a, a divine elegance. Double-story stained glass windows illustrating the Annunciation and the lives of the disciples shed a dusky colorful light on the pews below. Throw in a sustained choral note and voila!—enlightenment! The **Gäubodenmuseum**, Fraunhoferstr. 9 (tel. 818 11), off the main square, houses exhibits from the Early Bronze Age and from the "Roman Find" of 1950, as well as a collection of regional art and folklore. *(Open Tu-Su 10am-4pm. DM4, under 19 DM3.)* At the end of the street, turn right down Zollergasse and around to the late-Gothic **Karmelitenkirche**, Albrechtsgasse 21, with a stunning Baroque interior. Angels and disciples peer down from the lavish gold altar and stolid white columns.

One block down on Burggasse, the **Ursulinenkirche** suffers behind an off-putting white stucco facade. Built from 1736 to 1741 by the renowned Asam brothers as their last joint endeavor, the interior exhibits all the opulent, overbearing kitsch of Rococo. Peach marble columns snake up to the ceiling, lavishly covered in flashy gold and fanatic frescoes. Back down across Fürstenstr. on the banks of the Danube, parts of the **Herzogsschloß** date from 1356. Most of the palace interior is closed to the public, its innards clogged with the cholesterol blockage of bureaucracy. A few renovated floors house a new **state museum** (tel. 211 14) with a rather bland exhibition of images of worship from the 17th to the 20th century. *(Open W, F-Su 10am-4pm, Th 10am-6pm. DM4, under 1.9 DM3.)*

ENTERTAINMENT AND NIGHTLIFE For complete concert, live music, and club information, pick up the free magazine *in'said* at the tourist office and local bars. Nocturnal activity oscillates between bad and disco. **Max**, Hebbelstr. 14 (tel. 34 31), hidden in the shopping complex Gläuboden Park, is the place to trot to techno, trance, rap, and funk (cover DM10; beer DM4.50; open W, F-Sa 10pm-3am). From the train station, head left toward the post office, but follow the road to the left as it curves underneath the train overpass. The Gläuboden Park mall is ahead on the left.

Straubing recently opened an enormous outdoor swimming pool complex, **AQUA-therm,** Wittelbacherhöhe 50-52 (tel. 86 41 78 or 86 41 79), with an 80m waterslide, massage parlors, an indoor pool, a steam sauna, and a warm salt-water pool. Follow the tunnel to the left of the *Bahnhof* down Landshuterstr. and turn right onto Dr.-Otto-Höchtl-Str., which becomes Wittelsbacherhöhestr.; it's on the right. Or take bus #2 from Ludwigsplatz to "Aquatherm." (Open June-Aug.10 daily 8am-9pm; Aug.11-Sep. 14 8am-8pm. Closes 1hr. earlier Sa-Su. DM5, after 5:30pm DM3; students, seniors, and under 16 DM2, under 6 free.) **Bowl** yourself over at **Keglerhalle am Sportzentrum Peterswöhrd** (tel. 802 48), 20 minutes from the center of town (open daily 10am-midnight). Straubing hosts the only **zoo** in eastern Bavaria (tel. 212 77), with more than 1400 animals and a large aquarium. (Open Mar.-Sept. 8:30am-7pm; Oct.-Feb. 9am-dark. DM8, students and children 6-18 DM5, children under 6 DM3.)

Every four years in July, Straubing commemorates the 1435 death of Agnes Bernauer, the daughter of an Augsburg barber and wife of Duke Albrecht III of Straubing. Albrecht's father, Duke Ernst of Bavaria, was furious when he learned of his son's secret marriage to Agnes, a proletarian nasty. The senior duke condemned Agnes as a witch and sentenced her to drown in the Danube while his son was away. The people of Straubing passionately re-enact the tragic love story (minus the drowning) during the **Agnes Bernauer Festspiele** (next performance July 1999). Contact the Straubing tourist office for exact dates and details.

■ Regensburg

Located at the northernmost point of the Danube's passage to the Black Sea, Regensburg's *Altstadt* spills onto the islands dodged by the sinuous river as it converges with the Regen. A city of patrician homes and Imperial administrative houses, Regensburg lies close to two extraordinary sights: **Walhalla,** a tribute from King Ludwig I to German heroes, and the **Donaudurchbruch,** a deep gorge between high, grassy banks carved by the Danube. The city, which was originally a fortress built by Marcus Aurelius in AD 179, became the first capital of Bayern, then the seat of the Perpetual Imperial Diet (the parliament of the Holy Roman Empire, not an eating regimen for chubby monarchs; see **Worms,** p. 408), and finally the site of the first German parliament. But when the government opened a Bavarian university here in 1967, the steady flow of students through town saturated the *Altstadt* with cafes, bars, and shops, fostering a hipness that mixes well with Regensburg's Old World aura.

ORIENTATION AND PRACTICAL INFORMATION

Regensburg has easy train and bus connections to both Nürnberg and Passau. The historic *Altstadt* sprawls over a square-shaped cobblestone mecca; the Danube is to the north, the *Hauptbahnhof* and Bahnhofstr. to the south, Kumpfmühlerstr. to the west, and Maximilianstr. to the east. Maximilianstr. leads straight from the train station into the heart of the city.

Transportation
Trains: (info tel. 194 19). To Munich (1½hr., every hr.), Nürnberg (1-1½hr., every 30min.-1hr.), and Passau (1-1½hr., every 1-2hr.). Ticket office open M 5:30am-7:30pm, Tu-F 6am-7:30pm, Sa 6am-6:30pm, Su 7:30am-8:45pm.
Ferries: There's a boat to **Walhalla** Apr.-Oct. daily at 10:30am and 2pm with another departure May-Sept. Tu-Su at noon (45min.; one-way DM11, children DM5, families DM26; round-trip DM16, children DM7, families DM38). Call **Regensburger Personen Schiffahrt,** Werftstr. 8 (tel. 553 59 or 55359) for more info.
Public Transportation: Routes and schedules of Regensburg's new bus system are available at the *Presse & Buch* store in the train station (DM1). The transport hub is "Albertstr.," 1 short block from the station at the right. Single rides cost DM2.70. No night buses. Buy a **Tages Ticket** from the automatic machines at each major bus stop, which covers all-day transportation for 1 person, plus all-day transportation for 1 additional person after 9am (M-F DM6, Sa-Su DM4). On weekends, groups can buy 1 Tages Ticket for 4 people (DM4). A Tages Ticket purchased from a driver

costs DM1 more than one purchased from an *Automat*. People in the area Monday through Friday make out best by getting a **12-Streifenkarte** from the kiosk in the station *before* heading for the bus (DM10.50; punch 2 stripes each way per person plus one stripe per person for each extra zone outside the extra zone).
Taxi: tel. 194 10 or 570 00.
Bike Rental: Fahrradverleih PARK and BIKE, am Donaumarktpl. (tel. (0177) 831 12 34), right on the Danube by the *Altstadt*. Rental 10am-1pm, bike return 7-8pm. DM15-17 per day, children DM10 per day.

Tourist and Local Services

Tourist Office: Altes Rathaus, on Rathauspl. (tel. 507 44 10; fax 507 44 19). From the train station, walk down Maximilianstr. to Grasgasse and take a left. Follow it as it turns into Obermünsterstr., then turn right at the end to Obere Bachgasse; follow it 5 blocks down Untere Bachgasse to Rathausplatz. The office, to your left across the square, provides free maps, finds rooms (DM1.50 if inundated with tourists), and sells tickets to local events. 24hr. **private room** information number (tel. 194 14). Open Apr.-Oct. M-F 8:30am-6pm, Sa 9am-4pm, Su 9:30am-4pm; Nov.-Mar. M-F 8:30am-6pm, Sa 9am-4pm, Su 9:30am-2:30pm. Get info on the Bayerischer Wald at the **Tourismusverband Ostbayern,** Luitpoldstr. 20 (tel. 58 53 90; fax 585 39 39).
Lost and Found: At the Altes Rathaus (tel. 507 21 05).
Bookstore: Booox, Goldene Bärenstr. 12, entrance on Brückstr. near the Steinerne Brücke (tel. 56 70 14). Tons of discounted art booox, as well as disheveled comic books and English quick-reads (DM6). Ooopen M-F 9am-8pm, Sa 9am-4pm.
Women's Center: Frauen Gesundheits Zentrum, in the back building at Badstr. 6 (tel. 816 44). Information on women's rights and health. Open Tu 10am-1pm and 2-5pm, W 10am-1pm, Th 2-5pm.

Emergency and Communications

Emergency: tel. 110. **Police:** Minoritenweg (tel. 192 22). **Fire** and **Ambulance,** tel. 112.
Crisis Hotline: In case of rape or other trauma, contact **Caritas** (tel. 78 20).
Pharmacy: 24hr. service rotates among the city's pharmacies. To find out which pharmacy is on duty, visit **Maximilian Apotheke,** Maximilianstr. 29, 2 blocks from the train station. Open M-F 8:30am-6:30pm, Sa 8:30am-1pm.
Hospital: Evangelisches Krankenhaus, Obere Bachgasse (tel. 504 00), near the Thurn and Taxis *Schloß*, is the most centrally located.
Post Office: on Bahnhofstr., 93047 Regensburg, next door to the train station. They **exchange money** (DM2 fee for cash, DM6 per traveler's check). Open M-F 8am-6pm, Sa 8am-12:30pm.
Telephone Code: 0941.

ACCOMMODATIONS AND CAMPING

Most of Regensburg's cheap lodgings are centrally located, but they fill up in the summer. Reserve, reserve, reserve. If the hotels and *Pensionen* are full, the tourist office might find you a room in a private home. Otherwise, try the hotels in outlying parts of town—all are linked to the center by reliable bus service.

Jugendherberge (HI), Wöhrdstr. 60 (tel. 574 02; fax 524 11), on an island in the Danube. From the station, walk straight ahead up Maximilianstr. all the way to the end. Then turn right at the *Apotheke* onto Pfluggasse and immediately left at the Optik sign into the tiny Erhardigasse. At the end, take the steps down and walk left over the Eiserne Brücke (iron bridge), which becomes Wöhrdstr. on the other side. The hostel is 5min. away on the right (25min. total). Or bus #3, 8, or 9 from Albertstr. by the station to "Eisstadion." The hostel is a step ahead on the right. Recently renovated, it's pleasant but institutional. DM27. Big breakfast included. Dinner DM9. Sheets DM5.50. Key deposit DM5.50. Reception 6am-11:30pm. Check-in after 12:30pm. Curfew 1am. Reservations encouraged. Partial wheelchair access. Closed mid-Nov. to mid-Jan.
Spitalgarten, St.-Katharinen-Pl. 1 (tel. 847 74), inside the walls of the old hospital built by Bishop Konrad IV in the 13th century. Cross the Danube at the Steinerne

Regensburg

ACCOMMODATIONS

B Gaststätte Schildbräu
E Hotel Am Peterstor
F Hotel Apollo
C Spitalgarten
D Youth Hostel
A Campground

BAYERN

Bridge and go inside the gate to St. Katherine's on the left. Pass through another gate and go past the left side of the church. Or bus #12 from the station to "Stadtamhof." Head into the lively *Biergarten* and inquire about the *Pension* with the people behind the counter. Singles DM40; doubles DM80. Breakfast included. Showers in the hall. Reception until midnight. Call or write well ahead.

Gaststätte Schildbräu, Stadtamhof 24 (tel. 857 24), is over the Steinerne Brücke; follow the street for about 5min. and it's on the right. Or bus #12 from the station to "Stadtamhof." Clean and orderly rooms, each with bath and geraniums spilling from every window. Singles DM65; doubles DM110. Breakfast included. Reception 7:30am-midnight. Call ahead.

⊛**Hotel Apollo,** Neuprüll 17 (tel. 910 50; fax 91 05 70). From Albertstr. by the station, bus #6 (direction: "Klinikum") to "Neuprüll" (15min.; DM2.70) or walk 45min. Proximity to the university and lots of dee-luscious furnishings make it worth the trip. Rooms have cable TVs, radios, and telephones, and the hotel hooks you up with access to a pool, sauna, steam bath, and solarium. Singles DM55, with shower DM70, with bath DM78; doubles DM99, with shower DM110, with bath DM140. Non-smoking rooms available. Breakfast included. Reception 6:30am-11pm.

Hotel Am Peterstor, Fröhliche-Türken-Str. 12 (tel. 545 45; fax 545 42), 5min. from the train station. Walk straight ahead on Maximilianstr. and take the second left onto St.-Petersweg, which becomes Fröhliche-Türken-Str. around the corner. Rooms are neat and simple, with bath and TV. Singles DM65; doubles DM75. Breakfast DM10.

Camping: Azur-Camping, Am Weinweg 40 (tel. 27 00 25). From Albertstr. (1 block in front of the station), bus #11 (direction: "West Bad") to "Westheim." DM10 per adult, DM7 per child under 12; DM7 per tent; DM6 per car. Prices lower in the off-season (mid-Jan. to Mar. and Sept. to mid-Dec.). Reception 8am-1pm and 3-11pm.

FOOD

The 17th-century English dramatist and diplomat Sir George Etherege commented that Regensburg's "noble, serene air makes us hungry as hawks"—a laudable attempt to blame his swelling belly on the atmosphere rather than the heavy Bavarian fare and beer typical of the city. A tantalizing number of cafes, bars, and beer gardens await to tempt the Imperial Diet. A plethora of supermarkets in the city, however, will mend the proverbial holes in your pockets: **Tengelmann,** Untere Brückgasse 2, on the way to the tourist office from the train station, is a good starting point for the makings of a lazy picnic (open M-F 8am-8pm, Sa 7:30am-4pm). To stock up on fruit, vegetables, and other basics, head to the **market** on Domplatz (open Mar.-Oct. M-Sa 7am-6pm, Su 10:30am-6pm). Otherwise, join the rest of Regensburg at a beer garden for a meal of *Würstchen*, pretzels, and, of course, beer *vom Faß* (on tap).

University Mensa, on Albertus-Magnus-Str., in the park, on the university campus. Turn right from the train station and take the bridge over the tracks onto Galgenbergstr. Follow this street for about 20min. and take a right onto Albertus-Magnus-Str. As you emerge from underneath the parking structure, the stairs on the left will lead you up to the *Mensa*. Or bus #6 or #11 from the Altes Rathaus or Albertstr. (directions: "Klinikum" or "Burgweinting") to "Universität Mensa" (DM2.70). The cheapest meal in Regensburg, with a lively student crowd. Student ID will get you a Mensa card. Meals DM2.40-6. Open May-July and Nov.-Feb. M-Th 11:15am-1:45pm and 5-7pm, F 11:15am-1:45pm and 5-6:30pm, Sa 11:15am-1pm; Mar.-Apr. and Aug.-Oct. M-Th 11:15am-1:30pm and 5-6:30pm, F 11:15am-1:30pm and 5-6pm.

⊛**Hinterhaus,** Rote-Hahnen-Gasse 2 (tel. 546 61), off Haidplatz, down from Rathausplatz. A politically grooving grove of left-leaning tables. Excellent vegetarian dishes and salads (DM5-14). Exquisite *Kuchen* (DM4-7). Outdoor seating with occasional live jazz concerts. Open M-F 11am-1am, Sa-Su 6pm-1am.

Bistro Rosarium, Hoppestr. 3a (tel. 268 85). At the edge of the superbly landscaped Dörnbergpark. A Bavarian wood-framed restaurant with rose garden, umbrella-covered tables around a fountain, students, beer, and green trees. Pasta dishes (DM11-12), *Schnitzel* (DM13), fresh salads (DM7-13), and beer (DM4.60). Breakfasts start at DM7. Open daily 11am-1am.

Little Saigon, Dompl. 5, serves quick Pan-Asian cuisine with a Bavarian flair. Wide variety of vegetarian options. Rice noodles with vegetarian egg rolls, salad, ground nuts, and soy sauce (DM13.50). Fried noodles with mixed vegetables (DM10.90). English menu available. Open M-Sa 10am-midnight.

Beer Gardens

Goldene Ente, Badstr. 32 (tel. 854 55). Under magnificent chestnut trees on the banks of the Danube just across the Eiserner Steg footbridge upstream from the Steinerne Brücke. The oldest inn in Regensburg; during the summer the beer garden is packed with pleasantly pilsnered students. More complex menu inside. Steaks, *Würstchen,* and *Schnitzel* grilled for student-friendly prices (DM9-14). Salads DM5-11.50. Beer starts at DM3.90 for 0.5L. Open M-Sa 11am-2pm and 5pm-1am, Su 10am-1am. On a nice day, the beer garden is open all afternoon.

Kneitinger Keller, Galgenbergstr. 18 (tel. 766 80), to the right from the station and over the tracks (10min.). Regensburg's largest and most democratic beer garden (1200 seats). Devoted locals, large thirsty tourists, and intelligentsia-in-training alike follow their noses: the smell of beer has pervaded the entire area since the brewery was established in 1530. *Maß* DM7.80, six *Würstchen* with bread DM8.70, big pretzels DM3.30. Open daily 9am-midnight.

Wurstküche, Thundorferstr. (tel. 590 98), next to the Steinerne bridge with views of the river. A fun place to relax, gurgle a beer, and watch the 3000-ton ships drift by. The oldest operating fast food joint in Europe—the 12th-century workers who built the bridge broke for lunch here. Very busy and touristy, even though it looks like a wood shack with tables. Six small, delicious *Würste* from the smoky kitchen come with sauerkraut and bread (DM8.90). *Gulaschsoup* with bread (DM5.60). Open M 1-6pm, T-Sa 9am-6pm, Su 10am-6pm.

SIGHTS

Masonry walls, churches, and patrician homes in styles from Romanesque to Classical bear witness to Regensburg's 2000-year history. The **Porta Praetoria** (a Roman gateway) and ruins from its accompanying wall sketch a hazy outline of the city's original fortifications. They have been incorporated into a house located on Unter-den-Schwibbögen between the *Dom* and the Danube. One of the earliest documents of Regensburg's past is found on the front wall of the house—a flat foundation stone from the Roman fort of Castra Regina, inscribed in AD 179, when Marcus Aurelius was emperor. One block from the river on Niedermünstergasse lies the Domplatz, providing a stable foundation for the soaring high-Gothic **St. Peter's Cathedral** and the **Diocese Museum,** adjacent to the church (tel. 516 88). *(Cathedral open Apr.-Oct. daily 6:30am-6pm; Nov.-Mar. 6:30am-4pm. 1¾hr. tours given May-Oct. M-Sa 10, 11am, and 2pm, Su noon and 2pm; Nov.-Apr. M-Sa 11am, Su noon. DM4, students and children DM2. Museum open Apr.-Nov. Tu-Su 10am-5pm. DM3, students DM1.50, families DM7.)* Begun in 1276, the cathedral was finished in 1486, not counting the delicately carved 159m twin spires, which King Ludwig II added in typical grandiose style between 1859 and 1869. Once your eyes adjust to the dim lighting, the collection of richly colored stained glass windows will dazzle. Wheelchair access to the *Dom* is on the cathedral's northern side, via the "Eselturm." Inside the cathedral is the **Domschatz** (treasury; tel. 576 45), a priceless collection of gold and jewels purchased by the Regensburg bishops back in the days of indulgences and economic exploitation by the clergy. *(Domschatz open Apr.-Nov. Tu-Sa 10am-5pm, Su noon-5pm; Dec.-Mar. F-Sa 10am-4pm, Su noon-4pm. DM3, students DM1.50, families DM7. Ticket for Domschatz and Dom tour DM5.)*

Reclining in the western portion of the park across from the *Hauptbahnhof,* the **Fürstliches Thurn und Taxissches Schloß** (tel. 504 81 33), originally a Benedictine cloister, was the residence of the Duke of Thurn und Taxis after 1812. *(Tours Apr.-Oct. daily at 11am, 2, 3, and 4pm, Sa-Su an additional tour at 10am; Nov.-Mar. Sa-Su at 10 and 11am, 2 and 3pm. Joint admission to Schloß and Kreuzgang DM12, students DM10.)* Little remains of the Gothic cloister beneath later Baroque additions. The Thurn und Taxis family built a franchise, granted by Kaiser Maximilian in 1490, into a feudal postal empire that had a tight grip over much of Central Europe until the Prussian Post, backed by Bismarck's armies, cancelled it in 1867. This conflict was the proximate cause for a legacy of disgruntled postal workers the world over—it sure upset Oedippa Maas.

A few blocks away from the cathedral, the Gothic **Altes Rathaus** served as capital of the Holy Roman Empire until 1803. Four long iron rods are fastened onto the side of the Altes Rathaus. These were the official measurement standards (similar to our meterstick or yardstick today) by which the merchants traded in the Middle Ages. The impotent Imperial Parliament (the first of many similar bodies in German history) lives on in the **Reichstag Museum,** housed in the *Altes Rathaus.* The differing heights of the chairs reflect the political hierarchy of the legislators. *(Tours in German Apr.-Oct. daily every 30min. M-Sa 9:30am-noon and 2-4pm, Su 10am-noon and 2-4pm; Nov.-Mar. 1 per hr. English tours May-Sept. M-Sa at 3:15pm. DM5, students, seniors, and disabled persons DM2.50, families DM10.)*

The iconoclastic astronomer and physicist Johannes Kepler died of meningitis in 1630 at the site of the **Kepler Memorial House,** Keplerstr. 5 (tel. 507 34 42). *(Open Tu-Sa 10am-noon and 2-4pm, tours at 10 and 11am, 2 and 3pm. DM4, students and seniors DM2, families DM8, tour included.)* Period furniture, portraits, and facsimiles of Kepler's work are on display. Up the street at Keplerstr. 2 is **Keplers Wohnhaus,** a colorful house where he hung his hat and spent time with his family. **All-day museum cards** admit bearers to the Reichstag Museum, Kepler Memorial House, Regensburg Stadt Museum, and the town's modern art gallery; purchase them at the tourist office. *(DM10, students and seniors DM5, families DM20.)*

Down the river from Regensburg is **Walhalla** (tel. 96 16 80; fax 96 16 82), an imitation Greek temple poised dramatically on the steep northern bank of the Danube. *(Open Apr.-Sept. daily 9am-5:45pm; Oct. 9am-4:45pm; Nov.-Mar. 10-11:45am and 1-4:45pm. DM3.)* Ludwig I of Bavaria built the monument between 1830 and 1842 to honor Germans past and present whom he admired. Modeled after the Parthenon in Athens and named after the legendary resting place of Norse heroes, Walhalla stares imposingly down on the river as the boat from Regensburg approaches the dock (see **Practical Information,** p. 527, for ferry information). Ludwig called Walhalla "the child of my love." Hmm. The climb up the steep steps to the monument itself is tough going, but the view of the river and the opposite bank is a golden photo op. In the summer, these hallowed steps provide a lively evening hangout for students who venture here by bikes and car; probably not what poor Ludwig envisioned. Inside the monument are a series of busts of German leaders and military heroes, most of whom history left in oblivion. Take RVV bus #5 from the train station to "Donaustauf Wallhallastr." (25min. M-F every 20min.-1hr. 5:40am-11:20pm; buses return on a similar schedule 5:25am-10:53pm. On Saturdays, buses leave every 20min.-1hr. 6:30am-11:20pm; they return 5:40am-10:53pm; on Sundays every hr. 6:30am-11:20pm and return 6:53am-10:53pm. One-way DM3.50, children under 15 DM1.80.) See **Public Transportation,** p. 528, for info on special passes.

NIGHTLIFE

Many of the cafes and beer gardens listed above (see **Food,** p. 530) double as local nighttime haunts, and good bars raise inebriation to Walhallian heights. Ask at the tourist office for a free copy of *Logo* or *Stadtzeitung*—two monthly publications that list the liveliest events and addresses of the hippest bars and cafes in Regensburg.

Alte Mälzerei, Galgenbergerstr. 20 (tel. 730 33 or for tickets 757 49). Regensburg's official cultural center is in an old malt factory that hosts not only theater and musical events, but a ramshackle bar with pop, jazz, funk,"ethno," soul, reggae, and blues. Somehow it manages to stay "cool" despite its institutionalism. Summer student crowd opts for the outdoor beer garden; there's an awesome aerial view of the massive Kneitinger Keller. Beer DM4.20-4.90. Open daily 6pm-1am.

Cartoon, Bischof-Werner-Str., just around the corner from Alte Mälzerei. Postered with funny old illustrations, it serves pasta, chili, and *Schnitzel* (DM8-12). Vegetarian soups and crazy veggie dishes DM5-10. Cover DM5-20. Open M-F 11am-1am, Sa-Su 2pm-1am. For concert info call 757 38.

Wunderbar, Keplerstr. 11 (tel. 531 30).Young late-nighters pack into one of the only bars open after 1am, located just a few staggers from the Steinerne Bridge. Beer starts at DM4.20, but they specialize in extravagant mixed drinks like "Flying Kangaroos" and "Scorpions" (DM13.50-15). Cocktails DM3, cheaper Su-Th 10pm-midnight. Open M-Th and Su 10pm-3am, F-Sa 9pm-3am.

Filmbühne, Hinter der Grieb 8 (tel. 520 51). Keep an eye out for the staircase leading down just within a green gate. Regensburg's funkiest scene attracts a diverse and bizarre crowd. Old film posters, old fans, light bulbs, and strange art are scattered everywhere. Open daily 9pm-1am.

Südhaus, Untere Bachgasse 8 (tel. 519 33). One of Regensburg's best discos. Just behind Café Orphée through the little tunnel, past a gargoyle fountain and a huge stone angel with the "Südhaus" sign. Tuesday is "ultimate" alternative night. Thursday is gay night. Beer DM5.50 for 0.3L. Cover M DM3, Tu-Th DM5, F-Sa DM6. Open M-Th 11pm-3am, F-Sa 11pm-4am.

Scala, Gesandtenstr. 6 (tel. 522 93), located in the Pustet Passage between Rote-Hahnen-Gasse and Gesandtenstr. Flanked by 3 bars, hipsters bump and grind in this disco club. Open W-Th and Su 11pm-3am, F-Sa 11pm-4am.

■ Near Regensburg: Donaudurchbruch and Kloster Weltenburg

About 35km south of Regensburg, the **Donaudurchbruch** (Danube Passage) winds 5km through magnificent stretches of nature to **Kloster Weltenburg** (Weltenburg Monastery). The lush green slopes lining this sheltered length of the Danube River are dramatically interrupted every few hundred meters by gargantuan white cliffs, which have all been given names by the river captains of the past. (The phallic, free-standing rock has been paradoxically named *Jungfrau*—the virgin.) Gurgling ferries shuttle the oohs and aahs of visitors through the Donaudurchbruch from the docks at Kelheim to Europe's oldest Benedictine monastery, **Kloster Weltenburg** (founded AD 620). Squatting on a jut of land at a sharp bend in the Danube, the simple, red-roofed monastery encloses a surprisingly ornate church featuring a powerful, back-lit statue of St. George spearing the last life out of a screeching dragon. A huge fresco on the right shows Christopher Columbus (and the Virgin Mary) discovering America, while high above, a playful statue of the church's builder, Cosma Damian Asam (in the red coat), smiles down on all good tourists. The first 400 years of daily prayers in the monastery must have been a little, well, dull, for it wasn't until 1050 that the good brothers decided to found the world's first monastery brewery. Taste the product of their labor in the monastery's own beer garden—by far the most popular attraction for visitors (DM4.90 for 0.5L of the holy brew).

A visit to Kloster Weltenburg makes an excellent daytrip from Regensburg, but plan ahead. To do the trip in a day, take a train to Saal (20min., 1 per hr.) and from Saal take an RBO bus to Kelheim. Walk across the Kelheim parking lot to the Danube riverbank, and buy a round-trip ticket for the ferry (DM10, under 17 DM8.50, under 13 DM6 50, under 5 free, families DM28) which runs every 30-45 minutes daily from mid-March to October. The boat trip to the Kloster takes about 45 minutes; allow 35 to 40 minutes for the return. Pack a picnic lunch, and be sure to check schedules at the tourist office before you hop on the train.

BAYERISCHER WALD (BAVARIAN FOREST)

A coddled national treasure, the Bayerischer Wald is the largest range of wooded mountains in central Europe. These 6000 square kilometers of peaks (60 of which are over 1000m high) and countless rivers and creeks stretch from the Danube and the

Austrian and Czech borders to form a vast hook that lures hikers, campers, and cross-country skiers throughout the year. The **Bayerischer Wald National Park,** the first national park in Germany, strictly prohibits any activities that might alter the forest ecosystem—this includes camping and building fires outside of designated camp-grounds. Clearly marked trails lace 8000 hectares (20,000 acres) of forest. You can trek it alone or sign up for free guided hiking tours, botanical tours, natural history tours, or tours of virgin woodlands. To sign up for a tour (at least one day in advance) or for information and schedules, contact **Hans-Eisenmann-Haus,** Bömstr. 35, 94556 Neuschönau (tel. (08558) 961 50; open daily Jan.-Oct. 9am-5pm). For general information about the *Bayerischer Wald,* contact either the **Nationalparkverwaltung Bayerischer Wald,** Freyunstr., 94481 Grafenau (tel. (08552) 960 00; fax 46 90) or the **Tourismusverband Ostbayern,** Luitpoldstr. (tel. 58 53 90; fax 585 39 39), in Regensburg. Pick up a copy of the forest newspaper "Informationsblatt Nationalpark Bayerischer Wald" for the latest news about the forest, or a free **encyclopedia** of the Bayerischer Wald, which is filled to the brim with phone numbers, maps, and listings. Both are available at any tourist office in the forest.

The Bayerischer Wald is much more than just a verdant paradise; palaces, churches, and castle ruins are tucked away in tiny villages throughout the region. **Burgruine Hals,** an extensive castle ruin high on a woody cliff north of Passau, dates from the 12th century. The 18th-century **Wiesenfelden** (lush gardens) surround the ruins. For information contact the **tourist office,** 94344 Wiesenfelden (tel. (09966) 94 00 17). **Frauenzell's** 15th-century Benedictine church is lavishly *barockisiert* and *funkisient* (Baroquified and funkified), and parts of the **Annunciation Church** in **Chammünster** date from the 12th century.

The Bavarian region is famous for its crafts, particularly **glass-blowing,** associated with the forest for the past 700 years. The glass produced here is prized (and dropped) throughout the world, particularly the dark green *Waldglas* (forest glass). Every little forest village seems to have its own *Glashütte.* For more information, contact the **Bergglashütte Weinfurter,** Ferienpark Geyersberg (tel. (08551) 60 66), in Freyung, or the **Freiherr von Poschinger Kristallglasfabrik,** Moosauhütte (tel. (09926) 940 10), in Frauenau.

The remoteness of Bayerischer Wald towns attracts few English-speaking visitors, but the park maintains a heavy flow of Germans seeking healthy, sedate vacations. Use the towns below as springboards from which to explore the nooks and crannies of this mountain region. An impressive 17 **HI youth hostels** dot the forest; Regensburg's tourist office (see p. 527) has a helpful brochure as well as current addresses and phone numbers of the hostels. The towns of **Cham** and **Regen** can be reached by **train** (Cham from Regensburg or Nürnberg via Schwanndorf; Regen from Regensburg, Munich, or Passau via Platting). **Buses** run from Regensburg and Straubing to Cham and from Passau and Straubing to Regen. **Igel Buses** traverse four different regions of the national park proper; they run out of Grafenau, just outside the park.

■ Zwiesel

The abundance of train connections running through Zwiesel makes it an excellent hub for scouting the heart of the Bayerischer Wald. A skier's haven in the winter, in summer its focus flips to its 800-year history of glass-making, the modern-day incarnation of which is the production of postmodern wine glasses. Just north of town lies **Glas Park,** a village of glass-blowing houses that demonstrate to awed spectators how delicate fancies are created. Six buses per day shuttle to the Glas Park from the Stadtplatz (M-F beginning at 9:27am; last return at 6:37pm; check the tourist office). The **Waldmuseum** (forest museum), Stadtpl. 27 (tel. 608 88), behind the *Rathaus,* tells the tinkly tale of glass-making in the region. (Open May 15-Oct. 15 M-F 9am-5pm, Sa-Su 10am-noon and 2-4pm; Oct. 16-May 14 M-F 10am-noon and 2-5pm, Sa-Su 10am-noon; DM3, with *Kurkarte* DM2.50, disabled persons DM2, students DM1.) **Trains** run hourly from Plattling on the Nürnberg-Passau line (1hr., DM14.20). There is an information counter at the train station (open M 5:30am-12:10pm and 12:40-4:15pm,

The Woeful Decline of the ß

The story of the ess-tset ("ß") begins hundreds of years ago with the Goths, who devised a letter that efficiently did the work of a cumbersome double S with only one stroke, freeing more time for pillage and plunder. As time passed, the letter gained fame and renown, featuring prominently in the works of Goethe and Schiller. But once a lovable "letter" as *echt*-ly Germanic as *Gemütlichkeit* and morbid obesity, the ß may soon be a fugitive in its own land. It is only the most visible victim of a recent series of planned language and spelling reforms concocted by representatives of all of the German-speaking lands of Europe as "a systematic dismantling of anomalies." Other reforms standardize and Germanize the spelling of assimilated foreign words and other eclectically spelled words. Thus far, opposition in Germany has been most vocal, with legal challenges cropping up from Weimar to Wiesbaden. In Austria and Switzerland, however, all systems still appear to be go for the switch, and *Kinder* are already learning to spell ketchup "*ketschup.*" If the ess-tset is exterminated as planned, there will be no way of knowing whether somebody is drinking within limits *(in Maßen)* or excessively *(in Massen)*—so why not opt for the latter?

Tu-F 6:15am-12:10pm and 12:40-4:15pm, Sa 6:20am-12:40pm). The **tourist office,** Stadtpl. 27 (tel. 84 05 23; fax 56 55), in the *Rathaus,* provides maps and hiking information and finds **private rooms** for free (DM20-35). From the station, turn right and walk downhill on Dr.-Schott-Str. After a few blocks, veer left onto Innenriederstr. and cross the bridge, then take the gentle left onto Stadtpl.; the *Rathaus* is on the left. (Open M-F 8:30am-5:30pm, Sa 10am-noon; Nov.-Dec. M-F 8:30am-5:30pm.) The **post office,** Dr.-Schott-Str. 55, 94227 Zwiesel, **changes money** (open M-F 8:30am-noon and 2-5:30pm, Sa 8:30am-11am). There is a large **wheelchair-accessible public telephone** booth directly in front of the post office. The **telephone code** is 09922.

The **Jugendherberge,** Hindenburgstr. 26 (tel. 10 61; fax 601 91), is a 30-minute walk from the station. Follow the directions to Stadtplatz, continue past the *Rathaus,* and turn right onto Frauenauerstr. Continue straight for 10 minutes and turn left on Hindenburgstr. (one block after the "AOK" sign); the hostel is just over the hill. Or take bus #1 from the station to "Jugendherberge" (DM2; 1 per hr.). This clean hostel is the choicest accommodation in the Bayerischer Wald. "*Klein aber fein*" (tiny but shiny), repeats the proud hostel mother, and she's not talking about your nose. (DM20. Spacious doubles available. Sheets DM5.50. Breakfast included. Reception daily 5-7pm. Curfew 10pm, but they'll give you a key.) **Campingplatz TrööpplKeller,** TrööpplKeller 48 (tel. 17 09 or 603 91), is located on the Schwarzer Regen river, just 2km from the center of town. From the train station, turn right and walk downhill on Dr.-Schott-Str. After a few blocks, veer right onto Schlachthofstr., then turn right onto Langdorfer Str. and walk about 800m to TrööpplKeller on the left. All campsites come with running water. The **Elscafé-Pizzeria Rialto,** Stadtpl. 23, has a sweet bar and outdoor seating on a busy street; feed the hungry beast with pizza (DM7-11), pasta (DM7.50-9.50), or an ice cream confection (DM6-11). At the **Gasthaus MusicKanten-Keller,** 42 Stadtpl., imbibe a beer (DM4) as you feast on a large bowl of *Gulaschsuppe mit Nudeln* (DM8.50). Live music and dancing get the joint jivin' on the weekends. (Open Su-Th 9am-midnight, F-Sa 9am-1am.) **Lidl,** up the street from the tourist office at the intersection of Stadtplatz and Oberzwieslanerstr., is a convenient and extremely cheap supermarket (open M-F 8:30am-6pm, Sa 8am-1pm).

■ Bodenmais

Bodenmais, at the heart of the forest amid hills of velvet moss, can be reached by train from Zwiesel. The tourist-luring **Austen Glashütte,** on Bahnhofstr. (tel. 70 06), across from the *Rathaus,* showcases and sells wine glasses, jewelry, and cheaper fragile trinkets. A skilled glass carver will engrave your name on every purchased item for free. You can view the glass being blown, then enjoy a local brew in a personally-monogrammed souvenir *Stein* (DM3.90). **Hans und Hans'l,** two endearing Bavarians (complete with *Lederhosen*), sing and play the accordion on Fridays (1-5pm); please keep hands, feet, and objects to yourself. (*Glashütte* open M-F 9am-6pm, Sa 9am-4pm, Su 10am-4pm. Glass blown mid-May to mid-Oct. M-F 9am-noon and 1-6pm, Sa 9am-2pm, Su 10am-noon and 1-4pm; mid-Oct. to mid-May no glass blown on Sundays.)

Trains make the 20-minute journey between Zwiesel and Bodenmais roughly every hour (daily 6:25am-11:25pm to Bodenmais, 6am-10pm from Bodenmais; DM4.60 one way, DM9.20 round-trip). **Bus** #8651 also makes the trip to Bodenmais daily, leaving from the Zwiesel train station (25min., M-F 3:40pm, Sa 3:20pm). The same bus returns to Zwiesel from the Bodemais train station (M-Sa 8:40am). For a **taxi** call 484. Rent mountain **bikes** (DM20 per day) or **skis** at **Sport Weinberger,** Jahnstr. 20 (tel. 90 22 73), 10 minutes from the station down Bahnhofstr. Arriving from Zwiesel, the **Waldbahn** will drop you literally at the doorstep of the **tourist office,** Bahnhofstr. 56 (tel. 77 81 35; fax 77 81 50), in the modern *Rathaus*. The staff gives out a free book of accommodations and hiking trails, and offers a *Wanderpaß* (DM3) with tips and trails for hiking (open M-F 8am-6pm, Sa 9am-1pm, Su 9am-noon). Outside the tourist office is an impressive info center with a computerized room-finding service, a map of local alpine and nordic ski resorts, and a weather station. A public **fax** machine is located in the front of the tourist office lobby (DM2, plus normal telephone call charges; telephone cards only—no coins accepted). There are **weekly concerts** in the pleasant Bodenmais *Kurgarten*, behind the tourist office, with traditional Bodenmais music and clothing (May-Oct. Su 10:30am; free). The **post office,** Kötzinger Str. 25, 94249 Bodenmais, is a short walk from the station. After leaving the *Rathaus*, take a right on Bahnhofstr. and then veer right onto Kötzinger Str. (Open M-F 8:30am-noon and 2-5pm, Sa 8:30-11am.) The **telephone code** is 09924.

Bodenmais has 3600 inhabitants and almost twice that many hotel beds. Even so, this spa town fills quickly in summer and winter; call ahead. The **Jugendherberge,** Am Kleinen Arber (tel. 281; fax 850), is 8km from town in the mountains, a whopping 1½-hour uphill hike along a tiny paved road through a very beautiful part of the forest (DM20; breakfast included). Follow the Bahnhofstr. to the right and then turn right onto Scharebenstr. Hike up this narrow paved road for about 15 minutes and then take a right on Gr. Arbor at the "Ortsverkehr Markt Bodenmais" bus stop. From here it is about an hour's uphill climb—watch for the *Jugendherberge* signs. If you forgot your hiking boots at home, many of the private rooms and *Pensionen* in town are quite nice and fairly inexpensive (DM25-40). Try the computerized room-finding service (24hr.), or attack the tourist office's accommodations booklet with gusto. The **Penny Markt,** 70 Bahnhofstr., has cheap groceries (open M-F 8:30am-10pm, Sa 8am-4pm). The **Schmanterl Metzgerei Grillstube,** Bahnhofstr. 21, on the corner of Bergknappstr., serves *Leberkäs* with potato salad (DM8.90), *Curry-Wurst,* and fries (open M-F 7am-6pm). Grab a string of sausage, hop into **Müller,** the bakery next door, for *Brötchen*, and disappear into the forest—leave a trail of bread crumbs (bakery open the same hours as the Metzgerei).

■ Frauenau

Circumscribed by majestic wooded mountains, Frauenau, the "glassy heart of the Bayerischer Wald," is a fragile town in an idyllic location. Near the borders of the Czech Republic and away from the busier regions of Bayern, Frauenau remains virgin land, virtually untouched by tourists, with plenty of space for private exploration. The pristine waters of **Trinkwasser Talsperre,** a crystal-clear reservoir, can be easily reached by foot (a 3-4km walk). To get to the lake, take Hauptstr. up as it curves left, pass by the minigolf area on the right, and then take a right on Wasserhäuslweg (45min.). To continue on to Zwiesel, from the corner of Wasserhäuslweg and Zwieseler Str., follow the **bike** and **pedestrian path** next to Zwieseler Str. out of town. It is about a 7km bike ride to Zwiesel.

The **Glasmuseum,** Am Museumspark 1 (tel. 94 00 35), sprawled across a beautiful green landscape, holds 2500 years of glass treasures. (Open May 15-Oct. 31 Tu-Su 9am-5pm; Dec. 20-May 14 Tu-Su 10am-4pm. DM2.50, under 15 DM1, under 6 free.)

You can reach Frauenau by regular **train** from Zwiesel along the Zwiesel-Grafenau line (15min., 10 per day; to Frauenau 6:40am-10:23pm; from Frauenau 6:05pm-9:25pm; DM3 one way, DM6 round-trip). There is no train station office in Frauenau, but information about train transportation is available at the tourist office. Bus #8652 also runs to the Frauenau post office daily, leaving from the Zwiesel train station (14min.; M-F 11:23am, 2:20pm, and 3:23pm, Sa 11:23am, 2:15pm, and 5:23pm, Su 2:15pm). The extremely friendly **tourist office**, Hauptstr. 12, 94258 Frauenau (tel. 941 00; fax 17 99), provides information on hiking trails (trail map DM4), hotels, holiday farms (DM15-19), and *Pensionen* (DM20-30), and also rents bikes (DM10 per day). Turn left from the station and then right up Hauptstr. (Open M-F 8am-noon and 1:30-4pm; May 15-Oct. 15 also Sa 9:30-11:30am.) You can buy a pamphlet containing a map of the town and information about *Gasthäuser* and *Pensionen* from the **Automat** outside the tourist office (DM0.50). The **Jugendherberge** ("Haus St. Hermann"), Hauptstr. 29a (tel./fax 735), is in the same building as the **post office**, 94258 Frauenau (tel. 241), just uphill from the tourist office. The green hospital-like building is small and slightly cramped, but clean. (12-bed dorm rooms DM16.50. Breakfast included. Sheets DM5.50. Guest kitchen available for cooking.) Every Thursday there's a farmer's **market** from 7am to noon at the foot of the *Rathaus* on Hauptstr. If you arrive in town after noon, stop by the **Edeka Markt**, Hauptstr. 25, for groceries (open M-F 7:30am-6:30pm, Sa 7:30am-1pm). The **telephone code** is 09926.

■ Sleeping Around in the Bayerischer Wald

Jugendherberge Neuschönau (HI), Herbergsweg 2, 94556 Neuschönau (tel. (08553) 60 00; fax 829), nestles in the heart of the forest, a 20km bus ride from the train station at Grafenau on the bus coming from Spiegelau or Neuschönau. (DM24. Breakfast included. Sheets DM5.50.) **Jugendherberge Mauth (HI),** Jugendherbergestr. 11, 94151 Mauth (tel. (08557) 289; fax 15 81), is accessible from Passau (DM20; breakfast included; sheets DM5.50). Most Bayerischer Wald towns offer several *Pensionen* and *Gasthöfe* that cost DM18-30 per person (prices slightly higher in summer and around Christmas; breakfast included). The **Nationalparkverwaltung Bayerischer Wald** offers a big brochure on **camping** in the Bayerischer Wald. Drop by the office in Regensburg or write for it at *Info-Zentrum Nationalpark Hans-Eisenmann-Haus*, Böhmstr. 35, 94556 Neuschönau (tel. (08558) 961 50). For further info, contact the **Verkehrsamt Cham**, Propsteistr. 46 (tel. (09971) 49 33), or the **Haus des Gastes** in Regen (tel. (09921) 29 29).

■ Eichstätt

Sheltered in the valley of the Altmühl river and surrounded by the largest nature preserve in Germany, the **Naturpark Altmühltal,** the small university and Episcopal town of Eichstätt flaunts one of the most beautiful cobblestone market squares in Germany, as well as a **Jurassic Museum** with a renowned collection of 140-million-year-old fossils. The slowly drifting Altmühl river weaves a spell of relaxation and hospitality over the city's inhabitants, making Eichstätt one of the friendliest, most laid-back towns in Bavaria.

ORIENTATION AND PRACTICAL INFORMATION
The Eichstätt **train station** is a 15- to 30-minute ride from Ingolstadt (DM9.80). A little **train** shuttles the 5km between the Eichstätt *Bahnhof* and the Eichstätt *Stadt* station, leaving from track 1 (9min., every 30-40min. 5am-11:30pm, DM2.40). Rent **bikes** at the **Fahrradgarage**, Herzoggasse 3 (tel. 21 10 or 899 87), in the tiny alley that leads from the Marktplatz to the footbridge (DM13 per day; open daily 9-11:30am and 2:30-7pm). **Heinz Glas**, Industrie 18 (tel. 30 55), will rent you a **canoe** for a cruise down the Altmühl River (DM20 per day M-F, DM25 Sa-Su; under 12 50% off). The **tourist office**, Kardinal-Preysing-Pl.14 (tel. 988 00; fax 98 80 30), has free maps and helps find private rooms (DM25-30) for free. From the train station, walk right and follow the information sign

across the bridge (Spitalbrücke). Turn right on Residenzplatz and follow the bend left to Leonrodplatz, then bear right past the church until you reach Kardinal-Preysing-Platz on the left; the tourist office is up the street on the right. (Open Apr.-Oct. M-Sa 9am-6pm, Su 1-6pm; Nov.-Mar. M-Th 9am-noon and 2-4pm, F 9am-noon.) Tours of the town (1½hr., in German) leave from the tourist office (Apr.-Oct. Sa 1:30pm; DM5). When they're closed, go next door to the tourist information office for **Naturpark Altmühtal,** Notre Dame 1 (tel. 987 60). Cloistered in a former monastery, they provide information on trails and paths in the nature reserve (open Easter-Oct. M-Sa 9am-5pm, Su 10am-5pm). **Exchange money** at **Volksbank,** on the Marktplatz. (Open M-W 8am-4:30pm, Th 8am-5:30pm, F 8am-2pm. Service charge DM2 for cash exchange, DM2 per traveler's check with a minimum charge of DM5.) A convenient **pharmacy** is **Dom Apotheke,** Dompl. 16 (tel. 15 20; open M-F 8am-6pm, Sa 8am-noon). The **post office,** 85072 Eichstätt, awaits at Dompl. 7 (open M-F 8:30am-5:30pm, Sa 9am-noon). The **telephone code** is 08421.

ACCOMMODATIONS AND FOOD Eichstätt's **Jugendherberge (HI),** Reichenaustr. 15 (tel. 980 40; fax 98 04 15), is modern and comfortable. Follow directions to Willibaldsburg (see **Sights**), but turn right halfway up Burgstr. onto Reichenaustr. at the "Jugendherberge" sign. (Bed in 6-bed dorm DM24. Breakfast included. Sheets DM5.50. Reception 8-9am and 5-7pm. Lockout 10am. Curfew 10pm, but they'll give you a key if you want to party the night away. Closed Dec.-Jan.) To get to the university **Mensa,** Universitätsallee 2 (tel. 93 14 60), walk down toward the end of Ostenstr. and hang a right onto Universitätsallee; it's on the right. Buy a card (DM3) from the cashier on the first floor. (Cashier available noon-1:30pm. Student ID required. Meals DM2-4.40. *Mensa* open M-F 11:30am-2pm during term; in summer 11:30am-1:30pm; closed Aug. 5 to mid-Sept.) A relaxed **cafeteria** on the first floor has an outdoor garden (open M-Th 8:15am-7pm, F 8:15am-3pm; in summer M-F 8:15am-2:45pm). In town, **Ammonit,** Luitpoldstr. 19 (tel. 29 29), is a student hangout with beer (DM4-8) and other snackies (DM7-15; open M-F 9:30am-1am, Sa-Su 9:30am-2am). **La Grotta,** Marktpl. 13 (tel. 72 80 or 15 07), has affordable pizzas and pasta (DM8-15; open daily 11:30am-2pm and 5:30pm-1am; warm food served until 11pm). **Schneller's Backstube,** Markpl. 20a, provides inexpensive fresh bread and delicious pastries to quell carbo-cravings (open M-F 7am-6pm, Sa 6:30am-1pm).

SIGHTS The **Willibaldsburg** conspicuously watches over the town from its high perch across the river. To reach the castle from the train station, take a right; at the main intersection, turn right and follow the main street one block and turn left onto Burgstr. The 14th-century castle now houses the **Jura-Museum** (Jurassic Museum; tel. 29 56), filled with fossils from the Jurassic period found in the Altmühltal Valley, once covered by a vast prehistoric sea. See the earliest bird to ever catch a worm, the Archaeopteryx, who lived over 150 million years ago and whose fossil has been excellently preserved. Dinosaur movies (no Spielberg) are screened daily at 10:15am and 2:30pm. The **Museum für Ur- und Frühgeschichte** (tel. 60 01 74), also in the Willibaldsburg, picks up the story at the debut of *Homo sapiens* and continues it through the era of the Roman presence in the area. *(Both museums open Tu-Su 9am-noon and 1-5pm; Oct.-Mar. Tu-Su 10am-noon and 1-4pm. Jura-Museum DM5, students DM4, children under 15 free; Museum für Ur- und Frühgeschichte DM10.)*

Across the river, Eichstätt proper is built around the extravagant **Residenzplatz,** surrounded by the Rococo Episcopal palaces. The west wing has a particularly magnificent portal, and the interior is just as richly decorated. Free German-language tours of the **Residenz** (tel. 702 20) begin here if there are at least five people. *(Easter-Oct. M-Th at 11am and 3pm, F at 11am; Sa-Su every 30min. 10-11:30am and 2-3:30pm.)* In a corner of the Residenzplatz, in the middle of a fountain, stands the **Mariensäule** (Madonna Column). Behind the *Residenz* is the 14th-century **Hohe Dom** (High Cathedral), the product of the Romanesque, Gothic, and Baroque eras. *(Open to tourists M-Th 9:45am-1pm and 2:30-4pm, F 9:45am-3:30pm, Sa 9:45am-3pm, Su 12:30-5pm.)* The east apse features richly colored stained glass, and the north aisle shelters the intricate 15th-century stone **Pappenheim Altar.** On the other side of the high altar is the entrance to the **Mortuarium** (Mortuary), resting place of Eichstätt's bishops, in which the carved Gothic **Schöne Säule** (Beautiful Column) rises to meet the vault.

Also in the cathedral complex, the **Diözesan-Museum,** Residenzpl. 7 (tel. 507 42), examines the history of the diocese since its founding in 741 by St. Willibald. *(Open W-F 10:30am-5pm, Sa-Su and holidays 10am-5pm. DM2.50, under 18 free.)* Two blocks farther on Leonrodplatz is the Baroque **Schutzengelkirche** (Church of the Guardian Angel), built during the Thirty Years War, containing richly carved wooden altars and a striking golden sunburst above the high altar. Five hundred sixty-seven sculpted angels fly about the church's interior. Start counting.

■ Ingolstadt

Ingolstadt possesses the most important elements of a good *Bayerische Altstadt—* half-timbered houses and Renaissance facades. The site of the first Bavarian university from 1472 to 1800, this old Danube city is now best known as the home of the Audi. The name of this luxury car company was originally *Horch,* German for "eavesdrop," and the last name of auto innovator and entrepreneur August Horch. After WWII it was changed to the Latin *Audi* (listen) to help exports in an international market resistant to German-sounding products. It would take much more than a name change, however, to shake the traditional look of this old town. The *Stadtmitte* remains a tightly packed burst of old school architecture, enveloped by lush greenery with no evidence of dirty industry in sight.

ORIENTATION AND PRACTICAL INFORMATION Trains roll from Ingolstadt to Munich (1hr., 2-3 per hr., DM22); Augsburg (1hr., 2-3 per hr., DM16.20); and Regensburg (1¼hr., 2 per hr., DM19.40). To reach the tourist office and the rest of the old city from the distant train station, take bus #10, 15, 16, or 44 (DM2.70), from the station to "Rathauspl." (5 stops; every 10-20min.). You can also follow Bahnhofstr. on the right-hand side to Münchener Str, and head straight over the bridge down Donaustr. to the Rathausplatz (20min.). Public transportation **bus** routes center around the **Omnibusbahnhof,** located in the middle of the city (single fare DM2.70, *4-Farhtenkarte* DM10). The **Mitfahrzentrale,** Harderstr. 14 (tel. 194 40), arranges ride shares (open M-F 2-6pm). For a **taxi,** call 877 88. **Radverleih Fahrradinsel,** Münchener Str. 2, rents **bikes** for DM19 per day (tel. 730 27; open M-F 9am-12:30pm and 1:30-7pm, Sa 9am-4pm). Ingolstadt's **tourist office,** in the Altes Rathaus, Rathauspl. 4 (tel. 305 10 98; fax 305 10 99), hands out free maps, English-language brochures, bicycle maps covering the Donau river region from Ingolstadt to Passau (DM18.80), and a list of hotels and *Pensionen* in the area (open M-F 8am-5pm, Sa 9am-noon). They offer free German-language **city tours** on Saturdays at 2pm. **Exchange money** at **Volksbank,** Theresienstr 32 (open M-W 8am-4:30pm, Th 8am-5:30pm, F 8am-2pm). In an **emergency,** call 192 22. **Franziskus Apotheke,** Rathauspl. 13 (tel. 330 53), posts the name and address of the 24-hour **pharmacy** for any given night. The **post office,** 85024 Ingolstadt, is directly in front of the train station (open M-F 8am-6pm, Sa 8am-noon). The **telephone code** is 0841.

ACCOMMODATIONS Ingolstadt's superb **Jugendherberge (HI),** Friedhofstr. 4½ (tel. 341 77; fax 91 01 78), is located in a renovated section of the old town fortifications. From the tourist office, take Moritzstr. and make a left on Theresienstr. Follow it all the way to the Kreuztor, then walk through it and cross Auf-der-Schanz (10min.). Large echoing rooms and cavernous hallways, with private sinks and (massage) showers, not to mention a great location and a scrumptious breakfast—hosteling life rarely gets this good. (DM20. Sheets DM5.50. Curfew 11:30pm. Reception 3-9pm. Open Feb. to mid-Dec., but closed every 2nd and 4th weekend from Nov. 11-Dec. 15 and Feb. 1-Mar. 15.) **Pension Lipp,** on Feldkirchener Str. (tel. 587 36), down Schloßländestr. along the Danube and left up Frühlingstr., is pleasant if out-of-the-way. Still, it's the closest affordable *Pension.* (Singles DM40, with bath DM45; doubles

DM75, with shower DM85.) Campers can head out to **Campingplatz am Auwald-see** (tel. 961 16 16), but *a car is a must.* The site is off the E45/Autobahn A9, five minutes by car from the town center. (DM7.10 per person, under 12 DM4.90. DM5.10 per tent. DM9.90 per car. Open year-round.)

FOOD AND NIGHTLIFE The Kreuztor might represent the old, traditional *Ingolstadter Altstadt,* but it's also the epicenter of all that's hip and new in town. The local nightlife centers around Kreuzstr. (which turns into Theresienstr. toward the center of town). **Glock'n am Kreuztor,** Oberer Graben 1 (tel. 349 90), is the really loud cafe abutting the Kreuztor. It's especially popular in the summer when the benches and the kegs move outside. Daily dishes from pasta to pork run DM5-15. Save DM0.50 and buy a *Maß* (DM8.50 for 1L. Open daily 6pm-2am. 18+ admitted.) **Sigi's Café and Bistro,** Kreuzstr. 6 (tel. 329 52), a few steps down from Glock'n, is small, chic, and light green, with nice outdoor seating. *Wieners,* mozzarella sandwiches, and salads are all under DM11. (Open M-Sa 9:30am-2am, Su 2pm-2am.) **Restaurant Mykonos,** Ludwigstr. 9, dishes out Greek delights with a ritzy Bavarian tint—a beer garden out back. Omelettes (DM7.20) and Greek specialities (DM9-13) grace the affordable lunch menu. (Open daily 11am-3pm and 5pm-1am.) The budget-friendly **Norma supermarket,** Donaustr. 16, is on the *Altstadt* side of the Konrad-Adenauer-Brücke (open M-F 8:30am-6pm, Sa 8am-2pm).

　　Neue Welt, Griesbadgasse 7 (tel. 324 70), right off Kreuzstr., is home to the local artist and music crowd, with its own stage, the **Kleinkunstbühne.** Cabarets, alternative, and R&B concerts premiere regularly on Mondays, Tuesdays, and Fridays. Try the chili, a *Tsatsiki* (DM5.50), or vegetarian rigatoni with "special sauce" (DM8.80. Open daily 7pm-2am.) **Goldener Stern,** Griesbadgasse 2 (tel. 354 19), is just down a step from Neue Welt, in a light yellow house with big wooden tables. Self-proclaimed student-friendly prices are a joy, and an amicable staff sweetens the deal. Beer starts at DM4, and chocolatey and fruity crepes run DM4.50-6.50. Show up for the smoky crowds or relax in the beer garden. (Open daily 7pm-1am. 18+ admitted.)

SIGHTS AND ENTERTAINMENT The old city wall is magnificently represented by the turreted **Kreuztor,** topped by dainty stone ornamentation. Other remnants of the city's medieval fortifications (including numerous ponds—relics of the town moat) are scattered around the city. Just beyond the Kreuztor, outside the city wall, is the **Stadtmuseum,** Auf der Schanz 45 (im Kavalier Hepp; tel. 305 18 85), which explores the archaeological and cultural history of the area. *(Open Tu-Sa 9am-5pm, Su 10am-5pm. DM4, students and seniors DM2, Su free.)* Two blocks east of the Kreuztor stands the late Gothic **Liebfrauenmünster** (Minister of our Dear Lady), full of ornate altars and immense columns. A few blocks south on Anatomiestr., the **Deutsches Medizinhistorisches Museum** (German Museum of Medical History), Anatomiestr. 18-20 (tel. 305 18 60) is in the **Alte Anatomie,** an 18th-century university building. *(Museum open Tu-Su 10am-noon and 2-5pm. DM4, students and seniors DM2, Su free.)* It features an 18th-century "do-it-yourself" enema stool complete with a hand-operated water pump and a padded seat with a small protruding 3-inch-long pipe. That was a little more information than anyone needed to know. The "skeleton room" displays skinned human corpses with some of the dried-up muscles still attached, and an eerie collection of shrivelled guts and limbs. The goodness never ends. The staff will lend you a thick English guidebook to interpret the German-only exhibits. North of the *Münster* at the corner of Jesuiten and Neubaustr. is the **Maria-de-Victoria-Kirche** (Church of Our Lady of Victories; tel. 175 18), the "Rococo jewel." *(Open Tu-Su 9am-noon and 1-5pm. Ring for the caretaker. DM2.50, students and children DM1.50.)* This once spare chapel for students of the nearby Catholic school was rococoed with a vengeance in 1732, and an awe-inspiring frescoco now adorns the ceiling.

　　Across town on Paradeplatz is the 15th-century **Neues Schloß,** Paradepl. 4, a red-tiled castle that now houses a band of pierced-and-tattooed *Szene* kids and the less fascinating **Bayerisches Armee-Museum** (Bavarian Military Museum; tel. 937 70), collected under King Ludwig "If-I-weren't-crazy-I'd-be-dangerous" II. *(Open Tu-Su*

8:45am-4:30pm. DM5.50, students and seniors DM4, under 10 free. Joint admission to the main exhibit and to the special exhibit of armor and weapons used in WWI DM7.50, students and seniors DM5.50.) The brand-new **Museum für Konkrete Kunst** (Museum for Concrete Art), Tränktorstr. 6-8 (tel. 305 18 06), is right off Donaustr. near the Konrad-Adenauer-Brücke. *(Open Tu and Th-Su 10am-6pm, W 10am-2pm and 5-9pm. DM4, students DM2, children under 10 free.)* The neon lights and funkadelic designs in primary colors will make your head spin. Tours in German are given the second Wednesday of every month at 6:30pm (DM4). Have a burning fetish for automobiles? Call **Audi** for information on tours (tel. 89 12 41). Ingolstadt also has a fabulous outdoor **swimming pool,** Johnstr. 29 (tel. 802 77), just to the left beyond the Kreuztor (open May-Sept. M-Su 8am-8pm).

■ Augsburg

Founded by Caesar Augustus in 15 BC, Augsburg was the financial center of the Holy Roman Empire and a major commercial city by the end of the 15th century. The town owed its success and prestige mainly to the Fuggers, an Augsburger family that virtually monopolized the banking industry; Jakob Fugger "the Rich" was personal financier to the Habsburg Emperors. The third-largest Bavarian city also went down in history as a focal point of the Reformation and the birthplace of Bertolt Brecht. Today, Augsburg hides its age under a modern exterior of malls, cafes, and vibrant nightlife. Its huge pedestrian district is always hopping, especially at night when jazz music spills from the cafes out into the streets. The city's central location makes it an ideal train hub for travelers zig-zagging through Bayern.

ORIENTATION AND PRACTICAL INFORMATION Augsburg is connected by **train** to Munich (40min., 3-4 per hr.), Nürnberg (1½-2hr., 1-2 per hr.), Würzburg (2½hr. with a change at Treuchtlingen, 1-2 per hr.), Stuttgart (1½-2hr., 2-3 per hr.), and Zürich (5hr., 16 per day). The **Reisezentrum** (travel center) in the train station is open daily (M 5:15am-9:30pm, Tu-Sa 5:30am-9:30pm, Su 5:30am-10pm). Rent **lockers** at the train station (DM2-4). The infamous **Europabus** line, canvassing the Romantische Straße route, stops at the Augsburg train station (northbound 10:30am; southbound 6:20pm). The **Mitfahrzentrale,** Barthof 3 (tel. 15 70 19), arranges ride-shares for a small fee (open daily noon-9pm). The resourceful **tourist office,** Bahnhofstr. 7 (tel. 50 20 70; fax 502 07 45), off Königsplatz, about 300m from the train station down Bahnhofstr., sells excellent cycling maps and guides of the area and finds rooms (DM30-40) for a DM3 fee (open M-F 9am-6pm). A **branch** office at Rathausplatz (tel. 502 07 24) has weekend hours and free brochures and maps in English (open M-F 9am-6pm, Sa 10am-4pm, Su 10am-1pm). Walk straight from the station to the end of Bahnhofstr. and take a left at Königsplatz onto Annastr. Take the third right and you'll see Rathausplatz on the left; the tourist office is on the right. Walking tours of the city leave from the *Rathaus.* (Mid-May to mid-Oct. daily 10:30am; Dec. Su 10:30am; mid-Jan. to mid-May Sa 2pm. DM19, students and children under 15 DM12.) For medicinal wares, head to the **Rathaus Apotheke** on Rathausplatz, to your left as you face the *Rathaus* (open M-F 8:30am-6pm, Sa 8:30am-noon). Augsburg's **post office,** Halderstr. 29, 86150 Augsburg, exchanges cash (DM2 per transaction) and traveler's checks (DM6 per check); it's on your left as you face the station (open M-F 7am-8pm, Sa 8am-2pm, Su 10am-noon). The **telephone code** is 0821.

ACCOMMODATIONS Augsburg has a dearth of inexpensive, centrally located rooms, but a few do exist. To reach Augsburg's **Jugendherberge (HI),** Beim Pfaffenkeller 3 (tel. 339 09; fax 15 11 49), walk straight up Bahnhofstr. from the station to Königsplatz, bear left on Annastr., then right on Karlstr. Turn left onto the street across from Karolinenstr. which will soon become Hoherweg. Turn right after the church onto Inneres Pfaffengäßchen; follow the left side as it turns into Beim Pfaffenkeller. Bland, worn rooms feel like converted second-grade classrooms, but the hostel is central and the price is right. (DM20. Excellent breakfast included. Sheets DM5.50. Key deposit DM20 or an ID. Reception 7-9am and 5-10pm. Curfew 1am. Call ahead. Open late-Jan. to early-Dec.) Or try **Gasthof Lenzhalde,** Theolottstr. 2 (tel. 52 07 45; fax 52 87 61), located 750m from the station. From the *Bahnhof,* bear right onto Halderstr., take a sharp right onto Hermannstr., and cross the Gögginger bridge. Take the first right onto Rosenaustr. and follow it for several blocks; when it curves right at the traffic light the Gasthof is straight ahead. Very simple but tidy rooms overlooking a park. (Singles DM42, with shower DM50; doubles DM78; triples DM110.) More central but a tad more expensive is the **Jakoberhof,** Jakoberstr. 39-41 (tel. 510 30; fax 15 08 44). The room furnishings haven't quite made it to the 90s, but it's the cheapest you'll find in a central location. (Singles DM50, with bath DM75; doubles DM75, DM105.) To camp at **Campingplatz Augusta,** ABA Augsburg Ost, am Autobahnsee (tel. 70 75 75), take the bus (direction: "Neuburg") to "Autobahnsee" and follow the signs; the camp is about 400m away (DM8 per person, DM6 per tent, DM6 per car).

FOOD Don't miss the **Stadtmarkt** (farmer's market) between Fuggerstr. and Annastr., right past the St. Anna Kirche on Fuggerstr. (open M-F 7am-6pm, Sa 7am-1pm). Most corner joints sell the local beer, *Riegele Augsburg.* To stock up on basics, visit the **Penny Markt,** Maximilianstr. 71, to the right from the *Rathaus* (open M-F 8:30am-7pm, Sa 8am-2pm). **Tengelmann supermarket,** at the corner of Alte Gasse and Jesuitengasse, offers a little more variety (open M-Th 8:30am-6:30pm, F 8am-6:30pm, Sa 8am-1pm). A myriad of food stands line Maximilianstr. in the summer, but this *Imbiß* fare tends to be a bit pricey. The romantic **Don Camillo e Peppone,** on the corner of Theaterstr. and Ludwigstr., serves creamy soups (DM4.50-6), omelettes (DM7.50), and pizza (DM6.50) in wooden train compartment-like booths with plush cushions. (Open Tu-F 11am-2pm and 6pm-midnight, Sa 6pm-1am, Su 6pm-midnight.) For Chinese cuisine, head to **China Restaurant Liu** in the *Ludwigpassage* at Ludwigstr. 14 (tel. 305 69). Try the noodle and veggie dishes (DM12-14; open daily 11am-3pm and 5:30-11:30pm). New friends may be sitting along rough wooden banquet tables at **König von Flandern,** Augsburg's first *Gasthof*-brewery, 12 Karolinenstr. (tel. 15 80 50). Large portions of soup (DM4.70-6), salad (DM5-10), and meat (DM10-14) will satisfy ravenous Bavarian food fiends. (Open M-Sa 11am-1am, Su 5pm-1am.)

SIGHTS Germany's very own Daddy Warbucks, Jakob Fugger, founded the **Fuggerei** quarter in 1519 as the first welfare housing project in the world. The narrow cobblestone streets and little gabled houses are a haven for the elderly, who earn their keep by praying for the departed souls of the Fuggers and pay only DM1.72 (the equivalent of a "Rhine Guilder") rent annually. Budget travelers need not apply. To reach the Fuggerei from the *Rathaus,* walk behind the Perlachturm tower on Perlachberg, which becomes Barfüßerstr. and finally Jakoberstr., and turn right under the archway. The gates close at 10pm. The **Fuggerei Museum** documents this classic piece of urban planning, as well as the financial adventures of its patrons. *(Open Mar.-Oct. daily 9am-6pm. DM1, students and seniors DM0.70.)* Fugger was also responsible for building the **town palace,** Maximilianstr. 36-38, where the 1518 dispute between Martin Luther and Cardinal Cafetar ensured church schism. During that time, Luther stayed in the **St. Anna Kirche,** on Annastr. near Königsplatz, which served as the center of the Protestant revolutionary movement in Augsburg.

Augsburg's medieval past unfolds at the brightly frescoed **Guildhaus,** down Burgermeister-Fischer-Str., now part of the Marktplatz area. It lies down Bahnhofstr. from the train station along the edge of the park, past the streetcars. From the Guildhaus, a left down Maximilianstr. leads to the huge Renaissance **Rathaus.** *(Open daily 10am-6pm. Free.)* The brightly painted ceiling of the **Goldener Saal** depicts tradespeople, recalling the importance of commerce in Augsburg's history. *(DM3, children age 7-14 DM1, under 7 free.)* Down Hoher Weg to the left sits the **Hoher Dom,** the regional bishop's seat. *(Open M-Sa 6am-5pm; closed holidays.)* The cathedral, built in the 9th century, was renovated in the Gothic style in the 14th century and damaged in WWII. The chancel and high altar are intelligent examples of *Bauhaus*-inspired design, prevalent in German churches after the war. If you go to the left of the Perlachturm down Perlachberg and take a left onto Auf dem Rain, you'll arrive at the **Bertolt Brecht**

Haus, renovated in 1998, the 100th anniversary of Brecht's birth. *(Open May-Sept. Tu-Su 10am-5pm; Oct.-Apr. Tu-Su 10am-4pm. DM2.50, students and children DM1.50.)* It chronicles the life of one of the most influential 20th-century playwrights and poets through photographs, letters, and his poetry.

ROMANTISCHE STRAßE (ROMANTIC ROAD)

Between Würzburg and Füssen, in the Lechtal at the foothills of the Alps, expands a beautiful countryside of walled cities, castles, elaborate churches, and dense forests. In 1950, the German tourist industry christened these bucolic backwaters the **Romantische Straße,** and in recent years this area has become **the most heavily touristed region in Germany.** Deutsche Bahn's **Europabus** transports lots of families and elderly tourists daily from Frankfurt to Munich (Apr.-Oct., 12hr., change at Dinkelsbühl for Füssen) and back. Though this is the most popular way to travel the Romantische Straße, it is also one of the most inflexible—there is only one bus in each direction per day. Buses on the Frankfurt-Munich route leave from Frankfurt. Southbound and northbound buses leave daily at 8am and 9am respectively. Stops include (southbound 8am/northbound terminus 8:30pm), with stops in Würzburg (southbound 10am/northbound 6:45pm), Rothenburg (2:30pm/4:15pm), Dinkelsbühl (4:15pm/2pm), Nördlingen (4:55pm/12:15pm), Augsburg (6:20pm/10:30am), and Munich (7:50pm/9am). On the Dinkelsbühl-Füssen route, buses stop at Dinkelsbühl (southbound 4:15pm/northbound terminus 1:05pm), Augsburg (southbound 6pm/northbound 10:50am), Wieskirche (northbound only, 8:55am—with a 20min. stop for sightseeing), Hohenschwangau (Neuschwanstein Castle; 8:33pm/8:07am), and Füssen (8:40pm/8am)—this last bus does not stop in Munich. Check schedules with a tourist office before heading to the bus. The Europabus is also relatively expensive. (Frankfurt to Rothenburg DM59, to Dinkelsbühl DM71, to Munich DM116. Dinkelsbühl to Hohenschwangau or Füssen DM66, students and under 26 10% off, under 12 and over 60 50% off, under 4 free. Eurail or German Rail Pass holders ride free, but each traveling vagrant must pay a ridiculous one-time "registration" fee of DM7 in addition to a DM3 fee for the backpack for each daily departure.)

A more economical way to see the Romantische Straße for those without railpasses is to use the faster and much more frequent **trains,** which run to every town except Dinkelsbühl (take a tourist-free bus from Nördlingen or Dombühl). Those traveling the Romantische Straße by **car** may find themselves parking in large, specially built lots outside the old city walls of some towns, but will have easy access to many suburban budget hotels, *Privatzimmer,* and campgrounds that lie outside the reach of foot travelers. The Romantische Straße is an excellent opportunity for a leisurely **bike** journey, with campgrounds located merely 10 to 20km apart outside of almost every town. Tourist offices provide great cycling maps and information on campgrounds and bicycle shops located along the road. Some travelers reportedly hitch the route successfully; *Let's Go* does not recommend hitchhiking. For information or reservations call **Deutsche Touring** in Frankfurt, Am Römerhof 17 (tel. (069) 790 32 81; fax 790 32 19). For general information, contact the **Romantische Straße Arbeitsgemeinschaft,** Marktplatz, 91550 Dinkelsbühl (tel. (09851) 902 71; fax 902 79).

■ Rothenburg ob der Tauber

Rothenburg ob der Tauber is *the* Romantic Roadstop, touched by everyone—and we mean *everyone.* While Rothenburg is busy enjoying the same commercialized fate as its favorite December holiday, don't knock all the touristic pomp; this small town is probably your only chance to see a nearly intact medieval walled city in Bayern that doesn't contain a single modern building. That's right—not a single building in the entire town was built after the Middle Ages. At the end of the 19th century, locals blessed with kitschy foresight set up strict preservation laws in order to preserve their 16th-century town. However, in WWII, Rothenburg was devastated when 40% of the town was reduced to rubble by bombs. Amazingly, the center of the *Altstadt* endured and endured well. For historical charm and romantic enchantment, no other Romantic Road town comes close.

ORIENTATION AND PRACTICAL INFORMATION Trains run every hour from major cities to Steinach, where you can transfer for a quick trip to Rothenburg (15min.). Call 46 11 for **train information. Buses** also serve the route, sometimes in place of the train in the evening (see Europabus info, p. 550). The last bus leaves the train station for Steinach at 8:05pm. For a **taxi** call 20 00 or 72 27. Rent **bikes** at **Herrmann Kat's,** Galgengasse 33 (tel. 61 11; open daily 8am-7pm; half-day DM10, full day DM15), or at **Rad und Tat,** Bensenstr. 17 (tel. 879 84; DM20 per day; ID required; open daily 9am-6pm). Rothenburg's **tourist office,** Marktplatz 2 (tel. 404 92; fax 868 07; email info@rotherburg.de), supplies maps in English and books rooms (DM35-60), usually for free (DM2 during peak times). Walk left from the station, bear right on Ansbacher Str., and follow this street straight into the city to the Marktplatz (10-15min.). The tourist office is on your right, across the square. (Open May-Sept. M-F 9am-12:30pm and 1-6pm, Sa-Su 10am-3pm; Nov.-Apr. M-F 9am-12:30pm and 1-5pm, Sa 10am-1pm.) For a **24-hour room-finding service,** call 194 12. **Tours in German** depart from the steps of the *Rathaus* (90min.; Apr.-Oct. and Dec. daily 11am and 2pm; DM5). **English-language tours** meet daily at the *Rathaus* at 2pm (DM6). The "night watchman" leads a special tour with his candle-lit lantern and iron spear that is more entertaining than educating; it leaves from the town hall steps in the Marktplatz (English at 8pm; German at 9:30pm; DM6).

You can **exchange money** at the post office (DM6 per check, DM2 for a cash transaction). The **Wäscherei Then** (tel. 27 75) is a **laundromat** located at Johannitergasse 9. (Wash DM6.50, soap included. Dry DM3 per 25min. Open M-F 8am-6pm, Sa 8am-2pm.) The laundromat and Pension Then (see below) are owned by a father-son tandem; they *love* tourists. **Toppler-Apotheke,** Ansbacher Str. 15 (tel. 36 56), has a list in its window of opening times and addresses of all other **pharmacies** (open M-Tu and Th-F 8am-12:30pm and 1:30-6pm, W and Sa 8am-12:30pm). If you have **lost property,** contact *Fundamt*, Markpl. 1 (tel. 404 56). The main **post office** (tel. 941 50), 91541 Rothenburg, is at Bahnhofstr. 7 (open M-F 8:30am-noon and 2-5:30pm, Sa 8:30am-noon). In an **emergency,** contact the police (tel. 110). The **telephone code** is 09861.

ACCOMMODATIONS An incredible number of **private rooms** (DM20-45) not registered with the tourist office are available—they're marked by *"Zimmer frei"* signs. Just knock on the doors with the signs to inquire. Housed in medieval buildings, Rothenburg's two youth hostels share common management. Check in at the **Jugendherberge Rossmühle (HI),** on Mühlacker 1 (tel. 941 60; fax 94 16 20; email jhrothen@aol.com), at Rossmühleweg, a former horse-powered mill that shelters a modern set of carpeted rooms and a groovy staff. Amenities include ping-pong tables, a TV room where you can borrow movies, free storage lockers (DM5 deposit required), train schedules, and a weather board—this is what all hostels should be like. Follow the directions to the tourist office, take a left down Obere Schmiedgasse, and go straight until you see the *Jugendherberge* sign to the right. (DM22. Tasty breakfast included. DM9 dinner available. Sheets DM5.50. Reception 7am-midnight. Curfew midnight, but they'll give you an access code to the door.) The **Jugendherberge Spitalhof (HI)** exists as extra housing for Rossmühle, a mere stone's throw down the street (same reception, curfew, and hours).

Rothenburg has an unbelievable number of *Pensionen* for a town of its size, but most of them are expensive. For an exception, check out **Pension Raidel,** Wenggasse 3 (tel. 31 15), on the way to the hostel. Head down Obere Schmiedgasse and make a left on Wenggasse. Bright rooms and fluffy featherbeds, each one built and decorated by the owner, make this the most charming and authentic of the affordable *Pensionen* in the *Altstadt.* (Singles DM35, with bath DM69; doubles DM69, with shower

DM89. Breakfast included. Call ahead.) Included in the price of a room or apartment at **Pension Then,** Johannitergasse 8a (tel. 51 77; fax 860 14), in the proximity of the train station, is an insider's advice on the ins and outs of Rothenburg, an optional trip to the Wednesday night meeting of the local English conversation club, and a chance to go fishing on the Tauber with the owner, Willy Then. (Singles DM40; doubles DM70. Apartment with kitchen DM25 per person, 3-day minimum for 4-6 people.) From the station, turn left, then right on Ansbacher Str. and right on Johannitergasse.

FOOD With a cozy Christmas theme all year-round, it's not surprising that Rothenburg is famous for its delicious *Schneeballen* (snowballs): large balls of sweet dough dipped in chocolate, nuts, and powdered sugar, sometimes with a sweet center (often marzipan or amaretto). **Dillers,** Hofbronner-Gasse 16 or Hafengasse 4 (tel. 866 23), offers these doughy concoctions at industrially produced rates (DM2.40-5); you can also watch the bizarre snowball-making process there (open daily 10am-6pm). The **Roter Hahn,** Obere Schmiedgasse 21 (tel. 50 88) is the former home of the renowned wine-chugging Mayor Nusch whose tolerance for large doses of alcohol saved the town from destruction. This ancient restaurant caters to meat-lovers. (DM11-13; open daily 11:30am-10pm.) Those with a sweet tooth should try the *Apfelkuchen* (DM2.50) at the **Bäckerei-Café,** Galgengasse 6 (tel 33 59). The **Fränkisches Haus,** Golgengasse 13 (tel 34 39), offers regional food in a modern setting (DM10-17); they also proffer salads (DM7.50) and other vegetarian dishes (open M-F 8am-6pm, Sa 8:30am-6pm, Su 9am-6pm). **Pizzeria Roma,** Galgengasse 19 (tel. 45 40), serves hefty pasta dishes (DM8-13), pizzas (DM9-12), and fresh salads (DM4.50) long after the rest of town goes to bed (open daily 11:30am-midnight). Pick up fresh goods from vendors at the **Marktplatz** (open W and Sa 7am-noon). **Kapsch supermarket** is on the Rödergassen, inside the city wall as you enter the town (open M-F 8:30am-6:30pm, Sa 8am-1pm).

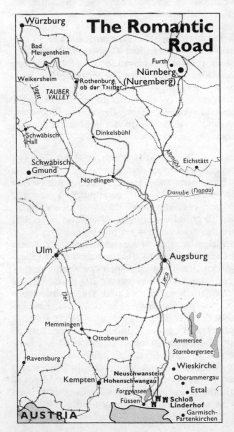

The Romantic Road

Würzburg
Bad Mergentheim
Weikersheim
Rothenburg ob der Tauber
TAUBER VALLEY
Tauber
Furth
Nürnberg (Nuremberg)
Schwäbisch Hall
Dinkelsbühl
Schwäbisch Gmünd
Nördlingen
Altmühl
Eichstätt
Danube (Donau)
Ulm
Iller
Augsburg
Lech
Memmingen
Ottobeuren
Ammersee
Starnbergersee
Ravensburg
Wieskirche
Neuschwanstein
Hohenschwangau
Kempten
Oberammergau
Forggensee
Ettal
Füssen
Schloß Linderhof
Garmisch-Partenkirchen
AUSTRIA

SIGHTS On the Marktplatz stands the Renaissance **Rathaus,** from whose 60m high tower you can scope out the town. *(Open daily 8am-6pm. Free. Tower open Apr.-Oct. daily 9:30am-12:30pm and 1-5pm; Nov.-Mar. M-F 9:30am-12:30pm, Sa-Su noon-3pm. DM1, children DM0.50.)* On this site in 1631, the conquering Catholic general Johann Tilly offered to spare the town from devastation if any local resident could chug a wine keg containing almost a gallon of wine. Mayor Georg Nusch successfully met the challenge, then passed out for several days. His saving **Meistertrunk** (master drink) is reenacted with great fanfare each year—live. The town clock acts out a *slooow* motion version of the episode over the Marktplatz. *(Hourly 11am-3pm and 8-10pm.)* Inside the courtyard behind the *Rathaus* are the **Historien-Gewölbe** (Historical Archways), which articulate the history of the Thirty Years War. *(Open May-Sept. daily 9:30am-5:30pm; Oct.-Nov. and Jan.-Apr. 10am-5pm; Dec. 1-4pm. DM3, students and disabled persons DM2, children DM1.)* Three gloomy stone cells lurk in the dungeon, where Mayor Heinrich Toppler and his son were once imprisoned by King Ruprecht. **Herrngasse,** the town's widest street, and **Schmiedgasse** are lined with old patrician homes. **Burggasse,** thought to be the oldest and darkest lane in town, was once affectionately referred to as "Höll" (hell) because it was partially built over by the Franciscan Monastery, secluding it from the rest of the city and adding to its dim and dusky image. **St. Jacob's Church,** Klostergasse 15, houses the Holy Blood Altar by Tilman Riemenschneider, a 5500-pipe organ, and 14th-century stained glass windows, that allow rivets of harlequin light into the church. *(Open Apr.-Oct. M-F 9am-5:30pm, Su 10:30am-5:30pm; Dec. noon-2pm and 4-5pm; closed Nov. and Jan.-Mar. DM2.50, students DM1.)* The **Reichsstadtmuseum,** Klosterhof 5 (tel. 404 58), housed in a former 13th-century Dominican convent, displays numerous rooms with contents preserved from the Middle Ages. *(Open Apr.-Oct. daily 9:30am-5:30pm; Nov.-Mar. 1-4pm. DM4, students DM3, children DM2.)* Adore the famous 12-panel painting of Christ's passion and the original wine *Krug* from the *Meistertrunk.*

The town's **Medieval Crime Museum,** Burggasse 3 (tel. 53 59), is definitely worth the entrance fee for anyone who can stomach the thought of iron-maiden justice. *(Open Apr.-Oct. daily 9:30am-6pm; Nov. and Jan.-Mar. 2-4pm; Dec. 10am-4pm. DM5, students DM4, children DM3.)* Take a picture of yourself in the stocks outside before heading into the dim, creepy basement for the **torture exhibits.** *Feel* the pain. The large rooms upstairs continue the fun, with exhibits on "eye for an eye" jurisprudence and the special punishments once reserved for bad musicians, dishonest bakers, and frivolous gossips. All displays are labeled in English.

Camp holds brazen sway at Käthe Wohlfahrt's **Christkindlmarkt** (Christ Child Market), Herrngasse 2, and the more extensive **Weihnachtsdorf** (Christmas Village), Herrngasse 1 (tel. 40-90). They're a must-see even if you *aren't* looking for a 4m-long nutcracker or a pea-sized porcupine. As your eyes glaze over like *Schneeballen,* head to the second floor of the *Weihnachtsdorf* for damaged items at 20-50% off; the cash registers never stop jingling, as more nutcrackers get sold than there are nuts on the planet to crack. *(Stores open M-F 9am-6pm, Sa 10am-4pm; Easter-Dec. also Su 10am-6pm.)* For some fresh air and impressive views of the *Altstadt,* skip along the 2.5km navigable city wall from Klingen Bastion to the Kobolzeller gate.

ENTERTAINMENT The **Figurentheater,** Am Burgtor at Herrngasse 38 (tel. 73 54 or 33 33), is Rothenburg's fantastically nonsensical puppet theater—better than the Von Trapp kid show. The guest book proudly displays Pablo Picasso's simple but elegant word of applause, *"Merveilleux."* (Shows June-Sept. M-Sa at 3 and 9pm; Oct.-Nov. and Apr.-May M-Sa at 3pm and 8:30pm. 90min. evening shows DM15, students DM10. 45min. matinees DM10, students DM8.) To go **fishing** in the Tauber River, give Herr Schmidt (the town tour guide and grave digger) a jingle at tel. 58 39.

Rothenburg prides itself on a tourist-friendly array of annual festivals. On Easter Sunday, the famed **Hans-Sachs-Spiele** (Hans Sachs play) and the **Schäfertanz** (Shepherd's Dance) are performed on the Marktplatz. The two displays celebrate, respectively, the shoemaker-cum-*Meistersinger* Hans Sachs, who wrote 208 plays, and the establishment of Shepherd's Day to honor the Shepherd's Guild. The historic **Meistertrunk** is re-enacted almost constantly during Easter weekend. The **Reichsstadt-Festtage** (City Festival) is held in the second week of September (Sept. 10-12 in 1999) with marches and festivals, as cattle traders, knights, and mutinous peasants all gather. Tickets for all events can be purchased at the *Reisebüro* (DM12-25). At Christmas, Rothenburg becomes a giant gingerbread house filled with mulled wine, Franconian *Bratwürst,* organ and brass band concerts, and nightly torchlight processions through the snow. A ski jump has been incorporated as part of the re-enactment of the *Meistertrunk.* But remember, the Rothenburgers are professionals who've been drinking wine and tumbling into snowbanks for centuries; do not try this at home.

■ Dinkelsbühl

Forty kilometers south of Rothenburg, the historical town of Dinkelsbühl boasts an impressive bevy of medieval half-timbered houses, a climbable 16th-century church-tower, and a navigable town wall with gateways, towers, and moats. Sound familiar? It is, though locals claim their town's superiority lies with Dinkelsbühl's authenticity; it houses the largest collection of original, unrestored structures on the Romantische Straße (repainting, of course, doesn't count). The Gothic **St. Georgskirche,** which dominates the Weinmarkt at the center of town, sprouts a Romanesque tower and striking fan vaulting. A tale for tourists explains why the houses along **Nördlinger-straße** are oddly-shaped—medieval superstition held that homes with right angles housed demons. Every summer the Dinkelsbühlers faithfully celebrate the salvation of their besieged town during the Thirty Years War with the **Kinderzeche Festival** (children's weeping festival; July 16-25 in 1999). The town tots' tears and the sweet voice of Lore, the beauteous daughter of the town sentry, reputedly persuaded the invading field commander of Swedish King Gustavus Adolphus II to spare Dinkels-bühl. A recreation of the event accompanies parades, fireworks, dances, and, of course, crying kids—a strangely satisfying experience for hosteling travelers. (DM4 for the required "festival badge"; seats at the various performances DM3-16.) The **Park Ring** around the *Altstadt* separates the old and new parts of town. New to the old town is the spiffy **3-Dimensional Museum** (tel. 63 36), housed in the Nördlinger Tor of the town wall (entrance through the gate and to the left). The only such museum in the world, it encompasses all the different ways (since the Middle Ages) that people have represented thick stuff in thin ways. (Open Apr.-Oct. daily 10am-6pm; Nov.-Mar. Sa-Su 11am-4pm. DM10, DM9 with tourist office coupon.)

The town's defunct **train station** now serves as a **bus station.** When traveling by bus to and from Dinkelsbühl, plan ahead. Regional buses go to Rothenburg (9 per day, 1-3 per day on weekends; transfer buses at Dombühl or Feuchtwangen), and to Nördlingen (7 per day, 4-5 per day on weekends). Schedules are posted at the tourist office and at the station. If you plan poorly, you might get stuck with the crowded and expensive **Europabus,** which takes tourists along the Romantische Straße (see p. 543). The **tourist office** (tel. 902 40; fax 902 79), on the Marktplatz, finds rooms for a DM3 fee and distributes free maps and schedules to the *Kinderzeche* festival. The office also **rents bikes** (DM7 per day, DM30 per week), and sells cycling and hiking maps (DM4.50). To get there, walk right from the *Bahnhof* and take the first left. Follow the footpath over tow bridges and into the city, then take the first right onto Nördlinger Str., which empties into the Marktplatz; the tourist office is in the rust-colored building with a bell tower on your right. (Open Apr.-Oct. M-F 9am-noon and 2-6pm, Sa 10am-1pm and 2-4pm, Su 10am-1pm; Nov.-Mar. M-F 9am noon and 2-5pm, Sa 10am-1pm.) **St. Paul's Apotheke,** Nördlinger Str. 7 (tel. 34 35), is the most convenient **pharmacy** (open M-F 8am-12:30pm and 2-6pm, Sa 8am-noon). For the **police,** call 888. The **post office,** 91550 Dinkelsbühl, is 100m to the right of the station (open M-F 9am-5pm, Sa 9am-noon). The **telephone code** is 09851.

Built in 1508 as a grain store, the **Jugendherberge (HI),** Koppengasse 10 (tel. 95 09; fax 48 74), is a huge, half-timbered house with wide wooden hallways furnished with bouncy lovechairs and creaking windows overlooking tiny cobblestone alleyways (great for people watching in the early morning). From the tourist office, head right up Nördlinger Str., and take a right onto Bahnhofstr. after passing the rust-colored *Rathaus.* At the first bus stop swing left onto Koppengasse; it's a large stucco building a few houses before the town wall on the right. (DM18. Breakfast included. Sheets DM5.50. Reception 5-10pm. Open Mar.-Oct.) **Pension Gerda,** Nestleinsberg-gasse 22 (tel. 18 60; fax 18 25), is a 10-minute walk away from the Marktplatz. (Doubles with bath DM35 per person; breakfast included.) Following the directions to the tourist office, take a left onto Turmgasse and then a right onto Nestleinberggasse by the city wall; it is set back off the road on the left side. A friendlier option closer to the hustle and bustle of the *Markt,* **Gasthof Zur Sonne,** Weinmarkt 11 (tel. 576 70; fax 75 48), has airy rooms with stunning pastel color themes to which you can stumble

after visiting their *Biergarten*. (Singles DM45-65; doubles DM75; triples DM102-120. Breakfast included. No hallway showers for those staying in rooms without showers.) Over the river, north of the city on Dürrwangerstr., is the **DCC Campingpark Romantische Straße** (tel. 78 17; DM6.50 per person, DM15 per tent and car).
Budget food is hard to find in touristy Dinkelsbühl. Head to **Selvi Döner**, Nördlinger Str. 8 (tel. 55 36 15), for burgers and *Würste* (DM3.50-8; open M-F 10am-midnight, Su 11am-1pm). **Café Rossini**, Nördlinger Str. 17 (tel. 73 70), is a favorite of locals and tourists alike, serving beer (DM3.40), elaborate ice cream concoctions (DM8-10), and portions of local cuisine (DM10-16; open M-Sa 9am-midnight, Su 1pm-midnight). **Tengelmann**, Nordlinger Str. 13 (tel. 35 09), conveniently fulfills **supermarket** needs (open M-F 8am-7pm, Sa 8am-2pm).

■ Nördlingen im Ries

About 15 million years ago, a stone meteorite, nearly one kilometer in diameter with an internal energy equivalent to about 250,000 Hiroshima bombs, crashed through the Earth's crust, creating an enormous crater upon which the present-day town of Nördlingen is perched. The medieval wall surrounding this perfectly circular town was built entirely from "Rieser Moonstones"—stones which formed as a result of the meteorite impact and which are very similar in consistency to rocks found on the moon. The only town in Germany where the original town walls are complete and can be navigated in their entirety, Nördlingen boasts a 90m Gothic bell tower nick-named "**Daniel**," from whose lofty height the town watchman has called down to the people below "So G'sell so!" every evening for the last 500 years. Those who climb up the 350 steps to the Keeper's chambers at the top of the "Daniel" are rewarded with a hawk's eye view of the circular city below. (Tower open daily Apr.-Oct. 9am-8pm; Nov.-Mar. 9am-5:30pm. DM2.50, children 6-16 years old DM1.50, under 6 free.) Elegant Gothic columns arch over the wide hall of **St. George**, dwarfing the people in the pews below (church open M-F 9am-noon and 2-5pm, Sa-Su 2-5pm). Explore the history of a medieval town and the construction of a town wall in Nördlingen's **Stadtmauermuseum**, in Löpsinger Gate. (Open daily 10am-4:30pm. DM2, children age 6-16, seniors, and disabled persons DM1, children under 6 free.)

Nördlingen can be reached by **train** from Augsburg (1hr., change at Donauwörth, 1 per hr., DM19.40), Nürnberg (1¾hr., change at Donauwörth, 8 per day), or Stuttgart (2hr., change at Aalen, 1 per hr.). The train station is open Monday 5:30-11:40am and 1-5:50pm, Tuesday through Friday 6:30-11:40am and 1-5:50pm, and Sunday 1:30-6:15pm. Buses also run from the Dinkelsbühl bus station to Nördlingen (45min., 8 per day, DM7.90). The **Europabus** (see p. 543) also stops in Nördlingen (departs from the *Rathaus* southbound 4:55pm, northbound 12:15pm). The **tourist office** (tel. 43 80 or 841 16; fax 841 13) distributes maps and brochures in English (DM0.50) and sells English guides to the *Altstadt* (DM7.80; open M-Th 9am-6pm, F 9am-4:30pm, Sa 9:30am-12:30pm). One-hour **German tours** of the town meet daily at the *Rathaus* (2pm; DM4, children under 12 free). **Einhorn Apotheke**, Polizeigasse 7, has a list of 24-hour pharmacies posted in the window (open M-F 8am-6pm, Sa 8:30am-noon). The **post office**, 86720 Nördlingen, to the right of the train station as you exit, exchanges traveler's checks (DM6 per check; open M-F 8:30am-5pm, Sa 9am-noon). The **telephone code** is 09081.

Nördlingen's **Jugendherberge**, Kaiserwiese 1 (tel. 841 09), a small, friendly hostel with tidy rooms, is just outside the city walls on the north side of town, 1.5km from the train station. (DM18. Reception 8-10am and 4-6pm. No new arrivals after 6pm.) **Drei Mohren Gasthof**, Reimlingerstr. 18 (tel. 31 13; fax 287 59), is located just inside the town wall. From the *Bahnhof*, walk left on Bgm.-Reiger-Str. and then take a right onto O.-Mayer-Str. which will curve to the left after one block. Head right on Romantische Str. which turns into Reimlingerstr. once you enter the stone gate. (Rooms DM35 per person.) **Gasthof Walfisch**, Hallgasse 15 (tel. 31 07), is located in the center of town near the Markplatz. From St. George Church's exit, head left onto Windgasse and then take a left on Hallgasse. (Singles DM30, with bath DM50; doubles DM60, with bath DM100.)

Nördlingen has an unbelievable number of small restaurants and street cafes located in romantic alleyways and quirky nooks of the city, but unfortunately the vast majority are expensive. An exception is the sprightly **Ciao Ciao Pizza Ristorante,** Luckengasse 15, which serves pizza (DM10-12) and pasta dishes (DM11-14) as well as super-cheap *Nördlinger Bier* (DM3.80) in a merry setting. (Open Tu-Sa 6pm-midnight, Su 5-10pm.) Treat yourself to a deluxe meal at the elegant **Hotel Sonne,** Markpl. 3 (tel. 50 67), next to the *Rathaus.* On a sunny day, refined and genteel diners sit under the shady street umbrellas, munching on tasteful salads (DM6.50) or slurping bowls of creamy soup (DM4.80-6). Daily specials run DM10.80-15.50. (Open daily 9am-1am.) If your grocery basket is empty, head to **Lidl,** Rübenmarkt 1, by the *Rathaus* (open M-F 8am-6pm, Sa 8am-1pm).

■ Würzburg

Surrounded by vineyard slopes and bisected by the Main River, Würzburg is the bustling center of the Franconian wine region and home to one of Germany's greatest palaces, the magnificent Baroque "Residenz." The imposing 13th-century Marienburg Fortress across the river provides a formidable backdrop for the palace, all but overshadowing it. Although the city has its origins as a religious center, Würzburg is now largely a *Uni*-town. More than 20,000 students attend the renowned Julius-Maximilans University, which numbers six Nobel Prize winners among its faculty. It was here that Wilhelm Conrad Röntgen discovered X-rays and their medical applications in 1895, for which he was awarded the first Nobel Prize six years later. Students and street performers contribute to the dynamic, artsy spirit of the pedestrian zone, which runs from the ornate Alte Marienbrücke bridge through the center of the city. Bicyclists, streetcars and skateboarders battle it out on these wide car-free zones, paved with pigeon feathers and lined with cafes, museums, and stunning Gothic cathedrals. Wartime bombing destroyed much of the town's 18th-century magnificence— all that remained intact in 1945 was the spire of Marienkapelle, pointing like an admonishing finger to heaven—but its older giants remain unchanged, making Würzburg a scenic portal for Germany's great tourist trail, the Romantische Straße.

ORIENTATION AND PRACTICAL INFORMATION

With its three separate tourist information offices (one situated right outside the train station), Würzburg is a traveler's dream come true. To get to the city's center at the *Markt,* follow Kaiserstr. straight ahead from the station, then take a right on Julius-promenade, and hang a left onto Schönbornstr., the main pedestrian and streetcar road; the *Markt* is a few blocks down and to your right. The Main River separates the rest of the city from the green, steep hills on which the fortress stands.

Tourist Office: Main Office, in the **Palais am Congress Centrum** (tel. 373 35), near the Friedensbrücke, where Röntgenring intersects the Main. Open M-Th 8:30am-5pm, F 8:30am-noon. Another branch in front of the **train station** (tel. 374 36) provides a packet with a free map and a hotel list for DM0.50; they also find rooms for DM5. Open M-Sa 10am-6pm. If it's past hours, grab a hotel list from the machine outside (DM0.50) or call the **24hr. accommodations hotline** at 194 14. A 3rd office is located in the **Haus zum Falken** (tel. 373 98), an ornamental yellow building on the Marktplatz. Excellent hiking maps (DM11.80), cycling maps of the Main River region (DM19.80), and city guide books in English (DM7.90) are sold here. Open M-F 10am-6pm, Sa 10am-2pm; Apr.-Oct. also Su 10am-2pm. 2hr. English-language tours around the city given mid-Apr. to Oct., Tu-Su at 11am. Tour fees (DM13, students DM10) includes entrance to the Residenz; meet at the Haus zum Falken tourist office. A German-language tour without the Residenz (1½hr.) is given daily at 10:30am (Apr.-Oct. DM9, students DM7). Free **Rathaus tours** (1½hr.) in German are given every Saturday at 10am and 4:30pm (Nov.-Dec. and Feb.-April 10am only). 2hr. **bus tours** in German depart from the Busbahnhof (M-Sa 2pm, Su 10:30am; DM14, students DM12).

Trains: At the *Bahnhof* (tel. 344 25). To: Rothenburg (1hr., 13 per day, change at Steinach, DM16.20); Nürnberg (1-1½hr., 2 per hr., DM 8); Frankfurt (1½-2hr., 1 per hr., DM37); Munich (2½hr., 1 per hr., DM75); Hamburg (3½hr., 1 per hr.).

Buses: Europabuses trace the Romantische Straße to Rothenburg (DM27) and Munich (DM84) daily at 10am, departing from bus platform #13 to the right of the station. Eurail and German Rail Passes valid (not the BahnCard). Students and youth under 26 get 10% off. The return bus to Frankfurt stops at Würzburg daily at 6:45pm. Reservations can be made 3 days in advance with the **Deutsche Touring Büro,** Am Römerhof 17 (tel. (069) 790 32 81; fax (069) 790 32 19).

Public Transportation: For info, call 36 13 52. **Streetcars** are the fastest and most convenient way around, but large sections are not covered. The **bus** network is comprehensive, though most routes do not run nights and weekends. Ask for **night bus** schedules at the WSB kiosk in front of the train station. Single fare DM2.30, 24hr. ticket covering zone K, zone A, and zone 1 (which is the city center) DM7.

Ferries: Schifffstouristik Kurth & Schiebe (tel. 46 29 82; dock kiosk tel. 585 73) and **Veitshöchheimer Personenschiffahrt GMBH** (tel. 915 53; dock kiosk tel. 556 33) depart from the Alter Kranen wharf near the Congress Centrum to the Veitschöchheim Castle (40min., DM8, round-trip DM13).

Bike Rental: Fahrrad Station, Bahnhofpl. 4 (tel. 574 45). DM17-20 per day, DM14-16 if you've traveled to Würzburg by train. When exiting the station turn left around the corner. Open Tu-F 9:30am-6:30pm, Sa 9:30am-1:30pm.

Mitfahrzentrale: Kiosk to the left of the station's exit (tel. 194 48 or 140 85). Ride shares to Frankfurt (DM15), Stuttgart (DM18), Munich (DM30), Berlin (DM46), and a sea of other cities. Open M-F 10am-6pm, Sa 10am-1pm, Su 11am-1pm.

Bookstore: Buchladen Neuer Weg, Sanderstr. 23/25 (tel. 355 90 18). Has a small but adequate selection of novels. Open M-F 9am-8pm, Sa 9am-4pm.

Pharmacy: Engel-Apotheke, Marktplatz 36 (tel. 32 13 40), lists night pharmacies on the door. Open M-F 8:30am-6pm, Sa 8:30am-1pm.

Emergency: Medical Aid, tel. 192 22. **Police,** tel. 110. **Fire,** tel. 112.

Post Office: Bahnhofpl. 2, 97070 Würzburg (tel. 330). Exchange money (DM2 fee) and cash traveler's checks (DM6 fee per check). Open M-F 6am-7pm, Sa 8am-1pm.

Telephone Code: 0931.

ACCOMMODATIONS AND CAMPING

The one drawback to this otherwise excellent city is the lack of budget accommodations. Finding single rooms for under DM45 is harder than finding Waldo. Würzburg's least expensive beds are around the train station, near Kaiserstr. and Bahnhofstr.

⊛**Jugendgästehaus (HI),** Bukarderstr. 44 (tel. 425 90; fax 41 68 62), near St. Burkard's Basilica, across the river from downtown. Streetcar #3 (direction: "Heidingsfeld") or 5 (direction: "Heuchelhof") to "Löwenbrücke," then backtrack; go down the stairs marked by the "Jugendherberge/Kappele" sign, turn right, walk all the way past 2 streets and a Sparkasse on the left, go through the tunnel, and it's immediately on your left. A modern, enormous villa, with views of the fortress and the Main River from the carpeted, spacious rooms. DM29. Full breakfast and sheets included. Reception 8am-10pm. Check-in 2-5:15pm and 6:30-10pm. Curfew 1am.

Pension Spehnkuch, Röntgenring 7 (tel. 547 52; fax 547 60), to the right of the *Bahnhof* down Röntgenringstr. Newly redone by the laid-back owner, rooms are very white and very bright. Singles DM50; doubles DM90. Breakfast included.

Pension Siegel, Reisgrubengasse 7 (tel. 529 41), a block down Kaiserstr. from the train station, on your left. Amateur murals of tropical isles lead up cramped stairs to small but comfortable and clean rooms. Nice singles DM46; doubles DM89. Breakfast included. Reception open before 2pm and 5-10:30pm. Call ahead.

Gasthof Goldener Hahn, Marktgasse 7 (tel. 519 41; fax 519 61), in a little golden building with green-checkered stained glass windows directly off the *Markt.* Clean rooms have phones and TVs. Singles DM40-50, with bath DM80; doubles with bath DM140. Hall shower DM3.

Camping Kanu-Club, Mergentheimerstr. 13b (tel. 725 36). Streetcar #3 or 5 (direction: "Heidingsfeld") to "Judenbühlweg." Right on the river. DM4 per person; DM3 per tent. Showers DM1.50. Reception noon-10pm.

FOOD AND ENTERTAINMENT

To sample some of the Würzburg region's distinctive wines, try **Haus des Franken-weins Fränkischer Weinverband,** Krankenkai 1 (tel. 120 93). The city's sweeter answer to Munich's *Oktoberfest,* the lively **Kiliani Festival,** is held during the first two weeks in July. The huge biannual **Wine Festival** takes place in early June and late September to early October. Adventurous souls should snoop around the bohemian back alleys of the city's south side, especially on Sandestr., the heart of the university sub-culture, where idiosyncratic people and curious food abound in smoky dens and grottoes. There is a **farmer's market** on the *Markt* (open Tu 6am-6pm, W 6am-4pm, F 6am-6pm, Sa 6am-2pm). For inexpensive foodstuffs, hit **Kapsch supermarket,** at the end of Kaiserstr. away from the station (open M-F 8:30-8pm, Sa 8am-4pm).

University Mensa, in the *Studentenhaus* on Am Exerzierplatz, at Münzstr.; through the doors to your left. Assembly-line eating. Würzburg University ID technically required for discounts, but even without one, it's cheap. Buy meal tickets at the machines outside the dining room. Meals run DM2.25 (with ID) to DM4.50 (without ID). Open mid-Oct. to mid-July M-F 11am-1:30pm, Sa 11:30am-1:30pm; evening meals M-Th 5:30-7:30pm; Feb.-Mar. closed Sa. Look for job offers, roommates, and cultural happenings.

Kult, Landwehrstr. 10 (tel. 531 43), right off Sanderstr., is one of the more visible bar-cafe-*Kneipen* for hip local alternatives. Mustard yellow interior, comfortable bar stools, Guns 'N Roses-look-alike waiters. Falafel sandwich with fresh "salad of the season" DM9.50. Mellow, but crowded at night. Open M-F 9am-1am (if too hot outside, open 9am-2pm and 6pm-1am), Sa 6pm-1am, Su 11am-1am.

Uni Café, Neubaustr. 2 (tel. 156 72), on the corner of Sanderstr. Relaxed student atmosphere and outdoor sidewalk seating with a great view of the Marienburg Fortress. Cakes, salads, breakfasts (DM3.50-9.50). Open M-Sa 8am-1am, Su 9am-1pm.

Cafehaus Brückenbäck, An der Alten Mainbrücke (tel. 41 45 45). From the hostel, turn left on Saalgasse and walk 2 blocks. Views abound: of the Marienburg, of the Main, and of the rabble in the pedestrian zone. Tasty *Apfelstrudel* (DM3.50), salads (DM6-13), and tons of liquid refreshments. Open M-F 8am-1am, Sa-Su 8:30am-1am.

La Clochard, Neubaustr. 20 (tel. 129 07). Crepes (DM5-8), sandwiches (DM7-11), and vegetarian dishes like *Jogurt-Kartoffeln* (potatoes topped with yogurt, cucumbers, and tomatoes, DM10.90) by a cozy corner fireplace. Old-World decor clashes with alternative music in this student hangout. Come by in the late afternoon to gawk at a throng of contented, caffeinated citizens enjoying "Happy Coffee-Crepe-Hour" (daily 3-5pm; 1 mug of coffee and a crepe for DM5.90).

Till Eulenspiegel, Sanderstr. 1a (tel. 134 73). Ivy-covered building with a beer garden out back. Funky rough wooden booths subverting the dominant layout and dimly lit with green candles. Beer and cocktails (DM3.40 and up). Entrees served M-Th until 9:30pm, F-Sa until 10:30pm (DM4-16). Open daily 6pm-1am.

Pepper La Pub, Bahnhofstr. 22, down and left as you exit the station. "House of 150 beers"—from the Czech Republic, Russia, Nigeria, Tahiti, and more. Also serves plain ol' Guinness on tap (DM3.20), sandwiches, soups, and pastas (DM6-14). Correctly match 6 mystery beers with their labels on Mondays at 6pm, and you can get smashed without paying a single *Pfennig*—test your prowess. Fridays **Karaoke** and "American Specials." Open M-Sa 11am-1am, Su 2pm-1am.

SIGHTS

Marienburg Fortress, the striking symbol of the city, keeps its vigil high on a hillside over the Main. The footpath to the fortress starts a short distance from the **Alte Main-brücke,** which is more than 500 years old and lined with statues of saints. German paintings, furniture, and *objets d'art* cluster in the **Fürstenbau Museum** (tel. 438 38). *(Open Tu-Su 9am-12:30pm and 1-5pm; Oct.-Mar. Tu-Su 10am-12:30pm and 1-4pm. DM4, students DM3, under 15 free if accompanied by adult.)* The fortress also houses the **Mainfränkisches Museum** (tel. 430 16), which features an extensive collection of works by Tiepolo and statues by Tilman Riemenschneider, the **Master of Würzburg.** *(Open Tu-Su 10am-5pm; Nov.-Mar. Tu-Su 10am-4pm. DM3.50, students DM2; pass to both museums*

DM6.) A genius of Gothic styling, Riemenschneider sided with the peasants in their 16th-century revolts against Luther and the powers-that-were. When the insurrection was suppressed, the sculptor's fingers were broken as punishment, and he could never work again. Masochists can make the climb to the fortress in under 30 minutes. Or take bus #9 from the "Spitäle" bus stop at the western end of the bridge (May to mid-Oct. every 30min. 9:43am-5:43pm, DM2). Weekend **tours** of the fortress depart from the Rundkirchekasse in the Fürsterbar. *(Sa-Su hourly 10-11am and 1-4pm.)*

In 1168, 12 years after he married in Würzburg, Friedrich Barbarossa raised the local bishop to the rank of "Prince." The **Residenz** palace (tel. 355 17 12), Neumann's masterpiece, was the base camp for Würzburg's prince-bishops during the Enlightenment. *(Open Tu-Su 9am-5pm; Nov.-March Tu-Su 10am-4pm. DM7, students and seniors DM4. Last admission 30min. before closing.)* It stands over the sweeping Residenzplatz, a 15-minute walk down Kaiserstr. and Theaterstr. from the station. The vibrant ceiling fresco by Johannes Zick in the first-floor garden room has never been restored; in fact, his use of extravagant colors got Zick fired. The Italian painter Giovanni Tiepolo was hired to finish the job in a more sedate style. His ceiling fresco in the grand staircase is the largest in the world, and certainly among the most ostentatious. Housed in the Residenz is the **Martin von Wagner Museum,** proudly displaying a collection of Greek and European painterly masterpieces. *(Open Tu-Sa 9:30am-12:30pm and 2-5pm, Su 9:30am-12:30pm. Free. Wheelchair accessible.)* The **Residenzhofkirche** is astounding— the gilded moldings and pink marble make this little church the apex of Baroque fantasy. *(Open Tu-Su 9am-noon and 1-5pm; Nov.-Mar. Tu-Su 10am-noon and 1-4pm. Free.)*

Behind the *Residenz* complex is the **Hofgarten,** a studiously laid-out park with meticulously manicured cone-shaped evergreens and a vast maze of thick bushes perfect for a thrilling game of hide-and-seek. *(Open dawn-dusk.)* In front of the *Residenz* down Hofstr. stands the 900-year-old **Dom of St. Killian,** Domstr. (tel. 536 91). *(Open daily 8am-7pm. Tours Apr.-Oct. M-Sa at noon, Su at 12:30pm. DM4, children DM2.)* It was rebuilt in the mid-1960s after being obliterated in 1945. Tilman Riemenschneider (see above) is responsible for the Gothic highlights of this large Romanesque cathedral.

■ Nürnberg (Nuremberg)

Although most of Nürnberg's historical landmarks were reconstructed after WWII and today few visible scars remain, the somber ghost of a disturbing past still haunts the streets of this vast city. Nürnberg played host to the massive Nazi party rallies held between 1933 and 1938, and lent its name to the 1935 Racial Purity Laws. Because of Nürnberg's close ties to Nazi power, the Allies chose this city as the site for the war-crimes tribunals. From the 14th until the 16th century, Nürnberg was a "free city," answering to no one lower than the emperor. Nürnberg's happy days came to an end as trade-routes shifted westward following the discovery of the Americas; furthermore, the Thirty Years War destroyed large parts of the city. As Hitler's power grew, money started rolling in with the Nazis' armament industry. WWII took its toll, though, and 90% of the city was reduced to rubble in 1945. Roughly half of that damage was a result of the bombings of January 2.

Today, Nürnberg, the second largest city in Bayern, jives with a steady German beat. Best known for its toy fair and Christmas market, its sausages and gingerbread, and its association with artists and former resident Albrecht Dürer, the city persists in both the historical and contemporary consciousness of the German landscape.

ORIENTATION AND PRACTICAL INFORMATION

The old city wall neatly circumscribes Nürnberg's thriving central district. From the train station, the main shopping district is across the street on Königstr. **Lorenzerplatz** and the **Hauptmarkt** lie just beyond the shopping district in the heart of the city. Much of the *Altstadt* lies within a pedestrian zone. The **Burg** perches on a hill, overlooking the town from the northernmost part of the *Altstadt.*

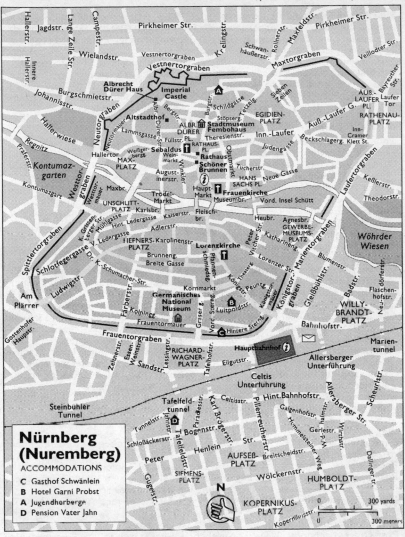

Nürnberg (Nuremberg)
ACCOMMODATIONS
C Gasthof Schwänlein
B Hotel Garni Probst
A Jugendherberge
D Pension Vater Jahn

BAYERN

Transportation

Flights: Flughafenstr, 100 (tel. 937 00), located 7km north of the city. **City-Airport-Express** (route 20) runs shuttles from the Herrnhütte underground station (20min., every 20-30min. 5:30am-11:30pm, DM6). To get there from the *Hauptbahnhof,* take U-Bahn #2.

Trains: Hauptbahnhof, Bahnhofpl. 9 (tel. 194 19). To Munich (1½-2hr., 2-3 per hr., DM53), Berlin (5½-6hr., every 1-2hr., DM132), Regensburg (1hr., 1-2 per hr., DM27), Würzburg (1hr., 2-3 per hr., DM28). A computer outside the *Reisezentrum* helps decipher the pesky details.

Public Transportation: Choose from U-Bahn, streetcars, buses, regional trains (known as *R-Bahn*), and S-Bahn. Single-ride tickets within the city DM3.30 (1½hr. with transfers). *Kurzstrecke* (short distance) DM2.50. 10 *Streifenkarte* (multi-use cards) DM12.90. Day or weekend card DM7.80. Maps at the tourist office.

Taxi: tel. 194 10.

Bike Rental: Fahrradkiste, Knauerstr. 9 (tel. 287 90 64), outside the southwest corner of the walled *Altstadt.* Basic wheels DM9 per day (DM200 deposit required). Mountain bikes DM15 per day (DM400 deposit). Foreign currency accepted as deposit. Open M-F 10am-7pm, Sa 10am-2pm.

Mitfahrzentrale: Strauchstr. 1 (tel. 194 44). Open M-F 9am-6pm, Sa 10am-1pm.

Hitchhiking: *Let's Go* does not recommend hitchhiking as a safe means of transportation. Hitchers headed to Munich and Austria: U-Bahn #1 or 11 to "Bauernfeindstr.," then bus #59 to "Am Zollhaus" and the *Autobahn* interchange. To Würzburg and Frankfurt: U-Bahn #1 to "Stadtgrenze" and walk to the A-3 interchange.

Tourist, Financial, and Local Services

Tourist Offices: Verkehrsverein (tel. 233 60; fax 233 61 611; http://www.nuernberg.de), is in the central hall of the *Hauptbahnhof.* Mailing address: Congress und Tourismus Zentrale, Frauentorgraben 3, 90443 Nürnberg. Free English-language city maps, brochures, and schedules of events, and finds rooms for a DM5 fee. Open M-Sa 9am-7pm. The **branch office** lies on the northern side of the Hauptmarkt. Open M-Sa 9am-6pm, Su 10am-1 and 2-4pm; Oct.-Apr. M-Sa 9am-6pm.

Tours: 2-5hr. English tours of the city depart from the Hauptmarkt tourist office May-Oct. and during *Christmasmarkt* daily at 2pm (DM12 plus castle admission price; children under 14 free if accompanied by an adult).

Budget Travel: abr Reisebüro, across from the tourist office in the train station (tel. 201 00), deciphers timetables. Open M-F 9am-6:30pm, Sa 10am-1pm.

Currency Exchange: The **AmEx** office is the cheapest option for those with or without The Card. If closed, head to the **Reisebank** (tel. 22 67 78) across from the tourist office in the train station. Exchange rates are decent; commission DM5 if exchanging less than DM100, commission 1% or DM7.50, whichever is higher, if exchanging more than DM100. Open M-Sa 7:45am-7:45pm, Su 9:15am-12:30pm and 1:30-5:15pm. Another good bet is the **post office** (DM2 for cash; DM6 per traveler's check). Beware the often absurd fees and rates at *Wechsel* stands.

American Express: Adlerstr. 2 (tel. 23 23 97), off Königstr., near Lorenzerplatz. Great rates and no service charges for changing cash and traveler's checks. All AmEx services for cardholders or those possessing traveler's checks. Open M-F 9:30am-5:30pm (cashier closed noon-2pm), Sa 9:30am-12:30pm.

Laundromat: SB Waschsalon, Spitzenbergstr. 2, near the University Mensa. Wash off the beer stains for DM6; suds run DM1. Open daily 6am-11pm.

Emergency and Communications

Emergency: tel. 110 or 192 22. **Police,** Jakobspl. 5, Nürnberg Mitte 1. **Fire** and **Ambulance,** tel. 112.

Rape Crisis: tel. 28 44 00. Counseling M 10am-noon, Tu 7-8pm, Th 4-6pm.

Pharmacy: City Apotheke, Königstr. 29. Open M-F 8:30am-6:30pm, Sa 9am-4pm. Check the notices in *Nürnberger Zeitung* for 24hr. pharmacies.

Hospital: Städtisches Klinikum, Flurstr. 17 (tel. 39 80). **Medical Assistance,** tel. 53 32 11 or 53 37 71.

Internet Access: In **Internetcafé Falkens Maze** (see **Food,** p. 555).

Post Office: Bahnhofpl. 1, 90402 Nürnberg. Cashes traveler's checks, **exchanges moolah,** and holds mail. Open M-F 8am-7pm, Sa 9am-2pm, Su 11am-2pm.

Telephone Code: 0911.

ACCOMMODATIONS AND CAMPING

You don't have to trek outside the *Altstadt* walls to hang your hat in an inexpensive *Pension,* but during the warmer months, you'd best phone first. If all else fails, the tourist office places dazed travelers in dazzling accommodations for a DM5 fee. Nearby Erlangen also offers an infrequently filled hostel/guest house (see p. 559).

Jugendgästehaus (HI), Burg 2 (tel. 230 93 60; fax 23 09 36 11). From the main hall of the train station, take the escalator down into the tunnel passage by the tourist office (marked "Königpassage" and "Zum Altstadt") and walk straight ahead, then left up to the sloping exit. Follow this main shopping street (Königstr.) through Lorenzerplatz over the bridge to the Hauptmarkt (10min.). Head in the direction of the golden fountain on the far left and bear right on Burgstr., then huff and puff up to the castle at the top of the hill (in the direction of the sign pointing to Burgerstr.; 20min.). Once a stable and grain storage house for the imperial castle, it's now a summer hotspot for the town's high school hipsters. The hostel's Romanesque arches, dizzying panorama over the city, and friendly desk staff (prone to playing with the loudspeakers) make for good hostellin' fun. 4-bed dorms DM29, but if ultra-booked they may stuff a mattress on the floor and charge you DM20. Reception 7am-1am. Curfew 1am. Theoretical quiet time 10pm-7am. Frequently booked solid; reservations strongly recommended.

Jugend-Hotel Nürnberg, Rathsbergstr. 300 (tel. 521 60 92; fax 521 69 54). Bus #212 to "Hernhütte," then bus #21 to "Ziegelstein." (25min.). Rustic and cheerful, but far from the action. Nice surrounding grounds complement the dorm rooms, all with bath. 3-bed dorms DM25 (DM22 for stays of more than 2 nights); singles DM37; doubles DM58. Breakfast DM7.50. Reception 8am-10pm. Call ahead.

Hotel Garni Probst, Luitpoldstr. 9 (tel. 20 34 33; fax 205 93 36), 5min. from the train station. Follow the underground passage from the train station to Königsplatz past Burger King on the left. The block is seedy; the location is central. It's a jolly family establishment with tiny, oddly shaped rooms. Singles DM40-62, with shower DM70, with bath DM75-85; doubles DM90, with shower DM100, with bath DM110-125. Breakfast included.

Gasthof Schwänlein, Hintere Sterngasse 11 (tel. 22 51 62; fax 241 90 08), 5min. from the train station. Take the underground passage from the main hall of the train station up to Königstr. and take an immediate left onto Frauentormauerstr. Follow the town wall as it curves right. The hotel is about 200m down on the left. The quiet hallways of the *Pension* are soothing, although rooms are slightly cramped. A small beer garden is out back. Singles DM40, with shower DM50; doubles DM70, with shower DM80. Reservations by post card or fax only.

Pension Vater Jahn, Jahnstr. 13 (tel./fax 44 45 07). From the west exit of the station, head straight on Ellgutstr. for 3 blocks (under the pedestrian underpass), then left under the heavily trafficked Tafelfeld Tunnel (8min.). "Vater Jahn" is written on the side of the tall *Pension*. Comfortable, tidy rooms. Singles DM43, with bath DM63; doubles DM75, with shower DM85, with bath DM95. Breakfast included.

Camping: Campingplatz im Volkspark Dutzendteich, Hans-Kalb-Str. 56 (tel. 81 11 22), behind the soccer stadium. S-Bahn #2 (direction: "Furth") to "Frankenstadion." DM9 per person. DM5 per small tent, DM10 per large tent. DM5 per car. Call ahead. Check-in 2-10pm. Open May-Sept.

FOOD

Nürnberg titillates the palate of any gourmet or brutally hungry pig. The city is famous for its speciality foods: *Rostbratwurst* (rough but delectable grilled sausage), boiled *Sauerwurst,* and *Lebkuchen,* a candied variant of gingerbread (traditionally devoured at Christmas, but always available at an *Imbtß* stand near you). For a super food, film, and beer extravaganza, bust a move to Cince Citta (see **Entertainment and Nightlife,** p. 558). If your wallet squeaks reprimands at you for constant splurging, **Aldi,** on Königstr. near the train station, will keep you feeling guiltless with cheap grocery options (open M-F 8:30am-6pm, Sa 8am-2pm).

Bratwurst Häusle, Rathauspl. 1, next to St. Sebald's Church, is the most famous and crowded *Bratwurst* spot in Nürnberg for good reason. As one local put it, "No one from Nürnberg comes here without a tourist." Six *Rostbratwürste* with *Sauerkraut* or potato salad DM9.50. Beer DM5-5.50. Open M-Sa 10am-9:30pm.

⊛**Internetcafé Falkens Maze,** Färberstr. 11 (tel. 23 23 84; email Max@maximum.de; http://www.maximum.de), at the corner of Frauengasse. Head up to the third floor of the *Maximum* complex; the cafe is on the right at the far end of the neon-lit hallway. Grab a soda or cup of coffee (DM3), then email or surf your night away. An amateur DJ mixes hardcore tunes as crazy cyber-punks fight over electronic machines—it's crowded here. 30min. connection DM5, DM8 per hr. (noon-4pm DM5 per hr.). Open M-Sa 11am-10pm.

Cafe Mohr, Färberstr. 3 (tel. 24 31 39), at the intersection with Karolinenstr. With an Art Deco-ish atmosphere overlooking a lively square, it's a fun place to meet and eat. Dark, smoky interior and funky outdoor seating. Crepes (DM4.50-8.50), healthy salads (DM6.50-11.50), pineapple shakes (DM5.50) and cappuccino lovelies, lovey (DM3.50). Open M-Th 9am-midnight, F-Sa 9am-1am, Su 2pm-midnight.

Enchilada, Hauptmarkt (tel. 244 84 98), behind the Frauenkirche. A popular Mexican restaurant and bar with a wide variety of vegetarian options. Nachos (DM10). Mexico salad (DM13), veggie quesadillas (DM16), and crazy cocktails (DM6-12). Open daily 11am-1am.

Bratwurst Röslein, Rathauspl. 6 (tel. 24 18 60), is a carnivorous paradise for flesh-eating, bone-crunching monsters. Enormous beer hall with long wooden tables and friendly waiters. Liver dumpling soup (DM4.50), roasted pig with dumplings smothered in dark beer sauce (DM10.95). No meal over DM11. Open daily 10am-midnight. Kitchen open 10am-11pm.

SIGHTS

Allied bombing left little of old Nürnberg for posterity. The churches, castle, and buildings were all reconstructed from the original stone between 1945 and 1966; most churches display post-war photos and feature empty pedestals where exterior statues were lost in the bombing. From the station, the closest part of the *Altstadt* is a walled-in area filled with cottages and shops; this is the **Handwerkhof,** a tourist trap masquerading as a historical attraction. The real sights lie farther up **Königstraße.**

Around the Altstadt and Castle

Nürnberg flaunts its opulence in the *Altstadt*'s three churches. The **Lorenzkirche** on Lorenzerplatz, originally Catholic like the town's other churches, later converted to Protestantism after Nürnberg became Lutheran in 1525. *(Open M-Sa 9am-5pm, Su 1-4pm. Tours in German M-F 11am-2pm.)* In WWII, all the transportable artwork was stashed in the cellar, while the church itself was completely destroyed except for the towers. The beautiful Gothic structure has been restored and once again displays priceless works of art. Of particular interest is the 20m high **tabernacle,** with delicate stone tendrils curling up into the roof vaulting. The large wooden carving hanging in front of the altar is Veit Stoß's 1517 masterpiece *Engelsgruß* (Angel's Greeting). Free tours of the church meet at the entrance.

Across the river on Hauptmarktplatz, rests the **Frauenkirche** (Church of Our Lady), constructed in 1352-61. *(Open M and W-Th 10am-1pm and 2-6pm, Tu and F-Sa 9am-1pm and 2-6pm, Su 12:30-1:30pm. Free summer tours M 12:10pm and W 6pm.)* The clock in the center of the facade is the site of the *Männleinlaufen* every day at noon: seven little **Kurfürsten** (nobles) circle three times around the seated figure of (Krazy) Kaiser Karl IV, the emperor who had the Frauenkirche built in 1350. Also on the Hauptmarkt is the **Schöner Brunnen** (Beautiful Fountain), which resembles nothing so much as the steeple of a Gothic church. Check out the 40 imaginatively carved figures, with Moses and the prophets way up top. On the side of the fountain facing into the market, a petite golden ring has been incorporated into the wrought-iron railing. The trick is that there is no seam or joint in either ring or rail. Legend has it that a young metal-worker fell in love with the king's daughter and fashioned the seamless ring-rail in tribute; her father was so impressed that he allowed them to marry. Nürnberg superstition says that if you turn it three times, your wish will come true.

Uphill and on the right from the Schöner Brunnen resides the **Rathaus.** Built between 1616 and 1622 in early Baroque style, sprinkled with a little Renaissance classicism, Nürnberg's *Rathaus* once held the largest council chamber in central Europe, until it was destroyed by fire in 1945. Beneath the building hides the **Lochgefängnisse** (dungeons; tel. 231 26 90), exhibiting juicy medieval torture instruments. *(Obligatory 30min. German tour every 30min.; English translation sheet available upon request. Open Apr. to mid-Oct. and during Christkindlesmarkt M-F 10am-4:30pm, Sa-Su 10am-1pm. DM4, students and children DM2.)* To continue your tour of the Nürnberg underground rat playground, meet at the nearby Albrecht-Dürer-Platz for a one-hour guided walk through the **Felsengänge**, Bergstr. 19 (tel. 22 70 66), in the *Altstadthof.* This web of passageways and cellars four to 25m below the *Altstadt* streets dates back over 100 years. *(Tours descend daily from the Dürer statue at 11am, 1, 3, and 5pm. DM7, students DM5, kids under 11 free.)* Bring a jacket; it's cold enough down there to store large barrels of beer. Across from the *Rathaus* stands the **Sebalduskirche.** *(Open Mar.-May daily 9:30am-6pm; June-Aug. 9:30am-8pm; Jan.-Feb. and Nov. 9:30am-4pm.)* The Catholic congregation morbidly celebrates the annual feast-day of St. Sebaldus by parading through town with his relics (that is, his corpse). During the other 364 days, he rests in his gilded cast bronze tomb in front of the altar. Up Burgstr. from the church is the fabulous **Fembo-Haus**, Burgstr. 15 (tel. 231 25 95), a lavishly ornamented patrician house which now contains the **Stadtmuseum.** *(Open Mar.-Oct. and during Christkindlesmarkt Tu-Su 10am-5pm; Nov.-Feb. except Christkindlesmarkt Tu-F 1-5pm, Sa-Su 10am-5pm. DM4, students and kids DM2.)*

Up the hill is the three-part castle: the **Kaiserburg** (Emperor's fortress), the **Burggrafenburg** (the fortress count's fortress), and the **Stadtburg** (the city fortress; tel. 22 57 26). Kaiser Konrad III in the 13th century originally erected the Kaiserburg and the next emperor, Friedrich Barbarossa, expanded it significantly. The spartan chambers of the Kaiserburg housed every Holy Roman Emperor after Konrad III—it was law that every German *Kaiser* spend at least his first day in office here. Since the castle had no heating, however, the *Kaiser*s usually spent their nights in the warm patrician homes of the *Altstadt.* Massive 40 ft. high and 20 ft. thick stone walls surround the castle and the manicured castle gardens. *(Gardens open daily 9am-8pm.)* Beyond the stone wall on the way up to the *Burg*, mysterious hoofprints were left by the steed of a German Robin Hood who escaped an execution. Inside lurk the Romanesque **Emperor's Chapel** and the imperial living quarters. *(Open daily Apr.-Sept. 9am-noon and 12:45-5pm; Oct.-Mar. 9:30am-noon and 12:45-4pm. Last morning tour noon; last afternoon tour Apr.-Sept. 4:30pm, Oct.-Mar. 3:30pm. DM5, children DM3.50.)* The 45-minute tour in German covers all parts of the Kaiserburg; the English-language tour offered by the tourist office also covers the castle (see p. 552). Maps in English cost DM2.50.

Ruins of the Third Reich

The ruins of **Dutzendteich Park**, site of the Nazi *Parteitage* (Party Convention) rallies in the 1930s, ring with a deserted disquiet and an unsettling non-presence, reminding visitors of a terrifying moment in German history. The annual rallies drew over 500,000 citizens. Take S-Bahn #2 (direction: "Freucht") to "Dutzendteich," then take the middle of the three exits, head down the stairs and turn left. Two hundred meters down the highway is a pink house and a hamburger stand; head left and follow the paved path around the pond until you see a large white stone stadium across the parking lot on the left. The museum entrance is around the back of the building, halfway down. **Zeppelin Field** sits on the far side of the lake near the massive marble platform from which Hitler addressed the throngs. The faint remains of a swastika stained into the marble is visible on the central promontory despite attempts to efface it.

The poles spaced intermittently along the desolate field once waved enormous banners, and were made infamous by Leni Riefenstahl's film **Triumph des Willens** (Triumph of the Will), which immortalized the 1935 Party rally in one of the most terrifying, enduring depictions of the "Fascist aesthetic." The overwhelming emotional power of Nazi events—injecting Wagnerian theater and Catholic ritual into Fascist grandiosity—can be seen in the exhibit *"Faszination und Gewalt"* (Fascination and Terror), located inside the **Zeppelin Tribüne** in the **Golden Hall** (entrance in rear; tel. 86 98 97). *(Open mid-May to Oct. Tu-Su 10am-6pm. DM5 with excellent German and English brochure about the exhibits, students DM4; without brochure DM2, students DM1.)* The exhibits cover the rise of the Third Reich, Nürnberg's role in the growth of National Socialism, and the *Nürnberg Prozesse* (Nürnberg War Trials of 1946). The photographs, depicting columns of uniformed Nazi troopers marching next to rows of concentration camp prisoners, are as frightful as they are moving. The gold mosaic swastika-like pattern on the ceiling of the tribune is still uncannily intact. The rest of the park envelops the Nazi-era **New Congress Hall** and the broad, untrafficked **Great Road.**

The predominant building style represents the apogee of Nazi architecture—massive and harsh, mixing modernist straight lines with Neoclassical pretension. The litter strewn about and the overgrowth on the paths and buildings define the mood today.

On the other side of town, Nazi leaders faced Allied military judges during the infamous war-crimes trials held in room 600 of the **Justizgebäude**, Fürtherstr. 22. Soon after the trials, in October 1946, 10 men were hanged for their crimes against humanity. The building still serves as a courthouse. Take U-Bahn #1 to "Barenschanze," and continue farther on Furtherstr., walking away from the *Altstadt.*

MUSEUMS

Albrecht Dürer Haus, Albrecht-Dürer-Str. 29 (tel. 231 25 68), uphill from the Sebalduskirche entrance, was the last residence of Nürnberg's favorite son during his final years (1509-1528). The *Fachwerk* contains period furniture along with Dürer's etchings and copies of his paintings (most originals are on display in Vienna, Munich, and Berlin), as well as an exhibit of Dürer-derived works by modern artists alongside the originals. Open Tu-W and F-Su 10am-5pm, Th 10am-8pm. DM5, students DM2.50.

Altstadthof, Bergstr. 19 (tel. 22 43 27), features an historic brewery. No free samples, but tempting 0.2 liter bottles of house brew cost a mere DM2.50. Hourly tours M-F 2-7pm, Sa-Su 11am-5pm; during *Christkindlesmarkt* daily 11am-7pm. DM4.50, children DM2.50.

Germanisches Nationalmuseum, Kartäusergasse 1 (tel. 133 10), is just across the river. From the Königstr. exit of the tunnel from the station, turn left through the archway onto Frauentormauer and right on Kartäusergasse. This huge, gleaming, modern building chronicles the last millennium of German art, with huge displays of medieval sculpture and painting and scientific instruments from Baroque and Renaissance Germany. A small floor is devoted to toys and dollhouses. Open Tu-Su 10am-5pm, W 10am-9pm. DM6, students and seniors DM3.

ENTERTAINMENT AND NIGHTLIFE

Nürnberg's nightspots run the gamut from ultra-traditional to hyper-modern—they take the fun-loving freak on a roller-coaster ride of sweet, diverse entertainment of all kinds. The *Altstadt* is packed with bars and clubs, and the teeny-bopper crowd hangs out at **Albrecht-Dürer-Platz** (uphill from Sebalduskirche). Pick up the weekly *Plärrer* (DM4), at **Deutsche Presse** in the train station; the region's best magazine, it lists musical events, cultural happenings, and addresses of bars, discos, and cafes. The free regional cultural guide *Doppelpunkt* is doled out at many bars and discos.

Cine Citta, Gewerbemuseumspl. 3 (tel. 20 66 60), packs seven cafes, 12 cinemas, and a disco into its multimedia mega-complex. The Italian joint, cappuccino bar, Tex-Mex place, and *crêperie* offer never-ending affordable options. Although most movies are in German, the weekly *Filmtips* provides a schedule of original language films (open Su-Th until 3am, F-Sa until 4am). The **Roxy,** Julius-Loßman-Str. 16 (tel. 488 40), shows more current English-language flicks, from trashy horror movies to love-sick romances. The **Planetarium,** Regiomontarsweg 1 (tel. 959 35 38), puts on old, new, and crazy shows. (Shows W 4 and 7:30pm, Th 7:30pm, and 2 weekends per month Sa 2:30pm, Su 11:30pm. Call for schedules. DM5, students DM3.50.)

Bars

Starclub, Maxtorgraben 33 (tel. 55 16 82), entrance is in the back—follow the graffiti and the parade of slouching high schoolers. No *paparazzi,* but a relaxed ramshackle garden house with rooms bathed in cool blue lights. Classy, diverse young crew creates a pocket of mischief in a residential area. Pinball, *Fußball,* TVs, and packed tables. Beer from DM3.90. Baguette DM5. Open M-F 9:30am-1am, Sa-Su 2:30pm-1am.

Saigon, Lammsgasse 8 (tel. 244 86 57), off Albrecht-Dürer-Str., across from the Burghotel. *The* trendy *Kneipe* at the moment, arguably the hippest place in town. Faddish, yet relaxing. Espresso DM3, cocktails DM10.50-12. Open daily 9pm-3am.

Treibhaus, Karl-Grillenberger-Str. 28 (tel. 22 30 41), in the west part of the *Altstadt,* a bit south of Westtor. Metal tables and dim lighting draw a slightly older crowd (i.e., no high-schoolers) to this bistro-bar. Killer cocktails with snacks, salads, pastas, and breakfast (DM5-16.50). Their speciality, *Milchkaffee,* gives "foam" a new meaning—be initiated. Open M-W 8am-1am, Th-F 8am-2am, Sa 9am-2am, Su 9am-1am. Kitchen daily until 10pm.

Café Ruhestörung, Tetzelgasse 21 (tel. 22 19 21), is a 5min. walk from the *Rathaus;* head right on Theresienstr., then left on Tetzelgasse. Relaxed atmosphere, though something of a scene—people-watch with a vengeance. Outdoor seating with patio furniture; the inside is black and green. Breakfast, sandwiches, salads (DM5.50-12.50), and warm meals like chili, pasta, and hamburgers (DM8.50-13.50). Beer on tap from DM4.50; Guinness DM6.50. Open M-W 7:30am-1am, Th-F 7:30am-2am, Sa 9am-2am, Su 9am-1am.

Cartoon, An der Sparkasse 6 (tel. 22 71 70), is a central, popular gay bar just off Theatergasse, near Lorenzplatz. Smallish, but stylishly awash in mahogany. Baguettes DM7. Beer DM4.30-4.50. Open M-Sa 11am-1am, Su 2pm-1am.

Dance Clubs

Mach I, Kaiserstr. 1-9 (tel. 20 30 30), in the center of the *Altstadt* near Karlsbrücke. Grooving patrons change size, shape, and drapery depending on the day. Thursday attracts the mellow "Best of the 70s to 90s" crowd; Friday swings with soul and hip-hop; Saturday signifies house. Cover DM10. Open Th-F 10pm-4am, Sa 10pm-5am.

Forum, Regensburger Str. 334. S-Bahn #2 to "Frankenstadion." Two dance floors assuage the musical needs of the cool. Friday is the night of nights—choose between hip-hop, hardcore, and experimental in the big hall, or progressive and trip-hop in the smaller hall. Techno parties and live music on Saturday. Some of the best bands around play at this joint. Open F-Sa and every second Th 9pm-4am.

Tolerant, Königstr. 39, Eingweikertsgäßchen. A mixed club, frequented by gays, lesbians, and heteros, centrally located. *Schlager* on Mondays—we warned you; W women only; Th 60s and 70s dance tracks; Sa "Saturgay night"; Su delicious dance mix. Cover DM10. Open F-Sa 9pm-5am, Su-Tu and Th 9pm-4am, W 8pm-4am.

■ Near Nürnberg: Erlangen

Once packed with craft-making Huguenots, today Nürnberg's little neighborhood buddy is an academic and industrial powerhouse. It's here that the elegant **Friedrich-Alexander-Universität** (founded in 1743), the second-largest Bavarian university, boasts eleven distinguished faculties and educates 28,000 students. Here, too, the German electronics giant **Siemens AG** conducts its most secret research. Designated "federal capital for environmental protection" in 1992, green Erlangen is the filial child of Mother Nature with an excellent network of bicycle paths, environmentally conscious city planning, and two expensive public gardens.

ORIENTATION AND PRACTICAL INFORMATION Erlangen can be reached by train from Nürnberg (20min., 2-3 per hr., DM5.80), Bamberg (30min., 1-2 per hr., DM9.80), or Munich (3¼hr., every hr., DM60). Walk one block straight ahead from the train station to reach the city's center, **Hugenottenplatz,** and its pedestrian artery (called **Hauptstraße** to your left and **Nürnberger Straße** a few blocks to your right). Rent **bikes** at **Fahrradkiste** (tel. 20 99 40) at the corner of Werner-von-Siemens-Str. and Henkestr. (Tour bike DM9 per day; mountain bike DM15 per day; ID and DM200 deposit required. Open M-F 11am-6pm, Sa 10am-1pm.) Erlangen's **tourist office,** Rathauspl. 1 (tel. 895 10; fax 89 51 51), cheerfully draws you into a sea of free brochures. They also find private rooms (DM20-45) for free. Walk one block straight ahead from the station, turn right at McDonald's, and continue straight until you see the ugly *Rathaus* high-rise on the left, just after the C&A mall; the office is straight up the open-air stairs. (Open M 8am-6pm, Tu-Th 8am-4:30pm, F 8am-12:30pm.) For a **pharmacy,** try **Schloß Apotheke,** Hauptstr. 32, which posts the name and number of the 24-hour "pharmacy of the night" in the window (open M-Tu and Th-F

8:15am-7pm, W 8:15am-6:15pm, Sa 8:30am-2pm). The **post office**, Güterhallenstr. 1, 91058 Erlangen, sits two blocks to the right of the station (open M-F 8am-6:30pm, Sa 8am-2pm). The **telephone code** is 09131.

ACCOMMODATIONS The **Jugendherberge**, Südliche Stadtmauerstr. 35 (tel. 86 25 55; fax 86 21 19), is central and convenient. Walk one block straight ahead from the station, turn right at the McDonald's, and take the second left onto Südl.-Stadtmauer-Str. The hostel is 10 minutes away in a stolid, square building. The sign reads *"Freizeitzentrum Frankenhof,"* and it's a central site for Erlangen's *Kinderkultur* with clubs and playing rooms. Spacious 4-bed rooms have hardwood bunkbeds. (DM18. Great breakfast included. Sheets DM5.50. Reception M-F 5-10pm, Sa-Su 7-11am and 4-10pm. Curfew 10pm, key available.) Inside the Freizeitzentrum you'll also find the **Gästehaus** for those 18 and over (same address and tel. as *Jugendherberge*). The Gästehaus has very simple but comfortable dorm-like rooms. (Singles with toilet DM37, with bath DM46; doubles with toilet DM50, with bath DM72; triples with toilet DM75.) **Camp** at **Naturfreunde Erlangen,** Wohrmühle 6 (tel. 253 03), on an island in the Regnitz river behind the station. Walk under the tracks from the station, right onto Münchener Str., left on Gerbereistr., and left just after the overpass onto Wohrmühlsteg (DM6.50 per person; DM5 per tent; open year-round).

FOOD This lively student town is packed with good cafes and affordable restaurants. One source of listings is Nürnberg's weekly magazine *Plärrer*. The Italian restaurant **Spago,** Hauptstr. 91 (tel. 20 30 81), flaunts a stylish decor and serves inexpensive, finger-lickin' good pizza (DM8-11; open Su-Th 11am-2:30pm and 5pm-midnight, F-Sa 11am-2:30pm and 5pm-1am). Plug-in, addicts, at the **Café Online,** at the Altstadtmarkt (tel. 89 76 32; http://www.c-online.de). Be careful not to spill your coffee (DM3), bits of your crepe (DM6-9), or your pasta (DM8-10) as you have electronic intercourse with friends back home (30min. connection DM6, 1hr. DM10; open M-Sa 10am-1am, Su 10am-10pm). A fresh produce **market** conquers the Marktplatz (M-F 7am-6pm, Sa 7am-2pm).

SIGHTS One block left up Hauptstr. from Hugenottenplatz is a large square whose left part is the Marktplatz, and whose right portion is the Schloßplatz. Entering the square, the **Palais Stutterheim** (tel. 86 27 35), built in 1728, looms behind you. *(Library open M, Tu, and Th-F 10am-6:30pm, Sa 9am-noon. Gallery open Tu-F 10am-6pm, Sa-Su 10am-5pm. Free.)* Once the town hall, it now shelves the town's books as official library and art gallery. The huge **Schloß** commands the right part of the square. Built in 1700 in half-Baroque, half-French Classical style, this castle was the home of Margrave Friedrich, the founder of the university. Friedrich never envisioned that his home would one day become the main administrative building of the university, housing stacks and stacks of paper and rooms and rooms of brow-furrowed bureaucrats. In front of the *Schloß* is an oversized green statue of Friedrich. Years of rough weather have bleached his face, leaving the eye-sockets black, as if the poor man's eyes had been gouged out. The *Schloß's* gray facade hides the vast 18th-century **Schloßgarten,** which begins in back of the building. *(Garden open daily 6:30am-8pm. Free.)* The beautifully manicured landscape and peaceful fountain attract many summer picnickers and other vacationers. Jazz and classical concerts are given in the garden during the summer. *(May-Aug. Su 11am, in front of the Orangerie.)* Around the left of the *Schloß* and past the semi-circular Orangerie lies the exotic **Botanical Garden,** cared for by the scholars at the Institute of Botany. *(Open M-W and F-Su 8am-4pm, Th 8am-6pm; Oct.-Mar. M-Sa 8am-4pm, Su 8am-noon; greenhouse open Tu-Su 9:30-11:30am and 1:30-3pm; Oct.-Mar. Tu-Sa 9:30-11:30am and 1:30-3:30pm, Su 9:30-11:30am. Free.)* The **Orangerie,** built in 1705, once sheltered citrus trees, shrubs, and exotic warm-climate flowers during the cold Erlangen winter months. To the left of the Orangerie, on the corner of Wasserturmstr. and Apfelstr., the late-18th-century tower was used to lock up naughty students; the room is free and open to the public.

NIGHTLIFE Groove, and we do mean groove, at **E-Werk,** Fuchsenwiese 1 (tel. 80 05 55; http://www.e-werk.de), a funked-up industrial building. Walk up Hauptstr. and left at Engelstr.—the building is straight ahead. Erlangen's *Kommunikationszentrum* leans left with musically and artistically hip folk. Inside the *E-Werk*, the **Tanz-Werk** (dance factory) cranks out indy on Tuesdays, while Wednesdays feature either *Männerdisco* (2nd W each month), or R&B (1st and 3rd W each month), and Thursdays challenge you to "all you can groove." Friday is hip-hop and pop, and Saturdays are either Frauendisco (4th F each month) or straight rock. On Sundays, oldies play. They also have films and jazz as well as weekly gallery exhibits. (Ticket office open M-F 10am-6pm, Sa 10am-noon; dance parties Tu and Th 10pm-2am, 1st and 3rd W 9:30pm-2am, 2nd W 8:30pm-2am, 4th W 9pm-2am, F 9pm-2am, Sa 10pm-4am, Su 9pm-2am.)

■ Bayreuth

Once you've turned off Tristanstr. onto Isoldenstr., walked past Walküregasse, and finally ducked into the Parsifal Pharmacy, there will be little doubt that you're in Bayreuth, the adopted home of **Richard Wagner** and the site of the annual *Festspiele*—an *en masse* pilgrimage of BMW-driving devotees coming to bask in his operatic masterpieces. Wagner retreated to Bayreuth in 1872 to escape his creditors and other folks he had burned. The remote town promised privacy, an 18th-century opera house, and an enchanting ego-fluffing concept—fans would now have to trek great lengths to experience a true Wagner performance. The grandiosity of it all has left Bayreuth a treasure trove of gorgeous buildings. An affection for pomp (or a well-founded desire to mock Wagner groupies) makes Bayreuth worthwhile even for those less-than-enthralled with the man and his music.

ORIENTATION AND PRACTICAL INFORMATION Bayreuth is pronounced "Buy Royt," *not* "Bay Ruth"; you will be scorched by lightning should you speak otherwise. The *Altstadt* lies five minutes south of the train station; exit to the left and walk down Bahnhofstr. The town is an easy daytrip from Nürnberg by hourly **trains** (1hr.; DM23.20); travelers from the north have to change in Lichtenfels. The **tourist office,** Luitpoldpl. 9 (tel. 885 88; fax 885 55), about four blocks to the left of the station, provides city maps, hotel listings, a monthly calendar of events, and city **walking tours** (DM8, students DM5; tours May-Oct. Tu-Sa 10am; Nov.-Apr. Sa only). **Private rooms** are only available during the *Festspiele* (DM5 fee); at other times, they will help you find a room in a hotel or *Pension* for the same fee. The office will also sell you tickets to Bayreuth's lively year-round theater, opera, and musical offerings. (Office open M-F 9am-6pm, Sa 9:30am-12:30pm.) **Exchange money** at **Citibank,** Maxstr. 46, which offers 24-hour bankcard service. (Open M and Th 8:45am-1pm and 2-6pm, Tu and F 8:45am-1pm and 2-4pm, W 8:45am-1pm and 1:30-4pm.) The **post office,** Bürgerreutherrstr. 1, 95444 Bayreuth (tel. 78 00), is across from the train station and to the right (open M-F 8am-7pm, Sa 8am-1pm). The **telephone code** is 0921.

ACCOMMODATIONS If you visit during the *Festspiele* and forgot to book your room last year, don't even try to stay in Bayreuth. Almost any other time, though, prices are reasonable and beds are available. Bayreuth's brand-new **Jugendherberge (HI),** Universitätsstr. 28 (tel. 25 12 62; fax 51 28 05), lies outside the city center past the Hofgarten near the university. Take bus #4 (DM2.30) from the Marktplatz to "Mensa," walk out of the *Uni* onto Universitätstr. and turn left. Or walk down Ludwigstr. from the city center, take a left onto Friedrichstr., then veer left onto Jean-Paul-Str., which merges with Universitätsstr. It's friendly but a tad regimented: at 10pm, *everything* locks up. (DM20. Breakfast included. Sheets DM5.50. Reception 7am-noon and 5-9:30pm. Lockout 9-11:30am. Curfew 10pm. Open Mar. to mid-Dec.)

   Gasthof Hirsch, St. Georgen 26 (tel. 267 14 and 85 31 42), is a 10-minute walk behind the train station, on a corner with a rainbow of geraniums spilling out the windows. Exit the train station in the back, just beyond track five; take a left as you exit, then right onto Brandenburger Str., and left onto St. Georgen. It's clean and crisp with 18 beds. (Singles DM35-40; doubles DM70-80.) At **Gasthof zum Brandenburger,** St. Georgen 9 (tel. 78 90 60; fax 78 90 62 40), the rooms are nice and sunny, as is the beer garden, and spiffy ivy wallpaper adorns the third floor (singles DM35, with shower DM60; doubles DM60, with shower DM130). **Gasthof Schindler,** Bahnhofstr. 9 (tel. 262 49), is close to the station. Clean rooms complement the restaurant with yellow tables in the basement (singles DM60; doubles DM95).

FOOD Fill 'er up at the **University Mensa** (tel. 60 81) for DM3-6; any student ID should do. Take bus #4 (DM2.30) from the bus station at the end of Luitpoldplatz on the right to "Mensa," then walk past the buildings straight ahead. The *Mensa* is to the right up the steps. It's an enormous, low-roofed building. Trade the cashier your ID and DM5 for a card. Put money on the card at the *automaten* in the hall, use the card to buy food, then get your DM5, plus any balance left on the card, back from the cashier. (Open Oct.-July M-Th 8am-6pm, F 8am-2pm; Aug.-Sept. M-Th 11:15am-1:30pm, F 11:15am-1:15pm.) **Braunbierhaus,** Kanzleistr. 15 (tel. 696 77), beyond Bayreuth's *Stadtkirche,* is an authentic delight nearly 900 years old. Share the authenticity with other authentic tourists while chewing on steak (DM20) or schnitzels (DM15-17). (Open M-F 5-10:30pm, Sa-Su 11am-2pm and 5-10:30pm.) **Gastätte Porsch,** Maximilianstr. 63 (tel. 649 49), serves humongous portions at great prices. *Schnitzels* and steak meals run DM11-17. (Open M-Sa 7am-8:30pm.) Across the road rests **Brauereischänke am Markt,** Maximilianstr. 56 (tel. 649 19), which dishes out *Bratwurst* with potato salad or *Kraut* (DM8.80; open M-Sa 11am-10pm).

Café Wundertüte, Richard-Wagner-Str. 33 (tel. 51 47 48), has a cup of coffee and a slice of raspberry *Torte* with your name on it (DM5.30), served in a wood-paneled atmosphere rounded out by small salads, noodles, *Wieners,* and cheeses (DM5-9.50; open M-Tu and Th-F 8am-6pm, Sa 9am-6pm). Fill up your basket at the **market** in the Rotmainhal near Hindenburgstr. (W and Sa 7am-5pm). **Norma,** right by Gaststätte Porsch, is the local **supermarket** with the fixings for a perfect picnic (open M-F 8:30am-7pm, Sa 8am-4pm).

THE WAGNER FESTSPIEL For Wagnerians, a devotional visit to Bayreuth is like a pious pilgrimage to Mecca. Every summer from July 25 to August 28, thousands of visitors pour in for the **Bayreuth Festspiele,** a vast and bombastic—in a word, Wagnerian—celebration of the composer's works. The music fills the **Festspielhaus** theater that Wagner built for his "music of the future." The world's operatic darlings, directors, and conductors have been taking on *The Flying Dutchman, The Ring of the Nibelung,* and *The Meistersinger* here since 1876. Judging from the number of German Wagner Societies and Clubs, the spectacle will probably continue for as long as the Holy Grail is old. Tickets for the festival (DM80-300, obstructed view DM40-50) go on sale several years in advance and sell out almost immediately. Write to Bayreuther Festspiele, 95402 Bayreuth, well before the September *seven years* before you wish to attend. Your request will be processed when it is received; you'll be notified some time after mid-November. Reserve a room in town as soon as you get tickets—Wagnerophiles just write **every year** and hope for the best.

SIGHTS If you're not a Wagner fan, feign appreciation for a day in this devoted opera-town. Wagner devotees visiting Bayreuth when the *Festspiele* is over console themselves with a **Festspielhaus** tour (tel. 787 80). To get there, go right at the station and up at the end of Siegfried-Wagner-Allee. *(Tours Sept.-Oct. and Dec.-May 10, 10:45am, 2:15 and 3pm. DM2.50.)* To fund the 1872 construction, the composer hit up sugar daddy Ludwig II, who was in the midst of his own egocentric building spree. Ludwig responded with modest amounts of cash, resulting in a semi-spartan structure—Wagner fans must endure cushionless seats and precious little leg room to catch a show.

Haus Wahnfried, which now contains the **Richard Wagner Museum,** Richard-Wagner-Str. 48 (tel. 757 28 16), was once the composer's home. *(Open M, W, and F 10am-5pm, Tu and Th 10am-8:30pm. July-Aug. DM5, students DM2; Sept.-June DM4, students*

DM2. *3-day passes for the Wagner Museum, the Jean Paul Museum, and Franz Liszt Museum available for DM6.*) It houses an inexhaustible and kitschy—yet valuable—collection of scores, costumes, and stage sets. See Wagner stamps, coins, and playing cards, as well as his spoons, mirror, and little *Wotan* and *Sieglinde* dolls (the Wagnerian Barbie and Ken). Three death masks provide morbid pleasure: Wagner's, composer Carl Maria von Weber's, and that of Wagner's friend Ludwig II. The thousands of exhibits are in German only—it might behoove you to pick up the melodramatic English guide-booklet (DM3). Wagner's compositions are played in the drawing room daily at 10am, noon, and 2pm; videos are shown at 11am and 3pm. Those who fail to appreciate his "Total Works of Art" (as he modestly referred to them) should recall Mark Twain's fiendishly accurate assessment of Wagner's music: "It's better than it sounds." Behind the house lie the graves of Wagner, his wife Cosima, and Russ, his big black dog.

Just to the left of the haughty Wagner Museum, the **Franz Liszt Museum,** Wahn-friedstr. 9 (tel. 757 28 18), exhibits the composer's pianos and music sheets and displays the room where he died (again, complete with death mask). In Bayreuth, Liszt is probably best known for fathering Wagner's wife—indeed, musical virtuosos also inbreed. Closer to the street, the **Jean Paul Museum,** Wahnfriedstr. 1 (tel. 757 28 17), celebrates the life of Bayreuth's greatest poet with an endless collection of notebooks and chairs. *(Both museums open daily 9am-noon and 2-5pm. DM3, students and seniors DM1. Ring to get in.)* Farther behind the Wagner house is the **Hofgarten,** an English-style park. Turn right as you enter and be led to the **National German Masonic Museum,** Hofgarten 1 (tel. 698 24). *(Open Tu-F 10am-noon and 2-4pm, Sa 10am-noon. DM2, students DM1. Ring to get in.)* If you've wondered what's inside those windowless temples or what the strange symbols mean, this is the place for you, complete with floor plans and pink roses. The bizarre rituals have transpired in Bayreuth for 225 years.

Just down Wahnfriedstr., enter the lovely gardens once again to wander down the primrose path to the 18th-century Baroque **Neues Schloß** (tel. 759 69 21), former residence of Friedrich the Great's sister, Margravine Wilhelmine. Considered one of Europe's most brilliant and cultured women, she married the Margrave of Bayreuth and ended up stuck in what must have seemed a provincial cow town. After a mysterious castle fire, she redecorated and rococoed like mad King Ludwig, and when she finished gilding the home furnishings, she swept her eyes across Bayreuth and strove to cosmopolitanize it. *(Castle open Tu-Su 10-11:20am and 1:30-4:10pm; Oct.-Mar. Tu-Su 10-11:20am and 1:30-2:50pm. DM3, students DM1.)* The lavishly ornate **1748 Margravian Opera House** is the tangible result of such frustration combined with more money than is good for a person. Wagner originally thought this theater's pomp appropriate for his production, but its 500 seats and stage proved way too small for his grandiose needs. *(Tours, including multi-media light show, every 30min. Open Tu-Su 9-11:30am and 1:30-4:30pm; Oct.-Mar. Tu-Su 10-11:30am and 1:30-3pm. DM7, students DM5.)* If you're sweating from all this palatial magnificence, make a splash in Bayreuth's fabulous outdoor pool, **Kreuzsteinbad** (tel. 661 07), and see that grand Wagnerian style is not limited to 18th-century opera houses. *(Open May-Sept. daily 7am-8pm. DM5, students DM2.50.)*

▨ Coburg

Coburg only joined Bayern in 1920 after spending years in Sachsen. This move fortuitously saved the city from inclusion in the GDR. The 1947 division of Germany shifted the town's geographical location from the heartland to the margins. Today, wealthy Coburg sits at the center again, but a brief trip north across the old GDR border reveals the vast incongruities the past 45 years have created. This 11th-century town has been beautifully preserved, thanks to an arbitrary line in the woods.

PRACTICAL INFORMATION From the Nürnberg-Berlin line, change at Lichtenfels to reach Coburg. From Coburg trains go to Nürnberg (2hr.; every hr.) and Sonnenburg

(30min.). From the train station, turn right on Lossaustr., left at the light onto Mohrenstr., around the large, central *Stadtcafe,* and right on Spitalgasse to reach the Renaissance **Altstadt** (15min.).Coburg's **tourist office,** Herrngasse 4 (tel. 741 80; fax 74 18 29), off the *Markt,* offers free maps and finds rooms (DM30-60) for free (open Apr.-Oct. M-F 9am-6:30pm, Sa 9am-1pm; Nov.-Mar. M-F 9am-5pm, Sa 9am-1pm). A **walking tour** in German departs from the *Denkmal* on the *Markt* (Sa 3pm; DM5). The **post office,** Hindenburgstr. 6, 96450 Coburg (tel. 910), to the left off Mohrenstr. on the way to the *Altstadt,* **exchanges money** (open M-F 8am-6pm, Sa 8am-noon). The **telephone code** is 09561.

ACCOMMODATIONS Jugendherberge Schloß Ketschendorf (HI), Parkstr. 2 (tel. 153 30; fax 286 53), rests in a sublime converted palace. The sight of play-school *Jugendherberge* furniture in the grand castle is a funny sight, but the modern rooms make spotless sense. Take bus #1 (from the Markt) to "DJH." Parkstr. is up on the left. Or walk on Ketschengasse to Ketschendorferstr., then all the way to Parkstr. to make a left (25min.). Ketschendorf proudly displays plaques proclaiming itself the "Best Bavarian Youth Hostel." Billiard tables and a disco back up the claim. (DM22. Breakfast included. Sheets DM5.50. Reception 5-6 and 8-9:30pm. Lockout 10am-noon. Curfew 10pm, but they'll give you a key. Hot showers available 7-9am and 3-10pm.) The **Gasthof Goldenes Kreuz,** Herrngasse 1 (tel. 904 73; fax 905 02), on the Marktplatz, offers clean, simple rooms and a restaurant downstairs (singles DM45, with shower DM50; doubles DM90, DM100). The **Münchner Hofbräu,** Kleine Johannisgasse 8 (tel. 750 49; fax 904 34), is both a hopping restaurant and *Pension,* two blocks from the Marktplatz off Spitalgasse. (Singles with bath DM55; doubles with bath DM105.) The restaurant serves just what you would expect, given the name—beer and plates of grilled sausages (DM8-14). Old clocks and stained glass windows add to the fun atmosphere. (Open daily 10am-midnight.)

FOOD AND NIGHTLIFE Two of Coburg's specialty foods are the *Thüringer Klößer* (dumplings) and the *Coburger Bratwurst.* Billowing clouds of smoke and the smell of grilled *Coburger Bratwürste* hang thick in the air over the market square, in which a **farmer's market** (W and Sa 7am-5pm) and a **fruit market** (Tu 7am-noon) take place. **Café Prinz Albert,** at the corner of Albertsplatz down Ketschengasse from the market (tel. 954 20), offers ice cream (DM4-7.80), sweet cakes (DM4), and small snacks (open M-Sa 8:30am-6:30pm, Su 10am-6pm). **Norma supermarket** lies on Hindenburgstr., across from the post office (open M-F 8:30am-6:30pm, Sa 8am-2pm).

For nightlife, **Café Filou,** Bahnhofstr. 11 (tel. 900 70), offers a relaxed atmosphere with funky round chairs and sepia-toned photographs. Try to grab a table in the greenhouse (pizza and pasta DM8.50-14.50; open M-Sa 9:30am-1am). **Café-Floh,** Herrngasse 12, off the Marktplatz, attracts students with its dark-wood environment, conducive to late-night philosophizing over beer. Fresh baguettes run DM3-7 (open daily 8pm-3am).

SIGHTS The huge 16th-century structure on the Marktplatz is the frescoed **Rathaus.** The old **Stadthaus** across the square was once the abode of the Coburg *Herzog* (Duke). The proud central statue is of **Prince Albert,** the Coburger husband of Queen Victoria. To the right down Herrngasse towers the part-Renaissance, part-neo-Gothic **Schloß Ehrenburg** (Castle of Honor; tel. 808 80), the town residence of the Coburg Dukes from 1547 to 1918. *(Tours Tu-Su 6 per day 10am-4:30pm; Oct.-Mar. Tu-Su 5 per day 10am-3:30pm. DM4, students and seniors DM3.)* When the *Herzog* built the palace, he did so without borrowing too much money and without grossly oppressing his peasantry. When the *Kaiser* toured the site, he remarked that it stood as a monument to the *Herzog's* honor, and the name stuck. The palace later fell to the Sachsen-Coburg-Gothas, and Albert spent his childhood within its walls. Victoria's private quarters can be toured.

Paved footpaths wind through the **Hofgarten,** a shaded, grassy expanse stretching from Schloß Ehrenburg to the 11th-century **Veste** (fortress). Allow 30 to 45 minutes to hike up the deceptively steep hill. Otherwise, take bus #8 from the *Rathaus* to

"Veste" (DM2.50) or the "Veste Express" which runs more often (DM3) and walk up about 50m. The 16th-century fortress, encircled by a double set of fortified walls, was inhabited until 1918, when Karl Eduard abdicated the dukedom. The **Coburg Art Museum** (tel. 07 90) is up at the Vest. *(Open Apr.-Oct. Tu-Su 9am-1pm and 2-5pm; Nov.-Mar. Tu-Su 2-5pm; DM5, students DM3.)* It houses all sorts of medieval goodies, from paintings by Cranach the Elder to a room occupied by Martin Luther, to an armor collection including miniature armor that really *was* worn by a midget. Back in town to the right of Herrngasse is the minty-green **Coburger Puppen-Museum** (Doll Museum), Rückertstr. 2-3 (tel. 740 47; fax 271 16). *(Open Apr.-Oct. daily 9am-5pm; Nov.-Mar. Tu-Su 10am-5pm. DM3.50, students DM3, under 14 DM2.)* In one of its 32 chronologically ordered rooms, following doll history from 1800 to 1955, spot Lilli, a curvy German doll from the 1950s intended for adults; the then-unknown American toy company Mattel bought the rights to her in 1958, and one year later young girls went Barbie-crazy, playing with an awkwardly shaped blonde. Contemplate the corporate toy world at the well-named **Café Hello Dolly.** South of Coburg stands the resplendent 18th-century **Vierzehnheiligen Kirche** (Fourteen Saints' Church; tel. (09571) 950 80), which was built on the spot where local villagers saw visions of the Christ Child and the "Fourteen Saints of Intercession" in 1445-46. *(Open daily 9am-6pm. Free.)* Take the train to Lichtenfels, then either walk or ride the infrequent bus to the church.

■ Bamberg

Be-yootiful, Bacchanalian Bamberg bangs back bounteous brews— 330 liters per capita per year, the highest consumption rate in the world. You would too if you'd come this close to complete destruction, not once, but *twice*. In the Thirty Years War, Bamberg survived two sieges by the formidable Swedish King Gustavus Adolphus II, and three centuries later, the city emerged from WWII with only minor bruises. Today, Bamberg's tourist office proclaims that the city "lives with history"…not to mention a hell of a hangover.

ORIENTATION AND PRACTICAL INFORMATION

The heart of Bamberg lies on an island between the Rhine-Main-Danube Canal and the Regnitz River (named for its location at the confluence of the Regen and the Pegnitz Rivers). Across the Regnitz from the island lie the winding streets of the *Altstadt*. To reach the *Altstadt* from the *Bahnhof*, walk straight on Luitpoldstr., cross the canal, and walk straight on Willy-Lessing-Str. until it empties into Schönleinsplatz. Turn right onto Langestr. and left up Obere Brückestr., which leads through the archway of the *Rathaus* and across the Regnitz (25-30min.). Or grab a city bus in front of the *Hauptbahnhof* for a quick ride into town (DM1.70). The **Bamberg Card** (valid for 48hr.) gives great discounts on public transportation in the city, a walking tour, and admission to four museums (1 person DM13, 2 people DM24, 3 people DM35).

Trains: The main station is on Ludwigstr. (tel. 194 19). Trains to Nürnberg (30min.-1hr., 2-4 per hr.), Würzburg (1¼hr., every hr.); Frankfurt (2hr. 10min., every hr.); Munich (2½-4hr., 1-2 per hr.).

Public Transportation: An excellent transportation net centers around the **ZOB (Zentral Omnibus Bahnhof)** on Promenadestr. off Schönleinsplatz. Ask at the tourist office for schedules. One-way bus fare DM1.70. Four-ride ticket DM5.

Taxi: call 150 15 or 345 45.

Bike Rental: Fahrradhaus Griesmann, Kleberstr. 25 (tel. 229 67). Walk straight on Luitpoldstr. from the train station, right on Heinrichsdamm after the bridge, left at the next bridge, and take the first right onto Kleberstr. DM12 per day. ID required. Open daily 9am-12:30pm and 2-6pm.

Tourist Office: Fremdenverkehrsamt, Geyerwörthstr. 3 (tel. 87 11 61; fax 87 19 60), on an island in the Regnitz. To get there, follow the directions to the *Altstadt*. Once through the *Rathaus*, take two lefts and re-cross the Regnitz on the wooden footbridge; the tourist office is on your right under the arches. You can avoid paying DM0.50 for their map by picking up a free hotel list or monthly program, which have better maps. A vending machine outside dispenses hotel lists and city maps for DM0.50. They also find rooms in hotels or pensions by mail or in person for a DM5 fee. Open Apr.-Oct. M-F 9am-6pm, Sa 9am-3pm., Su 10am-2pm; Nov.-Mar. closed Su. **Walking tours** of the city meet in front of the tourist office. Apr.-Oct. M-Sa 10:30am and 2pm, Su 11am; Nov.-Mar. M-Sa 2pm, Su 11am. DM8, students DM5. Tours of the cathedral and the *Neue Residenz* meet at the *Neue Residenz* and leave when there are "enough people." (Available Apr.-Sept. daily 9am-noon and 1:30-5pm; Oct.-Mar. 9am-noon and 1:30-4pm. DM8, students DM6.)

Currency Exchange: Citibank, on Schönleinspl. (tel. 332 21 11), accepts nearly any card. Open M-Tu and Th-F 9am-1pm and 2-6pm, W 9am-1pm.

Bookstore: Görres Bücher, Langestr. 24, stocks a small selection of contemporary novels in English on the top floor. Open M-F 9am-7pm, Sa 9am-2pm.

Laundromat: SB Waschsalon, in the Atrium mall left of the train station, 2nd floor (tel. 20 29 40). Wash DM8; dry DM1 per 8min. Open M-Su 7am-10pm.

Women's Resources: Every Tuesday evening in **Café Jenseits,** at Promenadestr. 5 (tel. 210 94), off Schönleinsplatz, a *Frauencafe* pops up with discussions of contemporary issues, films, and readings.

Emergency: tel. 110. **Police,** Schildstr. 81 (tel. 18 50). **Fire** and **Ambulance,** tel. 112. **Rape Crisis Line,** tel. 582 80.

Pharmacy: Einhorn Apotheke, Grüner Markt 3, just around the corner from Langestr., has a list of 24hr. pharmacies in the window. Open M-F 8:15am-6pm, Sa 8:30am-12:30pm.

Hospital: Klinikum Bamberg, Bugerstr. 80 (tel. 50 30).

Post Office: Hauptpostamt, Ludwigstr. 25, 96052 Bamberg (tel. 83 62 81), across from the train station, helps with telegrams and **currency exchange.** Also cashes traveler's checks (DM6 per check). Open M-F 8am-6pm, Sa 8am-12:30pm.

Telephone Code: 0951.

ACCOMMODATIONS AND CAMPING

Accommodations in Bamberg tend to be very expensive, largely because *Privatzimmer* are illegal to rent.

Jugendherberge Wolfsschlucht (HI), Oberer Leinritt 70 (tel. 560 02 or 563 44; fax 552 11). Bus #18 (from *ZOB*) to "Am Regnitzufer" (every 20min., DM1.50). Far from the city center, but the rooms are tidy. DM20. Breakfast included. Sheets DM5.50. Reception 4-10pm. Curfew 10pm. Because it's the only hostel in Bamberg, it fills up snap-crackle-pop quick; call very early for summer reservations. If full, try the hostels in Erlangen or Coburg. Open Feb. to mid-Dec.

⊛Maisel-Bräu-Stübl, Obere Königstr. 38 (tel./fax 255 03), 10min. from the station. Left off Luitpoldstr. Spacious, clean rooms with balconies overlook a pleasant courtyard. Big fluffy pillows. Singles DM39; doubles DM70, with shower DM80. Breakfast included. Delectable dinners from DM13. Reception 9am-midnight.

Hospiz, Promenadestr. 3 (tel. 98 12 60; fax 981 26 66). Large doubles, balconies, great breakfast—all in a central location, off Schönleinsplatz. Singles DM50, with bath DM70; doubles with shower DM80, with bath DM90-100; triples with shower DM108, with bath DM132. Reception 7am-9pm. Check-out 11am. Phone, fax, or mail reservations accepted. Call ahead.

Fässla, Obere Königstr. 19-21 (tel. 265 16; fax 20 19 89). 10-min. from the station. Go right off Luitpoldstr. Cozy and comfortable with TVs, phones, and bath. Singles DM63; doubles DM98; triples DM130. Breakfast buffet included. Parking DM5. Luggage storage available. Closed after 1pm on Sundays.

Camping: Campingplatz Insel, Am Campingpl. 1 (tel. 563 20). Bus #18 (direction: "Klinikum") to "Bug." Prime riverside locale. Showers, toilets, washing machines. DM6.50 per adult, DM4.50 per child, DM4.50 per tent, DM11 per car.

FOOD AND NIGHTLIFE

Bamberg boasts several breweries, but its most unusual specialty is **Rauchbier** (smoke beer). The daring can try its sharp, smoky taste (DM3.20 for 0.5L) at **Schlenkerla,** Dominikanerstr. 6 (tel. 560 60), Rauchbier's traditional home. The smoke brewery lies at the foot of the steps leading up to Domplatz. **Der Beck,** Hauptwachstr. 16, at Hauptwacheck, offers scrumptious snacks and pastries from the bakery (open M-F 6:30am-6:30pm, Sa 6:30am-2pm). The **Tengelmann supermarket,** Langestr. 14 (open M-F 8:30am-6:30pm, Sa 7:30am-4pm), sells groceries.

University Mensa, Austr. 37, off Obstmarkt, serves the cheapest edible meals in town for under DM5. Dine on yellow plastic trays (or put your meal on one). Menu changes daily. Any student ID will do. Open daily 11:30am-2pm. **Snack hall** open until 7pm. Check bulletin boards for jobs, rooms, and nightlife happenings.

Kachelofen, Obere Sandstr. 1 (tel. 571 72), in the Fränkisches Gasthaus. Roly-poly families pack in like sardines at the outside tables. Try the Leberknödel ("liver balls"—better than you might think) with Kraut (DM13), or other Bavarian specialities (DM13-26.50). Open daily 10am-1am (kitchen open until 11pm).

Polarbär, Judenstr. 7 (tel. 536 01). In the *Altstadt,* across the walking bridge and left a block or two. Small beer garden with aromatic atmosphere. Baguettes DM7.30. Salads DM5-11.30. Vegetarian dishes DM11-15. Open daily 11am-midnight. Kitchen open noon-3pm and 5-10pm. **Black Bar** open Su-F until 11pm, Sa until midnight.

Jazzclub, Obere Sandstr. 18 (tel. 537 40). Crowded, diverse student joint offers a funky mix of goth, alternative, punk, grunge, and mystic. F-Sa hosts the local jazz scene from 9pm-1am. Cover hovers at DM14, students DM11, DM4 on Tu. Open Tu and Th 9pm-1am.

Live Club, Obere Sandstr. 7 (tel. 50 04 58), offers varied disco. Scene changes with the days, mixing everything from R&B to hip-hop to hardcore. Stop by for a schedule. Open M and W 9pm-1am, Sa 9pm-2am.

SIGHTS

The **Altes Rathaus** guards the middle of the Regnitz River, the left arm of the Main, like an anchored ship. *(Open Tu-Su 9:30am-4:30pm.)* Built in the 15th century, its strategic location belied no preference for the church nor for the civic powers, each of which held a seat on opposite banks of the river. Stand on one of the two bridges to gaze at this half-*Fachwerk,* half-Baroque facade with a Rococo tower in between. You'll notice a number of visual oddities in the frescoes—painted cherubs have three-dimensional limbs and bodies that jut from the wall where sculpted stone has been attached.

Across the river and up the hill are the **Dom** (tel. 50 23 30) and the **Neue Residenz,** the former episcopal palace. *(Dom open daily 8am-6pm; Nov.-Mar. 8am-5pm—except during services. Also 30min. organ concerts May-Oct. Su noon. For info on tours see Practical Information, p. 565, or call 50 23 30.)* Founded by Emperor Henry II, the cathedral was consecrated in 1012, burned down twice, and was rebuilt in its present-day form in 1237. The most famous object within the *Dom* is the equestrian statue called the **Bamberger Reiter** (the Bamberg Knight), which dates from the 13th century and depicts the chivalric ideal of the medieval warrior-king. Many stories have grown up around the statue over the years, including one that the statue was a prophecy of Hitler's rise to power. The tomb of Heinrich II and Queen Kunigunde of the Holy Roman Empire lies near the east apse; Heinrich sponsored the construction of the cathedral and was later canonized. The **Diözesanmuseum** includes the **Domschatz** (cathedral treasures) and *Kaisermantel* (emperor's coat); enter through the *Dom. (Tours of the Dom and Domschatz gather Tu-Sa 10:30am inside the main entrance to the cathedral. DM3, students and seniors DM1.50.)* Across the square, the **Neue Residenz,** Dompl. 8 (tel. 563

51), strikes Baroque poses among roses; from its prim garden, the town stretches out in a sea of roofs. *(Open daily 9am-noon and 1:30-5pm; Oct.-Mar. 9am-noon and 1:30-4pm; last entry 30min. before morning and afternoon closing. DM4, students and seniors DM3. Tours of the Residenz meet at the cashier desk Apr.-Oct. daily. Tours DM4, students and senior DM3.)*

In town, the streets between the *Rathaus* and the *Dom* are lined with 18th-century Baroque houses, many of which are not yet renovated. At **Pfahlplätzchen,** the pink house on the corner of Judenstr., you can see the bay window from which Hegel peered while editing the proofs of the *Phenomenology of Spirit.* At the time, unable to find a university teaching position, the philosopher was serving as editor of the Bamberg newspaper (1807-08).

Böttinger Palace, on Judenstr., displays a 1713 facade inspired by a Venetian palace and a similarly exotic courtyard. Farther down the street, the lovely **Concordiahaus** is now the local Institute for Geochemical Research. Across the river at Schillerpl. 26 is the **E.T.A. Hoffmann House.** *(Open May-Oct. Tu-F 4-6pm, Sa-Su and holidays 10am-noon. DM2, students DM1.)* Author of the nightmarish *Sandmann,* Hoffmann wrote his uncanny stories in this rickety three-story house from 1809 to 1813.

Aschaffenburg

The Bavarian king Ludwig I affectionately referred to Aschaffenburg as his "Bavarian Nice." The city that served as a second residence for the Electors of Mainz still retains much of its past charm. Not even the near-total destruction of this Frankfurt suburb during WWII and its subsequent military occupation have frustrated the *Freundlichkeit* and hospitality of the locals. "Aschaffenburg Likes You!" proclaims a glossy brochure—and it's not kidding. After a cold spell in Frankfurt, don't be surprised if you're *Guten Tag*-ed frequently during your stay in "Ash-Monkey-Town."

ORIENTATION AND PRACTICAL INFORMATION Built on a high bank at a bend in the Main, Aschaffenburg is accessible by **train** from Frankfurt (1hr., 2 per hr., DM12) or Würzburg (1hr., 2 per hr., DM22). To reach the *Schloß* and the **tourist office,** Schloßpl. 1 (tel. 39 58 00 or 39 58 01; fax 39 58 02), bear right on Ludwigstr. in front of the station and walk down Duccastr.; cross the street to take a left down Friedrichstr., then take the next right down Erthalstr., and a final left onto Strickergstr. Stuck in an ultra-modern library, the office has a free room-finding service and sells excellent cycling maps of the Main River area (DM13.50) as well as city maps (DM1; open M-F 9am-5pm, Sa 10am-1pm). If the tourist office is closed, try one of the three smaller branches in town that will gladly shower you with glossy brochures. One information desk is located in the **Schloßmuseum** (open Tu-Su 11am-4pm), one in the restaurant at the entrance to the castle, the **Schloßweinstube** (open Tu-Su 11am-midnight), and another in the **Galerie Jesuitenkirche** in the **Stadt Galerie** (open Tu 2-5pm, W-Su 10am-1pm and 2-5pm). For a 1½-hour **tour** of the town in German (DM4, under 12 free), meet in front of the tourist office on Sunday at 2pm. A **laundromat, SB Waschsalon,** Beckerstr. 26, is on the corner of Kneippstr. close to the hostel (open M-Sa 9am-9pm; wash DM6, dry DM6, soap DM1). The **post office,** 63739 Aschaffenburg (tel. 36 90), to the left of the train station, **exchanges currency** and cashes traveler's checks (DM6 fee per check; open M-F 7am-6pm, Sa 8am-noon). The **telephone code** is 06021.

ACCOMMODATIONS AND FOOD Aschaffenburg's **Jugendherberge (HI),** Beckerstr. 47 (tel. 93 07 63; fax 97 06 94), is reached from the station by riding bus #40 or 41 to "Schroberstr." (DM1.70 one way). Head left up Kneippstr. and right onto Beckerstr.; the hostel is on the left. This is a quiet and friendly place with a die-hard *fußball* fan staff and access to quiet running and cycling paths through woods and meadows. (DM18. Breakfast included. Sheets DM5.50. Reception 8-9am, noon-1pm, and 5-7pm. Curfew 11:30pm.) Just outside the pedestrian zone, the cheerful owner of **Hotel**

Pape Garni, Würzburger Str. 16 (tel. 226 73; fax 226 22), provides a home-cooked breakfast with her rooms. From the Schloßplatz, follow Schloßgasse or Pfaffengasse and turn left onto Dalbergstr., which turns into Sandgasse and then into Würzburger Str. (Singles DM50; doubles DM90.) The friendly **Goldener Karpfen,** Löherstr. 20 (tel. 239 46; fax 20 02 54), provides a homey ambience, crooked rooms filled with cheery images of carp, and a "snug as a bug in a rug" bar in the hotel. (Singles DM50, with shower DM53; doubles DM96, with shower DM98; triples DM126, with shower DM135. Breakfast included.) Hidden just inside the city wall, **Zum Roten Kopf** has mastered hearty food—strong enough for Bavarians, but made for tourists: their specialties are *Wienerschnitzel* with salad (DM14.50), thick soups (DM3.50-5), and colorful salads (DM4.50). Beer runs DM2.70-4.50. From Schloßplatz, walk down Schloßberg to the right of the tourist office and turn left on Suicardusstr. (open M and W-Su 10am-midnight). Also convenient is the Bavarian restaurant and bar **Stadtschänke,** on your left as you exit the station. Daily menu options (DM7-15) include an entree and salad. (Open M-Sa 9am-midnight.)

SIGHTS After the annual winter hiatus, when *Fräulein* summer enters the stage, Aschaffenburg blossoms like a spring flower. Locals and tourists indulge in the city's home-brewed pride and joy, **Heylands Beer,** as they party with fireworks and merry-go-rounds for 11 days straight during the **Volksfest** in mid-June. In July, the **Kippenburg** and **Schloß wine festival** act as magnets for the city. The annual **Carillion-Fest,** held the first weekend in August, brings renowned ringers from around the globe and tintinnabulating tourists who come to swim in the musical swell.

Schloß-Johannisburg, the former domain of the Mainz bishops, is now an extensive museum of art by old Dutch and German masters. *(Schloß open daily 9am-noon and 1-5pm; Nov.-Mar. Tu-Su 11am-4pm. Museum open Tu-Su 9-11:30am and 1-4:30pm; Nov.-Mar. Tu-Su 11am-4pm; last entry 30min. before morning and afternoon closing. Museum admission DM5, students DM4.)* A set of 48 chromatically tuned bronze bells rings across the landscape daily at 9:05am, 12:05, and 5:05pm. The **Schloßgarten** possesses intricate pathways, ivy-canopied benches, and old town walls, forming a secluded haven for romance. *(Open daily until 9pm.)* Sweetly tucked behind the *Schloßgarten* is the **Pompejanum,** a Pompeii-style structure built for Ludwig I in the mid-19th century. *(Open mid-Mar. to mid-Oct. Tu-Su 10am-12:30pm and 1:30-5pm; last entry 30min. before morning and afternoon closing. DM3, students DM2.)* Walking south on Schloßgasse, turn left at Dalbergstr. to find the famous **Stiftskirche St. Peter and Alexander.** The repository of a millennium of cultural history, the **Stiftmuseum** (tel. 33 04 63) collection includes a 10th-century crucifix, Mathias Grünewald's painting *Beweinung Christi* (Mourning of Christ), and Vischer's *Magdalenenaltar. (Open M and W-Su 10am-1pm and 2-5pm. DM5, students DM2.)* Continuing down Dalbergstr. as it becomes Sandgasse, beautiful *Fachwerkhäuser* (half-timbered houses) pepper the path to the **Sandkirche,** a carefully preserved 1756 Rococo church.

Just past the tightly packed *Altstadt* lie the famous **Schönbusch Gardens** and the newly reopened **Schloß Schönbusch,** a country house built between 1778 and 1780 for the archbishop of Mainz. The view from the second-floor **Chamber of Mirrors** (preserved from the original house and hence a bit distorted) reveals the surrounding city basking in the rich backdrop of the Spessart forests. The archbishop allowed no vegetation between his summer home and Schloß-Johannisburg (3km away), and the two castles remain in that aristocratic see-you-see-me stance today. *(Castle open mid-Mar. to mid-Oct. Tu-Su 10am-12:30pm and 1:30-4:30pm. Admission and tour DM4, students DM3.)* The park itself was built by Elector Friedrich Karl Joseph in 1775 as an experiment in the novel English style of landscape architecture involving "naturalized" tree-scaping. Embellished with artificial ponds, islands, and bridges, as well as tiny buildings like the **Freundschafts tempel** (friendship temple) and the **Philosophenhaus,** the park reeks of fairy tale fallacy. If that prince on a white horse never shows up, navigate yourself to the *Schloß* after **renting a boat** at the **Unterer.** *(Rentals daily 10am-*

BAYERN

7pm. DM6 for 30min.) The **Irrgarten,** close to the restaurant at the park's entrance, is a maze formed by trimmed bushes, planted in 1829. To hedge the fate of the minotaur, climb the wooden tower to gain an overhead view before tackling the labyrinth. *(Open daily 9am-dusk.)* Watch out for David Bowie in tight, tight pants. Take bus #4 or 52 from the main station (DM1.70 one-way).

Appendix

■ Holidays and Festivals

OFFICIAL HOLIDAYS 1999

January 1	Neujahrstag	New Year's Day
January 6	Heilige Drei Könige	Epiphany
February 17	Aschermittwoch	Ash Wednesday
April 2	Karfreitag	Good Friday
April 4	Ostersonntag	Easter Sunday
April 5	Ostermontag	Easter Monday
May 1	Tag der Arbeit	Labor Day
May 13	Christi Himmelfahrt	Ascension Day
May 23	Pfingstsonntag	Whit Sunday (Pentecost)
May 24	Pfingstmontag	Whit Monday
June 3	Fronleichnam	Corpus Christi
August 15	Maria Himmelfahrt	Assumption Day
October 3	Tag der deutschen Einheit	Day of German Unity
October 31	Reformationtag	Reformation Day
November 1	Allerheiligen	All Saint's Day
December 25-26	Weihnachtstag	Christmas

FESTIVALS 1999

All Year	Europe's Cultural Capital	Weimar
All Year	Goethe's 250th Birthday	Nationwide
Late February to Early March	Film Festival	Berlin
February 11-15	Karneval	Köln
May 7-9	Hafensgeburtstag	Hamburg
Late June	International Film Festival	Munich
June 26	Christopher Street Day	Berlin
July-Aug.	Bach Festival	Leipzig
Mid-July	Love Parade	Berlin
Late July	Das Fest	Karlsruhe
July 25-Aug. 28	Wagner Festspiele	Bayreuth
Aug. 7-17	Gäubodenvolksfest	Straubing
Aug. 26-Sept. 4	Wine Festival	Stuttgart
Sept. 18-Oct. 3	Oktoberfest	Munich
Jan. 7-Feb. 16	Fasching (Carnival)	Munich
Dec. 24-27	Christmas Market	Nürnberg

■ Climate

Germany's climate is unexceptional. Rain is common year-round, though it is especially prevalent in the summer, when the weather can change with surprising disjointedness from one hour to the next.

Average Temp. Low-High	January °C	°F	April °C	°F	July °C	°F	October °C	°F
Berlin	-3-1	26-35	2-12	37-54	13-22	56-73	5-13	42-56
Dresden	-2-1	27-34	3-12	39-54	13-22	57-73	6-13	44-56
Frankfurt	-1-3	30-38	3-13	39-56	13-23	57-75	6-13	43-57
Hamburg	-1-3	30-38	2-11	37-52	12-21	55-70	6-12	43-55
München	-4-2	24-36	2-11	36-53	12-22	54-72	4-12	40-55
Stuttgart	-2-2	27-37	2-12	37-54	12-22	55-73	5-13	41-57

To convert from °C to °F, multiply by 1.8 and add 32. For a rough approximation, double the Celsius and add 25. To convert from °F to °C, subtract 32 and multiply by 0.55. For a rough approximation, subtract 25 and cut it in half.

°C	-5	0	5	10	15	20	25	30	35	40
°F	23	32	41	50	59	68	77	86	95	104

Average Precip (mm)	Jan	Feb	Mar	Apr	May	June	July	Aug	Sep	Oct	Nov	Dec
Berlin	48	40	36	41	50	68	75	73	48	51	47	44
Dresden	37	27	39	57	50	70	150	64	47	47	31	43
Frankfurt	45	40	53	58	60	73	60	73	53	55	58	55
Hamburg	60	40	50	45	55	73	81	78	68	60	66	71
München	48	43	53	71	101	124	127	111	83	60	53	50
Stuttgart	48	45	43	60	86	86	73	86	58	45	45	50

■ Time Zones

Germany uses West European time (abbreviated MEZ in German). Add six hours to Eastern Standard Time and one hour to Greenwich Mean Time. Subtract nine hours from Eastern Australia Time and 11 hours from New Zealand Time. Germany, like the rest of Western Europe, observes Daylight Savings Time.

■ International Calling Codes

In Germany, dial 00 to get an international line, then dial the country code, the city or area code (*without* the first 0), and the number. **Germany's country code is 49.**

Australia	Austria	Belgium	Czech Republic	Denmark	France	Hungary	Ireland
61	43	32	420	45	33	36	353

Luxem-bourg	Nether-lands	New Zealand	Poland	South Africa	Switzer-land	United Kingdom	U.S. and Canada
352	31	64	48	27	41	44	1

■ Telephone Codes

Aachen	Berlin	Bremen	Bonn	Braun-schweig	Dessau	Dresden	Düssel-dorf
0241	030	0421	0228	0531	0340	0351	0211

Erfurt	Essen	Frankfurt	Freiburg	Göttingen	Hamburg	Hannover	Heidel-berg
0361	0201	069	0761	0551	040	0511	06221

Kassel	Kiel	Koblenz	Köln	Leipzig	Magde-burg	Mainz	München
0561	0431	0261	0221	0341	0391	06131	089

Nürn-berg	Regens-burg	Rostock	Saar-brücken	Schleswig	Schwerin	Stuttgart	Weimar
0911	0941	0381	0681	04621	0385	0711	03643

■ Measurements

Like the rest of the rational world, Germany uses the metric system. Keep this in mind whenever you see a road sign, trailhead sign, or any other distance indicator—those are kilometers, not miles, so whatever distance is being described is not far away as Americans might think. Also, all German recipe books use metric measurements. And, unfortunately, gasoline isn't as cheap as it looks to those used to gallons: prices are *per liter.*

1 inch – 25 millimeters (mm)	1mm = 0.04 inch (in.)
1 foot (ft.) = 0.30 meter (m)	1m = 3.33 feet (ft.)
1 mile = 1.61 kilometers (km)	1km = 0.62 mile (mi.)
1 pound (lb.) = 0.45 kilogram (kg)	1kg = 2.22 pounds (lb.)
1 gallon = 4 quarts = 3.76 liters (L)	1 L = 1.06 quarts (qt.)=0.27 gallon

■ Language

Although the majority of the post-World War II generations in Germany speak English, you'll have many real face-to-face encounters with people who don't—especially traveling in Eastern Germany. German is a very rigidly structured language, following strict grammatical rules. Mastering the rules is quite an accomplishment in itself—"Life," Thomas Love Peacock said, "is too short to learn German." German uses three genders (*der, die,* and *das*), and has five ways of saying the simple (but oh-so-useful) word, "the." Before asking someone a question, always preface your query with a polite "*Sprechen Sie Englisch?*" (Do you speak English?).

PRONUNCIATION

Although you cannot hope to speak correct German without studying it, you can make yourself understood by learning only a little German. The first step is to master the pronunciation system. Unlike English, German pronunciation is consistent with spelling; once you learn the rules, everything is easy. There are no silent letters.

Consonants are pronounced as in English with the following exceptions: **C:** exists in German only in borrowed foreign words, and is pronounced like a K. **J:** always pronounced as a Y. **K:** always pronounced, even before an N. **P:** always pronounced, even before an F. **QU:** pronounced KV. **S:** pronounced as Z at the beginning of a word. **V:** pronounced as F. **W:** pronounced as V. **Z:** pronounced as TS.

The hissing, aspirant German CH sound, appearing in such basic words as "Ich" (I), "nicht" (not), and "sprechen" (to speak), is quite tricky for untrained English-speaking vocal cords. After A, O, U, or AU, it is pronounced as in the Scottish "loch." After other vowels, CH sounds like the English H in "huge" or "hubris" if you draw out this sound before saying the U. If you can't hack it, use an SH sound in the south and a KH sound in the north.

German has one consonant that does not exist in English, the "ß," which is alternately referred to as the "*scharfes S*" (sharp S) or the "*Ess-tsett.*" It is simply a shorthand symbol for a **double-S,** and is pronounced just like an English "ss." It appears in two of the most important German words for travelers: *die Straße,* "the street," which is pronounced "SHTRAH-ssuh" and abbreviated "Str."; and *das Schloß,* "the castle," simply pronounced "SCHLOSS." Note that the use of the "ß" is slowly being elimated from modern German in an effort to standardize spelling and create less confusion for German schoolchildren learning the language (see **That "ß" Thing, Plus A Few Necessary German Words,** p. 3 and **The Woeful Decline of the ß,** p. 535).

German vowel and dipthong sounds are also pronounced differently: **A:** as in "father." **E:** like the A in "hay." I: like the EE in "creep." **O:** as in "oh." **U:** as in "fondue." **Y:** like the OO in "boot." **AU:** as in "sauerkraut." **IE:** as in "thief." **EI:** like the I in "wine." **EU:** like the OI in "boil."

An **umlaut** over a letter (e.g., Ü) changes the pronunciation. An umlaut is often replaced by an E following the vowel, e.g., "schön" becomes "schoen." In the speech of most Germans, Ä is the equivalent of an American long A (as in "hay"). To make the Ö sound, round your lips to say "oh," freeze them in that position, and try to say "a" as in "hay." To make the Ü sound, round your lips to say "ooh," freeze them in that position, and try to say "ee" instead. Germans are very forgiving toward foreigners who butcher their mother tongue. There is, however, one important exception—place names. If you learn nothing else in German, learn to pronounce the names of cities properly. Berlin is "bare-LEEN," Köln is "KURLN," Hamburg is "HAHM-boorg," Munich (München) is "MEUWN-khen."

Once you've learned a bit of German, you can appreciate the startling differences among dialects. When both speak in the vernacular, a *Kölner* and a *Münchener* cannot understand each another. The Austrian and Swiss German dialects diverge even more strongly from the *Hochdeutsch* (High German) of the north. In general, linguistic distinctions in Germany follow the same pattern as in the U.S.; southerners speak in a more relaxed fashion, while the northern style is harsh and refined, with fully enunciated consonant sounds. For the purposes of the traveler, the crucial distinction is that southerners say "*zwo*" (TSVO) instead of "*zwei*" for the number two.

NUMBERS, DATES, AND TIMES

A space or period rather than a comma is used to indicate thousands, so 10,000 is written 10 000 or 10.000. Instead of a decimal point, Germans use a comma, e.g., 3.1415 is written 3,1415. Months and days are written in the reverse of the American manner, e.g., 10.11.92 is November 10, not October 11. The numeral 7 is written with a slash through the vertical line, and the numeral 1 is written with an upswing, resembling an inverted "V." Note that the number in the ones place is pronounced before the number in the tens place; thus "zweihundertfünfundsiebzig" (TSVEI-hun-duhrt-fuhnf-oont-ZEEB-tsikh) is 275, *NOT* 257. This can be very hard to keep in mind.

The months in German are *Januar, Februar, März, April, Mai, Juni, Juli, August, September, Oktober, November, Dezember.* The days of the week are *Montag, Dienstag, Mittwoch, Donnerstag, Freitag, Samstag/Sonnabend,* and *Sonntag.* Germany uses the 24-hour clock for all official purposes: 8pm equals 20.00. Thus, *vierzehn Uhr* is 2pm, *fünfzehn Uhr* is 3pm, etc. When Germans say "half eight" (halb acht), they mean 7:30; "three quarters eight" (dreiviertel acht) means 7:45 and "quarter eight" (viertel acht) means 7:15.

■ German-English Glossary

das Abendessen: dinner
ab•fahren: depart
die Abfahrt: departure
das Abteil: compartment of train
Achtung: beware
die Allee: avenue
die Altstadt: old city
die Anlage: park
an•kommen: arrive
die Ankunft: arrival
die Apotheke: pharmacy
der Ausgang: exit
die Auskunft: information
die Austellung: exhibit
das Auto: car
die Autobahn: highway
das Bad: bath
die Bahn: rail
der Bahnhof: train station
der Bahnsteig: train platform
der Beach-Volleyball: beach volleyball
der Berg: mountain
die Bibliothek: library
das Bier: beer
BRD (Bundesrepublik Deutschland): Germany
das Brot: bread
die Brücke: bridge
der Brunnen: fountain
der Burg: fortress castle
DJH (Deutsche Jugendherbergswerk): German youth hostel association
die Dusche: shower
der Dom: cathedral
echt: real
die Ehefrau: wife
der Ehemann: husband
der Eingang: entrance
der Eintritt: admission
das Essen: food
fahren: to go (by train, bus, ferry, auto, etc.)
der Fahrplan: timetable
das Fahrrad: bicycle
der Fahrschein: train ticket
der Flohmarkt: flea market
der Flughafen: airport
der Fluß: river
der Fremdenverkehrsamt: tourist office

das Frühstück: breakfast
die Fußgängerzone: pedestrian zone
der Garten: garden
die Gasse: alley
das Gasthaus: guest house
die Gaststätte: local bar with restaurant
der Hafen: harbor
der Hauptbahnhof: main train station
der Hauptpostamt: main post office
der Hof: courtyard
ICE: Inter-City Express train
der Imbiß: fast-food stand
der Insel: island
das Jugendgästehaus: higher quality hostel
die Jugendherberge: youth hostel
die Karte: ticket
das Kino: cinema
die Kirche: church
die Kneipe: student bar
der König: king
die Königin: queen
das Kreuz: cross
die Kunst: art
die Kur: spa or nature treatment for ailments
der Kurort: cure town
die Kurverwaltung: Kurort info office
das Land: state
die Lederhosen: traditional leather pants
die Lesben: lesbian
der Markt: market
der Marktplatz: marketplace
der Meer: sea
die Mensa: university cafeteria
die Mitfahrzentrale: ride-sharing service office
die Mitwohnzentrale: room-finding service office
das Münster: cathedral
das Museum: museum
die Neustadt: new city
der Notausgang: emergency exit
der Notruf: emergency phonecall

die Party: party
der Paß: passport
die Pfarrkirche: parish church
der Platz: square
die Polizei: police
der Postamt: post office
die Presse: newspapers and magazines
das Privatzimmer: room in a private home
die Quittung: receipt
das Rathaus: town hall
die Rechnung: bill
das Reisebüro: travel agency
das Reisezentrum: travel office in train stations
die Sammlung: collection
Scheiße!: shit!
das Schiff: ship
die Schiffahrt: navigation
das Schloß: castle
die Schule: school
schwul: gay
das See: lake
die Speisekarte: menu
die Stadt: city
der Strand: beach
die Straße: street
der Tal: valley
der Tor: gate
der Turm: tower
um•steigen: to make a connection
die Universität: university
der/die Vegetarier/in: vegetarian
die Vergangenheitsbewältigung: coming to terms with the past
das Volk: people
Vorsicht: caution!
der Wald: forest
wandern: to hike
der Wanderweg: hiking trail
der Weg: way
der Wein: wine
die Wende: "the turn"; November 1989, reunification, etc.
die Zeitung: newspaper
das Zimmer: room
der Zug: train

■ German Phrasebook

The following phrasebook is meant to give you only the very rudimentary phrases you will need in your travels. Nothing can replace a full-fledged phrasebook or a pocket-sized English-German dictionary. The German numbering system is especially confusing; look in the **Language** section above for further explanation.

English	German	English	German

PHRASES

English	German	English	German
Hello.	Guten Tag.	How are you?	Wie geht's?
Sorry/Forgive me.	Entschuldigung.	Yes/no	Ja/Nein
Thank you (muchly).	Danke (schön).	No thanks.	Nein, danke.
Good-bye.	Tschüß! (informal); Auf Wiedersehen! (formal)	No problem.	Kein Problem.
Good evening.	Guten Abend.	Good Night.	Gute Nacht.
Do you speak English?	Sprechen Sie Englisch?	Pardon? What was that?	Bitte?
When(what time)?	Wann?	What?	Was?
Why?	Warum?	Where is...?	Wo ist?
How much does that cost?	Wieviel kostet das?	Is...available?	Ist...erhältlich? (things) Ist...frei? (rooms)
I don't understand.	Ich verstehe nicht.	Do you understand (how bad I want you)?	Verstehen Sie (wieviel ich will dich)?
Please speak slowly.	Sprechen Sie bitte langsam.	How do you say that in German?	Wie sagt man das auf Deutsch?
Please repeat.	Bitte wiederholen Sie.	I can't speak German.	Ich kann kein Deutsch.
I would like...	Ich möchte...	I need...	Ich brauche...
I'm looking for...	Ich suche...	I need to find a doctor.	Ich muß einen Arzt finden.
What is your name?	Wie hei3en Sie?	My name is Sven.	Ich heiße Sven.
Where are you from?	Wo kommen Sie her?	I'm from Indiana. It's dreamy.	Ich komme aus Indiana. Es ist träumerisch.
Where is the restroom?	Wo sind die Toiletten?	How clean is the floor?	Wie sauber ist der Boden?
Can you please give me a rubdown?	Kannst du mich bitte abreiben?	Yikes! Gesundheit!	Jeiks! Gesundheit!
Now leave me alone. I want a cigarette.	Laß mich jetzt in Ruhe. Ich will eine Zigarette.	I lost my matches! Help!	Ich habe meine Streichholze verloren. Hilfe!

DIRECTIONS

English	German	English	German
(to the) right	rechts	(to the) left	links
straight ahead	geradeaus	Where is...?	Wo ist...?
How do I get to the underwear factory?	Wie finde ich die Unterwäschefabrik?	It's nearby. Why do you want to know?	Es ist in der Nähe. Warum willst du wissen?
I'm a model. And I need to get to work.	Ich bin ein Modell. Und ich muß zu Arbeit gehen.	Oh, well, it's sort of far away. Can I get a sneak preview?	Also, es ist ein bißchen weit von hier. Kann ich eine Vernissage haben?
When does the train leave?	Wann fährt der Zug ab?	Where is this train going?	Wo fährt dieser Zug hin?

NUMBERS

one	eins	two	zwei
three	drei	four	vier
five	fünf	six	sechs
seven	sieben	eight	acht
nine	neun	ten	zehn
eleven	elf	twelve	zwölf
fifteen	fünfzehn	twenty	zwanzig
twenty-five	fünfundzwanzig	thirty	dreizig
forty	vierzig	fifty	fünfzig
one hundred	ein hundert	one thousand	ein tausend

FOOD AND RESTAURANT TERMS

bread	das Brot	rice	der Reis
meat	das Fleisch	water	das Wasser
vegetables	die Gemüse	tap water	das Leitungswasser
cheese	der Käse	roll	das Brötchen
wine	der Wein	beer	das Bier
sausage	die Wurst	pork	das Schweinfleisch
chicken	das Huhn	beef	das Rindfleisch
potatoes	die Kartoffeln	french fries	die Pommes-frites
sauce	die Soße	coffee	das Kaffee
tea	das Tee	jelly	die Marmelade
It tastes good.	Es schmeckt mir gut.	It tastes awful.	Es schmeckt mir widerlich.
Check, please.	Rechnung, bitte.	I would like to order...	Ich hätte gern...
What time is breakfast served?	Wann wird Frühstück aufgetragen?	I'm a vegetarian.	Ich bin Vegetarier/Vegetarierin.
I'm a vegan.	Ich bin Veganer/in.	Give me chocolate.	Geben Sie mir Schokolade.

TIMES AND HOURS

open	geöffnet	closed	geschlossen
What time is it?	Wie spät ist es?	morning	der Morgen
afternoon	der Nachmittag	evening	der Abend
night	die Nacht	yesterday	gestern
today	heute	tomorrow	morgen
opening hours	die Öffnungszeiten	break time, rest day	die Ruhepause, der Ruhetag

OTHER WORDS

alone	allein	dead	tot
good	gut	bad	schlecht
happy	glücklich	sad	traurig
big	groß	small	klein
young	jung	old	alt
full	voll	empty	leer
hot	heiß	cold	kalt
dangerous	gefährlich	safe	ungefährlich

APPENDIX

Distances (km) and Travel Times (by Train)

	Aachen	Berlin	Bonn	Bremen	Dresden	D-Dorf	Frank-furt	Freiburg	Hamburg	Han-nover	Kassel	Köln	Leipzig	München	Nürn-berg	Rostock	Saar-brücken	Stuttgart
Aachen		642	90	387	649	80	263	541	484	351	307	68	576	650	503	638	274	450
Berlin	6hr.		608	390	214	565	564	827	285	285	388	583	192	587	431	219	791	652
Bonn	1½hr.	6hr.		349	570	78	181	422	450	317	273	26	497	588	399	604	269	357
Bremen	4hr.	4hr.	4hr.		488	298	467	700	119	133	281	324	370	745	573	297	694	657
Dresden.	9hr.	3hr.	8hr.	6hr.		568	471	724	485	371	337	578	124	494	346	474	655	572
Düssel-dorf	1½hr.	5hr.	45min.	3hr.	7½hr.		231	492	423	272	228	41	493	618	449	577	336	414
Frankfurt	3½hr.	5hr.	2hr.	4hr.	5½hr.	3hr.		272	497	362	194	192	398	399	223	651	200	216
Freiburg	5hr.	8hr.	4hr.	6hr.	8½hr.	4½hr.	3hr.		755	613	454	443	661	340	369	994	285	179
Hamburg	5hr.	2½hr.	4½hr.	1hr.	5hr.	4hr.	4hr.	8hr.		163	311	425	377	775	607	184	724	679
Hannover	4hr.	2½hr.	3hr.	1hr.	4½hr.	3hr.	3hr.	7hr.	1½hr.		176	292	263	640	478	338	589	565
Kassel	5hr.	3hr.	4hr.	2hr.	5hr.	3¾hr.	2hr.	3¾hr.	2hr.	1hr.		248	276	479	304	465	378	397
Köln	1hr.	5½hr.	20min.	3hr.	7hr.	30min.	2½hr.	4hr.	4hr.	3hr.	4hr.		505	579	432	579	289	379
Leipzig	7hr.	2hr.	6hr.	4½hr.	1½hr.	5½hr.	3½hr.	7hr.	4½hr.	2½hr.	4hr.	6hr.		422	274	366	582	499
München	7hr.	8hr.	5hr.	6hr.	7½hr.	6hr.	3½hr.	5hr.	6hr.	4½hr.	3½hr.	6hr.	6hr.		162	761	409	221
Nürnberg	5½hr.	6hr.	4½hr.	5hr.	6hr.	5hr.	2hr.	4½hr.	5hr.	3hr.	2hr.	5hr.	4hr.	2hr.		618	417	247
Rostock	7½hr.	3hr.	7hr.	3½hr.	6hr.	6½hr.	7hr.	9hr.	2hr.	4hr.	5hr.	6½hr.	5hr.	9hr.	7½hr.		878	833
Saar-brücken	4½hr.	8hr.	3½hr.	6½hr.	8hr.	4hr.	2½hr.	3¼hr.	7hr.	5hr.	3¾hr.	3½hr.	6½hr.	5hr.	5hr.	9hr.		201
Stuttgart	5hr.	6½hr.	3hr.	5hr.	7hr.	3½hr.	2hr.	2hr.	5hr.	4½hr.	3hr.	3½hr.	2½hr.	2½hr.	2½hr.	8hr.	3hr.	

Index

About Let's Go

THIRTY-NINE YEARS OF WISDOM

Back in 1960, a few students at Harvard University banded together to produce a 20-page pamphlet offering a collection of tips on budget travel in Europe. This modest, mimeographed packet, offered as an extra to passengers on student charter flights to Europe, met with instant popularity. The following year, students traveling to Europe researched the first, full-fledged edition of *Let's Go: Europe,* a pocket-sized book featuring honest, irreverent writing and a decidedly youthful outlook on the world. Throughout the 60s, our guides reflected the times; the 1969 guide to America led off by inviting travelers to "dig the scene" at San Francisco's Haight-Ashbury. During the 70s and 80s, we gradually added regional guides and expanded coverage into the Middle East and Central America. With the addition of our in-depth city guides, handy map guides, and extensive coverage of Asia and Australia, the 90s are also proving to be a time of explosive growth for Let's Go, and there's certainly no end in sight. The maiden edition of *Let's Go: South Africa,* our pioneer guide to sub-Saharan Africa, hits the shelves this year, along with the first editions of *Let's Go: Greece* and *Let's Go: Turkey.*

We've seen a lot in 39 years. *Let's Go: Europe* is now the world's bestselling international guide, translated into seven languages. And our new guides bring Let's Go's total number of titles, with their spirit of adventure and their reputation for honesty, accuracy, and editorial integrity, to 44. But some things never change: our guides are still researched, written, and produced entirely by students who know first-hand how to see the world on the cheap.

HOW WE DO IT

Each guide is completely revised and thoroughly updated every year by a well-traveled set of over 200 students. Every winter, we recruit over 160 researchers and 70 editors to write the books anew. After several months of training, researcher-writers hit the road for seven weeks of exploration, from Anchorage to Adelaide, Estonia to El Salvador, Iceland to Indonesia. Hired for their rare combination of budget travel sense, writing ability, stamina, and courage, these adventurous travelers know that train strikes, stolen luggage, food poisoning, and marriage proposals are all part of a day's work. Back at our offices, editors work from spring to fall, massaging copy written on Himalayan bus rides into witty yet informative prose. A student staff of typesetters, cartographers, publicists, and managers keeps our lively team together. In September, the collected efforts of the summer are delivered to our printer, who turns them into books in record time, so that you have the most up-to-date information available for your vacation. Even as you read this, work on next year's editions is well underway.

WHY WE DO IT

We don't think of budget travel as the last recourse of the destitute; we believe that it's the only way to travel. Living cheaply and simply brings you closer to the people and places you've been saving up to visit. Our books will ease your anxieties and answer your questions about the basics—so you can get off the beaten track and explore. Once you learn the ropes, we encourage you to put *Let's Go* down now and then to strike out on your own. You know as well as we that the best discoveries are often those you make yourself. When you find something worth sharing, please drop us a line. We're Let's Go Publications, 67 Mount Auburn St., Cambridge, MA 02138, USA (email: feedback@letsgo.com). For more info, visit our website, http://www.letsgo.com.

HAPPY TRAVELS!

Researcher-Writers

Kata Gellen *Berlin, Brandenburg, Niedersachsen, Sachsen-Anhalt, Hessen*
Dream R-W Kata knew all along that she and Deutschland were right for one another.
The solid, handsomely rugged face of the Harz mountains and twinkle of Berlin's
sparkling *Szene* reeled her in. Soon, Kata was smitten. A relationship blossomed, but
in harsh Hannover, she saw D-land's dark side. Did she really want to clean this country's bathrooms? Cook its breakfast every morning? Luckily, she recorded the passionate affair in her copy in meticulous, sensitive detail, learning through reflection that—
flaws and all—Germany had won her over. We never had any doubt.

Max Hirsh *Berlin, Mecklenburg-Vorpommern, Schleswig-Holstein*
Faster than a *schicki-micki* speedboat, wielding powers way stronger than convenient clichés, Max was no ordinary R-W—he was MetaMan! Outwardly a mild-man-
nered R-W, his five dispatches exposed his superhuman abilities. He infused his
copybatches with layer upon complicated layer of wit and irony, and he scoffed at
write-ups that couldn't keep themselves entertained, spanking them into self-aware
texts. His secret identity was confirmed during a call from a phonebooth in the midst
of a quick boot change. He opted for the pointy black leather ones.

Jamie L. Jones *Rheinland-Pfalz, Nordrhein-Westfalen, Niedersacshen, Hessen*
Once upon a time, in a land of dreamy castles and untouched isles, there was a
researcher named Jamie. But Jamie was no ordinary researcher; she was inspired. Her
magical pen danced across the pages of her delightful copybatches, singing praises of
every *Dorf* in all of Deutschland. So powerful was her gift that neither illness nor
rough seas could upset her magical stride. From the banks of the Rhine to the perfumed streets of Köln, she unearthed sparkling gems of prose, never failing to ensure
that her editors should live happily ever after.

Winnie Li *Frankfurt, Baden-Württemberg, Allgäu Alps, Rheinland-Pfalz*
Ok. So. Winnie rocked it. *Really* rocked it. Extracting every tiny detail from Baden-
Baden to the Bodensee, Winnie graced our office with page after page of penetrating
prose and the most beer coasters of any R-W. She braved Frankfurt's red light district
at 4am and scrutinized a hostel's bathroom floor, all for the sake of ultra-thorough
research. With endless energy, she bounded over the Schwarzwald hills and discovered on winding alpine roads the reasons why *Let's Go* does not recommend hitchhiking, prompting us all to pose the question: "Where's a Sven when you need one?"

Dáša Pejchar *Bayern*
Meticulous, thorough, and flat-out awesome, Dáša crafted copybatches that were a
joy to read. She blazed through Bavaria with skill and compassion, leaving a trail of
charmed German grandparents in her wake. Bionic Dáša left no vegetarians hungry
in Munich and no cow unloved in the Bavarian Alps. Neither *lederhosen*-wearing
trolls nor raucous frat neanderthals could stop Dáša from busting out copybatches as
beautiful as the dried Alpine flowers she sent back. Next Dáša brings her warm smile
(no bike!) to China, as her whirlwind round-the-world tour continues.

Mike Weller *Sachsen, Thüringen, Halle*
Mixmaster Maik-ee-Maik was our Eurotrash bad boy. Splicing Saxony's old-school
roots with Weimar's phatty birthday beats, he pumped out hi-fi copy with a dancehall
pulse. His *Superhits* include a tribute to his Leipzig 'hood and an experimental
blonde rendition. Not content to just remix the oldies, Maik-ee recorded the *über*-hip
in cities of the former East. He busted onto the Dresden scene with a brand new addition—to his nipple—and left a legendary figure of the underground. By the end, the
B-Boys got hip to the Maik-ee-Maik tip, and through it all Mike stayed chill.

Acknowledgments

Team Germany gives *Vielen Dank* to our kick-ass team of R-Ws; to Allison for her guidance and peanut butter bars; to A&S for TeutoNic Roo shenanigans; to Nic for Hooked on Classics and the beanbag; to Måns and Alex for forefatherly advice; to Anna for the big picture; to Jennifer, John, Ali, and Mike for typing skillz; to Anne, Tom, and the rest of reception for keeping things running smoothly; to Production and Mapland, for endless expertise; and to Tic Tac Toe, for findin' it *Scheiße*.**—GER**

Thank ya, thank ya Erica, for unwavering dedication, patience, and an eagle eye for improper infotext—you'll rock it in Scotland! Anna's enthusiasm was absolute, her observations impressive; Paris will find her fab. Allison got me started in the right direction and kept me going strong 'til August—*gracias... err, Danke!* Absolute thanks to Tommy, for everything, really; loving thanks to Swope House for so much damn fun ("Guiiilty!"); to Joyce for coming to Boston; to David, for anti-scarf solidarity; and to Mom, Dad, David, and Ryan, for helping me get here.**—DSM**

Thanks to Doug for hip editorial style and for listening to all my questions—from your answering service. Props to Anna whose boundless enthusiasm kept us swinging. *Danke* to Allison for the German lessons and the midnight oil. Love to Mom, Dad, and Mick for their patience and support…and the car, to Kristy for Fridays, Alyssa for late nights and phone schedules, marnie for a loved inbox, DT for NYC and night walks, Ona for always understanding, Justin for keeping me up, making me smile, and especially for asking, and to Sue, my inspiration, for believing.**—EAS**

Danke—danke—danke to the GER team, who never tired of my triple-checking. DJ Doug—strong, silent, hilarious. Erica, the *wunderbar* precise planning machine. Allison, who first taught me that it matters. Team FRA, my dark side, we be illin'. *Romantiques* represent. Ladies…proud, shake what your momma gave ya. Thanks for making this the summer of epic tank tops, a yellow kitchen table, and shadowy walks Home. Mom and Dad getaways are like surprise baskets of fruit. No Moogity—the best. **—AMSM**

Editor	Douglas Muller
Associate Editor	Erica A. Silverstein
Associate Editor	Anna M. Schneider-Mayerson
Managing Editor	M. Allison Arwady
Publishing Director	Caroline R. Sherman
Publishing Director	Anna C. Portnoy
Production Manager	Dan Visel
Associate Production Manager	Maryanthe Malliaris
Cartography Manager	Derek McKee
Design Manager	Bentsion Harder
Editorial Manager	M. Allison Arwady
Editorial Manager	Lisa M. Nosal
Financial Manager	Monica Eileen Eav
Personnel Manager	Nicolas R. Rapold
Publicity Manager	Alexander Z. Speier
New Media Manager	Måns O. Larsson
Map Editors	Matthew R. Daniels, Dan Luskin
Production Associate	Heath Ritchie
Office Coordinators	Tom Moore, Eliza Harrington, Jodie Kirschner
Director of Advertising Sales	Gene Plotkin
Associate Sales Executives	Colleen Gaard, Mateo Jaramillo, Alexandra Price
President	Catherine J. Turco
General Manager	Richard Olken
Assistant General Manager	Anne E. Chisholm

Thanks to Our Readers...

Mano Aaron, CA; Jean-Marc Abela, CAN; George Adams, NH; Bob & Susan Adams, GA; Deborah Adeyanju, NY; Rita Alexander, MI; Shani Amory-Claxton, NY; Kate Anderson, AUS; Lindsey Anderson, ENG; Viki Anderson, NY; Ray Andrews, JPN; Robin J. Andrus, NJ; L. Asurmendi, CA; Anthony Atkinson, ENG; Deborah Bacek, GA; Jeffrey Bagdade, MI; Mark Baker, UK; Mary Baker, TN; Jeff Barkoff, PA; Regina Barsanti, NY; Ethan Beeler, MA; Damao Bell, CA; Rya Ben-Shir, IL; Susan Bennerstrom, WA; Marla Benton, CAN; Matthew Berenson, OR; Walter Bergstrom, OR; Caryl Bird, ENG; Charlotte Blanc, NY; Jeremy Boley, EL SAL; Oliver Bradley, GER; A.Braurstein, CO; Philip R. Brazil, WA; Henrik Brockdorff, DMK; Tony Bronco, NJ; Eileen Brouillard, SC; Mary Brown, ENG; Tom Brown, CA; Elizabeth Buckius, CO; Sue Buckley, UK; Christine Burer, SWITZ; Norman Butler, MO; Brett Carroll, WA; Susan Caswell, ISR; Carlos Cersosimo, ITA; Barbara Crary Chase, WA; Stella Cherry Carbost, SCOT; Oi Ling Cheung, HK; Simon Chinn, ENG; Charles Cho, AUS; Carolyn R. Christie, AUS; Emma Church, ENG; Kelley Coblentz, IN; Cathy Cohan, PA; Phyllis Cole, TX; Karina Collins, SWITZ; Michael Cox, CA; Mike Craig, MD; Rene Crusto, LA; Claudine D'Anjou, CAN; Lizz Daniels, CAN; Simon Davies, SCOT; Samantha Davis, AUS; Leah Davis, TX; Stephanie Dickman, MN; Philipp Dittrich,GER; Tim Donovan, NH; Reed Drew, OR; Wendy Duncan, SCOT; Melissa Dunlap, VA; P.A. Emery, UK; GCL Emery, SAF; Louise Evans, AUS; Christine Farr, AUS; David Fattel, NJ; Vivian Feen, MD; David Ferraro, SPN; Sue Ferrick, CO; Philip Fielden, UK; Nancy Fintel, FL; Jody Finver, FL; D. Ross Fisher, CAN; Abigail Flack, IL; Elizabeth Foster, NY; Bonnie Fritz, CAN; J. Fuson, OR; Michael K. Gasuad, NV; Raad German, TX; Mark Gilbert, NY; Betsy Gilliland, CA; Ana Goshko, NY; Patrick Goyenneche, CAN; David Greene, NY; Jennifer Griffin, ENG; Janet & Jeremy Griffith, ENG; Nanci Guartofierro, NY; Denise Guillemette, MA; Ilona Haayer, HON; Joseph Habboushe, PA; John Haddon, CA; Ladislav Hanka, MI; Michael Hanke, CA; Avital Harari, TX; Channing Hardy, KY; Patrick Harris, CA; Denise Hasher, PA; Jackie Hattori, UK; Guthrie Hebenstreit, ROM; Therase Hill, AUS; Denise Hines, NJ; Cheryl Horne, ENG; Julie Howell, IL; Naomi Hsu, NJ; Mark Hudgklnson, ENG; Brenda Humphrey, NC; Kelly Hunt, NY; Daman Irby, AUT; Bill Irwin, NY; Andrea B. Jackson, PA; John Jacobsen, FL; Pat Johanson, MD; Russell Jones, FL; J. Jones, AUS; Sharon Jones, MI; Craig Jones, CA; Wayne Jones, ENG; Jamie Kagan, NJ; Mirko Kaiser, GER; Scott Kauffman, NY; John Keanle, NIRE; Barbara Keary, FL; Jamie Kehoe, AUS; Alistair Kernick, SAF; Daihi Kielle, SWITZ; John Knutsen, CA; Rebecca Koepke, NY; Jeannine Kolb, ME; Elze Kollen, NETH; Lorne Korman, CAN; Robin Kortright, CAN; Isel Krinsky, CAN; George Landers, ENG; Jodie Lanthois, AUS; Roger Latzgo, PA; A. Lavery, AZ; Joan Lea, ENG; Lorraine Lee, NY; Phoebe Leed, MA; Tammy Leeper, CA; Paul Lejeune, ENG; Yee-Leng Leong, CA; Sam Levene, CAN; Robin Levin, PA; Christianna Lewis, PA; Ernesto Licata, ITA; Wolfgang Lischtansky, AUT; Michelle Little, CAN; Dee Littrell, CA; Maria Lobosco, UK; Netii Ross, ITA; Didier Look, CAN; Alice Lorenzotti, MA; David Love, PA; Briege Mac Donagh, IRE; Brooke Madigan, NY; Helen Maltby, FL; Shyama Marchesi, ITA; Domenico Maria, ITA; Natasha Markovic, AUS; Edward Marshall, ECU; Rachel Marshall, TX; Kate Maynard, UK; Agnes McCann, IRE; Susan McGowan, NY; Brandi McGunigal, CAN; Neville McLean, NZ; Marty McLendon, MS; Matthew Melko, OH; Barry Mendelson, CA; Eric Middendorf, OH; Nancy Mike, AZ; Coren Milbury, NII; Margaret Mill, NY; David H. Miller, TX; Ralph Miller, NV; Susan Miller, CO; Larry Moeller, MI; Richard Moore, ENG; Anne & Andrea Mosher, MA; J. L. Mourne, TX; Athanassios Moustakas, GER; Laurel Naversen, ENG; Suzanne Neil, IA; Deborah Nickles, PA; Pieter & Agnes Noels, BEL; Werner Norr, GER; Ruth J. Nye, ENG; Heidi O'Brien, WA; Sherry O'Cain, SC; Aibhan O'Connor, IRE; Kevin O'Connor, CA; Margaret O'Rielly, IRE; Daniel O'Rourke, CA; Krissy Oechslin, OH; Johan Oelofse, SAF; Quinn Okamoto, CA; Juan Ramon Olaizola, SPN; Laura Onorato, NM; Bill Orkin, IL; K. Owusu Agyenang, UK; Anne Paananen, SWD; Jenine Padget, AUS; Frank Pado, TX; G. Pajkich, Washington, DC; J. Parker, CA; Marian Parnat, AUS; Sandra Swift Parrino, NY; Iris Patten, NY; M. Pavini, CT; David Pawielski, MN; Jenny Pawson, ENG; Colin Peak, AUS; Marius Penderis, ENG; Jo-an Peters, AZ; Barbara Phillips, NY; Romain Picard, Washington, DC; Pati Pike, ENG; Mark Pollock, SWITZ; Minnie Adele Potter, FL; Martin Potter, ENG; Claudia Praetel, ENG; Bill Press, Washington, DC; David Prince, NC; Andrea Pronko, OH; C. Robert Pryor, OH; Phu Quy, VTNM; Adrian Rainbow, ENG; John Raven, AUS; Lynn Reddringer, VA; John Rennie, NZ; Ruth B.Robinson, FL; John & Adelaida Romagnoli, CA; Eva Romano, FRA; Mark A. Roscoe, NETH; Yolanda & Jason Ross, CAN; Sharee Rowe, ENG; W. Suzanne Rowell, NY; Vic Roych, AZ; John Russell, ENG; Jennifer Ruth, OK; William Sabino, NJ; Hideki Saito, JPN; Frank Schaer, HUN; Jeff Schultz, WI; Floretta Seeland-Connally, IL; Colette Shoulders, FRA; Shireen Sills, ITA; Virginia Simon, AUS; Beth Simon, NY; Gary Simpson, AUS; Barbara & Allen Sisarsky, GA; Alon Siton, ISR; Kathy Skeie, CA; Robyn Skillecorn, AUS; Erik & Kathy Skon, MN; Stine Skorpen, NOR; Philip Smart, CAN; Colin Smit, ENG; Kenneth Smith, DE; Caleb Smith, CA; Geoffrey Smith, TX; John Snyder, NC; Kathrin Speidel, GER; Lani Steele, PHIL; Julie Stelbracht, PA; Margaret Stires, TN; Donald Stumpf, NY; Samuel Suffern, TN; Michael Swerdlow, ENG; Brian Talley, TX; Serene-Marie Terrell, NY; B. Larry Thilson, CAN; J. Pelham Thomas, NC; Wright Thompson, ENG; Christine Timm, NY; Melinda Tong, HK; M. Tritica, AUS; Melanie Tritz, CAN; Mark Trop, FL; Chris Troxel, AZ; Rozana Tsiknaki, GRC; Lois Turner, NZ; Nicole Virgil, IL; Blondie Vucich, CO; Wendy Wan, SAF; Carrie & Simon Wedgwood, ENG; Frederick Weibgen, NJ; Richard Weil, MN; Alan Weissberg, OH; Ryan Wells, OH; Jill Wester, GER; Clinton White, AL; Gael White, CAN; Melanie Whitfield, SCOT; Bryn Williams, CAN; Amanda Williams, CAN; Wendy Willis, CAN; Sasha Wilson, NY; Kendra Wilson, CA; Olivia Wiseman, ENG; Gerry Wood, CAN; Kelly Wooten, ENG; Robert Worsley, ENG; C.A.Wright, ENG; Caroline Wright, ENG; Mary H. Yuhasz, CO; Margaret Zimmerman, WA.

"A crash course that could lead to a summer job— or a terrific party." —*Boston Globe*

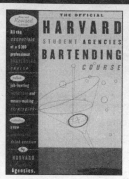

With **THE OFFICIAL HARVARD STUDENT AGENCIES BARTENDING COURSE**, you could find yourself mixing drinks professionally and earning great money, or at least, giving fabulous cocktail parties!

- Over 300 recipes for the most asked-for drinks— including a section on popular nonalcoholic beverages
- Tips on finding top-paying bartending jobs
- How to remember hundreds of recipes
- How to serve drinks and handle customers with aplomb

Please send me___copies of **THE OFFICIAL HARVARD STUDENT AGENCIES BARTENDING COURSE** (0-312-11370-6) at $9.95 each. I have enclosed $3.00 for postage and handling for the first book, and $1.00 for each additional copy.

Name

Address

City   State   Zip

Send check or money order with this coupon to:
St. Martin's Press • 175 Fifth Avenue • New York, NY 10010 • Att: Nancy/Promotion

---

ALSO AVAILABLE FROM ST. MARTIN'S PRESS

The only college guide written by college students is now better than ever with...

- Profiles of more than 300 schools in the U.S. and Canada, focusing on academics, housing and food, social life, student activities, and the campus and vicinity
- Insider tips on the application and admissions process
- Up-to-date statistics on tuition, acceptance rates, average test scores and more
- Plus: a College Finder, which picks the right schools in dozens of categories

VISIT THE BEST BET ON THE NET FOR TEENS www.cbnet.com

Please send me___copies of **THE INSIDER'S GUIDE TO THE COLLEGES** (0-312-18728-9) at $16.99 each. I have enclosed $3.00 for postage and handling for the first book, and $1.00 for each additional copy.

Name

Address

City   State   Zip

Send check or money order with this coupon to:
St. Martin's Press • 175 Fifth Avenue • New York, NY 10010 • Att: Nancy/Promotion

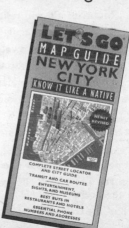

★Let's Go 1999 Reader Questionnaire★

Please fill this out and return it to **Let's Go, St. Martin's Press**, 175 Fifth Ave., New York, NY 10010-7848. All respondents will receive a free subscription to **The Yellowjacket**, the Let's Go Newsletter. You can find a more extensive version of this survey on the web at http://www.letsgo.com.

Name: _____

Address: _____

City: _____ **State:** _____ **Zip/Postal Code:** _____

Email: _____ **Which book(s) did you use?**_____

How old are you? under 19 19-24 25-34 35-44 45-54 55 or over

Are you (circle one) in high school in college in graduate school
employed retired between jobs

Have you used Let's Go before? yes no **Would you use it again?** yes no

How did you first hear about Let's Go? friend store clerk television
bookstore display advertisement/promotion review other

Why did you choose Let's Go (circle up to two)? reputation budget focus
price writing style annual updating other: _____

Which other guides have you used, if any? Fodor's Footprint Handbooks
Frommer's $-a-day Lonely Planet Moon Guides Rick Steve's
Rough Guides UpClose other: _____

Which guide do you prefer? _____

**Please rank each of the following parts of Let's Go 1 to 5 (1=needs
improvement, 5=perfect).** packaging/cover practical information
accommodations food cultural introduction sights
practical introduction ("Essentials") directions entertainment
gay/lesbian information maps other: _____

**How would you like to see the books improved? (continue on separate page,
if necessary)**_____
_____

How long was your trip? one week two weeks three weeks
one month two months or more

Which countries did you visit? _____

What was your average daily budget, not including flights? _____

Have you traveled extensively before? yes no

Do you buy a separate map when you visit a foreign city? yes no

Have you used a Let's Go Map Guide? yes no

If you have, would you recommend them to others? yes no

Have you visited Let's Go's website? yes no

What would you like to see included on Let's Go's website? _____
_____

What percentage of your trip planning did you do on the Web? _____

Would you use a Let's Go: recreational (e.g. skiing) guide gay/lesbian guide
adventure/trekking guide phrasebook general travel information guide

**Which of the following destinations do you hope to visit in the next three to
five years (circle one)?** Canada Argentina Perú Kenya Middle East
Caribbean Scandinavia other: _____

Where did you buy your guidebook? Internet independent bookstore
chain bookstore college bookstore travel store other: _____

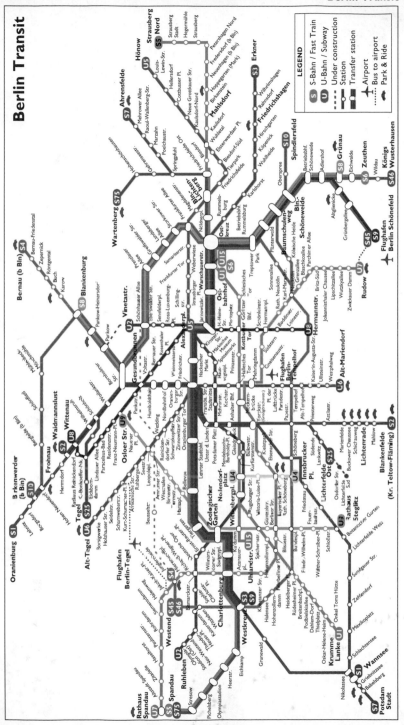

Berlin Transit

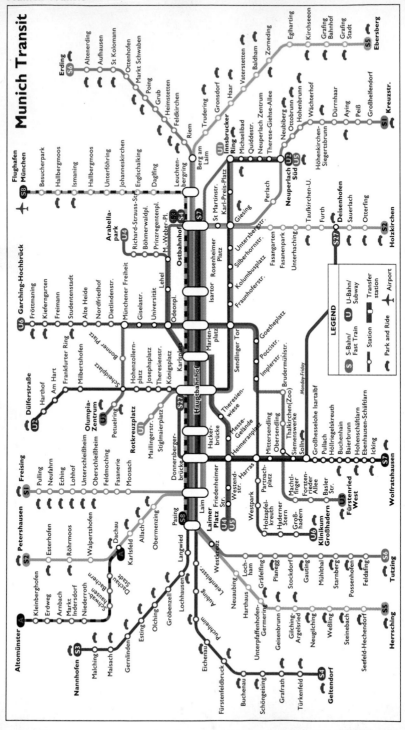

Munich Transit

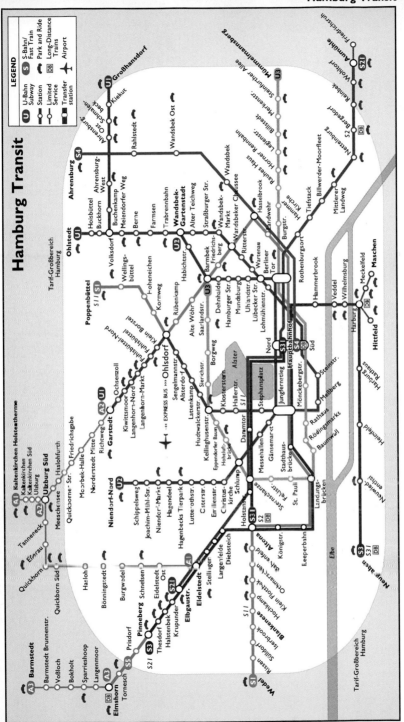

Hamburg Transit

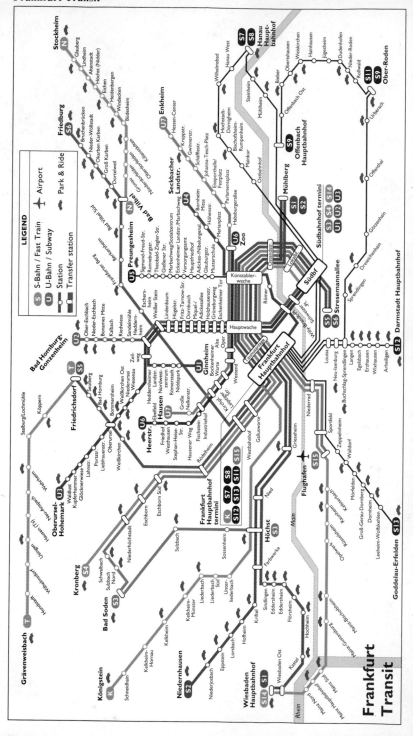

Frankfurt Transit